THE THEATRE OF CORNWALL.
SPACE · PLACE · PERFORMANCE

Also by Alan M. Kent

Poetry
Grunge
Out of the Ordinalia
The Hensbarrow Homilies
Love and Seaweed
Assassin of Grammar
Stannary Parliament
Druid Offsetting

Prose
Clay
Dreaming in Cornish
Cousin Jack's Mouth-organ: Travels in Cornish America
Proper Job, Charlie Curnow!
Electric Pastyland
The Cult of Relics/Devocyon dhe Greryow
Voodoo Pilchard

Drama
Ordinalia – The Cornish Mystery Play Cycle, a Verse Translation:
        The Beginning of the World
        Christ's Passion
        The Resurrection
Nativitas Christi: A New Cornish Mystery Play
Oogly es Sin
The Tin Violin
Surfing Tommies
A Mere Interlude

As Editor
Voices from West Barbary: An Anthology of Anglo-Cornish Poetry 1549-1928
The Dreamt Sea: An Anthology of Anglo-Cornish Poetry 1928-2004
Charles Valentine Le Grice, Cornwall's 'Lost' Romantic Poet: Selected Poems
Four Modern Cornish Plays

As Co-Editor
Looking at the Mermaid: A Reader in Cornish Literature 900-1900
Inside Merlin's Cave: A Cornish Arthurian Reader 1000-2000
Jack Clemo, The Awakening
The Busy Earth: A Reader in Global Cornish Literature 1700-2000
The Francis Boutle Book of Cornish Short Stories

Literary criticism
Wives, Mothers and Sisters: Feminism, Literature and Women Writers of Cornwall
The Literature of Cornwall: Continuity, Identity, Difference 1000-2000
Pulp Methodism: The Lives and Literature of Silas, Joseph and Salome Hocking

Dr Alan M. Kent M.Phil., M.Ed. was born in St Austell in 1967 and lectures in Literature for the Open University in south west Britain. A qualified teacher of Drama and Theatre Studies, he is also Visiting Lecturer in Celtic Literature at the University of La Coruña, Galicia, and a lecturer in Folklore for the Workers' Educational Association. His first collection of poetry appeared in 1994 and since then he has published poetry, prose, drama and literary criticism which have established him as one of the leading Cornish writers of his generation. His novels *Proper Job, Charlie Curnow!* (2005), *Electric Pastyland* (2007) and *The Cult of Relics/Devocyon dhe Greryow* (2010) have redefined the contemporary Anglo-Cornish novel. In 1998 he won the Charles Lee Literary Competition, in 1999 a European Union Euroscript Award and in 2004 the *Holyer an Gof* Literary Salver. His verse translation of the three plays of the *Ordinalia: The Cornish Mystery Play Cycle* was published to much acclaim in 2005. In 2007, his play *Oogly es Sin* was nominated for a Sony Regional Radio Drama Award, and he is twice winner of the Cornish Gorsedd Poetry in English Competition. His works have been performed in both Cornwall and England, and regularly feature on BBC Radio Cornwall. His most recent plays are *The Tin Violin* (2008), *Surfing Tommies* (2009) and *A Mere Interlude* (2010).

The Theatre of Cornwall:
Space · Place · Performance

Alan M. Kent

with a Preface by Mike Shepherd

WESTCLIFFE
BOOKS

First published in 2010 by Redcliffe/Westcliffe Books
81g Pembroke Road, Bristol BS8 3EA

info@redcliffepress.co.uk
www.redcliffepress.co.uk

ISBN 978-1-904537-99-1

British Cataloguing-in-Publication Data

A catalogue record for this book is available
from the British Library.

Front cover photograph: Kneehigh Theatre's *Tristan and Yseult*
at Restormel Castle, Lostwithiel, Cornwall, 2005. Courtesy
of Kneehigh Theatre and Steve Tanner Photography.

Cover design by Mark Cavanagh
Typesetting by Harper Phototypesetters Ltd
Printed by Hobbs The Printers Ltd, Totton, Hampshire

CONTENTS

To Chris Warner –
a Cornish theatrical visionary

ACKNOWLEDGEMENTS

Theatre is rarely the product of one individual. Contemporary high-quality drama is the result of an interaction between a dramatist, a director, actors and those people working backstage with sound, lighting, stage management, and the design and making of sets, costumes and props. Likewise, this book is based on that kind of interaction. Numerous people from very different backgrounds and places have helped me write this volume. Among these people are a group of scholars with whom I regularly debate Cornish and Celtic culture: Charles Thomas, Philip Payton, Brian Murdoch, Tim Saunders, Hildegard L.C. Tristram, Salikoko S. Mufwene, Nicholas Williams, Michael Everson, Garry Tregidga, Bernard Deacon, Kenneth MacKinnon, Frances Bennett, Myrna Combellack, John C.C. Probert, David H. Thomas, John Hurst, Melissa Hardie, James Whetter, Audrey Randle Pool, Antonio de Tores, Sydney Higgins, Neil Kennedy, Andrew C. Symons, Gerry Hones, Paul Manning, Chris Nancollas, Mina Dresser, Steve Patterson, Jane Costin, Gage McKinney, Briar Wood, Mick Paynter, Evelyn Newlyn, Shelley Trower, Gemma Goodman, Joan Beal, Aaron Cooper, Jackie Harding, Cheryl Hayden, Cath Camps, John Sinker, Hilary Orange, Antonio Raul de Toro, Farah Karim-Cooper, Ann Trevenen Jenkin, Gary German, John Reed, Joan Beal, Sabine Heinz, and Arthur Aughey.

From the world of theatre itself I would like to thank Chris Warner, Benjamin Luxon, Dean Nolan, John Hoggarth, Mbuguah Goro, Trevor Cuthbertson, Joanne Clare, Victoria Guy, Molly Weaver, Nikki Tout, Jackie Fergus, Jim Bloomfield, John Lee, Voirrey Kinrade, Simon Cartwright, Nick Lewis, Simon Turley, Iain Slade, Jacqueline Ball, John Trembath, Gerri Bonne, Tim Smithies, Barbara Tremewan, Tom Tremewan, Perran Tremewan, Sue Hill, Bill Mitchell, Carl Grose, Will Coleman, Hilary Coleman, David Wilmore, Emma Spurgin Hussey, Rory Wilton, Rick Worthy, Daniel Marchese Robinson, and Andy Martin. Especially helpful were Andrew Clare with his designs for the former Glasney College Site at Penryn, and Philip Vaughn at the Mount Pleasant Eco Park, Porthtowan.

A number of theatre companies and theatres have allowed me access to their archives, and for that I am very grateful. These include Kneehigh Theatre, Footsbarn Theatre, The Bedlam Theatre Company of Cornwall, Stiltskin Theatre Company, The Theatre Royal, Plymouth, The Minack Theatre, Porthcurno, and The Lane Theatre, Newquay, David E. Ivall and Truro Amateur Operatic and Dramatic Society, Margaret Goudge, Sheila

Lines and Newquay Dramatic Society, Freddie Rowe and staff at St Austell Arts Centre, Peter Woodward and the staff at Sterts Arts Centre, Upton Cross, the Georgian Theatre Royal, Richmond, North Yorkshire, and Bill and Gwen Phillips and the Cornish Association of Victoria. Ann Altree, and the Hypatia Trust at Trevelyan House Penzance, were particularly helpful in my research on the Georgian Theatre of Penzance. At BBC Radio Cornwall, I would like to thank Martin Bailie, Tim Hubbard, Matthew Shepherd and formerly of the station, Emma Lloyd and Christopher Blount for their support with this project.

Donald R. Rawe, D.M. Thomas, Ken George, Simon Parker and Jonathon Plunkett were equally helpful with material on their dramatic works. Gratis permission for inclusion of work by James Stock was granted by Nick Hern of Nick Hern Books, and for the drawing by F.E. Halliday, courtesy of Sebastian Halliday. Marigold Atkey, Bruce Hunter, and David Higham Associates were helpful in allowing permission for the writings of Charles Causley. On the 'playing places' of Cornwall, I am indebted to the earlier studies of Rod Lyon, Matthew Spriggs, and Oliver J. Padel. For the *An Darras* artwork, I am grateful to Leo Davey and Merv Davey. Drew Baker of the Theatron project at King's College, London was equally helpful with providing computer-generated images of Perran Round. My thanks too, to the trustees of the Tregellas Tapestry at the Cornwall Centre, Redruth and of the Gorseth Kernow archive. I am also grateful to Peter W. Thomas and Derek Williams, for allowing me to rework some of the material on Robert Morton Nance's drama contained in their volume *Setting Cornwall on its Feet: Robert Morton Nance 1873-1959* (2007). For the work of Nick Darke, I am grateful to Claire Weatherhead of Methuen Drama, an imprint of A.C. Black Publishers.

The following individuals, libraries and institutions have also been helpful in my research: the Morrab Library, Penzance, Michelle Brown of the British Library, the British Museum, the Victoria and Albert Museum, National Library of Ireland, the Bodleian Library, Oxford, Graham Thomas, Andrew Hawke and Anwen Pierce of the National Library of Wales, University College Cardiff Library, University of Bristol Library, the late Christopher Robinson and Heather Romaine, Keepers of the University of Bristol Theatre Collection, University of Exeter Library (in particular, Christine Faunch, Susan Inskip and Darren Bevin of the Special Collections section), Harvard University, the Library of the University College of St Mark and St John, Plymouth, Plymouth City Library and Museum, Plymouth and West Devon Record Office, Devon Record Office, Cardiff Central Library, Cornwall Record Office, Public Record Office, Cornish Family History Society, Gill Provis and Newquay Library, the Music and Drama Library, St Austell, Truro

Library, Paul Watts Photography, Steve Tanner Photography, St Nonna's Church, Alternun and Steve Skinner of Skinner's Brewery, Truro. As ever, I would like to thank Kim Cooper, Joanne Elliot, and the team of librarians at the Cornish Studies Library, Cornwall Centre, Redruth, and Angela Broome, Anne Knight, Robert Cook, Graham Bunney, Chistopher Bond and the late Roger Penhallurick at the Courtney Library, the Royal Institution of Cornwall. Terry Knight, formerly of the Cornish Studies Library, was always helpful in finding the most obscure texts for me. His contribution to my work has been long-standing and I am grateful for his time and energy over a number of years. Peter Hicks of Newquay Old Cornwall Society was also very helpful in my research and supplying photographs. L.C.G. Rogers and the Enys Estate kindly allowed me permission to quote from the remarkable *Truro Cordwainers' Play*.

Friends and family too have nourished and sustained the study. These include Barrie Kent, Clive and Glynis Kent, Danny and Jo Merrifield, Steven Curgenven, Chris and Kat Morford, Simon Baker, Ian Janes, Paul Annear, Paul Newman, Pamela Smith Rawnsley, Audrey Randle Pool, John Morford, Audrey Bryant, Mick Catmull, Pauline Barnes, Philip Davey, Andy Lobb, Jon Rosewall, Michael Chappell, Jim Pengelly, Jeremy and Lyn Le Grice, Les and Gill Goldman, Sue and Cliff Harris, Chris Davies, Lawrence Moody, Ann Gazzard, Gwyn Griffiths, Michael John Thompson, Peter Waverley, Charles Thurlow, and Clive Boutle and Kate Tattersall. Here too, I should like to mention Roger Ellis, formerly Senior Lecturer in the Department of English, University College Cardiff, who first encouraged me to study the theatre of Cornwall back in the mid-1980s. This book has much of its origins in his words and kindly advice.

I am also indebted to the Department of English at the Open University, who awarded me a substantial Research Affiliate award to complete the research for this volume. The support of David Johnson, Bob Owens, Dave Flatman, John Wolfe and Anne Ford is particularly appreciated. Finally, my thanks to Mike Shepherd for his insightful Preface, to Shirley Brown for her meticulous copy-editing, and to John Sansom of Redcliffe, whose belief and support in this publication has been there since I first suggested this project to him, a decade ago.

Alan M. Kent
Lanbrebois / Probus,
Kernow / Cornwall

Degol Stul / Twelfth Night, 2010

List of Illustrations

—

2. 'Devils and devices to delight as well the eye as the ear': Rounds, Rebellion and Recusants in Medieval and Tudor Cornwall, 1200-1600

3. 'Sure Mevagezy is a choice place': Renaissance, Restoration, Reform and… Pilchards - Ending the Stage of the Troyance Tongue, 1600-1800

4. 'The Locomotive Stage of Cornwall': Mining, Melodrama and Managers, 1800-1900

5. Treading the Boards beyond West Barbary: The World Stage of Cornwall, 1850-1900

6. 'The Protagonist St George and the Antagonist St Piran': Dramaturgy, Revival and Nationalism, 1900-1950

7. Performing Devolution: Dramatic Re-invention, New Theatre and New Belonging in Cornwall, 1950-2010

Conclusion: Recycling the *Plen-an-Gwarry* – Coming Full Cycle and Full Circle?

PREFACE

———

I grew up in Cornwall scrambling up and down cliffs when I shouldn't have, lighting fires where I shouldn't have, careering uncontrollably down hills on homemade dillies, getting lost, climbing trees and jumping off harbour walls. I remember being lagged in mud, soaking wet, covered in nettle rash and being told off. I largely ignored education, dreamt of far horizons and couldn't wait to get away. Cornwall gave me independence and a natural instinct for naughtiness. Infused with my Cornish childhood I stepped out into the world and didn't really 'fit'. The world of theatre I tried to enter seemed too often to be constrained by neurosis and the fear of 'having to get it right'. I had never been concerned with 'getting it right' and it wasn't long before I returned to Cornwall, which I thought of as a place where you could 'make it happen' – where you could be independent. It was 1978 and I have been making theatre ever since.

I don't know much about the history of Cornish theatre. What I do know is that Cornwall is rich in a tradition of theatre dating back to performances of the *Ordinalia* in *plen-an-gwarries*. I would like to think that historically, there has been a desire for the collective experience but there are very few village greens or town squares where communities have traditionally congregated. What there is though is a tradition and healthy desire for feast, festival and event. Whether it is Padstow's ancient and pagan Obby Oss or a recently created night of mayhem I witnessed in Stithians; now an annual event, born out of celebration for the departure of a nasty neighbour and featuring in 2008 a pig roast, splendid ales, lanterns in trees, animated film and an absurd pantomime horse race. There remains in Cornwall a sense of anarchy and independence. We are almost surrounded by sea so we look outward more often than inward; outward – where surprising connections can be made and stories of extraordinary experiences from across the seas – may be brought home.

I don't know much about Cornish theatre and I'm not sure that the Cornish are that 'fussed' about theatre, but I do know that the best theatre we make is influenced by Cornwall, and is irreverent, generous, brave and instinctive. If Health and Safety would allow it, I would have actors climbing trees, falling down cliffs, careering around on dillies, covered in mud and lighting fires in every show. Cornwall is a place to look to a giant horizon, strive to reach it and then come home before striking out again. Alan M. Kent's study of the history of theatre in Cornwall proves just that. I very much welcome this considered and enlightening study. It is something that is long overdue. In all this theatrical activity, I wonder what the next chapter will be... Here's to a relevant, innovative, anarchic and non-elitist international theatre of the future. May it continue to be grown in Cornwall.

Mike Shepherd
Kneehigh Theatre,
Lamledra Barns,
Gorran Haven,
Kernow / Cornwall

January 2010

INTRODUCTION

———

'Theatre... in oll Kernow' – Celticity, Crisis and Continuum

'Me yv duk in oll Kernow
    indella ytho ov thays
hag vhel arluth in pov
    hag vhel arluth in pov

[I am Duke in all Cornwall
    So was my father,
And a high lord in the country
    From Tamar to Land's End]'

Duke of Cornwall's speech from Whitley Stokes (ed. and tr.), *The Life of Saint Meriasek, Bishop and Confessor: A Cornish Drama,* 1872 [c.1504][1]

'Yes – it's lovely to be here in Kernow tonight – or as I prefer to call it, that little piece of shite off the coast of Ireland!'

Morholt's speech from Carl Grose and Anna Maria Murphy, *Tristan and Yseult,* 2003[2]

Of all forms of artistic expression, drama is perhaps the oldest. Since the earliest prehistoric and neolithic peoples realised that ritual or display could provoke a reaction in a given audience, humanity has both understood and demanded theatre. Since then, it has been spellbound by theatre's characters, spectacle, words and physicality. Maybe this is why we still remain fascinated with the locations and texts of Greek tragedies and comedies, so many centuries on from their first performances. Theatre and drama has an ability to interact with an 'audience' like no other art form. Unlike poetry and fiction, theatre is not a solitary experience: it is one to be shared by both performers and an audience. It is both participatory and engrossing, at the same time confirming and challenging one's identity – whether listening to the Duke of Cornwall in 1504, or hearing the words of the Irish champion and Cornish beater, Morholt – in 2003. We may be watcher, writer or performer, but theatre continues to delight us.

This book is about the theatre of Cornwall in all its manifestations. It is rarely acknowledged, but Cornwall – or *Kernow* (in the Cornish language) – has had, and continues to be, one of the most complex theatrical cultures in Western Europe, and it lays considerable claim to be *the* 'Celtic' theatrical territory.[3] Cornwall – whether one sees it as a Celtic nation or an English county – is a small territory, a peninsula jutting into the Atlantic Ocean on the edge of the British and Irish archipelago and on the western periphery of Europe.[4] Yet, over time, theatre in Cornwall has somehow, perplexingly, retained a lasting continuity: very often community-based, populist, and nearly always highly political. This volume examines not only the links between the geographical spaces and places where theatre in and about Cornwall has taken place, but also considers the changing tradition of performance located there over the centuries. To even the most casual of observers, Cornwall is a distinctly 'old' place, filled with an ancient landscape, language, literature, folklore, customs and traditions, and so it is perhaps apt that we are dealing with the oldest art form.

Within the confines of the work here, the core aims are to document, for both academic and popular readers, the history and story of that tradition, placing the theatre there in a Cornish, Celtic, British and European historical context. Alongside this, there has always been an innovative and progressive use of theatre space within Cornwall over several centuries, which merits a renewed investigation and enquiry. The journey we shall take within this volume will locate the theatre of Cornwall within several fields of study – among them Cornish studies, Celtic studies, performance studies, Cornish, Anglo-Cornish and Cornu-English literature, post-colonial studies and eco-criticism – since it is across the wide stage of these disciplines that our subject matter walks and talks. For the most part, this volume will consider theatre in Cornwall itself: that is, what texts, what venues, and what significant perform-ances have helped to shape our understanding of the historical process of theatre. We will also cross borders and boundaries to consider how Cornwall has been theatrically and literally 'imagined' elsewhere in these islands: a process that has occurred with all Celtic territories, and that has been of con-siderable interest to academics.[5] Theatre, above all else, is precisely the form to show the fraught interactions between ethnic, religious and national groups across the British and Irish archipelago: interactions ably documented by scholars such as Hechter, and Aughey.[6] Indeed, the shaping and perception of Cornwall in other territories – specifically England, though to a lesser extent also Europe, North America and Australasia – will have had implications on theatre at home.[7] These interactions are significant cross-cultural processes, at once inevitable and unstoppable. As John Kerrigan has argued, much

Anglophone writing is actually fascinated with the Celtic periphery.[8] The tradition of writing in English remains hugely intrigued by what happens on its borders and peripheries, and is actively concerned with both control and resistance – not only in the Celtic territories but also in others under imperial control in the world.

That said, such an investigation into the theatre of Cornwall will certainly involve investigating the particular nature of Cornish culture. It should not now be necessary to explain Cornwall's difference from England: given first the ongoing academic acknowledgement of this difference in several fields, encapsulated in the writings of a number of internal and external observers;[9] and second the increased popular notion of Cornwall's 'separateness'.[10] The agenda of this book necessitates that issues of Cornish difference are discussed in the context of theatre. Additionally, as I have argued elsewhere,[11] such a study must merit discussion of Cornish identity, values and ideology which, like all cultures, have changed over time in response to changes in the economy, religion, philosophy and society. This broadly 'cultural materialist' or 'historicist' approach to literature and theatre – developed initially by Marxist literary scholars such as Alick West and Raymond Williams,[12] then fine-tuned by Jonathan Dollimore and Alan Sinfield, and Scott Wilson,[13] – facilitates a mode of enquiry which disrupts and displaces traditional criticism (the so-called 'crisis' within literary and theatrical studies), and allows for 'historical context, theoretical method, political commitment and textual analysis' which offers study of the 'implication of literary texts in history'.[14] I believe that this methodology allows the best kind of investigation into the tradition of the theatre of Cornwall. It is a model that will be applied throughout the chapters that follow.

Tradition has been mentioned above, and it is a word that will inevitably recur in a study of this kind, though at present it is perhaps too 'folklore-ish' a term to describe the ongoing development of Cornish theatre. Even an awareness of the 'transforming nature' of this tradition will not suffice. A preferable term is that of the 'continuum' of Cornish theatre, which, like all continua, may have many links and even breakages, yet helps to define the way in which Cornish cultural history can be mapped and read. Importantly, Cornish cultural history is defined by a series of declines and revivals, related to external and internal agendas concerning preservation and modernisation.[15] We may even choose to consider the discontinuity of theatre in Cornwall, when particular genres and processes came to a complete halt, and when new formulations were put in place. Such discontinuity will be found at several points. Other markers are best put into position here too. To apply M. Wynn Thomas's compelling terms in relation to Wales,[16] we are also dealing with two 'corresponding cultures' in Cornwall: those of Cornish and English, which have historically vied with each other over the production of theatre, according to the conditions of production. We may go a stage further and argue that in modern Cornwall we are actually dealing with three corresponding cultures: Cornish, English and Cornu-English. As we go back in time we also contend with Latin, Norman French, and perhaps pockets of Breton. As we might expect, Cornish theatre throws much light on these cyclical processes of culture, being both part of the process itself, and a finely tuned commentator on that process.

To my knowledge, there have been several individual accounts which have considered particular time periods, or distinctive kinds of drama within Cornwall,[17] but there has been no readily available volume which seeks to pull all the distinctive strands of theatre in and about Cornwall together 'under one roof'. This means connecting early ritual and lost Cornish dramas to nineteenth-century English-language dramas in Cornwall; linking contemporary theatre on the protected Mining World Heritage Sites of Cornwall with fashionable Georgian drama in Penzance. It is a fine line to tread, but it is one that is important to walk if we are to continue to reassess and value Cornwall's cultural heritage. To clarify: we are treading on new boards here. In this author's view, although there had been considerable study of the Cornish-language theatrical texts of the medieval and Tudor periods, both in books and articles,[18] there has actually been very little study of 'theatre' itself through the centuries.[19] One could argue that there has been even less study of early modern, modern and contemporary drama, which have an equally important claim to academic treatment.

Some texts do come to mind, however, which have made considerable contributions to the field of theatre studies in Cornwall in the modern era. The first is a series of writings by the author Denys Val Baker (1917-84), who initially edited two series of the influential 'culture' periodical *Cornish Review*, and wrote *The Timeless Land: The Creative Spirit in Cornwall* (1973) and *The Spirit of Cornwall* (1984).[20] Both volumes contain chapters devoted to drama, in which Val Baker makes links between the medieval texts, spaces such as Perran Round amphitheatre at Perranporth, the Minack Theatre at Porthcurno, and festival and carnival culture in Cornwall, in many ways echoing the writings on comedy and festival of the Russian-born Shakespearean scholar Mikhail Bakhtin (1895-1975).[21] For example, one chapter in *The Timeless Land* has a notable section on Cornish opera, while *The Spirit of Cornwall* considers significant writers such as J.C. Trewin (himself a respected drama critic) and the playwrights Ronald Duncan and Donald R. Rawe. The second important contribution from the late twentieth century is a volume titled *Playbill: A History of the Theatre in the West Country* (1980) by Harvey Crane.[22] Crane's work contains some limited study of the Cornish-language dramas of the medieval and Tudor periods, but his real focus is on analysing work in the English urban centres of Plymouth and Exeter during the eighteenth, nineteenth and twentieth centuries. Occasionally, however, Crane does consider the indigenous drama of the 'West Country' [sic] – with some Cornish examples – but for the most part he tends to concentrate on touring shows, particularly when the great performers of each period performed at venues west of Bristol. Despite failing to recognise Cornish culture as different from the rest of the west of Britain, Crane's contribution is important since it does attempt to explore spaces and places, as well as to prompt an awareness of 'regional' difference within the context of England. His work remains the first real study of 'theatre in Western Britain'.

In terms of Cornish-language drama, the most important contributions of the past few years have been made by two scholars: Brian Murdoch and Sydney Higgins. Murdoch, Professor Emeritus of German at the University of Stirling, became interested in Cornish-language drama through his specialisation in medieval religious writings. Murdoch has published and commented on most of the major texts, and his 1993 work *Cornish Literature* and 'The Cornish Medieval Drama' (1994) remain the benchmarks to which all other studies must aspire.[23] *Cornish Literature*, in particular, takes a critical path through the central texts of the canon, which acknowledges their importance within European literature, but also places them within their local spatial context. Although Murdoch was writing before the discovery in 2000 of the 'lost' *Bewnans Ke* [*The Life of St Kea*] play, many of his theorisations and arguments are applicable to this text as well. Like Murdoch, Sydney Higgins made most of his theoretical interpretations of the Cornish-language canon before the discovery of *Bewnans Ke*. Higgins worked on the 1969 revival of the Cornish *Ordinalia*, with director Neville Denny, before lecturing on theatre studies at the University of Camerino, Italy. There, Higgins has not only co-ordinated European Medieval Drama conferences, but also written the important volume *Medieval Theatre in the Round* (1994)[24], which concentrates on the place and space of the Cornish plays, and the staging of *Bewnans Meriasek* in particular. Higgins's studies have transformed understanding of not only the staging of such texts, but also audience movement, and issues of promenade theatre and physicality of the performances. No study of the theatre of Cornwall can ignore the above scholars and texts in locating and defining the field. However, one significant volume has yet to be mentioned. This is one of a series of volumes contributing to the *Records of Early English* [sic] *Drama* (REED) series, co-ordinated by Alexandra F. Johnston at the

University of Toronto. The Cornwall edition (in the same volume as Dorset) contains a wealth of theatrical material, including records of performances, costings, costuming, staging and commentaries about early, medieval and Renaissance drama.[25] This volume, edited by Sally L. Joyce and Evelyn S. Newlyn, was the culmination of ten years of research, and it remains highly significant in terms of its comprehensiveness and eye for detail on all aspects of early theatre. Last, but by no means least, is the considerable contribution to the study of medieval theatre in Cornwall by Jane A. Bakere, especially in her work *The Cornish Ordinalia: A Critical Study* (1980).[26] In many ways, Bakere's volume set the course for the study of this period and culture, and in terms of depth and discussion on this cycle it is hard to surpass.

Theatrical research has also been published in the University of Exeter's Journal of the Institute of Cornish Studies, currently edited by Professor Philip Payton. Significantly, Payton has embraced new scholarship on Cornish theatre and literature.[27] On some level though, my book is still a reaction to the dominant and often unmoveable subject matter of Cornish Studies in general. Throughout the late twentieth century, particularly during the 1970s and 1980s, the initial focus of Cornish Studies tended to be on the Cornish language, sociolinguistics, archaeology and parish histories,[28] with the occasional article on theatre texts.[29] Outside of the Journal of the Institute of Cornish Studies, considerable academic energy was expended on documenting the industrial revolution in Cornwall, with a focus on technology, the economy and working conditions.[30] Folklore, literature and theatre were very much lower order concerns, and usually added for incidental detail rather than actual study.[31] It is important to see this as a developmental phase, and perhaps in line with other trends in the field of Celtic Studies and studies of other areas where industrialisation developed and then declined. More recently, under Payton's editorship, this energy has turned towards economic history, emigration and the Cornish Revival, but it is still only relatively recently that considerable strides in literature, theatre and cultural studies in general have been made. Thanks to a number of authors, the monolith of Cornish Studies is beginning to change, and more scholars are beginning to tackle other aspects of Cornish culture,[32] aside from what had broadly been an 'economic' base of the scholarship, and in particular the rise and fall of copper and tin mining.[33]

Within the wider field of Celtic Studies, Cornwall finds itself in a kind of 'double jeopardy'. Notwithstanding the fact that the territory is always considered of minority interest compared to the nation-states (and definers of modern Celticity) of Ireland, Scotland and Wales,[34] Cornwall's premier literary form – drama – is considered by mainstream Celticists to be at the bottom of the pile in terms of literary credibility. In this we have a division between what is considered 'high' art and what is 'low', but also a league table of Celticity judged by that territory's capacity for producing mythological and heroic literature. Interestingly, it seems that texts such as the Ossian cycle, *The Mabinogion*, and the exploits of Chuchulinn were early accorded a superior place in the hierarchy over the Brythonic narratives of King Arthur, Tristan and Yseult, and saints' lives. Even the most important scholars of Celtic Cornwall and Cornish – such as Nicholas Roscarrock, Edward Lhuyd, John Keigwin and Nicholas Boson – were conveniently left out of pan-Celtic collections, which often included writers of similar status in other territories. There may even be a sense that Goidelic Celtic culture assumes superiority over Brythonic Celtic culture. Magnus Maclean, a Professor of Celtic Studies at the University of Glasgow, encapsulates much of this wider feeling about Cornish literature and drama in his volume *The Literature of the Celts* (1902). He was highly dismissive of Cornish literature, principally, it seems, because so much of its content was dramatic:

> As for Cornwall, whose dialect is now extinct, she never produced much of a Celtic literature. What there is still extant is preserved in MSS. of the fifteenth century, representing possibly all the ancient literature she ever had, and dates from that or the preceding century. These pieces consist of one poem, entitled "Mount Calvary," and three dramas or miracle plays with nothing distinctly Celtic about them save the language. With the exception of these and another drama of the seventeenth century (1611), and the Lord's Prayer translated, the obsolete and defunct Cornish dialect has no literature to show, and therefore is not concerned with the special Celtic revivals characteristic of the literature in the other dialects.[35]

Maclean refuses even to recognise the existence of *Bewnans Meriasek* within his list (the three mentioned are presumably the three surviving plays of *Ordinalia*[36]), and remains ignorant of the rest of the literature in existence. Nevertheless, his focus for the rest of *The Literature of the Celts* remains resolutely on literary forms that were not dramatic. Within 'traditional' Celtic Studies, it is high epic narrative and poetry that have always been of paramount interest. Celtic drama does not have Celtic clout. Penguin's list of Celtic Studies features predominantly Irish, Welsh and Scottish material; Kenneth Hurlstone Jackson's *A Celtic Miscellany* has many Goidelic and Welsh sources, and yet only three Cornish texts – Edwin Chirgwin's version of 'Where Are You Going To, My Pretty Maid?', Cain and Abel from *The Creacion of the World*, and a section from *Bewnans Meriasek*.[37] In mainstream Celtic Studies, Cornish material is largely ignored.[38] This is a trend which began in the nineteenth century (perhaps because the prime movers in the Celtic Revival were all from Ireland, Wales and Scotland), and which has continued in contemporary scholarship, in which Cornwall and Cornish texts have, for the most part, been sidelined. Drama, perhaps because it is considered an inferior, more populist literary form, finds itself relegated to a lower position in the order. Seemingly, drama was too flexible, too piecemeal, too nebulous, and simply not heroic enough for Celticists seeking role-models and figures of resistance against a colonising English power.[39] This was all despite the fact that the stories being told by the Cornish texts were biblical and universal; or, if not that, then related to the mythological and magical events of saints' lives. We can now also consider these Cornish texts as ones which, in very sophisticated and clever ways, came to actively resist the English colonial project as an integral part of their performance. This position suited the larger Celtic territories because Celticists in powerful university institutions (both inside and outside of Celtic territories) had already decided the pecking order of Celticity, and the smaller territories of Cornwall and the Isle of Man (and, to an extent, Brittany, which was inaccessible and linguistically restrictive because most translations had been made into French and not English) were easily parked at the bottom. It was merely convenient for this view of the hierarchy that Cornwall's main literary form was drama, regardless of the fact that Cornwall's theatrical culture was highly advanced. The fact that Cornwall's historical status was confused – somewhere, as Deacon has argued, between Celtic nation and 'English' county[40] – added to the positioning. Cornwall, as I have elsewhere described, has 'an unresolved duality of place'.[41] Cornwall's alleged inferiority, in terms of its true 'Celticity' – apparently dead language, early destroyed independence, Celtic invention, Anglicisation, lack of separate church – matched its lower ranking in the field of literature.

However, there was not just a covert project to keep Cornish literature down; the problem was compounded by ignorance about what was available. This is partly due to the perceived subject matter of Celtic Studies. Because the major institutions of Celtic Studies have traditionally been located outside of Cornwall, Cornish Studies are usually presented as an adjunct or of minority interest when compared to the larger territories. In America, where many Celtic Studies courses are available, Cornwall is perceived as too distant, too small, and again of minority interest when compared to Ireland, Wales or Scotland. Cornwall must also accept some of the blame. It is only within the twenty-first century that Combined Universities in Cornwall has come into existence, and it still has a very small Celtic and Cornish Studies component.[42] There is, however, some hope that new impetus to the development of theatre arts within Cornwall will follow the relocation of Dartington College of Arts to the University College Falmouth campus at Falmouth/Penryn in April 2008.[43] Again, it has been relatively recently that many Cornish texts have been available in a format worthy of study in such institutions.[44] If we are honest, we must admit that the Cornish Revival as a whole, both pre-war and post-war, did a poor job of anthologising and circulating Cornish texts while Celtic Studies developed in the late nineteenth and twentieth centuries.[45] Happily, this situation is starting to change. As more writers and scholars from Cornwall have demanded a place within the field of Celtic Studies, there has been a concurrent rise in interest from the Celtic Studies community. Cornwall, it seems, is worth considering after all, in a world which has little new to say about Irish or Welsh texts. Its unresolved status – between Celtic nation and English county – apparently makes issues of Cornwall's identity, devolution, language, and theatricality all the more interesting. From a Celtic cultural-nationalist position, Cornwall's place makes the struggle for recognition twice as difficult. The other Celtic territories were at least operating from a position of some inherent 'nation-state-dom', or devolution. All of this concern with Celticity may seem irrelevant to some readers. After all, the bulk of the theatre we shall be looking at will in all likelihood be in English anyway. However, to use Hildegard L.C. Tristram's term, it is possibly the very importance of the 'Celtic-English'[46] connection in Cornwall that will come to define and best illustrate its theatrical experience and 'difference'.

Interestingly, there is comparatively little material documenting the history of drama in the other Celtic territories. This may reflect the nature of study in those fields. The Isle of Man appears to lack a dramatic tradition: Manx literature is given even shorter coverage than Cornish in Maclean's volume, and even contemporary indigenous scholarship appears to have little to say about the theatrical tradition there.[47] Although Brittany is comparable to Cornwall in very many ways, aside from the writings of Gwenolé Le Men and Yann Boussell du Bourg,[48] study of its theatrical culture beyond the 'mystery plays' seems very much in its infancy. Brittany's literature is now being disseminated in better ways, particularly amongst English-speaking territories,[49] but while knowledge of its folklore is relatively easy to access, the dramatic texts remain more obscure. Wales has a reasonably significant continuum of drama but, again, study of its texts – at least up until writers of the twentieth century – has been piecemeal. Dafydd Johnston has made some progress in disseminating a Welsh and Anglo-Welsh literature that now has drama at its core,[50] while Dedwydd Jones has reassessed the career of Twm O'r Nant,[51] broadly regarded as the father of drama in Welsh. Anwen Jones has also made significant study of the drama in Wales, relating it to a sense of shared, yet problematical, national consciousness.[52] Scotland, as we might expect, is better served than Wales, particularly by studies of playwrights in English.[53] It is less well-served by studies of those dramatists writing in Scots or Gaelic.

The exception to all of the above is Ireland (both in Éire and Northern Ireland), whose status in theatrical history is guaranteed by a number of significant dramatists operating both in and outside of Ireland during the twentieth century. Figures such as Bernard Shaw, W.B. Yeats, J.M. Synge, Sean O'Casey, Samuel Beckett, Brendan Behan and Brian Friel (writing mainly in English), as well as a number of texts in Irish, have helped to shape an Irish theatre, embodied in institutions such as the Abbey and Peacock Theatres, and now seen in historical context by a number of observers.[54] These have, in turn, prompted further studies of the historical development of theatre in Ireland, and have culminated in more radical interpretations than on offer elsewhere, many of which have looked at the country's complex political and religious identity.[55] Ireland does not, however, match Cornwall, in terms of its early, medieval and early modern theatrical culture. Its dramatic figures may be known on the world stage but, as this study will go on to show, writers such as W.B. Yeats and J.M. Synge have equivalents in Cornwall. Though the Cornish examples may not be as well known globally, they do help explain similar cultural developments of communities resisting English colonisation.

These Celtic examples are all interesting because they show other comparative examples of post-colonial literary and theatrical theory.[56] In the text you are now reading, the colonised is writing back at the coloniser and demanding an alternative reading of cultural experience. Both in terms of theory (texts such as this) and practice (contemporary Cornish drama), Cornwall is using post-colonial studies to assert its position over a domineering English presence not only in terms of historical experience, but also in contemporary theatre, art, culture, publishing, media and new technologies. According to a recent study by Leoussi and Grosby, it is these areas that are most important to assert when creating what they term 'ethnosymbolism' for the 'formation of nations'.[57] Post-colonial studies are also allied to nationalism, in the sense that 'conquered' territories of the past usually go on to reassert their own distinctive identities, which have somehow been buried by the 'conqueror'.[58] We should be looking to the theatre of Cornwall to examine both the moments where that colonisation took place and where it has been resisted, and how it might be overturned and reconsidered. The future must also be considered, for it is here where the new theatre of Cornwall will stake its claim in the process of resistance. Post-colonial studies have particular relevance to Cornwall, which has historically been one of the earliest of the Celtic territories to be 'accommodated' and integrated into what Bradshaw and Morrill have usefully termed the 'British state'.[59] Arguably, it is

Fig. 1. Celticity and Continuum in a Skinner's Brewery Poster advertising the 'Full Cycle' of *Ordinalia*, at St Just-in-Penwith, 2004. Courtesy of Skinner's Brewery, Truro.

this early accommodation which has given Cornwall its unresolved duality of place.

Performance studies have been enormously influential in my thinking on the theatre of Cornwall over several years. As we shall see, because of the unique cultural development of theatre in Cornwall, two critical works have been significant. These are Sandy Craig's *Dreams and Deconstructions: Alternative Theatre in Britain* (1980) and Baz Kershaw's *The Politics of Performance: Radical Theatre as Cultural Intervention* (1992).[60] Although published almost thirty years ago, Craig's book defines an alternative imagining of theatre space in Britain, which draws on open-air, amphitheatre style performance and reinterprets that tradition for a contemporary audience, using new spaces and places previously not used for performance. The volume has obvious relevance to anyone who knows how theatre in Cornwall currently operates, since small-scale, touring ensemble companies like Kneehigh, Miracle, Grinning Gargoyle, and BishBashBosh Productions provide a direct link back to the parish-based community performances of the medieval and early modern periods. Kershaw's book is equally important in that it offers an analysis of the social and political purposes of performance – for example, the inherent and clever digs made in Cornish at the English nation-state in the Tudor drama of Cornwall[61] – drawing on theories of ideological transaction (for example, the *Imagineers* project of

2008,[62] which sought to theatrically light the chimneys of the abandoned mine-stacks of the Great Flat Lode in order to promote ideological connection with the past), and highlighting cultural intervention and community action (for example in *The Cledry Plays* of Robert Morton Nance[63]), all of which are part of the continuum of drama in Cornwall. As we shall see, the political dimension of drama in Cornwall has always been significant, and continues to be so in the present. Both of these books provide a framework for the analysis here, since they are highly applicable to the kind of theatrical development seen. Although coming from a very different end of theatrical criticism, Michael Billington's *State of the Nation: British Theatre Since 1945* (2007) is also a significant text, since it looks at post-war Britain from a theatrical perspective.[64] Billington is not a theorist in the same sense as Craig or Kershaw; his credentials derive from his role as weekly theatre critic for *The Guardian* newspaper since 1971. Though Billington rarely draws on Cornwall, or even other peripheral territories of these islands (the text focuses almost exclusively on London, and more specifically the West End), he does examine the constant interplay between theatre and society from the resurgent optimism of the Attlee years, through the 1960s and 1970s and Thatcherism, to new growth in political theatre under Tony Blair and Gordon Brown in the post-9/11 period. This wider context is important to hold in mind, particularly in the later chapters of this volume, because although our focus is a Cornish one, we should not always restrict our perspective on theatre in Cornwall to the area west of the River Tamar.

In order to tell the story of theatre in Cornwall, it has been necessary to order and divide up my material. As in any historical study of this kind, dates and divisions allow us to keep a handle on the progression of time, though it should be remembered that many activities cross between the periods of time specified, and in that sense they should be regarded as artificial, albeit useful, boundaries. Whilst trying to outline the core developments of the theatre of Cornwall, I have, so far as I was able, given within each chapter a sense of several areas of study, including the history of particular theatres, how the theatre worked for audiences, the life and work of actors, behind the scenes, management, and the authors' works and plays. Holding all these in balance is a tricky juggling act, but I hope I offer enough to give some flavour of the past. Inevitably, we shall never quite know what it was actually like to sit and watch a performance of a play in Cornwall in 1504, or 1750, or 1928. All we can do is try to reconstruct as accurate a picture as possible. Additionally, there is the interaction of the terms 'theatre' and 'drama'. This book's title uses the former, though it might well have been the latter. In many ways, the two terms are interchangeable, and I hope the reader will see them as such. These days, theatrical histories tend to deal with the physical surroundings and buildings,

the parishes of Cornwall was simply not sophisticated enough to develop advanced theatrical culture, and suggests that there surely must have been borrowing, integrations and conversions from elsewhere in Europe – even from England itself. Even though this argument has been successfully countered by scholars such as James Whetter, and D.H. Frost,[78] it is one that still lurks beneath the surface of some scholarship. Any picture of Cornish culture that believes it cannot operate in an 'indigenous' state needs radically rethinking; yet we must also reassert Cornwall's 'internationalism'. There were no doubt influences from elsewhere in Europe (Brittany especially), and from England (for example, it could be argued that mystery play culture arrived in Exeter when the Cornish were there, and that they transported it back over the Tamar after Athelstan expelled them), but we must offset these against Cornwall operating with a remarkable sense of itself, and of itself as an 'international' player. Indeed, there may be a case not only for presenting Cornwall as one of the first western societies to undergo the industrial revolution, and therefore also to undergo industrial collapse, but also for beginning to see Cornwall as one of the hubs of European theatre operating whilst this economic process was taking place. It is a paradigm that I shall be testing during this volume, and which comes full circle in terms of how worldwide theatre operates today. Theatre in landscape, on a grand scale, in new locations, in communities, and in societies that are having to come to terms with either industrialisation or de-industrialisation – all of these have been tried and tested in Cornwall, not just between the post-war period and now, but over many centuries. We may go one stage further: perhaps in Cornwall, and the continuum of Cornwall's past theatre, we find the roots of much contemporary theatrical good practice.[79]

Although this volume intends to cover a wide range of theatrical activity related to Cornwall, it can in no way claim to be comprehensive. I am fully aware of its shortcomings. I could not, for example, explore detailed histories of all the amateur dramatic groups in the territory. Although some significant ones are touched upon here, there was simply not the space to cover them all. Perhaps this volume will prompt further study and enquiry. Likewise there have been a number of successful Cornish performers whom I could not possibly cover in depth. Those who expected further discussion of all the Christian symbolism of the mystery and saints' plays of Cornwall will be somewhat disappointed; that is another book for another time. A feminist reading of the cultural politics of Cornish theatre is very much needed, and although some of the issues are considered here, a full history of that field will be the concern of another scholar. Happily, some of the suggestions for enquiry made in my earlier works have been taken up by a number of researchers and writers, so my hope is that this will occur again.

This Introduction establishes the Celticity of theatre emerging from Cornwall, but locates that Celticity in a wider crisis of Celtic literature, of which Cornwall never quite seemed to be a part. In identifying this crisis, we are also able to make some elementary observations on the whole continuum of theatre in and about Cornwall. Chapter One builds upon this paradigm, noting that for many readers, observers and audiences, Cornwall is a particularly difficult 'Celtic drama queen' though she has a personality utterly rooted in ritual, landscape and community. It is here that I have attempted to document the origins of theatrical activity in Cornwall, relating them to icons, events and festivals, some well-known and also some that are more obscure or have been lost over time. Both proto- and para-theatrical activity are examined as precursors and links to theatrical practice, read in the context of the ritual year. Early texts, writers and practitioners also form part of the scope of this chapter, which comes to an end in the year 1200. Any reader of a book on the theatre of Cornwall would perhaps expect to see a section devoted to the drama of medieval and Tudor Cornwall, and this is precisely what Chapter Two offers. Read within a material context of playing places, rebellion and reformation, not only are the major works of Cornish-language dramatic literature considered, but so are a number of lost or 'shadowy' texts re-evaluated. The proliferation of theatrical culture in Cornwall during this phase is explored, as are some of the writers, and possible writers, of texts.

Given the collapse of Cornish culture in the Renaissance, it is the end of the stage of the Troyance tongue (Cornish) between 1600 and 1800 that is examined in Chapter Three, and yet this was also, paradoxically, a phase in which writers outside of Cornwall became fascinated with the concept of Cornish identity. As Cornish identity began to be recast within the context of the Civil War, the Restoration and the reforming processes of the eighteenth century, attention is also given to the texts, playwrights and theatres that emerged. I offer a vigorous reassessment of the presentation of Cornishness during this Age, which is usually seen as a difficult phase for Cornish identity. Much of the material in this section has not been fully considered by Cornish scholarship over the years. The cultural construction of Cornwall in places such as 'Mevagezy' shows a new relationship between London and the land of the West Britons. A number of texts and playwrights here show a profound understanding of the Cornish experience in the light of widespread linguistic, social, religious and political change.

In the opening half of the nineteenth century, reforming events of the period 1600-1800, coupled with the industrialisation of Cornwall, shaped a new kind of industrial drama for Cornwall. Chapter Four outlines the development of English-language drama about Cornwall in plays such as *The*

Fig. 2 A close up of the dragon, during a performance of Hal-an-Tow, in Helston, c.2000. Courtesy of Paul Watts Photography.

Great Hewas Mine and *John Bull*, and how the period between 1800 and 1850 also witnessed the great age of actor-managers such as James Dawson and Samuel Fisher, men at the front end of performance in Cornwall. The vast diversity of theatrical experience on offer both in Cornwall and elsewhere is considered.

While a number of touring shows were shaping popular taste in Cornwall, some texts kept an eye on events at home. Chapter Five examines how the second half of the nineteenth century saw Cornish subject-matter suddenly become fashionable on the wider British and European stage – ironically when a number of scholars of a Celtic twilight began to gather the fragments of the broken and seemingly unfixable 'medieval' drama. As emigration overseas simultaneously became a defining construct of the Cornish imagination, I analyse theatres, performers and texts from the culture of 'Cousin Jacks and Jennies'. Suddenly Cornwall was upon the world stage.

Developed in the context of two world wars, and massive industrial decline, the dramaturgy of the period 1900-1950 is examined in Chapter Six, with the focus being a Cornwall uncertain of its future development. Culturally, allegiances seem to be torn between a modernising, English-fixated culture of mass media, tourism and in-migration, and a small but significant group of writers, performers and scholars interested in using drama as a mechanism for cultural revival and political nationalism. The significance of theatre space such as the iconic Minack Theatre is considered, as well as the impact of dramatists such as Robert Morton Nance, Bernard Walke, Peggy Pollard, and Charles Causley. All that was wrong about the post-war cultural construction of Cornwall is considered by many of the dramatists who emerged in the late twentieth century. These dramatists, who were often politically nationalist, wanted a revised set of performance conditions in order to progress Cornish drama. On occasions, they were drawing on prior methods of performance for their inspiration, but there were also other groups looking back at festival, community and ritual for cultural reinvention. This is considered in Chapter Seven, along with the study of emergent voices in the Cornish theatrical continuum. Here, a concept of 'performing devolution' is offered. In the new devolved United Kingdom, Cornwall has not yet, despite protest and claim, achieved the kind of devolved power that has been accorded to Wales and Scotland and Northern Ireland. In this sense then, the cultural reinvention and new theatre of the past fifty years has, as yet, managed only to 'perform' that imagining. However, in terms of its ongoing quest for devolution, surely it is theatre that is asking the right kind of questions to create a new sense of belonging?

The Conclusion takes up a number of concepts from these chapters and reads them in context of several theatrical events occurring in twenty-first century Cornwall. It proposes that despite the changes and developments within the continuum, a pervasive sense of community, landscape and ritual persists in the readings and performances in Cornwall's theatrical spaces and places. Not only this, however. Given Cornwall's lead in all kinds of theatrical work through the centuries, it is perhaps not surprising to see the territory embrace all kinds of environmental and green theatre as part of contemporary ecocriticism. The theatrical history has therefore come full circle, as we witness new *plen-an-gwarries* being constructed from recycled car tyres. This should prove that Cornwall continues to be one of the most complex theatrical cultures in Western Europe, and it is *the* 'Celtic' theatrical territory.

In this volume, two strands are continually prevalent. The first is the connections across time and space between all kinds of theatrical activity in Cornwall: no sooner does a particular genre appear to wither away, than it comes back in a reconstructed form in a new period. Secondly, the concepts of space, place and performance repeatedly emerge in each of the phases explored. These are the central tenets of my argument. Inevitably, this book will be read in the light of my earlier publication, *The Literature of Cornwall: Continuity, Identity, Difference 1000-2000.* That book gave an analysis and historical overview of all forms of writing to emerge from Cornwall in a given time period. Within its remit, I could not examine theatrical culture in the detail that I wished. The current volume does take up a number of threads and themes explored in the earlier book, and also offers some alternative and new readings. My hope is that this volume will complement the other and expand our knowledge of drama.

From any book titled *The Theatre of Cornwall: Space, Place, Performance*, there will be several expectations. Readers may already have some awareness of the existing medieval and Tudor texts written in Cornish; they may also know something of theatrical events such as the Hal-an-Tow at Helston's Flora Day, Obby Oss at Padstow, or maybe even the spectacularly-located Minack Theatre at Porthcurno. In the past, they might also have attended a performance by the Kneehigh or Miracle theatre companies. The reality, however, is that these are mere snapshots of the theatrical culture of Cornwall over the past thousand years. The real picture of performance has been far more dynamic, far more interesting and far more bizarre, challenging and political than we might ever have imagined. The theatre of Cornwall is a show that has been locked away for a long time, and if I can offer some insight into this, then I will have done my job. Like the very best theatre, this volume will hopefully provoke intense discussion and debate. You, as an audience, are now settled. It is time to dim the lights. Let the play commence.

INTRODUCTION: NOTES AND REFERENCES

1. Whitley Stokes (ed. and tr.), *The Life of Saint Meriasek, Bishop and Confessor: A Cornish Drama*, London: Trübner and Co., 1872, p.126. Translation by the author.

2. Carl Grose and Anna Maria Murphy, 'Tristan and Yseult' in Kneehigh Theatre, *Tristan and Yseult, The Bacchae, The Wooden Frock, The Red Shoes*, London: Oberon Books, 2005, p.28. The text was first performed in 2003.

3. For a range of definitions of Celtic, see Malcolm Chapman, *The Celts: The Construction of a Myth*, Basingstoke: Macmillan, 1992; Simon James, *The Atlantic Celts: Ancient People or Modern Invention?* London: British Museum Press, 1999.

4. For useful histories, see Philip Payton, *Cornwall*, Fowey: Alexander Associates, 1996; Bernard Deacon, *Cornwall: A Concise History*, Cardiff: University of Wales Press, 2007.

5. Consider the arguments asserted in Murray G.H. Pittock, *Celtic Identity and the British Image*, Manchester and New York: Manchester University Press, 1999; David C. Harvey, Rhys Jones, Neil McInroy and Christine Milligan (eds.), *Celtic Geographies: Old Culture, New Times*, London and New York: Routledge, 2002.

6. Michael Hechter, *Internal Colonialism: The Celtic Fringe in British National Development, 1536-1966*, London: Routledge and Kegan Paul, 1975; Arthur Aughey, *Nationalism, Devolution and the Challenge to the United Kingdom State*, London: Pluto Press, 2001.

7. Of particular significance in the Cornish context are the territories to which the Cornish emigrated: North America, South America, Southern Africa and Australasia. The significant mobilisation of the contemporary Cornish overseas should not be underestimated.

8. John Kerrigan, *Archipelagic English: Literature, History and Politics 1603-1702*, Oxford: Oxford University Press, 2008.

9. See Philip Payton, *The Making of Modern Cornwall: Historical Experience and the Persistence of "Difference"*, Redruth: Dyllansow Truran, 1992; Ella Westland (ed.), *Cornwall: The Cultural Construction of Place*, Penzance: The Patten Press and the Institute of Cornish Studies, 1997; Malte W. Tschirschky, *Die Erfindung der keltischen Nation Cornwall: Kultur, Identität und ethnischer Nationalismus in der britischen Peripherie*, Heidelberg: Universitätsverlag Winter, 2006.

10. See John Angarrack, *Breaking the Chains: Censorship, Deception and the Manipulation of Public Opinion in Cornwall*, Camborne: Stannary Publications, 1999. Paradoxically, although Angarrack's writings are highly academic, he has nonetheless captured much popular sentiment within Cornwall. Another volume reflecting popular opinion is Derek Williams (ed.), *A Strange and Unquenchable Race: Cornwall and the Cornish in Quotations*, Mount Hawke: Truran, 2007. See

also Colin Robins and Bernard Deacon, *Merlin's Diner*, Tiverton: Cornwall Books, 1992; Jerry Clarke and Terry Harry (eds.), *Tales from Twickenham*, Redruth: Clarke and Harry, 1991.

11. Alan M. Kent, 'Scatting it t'lerrups: Provisional Notes towards Alternative Methodologies in Language and Literary Studies in Cornwall' in Philip Payton (ed.), *Cornish Studies: Thirteen*, Exeter: University of Exeter Press, 2005, pp.23-52.

12. Alick West, *Crisis and Criticism and Literary Essays*, London: Lawrence and Wishart, 1975; Raymond Williams, *Problems in Materialism and Culture: Selected Essays*, London and New York: Verso, 1980.

13. Jonathan Dollimore and Alan Sinfield (eds.), *Political Shakespeare: New Essays in Cultural Materialism*, Manchester: Manchester University Press, 1985; Scott Wilson, *Cultural Materialism: Theory and Practice*, Oxford: Blackwell, 1995.

14. Dollimore and Sinfield, op.cit., pp.vii-viii.

15. See the arguments in Alan M. Kent, *The Literature of Cornwall: Continuity, Identity, Difference 1000-2000*, Bristol: Redcliffe, 2000; Emma Mitchell, 'The Myth of Objectivity: The Cornish Language and the Eighteenth-Century Antiquarians' in Philip Payton (ed.), *Cornish Studies: Six*, Exeter: University of Exeter Press, 1998, pp.62-80.

16. M. Wynn Thomas, *Corresponding Cultures: The Two Literatures of Wales*, Cardiff: University of Wales Press, 1999.

17. See, for example, F.E. Halliday, *The Legend of the Rood*, London: Gerald Duckworth, 1955; Jane A. Bakere, *The Cornish Ordinalia: A Critical Study*, Cardiff: University of Wales Press, 1980.

18. For an overview of articles up to 1987, see Evelyn S. Newlyn (ed.), *Cornish Drama of the Middle Ages: A Bibliography*, Redruth: Institute of Cornish Studies, 1987; Robert Longsworth, *The Cornish Ordinalia: Religion and Dramaturgy*, Cambridge, Massachusetts: Harvard University Press, 1967; Graham Thomas and Nicholas Williams (eds. and trs.), *Bewnans Ke: The Life of St Kea – A Critical Edition with Translation*, Exeter: University of Exeter Press, 2007.

19. A notable exception is Bakere, op.cit.

20. See Denys Val Baker, *The Timeless Land: The Creative Spirit in Cornwall*, Bath: Adams and Dart, 1973, pp.53-64; *The Spirit of Cornwall*, London: W.H. Allen, 1980, p.87-105. Both of these chapters are very similar, with minor alterations. In the 1980 book, Val Baker confuses *Bewnans Meriasek* with the *Ordinalia*. Drama is given less prominence in the third of this series: *A View from Land's End: Writers against a Cornish Background*, London: William Kimber, 1982.

21. For a useful summary of Bahktin, see Michael Holguist, *Dialogism: Bahktin and His World*, London and New York: Routledge, 2002.

22. Harvey Crane, *Playbill: A History of the Theatre in the West Country*, Plymouth: Macdonald and Evans, 1980.

23. Brian Murdoch, *Cornish Literature*, Cambridge: D.S. Brewer, 1993, and 'The Cornish Medieval Drama' in Richard Beadle (ed.), *The Cambridge Companion to Medieval English Theatre*, Cambridge: Cambridge University Press, 1994, pp. 211-39.

24. Sydney Higgins, *Medieval Theatre in the Round: The Mutiple Staging of Religious Drama in England*, Camerino, Italy: Laboratorio degli studi Linguistici, 1995. See also (ed.), *European Medieval Drama 1996: Papers for the First International Conference on Aspects of European Medieval Drama*, Camerino: Universita Degli Studi Di Camerino - Centro Linguitico di Ateneo, 1996, and (ed.), *European Medieval Drama 1997: Papers for the Second International Conference on Aspects of European Medieval Drama*, Camerino: Universita Degli Studi Di Camerino – Centro Linguitico di Ateneo, 1997.

25. Rosalind Conklin Hays and C.E. McGee (Dorset), and Sally L. Joyce, and Evelyn S. Newlyn (Cornwall) (eds.), *Records of Early English Drama: Dorset / Cornwall*, Toronto: University of Toronto and Brepols, 1999. Most 'English' territories are now covered by this series.

26. Bakere, op.cit.

27. See, for example, Philip Payton, "a... concealed envy against the English': a Note on the Aftermath of the 1497 Rebellions in Cornwall' in Philip Payton (ed.), *Cornish Studies: One*, Exeter: University of Exeter Press, 1993, pp. 4-13; Jim Hall, 'Maximilla, the Cornish Montanist: The Final Scenes of Origo Mundi' in Philip Payton, (ed.) *Cornish Studies: Seven*, Exeter: University of Exeter Press, 1999, pp. 165-92; Paul Manning, 'Staging the State and the Hypostasization of Violence in the Medieval Cornish Drama' in Philip Payton (ed.), op.cit., 2005, pp.126-69.

28. Charles Thomas (ed.), *Cornish Studies / Studhyansow Kernewk* 1-15, Redruth: Institute of Cornish Studies, 1973-1987.

29. For example, see Andrew Hawke, 'A Lost Manuscript of the Cornish *Ordinalia*?' in Charles Thomas (ed.), *Cornish Studies / Studhyansow Kernewk* 7, Redruth: Institute of Cornish Studies 1979, pp.45-60.

30. This scholarship was embodied in particular in the publishing house of D. Bradford Barton Ltd of Truro.

31. A good example of this is Arthur Cecil Todd, *The Cornish Miner in America*, Spokane, Washington, 1995 [1967].

32. Representative examples of this change are Patrick Laviolette, 'Cornwall's Visual Cultures in Perspective' in Philip Payton (ed.), *Cornish Studies: Eleven*, Exeter: University of Exeter Press, 2003, pp.142-67; Jonathan Howlett, 'Putting the Kitsch into Kernow' in Philip Payton (ed.), *Cornish Studies: Twelve*, Exeter: University of Exeter Press, 2004, pp.30-60.

33. This is what I have termed elsewhere '56 Inch Cylinder Syndrome'. See Alan M. Kent, *Cousin Jack's Mouth-Organ: Travels in Cornish America*, St Austell: Cornish Hillside Publications, 2004, p.1.

34. See, for example, Magnus Maclean, *The Literature of the Celts*, London: Blackie and Son, 1908; J. E. Caerwyn Williams (ed.), *Literature in Celtic Countries*, Cardiff: University of Wales Press, 1971. The trend continues in more recent scholarship. For example, Helen Fulton (ed.), *Medieval Celtic Literature and Society*, Dublin: Four Courts Press, 2005, contains one essay on a Cornish text.

35. Maclean, op.cit., 1902, pp. 248-49. Maclean was not aware of *The Tregear Homilies* or *Bewnans Ke* since these were not discovered until 1949 and 2000 respectively. The 1611 text referred to is *The Creacion [sic] of the World*, written or transcribed by William Jordan. In 1902, the University of Glasgow was still known as the Technical College, Glasgow.

36. There is now considerable academic support for *Ordinalia* to have contained a childhood or nativity section after *Origo Mundi*. See Ken George, *Flogholeth Krist / The Cornish Ordinalia – the missing play: The Childhood of Christ*, Cornwall: Kesva an Taves Kernewek, 2006; Alan M. Kent, *Nativitas Christi / The Nativity: A New Cornish Mystery Play*, London: Francis Boutle Publishers, 2006.

37. See for example, Jeffrey Gantz (ed. and tr.), *The Mabinogion*, Harmondsworth: Penguin, 1976, and (ed. and tr.), *Early Irish Myths and Sagas*, London: Penguin, 1981; Kenneth Hurlstone Jackson (ed. and tr.), *A Celtic Miscellany: Translations from the Celtic Literatures*, Harmondsworth: Penguin, 1971, pp.221-2 and pp.300-304. A possible exception is Lewis Thorpe (ed. and tr.), *Geoffrey of Monmouth: The History of the Kings of Britain*, Harmondsworth: Penguin 1966. This does contain substantial Cornish material.

38. The following popular texts have a clear absence of Cornish material: Miranda Green, *Dictionary of Celtic Myth and Legend*, London: Thames and Hudson, 1992; John T. Koch, and John Carey (eds. and trs.), *The Celtic Heroic Age: Literary Sources for Ancient Celtic Europe and Early Wales and Ireland*, Malden, Massachusetts: Celtic Studies Publications, 1995; James MacKillop, *Dictionary of Celtic Mythology*, Oxford: Oxford University Press, 1998. Some changes have occurred however. The following publication contains detailed material on Cornish literature and drama: John T. Koch, (ed.), *Celtic Culture: A Historical Encylopedia*, Vols. 1-5, Santa Barbara, California and Oxford: ABC Clio, 2006. Successive scholars have also pushed for Cornish texts to be discussed at the forum of the annual conference of the Celtic Studies Association of North America. *Ordinalia's* 'Passion' was discussed for the first time in New York in 1999.

39. Ironically, of course, this is what W.B. Yeats (one of the prime movers of the Celtic Revival in Ireland) chose to confront English colonialism. See Richard

Allen Cave (ed.), *W.B. Yeats: Selected Plays*, London: Penguin 1997. For further background, see Robert Welch (ed.), *W.B. Yeats: Writings on Irish Folklore, Legend and Myth*, London: Penguin 1993.

40. Deacon, op.cit., pp. 1-3.

41. Kent in Payton (ed.), op.cit., 2005, pp.212-39.

42. See George Hoare and Alan Stanhope, *Towards a University in Cornwall*, Camborne: Cornwall College, 1998; Combined Universities in Cornwall, *Higher Education Opportunities in Cornwall: Full and Part-time Courses 2003-2004*, Penryn: Combined Universities in Cornwall, 2003.

43. For discussion of the merger see http://www.falmouth.ac.uk/138/the-college-8/dartingtons-merger-with-ucf-206.html

44. Examples include Alan M. Kent and Tim Saunders (eds. and trs.), *Looking at the Mermaid: A Reader in Cornish Literature 900-1900*, London: Francis Boutle Publishers, 2000; Tim Saunders (ed. and tr.), *The Wheel: An Anthology of Modern Poetry in Cornish 1850-1980*, London: Francis Boutle Publishers, 1999, and (ed. and tr.) *Nothing Broken: Recent Poetry in Cornish*, London: Francis Boutle Publishers, 2006; Thomas and Williams, op.cit., 2007.

45. Some of the problems of this are explored in Peter Berresford Ellis, *The Cornish Language and its Literature*, London and Boston: Routledge and Kegan Paul, 1974, pp.147-212. See also Kent, op.cit., 2000, pp.265-6.

46. See Hildegard L.C. Tristram (ed.), *The Celtic Englishes*, Heidelberg: Universitätsverlag Winter, 1997, and (ed.), *The Celtic Englishes IV: The Interface between English and the Celtic Languages*, Potsdam: Potsdam University Press, 2006.

47. Peter Davey and David Finlayson (eds.), *Mannin Revisited: Twelve Essays on Manx Culture and Environment*, Edinburgh: Scottish Society for Northern Studies, 2002.

48. Gwenolé Le Men, 'Celtic Drama: Breton Popular Theatre' in *The Celtic Pen*, Vol. 1, No. 1, 1993; Yann Boussell du Bourg, 'Breton Mystery Theatre: An Enduring Legacy' in *The Celtic Pen*, Vol. 2, No. 10, 1996.

49. See Ch. Le Goffic (ed.), *O.L. Aubert: Celtic Legends of Brittany*, Kerangwenn: Coop Breizh 1999 [1993]; Jacqueline Gibson and Gwyn Griffiths (eds. and trs.), *The Turn of the Ermine: An Anthology of Breton Literature*, London: Francis Boutle Publishers, 2006.

50. Dafydd Johnston, *The Literature of Wales*, Cardiff: University of Wales Press, 1994.

51. Dedwydd Jones, 'The Father of Welsh Drama: Twm O'r Nant' in *The Celtic Pen*, Vol. 2, No. 1, 1994.

52. Anwen Jones, *National Theatres in Context: France, Germany, England and Wales*, Cardiff: University of Wales Press, 2007.

53.   See, for example, Karen Marshalsay, *The Waggle of the Kilt: Popular Theatre and Entertainment in Scotland*, Glasgow: Glasgow University Library Studies, 1992; Alasdair Cameron and Adrienne Scullion (eds.), *Scottish Popular Theatre and Entertainment: Historical and Critical Approaches to Theatre and Film in Scotland*, Glasgow: Glasgow University Library Studies, 1995; John J. McGavin, *Theatricality and Narrative in Medieval and Early Modern Scotland*, Aldershot: Ashgate 2007.

54.   Nicholas Grene, *The Politics of Irish Drama: Plays in Context from Boucicault to Friel*, Cambridge: Cambridge University Press, 1999; Alan J. Fletcher, *Drama, Performance and Polity in Pre-Cromwellian Ireland*, Cork: Cork University Press, 2000; Christopher Morash, *A History of Irish Theatre 1601-2000*, Cambridge: Cambridge University Press, 2002. See also Abbey Theatre / Amharclann na Mainistreach, *Programme Autumn 08-Spring 09*, Dublin: Abbey Theatre / Amharclann na Mainistreach, 2008.

55.   Ó Caiealláin, Gearóid 'Irish Language Theatre: Drama Developments' in *The Celtic Pen*, Vol. 2, No. 1, 1994; Anne F. O'Reilly, *Sacred Play: Soul-Journeys in Contemporary Irish Theatre*, Dublin: Carysfort Press, 2004; Nicholas Grene and Christopher Morash (eds.), *Irish Theatre on Tour*, Dublin: Carysfort Press, 2005; Eugene McNulty, *The Ulster Literary Theatre and the Northern Revival*, Cork: Cork University Press, 2008.

56.   For useful overviews of post-colonial literary theory, see Bill Ashcroft, Gareth Griffiths and Helen Tiffin, *The Empire Writes Back: Theory and Practice in Post-Colonial Literatures*, London: Routledge, 1989; Seamus Deane (ed.), *Terry Eagleton, Fredric Jameson and Edward W. Said: Nationalism, Colonialism and Literature*, Minneapolis and London: University of Minnesota Press, 1990; David Bennett (ed.), *Multicultural States: Rethinking Difference and Identity*, London and New York: Routledge 1998; John Thieme, *Postcolonial Con-texts* [sic]*: Writing Back to the Canon*, London and New York: Continuum, 2001. For a consideration of the effect of devolution on Anglophone literary politics, see Robert Crawford, *Devolving English Literature*, Edinburgh: Edinburgh University Press, 2001. For the Cornish position, see Bernard Deacon, Dick Cole and Garry Tregidga, *Mebyon Kernow and Cornish Nationalism*, Cardiff: Welsh Academic Press, 2003.

57.   Athena S. Leoussi and Steven Grosby (eds.), *Nationalism and Ethnosymbolism: History, Culture and Ethnicity in the Formation of Nations*, Edinburgh: Edinburgh University Press, 2007, p.1-11.

58.   See John Angarrack, *Our Future is History: Identity, Law and the Cornish Question*, Bodmin: Independent Academic Press, 2002, and *Scat t'Larraps: Resist and Survive*, Bodmin: Independent Academic Press, 2008. This latter work is dedicated to the Cornish playwright Nick Darke.

59. Brendan Bradshaw and John Morrill (eds.), *The British Problem c.1534-1707: State Formation in the Atlantic Archipelago*, Basingstoke: Macmillan, 1996.

60. Sandy Craig (ed.), *Dreams and Deconstructions: Alternative Theatre in Britain*, Ambersgate: Amber Lane Press, 1980; Baz Kershaw, *The Politics of Performance: Radical Theatre as Cultural Intervention*, London and New York: Routledge, 1992.

61. See Payton, op.cit., 1993, pp.1-14.

62. *Imagineers* ran between 30 June and 4 July 2008 and promoted itself as 'a celebration of man, machine and land'. See http://www.antonywaller.com/imagineers.html

63. Robert Morton Nance, *The Cledry Plays: Drolls of Old Cornwall for Village Acting and Home Reading*, Penzance: The Federation of Old Cornwall Societies, 1956.

64. Michael Billington, *State of the Nation: British Theatre Since 1945*, London: Faber and Faber, 2007. Billington has regularly reviewed the work of Kneehigh Theatre.

65. See Thorpe, op.cit., For many of the legends and romances drawn on in Cornish drama, see Robert Hunt (ed.), *Popular Romances of the West of England: The Drolls, Traditions, and Superstitions of Old Cornwall (First Series)*, London: John Camden Hotten, 1865, *Popular Romances of the West of England: The Drolls, Traditions, and Superstitions of Old Cornwall (Second Series)*, London: John Camden Hotten, 1865.

66. Val Baker, 1980, op.cit., p.87.

67. Janet Wolff, *The Social Production of Art*, Basingstoke: Macmillan, 1992 [1981].

68. Ibid., p.1.

69. Ibid.

70. See Roger Penhallurick, *Tin in Antiquity*, London: Institute of Metals, 1986.

71. These views are found in most Anglo-centric histories. For a mid twentieth-century example, see G.M. Trevelyan, *A Shortened History of England*, Harmondsworth: Penguin, 1965 [1942]. Good contemporary examples of Anglo-centric scholarship are Marjorie Filbee, *Celtic Cornwall*, London: Constable, 1996, and also, to an extent, Richard Weight, *Patriots: National Identity in Britain 1940-2000*, London: Macmillan, 2002.

72. Even some Cornu-centric texts perpetuate this myth. See Catherine Rachel John, *The Saints of Cornwall: 1500 Years of Christian Landscape*, Padstow: Tabb House, 2001 [1981]. A more comprehensive picture is found in Nicholas Orme, *The Saints of Cornwall*, Oxford: Oxford University Press, 2000.

73. An argument presented in Amy Hale, Alan M. Kent and Tim Saunders (eds. and trs.), *Inside Merlin's Cave: A Cornish Arthurian Reader 1000-2000*, London: Francis Boutle Publishers, 2000.

74. Useful surveys are offered in James J. Wilhelm (ed. and tr.), *The Romance of Arthur: An Anthology of Medieval Texts in Translation*, New York and London:

Garland, 1994; Edward Donald Kennedy (ed.), *King Arthur: A Casebook*, London and New York: Routledge, 2002; Peter Goodrich (ed.), *The Romance of Merlin: An Anthology*, New York and London: Garland, 1990; Joan Tasker Grimbert (ed.), *Tristan and Isolde: A Casebook*, New York and London: Garland, 1995.

75.   For mermaids, see Barbara Leonie Picard, *French Legends and Fairy Stories*, Oxford: Oxford University Press, 1992 [1955]; Duncan Williamson, *Tales of the Seal People*, Edinburgh: Canongate, 1992; Elias Owen, *Welsh Folk-Lore: A Collection of the Folk-Tales and Legends of North Wales*, Felinfach: Llanerch, 1996 [1887]. For Lyonesse, see for example, Le Goffic (ed.), 1999 [1993] op.cit., and Lindsay Hunt, *Brittany*, Windsor: AA Publishing, 1995, pp.18-19. Cornish Pixies feature in J.K. Rowling, *Harry Potter and the Chamber of Secrets*, London: Bloomsbury, 1999. Cornish folklore travels with the Cornish: see Alan M. Kent and Gage McKinney (eds.), *The Busy Earth: A Reader in Global Cornish Literature 1700-2000*, St Austell: Cornish Hillside Publications, 2008.

76.   Donald R. Rawe, *The Trials of St Piran*, Padstow: Lodenek Press, 1971, and *Geraint: Last of the Arthurians*, Padstow: Lodenek Press, 1972; Grose and Murphy, op.cit., 2005; Kent, op.cit., 2006.

77.   See Maclean, 1902, op.cit.

78.   See James Whetter, *The History of Glasney College*, Padstow: Tabb House, 1988, pp.102-14; D.H. Frost, 'Glasney's Parish Clergy and the Tregear Manuscript' in Philip Payton, *Cornish Studies: Fifteen*, Exeter: University of Exeter Press, 2007, pp.27-89.

79.   Many aspects of dramatic theory with Cornish parallels are to be found in Richard Drain (ed.), *Twentieth Century Theatre: A Sourcebook*, London and New York: Routledge, 1995.

CHAPTER ONE

The Origins of a Celtic Drama Queen: Ritual, Landscape and Community, Pre-1200

'Earthen banks were frequently used... at the conveniency of the people, for their meeting together, in which they represented it, by grave actings, scriptural history, personating patriarchs, princes and other persons; and with great oratory pronounced their harangue, framed by art, and composed with heroic style, such as have been known to be of old in other nations.'

From 'Antiquities Cornuontanic' by William Scawen, 1680, in Davies Gilbert, *The Parochial History of Cornwall*, 1838[1]

'The draught from the sea sucked through the valley towards the Playing Place, two miles inland. There, between the villages, where the land broadened into tin streaming and deep mining country, the ground rose up by a few inches into an ancient Round, levelled by ploughing and by beasts, almost imperceptible now, except in the long shadows of dusk and dawn.'

From *The Playing Place: A Cornish Round* by Myrna Combellack, 1989[2]

Perran Round, a small feature in the landscape, some two miles east of the present-day surfing town of Perranporth, has good claim to be the oldest theatre in continual use in the island of Britain.[3] To the casual onlooker, there seems nothing particularly special about it: merely a grass-covered amphitheatre tucked in behind thick gorse and brambles. The imaginative visitor though, may observe two openings in the circular bank allowing performers to enter and exit, while a curious spoon-shaped ditch stretches from one side of the arena to the centre; perhaps some long-forgotten but highly creative theatrical device, which delighted the audience centuries ago. In its small,

Fig. 3. The Entrance to Perran Round, Perranzabuloe.

unassuming way, this *plen-an-gwarry* [English: playing place] is actually as important in the development of drama in Europe as, say, the Greek theatre at Epidauros, or even Shakespeare's Globe. The 'playing' places in Cornwall are that significant, that old. In such a structure as Perran Round, or the other well-preserved *plen-an-gwarry* at St Just-in-Penwith,[4] we see that Cornwall's theatrical roots can be traced back to time immemorial; and that as long as Cornwall has had a history, theatrical culture has been part of its very essence. We might say that about many societies both ancient and modern, but nowhere is theatre so intensely part of a people's history than in Cornwall. Nowhere in the world can be found in such a small territory — particularly in the medieval period — so intense a theatrical culture.

Present-day visitors to Cornwall perhaps see surfing, abandoned tin and copper mines, and the Eden Project as symbols of the place, but scratch the surface and you will find a vibrant history of drama and performance, as exciting as any tourist attraction. Indeed, most often, even contemporary theatre in Cornwall has its roots and origins in a world distant from the present, in the ancient past. Anyone who has either grown up in Cornwall or travelled there will recognise that. The Cornish imagination is ancient, multi-layered and highly distinctive. For some, Cornwall's historical experience —

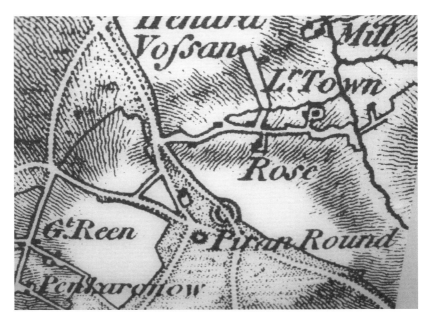

Fig. 4.   Perran Round on the 1865 Ordnance Survey Map. Note the pilgrim's pathway through the centre of the Round.

from Celtic nation to 'English' county and perhaps back again[5] – makes the place itself, in Denys Val Baker's words, 'the stuff of drama'.[6] Given Cornwall's 'difficult' status within the United Kingdom's geo-political structure, the territory has always been – dare I say it? – a 'drama queen', a tricky peripheral Celtic community for the centre to manage.[7] With a fiery, Celtic temperament, the Cornish and Cornwall were seemingly genetically built for performance. Our story will show how that Celticity here has been performed throughout the centuries in varieties of spaces and places, and how, despite changes in understandings and conceptualisations of that identity, a sense of distinctiveness has been maintained.

Where then, does this theatrical culture come from? Why, on a small granitic peninsula jutting into the Atlantic Ocean, does this flourishing dramatic culture arise? Just what are the origins of theatre in Cornwall? There is, unfortunately, no easy answer. Some of the origins of drama in Cornwall are identical to the origins of theatre and performance that are found across the globe. Others are more culturally and geographically specific; for example, maybe Cornwall's peninsula-formed isolation caused indigenous entertainment to establish quicker than elsewhere. For long periods of history, 'strolling' or travelling players would never have come to the far west of the island of Britain. Communities therefore began their own theatre as an organic, human process – as natural as laughter, sex or dance. This, however, is just one theory in a multitude of paradigms that might be applied to the origins of the Cornish theatrical experience. It is not my intention to answer all of these questions completely, but to provide some suggestions that you, as reader, must decide upon. No one theory of the origin of theatre in the land of the 'West Britons' will be correct. Very often, theories will collide and merge into one another. Such theories will also require an especial kind of multi-disciplinary approach to understanding cultural process. Boundaries and borders of usually distinctive disciplines will be crossed, and such an examination of the origins of theatre in Cornwall is bound to draw on archaeology, folklore, anthropology, ethnology, dramaturgy, theology and literary studies.

Two terms will help us understand the processes at work here. I use the terms *proto-theatre* or *proto-theatrical* to describe human activity, which may not necessarily be fully theatrical, but which displays early elements of performance. For example, archaeology has recently demonstrated the significance of late neolithic or early Bronze Age processional 'embanked walkways' between monuments in Cornwall; one found near Roughtor, on Bodmin Moor, is a particularly interesting example. In the sense that this would have shown what Caradoc Peters has termed 'embodied public religion',[8] we have a good, early example of proto-theatre. Although the event may not have led into theatre proper, some of its cultural styling is almost bound to have contained elements of processional or promenade theatre. Likewise, the terms *para-theatre* or *para-theatrical* will be used to describe activities related to theatrical activity of some kind, but which may have other cultural significance as well. 'Para-theatrical activity' can often describe apt conditions for the social production of drama, which may or may not result in actual drama. For example, numerous folkloric recorders in Cornwall have noted the para-theatrical activity of 'guizing', 'guising' or 'guise-dancing',[9] which always holds traditions of 'inversion' (dressing up) and carnival, and which sometimes – but not always – contained small, Christmas-themed dramas as well. These two terms will be used throughout this chapter and through this book, in order to delineate different kinds of theatrical activity.

The earliest proto-theatrical factor contributing to the origin of theatre in Cornwall is related to the landscape in which it takes place: the territory's unique geology.[10] It is perhaps a point that is ignored in most cultural studies of any territory;[11] that the geological distinctiveness of place has an all-pervading impact on the kinds of human activity which take place there. Although there are numerous other examples from around the world, Cornish culture has a very good claim to be highly influenced by the composition of its geological base. Indeed, this has led the Cornish poet and playwright D.M. Thomas (b.1935) to label Cornwall 'the granite kingdom';[12] and another poet, Peter Redgrove (1932-2003) in one of his most important poems, 'Minerals of Cornwall, Stones of Cornwall', to write of a case of mineral samples as being 'landscape in a box', with granite as 'rock of rocks'.[13] Of course, there are many other types of rock which make up the structure of Cornwall, such as sedimentary slate, sandstone and clays, yet igneous granite seems pervasive, developing over a period of thirty million years.[14] Distinctively, the peninsula of Cornwall is composed of cliffs, headlands, bays, estuaries, moors and tors, and according to Bristow has 'more hard-rock geological Sites of Special Scientific Interest' than anywhere else in Britain.[15] To the west of the mainland are the Isles of Scilly which, Charles Thomas argues, are relics from a 'drowned landscape'.[16] Given this, then the folk memory of the land of Lyonesse is not so surprising. Geology, mythology, legend and theatre are therefore intimately connected. Indeed, one of Cornwall's most distinctive theatre spaces, the Minack Theatre at Porthcurno, is hard to imagine without this geological base, for it is the rocks and cliffside that form both the auditorium and the scenery. Likewise, all the *plen-an-gwarries* which once existed were carved out and built from Cornish 'earths' which allowed their construction and development.[17]

Of course, it is this distinctive geology that has formed the valuable minerals in the earth which have been extracted by generations of Cornish people.[18] Without this continuum of mining and extractive industries, Cornwall would be a very different place, and indeed we would have no concept of Cornwall being the home of the 'industrial Celt'.[19] Themes of mining, of being underground, of refining and trading minerals have been part of Cornish theatrical activity for two thousand years. Whether this be tin, copper, clay, slate, or any of the other resources from the ground, it has created highly distinctive communities. Tin production can be traced back to prehistoric times, with accounts of trading found in classical Greek and Roman writings.[20] The mineral extractive industries have even brought about their own set of specific legends: tin from Cornwall was apparently used on Solomon's temple; the Phoenician Joseph of Arimathea not only traded for tin in Cornwall, but allegedly travelled there with Jesus Christ when he was a boy. Christ legends, in particular, pervade Creegbrawse Mine, near St Day.[21] It is not surprising then, that we find the story of Solomon's Temple in 'Origo Mundi [The Beginning of the World]', the first play of the *Ordinalia*,[22] and that Joseph of Arimathea is a central character in 'Resurrexio Domini [The

Fig. 5.   The arrival of the dove, during the Noah and the Ark sequence, from the 1969 production of *Ordinalia*. Courtesy of University of Bristol Theatre Collection.

Resurrection of our Lord]', the final play of the surviving trilogy.[23] Was it that such events were so ingrained in the imagination of the Cornish that they were a core part of the ideology of the dramas? Certainly, it would seem the case. For other examples, we can look at both 'Origo Mundi' and *The Creacion [sic] of the World* [*Gwreans an Bys*],[24] which both feature major sequences devoted to Noah and the building of the Ark. This story would have especial significance to Cornish mining communities, where it was believed that their mineral wealth was given to them by the redistribution of the earth's resources in the aftermath of God's cleaning of the world through the flood. *The Creacion of the World* is even subtitled 'Noye's Flude'.[25] This may also be the reason why so many para-theatrical folklore and superstitions have developed in the mining industries of Cornwall. Omens, taboos and mythological creatures accompany the Cornish underground;[26] not only in Cornwall, but to wherever the Cornish have travelled across the world.[27]

The distinctive geology of this part of Western Europe has made Cornwall into a peninsula. This 'peninsularity' has certainly contributed to its dramatic and theatrical culture in several ways. Being a peninsula contributed to Cornwall's separateness from the rest of the island of Britain, which allowed the original Brythonic language, and later Cornish, to survive into the modern era;[28] though paradoxically, its proximity to the forerunner of England and eventually England itself, made it 'accommodated' early on.[29] It is both this separateness and proximity which have made Cornish culture what it is. All theatrical activity is related to this paradox. Secondly, the peninsula juts into the Atlantic Ocean and, as a number of scholars have argued, this has meant cross-cultural contact not only with Ireland, Wales and Brittany, but with the Iberian Peninsula, and ships and peoples from the Mediterranean visiting the Isle of Britain.[30] The latter group included classical explorers, writers and traders. The former group has provided a cultural geographic base for saints' narratives, the starting point for so much of the dramatic tradition in Cornwall,[31] though not only this. Ongoing links and a commonality of 'Celticity' have survived into the contemporary era, with pan-Celticism just the latest thread of a long-standing process.[32] These maritime connections have allowed Cornwall to operate not as a periphery, but as an important economic and cultural unit in the world. In this way, dramatic narratives with their origins in Cornwall could spread across Europe, and Cornwall too could absorb and integrate other narratives from overseas.[33] Urban culture in this peninsula has been relatively late arriving. Therefore the human impetus for theatre has had to be expressed in a different way than in those territories that urbanised more quickly. Perhaps this 'peninsularity' is what has contributed to the distinctive medieval model of theatrical activity in Cornwall, which was spread across parishes; though even now, as we shall see, there are still residuals of this culture remaining. These three cultural processes may be directly connected to the geology of Cornwall.

What follows on from a place's geology is its landscape and weather. Landscape is the reason why tourists from all over the world come to Cornwall. The place is picturesque still, even at the start of the twenty-first century; and yet, Cornwall is not always picturesque. On many days of the year, it suffers from western weather fronts, bringing rain and mizzle.[34] Cornwall's climate, if not cold, is a wet one. The climatic influence on theatre is important; for at least in the first part of our story (and certainly for the bulk of its origins) large theatrical activity needs to take place in the summer months, with smaller scale events taking place indoors in the autumn and winter. The influence of the seasonal, and therefore ritual, year[35] will have major repercussions in our discussion of theatrical history in Cornwall. Weather therefore has a part to play in our story. Anyone watching a damp performance at the Minack Theatre in the middle of a typically wet British summer will tell you that. Landscape is related to weather, in that it is weather that shapes, erodes and deposits the landscape. The Cornish landscape has its iconic features. One thinks perhaps of the granite upland areas of Dartmoor (in a 'Greater Cornwall' or Dumnonian context at least), Bodmin Moor, Hensbarrow, Carn Brea, Carnmenellis and Chapel Carn Brea (West Penwith). All these places have many landscape features associated with ritual and alignments – proto-theatrical activity for ancient peoples, but also an ongoing sense of grand theatricality into the present. When we read Daphne du Maurier's *Jamaica Inn*,[36] the central character is not Mary Yellan or Joss Merlyn but Bodmin Moor itself. When Kneehigh Theatre play *Tregeagle* at Carn Marth quarry, near Carnmenellis, the backdrop is the granite intrusions all around. Put another way, landscape – whether surrounding a *plen-an-gwarry*, or as host to performance (say at the Sterts Theatre on Bodmin Moor, or on the arsenic flues of the Botallack mining complex) – is enormously significant. Could it be that this is one reason why 'outdoor' theatre has pervaded for so long in Cornwall? Why build a backdrop, when theatrical practitioners in, and operating in, Cornwall know that a spectacular one is to hand, just a few feet away. Despite the layeredness of landscape in Cornwall (prehistoric, post-Roman, medieval, pre-modern, industrial, post-industrial, contemporary, to choose but a few) – sometimes all in one place (at, say, Ballowal Barrow at St Just-in-Penwith, or the *Mên Scryfa* inscribed stone at Morvah) – there seems a ritual connection with it, that seems to draw out theatrical expression. Our theatrical origins therefore are not woolly nor 'New Age', but rather more ingrained from the outset. As we shall see, landscape will remain a significant factor in the origins of theatre in Cornwall.

The origins of theatre in Cornwall, therefore, are connected with all of the above physical and environmental factors and, perhaps too, an infusion, over time, of dramatic origins from its supposed beginnings in European culture: that of ancient Greece.[37] Indeed, it perhaps is all too easy to see a direct connection from the amphitheatres of Epdauros, Argos and Ephesus to, say, the Minack Theatre of Penwith.[38] However, it is harder to trace the direct fifth-century Athenian influences on drama in 'theatre' in early Britain. Obviously, over a longer period of time, Athenian conceptualisations of tragedy and comedy have certainly determined performance conditions, characterisation and narrative. This has come directly in the notion of protagonists, antagonists and, post-Sophocles,[39] the notion of a third actor, the tritagonist. Additionally, a core change might be seen in the way in which storytellers no longer just 'told' action: if the teller put on a mask, then he was now a character rather than a storyteller. Such concepts have tenuous echoes in all the medieval dramas of Cornwall, but precisely where and when they filter into the culture is harder to determine. As R.M. Wilson contends, even from the early medieval period, much information on these early dramas has been lost. He comments: 'Little is known of the drama in England before 1300, though presumably this country shared in the general development'.[40] Survivals might well have given us more indication of where the ideological notions of Athenian drama were integrated or contested. Likewise, Aristotelian influences on the nature of, for example, tragedy, comedy, poet, critic, scene, rhythm and catharsis,[41] surely travelled across the continent,[42] but we have no real way of knowing whether such ideas were transferred to manuscripts held at, for example, the Collegiate Church at Glasney, Penryn, or integrated into early drama operating in Cornwall.[43] There are some recognisable influences: satyr plays of fifth-century Athens have given to European culture a sense of parody and satire, combining dance and song into a whole, alongside cruder imagery which comes out in the devils, or the relationship between the Smith and his wife in the *Ordinalia*.[44] The buffoonery and clowning of the Greek comedies also have links forward into forms of theatre such as commedia dell'arte, which has been considerably important in, for example, the work of Kneehigh Theatre,[45] although there is no direct continuity. Perhaps however, the important contributions of fifth-century Athenian theatre were its focus on representing universal themes and ideas about human experience, and also the emphasis on language and scripting. Again, there is no way of being able to trace directly this influence in Cornwall, though presumably such processes did come to influence those writers of medieval Cornwall in conceiving of their work – purely because they were operating within a Latinate and pan-European scholarly culture; evidenced in, say, the experiences of the translator and possible playwright, John Trevisa (c.1342-1402).[46] A later influence is to be found in the Renaissance: particularly in the work of Richard Carew,[47] but also in nineteenth-century and contemporary playwrights.[48]

Although some scholars have argued for such pan-European gradual infusion of the tragic and comedic theory established in Ancient Greece[49] – spreading northwards and westwards – this does not seem sufficient for explaining *all* theatrical development in the island of Britain, and more especially in Cornwall. Gradually, alternative theories of theatre's origin have developed, which perhaps seem more in tune with Cornwall's specific history.

Fig. 6. Para-theatrical culture in Cornwall – featuring Obby Oss, Hal-an-Tow and Penglaz (the 'mast-horse'). Courtesy of http://leodavey.com

Ritual would therefore appear a significant shaping force in proto-theatre. This is because rituals are events that celebrate or confirm the shared customs, taboos and beliefs of a particular community. In early Cornwall, ritual must have formed part of community life and experience; otherwise we would not have the high number of ceremonial places which have survived into the modern age.[50] Of course, there could also be an equally high number of rituals performed which have left no remains – or which are yet to be uncovered or found. Rituals are a special kind of event in human society, for they have certain requirements in order to function. They require that all who are participating must believe in the significance of the ritual; otherwise it is rendered meaningless. A number of traditional rituals have survived from previous centuries in Cornwall, such as the Obby Oss at Padstow, the *Hal-an-Tow* at Helston and the Crying of the Neck ceremony. Other rituals have been invented in contemporary Cornwall: the annual 'Run to the Sun' festival in Newquay; Truro's City of Lights festival; or even Tom Bawcock's Eve at Mousehole. Obviously, ritual is necessarily linked to festival, though we shall consider the implications of festival in more detail later in this chapter.

Rituals do not always have to be spectacular. Some ritual is related to the conventions of normal life: for example, the way people say hello or goodbye to each other. However, we also know that ritual is often committed to transformation. This is usually completed through participation in some kind of symbolic act, though it requires those watching to believe that this process can occur. Specifically, this is the way ritual is related to the act of performance. Ritual is often associated with the process of transformation from childhood to adulthood; hence why so many cultures around the world contain processes that symbolise this progression. This may also be the reason why so many stories, narratives and dramas in Cornwall contain the story of a young man or woman's journey.[51] Importantly, rituals are not usually private events, which is something they have in common with theatre. Theatre, like ritual, is a community event: both comment upon and explain the culture they are aligned to. We may go further and suggest that both theatre and ritual are mechanisms for cultures to show their origins, and how they came to be – or, in Cornu-English parlance, how they 'belonged to be'. This transformational power is essential in all kinds of theatre and, because it is uniquely linked to community, then we have a model of origin that completely suits the experience of Cornwall. Sometimes ritual is viewed negatively, because it is deemed as repetitive and oppressive. However, we all recognise ritual in our lives, and much performance depends upon ritual for it to work. As brief examples of this, we should look at many of the component stories of, say, the medieval play 'Origo Mundi', which contains many ritualistic Christian

Fig. 7. Ritual and theatre merge in the Druid featured on Druid's Hall in Redruth, Cornwall. The Hall was built in 1859 on the site of the former Town Hall, which contained a theatre.

elements;[52] though, equally, ritualistic endeavour can also be found in, say, James Stock's *Star-Gazy Pie and Sauerkraut* from 1995.[53] Some theatre even accentuates these ritualistic elements, transforming them into repetitions, physical theatre or dance.[54] C-Scape are one Cornish physical theatre and dance company creating this kind of work in the twenty-first century.[55]

We can recognise in its present-day incarnation a long history of ritualistic behaviour in Cornwall. The territory has always been associated with the Druidic heritage of the island of Britain,[56] despite the fact that records of the period by writers such as Tacitus and Caesar show no connection with Druids in Cornwall.[57] However, over time, landscape, literature and folklore have transformed this situation. Related to Druidism is, of course, the bardic tradition in Celtic society, encompassed in the writing and legends surrounding the life of the sixth-century poet and scholar Taliesin.[58] There is one early example of ritualistic bardic activity in Cornwall, found in the Welsh Triads [*Trioedd Ynys Prydian*], which suggests that a 'Beisgawen' in 'Dyfnwall' was one of the three main Gorsedds which gathered in Britain.[59] 'Dyfnwall' may be seen as being Dumnonia, while one suggestion is that 'Beisgawen' is actually Boscawen Ûn stone circle in the parish of St Buryan.[60] If this was the place where a bardic order in Cornwall chose to meet, then there might have been, as Lyon suggests, 'ceremonies and contests for music, singing and literature'.[61] Judging by comparative information we have from other Celtic cultures,[62] this ceremony would have been highly ritualistic and formal, with a great deal of theatricality. The circle at Boscawen Ûn is dated to around 2000 BCE, so is not from the period when the Celts first arrived in Britain, or indeed Cornwall. However, as Chapman observes, this has not stopped generations of observers making connections between Celtic culture and such structures.[63]

Regardless of this Druidic heritage, the theatricality of bardism is something which may lie at the heart of the origins of dramatic culture in Cornwall, although it is hard to say for certain without any more concrete evidence. Such evidence was less important however, for the founders of the modern Gorsedd of Cornwall which, via Welsh 'reinvention' courtesy of the scholar Edward Williams (or, as he preferred, Iolo Morganwg [1747-1826]) in 1792, eventually found its way to revival – or complete invention – in 1928.[64] Significantly, the first modern Cornish Gorsedd took place at the supposed place of the original ritual – at Boscawen Ûn. If we view the Gorsedd as ritualised theatre, then there is a considerable thread of continuity here, and in the present-day ceremony of the Gorsedd – which takes place on the first Saturday of September every year – we may even have an echo of that original ritual (if one did occur). Before modern-day difficulties of mass spectators, parking and professionalism, the theatricality of the event also meant that past ceremonies would take place in 'ancient' locations, such as The Hurlers, The Merry Maidens or Castle Dore,[65] connecting present to past, via ritual. The language of the ceremony itself,[66] though part-based on the Welsh model and part-rooted, ironically (considering the Gorsedd is part of the Celtic empire 'writing back'), in the ceremonies of the Church of England, is highly ritualistic and displays considerable theatricality: for example, the *Offreyn Frutys an Nor* [The Offering of the Fruits of the Earth], *Arta ef a Dhe* [He shall come again] and *Cledha Myghtern Arthur* [The Sword of King Arthur] – the latter a staged moment when all bards unable to reach the sword lay a hand on a shoulder with one who is in contact with it. Any ancient Gorsedd would naturally have had many ritualistic elements, connecting humans to landscape, space and place. What is less clear, however, is who the community watching and celebrating are. Were such bards chosen locally, or did they travel a considerable distance from the rest of Dumnonia or Cornwall? Was the ritual watched by an audience similarly travelling distances – or was it more localised? Once formal ceremonies stopped, was there informal entertainment – of a kind where other forms of theatre might be expressed? These questions are unanswerable because the knowledge is lost, but we nevertheless need to ask them, in order to debate the origins of theatre in Cornwall. Inevitably, this kind of debate moves us into the realm of archaeology.

Archaeology in its traditional sense,[67] and its more ambitious 'intellectual' sense,[68] promoted by scholars such as Charles Thomas, may usefully be combined with some of the various neo-pagan scholarship to allow us to understand the nature of ritual behaviour in the Cornish landscape,[69] some of which may well have fed into the earliest forms of theatre. There is neither the time nor the space here to enter into the various debates over the nature and purpose of all the archaeological sites in Cornwall, but some specific examples at least give us an understanding of the general paradigm. Certainly, new forms of archaeological study are merging ever more closely with those scholars who attempt to uncover a more spiritual dimension to the Cornish landscape and, in many ways, aim to recreate and reinvigorate these early rituals – many of which have a theatrical base. When considering some of the dates in early Cornwall, it is sometimes hard to conceive of the time spans, let alone consider attempts at theatrical activity. We ought also to note that we are referring geographically not only to the area now known as Cornwall, but also to other parts of the western peninsula of Britain, extending into the South Hams, Dartmoor, and Exmoor.

What is known, as Peters, and Rowe argue,[70] is that during the paleolithic time period people tended to follow the migrations of animals since they formed the basis of their diet. This is the period some 400,000 to 10,000 years

BCE, and proto-theatrical activity and ritual contributed to the processes of hunting: perhaps hunters adopted certain practices to guarantee a good hunt, and there may well have been ritual celebration in communities once animals were killed. Particular animals may well have served as totems or spirit signs, which would have prompted ritualistic responses in the group. Paleolithic tools have been found in many locations across Cornwall, ranging from Newleigh in the north east, to Pendrea in West Penwith. From 10000 to 3500 BCE, society in this part of western Britain probably adapted to living in a more stable area, not only hunting but also gathering foods, both on land and at the seashore. During this mesolithic phase, as indicated by Peter Berridge and Alison Roberts,[71] it seems the society became more complex, perhaps indicating that rituals would have been more systematic and organised. In the late mesolithic, more stone technology was being used and, possibly, understanding of the seasons may have led to a notion of the ritual year and its effects.[72] It is possible that during this phase 'shamans' came to the fore, embodying broadly pagan beliefs – and, possibly, even demonstrating examples of proto-theatre as a kind of dramaturgy – designed to make that particular community successful. We cannot say that these groups of people followed the same religions or beliefs, for they probably practised their spirituality in very different ways. What is noticeable in Cornwall is that these communities seemed to favour coastal locations. Trevose Head, near Padstow, is one such site, where many mesolithic tools have been found,[73] and one can imagine mesolithic ceremonies taking place against the horizon of the ocean and the next set of headlands along the coast. Typically, many mesolithic communities were campsites, which were mobile, and perhaps based on seasonal movements. Again, it is not difficult to imagine both story and ritual being part of the dark evenings inside such camps.

Peters argues that neolithic culture in Cornwall occurs in the period between 3500 to 2700 BCE.[74] The main change in this period was that communities began to become more settled, and started to farm the landscape. Again, this would have tied them still further to the ritual year, and ritual dramaturgy, in order to generate and celebrate crop and animal successes. This community adapted to herding animals, instead of simply hunting them. We know also that communities first began to erect monuments and enclosures by using local stone.[75] Whereas the enclosures facilitated the herding of animals, the monuments suggest a new awareness of death, the afterlife and the significance of change. Maybe too, these communities developed a more complex relationship between rituals of life and rituals of death. It is this neolithic period that has left us the many portal dolmens (or quoits) which still dot the landscape of Cornwall today. Some of the more impressive examples include those at Lanyon, Zennor, Trethevy and Chûn.[76] At these chamber tombs, the outer structure (which once surrounded and covered the capstone) has worn away, leaving the quoit shape. They were once ceremonial burial places, where cremated remains were found. These burials must have been accompanied by ceremony and ritual. Other cists, carns and barrows also date from this period, and also formed part of the ritual landscape, no doubt giving rise to other rituals and processions. There is thus a complex relationship between people and nature, time and seasons.

As the late mesolithic Age merged into the bronze Age, between 2700 and 1500 BCE, the peoples of western Britain moved into a phase of burying valuable items with their dead, and developing stone erections to a new level, for this was the period in which many new megaliths and stone circles were created.[77] Sometimes, such stone circles and megaliths marked alignments with natural features or older monuments, but on occasions they were completely new structures. Archaeologists and others still debate their importance and significance to these communities, but they would seem to be sites of public and community ritual, again tied into patterns of alignments with the seasons and turn of the year. Many fine examples have survived into the twenty-first century: among them Boscawen Ûn, The Hurlers, The Merry Maidens and Tregeseal,[78] though there are numerous examples, stretching from Dartmoor to Land's End.[79] Even today, the stone circles carry with them a sense of theatricality, perhaps even once being sites of performance – proto-Rounds or *plen-an-gwarries* if you like. Put together they create a highly distinctive sense of sacred space and place. The highly distinctive menhirs that also form part of this ritual landscape were sometimes connected to other circles, but sometimes operated independently, having cists beneath them for burial purposes. Often their erectors had a great sense of theatre and design, locating them in enormously symbolic places: for example the St Austell longstone, high on Hensbarrow Downs, or the Mên Gurta upon St Breock Downs.[80] Elsewhere, other sites – such as Ballowall Barrow or Carn Gluze – were being developed and extended.[81] Such monuments clearly conveyed a sense of theatricality for their creators, and also for generations following. Barrows and cairns such as this are found all over Cornwall, in large numbers. Clearly this was a ceremonial and ritualistic society, strongly identifying with landscape and community, and 'performing' both rite and design. This was also the first age of craftwork in bronze and, given Cornwall's mineralogical background, metal was of supreme importance and status within this time period, embodied in finds such as the gold lunulae found at Harlyn Bay and St Juliot, the Trenoweth Collar from St Stephen-in-Brannel, and the Cup found at Riallaton. Such items may well have been used as the properties of proto-theatrical or para-theatrical activity. The other significant event during this phase is that a wider circle of trade began to take place between Cornwall and the rest of Europe, perhaps more fully circulating native narratives, and bringing in new stories.

It is in the next phase, 1500-200 BCE, that the Celts, having reached the island of Britain, spread their culture throughout the island – and specifically into Western Britain.[82] This is the age of forts, enclosures and roundhouses; for example, these include not only promontory forts at headlands and cliffs (probably developed from earlier structures, like at Treryn Dinas) but also enclosures such as Hall Rings and Round Wood, near Feock.[83] The finest examples of roundhouses are to be found at Chysauster and Carn Euny.[84] Such roundhouses usually had stone bases, with conical roofs. A hole in the roof allowed smoke to leave the building. The hill-forts and roundhouses were surely places of theatre, where stories were recounted. Long, dark winter evenings would have provided a captive audience. There may well also have been summer 'performances', when the light outside facilitated this kind of play – a seasonal dimension to theatre that has continued into the present age. Perhaps too, there were other para-theatrical ritual processes, again related to the turning of their year. Certainly, offerings and prayers would have been given for particular gods. Some structures have proven puzzling. Fogous (from the Cornish *fogou* [cave]) are underground passageways or souterrains with side chambers, and are often found near to roundhouse communities. Various theories about their origins have been expounded, ranging from them being birthing chambers, to ritual space. Perhaps they were for survival during attack, or to store food. Again, their very mystery gives them a certain theatricality. Despite not knowing their true purpose, we feel they may have been significant as performance space of some kind. Despite being a relatively short period, this Age is significant for it is one which in the popular imagination defines 'Celtic' as carrying with it a particular ideology and world order which, as we shall see, is sometimes correct, and sometimes wildly inaccurate.[85] Nevertheless, whether historically correct or not, the period evokes particular associations of theatricality and epic storytelling which have ramifications for our story here.

Cornwall is not quite Cornwall yet, though here we do see a version of what Robert Hunt later imagined as greater 'old Cornwall'.[86] This was the Roman concept of Western Britain, known as Dumnonia. As Pearce notes, in her 1978 study, Dumnonia included all of Cornwall, Devon and parts of western Somerset,[87] effectively the area into which the British Celts or Ancient Britons would be pushed back by the Anglo-Saxon peoples from the east. However, the period between 200 BCE and 400 CE was when Romans, if not occupying

Cornwall, certainly had an important presence within it. Roman finds have been discovered in Penwith; there is one example of a Roman fort at Nanstallon, near Bodmin; and another Roman style building is found at Magor, near Illogan. Exeter, meanwhile, was more fully Roman. Rome, as Banks and Harwood note, had a highly sophisticated theatrical culture,[88] parts of which may well have travelled with them, as the Roman Empire 'romanised' the periphery of Europe, Cornwall included. For example, the Roman civilization brought amphitheatres to Armorica (or later Brittany), which was part of Gaul.

At Nanstallon, excavations have revealed that the fort there did contain one larger public room, perhaps for some kind of entertainment or performance. Not for one minute am I suggesting that the kind of large Roman theatres found at, say, Rome itself, Athens, Ostia and Pompeii were operating in Western Britain, but perhaps there were smaller amphitheatres or places where Roman comedies were performed, even in the capital of Dumnonia, at Exeter. This makes even more sense given the proximity of Armorica. For comparison we should think of Caerleon in South Wales. There is a substantial Roman military amphitheatre there, which was once the headquarters of Legio II Augusta around 75 to 300 CE. As well as its Roman history, Caerleon is significant since Geoffrey of Monmouth makes Caerleon one of the most important cities in Britain, giving it a long and glorious history from its founding by King Belinus.[89] This may seem somewhat distant from the theatrical origins of Cornwall, but when one considers that the playwright or playwrights of *Bewnans Ke* [*The Life of St Kea*] incorporated much of this lore into their script,[90] then we see how origins feed and nourish the continuum in Cornwall. It is significant, of course, that in *Bewnans Ke* Arthur must face a Roman foe. Certainly, even if Greek theatrical tradition had little influence in Cornwall (aside from its ideas and concepts contained in medieval thought), there might be some case for citing a Roman influence in Cornwall, but we should be cautious in asserting this, because the link is still tenuous. A more productive way of seeing this Roman presence in Cornish culture might actually be in the transfer of ideas and technology for later use in staging and production. The other change the Romans brought was a force that would have enormous repercussions in the future theatrical development of Cornwall. This was the presence of Christianity. The process of converting the 'pagan' native West Britons was not altogether easy, however, since there is much evidence that earlier rituals continued to be conducted well into the late Roman period. Not everyone, it seems, felt the need to convert to the new order – a cultural resistance that was to continue into the Age of the Saints. It is the Age of the Saints (from around 400 CE onwards) that truly forms the starting point for much post-Roman and medieval drama in Cornwall;[91] we shall consider this phase (and the texts that were developed) in more detail later on.

For now, let us return to the earlier period in Cornwall and examine it from the perspective of other observers who comment on the proto-theatrical, ritualistic and sacred nature of the landscape. As observers such as James, and Stout have noted,[92] there has always been contention between more traditional archaeology and those groups which have viewed such features of the landscape of ancient Britain, and more specifically Cornwall, in non-traditional ways. This view of the landscape, once considered perhaps freakish and controversial, and promulgated originally in Cornwall by mid twentieth-century observers such as Ithel Colquhoun and even Aleister Crowley,[93] has since become much more normative and mainstream. The popular works of writers such as Nigel Pennick and Julian Cope have reinforced this connection,[94] reactivating the spiritual, symbolic and mytho-logical importance of ancient space and place, and its connection with ritual performance. Meanwhile, in studies of figures such as the St Merryn-based Ed Prynn, Cornwall's 'self-appointed Arch Druid', Rob Roy has demonstrat-ed the power and significance of the present megalithic revival – effectively the connection of twentieth and twenty-first century ritual and theatrical

Fig. 8. Para-theatrical culture embodied in the modern standing stones at the home of Cornwall's Arch-Druid, Ed Prynn.

space with that of the neolithic.[95] Following Colquhoun, and early ley-hunters such as Alfred Watkins,[96] much important work in this field was completed by John Michell (1933-2009). Michell had a view of 'sacred geometry' and 'archaeo-astronomy' which allowed him to theorise upon connections between sites in Cornwall. He first expressed these views in his influential 1969 volume *The View over Atlantis,*[97] but refined his position on Cornwall in his 1974 seminal work, *The Old Stones of Land's End.* The following probably seems like established knowledge in the twenty-first century, but his theories on the para-theatrical significance of these Cornish sites were, at the time, quite ground-breaking:

1. These were sited and orientated in accordance with the positions of the heavenly bodies as they crossed the horizon on certain days of the year.

2. From the central place of observations lines of stone or earth markers were extended over considerable distances in the directions thus astronomically determined.

3. Stone circles are built with extreme accuracy, the scheme of their ground plan being drawn in accordance with a synthetic canon of number and geometry such as was later used by the Pythagoreans. In some cases the astronomic sighting lines were arranged as extensions of construction lines within the geometrical scheme of a stone circle.

4. Most if not all megalithic sites are related geographically to others, with which they form straight alignments of three or more sites, each visible from the next in line. Every megalithic structure stands on one or more such alignments together with natural features, rocks, mountains and islands. Sometimes stretches of track for sacred or secular use follow these lines.

5. There is a connection between megalithic sites, and the earth's vital spirit. Centres of the magnetic current, associated with founts of underground water and geological faults, are marked by standing stones, dolmens or earthworks according to the geological peculiarities of the site.

6. Legends of old stones emphasise their magical character, as giving health and fertility, as marking scenes of mythological events, the abodes of heroes and local deities, the haunts of Spirits. Some are traditionally visited at certain seasons of the year in memory of a formal cycle or ritual in the past.

7. Stones and dolmens are sometimes associated with burials, either contemporary with the monument or of later date.[98]

It is point 6 that is most relevant to us here, though clearly the wider landscape is spiritually significant. This concept of the landscape holding 'songlines' is of enormous importance since, again, it suggests ritualised connections between space, place and performance.[99] Michell's theories were influential in two main ways. First of all, he prompted many post-war neo-pagans to reconsider their relationship with the historical nature of these Cornish sites (and those elsewhere in Britain) and re-enact or create from scratch theatrical rituals which were either inspired by or linked to Michell's 'songlines' across the Cornish landscape. Secondly, Michell's scholarship prompted further neo-pagan scholarship into the archaeological sites of Cornwall. This is best exemplified in works by writers such as Paul Broadhurst, Hamish Miller, Ian McNeil Cooke and Cheryl Straffon,[100] and also to an extent in the work of Robin Payne and Rosemarie Lewsey.[101] Straffon's significance comes in her own studies of the 'theatre' of sacred space in Cornwall, but also through her editorship of the magazine *Meyn Mamvro*, an enormously important publication in terms of disseminating a wider awareness of the 'ancient stones and sacred sites' of Cornwall.

Straffon and contributors to *Meyn Mamvro* show a considerable awareness of the significance of the ritual landscape, ritual and proto-theatre in Cornwall: whether on contemporary neo-pagan practice, or on historical study, the magazine's articles always convey an awareness of community dramaturgy. Some examples here will be helpful: Alan Bleakley has considered the bonfires associated with the Celtic midsummer, while Hugh Miners (a former Grand Bard of the Cornish Gorsedd) considers old pagan customs in Cornwall.[102] In an article in 1987 titled 'Where Stones touch the Sky', Helen Woodley examines theatrically-positioned stones at Tregeseal stone circle, in which she demonstrates that the stones were set in specific locations to connect to the rest of the landscape.[103] The intricate mazes found at Rocky Valley in North Cornwall are interpreted by Jeff and Deb Seward, while Ian McNeil Cooke and Cheryl Straffon consider the implications of the Celtic year.[104] The wider ritualised aspect of landscape is also found in a wide range of writings. Straffon considers rituals and rites at Cornish sites, while Paul Broadhurst sees Stowe's Hill (the site of the Cheesewring) as a significant 'ritual centre'.[105] Caeia March and Cheryl Straffon also note what they term 'the Calendar of the Land' when they explore a comparison between the 'Ritual Landscapes of Bodmin Moor' with Loughcrew in Ireland.[106] The apexes of these kinds of studies are found in Straffon's consideration of 'the Cornish Otherworld', Andy Norfolk's examination of Cornish 'songlines', and Joanna Tagney's examination of The Hurlers stone circle, which she views as 'sightlines to the sun'.[107]

At best, both of these forms of archaeological practice are combined to give the reader a full understanding of the structure of surviving material culture. One sees this in the work of Charles Thomas, when he debates the cryptic codex of burgeoning Christianity in Britain,[108] or in the studies of Stannon Down, St Breward, where Andy M. Jones considers the nature of 'settlement and ceremony'.[109] Likewise, Ann Preston Jones takes another look at Men-an-Tol in the light of neo-pagan interest in the structure.[110] Christopher Tilley has also shown the 'theatricality' of rocks within the Cornish landscape where he considers 'landscapes and power'.[111] All of these articles come from the field of archaeology but there are clear continuities from the more esoteric explorations of recent years. Such positions are usefully summarised in the work of the archaeologist John Barnett, who clearly recognises that to truly understand these early cultures, traditional archaeology needs to combine with the notion of 'sacred geometry':

> It is clear from the remains of ceremonial sites throughout Britain and the ritual deposits within them that as in most simple societies the viewpoints and explanations of the builders are likely to have been very alien to our own. There was probably a greater emphasis on symbolism, with magical and poetic belief systems as the motive forces geared towards spiritual entities and powers. We often do not understand this, dismissing prehistoric society as primitive and naïve. Many of the ideals and practices of the North American Indian may well be more intelligent than what replaced them.[112]

Ian McNeil Cooke also took a further look at the function and place of fogous. Whereas the 1961 study by Evelyn Clark had indicated thoughts about them being either 'places of hiding', 'a granary', 'a temple for religious use of the occupants of the fort' or having a 'sacred function',[113] Cooke goes further, convincingly arguing for 'an enactment of public and private ritual' which surely indicates both proto- and para-theatrical activity:

> The intended function of the fogou was therefore to form a physical bond between the Earth Mother and the Sun, her traditional son and consort, whereby there was the potential, through alignment, for a symbolic act of divine sexual union to take place during midsummer when the sun is at its most potent. Since the very existence of all plant and animal species is dependent on successful reproduction, the intention was to promote fertility though an act of sympathetic magic ensuring abundance of all animal, vegetable and mineral matter locked in the continual cycle of birth, growth, decay and death. The architectural features of the fogou provided a sacred space for enactment of public and private rituals and ceremonies associated with this cult – the more precise forms of which we are unfortunately never likely to know.[114]

This is an important statement, which helps us to understand the importance of ritual and the ritualistic origins of theatre in Cornwall. Related to this field are studies of early gods – both pre-Celtic and Celtic. We have no way of fully understanding what figures were worshipped and how this worship was conducted. However, a few tantalising leads have been suggested. John E. Palmer' relays the importance of the pagan god Brân.[115] Brân was widely worshipped through Cornwall and Wales as a 'magician King', and is well known for being called Brân the Blessed. Brân features in the Second Branch of the Welsh narrative epic *The Mabinogion*, where John T. Koch describes him as 'consistently honourable and heroic, but invariably reactive'.[116] In this part of the narrative, one of Brân's retinue, when forgetting an injunction, opens a magical door facing south towards Cornwall.[117] Brân means 'raven and/or crow' so it is perhaps significant that we find in West Cornwall a stone, the *Mên Scryfa* [English: Stone of Writing], which has upon it an inscription, *RIALOBRAN-CVNOVAL-FIL* (Rilalobran, son of Cunowal), which translates as 'Royal Raven' and 'Famous Chieftain', and probably dates from the sixth century CE. This has no likely connection to the 'Welsh' Brân above, but proves the significance of this creature as a symbol and totem. Other mythological figures may also have been worshipped in proto-theatrical fashion. Craig Weatherhill convincingly argues for the significance of horses in Celtic mythology, and therefore the place of Epona in ancient Cornwall.[118] Epona in Gallo-Brittonic means 'horse goddess', and Epona was the most abundantly worshipped Celtic deity of the Roman Empire. Here we perhaps also have a link forward to the mast horses and obby osses of the ritual year. Chris Jenkins, meanwhile, notes what he terms 'traces of the Goddess Sillana' with reference to the Isles of Scilly,[119] although there is less support for this view. Perhaps a more likely deity is that of Bride, whose connections are explored by March and Straffon.[120] Bride is usually seen as a pre-Christian goddess of fire, smithing, cattle, crops and poetry, who may well have been reinterpreted as the Celtic Saint Brigid.[121] Although primarily seen in the context of Ireland, there is some suggestion of a connection to Cornwall. The proto-theatrical worship of gods and goddesses naturally leads us to consider those individuals who led and organised response to deities in early communities in Cornwall. Often, these were shamanic figures.

Most studies concerning the history of drama usually list western shamanism as an important starting point for dramatic expression in ancient cultures.[122] The term 'shaman', as defined by Rozik, is of 'Siberian origin, and [was] initially used in the ethnography of Siberia… [it] applies to a class of medicine-men in various cultures who combine "healing", "mediumship" and "magic".'[123] The shaman is therefore a special kind of 'priest', 'sorcerer' or 'witch-doctor' who officiates in healing rituals or other kinds of rituals that benefit the community. Sometimes the shaman will enter into a trance by taking hallucinogenic drugs or by fasting and meditating. When in this physical and mental state, it is believed that powerful spirits take over the shaman; in other words, the shaman transforms into a spirit, with the spirit taking the physical form of the shaman. As Neelands and Dobson argue, this has two important connections with the origins of theatre:

> First, the Shaman brings the invisible word of spirits and demons into the actual world, which is also the ambition for some forms of non-realist and symbolic theatre. Second, the Shaman, from the audience's point of view, transforms into another character for the duration of the trance.[124]

Thus in Cornwall, like in several other cultures, many people are suspicious of the idea of spirits, demons and ghosts. One only has to look at the major folklore collections of Robert Hunt and William Bottrell to see this.[125] In fact, people tend to be scared of anything that can't be seen or heard, or proved to exist, but this has not stopped the theatre from trying to physically and visually represent both what Neelands and Dobson term 'the visible world and the invisible world of dreams, nightmares and fantasies'.[126] In Cornwall, these worlds can, of course, be pagan, Christian, an admixture of the two, or an alternative spirituality. The shaman is important in this way, but also in another role. When the shaman transforms into the spirit-being, then this is closely related to those forms of acting in which the actor is skilful enough to create the illusion that he or she has literally become the character he or she is portraying. This view of shamanism is supported by the work of Mircea Eliade, who observes that:

> of course, the Shaman is also a magician and medicine man; he is believed to cure, like all doctors, and to perform miracles of the fakir type, like all magicians, whether primitive or modern. But beyond this, he is psychopomp, and he may also be priest, mystic and poet.[127]

Rozik goes further, offering several pointers to the role and function of shamanistic figures, which have relevance to the origins of drama in Cornwall. The importance, he argues, of shamanism is that the shaman 'enacts' another being or inhabitant of another world. Usually too, 'the shamanistic act is performed in front of a community and in a well-defined area, whether outside or indoors'.[128] The shaman necessarily creates a spectacle and forces a relationship between him or herself and the audience. Indeed, some theorists of theatre believe that the transition from ritual to theatre occurred at the moment when participants in a ritual stopped being part of the ritual and became spectators[129]. The proto-theatrical activity of shamans creates 'belief' which is important to any theatrical performance, since all audiences are aware of the need for the 'suspension of disbelief' for a play to happen. Therefore shamans are not necessarily representations of naturalistic theatre, but are important in our understanding the duality of acting for a performer. Put another way, shamanism may even be considered, in Rozik's terms, as 'a prototype of acting'.[130] shamanism may also be related to the use of mask, in the sense that ritual masks represent 'reference to what is, or is supposed to be, a real entity'.[131] It may even be that masks and make-up were borrowed from ritual, and incorporated into theatre at some point.

Inevitably then, shamanistic behaviour is not necessarily a sign of early performance in Cornwall, though it may be that once participants in a ritual stop and become spectators, then they are doing something quite different. It could be that early peoples in Cornwall had members of their communities who were shaman types – operating as priests, mystics and poets – and using para-theatrical craft for ritualistic purposes. Nikolai Tolstoy takes this idea of shamanism in ancient Britain and Cornwall one step further in his volume *The Quest for Merlin*. Tolstoy strongly argues that the figure of Merlin in legend and literature ought to be re-evaluated as a shamanistc figure; Merlin is 'the trickster, the wild man and the prophet',[132] and displays many pan-cultural similarities to other shaman figures found across the globe (in Siberia, in Norse legend, and in the Bible). Folklore has presented Merlin as a wizard or enchanter,[133] but Tolstoy argues that there is sufficient evidence to show that he was a real figure living at the end of the sixth century CE. If this were the case, then the 'prophecy literature' attached to Merlin in both Geoffrey of Monmouth[134] and John of Cornwall seems to make more sense, given its sometimes rambling, impenetrable and esoteric nature. For example, the following is a section from John of Cornwall's *The Prophecy of Merlin* – a manuscript perhaps originally written in Cornish, and later translated into Latin.[135] In this text, many of the references, necessarily cryptic at the time, are now obscure beyond recovery, but clearly the prophecy calls upon the House of Arthur to unite against the incursions by other peoples into the islands of the Britons.

> May the weather be fine. Conan will sail the waves
> and may he who commands the East support Cadwaladr.
> A horseman whiter than snow loosening the reigns of his mount,
> all for duty having passed the whirlpool of Periron,

with a whitening rod snatches the streams in the middle of a circle,
and measures a mill over it.
After so many disasters and often stormy labours,
the Severn will hear so many triumphs,
so many of its battles to be mixed, your rivers laugh, O Tevi![136]

John of Cornwall reveals, in his glosses to the work, that his sources included documents in Old Cornish, demonstrating that Cornish literary traditions were thriving around 1150, despite the loss of native noble patronage in light of the Norman Conquest. Reading both the prophecy itself and its glosses makes considerable sense if we reconfigure the standard approach to Merlin, and replace it with an alternative notion of who he was. Tolstoy makes much of the 'trickster' nature of Merlin, putting forward a case that this kind of figure is 'buried in our unconscious mind since man first developed the power of rational thought'.[137] In this sense, given that Merlin was operating as this kind of figure, and presumably performed in front of a community, then there may also be a case for arguing that he was a proto-actor. This may also explain why, through the ages, his story has been retold, and that there are theatrical connections to his life.[138] This 'wild man' and 'trickster' notion of Merlin is given further validity in the work of Michael Dames, who asserts a comparative vision of Merlin with figures such as Suibne Geilte, his Irish counterpart, and supports Tolstoy's view of a shamanistic British landscape, in which Merlin operates between Cornwall, Wales and Scotland.[139] Further evidence of this 'shamanistic' proto-performer Merlin is to be found in Hale, Kent and Saunders' anthology of Cornish Arthuriana, *Inside Merlin's Cave* – notably in Richard Carew's satirical poem *A Herring's Tail* (1598) and in Thomas Heywood's *Merlin's Prophecies and Predictions* from 1651.[140]

Two significant points of origin are related to all of the above. Jo O'Cleirigh has drawn attention to what are termed 'milpreves – or adder's beads' in ancient British culture, in the light of Merlin being viewed as a shaman. Drawing on the work of Robert Graves, O'Cleirigh comments that 'an early Cornish poem [now lost] describes how the Druid, Merddin, or Merlin, went early in the morning with his black dog to seek the *glain*, or magical snake's eggs'.[141] According to Graves, these may actually have been fossilised sea-urchins, which were sometimes found in iron-age burials, and thought to have magical qualities. This myth reasserts a Brythonic Merlin figure with shamanistic needs, and an awareness of performance. Another notion of a 'Cornish shaman' figure with some similarities to Merlin as shaman, comes in the observations of Brendan McMahon.[142] Here, McMahon notes elements of shamanistic behaviour and clothing in the figure of Jack the Tinkeard in

Hunt's first series of folklore collections. The image of Jack strongly correlates with the costume of shamans in the Siberian and Nordic tradition:

> Tom's blows had no effect on the tinkeard, because he wore such a coat as was never seen in the West Country before. It was made out of a shaggy black bull's hide, dressed whole with the hair on. The skin of the forelegs made the sleeves, the hind quarters only were cut, pieces being let in to make the spread of the skirts, while the neck and skin of the head formed a sort of hood. The whole appeared as hard as iron; and when Tom hit the tinkeard, it sounded as if the coat roared like thunder. They fought until Tom got very hungry, and he found he had the worst of it. "I believe thee art the devil, and no man," says Tom.[143]

This certainly has parallels with shaman figures in those northern cultures, but also with some interpretations of Merlin figures in British culture.[144] The hood, the cloak and the spread all make him magical, while the tinkeard is in a shamanistic transformation. McMahon's theory of this being a small exemplar of ancient shamanism is significant, but in his 2006 work, *The Princess Who Ate People: The Psychology of Celtic Myths*, he offers a more sophisticated understanding of why and how Celtic mythology operates. McMahon chooses not to illustrate Cornish examples, and yet he offers a highly persuasive argument using other Celtic sources, stating that the success of Celtic mythology was because the stories anticipate modern dilemmas of alienation and, in considering themes of childhood, adolescence, courtship, death, personal identity and madness, the narratives help to restore integrity and identity to the group.[145] If this is the case, then we have perfect justification as to why such Brythonic and early Cornish stories were given 'theatricality' in the sense of proto-theatrical storytelling, or indeed proper theatrical performance. Certainly it is hard to define the moments of 'enactment' but there is indeed something significant in the link between such shamanistic figures as Merlin or Jack the Tinkeard, and the early development of theatre in Cornwall.

In many cultures around the world, the origins of theatre are linked to storytelling. Cornwall has a mass of stories that it has told over the centuries, some of which it continues to tell. Such stories have had an enormous influence over the dramaturgy of Cornwall. It perhaps seems an obvious thing to say, but both stories and storytelling (the way in which stories are told) have had a profound influence on the development of drama. The continuity of performance in Cornwall must, in part at least, have been based on the stories and storytelling styles of ancient times. Many playwrights have based their dramas on ancient stories. For example, the medieval playwrights of Cornwall had an interest in biblical narrative – a projection of the biblical world upon the local community – and in the stories of saints' lives, explaining the origin of the cultural-geography of the parish, its founder and its faith. Despite the worldly and epic nature of the story, its roots are locally grounded. However, ancient stories have continued to be retold and reinterpreted. As we shall see later, Carl Grose and Anna Maria Murphy's version of *Tristan and Yseult* (for Kneehigh Theatre) is the latest in a tradition of telling this story which goes back through Wagner's version, through Gottfried von Strassbourg, to an original Cornish telling, by a storyteller who intimately knew the narrative and the geography of Cornwall.[146]

Storytelling is influential in the construction of dramas of all kinds because most plays have a narrative in which there is a beginning, a middle and an end. This is significant because it is the way that most human beings comprehend the human experience. We all listen to other people's stories and gain a new sense of ourselves from hearing the experiences of others. Over the course of thousands of years, it is story that helps to shape our experiences in all sorts of ways. When stories are dramatised, the narrative is put into the context of a setting. Likewise, we are also introduced to the characters and how they operate within the story. This characterisation is significant because we find out who is involved in the story and project our own lives onto them. We wonder how we might behave in a similar situation. This question is enormously important in any piece of drama, but it is the conflict within a drama that interests us. Rarely does a play ignite the human imagination if everyone agrees. Therefore it is this 'difference of ideology' enacted within the context of the theatre that stimulates discussion and debate. Crucially, the debate over ideology is usually conducted in a peaceful environment, where the differences can be examined at a distance, on the stage.

At their best, stories appeal to our emotions. Most often the playwright, like the storyteller, has a particular intention to create emotions within us. Stories are told to arouse fear, pity, excitement, laughter, and anger within. Theatre has the same function. Similarly, the consummate storyteller offers a 'voice' or perspective on the particular events or people spoken about. If theatre follows this, then the playwrights, directors or creators of that theatre will stamp their own voice upon the piece of drama as well. This may be a single 'voice' or a set of multiple 'voices' (designers, makers, technicians, costumiers, choreographers etc). Such voices will certainly reveal the ideology of the people behind the creation of the work. In this way, storytelling in its widest sense has an influence over theatre and its moment of production. Another similarity between story-telling and theatre is that stories and plays are often told to explore a particular idea. However, although storytelling is in essence a proto-theatrical technique, the two are not the same. Because theatre involves a live performance, it also relies on dramatic elements such as time, space, physicality, lighting, sound, music and objects, in ways that storytelling does not have to. The use of dramatic elements such as these will inevitably affect the way in which an audience responds to a piece of theatre. Inevitably then, since theatre evolved to be 'live', it will always use more than just words to tell its stories. Two examples of this are readily found in the Cornish continuum of theatre. The word 'Ordinalia' (the usual titled afforded to the Cornish-language mystery play trilogy) in Latin means 'prompt book', and it has been suggested that a prompter read the lines to the performer, before he actually declaimed them in medieval Cornish theatre space.[147] Antithetical to contemporary work, and even post-medieval drama, this was perhaps a convention caused by the lack of mechanical reproduction of the text.[148] Thus, with such work, we have the 'storytelling' element of theatre; but it is the actor's physicality and use of space which makes the full performance. In this way, storytelling contributes to the whole, but it is not the whole. Similarly, the early twenty-first-century plays, reviving celebrations of St Piran around 5 March each year, contain many stylised story elements, but take place in a ritual landscape (Perran Sands), which contains a number of special components directly linked to the story.[149] The lighting is daylight, the style is promenade (followed by celebrants to a Celtic wheel-head cross), and a small lake in the sands acts as the Celtic Sea between Ireland and Cornwall. In this we have one medieval example and one contemporary example of the way in which storytelling continues to have an input into the dramaturgy of Cornwall.

With the advent of modern technology in the twentieth century, notions of traditional storytelling seemed to dissipate for a while, despite its centrality in the transferral to the next generation of culture and belonging. This is one thing storytelling strongly has in common with theatre: that passage of the ideology to listeners and watchers, so that group identity continues, despite historical change. It could be argued that storytelling has continued into the modern era – it is just the medium through which it is expressed that has altered: television, cinema, radio, and computer games all use storytelling as a core component of this transferral process. However, it is fair to say that a number of observers have remarked not only on the power of storytelling in inspiring young and old people alike, but also on the links between storytelling and theatre in ancient culture, and throughout the centuries. Therefore, academic interest in the importance of storytelling to both ancient and modern cultures has grown exponentially over the past few years. Rosen, and Maguire have shown the importance of stories working as proto-theatre within an educational context,[150] while Zipes sees the link between successful, identity-conscious communities and their ability to narrate experience.[151] Although considering primarily the art of the contemporary, professional storyteller, Wilson examines the long-standing connections between the performance art of the teller and traditions of narration within a theatrical context.[152] Contributors to John Beech's collection, *Oral Literature and Performance Culture*, trace both direct and indirect connections between orality and the development of theatre in different contexts.[153] This has implications in Cornwall, as Oliver Padel has shown. Padel argues that we should be carefully examining the link between oral and literary culture in medieval Cornwall, since this would have considerable bearing on what was being written. It is, however, complex, as he correctly contends:

> Although there is no reason why the authors of the medieval religious plays should necessarily have seen fit to include allusions to secular oral legends, it is clearly of interest to examine whether they did so; the converse, namely influence from literary traditions upon oral legends, would also be of interest, but would be much harder to detect because our knowledge of the legends themselves is so indirect.[154]

In a penetrating analysis, using a specific motif – in the form of Kyllywyk (the 'story' of the residence of King Arthur in Cornwall) – Padel argues there could be two origins of its inclusion in *Bewnans Ke*. It came, he argues, either from the 'oral tradition in Cornwall' or from the 'Welsh tradition, oral or literary'.[155] Given the limited understanding of the oral tradition in Cornwall, Padel seems to favour the latter.[156] Even so, his observations are not conclusive, and if the motif did arise from a Welsh source, then it gives more credence to the multi-cultural nature of early Cornish culture.[157] In short then, there is much cross-over and linkage, with theatre first borrowing from the tradition of the teller, but with tellers being influenced by trends in dramaturgy as well. Historically, there are many traditions of tellers operating in modern Cornwall, though the tradition stretches back several centuries before them. One example can be gleaned from the early 1580s. Following the execution of John Winslade of Tregarrick as one of the leaders of the 1549 rebellion,[158] according to Richard Carew, we know that his son, William Winslade 'led a walking life with his harp to gentlemen's houses' - probably working as a storyteller. Agnes Winslade had tried to get the property at Tregarrick transferred to William, but this did not happen, and so he became an impoverished Catholic exile, forced to travel as a teller, and known locally, as Carew notes, as 'Sir Tristam'.[159] Other tellers appear in the nineteenth century: Richard Nancollas of St Austell (popularly known as Rhyming Dick);

Anthony James of Cury; and the extempore Anglo-Cornish poets Stephen Langdon from St Mawgan-in-Pydar, and Billy Foss (or Frost) from Sancreed.[160] In the twentieth century, there was one Hope Johnson who told stories in the 1920s at St Hilary, near Marazion,[161] and according to Deane and Shaw, there were men such as Bill Chubb of Liskeard (d.1974), who combined life as a pedlar with storytelling.[162] In the present era, this ancient Cornish tradition is seen in the work of Trevor Lawrence (famed for his Cornu-English reinvention of popular motifs), Angie Butler, and the more postmodern style of Will Coleman (a teacher, writer, actor and storyteller).[163] Projects such as the mid-Cornwall-based *Tales from the White Mountains* and Verbal Arts Cornwall have also drawn upon the early storytelling tradition of Cornwall.[164] The tradition also continues to be popular in literary works by Michael Morpurgo, Michael Foreman, Charles Causley, Antonia Barber, and Nicola Bayley – all of which draw on early, and sometimes ancient, stories and which have para-theatrical origins and connections.[165]

For a picture of the range of narrative available, we should look to the anthologies of the nineteenth-century story collectors, such as Robert Hunt and William Bottrell (who will be considered in much detail later on in this volume), but collections such as those by Neil Philip, Philip Wilson, and Peter Berresford Ellis give insight into Cornwall as proto-theatrical narrative space within both a wider British, and a wider Celtic context.[166] As examples that work collectively as useful myths of origin, Ellis chooses Tewdrig, Tyrant of Treheyl (drawing on *Bewnans Meriasek*), The Lord of Pengersick, The Bukkys, *Jowan Chy-an-Horth*, *Nos Calan Gwaf* (an adaptation of Bottrell's 'An' Pee Tregear's Trip to Market on Hallan Eve') and *Lys-a-Gwrrys* (derived from a tale recorded by publisher Len Truran on the Lizard peninsula).[167] The work of Hale, Kent and Saunders has also suggested a pan-European 'Chinese whisper' of Cornish Arthurian narrative,[168] and there are several links between Breton and Cornish narratives due to the high level of interface between the two cultures.[169] This was particularly strong in the pre-Reformation period, but there have been ongoing links since. It may be that there were more 'high epic' narratives once told in Cornwall, as in other European sea-board cultures, but since none have survived (aside from the Arthuriana and Tristana) it is hard to say what these narratives might be, and how they would have contributed to the origins of theatre. We can perhaps only note vestigial remains within the main folktale collections, which have a flavour of this kind of culture. There were probably many lost dramas (written both in Cornwall and elsewhere in the islands of Britain) that set narratives in Cornwall. It is highly likely that more writers drew upon sources such as Geoffrey of Monmouth's *Historia Regum Britanniae [History of the Kings of Britain]*, which contains substantial

Cornish-related material. Some writers took this a stage further. There is, for example, the apocryphal lost 'Shakespeare' text based on the life of Vortigen or Vortigern, titled *Vortigern and Rowena*, which was actually authored by William Henry Ireland in 1796.[170] This is the kind of narrative space in which (had it survived, and been integrated into the real Shakespeare canon) we might look for early, and passed-down, Cornish material. Another surviving play – *The Birth of Merlin or The Childe hath found his Father* – also has a Cornish context, but even its dual authorship, apparently by William Rowley and William Shakespeare, is highly contentious.[171] Authorship apart, however, it is of interest to us that this 'matter of Britain' material does find a place in a wider British dramatic history. That Cornwall was integral in terms of defining that 'matter of Britain' shows its significance in the storytelling origins, and therefore in the theatrical origins of these islands.

Cornwall's presence within a wider European context is given attention in some origin stories that must have had some influence on conceptions of early theatrical imaginings of place. Two stories and their telling have significance here. The first is the legendary connection between Cornwall and Troy, which forms the first of the 'giant' stories collected by Robert Hunt.[172] The narrative is also found in Geoffrey of Monmouth's *Historia Regum Britanniae*,[173] and this is Hunt's likely original source. In summary, the story runs that in the aftermath of the fall of Troy, Brutus and Corineus travelled by sea to the island of Britain. On arriving at what is now Plymouth, the two Trojans and their men encountered the native people, but were 'pursued by several terrific giants'.[174] One of the giants, named Gogmagog, was injured, and taken back to Plymouth where he subsequently recovered. Negotiations for a peace deal between the natives and invaders were begun but, as part of the terms, Gogmagog suggested they 'try a fall' (wrestle). A wrestling match then began on Plymouth Hoe, between Corineus and the giant, with the Trojan eventually the winner: 'The giant fell on the rocks below, and his body was broken into fragments by the fall'.[175] This is why this mythic location is called Langoemagog or Gogmagog's Leap. According to Hunt, this legend has some archaeological basis, since in the digging of the foundations of the Citadel on Plymouth 'Haw' (Hoe), 'the great jaws and teeth therein found were those of Gogmagog'.[176] This is a neat coda to the narrative, which intrinsically also links Cornwall with the wider south west. Supposedly, Brutus landed at what is now Totnes, and went east to found the rest of Britain, while Corineus travelled west to found Cornwall. So embedded in previous centuries was this version of history that some writers – in particular, Oliver Oldwanton – continued to label Cornish the 'Troyance tongue' well into the early modern era.[177] Such a text gives an indication of how 'lost' texts may have conceived of the Cornish

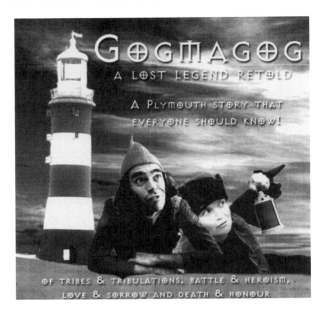

Fig. 9. Publicity photograph of *Gogmagog: A Lost Legend Retold*, as performed by Plymouth-based theatre company, Stiltskin, 2008. Courtesy of Stiltskin Theatre Company.

experience, drawing on the ideology contained in Geoffrey of Monmouth, and asserting the Trojan connection. As an origin myth for the Cornish, it is particularly apt, since it not only shows prowess against a foe, but neatly links to the long-established popularity of the sport of wrestling.[178] The story is also significant in that it forms a connection between ancient Mediterranean culture and Cornwall, and therefore provides a direct link to the mythology of the classical world.[179] Cornwall is therefore given a 'classical' origin within European culture; something which we shall see has ramifications within the wider conceptualisation of the territory within European thought.

Another 'origin' story connected to Cornish experience is the flooding of Lyonesse. The full mythos surrounding the 'flooding' is again recorded in the writings of Robert Hunt. The Cornish word for Lyonesse is *Lethowsow* and, according to Hunt, Lethowsow was 'a region of extreme fertility...[which] once united the Scilly Islands with Western Cornwall'.[180] One hundred and forty churches are supposed to have existed in the region, while the people there 'were remarkable for their industry and piety'.[181] Hunt makes much of the fact that the flooding of Lyonesse occurred on 11 November 1099, drawing on evidence from the Anglo-Saxon Chronicle, but the actual entry says: 'In this year also, at Martinmas, the incoming tide rushed up so strongly and did so much damage that no one remembered anything like it before; and on the same day there was a new moon'.[182] No actual location is given, and Hunt appears to assume this was the moment of flooding for Lyonesse. (The archaeological evidence is that the flooding of the Isles of Scilly took place much earlier at the end of the neolithic period.) Over time, there have been several folkloric notions of mariners hearing the bells of these churches under the waves, and trawling up pieces of masonry, though the Lyonesse myth is principally connected with two other components: the first is the story of how one of the ancestors of the Trevelyans (or Trevilians) escaped the flood by riding on a horse and landing at Perranuthnoe; the second is related to St Michael's Mount. The old Cornish name for this location is *Carack Looez en Cooz* [The Grey Rock in the Wood], and at one time the Mount did stand in a shore-line forest, which was probably flooded, like the Isles of Scilly, at the end of the neolithic period. Evidence of preserved wood has been found in Mount's Bay, and local legend suggests that the full extent of this landed area ran from Cudden Point to Mousehole, with Gwavas Lake (now the sea area just off Newlyn Harbour) a lake in the middle of that forest. Of course, archaeology has shown that the Isles of Scilly are the relics of a larger land area,[183] but it is still conjecture whether this is actually the Lyonesse imagined. However, Lyonesse has a para-theatrical significance because medieval, modern and contemporary writers have made Lyonesse the birthplace of Tristan. (If there were such a connection then, as Weatherhill and Devereux suggest, Leonois in Brittany is perhaps a more likely origin.[184]) Hunt's contemporary, the Reverend H.J. Whitfield also 'imagined' an Arthurian Lyonesse. In his version, Whitfield tells of the destruction of Lyonesse, but it is one in which Arthur's surviving army is pursued by Mordred in a westerly direction, across Cornwall and into Lyonesse.[185] Eventually, they founded a religious order on what is now the Island of Tresco, Whitfield neatly linking past and present, drawing on Tresco's history and the topography of the Isles, in which exist the islands of Great, Middle and Little Arthur. Again, the legend is significant. At once, it suggests that a more 'western' Celticity once existed in Cornwall, alongside a sense of loss over a greater territory and glory, reclaimed by nature. (In the contemporary context, it is perhaps a notable reminder of climate change on a cataclysmic scale.) Though not always explicit in drama, Lyonesse nevertheless forms part of the Cornish imaginative construct of themselves – a projection of space and place further into the Atlantic – that is more peripheral, more magical, and is ongoing, in the work of writers such as Thomas Hardy, Daphne du Maurier, Michael Morpurgo, Michael Foreman and myself.[186]

If Troy and Lyonesse offer a cultural-geographic perspective on para- and proto-theatrical experience in Cornwall, other storytelling influences have also had a pervading effect. Cornish people's connection to the sea is well-attested since neolithic times, and its imaginative construction of place is related to the mythology of the ocean. A key mythological component that has repeated references in literature and theatre is that of the mermaid. Probably the most famous narrative connected to mermaids is that of the Mermaid of Zennor, an image of which is found in the iconic bench-end carving at the church in Zennor. According to tradition, a mysterious woman attended church services in Zennor and nearby Morvah. The woman never aged, but became infatuated with local boy Matthew Trewelha, one day leading him down to the cliffs. Matthew and the beautiful woman were not seen again. Years later, the captain of a ship, who had put into Pendower Cove, was asked by a mermaid to lift up his anchor, since it was blocking her home. It was then that the people of Zennor realised what had happened to Matthew.[187] Other mermaid narratives persist at Lamorna, Seaton, Perranzanbuloe, Cury and Padstow.[188] The early integration of mermaid symbolism into Cornish theatre is proven in the theological exchange over the nature of Jesus, between the two doctors in the 'Passion' of the *Ordinalia*, a text with its origins in the fifteenth century. The First Doctor says:

> *doctor nynsv henna man*
> *n any il bos yn della*
> *den the uerwel yn certan*
> *awos cous lauarow da*
> *myreugh worth an vor vorvoran*
> *hanter pysk ha hanter den*
> *y vos dev ha den yn wlan*
> *the'n keth tra-na crygyans ren*

> [Doctor, that is not right at all,
> nor can it be so,
> that a man should die
> for saying such things.
> Look at the mermaid,
> half-fish and half-man,
> Let us believe the same thing of him,
> That he is clearly God and man.][189]

Fig. 10. The Mermaid bench-end at Zennor church in Cornwall.

This is proof enough that the authors of Cornish drama, even when considering 'world' subject matter such as the life of Jesus, were able to integrate secular, local symbols into the text, thus more readily connecting those watching and listening with the story. The result is that the biblical narrative has immediate effect on the local community, because the mythology of the local community appears to be integrated into the Bible: a perfect union of space, place and performance. This would be culture-specific enough if it were applied generally to Cornwall, but if the text of the *Ordinalia* were performed in a locale which had a specific mermaid legend, then the effect created on the audience would have been even more intense. We can perhaps speculate that if this were the convention of writing in medieval Cornwall, then maybe other parish-dependent mythological figures might also have been integrated as symbols into the 'universality' of the drama. Again we see a combination of secular, oral culture with universal biblical narrative. If the figures have a Celto-pagan origin, then all the better, since they were being integrated and used to demonstrate a Christian world view. Mermaid narratives are found in modern and contemporary theatre in Cornwall (for example, Pearl Peirson's 1951 production of *The Mermaid of Zennor* and the Bedlam Theatre Company of Cornwall's 1990 telling, *The Mermaid*), and probably featured in other performances over the centuries. The figure and the narratives are almost too good an icon of Cornish experience not to feature. Why then, should this figure and such narratives persist? Perhaps because mermaids are representative of the duality of Cornish experience: part-land, part-ocean. Like other parts of Britain, the mermaid may also be an interpretation of creatures of the natural world: perhaps seals or dolphins, which populate the coastline.[190] Thus we see a once para-theatrical narrative enter fully into the theatrical continuum.

Such a figure is therefore symptomatic of other iconic figures in Cornish folklore, which have had points of origin, and then have had repeated retellings on stage. Clearly, the maritime component of Cornwall's experience is important, but as indicated earlier in the chapter, the extractive industries of the territory have also formed a metaphorical base for drama. So ingrained in the ideology of Cornwall are the processes of mining that they are sometimes hard to disentangle from other aspects of experience. Indeed, we may argue that this is correct in that varieties of cultural materialist criticism suit this application, since all forms of cultural activity are intrinsically related to the economic base. Mining is crucial in Cornwall's economic base. Although there are no surviving early works that integrate processes of mining, early modern, modern and contemporary works make great use of mining as a metaphorical base for dramaturgy. There is, indeed, a specific vocabulary of mining,[191] which has its origins in the Cornish language, but has come to be perceived as a repository of Cornu-English expression. The Stannary institutions, although connected with all aspects of Cornish life, have their legal framework linked to the extractive industries from 'time immemorial'.[192] Therefore it was likely that, in the early theatre history of Cornwall, characters explored these aspects of experience – purely because they were reflecting the lived experience of audiences. No doubt, several early texts incorporated lore and legends from mining. Theatre and, more recently, television and cinema have often conceived Cornishmen as miners, or men with interest in mining.[193] This, I would posit, is age-old. Traces of this storied 'industrial Celtic' culture are therefore likely to be found along the way in our narrative.

Again, Robert Hunt is useful here in tracing elements of this extractive and industrial basis of Cornish culture. The Phoenician basis has already been considered in this chapter in relation to Joseph of Arimathea, but there are other ancient cultures that have purportedly had connections to Cornwall. Although probably pieces of anti-Semitic folklore, Jewish connections in the field of mining – both in the sense of Jews once working in the mines of Cornwall, and by a number of labels of workings and activities (Jews' houses, Jews' tins, and Jews' leavings) – have survived into the modern era.[194] Such a conceptualisation may well have influenced the portrayal of Jewish characters in the biblical dramas, though interestingly there is also reference to 'attall Saracen', possibly suggesting an Islamic or Arabic origin.[195] Perhaps this picture at least shows the multi-cultural nature of the mine trade in early Cornwall. St Piran, the patron saint of miners, is also a figure who may well have appeared in early dramas of Cornwall. Indeed, we should expect that if a drama was once performed at Perran Round, near Perranporth, it should feature the locally-connected saint himself. Like mermaids, the imagining of the underground mine spirits, the Knockers, has perhaps informed successive stages' imaginings of life underground, while warnings, omens and tokens of doom emanate from proto-theatrical ritual. Such spirits and superstition have travelled with the Cornish as they emigrated around the world, along the way providing new forums for expression of industrial lore.[196] Hunt also argues that at one time St Paul preached to the tinners on Dartmoor, and records that a cross on the road from Plympton to Princetown marks where this occurred. This merging of culture between Cornwall and Devon has significance, as we shall see next.

If orality and storytelling are significant in influencing dramaturgy in Cornwall from its earliest phase, then we might also return to that period of history associated with Dumnonia. Thus far, our concentration has been on Cornwall in its 'smallest' sense, after Athelstan's definition in the post-936 period. We ought also to be thinking of Cornish experience in a longer historical sense: that of the western Celts retreating away from Anglo-Saxon intrusion. Hunt comments on this by saying in his first collection that:

> ...When the task of arranging my romances was commenced, I found that the traditions of Devonshire, as far east as Exeter – the tract of country which was known as "Danmonium" [Dumnonia], or even more recently as "Old Cornwall" – had a striking family resemblance. My collection then received the name it bears, as embracing the district ordinarily known as the West of England.[197]

Such a comment is borne out in the work of scholars such as Sabine Baring-Gould (1834-1924), who actually notices that there is a good deal of folklore, story and song in common in the area from the River Exe to the west of Cornwall.[198] This might be a contentious argument for some Cornish nationalists, but it is one which has testified historical foundation. Thus, much of the folklore and proto-theatrical elements of Cornish theatre may have additional roots and origins in Devonian and Dartmoor lore, as well as in specifically Cornish folklore, due to the retreat of the 'Cornish' across the peninsula. In essence, this is also the reason why Breton folklore, theatre and literature has so many similar connections to those found in present-day Cornwall, since some of those peoples, retreating westwards, decided to head across the Channel to Armorica.[199] Indeed, some strikingly similar iconography and symbolism from Devon to that found in Cornwall and Brittany can be located. Eva C. Rogers' 1930 work, *Dartmoor Legends*, talks of an 'early and populous occupation' and of the 'Moormen during the Late Celtic period'.[200] She retells a version of the nymph Tamara, a creation story of the River Tamar, also recorded by Hunt.[201] Meanwhile, Druidic and bardic culture is emphasised in two stories: 'The Bards of the Wood of Wistman' and 'The Wrath of Taranis'.[202] In this we have a tangible connection to the early Cornish Gorsedd which supposedly met at Boscawen Ûn. Rogers offers, therefore, a wider Celtic imagining of the south-west peninsula. Not only is this found in the Druidic and bardic material, but also in tales of pixies and witchcraft,[203] thematic elements which form part of the corpus in Cornwall as well. Several shared folkloric elements are found recorded in the works of Ruth E. St Leger-Gordon, and Ralph Whitlock, which may indicate a 'pre-Tamar-as-border' defined Cornish commonality.[204] The shared linguistic heritage has also been considered in the work of Joseph Biddulph.[205] Although Biddulph's conceptualisation of Old Devonian has not been widely embraced by either nationalists or linguists, it remains an interesting field of enquiry, and one which demands more study.[206] Put together, this is a forgotten strand of wider south-western Celtic culture. Even more contentiously, this will also require us later to examine if and when there was an influence on Cornish theatre emanating from what is present-day England.[207]

So far we have looked at a number of components which have been influential in determining the origins of theatre in Cornwall. One that has been overlooked, however, is dance. The earliest human societies were entertained by dance, and would have incorporated dance into ritual and community events. This is still the case in Cornwall today. It is hard to imagine Helston's Furry Day without the processional Furry (or Flora) Dance.[208] Likewise, the movement of the Obby Oss at Padstow remains an integral part of the ceremony.[209] Dance also forms a large element of physical theatre activity by various contemporary theatre companies around Cornwall. Yet, as well as this, we know that when people go clubbing in Newquay on a Saturday night, they are actually doing something age old. Celebration via dance is a traditional part of many societies, and often the distinction between dance, drama and storytelling is a blurred line. The notion that dance and drama are different genres is, in fact, a relatively modern idea. In many non-European cultures, the boundaries between the two do not exist, so it is perhaps possible to conceive of such forms in early Cornwall. Even in the Renaissance, there were often no distinctions made between dancers, acrobats and actors – people in this profession were expected to be able to do all these activities. Dance, of course, has more recently had an influence on non-realist styles of theatre, though there is no reason to assume that it was not part of the earliest traditions of performance in Cornwall.

A flavour of this ancient input of dance into the theatrical culture of Cornwall can be found in the songs and dances collected by scholars such as Dunstan, Gundry, Davey and McGrady.[210] Although, for example, many of the songs collected by Dunstan were enshrined in their late nineteenth or early twentieth-century variants, most probably had more ancient origins, and therefore their musical motifs would have been strongly connected to community performance. This is certainly a model of scholarship for McGrady, who believes that many ballad carols written by Davies Gilbert and William Sandys have 'traces of ancient mystery' to them. Gundry even explicitly links the musical culture of Cornwall with theatre, by having the Obby Oss on the cover of his volume, demonstrating this age-old connection. He even considers whether there were connections between Cornish folk-song and the Latin chants of the Celtic church.[211] Although this is a somewhat tenuous connection, it cannot be wholly dismissed, considering, as Richard Rastall has considered, the music and associated dances within the Cornish mystery plays.[212] Bruch too, has examined the connections between verse structures and musical performance in *Bewnans Ke*.[213] Davey has done much to reassert the link between dance, music and popular culture in Cornwall which he interestingly terms 'from the mouths of the people',[214] suggesting a folk musical heritage, intrinsically related to performance. Davey has also established himself as the bagpiper of the Cornish Gorsedd, justifying, as Woodhouse offers, the link between ancient theatrical culture and Cornwall's musical and dance traditions.[215] Carvings of pipers on bench-ends at Alternun and Davidstow also assert the importance of piping. More recently, Davey has also completed considerable work on the difficulties of what he terms 'ancient traditions and modern sensitivities' based on the guizing continuum at Padstow's 'Darkie Days'.[216] Again, there is an established link between music and dance, and community performance and celebration.

Works by theatre theorists such as Victor Turner, and Celu Amderston have expressed the input of martial arts and traditional contests of skill and strength as being significant in the origins of some theatre across the world.[217] Since we have already noted that notions of conflict are of interest to an audience, then it is fairly easy to make the connection between exhibitions, contests and demonstrations of physical skill as a form of entertainment. Indeed, we know that in some Chinese and African cultures, the dexterity of a martial art is incorporated into a performance. Given Cornwall's propensity toward wrestling (or, to give it its more correct Cornu-English term, *wrasslin'*), it could certainly be theorised that there is a connection between the 'performance' of these feats of strength in competitions, and the development of theatre. Wrasslin' even has its own motto: *Gwary whek yu gwary tek* [Good play is fair play] – words spoken at the handshake between competitors, a notion which is in some ways related to the act of 'playing'. Consider the following observations of Richard Carew in the early seventeenth century:

> For performing this play, the beholders cast themselves in a ring, which they call making a place, into the empty middle space whereof the two champion wrestlers step forth, stripped into their doublets and hosen, and untrussed that they may so better commend the use of their limbs, and first shaking hands in token of friendship they fall presently to the effects of anger.[218]

Indeed, we also know that wrasslin' contests took place in the same locations as many *plen-an-gwarries*. Therefore, there is a long-standing connection and interaction between these forms of entertainment; perhaps even performed at the same time. The importance and endurance of Cornish wrasslin', not only in Cornwall but overseas, has been recorded by a number of observers.[219] This is all the more significant when it is discussed in the Trojan origin theory, as outlined earlier in this chapter. This connection is thrown into sharper light when we discover that the Globe and Rose Theatres of Shakespeare's time also held wrestling matches and bear-baiting contests alongside drama.[220] Clearly, this was pan-British too. Part of this ancient tradition of entertainment comes down to us in works by Charles Causley. Indeed, though now seen as politically incorrect and cruel, the traditions of entertainment provided by a dancing bear in his mother's youth are recorded by Causley.[221] Wrasslin' meanwhile continues to be a thread of contemporary Cornish drama.[222] The art of wrasslin' is therefore as important to defining a sense of community as the dramas.

This celebration of community is another important origin motif we have not yet fully considered. Such a celebration of community is intrinsically related to the ritual year. This can be in the form of a festival or a carnival. The theorist Bakhtin argues that the spirit of carnival is the full expression of a society's folk culture, and that it appears to oppose what is sacred and serious.[223] This temporary inversion or reverse of normal life facilitates an overthrow of what are established values and order. In effect, it tolerated anarchy and, in certain respects, gave working people a chance to 'let off steam'. This is likely to have been a recurring element of cultural experience for several millennia, perhaps even since the beginnings of humanity; though in early medieval Europe, such was the consolidation of religious ritual in life and the year, that festival culture paradoxically reinforced this tolerance of anarchy. In essence, the festival was legalised and sanctioned by traditions of the religious year. There was always, however, a fine line between enjoyment of the spectacle and its rebellious undertones: as witnessed in the authorities in Penzance in the late nineteenth century, who clamped down upon guizing activities, and, say, today in the various young people's music and surfing festivals which now take place regularly at Polzeath, and bring similar claims of disorder and inappropriate behaviour. Indeed, it was this very aversion to disorder that caused some non-conformist groups of the eighteenth and nineteenth centuries to frown upon festival and theatrical culture in Cornwall.

Mask and masque in its wider sense have been part of this process. As Rozik argues, masks have been used in festival and carnival across the globe for thousands of years, and whilst they are particularly useful in offering disguise from those watching (allowing a person to act in ways they normally would not), they are also perceived as dangerous, in the sense that masking again allows for illegal, disruptive and rebellious activity.[224] Masks, on such occasions, divert attention away from the face to the movement of the body, and thus enhance disruption and disorder. They also give us an understanding of characters' duality within a festival context. It could be that masks were used in early theatre in Cornwall, and even in some components of the mystery plays. Since none survive, it is hard to be conclusive though, as we shall see, echoes of them are found in contemporary festivals: for example, the person playing obby oss is not seen, and the dragon in *Hal-an-Tow* is also masked.

In recent years, there have been several studies that have related the origins of drama to particular events in the seasonal calendar.[225] Barber, and Bakhtin, for example, in famous studies of Shakespearean comedy, have shown how most of those comedies were related to a ritual moment in the year (for example, *Twelfth Night* and *A Midsummer Night's Dream*), and that these days were times when the normal order of society was inverted. Barber further demonstrates how such plays progress from an Old World, through a Green World to a New World. The Old World represents the old order, normally demonstrative of conservative and controlling forces within the drama, which by some event are thrown into disorder. This disorder manifests itself most specifically in 'green' space (normally a forest or a wood – where cultural isolation is possible), outside the confines of normal society. Confusion reigns and sometimes can even lead close to tragedy. However, events are turned around; a new order is gained, which reconfigures the world in favour of the main characters of the play.[226] Usually, this results in a set of multiple marriages. In considering this, we also need to realise that this model suits a predominantly non-literate audience, much like that which watched Cornish drama in the medieval and Tudor periods.[227] Drama allowed periodical alternatives to and inversions of the pattern of everyday life. Put another way: a subculture was tolerated by the dominant culture. We may go further: the Old World society was predominantly anti-comic and consisted of uninvolved spectators, whereas in the Green World, the confusion is both social and sexual (gender, as with Viola in *Twelfth Night*, is often hidden[228]).

There is now considerable academic weight in favour of the model that Shakespeare drew on the festival culture of Britain to demonstrate this 'topsy-turvy' culture.[229] If this is so, then we may understand that much drama across Britain (and logically in Cornwall) also draws on this aspect of cultural and seasonal life. It therefore becomes much easier to understand why Cornish mystery drama was performed at Corpus Christi and why, for example, mummers' plays and guizing took place at Christmas time – a direct link here, with the inverted order late-night partying of Feste, Sir Toby Belch and Andrew Aguecheek. Malvolio, as a Puritan (a group coming to full fruition under the auspices of Oliver Cromwell), is of course the antithesis of festival: he is the anti-comical, anti-carnival figure. Barber and Bakhtin's theories may have been made on Shakespearean comedy but they are crucially important for us in understanding the origins of theatre in Cornwall as well. Festival and theatre therefore occur

Fig. 11. Traditional festivals of the ritual year in Cornwall, as imagined in the Tregellas Tapesty. Courtesy of the trustees of the Tregellas Tapesty.

at these significant moments in the year, related to celebration, community and sense of place. Often they take place in a theatrical space that is significant in some way to the community. Cornwall has done much of late to recover and reinvent such festivals, which go back to earlier periods of history. Indeed, most communities in Cornwall now have a 'festival of inversion', directly related to the ritual year. A fine example is to be found at the present-day Golowan festival, or St John's Feast, in Penzance, where on 'Mazey Day' a mock mayor is chosen.[230] This is a classic demonstration of festival inversion culture, where the hegemonic social order is (for one day, at least) satirised. It is when the people mock the social order, enabling spontaneous parody; actor David Shaw one year offered spectators free cabbages and beer. There is universal displacement from top to bottom, from front to rear, and yet carnival and festival act as a safety valve, so dissipating opposition.

A couple of events in Cornwall fully demonstrate this festival culture and its relationship to drama. These are worth focusing upon because they truly show the interrelationship between festival, drama and community. The most obvious one (and it is one that we will constantly return to in this book), is the Obby Oss of May Day in Padstow. It is not possible to consider the whole of the evolution and development of Obby Oss here; thanks to scholars such as

Doc Rowe and others, one can find discussion of its wider place in traditional British festive culture.[231] Playwright and poet Donald R. Rawe has completed the most detailed study of the festival and, perhaps because of his theatrical leanings, has a keen understanding of the significance of the festival. He admits that the actual origins of the event are still shrouded in mystery, but does offer some material from a 1913 lecture by the Cornish historian Thurstan C. Peter, who makes the connection that 8 May was the beginning of the Celtic Beltane, when the coming of summer was observed with the lighting of fires. Therefore, this is the main source of the ceremony: to welcome the summer. Peter observes that:

> I believe the Hobby Horse and the Furry Dance alike to be ancient pagan festivals of revival and of fruitfulness, one of those forms of magic, not by any means implying the notion of invariable cause and effect, but an attempt to express in ritual the emotions and desires – and on this have been grafted on the one hand folk-lore and on the other Christian ceremonies, the history being still further confused by mistaken efforts of well-meaning persons to remove elements regarded by them as coarse.[232]

Thurstan, and Rawe argue for pan-British origins of such ceremonies, reflected in, as we have noted, other horses in Britain and Cornwall. However, in the drama of *Bewnans Meriasek*, broadly agreed to have been scribed at the start of the sixteenth century, Teudar mentions hobby horsing, and Rawe argues that this 'points to the conclusion that hobby-horsing was general in Cornwall at the time':[233]

> *Yv hemma ol an confort*
> *ambethe deworthugh wy*
> *ay serys yma thyugh sport*
> *pan vs dewen dymmo vy*
> *wel wel na fors*
> *re appolyn ev du splan*
> *kyns dyberth ny warth mas ran*
> *ma a pe dhe'n Hobyhors*
> *hay cowetha*
> *have that iiij lorel*
> *hag arta perthugh coff guel*
> *pendrellen tha comondya*

96

[Is this all the comfort
　That I should have from you?
O sirs, it is a sport to you
　When it is grief to me.
　　Well, well, no matter!
By Apollo, my bright god,
Before separating not a laugh but a cry
　I will pay to the hobby-horse
　　And her comrades.
Have that, ye four layabouts,
And again remember better
　What I may command.][234]

Therefore we have a picture of an ancient ceremony with proto- and para-theatrical elements. Events in the town have evolved and grown over time with, for example, a variety of different osses at different periods. Rawe also records the many personalities who, in living memory, have been involved with the evolution of the ceremony.[235] Certainly the May Day events of Padstow draw very closely on the elements of Bakhtin's theories on the origins of drama. The inversion of order takes place in an event on the eve of May Day when much decoration and preparation is given to the streets of Padstow, and once midnight has been struck then begin the well-known words of the 'Morning Song':

Unite and unite and let us all unite,
For summer is acome unto day,
And whither we are going we will all unite
In the merry morning of May.[236]

'Disorder' then is the business of the May Day, offering dramatic drumming, accordions, and dancing through the streets of the town. The person playing the oss is masked by the costume, and unseen by spectators. As Rawe observes, the people of Padstow remain highly guarded about the festival, since it represents a piece of genuine folk culture, which they have no desire to see marketed.[237] May Day at Padstow used to be a purely community-based event, harking back to an ancient time, when festival, drama and community were highly linked and very specialised, but thanks to television and radio, it is now widely attended, which in itself presents the town with problems. The original 'disorder' in a Bakhtinian sense of the word has sometimes been replaced with real disorder, where drunkenness has proven to be a problem for the Osses, the Teazers and those following the procession. May Day at Padstow took on an even greater political significance in the late twentieth and early twenty-first centuries, when it assumed the role of an act of resistance to second-home culture and the wider phenomenon of the town's environs being nicknamed 'Padstein' (referring to the influence of restaurants run by popular television chef Rick Stein) and nearby Rock being perceived at the time of writing as 'Kensington-by-Sea'.[238]

Less known, compared to May Day at Padstow, is the event that accompanies Helston's Furry Day: the *Hal-an-Tow*. Furry Day itself takes place on or around 8 May, and is perhaps best known for the genteel dances which take place during the day. The *Hal-an-Tow* originally took place in accompaniment to the dances but, after being revived in the 1930s by the Helston Old Cornwall Society, is now a separate event, being staged at several places (like medieval staging) from 8.30am onwards. The *Hal-an-Tow* is a much older piece of festival drama and, like Obby Oss at Padstow, it invokes the coming of summer. The event is actually a fairly typical example of a mummers' play though, as Deane and Shaw argue, there may well be some connections to local legends concerning a dragon and a devil.[239] Robin Hood and Mary lore, and perhaps fear of Spanish attack during the Renaissance, are also integrated into the song associated with the ceremony:

Robin Hood and Little John they both are gone to Fair-O,
And we will to the merry green wood to see what they do there-O,
And for to chase-O, to chase the buck and doe.
Hal-an-tow, jolly rumble-O,
For we are up as soon as any day-O
And for to fetch the Summer home, the Summer and the May-O,
For Summer is acome-O and Winter is agone-O.

Where are those Spaniards that makes so great a boast-O?
For they shall eat the grey goose feathers and we shall eat the roast-O.
In every land-O, the land where'er we go.

And as for that good knight St George, St George he was a knight-O,
Of all the knights in Christendom St George he is the right-O,
In every land-O, the land where'er we go.

God bless Aunt Mary Moses and all her power and might-O,
And send us peace in merry England both day and night-O,
And send us peace in merry England both now and evermore-O.[240]

Again, we see the Bakhtinian elements are prominent. The 'Green World' is noted, and the song suggests a clear deviance from the normal order of society because of the 'May-O'. In past times, the ceremony may well have had other ingredients to lengthen the performance, although the elements strongly match other summer mummers' events across Britain and, indeed, events at Padstow. In recent years, there have been attempts to build in St Piran as a character in the drama, as well as the event becoming more 'staged', spectacular and colourful than in previous years. The St Piran figure makes for a curious, more nationalistic imagining of the play, which traditionally contained standard 'English figures' such as St George, and mention of England rather than Cornwall. Nonetheless, the *Hal-an-Tow* is well-rooted in Cornish folklore and iconography, and gives us insight into how perhaps mummers' dramatic groups operated in the summer. Indeed, the same troupe was likely to have performed the winter guizing as well. There has been much debate over the meaning of the words *Hal-an-Tow*, but the probable derivation is from 'hal' meaning moorland, and *'tyow'* meaning houses. Thus, the chorus would mean something along the lines of 'in the country and in the town'.[241] This then makes a neat rhyme with the word 'rumble-O', meaning 'merrymaking'.

Both the Obby Oss at Padstow, and the *Hal-an-Tow* performance at Helston remain touchstones in the early theatrical culture of Cornwall, and integrate much of this chapter's main argument: that ritual, landscape and community in Cornwall remain tightly linked, and that all three provide significant contributions to the theatricality and dramaturgy of place. Whilst we are looking at early and primitive forms of drama, it may serve us well to explore one text in rather more detail. We may look at further examples of mummers' dramas in the chapters that follow, though it is appropriate now to examine how all of the elements discussed thus far can integrate and still be seen in vestigial form in a piece of text. The following drama from Camborne was recorded by the famous folklorist Cecil Sharpe[242] – sometime in the early twentieth century – from a J. Thomas of Camborne. This J. Thomas is very likely to be the same Jim Thomas who contributed many songs to Dunstan's collections of the 1930s.[243] R.J.E. Tiddy records Thomas's explanation of the drama:

There was little difference in the play in almost every district: but when I played it, Father Christmas was accompanied by two Merrymen or clowns who were making funny faces whilst Father was talking and singing old songs at intervals. And it would be they who would help the devil to carry the Turk out. And the Doctor would be a small boy of about twelve years old; he would have on a box hat, a frock coat, a pair of gloves too large for him, and a pair of spectacles on his nose with a hump on his back.[244]

This is a significant statement for it suggests that carrying on this age-old tradition was widespread in Cornwall, yet with contemporary adjustment according to circumstance. Its elements, though, were much older, and in line with some of the issues of ritual, storytelling, folklore, dance and community that have been discussed above. mummers' plays are, of course, related to the ritual year; though they are also pure farce, using crude imagery of struggle, death and resurrection to produce the necessary anxiety in the audience for cathartic purposes. In this sense, drama in Cornwall does have its origins in the Greco-Roman model. Rozik however, goes a step further, and argues that mummers' plays are even 'parodies of Shamanistic ritual'[245] – in particular, through the character of the Doctor. Given this, there may also be linkage to the 'Resurrection' play of the *Ordinalia*, where Jesus himself undergoes a 'shamanistic' revival after his death, which is echoed in the players' inability to bury Pilate's dead body. There are, according to Ernest T. Kirby, links here to characters and events that appear in the mummers' winter or spring-time ritual plays, and which can also be found in Cornwall:

(a) a doctor, who has travelled extensively to acquire his skills, performs the resurrection;

(b) a "cure" which is effected by extracting an object from the dead;

(c) a "presenter," who parallels the Shaman's "talker," repeats and/or interprets the unintelligible words of his master;

(d) a hobby horse, which derives "from the common Shamanistic belief that the Shaman rides a horse on his imaginary trance journeys to the other world."[246]

Clearly, if this is the case, then in Obby Oss, and in the Camborne Christmas Play that follows, we are drawing on ancient archetypes. Although an early twentieth-century incarnation of a Cornish mummer's drama, this Camborne play not only shows Camborne itself as a centre-point for Cornish and Anglo-Cornish drama, but also demonstrates how earlier and ancient elements were incorporated into its telling. To understand this, let us consider the narrative. The Knight and the Saint have two fights and in both, the Turkish Knight is killed. After the first mortal wound, the Doctor revives the Knight, but after the second, the Knight is pronounced dead, and is then taken out by the Devil.[247] The victor is promised a house for himself and God. The Christian overtones are straightforward enough. Although both characters boast of their power, Father Christmas admonishes only the Turkish Knight for his bragging. The audience clearly identify with the fact that Saint George is the patron saint of England, while the Knight is perceived as both an infidel and an enemy. It is worth us therefore considering the full text of the play:

The Page:

Here comes I the Page, I am come to ask you
to favour us with a few gallons of room in your house
For Father Christmas with his Pop and Touse,
For, friends, this is the time of the year
For Father Christmas to appear.

Father Christmas:

Here comes I old Father Christmas welcome or
welcome not;
I hope old Father Christmas will never be forgot.
We are not come here to laugh and geer
But come to taste your Christmas beer.
If your Christmas beer is all done
We are come to have a bit of fun;
But if for fun you are not inclined,
Before we leave we will taste your wine;
But if our fun you think it's right,
I call in the Turkish Knight.

Turkish Knight:

Here comes I the bold Turkish Knight.
I came from the Turkish land to fight:
First, I fought in England,
And then I fought in Spain,
And now I am come back to England.
To fight St George again.
If I could meet St George here,
I would put my spear in through his ear.
I would beat him and bale him
And cut him in slices
And take a small pot and make a pair of garters.

Father Christmas:

Bold talk, my child, bold talk, I am sure –
And St George is coming through the door.

St George:

Here comes I St George
A man of courage bold:
If thy blood is hot

I will soon make it cold,
As cold as any clay;
I will take thy life away.
Draw thy sword and fight or draw they purse and pay,
For satisfaction I must before I go away.

Turkish Knight: My sword is already drawn, no money will I pay,
For satisfaction you can have before you go away.

They begin to fight by crossing swords. After three leg-cuts and then three head-cuts, St George strikes a blow at the Turkish Knight and he falls to the ground. Father Christmas goes to him concealing some red ochre in his hand which he puts on the Turk's neck.

Father Christmas: Oh, oh, is there a doctor to be found
To cure this deep and deadly wound?

Doctor: Yes, there is a doctor to be found
To cure that deep and deadly wound.

Father Christmas: What can you cure?

Doctor: I can cure the itch, the specks, the spots and the gout –
If there's nine devils in, I can kick ten out.

Father Christmas: Wonderful cure, wonderful cure.

The doctor then gives the Turk a kick in the backside with the side of his foot.

Father Christmas: Is that all you can cure?

Doctor: No. I can cure the hipigo limpigo and no go at all.
The diseases of men big or small.

Father Christmas: Wonderful cure, wonderful cure.

The doctor, taking from his pocket a very large bottle and wooden ladle, pretended to pour some medicine into the ladle and to put it into the Turk's mouth.

Doctor: Now take a few drops of my helly com pain
And rise to fight St George again.

The Turk jumps up and has another fight with St George; but he soon receives his fatal blow and falls to the floor. Father Christmas goes to him and, shaking his head, says, My child is dead. Then the Doctor goes to him and takes hold of his foot to feel his pulse: he shakes his head and says, The Turk is dead.

The Devil:	Here comes I old Bealzibub,
	On my shoulder I carry my club,
	In my hand a frying pan:
	Don't you think me a jolly man?

Father Christmas:	How aren't you a jolly old man
	With a head like a pig
	And a body like a sow
	And a great long nose like the beam of a plough.

| The Devil: | I have a fire that is long lighted |
| | To put the Turk who was long knighted. |

With the help of the others, he gets the Turk on his back and goes out with him, saying,

> Here I goes old man Jack
> With the Turk upon my back,

The mason comes in with the trowel in his hand and a hod on his shoulder.

| The Mason: | Here comes I little Tom Tarter |
| | I am the boy for fixing marter. |

He takes St George by the hand and walks him out saying,

> With my trowel and my hod
> I will build a house for you and God.

The End.[248]

Various components of theatre's origins are integrated into this text. For certain, the play's origins lie in the ritual year. This is embodied in both the character of Father Christmas, and the sense of festivities brought on by the drinking of beer. The sheer farcical design of the piece appears to reflect some degree of medieval conception and style since, for example, the characters self-present ('Here comes I…'). It may well have been adopted and adapted from previous pagan culture, since it would have been relatively easy to change the names of the personages involved. There is also an aspect of seasonal myth here: the resurrection that occurs comes at a turning point in the year. If the play were presented close to the winter solstice, then the resurrection of light would have synchronised with the aims of the drama. However, the fact that the second resurrection of the Turkish Knight fails may symbolise both his failure in terms of his own spirituality and also, of course, a parody of earlier shamanistic culture. The Doctor here is a 'shaman' figure, but he is one that does not have the complete skills. This parody works because Christian culture has not encumbered it with the sacredness that one might find in early religious dramas in Cornwall and, indeed, in its fully formed medieval state. Of particular note here, is the way that Thomas' group of players conceptualised the Devil. The imagery is highly agricultural, suggesting a non-technical and non-industrial culture, and therefore perhaps of earlier origin. Secondly, Thomas also gives us an understanding of how the performance occurred, with the two clowns making funny faces while Father Christmas speaks. If Thomas' group were using this technique, which may have been passed down through generations, then we have another insight into early methods of performance. Clearly, satire is operating on a very sophisticated level, early on. Vestigial elements, therefore, of early dramatic culture of Cornwall can be noted in such a text. Cornishness itself, then, does not come out in theories of identity here: the conceptualisation is of a wider England (also matching the imagining in *Hal-an-Tow*, and other mummers' texts in Cornwall). It is perhaps the form and way that the drama was performed which defines its Cornishness more readily. This will prove crucial when we come to consider the universal themes of epic, biblical drama in Cornwall; and we will find parody, as developed here, also integrated into the two surviving saints' dramas, facilitating a stylised and important combination of the secular and the divine. Mummers' plays, like this one from Camborne[249] and the *Hal-an-Tow* from Helston, may come to us in their modern form, but their origins prove to be much older.[250]

Bewnans Meriasek and *Bewnans Ke* are the only surviving saints' dramas in the island of Britain. This must tell us something about the dramatic origins of Cornwall. As a genre, the lives of the saints offered fascinating subjects for early dramaturgy. Their survival would indicate something else: the sheer intensity of dramatic culture in Cornwall. Camborne and Kea are not that far apart geographically, and yet here are two very different plays with complex characterisation and dramaturgy. It is hard to know when theatre in Cornwall felt that the lives of saints were interesting potential sources for dramatic activity but, judging from later texts, clearly detailed records were kept of their works and association with particular places. As an example of this, we need only to look at Albert Le Grand's version of the Life of St Ke, which had been known about for a number of years before the rediscovery of the drama of *Bewnans Ke* in 2000.[251] There is likely, then, to be a high degree of correlation between the various endeavours of saints which have come down to us, and their imagining in dramatic form.

Our picture of how saints operated in the landscape and community of Cornwall from 400 CE is gained partly from their medieval lives collected by scholars from folklore, from archaeology and from history.[252] Ireland and Wales to the north, and Brittany to the south, play a significant part, since many core saints in Cornwall arrived on the northern coast, and then departed from the south. Some, however, were also indigenous to Cornwall. There are many memorial stones from the pre-Norman period that are Christian in nature, with their inscriptions and art confirming the displacement of an earlier pagan culture by a Christian one. From various accounts, the pattern would seem that saints, having converted local rulers, then journeyed to other locations, settling in these new places to create new centres of Christian life. Once that had been achieved, then it seems they either moved on (perhaps when still young), or stayed for the remainder of their lives. For the most part, such Celtic saints were working with populations which had seen a Roman influence on their lives, and thus were aware of so-called 'classical civilisation' but also knew the older Celtic gods. There is, indeed, considerable evidence of the transforma-tion of local Pagan deities into saints during this period, and that, over time, different lives and figures have been blended.[253] Likewise there is something of a link between community shamanistic figures and the tradition of saints in Cornwall[254] – a link that we shall never fully understand, but one that it is important to assert in our understanding of origins.

Some of the more famous saints in Cornwall are uniquely associated with places and communities. For detailed observations about their lives and works, then one of the most significant texts is Nicholas Roscarrock's *Lives of the Saints*. Roscarrock (*c.*1548-1634) was a Cornish Catholic, who suffered imprisonment and torture for his beliefs.[255] After being released from the Tower of London, he wrote a huge hagiographic dictionary, of which Devon and Cornwall form a large part. Roscarrock may offer us useful insights into a lost world of saintly lives and dramas. For example, his life of St Columba was apparently 'taken out of an olde Cornish Rymtha containing her Legend, translated by one Mr Williams, a Phisition there, but how Autentick it is I dare not saye, being loath to comptrowle that which I cannot correct'.[256] Such a statement is intriguing because it suggests the community of St Columb already had some kind of poetic or dramatic imagining of their saint in the

Cornish language, predating this period. He notes not only her Well, whose water would not boil (this sounds like a dramatic motif),[257] but also incidents in the lives of other saints which lend themselves to dramatic interpretation: the story of St Endelient tells of the incident of King Arthur and the cow,[258] while St Menfre threw her comb at the devil.[259] Orme describes these legends as 'picturesque';[260] but perhaps recast another way, they may be seen to be a Cornish theatre of 'origins', determined by local, yearly re-enactment. Roscarrock's writings have since been drawn on by a number of later scholars, among them Doble, John, and Orme, whose writings on saints in the modern era have helped to define their influence and place in Cornish history.[261] Of these, only John sees the significance of drama 'setting forth divine wonders and divine revelation' and observes that 'the plots might celebrate the local saint, Celtic, biblical or other... [with] majestic scenes showing forth God's work and his dealings with mankind from the Creation to the End of the World. These, in the vernacular, are shot through with biblical questions and allusions'.[262] John puts her finger on something important here: the vernacular. For indeed such drama needed to be composed principally in Cornish (though to an extent, we also see a creolization of language occurring, matching the socio-linguistic shift in Cornish history). It may even be that such drama never needed a script of the kind imagined from *Bewnans Meriasek* or *Bewnans Ke*, and that these two represent the full literary end of the spectrum. Some saints' lives may well have been learnt or extemporised from previous generations, without need for a book version. Indeed, this may well have suited many communities: illiterate, and isolated from book learning.[263]

One form of ritual landscape was established earlier in this chapter: the Cornish concern with ceremonial stone in specific landscape. The saints, then, offer an embellishment of that place, offering a new kind of 'sacred landscape' which will go on to inspire and develop new drama. In essence, to look at this dramaturgy in a materialist sense, it is at this point in history where the moment of production occurs. In understanding this, we may decide to consider saints' dramas in Cornwall as plays about community origins. Though only two survive, their survival gives us an impression about how other such dramas would have functioned in communities. Clearly, there are a number of leading saintly figures in Cornwall whose presence prompted dramatic inter-pretation;[264] but likewise, more obscure or minor saints may also have had dramas presented about them – depending on locale, population, and interest. Most saints' lives carry with them stories of miraculous deeds, some defeat of a greater evil and, very often, the founding of a holy well. The miraculous deeds lend themselves remarkably well to spectacle, while the battle between the hero of the drama and an evil force (whether the Devil or a local tyrant) makes for high-order conflict. The foundation of a Holy Well, as Broadhurst notes,[265] is of peculiar significance, for water is a life-giving element. It is needed for people to survive, and for health and comfort, so the founding of a well would have been of huge importance during this phase and after. That the well would still have been used by the people of the parish suggests an ongoing link back to the place's foundation origins. Community and past are therefore highly connected. Specific geographies of place may also have been incorporated into such dramas, localising the legend still further, and providing intimate understanding of the landscape for the community. If indeed the parish of Perranzabuloe did, at one point, present a play based on the life of St Piran, then the connection between its theatre space, its landscape and the saint's arrival via the ocean is highly charged. Saints' lives therefore have had a huge impact on culture in Cornwall, not only in the early and medieval period, but we still see their ongoing presence today. The poet John Betjeman continued to be fascinated with the lives of Cornish saints in works such as 'Trebetherick', 'Saint Cadoc' and 'North Coast Recollections'.[266] Indeed, this has led Payton to describe Betjeman's interest as 'one man's Celtic Quest'.[267] Donald R. Rawe's late twentieth-century dramas considered the lives of St Piran and St Petroc.[268] Clearly, he was making a connection between an imagined dramaturgy of the past and their contemporary relevance (especially in the new definition of a nationalistic St Piran in the twentieth century[269]). Thus, in the lives of saints, we see not only a face of the origins of theatre in Cornwall, but also their ongoing presence in the continuity of dramaturgy, that is perhaps not matched anywhere else (bar perhaps Brittany).

Having proposed some of the origins of theatre in Cornwall, and having arrived at an understanding of the interconnectedness of ritual, landscape and community, towards the end of this earliest phase of drama in Cornwall we do begin to witness the literary production of drama. Though the evidence is fragmentary and, in some cases, far removed from what we recognise now as dramatic texts or even scripts, these do inform us of how a literary-dramatic culture was operating in this period. The texts may be grouped in two main types: those that may have had their origins in Brythonic or Cornish, and those that have physically survived in Cornish. One of the former is *The Dialogue of Arthur and Eliud* by Taliesin. Taliesin should be considered in the light of bardic culture in Britain.[270] He may be viewed as a 'Welsh' poet associated with the territories of the Britons in the 'old North'; in some of his work he immortalised his most generous patron, Urien of Rheged, an area probably corresponding with modern Cumbria.[271] In later ages, prophetic poetry was often ascribed to him. Sometimes this kind of poetry was completed as a kind of dialogue, which may give an indication of early dramatic work completed in Cornwall. A conflict is produced between Arthur and his dead nephew Eliud, who appears before him in the form of an eagle: this is a motif that is very common in post-Roman Celtic literature.[272] Elements of Christian doctrine are debated, and here Arthur is portrayed as a man explicitly identified with the land of Cornwall. He is seen as a soldier, and one not fully acquainted with the fundamentals of Christianity:

Arthur

I marvel at it, since I am a poet,
before an oak tree with a beautiful top,
Why does the eagle stare? Why does it laugh?

Eliud/Eagle

O Arthur, who won long-lasting praise,
bear of the hosts, refuge of happiness,
the eagle has seen you before.

Arthur

I marvel at it, close to the seas,
and I ask it cautiously:
Why does it laugh? Why does the eagle stare?

Eliud/Eagle

O Arthur, whose career found long-lasting praise,
bear of the hosts, with a look of joy:
the eagle has seen you before.

Arthur

The eagle stands on the top of an oak:
if you sprang from bird-kind,
you would not be tame or gentle.

Eliud/Eagle

O Arthur, charging with sword in hand,
your enemies will not stand before your assault:
I am the son of Madog, son of Uthyr.

Arthur

O eagle, I do not know your kind
that travels the wood valley of Cornwall:
Madog the son of Uthyr is not alive.

Eliud/Eagle
O Arthur, of language and fierceness,
bear of men, anger will not preserve you:
I was once called Eliud.[273]

In essence, this is a Brythonic dialogue, which draws on an early imagining of
an Arthur figure. There are connections to material already discussed in this
chapter. Eliud is one of the names given to a shamanistic wild man figure and,
as we know, this archetype was also later applied to Merlin. Although Taliesin's
text was unlikely to be acted as a duologue as it might be now, Taliesin or other
bardic figures might have multi-voiced the piece.[274] Perhaps in such early
Brythonic poetry we see the initial literary construction of drama, with Arthur
as obvious – and perhaps even tragic – subject matter. Merlin himself can also
be viewed as a tragic figure; thus an audience, listening, would undergo
catharsis and understand hubris. Given, as we shall see below, the ideology of
bardic and poetic culture imagined in the *Vocabularium Cornicum*, perhaps this
is not too dissimilar to what may well have been developed in Cornwall.
Certainly the repetitive elements and the questioning structure of the piece
make it highly suitable for performance or recitation.

The ancient language of Cornwall is testament to a thriving culture of early
theatricality. We do, for example, have some insight into a lost Cornish
literature written in the eighth and ninth centuries. The first text to consider
is from an annotation on a ninth-century manuscript of *De Consolatione
Philosophiae* of Boethius, a text associated with the circle of King Alfred. The
annotation *ud rocashaas* appears to be Cornish and was written in a different
hand than other Latin and Old English comments.[275] This broadly translates
to 'The mind hated the gloomy places', which is perhaps a highly dramatic
observation, if not a full dramatic text. What is interesting is that this gloss
proves a link between indigenous Cornish culture and classical learning,
maybe indicating that theatrical material was passed on in a similar way.
Anicius Manlius Severinus, better known as Boethius (c.475-524) was born of
a Roman consular family and studied philosophy, mathematics and poetry. A
bold court minister and writer, he was deserted by his friends and supporters,
and was executed. His *The Consolation of Philosophy* shows how everything is
insecure, aside from virtue. The text became enormously influential in the
early Middle Ages, and may well have informed a good deal of learning and
writing in Cornwall. If this were the case, then themes of virtue would have
crept into the moments of textual production.

Formerly thought to have been the earliest source of written Cornish, the
nineteen glosses from Smaragdus's Commentary on Donatus date from

around the end of the ninth century. Aelius Donatus (*c*.354 AD) was one of the most famous Latin grammarians of late antiquity, while Smaragdus was Exarch (Emperor) of Ravenna between the years 585 to 589 and 603 to 611. They were originally thought to have been Old Breton.[276] Some scholars have believed that in 1907 Joseph Loth (1847-1934) demonstrated that they were Old Cornish. I submit that this is incorrect. The confusion perhaps shows the close cultural relationship between Old Cornish and Old Breton. It is, in fact, a Latin text that has been glossed by a Breton, but there are some striking similarities in five of the glosses to Old Cornish. The words are *Marchoc* [Horseman], *Fron* [Nose], *Mesin* [Acorn], *Toroc* [Tick (insect)] and *Cintil* [kinship group]. Again, we may reassert classical learning, as well as the age-old similarity between Breton and Cornish culture. Drama during this phase could have been performed in either territory with mutual understanding. Although the words are not dramatic, this was the vocabulary of performance that would have been used in the Old Cornish period.

Contained in the Bodleian library manuscript *Oxoniensis Posterior* are a limited number of Cornish glosses on *The Book of Tobit* (or *The Book of Tobias*).[277] *The Book of Tobit* is a book of scripture considered to be part of the Orthodox and Catholic biblical canon, and pronounced as canonical by the Council of Carthage in 397. Again, Breton and Cornish are hard to differentiate at this point in history. Speakers would have spoken a different dialect rather than a different language. All would have regarded themselves as speaking varieties of the British Language. The glosses are:

Cennen [Skin or membrane]
Drogn [Troop or gang]
Garn [Leg][278]

Again, these would have been used in performance. The word *Drogn* may be particularly relevant in describing a group of players. As well as these insights into a lost world of performance, throughout the territory of Dumnonia there are some inscribed stones which show examples of Old Cornish. One such example is found at Lustleigh parish church: *DXXTUIDOC CONHINOC* [Dettudioc, son of Conhinoc] The stone either marks a boundary or is a tombstone of Dettuidoc, son of Conhinoc. This section of Devon was not captured by the Saxons until sometime after 925, so this stone is further evidence of a wider south-western Celticity. The change in circumstances in the south west of Britain however, is documented in works such as the so-called *Bodmin Manumissions*, dating from around 960.[279] This document contains evidence of Saxon landowners in eastern Cornwall recording manumissions (or certificates of freedom) for serfs. Their method follows the custom to record legal transactions on the blank areas of sacred texts: thus ensuring honesty before God. In the *Bodmin Manumissions*, most of the lords have Saxon names while most of the serfs have Cornish names, showing how Cornwall was now under Saxon control. Though there is nothing particularly dramatic about this, issues of power and control over Cornwall were going to dominate theatrical culture in Cornwall for the next thousand years.

The best source of theatrical vocabulary, however, comes from the *Vocabularium Cornicum*, often referred to as *The Old Cornish Vocabulary*.[280] This Old Cornish-Latin thesaurus, dating from *c*.1100, was probably compiled by Ælfric, the abbot of Eynsham, It classified biblical and everyday terms for Cornish speakers learning Latin. In many respects, the vocabulary is perhaps the closest we shall come to understanding the language spoken during the age of Arthur. The vocabulary is logically presented, showing the ordering of the universe from God and Heaven downwards, and in its 955 entries, much of the known world is discussed.[281] Some of the entries are relevant to understanding this early theatrical world. The following, for example, all refer to parts of the body required for performance: *genau* [the mouth], *tauot* [a tongue], *stefenic* [palate], *gueus* [the lips], *briansen* [the throat], *sceuens* [the lungs], and *lau*, or *lof* [a hand or palm]. This is highly detailed, but consider the following terms, which delineate different kinds of speakers, who must have been witnessed in performance at some point: *creg* [a stammerer], and *stlaf* [lisping]. Clearly, in a predominantly oral society, people considered these as significant problems. The next terms are derived from the vocabulary of the Church, but also refer to degrees of orality and performance that accompanied religious functions: *profuit* [a prophet], *cheniat* [a singer], *canores* [a singing woman], *redior* [a reader] and *rediores* [a female reader]. This latter term prompts us to ask how likely it was that women giving the readings in a female religious community would have been admitted to the order of readers.

More political terms are also found, which may give us insight into some of the cultural-political make-up of early Cornish society. *Leid*, for example, refers to 'a tribe'. The implication therefore, is of a distant sub-community defined by common descent, which self-defines and has with it a set of narratives and stories defining that descent. *Chetua* means 'an assembly'. This probably refers to a political gathering, but such gatherings may have been witness to performances as well. *Datheluur* translates as 'a speaker, or orator'. In societies without a formal legal profession, and even in non-judicial proceedings in those societies where one exists, people with a gift for persuasive argument are often called upon to represent others in disputes and contentions. Likewise, speakers and orators used performance skills to create

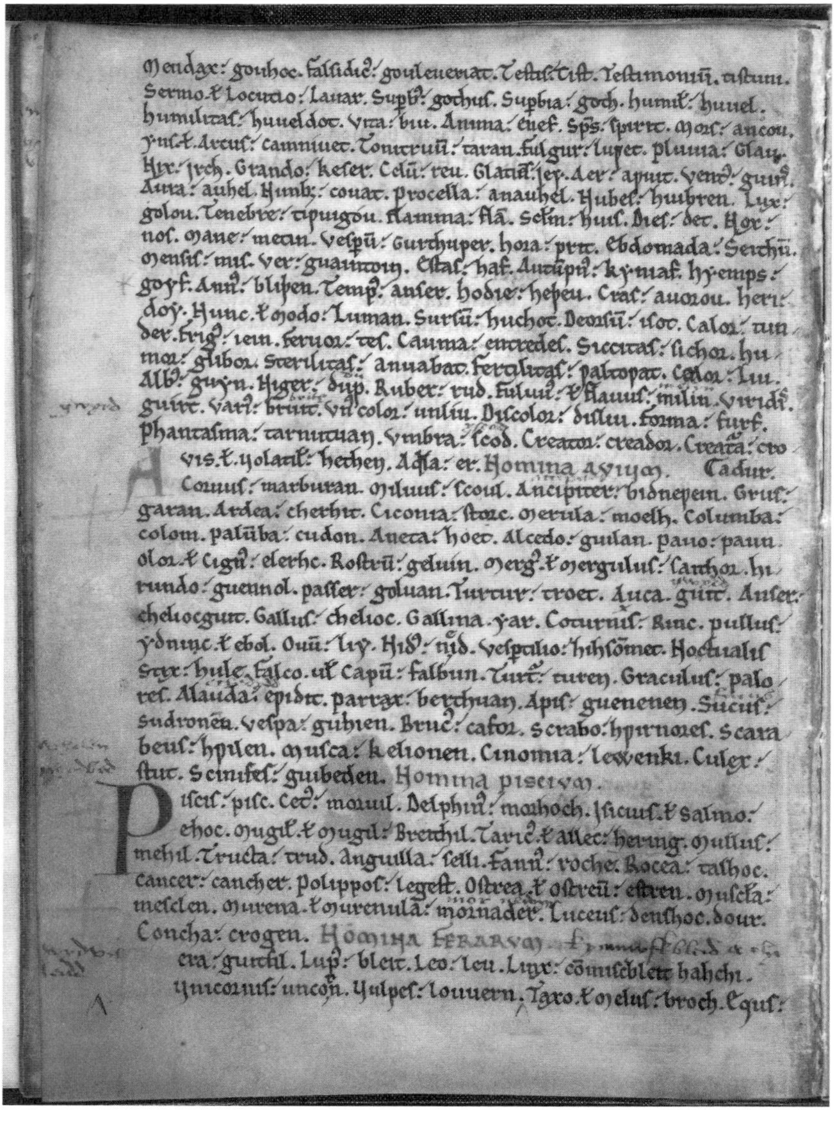

Fig. 12. A page of the *Old Cornish Vocabulary*, in the *Cottonian Vespasian A XIV*, featuring the colours, birds, fish and beasts. Courtesy of the British Library.

particular effects or to garner opinion. From a musical dramatic point of view, the *Vocabularium Cornicum* also contains many references to instrumentation and types of musicians, which may have accompanied or formed part of early performance. These are *corden* [a string], *teleinior* [a harper or harpist], *telein* [a harp], *barth hirgorn* [a trumpeter], *hirgorn* [a trumpet], *Piphit* [a piper], *Pib* [a pipe], *harfellor* [a fiddler], *(har)fellores* [a female fiddler], *harfel* [a viol], *cherniat* [horn-blower], corn [a horn], *Pibonoul* [pipe, flute or whistle], *keniat cobrica* [a hornpipe player] and *tolcorn* [a fife or flute].[282]

A more specific dramatic entry follows this list, with the word *pridit* meaning a poet. In the MS., this word has been underlined by a secondary scholar. Welsh has this word as *prydydd*, the root of which is related to the Welsh *pryd* 'shape, appearance' and the Irish *cruth* 'form'. The sense of it, then, is of one who creates or gives form to something. The evidence from Welsh and Irish Law is that the class of professional poets was divided in two ways. As was to be expected, the professional poet had to undergo a very long training, just like any other craftsman (women were excluded from the profession). The aspiring poet would attend a school run by a master, who would teach him the basic metres and set him tasks to perform. These would include praise poems, asking poems, elegies and battle songs. The higher the social rank of the person addressed, the more difficult would be the poetic forms used – and the greater would be the reward due to the poet. The other major division within the profession was between those who composed the poems and those who performed them. The performer was the other class of poet, but this was also related to music. In the Celtic languages, the vocabularies of music and of poetry are particularly hard to separate. The simplest explanation is that in performance a poem would have been chanted or sung.

With Cornwall's loss of external independence, and the placing of Saxons among the ruling classes, there would have been a loss of patronage for poets. The professional poets would then have lost their social status as privileged craftsmen.[283] In order to survive, they would have been forced to find an audience amongst the non-noble classes. Since that new audience would have possessed much less wealth, it would have been necessary for a composer of poetry to dispense with the services of a separate performer. They would probably have needed to reach a closer accommodation with the Church, whereas their colleagues in Wales, and even more so in Ireland and Scotland, were able to maintain their organisational independence for longer. The evidence from the middle Cornish period (broadly 1300-1540) is that this is exactly what happened. The literature of the time blends native and western Latin learning so completely that it is impossible to separate them. There are references in the early middle Cornish period (1100-1300) to scholars from Cornwall who had little or no English, but who nevertheless acquired enough learning to achieve high ecclesiastical office.[284] By the middle Cornish period, the Church (and centres of Christian learning like the Collegiate Church at Glasney) would have become the mainstay of native learning. However, at the time of the *Vocabularium*, this had not yet come about, and the 'poet' is listed with musical rather than clerical professions.

The word that follows *pridit*, is *barth*, meaning a 'mimick, or buffoon'. From when the Greek writers were first recording their observations of the Celts until recently, the clear sense of this word was 'somebody who recited poetry in public'. In a largely non-literate environment, people's only solitary uses of poetry would have been mainly in ritual or in work-songs. A mythology has grown up around the use of the word 'bard' in Celtic societies, not least in Cornwall where the post-1928 Gorsethow has encouraged use of the term. The word here suggests an alternative and perhaps more accurate depiction of who writes and 'tells' poetry and narrative in Cornish society c.1100. This is ironic, since clearly the contemporary Cornish Gorsedd ceremony seeks to 'imitate' aspects of an ideologically safe Celtic society, such as horns, harps, the calling of the quarters and allegiance to King Arthur.[285] Clearly, the actual meaning of 'bard' is much different to the popular imagining of such a Celtic ideal. Nevertheless, comedians fulfil important functions in all societies, not least in their satirical interpretation of events. Graves, meanwhile, persuasively argues for 'entertainer'.[286] Satire has always been an important function of poets in Celtic society. If praise was their chief duty, then anybody failing to meet the criteria meriting praise deserved blame. Native law attempted, with varying success, to regulate satire, prescribing who might do it and in what circumstances. However, by the time of the *Vocabularium*, it seems that the satirists would have lost their forensic function. They would have therefore needed to exercise their profession at less formal gatherings, such as fairs, feasts and revels. The musical context suggests that a satirist would have needed to sing and play an instrument, as well as deliver repartee, the latter probably often very earthy indeed. These core theatrical terms are followed by *lappior* [a dancer] and *lappiores* [a dancing woman] suggesting that both genders contributed to performances.

Some words follow in the *Vocabularium* that are, perhaps, less from the theatrical base, but contribute in para-theatrical ways to elements of performance in early Cornwall. *Chuillioc* refers to 'an augur, or a soothsayer': one who, at the beginning of an undertaking, foretold of the likely outcome by interpreting such phenomena as the flight of birds, or markings on the internal organs of sacrificial victims. The implication is that the *chuillioc* performed an office that a Roman might have regarded as of equivalent status. This may not have been an entirely accurate perception and, in addition, we must remember that this document was written several hundred years after Roman pagan beliefs, and indeed some native ones, had ceased to be held. *þurcheniat* means 'an enchanter'. The fact that both this and the previous word are placed in the context of words for harmful persons suggests the efficacy of pre-Christian magical procedures was accepted, but that their employment was not sanctioned. *Hudol* [a sorcerer] also falls into this category. Cornwall has a long folkloric tradition of 'pellers' [magicians].[287] *Cuillioges* [a divineress or female-soothsayer] is also recorded in the *Vocabulary*. Such figures were probably examples of latent proto- and para-theatrical practice, and made for obvious subject matter within drama.

Less harmful concepts related to drama are *scriuiniat* [a writer] and *scriuit* [a writing], though is hard to imagine just how much drama was actually written in this period. As indicated above, performers probably more often extemporised on a particular theme. The ritual year was well understood during this phase, and so there are terms for the seasons: *guaintoin* [the spring], *haf* [summer], *kyniaf* [autumn] and *goyf* [winter]. Ritual and performance to celebrate transitions between these seasons would have been established by this point. Not only was local culture understood though; clearly writers knew of other exotica. *Caur march*, for example, is the Old Cornish word for 'a camel'. Whereas most European languages have borrowed the original name via Latin, this coinage from native elements indicates a large quadruped, suitable for riding. Through maritime and trade activity, the early medieval Cornish may have been among the first peoples of these islands to observe these creatures.[288] Alternatively, they would also have been mentioned in biblical stories and community dramas. Another exotic entry is found in the word *oliphant* meaning 'an elephant'. Cornishmen and women travelling abroad may well have encountered elephants. In terms of theatricality, animal life on land does not get much larger, so presumably such animals also featured in native dramaturgy.

Cornish language writing and drama remains relatively quiet in the period immediately after the *Vocabularium Cornicum* although, as we have already noted, Geoffrey of Monmouth's *Historia Regum Britanniae [History of the Kings of Britain]* (1146), contains substantial Cornish material. Geoffrey called himself Goufridus Monemutensis, which suggests he was brought up in Monmouthshire, most likely not far from Caerleon-on-Usk, which is only twenty miles from Monmouth, and is a significant site in legendary and ancient Britain. From 1129 to 1151 he seems to have been at Oxford, most likely a canon of the secular college of St George's.[289] It was during this phase of his life that he assembled the *History of the Kings of Britain*, the 'Prophecies of Merlin' (originally conceived as a separate volume) and 'The Life of Merlin'. Later in 1151 he became Bishop Elect of St Asaph, North Wales and then, in 1152, a priest at Westminster. He died in 1155. Much of the *History of the Kings of Britain* is concerned with Arthurian material and, indeed, Geoffrey of Monmouth is one of the first surviving writers to promulgate the links between King Arthur and Cornwall. Geoffrey of Monmouth's book was written in Latin, though he interestingly refers to one British source for his narrative:

> Walter, Archdeacon of Oxford, a man skilled in the art of public speaking and well-formed about the history of foreign countries, presented me with a certain very ancient book written in the British language.[290]

A number of scholars have argued that this book, written in the 'British language' which, in effect, has given rise to all the narrative and dramatic constructions of Arthur through successive centuries, might well have been written in Cornwall, or perhaps even in the Brythonic south west of Britain.[291] What Geoffrey of Monmouth clearly did was to draw on this source text, but also to carefully create a compendium of mythological and historical narrative blending into a volume which displayed the glorious history of the Britons. The contribution this has made in much later drama has already been considered in the Cornish context. For example, the writer or writers of *Bewnans Ke* either knew of the *History* (or translation or adaptations of it),[292] or it had been so well-integrated into medieval thought that Geoffrey's version of events was taken as given. We must, however, also note the presence of figures such as Lear and Cymbeline in the work, which later inspired Shakespeare's versions.[293] Such plays are the surviving examples of Shakespeare's interest in Celtic Britain and, put alongside other more apocryphal texts,[294] they demonstrate that ancient Britain, and Cornwall in particular, were an imaginary construct of great interest to writers of the Renaissance.[295] This will be more fully considered in Chapter Three of this volume. 'The Prophecies of Merlin' section of the *History* contains much material of Cornish interest, and again likely inspiration for native drama. We are told that the 'Boar of Cornwall shall bring relief from these invaders, for it will trample their necks beneath its feet', that 'the Cornish oaks shall flourish' and that 'a soldier in a chariot will resist the Wolf and transform the Cornish people into a Boar. As a result the Boar will devastate the provinces, but it will hide its head in the depths of the Severn'.[296] Although it is now hard to make sense of these allusions, clearly the dramatic base is one of resistance to invasion. Although no text has survived, could it be that earlier dramatic variants of the *Bewnans Ke* Arthurian matter existed? According to Roscarrock, St Piran was the 'chaplyne of King Arthur who made the 8 Arch[bishop] of Yorke'.[297] Such a survival might suggest Arthurian matter in any play featuring St Piran, as well as the Arthurian material from St Endelient. St Endelient [St Endellion] is significant, because it is not that far from Tintagel. North Cornish playing-place evidence is thin compared to west and central Cornwall,[298] but this is not to say performances never occurred. Indeed, such was the 'effect' of Geoffrey of Monmouth's text (it was a 'best-seller' of its time) that Arthuriana may have been fashionably integrated into all early Cornish dramas, surviving through the middle Cornish period to the Renaissance. This paradigm of mass dramatic Arthuriana both before and after Geoffrey of Monmouth may seem tenuous to some observers, but further evidence (probably from an earlier period) can be gleaned from the related work of John of Cornwall. He seems probably to have been born in St Germans in the early twelfth century, studied in Paris, and died sometime around 1199. We have already noted the significance of John of Cornwall's work in terms of shamanistic origins for theatre in Cornwall, but since his text (*c.*1150) is so close to the date of Geoffrey of Monmouth's, it might indicate that 'prophetic writing' in the style of Merlin was then highly fashionable. The work was originally written in Old Cornish, and then translated and rerendered into Latin hexameters by John of Cornwall. The theme of resistance against Anglo-Saxon, Norman or 'English' control (which we will find again, four centuries later, in texts like *Bewnans Meriasek*[299]) is established here:

> Learn the way at last, Cornwall, learn the work.
> And our cradles shall bring back the Saxon mourning.
> Why is our hand so generous? Who thereafter will be thought free?
> Where the Great Bear looks, where the Tamar flows South,
> by the yoke of Brentigia, the French lord it everywhere.
> If you would continue to live, O Queen, you will so unplough,
> out of which rat-catchers and buck goats are multiplied in value.[300]

There is much of interest to us, in terms of dramaturgy, within the work. Among the points to which John of Cornwall refers are Cornish methods of counting, the ancestral lineage of Cornish characters, the achievements of Viscount Frewin and other Cornish who killed their enemies at a town called Truruf. He also makes reference to Bodmin Moor (then known as Brentigia), as well as the siege of the castle at 'Periron' called Tintagel. It is important to highlight the focus on ancestral lineage, since it also forms a significant section of the *Vocabularium Cornicum*. Performances in many ancient cultures around the world are dependent on families' actual allegiances and relationships.[301] This could well have been an issue for a western Brythonic culture that relied on lineage for status. The fact that John of Cornwall was probably from St Germans is equally interesting. St Germans as a centre of learning is often ignored in contemporary scholarship. Understanding of the cultural heritage seems to have given way to the dominance of Glasney College. This is perhaps understandable, given the purported close links of place-names and texts.[302] However, during the twelfth century, St Germans had an intellectual and creative class who may have constructed early drama, performed both in St Germans itself as well as elsewhere in Cornwall. Put another way: it was, in essence, a 'proto-Glasney'. Clearly, some observers have understood the cultural significance of St Germans: most famously John Whittaker (1735-1808). Whittaker was rector of Ruan Lanihorne and his study of *The Ancient Cathedral of Cornwall Historically Surveyed* asserts the significance of the ecclesiastical foundation, and the founding of the Cornish Bishopric at St Germans in east Cornwall.[303]

From this period emerges one other narrative which was to have a long-standing influence on the dramatic continuum of Cornwall: that of Tristan and Yseult.[304] Evidence for a Cornish origin of the narrative exists, despite the fact that during the twelfth and thirteenth centuries, various tellers, poets and scholars embellished the legend, assimilating material relevant to their audience,[305] and modifying it from its original moment of production. The narrative may have had a poetic origin, or a dramatic one. The piece may have evolved from a single storyteller, or a range of tellers, and may well have been a fashionable narrative. If 'bardic' culture survived in any form into the eleventh and twelfth centuries, then such a narrative would seem apt for the telling, but we have, of course, no way of knowing whether this was the case. In all versions of the narrative, Tristan saves Cornwall from paying a tribute to the Irish, and is embraced by King Mark into his retinue. A journey after he has been injured by the Irish Champion Morholt, takes Tristan to Ireland, where he meets Yseult and, after a feat of strength, swears to take her back to Cornwall to marry Mark in an arranged marriage. In some versions, Tristan and Yseult drink a love potion, which causes them to fall in love (though most scholars agree this was a convenient medieval addition to counteract the adultery). There follows the pain of a love triangle in which Tristan and Yseult try to deny their feelings. Eventually Tristan leaves for Brittany, meeting Yseult of the White Hands (presented through the dramatic device of *doppelgänger*), but never fully recovering from his love for Yseult. At the end, miscommunication results in their death, with Mark left alone. That a drama based on Tristan and Yseult (even in fragmentary form) did not survive is actually quite surprising, given the varieties of retellings that are extant. Certainly the piece lends itself to dramatic form, with antagonist, protagonist and tritagonist in place, and with a readily identifiable landscape and community as the cultural backdrop. The notion of the Irish raids and settlements upon the north Cornish coast matches real historical events of the eighth and ninth centuries,[306] while the link between Brittany and Cornwall shows how close the two territories were in terms of language, ideology and community.[307]

As I have argued elsewhere, the first scholar to assert that all the Tristan and Yseult narratives could be traced back to a single, original poetic source was Joseph Bédier (1864-1938).[308] From this source, other versions developed, and the tale began to diversify, whilst maintaining its Cornish base. Thomas, a French-writing poet of the twelfth century, prepared the oldest extant text, yet he is thought to have come from either Britain or Brittany, which may indicate a familiarity with Cornwall.[309] Gottfried von Strassburg (died c.1210) based his German version upon Thomas.[310] This is the text which then became the dominant 'European' version. However, an additional poet from the twelfth century, Béroul, about whom we know very little, completed a version of the romance (also in French) which inspired other later writers.[311] Arguments for the Cornish origin of the narrative are nevertheless persuasive. Henry Jenner (1848-1934) – basing at least some of his observations on the work of Joseph Loth[312] (1847-1934) – makes three significant points about the narrative which have impact on our understanding of early theatrical and literary culture in Cornwall:

1. That the author of the original story from which Thomas and Béroul derived their poems, and of the ground-breaking work on which the whole Tristan literature, whether in prose, verse or music, and whether in French, English, German or any other tongue, is built, was, if not actually a Cornish-man, a man well acquainted with Cornwall.

2. That he laid the scene of his story along the south coast of Cornwall from the Fowey estuary to St Michael's Mount, taking real and identifiable places for it, and not only real, but likely places.

3. That he wrote when French had been added to the Celtic and English, which had for some time been concurrently spoken in Cornwall.[313]

Jenner's comments are perceptive and reasoned, since we know that the geography of the earliest versions (such as that of Béroul) has a level of detail which suggests an intimacy with the landscape. If the 'author' was a Breton, we can perhaps consider this an artificial division because, as we have seen, Old Breton and Old Cornish were, in fact, enormously similar, and perhaps better viewed as different dialects of the same language. Inevitably, this leads us to a notion that Brythonic narrative, drama and poetry criss-crossed the British Channel, and that audiences in both Cornwall and Brittany experienced similar material. Jenner also suggests a multi-lingual world for Cornwall and Brittany, indicating the changes (from the east) occurring to these western territories, and also the presence of multi-lingual, multi-cultural performance.[314] The notion of Cornwall being completely Cornish-speaking is wrong-headed, and Jenner counters that here. Roberts has put forward additional material in support of Jenner's hypothesis, which provides a connection to Restormel Castle. He argues that Béroul:

> may have deliberately relocated a traditional Cornish legend into the Fowey area from a more western location, simply to heighten the drama for his patrons. He was probably writing to entertain members of the very powerful Cardinham family. Their estates lay beside the Fowey river, where Robert de Cardinham built the first castle at Restormel.[315]

The core concept here is the notion of 'heightening the drama' through a closer locality. When we consider this concept, we realise that it filters through the whole of the dramatic continuum in Cornwall, and Béroul (and/or other tellers) were simply creating a more effective telling, or performance, by adapting the piece to the immediacy of the community. This was the very same technique which would be used in the telling of epic, biblical narrative in the mystery plays of successive centuries;[316] and it would be used in the distant future as well, in nineteenth-century burletta and in twentieth- and twenty-first-century touring theatre. Restormel is, of course, a politically powerful location, closely allied to what is known about structures of control, jurisdiction and cultural creation in this period. It was a time that Bernard Deacon has described as being when 'Anglo-Norman colonization led to colonialism, [and] an earldom and diocese siphoned Cornish wealth off into southern England'.[317] Restormel is frequently posited as a likely repository of now lost Cornish language manuscripts because of its strategic and cultural dominance. It was ransacked and burnt by Parliamentarian troops in 1646 (alongside the Duchy Palace and church of St Bartholomew) during the War of Five Nations ('English' Civil War), and this is most probably when that collection was destroyed. However, in a remarkable piece of continuity, in 2005 – almost 900 years after a possible first telling or performance at the location – Kneehigh Theatre presented a spectacular dramatic version of *Tristan and Yseult* in the middle of Restormel Castle (ironically, now managed by English Heritage[318]), a stone's throw from the River Fowey.

It is important to assert here the orality of Béroul's text (even in translation), and therefore of the original base narrative. Structurally, he juxtaposes poetic episodes written in the so-called *jongleur* [or minstrel] style, with other sequences of stark simplicity and bare dramatic force. Again, these may have been a retelling of a Cornish original. Certainly, the construction leads us to be very aware of an audience. Consider the following conspiratorial section:

> Who can be in love for a year or two and not reveal it? For love cannot be concealed. Often one lover would wink at the other, often they would speak together both alone and in the sight of others. They could not find their pleasure anywhere and they had to meet many times. At Mark's court there were three barons – you never saw more wicked men![319]

The opening question here, and the emphasis on the collective 'you' in the audience, are markers of its 'telling' format. Other terms in the extant text make us aware of its orality. The appeal to listen, the self-commentary on the

Fig. 13. Kneehigh Theatre's *Tristan and Yseult*, at Restormel Castle, 2005. Courtesy of Kneehigh Theatre and Steve Tanner Photography.

narrative, and the notion of the audience missing out on the original actions are all embodied in the text: '*Hear now* of the hunch-backed dwarf Frocin...', 'In the leap which Tristan made the blood fell (*what bad luck!*)' and '*You should have seen* those lepers panting'.[320] In later versions, this orality disappears, and a more formalised method of narration is shaped.[321] Interestingly, the orality was later maintained in the Kneehigh Theatre version when Whitehand comments, 'Welcome to the club of the unloved... For what is love without these things? So, I welcome you to our story: We're all in it... all of us'.[322] As in the original, a connection is asserted between audience, teller and community.

The presence of this 'nation-defining' narrative in this early period shows how significant this text was. It has had, however, an ongoing presence in the historical development of drama inside Cornwall and related to Cornwall.[323] The legend could possibly have been integrated into saints' lives drama, particularly in localities associated with the narrative (north Cornwall, the Fowey Estuary, Moresk and Malpas[324]). There is also an echo of the love triangle motif woven into 'Origo Mundi', the first play of the extant *Ordinalia* – between David, Bathsheba and Uriah – which certainly draws on conventions of courtly love.[325] The legend also has a presence in Thomas Malory's *Le Morte Darthur* (1485),[326] and the notion of the significance of Tintagel and Castle-an-Dinas (part of the cultural geography of some versions) is also found in *Bewnans Meriasek* (*c.*1504).[327] Although the narrative fell out of fashion in the seventeenth and eighteenth centuries, by the nineteenth it appears to have been rediscovered, with Richard Wagner's opera of *Tristan und Isolde* premiered in 1865, and A.C. Swinburne's poetic telling, *Tristram of Lyonesse*, emerging in 1883.[328] Likewise, the twentieth century brought a host of literary and dramatic versions, among them A.S.D. Smith's 1951 Cornish-language version, *Trystan hag Isolt* (completed by D.H. Watkins in 1962),[329] Nora Ratcliff's play *Tristan of Cornwall* (1951),[330] and Arthur Quiller-Couch and Daphne du Maurier's *Castle Dor* (1962) – a transplantation of the narrative to Fowey in the nineteenth century.[331] Other contemporary tellings have emerged; not least those by the Bedlam Theatre Company of Cornwall and the Kneehigh Theatre version commented upon above. Outside of Cornwall, Kevin Reynolds produced a film version in 2006.[332] Other imaginings of the story have been developed using the base narrative as a starting point: for example in Jim Harrison's 1979 Cornu-American-themed novel, *Legends of the Fall* (1979),[333] while aspects were also incorporated into Caeia March's *Reflections* (1995), which offered a lesbian interpretation of the motifs.[334]

Beyond Tristana, as we move towards the thirteenth century, secular material was certainly still being written, but it was towards religious drama that Cornwall, as a whole, was moving. As Wickham, and Tydeman note,[335] this was not just a movement in Cornwall. It was a pan-European phenomenon based upon many of the origins already described in this chapter: religion and recreation based on the ritual year. A third factor was a growing awareness of the commercial and revenue-generating power of theatre. Religion would help develop a set of texts based on praising Christ and his humanity, on saints' plays, and upon morality dramas. In Cornwall, this would be combined with the social recreation brought about by moments in the ritual year. Commerce would allow for the shaping of community theatre for the community's benefit, but this would also see the later professionalisation of writing, acting, management and the funding of theatre. Although this process was occurring across the whole of the island of Britain, and within continental Europe, in the years 1200 to 1600,[336] Cornwall was to do it better, and more intensively, than anywhere else.

Intimately connected with this process of developing drama was the Collegiate Church of St Thomas at Glasney, Penryn. Although a number of other ecclesiastical institutions – many of them with Celtic Christian origins[337] – operated in Cornwall in the aftermath of the Norman Conquest, it was the

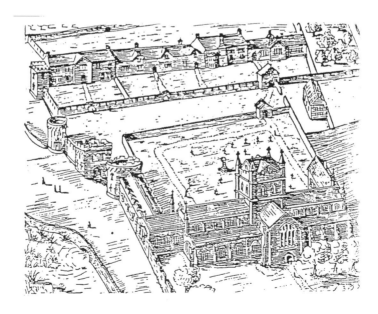

Fig. 14. A projected illustration of the Collegiate Church of St Thomas at Glasney, Penryn, *c.*1580 by Sir Ferdinand George.

Collegiate Church at Glasney which would dominate the Christian cultural landscape of Cornwall until its eventual dissolution and destruction in 1548. Many of the early ecclesiastical centres – such as Probus, St Buryan, St Michael's Mount, Launceston and Bodmin – may well have had personnel who developed liturgical and secular drama, but these were small institutions compared to what Glasney College would become. Whetter records that a possible reason for founding the College was the sudden proliferation of friaries in the middle of the thirteenth century, and that Bishop Walter Bronscombe of Exeter wished to counteract their progress and influence.[338] However, the College actually has a more mythical origin. In 1265 Bronscombe had been visiting Germany on behalf of Richard the Earl, and while he was taken ill in Canterbury, he had a vision of Thomas Becket, who informed him that he would recover, and that when he returned to the west he should found a collegiate college in the woods of Glasney in Penryn:

> This shall be to thee a sign. When thou comest to the place, Glasney, thou shalt search for a certain spot in it near the River of Antre, called by the inhabitants Polsethow, which Cornish name being interpreted is 'mire, or a pit' – which said place hath of old time borne such a name from the fact that wild animals in the neighbourhood when wounded by an arrow, were wont to run thither after the nature and custom of such animals, and to plunge into its depth, and arrows could never be discovered there. And thou shalt find in it a large willow tree, and therein a swarm of bees; and there thou shalt appoint the High Altar and ordain the fabric. Of which said place it hath been anciently prophesised: 'In Polsethow shall habitations, or marvellous things be seen'.[339]

In Cornish, this final sentence reads, *In Polsethow ywhylyr anethow*, which has the curious double meaning of both 'habitations [or dwellings]' or 'marvels'. If we understands these 'marvels' to mean drama and theatre, then we have quite an origin story for late medieval drama in Cornwall – directly connected, of course, to St Thomas the Martyr. Conveniently, perhaps, Cornwall may have already had a sophisticated dramatic culture up and running and, like so many prophecies, this may only pretend to promote events already occurring to give them higher status. That said, Bronscombe headed to Penryn and started to clear the site. By 1267, the Collegiate Church had been established, with the buildings erected and the site dedicated to St Thomas and the Virgin Mary. A constitution was devised, the first head of the College being Henry de Bollegh. The detailed development of Glasney College is not a matter for this volume; three major studies have already been completed by Whetter, Peter, and Palmer.[340] Suffice for us to say that, from its foundation in 1265, the institution developed steadily, increasing its influence, expanding its personnel and buildings, and developing a good deal of literature in Cornish.

Over time, a certain mythos has developed surrounding the connection between the Collegiate Church of St Thomas, and its involvement in the production of Cornish-language drama. As a number of scholars have proven, there is certainly a case for promoting this connection.[341] Glasney College had a number of literate, knowledgeable and creative Provosts, Priests and Masters to operate as an early 'university' in Cornwall.[342] The connection between texts such as the *Ordinalia* and the surrounds of Penryn and the Fal Estuary has also been asserted.[343] It was the literary centre of late medieval Cornwall. Not only did Glasney operate in this way, however; it also seemed to mediate and distribute other drama texts, from its feeder parishes. Thanks to the work of scholars such as Padel, and Frost,[344] we are now coming towards a more sophisticated understanding of the cultural processes behind the writing and development of drama in the late medieval period. We now better understand the relationship of secular narrative to liturgical drama, and the nature of writing in the parishes.

The 'Celtic drama queen' that was Cornwall now had an institution, and a set of affiliated writers in the surrounding parishes, that fed into Glasney's proto-university and communal-dramatic 'ensemble' culture. Ritual had transformed from its pagan roots to a Christian present, although much of the ritual year still informed the cycle of the seasons, interacting with remnants of Celtic Christianity, as well as the demands of the wider late medieval Church. No doubt secular dramas were ongoing as part of the ritual year, and the likelihood was that mythological, heroic, saintly and folkloric local elements (not least Arthuriana, Tristana, Britonnic and Bardic culture, Merlin-lore, fairie-lore and mermaids) were to be welded onto a growing liturgical drama of place. That drama would need to be performed in landscapes and communities in which the plays would be designed to carry a message to a broadly non-literate population, who were already forced to operate in a multi-cultural Cornwall. With its dramatic origins complete, Cornwall was about to move into a new highly-advanced and intensive theatrical phase. Perran Round was to be just one of a network of community theatre spaces across the territory, which would help define Cornish identity for the next three hundred years; yet ritual, landscape and community were still to be connected, in what William Scawen was to term the age of the 'great plays',[345] the so-called *guirremears*.

CHAPTER ONE: NOTES AND REFERENCES

1. William Scawen, 'Antiquities Cornuontanic' by William Scawen, 1680, in Davies Gilbert, *The Parochial History of Cornwall*, London: J.B. Nichols, 1838, pp.203-21.

2. Myrna Combellack, *The Playing Place: A Cornish Round*, Redruth: Dyllansow Truran, 1989, p.3.

3. This is at OS Grid Reference SW7790 5443.

4. Rod Lyon, *Cornwall's Playing Places*, Nancegollan: Tavas an Weryn, 2001, p.11.

5. Bernard Deacon, *Cornwall: A Concise History*, Cardiff: University of Wales Press, 2007, pp.1-3.

6. Denys Val Baker, *The Timeless Land: The creative spirit in Cornwall*, Bath: Adams and Dart, 1973, p.53.

7. See Michael Hechter, *Internal Colonialism: The Celtic Fringe in British National Development, 1536-1966*, London: Routledge and Kegan Paul, 1975; Mark Stoyle, *West Britons: Cornish Identities and the Early Modern British State*, Exeter: University of Exeter Press, 2002.

8. Caradoc Peters, *The Archaeology of Cornwall: The Foundations of our Society*, Fowey: Cornwall Editions, 2005, p.73. This feature was also examined by Channel 4's *Time Team*.

9. Tony Deane and Tony Shaw, *Folklore of Cornwall*, Stroud: Tempus, 2003, p.141-2.

10. See P.G. Embrey and R.F. Symes, *Minerals of Cornwall and Devon*, London: British Museum, 1987. See also E.B. Selwood, E.M. Durrance and C.M. Bristow, *The Geology of Cornwall*, Exeter: University of Exeter Press, 1998.

11. See Simon During (ed.), *The Cultural Studies Reader*, London and New York: Routledge, 1993. In this volume, only one article is devoted to geography. However, since the rise of cultural-geography as an area of study, there have been more articles on the subject.

12. D.M. Thomas, *The Granite Kingdom*, Truro: D. Bradford Barton, 1970.

13. See Alan M. Kent, *The Dreamt Sea: An Anthology of Anglo-Cornish Poetry 1928-2004*, London: Francis Boutle Publishers, 2004, pp.148-9.

14. For further discussion of the geological features of Cornwall, see Colin Bristow, *Cornwall's Geology and Scenery*, St Austell: Cornish Hillside Publications, 1996.

15. Ibid., p.iii.

16. Charles Thomas, *Exploration of a Drowned Landscape*, London: Batsford, 1985.

17. See Lyon, op.cit.

18. The classic work on the history of mining is A.K. Hamilton Jenkin, *The Cornish Miner: An Account of his Life Above and Underground from Early Times*, Newton Abbot: David and Charles, 1972 [1927]. For a new history, see Allen Buckley,

The Story of Mining in Cornwall: A World of Payable Ground, Fowey: Cornwall Editions, 2005.

19. See Alan M. Kent, *The Literature of Cornwall: Continuity, Identity, Difference 1000-2000*, Bristol: Redcliffe, 2000, p.280.

20. For Greek examples, see Audrey de Sélincourt and A.R. Burn (eds. and trs.), *Herodotus: The Histories*, Harmondsworth: Penguin, 1954, p.250; David N. Parsons, 'Classifying English Place-Names' in David N. Parsons and Patrick Sims-Williams, *Ptolemy: Towards a Linguistic Atlas of the Earliest Celtic Place-Names of Europe*, Aberystwyth: Department of Welsh, University of Wales, Aberystwyth, 2000, pp.169-78. This chapter, which has several Cornish references, unfortunately conflates 'English' with 'British'. For a range of Roman examples, see Roger Penhallurick, *Tin in Antiquity*, London: Institute of Metals, 1986. A creative exploration of this is found in Simon Young, *A.D. 500: A Journey through the Dark Isles of Britain and Ireland*, London: Phoenix Books, 2006 [2005].

21. See Deane and Shaw, op.cit., p.35.

22. See Edwin Norris, *The Ancient Cornish Drama*, London and New York: Blom, 1968 [1859], pp.1-219; Alan M. Kent, *Ordinalia: The Cornish Mystery Play Cycle – A Verse Translation*, London: Francis Boutle Publishers, 2005, pp.20-105.

23. Ibid., pp.1-201; ibid., pp.212-88.

24. See Paula Neuss (ed. and tr.), *The Creacion of the World: A Critical Edition and Translation*, New York and London: Garland, 1983. For a comparison with another cycle, see Richard Beadle and Pamela M. King (eds.), *York Mystery Plays: A Selection in Modern Spelling*, Oxford: Clarendon Press, 1984, pp.15-32.

25. See *Gwreans an Bys*, MS. Bodley 219, Oxford.

26. See Deane and Shaw, op.cit., pp.34-47.

27. See various examples in Alan M. Kent and Gage McKinney (eds.), *The Busy Earth: A Reader in Global Cornish Literature 1700-2000*, St Austell: Cornish Hillside Publications, 2008.

28. Paul Russell, *An Introduction to the Celtic Languages*, Harlow: Longman, 1995, pp.111-4.

29. See the general argument in Bernard Deacon, *Cornwall: A Concise History*, Cardiff: University of Wales Press, 2007.

30. See E.G. Bowen, *Saints, Seaways and Settlements in the Celtic Lands*, Cardiff: University of Wales Press, 1969; Barry Cunliffe, *The Celtic World*, London: Bodley Head, 1979, pp.186-93, and *The Ancient Celts*, Oxford: Oxford University Press, 1997.

31. See G.H. Doble, *The Saints of Cornwall: Parts 1-5*, Felinfach: Llanerch, 1997 [1960-1970]; Catherine Rachel John, *The Saints of Cornwall: 150 Years of Christian Landscape*, Padstow: Tabb House, 2001 [1981]; Ada Alvery, *In Search of St James: Cornwall to Compestella – A Mediaeval Pilgrimage*, Redruth:

Dyllansow Truran, 1989; Nicholas Orme, *The Saints of Cornwall*, Oxford: Oxford University Press, 2000. Cornwall has developed the only two surviving saints' plays in Britain.

32. See *Carn* magazine. See also Peter Berresford Ellis, *The Celtic Dawn: A history of Pan-Celticism*, London: Constable, 1993. The need for pan-Celticism is also debated in Marcus Tanner, *The Last of the Celts*, New Haven and London: Yale University Press, 2004.

33. A good example of this is the influence of Ruodlieb narrative on Cornish-language folktale, *John of Chyanhor*. See Brian Murdoch, 'Is *John of Chyanhor* Really a 'Cornish *Ruodlieb*'?' in Philip Payton (ed.), *Cornish Studies: Four*, Exeter: University of Exeter Press, 1996, pp.45-63.

34. For Cornish weather folklore, see K.C. Phillipps, *Westcountry Words and Ways*, Newton Abbot: David and Charles, 1976, pp.42-3.

35. For background here, see Ronald Hutton, *The Rise and Fall of Merry England: The Ritual Year 1400-1700*, Oxford: Oxford University Press, 1994, and *The Stations of the Sun: A History of the Ritual Year in Britain*, Oxford: Oxford University Press, 1996.

36. Daphne du Maurier, *Jamaica Inn*, London: Pan, 1978 [1936].

37. See Graham Ley, *A Short Introduction to Greek Theatre*, Chicago: University of Chicago Press, 1991; David Wiles, *Greek Theatre Performance: An Introduction*, Cambridge: Cambridge University Press, 2000; Marianne McDonald and Michael Walton (eds.), *The Cambridge Companion to Greek and Roman Theatre*, Cambridge: Cambridge University Press, 2007.

38. See Avril Demuth, *The Minack Open-Air Theatre: A Symposium*, Newton Abbot: David and Charles, 1968; Rowena Cade and Darrell Bates, *A Short History of the Minack Theatre*, Porthcurno: The Minack Theatre, 1971.

39. David Grene and Richard Latimore (eds. and trs.), *Greek Tragedies, Volume 1*, Chicago: University of Chicago Press, 1960, pp.107-228.

40. R.M. Wilson, *The Lost Literature of Medieval England*, London: Methuen, 1952, p.209. Although having England in the title, Wilson actually considers the whole of Britain.

41. See Malcolm Heath (ed. and tr.), *Aristotle: The Poetics*, London: Penguin, 1996.

42. See for example, Burgess Laughlin, *The Aristotle Adventure: A Guide to the Greek, Roman and Latin Scholars who transmitted Artistotle's Logic to the Renaissance*, Flagstaff, Arizona: Albert Hale, 1995; John David Lovelock, *The Function of Music in Greek Drama, and its influence on Italian Theatre, and Theatre Music of the Renaissance*, Milton Keynes: Open University Press, 1989.

43. See James Whetter, *The History of Glasney College*, Padstow: Tabb House, 1988. A classical influence is found however in the poetry contained in Tony Frazer

(ed.), *Poets of Devon and Cornwall: From Barclay to Coleridge*, Exeter: Shearsman Books, 2007.

44. See Jane A. Bakere, *The Cornish Ordinalia: A Critical Study*, Cardiff: University of Wales Press, 1980; Kent, 2005, pp.47-8 and pp.192-3.

45. Kneehigh Theatre's *The Ash Maid* was heavily influence by commedia dell'arte. See Kneehigh Theatre, *The Ash Maid*, programme, Truro: Kneehigh Theatre, 1994.

46. See David C. Fowler, *The Life and Times of John Trevisa, Medieval Scholar*, Seattle and London: University of Washington Press, 1995.

47. F.E. Halliday (ed.), *Richard Carew: The Survey of Cornwall*, London: Melrose, 1953. For a context, see Glanmoor Williams and Robert Owen Jones (eds.), *The Celts and the Renaissance: Tradition and Innovation*, Cardiff: University of Wales Press, 1990; Ceri Davies and John E. Law (eds.), *The Renaissance and the Celtic Countries*, Oxford: Blackwell, 2005; and Stephen Greenblatt, *Renaissance Self-Fashioning: From More to Shakespeare*, Chicago: University of Chicago Press, 1980.

48. See George Croker Fox (ed. and tr.), *The Prometheus of Aeschylus and the Electra of Sophocles, translated from the Greek, with notes intended to illustrate the typical character of the former*, London: Darton and Harvey, 1835, and *The Death of Demosthenes and other Original Poems, with the Prometheus and Agamemnon translated from the Greek*, London: John Bohn, 1839. Greek-style choruses are found in the work of Nick Darke and Alan M. Kent. See Nick Darke, 'The Body' (1983) in Andy Kempe, *The Script Sampler*, Cheltenham: Nelson Thornes Ltd, 2002, pp.124-37; Alan M. Kent, *The Tin Violin*, London: Francis Boutle Publishers, 2008. Darke has a chorus of farmers, whereas Kent has a chorus of fish-jowsters.

49. See R.A Banks, *Drama and Theatre Arts*, London: Hodder and Stoughton, 1985; John Ferguson and Kitty Chisholm (eds.), *Political and Social Life in the Great Age of Athens*, Bradford-on-Avon: Ward Lock Educational, 1978.

50. See John Barnett, *Prehistoric Cornwall: The Ceremonial Monuments*, Wellingborough: Turnstone Press Limited, 1982; Craig Weatherhill, *Cornovia: Ancient Sites of Cornwall and Scilly*, Penzance: Alison Hodge, 1989 [1985].

51. See those contained in Robert Hunt (ed.), *Popular Romances of the West of England: The Drolls, Traditions, and Superstitions of Old Cornwall (First Series)*, London: John Camden Hotten, 1865, and *Popular Romances of the West of England: The Drolls, Traditions, and Superstitions of Old Cornwall (Second Series)*, London: John Camden Hotten, 1865; William Bottrell (ed.), *Traditions and Hearthside Stories of West Cornwall: First Series*, Penzance: W. Cornish, 1870, and (ed.), *Traditions and Hearthside Stories of West Cornwall: Second Series*, Penzance: Beare and Son, 1873, and (ed.), *Traditions and Hearthside Stories of West Cornwall: Third Series*, Penzance: F. Rodda, 1880. For a context, see Joseph

Campbell, *The Hero with a Thousand Faces*, London: Fontana Press, 1993 [1949].

52. See Kent, 2005, pp.19-105.

53. See James Stock, *Star-Gazy Pie: Two Plays*, London: Nick Hern Books, 1995, pp.79-160.

54. The contemporary company Frantic Assembly are noted for this kind of work.

55. C-Scape's *Below* toured Cornwall in summer 2008.

56. The most famous exponent of this belief is William Borlase. See William Borlase, *Observations on the Antiquities Historical and Monumental of the County of Cornwall*, London: EP Publishing, 1973 [1754]. See also John Harris, *Luda: A Lay of the Druids*, London: Hamilton, Adams and Co., 1863. The writer and educational philosopher Rudolf Steiner has published extensively on the Druids. Steiner spent time at Tintagel in Cornwall. See Rudolf Steiner, *The Druids: Esoteric Wisdom of the Ancient Celtic Priests*, Forest Row: Sophia Books, 2001. For more on Steiner in Cornwall, see Richard Seddon, *The Mystery of Arthur at Tintagel*, London: Rudolph Steiner Press, 1990. For Druidry in Britain, see Stuart Piggott, *The Druids*, London: Thames and Hudson, 1968; Ronald Hutton, *Witches, Druids and King Arthur*, London and New York: Hambledon, 2003, and *The Druids*, London: Hambledon, 2007.

57. H. Mattingly and S.A. Handford (eds. and trs.), *Tacitus: The Agricola and the Germania*, London: Penguin, 1970; S.A. Handford and Jane F. Gardner (eds. and trs.), *Caesar: The Conquest of Gaul*, Harmondsworth: Penguin, 1982.

58. See J.E. Caerwyn Williams (ed.), *Ifor Williams: The Poems of Taliesin: Mediaeval and Modern Welsh*, Dublin: Dublin Institute for Advanced Celtic Studies, 1968. See also John Matthews and Caitlin Matthews, *Taliesin: The Last Celtic Shaman*, Rochester, Vermont: Bear and Company, 2002.

59. *Trioedd Ynys Prydian*, MS., Peniarth 16, NLW, Aberystwyth. For comment, see Chris Grooms, 'Trioedd Ynys Prydian' in John T. Koch (ed.), *Celtic Culture: A Historical Encylopedia*, Vols. 1-5, Santa Barbara, California and Oxford: ABC Clio, 2006, pp.1687-8.

60. Weatherhill, op.cit., p.92.

61. Rod Lyon, *Gorseth Kernow: The Cornish Gorsedd – what it is and what it does*, Cornwall: Gorseth Kernow, 2008, p.6.

62. See Dillwyn Miles, *The Secret of the Bards of the Isle of Britain*, Llandybie: Gwasg Dinefwr Press, 1992, pp.9-41.

63. Malcolm Chapman, *The Celts: The Construction of a Myth*, Basingstoke: Macmillan, 1992, p.v.

64. See Geraint H. Jenkins, *Facts, Fantasy and Fiction: Historical Vision of Iolo Morganwg*, Aberystwyth: University of Wales Centre for Advanced Wales and

Celtic Studies, 1998; Miles, op.cit., pp.42-59. For a Cornish perspective, see Hugh Miners, *Gorseth Kernow: The First 50 Years*, Cornwall: Gorseth Kernow, 1978, pp.10-11.

65. For a full list, see Lyon, op.cit., p.51-3. Of late, the Cornish Gorsedd has been forced to move away from this type of location.

66. See Gorseth Kernow, *Ceremonies of the Bards of Cornwall*, n.d. Leaflet handed out at annual Gorsedd ceremony.

67. Charles Woolf, *An Introduction to the Archaeology of Cornwall*, Truro: D. Bradford Barton, 1970; Caroline Malone, *Neolithic Britain and Ireland*, Stroud: Tempus, 2001; Toni-Maree Rowe, *Cornwall in Prehistory*, Stroud: Tempus, 2005; Lloyd Laing, *The Archaeology of Celtic Britain and Ireland c.AD 400-1200*, Cambridge: Cambridge University Press, 2006. See also Ronald Hutton, *The Pagan Religions of the Ancient British Isles: Their Nature and Legacy*, Oxford: Blackwell, 1991.

68. Charles Thomas, *And Shall These Mute Stones Speak? Post-Roman Inscriptions in Roman Britain*, Cardiff: University of Wales Press, 1994, and *Christian Celts: Messages and Images*, Stroud: Tempus, 1998.

69. Cheryl Straffon, *Pagan Cornwall: Land of the Goddess*, St Just-in-Penwith; Meyn Mamvro Publications, 1993, and *The Earth Goddess: Celtic and Pagan Legacy of the Landscape*, Poole: Cassell, 1997, and *Fentynyow Kernow: In Search of Cornwall's Holy Wells*, St Just-in-Penwith: Meyn Mamvro Publications, 1998; Nigel Pennick, *Celtic Sacred Landscapes*, London: Thames and Hudson, 2000 [1996]; Hamish Miller and Paul Broadhurst, *The Sun and the Serpent: An Investigation into Earth Energies*, Launceston: Pendragon Press, 1989.

70. Peters, op.cit.; Rowe, op.cit.

71. Peter Berridge and Alison Roberts, 'The Mesolithic period in Cornwall' in *Cornish Archaeology / Hendhyscans Kernow*, No.25, 1986, pp.7-34.

72. See Hutton, 1996, op.cit.

73. Donald R. Rawe, *A Prospect of Cornwall*, London: Robert Hale, 1986, p.17.

74. Peters, op.cit., pp.22-37.

75. See Roger Mercer, 'The Neolithic in Cornwall' in *Cornish Archaeology / Hendhyscans Kernow*, No.25, 1986, pp.35-80.

76. See Weatherhill, op.cit., p.103, p.112, p.39 and p.99.

77. See Patricia M. Christie, 'Cornwall in the Bronze Age' in *Cornish Archaeology / Hendhyscans Kernow*, No.25, 1986, pp.81-110.

78. Weatherhill, op.cit., p.92, p.35, p.105 and p.110.

79. John Barnett, 'Lesser Known Stone Circles in Cornwall' in *Cornish Archaeology / Hendhyscans Kernow*, No. 19, 1980, pp.17-29. See also Debbie Griffiths, *Guide to the Archaeology of Dartmoor*, Exeter: Devon Books, 1996.

80. Weatherhill, op.cit., p.118 and p.82.

81. Peters, op.cit., pp.62-3.

82. For background on migration and movement of Celtic peoples, see Laing, op.cit.; Simon James, *The Atlantic Celts: Ancient People or Modern Invention?* London: British Museum Press, 1999; Barry Cunliffe, *The Ancient Celts*, Oxford: Oxford University Press, 1997; John King, *Kingdoms of the Celts: A History and Guide*, London: Cassell, 1998.

83. Weatherhill, op.cit., p.34 and p.49.

84. Ibid., p.101 and p.96. See also Patricia M. Christie, *Chysauster and Carn Euny*, London: English Heritage, 1993.

85. See Chapman, op.cit.; James, op.cit.

86. Hunt, *(First Series)*, op.cit., p.28.

87. Susan M. Pearce, *The Kingdom of Dumnonia: Studies in History and Tradition in South West Britain AD 350-1150*, Padstow: Lodenek Press, 1978.

88. Banks, op.cit., p.19. James Whetter considers that Roman culture had a greater impact on Cornwall than had previously been imagined. The present A30 runs along the route of a Roman road (*magnum iter*). Spurs run off it from Fraddon to Carvossa and Golden hill forts. Another runs past St Stephen-in-Brannel, probably past the *plen-an-gwarry* at Gorran. Could it be that many playing places have a Roman origin?

89. Lewis Thorpe (ed. and tr.), *Geoffrey of Monmouth: The History of the Kings of Britain*, Harmondsworth: Penguin, 1966, pp.98-9.

90. Graham Thomas and Nicholas Williams (eds. and trs.), *Bewnans Ke: The Life of St Kea – A Critical Edition with Translation*, Exeter: University of Exeter Press, 2007.

91. For background on this period, see William Copeland Borlase, *The Age of Saints: A Monograph of Early Christianity in Cornwall with the Legends of the Cornish Saints*, Truro: Joseph Pollard, 1893; Thomas Taylor, *The Celtic Christianity of Cornwall: Divers Sketches and Studies*, Felinfach: Llanerch, 1995 [1916]; Orme, op.cit.

92. James, op.cit.; Adam Stout, *Creating Prehistory: Druids, Ley Hunters and Archaeologists in Pre-War Britain*, Oxford: Wiley Blackwell, 2008. See also Graham Harvey and Charlotte Hardman, *Paganism Today*, London: Thorsons, 1996.

93. Ithel Colquhoun, *The Living Stones: Cornwall*, London: Owen, 1957; Paul Newman, *The Tregerthen Horror: Aleister Crowley, D.H. Lawrence and Peter Warlock in Cornwall*, St Austell: Abraxas, 2005.

94. Pennick, op.cit.; Julian Cope, *The Modern Antiquarian: A Pre-millennial Odyssey Through Megalithic Britain*, London: Thorsons, 1997, and *Megalithic European: The 21st Century Traveller in Prehistoric Europe*, London: Element Books, 2004.

95. Rob Roy, *Stone Circles: A Modern Builder's Guide to the Megalithic Revival*, White River Junction, Vermont and Totnes: Chelsea Green Publishing Company, 1999, pp.103-22.

96. Alfred Watkins, *The Old Straight Track*, London: Abacus, 1994 [1925].

97. John Michell, *The View over Atlantis*, London: Harper Collins, 1969.

98. John Michell, *The Old Stones of Land's End*, London: Garnstone Press, 1974, p.124.

99. See Bruce Chatwin, *The Songlines*, London: Jonathan Cape, 1987.

100. Paul Broadhurst, *Sacred Shrines: In Search of the Holy Wells of Cornwall*, Launceston: Pendragon Press, 1991; Paul Broadhurst and Hamish Miller, *The Dance of the Dragon: An Odyssey into Earth Energies and Ancient Religion*, Launceston: Pendragon Press, 2000; Ian McNeil Cooke, *Mermaid to Merrymaid: Journey to the Stones – Ancient Sites and Pagan Mysteries of Celtic Cornwall*, Penzance: Men-an-Tol Studio, 1987; Straffon, op.cit.

101. Robin Payne and Rosemarie Lewsey, *The Romance of Stones*, Fowey: Alexander Associates, 1999.

102. Alan Bleakley, 'Fires of Bel: The Celtic Midsummer' in *Meyn Mamvro*, No.2, 1986, pp.14-17; Hugh Miners, 'Old Pagan Customs' in *Meyn Mamvro*, No. 3, 1986, pp.20-1.

103. Helen Woodley, 'Where Stones touch the Sky' in *Meyn Mamvro*, No.4, 1987, pp.7-10.

104. Jeff and Deb Seward, 'The Riddle of the Mazes' in *Meyn Mamvro*, No. 5, 1988, pp.15-19; Ian McNeil Cooke and Cheryl Straffon, 'The Celtic Year' in *Meyn Mamvro* No. 6, 1988, pp.16-19.

105. Cheryl Straffon, 'Rituals and Rites at Cornish Sites' in *Meyn Mamvro*, No.13, 1990, pp.6-9; Paul Broadhurst, 'Stowe's Hill: A Ritual Centre' in *Meyn Mamvro*, No.20, 1993, pp.6-10.

106. Caeia March and Cheryl Straffon, 'The Calendar of the Land: Ritual Landscapes of Bodmin Moor and Loughcrew' in *Meyn Mamvro*, No.24, 1994, pp.6-9.

107. Cheryl Straffon, 'The Cornish Otherworld' in *Meyn Mamvro*, No.45, 2001, pp.18-21; Andy Norfolk, 'Songlines: Legends in the Landscape' in *Meyn Mamvro*, No.62, 2007, pp.14-18; Joanna Tagney, 'The Hurlers: Sightlines to the Sun' in *Meyn Mamvro*, No.66, 2008, pp.8-11.

108. Thomas, 1998, op.cit.

109. Andy M. Jones, 'Settlement and ceremony: archaeological investigations at Stannon Down, St Breward, Cornwall' in *Cornish Archaeology / Hendhyscans Kernow*, Nos. 43-44, 2004-5, pp.1-140.

110. Ann Preston-Jones, 'The Men an Tol reconsidered' in *Cornish Archaeology / Hendhyscans Kernow*, No.32, 1993, pp.5-16.

111. Christopher Tilley, 'Rocks as resources: landscapes and power reconsidered' in *Cornish Archaeology / Hendhyscans Kernow*, No.34, 1995, pp.5-57.

112. Barnett, op.cit., p.30.

113. Evelyn Clark, *Cornish Fogous*, London: Methuen, 1961, pp.135-8.

114. Ian McNeil Cooke, *Mother and Sun: The Cornish Fogou*, Penzance: Men-an-Tol Studio, 1993, p.327. For further interpretations of fogous, see also Craig Weatherhill, 'The Riddle of the Fogous' in *Meyn Mamvro*, No 1, 1986, pp.5-9, and Jo May, *Fogou: A Journey into the Underworld*, Glastonbury: Gothic Image, 1996.

115. John E. Palmer, 'Bran the Blessed' in *Meyn Mamvro*, No.18, 1992, pp.16-19.

116. Koch, op.cit., p.236.

117. See Jeffrey Gantz (ed. and tr.), *The Mabinogion*, Harmondsworth: Penguin, 1976, p.81.

118. See Craig Weatherhill, 'Epona's Children' in *Meyn Mamvro*, No. 33, 1997, pp.14-16.

119. See Chris Jenkins, 'Traces of the Goddess Sillana' in *Meyn Mamvro*, No.35, 1998, pp.14-16.

120. See Caeia March and Cheryl Straffon, 'The Search for Bride' in *Meyn Mamvro*, No. 21, 1993, pp.20-22.

121. See the observations in James MacKillop (ed.), *Dictionary of Celtic Mythology*, Oxford: Oxford University Press, 1998, p.52.

122. Ronald Harwood, *All the World's a Stage*, London: Methuen, 1984; Phyllis Hartnoll (ed.), *The Oxford Companion to the Theatre*, Oxford; Oxford University Press, 1995. For insight into the origins of shamanism, see Ronald Hutton, *Shamans: Siberian Spirituality and Western Imagination*, London: Hambledon Continuum, 2007.

123. Eli Rozik, *The Roots of Theatre: Rethinking Ritual and Other Theories of Origin*, Iowa City: University of Iowa Press, 2002, p.69.

124. Jonothan Neelands and Warwick Dobson, *Drama and Theatre Studies*, London: Hodder and Stoughton, 2000, p.45.

125. Hunt, *(First Series)* and *(Second Series)*, op.cit.; Bottrell, op.cit.

126. Neelands and Dobson, op.cit.

127. Mircea Eliade, *Shamanism: Archaic Techniques of Ecstasy*, Princeton: Princeton University Press, 1972, p.4.

128. Rozik, op.cit., p.72.

129. This is the school of theatrical origin theory related to Arthur W. Pickard-Cambridge. See Arthur W. Pickard-Cambridge, *Dithyramb, Tragedy and Comedy*, Oxford: Clarendon Press, 1927. Pickard-Cambridge believes all Western theatrical activity has its origins in ancient Greece.

130. Rozik, op.cit., p.75.

131. Ibid., p.76.

132. Nikolai Tolstoy, *The Quest for Merlin*, London: Hamish Hamilton, 1985, pp.187-215.

133. See Peter Goodrich (ed.), *The Romance of Merlin: An Anthology*, New York and London: Garland, 1990.

134. See Thorpe, op.cit., pp.170-86.

135. *Prophetia Merlini*, Cod. Ottobonianus Lat. 1474, Vatican.

136. Amy Hale, Alan M. Kent and Tim Saunders (eds. and trs.), *Inside Merlin's Cave: A Cornish Arthurian Reader 1000-2000*, London: Francis Boutle Publications, 2000, p.47. Periron is the area in which Tintagel castle is located.

137. Tolstoy, op.cit., p.xvi.

138. See, for example, R.J. Stewart, Denise Coffey and Roy Hudd (eds.), *William Shakespeare and William Rowley: The Birth of Merlin, or The Childe hath found his Father*, Shaftesbury: Element Books, 1989. The latest is the 2008 BBC retelling of Merlin's childhood, titled *Merlin*.

139. Michael Dames, *Merlin and Wales: A Magician's Landscape*, London: Thames and Hudson, 2002.

140. Hale, Kent and Saunders, op.cit., pp.68-9 and pp.71-2.

141. Jo O'Cleirigh, 'Milpreves – or Adder's Beads: A Possible Connection with the Druids' in *Meyn Mamvro*, No 1, 1986, pp.10-11. The Graves text referred to is Robert Graves, *The White Goddess: A Historical Grammar of Poetic Myth*, London: Faber and Faber, 1961, p.39. I am unable to find the early Cornish poem to which Graves refers. However, according to Hunt, such information was contained in a letter written in 1701 by Edward Lhuyd. See Hunt *(Second Series)*, op.cit., pp.418-9. For Lhuyd's comment see R.T. Gunther (ed.), *Early Science in Oxford, Vol. XIV: Life and Letters of Edward Lhwyd*, Oxford: Oxford University Press subscribers' edition, 1945, p.464. It is interesting why these letters are not more often discussed in Cornish-language scholarship.

142. Brendan McMahon, 'A Cornish Shaman' in *Meyn Mamvro*, No.28, 1995, pp.9-11.

143. Hunt, *(First Series)*, op.cit., p.61.

144. See Tolstoy, op.cit., pp.168-9; Dames, op.cit., pp.36-9.

145. Brendan McMahon, *The Princess Who Ate People: The Psychology of Celtic Myths*, Loughborough: Heart of Albion Press, 2006.

146. See Henry Jenner, 'The Tristan Romance and its Cornish Provenance' in *Journal of the Royal Institution of Cornwall*, No.14, 1914.

147. See Halliday, op.cit., pp.144-5.

148. See Walter Benjamin, 'The Work of Art in the Age of Mechanical Reproduction' in Hannah Arendt and Harry Zohn (eds. and trs.), *Walter Benjamin: Illuminations*, London: Fontana Press, 1973, pp.211-44.

149. The performance usually takes place on the closest Sunday to St Piran's Day. Perran Sands is a ritual landscape. See E.W.F. Tomlin, *In Search of St Piran: An Account of his Monastic Foundation at Perranzabuloe, Cornwall, and its Place in the Western Celtic Church and Society*, Padstow: Lodenek Press, 1982. The present play was written by Simon Parker.

150. Betty Rosen, *And None of it was Nonsense: The Power of Storytelling in School*, London: Mary Glasgow Publications, 1988; Jack Maguire, The *Power of Personal Storytelling: Spinning Tales to Connect with Others*, New York: Jeremy P. Tarcher, 2000.

151. Jack Zipes, *Creative Storytelling: Changing Communities/Changing Lives*, London and New York: Routledge, 1995.

152. Michael Wilson, *Storytelling and Theatre: Contemporary Professional Storytellers and their Art*, London: Palgrave Macmillan, 2005.

153. John Beech (ed.), *Oral Literature and Performance Culture*, Edinburgh: John Donald, 2007. For interesting observations on the relationship between oral culture and theatre, see also Adam Fox and Daniel Woolf, *The Spoken Word: Oral Culture in Britain, 1500-1850*, Manchester: Manchester University Press, 2003.

154. Oliver Padel, 'Oral and literary culture in medieval Cornwall' in Helen Fulton (ed.), *Medieval Celtic Literature and Society*, Dublin: Four Courts Press, 2005, pp.95-6.

155. Ibid., pp.114-6.

156. Padel seems to favour a Welsh scribe for the play, as evidenced by an observation made at the Caroline Kemp Lecture given by Nicholas Williams, Institute of Cornish Studies, 13 September 2008.

157. For some perspectives on this, see Jon B. Coe and Simon Young, *The Celtic Sources for Arthurian Legend*, Felinfach: Llanerch, 1995. See also Paul Broadhurst and Robin Heath, *The Secret Land: The Origins of Arthurian Legend and the Grail Quest*, Launceston: Mythos, 2009.

158. See John Sturt, *Revolt in the West: The Western Rebellion of 1549*, Exeter: Devon Books, 1987; Stoyle, op.cit.

159. Halliday, op.cit., p.205.

160. See Deane and Shaw, op.cit. pp.116-31.

161. Bernard Walke, *Twenty Years at St Hilary*, London: Anthony Mott, 1982 [1935], p.184-5.

162. Deane and Shaw, op.cit.

163. See Trev Lawrence, *Songs, Poems and Legends: A Cornish Miscellany*, Paul: Sentinel, 1989; Angie Butler, *The Giants*, Penzance: West Country Giants, 2001; Will Coleman, *Tom and the Giant*, Cornwall: Brave Tales, 2005, and *Lutey and the Mermaid*, Cornwall: Brave Tales, 2005, *Madgy Figgy's Pig*, Cornwall: Brave Tales, 2005, and *Tales from Porth: The Box Set*, Cornwall: Maga, 2008. See also Craig Weatherhill, *Legends of Cornwall*, Tiverton: Halsgrove, 1998.

164. Mike Dunstan (ed.), *Tales from the White Mountains*, St Austell: Restormel Arts Clay Stories, 1993. Dunstan is the stage name of Mike Wilson. Verbal Arts Cornwall was a storytelling, drama and poetry project that ran in the late 1990s in Cornwall from Truro Library.

165. Michael Morpurgo and Michael Foreman, *Arthur: High King of Britain*, London: Pavilion, 1994; Charles Causley and Michael Foreman, *The Merrymaid of Zennor*, London: Orchard Books, 1999; Antonia Barber and Nicola Bayley, *The Mousehole Cat*, London: Walker Books, 1990. For a context to this, see Alan M. Kent, '"At the Far End of England...": Construction of Cornwall in Children's Literature' in *An Baner Kernewek / The Cornish Banner*, No.98, 1999, pp.16-21.

166. Neil Philip (ed.), *The Penguin Book of English Folktales*, Harmondsworth: Penguin, 1992; Philip Wilson (ed.), *Celtic Fairy Tales for Children*, Bath: Parragon, 1999. These collections contain a substantial number of Cornish stories. For comparative early narrative, and a notion of 'Atlantic'-arc story-telling, see Jane Smiley and Robert Kellogg (eds.), *The Sagas of the Icelanders: A Selection*, London: Penguin, 2000.

167. Peter Berresford Ellis, *The Chronicles of the Celts: New Tellings of their Myths and Legends*, London: Robinson, 1999, pp.349-430.

168. Hale, Kent and Saunders, op.cit.

169. See Ellis, op.cit., pp.433-524. See also F.M. Luzel, *Folktales from Armorica*, Felinfach: Llanerch, 1992 [c.1870].

170. See http://www.vortigernstudies.org.uk

171. R.J. Stewart, Denise Coffey, and Roy Hudd (eds.), op.cit.

172. Hunt, *(First Series)*, op.cit., pp.44-5.

173. Thorpe, op.cit., pp.53-74.

174. Hunt, *(First Series)*, op.cit.

175. Ibid.

176. Ibid. I can find no archaeological dig or date confirming this. A public house on the Barbican in Plymouth is now called *Gogmagog*.

177. Alan M. Kent and Tim Saunders (ed.), *Looking at the Mermaid: A Reader in Cornish Literature 900-1900*, London: Francis Boutle Publishers, 2000, p.82.

178. See Federation of Gouren, *Breton and Celtic Wrestling*, Brittany: Institut Culturel de Bretagne, 1985, pp.4-5.

179. Links attested in Charles Thomas, *Tintagel: Arthur and Archaeology*, London: English Heritage and Batsford, 1993.

180. Hunt, *(First Series)*, op.cit., p.190. *Lethowsow* means 'milky ones'. This is an alternative, earlier name for the Seven Stones.

181. Ibid. There is a similar Breton story concerning the lost city of Ys. See William Lewarne Harris, 'In Search of the Sunken City: The Birth of a Celtic Opera' in *An Baner Kernewek / The Cornish Banner*, No. 59, 1990, p.14.

182. See G. N. Garmonsway (ed.), *The Anglo-Saxon Chronicle*, London: Dent, 1975 [1953], p.235.

183. Paul Ashbee, *Ancient Scilly: From the First Farmers to the Early Christians*, Newton Abbot: David and Charles, 1974; Thomas, op.cit., 1985.

184   Craig Weatherhill and Paul Devereux, *Myths and Legends of Cornwall*, Wilmslow: Sigma, 1998 [1994], p.121.

185.   H.J. Whitfield, *Scilly and its Legends*, London: Timpkin, Marshall and Co., 1852, pp.12-24.

186.   James Gibson (ed.), *Chosen Poems of Thomas Hardy*, Basingstoke: Macmillan, 1975, p.46; Daphne du Maurier, 'East Wind' in Ella Westland, *Reading Daphne: A guide to the writing of Daphne du Maurier for readers and book groups*, Mount Hawke: Truran, 2007, pp.151-63; Morpurgo and Foreman, op.cit., p.15; Kent's press is called Lyonesse Press.

187.   See Bottrell, 1873, op.cit., pp.288-9.

188.   See Hunt, *(First Series)*, op.cit., pp.148-70. See also Causley and Foreman, op.cit.; Coleman, 2005, op.cit.; and Donald R. Rawe, *The Mermaid of Padstow: Stories and Poems*, Padstow: Lodenek Press, 1983.

189.   Kent and Saunders, op.cit., pp.78-9.

190.   See Duncan Williamson, *The Broonie, Silkies and Fairies*, Edinburgh: Canongate, 1985. Silkies are perceived to be sea people, sometimes taking the form of seals.

191.   W.G. Orchard (ed.), *A Glossary of Mining Terms*, Redruth: Dyllansow Truran, 1991.

192.   See George Harrison, *Substance of a Report on the Laws and Jurisdiction of the Stannaries in Cornwall*, London: Longman, Rees, Orme, Brown, Green and Longman, 1835.

193.   See Winston Graham, *The Poldark Omnibus*, London: The Bodley Head, 1991; Geoff Tibballs, *The Wycliffe File: The Story of the ITV Detective Series*, London: Boxtree, 1995; Nickianne Moody, 'Poldark Country and National Culture' in Ella Westland (ed.), *Cornwall: The Cultural Construction of Place*, Penzance: The Patten Press and the Institute of Cornish Studies, 1997, pp.129-36; Alan M. Kent, 'Screening Kernow: Authenticity, Heritage and the Representation of Cornwall in Film and Television' in Philip Payton (ed.), *Cornish Studies: Eleven*, Exeter: University of Exeter Press, 2003, pp.110-41.

194.   Hunt, *(Second Series)*, op.cit., pp.341-55. This is contested by Keith Pearce and Helen Fry (eds.), *The Lost Jews of Cornwall*, Bristol: Redcliffe, 2000.

195.   Ibid., p.343.

196.   A crème soda produced in Denver, Colorado is called Tommyknocker, inspired by Cornish miners taking part in the Colorado gold rush of 1859. See also Stephen King, *The Tommyknockers*, London: Hodder 2008 [1987]. Some information is also found in Hadley Tremaine, 'Cornish Folk Speech in America' in *Midwestern Journal of Language and Folklore*, Vol. 6, No.1/2, 1980, pp.17-25. For further background, see Paul Manning, 'Jewish Ghosts, Knackers, Tommyknockers and other Sprites of Capitalism in Cornish Mines' in Philip

Payton (ed.), *Cornish Studies: Thirteen*, Exeter: University of Exeter Press, 2005, pp.216-55. For other fairy lore in Cornwall, see Nigel Suckling, *Faeries of the Celtic Lands*, London: Photographers' Press, 2007.

197. Hunt, *(First Series)*, op.cit., p.28.

198. See Sabine Baring-Gould and H. Fleetwood Sheppard (eds.), *Songs from the West: Folksongs of Devon and Cornwall collected from the Mouths of the People*, London: Patey and Willis, 1889-1991; Sabine Baring-Gould, *A Book of the West; Volume 1 – Devon*, London: Methuen, 1899. For his imagining of place, see also Sabine Baring-Gould, *The Pennycomequicks: A Novel*, London: Collins, 1889, and *Urith: A Tale of Dartmoor*, London: Methuen, 1891. Pennycomequick is clearly a word of Brythonic derivation.

199. Pierre-Roland Giot, Philippe Guigon and Bernard Merdrignac, *The British Settlement of Brittany*, Stroud: Tempus, 2003.

200. Eva C. Rogers, *Dartmoor Legends*, London: The Pilgrim Press, 1930, p.7.

201. Hunt, *(Second Series)*, op.cit., pp.440-1. See also Alan M. Kent, *Druid Offsetting*, St Austell: Lyonesse, 2008, pp.66-80.

202. Rogers, op.cit., pp.65-111 and pp.217-39.

203. Ibid., pp.13-45 and pp.240-65.

204. Ruth E. St Leger-Gordon, *The Witchcraft and Folklore of Dartmoor*, London: Robert Hale, 1965; Ralph Whitlock, *The Folklore of Devon*, London: B.T. Batsford Ltd, 1977. See also Jack Simmons, *A Devon Anthology*, London: Anthony Mott, 1983 [1971]. For an interesting consideration of Celtic spirituality on Dartmoor, see H. Hugh Breton, *Spiritual Lessons from Dartmoor Forest*, Newton Abbot: Forest Publishing, 1990 [1929 and 1930].

205. See Joseph Biddulph, *A Handbook of West Country Brythonic: Old Devonian*, Pontypridd: Joseph Biddulph, n.d.

206. See the research on http://members.fortunecity.com/gerdewnansek

207. C.f. Matthew Spriggs, 'The Cornish Language, Archaeology and the Origins of English Theatre' in M. Jones (ed.), *Traces of Ancestry: Studies in Honour of Colin Renfrew*, Vol. 2, Cambridge: McDonald Institute Monograph Series, 2004, pp.143-61.

208. See Douglas Williams, *The Festivals of Cornwall*, St Teath: Bossiney Books, 1987; Ian Marshall, *The Amazing Story of the Floral Dance*, Dobwalls: Songs of Cornwall, 2003.

209. Ibid. See also Donald R. Rawe, *Padstow's Obby Oss and May Day Festivities: A Study in Folklore and Tradition*, Padstow: Lodenek Press, 1990 [1971]. In 2008 the thirtieth Lowender Peran Festival had a Festival 'Oss. This consisted of a circular structure around the performer tied with long colourful tatters. Such an arrangement was also reflected in the hat worn by the performer. See *The West Briton*, 23 October 2008, p.34-5.

210. Ralph Dunstan (ed.), *Cornish Dialect and Folk Songs*, Truro: W. Jordan, 1932; Inglis Gundry, *Canow Kernow: Songs and Dances from Cornwall*, Cornwall: The Federation of Old Cornwall Societies, 1972; Merv Davey, *Hengan: Traditional Folk Songs, Dances and Broadside Ballads collected in Cornwall*, Redruth: Dyllansow Truran, 1983; Richard McGrady, *Traces of Ancient Mystery: The Ballad Carols of Davies Gilbert and William Sandys*, Redruth: Institute of Cornish Studies, 1993. See also Merv, Alison and Jowdy Davey, *Scoot Dances, Troyls, Furrys and Tea Treats: The Cornish Dance Tradition*, London: Francis Boutle Publishers, 2009.

211. Ibid., p.4.

212. Richard Rastall, *The Heaven Singing: Music in Early English Religious Drama*, Cambridge: D.S. Brewer, 1996, and *Minstrels Playing: Music in Early English Religious Drama*, Cambridge: D.S. Brewer, 2001, pp.307-35, pp.336-46, pp.401-13.

213. See Benjamin Bruch, 'Verse Structure and Musical Performance in *Bewnans Ke*' in *Journal of the Royal Institution of Cornwall*, 2006, pp.57-66.

214. Davey, op.cit., p.11.

215. See Harry Woodhouse, *Cornish Bagpipes: Fact or Fiction?* Redruth: Dyllansow Truran, 1994. See also Pyba, *Ilow Koth a Gernow / The Ancient Music of Cornwall*, Withiel: Pyba, 1999; and Lyon, op.cit., p.29.

216. Merv Davey, "Guizing': Ancient Traditions and Modern Sensitivities' in Philip Payton (ed.), *Cornish Studies: Fourteen*, Exeter: University of Exeter Press, 2006, pp.229-44. C.f. Jason Semmens, 'Guising, Ritual and Revival: The Hobby Horse in Cornwall' in *Old Cornwall*, Volume 13, No. 52, 2005, pp.39-46.

217. Victor Turner, *From Ritual to Theatre: The Human Seriousness of Play*, New York: Performance Arts Journals Publications, 1987; Celu Amderston, *Deepening the Power: Community Ritual and Sacred Theatre*, Vancouver, British Columbia: Beach Holme Publications, 1995.

218. Halliday, op.cit., p.150.

219. See Federation of Gouren, op.cit.; W.F. Collier, 'Wrestling: The Cornish and Devonshire Styles' in *The Cornish Magazine*, 1898, pp.193-201; numerous examples in Kent and McKinney, op.cit.

220. See the observations on theatrical culture in Peter Ackroyd, *Shakespeare: The Biography*, London: Chatto and Windus, 2005, pp.323-88.

221. 'My mother saw a dancing bear' in Charles Causley, *Figgie Hobbin*, Harmondsworth: Puffin, 1985 [1970], p.95.

222. Kent has two Roman wrestlers, completing a hitch in a Cornish style in Alan M. Kent, *Nativitas Christi / The Nativity: A New Cornish Mystery Play*, London: Francis Boutle Publishers, 2006, pp.71-2.

223. See Mikhail Bakhtin, *Rabelais and His World*, Cambridge, Massachusetts, MIT Press, 1968 [1965]; David Shepherd, *Bakhtin: Carnival and Other Subjects*, Amsterdam, Georgia: Rodophi B. V. Editions, 1993.

224. Rozik, op.cit., pp.211-5.

225. See Glynne Wickham, 'The Beginnings of English Drama: Stage and Drama till 1660' in Christopher Ricks (ed.), *English Drama to 1710*, London: Penguin, 1987 [1971], pp.1-54; Hutton, op.cit., 1994.

226. See C.L. Barber, *Shakespeare's Festive Comedy: A Study of Dramatic Form and its relation to Social Custom*, Oxford: Oxford University Press, 1959; Bakhtin, op.cit.; Shepherd, op.cit.

227. For a perspective on this, see contributors to Huw Pryce (ed.), *Literacy in Medieval Celtic Societies*, Cambridge: Cambridge University Press, 1998; and Padel, op.cit.

228. Interestingly, the Green World in Trevor Nunn's film adaptation is 'Cornwall' which is the location for Illyria. Major sequences are filmed on the north coast, at Lanhydrock and at Cotehele. See Trevor Nunn (dir.), *Twelfth Night*, London: Fine Line Features, 1996.

229. See Malcolm Evans, 'Deconstructing Shakespeare's Comedies' in John Drakakis (ed.), *Alternative Shakespeares*, London and New York: Methuen, 1985 pp.67-94. For the background to criticism on Shakespearean comedy, and its eventual influence on Bakhtin and his followers, see Nevill Coghill, 'The Basis of Shakespearean Comedy' in Anne Ridler (ed.), *Shakespeare Criticism: 1935-1960*, Oxford: Oxford University Press, 1963, pp.201-27 and E.M.W. Tillyard, *The Elizabethan World Picture*, Harmondsworth: Penguin, 1988 [1943]. The influence of the work of Northrop Frye is also important.

230. See 'Golowan – John's Feast' in *Cornish World / Bys Kernowyon*, No. 6, 1995, pp.20-1.

231. See Doc Rowe, *We'll Call once more unto your house*, Padstow: Doc Rowe, 1982, and *May Day: The Coming of Spring*, Swindon: English Heritage, 2006; Williams, op.cit.; and Deane and Shaw, op.cit.

232. Rawe, op.cit., p.10.

233. Ibid.

234. Whitley Stokes (ed. and tr.), *The Life of Saint Meriasek, Bishop and Confessor: A Cornish Drama*, London: Trübner and Co., 1872, pp.60-1. Some adjustments in Stokes' transcription and translation have been made here.

235. Rawe, op.cit., pp.25-7.

236. Ibid., p.4.

237. Ibid., p.33.

238. See John Angarrack, *Scat t'Larraps: Resist and Survive*, Bodmin: Independent Academic Press, 2008, p.100.

239. Deane and Shaw, op.cit., pp.155-6.

240. Ibid., p.157. For a slightly alternative version, see Gundry, op.cit., p.12. Gundry notes that Nicolas Boson of Newlyn (writing *c*.1660) observed that a May Pole was

set up during the singing of the *Hal-an-Tow*. Another verse was also added by Robert Morton Nance post-1930: 'But to a greater than St George our Helston, has a right-O, St Michael with his wings outspread, the Archangel so bright-O, Who fought the fiend-O, of all mankind the foe', but has since been dropped. The Aunt Mary of the second verse may have some connection to the Cornish habit of referring to Mary, Mother of Jesus as Aunt Mary. See 'Modryb Marya – Aunt Mary' in Piers Brendon (ed.), *Cornish Ballads and Other Poems: Robert Stephen Hawker*, St Germans: The Elephant Press, 1975, p.26.

241. For discussion of this, see Deane and Shaw, op.cit., p.158; Gundry, op.cit.

242. Cecil Sharpe (1859-1924) was the founding father of the folklore revival in England. He spent a considerable amount of time collecting in Cornwall.

243. Dunstan, op.cit., p.11, p.18 and p.23.

244. R.J.E. Tiddy, *The Mummers' Play*, Oxford: Clarendon Press, 1923, p.144-47.

245. Rozik, op.cit., p.119.

246. Ernest T. Kirby, *Dionysus: A Study of the Bacchae and the Origins of Drama*, Ann Arbor: University Microfilms Int., 1982, p.52.

247. For a context, see Alan M. Kent, 'Some ancientry that lingers: Dissent, Difference and Dialect in the Cornish and Cornu-English Literature of Robert Morton Nance' in Peter W. Thomas and Derek Williams (eds.), *Setting Cornwall on its Feet: Robert Morton Nance 1873-1959*, London: Francis Boutle Publishers, 2007, pp.96-152. See also Robert Morton Nance, 'The Christmas Play of Saint George and the Turkish Knight' in ibid., pp.153-78.

248. Tiddy, op.cit. There is an intriguing connection here between the Devil of this play and pan-like structures found in the *plen-an-gwarries* of Perran Round and St Just-in-Penwith. The Devil mentions that he carries a 'frying pan'. Both the above locations have a theatrical device know as the 'Devil's spoon'. Is there some lost link?

249. It would be interesting to further consider any links between what Myrna Combellack calls 'The Camborne Play' and the Camborne mummers' play. See Myrna Combellack (ed. and tr.), *The Camborne Play: A verse translation of Beunans Meriasek*, Redruth: Dyllansow Truran, 1988. Brian Murdoch notes a parody of Mass in *Bewnans Meriasek*, which he terms a 'black mass'. See Brian Murdoch (ed.) *The Grin of the Gargoyle*, Sawtry: Dedalus 1995, pp.220-32.

250. This said, we need to maintain a healthy scepticism over supposed ancient origins of cultures. See Eric Hobsbawm and Terence Ranger (eds.), *The Invention of Tradition*, Cambridge: Cambridge University Press, 1992. See also Benedict Anderson, *Imagined Communities: Reflections on the Origin and Spread of Nationalism*, London and New York: Verso, 2006 [1983].

251. See Ken George (ed. and tr.), *Bywnans Ke*, Cornwall: Kesva an Taves Kernewek, 2006, pp.249-51.

252. See William Copeland Borlase, op.cit.; Taylor, op.cit.; Thomas, op.cit., 1994 and 1998.

253. See, for example, March and Straffon, op.cit., 1993.

254. For examples, see Hunt *(Second Series)*, op.cit., pp.261-83.

255. For a context, see Kent, op.cit., 2000, pp.55-9.

256. Nicholas Orme (ed.), *Nicholas Roscarrock's Lives of the Saints of Cornwall and Devon*, Exeter: Devon and Cornwall Record Society, 1992, p.68. See Nicholas Roscarrock, *Lives of the Saints*, MS. Add. 3041, Cambridge.

257. Orme (ed.), op.cit., p.67

258. Ibid., p.71.

259. Ibid., p.90.

260. Ibid., p.i.

261. Doble, op.cit.; John, op.cit.; and Orme, op.cit., 2000.

262. John, op.cit., p.21.

263. See Pryce, op.cit.

264. See map of sites in Charles Thomas and Joanna Mattingly, *The History of Christianity in Cornwall: AD 500-2000*, Truro: Royal Institution of Cornwall, 2000, p.14.

265. Broadhurst, op.cit.

266. John Betjeman, *Collected Poems*, London: John Murray, 1988, pp.52-3, p.81 and pp.135-40.

267. Philip Payton, 'John Betjeman and the Holy Grail: One Man's Celtic Quest' in Philip Payton (ed.), *Cornish Studies: Fifteen*, Exeter: University of Exeter Press, 2007, pp.185-208.

268. Donald R. Rawe, *Petroc of Cornwall*. Padstow: Lodenek Press, 1970, and *The Trials of St Piran*, Padstow: Lodenek Press, 1971.

269. See L.E.T. Jenkin, 'St Piran' in Myrna Combellack Harris (ed.), *Cornish Studies for Schools*, Truro: Cornwall County Council, 1989, pp.41-2.

270. See Williams, op.cit., 1968; Matthews and Matthews, op.cit. See also J. Gwenogvryn Evans (ed.), *The Book of Taliesin*, Llanbedrog: Privately published, 1910.

271. Alistair Moffat, *The Sea Kingdoms: The Story of Celtic Britain and Ireland*, London: Harper Collins, 2001, p.22.

272. See John T. Koch and John Carey (eds. and trs.), *The Celtic Heroic Age: Literary Sources for Ancient Celtic Europe and Early Wales and Ireland*, Malden, Massachusetts: Celtic Studies Publications, 1995.

273. Taliesin MS. 3, Jesus College, Oxford, 1-3a. For translation, see Hale, Kent and Saunders, op.cit., pp.35-6. The word Arthur is derived from the Brythonic word for a bear. Arthur is often described as a bear in Brythonic writings.

274. Cf. Koch and Carey, op.cit., pp.270-389.

275. http://www.admin.ox.ac.uk/po/news/2005-06/jun/15.shtml The Cornish within this text was discovered in 2006, following work by Malcolm Godden, Rohini Jayatilaka and Patrick Sims-Williams.

276. Donatus Glosses (BN MS. Lat. 13029 Paris [Bibliothèque Nationale], MS. Bodley 574, for 14 S.C. 2026 (3), Oxford). See Arbois de Jubainville in *Revue Celtique*, No.27, 1906. Translation by Alan M. Kent and Tim Saunders. I am indebted to the observations of Tim Saunders here.

277. Tobit-Glosses (Oxoniensis posterior) MS. Bodley 572, Oxford; Whitley Stokes *Old Breton Glosses*, Calcutta: Privately published, 1879; Joseph Loth (ed.), *Vocubulaire Vieux-Breton*, Paris: Privately published, 1884. See F. Madam and H.H.E. Craster (eds.), *A Summary Catalogue of Western Manuscripts in the Bodleian Library*, Oxford: Clarendon Press, 1922-55. For this I am indebted to the observations of Nicholas Williams.

278. Ibid. Translation by Alan M. Kent and Tim Saunders. The word *Garn* here is probably a transcription error, since *Gar* means 'Leg' in Cornish. *Cennin* would be a singulative of the collective *Cenn*; *Cenn* meaning 'skin'.

279. See Bodmin Manumissions (Bodmin Gospels, St Petroc's Gospels, BL Add. MS. 938, London). See Henry Jenner, 'The Bodmin Gospels' in *Journal of the Royal Institution of Cornwall*, No.70, 1922, pp.113-45, and 'The Bodmin Manumissions' in *Journal of the Royal Institution of Cornwall*, No.71, 1924, p.242.

280. *Vocabularium Cornicum* (Cottonian or Old Cornish Vocabulary, BL MS. Cotton Vespasian A XIV, London).

281. See also Norris, op.cit., pp.311-435; Eugene Val Tassel Graves (ed.), *Vocabularium Cornicum: The Old Cornish Vocabulary*, University of Columbia Ph.D. thesis, 1962; Ray Edwards, *Notes on Meaning and Word Usage on Examination of Old Cornish Texts*, Cornwall: Cornish Language Board, 1997. Publication of a new edition of the vocabulary, translated by Kent and Saunders, is anticipated in 2011.

282. In *The Romaunt of the Rose*, a Middle English text generally attributed to Geoffrey Chaucer, he makes reference to 'hornepipes of Cornewaile'. See F.N. Robinson (ed.), *The Complete Works of Geoffrey Chaucer*, Oxford: Oxford University Press, 1957, p.604.

283. When Cornish was coming into active use again during the recent period (1850-1970) the word *pridit* was not taken into general use. It is has therefore retained a certain rarified air, paradoxically like the word 'bard' in English. It is normally only used in poetic contexts. The most famous use of it was by Jack Clemo, who despite many reservations about the Gorseth, when he eventually joined, took the alternative bardic name *Prydyth An Pry* [Poet of the Clay].

284. See Whetter, op.cit.

285. Lyon, op.cit.

286. Graves, op.cit.

287. Hunt *(Second Series)*, op.cit., pp.319-26.

288. History tends to underestimate how far ancient peoples can travel. Two books which do not do this are Samuel Eliot Morison, *The European Discovery of America: The Northern Voyages AD 500-1600*, New York: Oxford University Press, 1971; E.G. Bowen, *Britain and the Western Seaways*, London: Thames and Hudson, 1972.

289. See Thomas Jones, 'The early evolution of the legend of Arthur' in *Nottingham Medieval Studies*, No.8, 1964, pp.3-21; Stuart Piggott, 'The sources of Geoffrey of Monmouth' in *Antiquity*, No.25, 1941, pp.269-86.

290. Thorpe, op.cit., p.51.

291. See Piggott, op.cit.; Peter Berresford Ellis, *The Cornish Language and its Literature*, London and Boston: Routledge and Kegan Paul, 1974, pp.22-3; Charles Thomas, 'Hardy and Lyonesse: Parallel Mythologies' in Melissa Hardie (ed.), *A Mere Interlude: Some Literary Visitors to Lyonesse*, Penzance: The Patten Press, 1992, p.15; Paul Broadhurst, *Tintagel and the Arthurian Mythos*, Launceston: Pendragon Press, 1992, p.44. Thomas notes that Geoffrey of Monmouth 'seems to have visited Tintagel'.

292. See Thomas and Williams, op.cit.; George, op.cit. Caerleon-on-Usk features in the play.

293. See Kenneth Muir (ed.), *William Shakespeare: King Lear*, London: Methuen, 1972; John Pitcher (ed.), *William Shakespeare: Cymbeline*, London: Penguin, 2005. For a context on these texts, see Andrew Hadfield, *Shakespeare, Spenser and the Matter of Britain*, London: Palgrave Macmillan, 2003 and David J. Baker, *Between Nations: Shakespeare, Spenser, Marvell and the Question of Britain*, Stanford: Stanford University Press, 2001.

294. Stewart, Coffey and Hudd, op.cit.

295. For background to this, see Davies and Law, op.cit., Williams and Jones, op.cit.; S.J. Connolly (ed.), *Kingdoms United? Great Britain and Ireland Since 1500: Integration and Diversity*, Dublin: Four Courts Press, 1999; John Kerrigan, *Archipelagic English: Literature, History and Politics 1603-1702*, Oxford: Oxford University Press, 2008.

296. Thorpe, op.cit., p.171, p.175 and p.184.

297. Orme, op.cit., p.106.

298. See Bakere, op.cit., p.29; Lyon, op.cit., 2001.

299. Philip Payton, 'a… concealed envy against the English': a Note on the Aftermath of the 1497 Rebellions in Cornwall' in Philip Payton (ed.), *Cornish Studies: One*, Exeter: University of Exeter Press, 1993, pp.4-13. See also James Whetter, 'Play recalls rebellion' in *An Baner Kernewek / The Cornish Banner*, No. 88, 1997.

300. Hale, Kent and Saunders, op.cit., pp.45-6. See also Michael Curley, 'A New Edition of John of Cornwall's *Prophetia Merlini*' in *Speculum*, No.57, 1982, pp.217-49. For a translation back into Cornish, see Julyan Holmes (ed. and tr.), *An dhargan a Verdhin gan Yowaan Kernow*, Cornwall: Kesva and Tavaes Kernewek, 1998.

301. For example, as the Dutch film-maker Rolf De Heer discovered in his work on the Aboriginal film, *Ten Canoes*, certain individuals could not be played or imagined, because they did not have the appropriate lineage. See Rolf De Heer (dir.) *Ten Canoes*, Los Angeles: Universal Pictures, 2007.

302. See Bakere, op.cit., pp.12-49

303. John Whittaker, *The Ancient Cathedral of Cornwall Historically Surveyed*, London: Stockdale, 1804. See also John E. Spence, *A Short Guide and History to the Church of St Germans*, St Germans: Privately published, 1966; and for an archaeological perspective, see Lynette Olson and Ann Preston Jones, 'An ancient cathedral of Cornwall? Excavated remains east of St Germans Church' in *Cornish Archaeology / Hendhyscans Kernow*, Nos. 37-8, 1998-9, pp.153-69. Textual sources have been found. See Richard Rutt, 'Missa Propria Germani Episcopi and the Eponym of St Germans' in *Journal of the Royal Institution of Cornwall*, Vol. 7, 1977, pp.305-9.

304. See E.M.R Ditmus, *Tristan and Iseult in Cornwall*, Brockworth: Forrester Roberts, 1979; Forrester Roberts, *The Legend of Tristan and Iseult: The Tale and the Trail in Ireland, Cornwall and Brittany*, Gloucester: Forrester Roberts, 1998. A useful base narrative is Hilaire Belloc and Paul Rosenfield (eds. and trs.), *Joseph Bédier: The Romance of Tristan*, New York: Vintage, 1945. See 308 below.

305. A selection is included in James J. Wilhelm (ed. and tr.), *The Romance of Arthur: An Anthology of Medieval Texts in Translation*, New York and London: Garland, 1994.

306. See Laing, op.cit., p.243-4.

307. This is asserted in A.S.D. Smith, *The Story of the Cornish Language: Its Extinction and Revival*, Camborne: Smith, 1947; Hilary Shaw, 'Celtic Drama: Cornish Miracle Plays' in *The Celtic Pen*, Vol. 1, No. 1, 1993; Jean-Pierre Le Mat, *The Sons of Ermine: A History of Brittany*, Belfast: An Clochán, 1996; Jacqueline Gibson and Gwyn Griffiths, (eds. and trs.), *The Turn of the Ermine: An Anthology of Breton Literature*, London: Francis Boutle Publishers, 2006.

308. See Kent, op.cit., 2000, pp.29-32; Joseph Bédier, *La Roman de Tristan*, Paris: Privately published, 1902-5.

309. For the text of Thomas's *Tristan*, see A.T. Hatto (ed. and tr.), *Gottfried von Strassburg: Tristan, with the Tristan of Thomas*, Harmondsworth: Penguin, 1967, pp.301-53.

310. Ibid., pp.40-300.

311. See Ernest Muret (ed.), *Le Roman de Tristan par Béroul*, Paris: Firmin Didot et Compagnie, 1903, and Alan S. Fredrick (ed. and tr.), *Béroul: The Romance of Tristan*, Harmondsworth: Penguin, 1970.

312. Joseph Loth, *Des Nouvelles Théories sur l'origine du Roman Arthurian*, Paris: Privately published, 1892.

313. Henry Jenner, 'The Tristan Romance and its Cornish Provenance' in *Journal of the Royal Institution of Cornwall*, No.14, 1914, pp.464-88.

314. For comment on this, see Kent, op.cit., 2000, p.22. This view is in contrast to some revivalist notions of Cornish culture.

315. Roberts, op.cit., p.6.

316. Bakere, op.cit., pp.32-49.

317. Deacon, op.cit., p.36.

318. For a perspective on this, see John Angarrack, *Breaking the Chains: Censorship, Deception and the Manipulation of Public Opinion in Cornwall*, Camborne: Stannary Publications, 1999, pp.445-6.

319. Fredrick, op.cit., p.60.

320. Ibid., p.54, p.64 and p.75.

321. See Hatto, op.cit., pp.40-300.

322. Kneehigh Theatre, *Tristan and Yseult, The Bacchae, The Wooden Frock, The Red Shoes*, London: Oberon Books, 2005, p.23, and *The Reviews*, Truro: Kneehigh Theatre, n.d., pp.3-4.

323. A variety of arguments assert this in Joan Tasker Grimbert (ed.), *Tristan and Isolde: A Casebook*, New York: Garland, 1995.

324. Malpas is not far from the cultural-geographic surrounds of the first half of *Bewnans Ke*. See Williams. op.cit.; George, op.cit. See also André de Mandach, 'Legend and Reality: Recent Excavation and Research in Cornwall concerning Tristan and Isolt' in *Tristania*, Vol.IV, No.2, 1979, pp.4-24.

325. See Norris, op.cit., pp.157-69; Robert Morton Nance, A.S.D. Smith, Ray Chubb, Richard Jenkin, Graham Sandercock (eds. and trs.), *The Cornish Ordinalia, First Play: Origo Mundi*. Cornwall: Agan Tavas, 2001, pp.149-62. For a critical commentary, see Brian Murdoch, 'Rex David, Bersabe, and Syr Urry: A Comparative Approach to a Scene in the Cornish *Origo Mundi*' in Philip Payton (ed.), *Cornish Studies: Twelve*, Exeter: University of Exeter Press, 2004, pp.288-304.

326. Helen Moore (ed.), *Sir Thomas Malory: Le Morte Darthur*, London: Wordsworth Editions, 1996.

327. Stokes, op.cit., p.126.

328. Hale, Kent and Saunders, op.cit., pp.123-6.

329. Ibid., pp.203-13; A.S.D. Smith, *Trystan hag Ysolt*, Redruth: J. & M. Roberts, 1951; D.H. Watkins, *Trystan and Ysolt*, Camborne: An Lef Kernewek, 1973.

330. This was part of the 1951 Cornish Drama Festival.

331. Arthur Quiller-Couch and Daphne du Maurier, *Castle Dor*, London: Dent, 1962.

332. Kevin Reynolds (dir.), *Tristan and Isolde*, Los Angeles: 20th Century Fox, 2006.

333. Jim Harrison, *Legends of the Fall*, New York: Delacorte Press, 1979.

334. Caeia March, *Reflections*, London: The Women's Press, 1995.

335. Glynne Wickham, *The Medieval Theatre*, Cambridge: Cambridge University Press, 1987; William Tydeman, *The Medieval European Stage 500-1550*, Cambridge: Cambridge University Press, 2001.

336. Harwood, op.cit., pp.77-100.

337. See Taylor, op.cit.

338. Whetter, op.cit., 1988, pp.1-2.

339. Ibid., pp.2-3; *Glasney Cartulary*, MS. Cornwall Records Office Dd R(S) 59; C.R. Sowell, 'The Collegiate Church of St Thomas of Glasney' in *Journal of the Royal Institution of Cornwall*, Vol. I, 1865, pp.21-34; John A.C. Vincent, 'The Glasney Cartulary' in *Journal of the Royal Institution of Cornwall*, Vol.6, 1878-81, pp.213-63. See also L.E. Elliot-Binns, *Medieval Cornwall*, London: Methuen, 1955.

340. Ibid.; Thurstan C. Peter, *The History of Glasney Collegiate Church*, Camborne: Camborne Printing and Stationery Co., 1903; June Palmer, *Searching for Glasney: The Evidence of the Records*, Cornwall: Friends of Glasney Occasional Paper, 1991.

341. Henry Jenner, *A Handbook of the Cornish Language: Chiefly in its Latest Stages with some account of its History and Literature*, London: David Nutt, 1904; Martyn F. Wakelin, *Language and History in Cornwall*, Leicester: Leicester University Press, 1975; Ellis, op.cit., 1974; Murdoch, op.cit., 1993; Kent, op.cit., 2000.

342. Whetter, op.cit., pp.102-14.

343. Bakere, op.cit., and *Glasney and Cornish Drama*, Penryn: Friends of Glasney, 1989; Mari Jones and Ishtla Singh, *Exploring Language Change*, London: Routledge, 2005, p.136.

344. D. H. Frost, 'Glasney's Parish Clergy and the Tregear Manuscript' in Philip Payton (ed.), *Cornish Studies: Fifteen*, Exeter: University of Exeter Press, 2007, pp.27-89; Padel, op.cit. For some further reflections on this issue, see D.H. Frost, '*Sacrament an Alter*: A Tudor Cornish Patristic Catena' and Malte W. Tschirschky, 'The Medieval 'Cornish Bible'' in Philip Payton (ed.), *Cornish Studies: Eleven*, Exeter: University of Exeter Press, 2003, pp.291-307 and pp.308-16.

345. Scawen, op.cit.

CHAPTER TWO

———

'Devils and devices to delight as well the eye as the ear': Rounds, Rebellion and Recusants in Medieval and Tudor Cornwall, 1200-1600

'Now there is coming more and more the big cycles of plays that are put on by the guilds. From Scotland to Cornwall it is happening, wherever people live together in numbers.'

From *Morality Play* by Barry Unsworth, 1995[1]

'The country people flock from all sides, many miles off to hear and see it, for they have therein devils and devices to delight as well the eye as the ear.'

From *The Survey of Cornwall* by Richard Carew, 1602[2]

Barry Unsworth's 1995 novel, *Morality Play* – about Nicholas Barber, a member of the clergy, turned travelling player – recognises the significant theatrical contribution of Cornwall and gives a remarkable insight into the theatrical culture of late fourteenth-century Britain. Right at the end of the period considered in this chapter, we see the observations of Richard Carew (1555-1634). It seems Carew was a man who, although embracing English literary and performance culture – having seen examples of 'the gwary miracles' – chose to give notes about their dramaturgy in his *Survey of Cornwall*. Carew's survey was some years in preparation (what he terms, 'long since begun, a great while discontinued, lately reviewed, and now hastily finished'[3]) so, although published in the early seventeenth century, it was in effect a sixteenth-century text. While Unsworth's words give some sense of the achievement of Cornish theatrical culture in the late medieval and Tudor periods, Carew's indicate a culture once again in transition. This chapter explores Barber's 'big cycles of plays' as well as how Cornish communities worked together to produce 'devils and devices to delight as well the eye as the ear'. The proto- and para-theatrical practice of the previous Ages was about to emerge confidently as a highly developed theatrical territory. We shall explore those developments here.

Given Cornwall's damp and wet climate, as well as the lack of any university-style institution in the aftermath of the Reformation, it is perhaps incredible that any textual sources have survived to demonstrate the theatrical culture of the period 1200-1600. The picture we have of this phase in the extant texts is a tiny sketch of the true complexity of the theatre of Cornwall during this phase. However, a fuller picture can perhaps be revealed through careful study of records of where *plen-an-gwarrie*s once existed, in textual records of performance, financial accounts, and a cultural-geographic examination of space and place. Without doubt, the somewhat singular concentration of theatrical activity in pre-Reformation Cornwall in the late medieval period stands as significant, not only in the islands of Britain, but also in European and world culture. Several continuities develop from previous Ages. The three strands of ritual, landscape and community continue to have an important shaping effect on the ways in which theatre expanded during these centuries. Likewise, although the end of this phase was to witness a catastrophic shutdown of theatrical culture (linked to a similar collapse of the Cornish language), its ideology would continue forward into successive phases, right up until the present day.

There are some unique difficulties in re-examining this phase. Firstly, of all the phases of theatrical history in Cornwall, it is this one that has received the most attention from scholarship, both inside and outside of Cornwall.[4] While negotiating a way to offer new perspectives, we must pay attention to the critical weight of observation and seemingly micro-analytical studies already completed.[5] The major Cornish-language texts will here be examined, not as a rock-face for linguistic mining, but as pieces of theatre. The discovery of *Bewnans Ke* offers us considerable potential,[6] because all previous substantial studies have been completed without that text in mind. Because the texts during this phase were, on the whole, written in Cornish (or mostly in Cornish), this area has been embraced by the field of Celtic Studies. However, as we have seen, 'normal' or traditional Celtic Studies have not really dealt with the Cornish theatrical continuum in an appropriate or sympathetic way. There has also been much debate over the years about how much of the theatrical continuum in Cornwall has been influenced by outside sources and traditions – both European (mainly Breton and French, though also German and Swiss) and, more contentiously, English – and, conversely, how much of the continuum developed organically in Cornwall.[7] Related to this has been a notion of English theatrical history appropriating the historical development of the *plen-an-gwarry* as part of its own theories of origin, leading towards the formation of such sixteenth-century theatre playhouses as The Swan and The Globe in London, and thus the forward trajectory of English theatre.[8] Moreover, many studies of the core texts in this period have been carried out under the auspices of English literary studies rather than performance studies.[9] One final point worth making about approaching this period with new methods of scholarship is, as indicated in Chapter One, to reappraise the significance of Glasney College as the centre of literary culture in Cornwall in the late medieval phase, when there was a growing notion of a more devolved pattern of writing, involving a wide range of writers across a larger geographical area.[10]

My approach to the medieval and Tudor period in the theatrical history of Cornwall will be the model used elsewhere in my work, and in the rest of this book: a cultural-materialist perspective.[11] Although this model has become the predominant way of looking at English Renaissance drama,[12] as well as other periods of literary development,[13] it has perhaps been embraced more slowly by medievalists, and in particular Celticists, than in other fields. As outlined earlier, it is my view that a cultural-materialist perspective is much needed in Celtic Studies, as a useful approach to re-examining literary and theatrical production. This new approach finds sympathy in Frantzen, who argues that medievalism (and therefore Celtic medievalism) needs to start speaking the same language as the rest of literary studies,[14] and Strohm, who wishes for more theory to be applied on the pre-modern text.[15] This position has been consolidated by the work of Schmitz, who has strongly argued that a historicist approach very much suits ancient texts.[16] Bar a few recent developments in the study of pre-modern Cornish-language drama,[17] this has not occurred, so an application here is timely.

As in the previous chapter, dates for texts and events are sometimes difficult. Usually texts are examined by archivists and scholars who explore the type of hand, parchment and vocabulary used, although this can sometimes be deceptive. We must realise that the extant Cornish-language dramas went through a series of hands, drafts and copies to be in their current 'preserved' form, and that we must be sceptical about assigning texts particular dates.[18] That said, there are, perhaps, more accurate records of performances that did occur, along with their dates, although the texts themselves have been lost. The picture throughout this chapter will remain, as elsewhere, generally chronological, although some crossings forwards and backwards will be made. The main textual sources for this phase are the three plays of the *Ordinalia* ('Origo Mundi', 'Passio Christi' and 'Resurrexio Domini'), *Bewnans Ke* and *Bewnans Meriasek*.[19] The sixth extant play *The Creacion of the World*, as scribed by William Jordan, will also be dealt with in this chapter; although in its manuscript manifestation[20] it is dated 1611, it more properly fits into this earlier period of development. There are, however, a number of smaller textual sources, which will be considered. These range from literary fragments to Account books, and they will help us reconstruct the breadth and range of work occurring. We should first examine the materialist context for performance before moving to the individual texts themselves.

The established model of literary and theatrical culture in Cornwall mainly operates in the following way: each parish or community appeared to have its own multi-functional performance space, the *plen-an-gwarry*;[21] over time, the community developed verse drama which was performed by a broadly illiterate group of actors, at significant dates in the ritual year. The text seems to have been developed by both the community and a literate priest figure (possibly with links to Glasney College), but is likely to be a 'developmental' piece of literature, meaning that it was adapted and extemporised for each performance. Acting appears to have been very different from how it is conceived now. Possibly performers rote learnt their lines (the rhyme helping them to do this), or the lines were whispered by a literate prompter (the so-called *ordinary*) for the actor then to declaim. The themes of such dramas usually displayed the origins of the parish and the community through a direct exploration of the life and works of the local saint, though, as Payton argues, under Tudor suppression there might also be political undertones.[22] Other dramas presented the core narrative components of the Bible, helping the community to celebrate the life and work of Jesus Christ. Some of the dramas seem also to feature legendary and folkloric components, ranging, for example, from Obby Oss (*Bewnans Meriasek*), Mermaids (the *Ordinalia*), and King Arthur (*Bewnans Ke*) to the so-called 'Legend of the Rood' (the *Ordinalia*).[23] Apocryphal stories also formed a component of the dramas, but these would have been even more harshly suppressed during the Reformation. The scale and size of the performance clearly depended on the parish and its resources. For example, it would seem right that Perran Round near Perranzabuloe is a large structure, for the saint being commemorated and celebrated there was St Piran, a well-known and popular Cornish saint, latterly perceived as the patron saint of Cornwall.[24] Clearly, infrastructural investment took place there over a number of centuries; this perhaps suggests that that particular piece of theatre drew visiting spectators from outside of the parish. A smaller example of a *plen-an-gwarry* has been located at Gorran in south Cornwall,[25] a compact theatrical infrastructure befitting celebrations of a more minor saint. For evidence of the kinds of infrastructure we need not look further than the observations made by Richard Carew at the end of the sixteenth century. Carew's points about the 'gwary miracle' give us a starting point from which we may project backwards to some of the texts we have, and to texts we believe existed:

> The gwary miracle, in English, a miracle play, is a kind of interlude, compiled in Cornish out of some scripture history, with that grossness which accompanied the Romans' *vetus comedia*. For representing it, they raise an earthen amphitheatre in some open field, having the diameter of [t]his enclosed plain some forty or fifty foot. The country people flock from all sides, many miles off, to hear and see it, for they have therein devils and devices to delight as well the eye as the ear. The players con not their parts without book, but are prompted by one called the ordinary, who followeth at their back with the book in his hand, and telleth them softly what they must pronounce aloud.[26]

As a starting point in our exploration, deconstructing Carew's classic account of the performance conditions of the typical 'gwary miracle' is an interesting process. Certainly, Carew is incorrect in describing the work as an 'interlude': as he well knew, interludes were technically something rather different. During this phase, the term 'interlude' was normally applied to short, moralistic pieces, sometimes with farcical comedy within them. In his qualification of this statement, 'a kind of interlude', he may be more correct; however, the ambition of the late medieval plays was never so small in scale. For one thing, the gwarry miracles had a much larger cast ('Origo Mundi', for example, has almost sixty different characters, with similar numbers for the 'Passion' and 'Resurrection') and, for another, told more epic stories. The 'grossness' which he then describes might fit some components of the action, but perhaps he was comparing the performance unfavourably with English-language drama, which he considered highly sophisticated.[27] His description of the Romans' *vetus comedia* is not really accurate either, although admittedly such comedy was similarly episodic and used everyday speech. His description of the amphitheatre seems more accurate, when compared to later observers,[28] and he seems more persuaded by the event's popularity. The description of the 'ordinary' himself, however, is more problematical. It is, as suggested above, now part of 'received' theatrical theory about Cornwall during this phase, though William L. Tribby believes that this late depiction of performance makes the drama look 'naïve and highly primitive', and we must consider the possibility that Carew's view may be wholly unreliable.[29] This is evidenced further in the rest of Carew's account since the prompter seems to have a very different agenda from the actor for the performance. Indeed the prompter's role would seem to equate more readily to a 'stressed' modern director:

> Which manner once gave occasion to a pleasant conceited gentleman of practising a merry prank; for he undertaking (perhaps of set purpose) an actor's room, was accordingly lessoned (beforehand) by the ordinary, that he must say after him. His turn came: quoth the ordinary, 'Go forth man, and show thyself'. The gentleman steps out upon the stage, and like a bad clerk in scripture matters, cleaving more to the letter than the sense, pronounced these words aloud. 'Oh (says the fellow softly in his ear) you mar all the play.' And with this his passion the actor makes the audience in like sort acquainted. Hereon the prompter falls to flat railing and cursing in the bitterest terms he could devise; which the gentleman with a set gesture and countenance still soberly related, until the ordinary, driven at last into mad rage, was fain to give over all; which trousse, though it break off the interlude, yet defrauded not the beholders, but dismissed them with a great deal more sport and laughter than twenty such gwaries could have afforded.[30]

Carew therefore, as Tribby contends, was watching the last gasp of the performance of such miracle plays of Cornwall (possibly a bi-lingual situation with the performance in Cornish but directed in English), and should be viewed very sceptically as the exemplar of performance method. This has not stopped it from being quoted at length. Certainly, although the *plen-an-gwarry* model of performance is the main method of theatre in this phase, it was not the only model of performance operating, so we need to be careful not to assert only one space and place to the detriment of the overall range of work being presented. Other models of performance will emerge as we progress. Carew stands at the end of this period of theatrical development. To understand its full unfolding, we need to look back in time to the thirteenth and fourteenth centuries.

The context for deconstructing the theatrical culture of Cornwall during this period comes from a number of observers. One of the central texts in any discussion of Cornwall during these centuries is L.E. Elliott-Binns' *Medieval Cornwall*.[31] Although published in 1955, his account remains a useful overview of the general social and cultural trends, as well as formulating a notion of a Cornwall that had many European connections and was multi-lingual: 'four different tongues were in use – Latin, French, English and Cornish'.[32] This was perhaps, in part, the antithesis of Rowse's later view that 'Cornwall in the Middle Ages was a little land very much on its own, living its own life, wrapped up in its Celtic tongue, and its dream of the Celtic past, rather a backwater, a dead end'.[33] In 1970, John Hatcher contributed a useful volume showing how a rural economy and society developed in medieval Cornwall,[34] with an eye on ancient extractive industries and emerging industrialisation. More recently historians have considered medieval Cornwall in new ways, with Payton arguing that it was the time of a 'first peripheralism – of territorial and cultural isolation' in what he terms the 'Celtic Duchy'.[35] Meanwhile, in his discussion of medieval Cornwall, Deacon had argued the significance of economic and demographic growth, accompanied by 'cultural distinctive-ness'.[36] In general, contemporary Cornish Studies have demonstrated how an aggrandising and imperialist English nation state had come to sedate the 'Celtic drama queen' via a period of accommodation, to full colonisation.[37] However, despite this apparent accommodation and colonisation, as observers such as Stoyle have proven, Cornish identity persisted into the early modern period,[38] as well as into the modern Age. The broader picture of this trend has been matched by the micro-studies of specific cultural and social change, exemplified in the work of W.M.M. Picken,[39] as well as the picture of the development of Christianity in Cornwall, as explored by Orme.[40] There are also histories of individual families and communities, with Whetter producing several ground-breaking works, including a detailed history of Glasney College.[41]

General literary trends in medieval Cornwall have been explored by both Murdoch, and Kent,[42] and further insight may be gleaned from comparison with both Breton and Welsh literary culture.[43] Newlyn, and Murdoch have done much already to document and disseminate major studies of drama and literature during this phase.[44] Likewise, Joyce and Newlyn's anthology of textual sources is very comprehensive, and can be read usefully alongside other comparative volumes from the *Records of Early English Drama* series.[45] It remains important to bear in mind that there is also a well-established academic base that has considered the development and performance of medieval drama, admittedly often set upon an English footing. Scholars such as Chambers, Southern, and Wickham established the field,[46] but more recent works from Higgins, Tydeman, and Davidson have added more sophisticated readings.[47] Beadle's collection of essays on medieval drama is also essential reading, notably containing an informative chapter by Murdoch.[48] Such texts inform our knowledge of medieval theatrical practice across the rest of Britain, and in continental Europe, and comparison with that practice is desirable. The social background to literacy, orality and literary production is also considered in works by Fulton, and Pryce.[49] Over the years, the observation and criticism of Cornish drama during this phase has been something of an intractable monolith, which is difficult to re-examine and question once again. This view of theatre, perhaps compounded by Carew's later observations, has given a particular slant to the scholarship thus far. Although work by Bakere, Longsworth and Harris has been ground-breaking,[50] some of it has been completed in isolation, without enough of a contextual reading of the rest of the theatrical culture surrounding the extant texts. As scholarship has continued, more texts and sources have been located. There is, then, a need for a re-examination clearly locating the surviving literary texts within the wider range of theatrical practice taking place. We shall first examine the framework in which theatre was working.

The connection between those of religious persuasion and those offering entertainment in early fourteenth-century Cornwall is reflected in the Episcopal Licence awarded to the small monastery at Tywardreath in mid-Cornwall in 1338. Clearly, the Benedictine monks at Tywardreath were worried about the number of attacks made by pirates along the coast, and so were seeking advice about possibly moving further inland. Although, as Bishop of Exeter, John Grandisson (1292-1369) appears sympathetic to this, he is worried that a move elsewhere might expose the monks to 'worldly and dissolute shows'.[51] Quite what kind of show he was referring to is unknown, but his comment suggests that there were performances occurring in Cornwall during this time featuring dramaturgy wholly inappropriate for monks. The earlier Diocese of Exeter records of 1287 also show a similar concern for clergy's well-being. In the Statutes of Bishop Peter Quinell, we learn of a dictate that forbids 'wrestling, round dances, or other improper pastimes in churchyards, especially on the eves and feastdays of the saints'.[52] Interestingly, in the same statute, Quinell expressed his concern for dramas as well, since 'the sacred canons [i.e. the canon law statutes] loathe for such stage-plays and shows of derision to be introduced, by which the decency of churches is polluted'.[53] Later, further advice is given: 'the way of life of clerics may appear in every way to be different from that of entertainers' and that 'we order that clerics not attend to entertainers and jugglers, play dice and knucklebones, nor be onlookers of or sharers with those who are playing, nor presume to attend public shows in order to watch [them]'.[54] Gambling, licentiousness and bad behaviour were linked to theatre; a trend noticeable this early on, and a view later extolled by Puritanism and Methodism.

All of these dictates are interesting to bear in mind because, certainly at some point, there must have been an ideological rethink about the ability of drama to communicate the message of Jesus Christ, given the then somewhat unexpected rise in 'gwary miracle' culture in the fourteenth century. The issue is, perhaps, that after the Church allowed drama to occur outside the walls of churches themselves (as can be seen in the dictates above), theatre developed rather more rapidly. Despite drama later being connected to the control of the Church, there was perhaps more flexibility in subject matter and characterisation. The success of Feast of Corpus Christi plays elsewhere in Europe must have been instrumental in inspiring their development in Cornwall. The dates of such performances are crucial. Depending on Easter, the date of the Feast is sometime between 23 May and 24 June. In Cornwall, this was especially suitable because of the warmer weather and long hours of daylight.

The ideological rethink may have been prompted by early performances, which led the religious leaders to realise how drama could be used to help educate the populace about the Gospel and its meaning. It was therefore to the Church's later advantage to have clerics (especially at the Collegiate Church of St Thomas in Glasney) assist in the development of performance, writing and dramaturgy. Perhaps, therefore, the model in the fifteenth century (the full age of the gwarry miracle in Cornwall) was to have representative presence at Glasney, to sanction and commission the writing of a text that would be used in the individual parishes (as with the cases of *Bewnans Ke* and *Bewnans Meriasek*), or one-off, larger presentations such as the *Ordinalia*, which could be performed near Glasney itself, or could 'travel' to other approved locations in Cornwall. A geographical disadvantage of this would be that sanction and approval would be rather easier for parishes close to Glasney (which benefited greatly from the income of St Kea, St Feock, Mylor, St Gluvias, Budoc, Manaccan, St Sithney, and also to an extent, St Allen, Lanmorek (Mevagissey), Gorran, St Colan and St Enodor) than ones in more distant places (say in Zennor or St Just-in-Penwith). It would be helpful if the creator of the text arose from nearby, or in the parish, because he would know local performance conditions, as well as the folklore, hagiography and community. Ritual, landscape and community again help shape the dramatic interpretations. We shall later see examples of some individual dramatists who appear to be operating under these conditions of production.

However, it would seem that, in the earliest years of this period, bishops such as Quinell were more sceptical about the power of drama. The subtext to all of this may be that approved religious-themed drama was somehow tolerated, but his concern seems more with secular work. Writing from Exeter, Quinell must have been aware of, or informed about, a range of secular stage plays around the wider geographical area of western Britain. There is further discussion to be had here. For example, during this period, how would touring troupes from England perform in front of broadly still-Cornish-speaking audiences? This leads us then to speculate on the possibility of Cornish-language secular drama also being performed at sundry locations, but not approved of by the church. One intriguing reference comes in Elliott-Binns' *Medieval Cornwall*, in which he states that 'in 1428 a certain Cornishman, Jakke Trevaill by name, is said to have presented various plays and interludes before Henry VI'.[55] The earlier activities of Trevaill would indicate a surviving and important secular tradition which, as Williams has suggested,[56] could be seen in later Cornish-language writers such as the shadowy Richard Angwyn of Bojewyan and 'another, Pendarvis by name' mentioned in John Ray's Itineraries of 1662 and 1667 respectively.[57] No texts by Angwyn or Pendarvis have been found. Perhaps Trevaill's position before the King was, in part, related to the Cornish contribution to Henry's father's success at Agincourt.[58] Since he governed with a Regent until 1437, it may have been Henry VI's advisors who felt it appropriate that Trevaill was presented. Trevaill remains an intriguing theatrical figure, about whom we would wish to know more.

A further interesting document that comes to light from the earliest phase of this period is an Episcopal Order to Glasney Collegiate Church dated around 1360.[59] The message from Grandisson gives advice to the church on the practice of events which may be deemed part of seasonal misrule around Christmas-time. This included boy bishop para-theatrical activity.[60] Clearly the bishop was

Fig. 15. The theatrical culture of medieval Cornwall, as imagined in the Tregellas Tapestry titled *Glasney*. Courtesy of the trustees of the Tregellas Tapesty.

worried about whether Glasney (like its sister colleges of Holy Cross at Crediton and St. Mary's in Ottery St Mary) had enough boys and youths in the community who might engage in such activities. The provost of Glasney College responds by commenting that he 'forbade them publicly and solemnly'.[61] The original order was written in Latin – being the 'Esperanto' of the medieval world – so that the Cornish-speaking community at Glasney would be able to understand it. This is somewhat ironic given Glasney's future development, but what we begin to see is that some dramatic activity was obviously appropriate, whilst other more anarchic versions were not. Thus theatre was not always tacitly sanctioned in the way that it appears in some accounts. There was clearly a tension and debate about its development and purpose that is too rarely considered. Such a debate would have far-reaching implications in the Reformation. However, as the fifteenth century unfolded, theatrical practice was permitted and it appears, in Cornwall at least, to have grown exponentially.

In the midst of this debate over secular and liturgical drama, we encounter the oldest surviving secular text of length, written in Cornish. Usually dated around 1380-1400, the so-called *Charter Endorsement* was discovered by Henry Jenner in 1877 on a land charter originally from the parish of St. Stephen-in-Brannel in mid-Cornwall.[62] The text contains forty-one lines of Middle Cornish rhymed strophic verse jotted down on the back of a charter which has been dated to 1340.[63] The initial section appears to be some kind of speech in which the speaker is offering marriage to a girl, who is praised as being very beautiful and would seem to make a good wife, though she is clearly quite young. This first part also makes reference to a bridge on the River Tamar, and how there is none like her on this side of it, a line which gives a nod towards Cornwall's territorial identity:

1.   *golsoug ty cowez*
        byz na borz mez
        dyyskyn ha powes
        ha zymo dus nes
5.   *mar cozes ze les*
        ha zys y rof mowes
        ha fest unan dek
        genes mar a plek
        ha tanha y
10.   *kymmerr y zoz wrek*
        sconye zys ny vek
        ha ty a vyz hy
        Hy a vyz gwreg ty da

zys ze synsy

15. *pur wyr a lauara*
   ha govyn worty
   Lemen yz torn my as re
   ha war an greyz my an te
   nag usy par

20. *an barz ma ze pons tamar*
   my ad pes worty byz da
   ag ol ze voz hy a wra
   rag flog yw ha gensy doz
   ha gaffy ze gafus hy boz

25. *kenes mes zymmo ymmyug*
   eug alema ha fystynyug

1. [Listen, you friend,
   never be ashamed;
   come down and rest,
   and to me come closer

5. if you know your own good,
   and to you I shall give a girl
   and a very beautiful one
   if she pleases you.
   O take her,

10. take her to be your wife;
   she will not seek to refuse you,
   and you shall possess her.
   She will be a good housewife
   for you to hold,

15. very truly I say,
   O ask her!
   Now into your hand I shall give her
   and on the Faith I swear it
   that there is not the like

20. on this side of the Tamar bridge
   I ask you: to her be good,
   and all your will she will do
   for she is a child and it is wise
   to get consent from her and me.

25. Although I am ashamed, kiss,
   go from here and hurry.][64]

This is high praise indeed, and quite clear in its objectives, yet the second part of the text is more difficult to draw meaning from. Here, it would seem there is perhaps another speaker, and now a woman is being told how to 'manage' a man. While control of this man would seem to be her objective, we also learn that the man himself is both gracious and considerate:

> *dallaz a var infrez dar war*
> *oun na porzo*
> *ef emsettye worzesy*
> 30. *kam ma vezo*
> *mar az herg zys gul nep tra*
> *lauar zesy byz ny venna*
> *lauar zozo gwra mar mennyz*
> *a wos a gallo na wra tra vyz*
> 35. *in vrna yz sens ze vez meystres*
> *hedyr vywy hag harluzes*
> *ras o ganso ren offeren*
> *curtes yw ha deboner*
> *zys dregyn ny wra*
> 40. *mar an kefyth in danger*
> *sense fast in della*
> [Begin early, quickly, be careful,
> of him who is not afraid
> so that to attack you
> 30. he will not dare at all.
> If he commands you to do something
> say to yourself, 'I never will.'
> Say to him, 'I shall if you wish.'
> Despite what he may be able to do, he will do nothing
> 35. then he will consider you as mistress and lady,
> while you shall live.
> He was gracious, by the Mass,
> he is courteous and well-mannered.
> To you, he will do no ill
> 40. if you have him in your power:
> Keep him firmly thus.][65]

When the text was first examined by Jenner, he viewed the language and spelling as Middle Cornish, 'differing hardly at all from those of the *Ordinalia* dramas and the Poem of the Passion'. However like Murdoch in later readings,

Jenner viewed the versification as 'very irregular'.[66] In exploring the content of the text, he makes a significant comparison with the similar mastery of wife over husband gained from drinking the waters of the Well of St Keyne,[67] so there may have been a wider pan-Cornish motif operating. If the text is part of a lost play, then it would appear to be something quite different from the rest of Cornish dramatic literature in this phase. As Jenner notes, 'some of those remarkable plays of the tenth-century Hroswitha of Gandersheim are frankly secular, and are modelled on Terence and Plautus in more ways than one, and there are others in various languages, but the general tendency of the medieval drama was religious'.[68] At the end of his analysis, Jenner makes the following important observations:

> If we could recover the whole of this play, it would probably be of more interest than the versified Scripture and Scripture legend which form so large a part of the *Ordinalia*, though to judge by this literary fragment the literary merit was not great. We cannot even conjecture what the rest of the story might have been. The allusion to 'pons Tamar', Tamar Bridge, might be taken as an indication that the story was a Cornish one, were it not that in the *Ordinalia* there are many instances of Cornish local colour introduced into events which took place in Palestine.[69]

Beyond value judgements on quality of literary production, Jenner makes an important point here about the story being 'a Cornish one'. Presumably he meant that it might have been a parish origin story (based on a saint or local figure) or an independent narrative or 'interlude' as presented later by figures such as Trevaill.[70] However, he does concede that the working model was to project Cornish topography onto a cultural geography. The view of the fragment as part of a longer play was promoted again in a 1963 article by Enrico Campanile.[71] Campanile examined the text again, and compared it with readings and translations by Jenner and Whitley Stokes. The nature of the verses suggested to him that this was a brief section from a longer work. However, he does ask how such a section could fit into the life of a saint or of Christ. A specific difficulty would be that in the medieval mind-set, the married state was regarded as inferior to celibacy. Therefore, it would be unlikely that a sacred drama would encourage two young people to marry. However, we do know that other medieval texts looked at such a theme, with characters starting off with good intentions, but being unable to resist love or carnal feelings.[72] Murdoch admits that 'we may be dealing with acting parts' but believes that the play/poem difficulty is unanswerable without more context.[73] He later noted the possibility of it being a 'bawd's part in a comedy, but there is too little of it for any certainty'.[74] Another difficulty is that we may divide up the speeches into further sections: for example, lines 31-33 might have been voiced by separate speakers. If this could be teased out further, then we clearly have more evidence of a play.

Alternative readings have been made. Toorians, who has perhaps completed the most comprehensive study of the *Endorsement*, has opined that it is most probably 'an independent poem'.[75] Meanwhile, Newlyn views the words as being spoken by a stereotypical female matchmaker;[76] Kent argues that the text offers us useful insight into the medieval literary construction of sexual politics.[77] Popular opinion has also viewed the text as a kind of 'best man's [or woman's] speech'; the lines casually written on the back of a discarded charter. A difficulty with that remains, however, because the versification is so artful. Intriguingly, given the connection to the parish of St Stephen-in-Brannel, Lyon has investigated the possibility of theatre space there.[78] Basing his reading on Charles Henderson,[79] he finds convincing evidence of a 'playing green' or 'wrestling' ring in the centre of the village of St Stephen, on the site of the old primary school. Because this is very close to the church, we can infer that the parish was presenting drama during the late medieval period. If the text presented was secular, then St Stephen-in-Brannel was unique. This does seem a slim possibility, but the *Endorsement* at least proves that a poetic/dramatic impetus could be found there around 1380-1400. Given Brannel's close proximity to other possible *plen-an-gwarry* locations, such as St Enoder (particularly associated, as we shall see, with one possible playwright, John Trevisa[80]), St Newlyn East (with connections later on to prose and homily translator John Tregear[81]), Ladock, and Probus, this whole area of mid-Cornwall would seem to be theatrically very active. There may be something in this, since another observer, Andrew Symons, has written on the 'curious concentration' of literary activity in mid-Cornwall, suggesting that, paradoxically, language transfer in the period 1500-1600 (and perhaps even earlier) actually prompted a new round of 'revivalist' creativity.[82] Symons' model is later than the context for the *Charter Endorsement*, but if theatrical activity continued after this phase, then it could be relevant to production conditions. Symons argues that language transfer has had longer term cultural-materialist implications in successive generations of writers arising from mid-Cornwall.

We need here to discuss the issue of possible sources for the 'gwarry-miracle' culture of Cornwall. Over time, I have discussed this with various colleagues; although significant suggestions and opinions have been put forward by Spriggs, Bakere and Murdoch,[83] the evidence is inconclusive.

Elsewhere in Britain during the late medieval period, such dramas appear to be predominantly an urban phenomenon, with the possible exception of East Anglia.[84] There is good evidence that Plymouth and the South Hams maintained vestigial Celticity into the early medieval period, which suggests that this area was part of the same intercourse with Brittany that Cornwall had. Considering this intercourse, could it be that certain travellers witnessed performances of such plays on the continent and, inspired by the idea, returned to the south-west of Britain ready to develop a similar method of performance? Certainly, we know that there was considerable economic, political and cultural interaction between the two communities since the period of time when the first Britons left west Britain for what has become known as Brittany.[85] The Britons there may have learnt from French (and perhaps even Swiss and German cultures[86]) of other forms of drama which were then reconfigured in the evolving Breton culture, and then once again passed back to Cornwall. This is one theory.

Another paradigm might be that, as the dramas were urban phenomena elsewhere, we ought to look more closely at 'urban' culture in the south west of Britain. Plymouth in the medieval period, as Walling argues, was hardly a town of such size to merit a fully operational guild and theatrical infrastructure.[87] However, Exeter might be a possibility, since its geography and cultural history point to development similarities with York, Chester and Coventry.[88] Exeter would have had in place guild structures that would facilitate the traditional medieval models of performance, such as 'pageant' wagons moving to particular performance points in the town. Although no cycle plays have been found associated with the city, there is a variety of surviving Anglo-Saxon and early medieval texts, indicating a once flourishing literary culture.[89] Indeed, it would be hard to imagine a city such as Exeter at this point in history without performances of this type. Related to this is the more contentious point: if travellers came to Exeter from Cornwall (and there is perhaps no reason why they may not have travelled to Exeter to witness such spectacle),[90] then this might have inspired communities further to the west to enact their own tellings of biblical events, as well as the dramatised life of their local saint. Such a 'fluid' reading of culture is controversial, but it is actually supported in the wider academy, by observers contributing to Bennett's collection. One of these observers, Homi K. Bhabka, argues that 'culture's in between'[91] – and this may be exactly the right model to apply to the wider theatricality of south-western Britain. Certainly, the nineteenth-century folklorist Robert Hunt would have lent much support to such a view. Likewise, Keith and Pile argue that such a 'spatial vocabulary becomes redundant' in situations like this.[92] Essentialist readings of cultural difference therefore need to be pared back here since they are politically and academically regressive, especially when considering this period of history.

Exeter, we should remember, had expelled 'Cornish' citizens (or rather Brythonic-speaking communities) from its boundaries under the edicts of Athelstan in CE 931,[93] but we know that the religious links were operational for much longer, embodied in the control of Glasney from Exeter.[94] This model is problematical for some, since it suggests an east-to-west distribution of culture, and that the Cornish were 'receiving' or even appropriating a more overtly 'English' model. Though contentious, this theory needs further consideration through an investigation of the Cornish in Exeter during the medieval period. Textual comparison would be helpful, but as no extant drama exists in Exeter, this is presently impossible. There is, of course, a third way: that is, as Chapter One asserted, that there was enough theatrical energy in Cornwall alone for such development to occur, and that although such plays were happening across the whole of the European continent,[95] the Cornish model of performance was going to be culturally unique (if not wholly unique, as we shall see, in terms of multiple-staging within Rounds). Indeed, an alternative model might even suggest that any urban theatrical performance in Plymouth or Exeter might actually owe its development to the advanced theatrical culture of Cornwall, and that travellers and observers took ideas eastwards. Put together, however, all of these factors may well have had an interconnected input into the development of cycle drama in Cornwall. Other permutations are possible. For example, it may well have been the south-western Celtic refugees who carried an already developed sense of theatricality across to Brittany and that, additionally, 'Celtic' or Brythonic theatrical energy was adapted and used in different ways by Anglo-Saxon culture. However, because of theatre's ephemeral nature, and the lack of medieval literary survivals in south-west Britain as a whole, the evidence still remains inconclusive, and we may never know. It is one area in our story that demands further investigation in the future.

Having explored some of the wider historical processes for the origin of Cornish drama during this phase, I now turn to an examination of staging and space. Here, this will be considered in general terms, with the staging of specific texts considered later in a more thorough examination of their operation. Given a certain caution in accepting Carew's comments on theatre space, it is to other commentators and observers that we should turn for detailed enquiry into the structure and functionality of the *plen-an-gwarry*. Carew, we must remember, was discrediting culturally recusant remnants of Roman Catholicism, and the Middle-Cornish dramas were seen as allied to that belief and ideology. So engaged was Carew with the modernist project of

Cornwall that he even saw fit to satirise that most symbolic of Cornish locations, Tintagel Castle (a bastion of high Celtic Arthuriana), in his poem 'A Herring's Tayle'.[96] Carew also came from the east of Cornwall, where Cornish language had already for a long time replaced English. Other figures knew the drama better. As Vice Warden of the Stannaries, William Scawen knew and understood Cornish culture well, and probably had insight into the folk memory of communities from the previous century. Although writing shortly after the Restoration, in 1680, in his *Antiquities Cornuontanic: The Causes of Cornish Speech's Decay*, Scawen attributes this decay to:

> the giving over of the Guirremears [*gwary myrs*, miracle plays], which were used at the great conventions of the people, at which they had famous interludes celebrated with great preparations, and not without shews of devotion of them, solemnized in open and spacious downs of great capacity, encompassed about with earthen banks, and in some part stone work of largeness to contain thousands, the shapes of which remain in many places at this day, though the use of them is long since gone. These were frequently used in most parts of the country, at the conveniency of the people, for their meeting together, in which they represented by grave actings, scriptural histories, personating patriarchs, princes, and other persons; and with great oratory pronounced their harangue, framed by art, and composed with heroic stile, such as have been known to be of old in other nations.[97]

Scawen's description is helpful, though we must be wary, for it may be tinged by his own romanticism and desire for revival. Several phrases stand out. He describes the gatherings as 'great conventions' which perhaps gives them greater status than just parish performances. The words 'solemnized' and 'grave actings' also suggest a commitment and seriousness of approach that seems missing in the notes of Carew. The stone work suggests craftsmanship in the production of lasting theatre space, rather than just adaptation of existing forts and enclosures. Scawen seems not to note any saints' plays, but does pay attention to 'scriptural histories'. Of interest is the fact that some secular characters are mentioned ('princes and other persons'). The plays are performed in 'heroic stile' which seems a comment on both dramaturgy and content (thus, broadly 'epic'), and Scawen also appears to write from a sympathetic position of knowing such performances happened elsewhere in Europe. This is an angle that Carew completely misses. Is Scawen exaggerating when he mentions that thousands attended? Perhaps he is, in some parishes, given estimates of population statistics,[98] but there is no doubt that some of the bigger venues could have coped with numbers of this kind. The works are also 'framed by art'. This is an interesting expression. Scawen could be talking about the language used, in that it was poetic and certainly framed as verse drama. However, this might also lead to us thinking about decorated performance stations – or multiple-stagings – inside the *plen-an-gwarry*, as well as costuming and special effects.[99] This comment is also perhaps linked to his observation of 'great preparations' suggesting a 'run' into performance that required practice, construction and organisation. Scawen's points here are supported by other comments in his text:

> This was a great means to keep in use the tongue with delight and admiration, and its continued also friendship and good correspondency in the people. They had recitations in them poetical and divine, one of which I may suppose this small relique of antiquary to be, in which the passion of our Saviour, and his resurrection, is described. They also had their Carols at several times, especially at Christmas, when they solemnly sung, and sometimes used, as I have heard, in their churches after prayers, the burden of which songs, "Nowell, Nowell, good news, good news of the Gospel," by which they kept use of the tongue the better.[100]

Scawen says something very significant here. The 'solemnity' of the Cornish is reinforced, something which is noted later in Cornish history,[101] but he talks enthusiastically about the social function of the theatre, and even a notion that it was the very act of theatre that kept the language alive in communities that were at least bi-lingual in most of Cornwall. This also points to the venues being used more widely than just for drama: for poetry readings and singing. We must be sceptical about this, for the poem mentioned (either part of the *Ordinalia*, or *Pascon agan Arluth*) is the only survival, and Scawen may be romantically interpreting this as a possibility.[102] However, the connection to Christmas customs certainly makes us think also of the traditions of Christmas dramas. It is impossible accurately to calculate the extent of non-theatrical usage, but Scawen's other notable point is the permanency of the space, since stone work on venues of this size would have been a considerable task for medieval stonemasons. For further comment on this, we must turn to the antiquary William Borlase. In his *Observations on the Antiquities Historical and Monumental of Cornwall*, first published in 1745, he records that:

> in these continued Rounds or Amphitheatres... the Britans [sic] did usually assemble to hear plays acted; these are called with us in Cornwall (where we have great numbers of them) *Plan an guare*; viz. the level place, or Plain of sport and pastime. The benches round were generally of Turf. We have one whose benches

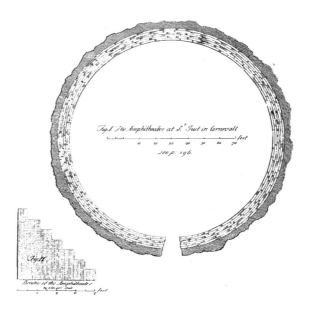

Fig. 16. Amphitheatre of St Just-in-Penwith. Borlase, *Observations*, plate xvi.

are of Stone, and the most remarkable Monument of this kind which I have yet seen; it is near the church of St Just, Penwith, now somewhat disfigured by the injudicious repairs of late years, but by the remains it seems to have been the work of more than usual labour, and correctness. It is an exact circle of 126 feet diameter; the perpendicular height of the bank, from the area within, now seven feet; but the height from the bottom of the ditch without, ten feet at present, formerly more. The seats consist of six steps, fourteen inches wide, and one foot high, with one on the top of all, where the Rampart is about seven feet wide.[103]

Borlase's comments are notable, for they suggest similar amphitheatres are found elsewhere, and that the 'ancient Britons' came to them to 'hear' plays acted. This might indicate at least a wider Dumnonian distribution of them, although he comments specifically on their intensity in Cornwall. Borlase's observations are matched by both a plan and sectional drawing of the space, and his description of the gwarry at St Just-in-Penwith resembles Scawen's. According to Higgins, Borlase's diagram of the theatre at first seems 'slightly inaccurate' because the outside of the circle is just an uneven line, with no mention of an outer bank or ditch.[104] However, this is clarified by a letter from

Fig. 17. 'Bivouacking gipsy-like in their tents.' The cast and crew of the 1969 production of *Ordinalia* recreate imagined medieval theatrical lifestyle. Courtesy of the Royal Institution of Cornwall.

the Reverend George Hadow, vicar of St Just, written in 1860 to one early translator of the *Ordinalia*, Edwin Norris. Hadow observes that:

> the old structure still remains in St. Just Churchtown, close to the principal inn; the clear outline of the circus is quite apparent, being formed externally by a stone wall of about four feet perpendicular height, whilst a green bank slopes inwards; there is now no outside ditch, nor are there any steps... a pathway leads right through it from the town to the market place.[105]

Thus, the stone formed a vertical wall. Also intriguing is the disappearance of the steps or benches. If the benches were made of stone slabs, then these might have been easily removed, but Borlase's comments and drawings display detailed accuracy about the steps; at some point after his text, they must have either naturally collapsed, or have been shaped into slopes. Disappointed by what he found there in 1934, Nance wrote that the St Just Round:

> was entirely encased in granite but even that had suffered injudicious repair, and since then the stone has gone, I believe to build a hedge not

so far away, in which its rectangular shapes still identify it, and what we have left is a mere stepless bank.[106]

Although Nance is dismissive, he ought to have been glad that so much of the round has still survived. Indeed, although much of the structure in the present era backs onto houses and other buildings, it is, in a way, quite well preserved. The stone nature of the Round at St Just-in-Penwith certainly suggests a permanence and sophistication that is lacking elsewhere. Perhaps its peripherality from the effects of the Reformation kept it in a workable state for longer. Certainly, it served its original purpose in a recent production of the *Ordinalia* (though that text might never have been performed there in original performance conditions).[107] Two more modern observers have commented on what it would have been like to have seen a production at a venue such as St Just-in-Penwith. In his analysis of medieval Cornish drama, which he titled *The Legend of the Rood*, F.E. Halliday offered the following view of performances in medieval Cornwall:

It must be remembered that these plays were written for an illiterate audience, for the most part even less capable of anything but inexplicable dumb-shows and noise than the groundlings of the Globe, and that to enforce the lessons of the scriptures and hagiology the lines had to be liberally spiced to make the matter savoury, and the grandest and loveliest episodes relieved by the crudest horseplay. Sometimes this is merely gross, and often brutal as well, and it is clear that, after the squib-throwing devils, the torturers or executioners, who are stock characters in all these Cornish plays, were the most popular performers. Frequently, however, the buffoonery is genuinely funny, and always it is vigorous and racy...[108]

Halliday may be right in some of his observations – in the sense of maintaining audience interest – but his views are perhaps tarnished by an 'arm's length', conventional, Anglo-centric view of the medieval audience in Cornwall. He seems to suggest an illiterate underclass were the only people watching. Considering some of the sophisticated theological concepts being dramatised on stage (in particular, for example, in *Bewnans Meriasek*[109]), this was clearly not the case. In all likelihood, such events would have drawn people from all classes of society. However, Halliday's observations do give us some feel of the stage-craft. Another slightly more romanticised perspective comes from Wilkie Collins. Collins, who was later to give a somewhat cynical account of theatre in nineteenth-century Cornwall, also imagines the environs at a 'gwarry miracle' (this time at Perran Round) in his *Rambles beyond Railways* (1851), drawing imaginatively on antiquarian studies of the spaces:

You approach nearer, and behold a circular turf embankment; a wide, lonesome, desolate enclosure, looking like a witches' dancing-ring that has sprung up in the midst of the open moor… Here the old inhabitants of Cornwall assembled to form the audience of the drama of former days. A level of grassy ground, one hundred and thirty feet in diameter, is enclosed by the embankment. There are two entrances to the area cut through the boundary circle of turf and earth, which rises to a height of nine or ten feet, and narrows towards the top, where it is seven feet wide.[110]

It is perhaps ironic that he should shape his account with such a pagan dimension, when the performance was so overtly Christian. He then describes an imagined audience, with liberal poetic licence:

Then imagine the assembling in the amphitheatre; the running around the outer circle of the embankment to get at the entrances; the tumbling and rushing up the steps inside; the racing of hot-headed youngsters to get to the top places; the sly deliberation of the elders in selecting the lower and safe positions… the universal speculations on the weather; the universal shouting for pots of ale; and finally… the gradual hush and stillness among the multitude; the combined stare of the whole circular mass of spectators on one point in the plain of the amphitheatre. And then the darkness coming on, and the moon rising over the amphitheatre, so silent and empty, save at one corner, where the poor worn-out actors are bivouacking gipsy-like in their tents, cooking supper over the fire that flames up red in the moonlight, and talking languidly over the fatigues and triumphs of the play.[111]

Although Collins' account might seem somewhat quaint and naïve (and, in his description of the aftermath, akin to a contemporary rock festival), there is a certain appeal in his imaginative reconstruction. While Collins was reflecting on medieval drama in this way, other observers were spotting more genuine architectural features inside the Rounds themselves. The drawings of stage plans from the *Bewnans Meriasek* manuscript indicate an area called the 'capella',[112] and this does have bearing on one of the features noted at St Just-in-Penwith. R. Halliwell, in his *Rambles in the West Country*, published in 1861, seems to notice a 'capella' there:

There are faint traces of a small circular spot in the centre, in which perhaps the prompter was located, and whence the actors issued to perform in the wide concentric space around it; a conjecture which seems to be supported by the diagrams in the Bodleian manuscripts of the Cornish mysteries.[113]

Halliwell's observation of this spot is important and it may well be an example of the kind of 'capella' seen in *Bewnans Meriasek*. Additionally, Halliwell seems to have read Carew and his notions about a prompter, but perhaps more convincing is that this might well have been the central area to which actors moved from their stations (or multiple stages), in order to give equi-projection to the whole of the audience. In this function, it may well have been convex and slightly raised, though if any prompter wished to be hidden, it would be concave. Halliwell's view of the Bodleian manuscripts seems confused. There is no diagram accompanying *The Creacion of the World*, and the three drawings in the *Ordinalia* indicate only the central playing area with no 'capella'.[114] It is certainly not small in any sense of the word. The capella reference perhaps bears more relevance to that other surviving *plen-an-gwarry* structure in Perranzabuloe, Perran Round. In a later work, *The Natural History of Cornwall* (1753), after mentioning St Just Round again, Borlase offers a description of the one at Perranzabuloe, which he describes as being 'a much larger one, of higher mound, fossed on the outside, and very regular… in the parish of Piran-sand'.[115] Like the drawing at St Just, Borlase presents a plan and sectional diagram which, over time, has become the iconic visualisation of what a *plen-an-gwarry* is meant to look like.[116] Borlase's

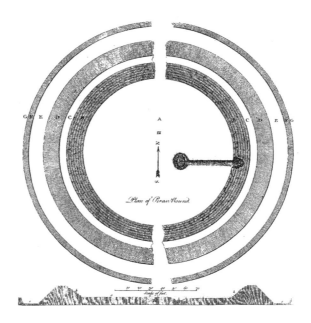

Fig. 18. Plan of Perran Round. Borlase, *Natural History of Cornwall*, plate xxix.

description is again highly detailed; the following feature is given prominence in the text:

> A circular pit 13 feet in diameter and 3 feet deep, the sides sloping, and half way down is a bench of turf so formed as to reduce the area of the bottom to an ellipsis; a shallow trench 4 feet 6 inches wide and 1 foot deep ran to the mound east, where it stopped at a semi-oval cavity, 11 feet, N. to S. and 9 ft. E. to W., which makes a breach in the benches.[117]

Here, the 'circular pit' and 'shallow trench' interest us the most. This may connect to the capella concept at St Just. In this case, it would be concave. There is no other example of such a 'pit' at any other locations. This trench and pit have come to be labelled 'the devil's spoon', though quite where this had arisen from is open to conjecture. There is no earlier textual mention of it. Such a device would, however, be very useful to dramaturgy. It would allow, for example, Adam and Eve to 'grow' out of the ground, by travelling along what Borlase labels the 'conveyor'[118] and to lie hidden under a grass-covered framework, then at an appropriate moment, when the lines dictated, suddenly emerge. Such medieval special effects could be applied to other such sequences. We have no knowledge that the *Ordinalia* was ever performed at Perran Round, but if a sequence such as 'The Death of Pilate' might be

Fig. 19. The so-called 'conveyor' or 'devil's spoon' at Perran Round.

enacted, then in Herod's burial, his body might be comically evicted from the depression. Certainly, the 'conveyor' in its present state is not nearly as deep as it once was. Although there is no example remaining in other locations, infill of the ground in those may have made it indistinguishable from the rest of the plain. No such device appears to have been used in the English plays of this type. Clearly, Borlase felt 'the Devil's spoon' was an inappropriate name for the device, and maybe he was basing his observations on some specific passages of *The Creacion of the World*:

> Adam and Eva aparlet in whytt lether, in a place apoynted by the conveyour, and not to be sene tyll they be called, and then kneel and ryse (Before line 343)

> Lett Adam laye downe and slepe wher Eva ys, and she by the conveyour must be taken from Adam is syde (Before line 393)[119]

Nance too, viewed the device as a secret passageway,[120] but Neuss has repudiated this claim.[121] The evidence suggests that Nance and Borlase were thinking along the right lines. Halliday has also looked at this feature, and he comments that 'half a dozen men could remain hidden until they were called upon to appear', and that 'traps in the stage along the line of the trench would offer opportunities for all manner of quaint devices'.[122] As well as noting the emergence of Adam and Eve, Halliday also proposes that it might additionally be used for Seth's burial, thus allowing the actor to crawl back to the side of the arena unnoticed.[123] We also note that Borlase describes benches at Perran Round, and although traces of them may still, in part, be seen, most have become sloped. The 1969 production erected a scaffolding structure, which imitated the benches, sitting on top of the surrounding mound, and gave the modern audience a higher perspective on the dramaturgy than the original productions there. Our understanding of theatre space in Cornwall is thus enhanced by consideration of these two survivals. For one thing, it demonstrates that although a model of performance style was endemic, construction of theatre space was nowhere near uniform. Put another way, it would seem that individual communities either adapted or constructed space according to specific requirements. Building methods varied according to the availability of materials, and size of audience/community obviously determined dimensions.

What is so significant about circularity as a design shape for a theatre? Higgins has argued that it is curious why the Cornish did not recreate the 'rectangular shape of their churches', though he admits that 'they may have been influenced by the ancient circular homesteads'.[124] This book has commented on how ritual space at stone circles may well have also shaped practice. Celtic art in Cornwall and elsewhere has also demonstrated an awareness of the use of circular symbolism, and knot-work uses continual and overlapping joined lines. Another possibility may be that, after the restrictions put on performance by the Church (as indicated at the start of this chapter), the option of open-air performance, not constrained by the Church or church buildings, was very appealing. Although the wooden construction of theatre space was fashionable elsewhere in Britain and Europe, the lack of trees in Cornwall may also have dictated round construction. After several centuries already of mining,[125] the Cornish were well practised in moving quantities of stone and earth, so this is another persuasive argument for such construction. Another link may, as indicated in Chapter One, be the Roman influence. The Romans had brought colosseums to the island of Britain for entertainment purposes, and remnants of this notion may have been embodied in the mind of the Britons, and thus the Cornish and the Bretons. Evidence of Breton performance conditions is less well known, but in Rouen, for example, the mystery play the *Actes des Apôtres* was performed in an amphitheatre in the early sixteenth century, described as 'que sa grandeur... approchait tout à fait celle du Colisée Roman [that in grandeur it approached the Roman Colosseum]'.[126] There was, however, an additional reason, embodied in the ideology of the medieval mind. This was, as Higgins argues, the 'symbol of the perfect circle', which is found throughout medieval Europe to illustrate and explain the world:

> When we look at medieval diagrams showing the movement of the stars, maps of the world, idealised plans of cities including both the ancient and New Jerusalem, illustrations of the Garden of Eden, the rose window in churches, we see fundamentally the same figure.[127]

This figure was the circle. Additional evidence for this world view may be gleaned from Hereford Cathedral's early fourteenth-century *Mappa Mundi*, which not only presents a circular map of the world, but also locates the circle of Jerusalem within it.[128] For the Cornish, a combination of all the above factors may have determined their original choice, after which the circular format may perhaps have become fashionable and dictated practice. There is sufficient evidence from many early dramas in England (particularly, for example, *The Castle of Perseverance* and in the *N-Town Mystery Plays*) that the Cornish-like model of multiple-staging, but within a Round, was used there too. Famous continental examples also show circular theatre space: the Callieau miniature of the 1547 Valenciennes *Passion* shows a line of stages, but the miniature can be seen as a way of getting over the problem of showing each of them in the Round. Sometime between 1452 and 1460, another French artist, Jean Fouquet, painted the famous illustration of *Le martyre de Saint-Apolline*, which also seems to show circular theatre space. Both these and the production at Rouen are broadly contemporary with the Cornish productions. Higgins comments that 'multiple staging was the norm for presenting open-air religious plays in Germany, Switzerland, the Low Countries, Spain and Italy'[129] so Cornwall was in good company. He is sceptical about all of them being presented in-the-round, but believes many of them to have been performed in this way.[130] Cornwall therefore was not unique in this sense: a longer and wider pan-European ideology determined shape, and therefore dramaturgy. Although writing slightly later in the seventeenth-century, the English writer John Milton offers an interesting commentary in his epic poem *Paradise Lost*. Considering Cornish dramas were presenting dramatic interpretations of the 'loss of Paradise', only regained when Jesus Christ (a second Adam figure) arrives, the following lines may be indicative of the philosophical reasoning behind *plen-an-gwarries* in Cornwall and 'in-the-round' open-air staging elsewhere:

So on he faces, and to the border comes
Of Eden, where delicious Paradise,
Now nearer, crowns with her enclosure green,
As with a rural mound, the champion head
Of a steep wilderness, whose hairy sides
With thicket overgrown, grotesque and wild,
Access denied: and over head up grew
Insuperable height of loftiest shade,
Cedar and pine, and fir, and branching palm,
A sylvan scene, and, as the ranks ascend
Shade above shade, a woody theatre
Of stateliest view.[131]

Milton appears to be arguing that such 'woody theatres' are the desired venue, paralleling, as they do, a notion of the original Paradise. This seems somewhat ironic in the light of the physical space of some Cornish theatre space (windswept, damp, and in the open, rather than in a wood) but nevertheless a model of best practice is reflected in Milton's words. The gaining of the 'stateliest view' seems not only to relate to the seriousness and solemnity of Cornish theatrical practice, but also suggests that this is simply the best way to view theatre; all people, and all classes of people, get the 'same' view. There is no gradation; hence the rise once again of theatre-in-the-round as

Fig. 20. Hubert Cailleau's sketch of the multiple staging of the Passion Play performed at Valenciennes in 1547. Courtesy of the Bibliothèque Nationale de Paris.

Fig. 21. Jean Fouquet's miniature of *Le martyre de Saint-Apolline*, painted 1452-1460.

Fig. 22. A survival of medieval theatricality? Playing Place road-sign near Truro, Cornwall.

theatrical practice in the 1960s and 1970s.[132] This would certainly match the long-term 'One and All' ideology of Cornwall, where equality is seen as a primary need.

Having considered the two best-surviving theatrical spaces from this phase in Cornwall, I now offer an overview of other attested and likely *plen-an-gwarry* theatre space. Over the years, a number of scholars have attempted to give accounts of such space across Cornwall, and I am here indebted to the work of observers such as Bakere, and Padel,[133] and also more recently to Spriggs, and Lyon.[134] Clearly, in a work of this length it would be impossible for me to give the precise justification for each of the following spaces. Suffice to say that unless the site has some specific physical remains, or remains that have been noted by previous observers, then others have been identified by local traditions, tithing maps and place-name evidence. Some observations are given but, as the reader will see, these are sometimes cross-referenced to textual sources or other evidence of theatrical activity. Precise locations (according to Ordnance Survey grid references) can be found in Padel, Spriggs and Lyon. In mapping all of the sites noted by these observers and others, we have, incredibly, some sixty sites, varying in size and design and, in all probability, origin as well. Can there be anywhere else in Britain that has so intense a theatricality in so small a territory? The answer is a firm no. Jenner, writing in 1930, comments that more than ninety of them had been found in west Cornwall, but does not provide further detail.[135] In 1969, Charles Thomas, however, offered a more startling statistic, which may at least contribute to the profusion of Rounds in Cornwall:

> Recent surveys suggest that rounds were spaced out over much of Cornwall at an average density of one per square mile, were surrounded by systems of little fields and grazing, and are most likely to have been the homesteads of free peasants or independent farmers... The total number of rounds in Cornwall may have been between seven hundred and a thousand.[136]

Thomas was writing about all Rounds, not necessarily those used for theatrical purposes, but even if only some of the seven hundred were adapted or converted into *plen-an-gwarries*, then this further supports our case for the intensity of medieval theatrical culture in Cornwall. New sites for past theatre space in Cornwall continue to be discovered;[137] given evidence of at least sixty, it is likely that there would have been many more locations which have simply been destroyed, built over, or ploughed out of fields.

Thus, to the reasonably complete theatre space at St Just-in-Penwith, and Perran Round, Perranzabuloe, we may add Cubert, Sancreed, Ruan Major, St Enodor, and St Stephen-in-Brannel. Perhaps the most obvious space in this category would be 'Playing Place' in the Parish of Kea, where Lyon notes two Rounds[138]. What theatre occurred in these locations? Cubert (who is probably synonymous with Gwbert, once of Cardigan in Dyfed) may, for example, have had his life dramatised, for he is said to have founded the well at nearby Holywell Bay. Sancreed, as we shall see later, also had a patron saint, as did Ruan (in 1277, there is a church of *Sanctus Rumonus Parvus*[139]), and Enodor (though little is known of his life[140]). St Stephen-in-Brannel has already been dealt with in the context of the *Charter Endorsement*. Kea Parish clearly mounted productions of *Bewnans Ke*, a text unheard of until its rediscovery in 2000. A linking of hagiography with theatre space is thus legitimate. Lyon also suggests Innis Downs, near Lanivet. This is a curious and interesting location, since it is not far from the church at Lanivet which, as Couch details, contains a small medieval wall painting, with Adam and Eve apparently walking out from the jaws of Hell.[141] This is a depiction of a classic moment from Cornish medieval drama: the Harrowing of Hell. It is known to people locally as 'The Whale', since the jaws appear to resemble a huge whale, and has similarities with the Hell Mouth in the

Fig. 23. T.Q. Couch's 1865 sketch of the Harrowing of Hell, from Lanivet Church, Cornwall. Courtesy of the Royal Institution of Cornwall.

Fig. 24. A sketch of Hell-Mouth for the 1968 production of *Ordinalia* at Perran Round. Courtesy of University of Bristol Theatre Collection.

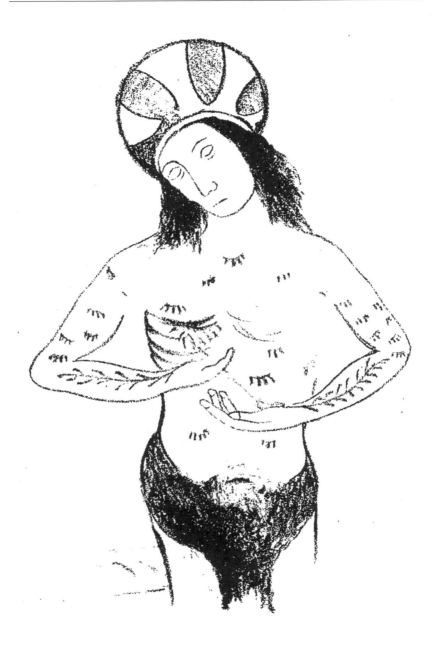

Fig. 25. Visualised theatricality? T.Q. Couch's 1865 sketch of 'Our Blessed Lord', from Lanivet Church, Cornwall. Courtesy of the Royal Institution of Cornwall.

Mystère de la Passion at Valenciennes. The painting is around two feet by two feet. The head of the Mouth is red coloured and, on the left, a hand appears to hold up an incomplete cross. There is also at Lanivet, as Couch observes, a figure of 'Our Blessed Lord', which perhaps offers a visual interpretation of what was being performed elsewhere in the parish. We also note the presence, not far away from the Round, of the fifteenth-century St Benet's Abbey (a former Benedictine monastery), which may also have had input into the dramaturgy.

The next group of amphitheatres are known performance spaces but contain few physical remains. Space here includes St Ives (which will be discussed in more depth below), Ruan Minor, Redruth, St Ewe, Sithney and two potential sites at Constantine: one at Trebah Wartha and another at Treglidgwith. These two sites at Constantine may mark changes in space and place usage over time. There could, however, be another explanation. 'Constantine' has a multitude of origins. One Constantine was the fourth-century Roman emperor who made Christianity a legal religion in the Empire. There was also a St Constantine, about whom not much is known except that he was a local landowner, becoming therefore both a 'king' and a saint. The so-called *Donations of Constantine* also links to the construction of *Bewnans Meriasek*.[142] Constantine was also a sixth-century King of Dumnonia, whom Gildas flatteringly described as the 'tyrannical cub of the filthy lioness Dumnonia'.[143] Given this, the folk memory of Constantine's achievements (apparently, he 'slaughtered two royal youths at the altar of a church'[144]) would have made a lively, indeed bloodthirsty drama. All or some of these stories may have been woven into the drama taking place there, with multiple identities and origins, perhaps matching multiple theatre space. We have already noted the 'layeredness' of Cornwall, and its concurrent 'peninsularity'.

Camborne is a notable location for drama, to which was attached, as we shall see later, its own extant play, *Bewnans Meriasek*. Padstow also shows evidence of a *plen-an-gwarry*, perhaps most obviously presenting a dramatisation of the life of St Petroc.[145] It has also, as we have seen, a significant para-theatrical tradition.[146] St Buryan meanwhile, had older ecclesiastical connections – there was a monastic-bishopric there[147] – and was a centre of scholarship. Therefore, some kind of performance emanating from there is not so surprising. According to Spriggs, there is reference to theatre space at Pendrea, near St Buryan, in 1716.[148] Other locations of this type include St Mabyn, Golant (St Sampson), Ludgvan and Germoe. Not only were there performances at the latter but, as we shall see, players from the village would perform elsewhere too. Another important location was the *plen-an-gwarry* at St Hilary, a location which was to have major influence on the writings of Bernard Walke, some six centuries later.[149] Of this group, perhaps the most significant is that of Stoke Climsland where, according to Spriggs, the Church Terrier in 1601 mentions 'the playing close, containing one acre or thereabouts'.[150] An acre would be an apt size for such theatre space, but the interesting thing about Stoke Climsland is that it is in east Cornwall, very close to the border with England, and would have experienced the loss of Cornish very early and, certainly, completely by 1300.[151] However, its presence suggests that some theatrical activity must have occurred there in the early medieval period and that some limited 'Protestant-approved' performance may have continued forward until around 1601.

Possible sites are also identified at Lezant, and interestingly two more east Cornwall locations, Talland (between Looe and Polperro), and Liskeard. Their use as performance space must have been abandoned fairly early, however. Interestingly, language transition may be noted at Talland because, as Lyon notes, the supposed site of the *plen-an-gwarry* is at Pleaton Park, 'Pleaton' being related to the Old English words for 'play': *plegian* and *pleghus*.[152] Cornish was lost from the Looe district around 1400, so this might indicate the change in nomenclature. In mid-Cornwall, we note possible performance too, at Ladock and, according to Spriggs, and Padel, two possible locations at Probus: one at Trewithen (noted also by Lyon[153]), and another at Candor.[154]

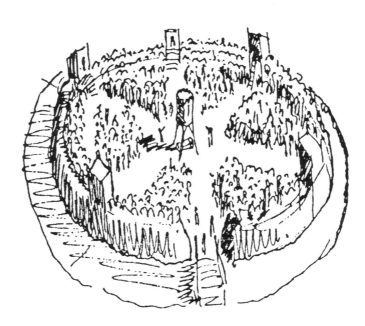

Fig. 26. Richard Southern's famous recreation of a performance in a *plen-an-gwarry*.

This proliferation may again be related to Probus's significance as a monastic-bishropic in previous centuries.[155] Para-theatrical culture has also been important in the parish, with large-scale hurling and wrestling competitions continuing into the nineteenth century.[156] Some other locations also offered two potential spaces. These are at Wendron and St Keverne. At the former, possible sites are offered by Lyon at both Halwyn and Churchtown,[157] while at the latter, Padel notes possibilities at Laddenvean and Tregoning.[158] Considering St Keverne's isolation, as well as its rebellious tendencies in the middle of this phase,[159] insight into the kind of drama performed there would be most interesting. Evidence for theatre space has also been noted at St Merryn, Gwennap Churchtown, Illogan (paralleling Redruth and Camborne on either side) and St Columb Major.

As sites worthy of more study, but with some *plen-an-gwarry* possibilities, both Lyon and Spriggs, note St Neot, Cardinham and St Erme.[160] The first place is significant because, as we shall see, its church windows depict several Bible scenes also found in the *Ordinalia*.[161] Cardinham is close by, which suggests an inter-related performance culture, while St Erme is located half-way between the more minor theatrical centres of Probus and Ladock, and those of Perran Round at Perranzabuloe and St Newlyn East. If work might be 'toured', or performed outside of the immediate parish, then these locations might seem places for it to happen. Rame in south east Cornwall is also viewed as a possibility by both Lyon, and Padel.[162] Lyon concludes his list of sites with the following: St Austell, Trelill (St Kew), St Issey, Crowan (the home of potential dramatist Radulphus or Ricardus Ton), Mylor, Piece, and Budock Water (a stone's throw from Glasney College).[163] Spriggs adds Mawnan (also close to Glasney College), Helston (an obvious omission from Lyon, considering William Jordan's text[164]), Sheviock, St Wenn, St Gluvias, Landewednack (distant and very isolated) and another intriguing possibility – that of another theatre space at Tresawen, in the Parish of Perranzabuloe.[165] Both Spriggs, and Padel also assert the importance of the Parish of St Allen (a fort there once had the name of *plyn en gwear*),[166] but this is not listed in Lyon. Likewise, these two observers also note the presence of a structure at Luxulyan,[167] with perhaps a life of St Sulian enacted. More modern amphitheatres are mentioned by Lyon in his listings.[168] These, famously at Gwennap, but also at Indian Queens, St Newlyn East and Whitemoor, are Methodist structures, built as 'preaching pits', though they might have been constructed on top of existing *plen-an-gwarries*. A difficulty here is that villages such as Indian Queens and Whitemoor only began to grow in the nineteenth century. However, there is no reason why some playing places cannot exist in isolated locations: one has only to look at Perran Round. Within this discussion, we might mention the surrounds of Glasney College itself at Penryn,[169] though, as I argued in Chapter One, performances are unlikely to have taken place inside the Church, or in its immediate locale – certainly in Glasney's earliest manifestation.

Although, as I have demonstrated above, theatrical space spreads across most of Cornwall, there are perhaps some areas where we might expect playing places to be located, but either they are not, or they are as yet undiscovered. A lack of them in far north-eastern Cornwall is perhaps logical, considering the early Anglicisation (though perhaps there might be an exception in Stratton). Somewhat more surprising is the absence of anything in Launceston, and also Lostwithiel, considering these were important geo-political centres: the first for the Normans; and the second for the Duchy and the Stannary Institutions. Perhaps the significant castles in both locations offered interior possibilities for theatre. The other surprising anomaly is Penzance. Penzance, as we have seen, has a proud festival and para-theatrical culture, but it has become quite urbanised, so any medieval structure is now very difficult to trace.[170] Considering the line of spaces coming from Germoe to St Hilary and on to St Buryan, lack of performance space here seems somewhat ironic in the sense that this part of Cornwall would become a centre-point for revivalist writings in Cornish in the late seventeenth and early eighteenth century.[171]

Given this materialist context for dramatic production, let us now turn our attention to the most famous texts of the late medieval canon of Cornish theatre. *Ordinalia* is the conventional title give to a Middle-Cornish dramatic trilogy written sometime at the end of the fourteenth century (c.1380) and composed of the following three plays: *Oridinale de Origine Mundi* ['Origo Mundi', The Beginning of the World], *Passio Domini Nostri Jhesu Christi* ['Passio Christi', Christ's Passion] and *Ordinale de Resurrexione Domini* ['Resurrexio Domini', The Resurrection of the Lord].[172] The first of these dramas contains 2,846 lines; the second 3,242 lines; and the third 2,646 lines. So the full trilogy is a large and substantial piece of work: 8,734 lines. The *Ordinalia* would appear to be the name applied to the text ever since the earliest work upon it by Keigwyn and Lhuyd, although this may not be the name by which its original audience knew it. *Ordinalia* is the plural of the Latin *ordinale*, meaning prompt or service book and, as we know from our discussion so far, it may well have been used as a prompt book, in the way conceived of by Carew,[173] or as the base copy from which the performance was developed. The text has, for many observers, come to represent all that is known and understood about medieval Cornish drama.[174] Even more so, it has perhaps become the best-known piece of Celtic literature to emerge from Cornwall (just as *The Mabinogion* is aligned to Wales, and *The Tain* to Ireland[175]), and has consequently been subjected to considerable misjudgement

Fig. 27. 'The Temptation' and 'The Oil of Mercy' in images from The Creation Window at St Neot's Church, Cornwall.

and incorrect scholarship.[176] That said, it is hard to summarise several centuries of developing work on the text, in addition to a number of critical papers and chapters looking at various aspects of language, performance and characterisation.[177] My remit here is, perhaps, not just to explore the *Ordinalia* as has been done in the past, but also to reconnect it to the wider historical process of theatre in Cornwall. By nature, this means looking not only horizontally across to other similar texts, but also vertically, back to those texts and performances that preceded it, and forward to those that followed. Given the number of lines in the *Ordinalia*, we know for certain that the work was ambitious. A three-day play cycle would have been a considerable undertaking for a religious community, or indeed a secular community linked to a religious one. If the *Ordinalia* was perhaps the exception (we know that *Bewnans Ke* and *Bewnans Meriasek* lasted for two days), then we begin to understand further that the work was not run-of-the-mill. That said, the *Ordinalia* and *Bewnans Ke* and *Bewnans Meriasek* may tell us that two or three day events were the norm, and that there may well have been other works which lasted as long or even longer. This picture is made all the more complex by a notion that, as we shall see, the *Ordinalia* itself may have been part of a longer work.

As indicated in Chapter One, texts such as the *Ordinalia* were permitted to grow and develop, as legislation changed over the right to perform drama. If performances were connected with the church, then obviously secular material would not have been in favour. Playwrights in Cornwall and elsewhere therefore turned to those moments in the Bible which offered the greatest drama.[178] It is obvious that key events such as the Flood, the Crucifixion and the Resurrection would be considered, though these are not easy moments to make into drama, considering the technology available to medieval theatre workers. Their ingenuity is therefore to be marvelled at, when we come to consider again not only the ambition of single works such as this, but their proliferation across the territory of Cornwall.

The *Ordinalia* survives in a single manuscript in the Bodleian Library, Oxford, known as Bodl. MS. 791.[179] There are two known copies made of this manuscript: one by John Keigwyn, also held in the Bodleian;[180] another, by Edward Lhuyd, held in the National Library of Wales.[181] Bodl. MS. 791 consists of eighty-three folios of text on parchment and, according to Longsworth, who has spent considerable energy examining the connection between religion and dramaturgy in the work, it is by two scribes.[182] By scribes we do not necessarily mean authors, since this may well have been a copy of an earlier version created by another author or set of authors. The authorship of the *Ordinalia* and other Middle-Cornish dramas is debated below. What is clear is that one hand carries the script to almost the end of 'Origo Mundi'. A second hand then takes over for the sequence at the end of this play, asking the audience to return tomorrow, and it is this hand that completes the remaining two plays. A further set of scribes have then gone through the manuscript at a later date, adding stage directions and making corrections to the text. The early hands have been dated to the early fifteenth century, suggesting that the original Middle Cornish of the late fourteenth century was here recopied. The later hands in the text are somewhat more difficult to date, although they presumably commented on the drama between this early fifteenth-century scribal process and Keigwyn's work upon it.

The *Ordinalia*'s provenance has been settled on as being Glasney College at Penryn, or at least connected to one of the canons or canons-in-training there. This consensus has come into place through three major strands. First of all, the evidence that virtually all the place names within the drama are from the immediate environs of the Fal Estuary, in which Penryn was located.[183] Secondly, Glasney College was perhaps the only institutional structure in medieval Cornwall that could facilitate the kind of dramaturgy and writing imagined in the *Ordinalia*.[184] Finally, the extended sequence in the third play, 'Resurrexio Domini', concerning 'Doubting Thomas', would indicate a Glasney

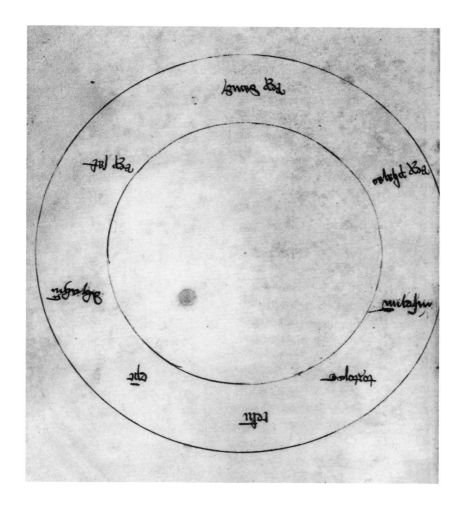

Fig. 28. Plan for the staging of *Origo Mundi*. MS. Bodl. 791, f 27. Reproduced by permission of the Bodleian Library, Oxford.

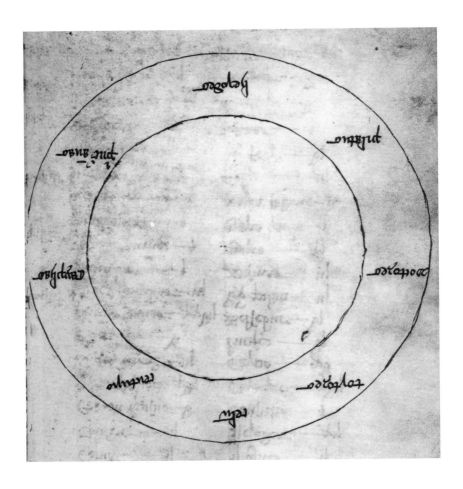

Fig. 29. Plan for the staging of *Passio Christi*. MS. Bodl. 791, f 56v. Reproduced by permission of the Bodleian Library, Oxford.

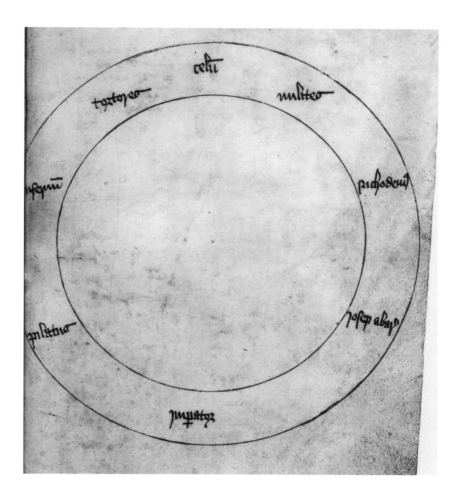

Fig. 30. Plan for the staging of *Resurrexio Domini*. MS. Bodl. 791, f 83. Reproduced by permission of the Bodleian Library, Oxford.

origin or connection.[185] This is because the full name of Glasney College was the Collegiate Church of St Thomas. To have a detailed characterisation of the very saint after whom the college was named provided an extra-special piece of dramatic recreation. Thus we can say with some degree of certainty that the *Ordinalia* was at some point presented either at Glasney or in its immediate vicinity, or somewhere around Penryn or Carrick Roads.[186] Whether the *Ordinalia* was presented elsewhere in Cornwall during this phase is a matter of conjecture: there was a 1969 version at Perran Round; and a 2004 millennial version at St Just-in-Penwith. We know that Glasney College had many connections to St Just-in-Penwith, and that St Just-in-Penwith has its own *plen-an-gwarry*, but this in itself is no guarantee that it was performed there. Likewise, as this chapter has shown, there are a number of other *plen-an-gwarries* around this area, which might be possible performance spaces for such a work, although there is no guarantee that they were delivered there. With the *Ordinalia*, we may even be looking at a completely different kind of performance space compared to some of the other locations. Evidence for this might be deduced from the stage diagrams in the manuscript, which give no sense of the capella found at the two locations above. The St Just-in-Penwith

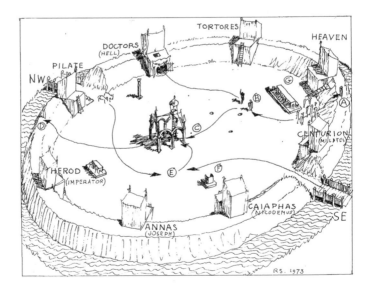

Fig. 31. A sketch of Day 3 (*Resurrexio Domini*) made in 1973 by Richard Southern from the 1969 production of *Ordinalia*. Courtesy of University of Bristol Theatre Collection.

Round suggested a more urban theatre, while that of Perran Round is more isolated. The *Ordinalia*'s original performance space may well offer a third way.

If the *Ordinalia* or variants of it were performed elsewhere in Cornwall, then there might be an argument that the base text could be adapted. The very specific Fal estuary locations could then be given local flavour, according to where it was being performed. Arguments which support this view include the fact that, in 'Passio Christi', the Smith and his wife are from Marghes jow (Marazion) – perhaps a vestigial component of an earlier or later draft.[187] This is certainly a view held by Bakere, who proposes that because one of the place-name references in 'Passio Christi' is seemingly to West Penwith (coupled with the exclusion of references to Penryn and to Trigg in north Cornwall), then this text is, in fact, older than either the first or third play.[188] The fact that *The Creacion of the World* [*Gwreans an Bys*][189] carries some structural and linguistic similarities to 'Origo Mundi', and was performed at Helston, may also demonstrate textual movement. In this case, Glasney may have provided such a base text, from which the Helston version was completed. It seems likely that Helston would have had a further day – or even three days – of performance, so this model might work. However, this theory is still conjecture. Detail about performances at, for example, Bodmin or St Ives would help to show whether this were the case, but such detail is not extant. There may even be a case for arguing that, in the summer months of Cornwall, it might have been possible to travel to several of the *guirremears* over a period of weeks, thus allowing the audience to compare spectacle, dramaturgy and Christian intent. If authors were known, and there is perhaps no reason why they should not be, then there may even have been a competitive element to writing them.

The language of the three plays of the *Ordinalia* is mainly Middle Cornish with around eighty strophic forms. Such a variety demonstrates considerable dexterity in the use of verse within drama. The rhymes naturally assisted the actor in memorising the lines, as well as helping to reinforce the message for the audience. At various places, French, English and Latin are also incorporated – indicating a multi-lingual Cornish theatre space. Certain elements of the revivalist and Cornish language movement in Cornwall sometimes suggest that medieval Cornwall was a 'perfect' Celtic environment, somehow 'unpolluted' by other language and culture, but if any text is an example of how this were truly not the case, then it is the *Ordinalia*. The place-names of the plays, which work to combine a biblical landscape with a Cornish one, would seem another indication of authorship at Glasney College. The merging of time and space is not much discussed in general *Ordinalia* scholarship but, in my view, it is one of the central mechanisms of dramaturgy of the entire trilogy. The drama juxtaposes this 'magical realist' vision of layered Cornwall

Fig. 32. The devils at work in the 1969 production of *Ordinalia* at Perran Round. Courtesy of the Royal Institution of Cornwall.

with the world of the Bible. As mentioned in Chapter One of this book, it is also reliant on localised metaphor, and a particular view of the biblical world so imagined in the medieval mind. The likelihood is that a number of ideological and spiritual metaphors, now lost on us, were very pertinent to the late medieval audience who watched its performance.

The *Ordinalia* is also a highly unified work, showing the fall and redemption of humanity. Many of its themes are derived from apocryphal sources including, in particular, in the second and third plays, the *Gospel of Nicodemus*.[190] However, the most important of these sources is the Legend of the Holy Rood; Murdoch argues not only that this strand has been neglected, but also that it was what made the Cornish cycle so unified and so distinctive.[191] In effect, the cycle follows the history of the cross, and begins with three seeds from the tree of life being placed in the mouth of the dead Adam by Seth, who is in search of the oil of mercy. The rods or saplings are encountered by Moses and David, and the same 'magical' wood is used to create the roof beams for Solomon's Temple, and eventually form the bridge at Cedron, leading to the same wood being used for the cross in 'Passio Christi'. We know that there was a good deal of interest in the legend of the cross during the late medieval period. It was fashionable at church festivals to have relics of consecrated wood within their midst. Indeed, Cornwall has a famous example of this kind of activity. There exists, in the British Library, a report describing the theft of a piece of the cross by a Cornish knight named Sir Roger de Wallysborough, who managed to secrete the item in his clothing. Part of the fragment of the cross was given to the church at Grade, previously known as 'cross parysshe' and the other part of it to St Buryan, the district in which de Wallysborough's lands lay.[192] Thus, the *Ordinalia* certainly reflects a concern with the wood of the cross, which was fashionable and, perhaps, towards the middle years of the sixteenth century, also dangerous. That is because such relics were looked upon as meaningless superstition by those activating the Reformation.[193] Numerous detailed investigations into the inspiration and sources for the work have been completed by Longsworth, Murdoch and others, and I suggest that the reader interested in the complex sources and religious background to the drama should consult those texts.[194] What is of interest to us here is the more immediate concern of where the *Ordinalia* fits into the wider continuum of drama from Cornwall, and how its dramaturgy was completed in practice.

The trilogy, like other pan-British and pan-European mystery plays is highly comic in places, with earthy humour. This was completely intentional, aiming to appeal to the common people and to entertain them whilst they were receiving the scriptural message. As we have seen, there is a good deal of intertextuality with most medieval texts, and the *Ordinalia* is no exception. Most often, *Pascon agan Arluth*[195] is seen as one of the sources for the dramatic trilogy, although some observers (among them David C. Fowler[196]) see it the other way round, with the poem using the drama as a source. Either way, the Christian message is imagined in a particularly Cornish way; whether poem or drama was first, the poem is, in many ways, conceived very dramatically, one being the 'mirror image' of the other. There is not time to enter into a full discussion of this text here, but suffice for us to say that it is productively read in tandem with 'Passio Christi'. Readers interested in the relationship between *Pascon agan Arluth* and the *Ordinalia* should see the scholarship of Murdoch, Edwards and Woodhouse.[197]

The action of 'Origo Mundi' – a dramatic consideration of key events in the Old Testament – is highly episodic. Despite, however, the obvious length of 'real time' between the episodes, the play has a real pace and vigour, and in many ways an almost Brechtian feel. This is because, in many respects, the style is 'epic' theatre rather than 'dramatic', and events are signposted, using the Rood as the signposting mechanism. This is extraordinarily artful. The need for ideological and spiritual education takes precedence over the desire to create credible characters and naturalistic action. The purpose is education and instruction, though this is to be achieved through the process of theatre. Longsworth sheds light on this by observing that 'The Cornish *Ordinalia* is, in fact, a splendid memorial to the pedagogical genius and integrity of the vernacular biblical dramatist who shaped it'.[198] To summarise then, structurally, the play is composed of the following elements:

The Creation, and Fall of Man
Cain and Abel
Seth, and the Death of Adam
Noah, and the Flood
Abraham and Isaac
Moses and the Burning Bush
Pharaoh and the Plagues
The Exodus, and the Crossing of the Red Sea
The Children of Israel in the Wilderness
King David and the Rods of Grace
David and Bathsheba
Solomon and the Building of the Temple
Maximilla[199]

The Holy Rood is central to the structure of 'Origo Mundi', which is comprised of multiple sections that form set pieces. These begin with the creation of the world, followed by Adam and Eve, Cain and Abel, Seth, Noah, and Abraham and Isaac. In the Moses section, he is given the role of planting the Rood saplings for the future. This is followed by Mary's discovery of the three rods, which will combine to form the Rood. After a love affair with Bathsheba, a remorseful King David writes his psalms and vows to place the three rods in a temple. After David's death, Solomon completes the construction of the temple, during which the Rood is used as a beam that comically refuses to fit anywhere in the structure. The first play concludes with the prophetess Maximilla, whose clothing inexplicably catches fire when she sits on the Rood, causing her to prophesy Jesus Christ, a crime for which she is duly executed.

At the start of the drama, two components are of considerable interest. These are Adam's naming of the beasts, and the temptation of Eve by the Devil. Adam's naming of the beasts is another moment in the *Ordinalia* where local detail coalesces with the biblical narrative. Although some of the animals are ones we might expect in any context, a few indicate the specific fauna of Cornwall:

yt'hanwaf bugh ha tarow
ha margh yw best hep parow
  the vap de rag ymweres
gaver yweges karnow
daves war ve lavarow
  hy hanow da kemeres

lemyn hanwaf goyth ha yar
a sensaf ethyn hep par
  the vygyens den war an bys
hos payon colom grwgyer
swan bargos bryny ha'n er
  moy drethof a vyth hynwys
y rof hynwyn the'n puskes
porpus sowmens syllyes
  ol thy'm gustyth y a vyth
leneswo ha barfussy
pysk ragof ny wra skvsy
  mar corthyaf dev yn penfyth

[I name cow, and bull,
And horse, it is beast without equal
  For the son of man to help himself;
Goat, steer, stag,
Sheep, from my words
  To take their names.

Now I name goose and fowl,
I hold them birds without equal
  For food of man on the earth;
Duck, peacock, pigeon, partridge,
Swan, kite, crows, and the eagle
  Further by me are named.

I give names to the fishes,
Porpoises, salmons, congers,
  All to me obedient they shall be;
Ling and cod,
A fish from me shall not escape,
  If I honour God perfectly.[200]

Such dramaturgy would connect with the audience watching, reinforcing the immediate connection between them and God. A more difficult piece of drama to mount would have been the section in the stage direction where '*Tunc iet pater ad celum et postea diabolus tanquam serpens loquitur ad euam in arbore scientic et dicit ad euam* [Then, God the Father shall go to heaven; and afterwards the Devil, like a serpent, speaks to Eve in the tree of knowledge, and he says wickedly to Eve]'.[201] The stage direction may be read literally, in which case the Devil would have to 'snake' his way across to Eve from Hell; or could be read as more of a metaphor for his persona, gestures and dialogue. Either way, such an image is depicted in the Creation Window at St Neot Church;[202] so this was clearly a pan-Cornish image (indeed pan-European), continually in the mind of those watching. Whichever way it is staged, the temptation offers the first large set piece to those producing and watching the drama. The following sequence is set in Paradise, and since this is not marked on the stage diagrams MS. 791, it is likely that the Devil's station was immediately below the station for Heaven. Spatially, there is considerable room for them to move from Paradise to where the rest of the audience is sat or stood, thus emphasising the theological point of the expulsion. There might be possible use of the capella in the next section where the stage direction reads, '*Et fodiet et terra clamat et iterum fodiet et clamat terra* [And he shall dig, and the earth cries: and again he shall dig, and the earth cries]'.[203] This is because a performer could be hidden in the dip so as to make the crying noises of the earth weeping as Adam digs.

Cain and Abel are not offered a station in the performance space, so it is less clear how they enter. Also less well demarked is where their altar space should be, although at the end of Abel's speech beginning '*certain goky os ha mad* [Simply thou art foolish and mad]', the direction reads '*Hic venient omnes in platea* [Here all shall come upon stage]'.[204] Presumably, '*platea*' here refers to the plain itself. It would then be relatively straightforward for the devils to cross over from Hell to claim Abel. Another dramatic difficulty is the issue of Eve becoming pregnant with Seth. It is solved in a subtle way by the dramatist: '*Et tunc recedat ab ea paucumper* [And then let him go away a little way from her]' and then '*et iterum veniet ad eam* [And again he shall come to her]' with Eve confessing that '*yma flogh genaf genys* [There is a child born to me]'.[205] The action swiftly transfers to the boy Seth, and his encounter with the Cherub during the sequence of the Oil of Mercy.[206] This scene is featured in one of the Creation Windows at St Neot Church.[207] In the play, the Cherub begins the legend of the Holy Rood with the following words:

kemer tyyr spus a'n aval
  a dybrys adam the das
pan varwo gorr'y hep fal
  yntre y thyns ha'y davas
Anethe ty a wylfyth
  tyr gvethen tevys whare
rag ny vew mo yes treddyth
  war lyrgh the vones the dre

[Take three kernels of the apple,
  Which Adam, thy father ate.
When he dies, put them, without fail,
  Between his teeth and his tongue.
From them thou wilt see
  Three trees grow presently;
For he will not live more than three days
  After thou reachest home.[208]

When this is completed, the devils fetch the body of Adam, which allows the drama to progress to Noah and the Ark. Clearly, this was a sequence intended for the plain rather than the stations, which is again fitting, because this section was a large set piece involving several characters. A stage direction here asks for 'men and cattle' to be loaded onto the ark, which is perhaps a practical possibility, the producers of the drama at least striving for some realism with the cattle, although this in itself would have brought about some logistical difficulties. The structure of the ark is more difficult to comprehend, though Shem does speak of covering the top of the ark with a cloth ['*guartha a'n gorhyl gans queth*'].[209] The sending out of the crow and the doves was presented in the 1969 production of the *Ordinalia* by painted images of the crow and the doves on pieces of wood, held by an actor; this may give us a clue as to how the dramaturgy was realised in previous Ages. God, meanwhile, is still positioned on his station as the ark is uncovered. The importance the Cornish put on the Flood has already been discussed, but its further theological significance is reinforced when the ark comes to rest on Mount Calvary. Here, the stage direction reads '*hic paratur altare et dues pater stet iuxta* [Here an altar is made ready, and let God the Father stand near it]'.[210] At this point then, God the Father has clearly descended from his station, and appears to be closer to the other characters of the Noah group.

Abraham, as befitting his status perhaps, is given a station. His entrance, however, comes while 'walking about [*hic pompabit Abraham*]', but then we learn that '*hic descendit* [Here he comes down]',[211] which suggests his initial perambulation was somewhere on his station. In terms of a transition from the Noah sequence, this is quite important, because presumably the audience focus would be away from the ark, and onto the station. This would also allow the actors of the Noah group to remove or cover the ark. In this way, the dramatist(s) behind 'Origo Mundi' are highly aware of the need for speedy scene changes, a point which further diminishes Carew's argument about the slowness of their delivery and performance. It is possible that the altar used by Noah could be doubled here, with Gabriel eventually coming down to him from Heaven's station. Once it is determined that Isaac is not to be sacrificed, Abraham decides upon a sheep. Again, it is unclear whether a mock-up or real animal was used.

So far, the dramaturgy inside the Round has occurred in the quarter mainly around Heaven and Abraham, but the sequence involving Moses probably involved considerable expansion across the plain. We know, for example, that Pharaoh is located in the west in the opposite quarter to much of the action so far. Moses' entrance is unclear, but there is an instant focus to his speech, since he observes the burning bush. This would presumably be relatively easy to create. More difficult is the miracle of the serpent turning into the rod. Considerable action takes place with the Pharaoh parading upon his station, while Moses moves across the plain to meet him. In terms of what modern theatre labels 'proxemics', again the dramatist and producers had a good eye on what would be visually stimulating for the audience. Of course Pharaoh, up higher, would have commanded status, with Moses on the level of the audience. Pharoah's status would presumably have been further enhanced by some form of exotic costuming. The proxemics only alter when 'Pharaoh goes down' and Moses '*ascendit super equum* [He mounts a horse]'.[212] In terms of theology, this is when things also start to change, so religion and dramaturgy are again operating in union. The sequence culminates in Moses 'smiting the sea', and the drowning of Pharaoh, his squire and his men. There is considerable ambition in this sequence and it is more difficult to theorise upon how this may have been achieved in the original performance conditions. The most likely mechanism would have been to have used cloths or drapes, which would have been positioned on the plain by other performers, and then moved vertically to indicate the sea being smitten. The cloth could then cover the Egyptian group as they passed through. Although relatively 'low tech', this way of representing water is still used on stage in the modern era.

The localisation process occurs again in the sequence where we see the children of Israel in the wilderness. First man [usually Caleb] has been spat on by a black toad, complaining that it occurred when '*ov coske yn haus yn hal* [sleeping down on the moor]'.[213] The use of the word '*hal*' here is interesting because it has very specific cultural-geographic meaning to anyone from Cornwall. The alignment therefore with the children of Israel in the wilderness would therefore be reinforced because there were areas of Cornwall in which this imagined 'wilderness' could be seen and experienced. This sequence leads into Moses striking the rock with his rod, causing water to exude. The physical nature of this would have required some effect at this point; the dramatic imperative of finding water is a common event on the late medieval stage in Cornwall. Such foundings of springs or wells are components in both of the saints' plays; this connects very firmly with community and landscape.[214] The text asks for Moses, having planted the rods at Mount Tabor, to die. Quite how this is presented is again problematical. Presumably, as before (between Adam and Abraham) the segue-way into the next episode (King David) provided the necessary distraction for Moses to die quietly upon the plain or bank.

The dramaturgy of the sequence with King David is enhanced by the comical roles of the Butler and Counsellor, who try to advise David for the best. The action here shifts away from Pharaoh's station to the immediate left of it, where David is initially positioned. Gabriel would therefore probably have to cross to David's station. Although there is energy created by David's encounters with the blind man, the lame man and the deaf man, it is really his affair with Bathsheba that forms the crucial part of the drama here. The David material is an innovative section, not found in any of the English cycles. Murdoch has recently argued that what we see in this sequence is a 'fairly radical biblical adaptation' and that, although it invites comparison with other medieval texts, the way it is imagined theatrically in 'Origo Mundi' is highly distinctive.[215] What is offered to the audience is a love triangle, and one which confronts medieval ideological conceptualisations of marriage and fidelity head on. Uriah is presented as a naïve but brave knight, thus embellishing the text with some courtly love components. Again, the use of horses made for spectacle. After Uriah's death, the notion of David's guilt is explored, resulting in him wishing for a penitential hymn for his sins. The building of the temple is then ordered. David's death could also result in some interesting dramatic movement. The Counsellor says '*dun goryn y gorf y veth* [Let us go and put his body in the grave]'.[216] One might see the possible use here of the capella, so that the framework might be pulled apart, and David's body placed within. However, the text complicates this by suggesting that, although they do bury him, the body is placed 'under some tent [*corpus sub aliquot tento*]',[217] which is somewhat unclear. Perhaps the tent referred to the structure over the capella or closer to the station. It is in the sequence involving David and Solomon that some of the most significant localisation of 'Origo Mundi' can be seen. The Messenger who goes to the masons to summon them for construction of the temple is rewarded as follows:

> *messyger rag the suruys*
> *the rewardye my a ra*
> *carn suyow ha trehembys*
> *chatur annethe thy's gura*

> [Messenger, for thy service
>   I will reward thee;
> Carnsew and Trehembys,
>   Make a charter for thyself].[218]

Jane Bakere has studied the cultural geography of such place-names in some depth, and notes that 'Carnsew and Trehembys are in the Parish of Mabe about a mile and a half from Glasney'. She further notes that 'The whole of the parish of Mabe formed part of the Manor of Penryn Foreign owned by the Bishop of Exeter while the great tithes belonged to Glasney College'.[219] A further set of place-names comes in Solomon's coronation sequence:

> *ha rag why thu'm kerune*
> *my a re thyugh bosuene*
> *lostuthyal ha lanerchy*

> [And to you, by my crown,
> I will give you Bosvene,
>   Lostwithiel and Lanerchy.][220]

Considering most of the other place-names in 'Origo Mundi' are within a ten-mile radius of Glasney, this reward is somewhat different. Bosvene, or modern Bosvannah, is in the Episcopal Manor of Penryn Foreign. This is found in the Parish of St Gluvias, about a mile from Glasney, but Loswithiel and Lanerchy (modern Lanner) are more distant. Lostwithiel was the long-standing capital of Cornwall (where the Stannary met), and so proves its significance. However, although Bakere suggests alternative parishes for Lanner, it is the one nearest Redruth that seems most likely.[221] Perhaps it was a fashionable location, but it may also have already been noted for its mineral wealth. This is not the end of the dramatic importance of place-names within the text however. When the masons complete their work on the temple, Solomon gives them reward:

dew vody tha ough yn guyr
ha rag bos agas wheyl tek
my a re thyugh ply vuthek
ha'n garack ruen gans hy thyr

[Two good bodies ye are, truly.
And because your work is fair,
I will give you the parish of Vuthek,
And the Carrack Ruan, with its land.][222]

Vuthek can of course be identified as Budock, which was also part of the Episcopal manor of Penryn Foreign. The 'Carrack Ruan' has prompted considerable debate. Initially, some observers have believed that it was a somewhat stingy gift, the rock being accepted as what is now known as the Black Rock. However, most observers, following Bakere, now believe it to be very generous because the Black Rock was, until the nineteenth century, the point of imposition of the tax of poll money on shipping arrivals.[223] This would certainly fit the response of the Second Mason who says, '*ha largys ha gromercy* [And largesse and thanks]'.[224] The dramaturgy of this is important because it would have shown to the audience that Solomon was already becoming a wise king. The sequence involving the temple is relatively straightforward dramatically, with the carpenters finding the Rood tree for the rafters, although there is comedy and confusion when the measurements and cutting of the wood variously cause it to be too short and then too long. In this sense, the dramatist is brilliantly outlining the magical and special nature of the wood, which is destined for greater things. Further localisation of the drama is apparent in Solomon's reward to the carpenters for the completion of their work. They are given charters of land in the vicinity of Penryn:

banneth a'n tas re ges bo
why as-byth by godys fo
  agas gobyr eredy
warbarth ol gueel behethlen
ha coys penryn yn tyen
  my a's re lemyn though why
    hag ol guer-thour
an enys hag arwennek
tregenver ha kegyllek
  annethe gureugh though chartour

[Blessing of the Father be on you!
You shall have, by God's faith,
   Your payment, surely;
Together all the field of Bohellan,
And the wood of Penryn, wholly,
   I give them now to you;
      And all their water courses.
The island and Arwinick,
Tregeaverm, and Kegellik,
   Make all of them a charter to you.][225]

These places were closer to Penryn, with most of them in the Episcopal Manor of Penryn Foreign. Only Bohelland is in the Parish of St Gluvias, at the head of Penryn creek, but still only half a mile from Glasney. Blending these locations into the drama would have given the text an impressive immediacy to those watching the performance. Place-names continue to be significant in the final section of 'Origo Mundi' when the prophetess Maximilla is killed by the torturers.[226] The dramaturgy has here shifted back to the original quarter of the Round (clockwise, closest to Heaven), for this is where the Bishop is located, and it is he who orders Maximilla's brutal execution:

awos henna nynsus vry
galas hy gobyr gynsy
   ha servyys yv del gothe
rag a's lafur why as beth
behethlan ha bosaneth
   eugh what th'aga seysee
      kyns ha bos nos
         my a rea
            thyyugh an dremma
hag ol chennary an clos

[Because that she was not obedient,
Her reward is gone with her,
   And she is served as she ought.
Because of your labour you shall receive
Bohellan and Bosaneth;
   Go at once and possess them,
      Before it is night.

I will give
  To you these places,
And all the Chennary of the Close].[227]

Here, we know that Bohellan has already been given out, so this merely shows the further evil of the Bishop, that the torturers or he may take it away from the carpenter, but Bosaneth – a farm in Mawnan, also contained in the Episcopal Manor of Penryn Foreign – has not previously been given out. The Chennary of the Close is interesting since it would appear to refer to the canonry of Glasney itself; an ironic comment on some topical issue perhaps. It is on this violent note that 'Origo Mundi' ends and, whilst it is not a happy conclusion to events in 'The Beginning of the World', there is no doubt that it would have whetted the audience's appetite for action and spectacle from the next day's performance. More recently Maximilla has come to be considered in new ways by one observer. Jim Hall has argued that Maximilla's execution reflects the growing religious turbulence of the period. Hall offers that this sequence of 'Origo Mundi' ought to be read in the context of the struggle for political power between Cornwall and England, and that Maximilla and the Bishop reflect this struggle: an argument, as we shall see, also applied by Payton on *Bewnans Meriasek*. Thus, he concludes that 'the cycle's careful ambiguities speak of an unstable and fractious audience whose faith… was often heavily compromised with persistent superstition and pagan vestiges'.[228] In this view, Maximilla is thus a deviation from conventional Catholicism by being, in effect, a Cornish variant of Montanism. Montanists believed that they superseded and fulfilled the doctrines proclaimed by the Apostles. Their belief was also in ecstatic prophecy, another function which Maximilla fulfils, therefore offering danger to the established order.

We then come to a significant issue within the text of 'Origo Mundi'. A number of observers, among them Harris, Kent, and George,[229] have identified a difficulty at this point. Textual evidence shows that the transition made between 'Origo Mundi' and 'Passio Christi' sometimes included a work based on Christ's childhood. Thus the lines *'flogholeth a his hep gortholeth* [the childhood of Christ, voluntarily]' could be inserted into Solomon's speech, if some now lost play was performed between those extant texts. This opens up the possibility (discussed later in this chapter) that the *Ordinalia* was originally a much longer work. A play that examined Christ's childhood would have been of immense interest to Cornwall, because there are long-standing connections between Christ, Joseph of Arimathea (as a tin trader) and travel to Cornwall. Such links inspired both Kent, and George to develop new dramas based on this knowledge.[230]

Having discussed much of the content and localised elements of 'Origo Mundi' as a whole, let us now turn to engagement with performance practice for this text. The model for performance of 'Origo Mundi' is the aforementioned 'multiple staging in the round'. When considered alongside the stage directions, and other manuscripts such as *Bewnans Meriasek*, this was the standard working practice for this kind of outdoor theatre. Thus, actors might begin their speech and performance at one of the eight stations constructed around the Round, and then move by some process (perhaps ladders or steps) to the plain itself. The performance here might feasibly involve movement across the Round to other stations or locations, in order to engage with other events or characters. The stations were obviously free-standing structures of some kind which, if built into a sloped bank, would require shorter construction at the back, and longer construction at the front, although there is no reason to assume that this was always the case. The structures might equally have been free-standing, though the stations in the diagrams from the *Ordinalia* manuscript would suggest that they are positioned in some way on the bank. Further evidence is gleaned from the manuscript and play text, which describes where, for example, the torturers are told both to descend and ascend.

We know that two of the stations were fixed for the three days of the *Ordinalia* cycle. The names of the stations are written around the Round, sometimes in a form of stage short-hand. The short-hand would appear to represent a kind of familiarity about positioning and space within the performance, and perhaps something that was familiar not only in this production but in others too. These are *celum* [Heaven] and *tortures* [torturers], and from the surviving diagrams we have some idea of their geographical alignment. The likelihood was that Heaven was associated with the east, with *infernum* [Hell] in the north. We might assume from their permanence (especially that of Heaven) that these stations could be quite elaborate and may well have been decorated in some way. Thus the torturers are placed geographically and symbolically between Heaven and Hell. Moving around the circle in a clockwise direction, we therefore find *celum* [Heaven], *episcopus* [bishops], *Abraham* [Abraham], *Rex Salamon* [King Solomon], *Rex dauid* [King David], *Rex pharo* [Pharoah], *infernum* [Hell] and *tortures* [torturers].[231] This would mean that Solomon performed directly opposite Heaven, while Pharaoh was next to Hell. This fits theologically. The plain itself remains unmarked in the diagram, and would thus presumably be used for other sequences, such as Paradise, Noah and the Ark, Moses and Maximilla.

Related to this is the positioning of the audience. A number of possibilities seem feasible. The entire audience could be sat on the bank watching from between the stations. This would be apt, since it would allow those watching to see the whole, across a panorama, whilst observing in more detail events to their immediate left or right at the stations. An alternative might be that although some of the performance could be watched in this way, it would also seem possible that some members of the audience followed the action of the drama in a promenade style. Thus the audience would move from the opening station to wherever the action of the play moved, for example, from the centre of the plain, back across to the next station, and across to the next, hence the play 'moving' from one player to another. This would require some areas within the Round being able to accommodate movement, and perhaps even, depending on numbers, some process of marshalling the audience. Another option would be that the audience operated entirely on this basis, though the former seems more likely, since it allowed multiple age groups to see the performance. The younger watchers could move with events, while more elderly viewers could sit.

To apply this theory, we might consider the opening sequence of 'Origo Mundi'. It must have begun at Heaven, with God the Father speaking. The audience then would have traced the making of Adam and Eve, perhaps from a capella (if one existed at the site(s) where the *Ordinalia* was performed), and then to Paradise. The Devil would then perhaps make his way from the Hell station across to the Garden of Paradise. Many characters within the trilogy are asked to 'parade' and this must mean they walk on the plain or *platea*. This would give the actors a good deal of freedom to roam in their performance, and possibly deliver lines close to the audience, and from within its ranks (perhaps extemporising, or involving audience participation). Other sequences within the trilogy require more space and development, events resoundingly more suited to the plain itself. For example, in the sequence involving David and Bathsheba, David is required to ride on horseback, as are Uriah and the messenger when they go off to war. Such a sequence could perhaps have been presented with real horses of some kind, which would have made this particular section quite spectacular. The stage directions of the opening of the play also offer us further insight into the construction and use of these stations, which the actors (and possibly the audience) moved between. It could be, for example, that there was a high level for God and the angels, with a lower structure in place for Paradise. This is indicated in the following stage direction: '*descendit Deus de pulpito* [God comes down from the upper stage]'.[232] Presumably, such stations were constructed of wood, and some form of fabric, and perhaps kept in the community for use again. This would certainly fit with the knowledge that we have of the construction of staging from Accounts of performance at St Ives, as we shall see later. The multi-stage model of performance within the Round was, as we have seen, a popular pan-European method of theatre, and in the stage plans of the

Ordinalia we gain a sense of its specific dramaturgy in Cornwall. Moving forward to the twentieth and twenty-first centuries, such stations are not dissimilar to some of the structures constructed by Kneehigh Theatre in their outside performances; so therefore 'stations' seem a supremely well-suited method of delivering outdoor performance, facilitating revelation of that character, providing a base or home for the character, and offering a place for the performer to go once their part has been delivered.

Having considered the dramaturgy, staging and audience of 'Origo Mundi', I now move to examine the material circumstances and performance conditions of 'Passio Christi'. Performance conditions of the second play of the trilogy, 'Passio Christi', can be discerned from the diagram contained in the manuscript of the *Ordinalia*. Again there are eight stations present, but because this drama does not call for the location of Hell, this is replaced in the north by the *Doctores* [Doctors]. Clockwise again, the stations from the east (top) are *celum* [Heaven], *centurio* [centurion], *Cayphas* [Caiaphas], *princeps annas* [Prince Annas], *herodes* [Herod], *pilatus* [Pilate], *Doctores* [Doctors] and *tortures* [torturers]. Therefore, Herod and Pilate are located in the west, opposite Heaven. The structure of 'Passio Christi' is different from 'Origo Mundi'. Although certain aspects of the drama are once again episodic, there is a unity and cohesion in terms of dramatic development, with each scene building upon the previous one, in a way that was not possible with the play of the first day. Therefore, the main action of 'Passio Christi' may be summarised by the following:

The Temptation of Christ
The Entry into Jerusalem
The Expulsion of the Traders from the Temple
The Healing of the Blind and the Cripple
Jesus at the House of Simon the Leper
The Conspiracy
The Last Supper
The Agony in the Garden, and the Betrayal
Christ before Caiaphas, Peter's Denial and the Buffeting
The Remorse and Death of Judas
Christ before Pilate
Christ before Herod
The Dream of Pilate's Wife
The Scourging and the Crown of Thorns
The Condemnation
The *Via Crucis* (Stations of the Cross)

The Forging of the Nails
The Crucifixion
The Two Thieves
The Last Words, and the Death of Jesus
Longius
The Deposition, Anointing and Burial.

We can begin to appreciate the complexity of the dramaturgy of 'Passio Christi' when compared to the thirteen major episodes of 'Origo Mundi'. There are twenty-two 'separate' units of drama here, which required immense organisation of space, place and performance in order to have the required dramatic effect. Unfortunately, there is not enough space here to examine all of the scenes. All we can hope to do within this volume is to examine some of the core moments of the dramaturgy at work. The drama opens with the temptation of Christ in the desert: Jesus is imagined standing in Mount Quarantena, near Jordan, looking between Jericho and Jerusalem. It would seem that even though this location is not mentioned in the stage diagram of the Passion, this would need to be somewhere higher, because the direction reads '*hic descendant omnes de monte* [Here let all descend from the mountain]'.[233] After discussion with Peter and Andrew, Jesus is confronted by Satan who, even at this point, is unsure whether he can tempt Christ, saying '*sur awos o low gallos / byth ny allaf yn ow ros / the wul pegh vyth y cachys* [Surely, notwithstanding all my power / I shall never be able, in my net / To catch him doing any sin].[234] Unsuccessful Satan retreats to Hell, and after God's request for his angels Michael and Gabriel to serve Christ, there begins a sequence where his disciples seek an ass and foal (which probably would have been real animals). A major sequence devoted to Palm Sunday follows, with the Hebrew boys welcoming him. The temple would appear to be in the plain itself as there is no note for it on the bank. Jesus's destruction of the market in the temple then allows the shopkeeper to travel across to the station belonging to Caiaphas, which inevitably sets in motion the events leading to the crucifixion. The miracles worked by Jesus on the blind and lame man would allow for specific dramatic moments of recovery from their afflictions. The sequence when Mary Magdalene washes Christ's feet follows; this too, was presumably completed in the arena.

Caiaphas, meanwhile, seeks advice from Prince Annas, whose station is the southern half. Annas moves swiftly down from his station, to then climb that belonging to Caiaphas, but only has to travel to the next station around in an anti-clockwise direction. Judas Iscariot is then positioned before them, accepting money to become Christ's traitor. In a major set piece, preparations for the last supper then start to be made, with Jesus washing the feet of his disciples. Characters such as Caiaphas and the Executioners all swear *By Mahound* [Mohammed] to display their 'irreligion'. To this Christian audience, Islamic belief meant 'pagan' and certainly non-Christian, so this method of declaring allegiance is used again and again in this drama, elsewhere in Britain, and in the other Cornish plays of the period. There is a great incident when Peter cuts off the ear of the executioner named Malchus, and then it is healed by Jesus. The temptation of Peter by the Portress is another moment of high drama, often ignored by other observers.

When it comes to the abuse of Jesus, the executioners are extraordinarily violent towards him and, although gruesome to watch, this is where the theology of the message is most reinforced. The torturers delight in their aggression and buffeting against Jesus, this sequence being juxtaposed with Judas Iscariot's taking of his own life. It is unclear how the actor playing Judas would have achieved the hanging, but presumably a stage gibbet could have been brought into the arena, and the mock suicide been presented there. In a neat twist, based on the medieval idea that the soul of the body left through the mouth, Satan observes: '*the enf plos casadow / ny vyn does dre the anow / rag the crist by the amme* [Thy soul, dirty villain, / Will not come through thy mouth, / Because thou hast kissed Christ]'.[235] This is a motive which is also seen in *Pascon agan Arluth*.

Structurally, the dramatist(s) of 'Passio Christi' have a keen eye on delaying the inevitable, in order to build expectation in the audience. It was not the conclusion of the drama in the form of the crucifixion that created the dramatic interest, but rather the way in which the audience were led there. Therefore, the extended debate by the two doctors contributes to this process, as does the slapstick humour of the gaoler and his boy/servant (to be revisited in 'Resurrexio Domini'), the executioners' torturing of Christ, and then the comedy of the Smith and his Wife. The gaoler's boy does mention one local place-name in passing: '*alemma bys yn tryger / war ow fay lacka mester / ny alsen y thyerbyn* [From this place to Treguer, / On my faith, a worse master / I should not be able to meet him]'.[236] This is probably a reference to Trigg, the name given to the north-easternmost hundred of Cornwall, which again gives us a notion of the locality of the drama spreading beyond the immediacy of Penryn.

In another part of the delaying process, the drama is enhanced when Beelzebub visits Pilate's wife whilst she is sleeping. In an elaborate but inevitably foolish wheeze, Beelzebub warns Pilate's wife that great harm will come to their children '*mar pyth an guyryon dyswrys* [if the innocent be destroyed]'.[237] In the sequence that follows, the executioners take great pains to explain what they will do to Christ. As Murdoch notes, much emphasis is placed on the thorns piercing the brain of Christ (a motif also seen in *Pascon agan Arluth* and *Bewnans Meriasek*),[238] the dramatist(s) clearly relishing the graphic reality of the process. The Second Executioner comments:

> *aban na fyn dowethe*
> *me a vyn y curune*
> * auel myghtern yethewon*
> *otte spern grisly gyne*
> *ha dreyn lym ha scharp ynne*
> * a grup bys yn empynon*

> [Since he will not end,
> I will crown him
>   As King of the Jews.
> See sharp thorns with me,
> And spines rough and sharp in them,
>   To pierce even to the brains.][239]

The run-up to the crucifixion is both brutal and comic, with the torturers delighting in their task. The link between Adam (the first Christ figure) and Christ is made by the finding of the Rood being used as a bridge at Cedron. Local detail is again added. We learn, for example, that when the executioners are called back by Pilate, the First Executioner admits that '*my re bye war ow ene / ov themloth may then pur squyth* [I was, on my soul, / Wrestling till I was very much tired]'.[240] There is a thread of continuity forwards here, for it was in the sixteenth century, as we shall see, that the London stage often presented the typical stage Cornishman as a wrestler. It is the Fourth Executioner who must call upon the Smith for the nails that are required. The Smith and his Wife are two excellent comic studies, the Smith himself being a dullard, whilst his Wife henpecks and gets on with the job, no doubt raising smiles from those women permitted to watch. Her down-to-earth ordering around of the Fourth Executioner is again a skilled piece of social realism, integrated into the wider story:

> *ty a whyth auel caugh guas*
> *whyth war gam vyngeans y'th glas*
> * ny dryk gryghonen yn fok*
> *powes lemmyn losel was*
> *ha knouk an horn tys ha tas*
> * mar ny wreth ty a fyth crok*

211

Fig. 33. Pilate's wife sleeps, while a devil tempts her, from the 1969 production of *Ordinalia* at Perran Round. Courtesy of University of Bristol Theatre Collection.

[Thou blowest like a dirty fellow.
Blow athwart, vengeance on thy maw,
  There remains not a spark in the forge.
Stop now, idle fellow,
And strike the iron, tick-a-tack;
  If thou dost not, thou shalt be hanged.[241]

The Smith and his Wife's stage time is relatively short, but it is just apt enough to draw back from the tragedy that is about to happen to Jesus. The fact that comedy can occur in tandem with the tragedy is not necessarily dramatically or theologically incorrect. It was simply emphasising the ignorance of humankind to Christ's suffering. The eventual crucifixion probably took place somewhere near the bank where the Centurion is positioned. Logically, this would be half-way between the station of Caiaphas, and Heaven. At the crucifixion itself, the dramaturgy calls for dramatic effects – the darkening over of the sun (an eclipse?),[242] and an earthquake – although clearly such demands would present production problems. 'Passio Christi' ends with two sections of drama that are not directly sourced from the Bible. The first is the legendary curing of the blind soldier Longeus [Longinus], whose eyesight is repaired after he thrusts his spear into Christ's side. Christ's blood runs down the spear and into his eye. Here, the dramatist(s) use four syllable verse units to express Longeus's wish for forgiveness: *'arluth thy'm gaf · del y'th pysaf · war pen dewlyn / an pyth a wren · my ny wothyen / rag ny wylyn* [Lord, forgive me · as I pray thee / On my knees: what I did · I knew not, / For I did not see]'.[243] The other non-Biblical scene is with Nicodemus, who will play a leading role in the final play. It is Mary, Joseph of Arimathea and Nicodemus who conclude events here.

'Resurrexio Domini' offers approximately the same number of sequences as that found in 'Origo Mundi'. It is of a similar length; if this was desired by the playwright(s), then it shows a certain awareness of structure and patterning. The text of 'Resurrexio Domini' is actually subdivided into three sections, and there may even be a case for presenting these as three separate dramas. If 'Resurrexio Domini' makes up the first half of the drama, this is then followed by *'morte pilati* [The Death of Pilate]', which lasts from Lines 1587 to 2360. The second sequence is then followed by a third component, which is named *'et incipit ascension Xti in celum* [And the Ascension to heaven begins]'. Therefore, although commonly titled 'Resurrexio Domini' as a whole, the final day of the *Ordinalia* is actually composed of three smaller sub-sections: the Resurrection itself, the Death of Pilate and the Ascension. 'The Resurrection' as a whole can be divided up in the following way:

The Imprisonment of Joseph of Arimathea and Nicodemus
The Harrowing of Hell
The Freeing of Joseph of Arimathea and Nicodemus
The Setting of the Watch
The Resurrection and Christ's Meeting with the Virgin
The Soldiers with Pilate
The Marys at the Tomb
Magdalene and the Gardener
Doubting Thomas, and Christ's appearance to the Apostles
The Journey to Emmaus
Christ's appearance to Thomas and the Other Apostles

These sequences are then followed by the Death of Pilate and the Ascension of Christ. One of the dramatic difficulties of 'Resurrexio Domini' for modern audiences is the seemingly disproportionate time spent on Doubting Thomas; this is the reason why, in two of the most recent performances of the drama (in 1969 and 2004),[244] the Thomas sequences were heavily cut. What must have been an intriguing debate for the late medieval Cornish audience is tiresome for contemporary onlookers, and is perhaps the only section of the drama where the pace drops. Because the play was connected with the Collegiate Church at Glasney, it was part of the conceptual integrity of the work that Thomas had to feature at length. The play itself neatly follows on from the Passion, with the release from prison of Nicodemus and Joseph of Arimathea, the Resurrection of Christ, the Harrowing of Hell, and (while disguised as a gardener) his encounter with Mary Magdalene, and the three Marys. Meanwhile, the protracted disbelief of Thomas contrasts with the ultimate faith of Mary Magdelene. The sub-plot to 'Resurrexio Domini', the death of Pilate, provided the producers of the play several opportunities for comedy and special effects when Pilate's corpse is rejected by the earth and the River Tiber. Eventually his body is carried off by the devils, while the play concludes with the Ascension. Another diagram in MS. 791 gives us an understanding of the dramaturgy in this play.[245] On the third day, Hell is again in its northern position, as in 'Origo Mundi', while the rest of the Round, clockwise, has the following stations: *Celum* [Heaven], *milites* [soldiers], *Nicodhemus* [Nicodemus] *Ioseph abarmathia* [Joseph of Arimathea], *Imperator* [Emperor], *pilatus* [Pilate], *infernum* [Hell] and *tortures* [torturers].

In the opening half of the drama the audience witness a series of miracles, which provide the dramatist with both challenges to stage-craft, and ways of accentuating the significance of Christ's resurrection. The play begins with Joseph of Arimathea arriving to speak to Pilate, who is on his station. Joseph of Arimathea is presented as assured and reasonable, probably what a Cornish audience would want of him. Both Joseph and Nicodemus are convinced of the imminent resurrection, and for this belief Pilate jails them. The exact location of the prison is not revealed but presumably, because no-one either ascends or descends, was probably somewhere in the arena. In a spectacular scene that follows, the Spirit of Christ accomplishes the Harrowing of Hell (in a dramatic presentation of what is seen as an image in a wall-painting at Lanivet Church[246]). Conceptually this is a very important sequence since it unites Adam and Eve with Christ and temporarily defeats the devils. Presumably this would have been a set-piece expected by the audience. Meanwhile, in the plain, Adam encounters two prophets, Elijah and Enoch, while the thief Dysmas confirms their suggestions as to what will happen next. Three bitter speeches follow from Tulfric, Beelzebub and Satan, the latter observing that '*gallas mur a enefow / a peyn hagh a tewolgow / ellas ellas* [Gone are the many souls / From pain and darkness. Alas! Alas!]'.[247]

One of the most spectacular events of the drama is the resurrection itself. The dramatic lead-in to the sequence features four soldiers who proclaim to Pilate their fear about Christ escaping from the tomb. This is actualised when the soldier sleeps and Christ rises from the dead. The stage direction reads '*iet*

Fig. 34. The costume designs for God, the Cherub, Adam and Eve, and a Devil imagined for the 1969 production of *Ordinalia* at Perran Round. Courtesy of University of Bristol Theatre Collection.

ubicunque voluerit [he shall go wherever he likes]'.[248] Jesus meets a comforted Mary, while the soldiers wake up. They are presented as incompetent fools, with Pilate labelling them *'fals merregion* [false knights]'[249] for letting Christ escape. The audience then witness the strength of the three Marys: Mary Magdalene, Mary, Mother of James and Mary Salome and, in a beautifully crafted sequence, Christ eventually comes to Mary Magdalene, disguised as a gardener. Here the four syllable units of verse work not only to make the sense breathless and immediate, but to reinforce the wonder of the resurrection. Christ speaks the following words of comfort:

> *maria myr · ov pym woly*
> *crys my the wyr · the thasserghy*
> *thy's y whon gras · rak the thesyr*
> *ioy yn ow golas · y fyth pur wyr*

> [Mary, see · my five wounds,
> Believe me truly · to be risen;
> To thee I acknowledge thanks · for thy desire,
> Joy in my land · shall be very truly.][250]

The following extended device of Thomas facilitates theological discussion about the nature of the resurrection, but the audience are expected to react with their own disbelief at Thomas's doubt. Fixing Thomas as the doubter had already been achieved in the Bible, but the dramatist uses this fact to connect with the immediate community of the Collegiate church. To have the symbolic figurehead of the local church be the biggest sceptic can be seen as a brilliant piece of dramatic irony. It takes two travellers, Cleophas and his Companion, who have met Christ, to try to convince Thomas that he is wrong. Even then, he is still doubtful, and only the risen Christ can make Thomas believe. He asks him: *'a Thomas doro the luef / yn woly guynys may fuef / dre an golon* [O Thomas, put thy hand / Into the wound where I was pierced / Through the heart]'.[251] Thus the resurrection is given reality for the audience, with the hand in the wound mimed.

The Death of Pilate sub-section has a clever compositional structure, for it balances the faith of the Emperor Tiberius (who is cured when he is shown an image of Christ by Veronica) and Pilate's fate to undergo a Christ-like trial. Pilate commits suicide, and here another parallel is shaped. The comical attempts to bury Pilate may be another opportunity to use the capella pit, since it could both accept the body and then, shortly afterwards, refuse it. The executioners who must now deal with Pilate fear he has the powers of a sorcerer;

indeed, in the way that Pilate's death is shaped by the dramatist, there is a sense that he is attempting to make Pilate 'magical'; only there is a kind of grossness to his end, which the audience must feel was justified. It is entirely fitting that the devils carry off his soul to Hell; all this to the accompaniment of a grotesque song. Pilate's acceptance into Hell then leads to the Ascension itself, with Jesus in Heaven with nine Angels beside him. Redemption has been granted to humankind. Jesus confirms this with *'map den my re wruk prenne / gans gos ow colon na fe / neop a wrussyn ny kyllys* [Mankind I have redeemed / With the blood of my heart, that there may not be / Any that we should lose]'.[252] It is the Emperor Tiberius who closes the play, and the whole trilogy, by summarising events and requesting celebration. Murdoch has usefully summarised the theology offered by the drama:

> Those who witnessed (as the audience has just witnessed) the miraculous events are saved, and the literal opening of Longinus' eyes underscores this; those who (again like the audience) witness only an image, like Tiberius, or are told of the events, like Thomas, can be saved. Only continued and obdurate rejection or complete despair leads to damnation, and the damnation is as real as Paradise.[253]

Presumably, although Murdoch's observation is about the *Ordinalia*, such a comment would be applicable to the numerous other dramas presented across Cornwall during the same phase. When one considers the power of the dramatic message in promoting the Christian faith, it is a very strong way of engendering faith. That kind of faith, which arose from the dramas, or at least was enhanced by them, had grown and developed throughout the previous two centuries, at least to the middle of the sixteenth century. We know, though, that despite the success of the genre, its days were somewhat numbered. However, before we move on from the *Ordinalia*, there is at least one other area of its dramaturgy worth considering. Richard Rastall has done much to heighten our understanding of the musical elements of the *Ordinalia*, showing that although 'aural effects did not play a large part in any of the thinking behind the cycle' there were nevertheless a number of stage directions, lines and passages of music which do contribute to the drama. In his work *The Heaven Singing: Music in Early English Religious Drama*,[254] Rastall outlines the philosophical and ideological framework of music within early drama, while in a companion volume, *Minstrels Playing: Music in Early English Religious Drama II*,[255] he offers a detailed consideration of musical motifs. In the opening of 'Origo Mundi', the dramatist pays considerable attention to the way Eve hears an angel singing to her. It is, of course, the devil trying to tempt her. The Devil also comments *'the behe may fe ellas / aga han kepar ha my* [so

217

that 'alas' may be / their song like as mine]',[256] with Satan then addressing Beelzebub with '*my a gan an conternot ha ty dyscant ym-kener* [I shall sing the counter note, And thou shalt sing descant with me]'.[257] Various observations are also made by Seth, the First Messenger and Moses about minstrels and noise, but one of the more famous sequences comes from King David, who rhetorically comments on events and calls out for minstrelsy:

wehthoug menstrals ha tabours
trey-hans harpes ha trompours
cythol crowd fylh ha savtry
psalmus gyttrens ha nakrys
organs in weth cymbalys
recordys ha symphony

[Blow minstrels and tabours;
Three hundred harps and trumpets;
Dulcimer, fiddle, viol and psaltery;
Shawms, lutes, and kettle drums;
Organs, also cymbals,
Recorders, and symphony.][258]

Such a speech comes when David is saying sorry to God. His counsellor advises that the only way forward for him is to build a new temple to the glory of God in order to atone for his sins. 'Noise' within the drama is seen as negative. At various points, characters complete tasks without noise, such as the Second Carpenter here, who explains that '*gurys yv the temple heb son* [the temple is done without noise]',[259] the implication being that it is done without commotion. In the English cycles, song is usually used as a mechanism to allow the release of the souls from Limbo, but here, as in this speech of Maximilla, it has another purpose: '*del vyth gans the gorf prennys / adam hag eva kefrys / ha gorrys the nef gans can* [As by the body redeemed was / Adam, and likewise Eve / And placed in heaven with song]'.[260] Clearly, here the dramaturgy is enhanced by the song, but it is Adam and Eve's placing in Heaven which is recalled rather than the release. Here the music motifs are, of course, operating metaphorically. Actual music comes at the end of the first day, when King Solomon shouts '*a barth a'n tas Menstrels a ras / pebough whare* [In the name of the Father; minstrels, Pipe immediately]'.[261] Thus the cue for celebration at the end of the drama is given; this is presumably accompanied by dancing and general merriment − of the kind indicated, as we shall see later, in the Accounts from St Ives.[262] Such a cue firmly places the *Ordinalia* in the ritual

218

year, and within the framework of wider entertainment. Although the play was religious in theme, it was clearly followed by more secular entertainment.

In 'Passio Christi' music is also important within the dramaturgy. This is most noticeably seen in the sequence when the seven boys spread olive branches, palm, bay and box, flowers and their own clothes before Jesus. There has been some debate here about whether the boys actually sing at this moment (particularly on '*bynyges yv map a ras / yn hanow dev devethys* [Blessed is the Son of grace / Who is come in the name of God]',[263] but it is unclear, since the text does not actually mention the dramatic entry into the City. Pilate asks Jesus about the children who are singing, so perhaps the actual song occurred between the boys' speeches and the address by Pilate to Jesus. Whatever way this was dramatised, the scene would have been quite spectacular, and somewhat touching for the audience to witness, particularly if the boys ranged in age. Presumably, boys were allowed to perform, though we have little under-standing of where they were recruited, or what further roles they had in the performance (although we know one probably performed with the gaoler). As we may expect, in the Passion, it is then the devils who use musical metaphor to good effect: Lucifer offers '*belsebub whek wheyth the corn / ha galwy dre a pup sorn / an thewolow* [Sweet Beelzebub, blow thy horn, And call through every corner / The devils]';[264] while Beelzebub himself says, '*me a whyth gans mur a grys / kymyuer dyaul vs yn beys / certan yn ta may clewfo* [I will blow with much force, Every devil that is in the world, Certainly, that he may hear well]'.[265] This volume has already commented on the significance of Joseph of Arimathea as an icon for the Cornish. The same may also be said perhaps of Beelzebub who, of all the devils, seems to have a particular resonance with the Cornish. We should note that is is Beelzebub who singularly manages to transfer himself as a character from plays such as the *Ordinalia* into a common figure of the Christmas mumming dramas of Cornwall. Later, in 'Resurrexio Domini', Beelzebub is heard to comment '*ha ty tulfryk pen pusorn / dalleth thy'nny ny cane* [And thou Tulfric, the end of a song / Begin to sing to us]',[266] with Tulfric responding with '*belsebub ha sattanus / kenough why faborden bras / ha me a can trebly fyn* [Beelzebub and Satan, You sing a great bass, / And I will sing a fine treble]'.[267] Such dramaturgy was clearly working as a parody of liturgical music, with Beelzebub as ultimate 'un-rule'.

One more unusual musical aspect of the drama also comes in 'Resurrexio Domini'. This comes in the song – or perhaps spoken ritual – of Mary Salome, which then encourages all three Marys to sing. Interestingly, this section is in English, and the complexities of how this chant is to be performed are debated at length by Rastall. One can only imagine that, in an alarmingly close similarity to what was to happen to Cornish on the London stage in the sixteenth and seventeenth centuries, the dramatist was here using English as something 'exotic', proving the 'otherness' of what the three Marys were experiencing:

> *ellas mornygh y syngh*
> > *mornyngh y cal*
> *our lord ys deyd that boghte*
> > *ovs al*

> [Alas! mourning I sing,
> > mourning I call,
> Our Lord is dead that bought
> > us all.][268]

An alternative resolution of this issue is that the refrain was too difficult to interpret or, perhaps, even by this stage was known commonly enough for it not to require translation. It already rhymed. In either case, the drama of the *cantant* which follows must have been emotionally charged. Fortunately, the satire of the devils is counteracted by the Fifth Angel at the end of the drama who, matching his lines, would be physically on the upper level of the station symbolising Heaven. Thus space, place and performance are intricately combined to sophisticated effect: '*joy del yl ov dythane / ny ny tywyn ow cane / Gloria in excelsis deo* [As joy may gladden me, / Let us not be silent, singing / Glory to God in the highest!]'.[269] According to Rastall, this kind of ending was a 'blessed' one, and as such gave legitimacy to move to the Emperor's lines of '*now minstrels pybygh bysy / may hyllyn mos the thonssye* [Now minstrels, pipe diligently, / That we may go to dance]'.[270] The celebration this time is more intense, because the audience has now witnessed the Death of Pilate, and the Ascension. In all, Rastall's work perhaps reinforces the fact that music is an underestimated part of the dramaturgy of works such as the *Ordinalia*, and that scholarship should pay more attention to the way in which music was used in dramas of this kind. Although recent conferences have tried to tease out more understanding of early music in Cornwall,[271] the area is in some ways even more shadowy than theatre and drama. There is, however, a connection backwards here – to several of the words from the *Old Cornish Vocabulary*.[272] Although it is harder, outside of the play texts, to locate and link performance with music, it surely must have happened in both this kind of context, and with touring performance as well.

So, we recognise the remarkable skill in dramaturgy of the *Ordinalia*. We also note, in contrast to many of the English cycle dramas, that it has a unified structure and pattern. The work, for all its compromises (apparent cheats in rhyme, moments of Anglicisation, pandering to low tastes), is actually progressive and multi-dimensional. Indeed, an alternative way of looking at the text would be to argue that its apparent weaknesses and compromises are its very strengths, that the *Ordinalia* successfully demonstrates not only 'materially' Cornish literary culture during this phase, but also the living socio-linguistics of its moment of production. As I have continued to argue, we need to move away from the model of production that promotes a mono-lingual state.[273] This feature of imagined Cornish history is certainly not the case, as can be clearly seen in the *Ordinalia*. The remaining question is who wrote it? In exploring this, it is interesting to examine the variety of writers operating in and around the theatrical culture of pre-Reformation Cornwall. However, whilst it is interesting to speculate, we should also be guarded in trying to answer such a question for inevitably it will be unprovable.

In all likelihood, we shall never truly know who composed the text, or who gave input to its evolution. However, the literary culture of this period is perhaps no better embodied than in the life and work of John Trevisa. According to David C. Fowler, who has spent considerable academic energy studying him, Trevisa (c.1342-1402) was probably born at St Enoder in mid-Cornwall.[274] Since the Parish of St Enodor was appropriated to Glasney Collegiate Church, it is likely that Trevisa began his education there, rising by 1360 to the position of clerk, for which the minimum age was eighteen. Finally, when he was about twenty years old, with the help of an influential patron (probably of the Berkeley family) he entered Exeter College, Oxford in 1362.[275] Trevisa was a Cornish speaker and writer, although his fame as a writer is usually derived from how he helped to save the English language. As Weatherhill has detailed, the Norman Conquest saw the status of English relegated to the role of the subjugated.[276] With Norman-French the language of the new rules, English was rapidly becoming extinct elsewhere in Britain. Trevisa wrote how John of Cornwall, a master of grammar, replaced French with English in grammar schools, and how he had taught English to a Cornishman, Richard Pencrych, who, in turn, taught others; thus English was revived.[277] Trevisa contributed to the process himself by translating Ranulf Higden's *Polychronicon*, providing the English with the largest history and encyclopedia of their history and culture in their own tongue. All this is perhaps quite ironic, seeing the fate of Cornish in the next few centuries. How much material, therefore, did Trevisa write in Cornish, and could he have developed a play? With St Enoder as an attested *plen-an-gwarry* site, a link is not impossible; neither is Trevisa's potential contribution from Oxford, when still a relatively young man.

Fowler has offered evidence (not all completely convincing) that Trevisa was responsible for the revisions of *Piers the Plowman* (now known as the B and C texts), with a considerable proportion of the evidence based on the 'very Cornish' aspects of the imagery used.[278] There is complex reasoning behind this theory, and it is surmised with thirty-eight pieces of evidence. One of the most significant is at XI, 332-253 of the B and C version of *Piers the Plowman*, where the list of God's creation (animals and birds) is near identical to that in 'Origo Mundi'. Other evidence includes the use of the Cornish word '*goky* [stupid]', and mention of a wrestling match, similar Ascension imagery, and other what Fowler terms 'southwesternisms'.[279] Obviously, if Trevisa were an author of the *Ordinalia*, then there might be even more evidence to assert this view. Fowler's position has been broadly dismissed by the establishment, but it does open up some interesting debate. Fowler himself indicates that in no way was Trevisa involved in either the writing or developmental construction of the *Ordinalia*, feeling that the cycle belongs to 'the third quarter of the fourteenth century' and was thus completed during the time that Trevisa was at Oxford, engaging in translation work and the recovery of English, steadily side-stepping his indigenous culture.[280] Other scholars have looked at this information anew. Symons, taking an altogether more controversial line, argues that Trevisa would singularly have been in the right place at the right time for the construction of at least the first draft of the *Ordinalia*, though perhaps not in the way traditionally imagined – as Cornish community playwright based at Glasney; hence, perhaps, the similar 'Cornishisms' in the B and C *Piers the Plowman* texts.

Symons's argument, however, is less related to Fowler's linguistic argument, and rather more to Trevisa's other achievement: the translation of the Bible into English. Work on the so-called Wycliffite Bible occurred between 1372 and 1376 at Queen's College; Trevisa, John Wycliff and Nicholas of Hereford were the lead translators.[281] However, a number of objectors tried to stop the process, among them Thomas Carlisle. It was Trevisa's involvement in the translation process that eventually led to him being expelled from Oxford due to his 'unworthiness'. From thereon, he took up a position as Vicar of Berkley Castle in Gloucestershire. This background is crucial to Symons's argument, which is worth reproducing at length:

> The *Ordinalia* is not a dramatization of scripture, the playwright takes consider-able liberties with scripture, but [offers] a theological interpretation of scripture. He is interpreting in accordance with his understanding of the theology of the time. A number of strands are discernible: a theology of salvation and grace; a theology of the Eucharist; a theology of the Trinity; a theology of the Church.

He is orthodox in the first but in the fourth he is antagonistic to the establishment. From Trevisa's other writings we know that he rejected the temporalities of the Church, and accepted the right of the secular authorities to dispossess. He also recognised the right of the laity to have the Bible in the vernacular and *sola scriptura*. In his various translations Trevisa shows himself willing to play fast and loose with the text so as to convey the meaning, and even to change the meaning for his own purposes. The various asides we find in *Ordinalia* are typical of the asides found in other writings.[282]

We therefore have a picture of Trevisa as quite a subversive and dangerous scholar for the establishment. This is borne out in Symons's further observations:

Did Trevisa translate the Bible? In his translations Trevisa was trying to construct an English capable of standing with French and Latin in expressive power. Whether he considered his achievements sufficient to go on to the Bible is questionable. Furthermore the academies of the time were deficient in Bible languages, even the Vulgates came in various forms; there was no standard. Translating the Bible into the vernacular held problems, both ways. There can be no question, however, that the Wycliffites at Oxford were working on a translation, but at a very foundational level. The authorities became scared: 1. because they feared a vernacular Bible which might challenge their interpretation; 2. because they knew that Trevisa and Wycliff would use it to challenge the Church temporalities. So they moved into Oxford and had Trevisa and his circle expelled. That is the reason, I suggest, behind the expulsions. I imagine that Trevisa was eventually allowed back because he had broken with Wycliff over the Eucharist, and possibly because he promised not to engage in Bible work while at Oxford. The translators of the King James Bible mention Trevisa in the introduction which has led people to hunt for a Trevisa Bible or has caused them to dismiss the acknowledgement. I think that Trevisa continued to work on the Bible while at Berkeley, but not in the form of a continuous narrative. His work was linguistic and interpretive. The King James scholars accessed this material and acknowledged Trevisa in the introduction. We must stop looking for a Trevisa Bible and start looking for something else.[283]

It is the phrases 'not in the form of a continuous narrative' and 'start looking for something else' alongside the above set of theological difficulties, which Symons believes possibly inspired Trevisa to write the *Ordinalia*, and which made the full cycle much longer than the extant version:

Did Trevisa translate the Bible into Cornish? The same problems arise as with translating into English. His answer was a dramatisation in which he tried to convey the meaning of the text, at least as he saw it, in a popular form. He set this out in terms of the readings of the Catholic year. The New Testament ones move from the incarnation at Christmas, through Lent to Easter. The New Testament section of the *Ordinalia* has the incarnation missing. Without it, the Catholic theology is truncated. There also needs to be a section on the Old Testament prophets and the captivity in Babylon, because they relate directly to the incarnation. Two sections have been lost. So it was a five day cycle. Were these performed on five consecutive days or on individual days throughout the year? It may be because they were performed in Cornish that the authorities failed to recognise the subversive elements.[284]

Certainly, there is more work to do here, and Symons's argument completely subverts received wisdom about the *Ordinalia*. The problem with the Trevisa argument is that we know he translated many texts into English and assisted with Bible translation, but beyond that the knowledge is too sketchy. The difficulties may be summarised as follows: firstly, Trevisa's input into the text would need to be further contextualised, because a far more likely author is obviously one of the canons at Glasney College. Secondly, although Symons comments on the unusual nature of the *Ordinalia*, the play itself has some unusual moments: for example, the David and Bathsheba story. Thirdly, the absence of the birth of Christ does not necessarily damage the overall theology. Here we need only look to the Gospels of St Mark and St John, which do not feature that either. Likewise, there are a number of other continental European works which also do not feature nativity sequences, one example being the *Osterspiele*.[285] Finally, it would need to somehow be proven that Trevisa could contribute to the motif of the Holy Rood, because that is what makes the *Ordinalia* so distinctive. At present, there is not enough evidence to prove this.

However, an argument such as Symons's does alter our conventional, somewhat safe reading of an anonymous *Ordinalia*, indicating that this was, in fact, a quite radical piece of theatre. Far from it being an ideologically-safe reading of scripture (as has been often promoted in the past[286]), it may well be something quite different. The subversion indicated here is also present in *Bewnans Ke* and *Bewnans Meriasek*,[287] so Symons's work has some support. A political and radical view of the nature of the Cornish canon would seem to continue to garner further support. Even if Trevisa was not connected to the *Ordinalia*, then he is still a writer in this period who would have been aware of the tradition, and would have encountered this kind of dramaturgy. His position as a Cornish scholar, but operating in a sometimes problematical English context, is the earliest manifestation of what we also see in later writers such as Arthur Quiller-Couch, A.L. Rowse and J.C. Trewin. Like Trevisa, what makes them interesting is that they stand for what Bhabha called 'culture's in-between'.[288] Trevisa may well be a bigger cultural force than we have previously imagined; but then again, he may also *not be;* there is no proof.

With Trevisa in the frame as a dramatist, we should also look elsewhere for potential playwrights. Elliott-Binns records the names of some other writers during the early medieval period. Among these were Robert Luc de Cornubia (who was at Oxford in the early 1320s), Michael Trewinnard, Thomas Trevett, Godfrey of Cornwall, and Michael of Tregury. Elliott-Binns gives little detail about them, or his sources.[289] The problem is that if they wrote at all, none of their texts have survived the ravages of time. If these scholars were educated in Cornwall, and then proceeded to Exeter College, Oxford, then they stand as possible creators and writers of drama. A little more is known, however, of Godfrey of Cornwall, and Michael of Tregury. Godfrey of Cornwall, who was alive in 1320, was born, interestingly, in St Stephen-in-Brannel, and was educated at Oxford and Paris, becoming Reader in Divinity at the latter.[290] He eventually joined the Carmelites and wrote in defence of that Order. William of Cornwall, Abbot of Newenham in 1272, is believed to have been his brother. From lowly origins in Cornwall, both of these men seem to have had a pan-European influence. Of course, it is hard to think of Godfrey without thinking of the *Charter Endorsement*. He is a bit early to be its creator, since the *Endorsement* is usually dated around 1380, but is closer to the Charter itself (from 1340).

Michael of Tregury – or just Michael Tregury – is a more spectacular example of Cornish academic and religious success. Tregury was born in the mid-Cornwall parish of St Wenn, and educated at Exeter College, Oxford.[291] Certainly, he would have been a Cornish speaker and writer, though he became a distinguished scholar and cleric. First chaplain to Henry VI, then rector of the University of Caen in 1440, he eventually became the Archbishop of Dublin in the years 1450-1471.[292] This was a quite meteoric rise, but it is possible that his earliest written work may have been dramatic. St Wenna (d. 18 October 544) was a Cornish saint and Queen, who may have made good subject matter.[293] Another early writer was Girard of Cornwall (Girard Cornubiensis) who was certainly operating around 1350, writing *De gestis Britonum* and *De gestis Regum West-Saxonum*,[294] but he seems to have been rather more of a historian than a playwright. These two texts might offer further insight into the development of post-Roman and early-medieval Cornwall, but appear to have been lost. A final early writer is William de

Grenfild (Grenville), who was the son of Sir Theobald Grenville of Stowe in North Cornwall. Grenville became Dean of Chicester, eventually Chancellor of England when he was elected Archbishop of York in 1304.[295] He was probably middle-aged by the time he gained this position, so we can infer that he would have been born around 1260, when Cornish had already retreated beyond a line from Crackington Haven to Launceston. Therefore, although an interesting figure, he is unlikely to have been a Cornish-language dramatist of any note. It was also a period before dramatic work was legitimised for the clergy. The emerging pattern is that if these men were writers of Cornish-language drama, then they would most probably have to have completed it when they were younger, because their careers take them outside of Cornwall in their early twenties. Perhaps the production of a Cornish-language drama was even a rite-of-passage event.

Other names of playwrights have, however, been considered, especially in the fifteenth and sixteenth centuries. Among these is Master John Pascoe, who was ordained as an acolyte at Clyst on 23 February 1426, and received his tonsure at Helston on 19 August 1427. He later became subdeacon at Chudleigh in 1429, and a priest at Crediton in 1430. On 18 February 1451 'Master John Pascowe, rector of Camborne' was licensed to receive penances and hear confessions, while also working for a while at Lanreath. Sometime before 1463, he must have gained a prebend at Glasney, but by 1497 had resigned this role, on being collated to provostship. As quite an old man, he must have exerted considerable leadership over activities at Glasney College. Whetter observes that 'it must have been under the old, venerable provost that productions of the plays were fostered and fortunately and unusually committed to paper'.[296] Given Pascoe's links to Camborne, Whetter also feels that the play of *The Life of St Meriasek* was actually a response to Bishop Bronescombe's desire to replace the older Celtic saints with Latin ones.[297] Pascoe may have been important in using the drama as a method of counter-acting this practice.

Pascoe's successor was Sir John Oby, who had previously held the sacristianship.[298] Oby's origins are not known, but on Pascoe's resignation he was collated provost. He was also vicar at St Gluvias, and there is some physical evidence of performance taking place there.[299] However, Oby seems less of a playwright, and more of an administrator. In 1497 he was unpopularly acting as a tax collector, and was later murdered in Somerset. In terms of his support for Cornish-language theatre, he seems to have been a less sympathetic figure than John Pascoe. Two other figures also enter the frame as possible playwrights. These were Master John Nans and Alexander Penhylle.[300] Nans was Cornish, intellectually gifted, and attended the University of Oxford, where he became doctor of law He travelled to Bologna, becoming rector of both universities there, demonstrating the pan-European nature of Cornish intelligentsia during this period. He also spent time in Herefordshire, but by the early 1490s he was back in Cornwall, installed as the vicar of Gwennap, and gaining a prebend at Glasney. Like Oby, Nans also suffered in the political upheaval of the rebellions of 1497, and seems to have resigned in 1501. For a while (1504-05) Nans became rector at Redruth, but by 1509 he was dead. Significantly, Gwennap and Redruth are both possible *plen-an-gwarry* locations,[301] so perhaps Nans was active as a dramatist. He certainly would have had the intellectual capability for the task. Whetter observes that he was 'probably a supporter of the Cornish literary revival at Glasney'.[302] Penhylle, meanwhile, had graduated from Exeter College, Oxford. Appointed rector at Illogan church, he was instituted as a prebend at Glasney in 1495. Whetter, however, thinks Penhylle less likely to be a dramatist,[303] and more likely to have been a supportive and sympathetic head of the college, creating the right kind of conditions for performance. Thus, Whetter concludes that:

> it is probably to the lesser ranks in the college that one should look for the answer [to who was writing drama], to members of full-time staff, for instance, vicars associated with Radolphus Ton, who spent time in the scriptorium and were involved in the life of the local community, particularly in the production of plays.[304]

The figures of Pascoe, Oby, Nans and Penhylle may not have been playwrights themselves, but they certainly would have been actively involved in promoting the genre. This observation and knowledge brings us back to two central observations: first of all, that the writing of drama was perhaps deemed a young man's activity, in order to gain cultural and theological understanding; secondly, that there was – as perhaps demonstrated by events in Camborne – quite a degree of devolved literary activity away from Glasney. One thus gains an impression of texts sometimes being generated outside of the confines of the Glasney scriptorium but taken to men such as Pascoe, Oby, Nans and Penhylle for approval. In this way, there would be an operative blending of the community with the intellectual and theological centre of Cornwall. Frost, although looking at a slightly later period, concerned with the translation of Bishop Bonner's homilies by John Tregear, appears to argue that, in the sixteenth century, ecclesiastical writing conducted under the aegis of Glasney was actually undertaken in the nearby parishes of mid- and west Cornwall, rather than at the college itself. Frost therefore argues that it 'was the humble clergy that ran the parishes in west Cornwall from which Glasney drew its tithes' who performed much of 'the work to preserve traditional religion through the medium of Cornish'.[305] Frost's analysis would appear to confirm much of what has been said above, and during the course of this chapter. In the process, Frost identifies a number of other possible writers – among them Thomas Stephen, Ralph Trelobys and interestingly, a Richard Ton – the latter perhaps the mysterious Rad Ton, as discussed next.

More is known of the origins of *Bewnans Meriasek* [*The Life of St Meriasek*]. The manuscript, titled *Ordinale de Meradoc, espiscopi et confessor*, would seem to have been completed by one Dominus Hadton (or Rad [olphus] or Ricardus Ton) in 1504. His name is found at the end of the manuscript: '*Finitur per dominum Hadton anno domini ML VC IIII* [completed by Master Hadton in 1504]'.[306] It was Gilbert Doble who first proposed that Hadton was a misreading for Rad Ton, and therefore Radolphus, or Ricardus.[307] Ton was believed to have been a Canon at Glasney, though probably with connections to Camborne, where Meriasek (or Meriadoc[308]) is one of the patron saints. A difficulty with this reading is that the first ten pages of the manuscript are not in the hand of Radolphus or Ricardus Ton, and are intriguingly written without the necessary stage-directions for performance.[309] Therefore Ton, in following other survivals, seems to have been engaged in the process of making some form of prompt copy.[310]

What makes the link to Camborne more convincing is that there are several references in the text to places and and events in west Cornwall, Penwith and Kerrier. Notably too, one of the main characters in the drama, the pagan tyrant King Teudar, had many associations with the Hayle area,[311] not too far distant from Camborne. The use of King Teudar as a stage villain also had other implications. The play was constructed when Henry Tudor was on the throne and, as Whetter notes, following the 1497 rebellions and 'the banishing of popular figures such as Henry Bodrugan',[312] the new king was not popular with the Cornish people. When Teudar is made to look a fool in the drama, the 184 'manucaptors', who represented almost every parish in Cornwall, must have enjoyed hearing about the play's narrative. In creating a character like Teudar – who would have been understood by those watching, but more difficult to understand by non-speakers of Cornish – the writer has employed skilful dramaturgy, and developed one of the finest pieces of political theatre from Cornwall.[313]

Although there is some doubt regarding Ton's authorship of the drama, and we must be careful in assigning him full authorship when he may well have only been the scribe, it is perhaps interesting to consider the play's origins. We know that such dramas were popular in Brittany as well as in Cornwall, and it becomes very clear that the author(s) of *Bewnans Meriasek* have fairly intimate knowledge of Breton traditions. Whetter certainly feels that 'the Cornish author must have had before him a copy of the Breton life of the saint, whose memory was cherished in the diocese of Vannes'.[314] Given the fusion of linguistic and liturgical culture between Brittany and Cornwall, however, this cultural duality is not entirely impossible. Indeed, there must have been a good deal of cross-fertilization of culture between the two territories. Whetter observes the following:

> From a complaint of a Truro custom-house officer, Alexander Carvennel, in 1537, it is known that in that year a party of Cornishmen, accompanied by the vicars of Newlyn East and St Agnes, were on a 'pope-holy pilgrimage' to Lantreger (Treguier) and undoubtedly such visits were common before the Reformation. Perhaps on one such pilgrimage a canon of Glasney, either at Treguier or Saint Jean-du-Doigt (a famous pilgrimage chapel sited on the coast and known to have possessed a copy a life of St Meriadoc) may have seen and made a copy of the life.[315]

Whetter also importantly notes how in the fifteenth-century links had grown up between the parish and Glasney, again supporting the more devolved method of writing outlined above.[316] Powerful Cornish families such as the Bassetts of Tehidy, claiming Norman ancestry, would have had no real interest in promulgating the Cornish language, but might have bowed to local pressure in funding and supporting those who wrote. Whetter goes further, offering that such families might also have been more supportive towards such projects if the material also encompassed Britain's Arthurian and Celtic inheritance, because it offered them legitimacy.[317] *Bewnans Meriasek* does contain this kind of material[318] and, as we shall see, it may be even more relevant to consider in the light of *Bewnans Ke*, which contains substantial Arthurian matter. Whetter observes that 'in Richard II's reign men from outside of Cornwall such as the Herle, Colshull, and Assheton families, acquired positions and estates in Cornwall, and it could be that the older-established gentry tended to emphasise their local links'.[319] This may explain why there was something of a literary revival.

All of this gives a useful materialist context for discussing *Bewnans Meriasek*.[320] The drama is both a miracle and a saint's play written in Middle Cornish, though perhaps with leanings toward 'Tudor'-period Cornish.[321] The newly-discovered *Bewnans Ke* (discussed below), and *The Life of St Meriasek* are the only two surviving vernacular plays in Britain dealing with the lives of saints. In terms of structure, content and versification, there are considerable similarities between them. The 4,569 lines, in seven- and four-syllabled verses, form an exuberant and multi-dimensional weaving together of historical and legendary characters from different centuries, with strong undertones (as noted above) of contemporary Cornish politics. Some 120 characters are required, with 99 speaking parts and, as Grigg notes, numerous properties, and multiple locations.[322] The work was performed over two days, in-the-round, offering, as Murdoch details, the twin soteriological themes of conversion and healing through miracles involving Meriasek, Sylvester, and the Virgin Mary – an important cult at both Glasney and Camborne.[323] It is, as he succinctly posits, a drama about 'church, state and salvation'.[324] Characters self-present – suggesting elements of an older dramaturgy – but what is spectacular about the work is both the range of characterisation and the sophistication in its construction. Within its complexity, there is a consistency of approach, suggesting a highly-skilled dramatist. That said, the work was doomed for performance in the second half of the sixteenth century because of its explicit Marianism, and only one manuscript copy of the drama has survived into the modern era. It was originally in the collection of the Welsh antiquarian Robert Vaughan (1592-1667), though how he obtained the manuscript is unclear. The manuscript was then inherited by W.W.E. Wynne of Peniarth in 1859, and was subsequently studied by the Reverend Robert Williams[325] and Whitley Stokes, eventually being donated in 1909 to the National Library of Wales, where it has remained ever since.[326]

According to tradition, St Meriasek lived in Brittany in the seventh century and is one of the patron saints of Camborne (the other being St Martin). Fitting the origins of the saint, about half of the drama is set in Brittany, with the remaining half split between Cornwall and Italy. In summary, the first day of the drama begins with Meriasek's education in Brittany. This is a highly comic sequence with a schoolmaster who is permanently drunk, and so immediately wins the audience's attention.[327] The Breton King, Conan, arranges a marriage to his daughter for Meriasek but his mind is set on rejecting worldly comforts. Meriasek chooses instead to join the priesthood. He travels as a Christ-like missionary to Cornwall, on the way calming a storm that almost wrecks the boat he is travelling in. In the following lines, Meriasek comforts the crew, his actions prompting praise from a sailor:

Mereadodus
A bethugh a confront da
crist agen gueres a ra
ha me a vyn y pesy
mar pe y voth indella
na rella den peryllya

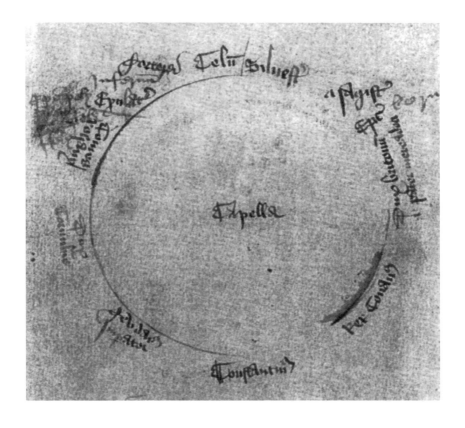

Fig. 35. Bewnans Meriasek: Peniarth, MS. 105, p.98. Reproduced by permission of the Llyfrgell Genedlaethol Cymru / National Library of Wales.

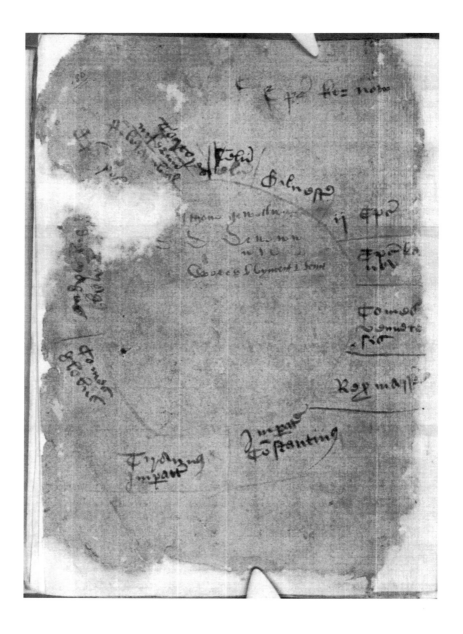

Fig. 36. Bewnans Meriasek: Peniarth, MS. 105, p.180. Reproduced by permission of the Llyfrgell Genedlaethol Cymru / National Library of Wales.

in tyr na mor in bysma
   mar creya war crist ha my

   Navta
Meryasek gorthys reby
drethos ol sawys on ny
   a peryl sur in torma
kegy in tyr a dremas
in kernov the ihesu gras
   theth desyr ty re dufa

   [*Meriasek*
O be ye of good comfort!
Christ will help us.
   And I will beseech him,
If such were his will
no man would be endangered
   If he called on Christ and me.

   The Sailor
Meriasek, worshipped be thou
Through thee we all are saved
   From peril surely at this time.
Go thou on land, O honest man.
In Cornwall, thanks to Jesu,
   According to thy desire thou hast come.][328]

Although comparatively short textually, this would presumably have been a moment where a boat would have been wheeled into the plain. The storm might have lent itself to various special effects, so this sequence would have maintained audience interest because of its spectacle. The above text also gives us a feel of the verse form, and the distinctive Cornish of *Bewnans Meriasek*, to which a number of observers have drawn attention.[329] When he arrives in Cornwall, Meriasek is able to cure the sick. After establishing an oratory or chapel at Camborne, he comes into conflict with the tyrant Teudar. Teudar is presented as a ranting pagan, in what Murdoch has called a 'composite of non-Christian elements' (Mahommed, Apollo, Jove, Sol as well as the demons Belsebuc and Monfras).[330] Appropriately, considering the importance of the Marian cult in Camborne, Meriasek and Teudar then debate the Virgin birth. Teudar is a cynic, whose verbosity and pride would have made him a detestable figure:

Sevys oys a woys worthy
  meryasek beth avysyys
rag dovt cafus velyny
  na govs tra na fue guelys
  me a lener
erbyn reson yv in beys
heb hays gorryth thymo creys
bones flogh vyth concevijs
  in breys benen heb awer

[Raised art thou of worthy blood.
  Meriasek, be advised.
For fear of getting disgrace,
  Speak not aught that has not be seen
  I say,
It is against all reason
Without a man's seed, believe me,
That a child is ever conceived
  In a woman's womb without difficulty][331]

Meriasek deftly counters Teudar's arguments, offering as analogy the poetic image of the sun passing through glass. Teudar, however, is still an unbeliever and he tries to tempt Meriasek. This is clearly a scene with echoes of the temptation of Christ; given all his other deeds, Meriasek is to be perceived by the audience in this way. Meriasek at first hides in a rock ('*carrek veryasek* [Meriasek's rock]'),[332] then returns to Brittany, where he becomes a hermit, performing a number of other miracles, including the taming of a wolf. In this, one can see the fast-paced nature of the drama, as well as the use of multiple locations and characters. The play then takes a change in direction because it now shifts to Italy. Some observers have commented on the difficult reconciliation of time periods in the drama, but in a way this does not matter, because all of the events are happening in a blended remote past. The past is connected via place. Again, it is a drama of landscape and community.

The focus then shifts on to St Sylvester, who heals a leprosy-stricken Constantine, who has plans to heal himself by bathing in the blood of children. This sequence (originally found in the *Legenda Aurea* [Golden Legend][333]) is where the unity of the drama is more fully developed, because again there is the symbolism of pagan and Christian belief. The blood of the children is contrasted with the baptism and healing of the Emperor. Sylvester, therefore, works as a link to both Meriasek and Christ, symbolically uniting the two across time and place. Considering the seriousness of events here, it is perhaps not surprising that the playwright uses two comic characters – a quack Doctor, and a Clerk named Jankyn – to offset events, and maintain the comic thread. This strand is then counter-balanced with Meriasek seen back in Brittany. There, he preaches holy poverty and, by prayer, generates fire to fall from the sky which ignites the forest. This frightens a group of outlaws, who are then converted to Christianity. An earlier thread is then revisited, when the drama returns to events in Cornwall, where the Duke of Cornwall (somewhat reminiscent of King Arthur), challenges Teudar's reign:

> Me yv duk in oll kernow
> > indella ytho ov thays
> hag vhel arluth in pov
> > a tamer the pen van vlays
> tregys off lemen heb wov
> > berth in castel an dynas
> > > sur in peddre
> ha war an tyreth vhel
> thym yma castel arel
> a veth gelwys tyndagyel
> > henna yv ofen tregse.

> [I am Duke in all Cornwall:
> > So was my father,
> And a high lord in the country
> > From Tamar to the Land's End.
> I am dwelling now, without a lie,
> > Within the castle of Dynas
> > > Surely in Pidar,
> And in the high land
> I have another castle,
> Which is called Tyntagel:
> > That is my chief dwelling seat.][334]

We note in this the explicit links to Arthurian sites (Castle-an-Dinas and Tintagel) and so, too, we observe a writer who was drawing on mythological connections. The cultural-geographic context of space is also alluded to, in defining the bounds of Cornwall. We can also read here the demands and importance of lineage ('So was my father'), so supporting the view that Teudar is a kind of interloper within a wider and longer historical pattern – paralleling the remote, but linked, nature of the whole of the play. In the build up to the battle, one of the Stewards informs the Duke of the whereabouts of Teudar. Although a relatively inconsequential speech, it is here that we see the cleverness of the way *Bewnans Meriasek* is developed, for the playwright laces the rhyme with local detail and place-names, which would have increased the immediacy of the performance:

> *Tregys vue in lestevdar*
> *honna yma in menek*
> *sav plas aral sur heb mar*
> *us then tebel genesek*
> *berth in porder*
> *honna veth gelwys goddren*
> *ena purguir en poddren*
> *thotho prest re ruk harber.*

> [He was dwelling in Lostowder.
>   This is in Meneage;
> But another place surely without doubt,
>   there is, native to the devil,
>   Within Powder,
> This is called Godren:
> There right truly the rotten fellow
>   Has made for himself a harbour.][335]

As Rastall details, the end of the play comes when Teudar is defeated, the Duke of Cornwall encouraging the audience to celebrate with drinking and dancing.[336] The defeat of Teudar at this stage in the two days is highly important in terms of the structure. Not only is the stage Henry Tudor mocked, but the very fact that the blessings of Christ and Mary are given suggests somehow that a natural and God-given order has returned. The celebration and music, like the territorial destiny, are completely consistent with the morality of the play. However, the audience are reminded that events are not finished, and that there will be more to see tomorrow. If the first day of *Bewnans Meriasek* is an example of the kind of epic drama being delivered in Cornwall, then we can quickly see that the themes, characterisation and action – and indeed its political undertones – are far more complex than much other drama occurring in the whole of Britain during this phase. This is often forgotten.

The direction of the second day of the drama not only builds upon the first day's events, but offers a series of reflections and ironic comments on what has already occurred. Given that the first day culminated in a battle, and that devices of spectacle such as miracles, ships and fire have already been used, the dramatist(s) needed to find other methods of developing the dramaturgy. This, I would offer, he achieves with considerable success. The action first begins in Italy with Constantine offering a recapitulation of events, but then returns to Brittany. Meriasek heals the blind Earl Globus (seemingly a non-historical invented character), a deaf man, a leper, and a demoniac. A sequence is then developed in which, after the Bishop of Vannes dies, Meriasek is chosen to succeed as bishop, first resisting, but eventually agreeing to the task. A link to Italy is offered because patents for this are sought from the now Pope Sylvester in Rome. In this way, the strands of the drama are united. The dramaturgy of Meriasek's resistance is conducted through debate, significantly, with the Bishop of Kernov (this would conveniently stand for both the district in Brittany [Cornouailles]) as well as Cornwall itself, so unifying the two places.

The next major sequence in the play, often called 'the woman and her son', has been described as a 'sub-plot' or even 'padding',[337] but this is not really the case, for it is intimately connected with the other themes of the drama, and more especially the interest in Marianism at Camborne. Put simply, a boy is imprisoned by a tyrant, and his mother prays before a statue of Mary, taking home the image of the infant Jesus when her supplications seem of no avail. Mary, with Jesus's blessing, frees the boy and, when he returns home, his mother restores the image of the baby to the statue.[338] The pagan tyrant is unnamed this time, though clearly there are echoes of Teudar in his behaviour. He is pitted against a King Massen, another Christian king, so echoing and developing the earlier themes. At the end of the sequence, the Mother expresses her thanks through prayer, but this is counter-pointed by other dramaturgy. The distinctive section is a mock black mass. As Murdoch observes, this may be 'viewed as a grotesque conglomerate of Satanism, a mis-understood and (since it is actually not polytheistic) ignorantly maligned Islam, and classical mythology'.[339] The pagan tyrant king's bullying torturers are devil-worshippers; in the temple, alongside the tyrant, they encounter some demons:

> *Primus Demon*
> *Duen ny lemmen then tempel*
> *an turant a vyn cowel*
> * gul sakyrfeys*
> *may hallo guthel moy druk*
> *myryn orto vn golok*
> * kyn na vo hy rag y leys*

First Demon
[Let us come now to the temple,
The tyrant will completely
  Make sacrifice
So that he may do more evil.
Let us look at him one look,
  Though that be not for his advantage][340]

The torturers bring various items, including a ram's head, a horse's head, and three ravens, the Tyrant himself offering '*omma pen tarov shylwyn* [Here a white bull's head]'.[341] Given all these items, the mock ritual of the black mass must have looked theatrically very impressive. What is so highly crafted about the sequence is that all this demonology is rounded off with a resoundingly comic note. Calo, the tyrant's skivvy or drudge, brings in a tom cat from 'Morville':

Thum du iovyn in y fath
me a offren lawen cath
  ny yl boys guel legessa
me as droys a voruelys
le may fue an iovle elys
  degens ytte om hascra
pen bogh ha gaver pelys
  ov du lemen thyn grassa

[To my god, Jove, in his face
I will offer a tom-cat:
  There cannot be better to catch mice,
I have brought it from Morville
A place where the devil has been anointed
  Let him take them, behold them in *my* bosom,
A buck's head and a skinned goat,
  May go, now thank us for it.][342]

This undercutting of the high ritual displays much skill, not only in terms of humour for the audience watching, but also for an understanding of how drama in this phase could function. There is a certain modernity in this, which is lacking in the *Ordinalia*. By the time *Bewnans Meriasek* was written, the dramas being assembled clearly incorporated lots of motifs, legends and humour, which deviated from earlier practice. Such modernity would be noticeable elsewhere on the stages of Britain. We may go further. It is such an awareness of the opportunities for ritual in performance that make the dramatist(s) of *Bewnans Meriasek* stand out. Throughout the two days there is a consummate awareness not only of Christian ritual, but also of more pagan – or even diabolical – activity. There is another point, however, behind this. The dramatist seems to sense the importance of the ingredients of ritual in the drama. He was, therefore, operating in a continuum from the earliest performance in Cornwall. When we consider the layers of the play – the other narratives, the ritual and classical shaping of the drama – then we really begin to understand the sophistication of its construction.

As in many sections of the drama, miracles bring about conversion. The boy's miraculous escape brings about the conversion of the gaoler, and puts the black mass into perspective. All of this is brought about by what Murdoch calls 'Marian intercession'.[343] The play then progresses onto a second narrative from the life of Sylvester. A dragon has been terrorising the local people, and its presence has been blamed for the development of Christianity there. In performance, there is very little else that is so dramatically interesting as a fire-breathing and menacing dragon. Sylvester manages to tame the dragon, along the way resurrecting the two dukes who were killed by it. The dragon is then sent away and, as Murdoch concludes, 'as with Meriasek's removal of the wolf and the robbers, secular authority is dependent upon the church'.[344] This is a core concept through the play. The play then ends with Meriasek's death and, appropriately, his soul ascends to heaven. It is the Earl of Vannes who provides the epilogue:

Dywhy banneth maryasek
ha maria cambron wek
  banneth an abesteleth
evugh oll gans an guary
ny a vyn agis pesy
  kyns moys an plaeth

[To you the blessing of Meriasek,
And of sweet Mary of Camborne,
  The blessing of the apostles!
Drink ye all with the play
We will beseech you
  Before going from the place.][345]

As for the diagram of the first day of the play of *Bewnans Meriasek*, it notes thirteen stations.[346] The way the diagram is shown in the manuscript has *Celum* [Heaven] at the top, which was probably in the east. Proceeding clockwise, the stations are *Siluester* [Sylvester], *Magister* [Schoolmaster], *Episcopus Kernov* [Bishop of Kernou], *Dux brittonum id est pater mereadoci* [Duke of Brittany], *Rex Conanus* [King Conan], *Constantinus* [Constantine], *Tevdarus Imperator* [Teudar], *Dux Cornubie* [Duke of Cornwall], *Comes rohany* [Earl of Rohan], *Exulatores* [Outlaws], *Infernum* [Hell] and *Tortores* [Torturers]. We might raise this number to fourteen if the Bishop Poly also had a position, probably located between the Earl of Rohan and the Outlaws. There was also the *capella*, which probably featured a chapel of some kind. What is interesting about this layout is that it reflected imagined cultural geography: for example, Constantine and Brittany are in the south, while the Duke of Cornwall is most obviously placed in the west. The complexity of the action in *Bewnans Meriasek* is reflected in this diagram. The fact that the diagram looks somewhat over-written suggests active revision of this by the final hand.

This complexity is also reflected in the second day.[347] There would appear to be fifteen stations altogether. However, because a large piece of the upper left arc is missing from the manuscript leaf, the names of not all of the stations are visible. Fortunately, Stokes seemed to have had access to the manuscript before this damage, and it is to him we should look to provide the complete set. Beginning again at the top, at the east, and working in a clockwise direction, we thus have *Celum* [Heaven], *Siluester* [Sylvester], *ij Episcopus* [Second Bishop], *Episcopus Kernov* [Bishop of Kernou], *Comes vennetensis* [Earl of Vannes], *Rex massen* [King Massen], *Imperator Constantinus* [Constantine], *Tirannus Imperattor* [Tyrant], *Comes globus* [Early Globus], *Primus Dux Magus* [First Duke], *Secundus Dux Magus* [Second Duke], *Episcopus Poly* [Bishop Poly], *ffilius Mulieris* [Woman's son], *Infernum* [Hell] and *Tortores* [Torturers]. It seems, however, that the First and Second Duke would be on the same station and, of course, some of the characters may have shared points of departure and return. There would again probably have been a chapel in the middle of the capella. We note the southern positioning of Constantine and the Breton characters. A curious aspect of the second day's diagram is that some of the characters are segmented off. This may be just to provide clarity in an otherwise cluttered diagram, but it does give a further notion of the special dimension of the stations. The quantity of characters in these diagrams suggests quite a large playing area for the event. Indeed, the directions indicate that the stations must have been of considerable size. For example, in the battle between the Duke of Cornwall and Teudar, a number of men must have been on stage, and may also have been riding horses. We might also consider the fact that certain devices (such as Meriasek's ship or the dragon) might need to be rolled in or wheeled on. When the audience is factored into this, one begins to realise that the dramaturgy of *Bewnans Meriasek* demanded larger and more complex space than even the *Ordinalia*.[348]

Given the complexity of the dramaturgy of *Bewnans Meriasek*, it would clearly be impossible to fully examine its stage-craft in the space here. However, in a series of works, Higgins has tried to resolve some of the major issues of performance, and these are helpful to consider.[349] Some of the core elements make for useful exploration. Considering the textual details, Higgins believes that a gap in the Round was most likely found between King Conan and the Duke of Brittany on the first day of the play, and notes that, since time passing is required between Meriasek as a boy and as a man, the lines of Conan spoken at this station could indicate this. The stage direction for the feast at the Duke of Brittany's castle indicates that it took place in the plain. Considerable use of stage-hands would have been required here, not least in how Meriasek obtains his priest gown. It may well have been hidden 'on stage' but he would still need to put it on. Higgins also notes that a multi-functional location in the drama may well be the rock, which could double for several places, among them the cave, the hermitage, and the tomb, with the audience, therefore, having to make the conceptual and geographic transition – a technique also used in modern theatre. Clearance of the feasting event would then facilitate the entrance of the boat, the one thing 'covering' the movement of the other. It is a little unclear how Cornwall would be presented when Meriasek lands there, after the storm, though presumably he would simply step down onto the plain itself. This would allow an easy transition to the chapel. Importantly, the chapel would probably have had to physically resemble the real chapel found in Camborne.

Given Teudar's stage energy, it would suit to have him parading in front of his station, the rhythm of his walking matching the anger of his lines. After the Teudar sequence, the torturers' leaving would allow the boat to be brought back in for the journey to Brittany. The issue of the mountain, just after the wolf section, is probably solvable by use of the banks of the Round itself. The action changes now, however, for events move to the southern section of the Round to match the geographical location for Constantine. In this section, there is a good deal of energetic movement, to match the proxemics of the characters. Some properties would be required for use by the Doctor, in his examination of Constantine's urine, but this was presumably easy enough to stage-manage. The torturers' boasting has strong elements of the 'Slaughter of the Innocents', probably known from other biblical dramas, and there was probably a good deal

Fig. 37. Musicianship at the end of *Bewnans Meriasek*. A fiddle player bench-end, from Altarnun Church.

Fig. 38. Another example of musicianship at the end of *Bewnans Meriasek*. A piper bench-end from Altarnun Church.

of audience interaction here. A more difficult effect to achieve is the direction reading '*enituit splendor lucis* [a marvellous splendour of light]' at line 1835,[350] during the sequence when Contantine is being baptised. Equally challenging would be the presentation of the fire in the forest in Brittany.

Higgins has noted some processional qualities to the structure of the first day, which appear to demark the various sections. Thus, Section One (lines 1-595) ends with the boat moving around the central area, Section Two (lines 596-1081) ends with the boat again moving around the central area, Section Three (lines 1082-1865) ends with a holy procession, while Section Four (lines 1866-2512) ends with the battle between the Duke of Cornwall and Teudar.[351] In this way then, the mechanics of the performance are measured and controlled, with set pieces being punctuated by these larger movements. On the second day, Higgins notes that types of characters were consciously positioned in the same space in the *plen-an-gwarry*, to assist with the overall harmony of the dramaturgy.[352] Thus, the second tyrant occupies the same station as Teudar, and King Conan is replaced with King Massen. The important financial and logistical point of this was that it would have been unnecessary to make any changes to the stations. The Constantine sequences are reasonably clear, and the stations for the bishops are established. It would appear that during the section with the Tyrant the whole of the *platea* could be used for the hunting sequence, while a spectacle would be generated by the demons coming out of Hell. When Massen and the Tyrant's armies collide, it was presumably the demons that carried off the dead. One unresolved difficulty was the position of the gaoler. This remains somewhat unclear in the manuscript. What we know for certain is that the icon of the gaoler and his boy seems to be an established feature of Cornish drama; they also occur in a more developed role in the *Ordinalia*. Another was the difficulty of presenting the dragon. It needed to be impressive, and also demanded certain special effects: '*her a gonn yn y dragon ys mouth aredy & fyr* [Here a gun ready in the dragon's mouth and fire]'.[353] We also learn that '*sum of ye sovdrys y sowlyd* [some of the soldiers are swallowed]'.[354] The likelihood then, as Higgins contends, was that the dragon needed to be 'very large' and 'to be manoeuvrable, it most probably was on wheels'.[349] The dragon would seem to be one of the most spectacular stage effects in late-medieval Cornish drama. As on day one, a similar processional patterning sub-divides the drama: Section One (lines 2513-3098) ends with people who attended Meriasek's consecration returning to their stations; Section Two (lines 3099-3542) ends with the fight between the two armies; Section Three (lines 3542-4180) ends with a holy procession; and Section Four (lines 4181-4568) ends with the dispersal of the crowd who attend Meriasek's burial.[355] Doubling would have been permissible because:

1. Although there are 99 speaking parts in St Meriasek, there are only 62 on Day One and 54 on Day Two.
2. Only 16 characters appear on both days.
3. 71 out of the 99 characters appear in only one section of the play.
4. 75 of the characters have less than fifty lines.[356]

The comparatively small number of characters (16) who appear on both days would therefore have required most rehearsal but, even considering the doubling or tripling of certain characters, rehearsals for the event must have been huge and very demanding. This does not even begin to appreciate the backstage work required for the event: the assembly of the scaffolding for the stations, the costuming, the construction of wheeled devices, such as the boat and dragon, and the general materials needed for set construction. That said, there must have been a considerable infrastructure surrounding the play, catering for not only the performers, but also those who travelled to see the event: food, drink, accommodation, washing and toilet facilities must all have been required for onlookers. This again demonstrates how massive an event any production of *Bewnans Meriasek* must have been. In this sense, it completely negates the observations of Carew about rehearsal and performance technique.[357] Bearing this in mind, one might even suggest that *Bewnans Meriasek* was such a spectacle that it commanded audiences travelling some distance. It would therefore have had a peculiarly important status within Cornwall, and the wider south-west of Britain, one which saw it rise above the perhaps less spectacular dramas of other parishes. What is certain is that rather than it being, in Ellis's somewhat surprising words, 'very long and ill-constructed',[358] it is, as this chapter has demonstrated, epic and structurally harmonious.

It is, therefore, surprising that *Bewnans Meriasek* has not prompted as much discussion or academic debate as one might expect. This may be partly attributed to the complexity of the text, and the many dense theological issues it contains. However, once one begins to see the various strands contributing to the whole, then the drama becomes easier to follow. In some ways, discussion and criticism about *Bewnans Meriasek* is still in its infancy when compared, for example, to the *Ordinalia*.[359] A lead scholar of the work in the past twenty-five years has been Myrna Combellack who, as well as studying numerous aspects of the drama, has produced a useful verse translation.[360] However, the expert on wider medieval performance, Wickham, has considered the drama in the light of the staging of saints' plays (though confusingly conflates Cornwall with England),[361] while Grantley has viewed the significance of 'producing miracles' within the dramaturgy.[362] Turk and Combellack based an article on the importance of doctoring and disease in the drama, considering in some depth Constantine's doctor, and the curing of lameness, mental illness and leprosy. They indicate that, given the material circumstances of its production, the possibility in the drama of a cure for such illness offered hope to those watching from within a suffering community: as late as 1590, three lepers were buried at Redruth.[363] Crawford has examined in some detail the connections between social status and stanza forms within the text, confirming the general view now that the higher-class characters speak in a more developed and complex stanza form than those of lower class.[364] Parts of the text have featured in anthologies of Celtic literature and Cornish literature.[365] The best criticism and study has come from Brian Murdoch, in a number of works,[366] while Grigg's recent account provides, for the uninitiated, an accessible way into the drama.[367] Rutt, meanwhile, in a feisty response to the political readings of observers such as Payton, argues the following:

> The Marian content of *Bewnans Meryasek* is of remarkable tenderness. The story of the women bargaining with Our Lady by stealing the image of the Baby Jesus from the statue in church, for all that it had become a commonplace, must be seen as tender. Tenderness does not come across easily when it is declaimed in circular arena against a Cornish wind: but it gets through by the sheer insistence and volume of the repeated message. Likewise, one miraculous healing would make no impact. The many healings that seem repetitious when the play is done in a church or hall got their effect from their sheer number in the plain-an-gwarry. The more so since the audience would be largely illiterate.[368]

Rutt may have a point here. He notes the intimacy required in the performance of *Bewnans Meriasek*, yet we also see a thread of modernity, which paradoxically pulls away from the Marianism of the play. This is because, despite the epic drive of the production, a certain closeness is needed (a kind of theatrical 'pull focus') on its more intimate moments. How this was actually achieved is still to be debated. Rutt was writing in response to Payton, and to a growing sense that criticism about the play was moving, in his view disturbingly, in a political and cultural-nationalist direction. However, it is Payton (following observations by Lynette Olson on tyranny in the drama[369]) who has reactivated discussion on the political aspects of the drama and, to a great extent, reignited interest in the work. Payton, arguing for what he terms its 'special resonance in post-1497 Cornwall',[370] also cites the important observations of Wooding:

[Teudar's] defeat by the Duke of Cornwall may well have been a statement of the locals' disillusionment with the distant king. The fact that the play itself was in the local language, probably not understood by English onlookers, might serve to reinforce the "underworld", or slightly subversive quality of it.[371]

The analogy would appear to be correct, particularly when we consider some of the more famous speeches of Teudar in the first day of the drama:

Tevdar me a veth gelwys,
  arluth regnijs in kernov
may fo mahum enorys
  ov charg yw heb feladov
  oges ha pel
penag a worthya ken du
y astev paynys glu
  hag inweth mernans cruel

[Teudar I am called,
  Lord reigning in Cornwall.
That Mahommed be honoured
  Is my charge without fail,
  Near and far.
Whosover worship another god,
They shall have keen pains,
  And likewise a cruel death.][372]

Later, he also comments:

Duk Kernov hag oll y dus
indan ov threys me as glus
  poran kepar ha treysy

[Duke of Cornwall and all his folk,
Under my feet I will crush them
  just like grains of sand.][373]

Because this Teudar is an interloper, such speeches attracted not only theological but also 'nationalist' resentment. What is important about this is that it reconfigures 'safe' readings of miracle or saints' plays as something more than purely dramatic evocations of Christian belief. Other ideological perspectives were considered, and it is interesting to speculate on whether other dramas featured similar guarded political messages, as would certainly seem the case with *Bewnans Ke*. Payton was to conclude that:

> the extent to which the collation (and presumed public performance) in 1504 of an edition of *Beunans Meriasek* did reflect an underlying resentment in Cornwall is certain to attract more extensive academic debate and further research. However, taken with other glimpses and evidences, and set alongside the important fact of the Charter of Pardon of 1508, it does begin to hint at a Cornwall that was indeed restless and – from the perspective of a 'centre' that had already been challenged seriously from the Cornish – in need of renewed accommodation.[374]

The perspectives of both Rutt and Payton are valid within the drama, because of its multi-layeredness and complexity. The precise dramaturgy of *Bewnans Meriasek* does merit further examination. The last major performance of a 'full' version of *Bewnans Meriasek* took place at St Paul's Church, Truro in February 1986. This was produced with a mixture of amateur, professional and student actors, but was not in any sense like the original performance conditions. The acting text was Myrna Combellack's English-language verse translation. Usefully, in order to lessen the complications of performance, the pages of her 1988 printed English verse translation are coded, matching the page colours with significant episodes.[375] Although the extant manuscript copy of *Bewnans Meriasek* dates from 1504, it seems the play – and, despite the ravages of the Reformation, some form of it, or another kind of interlude – continued to be performed at least up until the early 1580s. The Churchwardens' Accounts of St Meridocus and St Martin detail, in June 1539-40, how one Thomas John Harvy gave over an item (probably money) that 'he receuyed at the play that the young men mad[e]'.[376] We might infer that the performance of drama in Camborne seems exclusively a young man's activity. Receipts for such money are also recorded in the June 1542-3 Accounts.[377] Performance seems to be still ongoing in 1549, when a 'pyper yn the playe' is paid.[378] The expenses incurred by the 'interlude players' are also detailed in 1577 and in 1582;[379] though by this time, an interlude sounds quite a different prospect to what was perhaps intended with the full script of *Bewnans Meriasek*. Things seem to have completely altered by 1595, however, when the only entertainment alluded to was Morris dancing. Perhaps the full force of the Reformation had settled things. However, we should not think of this Morris as it is presently conceived.[380] 'Guizing' would be a more accurate description for this, and other later Morris mentioned in this chapter. Charles Thomas has spent some time investigating possible *plen-an-gwarry* sites in Camborne. In his *Christian Antiquities of Camborne* (1967) he quotes Edward Lhuyd's observations on some entrenchments titled 'Plains'.[381] Thomas's preference for the site is at Race Farm, where one of the fields was called Ring Close. This would connect with the play's interest in Teudar, since Race Farm lay between Camborne and Hayle. Lyon, however, also puts forward another possible location at Lower Rosewarne.[382]

Elsewhere, through the fifteenth century, other drama had been developed. *Bewnans Ke* [*The life of St Ke*] is another saint's play written in Middle Cornish.[383] The present manuscript edition of the play dates from the late sixteenth century, but it was clearly created and performed earlier. It only came to light in 2000, among the papers of the late Welsh scholar Professor J.E. Caerwyn Williams, which were donated to the National Library of Wales, and was then discovered by the archivist Graham Thomas.[384] The rediscovery of this text is not only a major milestone for Cornish language and literature, but also impacts considerably on our understanding of Cornish-language drama. Its finding effectively increases the dramatic corpus by one sixth, and it represents a very considerable contribution to our understanding of medieval drama within these islands. As we shall see, because of the nature of the subject matter of the play – part hagiography, part Arthurian legend – the drama ties together a number of strands which, although predicted over time by some scholars,[385] could not be evidenced. The Arthurian material in particular meant that perhaps, finally, Cornwall could have claim to a substantial medieval text that considered this matter. Considering Cornwall's historical cultural continuum with Arthurian matter, this was no small thing. *Bewnans Ke* was the first 'new' major Cornish-language text to have been found since the discovery of John Tregear's *Homilies* in 1949.[386] The finding of the text generated considerable excitement, not only amongst Cornish-language enthusiasts, but also in the theatrical community. Fundamentally, observers and scholars had another text that both justified the complexity of the theatrical continuum in Cornwall and also asked the question: if such a work as *Bewnans Ke* could apparently 'come out of nowhere', then what other dramas have survived, still hidden in the cupboards, shelves and libraries of the world?[387]

The play offered observers some new insights into dramaturgy, providing scholars with a range of new words and confirmation of derivative forms, as well as insights into place-names and the cultural geography of the area to which much of the play refers: the Parish of Kea in mid-Cornwall, located on the banks of the River Fal.[388] The play, however, is not only parochial, for in places it deals with both pan-British and pan-European events. A village

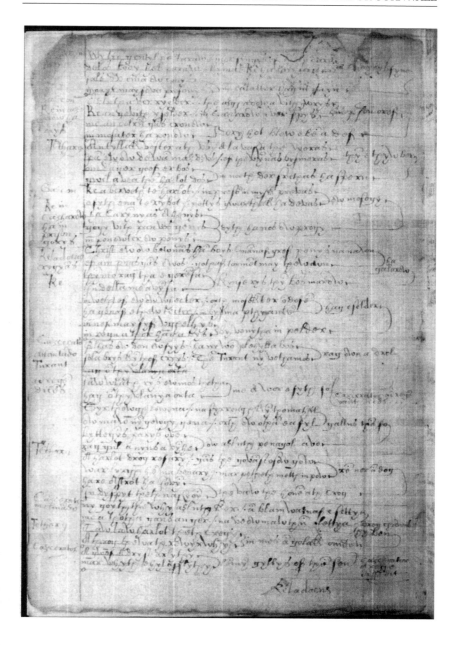

Fig. 39. One of the opening pages of *Bewnans Ke*: MS. 23849D. Reproduced by permission of the Llyfrgell Genedlaethol Cymru / National Library of Wales.

located in Kea Parish, now called 'Playing Place', is the probable theatrical venue for the drama. We know from observers such as Lyon that there were, in fact, two possible sites for theatrical activity there: two earthworks exist, only some fifty metres apart.[389] In a very real sense, the imagining of the theatrical community surrounding the drama became a fascinating piece of detective work. As we know, Kea Parish is not very far from Glasney College at Penryn, so there is a likely link. Thomas and Williams remind us that Kea paid its tithes to the Canons there.[390] As we shall see, there are a number of similarities between *Bewnans Meriasek* and *Bewnans Ke*. However, while the former, as we have seen, is just about complete, the latter is not, which does create some difficulties for us. To have *Bewnans Meriasek* as a comparative text is extremely useful, because that drama gives us much insight into the dramaturgy of *Bewnans Ke*. That said, the dramaturgy of *Ke* is much less clear, and observers are only just beginning to examine the performance conditions and staging of this work. The manuscript of *Bewnans Ke*, like *The Creacion of the World*, contains no stage diagrams. At this point, we must also be guarded. It is likely that *Bewnans Ke* was mounted in ways similar to the other texts in the corpus, but there may have been some notable and important differences.

It is somewhat puzzling why J.E. Caerwyn Williams did not release the text earlier into the academic community. Considering the paucity of Cornish-language texts, and craving for their existence, one might have hoped the text would have come to light earlier. We do know that Williams began a process of translation, but this was abandoned. It still remains unclear how the text came into his possession to begin with. We do, of course, recognise that works such as *Bewnans Meriasek* appear to have ended up in Wales because at first glance they must have appeared to look like Welsh. Photographic images of the manuscript are available on the website of the National Library of Wales;[391] Oliver Padel has completed a useful provisional transcription of the manuscript.[392] Effectively, three critical editions of the play now exist. A provisional translation was made by Michael Polkinhorn,[393] followed by *Bywnans Ke* edited by Ken George (2006),[394] and *Bewnans Ke: The Life of St Kea – A Critical Edition with Translation*, edited by Graham Thomas and Nicholas Williams (2007).[395] Of these, the latter is the most helpful, since it contains only the original text with a translation (the lack of which, as we have learnt, is elsewhere a considerable problem for Cornish-language drama). The text itself is anonymous, written in what is generally termed the Bookman Old Style of script. Although the editors and translators have deciphered many of the lines, there are still a number which remain obscure or difficult to translate. The manuscript of the drama is incomplete, with the beginning and ending missing (some five leaves), as well as several internal pages. The original work is thought to contain thirty-four leaves. The extant lines presently total approximately 3,300, giving an estimate for the full work, of some 5,600 lines.[396] This would make the drama slightly longer than *Bewnans Meriasek*, which has 4,568 lines.

As a whole, the play can be divided into two sections equating to the two days of performance: the first dealing with the life of the saint; the second dealing with Arthurian matter closely related to material from Geoffrey of Monmouth's *Historia Regum Britanniae*.[397] Fortunately, evidence for the full life of St Ke is to be found in Albert Le Grand's *La Vie* [*The Life*],[398] which adds Arthurian matter to his life, and thus compares very well to the play's narrative, with St Ke returning at the end (missing in the manuscript). Le Grand's *Life* therefore, can be used to fill in the gaps at the beginning and the end of the play. In order to understand the opening of the drama, then we must look to *La Vie*:

> Saint Ké or Kenan, surnamed Colodoc, was born in the Isle of Britain of noble parents, his father's name was Ludun and his mother's Tagu. Because of his knowledge in all kinds of sciences, he is admitted to the priesthood and raised to the dignity of a bishop in one of the cities of his country.[399]

This is what we might expect to see in the opening of the drama. Whether as much of his childhood would be shown as Meriasek's is not clear, but certainly the *Life* would give the dramatist(s) plenty of opportunity to demonstrate Ke's abilities. We also learn that Ke gives people both spiritual and material 'bread', but 'finds the episcopal office too much to bear' and thus resigns and 'goes into the country of Cambria'.[400] This provides something of a difficulty, because Cambria translates as Wales. Two possibilities might be operating here. Le Grand himself may have known little of Cornwall, and so mistakenly used the word Cambria, believing that it was where the action of the narrative took place; it could be that Cornwall was merely perceived by him as being 'West Wales' and therefore apt. This action suggests a starting station for Ke and his parents, and then a step down into the plain in order to journey. A dramatic difficulty is that it is actually not a part of the same island, so this would be somewhat more difficult to show than, for example, the different locales of *Bewnans Meriasek*.

However, in Le Grand, the next episode is clearer to show. Ke is destined to obtain a bell, and to travel with it. The bell will ring by itself when he reaches a place called Rosené (Rosewa). He goes to a man named Gildas, a 'skilful bell-founder'. So Le Grand informs us, 'By the sign of the Cross, Ké is able to increase the small amount of metal to such a size that after the bell is made there is still enough payment for the work'. Probably this action could still be completed in the plain of the Round. Travelling with other holy men, Ke then comes to 'rest on the grass near an arm of the sea called Hildrech'[401] and it is here that he hears a man shout the name of Rosené. This is beautifully complemented by a moment of social realism in which a man is seeking his cows – animals remain very important in the dramaturgy here. Hearing the shout, Ke goes down to the shore, which is from thereon known as Krestenn Ké (the Shore of Ke). We are told that 'here, he strikes a rock from which gushes water for his thirsty disciples to drink, and to this day the sick who drink this water in faith are restored to health'.[402] Elements of this are very similar to those of *Bewnans Meriasek*: the rock with the holy well is an important stage device there, as is its ability to cure; the same issues noted in Turk and Combellack are apparent here.[403] In terms of the dramaturgy, the only observation here is that, given the complexity of this initial narrative, the playwright only has some ten pages to get Ke to this point. Therefore, the action at the beginning would necessarily have to be quite compacted.

Once the bell rings, Ke knows this is the place to stop, and this is really where the life and drama begin to converge. Here, Ke builds himself a chapel, perhaps in a similar way to Meriasek. We may then turn to the surviving text of the manuscript. In the next section of the play, Ke initially restores a shepherd to life in the forest near Gudrun [Goodern] castle (Goodern is a present-day farm within Kea parish), and encounters one of Teudar's foresters; Teudar has a presence in the very same location in *Bewnans Meriasek*. Teudar is a similar tyrant to the one found in that drama, and perhaps another not so subtle commentary upon Henry Tudor. He would presumably have had a station to parade upon. Already though, we see a quite different kind of dramaturgy than in the other dramas. There are not so obviously the stations of Heaven and Hell; while, in the previous dramas, local place-names formed a cultural-geographic backdrop, here they are much more integrated into the action, with perhaps a station such as Goodern located geographically in the same direction in the Round (i.e. to the north-west). Teudar, meanwhile, seems a character type in Middle-Cornish drama, ranting, and always questioning whatever individual he encounters. Again, he is Murdoch's 'composite of non-Christian elements',[404] the difference this time being that Ke is an interloper:

> *Teutharus*
> *Te javal, ew henna gwyr?*
> *Lavar heb gow!*
> *A bele teta the'n tyr?*
> *Menyk the bow*
> *whath ha'th tyman!*

Ho ys thy lord? tel me that!
Ase rusta hager prat!
Gogy dyndy! kimmes blam!

[*Teudar*
You scoundrel, is this true?
Speak without lie!
From whence do you come to the region?
Declare your country
and further your domain!
Who is your lord? tell me that!
What an evil trick you have done!
Woe to you for deserving so much blame!]⁴⁰⁵

There then follows a section of theological debate and Teudar orders Ke to be placed in prison. Again, this is an established event of the Middle-Cornish stage, with a world-weary gaoler and quick-witted boy. In other dramas, the gaol is generally not a station, so we may accept the same here. However, in a departure from other texts, it is the boy who promises to torture Ke. Teudar's machinations fail, however, when the boy reports that there is a 'sweetness' about Ke, the direction reading '*whecter sawer gans Ke* [Kea has fragrance of smell]'.⁴⁰⁶ This extended sequence provides considerable opportunity for comedy and slapstick though, at the end of it, Teudar seems somewhat 'brow-beaten', agreeing to give Ke some land, but still wishing to hunt there. A section follows with the torturers, but the manuscript is badly mutilated at this point, and so the action is less clear here. Again, though, the torturers would probably have their own station, close to that belonging to Teudar. Le Grand's *Life* remains unclear on them as well, but we know their function on the late-medieval stage. If we follow Manning's arguments, and apply them to *Bewnans Ke*, then they are representative of a wider kind of social violence inflicted on Cornwall during this phase, perhaps even developed further during the post-1497 period.⁴⁰⁷ Despite the fragmentation of the text, their aim is clear – to do violence to Ke, Fourth Torturer menacingly saying '*gul afruthow ny a vyn* [we will make a deformation]'.⁴⁰⁸ Interestingly, at this point, Teudar labels Ke '*A lobbry Sous!* [O filthy Englishman!]',⁴⁰⁹ which is intriguing because it suggests Teudar is aware of Ke's ethnicity, compared to his own. However, despite perhaps problems with how the English were accommodating Cornwall, clearly Ke is presented in a sympathetic light to the Cornish watching; thus they would have empathy with him.

To summarise the next phase of the drama: Ke protects a stag, but Teudar and his torturers steal Ke's oxen; Ke asks for their return, but in a moment of violence, the torturers break three of Ke's teeth and we learn that *'Pen Ke a ve terrys bys i'n grogan* [Kea's head was broken into the skull]'.[410] This stage violence is clearly a strand of performance deemed necessary to generate appropriate sympathy for the main character and, of course, to engender further hatred towards Teudar. Ke causes a holy well to develop, cures a leper (through an extended piece of Marianism), and then a pair of stags plough Ke's land in place of the oxen. Kelliow (now Killiow), also mentioned in the text here, is found some four kilometres south west of Truro, between Goodern and Playing Place. There are some splendid touches of detail in this section: for example, the names of the two stags:

> *Arator*
> *In rag, Kyrnyk ha Kella!*
> *In hanow Du uhella,*
>   *gonethough heb bysmeras.*
>   *Me a lever, ru'm besow!*
>   *neffra ny'n gevyth esow*
>   *a venna Du e weras.*

> *Ploughman*
> Forward, Kyrnyk and Kella!
> In the name of the highest God,
>   plough without reproach.
>   I say, by my ring!
>   never will he be in want
>   whom God wishes to help.[411]

It is hard to tell whether real deer would have been used here. Considering their skittish nature, this might seem impossible. Oxen would have been easier to control. Perhaps the roles of the stags may have been played by humans. Following discussions with his Advisor (a component seen in other drama of the period) Teudar eventually agrees that Ke can have whatever land he can impark (enclose). In a later comic sequence, Teudar is bathing and asks the maiden Oubra to find a potion. Oubra is a highly-distinctive character: part-herbalist, part-witch and seemingly also part-seductress. Oubra explains the ritual processes behind the potion, no doubt an admixture of invented mumbo-jumbo and real folklore:

    Oubra

Atomma drogga dryton.

Ny sowrd clevas in mab pron

  na ra rewgh e lawsa.

  Fit ex canis mordula

   ha leth an wheghyth gafna

   na's teva leugh a vys Mee.

Henna ew gwastell vynnys

dyghtys a gyk herynnys

  ha blonak ha gwygh unlew,

  fryys war tan i'n padal

  ha gansa leth a'n ladal,

  ha sof pot hag oyow bew.

    [*Oubra*

Here is dog's excrement.

No illness occurs in a human being

  that it will not simply assuage.

   It is made from the bite of a dog

   and the milk of the sixth calfless cow

   that has had no calf since the month of May.

That is a little cake

prepared from the flesh of herrings

  and lard, and winkles of one colour,

   fried in a pan over the fire

   together with milk from the ladle,

   potted suet and fertilized eggs.][412]

Unfortunately, the potion causes Teudar to become stuck in the bath. Probably, the bath would have been in the middle of the plain, and perhaps made from a hollowed-out tree trunk. Ke is then able to take a large portion of Teudar's land. The relationship between Oubra and Teudar is very ambiguous. Teudar is clearly attracted to her, but she seems to aid Ke's cause. In the next sequence, Teudar asks for protection and curses Ke. Ke approaches a king, but the next two leaves, which link to the Arthurian matter of the play, are missing. The place-names of this latter section refer to a specific geographic area: Kewnans is most likely to be Cowlands, Tremustel is Trevaster, and Penpol (now Penpoll) is at the end of Lambe Creek. In this way, the tight geography of the first day of the play is maintained. It is uncertain whether there would be any kind of musical celebration at the end of *Bewnans Ke*, like that found in

Bewnans Meriasek. On the face of it, the ending would seem somewhat downbeat, though this is not to say music did not occur. Although Bruch has identified passages in the second day of the play where some form of musical refrain may have been used,[413] the first day shows little engagement with song or musicianship. Indeed, this may be part of the intended dramatic effect – because the grand, world-shaping events of the second day were more aptly accompanied by music, or delivered in 'song'.

On the face of it, events in the opening day of *Bewnans Ke* may not sound that spectacular when one compares them to, for example, *Bewnans Meriasek*. However, this view needs questioning. First of all, *Bewnans Ke* is one drama that firmly demonstrates the central theme of this book: issues of space, place and performance. The saint's story is remarkably contained within the surrounds of the playing place, and the performance is highly connected to the natural fauna and flora of the riverside parish. Much local reference (albeit some of it lost) is contained within the script, which suggests a dramatic community using the drama to help define its identity and origins. If the writer were connected to the Collegiate Church at Glasney, then he perhaps knew intimately the landscape being constructed in the dramaturgy, as well as

Fig. 40. Old Church, Kea in Cornwall, dedicated to St Ke.

having the life of Saint Kelodocus before him. The way in which the drama is shaped, therefore, demonstrates a profound understanding of ritual, community and landscape, perhaps more wholly embedded than even that of the play at Camborne.

The four pages missing in the middle of the manuscript mean that the start of the Second Day is unclear. However, it seems likely that, following Le Grand's *Life*, somewhere here Ke has travelled to Brittany. The *Life* points to an episode involving a merchant and corn,[414] though, given the quantity of pages missing, this would seem too complex a narrative to develop at this point. The cultural and political significance of the dramatisation of King Arthur in a Cornish-language text is not to be underestimated, for it uniquely links dramaturgy to identity, and therefore historical experience.[415] The Arthurian matter of *Bewnans Ke* is lengthy and complex; within the remit of this volume, I am able to offer only relatively brief discussion of the action; suffice for me to say that the presentation of the drama in a *plen-an-gwarry* would necessitate a high degree of spectacle, a number of characters, and a good deal of epic action. Again, this is not the world of Carew, but there is perhaps something of the words of Scawen here: 'patriarchs, princes... framed by art, and composed with heroic style'.[416] Scawen's term 'heroic style' inevitably also makes us think of the genre of 'courtly love' and, to some extent, even with passages of Modred and Guinevere, there is an element of that here as well.

The likely organisation of the Round on the second day would be a similar revision to that found on the second day of *Bewnans Meriasek*, with the stations of the earlier 'evil' characters being similarly replaced. We may then, begin to imagine Modred, or perhaps the Emperor Lucius, occupying similar space to Teudar. That said, however, there would probably be enough other stations free (from the first day) to enable further delineation of the stations. The second day deliberately changes from the intimate feel of the first day to explore pan-European events, with a host of different and often legendary characters. The day opens with a coming together of leaders and bishops from across the islands, with Cador, the Duke of Cornwall, leading the discussion. Cador would probably have had a station, to match his status. Much is made of Arthur's headquarters in Cornwall – at Gyllywyk [Kellywyk].[417] Here we see the Cornish-speaking 'warriors' of the court of Arthur, whose legitimacy of control is paralleled by the Bishops' praise to Mary. An interesting stage direction is given in this opening sequence: '*Tunc ambulant circa theatrum omnes bini et trini* [Then they all walk around the theatre in twos and threes]'.[418] This is interesting because it suggests a naturalism in approach: the characters are walking naturally and discussing events, but the word 'theatrum'

– used here but not elsewhere – very definitely defines the space in which we are operating. Such a term is not used elsewhere in the corpus. Arthur himself has a curious entrance. He is described as *Arthurus Rex Britannie*, but the dramatist qualifies this with '*que nunc Anglia dicitur* [which is now called England]',[419] seemingly showing a contemporary Britain undergoing restructuring. Arthur's speech here is much as we should expect, though interestingly it opens with English:

Peys! Syth Y hot wyld and tam,
  dem ha best peswartrosak,
I say Arthur is my nam
  myghtern bras ha galosak
    ha conqueror.
    Mara tof ha trewelas,
      ny vyth mab den ou gwelas
rag †arsevnanst ha terrur.

[Peace! Since I command wild and tame,
  man and four-footed beast,
I say Arthur is my name,
  a great and powerful king
    and a conqueror.
    If I happen to be angry,
      no human dare look on me
for †uneaset and terror.][420]

Initially then, within the dramaturgy, we see Arthur receiving Duke Cador and Augelas, various squires, bishops, Beduer, Syr Kay, Hoel, seven kings (Orkney, Norway, Dacia, Iceland, Gotland, Krakow, and Castile), Modred, Gawain, and knights.[421] All offer him great praise. It is unlikely that each of the kings would have had their own stations, but presumably their collective entrance could have been quite spectacular. Quite how aware the audience and performers would have been of their spatial geography is difficult to surmise, but there might have been some sense of them arriving from the north. In summary, in the next sequence, the Roman Emperor Lucius learns that Arthur refuses to pay tribute to him and so sets forth twelve legates to speak to him. Given his imagined world, and if the author here was following convention, then Lucius's station would be in the south. If Arthur is imagined at Caerleon, then this would also be a station. We know that he has a tent: '*Clauditur tentum Arthuri* [Let Arthur's tent be close]',[422] but the welcoming of the large quantity of legates would suggest a banquet or feast of some kind in the middle of the plain. This is confirmed when Arthur '*descendit* [goes down]', saying the following lines:

> *Dun, ow amors ha'm cuvyon,*
> *gans solas hag englynnyon,*
> *ha merth ha melody whek,*
> *Th'agan palas gwel ew thyn*
> *revertya gans cannow tek*
> *ha predery, ren Austyn!*
> *a'gen gwayow.*
> *Nyns a ancof.*

> [Come, my friends and my dear ones,
> with entertainment and verses,
> and mirth and sweet melody
> It is better for us
> to return to our palace with sweet songs
> and to consider, by St Augustine!
> our moves.
> He will not be forgotten.][423]

Williams has commented on the significance of these lines of Arthur, suggesting as they do an assertion of an earlier literary tradition, extending the use of the well-attested *englyn* form in Cornish.[424] The legates, however, fail to persuade Arthur to pay the tribute and so the Emperor leaves for France. Notably, Modred's indication of failure seems a prediction of future events, while two of the legates debate Arthur's power and control, and posit a trap. Arthur also leaves for France, and they battle there. Lucius recruits an army to support him. Lucius is then killed, and his head sent to Rome. The sheer range and diversity of characters speaking here guarantees an almost continual flow of action; it seems that the plain may have been the central area for action on the second day. This would be even more likely if the dramatist wanted to simulate more of the conflict. In this sense, the *plen-an-gwarry* shows here its variety of use. It can deal with localised action, as well as spectacle and, as we shall see, also cope with more intimate moments, such as the affair between Modred and Guinevere.

So far, this is but one strand of the Arthurian thread, and shows how the playwright is skilfully (like the author of *Bewnans Meriasek*) able to juggle a number of concurrent narratives. Arthur, meanwhile, has left Guinevere at home, and Modred is in charge. They begin an affair. This is structured in a similar way to events surrounding David and Bathsheba in 'Origo Mundi'. News of this reaches Arthur, while Modred enlists a Saxon, Cheldric, to assist. Arthur and Modred's forces meet, while Guinevere's handmaidens threaten to reveal details of her affair to Arthur. Arthur then offers the governorship of Britain to Modred, and leads his army to face the warriors of Lucius. Lucius is killed, and his army flees from Arthur's forces. A messenger takes the news of this to four senators, and they thank him for it. Some Cornish colour is offered to this section when one of the Senators blesses the messenger with Saint Cleer and Saint Ia, saints who perhaps had their own origin dramas in Cornwall. At the end of the play, Modred and Guinevere discuss their feelings. Guinevere relays her guilt, but Modred turns on the charm, and says he will commit suicide if their love ends. Guinevere relents and they head to the chamber. The handmaidens gossip about them, while Modred is visited by the Bishop in order to crown him king of Britain. Another messenger gives Arthur the news of their affair and of Modred's rise to power. Modred and Guinevere have betrayed Arthur at his moment of glory. The rest of the play text is missing but, following Albert Le Grand's *Life*, presumably Ke operated as something of a peace-maker between them. This seems to be achieved through the following: 'St Ké, realizing that any negotiation is impossible, returns to Brittany, but not before comforting Queen Guenaran (Guinevere) and persuading her to enter a convent'.[425] Ke meanwhile, travels to Cleder, and dies on the first Saturday in October 495. It is unclear whether the ending of the drama works in the same way. For modern audiences at least, the non-resolution of the conflict and Guinevere's entry into a convent are not particularly satisfactory conclusions. The latter, however, may have been a realistic outcome for someone who had committed adultery. The resolution of the territorial conflict may perhaps reflect the wider debate over the accommodation of Celtic Britain. Proportionally, much more of Le Grand's *Life* of Ke is devoted to his conflicts with Teudar in the parish, with the events of Arthur's troubles somewhat compacted in comparison.

A range of discussion has built up about the play. Williams has recently suggested that the play gives us a tangible insight into the wider literary culture of medieval Cornwall. As he sees it, aspects of the drama are a good example of how educated clerics, writing in secular Brythonic, could have continued to operate in Cornwall for quite some time after the Norman Conquest.[426] Thus, writers such as Richard Angwyn and 'Pendarvis' were the last of this type.[427] Drawing on textual evidence, based upon the War of the Roses, Thomas and Williams observe that 'our play was written at some time during the years 1453-60 when the Lancastrian Henry VI was king but was rendered impotent by insanity and captivity and when the real power in the land was in the hand of the Yorkists'.[428] The author clearly supports the Yorkists. This means that the Middle Cornish of the drama is very much comparable with that found in the *Ordinalia*. However, there is not the space here to enter into a full discussion of the work's textual transmission. What is noted is that the scribe of the surviving manuscript is not very accomplished at copying Cornish correctly. For discussion on this, and further phonological debate, I refer the reader to Thomas and Williams's edition.[429] Certainly, this inability to copy Cornish correctly has caused some observers, such as Padel, to feel that the present manuscript's origins were actually in Wales – matching also its discovery there[430] – though others have dismissed this claim.[431] In his studies, George concludes that it is a copy of a copy,[432] but Williams recently noted that the surviving manuscript may, in fact, be a copy of a copy of an original.[433] Thus there would have been the original, a copy completed by a good Latinist, and then a copy by the scribe of the present manuscript. Travelling forward in its transmission, George usefully further observes that 'accepting the statements of experts on handwriting that the copy dates from the second half of the sixteenth century, it became clear to me that this was not a copy for performance'.[434] Such a rationale differs from received wisdom about the other extant dramas, which appear to be made for some form of performance. George therefore concludes that 'it may well have been copied by a Catholic wishing to preserve a relic of the age before 1549, perhaps a member of a family living at Killiow in the parish of Kea'.[435] *Ke's* Marianism is, in many ways, not as explicit as that found in *Bewnans Meriasek* (which was, after all, publicising a Marian centre). However, several folkloric texts refer to King Arthur carrying into battle a shield with the image of Mary and the child Christ upon it – a central strand of Marianism in *Bewnans Ke*.

Intriguingly, the Arthurian matter of the Second Day of the play closely follows the narrative given in Geoffrey of Monmouth's *Historia Regum Britanniae* [*The History of the King of Britain*]. Considering the widespread circulation of this text since its completion in 1136 – and there is perhaps good reason to assume that a copy was held at Glasney College – one can see that the playwright(s) clearly had knowledge of Geoffrey's history. Mention has been already made in this chapter of John Trevisa's lost work, *Book of the Acts of King Arthur*, and this may also have been a source for the author. The likelihood is that if Trevisa's book did exist, he would have made a Cornish-language version of Geoffrey's history – something of an irony, considering that Geoffrey admits his source was an old manuscript in the British tongue. There may be evidence for this, but a central difficulty here is that the names of the Arthurian characters in the play are not often offered in their Cornish form, which indicates the lack of a filtering process. That said, if the playwright was drawing on Trevisa, then Trevisa himself may not have Cornishised his version of Geoffrey of Monmouth. We may, however, have had more evidence of a link if the names were in more Cornish forms. The links are intriguing, but presently unclear. Three final observations on Geoffrey of Monmouth's *Historia* and its relationship to *Bewnans Ke* are worth making. Firstly, although Geoffrey spends considerable energy on pointing out Arthur's Cornish provenance at Tintagel, this place appears not to feature within the extant *Bewnans Ke*; secondly, a strong link to Merlin is propounded in *Historia Regum Britanniae*, but not in any of the play-text; and finally, it is somewhat significant that the dramatist elects to focus only on Arthur's battle with the Romans – when a strong component of the Brythonic tradition about Arthur, was his countering of the Saxons.[436] To some extent, both the Romans and Saxons represented the 'Other'.

Although I have tried to give a flavour of some of the original performance conditions and material environment of performances of *Bewnans Ke*, there are considerable difficulties in developing such a reconstruction. This is due partly to the lack of stage diagrams, and partly to the incomplete nature of the manuscript. Unlike *Bewnans Meriasek* and the *Ordinalia*, there have, as yet, been no modern performances of the work. Until this is attempted, we are inevitably operating only with guesswork. Since the publication of the main editions of the work, there has not been much discussion of the staging of *Bewnans Ke*. One has hope that such discussion here will prompt further and more detailed enquiry. Given *Bewnans Ke*'s comedy and its Arthurian dimensions, a performance revival would seem possible at some point; although it might be reasonable to edit some of the more discursive moments of the Second Day, which would be hard for a modern audience to digest. Certainly, a suitable beginning and ending for the work could be devised. In some ways, however, the lack of diagrams also makes us rethink because, if anything, the presence and integration of *Ke* into the corpus proves further the considerable variety of Cornish drama under the genre of the 'gwarry miracle'. Kea itself is still dominated by the two churches (St Kea Church and Old Kea Church) which were founded by the play's protagonist.

In very many ways, although the *Ordinalia* may stand as the high watermark of medieval literary Cornwall, both *Bewnans Ke* and *Bewnans Meriasek* offer much more of interest to both scholars and performers. This is because the authors of both texts interweave many more strands and legends, and because the characterisation is better developed. At times, the characters of the *Ordinalia* are rather two-dimensional (perhaps necessarily so in a direct dramatic interpretation of the Bible), while the two saints' plays offer foils and foibles of the individuals being dramatised. Both of these dramas also assert a conscious vision of Cornishness and, although taking on some often complex liturgical themes, they nevertheless continue to foreground local identity. This is obvious in the language itself, and also in the various local elements that are dropped into the dramaturgy at various points. We again have no real idea whether these two dramas represent the very top quality drama being written during this phase, or whether they represent perhaps more the middle ground of creativity. Certainly, considering their ambition, their authors were no small-time writers since both texts are complex. We have more obvious clues to the authorship of *Bewnans Meriasek* than *Bewnans Ke*. What is significant is that Kea Parish is comparatively close to Penryn, and therefore Glasney College: they are separated by only a day's walk. *Bewnans Ke* also fits into a wider cultural-geographic imagining of Cornish space, since the Cornish place-names in the text, like those of the *Ordinalia*, match the surrounds of the Fal Estuary and River. Outside of their medieval material circumstances, these three plays (once *Bewnans Ke* had become known) have gone on through successive centuries to become a symbol of both literary and theatrical development in Cornwall. As can be seen above, in no way was their dramaturgy backward looking or un-progressive. Indeed, the *Ordinalia's* dramatic solutions to the problems of staging the Legend of the Rood are spectacularly successful, and highly innovative. Their survival allows us a certain degree of insight into what other dramas might have been developed in Cornwall during this phase, and it gives an indication of the direction in which native Cornish drama was heading, had it not subsequently collapsed during the processes of the Reformation. We now begin to see how sustained the Cornish theatrical continuum is, when read alongside the intensive *plen-an-gwarry* culture of the period.

While performances of texts such as the *Ordinalia*, *Bewnans Meriasek* and *Bewnans Ke* were ongoing, early records in Cornwall do demonstrate some touring activity. The 1404-5 Borough Accounts of Launceston, some twenty-five years after *Ordinalia's* proposed date of composition, list the travelling expenses of a group of players who travel via Tavistock to Plympton and back again on three separate occasions. Costs included 'the plays at supper, wine and beer, hay and fodder, horseshoes, wine and alms'.[437] Sadly, no mention of the subject matter of the play is given. Through the following decades of the century, the Borough Accounts also give much time to detailing para-theatrical activity on St Mary Magdelene's Eve on 25 November. The 1440 entry gives a good impression of this, listing the 'confraternity of minstrels'[438] and then, in 1459, the 'four gallons and one potell of wine and for bread' used by 'the mayor and his fellowes'.[439] Celebration on St Mary Magdelene's Eve (linking to the characterisation of Mary Magdelene in the *Ordinalia*) continued through the fifteenth century, and well into the first half of the sixteenth: for example, the 1520-1 Borough Accounts list wine paid for a juggler, and the external expense of a bearward [a bear-keeper/trainer], and 'one beast called a camel this year'.[440] Changes seem to occur in the latter end of the sixteenth century when we learn in 1572 of summer-time payment made to the 'venesicians [actors or dancers] that were here & plaid here whereof there was gathered' suggesting a community gathering[441] and, in the following year, payments were given for 'the players of Mylton', 'a singing man which came from South Tawton', and a 'beere hearde'.[442] In 1574 greater sophistication comes to the town in the form of 'the players one Maie day' then later, in September, payment made to 'the Enterlude players' and to 'the poppet players'.[443] 1574 brings the Interlude players back in form of 'my Lord Staffordes men, by master maior's commandment'.[444]

In the latter end of the fifteenth century, some of the more famous houses and families of Cornwall were clearly taking part in theatrical activities. At Catholic Lanherne, in the house of the later recusant Arundells, Sir John Arundell's Stewards' Accounts give details of various costumes and 'paper for disgysyes' in 1466.[445] These disguises (guizing) were probably for mumming-type activities. 'Red lead' and 'white lead' are also recorded, which were perhaps used for some kind of make-up. 'Gold foyll' and 'glewe' are also mentioned, suggesting much energy in the creation of costuming.[446] Later, in the early sixteenth century, 'egupcians' danced there,[447] with later wills and inventories showing something of an active performance/musical culture.[448] Although there is no evidence in the Accounts, Bakere suggests that the players probably not only performed at Lanherne, but might also have travelled to other manor houses.[449]

If texts such as the *Ordinalia*, *Bewnans Meriasek* and *Bewnans Ke* could be developed in the west of Cornwall, surely other communities would want as spectacular an event? Given Bodmin's connections to St Petroc, it is perhaps not surprising to see theatrical activity taking place there in the late fifteenth century. The St Petroc's Church Building Accounts for 1470-1 show receipts for 'the players yn the church hay William Mason and Iis fellowes v s.'[450] Clearly a continuity of performance took place here, since the General Receivers' accounts of 1494-5 also make reference to payment to 'Wyllyam Capynter for syluer and the making of [a] Garnement and for colours ocupyed for dyademys & crownys & such oder (longyng to Cor…) Christi game and for tynfoyle that Iohn Wythyall had of Rafe Stayner'.[451] The energy put into the costuming and design clearly shows a drama of some significance here. Meanwhile, we learn that sometime at the beginning of the sixteenth century (probably between 1501 and 1513) a minstrel was paid for his services.[452] As this was part of the Town Receivers' Accounts, this may not have been connected to the church. The General Receivers' Accounts between 1504 and 1505 show payment 'onto harry Kyngge and his Cumpaney for ther disportes in the Ilde halle' which perhaps refers to more secular drama. At the same time a 'Berewarde' is also given reward'.[453] As Harry Kyngge crops up in other locations in the same period, it would seem to indicate a travelling troupe. On 4 October of the next year, the same set of Accounts lists payment to 'the Minstrelles of My Lord of Devynshire', and makes reference to a 'daunce Seynt Erme Botrescastelle' showing some festivities and dancing imported from Saint Erme, and Boscastle.[454] In 1505-6 we also see reference made to a Robin Hood play in October's Accounts from the Berry Tower Building.[455] This tower was built between 1501 and 1504, as part of the chantry church of the Holy Rood. According to Joyce and Newlyn, there were three guilds who operated in Bodmin: the New, the Holy Rood (again evidence of the importance of this legend in Cornwall); and the St Christopher,[456] who appear to have organised performances.

More detailed expenditure comes in the General Receivers' Accounts of October 1509-10, where we learn about the 'showe of Corporis Christi'. Cloth for the manufacture of the costume of Jesus, is mentioned, as are other garments and linen.[457] Here, then, we see that a Corpus Christi drama based around the life of Jesus was enacted in Bodmin in the opening decades of the sixteenth century. There were also payments made slightly earlier (in 1503-4) to the civic musicians, or 'waytes' of Bodmin.[458] Such musicians were likely to be involved in the Corpus Christi play as well. Certainly, in the next decade – from 1510 to 1520 – similar theatrical activity seems to be occurring in the town, because 'thynges for the showe' still need to be made in 1514-15, and the waytes musicians performed again in 1519.[459] Construction was still required in 1529,[460] at which point the play had been performed for some thirty years into the new century. We also know that plays from elsewhere were performed in Bodmin. For example, the Town Receivers' Accounts (c.1515-39) detail the '16d given to the play from Tywardreath'.[461]

It seems that at Bodmin, in previous times, the Corpus Christi drama was produced by a combination of both civic and church leadership. This is fully noted in 1539 when St Petroc's Inventory of Church Goods lists Jesus's 'cotte of purple scarenett'[462] as well as, in 1566, '4 tormenteris cotes' and 'toe develes cotes'. A distinctive 'crowne of black' (clearly connected with the devils) is also mentioned here.[463] However, we know that the dissolution of Bodmin Priory took place in the same year, so this probably indicates a catalogue of goods for the investigating commissioners. Rowse believes that such costumes were used for performance on Good Friday, but it is likely they would have been used both for this and at other times during the ritual year.[464] With this we at least have a notion that the Bodmin Corpus Christi drama featured a torturer's sequence, leading to the crucifixion. The costumes for Jesus, the tormentors and the devils are mentioned in 1566, but by this time the religious drama had been more or less completely shut down.[465]

Although the parish records stop recording such information in the period after 1566, theatrical activity must have carried on for some time. Carew, gathering material in the later decades of the sixteenth century, mentions the para-theatrical activity that took place at Halgavor [English: Goat's Moor]. This is where boxing matches were staged, and perhaps the same place was used for performances as well. According to Carew, this is where the expression 'He shall be presented in Halgavor Court' arose.[466] The one problem with this theory is that the site is described by Carew as being a quagmire, so it would seem unlikely to have theatrical use. The Cornish Record Office also contains a document showing a lease to one William Collier around 1603. This mentions a place in the south-eastern part of the town which is called 'The Ffryers [Friars]'.[467] Apparently there was 'nowe a Cocke pitt built' which might indicate a *plen-an-gwarry* structure, but neither Spriggs nor Lyon lists this.[468] It begins to sound as though the Corpus Christi play in Bodmin was a much more urban affair than elsewhere in Cornwall; however, it being one of Cornwall's premier ecclesiastical centres, this would seem apt.

In contrast to more central and westerly parishes of Cornwall, Stratton, in the north east, lost Cornish comparatively early. Certainly not much Cornish would have been spoken there in the period after 1200. However, this did not hinder the development of theatrical activity in the sixteenth century. The earliest records from St Andrew's Churchwardens' Accounts come from February in the years 1522-3, when money was received by some performing 'Eygppcions for the church howse'.[469] Entertainment in the form of a bear also came in 1527,[470] while in 1535 we have detail of 'Robynhode & all of hys fellows', the money collected by one I. Greeby.[471] John Mares and 'hys company that played Robyn hoode' gave monies to the church in 1536,[472] and such a pattern of performance appears to continue to 1544.[473] In the Accounts running from 1559 to 1562, there is curious reference to 'Iepcyons', which again suggests a performing gypsy group.[474] Performances seem to last until at least the end of the 1560s, when monies were transferred for a 'mynyster to helpe playe and sing' and to 'Cottell for the bull ryng'.[475] This might indicate some kind of performance space, but probably not a *plen-an-gwarry*.

Although no surviving evidence has been found of a *plen-an-gwarry*, as we might expect, there seems to have been a good deal of theatrical and para-theatrical activity operating in Lostwithiel in the 1530s. The 1536-7 St George's Guild Stewards' Accounts receipts give some flavour of this. The main para-theatrical activity appears to have been St George's Riding to a certain shrine (an event with continuity forwards to Robert Morton Nance's interest in St George iconography). Although details are sketchy from the Accounts, a great deal of energy and expense is given over to the 'skowring of St George's harnes'.[476] The activity was obviously connected to the church at Lanlivery, since the vicar there is mentioned in the Accounts. Another significant entry is that of Nicholas the Britton [Breton] who was paid for the fastening of St George's harness.[477] The theatricality of what was probably a development of this ceremony is found in the observations of Carew:

> Upon little Easter Sunday the freeholders of the town and manor, by themselves or their deputies, did there assemble; amongst whom, one (as it fell to his lot by turn) bravely apparelled, gallantly mounted, with a crown on his head, a sceptre in his hand, a sword borne before him, and dutifully attended by all the rest on horseback, rode through the principal street to the church; there the curate in his best beseen solemnly received him at the churchyard stile and conducted him to hear divine service; after which he repaired with the same pomp to a house fore-provided for that purpose, made a feast to his attendants, kept the table's end himself, and was served with kneeling, assay, and all other rites due to the estate of a prince: with which dinner the ceremony ended, and every man returned home again. The pedigree of this usage is derived from so many descents on ages that the cause and author outreach remembrance: howbeit, these circumstances offer a conjecture that it should betoken the royalties appertaining to the honour of Cornwall.[478]

Now long forgotten, this ceremony would seem to be of considerable importance, and the procession may have an undercurrent of related theatrical activity. During the middle decades of the 1500s, St Olaf's Church at Poughill clearly had some kind of theatrical entertainment occurring, for the 1550-1 Church-wardens' Accounts make reference to payment made to 'the Kynges enterluyd plaers & for there dener'.[479] In the immediate decades after this, we learn of much theatre taking place at St Breock. Around 1557, some dancers 'made their accounte & hath payed in clere gaynys', an intriguing and tantalising reference is made to a 'Svsnana ys Playe [Susanna Play]' and 'Chrystoffer Rvychard made hys accounte & hath payed to the store clere'.[480] Later, in 1565, 'Lydwan [probably Ludgvan] dancers' were paid.[481] The following year we learn of the 'enterlwd players of Saint denys' having performed there,[482] and in 1567, payment is also made for the 'daunce of gramputh [probably Grampound]'.[483] In 1573, in the period April to May, we learn of receipts from 'Robyn Hoode & hys Cumpayne' – perhaps indicating a May event.[484] Clearly St Breock seemed to be quite adept at importing dancing and drama from elsewhere in Cornwall. 1574 brought dancers from St Evel, while the 1590s had 'players of Robyn Hoode that came from St Cullombe the Lower [Minor]'.[485] Given the close proximity of these two parishes, one can see how this might work. Clearly, however, there were rival productions, for in 1591 St Breock welcomed 'the Robyn Hoode of Maugan [St Mawgan]'[486] which again is close to St Breock.

It is perhaps not surprising to observe a significant amount of theatrical activity in nearby St Columb Major. This book has already alluded to the potential drama of St Columba, as mentioned by Nicholas Roscarrock (c.1550-1634), who writes about 'an olde Cornish Rhyme (possibly a verse drama?) containing her Legend, translated by one Mr Williams, a Phis[it]ion there, but howe authentick it is I dare not say'.[487] Considering the fact that Roscarrock was gathering material around the same time as some of the drama that follows, there may well have been a link, but it is difficult to prove. In St Columb Major it is in the 1580s and 1590s that we find most evidence of theatre at work. The Churchwardens' Accounts of St Columba the Virgin carry a range of information. In 1584, there is mention of the following items: 'coates for dancers, a ffryer's coate, 24 dansinge belles, a streamers of red moccado and [boc] locram, and 6 yards of white woollen clothe'.[488] This certainly makes for some kind of spectacle within the town. By 1587 the dancers' coats appear specifically to be for Morris work, since 'morrishe coates' are then listed.[489] These entries in the so-called *St Columb Green Book* continue into the 1590s, although in 1594 we learn of 'Rychard beard owethe to be payd at our ladye day in lent x.s. of Robyn hoodes monyes', and that 'Robert calwaye owethe for ye same'.[490] The Morris coats continued to be mentioned in later accounts, from 1595 to 1597. It would appear, then, that some kind of performance took place in St Columb Major which involved a Morris/guizing-styled interpretation of Robin Hood. A few fragments of Robin Hood plays have survived in the English canon, and some flavour of what occurred in St Columb Major and Minor during the sixteenth century may be discerned from the following, as sourced in Tickner. One of the English stage versions of Robin Hood from the same period has him encounter a potter:

Robin: Listen to me, my merry men all,
            And hear what I shall say;
            Of an adventure I shall you tell,

That befell the other day.
With a proud potter I met
And a rose garland on his head,
The flowers of it shone marvellous fresh;
This seven year and more he hath use this way,
Yet was he never so courteous a potter
As one penny passage to pay.
Is there any of my merry men all
That dare be so bold
To make the potter pay passage
Either silver or gold.[491]

Little John denies the request, knowing how strong the potter is, but later Robin and the potter fight, with the theme of payment for passage:

Robin: Passage shalt thou pay here under the greenwood tree.
Potter: If thous be a good fellow, as men do thee call,
            Lay aside thy bow,
            And take thy sword and buckler in thy hand
            And see what shall befall.
            [*They fight, and the Potter uses his quarter-staff with such goodwill that Robin is forced to call his band.*][492]

This text is only a fragment, so presumably the potter later gave in, at the appearance of superior numbers. According to Tickner, the story goes that Robin then borrows the potter's wares for the day and, dressed up in his clothes, travels on to Nottingham Market.[493] Perhaps some local adaptation of this type of narrative would have been made. Although this is clearly not the text used at St Columb Major and Minor, it does give a suggestion of the dramaturgy in operation, and plays there may have had a similar scope. The rhyme certainly matches Cornish verse drama, while the feel is of other Cornish mumming texts, albeit without their self-declamation. One of the classic ingredients of all Robin Hood narratives is the fight with a quarter-staff, usually over a river; this would obviously suit a Morris/guizing interpretation because many sides use staffs or sticks as part of the performance and dance. St Columb Major and Minor is not too distant from Padstow and, as Davey had proven, there is a tradition there of winter-time Morris/guizing, including, somewhat controversially in the modern era, with blackened faces.[494] Therefore, this could be a wider trend in this part of Cornwall. One final point is worth making. In the proud aftermath of Agincourt, where

Cornish archers made a notable contribution, bow-craft and archer-lore would have been highly respected in Cornwall. Therefore, having a hero who is an expert with a bow would have greatly appealed to young men. The latest reference to 'the young men of the parish which plaide a stage play' comes in the 1615-16 Accounts, so clearly performance of some kind continued on into the seventeenth century.[495] It is significant that no later Accounts are drawn up for such performance, yet St Columb Major continues to hold its para-theatrical hurling competition. Clearly, the Robin Hood theme was very fashionable during the closing years of the sixteenth century, perhaps because it was also apolitical and a safe narrative. That said, the narrative continued to be popular in the twentieth- and twenty-first centuries.[496] According to Lyon, St Columb Major may possibly once have had a *plen-an-gwarry*. This he deduces from the Church Terrier of 1727, which records 'The Playing Meadow, 1a. bounded on the E by the Bowling Green and on the W by a lane', and 'Williian [William] Berry's Garden was taken out of the Playing Meadow and is now set in it'.[497]

In Antony Parish in south-east Cornwall, there was considerable theatrical activity happening during the middle years of the sixteenth century. In Millbrook in 1548-9, the Churchwarden's Accounts indicate payment to the players there. In 1553-4 during the month of August reference is made to an item 'receyved of Robyn Hodd & the maydyns' indicating that a drama of Robin Hood was played there.[498] Similar records occur between 1554 and 1559, which demonstrates at least ten years of performance. Two of the performers during this phase appear to be Iohn [sic] Rowe and Elizaberth [sic] Serell. Another intriguing reference to performance in south-east Cornwall is found in the 1582-3 Mayors' Accounts from West Looe where reference is made to an 'Item to Colakote tow shellinges yo goe to the showes'.[499] Joyce and Newlyn argue that the shows there may well have a connection to a narrative that they term 'A Merry Tale of the Queen's Ape in Cornwall'.[500] The tale is too long to quote in full here, but the most relevant section would appear to be the following:

> In the reign of Queen Elizabeth, a fellow who wore his hat buttoned up on one side, and a feather therein, like a tooth-drawer, with the rose and crown on his breast for a badge, had obtained a licence from the Lord Chamberlain, to make a show of a great ape about the country, who could perform many notable tricks; and by going to markets and fairs, his master picked up a great deal of money. The ape usually rid upon a mastiff dog, and a man beat a drum before him. It happened that these four travellers came to a town called Loo in Cornwall, where, having taken an inn, the drum beat about the town to give notice, that at

such a place was an admirable ape, with very many notable qualities, if they pleased to bestow their money and time to come to see him; but the towns-people being a sort of poor fishermen who minded their own employments, none of them thought it worth their while to see this worthy sight, at which the fellow being vexed, resolved to put a trick upon them.[501]

Clearly, this might have been the kind of show that Looe witnessed, with the fellow threatening to drive everyone out of the town. Events in the tale are absurdly comical, with the mayor, after having to watch the ape pucker his lips to kiss his wife, eventually inviting the fellow for supper. Certainly, such touring creature shows came to Cornwall, so there may be some measure of truth in the connection.

One of the families in most trouble during this period of religious reformation was the Tregians of Golden, near Probus. As Rowse, and Kent and Merrifield have detailed,[502] events surrounding the arrest, incarceration and trial of the recusant Francis Tregian demonstrate the troubling religious changes of the period. A Treatise written about his trial has a significant theatrical connection. During Tregian's first trial at Launceston in 1578, one of the witnesses was a man named Twigge, who had arrived at Golden at Christmas 1575 to perform an interlude there. Admitting that he had been 'runninge aboute the Countrye from place to place, with a balde Enterclude',[503] Twigge gave evidence connecting Tregian to Cuthbert Mayne. From the Treatise no suggestion of the content of the interlude is given, though it seems to have been a one-man show. Probus is itself of interest, for as well as being an important early ecclesiastical centre, in prior times it also had two potential *plen-an-gwarries*, suggesting a drama which may have presented the story of the parish's two saints: Probus and Grace.[504] Ironically, Golden is only a stone's throw away from the site at Trewithen, where Lyon identifies one location.[505] The fact that interludes continue to be performed just down the road may suggest a continuity of travelling performers over a longer period of time. Not far from the playing-places of Probus, and close to the ones at Kea, is Truro. Documentation does seem to indicate that there was, at one time, some kind of playing-place structure within Truro. John Leland, who would sometimes have visited Truro between 1535 and 1543, indicates the following: 'There is a castelle a quarter of a mile by West out of Truru longing ti the earle of Cornwale now clene doun/the site of which is now usid for a shoting and playing place.'[506] Lyon believes that this is marked on the 1809 Ordnance Survey map, and was perhaps used 'for the possible performance of miracle plays'.[507] It is interesting to speculate on what kind of text would have been performed in Truro, since no saintly life comes to mind. However, it is not that far (especially by river) from Glasney, so there could be a connection there.

In the final quarter of the sixteenth century and the opening half of the seventeenth century, the Borough Accounts of St Ives Guildhall give considerable insight into the developed theatrical culture of the town. Like many of the other examples in this chapter, the dramas examined probably carried on for many years before they appeared in Account records. In St Ives, considerable academic enquiry has also been made into the personnel behind the Accounts, and interested readers may follow-up that enquiry.[508] My purpose here is not to document those individuals but rather to show St Ives as a significant theatrical centre, certainly in the years 1571-2, when the Borough Accounts list detailed monies received for 'a playe' which seemed to run for six days.[509] From the Accounts, it is unclear whether this was the same play run on six days, or rather six days of a cycle, with a different play each day. The former seems more logical, although little detail is given about the subject matter of the drama. Bakere argues that more revenue comes in as word about the play spreads.[510] We learn also for example of the 'drincke money after the playe' and that 'somer games' occurred at the same time. The drinking afterwards also seemed to have brought in a fair amount of money, so was obviously an important part of the proceedings, possibly financing the production. Considerable construction seems to have been required, however, for payment also went for 'iiij trees' and the use of a carpenter. One Thomas Hicks delivered to a Mr Trinwithe 'things for the playe' and 'halfe a dosin of white lambes skyns' were also employed. Importantly we also see reference to 'the carpenters yat made hevin [Heaven]'.[511] The latter references would seem to indicate a religious drama of some kind. Theatre was still occurring in the following year (1572), when we learn of the 'Kinge & Quene of ye sommer ga[mes]', played by Harries Sterrie and Jane Walshe. The Accounts for this year also detail items received for 'ye interlude', while some 'elme bordes' are required in 'ye playing place'. There is some notion here that a wooden construction of a 'station' may have been made, but the Accounts suggest a few rather than the many that would be needed, if they were to be made of wood. John William also receives payment for 'things which he delyueryd aboute the laste playe' while Thomas Trinwith pays 'co[…] of Trewro [Truro?] for lyneclothe'.[512] In successive years, various other people play the King and Queen of the Summer Games right up until 1634.[513] However, there is then less mention of drama itself. Only in 1586 do we learn that payment was made for 'the players of Germal [Germoe] which gathered for yeir church',[514] but there seems not to be the complexity of performance or such a long performance schedule as in 1571-2. The obvious subtext of this is that Reformationist activity had colluded to shut down the large event. The Germoe reference is intriguing, however, for this village is located twelve miles

Fig. 41. The merging of knightly and Biblical culture in *Pascon Agan Arluth*.

away from St Ives. As Bakere notes, they must have been of 'a sufficiently high standard' to perform in a larger town.[515]

Likewise, 1587 saw payment made to 'Robin howde of St colloms the lower by the appointment of Mr Tregera',[516] another piece of imported drama, this time from the east of the territory. By 1633, drama seems to have disappeared altogether, although we do learn that part of the function of the King and Queen of the Summer Games was to collect money for the poor, since monies would be 'delivered to the overseers of the poore for this yere'.[517] Lyon believes that a *plen-an-gwarry* once existed in St Ives and that the location is where the old Stennack primary school now stands. His evidence for this comes from Matthews, who in 1892 observes that 'The name Plain an Gwarry is given to a piece of land at the Stannack in a deed of 1808, but has long been forgotten. At that date, the land in question was an orchard'.[518] If the location was an orchard (or at least an area containing apple trees), then this would make an appropriate setting for the King and Queen of the Summer Games. Hutton observes that such Kings and Queens of Summer were replaced elsewhere in the islands of Britain by Robin Hood as the centre of the revels sometime between 1450 and 1550.[519] If this were the case, then St Ives was running an older model,[520] whereas St Columb Minor had become more contemporary. This was also probably couched in linguistic terms, with St Columb Minor using English and St Ives still using Cornish. However, we must also be sceptical of Robin Hood as only an English import. Similar such dramas were run all across Europe, and may have also developed organically in Cornwall.

Sancreed is one location already connected with Cornish-language literature, in that the earliest of the extant manuscripts of *Pascon agan Arluth* was found in the church there.[521] We also know that portions of the poem resemble sequences within 'Passio Christ' from the *Ordinalia*, so there is an important dramatic connection.[522] Additionally, the story of St Sancred is highly dramatic in the sense that, after he accidentally killed his father, the saint went in remorse and penance to work as a swine-herder, which gave him the opportunity to work with nature.[523] There is also considerable evidence pointing toward a *plen-an-gwarry* at Sancreed. Lyon cites Pool, in his discussion of *The Penheleg MS*, which he dates as 1580,[524] but which others dated slightly earlier as being from 1558.[525] It features some early evidence of performance at the *plen-an-gwarry* in Sancreed, from *the Deposition of John Veal et al.*[526] The June 1568 deposition concerns a murder which took place some time between 1498 and 1505, at a period when the miracle play seemed to be fully operational. The important part of the account is the following sequence:

> It fortuned within a while after there was a Mirable [Miracle] Play at Sanckras Parish divers Men came to the play amongs whom came a Servant of this Mr. Trevrye [the murderer] – named Quenall and (in the Place before the Play began) the said Quenall fell at Variance with one Richard James Veane & so both went out the Play and fought together the said Quenall hadf a sword & a Buckler, and the other had a single Sword the said Quenall was a very tall Man in his Hight; the other gave back and fell over a Mole Hill and e're he could recover himself: the said Quen[all] thrust his sword through him and so immediately dyed and Quenall taken and bound to the End of the Play: and before the Play was done his Master hearing thereof came to the Place with other Sanctuary Men and by force would have taken him away from his said Grandfather Mr. Veal and others but he was not able so to do with a Sufficient Guard he was Carried to Conertone Gaol Where he was after hanged on the Gallows in Conerton Down and so was more in his Time for there was no prisoner than Carried to Launston Gaol.[527]

Several elements make this account interesting. Not only is the drama offstage perhaps more significant than that on-stage, but it also gives an indication of the diversity of the population who would travel to such an event. Actions to deal with Quenall seem to have occurred only after the play had finished, to avoid creating too much of a disturbance. As Veal himself would have been around ten years old when all of this happened, his memory serves him well. However, we might still have preferred him to have recalled the drama itself rather than the events of the murder; does this suggest either that the drama was not very memorable, or that it was simply taken for granted? In terms of the place itself, it is striking that such a crime should have occurred in the very parish associated with its origin saint committing a murder as well. As Bottrell later notes, it is interesting that Veal still pronounces Sancreed as *Sanckras*,[528] indicating operational Cornish-language culture in 1568.

So far in our account, the focus has been on purely 'mainland' theatre, but it is perhaps worth pausing to look at two other places where drama may potentially have occurred: these are the island of Lundy and the Isles of Scilly. Although carrying their own identities for many years, both island groups have an age-old relationship with Cornwall. Lundy is perhaps presently more connected to Devon in England than it is to Cornwall, although this had not always been the case. Significantly, although barely populated, Lundy presumably had similar early proto- and para-theatrical activity continuing there, and certainly a sense of ceremony, as discussed by Langham in his observations of its early history.[529] We know also, for example, that Lundy was used as a base by the Welsh Prince Madoc around the year 1170, but it was perhaps after 1199, when the Norman de Marisco family assumed control of the territory, that the island's story really developed.[530] Although the sixteenth century brought liaisons with the famous Cornish families of the Arundells and the Grenvilles, the records have little of note that is directly related to theatre or performance. Presumably, however, the various garrisons stationed there over this period told stories and created their own entertainments, since there was not much else to do.

One might have felt that, as a last point of Celticity, the Isles of Scilly might also have developed their own dramas. Again, however, the records are curiously devoid of any kind of performance being presented there. It is well known that despite their Celticity, successive observers have argued for their comparatively early Anglicisation (Scilly was effectively repeopled under the edicts of Henry VII and Elizabeth I),[531] so this may be one reason why the traditions of mainland Cornish drama never developed there.[532] Matthews, however, does offer some insights. He notes that Scillonians did take part in feasts up until relatively modern times; such feasts may have involved pageants or some kind of performance. One he identifies was the so-called 'Feast of Nickla Theis', which was an older medieval custom, later transformed into a modern harvest festival.[533] Guizing did occur, however, and was likely to have been introduced to the islands from west Cornwall. The guizing was accompanied by dancing, sometimes with the men of successive garrisons 'disguising' their identity. Shrove Tuesday brought a custom of bombarding the doors of houses with stones, asking for 'money, pancakes or stones'.[534] Curiously, this topsy-turvy festival culture is all of which we have evidence, as one might have expected either fishermen or travellers to have been in Cornwall while 'gwarry miracles' were being performed, particularly as this was a summer phenomenon on the whole, and the season permitted easier travel. However, for most residents of both Lundy and the Isles of Scilly during the late medieval and Renaissance periods, theatre in the sense that it is explored through this chapter must have seemed highly exotic and somewhat unachievable.

Other Cornish-linked texts were being created elsewhere, however. One text usually examined in the light of this period is *The Image of Idleness* by Oliver Oldwanton. Often a footnote in most other publications, Oldwanton's text has several reasons for being significant here. First of all, although the text has, in the past, been viewed as a drama,[535] it is in fact a monologue, written in the form of a treatise containing, as Murdoch notes, 'stories in a pseudo-epistolary form'.[536] There is every reason to assume that sections of it could be performed or declaimed, although it is not quite a drama in any conventional way. Secondly, although the text contains some Cornish material, it was most probably written for the amusement of young, learned gentlemen of London sometime between 1550 and 1570, ending up in a published form in 1574, its full title being *A little Treatise called the Image of Idlenesse, containing certaine matters mooued between Walter Wedlock and Bawdin Bachelor, translated out of the Troyan or Cornish tung into English.*[537] For the most part, the text is quite impenetrable for the modern reader, being full of contemporary allegory and puns, as well as what Ellis has described as 'a series of moral (or rather immoral) platitudes of a conventional type on love and marriage'.[538]

However, the story is familiar enough: it is basically an early version of Pygmalion, where the King of Cyprus fell in love with his own sculpture; followed by Aphrodite endowing the statue with life and transforming it into the flesh and blood of Galatea. In Ovid's version, the statue transforms back into ivory, but here the writer chooses instead alabaster – a more contemporary material. What Oldwanton does is to adapt the morals of this story to make them relevant to contemporary London. The reasoning behind the Cornish reference would seem to come from a sequence mid-way through, when the narrator explains the old name for London:

At one time a Gentleman of the West parts (who shall remain nameless) at Charing Crosse in his way homewardes from London (then called Troynouant) over took a certain fair mistresse whome when he had saulted, and by communication did perceive that she would ride foure or five dayes in his company, he was wonderful glad thereof.[539]

Here, Oldwanton is very obviously making the link between the Troyance tongue (Cornish) and the town of London (Troynouant). Troy was ancient territory which would offer a link to the classical age in which the narrative first arose. Cornwall was first allegedly occupied by refugees from Troy, a myth that had been developed by Geoffrey of Monmouth, but was still apparently ongoing at the end of the sixteenth century. It would therefore then be apt for the text to contain Cornish language, as well as some Cornish characters. However, the amount of Cornish is very limited, and the three Cornish characters later mentioned are not really developed. The line of Cornish comes in Chapter Seven, when the classical world and the Cornish world are blended together:

> Tyll at length this Pigmalion died and then was his wife turned agayne into an image of alabaster which to this day so remayneth and is accompted throughout all Greece theyr best and chiefest Pylgremage for to remove or expel the passion and paynes of ielousy. The Princes of Tarent (but after some bookes, of Ottronto) finding by inmissable proof that her husband had been behaving badly towards her 'being warned by a vision to repayre unto this blessed image for helpe, did avowe her Pylgrymage thither and received the Oracle, *Marsoye these duan Guisca ancorne Rog hatre arta* [if there is to thee grief to wear the horn, give it home again], being expounded by the prestes of that Temple to this effect in Englyshe. If to weare the horne thou fynde thy selfe agreed, gyve hym back agayne and thou shalt sone be eased.[540]

Thus, in this section, the Princess of Tarent of Ottronto finds out that her husband has a mistress, but the whole of the end of this sequence is broadly based on a contemporary joke based around the theme of wearing horns, which must surely have been related to phallic imagery. What is most intriguing though is how Oldwanton knew this piece of Cornish. He was probably not a native speaker, unless he himself had come from Cornwall, but considering the quality of his secular written English, we can probably dismiss this. The likely explanation in this century, and the ones that followed, was that certain pieces of Cornish were known in London, or that there was a Cornish community operating in London that could supply such material. Perhaps these could even be pieces of 'stage' Cornish that emphasised a convenient difference for the writers of such texts: in effect, a convenient gag from the periphery of Britain. It is interesting too that it is the Oracle that uses

Cornish. This would be apt because Oldwanton was seeking a language that sounded completely different to English, and in this case opts for Cornish because of its apparent classical origin. The phrase 'to this effect in Engylyshe' is important, because we know that around the islands of Britain, several native languages were being forced to rerender themselves in this way. No further Cornish is used. Many of the rest of the sequences offer guidance for young men on the wiles of relationships, the following being a good example: 'Heer Bawdin to proove that women are never so much addit to bent to heir owne will and opinion, but that by wisdom and good policy they may easily be broken therof, shevveth a lively example of late experience'.[541]

Three Cornish characters are also mentioned in a small and scandalous story of a priest named John Polmarghe of Penborgh (presumably a version of Glasney at Penryn), as well as Maister Jewgur and Syr Ogier Penkeyles, but these seem to be merely background material, to enhance the text's Cornish credentials, rather than contributing to the plot. The concept of the translation of the work from Cornish is an intriguing one. Ellis offers that 'we do know that several manuscripts of Cornish have been lost and it could be that *The Image of Idleness* was one such piece. Comparison with some 'bawdy' Irish and Welsh tales shows that such a tale was not alien to Celtic literary tradition'.[542] However, Ellis' argument is not convincing. As this book has shown, the Cornish literary tradition, certainly by this phase, was unallied to other Celtic traditions (bar Brittany) and, as argued above, the piece would seem more a work that included Cornish as a device, rather than a survival from an earlier text. This was Henry Jenner's view as well.[543]

A flavour of performance in the late fifteenth and early sixteenth centuries is to be found in two contrasting sources from the period. James Whetter, in his account of the Bodrugan family, informs us that Henry Bodrugan maintained a very large household at Bodrugan (between Mevagissey and Gorran) on the south coast.[544] In the manorial Accounts of 1468, Roger Jak Thomas, the reeve, paid him two sums amounting to £37.8s.3d, 'for the costage and expenses of his hospicium at Bodrugan'.[545] As Whetter notes, this was a very large amount of money, and must have indicated a good deal of entertainment, and probably performance of some kind.[546] The likely performance was minstrelsy (lute-playing, singing and the recitation of poetry), although by no means did this exclude drama. Indeed, as Southworth proposes, in this period, fools and jesters often co-ordinated small-scale dramatic activity within court,[547] so probably served the same function in grander families as well. Indeed, 'player fools' were actually instrumental in shaping much secular theatre during this period. We also know that when Bodrugan travelled across the Tamar, he requested similar entertainment. In

Barnstaple, the town Accounts of 1476 and 1477, show payments of 4d were made on two occasions to 'minstrels of Henry Bodrugan'.[548] The minstrels are likely to have continued working into the next century as well.

Clearly, the importance of minstrels and 'foolery' continued in Cornwall long after Henry Bodrugan's time. In east Cornwall, at the Church of St Nonna in Alternun (popularly known as the 'Cathedral of the Moor') we find a number of para-theatrical carved bench ends.[549] Totalling seventy-nine in number, they were carved by Robert Daye, sometime between 1510 and 1530, and they are an outstanding feature of the church. The bench ends feature a variety of subjects including sheep on the moor, parish worthies and religious subjects, but also a fiddler and a man playing the Cornish bagpipes – perhaps an image of those found playing at the end of the 'guarry miracles'.[550] Most significant to our story here is the carving of a jester. It is intriguing to wonder whether the figure, standing with legs akimbo, and somewhat gangly in appearance, was generic or based on a local man. Motley patterned clothing is visible on the carving, and the figure seems to be wearing the distinctive hat of the jester: the characteristic cap 'n' bells or cockscomb. One top liliripe (floppy point with a bell) is visible, and the others dangle onto his chest. He also appears to be carrying a mock

Fig. 42. The Jester bench end at Alternun in Cornwall.

sceptre. In this age, jesters were supposed to speak 'frankly' and 'honestly', which meant that the fool often walked a thin line and had to exercise careful judgement in how far he might go. The survival of the jester at Alternun betokens an early theatrical culture, which it is perhaps curious to see survive. This is because the tradition of jesters, whether in communities or at court, was overthrown during the Civil War. In a Puritan Christian republic, under the Lord Protector Oliver Cromwell, there was no place for such fripperies as jesters. This vestigial survival must have been missed. It perhaps, however, indicates a wider pattern of performance beyond purely mystery play culture.

Although the surviving text is dated from the next century, the text known fully as *The Creacion of the World, with Noye's Flood*, is probably from the middle period of the sixteenth century. Although it emerged from the opposite end of the territory to the jester at Alternun, it nonetheless contains several comic elements. The text has also come to be known as *Gwyrans an Bys*,[551] although this would seem to be a later translation back into Cornish, the English title being somewhat uncomfortable for even some of its earliest observers and translators.[552] In very many ways, *The Creacion of the World* is seen as a kind of afterthought or footnote in many studies;[553] while considerable attention has been paid to the *Ordinalia* and *Bewnans Meriasek*, this drama is perceived as less significant, and sometimes only as a reworked 'Origo Mundi'. This is a pity since, as I will show, the text is highly interesting, and deserves to be more widely appreciated. So let us make some general observations about its position in the continuum of theatrical activity in Cornwall.

What we know is that *The Creacion of the World* is a biblical-themed drama that was probably written for outdoor performance in or near Helston, and would appear to be part of a larger work, similar to the *Ordinalia*. Given Helston's history of para-theatrical pageant (seen in the contemporary *Hal-an-Tow* and Furry Day[554]), it may be linked to long-term festival activity there. A short colophon reveals that the text was scribed by William Jordan (of whom we known very little, only that he may have come from the parish of Madron), and is dated 12 August 1611, but this is probably just a transcription, with the original text being written much earlier. Therefore Jordan is the scribe rather than the author of the text. The likelihood is that it represents a pageant master's working or prompt copy. The original *The Creacion of the World* exists in one manuscript, known as Bodleian MS. 219.[555] This is a paper manuscript of 95 folios, around $12\frac{1}{2}$ inches by $3\frac{3}{4}$ inches. As well as this original, there are some four other manuscript versions;[556] the play has had a lively printed history,[557] with a section of it even finding its way into Jackson's mainly 'anti-Cornish' miscellany.[558] What is remarkable about the play is its size. It has over two and a half thousand lines, which means that it is twice as

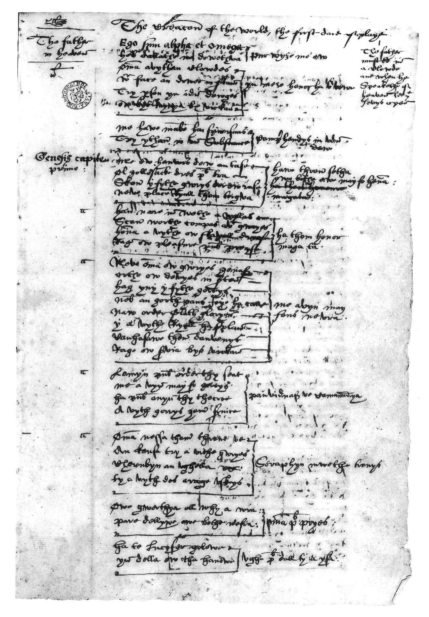

Fig. 43. The first page of the manuscript of *The Creacion of the World*, MS. Bodley 219. Reproduced by permission of the Bodleian Library, Oxford.

long as the corresponding section in 'Origo Mundi'. This is often not recognised. Joyce and Newlyn offer a useful summary of the way in which Cornish-language drama is laid out upon the page, with *The Creacion of the World* being a good example:

> The manuscripts of the Cornish play-texts use a curious layout, which is easy to follow if the manuscript is being read in extenso but is difficult to reproduce in print, and hard to comprehend if reproduced... The manuscript layout was designed to display the rhyme schemes of the stanzas, often *aabccb*; this was achieved by placing the rhyming pairs (*aa* and *cc*) below one another, with the pair of non-adjacent rhyming lines (*b... b*) offset to the right, each of these lines of poetry attached by a drawn line to the couplet which it was intended to follow.[559]

It is a point worth noting, because clearly there was a standard procedure of layout for the Cornish dramas of this period. It is certainly followed in the *Ordinalia*, and *Bewnans Meriasek*, but is usefully seen here as well. Therefore, although the text was quite late, Jordan seemed to be following an established model, which worked for the actors, the scribe and the director or prompter. Related to this method is the content: the incorporation of the Rood legend (relating to the Cross) and Adam's consignment to Limbo indicate an originally strongly Catholic work, while the likely presence of the story of the Virgin in any second play would have contributed to the rest of the cycle's loss and destruction at the time of the Reformation. As noted above, there are marked similarities to 'Origo Mundi',[560] either formulaic or borrowed, but *The Creacion of the World* contains some additional sequences. For example, Lamech (a descendant of Cain, the author of moral deterioration, and the first polygamist), an apparently poor-sighted huntsman, meets his infamous forebear and kills him by accident. Additionally, the play contains the developed rebellion of Lucifer, and the unusual character of Death, who offers a pivotal homiletic speech. *The Creacion of the World* is sub-titled 'The First Daie of Playe' and, because the character of Noah invites the audience to attend again the next day, and to see redemption, it seems highly likely that the play was the first section of a longer cycle play, perhaps with a separate larger title:

Dewh a vorowe a dermyn:
Why a weall matters pur vras,
Ha redempcion granntys
Der vercy a Thew an Tase,
  Tha sawya neb es kellys.

[Come tomorrow, in good time:
you will see very great matters,
and redemption granted
all through the mercy of God the Father,
  to save whoever is lost.][561]

The standard edition of the play is Paula Neuss's translation, although there have been several other editions over the years. In many ways, as Neuss demonstrates, the play is more structurally and linguistically sophisticated than 'Origo Mundi'.[562] The 7-syllable line is not strictly followed in the text, but 8-syllable lines would become 7-syllable in actual speech, if the elision of vowels is recognised. As mentioned earlier, Kent and Saunders have argued that, though common to many dramas across Europe, the title of the work 'with Noye's Flood' may had have special significance to Cornish mining communities, where it was believed that their mineral wealth was given to them by the redistribution of the Earth's resources in the aftermath of God's cleansing of the world through the Flood.[563] The emphasis in the title is more fully understood if this Cornish world-view is held in mind. This also proves that *The Creacion of the World* is much more intense a work than 'Origo Mundi': in the latter play we still have the episodes involving Abraham and Isaac, Moses and Pharoah, David and Bathsheba, Solomon, and Maximilla to go, but the Helston play concentrates only on the period from Adam and Eve to the Flood. Considering Noah's exhortation to return, it would appear that the cycle would then jump to later biblical history, although perhaps it was still possible to show further Old Testament material. However, the play does have a unified theological structure, as witnessed in the choral comments of Noah at the end, when he observes:

Why a wellas, pub degree
Leas matter gwarryes,
  Ha creacion oll an byse.

In weth oll why a wellas
An keth bysma consumys

[You have seen, every one of you,
many matters played
  and the creation of all the world.

Also you have all seen
the same world consumed.][564]

Perhaps the most singular amazing thing about *The Creacion of the World* is that it is the latest surviving example of a miracle play in Britain. Centrally, the drama works on basic moral debates and asks the audience to question issues of life and death and good and evil. Within this play, there is actually quite a lot of advice given to the audience, and this is not very common. Normally, audiences would have taken the message just from watching, but in *The Creacion of the World* there is a considerable amount of direct audience address, of the kind indicated above. The structure of the drama is composed of the following elements, although these merge much more smoothly together compared with the more episodic structure of 'Origo Mundi' where each episode is almost a distinct entity. Neuss notes that 'although the scene constantly shifts between different sets of characters, figures used in one scene reappear later in another'.[565] Thus, we have:

The Creation of Heaven, the Angels, and the Fall of Lucifer
The Creation, Temptation and Fall of Man
The Expulsion and coming of Death
Cain and Abel
Seth's birth
Cain and Lamech
Seth's visit to Paradise and the death of Adam
Translation of Enoch
The Making of Pillars
Noah's Flood
Epilogue.[566]

Within the manuscript of *The Creacion of the World*, there is no diagram of the stage layout (as in the *Ordinalia* and *Bewnans Meriasek*), so it is less clear where the stations were organised. Presumably, the drama was presented in the same way as other Cornish miracle plays. We know that the performance is constantly shifting from one area of the Round to the next, and this shifting action is useful since it means that the playwright does not always have to rely on biblical structure alone for performance. To this extent, *The Creacion of the World* is a much freer adaptation, perhaps reflecting its later construction. Structurally, too, the drama is composed of many more polar opposites than 'Origo Mundi', with good characters pitted against bad ones: for example Abel versus Cain, Seth versus Lamech, and Enoch versus Tubalcain. In many ways, this understanding of an axis of conflict makes for a more modern text, in that the original dramatist(s) recognised that 'conflicts' make for interesting performance. The conflict is not so well

Fig. 44. Sketch of an imaginary performance in a Cornish Round by F.E. Halliday. Courtesy of Sebastian Halliday.

defined in 'Origo Mundi', where the playwright more literally follows the Bible.

In terms of the moral positioning of the drama, we know from the *Ordinalia* that figures such as Adam, Abel, Seth, Enoch and Noah are all types of proto-Christ figures, who pave the way for the eventual emergence of Christ in the second play. Similarly, the evil characters are all forms of lineage from Lucifer. Neuss goes one step further. She believes that the playwright(s) consciously included echoes of previous speeches to reinforce these connections.[567] A good example is the way Cain says similar words to Lucifer. Thus, Lucifer comments:

> *Nynges thymo remedy;*
> *An trespass ytho mar vras,*
> *Ny amownt whelas mercye;*
> *My a wore ny vyn an Tase*
>   *Ov foly ymmo gava.*

> [There's no remedy for me;
> the sin was so great.
> It does no good to seek mercy;

I know God will not
    forgive me my folly.][568]

Later, Cain expresses similar sentiments:

Ow folly ythew mar vras,
Haw holan in weth pur browt;
Ny vanaf tha worth an Tase
Whylas mercy, sure heb dowte,
    Kynnamboma lowena.

[My folly is so great,
and also my heart very proud;
I won't seek mercy from the Father,
that's certain,
    although I'm unhappy.][569]

This again would suggest a sophisticated compositional structure, where echoes link and fuse characterisation – a more modern theatrical trait. Neuss interestingly observes that the evil characters in the drama go through what she terms a 'progressive degradation',[570] similar to the way Milton handles the fate of Satan in *Paradise Lost*.[571] It is quite intriguing that there is only some thirty years' difference between the final version of the Helston play and Milton's text that was drafted as early as 1640, though it did not emerge until 1667. Again, *The Creacion of the World* would seem to point forwards rather than backwards in its morality and characterisation. Lucifer's degradation is complete, but it is expressed in a new way with the character of Cain. The author(s) of the text have shaped Cain as a highly comic figure, who endears himself to the audience, consequently enhancing Abel's self-righteousness. This displays a somewhat more sophisticated interpretation of their relation-ship, and one which challenges 'traditional' audience response to the moral position. This, again, would seem to be the playwright's desire.

The work progresses further in the development of the character of Lamech. He begins as a bully, but by the end of his sequence he is viewed as a comic figure, groping around trying to locate his great-great-great-great grandfather. However, when Lamech murders his servant, he destroys any growing sympathy the audience may have had for him. Lamech's place in the development of characterisation in Cornish drama is important. This is because he is not a simple two-dimensional representation of evil. In essence, his buffoonery makes him more dangerous, and shows that evil can come in different, non-traditional forms. Lamech also makes structural nods forward to the self-defining 'Renaissance individuality' of the stage in the next century.[572] Again, he is very much a transitional character. *The Creacion of the World* is the only drama of the medieval period in the British Isles, in which the character of Lamech is featured. He is therefore, highly distinctive. Lamech is more evil than Cain. To emphasise this, the dramatist wittily turns him into a flagrant polygamist and womaniser:

Mo yes un wreag thym yma
Thom pleasure rag gwyll ganssy.
Ha sure me ew an kensa
  Bythqwath whath a ve dew wreag.

Han mowyssye lower plenty
Yma thym; nyngens dentye,
Me as kyef pan vydnaf ve;
Ny sparyaf anothans y,
  Malbew onyn a vo teag.

[I have more than one wife
to take my pleasure with.
And surely I'm the first
  ever yet to have two wives.

And I have young ladies in plenty,
they aren't choosy.
I have them whenever I like.
I never keep away from them,
  damn well not from one that's pretty.][573]

As we might expect, the Noah sequence of *The Creacion of the World* is better developed than that found in 'Origo Mundi'; the morality of this sequence displays a sophistication not found elsewhere. Tubalcain (the son of the Cainite Lamech) mocks Noah, believing the ark will never be finished, but Noah remains stoic and committed to the project. The theological debate here is quite complex, because although the audience have just seen God say that he does not want to flood the world, it is sinners like Tubalcain who will force him to do so. By the end of the drama, we have witnessed what Neuss terms a 'chain of sin that leads from creation to destruction'.[574] Good, in the form of Noah and his family, will survive, and provide a footing that will eventually lead into redemption. There are hints of this earlier on in the drama.

After Lamech, another unique component of this drama is the figure of Death [Cornish: *Ankow*]. Death is a highly symbolic character, demonstrative of what humans have brought upon themselves through their weakness. Unlike so many characters in this drama, Death is less forward-looking and represents more of the morality-play nature of previous drama. Indeed, the figure is perhaps similar to, or inspired by, Brythonic culture of an earlier period; Breton folklore, for example, is laced with the figure of *Ankou* [Death's Coachman],[575] and there might even be a cross-Channel link. Certainly, Death would be a fascinating figure to play within the drama. His major sequence is his appointment by God to kill everyone with his dart, eventually taking the life of Adam. Death offers a powerful homily:

Yn della ythew poyntyes
Tha vyns a vewa in byes
  Me the latha gans ow gew.

Adam na Eva pegha
Ha deffan an Tas terry,
Mernans ny wressans tastya
Mes in pleasure venarye
  Y a wressa prest bewa.

Omma eve ytho poyntyes
Chief warden war Pardice,
Ha der pegh a Coveytes
Oll y joye ythew kellys,
  May fetha paynes ragtha.

Gans an Jowle yfowns tulles
Der an Serpent malegas,
  Dell welsowgh warbarth omma.

[Thus it is appointed
to all who shall live in the world
that I shall kill them with my dart.

Had Adam and Eve not sinned
and broken the Father's command,

they would not have tasted death,
but they would live for ever
in eternal pleasure.

Here he was appointed
chief warden over Paradise,
and through the sins of Covetousness
all his joy is lost,
that he shall have punishment for it.

They were deceived by the Devil
through the cursed Serpent,
as you have seen together here.][576]

Other components of the dramaturgy make *The Creacion of the World* a fascinating proposition for performance.[577] At the front-end of the play, we learn of the human-headed serpent that tempts Eve; a very unusual component. As noted earlier, structural repetition occurs throughout the piece, which gives a highly unified effect in terms of performance. As in 'Origo Mundi', the devils have great fun in the performance, often travelling to Hell with 'great noyse'.[578] The language of *The Creacion of the World* has often been seen as a problem. It is not a 'pure' Celtic text and, indeed, the Cornish of it is crammed with several bi-lingual puns, suggesting a community in linguistic and cultural transition. The puns are used, however, to great effect, and we should not view them as just a kind of 'corruption'. The rest of the Cornish is quite similar to that found in the *Homilies* translated by John Tregear,[579] so its inception must have come from a similar phase, broadly being 'late Cornish'. If we go by Tregear, then we are probably talking about 1560 as the moment of original production. However, this date is not the only one in contention. The general language of the text means that it cannot have been written earlier than 1500, and Nance locates it closer to 1530.[580] Hooper notes that Nance and Smith eventually agreed on a date somewhere between 1530 and 1540.[581]

There is not time here to enter into a full discussion of the similarities between 'Origo Mundi' and *The Creacion of the World*. It perhaps suffices to say that there are some notable similarities, both structural and linguistic, between the texts, and that the interested reader will find these debated in detail by both Murdoch, and Neuss.[582] What is perhaps more interesting is how such similarities occurred. *The Creacion of the World* is obviously a later text, which might indicate some structural borrowings from either performances or literary versions of the earlier play. This is what Neuss has termed 'memorial reconstruction'[583] – arguing that the playwright(s) of *The Creacion of the World* had observed the earlier text in operation, but chose both to use and adapt elements for the play attached to the community around Helston. It is therefore a kind of mnemonic extemporisation, perhaps offered by actors as well as the writer(s). This would explain both the similarities and the new insertions (Lamech, Death and Enoch). Some of the lines from 'Origo Mundi' are taken virtually verbatim, occurring in three major moments: the Creation and Fall, the Cursing of Cain, and the Noah sequence.[584] Another important and distinctive component not contained in 'Origo Mundi' is the mark of Cain. In the text a stage direction calls for this to be marked by the letter *omega*, and observers such as Neuss have linked this to the horns that often make up the mark. Cain himself refers to this in his line 'in Corne ow thale [on the horns of my forehead]'.[585]

In terms of staging, a number of points are worth mentioning. The modernity of the text is perhaps also seen in the degree of detail found in the English-language stage directions of the manuscript. It is a general trend within drama that stage directions have become more complex as drama has developed – consider, for example, the difference between Shakespeare and Harold Pinter; certainly much more instruction is given in *The Creacion of the World* than in the *Ordinalia*. The manuscript, and the stage time given to both Heaven and Hell, suggest that these 'multiple stages' must have been quite elaborate and spectacular. Hell would appear to have two levels; in one section, the term *gegen* [kitchen][586] is used, which might indicate some kind of symbolic pot or pan. Paradise is also given a lot of attention in the stage directions, but relatively few other stations are noted. Lamech would probably have had a tented structure, because a number of sources refer to this, although it is slightly less clear, for example, where Noah might emerge from. That said, despite Noah being a central character in 'Origo Mundi', there he has no base. From this we may conclude that, although some elements of the staging would appear to match the other surviving Cornish drama, and those written about but not extant, *The Creacion of the World* might seem the exception to the rule. In all likelihood, the performance area required for this text would have been smaller than those required for the *Ordinalia, Bewnans Meriasek* or *Bewnans Ke*. We also know that the stage directions refer mainly to events in the plain, rather than on the periphery, so this suggests a slightly different method of performance. Another point worth making is that whilst the Legend of the Holy Rood would seem a particularly important Cornish legend to incorporate into the drama, the picture of it here is much less clear,[587] principally because we do not know the direction it takes on the Second Day.

The most comprehensive picture of the staging of *The Creacion of the World* is offered by Higgins in 1996.[588] Higgins recognises the difficulties of assessing notions of permanent stations with the piece, and also the accuracy of the stage directions, given the difficulties alluded to in the layout of the manuscript (as outlined by Joyce and Newlyn above). Despite these issues, and drawing on the initial speeches of the characters, the stage directions, and comparison with the *Ordinalia* and *Bewnans Meriasek*, Higgins proposes the following layout. Heaven would be positioned in the east, at the furthest point in the circle; then, following in clockwise order would come Enoch, Noah, Tubal, Adam, Lamech, Hell and Death. Adam would be located in the west, with Hell at the northernmost point, and Tubal and Noah in the south. Paradise is therefore located in the centre of the Round.[589] Higgins also notes the dramatic entry of God at the beginning of the play. He proposes that the upper part of Heaven would be shrouded in cloud. This would be represented with folding 'leaves' so that the upper clouds part to reveal him before he begins to speak. As noted by Neuss, the verticality of the Heaven structure is important in the *Creacion*, because of the expulsion of Lucifer, an event less considered in the *Ordinalia*. We thus have a picture of a more compact stage, with a higher vertical dimension. In contrast to Neuss, Higgins also feels that there was a more conscious development of stations in the mid-sixteenth century, and that more lines were delivered from the stations.[590] This would seem feasible as, over time, drama has intrinsically travelled towards a more single stage – though this is not to deny the subsequent developments of multiple-stages or theatre-in-the round, in the twentieth century. This theory proposes a very different way of marshalling and moving the audience from that used in the *Ordinalia*. Higgins also proposes that a more elaborate vision of Hell was constructed, Hell having not only a gaping jaw, but also a pit, a kitchen, and probably Limbo. There is also some evidence, Higgins feels, for inferring use of machinery in the play, which would match other theatrical developments across Britain. Such machinery would counteract the components of the drama that Neuss found 'inexplicable'.[591]

Aware that such stations do not explain the whole of the action in *The Creacion of the World*, Higgins also believes that what he terms 'temporary stations' were part of the dramaturgy.[592] Five are proposed: Mount Tabor, the place of sacrifice where Abel was slain; the Forest, where Cain was killed and we have the tomb where Adam was buried; the two Pillars, erected by Seth; Noah's ark; and an altar for Noah. We may read these as mere scenic devices, either hauled on or positioned at an appropriate time, and possibly – as at Perranzabuloe – through a gap in the Round. Eventually, Higgins concludes that, just as in *Bewnans Meriasek*, the performance pattern followed a series of segmented areas of the Round, which corresponded with the action of the drama and audience movement. Higgins and Neuss deviate in some of their interpretations, but this does not mean that there are strongly contrasting views about this performance. Indeed, both are committed to showing the more vertical aspect of performance, the progression through segments of the arena, and the more compact space in which the performers were working. Relatively little experimentation has occurred with *The Creacion of the World*, when compared to the *Ordinalia* and *Bewnans Meriasek*. Donald R. Rawe used an English-language version of the text at Perran Round in 1973, taking his cue for performance from his own modern dramas, as well as the 1969 *Ordinalia* production.[593] In 1977, Bodmin Church also held a production, but this was not presented 'in the round'. To date, there have been no further productions, and *The Creacion of the World* is ripe for revival. Jenner observed that 'William Jordan may well have arranged his Creation for performance in Crasken Round or the Plan-an-Gwary at Ruan of St Hillary [sic] under the auspices of the clergy of Meneage. But of this we know nothing'.[594] Jenner's theory is not an impossibility, but it does seem a rather long way from Helston at St Hilary (although there are continuities forward here, to the work of Bernard Walke). Neuss has also drawn attention to the observations of Tubalcain, who criticises Noah for building the Ark '*In creys powe, tha worthe an moare* [in the middle of the country, away from the sea]',[595] which may give indication of an inland performance, but may just as well serve for somewhere in the middle of the *plen-an-gwarry*. Conclusions are, therefore, hard to come to. Jenner further observes that *The Creacion of the World* has much more literary merit than 'Origo Mundi'. He furthermore notes the use of English by Lucifer and his angels, and that 'they only spoke Cornish when on their best behaviour'.[596] This is an interesting linguistic twist considering that the audience, probably then bilingual, was speaking Cornish less often, and in specific contexts.

Rastall, meanwhile, following his work on the *Ordinalia* and *Bewnans Meriasek*, has also noted the importance of music in *The Creacion of the World*. He concludes that aspects of the liturgy were sung during the performance, and that song is used within the performance with the explicit aim of praising God. As in the other dramas, he also notes the presence of minstrels, concluding that the cast and the audience dance together at the end of the production, and that the particular form of dancing used was something of a 'custom', though it remains unclear what that custom was.[597] Given Helston's musical and dance heritage, there may well be some links here – not only with the Furry Day celebrations but maybe even through *Hal-an-Tow*. The connection remains hidden, but nonetheless intriguing.

In his lengthy studies of *The Creacion of the World*, Murdoch has noted that during the Reformation the core difficulty in the play would have been the concept of Limbo. He relates that Limbo would have been an issue considered in the *Henrician Ten Articles* of 1536, as examined in studies by Dickens and Carr, and Parker.[598] Therefore, he observes of the text that 'Like earlier plays, we find in *Gwreans an bys* elements from those medieval legends dismissed by Reformers, although even Protestant dramatists kept some non-biblical elements, such as the fall of the angels, in spite of the *sola scriptura* precept'.[599] He thus concludes that 'there is very little in the work that might have been offensive to the Reformation, as for example, excessive Marianism' though he does note that 'what was in the lost second part, of course, we cannot say'.[600] If there was a certain dramaturgy about the Virgin in the second day's play, then this would account for its destruction. Murdoch also offers observations on the apocryphal origins of components of the drama, most notably from the Golden Legend and the Gospel of Nicodemus, which clearly had a structural input into the text.[601] Murdoch notes that Jordan may not even have had the second day of the play before him, to make a copy.[602] He also offers the following observation:

> At all events, the play stands at the end of the tradition of biblical adaptation in dramatic form in Europe, comparable most readily with the French *Mistére* and to an even greater extent, with works like Ruf's *Adam and Heva*, however remote in real terms. *Gwreans an bys* looks in some ways like a Protestant drama, and certainly it stands at the very least on the fringe of the Reformation.[603]

In such a statement, although Murdoch notes the Catholic element, he also notes a certain modernity, a view I have expressed above with regard to the characterisation and dramaturgy. Murdoch adds that 'the solifidian Reformation would have been hard-pressed to object to the presentation of good works and the stress on the word of God in the play, even if it effectively put an end to the practice of mystery-plays in general as a means of communicating that word'.[604] In this sense, then, the reason for the survival of the first play of *The Creacion of the World* may be connected with its very modernity, and the notion that lines such as the following would be appropriate still within a Reformed Britain:

> *Ymadge dean gwrega shapya:*
> *Mar an kerowgh dell gotha*
> *Why a wra orthaf cola.*

[I shaped the image of man
If you love me as you should,
You will hear me.][604]

Somehow then, this particular drama managed to survive in a world that had undergone Protestant reform. In the year 1611, when Jordan as copying the surviving manuscript of *The Creacion of the World* in Helston, Shakespeare was in London writing the Celtic-themed *Cymbeline: King of Britain* and *The Tempest*, a play devoted to the issue of colonialism. But the linguistic and cultural landscape of Britain had undergone much change, as we shall see below. Symbolic of this was the successful unifying of the island of Britain under the English-language King James Bible. Before we turn to the next phase of the continuum, it is perhaps worth noting further the direct issues surrounding the Reformation in Cornwall. The state of Cornish-language drama is put into perspective by, for example, the observations of Andrew Boorde in 1542. In his *Fyrst Book of the Introduction of Knowledge* (eventually published in 1547) he notes that, 'In Cornwall is two speeches; the one is naughty Englysche, and the other Cornyche speche. And there maybe men and women the which cannot speake one worde of Englysche, but all Cornysche'.[606] Boorde's observations denote a territory in linguistic and spiritual upheaval.

By the middle of the sixteenth century, the Reformation was in full operation in Cornwall, and was to prove the real factor in the decline of Cornish during this phase. The miracle plays, so much a core plank of Cornish identity, were immediately suspect for their theology and Marianism, and so were suppressed in the communities that had long supported them. Alongside this, contact with Brittany – which had in part provided the subject matter of some of the dramas, and which had kept a shared linguistic commonality – ceased, since France, to which Brittany had been politically linked since 1532, was hostile to the aims of the Reformation.[607] More boldly perhaps the old Latin language of the church services in Cornwall was to be replaced with English. Such an Anglicisation project on church services became the focus of Cornish people's resentment about the imposition of new religious practices. As detailed by Rowse, Sturt, and a number of other observers,[608] the first Act of Uniformity, which introduced English in all church services in 1549, was met with hostility and rebellion in Cornwall and west Devon. In an echo of earlier rebellions around 1497, the Cornish took up arms and marched eastwards, setting down their demands over language and religiosity to King Edward:

Item we wil not receyue the new seruyce because it is but lyke a Christmas game, but we wull have oure olde seruice of Mattens, masse, Euensong and procession in Latten, as it was before. And so we the Cornyshe men (whereof certen of vs vnderstande no Englysh) vtterly refuse this new Englysh.

By vs

Humphrey Arundell
Thomas Underhyll
John Slowman
William Sagar *Chief Captaynes*
John Thomson *Pryeste*
Henry Bray *Maior of Bodma*
Henry Lee *Maior of Torrinton*
Roger Barret *Prieste*[609]

Arundell's family had a history of theatrical activity, and it is likely that most of the others had encountered the culture of 'gwarry miracle' as they were growing up. The response of the authorities to all of this was not sympathetic. The Cornish had some initial victories, but at Fenny Bridges and Clyst Heath, near Exeter, they met the full force of Lord Bedford's army. Many Cornish were slaughtered, and after this the army moved into Cornwall, continuing the processes of the Reformation.[610] Under the leadership of the Provost Marshall, Sir Anthony Kingston, burnings, hangings and destruction were carried out in Cornwall. Undoubtedly, many Cornish-language dramas were destroyed during this phase, also contributing to a less-than-secure theatrical environment. Putting on theatre during this phase was highly dangerous, particularly if the drama did not convey the appropriate theological message. Interestingly, the metaphor chosen for their complaint was that of 'A Christmas Game' which again gives some indication of para-theatrical activity, and again reinforces the seasonal nature of the Cornish dramatic continuum (perhaps the game was guizing?).[611]

However, ironically enough, it was an enlightened playwright, one Nicholas Udall (1504-56), the author of one of the first classical plays in English, *Ralph Roister Doister* (1552), who wrote a pamphlet suggesting that the new Protestant service, the Bible and Prayer Book ought to be made available in Cornish.[612] Unfortunately, Udall's suggestion was more or less ignored, and 'the Prayer Book became a chief instrument in the spread of the English language in Cornwall'.[613] Despite a 1560 resolution at a conference of the Anglican Church that 'it may be lawful for such Welsh or Cornish children as can speak no English to learn the Premises in the Welsh tongue or the Cornish language',[614] translations were not made available. Cornish language and Cornish theatre were therefore in meltdown. This was, as Pool details, despite the best efforts of individuals such as Dr. John Kennal (d.1592),[615] the influential and pluralist parson of St Columb Major, an ecclesiastical laywer with whom, according to Carew, lay buried 'the principal love and knowledge of this language',[616] and Richard Pendrea who, as a Catholic priest in exile, preached in Cornish before King Philip III of Spain in Valladolid in 1600.[617] Both Kennal and Pendrea surely had knowledge of Cornish-language dramas.

The writing was on the wall for the demise of Glasney College, which had been the filter and funder of Cornish dramatic activity for three centuries. As Whetter has detailed, in 1548 William Body had purchased the archdeaconry of Cornwall, provoking much trouble in the west. Body gave the impression that the confiscation of church goods was for the crown, but this was a ruse to show antipathy to the old Catholic order.[618] The priories of east Cornwall had already been dissolved in 1536, under earlier edicts of reform. Attention was then paid to the remaining large establishment: Glasney College. In the aftermath, the buildings at Glasney deteriorated, and stone was removed for construction of other properties. The devastation that came with both the hard-handed centralist approach to the rebellious Cornish, as well as the shut-down of established methods of theatrical practice, was to have a devastating effect on a continuum which had been in place for at least four hundred years. The effects of such rebellion were felt strongly in Cornwall, and upon the centralist authorities, as well as on numerous other future playwrights and observers. This would be seen again and again in the centuries that followed. The manuscript of *The Creacion of the World* was clearly a last gasp of native, yet progressive, Cornish theatre. While this was being transcribed by William Jordan, a new phase of Cornwall's theatrical history unfurled, distant from the multiple stages and gwarry miracles that once dominated west of the River Tamar.

CHAPTER TWO: NOTES AND REFERENCES

1. See Barry Unsworth, *Morality Play*, London: Hamish Hamilton, 1995, p.51.
2. F.E. Halliday (ed.), *Richard Carew: The Survey of Cornwall*, London: Melrose, 1953, p.144.
3. Ibid., p.75.
4. See, for example, Martyn F. Wakelin, *Language and History in Cornwall*, Leicester: Leicester University Press, 1975; Jane A. Bakere, *The Cornish Ordinalia: A Critical Study*, Cardiff: University of Wales Press, 1980; Sydney Higgins, *Medieval Theatre in the Round: The Multiple Staging of Religious Drama in England*, Camerino, Italy: Laboratorio degli studi Linguistici, 1995; Brian Murdoch, *Cornish Literature*, Cambridge: D.S. Brewer 1993; Alan M. Kent, *The Literature of Cornwall: Continuity, Identity, Difference 1000-2000*, Bristol: Redcliffe, 2000.
5. A recent range includes Jim Hall, 'Maximilla, the Cornish Montanist: The Final Scenes of *Origo Mundi*' in Philip Payton (ed.), *Cornish Studies: Seven*, Exeter: University of Exeter Press 1999, pp.165-92; Paul Manning, 'Staging the State and the Hypostasization of Violence in the Medieval Cornish Drama' in Philip Payton (ed.), *Cornish Studies: Thirteen*, Exeter: University of Exeter Press, 2005, pp.126-169; Benjamin Bruch, 'Verse Structure and Musical Performance in *Bewnans Ke*' in *Journal of the Royal Institution of Cornwall*, 2006, pp. 57-66.
6. Graham Thomas and Nicholas Williams (eds. and trs.), *Bewnans Ke: The Life of St Kea – A Critical Edition with Translation*, Exeter: University of Exeter Press, 2007.
7. For discussion, see Peter Berresford Ellis, *The Cornish Language and its Literature*, London and Boston: Routledge and Kegan Paul, 1974.
8. Two texts that propound this view are F.E. Halliday, *The Legend of the Rood*, London: Gerald Duckworth, 1955, and Richard Southern, *The Medieval Theatre in the Round: A Study of the Staging of The Castle of Perseverance, and related matters*, London: Faber and Faber, 1957. For response to these and others, see Matthew Spriggs, 'The Cornish Language, Archaeology and the Origins of English Theatre' in M. Jones (ed.), *Traces of Ancestry: Studies in Honour of Colin Renfrew*, Vol. 2, Cambridge: McDonald Institute Monograph Series, 2004, pp.143-61. Although surprisingly not citing specifically Cornish examples, other theatre-in-the-round is also considered in Richard Leacroft, *The Development of the English Playhouse: An Illustrated Survey of the Theatre Building in England from Medieval to Modern Times*, London: Methuen, 1973.
9. See, for example, Halliday, op.cit.; F.J. Tickner (ed.), *Earlier English Drama: From Robin Hood to Everyman*, London and Edinburgh: Thomas Nelson and Sons, 1929. The focus on literary rather than performance studies is also endemic

in Rosalind Conklin Hays and C.E. McGee (Dorset) and Sally L. Joyce and Evelyn S. Newlyn (Cornwall) (eds.), *Records of Early English Drama: Dorset / Cornwall*, Toronto: University of Toronto and Brepols, 1999. Although problematically titled, this is a most useful volume.

10. See D. H. Frost, 'Glasney's Parish Clergy and the Tregear Manuscript' in Philip Payton (ed.), *Cornish Studies: Fifteen*, Exeter: University of Exeter Press, 2007, pp.27-89. This devolved pattern certainly seems to be in place by the time of the Tregear Manuscript (c.1550-60).

11. See Scott Wilson, *Cultural Materialism: Theory and Practice*, Oxford: Blackwell, 1995; Alan M. Kent, *The Implication of Texts in History: The Rise, Development and Some Applications of Cultural Materialism*, University of Exeter M.Phil. thesis, 1991.

12. Jonathan Dollimore and Alan Sinfield (eds.), *Political Shakespeare: New Essays in Cultural Materialism*, Manchester: Manchester University Press, 1985.

13. George Wootton, *Thomas Hardy: Towards a Materialist Criticism*, Lanham: Rowan and Littlefield, 1985.

14. Allan J. Frantzen, *Speaking Two Languages: Traditional Disciplines and Contemporary Theory in Medieval Studies*, Albany: State University of New York Press, 1991. A 'Celtic' materialist criticism is much needed.

15. Paul Strohm, *Theory and the Pre-Modern Text*, Minneapolis: University of Minnesota Press, 2000.

16. Thomas A. Schmitz, *Modern Literary Theory and Ancient Texts*, Oxford: Blackwell, 2007.

17. See Oliver Padel, 'Oral and literary culture in medieval Cornwall' in Helen Fulton (ed.), *Medieval Celtic Literature and Society*, Dublin: Four Courts Press, 2005, pp.95-116. Fulton writes from a materialist perspective. Padel (usually a medievalist) takes a more materialist approach here.

18. For commentary on this, see Thomas and Williams, op.cit. See also the observations of Paula Neuss (ed. and tr.), *The Creacion of the World: A Critical Edition and Translation*, New York and London: Garland, 1983.

19. The manuscript sources for these are *Ordinalia*. MS. Bodl. 791, Oxford; *Bewnans Meriasek*. MS. Peniarth 105, NLW, Aberystwyth; *Beunans Ke*. MS. 23849D, NLW, Aberystwyth.

20. See *Gwreans an Bys*. MS. Bodley 219, Oxford.

21. Rod Lyon, *Cornwall's Playing Places*, Nancegollan: Tavas an Weryn, 2001; Spriggs, op.cit., pp.160-1.

22. See Philip Payton, 'a...concealed envy against the English': a Note on the Aftermath of the 1497 Rebellions in Cornwall' in Philip Payton (ed.), *Cornish Studies: One*, Exeter: University of Exeter Press, 1993, pp. 4-13.

23. For the later concept, see Halliday, op.cit.

24. See Nicholas Orme, *The Saints of Cornwall*, Oxford: Oxford University Press, 2000, pp.221-223.

25. See James Whetter, 'The Search for Gorran's Playne-an-Gwarry' in *Old Cornwall*, Vol.11, No.4, 1993, pp.157-62. For further reflections on this, see 'Miracle Plays at Gorran' and 'St Goran' in James Whetter, *Essays Ancient and Modern*, Gorran: Lyfrom Trelyspen, 2005, pp.109-12. According to Whetter, in 1478, William Worcester found Woronus, confessor, in the kalender of Bodmin Priory under 7 April – the date probably commemorates the date of his death. Gorran feast was celebrated on the Sunday after Easter, which comes at about the same time. Given other theatrical culture operating in Cornwall at the same time, this date would seem apt for a play at Gorran.

26. Halliday, op.cit., pp.144-5.

27. This view is given support by Carew's essay on 'The Excellency of the English Tongue', ibid., pp.303-8.

28. See, for example, William Borlase, *Observations on the Antiquities, Historical and Monumental of the County of Cornwall*, London: EP Publishing, 1973 [1754], plate xvi, and William Borlase, *The Natural History of Cornwall*, Oxford, 1758, plate xxix.

29. William L. Tribby, 'The Medieval Prompter: A Reinterpretation' in *Theatre Survey*, Vol. 5, No. 1, 1964, pp.71-8. However, see also Butterworth, who contends that Carew is correct. Philip Butterworth, 'Book-carriers: Medieval and Tudor Stage Conventions' in *Theatre Notebook*, 24, 1992, pp.12-28.

30. Halliday, op.cit., p.145.

31. See L.E. Elliott-Binns, *Medieval Cornwall*, London: Methuen, 1955.

32. Ibid., p.398. Breton may be a fifth, though at this time Breton and Cornish were probably seen by speakers as different dialects of the same language.

33. A.L. Rowse, *The West in English History*, London: Methuen, 1949, p.67. Such a view might also be disputed by the fact that in 1498 Breton and Cornish fishermen were operating off the coast of Newfoundland. See Samuel Eliot Morrison, *The European Discovery of America: The Northern Voyages A.D. 500-1600*, New York: Oxford University Press, 1971, p.225.

34. John Hatcher, *Rural Economy and Society in the Duchy of Cornwall 1300-1500*, Cambridge: Cambridge University Press, 1970. See also John Hatcher and Mark Bailey, *Modelling the Middle Ages: The History and Theory of England's Economic Development*, Oxford: Oxford University Press, 2001.

35. Philip Payton, *The Making of Modern Cornwall: Historical Experience and the Persistence of "Difference"*, Redruth: Dyllansow Truran, 1992, pp.43-72.

36. Bernard Deacon, *Cornwall: A Concise History*, Cardiff: University of Wales Press, 2007, pp.30-61.

37. See the argument in John Angarrack, *Our Future is History: Identity, Law and the Cornish Question*, Bodmin: Independent Academic Press, 2002.

38. Mark Stoyle, *West Britons: Cornish Identities and the Early Modern British State*, Exeter: University of Exeter Press, 2002.

39. Oliver Padel (ed.), *W.M.M. Picken: A Medieval Cornish Miscellany*, Chichester: Phillimore and Co., 2000. Of most relevance here are 'The Patron Saints of Poundstock and Helland Churches' and 'St German of Cornwall's Day', pp.113-4 and pp.115-20 respectively.

40. Nicholas Orme (ed.), *Unity and Variety: A History of the Church in Devon and Cornwall*, Exeter: University of Exeter Press, 1991, and *Cornwall and the Cross: Christianity 500-1560*, Chichester: Phillimore and Co., 2007.

41. See James Whetter, *The Bodrugans: A Study of a Cornish Medieval Knightly Family*, Gorran: Lyfrow Trelyspen, 1995, and *Cornwall in the 13th Century: A Study in Social and Economic History*, Gorran: Lyfrow Trelyspen, 1998, and *The History of Glasney College*, Padstow: Tabb House, 1988.

42. Murdoch, op.cit.; Kent., op.cit.

43. See, for example, Jacqueline Gibson and Gwyn Griffiths (eds. and trs.), *The Turn of the Ermine: An Anthology of Breton Literature*, London: Francis Boutle Publishers, 2006; Dafydd Johnston, *The Literature of Wales*, Cardiff: University of Wales Press, 1994.

44. Evelyn S. Newlyn (ed.), *Cornish Drama of the Middle Ages: A Bibliography*, Redruth: Institute of Cornish Studies, 1987; Brian Murdoch (ed.), *The Medieval Cornish Poem of the Passion: A Bibliography*, Redruth: Institute of Cornish Studies, 1979.

45. Joyce and Newlyn, op.cit; John M. Wasson (ed.), *Records of Early English Drama: Devon*, Toronto: University of Toronto and Brepols, 1986. This text makes a good comparison to Cornwall. The medieval and Renaissance period is slight by comparison. No cycle dramas have survived in Devon. For a wider literary comparison, see Jack Simmons (ed.), *A Devon Anthology*, London: Anthony Mott, 1983 [1971]. No drama is featured.

46. E.K. Chambers, *The Mediaeval Stage*, Oxford: Oxford University Press, 1903; Southern, op.cit., 1957; Glynne Wickham, 'The Beginnings of English Drama: Stage and Drama till 1660' in Christopher Ricks (ed.), *English Drama to 1710*, London: Penguin, 1987, pp.1-54, and *The Medieval Theatre*, Cambridge: Cambridge University Press, 1987.

47. Higgins, op.cit., and (ed.), *European Medieval Drama* 1996: *Papers for the First International Conference on Aspects of European Medieval Drama*, Camerino: Universita Degli Studi Di Camerino – Centro Linguitico di Ateneo, 1996, and (ed.), *European Medieval Drama* 1997: *Papers for the Second International Conference on Aspects of European Medieval Drama*, Camerino: Universita Degli Studi Di Camerino – Centro Linguitico di Ateneo, 1997; William Tydeman, *The Medieval European Stage 500-1550*, Cambridge: Cambridge University

Press, 2001; Clifford Davidson (ed.), *Material Culture and Medieval Drama*, Kalamazoo, Michigan: Western Michigan University Press, 1999.

48. Brian Murdoch, 'The Cornish Medieval Drama' in Richard Beadle (ed.), *The Cambridge Companion to Medieval English Theatre*, Cambridge: Cambridge University Press, 1994, pp.211-39.

49. Fulton, op.cit.; Huw Pryce (ed.), *Literacy in Medieval Celtic Societies*, Cambridge: Cambridge University Press, 1998.

50. Bakere, op.cit.; Robert Longsworth, *The Cornish Ordinalia: Religion and Dramaturgy*, Cambridge, Massachusetts: Harvard University Press, 1967; Markham Harris (ed. and tr.), *The Cornish Ordinalia: A Medieval Dramatic Trilogy*, Washington D.C.: Catholic University of America Press, 1969, and (ed. and tr.), *The Life of Meriasek: A Medieval Cornish Miracle Play*, Washington D.C.: Catholic University of America Press, 1977.

51. DRO: Chanter 4, 18 April.

52. See Diocese of Exeter, *Statutes of Peter Quinell*, 16/4, Chapter 13, as translated by Abigail Ann Young, in Joyce and Newlyn, op.cit., pp.579-80.

53. Ibid.

54. Ibid., Chapter 17, p.80.

55. See Elliott-Binns, op.cit., pp.403-4. Elliott-Binns wrongly credits William Sandys (Uncle Jan Trenoodle), *Specimens of Cornish Provincial Dialect*, London: John Russell Smith, 1846, with this information. No further reference to this has been found. Trevaill's performance before Henry VI was certainly an exception to the rule. Southworth argues that advisors to Henry VI usually discouraged such activity, especially with regard to fools. See John Southworth, *Fools and Jesters at the English Court*, Stroud: Sutton, 2003 [1998], pp.77-8.

56. A remark in response to an audience question, made by N.J.A. Williams speaking on 'The Language of Bewnans Ke' at Universities of Cornwall, Tremough, 13 September 2008. See N.J.A. Williams, *The Language of Bewnans Ke*, Unpublished paper, 2008.

57. See Edwin Lankester (ed.), *Memorials of John Ray, consisting of his life by Dr [William] Derham, biographical and critical notes by Sir J.E. Smith and Dupetit Thouers with his itineraries, etc*, London: Ray Society, n.d. John Ray (1627-1705) was one of Britain's first naturalists, with a keen interest in philology.

58. Many Cornish made up the contingent of archers. See Jan Gendall, 'Fifteenth-Century Archery: New Perspectives' in *Journal of the Royal Institution of Cornwall*, 2008, pp.71-80.

59. DRO: Chanter 3.

60. For background on this, see Ronald Hutton, *The Rise and Fall of Merry England: The Ritual Year 1400-1700*, Oxford: Oxford University Press, 1994, pp.10-12 and pp.53-54.

61. DRO, op.cit.

62. For a history, see T.J. Olver, *An Account of the History of St. Stephen-in-Brannel*, St. Stephen-in-Brannel: St. Stephen-in-Brannel Church, n.d.

63. Henry Jenner, 'The Fourteenth-Century Charter Endorsement' in *Journal of the Royal Institution of Cornwall*, No. 20, 1915-1916, pp.41-48. The Charter itself reads, 'Fine made at Westminster in the Quinzaine [i.e. fortnight] of St. Michael, in the 14th year of King Edward III, whereby Thomas Leghe of Rosugou [Resugga] and Margery his wife convey to Nicholas, son of John of Menleder [Meledor], in tail at a rent of 20s., lands in Menleder'.

64. Alan M. Kent and Tim Saunders (eds. and trs.), *Looking at the Mermaid: A Reader in Cornish Literature 900-1900*, London: Francis Boutle Publishers, 2000, pp.30-31.

65. Ibid., pp.30-33.

66. Jenner, op.cit. A similar view is also taken by Nance. See Robert Morton Nance, 'The Charter Endorsement in Cornish' in *Old Cornwall*, 1947, pp.34-6.

67. This piece of folklore may be summarised by the following: Local legend says that whoever first drinks water from the well after they are married will have control of the other. After the ceremony, the groom runs to the well as fast as possible in order to drink the water. The bride stays still and calmly produces a bottle filled with water from the well, then drinks from it. See Richard Carew 'The Well of St Keyne' in Alan M. Kent (ed.), *Voices from West Barbary: An Anthology of Anglo-Cornish Poetry 1548-1928*, London: Francis Boutle Publishers, 2000, p.29.

68. Jenner, op.cit. Hroswitha [or Hrotsvitha] of Gandersheim, Germany (c.935 to c.975) was a Canonness of the Benedictine Order, a poet and a dramatist. Her plays drew on apocryphal gospels.

69. Ibid.

70. For some perspectives, see Evelyn S. Newlyn, 'The Middle Cornish Interlude: Genre and Tradition' in *Comparative Drama*, 30, 2, 1996, pp.266-81.

71. Enrico Campanile, 'Un Frammento Scenico Medio-Cornico' in *Studi e Saggi Linguistici*, Vol.3, 1963, pp.60-80.

72. See the observations in Ray Edwards, 'The Charter Fragment: Play or Poem?' in *The Celtic Pen*, Vol.2, No.1, 1995, pp.17-19. Edwards notes this in Libro de Buen Amor [The Book of Good Love]. See http://www.gutenberg.org/ebooks/16625. See also Ray Edwards (ed. and tr.), *The Charter Fragment*, Sutton Coldfield: Kernewek Dre Lyther, 1991.

73. Murdoch, op.cit., 1993, p.13.

74. Murdoch, in Beadle (ed.), op.cit., p.8.

75. Lauran Toorians (ed.), *The Middle Cornish Charter Endorsement: The Making of a*

Marriage in Medieval Cornwall, Innsbruck: Institut für Sprachwissenschaft der Universität Innsbruck, 1991.

76. See Evelyn Newlyn, 'Between the Pit and the Pedestal: Images of Eve and Mary in Medieval Cornish Drama' in Edelgard E. DuBruck (ed.), *New Images of Medieval Women: Essays Towards a Cultural Anthropology*, Lampeter: The Edwin Mellen Press, 1989, pp.121-64.

77. Alan M. Kent, *Wives, Mothers and Sisters: Feminism, Literature and Women Writers of Cornwall*, Penzance: The Jamieson Library, 1998, pp.8-9.

78. Lyon, op.cit., pp.21-22.

79. Charles Henderson, *Parochial Antiquities*, Vol, V, 1915. MSS. in Charles Henderson Collection, Courtney Library, Royal Institution of Cornwall.

80. See David C. Fowler, *The Life and Times of John Trevisa, Medieval Scholar*, Seattle and London: University of Washington Press, 1995.

81. See Ray Edwards (ed. and tr.), *The Tregear Homilies*, Sutton Coldfield: Kernewek Dre Lyther, 1994; Frost, op.cit.

82. See Andrew C. Symons, 'She, 'Er and 'Un: Study II in Language and History' in *An Baner Kernewek / The Cornish Banner*, No. 94, 1998, pp.6-7. For a wider consideration of language change in Cornwall during this period and afterwards, see Andrew C. Symons, 'Models of Language Transfer' in *An Baner Kernewek / The Cornish Banner*, No. 96, 1999, pp.6-9.

83. Spriggs, op.cit.; Bakere, op.cit.; Murdoch, op.cit. All of these scholars have debated such origins with me with keen interest, and I am very grateful to them.

84. See Richard Beadle, 'The York Cycle', David Mills, 'The Chester Cycle' and Alan J. Fletcher, 'The N-Town Plays' in Beadle, op.cit., pp.85-108, pp.109-133 and pp.163-88 respectively.

85. See Pierre-Roland Giot, Philippe Guigon, and Bernard Merdrignac, *The British Settlement of Brittany*, Stroud: Tempus, 2003. For long-surviving cultural similarities, see R.A.H. Bickford-Smith, 'The Celtic Drama Revived: Buhaz Sant Gwennole at Morlaix' in *The Cornish Magazine*, November 1899, and Yann Boussell du Bourg, 'Breton Mystery Theatre: An Enduring Legacy' in *The Celtic Pen*, Vol. 2, No. 10, 1996, pp.17-18. Boussell du Bourg indicates a Cornish connection. A full study comparing Breton and Cornish drama is yet to be written.

86. Such a connection is explored in Brian Murdoch, 'Is *John of Chyanhor* really a 'Cornish *Ruodlieb*?' in Philip Payton (ed.), *Cornish Studies: Four*, Exeter: University of Exeter Press, 1996, pp.45-63.

87. R.A.J. Walling, *The Story of Plymouth*, London: Westaway Books, 1950, pp.17-28.

88. See Todd Gray, *The Chronicle of Exeter*, 1205-1772, Exeter: The Mint Press, 2005; Nicholas Orme, *Exeter Cathedral As It Was: 1050-1550*, Exeter: Devon Books, 1986.

89. See Kevin Crossley Holland (ed.), *The Exeter Book Riddles*, Harmondsworth: Penguin, 1979. When Leofric, first Bishop of Exeter, died in 1072, he bequeathed to the Cathedral library, the *Codex Exoniensis*, or Exeter Book. The University of Exeter's Department of English has reignited this tradition with its series of Exeter Medieval English Texts and Studies series. Although publishing a range of pan-British texts, Cornish ones have thus far been ignored.

90. See Maryanne Kowaleski, *Local Markets and Regional Trade in Medieval Exeter*, Cambridge: Cambridge University Press, 2003. For some sense of the possible links and routes, see Katherine Barker and Roger J.P Kain, *Maps and History in South-West England*, Exeter: University of Exeter Press, 1991.

91. Homi K. Bhabka, 'Culture's in between' in David Bennett (ed.), *Multicultural States: Rethinking Difference and Identity*, London and New York: Routledge, 1998, pp.29-36. Such a theory would also need to draw on Frantzen, op.cit., and Schmitz, op.cit.

92. See Michael Keith and Steve Pile (eds.), *Place and the Politics of Identity*, London and New York: Routledge, 1993, pp.2-3.

93. Peter Berresford Ellis, *Celt and Saxon: The Struggle for Britain AD 410-937*, London: Constable, 1993, p.266.

94. Whetter, op.cit.

95. See Ronald Harwood, *All the World's a Stage*, London: Methuen, 1984, pp.77-100.

96. Halliday, op.cit., 1953, pp. 281-99. The poem is about a snail making its way up one of the castle's imagined spires.

97. Cited in Kent and Saunders, op.cit., p.282. Scawen was a Vice Warden of the Stannaries, in effect, Chief Justice of Cornwall. For background, see Matthew Spriggs, 'William Scawen (1600-1689) – A Neglected Cornish Patriot and Father of the Cornish Language Revival' in Philip Payton (ed.), *Cornish Studies: Thirteen*, Exeter: University of Exeter Press, 2005, pp. 98-225.

98. See Deacon, op.cit., pp.38-41; Hatcher, op.cit.

99. The most famous example of these kind of stations is found in the sixteenth-century setting for the Mystère de la Passion at Valenciennes. See Harwood, op.cit., pp.92-93.

100. Kent and Saunders, op.cit.

101. See Robert Louis Stevenson's comments on Cornish Miners in North America in 1879. See A.L. Rowse (ed.), *A Cornish Anthology*, Penzance: Alison Hodge, 1990 [1968], p.7.

102. This essay is also titled 'Observations on an Ancient Manuscript, entitled *Passio Christi*'. A separate 'Passio Christi' from the rest of *Ordinalia* does not seem likely, although Bakere has indicated that the Passion may have west Cornwall origins.

103. William Borlase, *Observations on the Antiquities Historical and Monumental of the County of Cornwall*, London: EP Publishing, 1973 [1754], pp.195-6. See a more recent survey in A. Guthrie, 'The Plan-an-Gwarry, St. Just, Cornwall: Report on an Exploratory Excavation' in *Proceedings of the West Cornwall Field Club*, 2, 1, 1956-7, pp.3-7.

104. Higgins, op.cit., p.25.

105. Edwin Norris, *The Ancient Cornish Drama*, London and New York: Blom, 1968 [1859], p.455.

106. Robert Morton Nance, 'The Plen an Gwary or Cornish Playing-Place' in *Journal of the Royal Institution of Cornwall*, 24, 1935, p.192.

107. Ordinalia Company, *Ordinalia: The Full Cycle*, Penzance: Three S Films, 2004.

108. Halliday, op.cit., 1955, p.18.

109. See Murdoch, op.cit., pp.99-126.

110. Wilkie Collins, *Rambles beyond Railways, or Notes in Cornwall taken a-foot*, London: Westaway Books, 1948 [1851], p.130.

111. Ibid., pp.138-40. The gypsy image is intriguing since many of the touring performers of this phase are described as 'Egyptians'.

112. *Bewnans Meriasek*. MS. Peniarth 105, op.cit., p.98.

113. R. Halliwell, *Rambles in the West Country*, London: n.p.,1861, p.118.

114. See *Gwreans an Bys*. MS. Bodley 219, ibid.; *Ordinalia*. MS. Bodl. 791, f. 27, f. 56v, f. 83.

115. William Borlase, *The Natural History of Cornwall*, Oxford: Oxford University Press, 1758, p.295.

116. For extemporisation of this design, see the cover of Alan M. Kent, *Out of the Ordinalia*, St Austell: Lyonesse, 1995.

117. Borlase, op.cit.

118. Ibid.

119. Neuss, 1983, pp.28-29 and pp. 32-33.

120. Nance, op.cit., p.204.

121. Paul Neuss, 'The Staging of The Creacion of the World' in P. Happé (ed.), *Medieval English Drama*, London: Macmillan, 1984, p.197. Neuss comments that 'Nance's suggestion seems invalid…, for the second mention of the conveyor indicates an agent or instrument: *by* cannot mean 'beside', or even 'via'.'

122. Halliday, op.cit., p.29.

123. Ibid.

124. Higgins, op.cit., p.33.

125. See Roger Penhallurick, *Tin in Antiquity*, London: Institute of Metals, 1986.

126. R. Lebègue, *Le Mystère des Actes des Apôtres. Contribution à l'étude de l'humanisme et du protestantisme français au XVIe siècle*, Paris, n.p.,1929, p.78.

127. Higgins, op.cit., p.35.

128. Gabriel Alington, *The Hereford Mappa Mundi*, Leominster: Gracewing, 1996.

129. Higgins, op.cit., p.37.

130. Ibid.

131. Gordon Campbell (ed.), *John Milton: The Complete Poems*, London: Dent, 1980, p.219.

132. See Harwood, op.cit., p.308.

133. Bakere, op.cit., pp.28-30; Oliver J. Padel, 'Ancient Parishes with Possible Examples of the Plain-an-gwarry' in Joyce and Newlyn, op.cit., pp.558-63.

134. Spriggs, op.cit.; Lyon., op.cit.

135. See Henry Jenner, 'Perran Round and the Cornish Drama' in *The Seventy-Eighth Annual Report of the Royal Cornwall Polytechnic Society*, 1, 3, 1911, p.38.

136. Charles Thomas, 'Piran Round and the Medieval Cornish Drama' in K. G. Foster (ed.), *Piran Round, Perranporth: Souvenir Programme*, Cornwall: Cornwall County Council, 1969, pp.6-9.

137. Whetter, op.cit., 1993.

138. Lyon, op.cit., p.14.

139. Oliver J. Padel, *A Popular Dictionary of Cornish Place-Names*, Penzance: Alison Hodge, 1988, p.151.

140. St Enodor was the birthplace of John Trevisa, who may have had an input into theatrical work there.

141. It was discovered by T.Q. Couch. See William Sandys in *Journal of the Royal Institution of Cornwall*, Vol. 1, No. 4, 1865, p.78. Sandys comments that 'Close under the wall-plate and near the upper door of the roof-turret, was the head of a monster painted in red, from whose jaws issued several human figures'. The church is dedicated to St Nevet. There are equivalent dedications in Brittany.

142. Murdoch, op.cit., p.102.

143. Padel, op.cit., 1988, p.72.

144. Ibid.

145. For a modern play on this saint, see Donald R. Rawe, *Petroc of Cornwall*, Padstow: Lodenek Press, 1970.

146. Donald R. Rawe, *Padstow's Obby Oss and May Day Festivities: A Study in Folklore and Tradition*, Padstow: Lodenek Press, 1990 [1971].

147. Thomas Taylor, *The Celtic Christianity of Cornwall: Divers Sketches and Studies*, Felinfach: Llanerch, 1995 [1916], pp.65-66.

148. Spriggs, op.cit., p.160.

149. See Bernard Walke, *Twenty Years at St Hilary*, London: Anthony Mott Ltd, 1982 [1935], and *Plays from St Hilary*, London: Faber and Faber, 1939.

150. Spriggs, op.cit.

151. Craig Weatherhill, *Cornish Place Names and Language*, Wilmslow: Sigma, 1995, pp.8-9. For a perspective on language change at the border, see Andrew C.

Symons, 'Language Transfer in Cornwall' in *An Baner Kernewek / The Cornish Banner*, No. 127, 2007, pp.15-16.

152. Lyon, op.cit., pp.74-5.

153. Ibid. pp.78-9.

154. Padel, op.cit., 1999, p.561.

155. Alan M. Kent and Danny L.J. Merrifield, *The Book of Probus: Cornwall's Garden Parish*, Tiverton: Halsgrove, 2004, pp.23-26.

156. Ibid., pp. 225-9.

157. Lyon, op.cit., pp.75-77.

158. Padel, op.cit., p.562.

159. Deacon, op.cit., pp.65-7.

160. Lyon, op.cit., p.7-8; Spriggs, op.cit., p.160-1.

161. Patricia Bourke, 'The Stained Glass Windows of the Church of St. Neot, Cornwall' in *Devon and Cornwall Notes and Queries*, 33, 1974-8, p.65; Evelyn S. Newlyn, 'The Stained and Painted Glass of St. Neot's Church and the Staging of Middle Cornish Drama' in *Journal of Medieval and Renaissance Studies*, 24, 1994, pp.89-111. See also Robert Morton Nance, 'Painted Windows and Miracle Plays' in *Old Cornwall*, 5, 1955, pp.244-8.

162. Lyon, op.cit.; Padel, op.cit., p.561.

163. Lyon, ibid.

164. Neuss, op.cit.

165. Spriggs, op.cit.

166. Spriggs, op.cit., p.160; Padel, op.cit., p.562.

167. Spriggs, op.cit., Padel, op.cit., p.561.

168. Lyon, op.cit., p.8.

169. See Deborah Wingfield, *Penryn: Archaeology and Development – A Survey*, Redruth Institute of Cornish Studies and Cornwall Committee for Rescue Archaeology, 1979.

170. Some of the difficulties in dealing with early archaeological survivals in Penzance can be seen in Charles Thomas, *Penzance Market Cross, A Cornish Wonder re-wondered*, Penzance: Penlee House Gallery and Museum, 1999.

171. See numerous examples in Kent and Saunders, op.cit., pp. 224-45.

172. See Edwin Norris, *The Ancient Cornish Drama*, London and New York: Blom, 1968 [1859]. Although Norris' text contains some errors, it does attempt to present the original text with an English translation, and so will be used here. A Unified Cornish version of the trilogy is found in Robert Morton Nance, A.S.D. Smith, and Graham Sandercock (eds. and trs.), *The Cornish Ordinalia, Second Play: Christ's Passion*, Cornwall: The Cornish Language Board, 1982, and (eds. and trs.), *The Cornish Ordinalia, Third Play: Resurrection*, Cornwall: The Cornish Language Board, 1984; Robert Morton Nance, A. S. D. Smith, Ray Chubb,

Richard Jenkin, and Graham Sandercock (eds. and trs.), *The Cornish Ordinalia, First Play: Origo Mundi*, Cornwall: Agan Tavas, 2001. Although not the original Cornish of the manuscript, the text nevertheless has a useful translation. For a modern English-language verse translation, see Alan M. Kent, *Ordinalia: The Cornish Mystery Play Cycle – A Verse Translation*, London: Francis Boutle Publishers, 2005.

173. Halliday, op.cit., 1953.

174. See Magnus Maclean, *The Literature of the Celts*, London: Blackie and Son, 1908.

175. See Jeffrey Gantz (ed. and tr.), *The Mabinogion*, Harmondsworth: Penguin, 1976, and (ed. and tr.), *Early Irish Myths and Sagas*, London: Penguin, 1981.

176. Maclean, op.cit. See also A.W. Ward and A. Waller (eds.), *The Cambridge History of English Literature, V: The Drama to 1642 Pt 1*, Cambridge: Cambridge University Press, 1970 [1910], p.16; J.R. Piette, 'Cornish Literature' in *The Penguin Companion to Literature I*, Harmondsworth: Penguin, 1971, p.119.

177. The current academic consensus is found in Longsworth, op.cit.; Bakere, op.cit., 1980; Murdoch, op.cit., 1993, pp. 41-74, and op.cit., 1994, pp.211-39; 'Introduction' in Kent, op.cit.; Higgins, op.cit.

178. See the various contributors to Beadle, op.cit.

179. See *Ordinalia*. MS. Bodl. 791, Oxford. For commentary, see 'MS. 791' in Alan M. Kent, *Assassin of Grammar*, Penzance: Hypatia Publications, 2005, p.37.

180. Bodl. MSS. 28556-28557, Oxford.

181. Peniarth, MS. 428E. For a perspective on these two manuscripts, see Andrew Hawke, 'A Lost Manuscript of the Cornish *Ordinalia*?' in Charles Thomas (ed.), *Cornish Studies / Studhyansow Kernewk 7*, Redruth: Institute of Cornish Studies, 1979, pp.45-60.

182. Longsworth, op.cit., p.5.

183. See Bakere, op.cit., pp.12-49.

184. See Whetter, op.cit., 1988.

185. Norris, Vol. II., op.cit., pp.74-121.

186. See T.D. Crawford, 'The Composition of the Cornish *Ordinalia*' in *Old Cornwall*, 9, 1979-1985, pp.145-53 and pp.166-7; David C. Fowler, 'The Date of the Cornish *Ordinalia*' in *Mediaeval Studies*, 23, 1961, pp.91-125.

187. Norris, Vol. I, op.cit., pp.432-3.

188. Bakere, op.cit., pp.42-3.

189. See Neuss, op.cit.

190. For discussion on this, see Murdoch, op.cit., 1983; Bakere, op.cit., pp.76-108.

191. Brian Murdoch, 'Legends of the Holy Rood in Cornish Drama' in *Studia Celtica Japonica*, Vol. IX, 1997. The initial discussion of this area of enquiry was shaped by Halliday. See Halliday, op.cit., 1955.

192. This is discussed in Longsworth, op.cit, p.47, but see also BL: MS. Harl. MS. 2252, folios 50b-51b and Henry Jenner and Thomas Taylor, 'The Legend of the Church of the Holy Cross in Cornwall' in *Journal of the Royal Institution of Cornwall*, 20, 1917-1921, pp.295-309.

193. For a context see Robert Whiting, *The Blind Devotion of the People: Popular Religion and the English Reformation*, Cambridge: Cambridge University Press, 1989; Laurence Snell, *The Suppression of the Religious Foundations of Devon and Cornwall*, Marazion, n.p., 1967.

194. See Longsworth, op.cit.; Murdoch, op.cit., 1983; Robert T. Meyer, 'The Liturgical Background of Medieval Cornish Drama' in *Trivium*, 3, 1968, pp.48-58; Henry Jenner, 'The Sources for the Cornish Drama' in Jenner Papers, Royal Institution of Cornwall, Truro.

195. Ray Edwards (ed. and tr.), *Pascon Agan Arluth / The Poem of Mount Calvary*, Sutton Coldfield: Kernewek Dre Lyther, 1993; Murdoch, op.cit., pp.19-40.

196. Fowler, op.cit.

197. Murdoch, op.cit.; Edwards, op.cit.; Harry Woodhouse (ed.), *The Cornish Passion Poem*, Cornwall: Gorseth Kernow, 2007. For a detailed list of criticism see Murdoch (ed.), op.cit., 1979. See also Brian Murdoch, 'Pascon Agan Arluth: The Literary Position of the Cornish Poem of the Passion' in *Studi Medievali*, Series 3, Vol.12, No.2, 1981.

198. Longsworth, op.cit., p.124.

199. These episodes are usefully compared with other dramas of the same period. See Beadle, op.cit. See also Gloria J. Betcher, 'Makers of Heaven and Earth: The Construction of Early Drama in Cornwall' in Davidson, op.cit.

200. Norris, op.cit., pp.10-11.

201. Ibid., pp.12-13.

202. Newlyn, op.cit., 1994. Although much of the metaphorical base is contained within the Creation Window at St Neot, an image of Christ's resurrection is also found in the Calloway Window. See Kent, op.cit., 2005, p.10.

203. Norris, op.cit., pp.28-9.

204. Ibid., pp.36-9.

205. Ibid., pp.50-1.

206. For background on this, see Esther Casier Quinn, *The Quest of Seth for the Oil of Life*, Chicago: Chicago University Press, 1962.

207 Newlyn, op.cit.

208. Norris, op.cit.,pp.63-3. There has been considerable debate over this naming sequence, with Fowler using it to justify John Trevisa's involvement in the writing of the B and C texts of *Piers the Plowman*. See Fowler, op.cit., pp.241-47.

209. Ibid., pp.80-1.

210. Ibid., pp.88-9.

211. Ibid., pp.96-97.

212. Ibid., pp.122-3. For further insight into the use of the arena, see Neville Denny, 'Arena Staging and Dramatic Quality in the Cornish Passion Play' in Neville Denny (ed.), *Medieval Drama*, London: Stratford-upon-Avon Studies 16, 1973, pp.125-53; Crystan Fudge, 'Aspects of Form in the Cornish *Ordinalia* with special reference to 'Origo Mundi' in *Old Cornwall*, 8, 1973-79, pp.457-64 and pp.491-98.

213. Ibid., pp.134-5.

214. See Paul Broadhurst, *Sacred Shrines: In Search of the Holy Wells of Cornwall*, Launceston: Pendragon Press, 1991.

215 Brian Murdoch, 'Rex David, Bersabe, and Syr Urry: A Comparative Approach to a Scene in the Cornish *Origo Mundi*' in Philip Payton (ed.), *Cornish Studies: Twelve*, Exeter: University of Exeter Press, 2004, pp.288-304.

216. Norris, op.cit., pp.178-9.

217. Ibid., pp.180-1.

218. Ibid., pp.174-5.

219. Bakere, op.cit., p.34. There were two parts of the manor. One was Penryn Home and this related to the manor covering the town of Penryn. Penryn Foreign refers to the lands outside the town. I am indebted to James Whetter for the information here.

220. Norris, op.cit., pp.182-3.

221. Bakere, op.cit., pp.35-6.

222. Norris, op.cit., pp.186-7.

223. Bakere, op.cit., p.37.

224. Norris. op.cit.

225. Ibid., pp.196-7.

226. For the function of the torturers see Sally Joyce Cross, 'Torturers as Tricksters in the Cornish *Ordinalia*' in *Neuphilologische Mitteilung*, 84, 1983, pp.448-55. For another consideration of the function of the torturers and executioners, see Manning, op.cit. In summary, Manning suggests that the violence of the stage in both *Ordinalia* and *Bewnans Meriasek* reflects the violent period of religious and cultural history which Britain endured under the Reformation. The violence of the real world was matched by violence on stage. While some of this may be correct, it does not account for the violence against Jesus recorded in the Gospels.

227 Norris, op.cit., pp.210-1.

228. Hall, op.cit.

229. See Phyllis Pier Harris, *Origo Mundi, First play of the Cornish mystery cycle, the Ordinalia: a new edition*, University of Washington: Ph.D. thesis, 1964; Alan M. Kent, *Nativitas Christi / The Nativity: A New Cornish Mystery Play*, London: Francis Boutle Publishers, 2006; Ken George, *Flogholeth Krist / The Cornish*

Ordinalia – the missing play: The Childhood of Christ, Cornwall: Kesva an Taves Kernewek, 2006.

230. These are discussed further in Chapter Seven.
231. See *Ordinalia*. MS. Bodl. 791, Oxford, f. 27. Bakere also pays considerable attention to the staging process. See Bakere, op.cit., pp.150-69. Further useful material is found in Ian Love, *Hic Descendit Deus Pater: Miracle Play Performance in Late Mediaeval Cornwall*, University of Cambridge, BA Dissertation, 2002.
232. Norris, op.cit., pp.4-5.
233. Ibid., pp.224-5.
234. Ibid., pp.226-7.
235. Ibid., pp.344-5.
236. Ibid., pp.404-5.
237. Ibid., pp.376-7.
238. Murdoch, op.cit., 1994, p.220.
239. Norris, op.cit., pp.390-1.
240. Ibid., pp.420-1.
241. Ibid., pp.436-7.
242. This was one reason why the Ordinalia Trust wished to mount a production of 'Passio Christi' in August 1999, because during that year Cornwall experienced a solar eclipse.
243. Norris, op.cit., pp.462-3.
244. Neville Denny (dir.), *Performance Texts for the Cornish Ordinalia*, 1969; Ordinalia Company, *Ordinalia: The Full Cycle*, Penzance: Three S Films, 2004.
245. *Ordinalia*. MS. Bodl. 791, Oxford, f.83.
246. Couch, op.cit.
247. Norris, op.cit., Vol. II, pp.24-5.
248. Ibid., pp.34-5.
249. Ibid., pp.48-9.
250. Ibid., pp.68-9.
251. Ibid., pp.116-7.
252. Ibid., pp.196-7.
253. Murdoch, op.cit., 1994, p.224.
254. Richard Rastall, *The Heaven Singing: Music in Early English Religious Drama*, Cambridge: D.S. Brewer,1996.
255. Richard Rastall, *Minstrels Playing: Music in Early English Religious Drama II*, Cambridge: D.S. Brewer, 2001.
256. Norris, op.cit., pp.24-5.
257. Ibid., pp.42-43.
258. Ibid., pp.150-1.
259. Ibid., pp.196-7.

260. Ibid., pp.200-1.

261. Ibid., pp. 216-7. On this, see J.R. Moor, 'Miracle Plays, Minstrels and Jigs' in *Proceedings of the Modern Language Association of America*, 48, 1933, pp.943-45.

262. See Borough Accounts, St Ives Guildhall.

263. Ibid., pp.240-1.

264. Ibid., pp.464-5.

265. Ibid.

266. Ibid., Vol. II, pp.176-7.

267. Ibid., pp.178-9.

268. Ibid., pp. 58-9.

269. Ibid., pp.190-1.

270. Ibid., pp.198-9.

271. For example, the Cornish Music Symposium held at the Institute of Cornish Studies, Combined Universities of Cornwall, in 2008.

272. Ibid., pp.311-435. See also Eugene Val Tassel Graves (ed.), *Vocabularium Cornicum: The Old Cornish Vocabulary*, University of Columbia, Ph.D. thesis, 1962.

273. A view asserted in Crystan Fudge, *The Life of Cornish*, Redruth: Dyllansow Truran, 1982. With such a text, it is perhaps what is *not said* about the culture that leads me to suspect this view as being untenable.

274. David C. Fowler, *The Life and Times of John Trevisa, Medieval Scholar*, Seattle and London: University of Washington Press, 1995, p.23. A slightly alternative perspective is found in David C. Fowler, *John Trevisa*, Aldershot: Variorium, 1993.

275. Ibid., pp.24-83.

276. Craig Weatherhill, *Cornish Place Names and Language*, Wilmslow: Sigma, 1995, p.82.

277. Useful commentary on the process is found in David Crystal, *The Cambridge Encylopedia of The English Language*, Cambridge: Cambridge University Press, 1995, p.35.

278. See Fowler, op.cit., pp.241-7.

279. William Hals also refers to a '*Book of the Acts of King Arthur* by John Trevisa'. See William Hals, *The Compleat History of Cornwall*, Truro, c.1736, p.103. A copy is held in the Courtney Library, Royal Institution of Cornwall. Could this text have had an input on the shape of the Arthurian matter of *Bewnans Ke*?

280. Fowler, op.cit., p.18. For a more detailed discussion, see David C. Fowler, 'The Date of the Cornish "Ordinalia"' in *Mediaeval Studies*, 23, 1961, pp.91-125.

281. For background, see Crystal, op.cit., p.48.

282. Andrew C. Symons, *Trevisa: Further Reflections*, Unpublished paper, 2008, p.1. It is important to assert that this is not Symons' full position. He is merely exploring possibilities.

283. Ibid., p.1-2.

284. Ibid., p.2.

285. Several scholars have discussed the Trevisa issue with me, and I am indebted to all of their input. Brian Murdoch has been most helpful in clarifying the medieval liturgical issues, and for his suggestions of similar texts. For an exploration of Trevisa's link to the medieval Cornish Bible, see Erik Grigg, 'The Medieval Cornish Bible: More Evidence' in Philip Payton (ed.), *Cornish Studies: Sixteen*, Exeter: University of Exeter Press, 2008, pp.19-25. Grigg is clearly drawing on a similar conceptualisation to Symons.

286. See Norris, op.cit.

287. Payton, op.cit., 1933.

288. Bhabka, op.cit.

289. Elliott-Binns, op.cit., pp.406-9. An officer at Exeter College in 1417 was Walter Treugof [or Trengof]. See University of Oxford (ed.), *The Historical Register of the University of Oxford, completed to the end of Trinity Term, 1888*, Oxford: Clarendon Press, 1888.

290. See http://freepages.genealogy.rootsweb.ancestry.com

291. See Thomas Walsh, *History of the Irish Hierarchy*, New York: D. & J. Sadlier and Co., 1854, p.119.

292. Tregury is buried at Dublin Cathedral. His epitaph reads *Perasul Metropolis hic Dublinenus, Marmore tumbatus, pro me Christum flagitetis* [Here's Michael the Prelate of Dublin See, In Marble intomb'd, invoke Christ for me].

293. Notably, there was, on nearby Rosenannen Downs (formerly called Carenza Wortha), a chapel dedicated to St Mary Magdalene, which was destroyed in the War of Five Nations (Civil War). Other Magdalene para-theatrical traditions occur in Launceston.

294. See http://freepages.genealogy.rootsweb.ancestry.com. The only other reference I can locate about this author and his work is in W.H. Stevenson, '*Dr Guest and the English Conquest of South Britain*' in *The English Historical Review*, Vol.17, No.68, 1902, pp.625-42.

295. Ibid.

296. Whetter, op.cit., 1988, p.108.

297. Ibid.

298. Ibid

299. See Spriggs, op.cit., p.160-1.

300. Whetter, op.cit., p.109.

301. Spriggs, op.cit.

302. Ibid., p.110.

303. Ibid., p.111.

304. Ibid.

305. Frost. op.cit. The Rad Ton might in fact, be Ricardus. According to Ellis, op.cit., there was a priest at Crowan, near Camborne, named Dominus Ricardus Ton.

306. *Bewnans Meriasek*. MS. Peniarth 105, NLW, Aberystwyth. An on-line version is available. See http://www.llgc.org.uk/drych/drych_s074.htm

307. See G.H. Doble, 'Saint Meriadoc: Bishop and Confessor' in *Cornish Saints Series*, No. 34, 1935; Whetter, op.cit., p.109.

308. A name subsequently used by J.R.R. Tolkien to name one of the hobbits in *Lord of the Rings*, demonstrating Tolkien's awareness of Cornish and Breton Celtic culture. The theme of Meriasek continues to inspire writing. See, for example, Neil Kennedy, 'Meriasek' in Tim Saunders (ed. and tr.), *Nothing Broken: Recent Poetry in Cornish*, London: Francis Boutle Publishers, 2006, pp.146-7. Camborne people are known by the nicknames of 'merry geeks, merry jacks or merrysickers'. See Jan Gendall, *Scat-Ups, Scabs, and Shagdowns: A Glossary of Cornish Community Nicknames*, Menheniot: Teer ha Tavas, 1995, p.2. Camborne has the only dedication to Meriasek in Britain.

309. *Bewnans Meriasek*. MS. Peniarth 105, NLW, Aberystwyth.

310. The archivist David Thomas believes he has located another contender for authorship of the drama. This will be discussed in a forthcoming article by him.

311. See Henry Jenner, 'King Teudar' in Trelawney Roberts, Charles Henderson and Leonard Seldon (eds.), *Tre, Pol and Pen: The Cornish Annual*, London, 1928, pp.29-34; W. H. Pascoe, *Teudar: A King of Cornwall*, Redruth: Dyllansow Truran, 1985.

312. Whetter, op.cit., p.105.

313. For detailed examination of this, see Payton, 1993b. See also Joyce Youings, 'The South-Western Rebellion of 1549' in *Southern History*, 1, 1979, pp.99-122.

314 Whetter, op.cit., p.106. Thurstan C. Peter goes further, believing that the play is actually a translation of a Breton original. He also suggests John Nans as the translator. Part of his reasoning for this is that the saint's name appears in the text as both Meridoc (Breton) and Meriasek (Cornish). See Thurstan C. Peter, *The Old Cornish Drama*, London: Elliot Stock, 1906.

315. Ibid.

316. Ibid. See also F.A. Ginever, 'The Tale of Camborne's Patron Saint' in *Camborniana*, 1897, pp.5-22.

317. Ibid.

318. A point made in Amy Hale, Alan M. Kent and Tim Saunders (eds. and trs.), *Inside Merlin's Cave: A Cornish Arthurian Reader 1000-2000*, London: Francis Boutle Publishers, 2000.

319. Whetter, op.cit.

320. The standard edition is Whitley Stokes (ed. and tr.), *The Life of Saint Meriasek, Bishop and Confessor: A Cornish Drama*, London: Trübner and Co., 1872. Useful

corrections to this edition were offered by Ray Edwards in 1996. For English-language versions, see Markham Harris (ed. and tr.), *The Life of Meriasek: A Medieval Cornish Miracle Play*, Washington D.C.: Catholic University of America Press, 1977; Myrna Combellack (ed. and tr.), *The Camborne Play: A verse translation of Beunans Meriasek*, Redruth: Dyllansow Truran, 1988. See also Whitley Stokes, 'A Glossary to the Cornish Drama, *Beunans Meriasek*' in *Activ für celtische Lexigraphie*, 1, 1898-1900, pp.101-42.

321. For a context, see Clifford Davidson (ed.), *The Saint Play in Medieval Europe*, Kalamazoo, Michigan: Medieval Institute Publications, 1986.

322. See Erik Grigg, *Beunans Meriasek / The Life of St Meriasek: A Study Guide*, Cornwall: The Cornish Language Board, 2008, pp.23-5.

323. Murdoch, op.cit., 1993, pp. 99-126.

324. Ibid.

325. See Robert Williams, 'Cornish Literature' in *Archaeologia Cambrensis*, 3, 15, 1869, pp.408-9.

326. See W. Davies, *Cornish Manuscripts in the National Library of Wales*, Aberystwyth: National Library of Wales, 1939.

327. For commentary on this, see Nicholas Orme, 'Education in the Medieval Cornish Play *Beunans Meriasek*' in *Cambridge Medieval Celtic Studies*, 25, 1993, pp.1-13.

328. Stokes, op.cit., 1872, pp.36-7.

329. For a range, see Ken George, *A Phonological History of Cornish*, University of Western Brittany, Brest, Ph.D thesis, 1984; Richard Gendall, *1000 Years of Cornish*, Menheniot: Teere ha Tavaz, 1994; N.J.A. Williams, *Cornish Today: An Examination of the Revived Language*, Sutton Coldfield: Kernewek dre Lyther, 1995.

330. Murdoch, op.cit., 1994, p.231.

331. Stokes, op,cit., pp.48-9.

332. Ibid., pp.60-1.

333. See W.G. Ryan (ed. and tr.), *The Golden Legend by Jacobus de Voragine*, Vols. 1 and 2, Chichester: Princetown University Press, 1993.

334. Ibid., pp.126-7.

335. Ibid., pp.130-1.

336. Rastall, op.cit., 2001, pp.401-13.

337. See Grigg, op.cit., p.11; Murdoch, op.cit., p.233.

338. For a detailed exploration of this, see Brian Murdoch, 'The Holy Hostage: "*De filio mulieris*" in the Middle Cornish play *Beunans Meriasek*' in *Medium Acvum*, 158, 1989, pp.258-73.

339. Brian Murdoch (ed.) *The Grin of the Gargoyle*, Sawtry: Dedalus 1995, p.229.

340. Stokes, op.cit., pp.196-7.

341. Ibid.

342. Ibid., pp.198-9.

343. Murdoch. op.cit., 1994, p.234.

344. Ibid.

345. Stokes, op,cit., pp.264-5.

346. See *Bewnans Meriasek*. MS. Peniarth 105, NLW, Aberystwyth, p.98. The short-hand Latin of the original diagram has been elucidated here.

347. Ibid., p.180.

348. Cf. Bakere, op.cit.

349. See Sydney Higgins, 'The Action of St Meriasek – Day One' in Higgins, op.cit., 1995, pp.73-122. See also Sydney Higgins, *Medieval Staging in Cornwall with Special Reference to St. Meriasek*, University of Bristol, M.Phil. thesis, 1974.

350. Stokes, op.cit., pp.104-5.

351. Higgins, op.cit.

352. See Sydney Higgins, 'The Action of St Meriasek – Day Two' in Higgins, op.cit., 1995, pp.123-44. Elements of Higgins's M. Phil thesis are incorporated into this.

353. Stokes, op.cit., pp.228-9

354. Ibid.

355. Higgins, op.cit., p.114.

356. Ibid., pp.119-20.

357. Halliday, op.cit., 1953, p.144.

358. Ellis, op.cit., p.40.

359. Twentieth-century studies include Robert T. Meyer, 'The Middle-Cornish Play: *Beunans Meriasek*' in *Comparative Drama*, 3, 1969, pp.54-64; Robert Morton Nance and E.G.R. Hooper, 'Notes on the *Beunans Meriasek* Manuscript' in *Old Cornwall*, 9, 1979-1985, pp.34-6. Hooper was editing Nance's earlier notes. A useful volume is Graham Sandercock, *Meryasek yn Kernow*, Cornwall: Kesva an Taves Kernewek, 2000.

360. See Myrna May Combellack-Harris, *A Critical Edition of Beunans Meriasek*, University of Exeter, Ph.D. thesis, 1985; Combellack, op.cit., 1988.

361. Glynne Wickham, 'The Staging of Saint Plays in England' in Sandro Sticca (ed.), *The Medieval Drama*, Albany: State University of New York Press, 1972, pp.115-18.

362. Darryl Grantley, 'Producing Miracles' in Paula Neuss (ed.) *Aspects of Early English Drama*, Cambridge and Totowa, New Jersey: D.S. Brewer, 1983, pp.78-91.

363. Frank A. Turk and Myrna M. Combellack, 'Doctoring and Disease in Medieval Cornwall: Exegetical Notes on Some Passages in *Beunans Meriasek*' in Charles Thomas (ed.), *Cornish Studies / Studhyansow Kernewk* 4/5, Redruth: Institute of Cornish Studies, 1976-1977, pp.56-76.

364. T.D. Crawford, 'Stanza Forms and Social Status in *Beunans Meriasek*' in *Old Cornwall*, 9, 1979-1985, pp.431-39.

365. Significant sequences are featured in Kent and Saunders, op.cit., pp.118-85. A sequence from St Meriasek's arrival in Cornwall also features in Kenneth Hurlstone Jackson (ed. and tr.), *A Celtic Miscellany: Translations from the Celtic Literatures*, Harmondsworth: Penguin, 1971, pp.304-5.

366. Murdoch, op.cit., 1993, 1994.

367. Grigg, op.cit.

368. Richard Rutt, 'Love and Tears at the Camborne Play' in *The Celtic Pen*, Vol. 2, No. 1, 1994, p.18.

369. Payton's discussion with Olson eventually resulted in Olson's article. See Lynette Olson, 'Tyranny in *Beunans Meriasek*' in Philip Payton (ed.), *Cornish Studies: Five*, Exeter: University of Exeter Press, 1997, pp.52-9.

370. Payton. op.cit., 1993. p.10.

371. Jonathan Wooding, *St Meriasek and King Tudor in Cornwall*, Sydney: n.p., 1992.

372. Stokes, op.cit., pp.44-45.

373. Ibid., pp.136-7. Edwards offers a different translation of this: 'Under my feet I will stick them with bird-lime, just like starlings.'

374. Payton, op.cit., 1993, pp.11-12. See also Mark Stoyle, 'The dissidence of despair: Rebellion and identity in early modern Cornwall' in *Journal of British Studies*, 38, 4, 1999, pp.423-44.

375. Combellack, op.cit., 1998. Combellack's work on drama from this phase inspired much of her later fiction. See Myrna Combellack, *The Playing Place: A Cornish Round*, Redruth: Dyllansow Truran, 1989.

376. CRO: PD/322/1.

377. Ibid. The money was in the hands of Richard Crane, who was a churchwarden and warden of the Mid-Lent Guild. For background on guild organisation in Cornwall during this phase, see Joanna Mattingly, 'The Medieval Parish Guilds of Cornwall' in *Journal of the Royal Institution of Cornwall*, 10, 3, 1989, pp.290-329.

378. Ibid. Bakere, op.cit., p.21, logically connects this with the lines at the end of both the first and second days of *Bewnans Meriasek*, which mention pipers and minstrels. See Stokes, op.cit., p.144 and p. 264.

379. Ibid., CRO: PD/322/2.

380. Ibid. A useful perspective on this is found in John Forrest and Michael Heaney, 'Charting Early Morris' in *Folk Music Journal*, 6, 2, 1991, p.177. The Morris under consideration is not that conceived of after the work of Cecil Sharpe, one of the founders of the English Folk Revival. For examination of past and present Morris, see Georgina Boyes, *The Imagined Village: Culture, Ideology and the English Folk Revival*, Manchester: Manchester University Press, 1993, and contributors to Boyes (ed.), *Step Change: New Views on Traditional Dance*,

London: Francis Boutle Publishers, 2001. It could be that Morris/guizing developed in Cornwall and passed to England. Guizing of this kind is a pan-European phenomenon. I am indebted to Merv Davey for his observations here.

381. See Charles Thomas, *Christian Antiquities of Camborne*, Cornwall: H.E. Warne, 1967, p.171.

382. Lyon, op.cit., p.43.

383. *Bewnans Ke*. MS. 23849D, NLW, Aberystwyth.

384. See Thomas and Williams, op.cit., p.x. The papers were donated by Mrs Gwen Caerwyn Williams.

385. See Henry Jenner, 'Some Possible Arthurian Place-Names in West Penwith' in *Journal of the Royal Institution of Cornwall*, 1912, and 'Tintagel Castle in History and Romance' in *Journal of the Royal Institution of Cornwall*, No.74, 1927; Hale, Kent and Saunders, op.cit.

386. See Edwards, op.cit.

387. A number of scholars have taken up this call – among them, Matthew Spriggs and myself.

388. See I.M.G., *Old Kea Church*, Kea: Old Kea Church, 1991.

389. Lyon, op.cit., pp.13-14. Could it be that two rounds operated here for each of the days? If so this would be a novel division of dramatic activity. I am indebted here to Philip Davey for discussion on this, and theatre at Playing Place.

390. Thomas and Williams, op.cit., p.xliii.

391. http://www.llgc.org.uk/drych

392. http://www.asnc.cam.ac.uk/resources

393. http://www.bewnanske.co.uk

394. Ken George (ed. and tr.), *Bywnans Ke*, Cornwall: Kesva an Taves Kernewek, 2006.

395. Thomas and Williams, op.cit.

396. Both George, and Thomas and Williams give considerable discussion to this.

397. See Lewis Thorpe (ed. and tr.), *Geoffrey of Monmouth: The History of the Kings of Britain*, Harmondsworth: Penguin, 1966.

398. This is contained in Thomas and Williams, op.cit., pp.xii-xiv. Another translation is found in George, op.cit., pp.249-51.

399. Ibid., p.xii.

400. Ibid.

401. Ibid.

402. Ibid.

403. Turk and Combellack, op.cit.

404. Murdoch, op.cit., 1994, p.231.

405. Thomas and Williams, op.cit., pp.10-11.

406. Ibid., pp.52-3.
407. Manning, op.cit.
408. Thomas and Williams, op.cit., pp.68-9.
409. Ibid.
410. Ibid., pp.76-7.
411. Ibid., pp.90-1.
412. Ibid., pp.116-7. Professor Williams kindly offered a corrected transcription and translation of these lines. Dog excrement was used as a folk remedy.
413. Bruch, op.cit.
414. Thomas and Williams, op.cit., p.xiii.
415. For a range of texts that comment on this, see Hale, Kent and Saunders, op.cit.
416. Scawen, op.cit.
417. Thomas and Williams, op.cit., pp.130-1. This is generally perceived to be Callington. For discussion here, see Padel, op.cit., 2005.
418. Ibid., pp.144-7.
419. Ibid.
420. Ibid., pp.146-147. The † shows this transcription may not be accurate.
421. For a response to this, see Alan M. Kent, *Stannary Parliament*, St Austell: Lyonesse, 2006, p.23.
422. Thomas and Williams, op.cit., pp.168-9.
423. Ibid., pp.206-7.
424. See Nicholas J.A. Williams, 'The Cornish Englyn' in Philip Payton (ed.), *Cornish Studies: Fifteen*, Exeter: University of Exeter Press, 2007, pp.11-26.
425. Thomas and Williams, op.cit., p.xiv.
426. Nicholas J.A. Williams speaking on 'The Language of Bewnans Ke' at the Combined Universities of Cornwall, Tremough, 13 September 2008.
427. See the observations of John Ray, cited in Kent and Saunders, op.cit., p.276.
428. Thomas and Williams, op.cit., pp.xliv-xlvi.
429. Ibid. A range of linguistic and phonological issues is debated here. George has also offered a supplementary word list based on *Bewnans Ke*. See Ken George, *Rol dewisys a eryow nowydh po kevys namenowgh, a-dhiworth Bywnans Ke*, Cornwall: Cornish Language Board, 2006.
430. This point is made in Padel, op.cit., 2005, and reiterated on 13 September 2008.
431. This view was dismissed by Williams on 13 September 2008.
432. See George, op.cit., 2006, p.6.
433. Williams, 13 September 2008.
434. George, op.cit.

435. Ibid.

436. The Roman component of Arthuriana is a curious addition to the corpus. However, this does feature in Hals's version of the story (c.1736). See Hale, Kent and Saunders, op.cit., pp.73-80.

437. CRO: B/Laus/135.

438. DRO: Chanter 11 f. ccxiii verso.

439. CRO: B/Laus/143. There is remarkable continuity from this to the concerns of the Anglo-Cornish dramatist and poet Charles Causley. See 'Mary, Mary Magdelene' in Charles Causley, *Collected Poems 1951-1975*, London: Macmillan, 1975, pp.239-40.

440. See CRO: B/Laus/147. See Causley, ibid., p.241.

441. CRO: B/Laus/170.

442. CRO: B/Laus/173-78. The term *venesicians* may have a link to the word Egyptians [gypsies].

443. Ibid.

444. Ibid. For full background here, see Richard Peter and Otto Barhurt Peter, *The History of Launceston and Dunheved in the County of Cornwall*, Plymouth: W. Brendon, 1885.

445. See Sir John Arundell's Stewards' Accounts: HK/17/1 in Courtney Library, Royal Institution of Cornwall. See also H.L. Douch, 'Household Accounts at Lanherne' in *Journal of the Royal Institution of Cornwall*, 2, 1, 1953-4, pp.25-32.

446. Ibid.

447. CRO: AR/26/2.

448. See CRO: AR/21/21/2 and CRO: AR/21/22.

449. Bakere, op.cit., p.20.

450. CRO: B/Bod/244.

451. CRO: B/Bod/314/3/10.

452. CRO: B/Bod/314/2/15.

453. CRO: B/Bod/314/2/21.

454. CRO: B/Bod/314/3/21 and 22.

455. CRO: B/Bod/314/1/6.

456. See Joyce and Newlyn, op.cit., p.595.

457. CRO: B/Bod/314/2/26.

458. CRO: B/Bod/314/2/20.

459. CRO: B/Bod/314/3/32 and 39.

460. CRO: B/Bod/314/3/51. This was for construction of a 'barrys'.

461. CRO: B/Bod/314/2/12.

462. See John Wallis (ed.), *The Bodmin Register: Containing Collections Relative to the Past and Present State of the Parish of Bodmin*, Bodmin, 1827-38. More recent

ceremonies may have their roots in the drama and customs here. See Pat Munn, *Bodmin Riding and Other Similar Celtic Customs*, Bodmin: Bodmin Books Limited, 1975.

463. CRO: B/Bod/233.

464. Rowse, op.cit., p.261 and p.147. Reflection on this period is given in H. Michell Whitley, 'The Church Goods of Cornwall at the Time of the Reformation' in *Journal of the Royal Institution of Cornwall*, 7, 1881-2, pp.92-135.

465. CRO: B/Bod/233. There is an intriguing reference in the diary of William Carnsew of Bokelly regarding performance in Bodmin in 1576. On 29 July, he notes: 'I am wrytyn to to [sic] meett Mr Mohan att bodman playes spent ther 12 s. wherof I gaue wrestlers 5 s.' See PRO: SP 46/16. It seems therefore that performance in Bodmin continued until this date. Halgavor is close to Bokelly.

466. Halliday, op.cit., 1953, p.197.

467. CRO: B/Bod/20.

468. Spriggs, op.cit.; Lyon, op.cit., p.105. Lyon does note a possible site at Cardinham called Place Green Field at Lower Haygrove.

469. BL: Additional MS. 32243. For background here, see Edward Peacock, 'On the Churchwardens' Accounts of the Parish of Stratton, in the County of Cornwall' in *Archaeologia*, 46, 1, 1880, pp.195-236.

470. Ibid.

471. BL: Additional MS. 32244.

472. Ibid.

473. Ibid.

474. See BL, op.cit. 32243.

475. Ibid.

476. PRO: E 31/122. For detail on 'Riding' ceremony, see Munn, op.cit.

477. This is clearly significant. Both Rowse, and Cornwall comment on the high proportion of Breton people living in Cornwall during this phase. See Rowse, op.cit., pp.95-96, and Julian Cornwall, *Revolt of the Peasantry 1549*, London: Routledge, 1977, p.42.

478. Halliday, op.cit., p.212.

479. CRO: P/192/5/1.

480. CRO: P/19/5/1.

481. Ibid.

482. Ibid.

483. Ibid.

484. Ibid. We know that the Robin Hood players from St. Columb Minor also performed in St Ives in 1587-8. For background on Robin Hood plays, see David Wiles, *The Early Plays of Robin Hood*, Cambridge: Cambridge University Press, 1981.

485. Ibid.

486. Ibid.

487. Nicholas Orme (ed.), *Nicholas Roscarrock's Lives of the Saints of Cornwall and Devon*, Exeter: Devon and Cornwall Record Society, 1992, p.68.

488. CRO: P/36/8/1.

489. Ibid.

490. Ibid.

491. Tickner, op.cit., p.20.

492. Ibid., p.23.

493. Ibid.

494. Merv Davey, "'Guizing': Ancient Traditions and Modern Sensitivities' in Philip Payton (ed.), *Cornish Studies: Fourteen*, Exeter: University of Exeter Press, 2006, pp.229-44.

495. CRO: P/36/8/1.

496. See, for example, Ian Sharp (dir.), *Robin of Sherwood*, Bristol: HTV/Goldcrest, 1984; Kevin Reynolds (dir.), *Robin Hood: Prince of Thieves*, Los Angeles: Warner Bros, 1991; Dominic Minghella (dir.), *Robin Hood*, London: BBC, 2006.

497. Lyon, op.cit., p.85-87. According to Lyon, this is the 'site now covered by Halveor Close, immediately opposite the property 'Lanherne''. Useful information on the development of the church in St Columb Major is given in Charles Henderson, *St Columb Major Church and Parish*, Long Compton, n.p., 1930, and in R.M. Serjeantson, 'The Church and Parish Goods of St Columb Major, Cornwall' in *The Antiquary*, 33, 1897, pp.344-6.

498. See CRO: P/7/5/1.

499. CRO: B/WLooe/21/1. For background, see Austin L. Browne, *Corporation Chronicles: Being Some Account of the Ancient Corporation of East Looe and of West Looe in the County of Cornwall*, Plymouth: John Smith, 1904.

500. This tale is found in Thomas Bond, *Topographical and Historical Sketches of the Borough of East and West Looe in the County of Cornwall*, London: J. Nichols and Son, 1823, pp.281-5. See also Joyce and Newlyn, op.cit., pp.574-6. The author of the tale remains unclear. A possible contender is Richard Peter.

501. Ibid.

502. See Rowse, op.cit., pp.342-79; Kent and Merrifield, op.cit., pp.47-50.

503. *Treatise on the Trial of Francis Tregian*, St Mary's College, Oscott: MS. 545, pp.89-94.

504. Kent and Merrifield, op.cit., pp.18-19.

505. See Lyon, op.cit., pp.78-80. Lyon locates the *plen-an-gwarry* in the north-eastern corner of Sorn Field. This was also used for wrestling matches.

506. See John Leland, 'The Itinerary: So far as it relates to Cornwall' in Davies Gilbert, *The Parochial History of Cornwall*, London: J.B. Nichols, 1838. For background, see John H. Chandler, *John Leland's Itinerary: Travels in Tudor England*, Stroud: Sutton, 1993.

507. Lyon, op.cit., pp.58-9. Lyon locates this as being on the present site of the Courts of Justice.

508. See Joyce and Newlyn, op.cit., pp.603-7. See also J. H. Matthews, *History of St Ives, Lelant, Towednack and Zennor*, St Ives Trust and St Ives Library, 2003 [1892]; W. Badcock, *Historical Sketch of St Ives and District*, St Ives: W. Badcock, 1896.

509. Borough Accounts, St Ives Guildhall, f.3.

510. Bakere, op.cit., p.16.

511. Ibid.

512. Ibid., f.6.

513. Ibid., f. 7v, f. 10, f. 13, f. 56, f. 17v, f. 22, f. 19, f .51, f. 61, f. 79.

514. Ibid., f 16.

515. Bakere, op.cit. p.17.

516. Borough Accounts, St Ives Guildhall, f.17v.

517. Ibid., f. 79.

518. See Lyon, op.cit., p.29. This location is not too far away from the present-day Kids R Us Theatre in St Ives.

519. Hutton, op.cit., p.31.

520. Confirmed by the Borough Accounts of 1640-1. See Borough Accounts, ibid., f 4.

521. This is BL: MS. Harley 1782 London. See Ray Edwards (ed.), *Pascon Agan Arluth / The Poem of Mount Calvary*, Sutton Coldfield: Kernewek dry Lyther, 1993; Ellis, op.cit., p.44.

522. See Murdoch, op.cit.

523. Above the main entrance to the church, a small (modern) statue of St Sancred and a piglet can be observed.

524. See P.A.S. Pool (ed.), 'The Penheleg Ms' in *Journal of the Royal Institution of Cornwall*, III, 3, 1959, pp.163-228. Lyon argues also that 'The Tithe and Apportionment for the Parish of Sancreed in the Churchtown tenement names field No.426 'Plain Gwarry'. See Lyon, op.cit., pp.16-17.

525. See Joyce and Newlyn, op.cit., p.519.

526. CRO: X/50/5. This is the Penheleg Ms.

527. Ibid.

528. William Bottrell (ed.), *Traditions and Hearthside Stories of West Cornwall: Second Series*, Penzance: Beare and Son, 1873, p.269.

529. A.F. Langham, *The Island of Lundy*, Stroud: Sutton, 1994, p.4-5.

530. Ibid., p.11.

531. See G. Forester Matthews, *The Isles of Scilly*, London: George Ronald, 1960, pp.9-13; David W. Moore, *The Other British Isles*, Jefferson, North Carolina and London: McFarland and Company, 2005, pp.168-176.

532. Curiously, Scilly, though not holding much of a literary or theatrical canon, is often recorded in some of the Scandinavian Sagas: in particular, the Heimskringla Saga (c.1230) and the Orkneyinga Saga (c.1200). See Herman Palsson and Magnus Magnusson (eds. and trs.), *King Harald's Saga from Snorri Sturluson's Heimskringla*, London: Penguin, 2005; Herman Palsson and Paul Edwards (eds. and trs.), *The Orkneyinga Saga: The* History *of the Earls of Orkney*, London: Penguin, 2004.

533. Matthews, op.cit., p.202.

534. Ibid., pp.28-9.

535. Ellis, op.cit., p.67.

536. Murdoch, op.cit., p.9.

537. Walter Wedlock (Oliver Oldwanton), *A little Treatise called the Image of Idlenesse, containing certaine matters mooued betwen Walter Wedlock and Bawdin Bachelor, translated out of the Troyan or Cornish tung into English*, London: William Seres, 1574. The British Library catalogue lists the author as Wedlock, but it is in fact Oldwanton.

538. Ellis, op.cit., p.68.

539. Oldwanton, op.cit., p33.

540. Ibid., p.46.

541. Ibid., p.32.

542. Ellis, op.cit., p.69.

543. See *Annual Report of the Royal Cornwall Polytechnic Society*, 1929.

544. Whetter, op.cit., 1995, p.53.

545. Ibid.

546. Ibid.

547. Southworth, op.cit., pp.154-72.

548. PRO: CI 46/388.

549. See Pat Munn, *The Story of Cornwall's Bodmin Moor*, Bodmin: Bodmin Books, 1972. The Vicar of Alternun is the villain in Daphne du Maurier's novel *Jamaica Inn*. See also Parochial Church Council of Alternun, *St Nonna of Altarnon*, Alternun: Church of St Nonna, Altarnun, n.d.

550. For a discussion, see Harry Woodhouse, *Cornish Bagpipes: Fact or Fiction?* Redruth: Dyllansow Truran, 1994. There were, in fact, several types of Cornish bagpipes. Cornish use of pipes is mentioned in Geoffrey Chaucer's *The Romaunt of the Rose*. See F.N. Robinson (ed.), *The Complete Works of Geoffrey Chaucer*, Oxford: Oxford University Press, 1957, p.604. The contemporary musician and

ethno-musical scholar Merv Davey plays Cornish bagpipes at numerous theatrical and para-theatrical events. The storyteller Will Coleman also uses Cornish bagpipes in performance.

551. *Gwreans an Bys.* MS. Bodley 219, Oxford.

552. See Neuss, op.cit., 1983, pp.lxxxvi. She lists the following four additional manuscripts: Bodleian MS. Corn. e. 2 (This is dated 1691 and is probably in Keigwyn's autograph; later revised by Thomas Tonkin and William Hals); British Library Harl. MS. 1867 (This manuscript also contains some of Edward Lhuyd's letters and a collection of Welsh proverbs); a copy transcribed by John Moore in 1698, in the Gatley Collection (Gatley MS.) bequeathed to the Royal Institution of Cornwall in 1885; and a copy of Keigwyn's version also containing the Cornish Passion poem, originally in the collection of Davies Gilbert, and used by him in his edition of the play (This copy was sold at Sotheby's on 22 March 1917, to a buyer named 'Potter').

553. It barely features in Ellis, op.cit., 1974.

554. See Ian Marshall, *The Amazing Story of the Floral Dance*, Dobwalls: Songs of Cornwall, 2003.

555. See *Gwreans an Bys*, op.cit.

556. See Neuss, op.cit.

557. Davies Gilbert (ed.), *The Creation of the World with Noah's Flood, written in Cornish in the Year 1611 by Wm. Jordan, with an English Translation by John Keigwin*, London, J.B. Nichols, 1827; Whitley Stokes (ed. and tr.), *Gwreans an Bys: The Creation of the World*, London and Edinburgh: Williams and Norgate, 1864; Robert Morton Nance and A.S.D. Smith (eds. and trs.), *Gwyrans an Bys*, Padstow, Federation of Old Cornwall Societies, 1959; E.G. Retallack Hooper (ed.), *Robert Morton Nance and A.S.D. Smith (eds. and trs.), Gwyrans an Bys*, Redruth: Dyllansow Truran, 1985. See also Oliver J. Padel, 'Review of *Gwyrans an Bys* or *The Creacion of the World* in *Old Cornwall*, 10, 1985, pp.98-99; Donald R. Rawe, *The Creation of the World*, Padstow: Lodenek Press, 1978. The editions here mark a peculiar problem for Cornish-language drama. Although Neuss' work is the standard critical edition, it suffers from poor typesetting. Gilbert and Stokes' editions suffer from some mistakes in translation, while the Nance and Smith editions do not use the base manuscript text (it has been converted to Unified Cornish). The need is for more critical editions of the works with the Cornish in original spelling with translations into English.

558. 'The Murder of Abel' in Kenneth Hurlstone Jackson (ed. and tr.), op.cit., 1971, pp.300-3. A substantial section of Lamech and Noah is also contained in Kent and Saunders, op.cit., pp.186-211.

559. See Hays, McGee, Joyce and Newlyn, op.cit., p.456.

560. See Appendix II in Neuss, op.cit., pp. 241-5. See also Paula Neuss, *The Creacion of the World*, University of Toronto, Ph.D. Dissertation, 1970.

561. Neuss, op.cit., 1983.

562. Ibid., pp.xviii-lxxxii.

563. See Kent and Saunders, op.cit., p.345.

564. Neuss, op.cit., pp.204-5.

565. Ibid., p.xxi.

566. See *Gwreans an Bys*, op.cit.

567. Neuss, op.cit., pp.xxiii.

568. Ibid., pp.36-37.

569. Ibid., pp.124-5.

570. Ibid., pp.xxiv-xxv.

571. See Campbell, op.cit.

572. See the observations in Stephen Greenblatt, *Renaissance Self-Fashioning: From More to Shakespeare*, Chicago: University of Chicago Press, 1980.

573. Neuss, op.cit., pp.118-9.

574. Ibid., p.xxx.

575. See O.L. Aubert, *Celtic Legends of Brittany*, Kerangwenn: Coop Breizh, 1993.

576. Neuss, op.cit., pp.84-5.

577. For some perspectives on this, see Paula Neuss, 'The Staging of The Creacion of the World' in P. Happé (ed.), *Medieval English Drama*, London: Macmillan, 1984, p.197, and 'The Staging of the 'Creacion of the World' in *Theatre Notebook*, 33, 1979, pp.116-25.

578. See Neuss, op.cit., 1983, pp.138-9.

579. For a text, see Edwards, op.cit., 1994. For a critical reassessment, see Frost, op.cit.

580. Neuss, op.cit., p.lxxii.

581. Hooper, op.cit., p.5.

582. Murdoch, op.cit., 1993, pp.75-98, and op.cit., 1994, pp.224-30; Neuss, op.cit., pp.xxxvii-xlix.

583. Paula Neuss, 'Memorial Reconstruction in a Cornish Miracle Play' in *Comparative Drama*, 5, 2, 1979, pp.129-37.

584. Neuss, op.cit., 1983, p.xxxix.

585. Ibid., pp.132-3.

586. Ibid., pp.162-3. For a perspective on this, see Brian Murdoch, 'Creation, Fall and After in the Cornish *Gwreans an Bys*: Some Comments on a Late Medieval Mystery Play' in *Studi Medievali*, Series 3, Vol.19, No.2, 1988.

587. C.f. Halliday, op.cit., 1955.

588. Sydney Higgins, 'Creating the Creation: the staging of the Cornish medieval play *The Creation of the World* in Sydney Higgins (ed.), op.cit., 1996, pp.67-96.

589. Ibid., p.74. Useful comparison may be made to Higgins' diagrams for *Bewnans Meriasek*.

590. Ibid., p.78. Higgins gives tablature of this.

591. Neuss, op.cit., 1983, pp.lx-lxi.

592. Higgins, op.cit., p.82.

593. Rawe, op.cit.

594. Henry Jenner, 'The Cornish Drama' in *Celtic Review*, III, 1906-7, p.373.

595. Neuss, op.cit., pp.186-7.

596. Jenner, op.cit.

597. Rastall, op.cit., 2001, pp.336-46.

598. See A.G. Dickens and D. Carr, *The Reformation in England*, London: Hodder Arnold, 1967, p.77; T.M. Parker, *The English Reformation to 1558*, Oxford: Oxford University Press, 1966, p.90f.

599. Murdoch, op.cit., 1993. p.75.

600. Ibid., p.76.

601. Ibid., pp.88-91. See also Ryan, op.cit.

602. Ibid., p.96.

603. Ibid.

604. Ibid., p.98.

605. Neuss, op.cit., pp.202-3.

606. Kent and Saunders, op.cit., p.265.

607. See the observations in Gibson and Griffiths, op.cit., and in Jean-Pierre Le Mat, *The Sons of Ermine: A History of Brittany*, Belfast: An Clochán, 1996.

608. A.L. Rowse, *Tudor Cornwall*, Redruth: Dyllansow Truran, 1990 [1941], pp.253-219; John Sturt, *Revolt in the West: The Western Rebellion of 1549*, Exeter: Devon Books, 1987; Ann Trevenen Jenkin, *Notes on the Prayer Book Rebellion of 1549*, Leedstown: Noonvares Press, 1999; Chris Morgan, 'The Rebellions of 1549 in Tudor England' in *History Review*, No.19, 1994, pp.1-5.

609. Kent and Saunders, op.cit., p.267.

610. For the wider historical significance of this event, see the arguments in John Angarrack, *Our Future is History: Identity, Law and the Cornish Question*, Bodmin: Independent Academic Press, 2002. For another position, see Deacon, op.cit., 2007, pp.77-9.

611. For a new examination of this period, see Cheryl Hayden, '1549 – The Rebels Shout Back' in Philip Payton (ed.), *Cornish Studies: Sixteen*, Exeter: University of Exeter Press, 2008, pp.206-28. Interestingly one of the characters in Hayden's novel 'A Christmas Games' is the para-theatrical figure of William Winslade (Sir Tristam).

612. See Ellis, op.cit., p.63.

613. Rowse, op.cit.

614. Ellis, op.cit. Resistance was found in the work of John Tregear. See Edwards, op.cit., and Frost, op.cit.

615. See P.A.S. Pool, *The Death of Cornish*, Cornwall: Cornish Language Board, 1982, p.7.

616. Halliday, op.cit., 1953, p.127.

617. Pool, op.cit. For text, see Kent and Saunders, op.cit., p.270.

618. Whetter, op.cit., 1988, pp.112-4.

CHAPTER THREE

'Sure Mevagezy is a choice place': Renaissance, Restoration, Reform and... Pilchards: Ending the Stage of the Troyance Tongue, 1600-1800

'Leroi? A Cornish name. Art thou of Cornish crew?'

Pistol, in Act IV, Scene i, from *Henry V* by William Shakespeare, 1599-1600[1]

'Never credit me for I will spurt some Cornish at him: *Pedn bras vidne whee bis creegas.*'

Nonsense, in Act V, Scene viii from *The Northern Lasse* by Richard Brome, 1632[2]

The period 1600-1800 witnessed some major changes in the history of the theatre of Cornwall. As the sixteenth century changed into the seventeenth century, the effects of the Reformation were still being felt upon the stage in Cornwall, as well as upon how Cornwall and Cornishness were presented elsewhere. In the sixteenth century, the rise of Puritanism, as a direct consequence of events in the Reformation, had had drastic effects on theatre in general, eventually causing the virtual shut-down of all forms of theatrical activity. Puritans, though of different sects and persuasions, all felt that the Reformation in Britain had not gone far enough, and that the Church of England was still too tolerant of the practices associated with the Church of Rome.[3] Likewise, the so-called 'Troyance tongue' of Cornwall (mythically brought by the Trojan refugee Corineus) would have a further period of decline, culminating in the late eighteenth-century collapse of the language.[4] The conditions for this collapse, however, had been established during the reforming years of the Tudor period,[5] and the consequent wish by England (and inevitably Cornwall itself) for Cornwall to use more English.

In the wake of this, theatre clearly progressed in both Cornwall and London, but it met with an even greater clampdown during the years of the War of Five Nations [Civil War] and the Interregnum, between 1642 and 1660. Although the Restoration of Charles II brought about a change of cultural attitude in Britain, in terms of theatre, this was really felt initially only in London,[6] and no texts or performances in Restoration theatre seem to have considered Cornwall and the Cornish worthy of dramaturgy. This position changes in what we may term the post-Reformation period, between 1700 and 1737 when, although there is scant evidence of indigenous theatre, the Cornish started to be considered once again upon the stage. The material conditions for this to happen necessitated that the restored theatre also needed to be internally reformed in order for it to evolve. It took the final sixty years of the eighteenth century for dramatists to feel confident about presenting Cornwall as a theatrical space and place, where, to paraphrase Samuel Foote, Mevagezy could be 'a choice place' again. It is at the end of this century that we see some of the surviving indigenous Anglo-Cornish texts re-emerge, as well as the growth of urban theatre in Cornwall. Although the changes in this period are vast, and the intricacies of the political, social and economic conditions of production difficult to summarise, it is really here that a modern theatre of Cornwall is formed. This development is neatly summarised by the quotes at the head of this chapter: Pistol's famous question in Shakespeare's *Henry V*, regarding the 'Cornish crew'; and the fascinating, slightly later 'spurt' of stage Cornish language, when the character of Nonsense speaks in Richard Groome's 1632 play *The Northern Lasse*. On the one hand, Shakespeare appears to be suggesting an even greater accommodation of the Cornish was in hand; on the other hand, Broome realised that Cornish difference was being maintained, even if it was explored through comedy, and was hardly the most flattering picture of a stage Cornishman. There were other imaginings of Cornishness, which we shall also consider here.

The opening forty years of the seventeenth century still saw some indigenous theatrical activity in Cornwall but, overall, the stage of the Troyance tongue itself was over. In Richard Carew's account of a performance of a gwarry miracle in his *Survey of Cornwall*, we perhaps witness the last gasp of that larger dramatic event.[7] There were clearly some survivals though, as we know from the 1611 copy of the probably Helston-based *The Creacion of the World*, scribed by William Jordan.[8] What is more difficult to know is whether such texts continued to be performed in communities across Cornwall. If they were, it is most likely that they would have been a shadow of their former selves, and that such activities would continue to be monitored by the authorities. It could even be that some aspects of recusant performance might still have taken place 'behind closed doors'. However, the modernising effects of the previous century had certainly taken their toll, and it would appear there was no institution within Cornwall, with the possible exception of Restormel Castle, that could care for and preserve any surviving dramatic texts. The texts were therefore scattered. Besides that, there is a sense, both in Carew, and in the later writings of Scawen in 1680, that no-one in Cornwall really cared.[9] The severance of ties with Brittany only contributed further to the problem.[10] Paradoxically though, just as theatre was declining at home, playwrights on the London stage had begun to become fascinated with Cornwall, and the early decades of the seventeenth century saw a series of dramas in which aspects of both contemporary and historical Cornishness were being staged. Clearly, as a territory and people, the Cornish provided a degree of 'otherness' for the London stage, combined with interest in Cornwall's proximity to Spain, its customs and sports, and their general difference from what had become by now, 'the rest of England'.

Before we turn to this London stage, let us give one last look at the surviving strands of theatre in Cornwall during this period. Some of the theatre operating is a direct continuation of that found in the previous century. As we know, records for the survival of drama in east Cornwall have not survived well. In Calstock, in 1601, we learn of the will of one Richard Clare, which mentions him bequeathing both his harps to two blind boys, and his trumpet to a 'meheamed' [maimed] man.[11] This in itself is not really sufficient evidence for any theatrical activity occurring, but might at least indicate some performance work continuing there. Better evidence comes from Liskeard. In the 1575-6 Mayors' Accounts there we learn of 'nyne Enterlude players this yere',[12] and after something of break in the 1590s, theatrical activity reappears in the Accounts from 1604 onwards.[13] The same Accounts also make note of the '12s received from Peter Hambly and John Harrell for a licence to sell drink and to play in the guildhall on Pentecost this year'.[14] Although a small reference to theatre, the Accounts are interesting, for they suggest not only the need for licensing to ensure apt and appropriate performance, but also that theatre still had an ongoing connection to the ritual year, since the licence was for Pentecost, the Whit Monday holiday date. Given Liskeard's cultural-geographic position, the performance would have probably been delivered in English, but it is hard to glean any sense of what kind of drama this might have been.

It seems that theatre in Cornwall also carried on at quite a professional level. The power and realism of that theatre is explained in a 1612 document titled *An Apology for Actors*, written by Thomas Heywood (*c.*1574-1641). Heywood, who had been born in Lincolnshire, was a dramatist of some merit, writing over 200 plays, most of which have now been lost. His 1612 text, however, is one of the best Jacobean summaries of traditional arguments in favour of the stage. It is full of interesting and amusing anecdotes, one of which arises from a performance in Penryn. Clearly what happened was that the scene on the stage was so realistic that the invading Spanish really thought there was a counter-attack. Given the sensitive times of this Age – and the tenuous relationship between the western approaches and the Spanish Fleet – it is perhaps easy to see why the following came to pass:

> As strange an accident happened to a company of the same quality some 12 years ago, or not so much, who playing late in the night at a place called Pe[n]rin in Cornwall, certaine Spaniards were landed the same night unsuspected, and undiscovered, with intent to take the town, spoyle and burn it, when suddenly upon their entrance, the players (ignorant as the townes-men of any such attempt) presenting a battle on the stage with their drum and trumpets strooke up a lowd alarme: which the enemy hearing, and fearing they were discovered, amazedly retired, made some few idle shots in a brauado, and so in hurly-burly fled disorderly to their boats. At the report of this tumult, the townes-men were immediately alarmed, and pursued them to the sea, praysing God for their happy deliverance from so great a danger, who by his providence made these strangers the instrument and secondary meanes of their escape from such imminent mischief, and the tyranny of so remorceless an enemy.[15]

Writing in 1865, Williams Sandys (1792-1874), the musical and Cornu-English scholar, felt that the incident referred to a play about Samson, performed at a barn in Penryn in 1587.[16] He conjectures that the Spanish arrived in town exactly at the dramatic moment when Samson attacked the Philistines. Heywood dates the performance somewhat later than Sandys. Drama, it seems, rather than reality, saved the day. Even if the date of the performance is slightly earlier, then performances such as this probably continued into the opening years of the seventeenth century. Later Accounts become very scant for theatrical activity in Cornwall, which would indicate a further shutdown of activity. The same pattern was affecting other parts of Britain,[17] but considering the intensity of Cornish theatrical culture, the effect must have been felt more readily, with communities feeling the destruction and displacement of an earlier ideology of performance.

The same worries of the authorities, over the place and purpose of theatrical entertainment, were also affecting the stage in London, where

William Shakespeare (1564-1616) and his contemporaries were similarly coping with Puritanical ideology wanting to close theatres. We need not cover here the life and work of Shakespeare, which has already been considered by a number of observers.[18] Some observers of the history of the development of the 'English playhouse' (particularly its incarnation as the 'wooden O' of the Globe and the Swan in early sixteenth-century London) have suggested that its origins may lie in the 'multiple staging within a round' of the *plen-an-gwarry*, and that somehow, through some undetermined process, this became imported into English theatrical culture in the previous century.[19] Although there are similarities, such a link is harder to prove. Spriggs, meanwhile, is dismissive of this view, arguing that English theatrical historians simply appropriated a separate Cornu-Celtic tradition.[20] The interest in Celticity does, however, match a wider interest in some of the writing from this period, which looked to the peripheries of Britain,[21] and often brought peripheral characters to the stage as 'comical oddities' who had not yet quite attuned themselves to the project of an English-speaking Britain. However, this is perhaps at odds with some new scholarship which is beginning to understand in more detail the effect of the Renaissance on Celtic territories, and argues that far from being backwaters of cultural development, they actually offer much innovation, scholarship, and an unexpected embracing of the ideals of the period.[22] However, such a view does not match stereotypical and popular opinion of characters on the London stage. A few of Shakespeare's plays contain Cornish subject-matter. This is of direct interest to us, for it shows how the London audiences of this period perceived Cornwall and Cornishness. It is perhaps a pity that the Cornish are not more imagined in his work, perhaps akin to some of the Welsh characters in his dramas, for we would then have better insight into how Cornish Celticity was perceived during that phase.

As indicated at the start of this chapter, one of the plays with Cornish subject matter is *Henry V*; almost certainly written in 1599, but printed in 1600. The play opens with the newly-ascended Henry astonishing both courtier and clergy alike with his state-craft and piety, compared with the anarchic Prince Hal of old. The Archbishop of Canterbury demonstrates, via the 'Salic Law', that the Welsh-born Henry – as king of England – has good claim on the throne of France, and thus begins his quest for rule there. After besieging and capturing Harfleur, he then achieves a resounding victory at the battle of Agincourt (1415). In Act IV, Scene i Henry walks around the 'English' camp on the night before the battle at Agincourt, chatting to his soldiers to test the mood. There he encounters the character of Pistol, who is on guard. In Falstaff's dubious military adventures, Pistol is his 'ancient' (i.e. second officer), and he is a mountebank, a fanatical swashbuckler and braggart, full of braggadocio. Pistol demands to know who the stranger is, and Henry replies with 'Harry Le Roy'. Pistol then asks, 'Leroi! A Cornish name: art thou of Cornish crew?'.[23] I have argued that although Pistol's view on the Cornish is somewhat ambiguous, it suggests that the Cornish have reached terms of accommodation which suited the English more favourably, but the English still had some sympathy for Cornish identity, as witnessed in the ongoing jurisdiction of the Stannary. The Cornish in the play are not presented in comic terms like the other Celtic characters – the Scottish Captain Jamy, the Irish Captain Macmorris and the Welsh Captain Fluellen; nor are they presented as the Cornish are in other early seventeenth-century plays. Part of the reasoning for this would be the fact that the Cornish had served Henry V so well in his Agincourt victory that it would be incongruous to have presented them in any other way; hence my justification for their 'proud inclusion'.[24] Payton, in summarising my argument, observes that 'the Cornish are afforded special treatment' and that 'Cornwall had become a sort of manageable junior partner'.[25] The historian Mark Stoyle has recently taken an interesting different view. He feels that the context of Pistol's discussion ('ultra-nationalist Englishman's disdain') and his use of the term 'crew' display a general dislike of the Cornish (who are presumably still unhappy about their accommodated position), shared by Pistol who, as an English soldier, regarded the Cornish as 'lesser' beings and base and inferior. In his view, this reading matches other evidence from the same period.[26] My response to this is that such a reading is perhaps politically desirable (especially in the light of the rest of Stoyle's argument), but does not fully match the relationships in Henry V's army, nor the true picture of cultural interaction in Renaissance Britain. In essence, despite their differences of approach, both readings show a similar understanding of the problem of the Cornish during this phase – accommodation moving towards a more full imperialism – that was, to an extent, being depicted on the English stage. We must also consider that this is only one line within a much longer text.

Within my first look at *Henry V*, I also commented on the possible significance of the character of Williams.[27] Williams has a number of characteristics that might indicate that he was also Cornish, despite his Welsh-sounding name. He does not have the stage Anglo-Welsh-isms of Fluellen. Certainly, his dialogue with the disguised King Henry V smacks of Cornish logic and, unlike the Welsh, Irish and Scottish, the Cornish had less of a stage persona (particularly at the start of the sixteenth century) since their 'skills in the art of war need not be discussed – they are taken for granted'. Perhaps the most curious aspect of *Henry V*, however, is neither Pistol's attitude nor Williams's identity, but the fact that although the other Captains are engaged in the 'mines' at Harfleur, the Cornish (renowned even then for their mining skills) are not featured.[28] This was quite possibly because in the popular imagination they had already established their position at Agincourt as archers, as in the Cornish reference in the caption to Henry V's portrait over the south gate in Launceston:

> He that will do aught for mee
> Let him love well Sir John Trelawnee.[29]

The representation of the Cornish in *Henry V* focuses on their role in and contribution to a medieval army, though it is filtered by Shakespeare through late sixteenth- and early seventeenth-century eyes. A similar filter is found in the tragedy of *King Lear*, though this time the gaze was towards ancient Britain. *King Lear* probably dates, in its first version, from 1605, and we know that it was performed at Court in 1606.[30] The play's sources include a chronicle play, *King Leir* (performed around 1594), and the chronicles of Raphael Holinshed (1577); the Gloucester sub-plot was probably derived from Sir Philip Sidney's *Arcadia*.[31] However, in looking at Holinshed, it is quite obvious that he was drawing upon Geoffrey of Monmouth's *Historia Regum Britanniae / History of the Kings of Britain*, in which a substantial section is devoted to the telling of Lear's story.[32] In the drama, Lear, an elderly king of Britain, has three daughters; Goneril, wife of the Duke of Albany; Regan, wife of the Duke of Cornwall; and Cordelia, for whom the King of France and the Duke of Burgundy are suitors. Intending to divide his kingdom among his daughters according to their affection for him, he asks them to say which loves him most. Goneril and Regan profess extreme affection, but Cordelia, disgusted by their hollow flattery, says that she loves him according to her duty only, no more, no less. This premise begins the lapse into tragedy.

The Duke of Cornwall's part is small, but is enhanced by his marriage to Regan, with the audience making the territorial association. In the play, he really operates in only one mode: cold-hearted cruelty. His highhandedness toward Kent (putting him in the stocks for quarrelling with Oswald) is matched by his murderous rage against the servant who tries to stop him from blinding Gloucester. Most famously this cruelty is seen in the details of the blinding itself when he comments: 'Out, vile jelly! / Where is thy lustre now?'[33] A number of observers have commented that as the moral ambiguity of the play increases, he vanishes, apparently killed by his own servant.[34] There is no place for him in a world of randomness, and of making the right choice for good. Alternatively, his disappearance might be read as the servant realising that he represents an inappropriate aspect of Cornwall, and that his death will allow the dukedom to start afresh. In effect, Regan is Cornish by association. Although the least characterised of the three sisters, we find her haughty, distant and taciturn. In the argument scene between Oswald and Kent, she takes no part, but stands silently approving of her husband's treatment of Kent, until the very end, when she gives the order for stocking Kent: 'Put in his legs'.[35] In the same cruel way, she watches impassively as Gloucester is bound, and then suddenly exhorts the soldiers to fasten him, 'Hard, hard!'[36] She joins in with his interrogation ('To whose hands have you sent the lunatic king? / Speak.'[37]), stabs the servant who tries to stop Cornwall blinding him, and sends Gloucester into the storm ('Go, thrust him out at gates, and let him smell / His way to Dover'[38]). In her plotting with Oswald (to kill Gloucester) and with Edmund (to supplant Goneril), she continues to be evil until the very end. Neither character presents a positive picture of Cornishness.

Modern readings of the play have often commented upon the text as being a dramatisation of a project for a 'politically-devolved Britain',[39] with the Duke of Cornwall and Regan commanding that part of the island which included Cornwall. Such a reading puts Lear himself into a new light: a man with an awareness of the separate historical identities of the island, an abdication of the throne (perhaps looking forward to events of the Civil War), and a notion that kingship was no longer a way to run a 'country'. The fact, however, that this division of Britain leads to such tragedy and chaos would seem to indicate a latent desire in Renaissance Britain to integrate and combine, rather than devolve. The Duke of Cornwall and Regan both have prominence in the plot, suggesting that in the English public mind, Cornwall still had a separate identity. Their quarrelsome nature however (even with the king), would suggest that Cornwall was still a tricky periphery to be managed by the centralist state, and that – though presented in 'ancient Britain' – the issue of Cornwall was still a topical one. We may go further: the frankly loathsome nature of their Cornishness may suggest that Cornwall was also to be read this way. Such a position would therefore support the general argument of Stoyle's reading of the presentation of Cornwall and Cornishness during this phase.[40]

Ancient Britain was also mined in *Cymbeline: King of Britain*, recorded as being performed in 1611, perhaps at the Globe.[41] The plot was again from Geoffrey of Monmouth's *History*, based on legends concerning the early Celtic British king Cunobelinus.[42] Its relevance to Cornwall, compared to *Henry V* and *Lear*, may be slightly more tangential, but in the sense that it is an origin story of the Western Celts of Britain (of which the Cornish were a part), it does bear some relevance. Cunobelinus was the last Celtic British king to stand against the Romans, and the father of Caratacus, whose heroism and defiant nobility won the admiration even of the enemy who paraded in Rome in triumph. This, however, has little to do with Shakespeare's drama, for he makes Cymbeline a fool, an absolute ruler whose decisions are arbitrary (again predicting some of the concerns over the rule of Charles I). These decisions have devastating effects on both him and those he loves. While the plot of the drama has no direct Cornish connections, its significance lies in its depiction of a Celtic Britain. In various ways, the play seems to present Cymbeline as a kind of un-understandable enigma, but there is a kind of restlessness and danger within his lines. Again, this might be a wider metaphor for how Shakespeare was perceiving contemporary Celtic Britain – another example of the 'enigma' of the Celts, despite the fact that Shakespeare would not have conceived of the Britons, Cornish or Welsh in latter-day Celtic terminology.[43] Such a reading of *Cymbeline: King of Britain* would support the observations of John Kerrigan, who in a recent work has disproved how 'literature in Britain' should be thought of in narrowly English terms.[44] His correction has been achieved by devolving Anglophone writing, particularly from the seventeenth century. The argument demonstrates how much remarkable work was produced in and about the Celtic territories, and how preoccupied writers and dramatists were with the often fraught interactions between ethnic, religious and national groups around the British-Irish archipelago. Canonical texts such as *Cymbeline*, *King Lear* and *Henry V* clearly fit Kerrigan's hypothesis. As we shall see later in this chapter, there are a number of texts which look at the same fraught interaction, but which have become neglected because they do not fit the Anglo-centric paradigm. The various crises of the seventeenth century influenced intellectual thought, but the thrust of the century, and that of the eighteenth century, as Linda Colley has shown, was towards unionism.[45]

Into Kerrigan's theories on this period, we may also add another text, *The Birth of Merlin, or, The Childe Hath Found His Father*.[46] This Jacobean play was first performed in 1622 at the Curtain Theatre in Shoreditch, London, and is a text with more closely connected Cornish material. The play is a comedy, depicting the birth of a fully-grown Merlin to a country girl named Joan, and also features various figures from Arthurian legend, including Uther Pendragon, Vortigern and Aurelius Ambrosius. The play, as Stewart, Coffey and Hudd have demonstrated, was first published in 1662, in a quarto printed by Thomas Johnson for the booksellers Francis Kirkman and Henry Marsh. That first edition attributed the play to William Shakespeare (perhaps for promotional purposes) and William Rowley.[47] However, most scholars reject the attribution to Shakespeare and believe that the play belongs to Rowley, although he may well have worked with another collaborator.[48] As we shall see later in this chapter, Rowley is an interesting figure for the theatre of Cornwall, for he both develops this text, and collaborates with Thomas Middleton on another play (*A Fair Quarrel*) which looks at plenty of Cornish material. The origins of William Rowley (c.1585-1626) are not known, though he would appear to have been English, and to have begun his career as an actor-playwright who specialised in playing comic characters. He was probably quite a large man, since his forté lay in fat-clown roles, providing a variety of plays with this kind of low comedy. This is one piece of evidence which supports his contribution to *The Birth of Merlin*, since within the play, the unnamed Clown was probably written by Rowley, with himself in mind to play the part. As well as his acting career – working initially with the Queen Anne's Men at the Bull Theatre, and eventually with the King's Men (Shakespeare's famous company) – Rowley was also a prolific dramatist, producing some sixteen surviving plays, as well as a number which have been lost. It seems he frequently collaborated with others, lending his comic talent to the development of scripts.

The Birth of Merlin would appear again to be based on Geoffrey of Monmouth's *History*, as well as a number of other British chronicles.[49] This volume has already demonstrated the significance of Merlin as an archetype within the theatrical origins of Cornwall, so it was perhaps apt, considering the development of the concept of Britain in the early seventeenth century, that a play about his life would emerge. Rowley was writing not for a Cornish audience, but for a London one, though it was a London which probably had some awareness that the character of Merlin was associated with mythic, ancient Britain, and that 'exotic' Cornwall might appear somewhere in the plot. As Levin argues, a number of plays from this period show a three-level plot,[50] and *The Birth of Merlin* is no exception. Such a three-level plot works in the following way. On the first level, the characters are royal or noble, and their concerns are of 'national' importance. On the second level are characters who are usually aristocratic and genteel, and are coping with some form of personal fulfilment, while the third level deals with comic sub-plot. Whilst this was the same for a number of plays in this period, the difference with *The Birth of Merlin* is its spectacle (prophecies, the devil, dragons and comets) and its fast pace; the piece requires visual effects and quick-witted actors. The drama opens with the second-level characters. Here we see the noble Donobert, his daughters Constantia and Modestia, and their suitors Cador (a Cornishman) and Edwin. Modestia wants a religious vocation, but has pressures upon her to marry. Constantia is more willing to marry, and debates her relationship with Cador:

Constantia:	I was content to give him words for oathes, he swore so oft he love'd me.
Donobert:	That thou believest him?

Constantia:	He is a man I hope.
Donobert:	That's in the trial Girl.
Constantia:	However I am a woman, sir.
Donobert:	The law's on thy side then, sha't have a Husband and a worthy one. Take her brave Cornwall, and make our happiness great as our wishes.
Cador:	Sir, I thank you.[51]

Events of greater magnitude are introduced in the Second Act, when we encounter King Aurelius and the British Court. The British are in celebratory mood due to a clear victory over the invading Saxons, though they are troubled that the King's brother Uther Pendragon (of Cornwall) is missing. When a peace is negotiated with the Saxons, Aurelius falls in love with the Saxon princess Artesia. Because of this, he grants the Saxons generous peace terms despite the many objections of his court; Donobert reacts with 'Death! he shall marry the devil first, marry a Pagan, an Idolater'.[52] Before the scene ends, Modestia explains to a hermit her own difficulties. Act II of the drama introduces the Clown, and Joan, 'his sister great with childe'.[53] The audience learn that Joan has gotten herself pregnant through the advances of a mysterious stranger. After comic dialogue between them about the nature of the clown's 'bastard cousin' they come upon Uther, who has been wandering in the wood, disconsolate, after catching sight of a beautiful woman, with whom he had fallen in love. Seeing an opportunity, the Clown tries to marry off Joan to him, but Uther is outraged by this. Courtiers from Aurelius find Uther and carry him back to the Court, while the Clown and Joan continue their search for the child's father.

Back at the court, Aurelius's infatuation has resulted in a sudden marriage with Artesia, but not all of his courtiers are happy with this. One British noble, Edol, is so outraged that he leaves. The Court is now forced to blend Celto-British culture with Saxon culture, though this does not go smoothly. However, conventional spirituality does win through, because the Christian hermit wins a complex contest fought with a pagan Saxon magician. We also learn that the woman he was infatuated with – Artesia – is now his brother's wife. Meanwhile, the Clown and Joan have also reached the Court, asking various courtiers if they are the father of the child. Finally, in a spectacular sequence, Joan sees the father, who she believes is very handsome, but whom the Clown can only see as the devil. During a storm, the stage direction reads, 'enter the Devil in man's habit, richly attired, his feet and his head horrid'. The Devil comments:

She calls me, and yet drives me headlong from her,
Poor mortal, thou and I are much uneven,
Thou must not speak of goodness nor of heaven,
If I confer with thee: but be of comfort,
Whilst men do breathe, and Brittains name be known,
The fatal fruit thou bear'st within thy womb
Shall here be famous to the day of doom.[54]

Such a piece of dialogue works as a prophecy, and this is apt, since early Merlin stories are heavily laden with prophecy. Rowley clearly knew this and so integrated it into the Devil's speech. The devilry here is matched by the other plot concerning the two daughters. Modestia's defence of Christian life is so persuasive that Constantia is also converted. Perhaps we see here a piece of dramatic instruction to the audience, and something that might placate the religious complaint about the immorality of theatre. Even so, their father Donobert is outraged, but urges the two suitors not to give up. Back in the forest the Devil assists in the birth of Merlin, by summoning Lucina and the Fates to Joan's side. Merlin is born fully-grown, with a beard, and is eventually met by the Clown. However, events in the three plots now become further connected because the Devil predicts a dramatic future for his new-born son. In the next scene, we learn that the Saxons are plotting treason, while the Celto-British order fragments when Artesia causes a split between Aurelius and Uther. The knowledge that a Saxon ally, Vortigern, is building a castle in Wales sharpens the minds of the Celto-British, and eventually Edol and Uther lead a victory against him. Vortigern's castle keeps collapsing and, to guarantee success, the Welsh must sacrifice a fiend-begotten child. They are pleased and relieved when Merlin appears, but he has no intention of being sacrificed, and instead prophesises (through a comet) Vortigern's defeat. The final act of the play offers swift resolution to the three threads of plot. Merlin seals his devil father in the earth, and leads Joan to a life of repentance. A similar Christian theme is followed with Modestia and Constantia, who are allowed by Donobert to commit to a celibate life. Uther then takes control of Britain, presumably pre-figuring the arrival of King Arthur.

Although *The Birth of Merlin* is not well known, it is one text which fully commits to a consideration of Celtic Britain, eventually leading to unity amongst a Celtic group, who are initially at odds with one another. Differences are put aside to fight a greater foe, and there may be something of the constant threat of the Spanish in some of Rowley's imagination here. In many ways, the text offers a similar investigation of the theme of 'bastardy' in Renaissance Britain, as found in *King Lear*, in the character of Edmund.[55] Characters such

340

as Edmund were challenging the world view by showing that old allegiances and the old hierarchy would not restrain ambition in the way that they had done in the past. Stephen Greenblatt has labelled this new ideology as 'Renaissance self-fashioning',[56] while Merlin might also stand for what A.L. Beier has termed 'masterless men' – men who do not have the allegiance or servitude of old.[57] To an extent, the bastard Merlin is another representation of both of these, but he is also endowed with magical powers. Another issue is the forging of a union of the different ethnic groups of Britain. It is interesting that early on in the drama Rowley views the combined Saxon and Celtic British Court as unstable. We are at first uncertain which side he will come down upon, but in the end he elects to be sympathetic to the Celtic cause, because it is the Saxons who commit treachery by assassinating Aurelius. It is likewise significant that Uther Pendragon, aided by Merlin, is declared king of Britain at the end of the play. Rowley seems to be asserting that the old order was worth preserving, and that the sensibilities and morals of the Celtic-British defeat the incoming Saxons. In a way, Rowley's vision is controversial, for it seeks an imagining of Britishness based on older Cornu-centric readings of culture. One might have thought that he would wish to show the Court negotiating a peace between the two groups, and the Saxons leading, but this is not the case. *The Birth of Merlin* is therefore an intriguing text, which perhaps should be better known. However, its Shakespearean providence is much less certain. Although it may seem something of a paradox, considering the high status that Shakespeare has in English culture, the writer and Cornwall were to have an ongoing relationship over the next few centuries. Certainly, many of Shakespeare's dramas were performed in Cornwall in the nineteenth century, and the territory even developed its own festival of his dramas in the middle of the twentieth century. Scholars such as A.L. Rowse and J.C. Trewin have continued to champion the power of his work; moreover, at the start of the twenty-first century, the Cornwall Theatre Collective presented a Cornish-ised version of *Macbeth*, titled *Mapbeth: Son of the Grave*.

During the opening phase of the seventeenth century, though, a number of other theatrical activities were happening, which are worth exploring at this point. George Clement Boase and William Prideaux Courtney's *Bibliotheca Cornubiensis* gives insight to several performances, writers and texts which, though lost, give a flavour of Cornu-centric, or related work. The *Diary* of the Elizabethan theatrical entrepreneur Philip Henslowe (c.1550-1616) gives an account of a performance of a play titled *Harry of Cornwall*.[58] This intriguing title was performed by the Lord Strange's Men in both 1591 and 1592, but the text was never printed. It nevertheless gives an indication that Cornish material could be popular on the cusp of the next century. We also know that a play was produced in 1634 titled *The Chronicle History of Perkin Warbeck: A Strange Truth*. This was written by one John Ford, the son of Thomas Ford of Islington in London, who was born on 17 April 1586 and died c.1639. According to Boase and Courtney, this was 'acted (sometimes) by the Queenes Majesties Servants at the Phenix in Drurie Lane, London'. It was also printed and sold by 'Hugh Beston… at his shop neere the Castle in Cornhill' and ran to some forty-four pages. Act IV, Scene v of the drama was set on the 'coast of Cornwall' while Act V, Scene i, was set at 'St Michael's Mount'.[59] The play is a retelling of the events in the life of Perkin Warbeck (1474-1499) who, as Arthurson has detailed, was a 'pretender' to the English throne during the reign of King Henry VII.[60] Warbeck's claim to the throne is complex, with some claiming that he was an impostor, pretending to be Richard of Shrewsbury, 1st Duke of York, and therefore the young son of King Edward IV. Others believed his claim, among them many Cornish. On 7 September 1497, travelling from Ireland, Warbeck landed at Whitesand Bay, near Land's End, hoping to capitalise on the Cornish people's resentment in the aftermath of their uprising some three months earlier. He found a good deal of sympathy in Cornwall, given that he claimed he would put a stop to the taxes levied to help fight a war against Scotland, and on Bodmin Moor he was declared 'Richard IV'. A 6,000 strong Cornish army then advanced on Exeter before heading towards Taunton.[61] However, at word that Giles, Lord Daubeney, was ready to attack, he deserted the Cornish, leaving them to face the might of Henry VII alone on 4 October 1497. Eventually, Warbeck was captured and after reading a confession was executed in 1499. What is intriguing about this drama is that it clearly featured a good deal of Cornish material and shows that the London populace still held a fascination with the Perkin Warbeck conspiracy even though the events took place over a century ago.

Ford's drama ought to be better known for it contains substantial Cornish material. The dramaturgy is also epic, with a large-sized cast, equivalent in range and class to some of Shakespeare's Histories. The play begins with a description of 'the Scene', which we are told is 'the continent of Great Britayne'. This geography matches an island-wide cast including Henry VII, Dawbney, Sir William Stanley, Oxford, Surrey, the Bishop of Durham, the Chaplain to Henry VII, Sir Robert Clifford, Lambert Simnell, Hialas (a Spanish agent), James IV (King of Scotland), the Earle of Huntley, the Earle of Crawford, Lord Daniell, Marchmount (a Herald), Frion (Warbeck's Secretary), the Mayor of Cork, Heron (a mercer), Sketon (a taylor), Astley (a scrivener), as well as Perkin Warbeck himself. Supporting this cast are Ladie Katherine Gourdon (Warbeck's wife), the Countesse of Crawford, Jane Douglas (Lady Katharine's mayd), and various constables, officers, servingmen and soldiers (many of whom play the Cornish). The drama itself was dedicated to the rightly honourable William Cavendish, with Ford noting that 'out of the darkness of a former Age (enlighten'd by a late, both learned, and an honourable pen) I have endeavoured to personate a great Attempt, and in It, a greater Danger'.[62] Early on in the text is a flavour of the 1497 Rebellion, with the urgency of Henry VII's request for news from the west, but also his reluctance to let his sleep be disturbed:

King Henry: Dawbney's voyce, admit him.

                What new combustions huddle next to keepe

                Our eyes from rest? – the newes?

Daw: Ten thousand Cornish grudging to pay your

                subsidies have gathered a head led by a

                Blacksmith, and a Lawyer, they make for London,

                And to them is joyn'd Lord Audlie, as they march,

                Their number daily encreases, they are –

King Henry: Rascalls – talke no more;

                Such are not worthie of my thoughts tonight:

                And if I cannot sleep, Ile wake: – to bed.

                When Counsailes faile, and theres in man no trust,

                Even then, an arme from heaven, fights for the just.[63]

This is good-quality writing, touching Shakespeare's as a historical dramatist. When the Cornish Rebellion progresses to Blackheath, we hear of Henry's strategy in a soliloquy, the last line here as powerful anything Shakespeare wrote in *Richard III*:

King Henry: Rage shall not fright

                the bosome of our confidence, in Kent

                our Cornish Rebells cozen'd of their hopes,

                Met brave resistance by the Countryes Earle,

                George Aburgeniem, Cobham, Poynings, Guilford,

                And other loyal hearts, now if Blackheath

                Must be reserved the fatall tombe to swallow

                Such stifneckt Abjects, as with wearie Marches,

                Have travailed from their homes, their wives, and children,

                To pay in stead of subsidies, their lives.[64]

As well as such compelling speeches Ford is also able to control more intimate moments in the drama; this is most tellingly seen in the sequences between Perkin Warbeck and his wife Katherine. When the plot unfolds to arrive in Cornwall, Warbeck explains his wishes for her:

Warbeck: But there are chimes for funeralls, my businesse
      Attends on fortune of a sprightlier triumph;
      Eor lone and Majestie are reconcil'd
      And vow to crowne thee Empresse of the West.[65]

This claim to 'sprightlier triumph' is supported by information provided by Frion, who explains to Warbeck how he will be received there. Clearly, this text is of crucial relevance to our understanding of the presentation of a 'stage' Cornwall during this phase, though it was extremely unlikely that many people in Cornwall would even have known of Ford's drama. His secretary Frion explains the support he would receive there:

Frion: I tolde yee
      Of letters that come from Ireland, how the Cornish
      Stomack their last defeate, and humblie sue
      That with such forces, as you could partake,
      You would in person land in Cornwall, where
      Thousands will entertaine your title gladly.

Warbeck: Let me embrace thee, hugge thee! tha'ast revivd
      My comforts, if my cosen King will sayle,
      Our cause will never, welcome my tride friends.[66]

The crucial scenes of the drama, as noted by Boase and Courtney, are those upon Bodmin Moor where Warbeck explains his relief to arrive in Cornwall, and Sketon, in a fantastically vivid description, declaims Cornish support for him:

Warbeck: After so many stormes as winde and Seas,
      Have threatened to our weather-beaten Shippes,
      At last (sweet fayrest) we are safe arriv'd
      on our deare mother earth, ingratefull onely
      To heaven and us, in yeelding sustenance
      to slie usurpers of our throne and right.

Sketon:	Save King Richard the fourth, save thee King of hearts? the Cornish blades are men of metall, have proclaimed through Bodnam [Bodmin] and the whole Countie, my sweete Prince, Monarch of England, some thousand tall, yeomen, with bow and sword alreadie vow to live and dye at the foote of King Richard.
Warbeck:	To Exeter, to Exeter, march on. Commend us to our people; we in person Will lend them double spirits, tell them so.[67]

What is so sophisticated about Ford's drama is that he juxtaposes this with a scene at the Mount, where Katherine and Jane are talking. Jane seems to have a second sense about the doom that Warbeck will meet. Her advice is 'To your shippes deare Lady: and turn home'.[68] In such ways, the pace and direction of the dramaturgy is maintained. Jane's prophecy of course comes true, when Daliell arrives with news that the attempt for the throne has failed, and that:

> All the Cornish
> At Exeter, were by the Citizens
> Repulst, encountered by the Earl of Devonshire,
> And other worthy Gentlemen of the Countrey.
> Your husband marcht to Taunton, and was there
> Affronted by King Henrie Chamberlayne.
> The King himselfe in person, with his Arme
> Advancing neerer, to renew the fight
> On all occasions.[69]

News comes shortly afterwards that Warbeck is 'put into a pair of stocks'[70] and will be put to trial. Order is therefore maintained. The Epilogue is well-written, linking the political purpose of the drama to the nature of theatre and poetry itself:

> Here has appear'd, though in a severall fashion,
> The Threats of Majestie; the strength of passion;
> Hopes of an Empire, change of fortunes, All
> What can to Theaters of Greatness fall,
> Proving their weake foundations: who will please
> Among such severall sights, to censure these
> No birth's abortive, nor a bastard's brood
> (Shame to a parentage, or fatherhood)

May warrant by their loves, all just examples,
And often finde a welcome to the Muses.[71]

The play seems not to have been shown any more during the century: perhaps
the issue of 'true' and 'false' royalty would be too near to the bone for the
decades which followed. It seems that Ford's presentation of the Cornish is not
very positive in such a text, because the drama would have shown not only the
beaten Cornish ready for another crack at Henry VII but also, again, that they
were a difficult 'Celtic drama queen' to manage from the centre. This is
perhaps as openly a 'nationalist' text (if one can have such a text during this
time) as we might find during this phase. It is a pity too, that the drama is not
better known, although maybe this volume will start to work an important
corrective.

A Cornish writer operating within the context of London in the middle of
the sixteenth century was Sir William Lower. Little of his life is known, but it
seems he was a fairly prolific playwright. He was born at Tremere, St Tudy in
north Cornwall, probably around 1600, and died in London in 1662.[72] Lower
wrote some ten plays, of which we know only a little. His first work was *The
Phoenix in her Flames*, said to have been 'a tragedy in four acts and in verse'
with 'the scene set in Arablia [sic]'.[73] It was performed sometime in 1639. In
the early part of his career, Lower's line seems to have been in the translation
of French works, and the reimagining of Roman tragedy. Therefore we see *The
Innocent Lady*, translated from the French of Rene de Ceriziers (1603-1662)
written in 1654, followed in the year after by *Polyeuctes the Martyr* (about the
Roman saint), translated from Piere Corneille (1606-1684). The same year
brought about *The Innocent Lord*, and in 1656 two of Lower's plays: *The
Triumphant Lady* and *Horatius, A Roman Tragedy*. A change of mood came in
1657 with a comedy titled *The Three Dorothies*, and this different atmosphere
continued with a drama titled *The Enchanted Lovers*, which was apparently
aired in 1659. The final two plays of his career were *The Noble Ingratitude* and
The Amorous Fantasme, both from 1661. Of course, by the time Lower was
completing his work, the Puritanical shutdown of the London theatres, as well
as all other theatrical and festival entertainment, was underway – so it would
seem that his work perhaps did not receive adequate exposure, and hence his
loss from the general canon. Considering he was also active as a writer during
the Civil War, Lower's circumstances could hardly have been worse. He is one
figure who may well have embodied the mid-seventeenth-century Cornish
dramatist. Certainly by the time the Restoration had occurred and Restoration
theatre truly begun in its aftermath, new playwrights were making headway.
Doubtless his texts would probably have been consigned to an earlier era,

although given the title of *The Amorous Fantasme*, perhaps this was more in line with the liberated new age after the restoration of Charles II.[74]

Back in London, there were other writers who at least had knowledge of the Cornish, even if they only featured in a very small way in their drama. One such writer was Ben Jonson (1572-1637). Educated at Westminster, Jonson served as a soldier in the Low Countries before beginning to work as a player and playwright in 1597.[75] Jonson's *Bartholomew Fair* was performed by the Lady Elizabeth's Men at the Hope Theatre on 31 October 1614. Fitting our conception of drama based on the ritual year, the play is set at the pre-eminent fair which took place at Smithfield on 24 August, St Bartholomew's Day. Smithfield was a site of public executions and slaughterhouses, so it was a fitting location for a fair, for audiences had been previously entertained in other ways. At the fair, people traded cloths and other goods, but also indulged in entertainment. The drama follows the fortunes of the various visitors to the fair, to whom many mishaps and misunderstandings occur, Jonson using his characters to comment on social, religious and political aspects of London society in Jacobean Britain. The Cornish component of the drama is slight, but significant. It is voiced by Edgworth, a cutpurse, who is in discussion with Winwife and Quarlous (base characters who jeer at the fair people). When Edgworth enters, Winwife calls him a 'lime-twig' (a thief) and asks 'Hast thou touched?'. Edgworth explains who he had encountered, mentioning how 'they ha' got in a northern clothier, and one Puppy, a western man, that's come to wrestle before my Lord Mayor anon'.[76] Clearly, the western man is a Cornishman, who has come to display his skill before the Mayor in London, where, according to Jamieson, a wrestling contest was held in front of the tent of the Lord Mayor, Alderman and sheriffs, this being one of the main events of the fair.[77] It is perhaps interesting though, how Edgworth singles out these characters for he indicates they are ripe pickings for thieves. We therefore conclude that 'western' men and northern English people were regarded by the character as somewhat naïve in the confines of the fair. However, at the same time, the distance travelled by western men demonstrates both how highly regarded wrestling was as a skill and also knowledge of such London fairs back in Cornwall. Clearly, Jonson notes that the Cornish characteristically wrestle: this defines the group. The grammar of Jonson's writing makes it unclear whether Puppy is the name of the Cornishman, or if it is connected to the previous reference to the clothier. If Puppy is his name, then it is perhaps further indication of the naïvety of the Cornish. It may also comment on the lack of fierceness in his wrestling prowess.

If Lower's work remains in obscurity, and Jonson's minimalist look at the Cornish is still somewhat hidden within theatre scholarship, then two other

A Faire Quarrell.

With new Additions of Mᶜ. *Chaugh* and *Trimtram* Roaring, and the Bauds Song.
Neuer before Printed.

As it was Acted before the King, by the Prince us Highnesse Seruants.

{ Written by *Thomas Midleton*, } Gent.
{ and *William Rowley*. }

Printed at London for *I. T.* and are to be sold at Christ Church Gate. 1617.

Title-page of Middleton and Rowley's
" Fair Quarrel," 1617

Fig. 45. The frontispiece of an early edition of *A Fair Quarrel* by Thomas Middleton and William Rowley.

texts from slightly earlier in the century deserve considerable discussion in this chapter. The first of these is a Jacobean tragi-comedy titled *A Fair Quarrel*, a collaborative text written by Thomas Middleton and William Rowley.[78] Rowley, we have already seen, appears to have had some degree of interest in Cornish subject-matter, but Middleton's involvement in the development of this text is of interest to us. Thomas Middleton lived between 1580 and 1627, and of all the dramatists operating in this period, he was among the most successful and most prolific, partly due to his writing in a range of genres, and also due to a series of successful collaborations with other performers and writers. He was born in London, the son of a bricklayer, who had interestingly bought property adjoining the Curtain theatre in Shoreditch. This location obviously influenced his future career. He attended Queen's College Oxford, matriculating in 1598, but he did not graduate, favouring instead to spend his time writing long Elizabethan-style poems.[79] One of his early satires ran afoul of the Anglican Church's ban on such work, and it was apparently burned. Middleton furthered his career in the early 1600s by writing topical pamphlets, though his success as a dramatist really began in the period after 1610, when he began a very fruitful collaboration with the actor-writer Rowley, but also developed his own pieces: among them *The Revenger's Tragedy*, *Women Beware Women* and the satirical city comedy, *A Chaste Maid in Cheapside*.[80] The collaboration with Rowley most successfully bore fruit with *The Changeling* and *Wit at Several Weapons*, but it is the play they collaborated on titled *A Fair Quarrel* that is of interest to us here, because it features substantial and important Cornish material.

Like *The Birth of Merlin*, the play has three interconnected plots[81] and, as was the usual collaborative practice of Middleton and Rowley, the former took responsibility for the serious main plots, while the latter handled the comic sub-plot. However, it seems this was not always rigidly followed, and that there was also a good deal of crossover between them. The main plot here tells the story of Captain Ager and his mother; the second-level plot deals with Fitzallen and Jane; the third is the overt comedy material about the two Cornish clowns, Chough and Trimtram. Chough is presented as a Cornish wrestler[82] – perhaps drawing on the legacy and ideology found in Jonson's presentation of the Cornish – and was most likely to have been a role written for him to play. Much of the plot concerns the issue of duelling, which was highly topical in the period in which the play was presented. King James's first proclamation against duelling was issued in 1613. The play emerged sometime between 1615 and 1616, with the text being published in 1617. The long opening scene of the drama sets up later events for Chough and Trimtram.[83] A wealthy citizen named Master Russell is concerned about the marriage of his only child, his daughter Jane. She has been courted by a young man named Fitzallen; Russell is concerned that he does not have any money, and so attempts to prevent the marriage. To do so, he stages a false arrest of Fitzallen, clearing the way for a suitor of his own choosing. The rich prospective husband he has picked out for her is Chough, presented throughout as a crude and offensive fool. What complicates matters, however, is that Jane and Fitzallen have, unbeknown to her father, entered into a nuptial precontract – a *de praesenti* betrothal – which meant that the two lovers could engage in sexual contact, and that their child would be legitimate.[84]

For the James I-era audience watching *A Fair Quarrel*, there would have been certain expectations of what Chough and Trimtram would be like. The characters' names are clearly important. While Chough (pronounced 'Chuff') is a clear enough symbol of Cornish identity (choughs could be found on the coast of Cornwall, the bird featured on a number of coats of arms of Cornish families, and the spirit of King Arthur was believed to be embodied in the creature[85]), in the sixteenth century, the word had a secondary meaning. From an English point of view, in the late medieval and early modern period, the word 'chuff' also meant a rustic boor [sic].[86] Therefore, this conveniently seemed to summarise a view of the average Cornishman of the Age: that, whilst having this heroic background, they were actually quite boorish. Middleton and Rowley were therefore cleverly manipulating the audience to respond to Chough in a certain way. Though he has pretensions of gentility, and even 'Arthurian' qualities, his stage presence denotes a character struggling to cope with the manners and mores of London 'society'. Stoyle argues that the term 'Cornish Chough' was a common derogatory expression,[87] and perhaps it remained in the ideology of the rest of Britain from Cornwall's rebellious nature of previous centuries. In other plays of the period, there is also an indication that the name implied obesity and largeness,[88] which would suit Rowley's frame. Chough's servant, too, has an interesting name: Trimtram. Its comic sing-song is only a short step away from that most Cornish of knights Sir Tristram, or Tristan, of the earlier Celtic Romance,[89] which, as we have noted, most probably had its origins on the south coast of Cornwall. Giving this name to a servant therefore undercuts all previous heroic and romantic imaginings of the character, enhancing the boorish and unsophisticated nature of Chough. His copying of Chough is probably derived from the proverb 'Trim tram, like master, like man'.[90]

Considering the fact that Chough and Trimtram are some of the few surviving representations of stage Cornishness, it is worth considering their dramaturgy in some degree of detail. To an extent, they symbolise the wider way in which Cornwall was represented on the London stage in the early seventeenth century.

When Russell enters with Chough and Trimtram, he introduces them to Jane. The cloddish behaviour of Chough is instantly recognised when he attempts to kiss Jane. He comments, 'I'll show her the Cornish hug, sir.'[91] The 'Cornish hug' was a pun on the wrestling move of the squeezing first grip, but also with a double meaning.[92] A hug suggests something physically comforting whereas for the rest of Britain it was a fight move, or an act of aggression. Alongside this, such a wrestling move is inevitably designed for deception, to engender a throw or fall. It is therefore woefully inappropriate for the purposes of seduction, and presumably much comic mileage would have been found in Chough's move on Jane being like a wrestle rather than an embrace. This is supported by his comment 'I never do any kindness to my friends but I use to hit 'em in the teeth with it presently'.[93] Meanwhile Trimtram is introducing himself to Jane's confidante Anne in the same way, commenting 'My name is Trimtram, forsooth, what my master does, I use to do the like'. He comically mirrors Chough's moves but Anne's retort keeps him in check: 'You are deceived, sir; I am not this gentlewoman's servant, to make your courtesy equal.'[94]

In an aside to the audience, Jane comments that she 'will learn too soon' about Chough, who comments 'My name is Chough, a Cornish gentleman; my man's mine own countryman too, i'faith. I warrant you took us for some small islanders'.[95] There is quite a lot of subtext to this statement. Chough instantly sits with 'rough' which is in turn ironic, considering he views himself as a gentleman. There is, however, a notion of Cornwall still having territorial identity, since Trimtram is described as being his 'countryman', but there is something more here. It seems that in this text, and in later eighteenth century texts, Cornish characters often used the epithet 'i'faith' to justify and qualify what has been said. This seems a way of demonstrating a specifically Cornish Christianity. The confusion over small islanders refers to the Scots and the Irish. At this suggestion, Chough responds with 'Red Shanks?' This was a term of contempt for Scottish Highlanders and the Irish, but it is also self-mocking, because the chough has highly distinctive red legs. The genuine quality of their intent is described by Chough thus: 'No, truly, we are right Cornish diamonds.'[96] Whilst this may sound good, the probable inference to the audience is that they are counterfeits and fraudsters. A pun follows on the title of the play when Trimtram offers: 'Yes, we cut quarrels, and break glasses, where we go', which, considering their behaviour so far, the audience has no reason to doubt. Once introductions have been made, Russell begins the marriage negotiations:

Russell: How do you like her, sir?

Chough: Troth, I do like her, sir, in the way of comparison, to anything

	that a man would desire: I am as high as the Mount in love with her already, and that's as far as I can go by land; but I hope to go further by water with her one day.
Russell:	I tell you, sir, she has lost some colour
	By wrestling with a peevish sickness now of late.
Chough:	Wrestle? Nay, and she love wrestling. I'll teach her a trick to overthrow any peevish sickness in London, whate'er it be.
Russell:	Well, she had a rich beauty, though I say't;
	Nor is it lost: a little thing repairs it.[97]

Much of this scene is laden with sexual innuendo, though Middleton and Rowley develop this through a further set of wrestling imagery. Chough's insensitive response to her sickness is, of course, love-making, which in his view is analogous to wrestling. The Mount referred to is St Michael's Mount in west Cornwall, which was probably a known enough symbol of Cornwall. Russell's unknowing statement about a 'little thing' reminds the audience of her baby. Chough continues the bawdy innuendo in the next section of dialogue ('I'll show you a trick that you never saw in your life'[98]), but there are also some witty puns by Middleton and Rowley on wrestling terminology and rules: 'I will not catch beneath the waist, believe it: I know fair play.'[99] Of course, it is Chough's desire to catch Jane beneath the waist, while the end of the line is a pun on the age-old motto of Cornish wrestlers: 'Fair play is good play'.[100] Even so, for Middleton and Rowley to know this suggests that the Cornish penchant for wrestling, and its terminology, had pan-British status at this point; otherwise many of the gags would have been lost on the audience. The humour continues with Chough's statement: 'I'll never believe that: the hug and the lock between man and woman, with a fair fell, is as sweet an exercise for the body as you'll desire in a summer's evening' and lots of puns on 'inturn' (the manoeuvre of putting one leg between the opponent's leg to overthrow them) and 'green' (clothing stained by grass, due to wrestling or sexual intercourse).[101] When Jane retires, already bored with Chough's attempts to woo her, Chough responds with what seemingly a man from the south-west of Britain would say: 'I will part at Dartmouth with her, sir.'[102]

When the others have gone, Chough and Trimtram are left to discuss the concept of 'roaring'. During the period 1610-20, roaring was a fashionable trend of riotous behaviour by gallants with a penchant for machismo quarrelling (often through competitive dialogue) and duelling. When seen in Chough and Trimtram, this is highly comic. Chough is unconvinced of the concept, preferring instead to have a wrestling school in London but, as Trimtram offers, success in the city is dependent upon it: 'You must learn to roar here in London, you'll never proceed in the reputation of gallantry else'.[103] Following another set of bawdy puns ('a fire of her touch-hole') on a canon named Roaring Meg (conflating the famous roarer Long Meg with the Edinburgh canon *Mons* Meg), the pair then reflect on the heroic past of wrestling. The origin myth of Corineus is considered, though comically Chough confuses this with Hercules and Mount Olympus. In a final work-out of stupidity in this scene, the pair confuse and conflate history and dates, feeling that this was not that long ago; perhaps displaying a Cornish 'national' characteristic of making events of the past seem extremely significant to the present.

One later scene that shows the significance of Chough and Trimtam is Act IV, Scene i. Here the pair are shown taking 'roaring' lessons from an English soldier turned con-artist, so that they can learn to be fashionable 'roaring boys'. Clearly the soldier (the Colonel's friend) is somehow aware of their difference, because he asks them 'tell me in what language I shall roar a lecture to you'.[104] The conversation is steered in the direction of the Sclavonian [Slavic] language, but the Londonian roar is considered most relevant since Chough only wishes to 'use all my roaring here in London: in Cornwall we are all for wrestling, and I do not mean to travel over sea to roar there'.[105] The Londonian roar is taught using classical mythology, which both Chough and Trimtram confuse. At this point, Trimtram is nearer Chough's equal than his servant: whilst learning, an argument breaks out between them, demonstrating that in fact they are related. The argument is a perfect imagining of what 'roaring' at each other should be:

Chough:	Wilt thou not yield precedency?
Trimtram:	To thee? I know thee and thy brood.
Chough:	Know'st thou my brood? I know thy brood: thou art a rook.
Trimtram:	The near akin to the choughs!
Chough:	The rooks akin to the choughs?
Colonel's Friend:	Very well maintained.
Chough:	Dungcart! Thou liest!
Trimtram:	Lie? Enucleate the kernet of my scabbard!
Chough:	Now, if I durst draw my sword, 'twere valiant, i'faith.
Colonel's Friend:	Draw, draw, howsoever.
Chough:	Have some wine ready to make us friends, I pray you.
Trimtram:	Chough, I will make thee fly and roar.
Chough:	I will roar if thou strik'st me.
Colonel's Friend:	So, 'tis enough; now conclude in wine. I see you will

	prove an excellent practitioner: wondrous well
	performed on both sides!
Chough:	Here, Trimtram, I drink to thee.[106]

As we see, the mock duel/quarrel is resolved, but the dialogue gives us insight into the ramifications of lineage and identity for the Cornish. The rook is obviously a bird, of the crow family, but not a chough itself. A rook was also somebody who was a cheat, a gull or a fool, so though 'brood-ship' with Chough is claimed, Chough feels Trimtram a rook to his more iconic bird. The sequence is also another undercutting of the image of the 'Arthurian Knight', because although their confrontation is meant to be heroic, the entire episode is supremely comic, with the Cornish pair arguing amongst themselves. However, they are now trained in the act of 'roaring'. In Scene iv of Act IV, Chough and Tristam absurdly set up their own 'roaring' school, with intentions of educating others in how to do it. The scene shows them indulging in highly comic verbal fantasy of their own 'roaring talk'. In all of this, there may well be a subtext that the Cornish need lessons on how to talk, because they are still apparently new to speaking English anyway.[107] Such a hypothesis is borne out later in the drama, but here Chough and Trimtram try to run 'roaring' rings around the other characters. Trimtram uses his learning: 'I mean to confront thee, cyclops'.[108] Captain Albo, who has to deal with them, notes they are raw and unpractised at 'roaring' when he terms them 'freshwater friends'.[109] Chough here delivers lines such as 'I would enucleate my fructifier' and the response from Albo is that he 'has eaten pippins' (pippins being a variety of apple apparently favoured by Celtic peoples), with the implication that the pair are drunk.[110] It takes an onlooker, a bawd who they have come to know, called Meg, to calm things down. After a song, Chough and Trimtram ludicrously parry over-the-top praise, which is wholly comic, considering how they were at the start of the drama:

Chough:	Melodius minotaur!
Trimtram:	Harmonious hippocrene!
Chough:	Sweet-breasted bronstrops!
Trimtram:	Most tunable tweak!
Chough:	Delicious duplar!
Trimtram:	Purefactious panagron!
Chough:	Calumnious calicut!
Trimstram:	And most singular sindicus![111]

The scene concludes with Chough and Trimtram discussing the bawdy nature of the streets of London, with the implication that they, as rural bumpkins, are enjoying its pleasures of sexual commerce. Act V then leads to the confrontation between Chough and the Physician. The Physician tells him that Jane is 'naught' and that his 'intended bride is a whore'.[112] Chough becomes worried he will catch the 'pox' from her and comments that he will now 'wrestle a fall with her father' for having deceived him. At the arrival of Russell, Chough asks, 'Came I from the Mount to be confronted?'[113] There follows a sequence where he and Trimtram attempt to explain in 'roaring' speak that Jane is a whore; the meaning of which completely passes over Russell. His request is 'Good sir, speak English to me' because the implication is that the confusing 'roaring' speak is in the Cornish language. Chough's response to this is 'All this is Cornish to thee; I say thy daughter has drunk bastard in her time'.[114] For the audience, the language being spouted on stage must have implied to them what Cornish sounded like: a bizarre and strange gibberish.[115] Chough and Trimtram then reflect that they have travelled all these miles for a London whore, when one might have been found much closer to home:

Chough:	I could have had a whore at Plymouth!
Trimtram:	Ay, or at Pe'ryn [Penryn].
Chough:	Ay, or under the Mount.
Trimtram:	Or as you came, at Evil [Yeovil].
Chough:	Or at Hockey [Wookey] Hole in Somersetshire
Trimtram:	Or at the Hanging Stones in Wiltshire.[116]

The mention of Plymouth is interesting, because this was the period in which that city expanded greatly as a centre of trade and exploration;[117] and the implication might be that this was where Chough made his money. Pe'ryn is one place in Cornwall that, as we see here and later, seems to have been well-known (as being in Cornwall) from the perspective of elsewhere in Britain. The locations clearly match their imagined route to London, and there are shades here of the route that the rebellion of 1497 followed;[118] Middleton and Rowley seem to be thinking along the lines of this is how the Cornish would travel to London. Jane is facing marriage to Chough, but the Physician, whose earlier advances upon her she had spurned, turns up at the event and makes an accusation about the shame of her illegitimate child.[119] Shocked by this revelation, Chough backs out of the ceremony, with Russell reconciling himself to Fitzallen as a son-in-law. The alternatives, it would seem, are far worse.

There is more Cornu-centric material to follow however. In a quite brilliant linguistic turn around (after all the pretend Cornish of the 'roaring'),

Middleton and Rowley then use a small piece of real Cornish language, as Chough orders around the Physician: 'Phy-si-ci-an! *Mauz avez*, physician!'.[120] If it were Rowley performing the part of Chough, then clearly, he knew enough Cornish to integrate at least a small phrase into the text, *Mauz avez* is probably Rowley's phonetic rendering of *môs* [to move, go] and *aves* [out, outside]. The intention of this is unclear, however, because if Chough was ordering the Physician around, then he would not enter in the next piece of stage direction. The implication, therefore, is that he means something along the lines of 'hurry up', but the Cornish does not quite read in this way.[121] Though also grammatically incorrect (it should be *kejy* or *kehejy* if in the imperative), it is an interesting dramatic spin, which shows perhaps more awareness of identity than the rest of the boorish imagining of the Cornish in the rest of the play. Events seemed to have shaped Chough and Trimtram into something different. Chough offers, 'Pray you, think I know as much as every fool does' while Trimtram responds with, 'Let me be Trimtram: I pray you too, sir'.[122] Here then, Trimtram appears to be saying let me be myself now, and not the fool that Chough has just classified himself as. Considering that, earlier on, Trimtram was 'like master, like man', the difference is marked. Chough's comment displays an admission of foolishness, which whilst showing he is still a bumpkin, at least demonstrates an awareness of his weakness: a quality which should, at the end, endear him to the audience. The linguistic difficulties of the Cornish are perhaps encompassed in Chough's lines to Russell, 'I'll not speak another word, i'faith' which seems to show him now afraid to put his foot, so to speak, yet again, in someone's mouth.[123] Yet, the wider implication is that the Cornish are still negotiating their linguistic and cultural presence in a Britain that finds that difference hard to endure and tolerate. Later, Chough observes 'I will reveal it, and yet not speak it neither'.[124] Their singing of some of the roaring lines at the end of the drama indicates them trying to fit, but perhaps failing to do so. In the end, Chough will 'bid myself a guest, though not a groom'.[125] The quarrels of the play that have been engendered by Russell are resolved, but the wider quarrel of England and Cornwall remains unresolved. Although the presentation of Chough and Tristram is highly derogatory in many senses, clearly Middleton and Rowley knew something about Cornish history and identity in this phase. The picture we have is far more detailed than anything in Shakespeare and, as we shall see, such imaginings of stage Cornishness outside of Cornwall did not much alter in the next century. Such dramas clearly set the standard of how Cornwall and Cornish characters were to be conceived.

Some fifteen years later, there emerged another text which again looked at a stage imagining of Cornishness. This was Richard Brome's *The Northern*

Lasse, which was first performed in 1632. Brome's drama is cited by a number of observers for containing one line of Cornish language.[126] Although this is significant, the play actually offers a lot more insight into a similar kind of stage Cornishness, as expounded by Middleton and Rowley in *A Fair Quarrel.* Brome (c.1590-1653) was a servant and then perhaps secretary to Ben Jonson, whose friendship he later enjoyed. Of Brome's surviving fifteen plays,[127] *The Northern Lasse* is the earliest; it was also the most popular, and the work defined his reputation and style. In many ways, Brome appears to have been much influenced by the dramas of Jonson, and there are certain stylistic similarities in their comedies. However, Brome's work is a lot kindlier than Jonson's; his texts are less satirical, and much more romantic. The principal difficulty of this drama for modern readers is the way in which Brome conceives of Constance, the northern lass. As a character she is thinly drawn, and her "northern" speech is, for the most part, clumsy and awkward. However, it was probably sufficient for the London stage (it was performed both at the Globe and Blackfriars theatres) to denote her difference from the sophistication of the south.[128] Brome, however, wanted to show aspects of 'other' cultures of Britain within the drama, and this is where the Cornish character comes in.

The play's plot is relatively straightforward: Sir Philip Luckless is about to marry the rich London widow Fitchow, but receives a letter from a woman named Constance, reminding him of her love for him. Luckless mistakenly thinks that the writer is another Constance of low reputation, and so he disregards the letter as unimportant. He discovers this mistake too late, after he has married Fitchow. The rest of the play is then concerned with the mechanisms which Luckless tries to induce a divorce from her. Fitchow's foolish brother, whom she tries to marry to Constance, is fobbed off with an inferior substitute, and Luckless and the true Constance are eventually reunited. The most famous scene, from a Cornish point of view, is Act V, Scene viii. Here, Cornwall is presented as being close enough to Spain, or, put another way, almost remote enough from England, for a Spaniard to understand Cornish:

Bullfinch: Alasse, what shall we doe then? Gentlemen, have any of you any Spanish to help me understand this strange stranger?

[*They all disclaim knowledge*]

Bullfinch: What shiere of our Nation is next to Spain? Perhaps he may understand that shiere of England.

Tridewell: Devonshire or Cornwall, sire.

Nonsense: Never credit me but I will spurt some Cornish at him: *Pedn bras vidne bis creegas.*[129]

The garbled Cornish here broadly translates to 'Big head, will you be hung?' The 'Big head' would appear to be Luckless's serving man, Tridewell, who is trying to 'tread well' around the odd 'Celt', Nonsense. In reality, however, this sequence has much historical resonance. Cornwall was the first line of defence against Spanish naval attack, and the threat, as alluded to in Carew's *The Survey of Cornwall*, was very real.[130] In 1595 (thirty-seven years earlier) Paul, Newlyn and Penzance were sacked by the Spanish,[131] and the Spanish Armada's defeat, under Lord Howard of Effingham in 1588, was still fresh in the memory. Although this section has been often discussed, what is generally not recognised is the further Cornish material in the drama. Earlier, Bullfinch, in discussion with the character Squelch, talked sarcastically about a young man called Nonsense:

> I apprehend him to be Master Salomon Nonsense, Son and Heire to my right worthy friend, Sir Hercules Nonsense of Cornwall. If you be not hee sir, I am sure it is you. I may bee deceivd, but I am certaine tis he.[132]

Nonsense therefore, is established early on as a Cornish character, one who has no social skills and throughout the play speaks 'nonsense' – the Cornish that he does speak only reinforcing this. Brome also gives Nonsense a catchphrase: 'Never credit me...' which would appear again to support this nonsensical way of speaking. Widgine even goads him into oration: 'Speake Master Nonsense... A speech of yours would do't'.[133] Such coding throughout the play was perhaps immensely funny for the audience in London: it allowed them to laugh at the unsophisticated nature of the linguistic map of the rest of Britain. When Nonsense is placed before Constance to woo her, he struggles, and she can only conclude that 'Your mouth's not wide enough for your words',[134] since he is trying too hard. Nonsense himself admits, 'Shee understands nothing that I can speake'.[135] Although it is not stated, this is clearly a Cornishman already struggling to cope with a recently-acquired 'new' tongue and then having to deal with the fashions of London English.[136] When Nonsense speaks his line of Cornish later in the play, Squelch is forced to respond with: 'Am I transformed utterly? Is my language alter'd with my apparel, or are you all mad? What unspeakable misery is this?'[137] Although his comment is said in jest, the subtext is more serious: that the centre wishes conformity, and those who subvert this are 'mad' and bring 'misery'. Nonsense is therefore the polar opposite of Luckless, who speaks good-quality English, and who, although initially luckless in marriage, uses the conventions and humours of the day to transform his situation. Nonsense can only ever be naïve and unsophisticated, although the audience probably warmed to him, because his ineptitude is very human. In a witty conclusion, Brome uses Nonsense as his character to sum up the nonsensical and therefore comic nature of the play, but also he declares that events might inspire him to write a play about it, back in Cornwall:

> Never credit me, but I have had sport enough o'conscience, and I doe not make a Stage play on't, when I come into Cornewall: I protest and vow then say there was Nonsense in this.[138]

This is a highly interesting speech, since two constructions of Cornwall are operating: it would be amusing for the audience to consider such an incompetent character as Nonsense devising a play, and entering into the profession of the playwright. The fact that Nonsense is Cornish, and would write a nonsensical play is, for the London audience, pure logic, of the ideology of the centre at least. However, underneath this, despite this snobbery, is perhaps a view that supports the central argument of this book: that Cornwall has a long association with drama and, however tiny a reference, here it is once again, on the London stage, in 1632. Plays were mounted in London, but there was enough knowledge from Brome, that dramas (although perhaps not as sophisticated) also occurred in Cornwall, or at least had done so within the recent past. Considering Jonson's understanding of visiting Cornish culture to Bartholomew Fair, then there is no reason to doubt that Brome also knew something of Cornwall. Although the line of Cornish is not perfect, he also had enough awareness of the language to assert that other parts of Britain had a different language than English. Despite the satire about the figure of Nonsense, and therefore, by extrapolation, the Cornish elsewhere, Broom shows that the linguistic politics of Britain, and their representation on the Renaissance stage, are a good deal more complex than we might imagine. This position lends further credence to a wider paradigm about the nature of the stage representation of the Cornish during this phase: one found in Ford, Middleton and Rowley, and Brome, and also found later in the work of George Lillo and, to an extent, also in the work of Samuel Foote.

The Puritan ethic, which had so railed against the theatres of the Elizabethan period, was to find success in the middle years of the seventeenth century. In 1642 the theatres were closed by Parliament, as part of the general disputes which were occurring between King Charles I and Parliament. Much of this was governed by a conflict between high Churchmen and Puritans, over several issues. Charles's idea that the 'Divine Right of Kings' (the very debate of a number of Shakespeare's dramas) put him above the law annoyed a defiant Parliament, which he dissolved three times. He favoured bishops, while others, especially the Scots, wanted a more Puritan worship. In desperate need of money for armies, Charles I imposed taxes which provoked stern resistance. Parliament raised an army and civil war broke out across Cornwall, England, Wales and Scotland, eventually also embroiling Ireland into the conflict.[139] Charles scored many victories at first, but in 1644 the Parliamentarians gained the upper hand over the Royalists. Two final defeats in 1645 led Charles to surrender to the Scots, who handed him over to his enemies. In 1649 he was tried for treason, condemned and beheaded. From then on, the army rather than Parliament assumed control, under a leading general, Oliver Cromwell (1599-1658).[140] The ramifications of the conflict in Cornwall have been considered by a number of scholars, among them Mary Coate, whose work defined many subsequent studies.[141] In the new Cornish historiography, however, the Civil War has more recently come to be read in a different way by a number of historians.[142] The alignment of many Cornish nobles and families to the king and the Royalist cause, is to be seen in the light of the unique geo-political position of Cornwall, whose territorial independence had always been given special dispensation by a long line of rulers, not least in the way in which Cornwall's jurisdiction was maintained by the Stannary system. Put simply, support for the king against the Parliamentarians was, paradoxically in their view, a way of maintaining independence. As Stoyle has shown, propaganda was in widespread use during the conflict, with many Parliamentarian pamphlets and literature directed against the Cornish.[143] The conflict and the subsequent Interregnum were also to have a major effect on the further shut-down of Cornish-language drama, community performance, and other markers of the ritual year.

One writer who had been active before the conflict was Sir John Mohun. Mohun was not Cornish: he was, in fact, born in Okehampton, on 15 April 1592.[144] His only known surviving play was a tragi-comedy titled *The Emperor of the East*, which seemed to have a considerable degree of success in its day, because it was performed at both the Blackfriars and Globe playhouses by the King's Majesties Servants in the early 1630s, being printed by Thomas Harper in 1632. Little is known of the content, but the drama was set in Constantinople, showing it had a degree of ambition, if not any south-western connections. Although Mohun was not Cornish himself, his family had connections to Tavistock on the Cornwall-England border,[145] and political allegiances to Grampound, and when the Civil War began, he became one of the commanders for the king in Cornwall. This would seem to indicate that he had further connections to Cornwall, and an affinity with both the people and popular opinion there. Mohun was clearly active as a writer on the London stage, and so is included here, because he may well have contributed other texts which perhaps had had more Cornish content. Mohun died early on in the conflict, in 1644, aged fifty two, but it is unclear whether this was through natural causes or through injuries inflicted by Parliamentarian forces.

While the Civil War was occuring, one Cornish writer continued to write drama. This was Sir William Killigrew (1606-1695). During the War, he had been Governor of Pendennis Castle; in the Restoration, he eventually became Vice-Chamberlain to the Queen. Little is known of his origins in Cornwall, but he eventually died in London, having risen to become an important member of Court. Killigrew is a both frustrating and interesting figure within the continuum of dramatic writing to emerge out of Cornwall. In the Restoration phase, it simply would not do to develop contemporary drama, because current themes were likely to offend someone. Therefore his work tended to be set in foreign or mythical locations, with somewhat ludicrous plots. A drama which escaped the problems of the day was fashionable. However, such a dramaturgy means that his plays are unlikely to be revived simply because they were so indicative of the Age in which they were constructed. His first work was published in 1653, after the anti-theatrical ethos of the Interregnum had been established, although it remains unclear where the work was performed. This was *Ayres and Dialogues for one, two and three voyces*.[146] Four major tragi-comedies emerged between 1653 and 1666.[147] The first collated work was *The Seege of Urbin*. Set in Pisa, this follows the experiences of a woman named Celestina, with an opening bedchamber scene where 'she is seen sitting by a table, in a rich night-gown, a scarfe over her head, holding a dagger in her handkerchief.'[148] With a foreign setting for the drama, Killigrew could not possibly offend anyone. In many ways, this matched the number of Royalist supporters living in exile elsewhere in Europe. However, it seems he altered his play *Pandora, or The Converts* from a tragedy to a comedy because it was not approved on the stage. The drama was set in Syracusa. Such a development perhaps led to him more fully embracing the tragi-comic form. *Selindra* is set in the Emperor's Palace in Bizantium [sic], moving the action between Hungary and Greece, while *Love and Friendship* is set on the Island of Cithera, and was an elaborate historical fantasy. Two further plays followed: *Ormasdes* (a similarly fantastical tale),[149] and finally what his publishers described as *The Imperial Tragedy*, 'taken out of a Latin play, and very much altered, by a Gentleman for his own diversion'.[150] This was apparently acted at the Nursery in the Barbican. However, despite his political rise to power, it seems that after 1669 Killigrew stopped writing drama, perhaps because of the difficulties over *Pandora*, and possibly because of the failure of *The Imperial Tragedy*. Sadly, although Killigrew negotiated his way through the cultural minefield of the aftermath of the Civil War, he never saw fit to develop a Cornish-themed work. There are no traces of his ethnicity within the extant texts either.

Killigrew was very connected to Falmouth, and around the same time as the development of his exotic dramas, other kinds of performances were occurring on the streets of Falmouth and Penryn. In the Mayor of Penryn's Cash Book for 1666, there is the following entry: 'Received by Mr. Tomblyn the Mountebancke for leave to make his stage before the Dolphin and Angell Inn 1s. 6'.[151] The word 'mountebank' is an interesting choice here. It is derived from the Italian *montambanco* or *montimbanco*, based on the phrase *manta in banco* (literally the notion of a quack medicine seller getting up onto a bench to address his audience). Whilst this might seem unconnected with theatre, many sellers of medicine would combine their desire for sales with the development of an outdoor stage show, which would impress onlookers to buy the product. In some cases, the show often took precedence over the selling, and such performers could gain more money in this way than through the sale of pseudo-medicine. Thus, in the late seventeenth century, the term came to mean a kind of dubious street performer, who attracted the public, but was essentially problematical for the authorities; hence the fee levied upon Mr Tomblyn [Tamblyn?], who sounds as if he is a Cornish mountebank. Another entry from 1669 says: 'Disb. pd. tumblers wiffe, which came with the Mountebancke for her reliefe beinge going to London 2s. 6d'.[152] This entry is somewhat unclear. It seems that acrobatic performance was on offer in the streets of Penryn, and that the company of performers were, in some capacity, travelling to London. Given Ben Jonson's understanding of events such as Bartholomew Fair, then this seems a likely journey and, put against the active theatrical culture after the Restoration, entirely logical as well.

The return from exile of Charles II was to change things greatly. At three o'clock in the afternoon of 25 May 1660, King Charles II left his ship, the *Royal Charles*, and was rowed ashore to Dover, where he knelt to thank God for this safe return. Four days later, he entered London, and his subjects rejoiced. In this moment, so begins what we might legitimately call the 'modern' theatre of Britain. This development was in response to the end of nine years of royal exile, and eleven years of Puritan government, during which time the Puritan ethic had been translated into law. The Puritans' approach was less directly political, and more subtle. In a way, it seemed to say that plays are art, art is beautiful, the beautiful is pleasant, and the pleasant damnable. Alongside this was a distrust of the theatre's powers of seduction. Back in 1642 the Puritans had closed all theatres and outlawed events relating to the ritual year (such as maypoles and Morris dancing).[153] However, their efforts were not completely successful, for plays were still mounted, almost as a challenge, in public houses, inns and private homes, although there was always a danger of being raided by the military. However, with the collapse of the

Commonwealth and Puritan control, the restoration of Charles II might well be seen more cynically as less the restoration of the old order, and more the outcome of a piece of political improvisation in a country which was losing control of itself.

Charles II's magnanimity at the start of his reign was politically brilliant. He relished the power to enhance the prospects of those who had smoothed his path to the throne, and also those Royalists who had remained loyal to him during his exile. In Cornwall, the many figures and families who had supported him were thus rewarded. King and Court had a renewed confidence they had not felt since the previous century, and there were new currents of moral licence and intellectual enquiry. Although the king was supportive of scientific enquiry, and thus the rejection of superstition, Charles II was also committed to reinstating the theatre. This institution was to encourage the ebullient pursuit of pleasure, with wit, outrageous romps and satire aplenty. Two individuals were nominated by the king to be at the forefront of this development: Thomas Killigrew (1612-83), and Sir William Davenant (1606-68).[154] Killigrew was appointed as overseer of his own company of players, the King's Men, while Davenant controlled the servants of the king's brother and were named the Duke's Men. Henry Herbert, meanwhile, was reappointed as the Master of Revels, and Killigrew and Davenant effectively ran a duopoly of performance in the opening years of the Restoration. While this was occurring in London, little was happening in Cornwall or, for that matter, in the rest of Britain. It would take some time for the changes at the centre to 'filter out' to the periphery.

It took a while for Restoration drama to develop fully, but the period 1660-1700 tends to be dominated by the genre of 'Restoration comedy' – a kind of comedy of manners, whose predominant tone was witty, bawdy, cynical and amoral. The plays were mainly written in prose, with some of the more romantic moments in verse. The plots were complex, usually double, and sometimes triple. Repartee and discussions of marital behaviour formed much of the interest in the dramaturgy, with the characterisation composed of fops, bawds, scheming valets, sexually voracious young widows and older women.[155] Another crucial character was the unmannered and uncultivated country squire. Frustratingly, it would appear there are no surviving Restoration comedies that feature Cornwall or Cornish characters. Had some emerged, however, they would surely have featured Cornish squires coming to London, to operate in this world of sexual intrigue, money and fashion. The trend towards this form of characterisation is one we note in the remainder of the eighteenth century, so the peripheral character amongst the genteel centre is one we should expect to see. Thus, advanced, witty conversation was an urban phenomenon and life in the country was its butt. The social clumsiness of rural immigrants to London remained a regular comic theme. The prospect of a prolonged rural residence (in somewhere like Cornwall) was thought of as being unspeakably grim.[156]

Considering the sexual and bawdy themes of the drama, as Restoration comedy grew, respectable citizens avoided the theatres (in something of an overhang of the Puritan ideology) and the plays were seen, by some at least, as a source of corruption, frivolity, blasphemy and immorality. This argument was most famously articulated by Jeremy Collier's 1698 attack titled *A Short View of the Immorality and Profaneness of the English Stage*.[157] Specifically, Collier criticised playwrights such as John Dryden, William Wycherley, William Congreve and John Vanbrugh for the way in which they presented the clergy and for the theatre's general immorality. Such a work undoubtedly became embedded in the minds of the future Methodist movement, but the broadside had more lasting consequences in this Age. Certain actors and actresses were fined, and playwrights, in turn, had to alter the way their dramas were constructed. This put an end to the classic period of Restoration comedy, and the plays had to take a new direction: the 'reformed' dramas of the immediate post-Reformation Age (broadly between 1700 and 1737). It was here that a Cornish voice emerged once again.

The Reformation had another crucial impact on the theatre. While it would appear that both female and male actors performed in medieval Britain, the Tudor Age had prompted a clampdown on women upon the stage; certainly, in the Renaissance, no women were allowed to perform. Since the new reign welcomed innovation, women were allowed both to perform and write for the theatre.[158] On stage at least, women were treated as intellectually equal to men, and in some cases as intellectually superior. However, their openness in discussing sexual manners was fuel to the flame of the theatre's critics, such as Collier. Therefore, the emancipation of women in the theatre had to be achieved in a somewhat guarded way. This is particularly true of the kind of comedy of manners that evolved. Here lies the cool paradox that passion needs to be treated dispassionately in the acutely observed social context of the period. Certainly this emancipation of the stage for women would have consequences for female actors in Cornwall. The difficulty for the Age was that theatre was not always attended for the drama itself. It was a place to be seen and heard. Whisper and gossip in the audience were as important as events onstage. Therefore it is not surprising that the audience's obsession with actresses and their supposedly spicy lifestyles sometimes spilled over on to the stage itself, compromising the integrity of the plays. Ironically, part of the original justification for allowing women on the stage had been the moral wish to cleanse the theatre of 'cross-dressing'. However, this project failed, because many of the plays called for female actors to dress as men, with some actresses flaunting normally concealed parts of their bodies.

The first theatre to open outside of London was in Smock Alley in Dublin. This was in 1662. Taste there, however, was dominated by that from London, for companies would often tour there in the summer. Theatre in the rest of the islands was slow to develop. Bristol, for instance, rejected a bid to build a new playhouse until after 1730, despite fashionable Bath already developing a venue. These south-west venues probably dictated the kind of work which was shown any further towards the west, although there is no evidence of theatre building or performances. Presumably Cornwall would still have been dependent on touring companies, roughing it out, on a road system that would not be greatly upgraded until the economic boom of the 1750s. We know very little about the content of such productions, the venues they played in, or the audiences they attracted. Presumably, however, centres in Cornwall looked to places such as Bristol and Bath to determine taste and fashion. The touring companies would have struggled to make it into the far depths of Cornwall, although there is no reason to assume that they did not merge with a somewhat reinvigorated post-Cromwellian 'feast' and festival culture. However, the ritual year had inevitably been damaged by the Puritan shut-down, so there were perhaps fewer venues and audiences. Territories such as Cornwall were in essence still viewed as separate entities for London managers and promoters. Sadly, very few dramas of peripheral provenance come to have any impact on the Britain-wide repertoire.

In London, meanwhile, dramas of the past were also mined as a source. Shakespeare and his contemporaries were re-evaluated, and adapted for current tastes. Not surprisingly, the adaptations made all kinds of compromises and changes to suit soft-centred morality. Nathum Tate took his hand to the Cornish and 'devolved Britain'-flavoured *King Lear*, omitting the Fool, preserving Cordelia to survive and marry Edgar, and ending the play with Lear living to a ripe old age. Much of the blame for this kind of work fell on the two great theatres: Drury Lane and Covent Garden. There was enormous rivalry between them, and each would do anything they could to see that seats were filled. One south-western writer (if not a Cornish one) turned this rivalry within London to advantage. This was the Barnstaple-born John Gay (1685-1732), who took his ballad opera *The Beggar's Opera* to Drury Lane. Drury Lane rejected it, but in 1728 John Rich's theatre in Lincoln's Inn Field produced Gay's work to phenomenal success. Gay shows how a dramatist from the south west could develop work in London, and that he knew how to play off the theatres against one another. The political satire of *The Beggar's Opera* was not quite light-hearted enough for some however. In the drama, Sir Robert Walpole's government had been satirised, and the following year he had Gay's sequel, *Polly*, suppressed.

Perhaps because of such difficulties, and ones which followed, in 1737 the infamous Licensing Act was passed to ensure that all new dramas were submitted for approval to the Lord Chamberlain, and only two Patent houses (Drury Lane and Covent Garden) were allowed to operate as places of entertainment. Many nervous owners of smaller theatres shut their doors. However, promoters and managers realised that there were ways around this legislation. Instead of promoting straight plays they advertised 'Concerts of Vocal and Instrumental Music' divided into two parts. It looked innocent enough, but between the two parts of the concert were plays 'performed gratis by persons for their diversion'. Thus, the theatrical world was once again able to subvert authority. The fickle application of theatrical law is a running theme throughout the eighteenth century. The historian Paul Langford has argued that the Stage Licensing Act of 1737 was 'the one undoubted and comprehensive victory in Walpole's extended warfare with the intellectuals of his day' but also notes that 'the British reputation for passing law which nobody bothered to observe was so marked that it was considered an important element in the libertarian tradition'.[159] Thus, there is general agreement that the Act arrested the development of theatre in Britain, but such an agreement should be tempered with the view that it was frequently ignored throughout the rest of the (dis)united Kingdom.[160] As we shall see later, unsanctioned playhouses proliferated, particularly in territories like Cornwall, but because the only records of drama contained in the British Library are the ones sanctioned by the Lord Chamberlain, this gives a skewed picture of what performance was actually occurring. Performance at fairs, festivals and at other points in the ritual year must have continued, suggesting that there was an undercurrent of theatrical subversion in spite of the wish to reform and 'tame' the theatre. That said, the Act of 1737 did steer dramatists away from political satire, and onto either adaptations of 'safe' past narratives or to observations of human behaviour, all this despite the fact that Britain would almost constantly be at war for the remainder of the century. The only apparent reference to this state of affairs was that many of the characters in such dramas were soldiers or sailors on leave. The complexity of life within Britain or Cornwall itself was barely touched. Nevertheless, as Whetter demonstrates in his survey of notable individuals of the eighteenth century (William Hals, James Gibbs Junior, Warwick Mohun, Thomas Tonkin, Admiral Boscawen, William Borlase, Admiral Pellew, John Opie, Harry Carter and Christopher Wallis), there were important and significant social, political, cultural and economic changes occurring on a large scale[161] – not least of which were the expansion and development of the extractive industries in Cornwall,[162] and the move to unite the 'Kingdom' in the Act of Union of 1801.

Theatre in the periphery developed in the light of flowering urban culture there, and by the construction of a pan-British road network, primarily through the Turnpike Acts (of which there were some 340 between 1750 and 1770 alone). Thus Cornwall, too, had a turnpike network feeding into a pan-British system, facilitating a new kind of mobility for theatrical practitioners. Regional touring circuits were established, permitting seasonal visitations from the centre. The London repertoire continued to dominate, though the notion of rewriting to cater for non-metropolitan practice began to filter through. There were therefore rich pickings to be had by the London stars. The regional circuits were 'un-policed' compared to London. Roger Kemble (operating between 1766 and 1781) toured his company as far in to the south-west peninsula as Exeter,[163] while Thomas Jefferson (1732-1807), founder of one of the most famous theatrical dynasties in America, ran his operation from a base in Plymouth for some thirty years, from 1765 to 1795.[164] If smaller companies made it to Cornwall, then they would have aligned themselves, as ever was the case, to fairs, festivals and feasts.

The aftermath of the Interregnum brought about a well-documented further decline in the use and promotion of the Cornish language, contribut-ing factors of which were discussed in some detail in William Scawen's *Antiquities Cornuontanic: The Causes of Cornish Speech's Decay*, published in 1680.[165] Scawen strongly argued, as we already know, that the loss of the miracle plays was a massive factor in the decline of the language. Crucially also, however, the loss and burning of ancient Cornish records at Restormel during the Civil War, as observed by Scawen, had implications for theatre. The likelihood is that the castle would have housed some texts of dramatic interest, possibly even connecting back to Tristania. Further suppression of any remnants of Celticity from church services during the Puritanical years of Cromwell would also have precluded the survival of any remaining community dramas. A few writers, however, as detailed by Ellis, Weatherhill, and Kent and Saunders, were actively trying to fire interest in the language and its literature.[166] The ending of the use of the 'Troyance Tongue' on the stage had really stopped at the start of the seventeenth century, but alongside the linguistic shift was also a cultural one. Amongst the group of writers active in this late renaissance of writing in Cornwall, none seemed particularly interested in writing drama. This is a curious moment because, given the continuity of drama in Cornwall (as a literary medium), we might expect to see this group of writers re-engaging with the genre. Possible reasons for this lack of engagement are the fact that the tradition in Cornwall used verse drama, and this group of writers was simply not competent in this form, or, alternatively, that they saw the genre as, frankly, outmoded and maybe even believed that drama had inadvertently contributed to the decline of Cornish language and literature. It is therefore not surprising that the genres they did choose were, on the whole, not dramatic. Instead it was folktale, poetry, translation (particularly of sections from the Bible), and proverbs that dominated.[167] The writers were actually taking their cues from other pan-European literary forms; ironically anything but drama. The group of writers was actually also quite small, and concentrated for the most part in the far west of Cornwall. Among them were Nicholas, John and Thomas Boson, Oliver Pender from Mousehole, William Gwavas of Paul, the Sancreed-based William Rowe, and Henry Usticke and John Tonkin from St Just-in-Penwith. Further to the east, at St Agnes, lived Thomas Tonkin, who also formed part of this group.

Some themes were, however, retained. *A Cornish Song to the Tune of the Modest Maid of Kent*,[168] written by John Tonkin (c.1695), advises hard work and trust in God: issues which had always been the message in the earlier dramas. The various versions of *John of Chyanhor* (recorded by Edward Lhuyd and Nicholas Boson[169]) suggest, according to Brian Murdoch, a European influence from Germany,[170] again pointing to the multi-cultural dimension of Cornish writing. Various poems and advice on marriage by this group (in particular work by William Allen and James Jenkins) were linking to a continuity (of which they were most probably unaware) stretching back to the *The Charter Endorsement*. Perhaps the only real exception to the general trend away from work on drama was the activities of John Keigwin (1641-c.1710) of Mousehole. Keigwin was Scawen's nephew, a native speaker and scholar of the language, who had been given three Cornish manuscripts by Sir Jonathan Trelawny, the Bishop of Exeter. Trelawny had asked Keigwin to translate them into English, and it is perhaps at this moment that modern translations of earlier Cornish-language drama first emerge. Evidence for this comes from Edmund Gibson's additions to William Camden's *Britannica* in 1695. In the Cornwall section we learn that:

> three books in Cornish are all that can be found. One is written in an old court-hand on Velam, and in 1036 verses contains the History of the Passion of our Saviour... The other two are translated out of the Bodleian Library; one is translated, and the other is now a translating by Mr. Keigwin, the only person perhaps that understands the tongue.[171]

The first book referred to here is *Pascon Agan Arluth* or *Sacrament an Alter*, while the second two are clearly the *Ordinalia* and *The Creacion of the World*. Keigwin has also offered a translation into Cornish of the letter from Charles I, thanking the Cornish people in 1643 for their services and support during the Civil War, which is presently preserved in English in a number of churches throughout Cornwall. If anyone were to write original drama on the scale of the above work, then it perhaps would have been Keigwin, but sadly, it seems, he did not write original work. If he did, then none has survived.

Contemporary with Keigwin was Edward Lhuyd (1660-1709). Lhuyd had Welsh parents, but was born in Shropshire.[172] He rose to become Keeper of the Ashmolean Museum at Oxford, and between 1697 and 1701 carried out philological study in all the Celtic territories, visiting Cornwall, as Williams details, in 1700.[173] It was Lhuyd who used Keigwin's translations of the *Ordinalia* and *The Creacion of the World* to assist in the composition of his *Archaeologia Britannica*, but who also identified the 'Vocabulary' in the Cottonian Library in London as being Old Cornish. This document, as we know, contained a number of theatrical and para-theatical terms. Compared to the indigenous writers in Cornwall, Lhuyd was also something of an exception in the literary construction of Cornish. For some reason, he had identified the importance of the use of the *englyn* (a three-lined unit of verse) within the Cornish literary tradition, a concept later confirmed by the work of Nicholas Williams on *Bewnans Ke*.[174] Lhuyd's poem, *On the Death of King William III a British Song in the Cornish Dialect; according to the pattern of the poets of the sixth century* (1703), was a spirited elegy in support of the Protestant cause, for which Cornish soldiers fought at the Battle of the Boyne. If *englyns* or sustained *englyns* (*englynion*) has been part of the verse dramatic traditions in Cornwall, then Lhuyd was certainly working along the right lines to recreate it. The sad fact was that in reality, however, as far as extant texts go, new Cornish-language drama was apparently silent from 1600 to 1900. New energy in the dramatic genre had to come from writers using English, and it was coming both from indigenous writers and from those outside of Cornwall. Lhuyd's work, however, was of crucial importance in the twentieth century for the active revival of dramatic writing in Cornish.[175]

All of this preservation work clearly caught the eye of one dramatist operating in Exeter. This was Andrew Brice (1690-1773), who early in his life was an apprentice printer but in his thirties turned his hand to playwriting, developing in 1727 a drama titled *The Exmoor Scolding*.[176] Brice's drama was highly attuned to the dialect and accent of Exmoor, and there is a pervading interest throughout the work in the preservation of this old socio-linguistic culture. Brice's fear seems to be that because of modernity, this will soon be lost. To advance his argument, in the preface to the drama he comments, with some degree of wonder, that the Bible was being translated into Cornish:

> As it's natural and full of Honour to love one's Country so it's natural (and why not as praiseworthy) to love its language. And I hear of a Gentleman in Cornwall (in Antique Renowned for Love to Saints and Shipwrecks) who has taken noble mighty pains in translating the Bible to Cornish or Cornubian Welch.[177]

It would seem that Brice got hold of the wrong end of the stick. Although writers such as William Rowe were translating parts of the Bible in Cornish, the full text was, in fact, a long way off. Brice would seem to be thinking of John Keigwin, but Keigwin was involved in translating several Bible-inspired manuscripts, and not the Bible itself. Still, it would seem the fame of this endeavour had spread to Exeter and its surrounds (perhaps through the endorsement of Sir Jonathan Trelawny). Brice qualifies Cornish for his readership, perhaps thinking that it would not be understood; therefore adding the phrase 'Cornubian Welch'.[178] Richard Polwhele felt that Brice's drama was an interesting comparison to Cornish drama, and that in his view, there were useful Cornu-English similarities:

Thomasin:	Lock! Wilmot, vor why vor ded'st roily zo upon ma up to Challacomb Rowl? – Ees dedent thenk he had'st a be zich a Labb o' tha Tongue. – What a Vengance! wart betwatled, or wart tha baggaged; – or hadst tha took a shord, or paddled?
Wilmot:	I roily upon tha, ya gurt, banging, muxy Drawbreech? – Noa, 'twas thee roilst upon me up to Daraty Vogwill's Upzitting, when tha vung'st (and to be hang'd to tha!) to Rabbin – 'Shou'd zem tha wart zeck arter Me-at and Me-al, – And zo tha merst, by ort es know, wey guttering; as gutter tha wutt whan tha cam'st to good Tackling. – But zome zed Shoor and shoor tha ded'st bet make wise, no zee nig tha young Joey Heaff-filed wou'd come to zlack thy Boodize and whare awou'd be O vore or no. – Bet 'twas thy old Disyease, Chun.[179]

Brice does provide us with such a sample of Exmoor-based drama of this period, but Polwhele wanted more of a Celtic connection from it. In reality, however, Polwhele's scholarship was flawed: there is a good deal of difference between the Cornu-English of Cornwall (which has a visible and coherent sub-strata of Cornish) and what he observed in Brice – the Exmoor dialect of English having little Celtic substrata. Polwhele admitted some of the difficulties, eventually noting that, 'The natives of the Southams greatly differ in their phraseology and pronunciation from those of the North of Devon. They have more of the Cornish, than the Exmoorian, in their language and conversation'.[180]

The stage was therefore set for the further transfer of Cornish to English. One important English writer to emerge in this Post-Reformation period of change was George Lillo (1693-1739). Lillo appeared to have an interest in Cornwall, and decided to develop a new play named *The Cornish or Penryn Tragedy, or The Fatal Curiosity*. The origins of his play lay in a so-called 'black letter' printed chapbook from 1618 which was originally titled *News from Pe[n]rin in Cornwall*.[181] The story is a moral tale, drawing on some of the central narratives of European folk literature,[182] such as wicked stepmothers and over-ambition. The story is characterised by what I have termed elsewhere as 'a Renaissance Cornishman, who consciously decides to alter his fate, rather than be a victim of it'.[183] Lillo's reformed world is one of modernity and exploration projected back onto the Elizabethan Age. Growing economic activity and trade are central to the story's themes:

A Most Bloody and Un-exampled Murder Very lately committed by a Father on his owne Sonne (who was lately returned from the Indyes) at the Instigation of a Mercilesse Step-mother together with their severall most wretched endes, being all performed in the Month of September last Anno 1618.[184]

Lillo was said to be originally a jeweller of Flemish descent, although he went on to write what was one of the most successful prose domestic tragedies of his Age, *The London Merchant, or The History of George Barnwell*. *The Fatal Curiosity* was first produced by the theatrical innovator Henry Fielding (1707-1754) in 1736,[185] and it must have remained a popular drama on the stage in Cornwall and elsewhere. Although certainly performed in this century in Cornwall, it was really in the early nineteenth century that the text rose to the height of its fame.[186] Lillo was one of the earliest dramatists to recognise that the exotic, peripheral and strangely Celtic aspects of Cornwall could be employed in his chosen art-form. According to Davies, 'the fable is founded on a melancholic fact which happened in a village on the western coast'.[187] The drama was written in blank verse, and this must have seemed quite archaic for the later nineteenth-century Cornish audience. However, the plot is so archetypal that its popularity continued, and has done so, well into the twentieth and twenty-first centuries.[188]

In Lillo's version, Old Wilmot (the father) is feeling the stress of poverty and so, under the encouragement of his wife Agnes, murders the stranger who has left a casket with them. The stranger is his son (Young Wilmot), whom he thought had perished in a shipwreck. Lillo is a skilled playwright, and the text offers a good deal of insight into Cornish identity, ideology and imagination during the period. He also has a sense of place in the piece. In the opening of the play Old Wilmot philosophises about the movement of the sun, eventually asking his servant Randal where he has been. Randal responds with news of the previous night's storm, which is the ignition point of the tragedy:

Randal:	Not out of Penryn, sir; but to the strand,
	To hear what news from Falmouth since the storm
	Of wind last night.
Old Wilmot:	It was a dreadful one.
Randal:	Some found it so. A noble ship from India
	Ent'ring in the harbour, run upon a rock,
	And there was lost.
Old Wilmot:	What came of those on board her?
Randal:	Some few are sav'd, but much the greater part,
	'Tis thought, are perished.[189]

This gives the audience a context for events, when in the real world Sir Walter Raleigh had been betrayed by Sir Lewis Stuckley. This is important, since it demonstrates that the domestic tragedy matches a wider political tragedy of the Age in which the play is set. The female heroines of the play are Charlot and Maria, who spend much time lamenting the fact that the coast is a dangerous and tragic place, Charlot noting: 'What terror and amazement must they feel, Who die by ship-wreck!'[190] Charlot is pining for the Young Wilmot who has travelled overseas, but is put in her place by Agnes, when she says: ''Tis just as likely Wilmot should return, As we become your foes.'[191] The play then changes scene to the 'port of Penryn' where we meet Young Wilmot, dressed in 'foreign habit', who has survived the shipwreck. However, the young man is perhaps a little wary of Cornwall's barbarity (which might have prompted some laughter in performance), suggesting that some reform (as elsewhere) might be in order, but also seemingly indicating that the Cornish are treated with a rough hand:

Y. Wilmot:	It is a scandal,
	Tho' malice must acquit the better sort,
	The rude unpolisht people here in Cornwall
	Have long laid under, and with too much justice:
	Could our superiors find some happy means

> To mend it, they would gain immortal honour:
> For 'tis an evil grown almost invet'rate,
> And asks a bold and skilful hand to cure.[192]

As we might expect from a text from this period, England and Cornwall are often conflated, especially when Young Wilmot remarks on the land being a 'seat of plenty, liberty and health',[193] all of which forms heavy irony later on. The Second Act follows with a neat piece of disguise, with Charlot meeting the stranger, but not recognising him as Young Wilmot.[194] She feels he has forgotten her, and comments, 'Would'st thou die, my Wilmot!' Randal meanwhile learns of Young Wilmot's return, though the latter's wish to return to his parents as a stranger to 'improve their pleasure by surprise'[195] is clearly an unwise move. Randal is perhaps the key character in the entire drama, since he is the one caught between telling the truth to Charlot and Old Wilmot, and the wishes of Young Wilmot. In a political sense, he is also the most aware character, and perhaps the one upon whom the Cornish audience may have modelled themselves. At one point he thinks he must leave Penryn, aware that 'this is the native uncontested right, The fair inheritance of ev'ry Briton, That dares put in his claim'. Randal comments that his 'choice is made' for he alone can see the chaos that will occur. Lillo also appears to make him purposely astute, noting the difference in status of Cornwall and England. He comments, 'A long farewell to Cornwall, and to England!'[196] This contrasts with the tragic naïvety of Young Wilmot, who does not understand the geo-political relationship of the 'western coast'. Because of his desire to remain incognito, Young Wilmot then hands Agnes the casket of treasure. Lillo then writes a powerful soliloquy for Agnes, in which she contemplates events:

Agnes: Who should this stranger be? And then this casket – ,
          He says it is of value, and yet trusts it,
          As if a trifle, to a stranger's hand –
          His confidence amazes me – Perhaps
          It is not what he says – I'm strongly tempted
          To open it, and see – ...
          ... – Must I resign it? Must I give it back?
          Am I in love with misery and want? –
          To rob myself, and court so vast a loss? –
          – Retain it then – But how? There is a way –
          Why sinks my heart? Why does my blood run cold?
          Why am I thrill'd with horror? 'Tis not choice,
          But dire necessity suggests the thought.[197]

Agnes, therefore, is Cornwall's Lady Macbeth. She is evil personified on the streets of Penryn. When contemplating the murder of the stranger, she shows a cool and calculating personality, although Lillo chooses to present the actual murder somewhat farcically – with the dagger being dropped before the stabbing occurs offstage, in another room. The gory finale is made all the more dramatic by the words of Charlot: 'To wretched mortals be not quite extinguish'd, And terrors only guard your awful thrones',[198] with Old Wilmot stabbing Agnes, and Randal offering his condolences to the father and Charlot, ending with words of advice for the audience: 'The ripe in virtue never die too soon.'[199]

One dramatist operating on this reformed early- to mid-eighteenth-century stage was the Truro-born dramatist, actor and theatre manager Samuel Foote (1720-1777). Foote stands as one of the most important figures in the story of the theatre of Cornwall, and yet Cornish cultural history has seemingly, so far, chosen to ignore him.[200] There are perhaps two reasons for this. In his day, Foote was a highly controversial figure, with many of his satirical plays purposefully causing trouble and mischief, which meant that after his death, Cornwall did not champion him as one of its greats. Radical thought in this sense, is hardly one of Cornwall's general contributions to culture. Paradoxically, of course, that is what now makes him so interesting and important to consider. The second reason he has been forgotten is that earlier Cornish literary scholars looked at his dramas, and apparently saw nothing remarkably Cornish about them, and so have dismissed his work as Anglo-centric and therefore of little relevance.[201] This, I would argue, is wrong-headed, because a closer look at his work demonstrates some highly interesting examples of eighteenth-century stage Cornishness, as well as an engagement with that most Cornish of eighteenth-century faiths: Methodism. Far from dismissing Foote as insignificant to our story, he stands as a figure coming out of Cornwall to become one of the most influential dramatists writing for the British stage. Put another way, there would seem to be no-one in the entire Anglo-Cornish theatrical history who matches his output, or his success. Those are two very good reasons why Foote's name should be foregrounded and his Cornishness more often celebrated. A 'nationalist' literary critique of Cornwall has not, of course, served Foote any better; he is too quickly viewed as someone ignoring his cultural roots and identity, and preferring betterment in London, in England. This view should also be overturned, however, for in some ways his writing outlines a nationalist view of Cornwall far better than previous dramatists, or those who came after him.

Foote's life itself was huge drama. He was born at Truro into a wealthy family, his father being John Foote, who at various times held the positions of

SAMUEL FOOTE Esqr

Printed for J. Hinton, at the King's Arms in Paternoster Row.

Fig. 46. An engraving of Samuel Foote (1720-1777).

Mayor of Truro, Member of Parliament for Tiverton, and a Commissioner in the Prize Office. His mother was Eleanor Goodere, the daughter of baronet Goodere of Hereford. Goodere's family were 'eccentric… whose peculiarities ranged from the harmless to the malevolent', and there is a suggestion from at least one of his biographers, Douglas Howard, that he may have inherited these qualities.[202] His early education was in Truro, but he was later educated at the collegiate school at Worcester, and then at Worcester College, Oxford. On coming of age, Foote inherited a fortune when one of his uncles, Sir John Dinely Goodere, was murdered by another uncle, Captain Samuel Goodere. It was this inheritance that bankrolled his academic career. It was while at Oxford that Foote first showed signs of comic genius, mimicking his tutors and fellow students, although missing many of his classes. Oxford dis-enrolled him on 28 January, 1740 and Foote left without taking his degree. He had spent three years there, where he dissipated his fortune. However, the experience had not been without its benefits. He had, while at Oxford, gained a classical education, which obviously assisted his later ingenious prose style. His next move was to study law at the Middle Temple in London, and despite him engaging with the banter of the legal world, one anonymous later observer says that he 'found it dull'.[203] Finding himself in debt, Foote married one Mary Hickes (or Hicks) on 10 January 1741. Hickes came with a sizeable dowry and so he was able to continue in the style to which he was accustomed. The marriage seems a convenience for him, however, since his contemporaries say that he mistreated her, and then left her when his own financial situation improved.[204]

By this time Foote had been attracted to the trendy Bedford Coffee House in Covent Garden, and to the world of London theatre, his period in the debtor's prison in 1742 possibly forcing his hand. Fortunately Foote came under the tutelage of the notable Irish-born actor Charles Macklin (c.1690-1797). Macklin taught Foote the basics of performance, and it seems he was a swift learner, for less than a year later Foote was starring opposite Macklin's Iago, playing Othello at the Haymarket Theatre in February 1744. This performance was not particularly successful but it did lay the ground for Foote's own acting career, in that he was quite adaptable, and could perform a variety of roles – including women. What is noticeable about this version of *Othello* was that it was illegally produced under the Licensing Act of 1737, which lay down, in the most forceful terms, the conditions of performance. The Act clearly forbade the production of plays in theatres not holding letters patent, or approved by the Lord Chamberlain. During his career, the Licensing Act's regulations were something Foote was to run into on numerous occasions. As we know, the way the Haymarket, and other theatres of the Age, got around the Act was to hold musical concerts, with the plays thrown in for free. After performing in Dublin in the summer of 1744, Foote then returned to London, joining the company at the Theatre Royal, Drury Lane, where he worked alongside some of the most famous actors of the Age – Peg Woffington (c.1720-1760), Spranger Barry (1719-1777) and David Garrick (1717-1779) – enjoying roles in George Farquhar's *The Constant Couple* and John Vanbrugh's *The Relapse*. In these plays, Foote began to show his talent for mimicry.

An important development came in 1746, when Foote obtained the lease for the Haymarket Theatre (then called the Little Theatre). The Haymarket was where he and Macklin had illegally produced *Othello*, but with his managerial status in place, Foote could now properly begin to write and produce drama. His first play to open there was *The Diversions of the Morning or, A Dish of Chocolate* – a one-man show, with Foote taking the lead in a comic satire on contemporary public figures and actors. One of the people satirised was the famous surgeon, Chevalier Taylor, who rode from court to court in Europe selling his skill, and was often presented as a quack doctor or 'mountebank'. A commentator observed that:

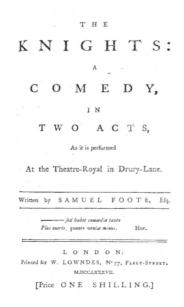

Fig. 47. A frontispiece for a published version of *The Knights*, Samuel Foote's Cornish-themed drama.

The Diversions of the Morning was first met with some little opposition from the civil magistrates of Westminster, under the function of the act of parliament for limiting the number of playhouses, but our author being patronised by many of the principal nobility and gentry, the opposition was over-ruled, and after altering the title to that of *Giving Tea*, representing it through a run of upwards of forty mornings to crowded and splendid audiences.[205]

His second drama, was *An Auction of Pictures*, which opened at the Haymarket in 1748. This play was a satire of the dramatist and novelist Henry Fielding (1707-1754), and the production commenced a war of words between the two. Clearly Foote was out to make a name for himself. Again, Foote played all the characters in the piece: among them, 'Sir Thomas de Veil, then the acting justice of peace for Westminster, also Mr. Cock, the celebrated auctioneer and the famous orator Henley'.[206] His next work was the more ambitious *The Knights* (1748), a play which will be examined in further depth below, since it was a vehicle to satirise Italian opera as well as, significantly for this volume, the gentry of Cornwall. *The Knights* was a considerable success, helping to deflect the previous criticism, and earning enough to fund time for him in fashionable Paris. However, Foote had another target in mind: the burgeoning market of art and antiques. This he aimed at in 1752, with *Taste*, a play in which 'the general intention of it [was] to point out the numerous impositions that persons of fortune and fashion daily suffer in the pursuit of what is called Taste... from the tricks and confederacies of painters'.[207] One of the central characters in it was the very Cornish-named Lady Pentweazel. She was played by Foote (looking, in a painting at the time by Robert Quirke, quite the ugliest Lady ever[208]), who wore a large headdress (satirising the elaborate headdresses of the day), with feathers that fell out through the course of the play. The piece had a prologue written for it by Mr Garrick, who seems to extol the superiority of the Briton or Britain:

> Before this Court, I Peter Puff appear,
> A Briton born, and bred an auctioneer;
> Who for myself, and eke a hundred others,
> My useful benefit, learned bawling Brothers,
> With much Humility and Fear implore ye
> To lay our present Desp'rate case before ye.[209]

Although a high burlesque comedy of some note, with savage satire of the foibles of predatory dealers, its run was not successful. It was performed on only five occasions. The rethink came in the form of *The Englishman in Paris*.

This was a comedy in two acts, first performed at Covent Garden in 1753, full of the kind of topical allusions which characterised the whole of Foote's work. Starring Macklin in the part of Buck, and 'Miss Macklin' (Mary Macklin [c.1734-781], his daughter) as Lucinda (in which she showed 'her various qualifications of music, singing and dancing in all which she obtained universal applause'[210]), the piece satirised the boorish behaviours of the 'English' gentleman abroad, and was viewed by one later observer as being 'designed to expose the absurdity of sending our youth abroad, to catch the vices and follies of our neighbouring nations'.[211] Interestingly, the same observer notes critically that it was 'somewhat an inconsistency in the portrait of the Englishman, that scarcely renders the execution answerable to the intention'.[212] Was this, we may ask, Foote, the Cornishman, not quite being able to match the 'English' intention of it? Perhaps this was the case. Despite the thoughts of this reviewer, this play was generally deemed highly successful. Around this time Charles Macklin had opened his London School of Oratory for budding actors. Foote, never one to miss a chance, opened a mock one of his own at the Haymarket, and wrote one of his most famous pieces, to test Macklin and his ilk, which has come to be known as 'The Great Panjandrum':

> So she went into the garden to cut a cabbage-leaf to make an apple-pie; and at the same time a great she-bear, coming up the street, pops its head into the shop. "What! No soap?" So he died, and she very imprudently married the barber; and there were present the Picninnies, and the Joblillies, and the Garyalies, and the grand Panjandrum himself, with the little round button at top, and they all fell to playing the game of catch-as-catch-can till the gunpowder ran out at the heels of their boots.[213]

The conflict became real when Macklin himself appeared at one of the sessions, but both Foote and Macklin appear to have revelled in the banter. Given the success of *The Englishman in Paris*, it was not long before he returned with a sequel. This was *The Englishman returned from Paris* (1756) at Covent Garden. An observer of the time wrote of it: 'Wherein the Englishman who was a brute, is now a coxcomb, from being absurdly averse to anything foreign, he is grown into a detestation of every thing domestic; and rejects the very woman, now possessed of every advantage, whom he before was rushing headlong into marriage.'[214] A now lost play followed. This farce was *The Green-Room Squabble or a Battle Royal between the Queen of Babylon and the Daughter of Darius*. It is generally thought to have been a satire on Nathaniel Lee's *The Rival Queens*, a play that was very popular in Cornwall in the early part of the next century. In one production of Lee's epic, the two performers Peg Woffington and George Anne Bellamy (c.1731-1788) conflicted over costumes. Apparently, Bellamy's Parisian fashions made Wofffington drive her off stage using a dagger.

Having satirised others, Foote's next work, *The Author*, which played at Drury Lane in 1757, turned its focus onto the world of writing. The plot concerns the father of a poor author, who disguises himself in order to spy upon his son. Foote created the role of Cadwallader for himself, using it to satirise John Aprice, a renowed patron of authors. The name Cadwallader is interesting, since he was historically the king of Gwynedd of the seventh century, the last Welsh king to lay claim to lordship over all of Britain, a figure still known enough in the English public's imagination to invite ridicule.[215] A critical reviewer wrote of the piece that 'it was written only for the sake of affording to the writer of it an opportunity of exerting his talents of mimickry, at the expense of a gentleman of fame and fortune, Mr Aprice, whose particularities of character, although entirely inoffensive, were rendered the butt of public ridicule in the part of Cadwallader'.[216] Audiences flocked to the theatre, but the content was considered too controversial, and so it was soon shut down by the Lord Chamberlain. The wit of the piece has not much dated however. In one section, the character Vamp comments, 'Books are like women... To strike they must be well-dressed; fine feathers make fine birds; a good paper, an elegant type, a handsome Motto, and a catching title, has drove many a dull treatise thro' three editions'.[217]

His most famous play, *The Minor* (1760), was a satire directed against Methodism, in which Foote mimicked George Whitefield (1714-70) the popular evangelical preacher who had been under the influence of John and Charles Wesley while at Oxford.[218] After a trip to Georgia with the Wesleys, he attracted much attention at large open-air meetings with his fervent and emotional sermons. Interestingly, Whitefield, the son of a widow innkeeper at Gloucester, had actually been very interested in the theatre, and used theatrical methods to enact his sermons – something at which it was obviously difficult for Foote to resist poking fun. He was also cross-eyed (having Strabismus vision), though thousands flocked to hear him preach because of his dramatic style. Whitefield's views eventually diverged from the Wesleys and he became increasingly Calvinistic, later founding 'Lady Huntingdon's Connection', a Calvinistic Methodist group.[219] Foote called his stage 'Whitefield' Dr Squintum (following his ocular difficulties) and the play remains Foote's most powerful work. Foote must, by this point, have known the influence of Methodism in certain parts of Britain, and especially Cornwall.

This three-act comedy is worth looking at more closely. An earlier version of the play was presented in Dublin in January of 1760, with a young, new mimic named Tate Wilkinson (1739-1803). The play was a failure, but Foote

The MINOR.

Fig. 48. An illustration of Samuel Foote in the Methodist-themed play *The Minor*, playing the role of Mrs Cole.

returned to London, redrafting and expanding the original content. When the play opened in London, condemnation came from many quarters but, as Foote realised, this controversy contributed to its success; it eventually ran for thirty-eight nights, playing to full houses at the Haymarket. Though 'performed entirely by a young and inexperienced company',[220] the receipts from it made Foote a rich man again. Although it was Foote's greatest success, the evolution of the play was painful. As an article in *Universal Magazine* recalls, before its premiere in London, Foote showed the text of *The Minor* to Thomas Secker (1693-1768), the Archbishop of Canterbury, to seek his advice and approval. Secker objected to several passages, but there was one in particular to which he objected. This was the sequence when Mrs Cole refers to herself as a 'lost sheep'. Apparently, Secker viewed this as being inappropriate since it was a sacred passage. Wishing the piece to be successful, Foote asked Secker to strike through any other objectionable passages, with the piece, upon publication, having a note attached: 'Revised and Corrected by the Archbishop of Canterbury.'[221] It was perhaps such attacks that later caused the Methodist movement to be so averse to theatre (an aversion particularly felt in Cornwall). The holier-than-thou attitude of the Methodists is represented in several other characters in the play. Here is just one example of Sir George's high-handed approach in response to Mrs Cole:

> Sir George: I am, madam, treating your friends here with a cold collation, and
> you are opportunely come for your share. The little gentlewoman
> is safe, and in much better hands than you designed her.
> Abominable hypocrite! who tottering under the load of irreverent
> age and infamous diseases, inflexibly proceed in the practice of
> every vice, impiously prostituting the most sacred institutions to
> the most infernal purposes.[222]

One place where Foote's satire works particularly well in this drama is the Epilogue. In such lines, one can easily see Foote's willingness to satirise himself as well as others. This is coupled with a supreme awareness of the theatre being consigned to the same physical space as the Devil. However, there is a sting in the tale, since Foote promises that any monies that are collected would, Methodist-like, be given to the poor. This enabled the dramatist to pile irony upon irony, and the following speech, in which the character Shift addresses Sir George, summarises how much Foote had sharpened his dramaturgy:

Shift: Ay, that might be, ye cry, with those poor souls;
But we ne'er had a rasher for the coals,
And d'ye deserve it? How d'ye spend your days?
In pastimes, prodigality, and plays/
Let's go see Foote? ah, Foote's a precious limb?
Old Nick wil soon a football make of him!
For foremost rows in side-boxes you shove,
Think you to meet with side-boxes above?
Where giggling girls and powder'd fops may sit,
No, you will all be cramm'd into the pit,
And crowd the house for Satan's benefit.
Oh, what you snivel? well, do no more,
Drop, to atone, your money at the door,
And, if I please, – I'll give it to the poor.[223]

Other works came in quick succession in the 1760s: *The Lyar* (1762), first presented at Covent Garden, had 'some strokes of humour in it' but 'its success was indifferent' there being 'not a sufficiency of incident and sentiment to engage the audience's hearts'.[224] *The Orators* (also 1762) met with considerable success, again performed at the Little Theatre in the Haymarket. It apparently had a great variety of characters, notably a Printer from Ireland, who we are told had all 'the disadvantages of age, person, and address, and even the deficiency of a leg' (the latter a somewhat ironic point of characterisation considering the accident that would later befall Foote).[225] *The Mayor of Garrat* followed in 1763, with Foote taking the title role himself – a city militia officer named Major Sturgeon – while 1764 brought a performance of *The Patron*, again at the Haymarket. One of Foote's ongoing targets was antiquarians (whom presumably he had encountered on several occasions in Cornwall). Foote believed that such individuals were keenly out of step with the modern world of the 1760s, and so this text examined another 'superficial pretender to wit and learning, [who] affords his countenance to the protection of a set of contemptible writings, for the sake of the incentive offered by money'.[226] This theme was continued in *The Commissary* in 1765.

1766 brought about a change of circumstances; sadly, a case of life mirroring art. When he had joked about his character of the one-legged Irish printer, it was unlikely that he knew the same injury would come to him. Foote had been out riding with Prince Edward Augustus (1739-1767), Duke of York and Albany, when he was thrown from his horse, with the injury costing him his leg. Such a disability was not going to stop Foote. Indeed, as ever, he used the problem of his new wooden leg to his advantage, writing the self-deprecating

The Devil upon Two Sticks for the Haymarket in 1768. Drawing on the publicity of his riding accident, the play was a marked success abounding with 'wit and humour'.[227] Another similarly themed work was *The Lame Lover*, a comedy about the adventures of Sir Luke Limp, the Serjeant, and his son. *The Maid of Bath* premiered in 1771, in which Foote pilloried Squire Long, the unscrupulous sexagenerian lover of Miss Elizabeth Linely, who was to marry Richard Brinsley Sheridan (1751-1616), the eventual author of *The School for Scandal* (1777). As an observer put it: 'The ground work of this very interesting performance is taken from a transaction which happened at Bath, in which a person of fortune was said to have treated a young lady celebrated for her musical talents in a very ungenerous manner.'[228] *The Nabob* (1772) was aimed at the directors of the East India Company where 'the character of Sir Matthew Mite was intended for a gentleman who had risen from the low situation of a cheese-monger'[229] and *Piety in Patterns* (1773) ridiculed sentimental comedy and Samuel Richardson's *Pamela* (1740-1). Three other major works were developed. These were *The Bankrupt*, again at the Haymarket in 1776 – though this was rather a collection of sketches than a full play – *The Cozeners* (Haymarket, 1774), and *A Trip to Calais*. This latter play was intended for presentation at the Haymarket in 1776, but 'containing a character designed for a lady of quality, she had interest enough to prevent it obtaining a licence'.[230] Therefore, this text had to be revised, eventually appearing at the Haymarket later in 1776 under the title of *The Cupuchin*.

Toward the end of his life, due to ill health, Foote was forced to enter an agreement with George Colman (the Elder [1732-1794]), the father of George Colman the Younger (whose work would become highly popular on the stage of nineteenth-century Cornwall). This agreement was for the patent of the theatre, according to which he was to receive from Colman the Elder 1600 £1. per annum, besides a stipulate sum whenever he chose to perform.[231] Foote had cut a good deal, and he continued to live luxuriously, travelling again to France in 1777. While *en route*, he had a stroke and died. He was fifty-six years old. Foote was privately interred in the cloisters of Westminster Abbey, and he left a son, who gained his fortune. A wit at the time wrote of him:

> Foote from his earthly stage, alas! is hurl'd,
> Death took him off, who took off all the world.[232]

This pithy comment is actually quite apt, considering his general achievement. Another observer made the following commentary some ten years after his death, trying to evaluate Foote's contribution to the British stage:

All Mr Foote's works are to be ranked only among the *petites piéces* of theatre. In the execution they are somewhat loose, negligent, and unfinished; the plans are often irregular, and the catastrophes are not always conclusive; but with all these deficiencies, they contain more strength of character, more strokes of keen satire, and more touches of contemporary humour, than are to be found in the writings of any other modern dramatist. Even the language spoken by his characters, incorrect as it may sometimes appear, will on a close examination, be found entirely dramatical, as it abounds with those natural minutiae of expression, which frequently form the very basis of character, and which render it the trueist mirror of the conversation of the times in which he wrote and published them.[233]

Although in places critical, the assessment is quite a fair one. His pieces were small works, but the notion of them being 'loose, negligent and unfinished' is an interesting observation. Looking back on this from the twenty-first century, we see that Foote was probably creating more of an improvisational and extemporising comedy than many of his fellow dramatists. Perhaps this is why he was known as 'the English Aristophanes', for the Greek comic playwright of c.446 BCE–c.386 BCE operated in the same way, loving timing and mimicry. To this extent, Foote's work points far forward, to well beyond nineteenth-century drama, and perhaps even into the post-war period of British and European drama. The problem with Foote's works now is that they are so littered with topical allusions and contemporary satires of his Age that their full impact is somewhat lost upon us, and it is hard responding to jokes which always require detailed knowledge of the culture of eighteenth-century London society. He is therefore dissimilar to his peer Oliver Goldsmith (1730-1774) and the slightly later Sheridan (1751-1816), whose works are more timeless, because they do not carry the same level of allusion to contemporary figures. This does not, however, stand to criticise or belittle Foote. As an observer wrote: 'Our author has now become a great[er] favourite of the town than ever; his very laughable pieces, with his more laughable performances, constantly filled his house, and his receipts were for some seasons almost incredible'.[234]

I have purposefully left one of Foote's plays for separate discussion, since it is, I believe, a highly significant text in the canon of theatre from Cornwall. As indicated above, *The Knights*, dated 1748, is something of a lost gem – a work that ought not only to be better known in Cornish letters – but to be more celebrated within wider pan-British drama. However, for our history of theatre of Cornwall, *The Knights* is important because it is one of the few surviving eighteenth-century texts that looked directly at Cornish subject matter and, additionally, stage Cornishness of this period. The plot of the play is quite complex: three members of Cornish gentry, Sir Gregory, Timothy and Master Jenkins, are travelling 'abroad' in England, and find the company of Hartop in Herefordshire highly conducive. Sir Gregory, Timothy and Master Jenkins are the eighteenth-century incarnations of Chough and Tristram, perhaps without the linguistic subtlety of the Middleton and Rowley conceptualisation. Hartop later plays the role of Sir Penurious Trifle in a farcical plot in order to prevent an arranged marriage happening to Timothy. Foote played Hartop/Trifle in the performance. An observer commenting on the play wrote:

> Sir Penurious Trifle and Sir Gregory Gazette, the first of which has a strong passion for perpetually entertaining his friends with a parcel of stale, trite, indulgent stories, and the latter, who is possessed with a most insatiable thirst for news, without even meaning capacity sufficient to comprehend the full meaning of most familiar paragraphs in a public journal. The first of them received additional life from the admirable execution of the author in his reproduction of the character, in which indeed, it has been reported that he mimicked the manners of a certain gentleman in the west of England.[235]

However, this does not tell the full story, for Foote was clearly basing his ideas on Cornishmen that he knew. He writes in the introduction to the published version of the play that:

> The three principal characters I met with in a summer's expedition; they are neither vamped from antiquated plays, pilfered from French farces, nor the baseless beings of the poet's brain. I have given them in their plain natural habit; they wanted no dramatic finishing.[236]

This indicates the imagined individuals required little input from Foote; he merely wrote how he heard and saw them. Although Foote was some way into his London career, clearly he was still returning to Cornwall on a regular basis – probably each summer. A second concept perhaps underlies the title of the play. For the London audience of 1748, any knightly association with Cornwall – which most would not have visited – was bound to bring to mind images of King Arthur and Tintagel, conjuring up a certain ideology, which was clearly Foote's intention. He would then undercut their romantic image with the reality of the three characters on the stage, in a way not too dissimilar to the poetic energy of the earlier Richard Carew. Cornish material is first explored in the first act, when after a lengthy discussion Sir Gregory asks their friend Hartop about the latest news. The way in which Sir Gregory is imagined suggests that, in Cornwall, the latest news is hard to come by, and therefore he constantly seeks gossip about contemporary events. Hartop has by now realised this behaviour, so chooses to poke fun at Sir Gregory by inventing a Papal deal over parts of Cornwall, the Isles of Scilly, and for good measure, the Needle Rocks off the Isle of Wight. The piece is introduced by their common knowledge of another individual named Killigrew, and the not too distant memory of Cornwall being in the front-line against Spain:

Sir Gregory: May be so, may be so! The Fool! Ha, ha, ha! well enough! a queer dog, and no fool, I warrant you! Killigrew, ah, I have heard my grandfather talk much of that same Killigrew, and no fool! But what is all this to news, Mr Hartop? Who gives us best account of the king of Spain, and the queen of Hungary, and those great folks? Come now, you could give us a little news if you would; come now! – fang! – nobody by! – good now do; come, ever so little!

Hartop: Why, as you so largely contribute to the support of the government, it is not fair you should not know what they are about. – We are at present in a treaty with the pope!

Sir Gregory: With the Pope! Wonderful! Good now, good now! How, how?

Hartop: We are to yield him up a large tract of the *Terra Incognita*, together with both the Needles, Scilly-rocks, and the Lizard-point, condition that the pretender has the government of Laputa, and the bishop of Greenland succeeds to St. Peter's chair...[237]

All of this, the naïve Sir Gregory seems to accept. There is perhaps something else at work here, which reminds us too of the naming, in the *Ordinalia*, of the land charters as reward for the torturers. The Pope is to receive the Scilly rocks, which, of course, barely have any use, and also just the Lizard-point, the most southerly point of mainland Britain, where there is nothing of any value. In 'Origo Mundi' in the *Ordinalia*, one of the charters awarded to the masons from Solomon is for *garrak ruan* [probably the so-called Black rock], in the middle of Carrick Roads, which is a remarkably similar image.[238] Of course, Foote would perhaps have cared little or not even known of his Cornish-language dramatic heritage, but it seems a similar method nevertheless: that of giving out land which is apparently worthless. The plot of the drama moves on to Timothy's situation. Hartop, now fed up with the boorish Sir Gregory, turns his attention to the young Cornishman. Timothy is, without doubt, the best example of stage Cornishness in the eighteenth-century, yet as we shall see, Foote knew the culture well, and litters this section with well-attuned examples of 'West-Briton' identity. We notice too, that Hartop is allowed 'native country'. This is hardly a statement of nationalistic awareness, but it could be read as Foote/Hartop knowing that Cornwall retained, even into this era, a sense of territorial distinctiveness:

Hartop:	I am glad to see you in Herefordshire. Have you been long from Cornwall?
Timothy:	Ay, sir, a matter of four weeks or a month, more or less.
Sir Gregory:	Well said Tim! Ay ay ay, ask Tim any questions, he can answer for himself, Tim, tell Mr Hartop all the news about the elections, and the tinners, and the tides, and the roads, and the pilchers: I want a few words with my master Jenkins...
Hartop:	You have been so long absent from your native country that you have almost forgot it.
Tim:	Yes sure; I ha' been at uncle Tregeagle's a matter of twelve or a dozen year, more or less.
Hartop:	Then I reckon you were quite impatient to see your papa and mamma.
Tim:	No sure, not I. Father sent for me to uncle, sure Mavagezy is a choice place! And I could a'stayed there all my born days, more or less.[239]

Sir Gregory's speech here is wonderfully well-crafted, with just the right level of material detail about Cornwall to flag up its cultural difference. The elections are highly significant. Cornwall's 'rotten boroughs' corruption – sending a higher proportion of Members of Parliament to London – is well-known, and after The Great Reform Act of 1832 would have been part of the cultural and political dialogue of the time.[240] In some ways, it also harks back to the older concept of the rebellious Cornishman in London to 'try the law'.[241] The industrial infrastructure is considered as well, and since prospecting back home in Cornwall was partially English-financed, this image is also apt.[242] The tides are a more obvious one – Cornwall is surrounded by the ocean – but the road is also an interesting one, perhaps insinuating how bad travel was, back and forth between Herefordshire and Cornwall. The story of Tregeagle would probably have been known to Foote, though here he reuses the name for a Cornish family. For the stage, Tregeagle is ultra-Cornish, and therefore apt as Timothy's uncle. Mevagezy may be one Cornish place that Londoners may have heard of, but even if they hadn't, the sound of the word is alien enough. That it is 'a choice place' for Timothy is again amusing for fashionable London, because for them it most certainly would not have been. In this small sentence therefore, we see all that is apt and relevant about the cultural politics between Cornwall and England in this Age. Foote's language is sparse, but he completes the trick faithfully. In the list of newsworthy items, the final concept of pilchard-fishing is also significant. As Whetter has argued, the pilchard industry had grown steadily since the Elizabethan period, but by this point was growing enormously.[243] Cornish pilchards were being shipped all over Europe, but particularly to some of the Mediterranean Roman Catholic countries for Lent. The symbol and importance of the pilchard would therefore, have been very well known. At home, only some forty years earlier, John Boson (1665-c.1720) had written his Cornish-language Pilchard Curing Rhyme:

Blethan ha bletha Gra Gorollion toas
Ha gen Hern lean moas ort Dour Gawvas
Wor duath Gra Gwenz Noor East wetha pell
Rag en Poble pow tooben debra ol
Ma Pearth Hern pokar ol an Beaz
Moy Poble Bohodzack vel poble Broaz.

[Year after year ships will come
And they will leave Gwavas Lake full of our pilchards
At last, the North East wind will blow far
For the people of hot countries will eat them all.
The wealth of pilchards is like the world:
More poor people than rich.][244]

Thus, the stage Cornishman would be one who would talk about pilchards, and Foote, with his ear very much to the ground, knew what London society expected. There was probably enough awareness of him too being from Cornwall, so the satire would be doubly funny. In this next section of dialogue, Foote continues to remind the audience of Cornwall's difference by considering culturally distinctive amusements and pastimes. In this section, the audience also learns of imagined Cornu-English speech patterns. Presumably to emphasise rurality and lack of sophistication in his responses, the Cornishman replies twice with 'Nan?' and also the expression 'fath and soul' is repeated twice. The latter may well have been indicative that he was of Methodist persuasion, something the London audience would also have understood:

Hartop:	Pray, sir, what were your amusements?
Tim:	Nan? What do you say?
Hartop:	How did you divert yourself?

Tim:	Oh, we ha' pastimes enow there: we ha' bull-baiting, and cock-fighting, and fishing, and hunting, and hurling, and wrestling.
Hartop:	The two last are sports for which that country is very remarkable: those, I presume, you are very expert?
Tim:	Nan? What?
Hartop:	I say you are a good wrestler?
Tim:	Oh! Yes, sure, I can wrestle well enow; but we don't wrestle after your fashion; we ha' no tripping fath and soul! We all upon close hugs or the flying mare, Will you try a fall, master? I wan't hurt you, fath and soul.[245]

The fact that Tim outlines how the Cornish 'don't wrestle after your fashion' seems to outline a fairer approach to the sport, and Tim is only too keen to demonstrate his 'throws' upon Hartop. Cleverly, Foote develops a scene later on that is an echo of this one, where Sir Gregory asks what amusements may be found in London. With his words 'no distress' Hartop seems to express his weariness of what is available:

Sir Gregory:	But pray, cousin, what diversions, good now! Are going forward in London?
Hartop:	Oh, sir, we are in no distress for amusements; we have plays, balls, puppet-shows, masquerades, bull-baitings, boxings, burlettas, routs, drums and a thousand others…[246]

It is with such dramaturgy that one begins to note Foote's skill as a dramatist. The comic high-point of Timothy and Hartop's discussion however, comes in the scene after the discussion about hurling and wrestling. Hartop is trying to investigate if Timothy has a sweetheart at home, though Timothy confuses this with the name of his bitch and dog. The dog is given a seemingly Cornu-English name, Jowler, which compares well to Cornish words such as *jowster* [fish hawker] and *jowds* [rags]. At this point, the scene transforms into bawdy comedy as we learn how they 'tugge'd it all the way up'. Another place is also mentioned here. As long-term capital of Cornwall, Lanston (it is written in a Cornu-English manner) may have been another location heard of by the London audience. This joke about confusing his dog with his sweetheart then forms the launch for the rest of the action: Dame Winifred sounding dull and 'English', while Mally Pengrouse (although having an unappealing surname [to London sensibilities at least]) sounds sexy and alluring, particularly since her face is given such honest Cornish poetic description. The section is worth quoting in full:

Hartop: We had as good not venture though – But have you left in Cornwall nothing that you regret the loss of more than hurling and wrestling?

Tim: Nan? What?

Hartop: No favourite she?

Tim: Arra, I coupled Favourite and Jowler together and sure they tugg'd it all the way up. Part with Favourite! No I thank you for nothing: you must know I nursed Favourite myself, uncle's huntsman was going to mill-pond to drown all Music's puppies; so I saved she: but, fath, I'll tell you a comic story: at Lanston they both broke loose and eat a whole loin-a'-veal and a leg of beef: Crist! How landlord swear'd! fath, the poor fellow but hut came you to know about our Favourite?

Hartop: A circumstance, so material to his son, could not escape knowledge of Sir Gregory Gazette's friends. But here you mistook me a little Squire Tim; I meant whether your affections were not settled upon some pretty girl; has not some Cornish lass caught your heart?

Tim: Hush! 'god, the old man will hear; jog a tiny bit this way; – won't a tell father?

Hartop: Upon my honour!

Tim: Why then I'll tell you the whole story, more or less. Do you know Mally Pengrouse?

Hartop: I am not so happy.

Tim: She's uncle's milkmaid; she's as handsome lord! Her face all red and white, like the inside of a shoulder of mutton: so I made love to our Mally; and just, fath, as I had got her good will to run away to Exeter and be married, uncle found it out and sent word to father, and father sent for me home; but I don't love her a bit the worser for that: but, 'icod, if you tell father, he'll knock my brains out, for he says I disparage the family, and mother's mad as a March hare about it; so father and mother ha' brought me to be married to some young body in these parts.

Hartop: What, is my lady here?

Tim: No sure, Dame Winifred, as father call her, could not come along.[247]

This is another successful section, well-crafted by Foote, in order for his audience to be sympathetic towards Timothy's wishes. There is also a good deal of Cornu-English dialect in this section, or at least how Foote imagines it to be spoken in the middle of the seventeenth century. The writing does not really equate that well with even nineteenth-century dialecticians, let alone those from the twentieth-century. It seemingly does bear more of a resemblance to work by earlier writers of Cornu-English, such as Andrew

Boorde.[248] We have to remember, however, that even Boorde's work was a 'guidebook' and perhaps nowhere near the reality of speech. It is also the case that Foote is filtering the work. Too much unconventional grammar and too many Cornishisms will alienate his audience. The line he appears to have walked is just about right. It is easy, perhaps, now to view Foote's work and complain about it: that the characters are simpletons, and peripheral, unsophisticated stereotypes, who really do not know how to behave in this kind of society. To his credit, however, there is believability about a character such as Timothy that makes him stand out from other characters on the stage of this Age. Therefore, if Foote's aim is to highlight cultural, political and linguistic difference, then he has achieved it. Throughout the play, Timothy carries with him a certain logic, naïvety and gravitas that must have appealed to the London audience, so as well as being wholly Cornish, he is an 'everyman' figure. This is a difficult trick to pull off, but Foote manages it.

Once Dame Winifred is mentioned, events in the play speed up markedly. Hartop disguises himself as Sir Penurious Trifle and, in a wonderful sequence, harking back to the days of the Civil War, manages to satirise Puritans and anti-Royalists. He observes the following: 'What does a Puritan do – the Puritans were friends to Noll – but he puts up the sign of an owl in an ivy-bush, and underneath he writes "This is not the royal oak!"'[249] We soon learn that that 'Tim has na gone and married Mally Pengrouse' to which Sir Gregory responses with 'Who the dickens is she?'[250] In order to keep the peace, the characters then indulge in changing identities, with Jenkins playing Sir Gregory Gazette, and Hartop as Timothy.[251] Further chaos ensues, until the Cornish gentry continue on their travels: this time from Herefordshire to Wales, presumably to cause further chaos there. For anyone interested in the theatrical history of Cornwall, *The Knights* is a worthy read, and certainly, the play should be much better known. In this work, and perhaps in *The Minor*, we see the scale of Foote's achievement. It is therefore a pity that not more Cornish characters feature in his work, though compared to the rest of the century, this represents the best imagining of a stage Cornwall. *The Knights* also provides us with continuity back to Lillo's *Fatal Curiosity* of 1736, and prefaces much of the early nineteenth-century indigenous drama of Cornwall.

Foote was operating too early in the eighteenth century to witness the opening of two major urban theatres in Cornwall: the Penzance theatre and the Assembly-Room Theatre at Truro. While some critical attention has been paid to the theatre at Truro,[252] rather less is known about the Penzance theatre. It also had a shorter lifespan, and although relics of the structure have survived until the present day, the theatre seems set to decay further, despite the efforts of various individuals and organisations.[253] Because of its period of operation, the theatre in Penzance is known by many as the 'Georgian Theatre', and it is to be found between Chapel Street and New Street, at the rear of the present-day Union Hotel. In the late 1780s, the Union Hotel was then known as the Ship and Castle Inn,[254] and was owned by John Stone. On 29 February 1786, the residents of Penzance read a short article in *The Sherbourne Mercury* newspaper about plans for the Inn and its letting. The article gives a sense not only of the period, but also the material conditions of the day:

> To be lett for a term of years, and entered upon at Lady-day next, all that ancient and reputable and well accustomed inn and Tavern known by the name of The Ship and Castle Inn in the town of Penzance, in the county of Cornwall; consisting of sixteen lodging rooms, besides servants apartments, a most spacious dining room, five parlours, a most excellent kitchen, wash-house, brewing house, laundry, roomy beer-cellars and wine-cellars, stabling for thirty horses, and every other requisite for a commodious Inn and Tavern. The premises have long been in the possession of Mr. John Stone, the owner, who has carried on the business for many years with great reputation and success, and whose ill health now obliges him to decline.
>
> The assemblies, promenade &c, are always held in the Ship and Castle. There is a cock-pit adjoining, in the garden; and an elegant theatre is now about to be built by the manager of the Exeter company of comedians, in the yard behind the house. The house and premises are completely furnished with all necessary stocks, genuine liquors, &c, which may be had at a fair appraisement; and the business will be continued till the house is taken. Apply for particulars to the said John Stone.[255]

Thus steps were taken to construct a new theatre for Penzance over the old stables at the rear of the Inn. Keith Kennedy has estimated that 'the theatre itself was a simple rectangle 60 feet by 29 feet with a stage 21 feet deep, and was painted blue and white'.[256] Such a design is comparable with the surviving and now restored (in 2003) Theatre Royal, Richmond in North Yorkshire, which is perhaps the closest extant model to what the Penzance theatre would have looked like in its day. The theatre there was built by the actor-manager Samuel Butler in 1788, though there is no record of the architect.[257] Given the date, however, and the similarities between the two structures, it would certainly seem that the two were designed by the same person, and that the Penzance theatre may well have been the model for the one at Richmond, being constructed just two years later. Kennedy notes that 'at its peak it held

500 people for the more popular performances but this was in extremely overcrowded conditions'.[258] Modern theatre regulations would probably allow an audience of only two hundred people in the space.

The precise date of the opening of the new theatre is not known. However, we do know that the theatre was definitely open by May 1787. The diary entries of a William Veale from Trevaylor observe that: 'Mrs Veale and I drank tea and supp'd at Mrs. Jenkins' in Penzance. After we viewed at the theatre *The Suspicious Husband* with *The Agreeable Surprise*. Bill: Play Mrs. Veale and Self 8s and 6d.'[259] The former is probably the 1747 play by Dr Benjamin Hoadly (1706-1757) which, despite it being his one and only play, has been very popular, while the latter was a popular comic opera. The individual responsible for the development of this material at the theatre was Richard Hughes. Hughes was originally from Birmingham, but had moved to the south-west of Britain to marry the daughter of the manager of the Plymouth Dock Theatre. This arrangement set him on a career path which would see him as one of the more important actor-managers of the Age. Hughes also established a method of working which would be the model for the later actor-managers of Cornwall in the opening decades of the nineteenth century. Hughes was certainly successful in Penzance and elsewhere, for he eventually became owner and manager of the Sadler's Wells Theatre in London, as well as controller of the theatres in Weymouth, Plymouth, Exeter, Devonport, Truro – and even one on the island of Guernsey. By the time of his death in 1814, he had come to be known as the 'Father of Provincial Drama'[260] – a heady function and responsibility. As we shall see more fully in Chapter Four, each theatre was open for several months of the year, and Mr. Hughes' Company of Players moved from one theatre to the next to perform their repertoire. This was a lucrative process, since it meant that one play could be worked up and marketed throughout the peninsula, usually during the winter season.

After Hughes's death, management of the theatre passed to his son John, and this continued for some time, until Hughes junior became more involved in the London scene through the purchase of Vauxhall Gardens at Kennington.[261] The control of the theatre then passed to a set of figures about whom we shall learn more later in this volume: Samuel Fisher of Falmouth (John and he formed a partnership in 1804), Mr Osbaldiston (first of Exeter, but then later heavily involved with the Assembly-Room Theatre at Truro), and finally James Dawson,[262] who managed the theatre until its closure in 1831. In the archives of the Morrab Library, the Courtney Library, Truro, and Penlee House and Gallery are to be found, in total, some 187 playbills, which trace early performances in the theatre (in 1787) to the final performance on 10 January 1831. These were mainly printed by Mr Vigurs, though some others were from G. Cok and Mr Thomas of Penzance. Ann Altree, who has completed a substantial study of the theatre, informs us that:

> seating was available in the pit, gallery and boxes. In June 1787, the boxes cost 3s per person, the pit 2s per person, and the gallery 1s. A reduction in price was given at about 8.30pm, which brought the cost down to 2s, 1s and 6d respectively. Children under 12 were charged half price. The theatre would have been patronised by the elite and middle-class of Penzance. The average wage for a miner at this time was about 6s a week, so the prices quoted would have been a lot for the working class in Penzance to pay.[263]

Many of the dramas mounted were 'standards' of the period, with several pieces continuing to be popular as the nineteenth century unfolded. The Penzance theatre did, however, mount a tremendous variety of performances, ranging from works such as *John Bull: An Englishman's Fireside*[264] to Shakespeare, melodrama, opera, comic opera, songs, circus acts and various child prodigies. Kennedy also notes that, in line with many other theatres across Britain, technical attempts to achieve spectacle also developed. These included 'falling rocks, torrents of water, hogsheads of fire, smoke, thunder and lightning, and other sensations being much in demand'. According to Altree, 'the doors of the theatre opened at 6.30pm, with performances beginning precisely at 7pm'.[265] She also details an early show from 1787, which was:

> a comic opera *The Duenna*, or *Double Elopement* with Mr Hughes in the leading role, then came *Fal Deral* (believed to be dance music) and a hornpipe from Master Hughes. This was followed by a hunting song and the evening concluded with a farce: *Patrick in Prussia, or Love in the Camp*.[266]

Three detailed illustrations of the Penzance theatre exist. The first is in the collection of Harvard University, and is a sketch of the exterior of the building, clearly showing the stabling and coach-house below.[267] Here can be seen a rectangular, rubble-stoned building, with granite dressed quoins, doors and windows, with a slate roof.[268] Two sketches of the theatre were also made in 1987.[269] These drawings give a good impression of the internal and external structure, showing the sloping stage floor (at the south end) with four trap doors, the gallery floor, the partition framing under the gallery (which formed the foyer, at the north end), and the sloping pit floor structure.[270] Decorated pillars supported the galleries. There would also probably have been a lean-to dressing room at the rear of the stage. Socket holes in the building confirm

Fig. 49. A watercolour painting of the Penzance Theatre. Courtesy of Harvard University.

the presence of a proscenium opening for the stage. Judging by comparison to the theatre at Richmond, the stage itself was movable so that boards might be inserted or taken away from the stage, to reveal more or less of the pit. It was common practice for such staging to allow the entrance of mythological characters: for example, as evidenced below, the witches in *Macbeth*. The drawings thus indicate a multiple-use space (just like the *plen-an-gwarry*) and, although compact by modern standards, the physical nature of the building and its architecture must have made for innovative performance. Clearly the two levels of panelled galleries were for richer members of the audience, while the simple benches allowed less well-off members of the community to attend. Such was the importance of the theatre that in March 1960 the venue was visited and commented upon by the theatre-historian Richard Southern (instrumental in the reuse of the theatre at Richmond in 1963), who completed an early sketch of the interior.[271] Southern spoke at the Penzance Playgoers' Theatre Club and, according to *The Cornishman* newspaper of the time, made the following core observation on what he said about the theatre:

The Georgian theatre was different from any other because it came at a time when its designers had settled their ideas once and for all, and knew exactly what

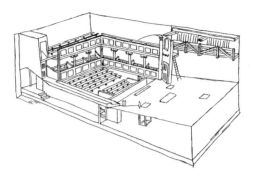

Fig. 50. A sketch of the overall view of the interior of the Penzance Theatre.

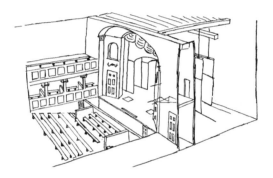

Fig. 51. A sketch of the view of the stage and proscenium arch at the Penzance Theatre.

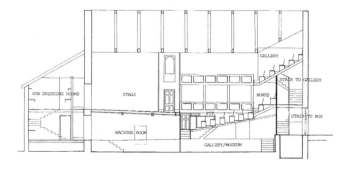

Fig. 52. A longitudinal section through the Georgian Theatre at Penzance, if it were re-built. Courtesy of Renton Howard Levin Partnership.

they wanted… [In Penzance] the original stage was still there, above the garage, and there he had seen four traps, including one which was quite unique, the so-called 'cauldron trap' at the rear of the stage, used mainly for the Witches Scene in *Macbeth*. Remaining to the view also was the trough into which were stuck the oil wicks which served as the footlights.[272]

Clearly, the Harvard drawing suggests that the theatre was, in some ways, a conversion of the stables. In late eighteenth-century Cornwall, this seems to have been a trend which occurred from the River Tamar to Penzance, since Robert Dyer, in his account, titled *Nine Years of an Actor's Life* (published in 1833, but about the end of the previous century), indicates this:

> The second probationary year began in the stable of the Kings Arms at Launceston which, surely having undergone sundry alterations was named a theatre, and surely such a theatre had never before had existence. Its breadth (the stage) might have been eight feet, its depth the same, its height not more than six feet five inches, for our opening night the nodding plumes I wore as Aranza absolutely were hid in the flies. The entrance behind the scenes passed over a large granite water trough, and through a window about one yard square. The gentlemen had access to their dressing room by a common ladder, while everything was conducted with the strictest regard to ceremony, and the duties of the prompter, scene shifter, property man and candle snuffer were performed by Mr Dawson Snr. I have seen him speak the tag of a piece in the corner of the stage, whilst with one hand offstage rang the bell and lowered the curtain when the play had ended.[273]

Conditions at Penzance were probably a little more sophisticated, but in his account Dyer does offer a flavour of the period. Such ad hoc touring circumstances are expressed elsewhere in his account, as well as the notion of barn/stable-to-theatre conversion:

> Never can I forget the truly Thespian mode of journeying to the west. As an especial favour, manager Dawson invited me to join his family party. We started in a wagon, the back part of which received the extensive scenery, machinery, dresses, decorations, etc. of the erratic company and on the whole lay the inebriated body of Mr. − and the huge carcase of Triton a mixed Newfoundland dog. In front sat Mr and Mrs Dawson Jr and their infant son; Mr and Mrs Sally Scholey sat next and in the background I jolted on, and this load of sin and scenery was drawn by a pair of half starved horses. We had plentiful supply of provisions, the manager was facetious and with an eye to business examined every barn we passed on its convertible capabilities should he ever be tempted to open a theatre there.[274]

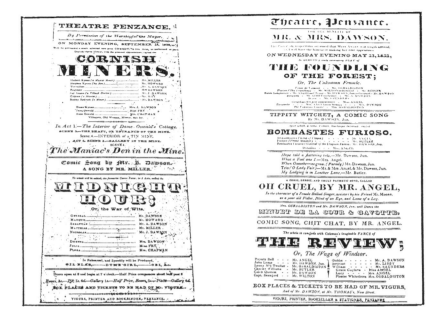

Fig. 53. A play-bill for the drama 'The Cornish Miners' at the Penzance Theatre, *c*.1821.

Comparatively then, Penzance must have seemed something of an oasis of grandeur. We know, however, from accounts from Collins,[275] and from Dyer, that the theatre in Redruth was held above the stables. Dyer observes that the theatre in Redruth was a 'spacious loft erected over an eight stalled stable'. Likewise, the 'rural theatre' in Bodmin was also used as a stable out of season, and the dressing rooms there, were located in the hayloft.[276] Interestingly, Dyer originally labels the theatre in Penzance as 'The Stable'. In this period, only Liskeard seems to have been different from the stable theatre concept, since performances there took place in the Town Hall. We also know that James Dawson related the conditions of performing above the stable at Penzance in his autobiography. Dawson comments that:

> the aroma [of horse manure] made our host sneeze and one evening when Hamlet conjures Horatio and Marcellus to 'Swear by my sword' the ostler underneath roared to his horse, 'Come up you boogger, or I'll scat the brains out of tha!... This unexpected salutation acted like an electric shock on the nerves of

Hamlet who rushed offstage exclaiming 'Oh Day and Night, this is wondrous strange'.[277]

Clearly the activities beneath the stage were a problem for touring companies. Altree lists another example of this. An observer named Edward Smith noted that the voices of actors were sometimes not audible owing to the kicking of the horses. It may be that such stories were part of the 'legend' of playing such theatres. However, there is other evidence that supports the notion that this was a particular problem in Penzance: a player named Cross, performing *Richard III*, appeared on stage one night, declaiming the famous line 'A horse, a horse, my kingdom for a horse'.[278] The ostler below, apparently speaking loud enough to be heard, replied with: 'Do you think I am going to lend you a horse for your May games? No, you may borrow from elsewhere.' It seems the ostlers at Penzance were well-known for this kind of commentary, perhaps inspiring the following doggerel:

The Manager whose name was Cross
Dressed out in Richard cried, '*A horse!*
A horse! My Kingdom for a horse.'
The Ostler heard, '*Zoosts Master Cross*
D'ye think to fool me here below
And make partner in your show?
What! Bring a horse upon the stage?
Here's one indeed that's blind with age.
A horse! No, 'tis a Mare by gee,
A stumbling toad, with broken knee.'
Then crooked-backed Richard knit his brow
And loast his Part... I can't tell how,
But cried again with vacant Stare,
'*A Mare! My Kingdom for a Mare!*'
The Gallery would not let this pass,
They all exclaimed, '*an Ass! an Ass!*
An Ass – My Kingdom for an Ass!'[279]

Not only were regular companies touring Penzance, but a number of famous performers came to Penzance to work. One of them was the tenor Charles Benjamin Incledon (1763-1826). Incledon was a Cornish singer, the son of a doctor from St Keverne, who began his singing career as a choirboy at Exeter but, after a spell in the navy, turned his attention to the stage, working in the south west of Britain, before great success in 1790 at Covent Garden. From thereon, he was perhaps the most famous tenor of his day, singing both opera and oratorio, and a number of popular ballads, such as *Sally in our Alley*, *The Arethusa* and *Black-eyed Susan*. Incledon certainly performed in Penzance in the early part of his career, but probably also returned when he retired in 1822, and toured the regions of Britain with an entertainment called *The Wandering Melodist*. Another visitor was Edmund Kean (1789-1833), one of the most famous actors of this phase.[280] In his early career, Kean was a member of the Exeter Company, so almost certainly played at Penzance, with Hughes supporting his development, though in August 1826 he returned to play the role of Othello. In 1828, he was back, this time playing Shylock in *The Merchant of Venice* in his last tour of the south-west of Britain. Not only was theatre being imported *to* Cornwall; in June 1812, theatre was exported *from* Cornwall, when the Penzance Players took part in a foreign tour, entertaining Wellington's troops in Portugal and Spain, where they were fighting Napoleon's forces.[281] This is perhaps the earliest record of a company from Britain touring overseas. The Penzance theatre was the institution to which the Players attached themselves, and most likely where they rehearsed and gathered.

Kennedy notes that 'audiences started to dwindle in the 1820s as public opposition to theatrical performances grew throughout the provinces, mainly in line with the increase in Methodism'.[282] Although Kennedy notes the importance of Methodism's oppositional ideology, such a decline did not happen elsewhere until the middle of the century. It is perhaps more likely that Penzance declined simply because of its peripherality. While good road connections now existed to Truro, and to Falmouth (two towns that were also growing), Penzance was that much further for the companies to travel to[283] and, as an urban centre, it was not growing with the same pace as Truro and Falmouth.[284] Upon closure in 1831, the theatre was moth-balled for several years, before it was more fully dismantled in 1839. Theatrical events did not stop completely however. As Altree details, events continued in the assembly room of the Hotel: 'there is a playbill dated 1842, advertising the Grossmith brothers [with a programme including] the *Ghost of Hamlet's Father*, *Odd Propensities, or Say's Romance*, *Freaks of Fate, or O'Callaghan's Last*, and *My Uncle John, or the Ball Night*'.[285] J.S. Courtney also observes seeing a conjurer named Jacobs perform in the assembly room around the same time – so there is at least a continuity of theatricality forward into the rest of the century.[286]

Over the years, the old theatre building has had a variety of uses, including being a billiard hall, a Masonic Lodge, a meeting room, a travellers' rest, an ice house, a place for furniture storage, and headquarters for the Brownies. 1881 brought the most serious change, when the roof was lowered some six feet,[287] and over the passage of time the building has deteriorated even further. In the 1990s and early twenty-first century, there have been various efforts to reconstruct the theatre, including a detailed architectural restoration,[288] but following somewhat negative responses from English Heritage,[289] the project has stalled. Given the importance of the Penzance theatre – it is certainly the oldest surviving theatrical building in these islands – it seems a pity that the response was negative. Perhaps more scarily, although some of the original fittings and fixtures still survive inside, the present owners appear to be thinking of a conversion into flats. The Union Hotel is perhaps now famous for being the location at which the announcement was made in October 1805 regarding the death of Horatio Nelson. Folklore in and around the hotel suggests that the earliest announcement was made from the gallery in the assembly room of the hotel by Mayor Giddy. However, research suggests that this was wrong, and that the earliest announcement was made at the Penzance theatre, as recorded by the folklorist Margaret Ann Courtney:

> It is a fact, however, that the news of Nelson's death was first heard here. It was brought into the port by two fishermen, who had it from the crew of a passing vessel. A small company of strolling actors were playing that night at the little theatre then standing over the stables in Chapel Street (behind the Union Inn) and the play was stopped for a few moments whilst once of the actors told the audience.[290]

Such information is perhaps a further reason for the wider significance of the theatre in Penzance. Alongside other theatrical space, such as Perran Round, it is why the theatrical history of Cornwall is so important. 1787, however, witnessed not only the opening of the Penzance theatre, but also a new Assembly-Room Theatre for Truro. There are considerable similarities between the theatre in Penzance and the one at Truro. However, as we shall see, the one in Truro was far more influenced by subsequent reaction to and reformation of the 1737 Stage Licensing Act and, in a way, it had more multifunctional space than the 'stable' theatre in the west. As this chapter will later explore, folk drama was ongoing within Truro and its surrounds, but as H.L. Douch suggests, other performances were obviously taking place in the town in the latter decades of the century:

> In Truro during the eighteenth century, the occasional theatrical performance would be given in the Town Hall or the Coinage Hall. It was in the large chamber above the Coinage Hall that Prince William Henry, from the frigate

Hebe, witnessed a performance in 1785; so many people were anxious to see him, if not the play, that the floor was in danger of giving way.[291]

Thus an elegant little theatre and assembly rooms were opened in High Cross around 27 September 1787;[292] the palladian façade remains, presently looking upon the square in front of the western front of Truro Cathedral. Howell has considered the development of the Assembly-Room Theatre in Truro in the light of the legal position of theatre in Britain during this period. The 1737 Licensing Act tends to be noted in theatrical scholarship for causing the loss of status to so-called 'strolling players',[293] but it also had an effect on the development of new theatres. Howell observes that:

> the 1737 Licensing Act made professional acting and buildings for that purpose illegal outside Westminster unless theatre companies gained a Royal Patent by Act of Parliament. Enforcement of the Licensing Act varied, depending on the support players cultivated from influential patrons. At Richmond, Yorkshire, for example, players gained permission to illegally erect a purpose-built theatre, in November 1787. These conditions remained in force until the 1788 Licensing Act restored the power of local authorities to license theatres, albeit for strictly limited seasons. Under such conditions the players' needs and purposes invariably determined the nature of theatre building.[294]

Clearly, then, the shareholders at Truro (two of which were Francis Enys and Thomas Warren) had an eye on these legal developments, and knew that the law was likely to change. The extant evidence for the theatre's construction and use falls into three main categories: a) eye-witness accounts including correspondence, diaries and newspapers; b) drawings by the architect Christopher Ebdon, dated April 1786; c) photographs taken by Truro company A.W. Jordan, just before the theatre's demolition in 1923. Eye-witness accounts demonstrate how, from the outset, the proprietors conceived the building as an assembly room rather than a theatre, to evade the 1737 Act. The building's earlier known documentation exists in a letter dated 26 May 1796 from Francis Enys to Thomas Warren:

> We have at last, after many tedious delays, finally adjusted our assembly rooms plan, Andrew Stephens [the builder?] gave in the lowest estimate for £1057, which, with the purchase money of £500 and sundry other matters will, I apprehend, amount to at least £1700 of which 1500 or 1550, I forget which, is already subscribed, and we have agreed to trust to providence for the remainder, and so proceed as fast as possible with the building.[295]

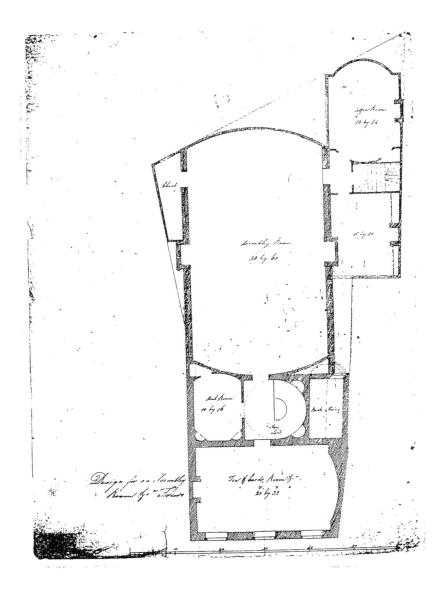

Fig. 54. A design for the Truro Assembly-Room Theatre without theatrical fixtures, by Charles Ebdon, 1786. Courtesy of the Royal Institution of Cornwall.

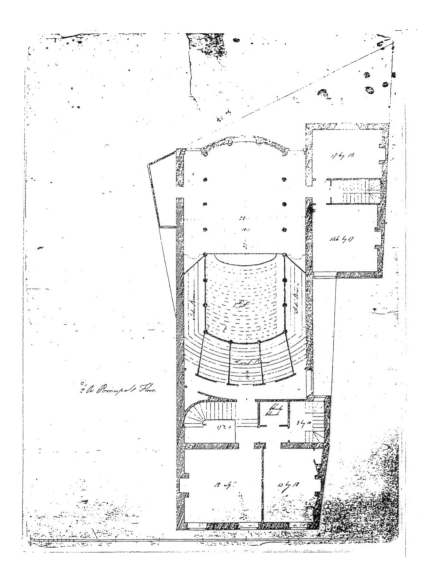

Fig. 55. A design for the Truro Assembly-Room Theatre with theatrical fixtures, by Charles Ebdon, 1786. Courtesy of the Royal Institution of Cornwall.

The architect appointed for the project was Christopher Ebdon.[296] Ebdon was a clever visionary who was trying to balance the needs of his clients with the legal requirements. One drawing shows Ebdon's design for an assembly room, devoid of any theatre fittings, while others show an alternative scheme for a theatre with similar exterior walls to the assembly room. Intriguingly, thus far the correspondence makes no reference to a theatre, indicating the proprietors' flexible attitude. The correspondence date of May 1786, however, suggests that Ebdon's plans, made a month earlier in April were "adjusted". Thomas Warren's draft reply scribbled on the same letter supports this view:

> When I left Truro I did not subscribe myself as the original plan was altered and several other… things have been done which I disapprove of. However, I shall pay my subscription upon my return as I think it will be an ornament to the town.[297]

As Howell, notes, 'the added respectability very likely contributed to the Truro shareholders' evasion of the 1737 Act'.[298] Perhaps the design alteration, which aroused Thomas Warren's disapproval in the above letter, included a notion of the assembly room's adaptability to a theatre. If so, the assembly room guise worked well, since Warren's support was based on his opinion that the building "will be an ornament to the town", even though it contained an illegal theatre. Thus, the explicit aim of the building was to be a respectable assembly room, though in anticipation of the law changing, it might be adapted quickly to a theatre. The multi-use nature of the building would also make it more lucrative financially: theatre was not available all the time, either from indigenous players, or from touring companies. Balls, galas and musical events could thus be held in one of the building's formats. Howell notes this adaptability in his observations:

> The façade certainly presents a prominent, genteel exterior. Seventeen of the surviving proposal drawings show alternative treatments of the façade, one of which remains the only surviving drawing actually executed. In its theatre format, if the entrances from the street were executed as proposed… separate doors served each class of spectator. The left-hand doorway led to the staircase for the more expensive boxes, whilst the right-hand entrance led to the tap room, gallery staircase and pit passage. In its assembly room format, the former led to the main assembly room, whilst the latter led to a tap room and the gallery staircase. Not surprisingly the assembly room interior presents no apparent theatre fittings, but, as the 1795 diarist points out, the general arrangement of galleries on three sides of a long room reminds us of eighteenth-century provincial theatre interiors, such at that surviving at Richmond, Yorkshire,

together with the larger, more elaborate version at King Street (later the Theatre Royal) Bristol.[299]

There were some similarities in the design of the assembly room theatre at Truro, with that of Penzance, and the theatre at Richmond. Conversion to a theatre was actually quite simple. Removing one half of the floor revealed the pit, which had fixed benches on a raked floor. When this was revealed it would simultaneously create a raised stage. The benches are clearly visible in the photographs taken just before it was demolished.[300] Such a method of operation is supported in the view of a contemporary observer, who was visiting Truro in 1795. He comments on the flexibility of the space:

> We went to the assembly room which is elegantly neat... It is so built that when wanted for a play part of the floor is taken up and in many other respects has the appearance of a theatre, having galleries around the room.[301]

Thus the entrepreneurs had succeeded in evading prosecution, and once the law altered, they could be more open about its use. The adaptation of 'stables' for this purpose was again part of the evasion of the law: exactly what had

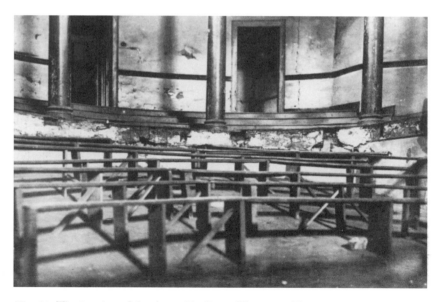

Fig. 56. The interior of the Assembly-Room Theatre at Truro, revealing the pit and benches. This photograph was taken in 1923 before the demolition process. Courtesy of the Royal Institution of Cornwall.

happened in both Bodmin and Penzance. Concealment was part of the agenda. In Truro, paradoxically, it was its elegance and respectability that provided the subterfuge. Howell concludes that:

the Truro assembly-room's dual purpose design illustrates one solution to the problem of erecting unlicensed purpose-built theatres in England between 1737 and 1788. It served the needs of the players who used it both by attracting a respectable clientele to support their evasion of the act, and a simple room easily adaptable to a theatre which focused on the players, drama, and the audience, not on painted scenery. In this light, rather than continuing to approach long rooms, as in the words of Arnold Hare describing the Vinc Inn Salisbury long room, "neither adequate nor convenient" theatres, it may be more useful to regard them as precedents in a theatre building tradition under the direct influence of the players that used them. This tradition is traceable in the similar player-spectator relationships within the adapted (as in Truro) and purpose-built (as at Richmond, Yorkshire) illegal theatres, and its influence is also evident (as at Bristol) in plans of legal Theatres Royal designed by carpenters and masons.[302]

Some theatrical historians have argued that all provincial Georgian theatres provided adaptable buildings specially designed to serve as community centres and for the local population and theatres for touring companies.[303] Clearly, this view is not really correct, and Truro is perhaps the exception that proves the rule. Interestingly, the photographic evidence of the building at the end of its life actually shows that the theatre in Truro differs little from other eighteenth-century theatres in Britain, used solely for drama. It certainly has the traditional constructive geometry one sees elsewhere and has benches curving in line with the rear pit wall. Another important observation about the space at Truro was that in all likelihood drama there, at least until the early years of the nineteenth century, did not employ changeable painted scenery. The space created, however, must have given intimate contact between the performers and the audience, and this would have lasted well into the nineteenth century. The Rooms, as we might expect in this era, were elegant and neat, and it is believed to have been the only assembly room in Britain that doubled as a playhouse.

The theatre at Truro came into its own during the Napoleonic Wars. There were many officers about, as well ladies ready to be pursued by officers, and so the stage, the balls, and the card rooms were no doubt well-patronised. As Palmer notes, this was also matching the expansion and growth of Truro.[304] Douch observes that when the Wars came to an end 'the theatre was less well used',[305] but as we shall see in Chapter Four, this was not completely the case.

Fig. 57. An early twentieth-century photograph of the exterior of the Assembly-Room Theatre in Truro. Courtesy of the Royal Institution of Cornwall.

Fig. 58. The surviving façade of the Assembly-Room Theatre in Truro in 2008.

Theatres of this type continued to the middle of the century at least, and by then there were other reasons for its decline. Douch does, however, include the reminiscences of an individual named Heard, who wrote a Gazetteer for the period and, although writing somewhat later in 1817, he perhaps captures some of the early energy of the Truro venue. Interestingly, he seems unconvinced about the façade of the building:

> The theatre contains no exterior beauty but is so judiciously contrived within to be either perfectly adapted for scenic representations or easily converted into an elegant ball room, connected with which are card-rooms and apartments for refreshments. The amusements of the inhabitants are occasionally diversified by visits of a migratory company of players who, however, seldom come here above once in three years; but assemblies are held here monthly during the winter season and three public concerts take place here annually.[306]

Clearly Heard was being sarcastic about the migratory companies, because the newspaper and playbill evidence suggest otherwise; although even he notes the genius of Ebdon's interior design. Viv Acton, who has examined the Truro theatre in the early years of the nineteenth century, comments that one observer notes, in 1824, that 'for a provincial theatre at so remote a distance, [it] was still the centre of attraction for the beauty and fashion of Truro and its vicinity'.[307] This had obviously been the case in the final decade of the eighteenth century as well. One is still able to note some of this beauty and fashion in the remaining ashlar façade at High Cross, exemplified in the profile busts of William Shakespeare and David Garrick in circular frames. The tympanum of the pediment contains a circular plaque with a draped female figure holding a mask and a mirror, while the three tall sash windows at the first floor level have finely carved reliefs over two gryphons supporting a tripod within a rectangular frame over the central window.[308]

While fashionable drama was being presented at the Truro Assembly Rooms at the end of the eighteenth century, other folk drama was happening elsewhere in the area. One play which can be dated to around 1780-90 is the so-called Truro Cordwainer's Play, which can be found in the Enys Memoranda at Cornwall Record Office.[309] It is titled thus because the play would have been performed by a collection or perhaps guild of cordwainers – craftsmen who made shoes and other articles from soft leather.[310] The Enys Memoranda is a miscellaneous collection of charters, documents and letters from the Enys family and the Enys mansion from around the time of Elizabeth I onwards. Enys is located between Penryn and Mylor on the western side of the River Fal. The Truro Cordwainer's Play appears to have

Fig. 59. A profile bust of William Shakespeare on the surviving façade of the Assembly-Room Theatre in Truro.

Fig. 60. A profile bust of David Garrick on the surviving façade of the Assembly-Room Theatre in Truro.

first come to light through the friendship between the Cornish scholar
Thurstan C. Peter and John Davies Gilbert Enys in the early twentieth
century. Enys was born in 1837 at St Gluvias, Penryn and, after a successful
career in New Zealand, returned to the family mansion there, on the death of
one of his brothers. He then became a councillor for the Mylor division of
Cornwall, dying in 1912. Peter completed a transcript of the play labelled in
the Cornwall Record Office as 'Text of a Christmas mummers' play with the
names of the persons taking the various parts n.d., eighteenth century' in
1905.[311] The transcript of this is now contained in the Courtney Library, Royal
Institution of Cornwall, where he writes in his notebook the following
observation:

> The libretto is from a MS. in the possession of John D. Enys (1905) who got it
> from Mylor. The original is written by a very illiterate man, but I have followed
> it closely for fear of wrong conjecture. For the same reason I have kept the lines
> of the original.[312]

This is why the play was initially known as the Mylor Play, but following the
work of Millington, who has researched the drama in great detail,[313] it is
perhaps better placed in Truro. In principle, Millington's theory is that the
actors have closer connections with Truro than they do with Mylor, so his
relabelling of the text is, in essence, just. His examination of the actors' lives
as what he terms a 'single synchronic generation'[314] also enables him to date
the play to the period above, making it one of the earliest recorded mummers'
plays in Britain. His evidence also draws on the fact that the earliest historical
allusion in the text comes from 1759, which might give the text an even
earlier provenance. I have studied both the original MS. in the Enys
Memoranda and Peter's transcript. Unlike some other mummers' plays, where
the character parts precede the lines, one difficulty about this play is that the
names of the actors precede the parts. Five actors are actually named. These
are William Solomon, who had forty-eight lines, John Rowe (alias F. Rowe),
who had ten lines, Pentecost Langdon (alias Penty Landin), who has sixty-six
lines, William Williams, who has forty-eight lines and Henry Crossman,
who has eighty-two lines. Given this, it would seem that the better
performers were Langdon, and Crossman, since they had the most lines to
learn.

Within the text, Solomon plays the narrator, Little Man John, and King
of France; Rowe, Father Christmas, Sampo, and Beelzebob; Langdon, Bing
Bing and the Turkish Knight; Williams, the King of Egypt, a Bloody
War[ri]or and the Doctor; and Crossman, Vornal Bould, King Henry and

Saint George. As can be seen, the multitude of characters and the doubling and tripling of parts makes for a more complex narrative than some other Cornish and British mummers' dramas. After study of the Constable's list for Truro,[315] Millington places the performers there, rather than at Mylor. This would make sense, for probably Truro could have maintained a guild of cordwainers. Millington observes that the text is 'relatively long and sophisticated for a folk play, and probably required actors of mid-teenage to late teenage as a minimum'.[316] Such an observation fits Millington's general observations about the age and background of the performers, but perhaps also tells us something else: that this kind of 'guizing' was usually a young man's activity, and this is probably historically the case across the rest of Cornwall during this time, and into the next century. How the text ended up in Mylor is perhaps more obvious: one of the descendants of the actors simply moved there and took the text with him. While this appears to explain where it was performed and where the text ended up, the text of the play throws up some interesting observations:

40% of lines, found in other folk play texts.
15% of lines, Addison's (1707) Rosamond: An Opera.
10% of lines, the balled King Henry Fifth's Conquest of France (c.1730).
35% of lines, not yet found elsewhere in folk plays or in literary sources.[317]

This perhaps makes us rethink the composition of mummers' plays in Cornwall. There is a tendency to believe in their organic origins, but on the evidence of this we see Cornish performers synthesising outside texts for local use. This is not, however, just peculiar to Cornwall. Such borrowing occurred elsewhere in Britain as well, and it should not demean the intention of the performance. Curiously, Millington also notices some Irish parallels. His implication is that fast Falmouth packet shipping facilitated swift movement of culture across the Atlantic periphery.[318] However, considering that the Irish models were already borrowings of English culture, the argument seems moot. Structurally, the drama is very similar to other mummers' plays considered in this volume; the script being a combination of verse and prose. The main difference from the other Cornish plays is the contemporary inclusion of the King of France, and an extended sequence with the doctor; the main similarities with the Irish plays are the part of Beelzebub and Saint George's introductory speech, which may be compared here:

Truro Cordwainer's Play

Here comes I son George
    from England have I sprung
sum of my worndas works now for to begin
first into a Closat I was put
then into a Cave was lock
I sot my foot upon a Rokke Stone
their did make my sad an griveus mone
how many men have I slew
and rund the firehe dragon thrue

I fought them all Corragesly
and stil got of thire victory
England's right England's admorration
now ear I drow my blood meepon
ho is the man that doth be fore me Stand
I will cut him down with my Courrageus hand

Christmas Rime in Smyth and Lyons

Here comes I knight George
    from England have I sprung
one of those noble deeds of valour to begin
seven long Years in a close Cave have I been kept
and out of that into a prison leapt
and out of that unto a rock of Stone
where there I made my sad & grievous moan
Many a Giant I did subdue
I run the fiery Dragon thro' & thro'
I freed fair Sabra from the stake
what more could mortal man then undertake
I fought them all courageously
and still have gained the victory
and will always fight for LIBERTY
here I draw my bloody weapon
shew me the man that dare me stand
I'll cut him down with my courageous hand[319]

The major differences appearing in the Truro play are the loss of the section about rescuing Sabra, and the fight for liberty. Otherwise the two are remarkably similar: Millington agrees that the Anglo-centric theme actually made little difference to them being embraced in Ireland, and therefore, as argued in this volume, in Cornwall. A difficulty in the Truro MS. is that many of the lines run on into each other (particularly in the doctor sequence), while the lexical and spelling difficulties of the hand, make it hard to understand the full meaning. This can be evidenced in the opening scenes:

William Solomon, first part
Rume rume Galants rume Give me a rume to rime,
For in this house i mine to some of my past time
now gentlemen an Lady it is christmas time
i am a blade that knew my trade all people doth a dear me
i will swager an banter an I will drive the town be fore me
if I am naked or if I am priet I will give aman an answer
the very first man or boy i mits my Soard shall be is fencer
be hind the doar thare lye a score pray Git it out if you can sur
i walke away have nothing to pay, an let in the swagering man sur

John Rowe, second part
hare comes I ould father christmas welcom or welcom not,
i hope ould Father Christmas will never be forgot.
ould father christmas a pair but woance a yare
he lucks like an ould man of 4 score yare

Penty Landin, part the third
hopen the door and Lat me in.
i hope your favour i shall wind.
wether irise or wether ifoll,
i will do my endeavour to please you all.
St George is at the doar and Swear he will com in
with soard an buckler by is side i fear he will purs my skin
i now he is no fool
i now he will say more by wan inch of candle
than ican perfoe white ten pound born out
and if you would not believe what i say
let the king of eagipt com in and clare the way[320]

The repetition of the same words for certain rhymes (time, yare) would indicate a less sophisticated hand in the text's construction, and yet the parts do convey the energy of the first performance, with the typical request to make space for the actors. The combat section is slightly extended, and there may be some evidence, supported by Millington, that it could have connections back to the subject matter of the Tudor Robin Hood dramas (popularised in particular at St Columb Minor and Major) because these featured similar ritualised combat sections, where threats are made before the development of the conflict:

> *Henry Crossman [St George]*
> Thee come so far a way to fight such man as I
> I will cut thy dublats full of Hylent holes
> and make thy buttuns fly

> *Pentry Laudin [Turkish Knight]*
> I am a man of vallour I will fight untill I die
> sun George thou never will face me but away from me will fly[321]

There is a more obvious connection here, however, to the Robin Hood texts, with the brief use of the character Little Man John. The play's other major difference is the incorporation of King Henry and the King of France, which may again suggest an earlier origin. One of the most impressive sections of the drama is the delusional poetic voice of the Turkish Knight, which is worth reproducing in full:

> What places is are
> what seens appare
> whare ever itorn mine eye
> tis all around
> in chantin ground
> and soft delusions rise
> floury mountains
> mosy fountains
> what will veriety surprise
> tis on the alow walk we walks
> an hundred ecos round us stock
> from hils to hils the voices tost
> rocks rebounding
> ecos resounding
> not one single words was lost[322]

Certainly the Truro Cordwainers' Play has much to offer the sub-genre of the hero-combat mummers' play in Britain. The manuscript in the Enys Memoranda gives no indication of when such a script would be performed, or where it was performed. Presumably, it was presented around Christmas time, around the streets of Truro, when guizing was still popular there. A more recent article by Tom Pettitt has confirmed the influence of the *Rosamond* opera (1707) on the shaping of the Truro Cordwainers' Play.[323] Pettitt argues that the differences in the textual sources may be put down to 'the course of writing down from recitation or memory', what he terms the 'living transmission'.[324] He further posits that possibly the play had older origins but that the *Rosamond* sequences were added when that text was fashionable. He finally suggests that *Rosamond* was likely to have been part of the local repertoire of the theatre of Truro and its surrounds; perhaps before the opening of the Assembly Rooms redefined theatrical conditions there. In this sense, *Rosamond* would seem to have been an imported text, but then given local Cornish spin. Given this, we perhaps have a longer period of time where the Truro Cordwainers' Play was in development, so that its 1780-1790 incarnation may well have been a preservative attempt to record what had occurred before. The play certainly seems to drop out of public knowledge by the middle of the nineteenth century, and although other such mumming dramas are mentioned towards the end of the next century, it is not really until the opening decades of the twentieth century that the form is given any such impetus to revive.

Returning to the title of this chapter, Truro would have been 'a choice place' for theatre since it was available at the Assembly Rooms and on the streets; in the end, therefore, offering theatre for all classes. In that sense, Truro stands, momentarily at least, as shaping Shepherd's wish of relevant, innovative, anarchic and non-elitist international theatre.[325] Just like the texts of Foote's dramas, the Truro Cordwainers' Play may be of greater significance than we first imagined, with it absorbing outside influences but repackaging them for the indigenous folk tradition. That interface would have ramifications for the next phase of the theatre of Cornwall's development. Likewise, the temporary ending of the Troyance Tongue on stage was accompanied by an English-language replacement, enjoying the presentation of Cornish stereotypes upon the stage in the 'centre' of these islands. Meanwhile, the Civil War, the Restoration, and reforming Age of the early eighteenth century had also helped to shape the material culture, the play-scripts and the acting of the rest of the eighteenth century. Space, place and performance were proving just as important as before. The industrialisation of Cornwall was also a contributing factor to how Cornwall was to be imagined in the future theatre. In the background, resistance to the dominance of the Anglican Church had found ongoing favour in the reforming movement of Methodism. The theatre of Cornwall was entering a new phase of development, with space, place, and performance reinvented once again.

CHAPTER THREE: NOTES AND REFERENCES

1. Gary Taylor (ed.), *William Shakespeare: Henry V*, Oxford: Oxford University Press, 1982, p.209.

2. Alan M. Kent and Tim Saunders (eds. and trs.), *Looking at the Mermaid: A Reader in Cornish Literature 900-1900*, London: Francis Boutle Publishers, 2000, pp.275-6. The Cornish here translates to 'Big head, will you be hung?'

3. See Christopher Haigh, *English Reformations: Religion, Politics, and Society under the Tudors*, Oxford: Clarendon Press, 1993; John Adair, *Puritans: Religion and Politics in Seventeenth-Century England and America*, Stroud: Sutton, 1998.

4. See P.A.S Pool, *The Death of Cornish*, Cornwall: Cornish Language Board, 1982; Richard Gendall, *1000 Years of Cornish*, Menheniot: Teere ha Tavaz, 1994.

5. Mark Stoyle, *West Britons: Cornish Identities and the Early Modern British State*, Exeter: University of Exeter Press, 2002.

6. See Ronald Harwood, *All the World's a Stage*, London: Methuen, 1984, pp.177-96; Robert G. Lawrence (ed.), *Restoration Plays*, London: J.M. Dent and Sons, 1976.

7. F.E. Halliday, (ed.), *Richard Carew: The Survey of Cornwall*, London: Melrose, 1953, pp.144-5.

8. Paula Neuss (ed. and tr.), *The Creacion of the World: A Critical Edition and Translation*. New York and London: Garland, 1983.

9. William Scawen, 'Antiquities Cornuontanic: The Causes of Cornish Speech's Decay' in Kent and Saunders, op.cit., pp.281-93.

10. Ibid.

11. CRO: AP/C/118/1.

12. CRO: B/Lis/266.

13. CRO: B/Lis/268.

14. CRO: B/Lis/272.

15. See Thomas Heywood, *An Apology for Actors*, London: Nicholas Okes, 1612, cited in A.W. Pollard and G.R. Redgrave (comps), *Short Title Catalogue, 1475-1640*: 13309.

16. Williams Sandys, 'On the Cornish Drama' in *Journal of the Royal Institution of Cornwall*, 3, 1865, p.18.

17. See Ronald Hutton, *The Rise and Fall of Merry England: The Ritual Year 1400-1700*, Oxford: Oxford University Press, 1994, pp.153-99.

18. For biography, see, for example, A.L. Rowse, *Shakespeare the Man*, London: Macmillan, 1973; Peter Ackroyd, *Shakespeare: The Biography*, London: Chatto and Windus, 2005. For critical studies, see John Drakakis (ed.), *Alternative Shakespeares*, London and New York: Methuen, 1985; Jonathan Dollimore and Alan Sinfield (eds.), *Political Shakespeare: New Essays in Cultural Materialism*, Manchester: Manchester University Press, 1985; Gary Taylor, *Reinventing*

Shakespeare: A Cultural History from the Restoration to the Present, London: Vintage, 1991. See also contributors to John Russell Brown and Bernard Harris (eds.), *Elizabethan Theatre*, London: Edward Arnold, 1974 [1966].

19. See, for example, F.E. Halliday, *The Legend of the Rood*, London: Gerald Duckworth, 1955; Richard Southern, *The Medieval Theatre in the Round: A Study of the Staging of The Castle of Perseverance, and related matters*, London: Faber and Faber, 1957; K.M. Dodd, 'Another Elizabethan Theatre in the Round' in *Shakespeare Quarterly*, 21, 1970, pp.125-56.

20. Matthew Spriggs, 'The Cornish Language, Archaeology and the Origins of English Theatre' in M. Jones (ed.), *Traces of Ancestry: Studies in Honour of Colin Renfrew*, Vol. 2, Cambridge: McDonald Institute Monograph Series, 2004, pp.143-61.

21. For a perspective, see contributors to Brendan Bradshaw and John Morrill (eds.), *The British Problem c.1534-1707: State Formation in the Atlantic Archipelago*, Basingstoke: Macmillan, 1996; Michael Hechter, *Internal Colonialism: The Celtic Fringe in British National Development, 1536-1966*, London: Routledge and Kegan Paul, 1975; Murray G.H. Pittock, *Celtic Identity and the British Image*, Manchester and New York: Manchester University Press, 1999.

22. This was begun by David Mathew, *The Celtic Peoples and Renaissance Europe*, London, Sheed and Ward, 1933, but for a new consideration see Ceri Davies and John E. Law (eds.), *The Renaissance and the Celtic Countries*, Oxford: Blackwell, 2005.

23. Taylor, op.cit., 1982.

24. Alan M. Kent, 'Art thou of Cornish crew? Shakespeare, *Henry V* and Cornish Identity' in Philip Payton (ed.), *Cornish Studies: Four*, Exeter: University of Exeter Press, 1996, pp.7-25.

25. Payton, op.cit., p.2.

26. Stoyle, op.cit., pp.36-7.

27. Kent, op.cit.

28. See Taylor, op.cit., pp.163-70. For a comparison, see Trevor Lloyd, 'Alexander the Pig: Shakespeare and the Celts', unpublished paper read at Sixth Australian Celtic Conference, 2007.

29. A.L. Rowse (ed.), *A Cornish Anthology*, Penzance: Alison Hodge, 1990 [1968], p.114.

30. See Kenneth Muir (ed.), *William Shakespeare: King Lear*, London: Methuen, 1972, pp.xiii-lviii.

31. See Philip Sidney in Gerald Bullet (ed.), *Silver Poets of the Sixteenth Century*, London: Dent, 1984, pp.173-280.

32. Lewis Thorpe (ed. and tr.), *Geoffrey of Monmouth: The History of the Kings of Britain*, Harmondsworth: Penguin, 1966, pp.81-4.

33. Muir, op.cit., p.135.

34. Ibid., pp.xiii-lviii.

35. Ibid., p.74.

36. Ibid., p.131.

37. Ibid., p.132.

38. Ibid., p.135.

39. See Andrew Hadfield, *Shakespeare, Spenser and the Matter of Britain*, London: Palgrave Macmillan, 2003; Joan Fitzpatrick, *Shakespeare, Spenser and the Contours of Britain: Reshaping the Atlantic Archipelago*, Hatfield: University of Hertfordshire Press, 2006. The devolution of the map is shown well in the 1984 television production, starring Laurence Olivier as Lear, and directed by Michael Elliott.

40. Stoyle, op.cit.

41. See John Pitcher (ed.), *William Shakespeare: Cymbeline*, London: Penguin, 2005. For a modern adaptation from an Anglo-Cornish dramatist, see Emma Rice and Carl Grose, *Cymbeline*, London: Oberon Books, 2007.

42. Spence, op.cit., p.119.

43. For a similar but later view, see Matthew Arnold, *The Study of Celtic Literature*, London: Smith and Elder, 1867.

44. John Kerrigan, *Archipelagic English: Literature, History and Politics 1603-1702*, Oxford: Oxford University Press, 2008.

45. Linda Colley, *Britons: Forging the Nation 1707-1837*, New Haven and London: Yale University Press, 1992. See also Bradshaw and Morrill, op.cit.

46. R.J. Stewart, Denise Coffey and Roy Hudd (eds.), *William Shakespeare and William Rowley: The Birth of Merlin, or The Childe hath found his Father*, Shaftesbury: Element Books, 1989.

47. Ibid., pp.1-54.

48. For the debate, see Mark Dominik, *Shakespeare and 'The Birth of Merlin'*, Beaverton, Oregon: Alioth Press, 1991.

49. See Thorpe, op.cit., pp.170-85, and John of Cornwall, *Prophetia Merlini*, Cod. Ottobonianus Lat. 1474, Vatican. For further background, see Nikolai Tolstoy, *The Quest for Merlin*, London: Hamish Hamilton, 1985, and Michael Dames, *Merlin and Wales: A Magician's Landscape*, London: Thames and Hudson, 2002.

50. Richard Levin, *The Multiple Plot in English Renaissance Drama*, Chicago: University of Chicago Press, 1971.

51. Stewart, Coffey and Hudd, op.cit., p.69.

52. Ibid., p.75.

53. Ibid., p.79.

54. Ibid., p.100.

55. Muir, op.cit., pp.22-24.

56. Stephen Greenblatt, *Renaissance Self-Fashioning: From More to Shakespeare*, Chicago: University of Chicago Press, 1980.

57. A.L. Beier, *Masterless Men: The Vagrancy Problem in England 1560-1640*, London: Methuen, 1985.

58. George Clement Boase and William Prideaux Courtney (eds.), *Bibliotheca Cornubiensis*, London: Longman, Green, Reader and Dyer, 1874, 1878 and 1882, p.967. Boase and Courtney offer that J.P. Collier's edition of the Diary published by the Shakespeare Society has the references on p.21, p.23, p.26 and p.27.

59. Ibid., p.158.

60. Ian Arthurson, *The Perkin Warbeck Conspiracy 1491-1499*, Stroud: Sutton, 1997. Though a useful book, Arthurson takes up an Anglo-centric position, and mistakenly lessens the significance of the rebellions of 1497.

61. Ibid., p.181-8.

62. John Ford, *The Chronicle Historie of Perkin Warbeck: A Strange Truth – A Tragedy in Five Acts and Chiefly in Verse*, London: T.P. for Hugh Beeston, 1634, p.iii.

63. Ibid., p.12.

64. Ibid., p.22.

65. Ibid., p.27.

66. Ibid., p.37.

67. Ibid., pp.43-4.

68. Ibid., p.45.

69. Ibid., p.46.

70. Ibid., p.53.

71. Ibid., p.60.

72. Boase and Courtney, op.cit., p.327.

73. Ibid.

74. For a fictional consideration of theatrical culture in the Restoration, see Rose Tremain, *Restoration*, London: Hamish Hamilton, 1989. Tremain is not Cornish and was born Rosemary Thomson.

75. For background on Ben Jonson's work, see Jonas Barish, *Ben Jonson and the Language of Prose Comedy*, Cambridge, Massachusetts: Harvard University Press, 1960.

76. Michael Jamieson (ed.), *Three Comedies: Volpone, The Alchemist and Bartholomew Fair*, Harmondsworth: Penguin, 1966, p.416.

77. Ibid., p.486.

78. Roger Victor Holdsworth (ed.), *Thomas Middleton and William Rowley, A Fair Quarrel*, London: Benn, 1974. An on-line version of the text is found at http://www.tech.org/~cleary/fairq/html.

79. See Mark Eccles, 'Middleton's Birth and Education' in *Review of English Studies*, 7, 1933, pp.431-41.

80. Bryan Loughrey and Neil Taylor (eds.), *Thomas Middleton: Five Plays*, London: Penguin, 1988.

81. See Levin, op.cit.

82. See the observations of Carew on Cornish wrestling in Halliday, op.cit., 1953, pp.150-1. See also Federation of Gouren, *Breton and Celtic Wrestling*, Brittany: Institut Culturel de Bretagne, 1985.

83. This scene lasts for the whole of Act I. See Holdsworth, op.cit., pp.1-29.

84. This could be seen as a kind of 'hand-fasting'. Such conditional agreements were popular in the seventeenth century.

85. See Jas. L. Palmer, *The Cornish Chough through the Ages*, Penzance: Federation of Old Cornwall Societies, n.d. See also the observations throughout in Amy Hale, Alan M. Kent, and Tim Saunders, (eds. and trs.), *Inside Merlin's Cave: A Cornish Arthurian Reader 1000-2000*, London: Francis Boutle Publishers, 2000.

86. Oxford English Dictionary.

87. Stoyle, op.cit., pp.37-8.

88. See William Shakespeare, *Henry IV*, II, ii, Line 86. *The Honest Ghost*, by R. Braithwaite, 1658, also features the lines 'a Country Gull,/Whose fathers death had made his pockets full,/… this Cornish Chough mourns for his father/In a *Carnation feather*'. See http://www.tech.org/~cleary/fairq/html. These lines link both the rustic and Cornish usage.

89. Joan Tasker Grimbert (ed.), *Tristan and Isolde: A Casebook*, New York and London: Garland, 1995.

90. Holdsworth, op.cit., p.47.

91. Ibid.

92. See also the observations on this in Philip Payton, *Cornwall*, Fowey: Alexander Associates, 1996, pp.149-76.

93. Holdsworth, op.cit.

94. Ibid.

95. Ibid., pp.47-8.

96. Ibid., p.48.

97. Ibid., p.48-9.

98. Ibid., p.50.

99. Ibid.

100. In Cornish: *Gwary tek yu gwary whek*. Wrestling matches in Cornwall always begin with the competitors shaking hands.

101. Holdsworth, op.cit.

102. It seems that both medieval and Renaissance literature imagined 'Dartmouth' as symbolic of wider south-west Britain. The Shipman in *The Canterbury Tales* is also from there. See F.N. Robinson (ed.), *The Complete Works of Geoffrey Chaucer*, Oxford: Oxford University Press, 1957, p.21.

103. Holdsworth, op.cit., p.52.

104. Ibid., p.75.

105. Ibid., p.78.

106. Ibid., p.83.

107. For issues affecting language transition, see Martyn F. Wakelin, *Language and History in Cornwall*, Leicester: Leicester University Press, 1975; Andrew C. Symons, 'Models of Language Transfer' in *An Baner Kernewek / The Cornish Banner*, No. 96, 1999, and 'Language Transfer in Cornwall' in *An Baner Kernewek / The Cornish Banner*, No. 127, 2007.

108. Holdsworth, op.cit., p.100.

109 Ibid., p.101.

110. Ibid., p.102.

111. Ibid., p.104-5.

112. Ibid., p.113 and p.114.

113. Ibid., p.116.

114. Ibid., p.117.

115. Carew notes that Cornish is 'easy to be pronounced and not so unpleasing in sound, with throat letters, as the Welsh'. See Halliday, op.cit., p.126.

116. Holdsworth, op.cit., pp.117-8. Is it Middleton and Rowley's intention to make these place-names sound amusing? The final location obviously refers to Stonehenge.

117. R.A.J. Walling, *The Story of Plymouth*, London: Westaway Books, 1950, pp.69-100.

118. See A.L. Rowse, *Tudor Cornwall*, Redruth: Dyllansow Truran, 1990 [1941], pp.141-2.

119. It is curious that illegitimacy is also a theme in *The Birth of Merlin*. Was this Rowley's input?

120. Holdsworth, op.cit., p.118.

121. Tim Saunders offers 'Go out' or 'Go away'. I am indebted to him for discussion here.

122. Holdsworth, op.cit., p.120.

123. Ibid., p.123.

124. Ibid., p.124.

125. Ibid., p.128.

126. See Kent and Saunders, op.cit.; Peter Berresford Ellis, *The Cornish Language and its Literature*, London and Boston: Routledge and Kegan Paul, 1974, p.76.

127. His other major plays included *The Antipodes, The Sparagus Garden, Covent Garden, Weeded, The New Academy or The Exchange, The Damoiselle*, and *The Court Beggar*.

128. This early division is rooted in pre-history but grew in the Early Modern Period. See Helen M. Jewell, *The North-South Divide: The Origins of Northern Consciousness in England*, Manchester: Manchester University Press, 1994.

129. See http://www.letrs.indiana.edu/cgi-bin/eprosed, p.31. This is a useful on-line version of the play. The page numbers refer to sections of the play as on the website, and are numbered in the individual Acts only. The full title of the play is *The Northern Lasse, a comedie. As it hath beene often Acted with good Applause, the Globe, and Black-Fryers. By his Majesties Servants*. The other main characters are Anvile, Widgine, Pate, Mistress Trainewell, Beavis, and Howdie. See also Harvey Fried (ed.), *A Critical Edition of Brome's "The Northern Lasse"*, New York and London: Garland, 1980.

130. See Carew, op.cit.

131. This invasion was subject to a supposed prophecy from an earlier period: '*Ewra teyre a war meane Merlyn, Ara lesky Pawle Penzanz ha Newlyn* [They shall land on the Rock of Merlin, Who shall burn Paul, Penzance and Newlyn]'. See Kent and Saunders, op.cit., pp32-3.

132. http://www.letrs.indiana.edu/cgi-bin/eprosed, p.25.

133. Ibid., p.38.

134. Ibid., p.12.

135. Ibid., p.23.

136. Numerous scholars note the rapid decline of Cornish in mid-Cornwall during this phase.

137. http://www.letrs.indiana.edu/cgi-bin/eprosed, p.31.

138. Ibid., p.41.

139. For context, see Charles Carlton, *The Experience of the British Civil Wars*, London and New York: Routledge, 1992; Trevor Royle, *Civil War: The Wars of the Three Kingdoms 1638-1660*, London: Abacus, 2006. For various statements of positions in the run-up to the conflict, during the conflict, and the aftermath, see sources in Christopher Hampton (ed.), *A Radical Reader: The Struggle for Change in England 1381-1914*, Harmondsworth, Penguin, 1984, pp.149-286.

140. See Christopher Hill, *God's Englishman*, London: Weidenfield and Nicholson, 1970; Jessica Saraga, *Cromwell*, London: Batsford, 1990.

141. Mary Coate, *Cornwall in the Great Civil War and Interregnum, 1642-1660*, Truro: D. Bradford Barton, 1963 [1933]. For a dramatic recreation of the Cornish in the Civil War, see Alan M. Kent, *Oogly es Sin: The Lamentable Ballad of Anthony Payne, Cornish Giant*, London: Francis Boutle Publishers, 2007.

142. See Payton, op.cit., 1996, pp.153-66; Bernard Deacon, *Cornwall: A Concise History*, Cardiff: University of Wales Press, 2007, pp.88-9. This general view needs to be tempered by the fact that not all Cornish gentry took the Royalist

position. For an exploration, see Anne Duffin, *Faction and Faith: Politics and Religion of the Cornish Gentry Before the Civil War*, Exeter: University of Exeter Press, 1996. Duffin's work is Anglo-centric but offers useful insights.

143. Stoyle, op.cit., pp.66-112.

144. Boase and Courtney, op.cit., p.364.

145. Mining culture existed in a similar way in West Devon and Dartmoor to that west of the River Tamar.

146. William Killigrew, *Ayres and Dialogues for one, two and three voices*, London, 1653.

147. William Killigrew, *Four New Playes, viz. The Seege of Urbin, Selindra, Love and Friendship: tragy-comedies, Pandora, comedy*, Oxford: Oxford University, printed by Henry Hall, 1666.

148. Ibid., p.vi.

149. William Killigrew, *Three New Playes, viz. Selinda, Pandorea, Ormasdes*, London, 1674.

150. William Killigrew, *The Imperial Tragedy, taken out of a Latin play, and very much altered, by a Gentleman for his own diversion*, London: William Wells and Robert Scott, 1669.

151. Penryn Borough Records Mayor's Cash Book 1657-8, cited in James Whetter, *The History of Falmouth*, Gorran: Lyfrow Trelyspen, 2004 [1981], p.79.

152. Ibid.

153. See Ronald Hutton, op.cit., pp.200-27.

154. For further discussion of the role of these individuals, see Harwood, op.cit., pp.178-9.

155. See Lawrence, op.cit.

156. This imagining has persisted. See, for example, Raymond Williams, *The Country and the City*, St Albans: Paladin, 1975 [1973]. In the late twentieth-century, however, this construction was usually perceived along 'centre-periphery' lines. See, for example, Michael Keating, *State and Regional Nationalism: Territorial Politics and the European State*, London: Harvester Wheatsheaf, 1988, and contributors to Tony Brown and Russell Stephens (eds.), *Nations and Relations: Writing Across the British Isles*, Cardiff: New Welsh Review, 2000.

157. For an exploration of this, see Robert Markley, 'The Canon and its Critics' in Deborah Payne Fisk (ed.), *The Cambridge Companion to English Restoration Theatre*, Cambridge: Cambridge University Press, 2000. Collier's short view was, in fact, extremely long.

158. One of the most important playwrights was Aphra Behn (1640-1689). See W.R. Owens and Lizbeth Goodman, 'Remaking the Canon: Aphra Behn's *The Rover*' in W.R. Owens and Lizbeth Goodman (eds.), *Approaching Literature: Shakespeare, Aphra Behn and the Canon*, London: Routledge, 1996, pp.131-92.

The Rover was first performed by the Duke's Company at the Dorset Garden Theatre in March 1677.

159. Paul Langford, *A Polite and Commercial People: England 1727-1783*, Oxford: Clarendon Press, 1999, p.49.

160. This view is supported by a number of contributors to S.J. Connolly (ed.), *Kingdoms United? Great Britain and Ireland Since 1500: Integration and Diversity*, Dublin: Four Courts Press, 1999.

161. James Whetter, *Cornish People in the 18th Century*, Gorran: Lyfrow Trelyspen, 2000. For observations on social change, see John Rule, *Cornish Cases: Essays in Eighteenth and Nineteenth Century Social History*, Southampton: Clio Publishing, 2006.

162. Allen Buckley, *The Story of Mining in Cornwall: A World of Payable Ground*, Fowey: Cornwall Editions, 2005, pp.62-90.

163. Roger Kemble was the father of John Philip, Charles, Stephen and Sarah [Siddons] Kemble. See Peter Thomson, *The Cambridge Introduction to English Theatre, 1660-1990*, Cambridge: Cambridge University Press, 2006, p.132.

164. Ibid., p.132. See also Harvey Crane, *Playbill: A History of the Theatre in the West Country*, Plymouth: Macdonald and Evans, 1980, p.43.

165. William Scawen, op.cit. Useful context for Scawen's intellect is found in the following volumes: Williams and Jones, op.cit., and Davies and Law, op.cit.

166. This group is well known, and individual biographies and dates are found in Ellis, op.cit.; Craig Weatherhill, *Cornish Place Names and Language*, Wilmslow: Sigma, 1995; Kent and Saunders, op.cit.

167. For a selection see Kent and Saunders, op.cit.

168. Ibid., pp.226-9.

169. Ibid., pp.212-19. For commentary on the versions, see Oliver Padel (ed.), *The Cornish Writings of the Boson Family*, Redruth: Institute of Cornish Studies, 1975.

170. Brian Murdoch, 'Is *John of Chyanhor* Really a 'Cornish *Ruodlieb*'?' in Payton, op.cit., 1996, pp.45-63.

171. See Edmund Gibson (ed.), *Camden's Britannica*, Newton Abbot: David and Charles, 1975 [1695], column 17. A translation of the New Testament was completed in 2002. See Nicholas Williams, *Testament Noweth agan Arluth ha Savyour Jesu Cryst*, Redruth: Sprys a Gernow, 2002.

172. For a biography, see entry in John Koch (ed.), *Celtic Culture: A Historical Encylopedia*, Vols. 1-5, Santa Barbara, California and Oxford: ABC Clio, 2006, pp. 1152-3.

173. Derek Williams, *Prying into Every Hole and Corner: Edward Lhuyd in Cornwall in 1700*, Redruth: Dyllansow Truran, 1993. Lhuyd's Cornish Notebooks are being prepared for publication by Ken George.

174. See Nicholas Williams, 'The Cornish Englyn' in Philip Payton (ed.), *Cornish Studies: Fifteen*, Exeter: University of Exeter Press, 2007, pp.11-26.

175. Lhuyd's work was felt by Jenner the best point to base the revived language upon. Subsequent work failed to recognise the impact of Lhuyd's scholarship until more recently. For a debate, see Michael Everson, Craig Weatherhill, Ray Chubb, Bernard Deacon and Nicholas Williams, *Form and Content in Revived Cornish*, Westport: Evertype, 2007. Richard Gendall describes Lhuyd's grammar as having 'a strong sense of familiarity about it, relating it to the present day'. See Richard Gendall, *A Practical Dictionary of Modern Cornish, Part One: Cornish – English*, Menheniot, Teere ha Tavza, 1997.

176. Andrew Brice, *The Exmoor Scolding*, in *Brice's Weekly Journal*, No.52, 1727.

177. Ibid.

178. Cornwall was known as West Wales and the Cornish as the West Welsh even up to the Tudor period. See Philip Payton, *The Making of Modern Cornwall: Historical Experience and the Persistence of "Difference"*, Redruth: Dyllansow Truran, 1992, p.46.

179. Brice, op.cit.. See also Richard Polwhele, 'The Language, Literature and Literary Characters of Cornwall' in *The History of Cornwall*, London: W. Davies, 1806, p.6. Brice wrote an additional play titled *An Exmoor Courtship*, See Polwhele, pp.29-33.

180. Polwhele, op.cit., p.24 and p.4. He also notes that 'The Cornish language was current in a part of the South-Hams, (which I have called East-Cornwall) in the time of Edward the First; and long after, in all the vicinities of the Tamar. In Cornwall, it was universally spoken'. See p.6.

181. *Black Letter Pamphlet: News from Pe[n]rin in Cornwall of a most Bloody and unexampled Murder*, Quarto, Bodley, 4 M G29 (2), Oxford.

182. Lillo's version later influenced German so-called 'fate drama'.

183. Alan M. Kent, *The Literature of Cornwall: Continuity, Identity, Difference 1000-2000*, Bristol: Redcliffe, 2000, p.60. For further insight into this Renaissance individuality, see Greenblatt, op.cit.; Beier, op.cit.

184. *The Black Letter Pamphlet: News from Pe[n]rin in Cornwall of a most Bloody and un-exampled Murder*, op.cit.

185. Thomas Davies (ed.), *Lillo's Dramatic Works Vol. 2: Fatal Curiosity, Marina, Elmerick, or Justice Triumphant, Britannia and Batavia, Arden of Feversham*, Whitefish, Montana: Kessinger Publishing, 2008, p.7. A prologue was written for the drama by Henry Fielding.

186. After 1736, Lillo's text was actually withdrawn from the stage until the summer of 1782, when it was revived by George Colman.

187. Davies, op.cit., p.6.

188. See Donald R. Rawe, *Murder at Bohelland*, 1991. Another version of the story,

Bohelland, was the first new play written by Justin Chubb for the Cornish Theatre Collective in 1997, as part of the Lady Jane Killigrew Festival. The play was also revived in Penryn in 2003.

189. Davies, op.cit., pp.10-11.

190. Ibid., p.14.

191. Ibid., p.20.

192. Ibid., p.22.

193. Ibid.

194. This has an interesting parallel to *Ordinalia*'s 'Resurrection' play, where Jesus is disguised as a gardener and Mary does not recognise him as her son. Lillo is probably more influenced by Shakespeare's *Twelfth Night*.

195. Davies, op.cit., p.33.

196. Ibid., p.32.

197. Ibid., pp.39-40.

198. Ibid., p.45.

199. Ibid., p.49.

200. Foote's work is not explored in either the First or Second Series of *Cornish Studies*. His plays are not considered in any of the works by Denys Val Baker. He gets a very brief mention in Harvey Crane's *History*. He is featured as an entry in Maurice Smelt, *101 Cornish Lives*, Penzance: Alison Hodge, 2006, pp.88-90. Smelt comments that 'Like Lord Byron, Samuel Foote was mad, bad and dangerous to know'.

201. The present author holds up his own hands. Kent, op.cit., 2000, following type, does not feature Foote. Foote is not seen as influential in the modern era. See John Hurst, 'Literature in Cornwall' in Philip Payton (ed.), *Cornwall Since the War: The Contemporary History of a European Region*, Redruth: Institute of Cornish Studies and Dyllansow Truran, 1993, pp.291-308. It is hoped this chapter will stand as a correction.

202. See Douglas Howard, 'Samuel Foote' in Paula Backschneider (ed.), *Dictionary of Literary Biography, Volume 89: Restoration and Eighteenth-Century Dramatists*, Detroit: Gale Research, 1989, p.131.

203. Cited in Samuel Foote, *The Dramatic Works of Samuel Foote*, Vol. I, London: J. F. Rivington, C. Rivington, R. Baldwin, and S. Bladon, 1788, pp.1-23.

204. Howard, op.cit.

205. Cited in Foote. op.cit., p.5.

206. Ibid.

207. Ibid., pp.7-8.

208. The picture is in Mary C. Murphy, and Gerald S. Argetsinger, 'Samuel Foote' in Carl Rollyson and Frank N. Magill (eds.), *Critical Survey of Drama*, Vol. 2, Pasadena, California: Salem Press, 2003, p.1103.

209. Foote, op. cit., p.x.

210. Ibid., p.8.

211. Ibid.

212. Ibid.

213. See http://www.worldwidewords.org/weirdwords/ww-pan2.htm. The name 'Panjandrum' was later adopted during the Second World War, for an explosive device developed by the British military.

214. Foote, op.cit., p.10.

215. This may also be a reference to Shakespeare's Act V, Scene i in *Henry V*, when Pistol responds to Fluellen with the line, 'Not for Cadwallader and all his goats'. See Taylor, op.cit., p.262. Foote may or may not have known of the Cornish-Welsh link, but he does appear to use it for satiric effect.

216. Foote, op.cit., p.11.

217. Foote, op.cit., Vol. IV, p.16.

218. For background, on this, see Rupert Davies, *Methodism*, Peterborough: Epworth Press, 1985 [1963].

219. See A. Brown-Lawson, *John Wesley and the Anglican Evangelicals of the Eighteenth Century*, Durham: The Pentland Press, 1994, pp.91-96.

220. Foote, op.cit., Vol. I, p.12.

221. See *Universal Magazine*, December, 1778, p.316.

222. Foote, op.cit., Vol II, p.73.

223. Ibid., p.79.

224. Foote, op.cit., Vol. I, p.13.

225. Ibid., p. 14.

226. Ibid., pp.14-15.

227. Ibid., p.15.

228. Ibid., p.16.

229. Ibid., p.17.

230. Ibid., p.18. Foote also put his name to a work entitled *The Comic Theatre* (in five volumes), being a translation of a number of French comedies. Of these, only the first play, *The Young Hypocrite*, is attributed to him.

231. Ibid., p.21.

232. Ibid., p.23.

233. Ibid., pp.18-19. Another assessment is found in Jon Lee, 'An Essay on the Life, Genius and Writings of the Author' in John Lee (ed.), *The Works of Samuel Foote Esq*, London: Sherwood, Gilbert and Piper, 1830, pp.i-cxiv. Lee may be the anonymous observer of the first anthology of Foote's writings, though no name is given there.

234. Ibid., p.19.

235. Ibid., p.9-10.

236. Ibid., p v.

237. Ibid., pp.13-14.

238. This may not be quite what it seems. The Black Rock was, in fact, used as the point of imposition of the tax of poll-money for shipping arrivals, in which case it would have been highly lucrative. For more on this, see Jane A. Bakere, *The Cornish Ordinalia: A Critical Study*, Cardiff: University of Wales Press, 1980, pp.36-7.

239. Foote, op.cit., p.16.

240. Payton, op.cit., 1992, pp.84-5.

241. As seen in the writings of Andrew Boorde, *c.*1547. See Kent and Saunders, op.cit., p.265.

242. This period is well imagined in the first Poldark novel: *Ross Poldark*. See Winston Graham, *The Poldark Omnibus*, London: The Bodley Head, 1991. See also Buckley, op.cit., and John Rowe, *Cornwall in the Age of the Industrial Revolution*, St Austell: Cornish Hillside Publications, 1993 [1953].

243. James Whetter, *Cornwall in the Seventeenth Century: An Economic Survey of Kernow*, Padstow: Lodenek Press, 1974, p.176. See also Payton, op.cit., pp.105-6.

244. Kent and Saunders, op.cit., pp.236-7.

245. Foote, op.cit., p.18. This list in here has a remarkable similarity to the list of Cornish pastimes referred to in George D. Marsh, and the Writers' Project of Montana, *Copper Camp: The Lusty Story of Butte, Montana, The Richest Hill on Earth*, Helena: Riverbend Publishing, 2002 [1943]. Continuity is there some 150 years later and on a different continent.

246. Ibid., pp.21-22.

247. Ibid., pp.18-19.

248. Kent and Saunders, op.cit. See also Brian Murdoch (ed.), *The Grin of the Gargoyle*, Sawtry: Dedalus, 1995, pp.201-2.

249. Foote, op.cit., p.30.

250. Ibid., p.40.

251. Ibid., p.43.

252. See Mark A. Howell, 'Planning Provincial Theatres Under the 1757 Stage Licensing Act' in *Theatre Notebook: A Journal of the History and Technique of the British Theatre*, No. 3, 1989, pp.104-118.

253. The Friends of the Georgian Theatre, Penzance were formed on 27 April 1986, with the aim of the organisation 'to restore the Georgian Theatre, Penzance to its original condition as a fully operational live theatre for the benefit of the Town, the County [sic] and the Nation'. See F. Keith Kennedy, *A Brief History of the Georgian Theatre Penzance*, Penzance: Union Hotel, n.d., p.1.

254. For background, see P.A.S. Pool (ed.), *George Clement Boase: Reminiscences of Penzance*, Penzance: Penzance Old Cornwall Society, 1976, pp.47-8.

255. *The Sherbourne Mercury*, 28 February 1786.

256. Kennedy, op.cit.

257. See Richard Southern and Ivor Brown, *The Georgian Theatre, Richmond, Yorkshire*, Richmond: The Georgian Theatre, Richmond Trust, 1973. See also http://www.georgiantheatreroyal.co.uk

258. Kennedy, op.cit.

259. Cited in ibid.

260. Ibid.

261. Vauxhall Gardens was one of the leading public venues for entertainment in London from the mid seventeenth century to the mid nineteenth century. See Walter Sidney Scott, *Green Retreats: The Story of Vauxhall Gardens 1661-1859*, London: Odhams Press, 1955.

262. See James Dawson, *The Autobiography*, Truro: J.R. Netherton, 1865.

263. Ann Altree, 'The Georgian Theatre' in June Palmer and Ann Altree (eds.), *Treasures of the Morrab: A Library that has more than Books*, Penzance: The Morrab Library, 2005, pp. 43-8. This book was developed by Penwith History Group. I am indebted to Ann Altree for her conversations with me about the Penzance theatre.

264. In his history of Penzance, Peter Pool notes that the Anglo-Cornish poet Charles Valentine Le Grice (1773-1858) reprinted a letter he had sent to the Royal Cornwall Gazette in 1803, following a visit to the theatre to see a new comedy by a Mr. Colman, *John Bull*, which was set in Penzance: 'Imagine my surprise at finding the vicinity of Penzance represented as a desert moor, and that too with the uncouth denomination of Muckslush Heath! I know that an idea prevails, that around Penzance every wind that blows is a storm, that the few houses which are above ground are built of wrecked timber, that the underground inhabitants are the most numerous, that the above-ground gentlemen are all smugglers, and that every horse at night is a kind of will o'whisp, and carries a lantern at his tail to decoy the coasting mariner. Now I beg leave to inform Mr. Colman that Penzance is a very different place from the commonly received opinion. We have cards for the sedentary, books for the lounger, balls for the light-heeled, clubs for the convivial, and picnics for the gay and thoughtless. Turbot and mullet swim almost at our doors; our fields are perfect gardens; our bay is inferior only to the Bay of Naples; and as for our climate, from the rarity of ice not a boy here can slide, and a pair of skates would be a matter of as much astonishment as an air-balloon.' See P.A.S. Pool (ed.), *The History of the Town and Borough of Penzance*, Penzance: The Corporation of Penzance, 1974, pp.118-9. This event prompted Le Grice to write a poem titled *The Petition of an Old Uninhabited House in Penzance to its Master in Town, with Hints to the Author of John Bull, A Comedy*. For a collection of Le Grice's work, see

Alan M. Kent (ed.), *Charles Valentine Le Grice – Cornwall's Romantic Poet: Selected Poems*, St Austell: Lyonesse, 2010.

265. Altree, op.cit.

266. Ibid.

267. Harvard University Theatre Collection. I am indebted to Melissa Hardie and David Wilmore for bringing this to my attention.

268. A useful architectural survey is found in Renton Howard Wood Levin Partnership, *The Georgian Theatre, Union Hotel: A Feasibility Study for the Reconstruction*, 1989. See also Peter Waverley, 'The Lost Georgian Theatre', Article in the Hypatia Trust Archive, n.d.

269. These sketches were made by an artist with the initials P.G.H. They belong to the archive of Joan Leeds whom, despite considerable effort, I have been unable to trace.

270. Similar structures are described in Harwood, op.cit., and in Thomson, op.cit.

271. Southern's sketch is found in Renton Howard Wood Levin Partnership, op.cit., p.20.

272. *The Cornishman*, 17 March 1960.

273. Robert Dyer, *Nine Years of an Actor's Life*, London: Rees, Orme, Brown, and Co., 1833, p.22. Dyer describes himself on the title page as being 'Late of the Theatre Royal, Plymouth, Worcester, Derby, Nottingham, Taunton, Barnstaple, &c, &c' but neglects mentioning his Cornish period. The volume was written in Plymouth and many of his subscribers were from there. However the subscription list does mention four Cornish names: Peter Brendon and Mr Hamblyn, both of Launceston; and Mr William Hicks and Edward Mountsteven Wright, both of Bodmin. Dyer was also a talented poet and dramatist. His poems included *Dunmere, Eliza, Robert: A Fragment, The Bard's Last Lay, Faith, Hope and Charity, Belles Lettres*, and *Epitaph on James Shatford*. See pp.26-32 and pp.80-1. The drama *Scenes of Passions* is found on pp.159-89.

274. Ibid., pp.34-5. Dyer met his wife in Penzance. However, on one tour, a critic did not like his performance: 'My acting in Penzance did not give general satisfaction, inasmuch as a critic took exception to my style, and made a violent anonymous attack on me in the pages of the Dramatic magazine. I have not the number to refer to, in which his remarks have a place, but they had a withering influence on my spirits, and almost determined me on leaving the stage. He abused my personal and mental pretensions – compared my head to a mop – my mouth to a vast cavern – ridiculed my attempts at elegance in Corinthian Tom – and insisted that Nature designed me for an Irish Watchman!' See p.35.

275. Wilkie Collins, *Rambles beyond Railways, or Notes in Cornwall taken a-foot*, London: Westaway Books, 1948 [1851], pp.118-28.

276. Dyer, op.cit. Dyer writes the following observation: 'The Theatre-Rural, Bodmin, stood in Back-Lane, and when the players were gone was converted to a stable. The dressing-rooms were in the hay-loft. On the second season we had better accommodation in a pig-stye, but of which I did not avail, as a chandler-friend allowed me to dress in his melting-shop – no bad proof, as the actors said of my love for fat. Our stage has little depth, and less breadth, while the room behind the scenes was proportionally less, and I remember that in Falstaff, Manager Dawson was obliged to unpad, as, with his artificial corpulence, he could not pass between the wings and the wall; – and that subsequently on a fat lady's joining the company, she had certainly received her discharge had she been one hair's breath stouter, for moving the wings nearer each other would have "cabined, cribbed, confined" us, beyond endurance, and to knock down the walls was thought too expensive'.

277. Dawson, op.cit., pp.95-6.

278. This is from Act V, Scene iv.

279. Edward Smith, 'Reminiscences' in *The Cornishman*, 25 October, 1883. I am indebted to Ann Altree for referring me to this source. Cross was more a leading actor than the general manager.

280. For a biography, see Raymond Fitzsimons, *Edmund Kean*, London: Hamish Hamilton, 1976. As Altree details, Kean's son Charles maintained links with Penzance. There is, in the Morrab library archive, a letter from him to one J.J. Boase of Penzance, dated 5 January 1862. Kean was staying at the Union Hotel, and the correspondence references a section from Shakespeare's *All's Well that Ends Well*. See Altree, op.cit., p.46.

281. This is detailed in Kennedy, op.cit.

282. Ibid.

283. This point is made in Renton Howard Wood Levin Partnership, op.cit., p.10. They comment that 'during this period travelling conditions were extremely difficult'.

284. An alternative view is found in Pool, op.cit.. He comments that 'Penzance has indeed become a social centre, second in Cornwall only to Truro. From 1770 onwards fortnightly assemblies had been held from October to March at the "Ship and Castle" (now the Union), and by 1791 these had so grown as to require the erection of new premises, the assembly room being built by subscription in the hotel garden and the first assembly held there on 24 October, the season culminating with an Easter Ball in April 1792'. However, Falmouth grew rapidly in the aftermath of this period.

285. See Altree, op.cit., p.48.

286. See observations in Louise Courtney, *Half Century of Penzance 1825-1875 – from notes by J.S. Courtney*, Penzance: Beare and Son, 1878.

287. 'Penzance Little Theatre' in *The Cornishman*, 1 November 1945.

288. See the positive response to this in the *Cornish Buildings Group Newsletter*, 2004, p.1.

289. Letter from Territory Co-ordinator West, Miss Daniella Lipscombe, English Heritage: South-West Region to Dr Melissa Hardie, The Hypatia Trust, New Mill, Penzance, 9 February 2007. Lipscombe comments that 'the degree of alteration and loss of fabric is, however, too great for it to merit listing at a higher grade'. Such a comment prevented the building reaching Grade I listing, and no funding was forthcoming. I am indebted to Melissa Hardie for giving me sight of this letter. Such correspondence can be viewed against the supportive findings in Eric Berry, 'The Old Theatre, Penzance: Preliminary Findings for Sensitivity Study', 2006, unpublished notes in the Hypatia Trust Archive.

290. Margaret A. Courtney (ed.), *Cornish Feasts and Folklore*, Exeter: Cornwall Books, 1989 [1890], pp.81-2.

291. H.L. Douch, *The Book of Truro*, Chesham: Barracuda Books, 1977, p.120.

292. *The Sherborne Mercury* 24 September 1787.

293. See the observations in Sybil Marion Rosenfeld, *Strolling Players and Drama in the Provinces 1660-1765*, London: Octagon Books, 1970, p.5-9.

294. Howell, op.cit. As well as Howell, I am indebted to the researches here of Mr T.H. Clark of Truro who first researched the Truro Assembly-Room Theatre in the 1970s. After demolition of the rear, it became 'The Delectable Duchy Tea Room' and then turned into retail premises, firstly an estate agent and then, more recently, a bakery.

295. CRO: DD EN906/1.

296. See Christopher Ebdon, Plan of the Assembly Rooms (High Cross, Truro): 14 designs submitted "for the erection of the Old Assembly Rooms at Truro" in Courtney Library, Royal Institution of Cornwall, Truro. This was not the first proposal for a dual-purpose assembly-room theatre. Plans dated 7 April exist for one at Bath that was never built. For comparison to other areas, see Arnold Hare, *The Georgian Theatre in Wessex*, London: Phoenix House, 1958, p.99, and Cecil Price, *The English Theatre in Wales*, Cardiff: University of Wales Press, 1948, pp.11-15.

297. CRO: DD EN906/1.

298. Howell, op.cit.

299. Ibid.

300. These are available in the photographic archive of the Royal Institution of Cornwall. Useful comparison can be made to the following pieces of research: Richard Southern 'The Lost Remains at King's Lynn' in *The Revels History of Drama in English*, 1975, No. 6, p.67; Ian Mackintosh, 'Rediscovering the Courtyard' in *Architectural Review*, April, 1984, p.67.

301. CRO: AD43 Anon, *Journal of a Tour of Cornwall*, unpublished ms. diary.

302. Howell, op.cit.

303. A general argument found in Ian Mackintosh, *Architecture, Actor and Audience*, London and New York: Routledge, 1993.

304. June Palmer, *Truro in the Eighteenth Century: Interlocking Circles*, Truro: June Palmer, 1990.

305. Douch, op.cit.

306. Ibid.

307. Viv Acton, 'Truro – Leisure and Entertainment' in June Palmer, (ed.), *Truro in the Age of Reform: 1815-1837*, Truro: June Palmer, 1999, pp.41-7.

308. A thorough restoration of the façade was completed in 1975. It received a European Architectural Heritage Year Award for this.

309. Enys Memoranda (n.d.) at Cornwall Record Office, f.22. I am indebted to the Enys Estate for allowing me permission to quote from this text.

310. A forthcoming article by Joanna Mattingly looks at Guild structures in this part of Cornwall.

311. There are two main interpretations of the origin of the word 'mummers'. As Hutton offers, the term may have its origins in the Greek word *mommo*, meaning a mask, the wearing of which became popular at royal functions in the fourteenth century, the practice being termed *momerie*. The fashion spread out of the court and upper class houses, where it caused many problems as revelry by night offered society concerns over 'masterless men' and the crime they might commit. Some towns would ban 'Momerie' for such a reason. See Ronald Hutton *The Stations of the Sun: A History of the Ritual Year in Britain*, Oxford: Oxford University Press, 1996, p.13. A second equally convincing explanation is that 'mummers' may come from the Middle English *mum* meaning 'silent', and since the plays were originally mime or dumb shows, the term seems convincing. See Walter W. Skeat (ed.), *An Etymological Dictionary of the English Language*, Oxford: Oxford University Press, 1963.

312. Thurstan C. Peter Collection, Box 1, Notebook 2, Courtney Library, Royal Institution of Cornwall. See also Thurstan C. Peter, 'Replies: St. George Mumming Play' in *Notes and Queries*, Series 12, Vol. I, 1916, pp.390-393. The references below refer to Notebook 2.

313. Peter Millington, 'The Truro Cordwainers' Play: An Eighteenth-Century Christmas Play' in *Folklore*, Vol. 114, No. 1, 2003, pp.53-73.

314. Ibid., p.58.

315. See Constables List. Schedule B: *Constables List of the Borough of Truro*, Courtney Library, Royal Institution of Cornwall, Ref. N/80, 1803; Schedule B: *Constables List of the Borough of St Clement*, Courtney Library, Royal Institution of Cornwall, Ref. N/73, 1803.

316. Millington, op.cit., p.62.
317. Ibid.
318. Ibid., p.66. For background, see Tony Pawlyn, *The Falmouth Packets*, Mount Hawke: Truran, 2003.
319. See Peter, op.cit; Joseph Smyth and David Lyons, *Christmas Rime, or, The Mummer's own Book*, Belfast: Smyth and Lyons, 1803-18.
320. Peter, op.cit.
321. Ibid.
322. Ibid.
323. For the opera, see A.C. Guthkelch (ed.), *The Miscellaneous Works of Joseph Addison*, 2 Vols, Vol. 1, London: C. Bell and Sons, 1914.
324. Tom Pettitt, 'From Stage to Folk: A Note on the Passages from Addison's Rosamond in the "Truro" Mummer's Play' in *Folklore*, Vol. 114, No. 2, 2003, pp.262-70.
325. See Shepherd, in the Preface to this volume.

CHAPTER FOUR

'The Locomotive Stage of Cornwall': Mining, Melodrama and Managers, 1800-1850

'I can only say, as the result of my own experience at Redruth, that if the dramatic reforms which are now being attempted in the theatrical byways of the metropolis succeed, there would be no harm in extending the experiment as far as the locomotive stage of Cornwall.'

From 'The Modern Drama in Cornwall' by Wilkie Collins, *Rambles Beyond Railways, or Notes in Cornwall taken a-foot*, 1851[1]

'In Plymouth they only laugh occasionally, but we always got louder laughs in Cornwall.'

James Dawson, Actor-Manager of the Truro Assembly-Room Theatre, *c.*1840, cited in Harvey Crane, *Playbill: A History of Theatre in the West Country*, 1980[2]

The theatre of nineteenth-century Cornwall formed a cultural backdrop to one of most industrialised nations on the earth.[3] Although the Licensing Acts of 1737 and 1788 continued to have ramifications,[4] most theatrical entrepreneurs were able to operate 'legally' by bending the rules, just as the Assembly-Room Theatre in Truro had done at the end of the eighteenth century. The Licensing Acts were, in some ways, very damaging to the development of drama outside of London (only Covent Garden and Drury Lane still had permission to give straight performances), so the entrepreneurs and actor managers found ways in which other forms of theatre could be employed to keep their venues busy, thus securing financial viability. In this sense, provincial theatre operating in Cornwall had again to be innovative and creative to survive. Legal shutdowns had occurred before, but this situation alone was not going to stop dramatic activity. Indeed, the rebellious and dissident nature of 'barely legal' performance probably enhanced the dangerous appeal of the theatre. Some of Cornwall's by now developed urban theatres – at Falmouth, Truro, Redruth and Penzance (licensed by local authorities, albeit for limited seasons) – turned to farce, pantomime and opera to keep revenue flowing in. With a few exceptions, the season for urban theatre generally lasted from November to March.

However, there were also legal loopholes that could be exploited by the actor managers and promoters. For example, some plays could be performed if they contained at least five songs. Such loopholes gave rise to burlesque plays, which were usually parodies, or shorter adaptations of straight plays. Such dramas were already in the urban dramatic continuum of Cornwall by the turn of the nineteenth century, and those venues that had developed at the end of the eighteenth century usually had a stock set of burlesque, which could be drawn upon by both a few internal players and touring companies. Another highly popular genre – burletta – developed. These were straight plays with five songs in them, and a favourite format in early nineteenth-century drama in Cornwall. Across Britain such a format marks the beginning of musical theatre in the sense we know it at the beginning of the twenty-first century. Performances of Shakespeare could also be adapted to this format. Indeed, Shakespeare's plays were remarkably rich sources for players and promoters to draw upon in this period. They were out of copyright, which facilitated easy and convenient changes in plot (tragedies were still being rewritten to have happy endings). Songs or a chorus could be added, so using the legal loophole. Local colour was important, so the period standards were adapted to fit Cornish circumstances. For example, songs could be adapted to feature particular places or events, or jokes and comedy given a Cornish twist.

It was not until the Theatre Act of 1843 that abolition of the licence needed to perform straight plays was made law,[5] but by this time many of the conventions of how to present drama in Cornwall were fully established. Judging by newspaper accounts and advertisements for drama post-1843, it seems the shock of the abolition of the licence caused considerable impact upon the theatrical community, for after this date, theatre in Cornwall hardly knows what to do with itself. One impact was that although audience demand was for the old-style burletta and farce, promoters (with an eye on the major urban centres of Plymouth, Bristol and London) were looking to mount productions of the by then more fashionable straight plays, but it seems audiences stayed away. Another impact on theatrical activity was the economic situation of Cornwall during the 1840s. In what historians now call the 'hungry forties',[6] Cornwall experienced considerable social and economic turmoil, brought about by the twin economic factors of crop failure and industrial decline. The 1840s was also the great decade of popular emigration overseas,[7] with a resultant collapse of the working-class audience.

The picture one receives of urban theatre in Cornwall in the early half of the nineteenth century is of a very creative and dynamic period, still drawing in part on the success and style of late eighteenth-century drama. Many of the plays popular in the previous century were still being performed, and most drew stylistically on this earlier phase. Anglo-centric scholarship may see this as some kind of cultural lag, and that the London and Bristol theatres had already progressed in terms of style, form and genre, though a more enlightened view might argue that Cornwall was, in a sense, following its own path, with much of the style kept from the previous period, but with a more resolutely Cornish subject matter being portrayed. Key to this was also the rise of the performance style known as melodrama (this literally means 'song drama'), which was key to understanding burletta and burlesque plays. The performers of the late eighteenth and early nineteenth centuries developed an acting style which allowed them to cope with both dialogue and song. This meant many of the grand gestures and posture of opera became part of the delivery in more mainstream theatre.

Although, as we shall see, the theatres of urban Cornwall continued to attract different social groups (seating them, as elsewhere in Britain, in different parts of the theatres), their demand for action, emotion and spectacle

Fig. 61. The last scene of *Tom Thumb the Great* from the Scarborough Theatre, in 1821, as engraved by Thomas Rowlandson. Theatre in Cornwall during this phase would have looked very similar. Courtesy of the University of Bristol Theatre Collection.

was very much the same. Melodrama suited early nineteenth-century audience needs. The plays were quite two-dimensional, the dialogue was simple, and there was room (within the technical confines of this period) for action and spectacle. The 1843 Act caused this to change: after a period of theatrical unrest, audiences came to demand less romance and exotica, and favoured material containing stories they could relate to. This, in turn, caused its own revolution in theatrical activity at the end of the century. In this, Cornwall was no different to anywhere else in Britain. Theatre again had to change to fit audience demands.

As well as theatrical activity at home, during the nineteenth century, Cornwall and Cornish subject matter, as we shall see, becomes a very important element within drama being presented elsewhere in Britain. We should not be surprised at this, for as our story has shown, it was always the case. However, the presentation came with both a new revitalisation and a new set of conventions. Therefore, the picture we have in the nineteenth century is that as the century progresses, indigenous and touring drama in Cornwall somewhat declines – certainly after the 1840s – but the thematic thread of Cornwall is taken up by a number of dramatists operating elsewhere in Britain and Europe. This is seen no better than in W.S. Gilbert and Arthur Sullivan's comic operas *The Pirates of Penzance, or Love and Duty* (1879), and *Ruddygore, or The Witch's Curse* (1887),[8] and Richard Wagner (1813-83) in his operas *Tristan and Isolde* (1865), and *Parsifal* (1882) – the latter with its Arthurian Holy Grail theme.[9] The peculiar nature of Cornwall, alongside its Celticity, would eventually come full circle: as its cultural distinctiveness was being more fully recognised on the world stage, cultural revivalists back home noticed, and would come to reassert that Celticity and identity for the modern era. Put another way, the original theatrical culture (of Arthuriana, of Tristan, of piracy, of paganism) was about to be redefined in new ways.

Not only was this Celticity to be redefined on the stage, but dramatists operating outside of Cornwall were finding other aspects of Cornish culture interesting. Although mining in particular had been a strand throughout the earlier phases, Cornwall's industrial powers were reaching new heights at the start of the nineteenth century. We should, therefore, not be surprised by the emergence of one play by the shadowy George William Downing, which considered this area in depth. This was his drama, *The Great Hewas Mine, or The Humours of Cornwall*, which although published around 1816,[10] probably emerged a little earlier. Not much is known about Downing, though from Boase and Courtney we learn that he was born in Plymouth around 1778, dying eventually on a voyage to the Cape of Good Hope in 1820. The son of a purser in the Navy, it seems he pursued a career as a wine merchant before

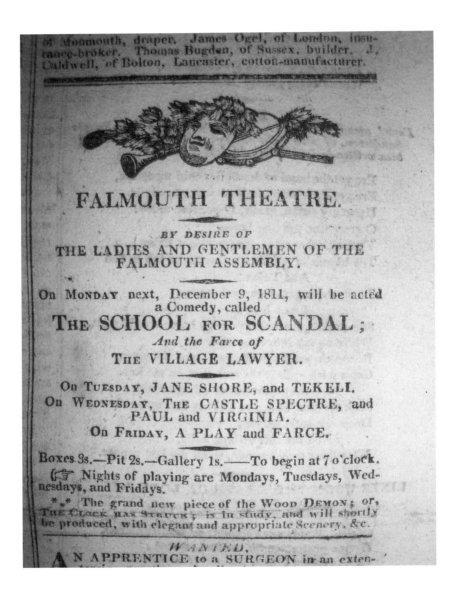

Fig. 62. An advertisement for the Falmouth Theatre, found in *The Royal Cornwall Gazette and Falmouth Packet.*

turning his hand to play-writing.[11] However, *The Great Hewas Mine* appears to be his only work. We can perhaps forgive him for the lack of any further plays, because this sole text is one of the most important pieces of dramatic writing within the Anglo-Cornish canon.

There are some initial observations we may make about Downing. Coming from Plymouth, and having a Naval background, Downing certainly knew a great deal about shipping and the coast of south-west Britain. This comes across strongly in the drama. He also understood many of the processes and technologies of the mining industry, which suggests he spent considerable time in Cornwall. Likewise, as we shall see, Downing also understood the linguistic heritage not only of Cornwall, but also of London, indicating considerable time spent in the latter location as well (we know that he lived at Tower Street[12]). That the work was produced at the Theatre Royal, Covent Garden, indicates that it had considerable status in its day, although perhaps lack of success with this text or others prompted him to try his luck overseas. Without doubt, however, Downing's work should be much better known within Cornwall, for what he presents is a complex and ambitious industrial drama of Cornwall: in essence, exactly what we might expect at this point in the material development of theatre in and about Cornwall.

Certainly the play had considerable status in London, with a cast of major performers of the day, including Charles Kemble in the role of Charles Andrews. Indeed, judging by the name, it seems the part may even have been written by Downing especially for Kemble. The full names of the actors are not listed in the surviving edition of the play, but the following should give an idea of the other parts and performers: Dick Andrews (Matthews), Timothy Gammamiel Stirabout (Liston), Harry Shark (Simonds), Captain Toplift (Braham), Jan Drury (Blanchard), Sukey Lile (Miss Stephens), Jenny Birch (Mathews), Polly Drury (Foote) and Mrs Drury (Mrs Davenport). A number of miners, constables and peasants are also part of the dramaturgy, although one important figure, Lile, the Superintendent, is not listed here. The play is a comedy, much related to earlier theatrical conceptualisations of Cornwall, with the action surrounding the Great Hewas mine, located in mid-Cornwall. Great Hewas, alongside the Polgooth mine, yielded a number of ores at the end of the eighteenth and beginning of the nineteenth century, raising tin to the value of nearly a million in sterling. Hewas was also well known for having some reserves of gold and, apparently, even had remains of so-called Phoenician workings, so it had clearly been mined for some centuries. Downing, therefore, had carefully selected this site for the location of his drama; the likelihood was that the mine would have had a pan-British reputation as well.

The drama is connected to London through a pretentious young Cockney character called Timothy Gammamiel ('Gammy') Stirabout. Stirabout is his name and 'stirabout' is his nature, for it is he who sets up many of the comic devices in the drama – often at his own expense. The audience sees him cuckolded on several occasions, by other characters who have a better under-standing of the mores and morals of the Age. In many senses, Stirabout is a Chaucerian character-type, who is rather like the foppish and fastidious parish clerk Absolon from *The Miller's Tale*. He opens the play: '*Act I, Scene i: An extensive tin-mine, with steam engine and stamping mills at work. Time, early morning, The Sun rising. Enter T.G. Stirabout, dressed in short jacket and check apron, with one end of which he is wiping his eyes, apparently in great distress*'.[13] Downing has constructed Stirabout to represent the outsider view of Cornwall. He is not happy that he has been sent to Cornwall by his father to learn about mining. We also note his linguistic difference, his Cockney accent coming across strongly in all his dialogue:

Gammy: Who on earth vould ever have had a father, I says – but –
           but mother says, I must have had vone, – and she knows best,
           bless her heart. But then to have had sitch a surley,
           black looking, cross beast as he is; – vy, vy, his scoul voud –
           vy it vould make you shiver, quite shake to look at him.
           I believes it all now, vat the folks says about rum freezing in
           Canada; if the inhabitants of that there outlandish place do
           make sitch shocking ugly faces as he can.[14]

The implication is that Canada would be a better place than being in Cornwall. This is reinforced in a later confession to the audience about the devious nature of the Cornish miners:

Gammy: Then to think, ven she went down to Margate to introduce
           Meggenini into the world, and to shew off her best bonnet, and
           to play at Lew; vat the deuce does my father do, but send me
           down here in the coach. "Go," – says he vone morning – "go
           Gammy down to Cornwall, and try if you can't find out the
           tricks of the Cornish miners – they'd cheat the very devil
           himself! But I think," says he, "that I've put you up to a few in
           our waults.[15]

His apprenticeship in the tin mine at Hewas allows Downing to render a piece of industrial drama, connected to the already established idea of having to have an ugly face to work in such conditions. Steam and stamps form part of the dialogue:

Gammy: Made me stoker to the steam engine fire, till my face was all
           srivell'd up like a roasted taty. Afterwards vent vith the
           ingineer to oil the steam engine, and nearly lost an arm by vone
           of the cursed Snapps! – vas as black and stunk of oil like a lamp
           lighter... Eh! Vat vas that there? [*listening to a noise*] Oh, it's
           only the Stamps at work.[16]

Gammy's pretensions and wishes not to be like other Cornishmen are contrasted with the hero Cornishman of the play, Dick Andrews. Andrews is every inch the Cornishman figure we might expect – witty, well-travelled, industrially-aware, and able to seize good from a situation:

Dick: Aye, aye! Pretty well! thanks to my fortunate stars! in my own
           country again! Landed from a mackrel boat in Plymouth; paid
           my passage by an order on the prefect of the department,
           written by myself: – gave out that I was one of Napoleon's
           private secretaries and physicians extraordinary!... Sent my boy
           on to St Austle to hire lodgings, while I disguised myself as
           a Jew Pedlar, and came by sea to Falmouth. So here I am...
           Oh – a tin mine I see! pretty enough. But who in the name
           of all the saints at once, is that up so early and at work? [*takes
           out his glass*] As I live! my old master's son, Gammamiel
           Stirabout.[17]

This text is interesting. It contains standard anti-semitic lore of the Age, but also we note Andrews' ability to work overseas. The cultural geography of the piece is also accurate. St Austell is the closest major town to the mine at Hewas, and clearly he had travelled down the southern coast. For fun, Andrews decides to disguise himself for much of the play as a travelling Frenchman, although there are also other moments when he uses deception: for instance, in a scene when he is disguised as an old woman, asking about a missing donkey. Andrews' adaptability, European awareness and general manliness are contrasted with Gammy's effeminate nature: 'The ugly Captin vill be here at six, and then they'll make me go down the Mine, vether I likes it or not! Oh dear! oh dear! [*sits down crying*]'.[18] We note how Gammy describes much of the Cornish world as 'ugly'. In a brilliantly-conceived next section, this 'ugliness' is given face by the arrival of some miners. All are described as captains, which is probably a mistake on Downing's part, confusing the precise nature of industrial lore in Cornish mining. Each shift would usually have only one captain. However, their attitude towards their profession is upbeat and a direct contrast to Gammy's London sensibilities:

First Captain: Come, my boys, let's have a drop of the right sort before we go below; – those confounded protection boats won't allow us poor miners hardly a keg of gin or brandy without duty.

Second Captain: - No: – what with them, and those red coated fellows, it's hard to get a drop to prevent the damp settling on our stomachs.

Third Captain: - The prince, – God bless his majesty, has never been among us, or he'd alter that matter, I dare say.

First Captain: - Now then my boys, the Prince and Old England; and the old Cornish toast of tin, copper, and fish: – then a song, and to our work all hands.[19]

This section allows Downing to raise another theme: that of 'free-trading' and 'protection', which is explored later on in the drama. Their 'ugliness' is, however, removed for the audience, by their then singing a Cornu-English trio about the ancient nature of their work:

Tho' many take pride in their gold,
And in boasting don't think it a sin;
We miners may zure make so bold,
Az to zay a few words about tin.

To Cornwall, the subject from Tyre,
Sent vessells so gailey and trim,
And all they could rap, read and hire,
They'd exchang'd for the pure Cornish tin.

Where's the mortal vrom peasant to prince,
Vrom Russia to famous Pekin?
Who prefers not to hash, stew or mince,
In Cornwall's pure native grain tin.[20]

The song trio is followed by the entrance of Lile, the Superintendent. In this character, Downing is probably trying to present a picture of the standard Cornish mining captain, for 'captain' was the alternative name for a Superintendent. Lile is an important character, for he outlines a number of the plot ingredients at this point, expressing concern over Jenny Strawberry, a local cunning woman or witch. Lile's daughter Sukey is also a major love interest in the work. Lile also understands the nature of funding of the mines in Cornwall, from London:

> Lile: Good morning, Captains, all of ye! – Now then, my lads, the concern looks well, we shall set a Steam Whim to work soon, and more Stamping mills. The proprietors in London don't want for money: – and when money is not wanting in Cornwall, - there's no deficiency of willing hands to earn it; even if it should be at the risk of their lives![21]

Although Downing is keen to point out the camaraderie of the mining environment in Cornwall, he is not presenting a naïve picture. In one sequence that follows, Andrews and his friend Harry encounter a number of invalids, who have all been hurt somehow while working underground. Harry observes: 'Tis he made nothing of; and on his return, restored the sight to two, whose eyes were blown out by gunpowder in the mines! – put one man's neck in again that had been hung and gibetted for a fortnight'.[22] Jenny Birch, meanwhile, argues that Gammy has brought shame upon her, because although he seems in many ways to like her, he also considers her beneath him for marriage. The implication is that Gammy has used her:

> Jenney: You cruel hard hearted man! why you know when we us'd to buddle the tin together, – you promised to marry me, – you know you did.
>
> Gammy: Aye, cure the buddling! I says, But marry you! my poor simple girl! – Lord bless you, vy ven I goes back to Lunnun I shall be quite another kind of a cretur, then.[23]

As we can see, *The Great Hewas Mine* is no small-scale drama. Indeed, it was rather the opposite: an attempt to document dramatically the real situation in Cornwall. Again here, Downing shows his observational skills. He understands the processes of buddling tin,[24] identifying that this was the work of the mining women or bal-maidens[25] and, by implication, the effeminate Gammy. The connection to wrecking and plundering, and by implication the 'wildness' of Cornwall, is made in Act II. Here Captain Toplift's vessel has run aground in Mount's Bay during tempestuous weather, the crew having to haul their ship up the beach. Quite how this was presented in the theatre space is not known, but it looks as if Downing was trying to develop a piece of spectacle for the audience.[26] Here, in the conversation between Toplift and his Steward, we gain a sense of the debate offered by the drama: are the Cornish hospitable or not? In essence, therefore, what Downing considers is the 'representation' of the Cornish:

Steward:	Why to be sure, captain, it's some consolation as you say, to be in one's own country; but if our bones are to be pick'd, I don't see for my part much odd who does it! This is the Cornish coast, and I've heard that they don't stand about trifles; – rare hands at plunder! – What would I give just now for a mess of lobscouse; or a piece of broil'd shark, or a famous bowl of pea soup with a piece of pork in it?
Toplift:	Come, let's pipe a stave or two – and bid her farewell? and then weel see whether the Cornish men are really so inhospitable as they've been represented.[27]

Perhaps more artistic licence is taken by Downing in the next part of the drama, where the crew of the shipwreck encounter Jan Drury and his family. Drury's wife is uncertain who the crew are. She fears them, thinking they are the 'protection boats to zarch and ruinate us'.[28] Toplift and the Steward, however, assure them they are not the 'Protection' and merely wish, now that they are shipwrecked, to visit the Great Hewas Mine. Notably, Drury (who is positioned here as a reformed plunderer) offers the following in response to their request: 'The Great Hewas Mine! why it be about seven miles off. Ztay, I'll put thee in the way; and az voor the boats crewe, they zhall stop at my cot, and be ready to take care ov what comes vroom the wreck.'[29] Artistic licence is taken at this point, because the mine was, of course, a lot further to the east. Andrews and Harry, meanwhile, are in the surrounds of that by now established Cornish location (for London audiences at least), Mevagissey, still pursuing the theme of disguise in the drama, with the former dressed as an old soldier, in rags, and having a fiddle, led by a dog, with the latter in mining work dress. There follows a song from Andrews; such songs were perhaps still useful to ensure the legality of the performance:

Jan Smaalgrove was a miner bold, a zeemly lad waz he;
He'd work with any man o' the world, whoever he might be;

All on a time, aye, in the mine, gunpowder blew ov his head!
And Nell, poor zoul, took grief full zore, to vind that he was dead!
Alas poor Jan and Nelly, Nell and Jan Oh Oh.[30]

It is in such sequences that we gain an impression of what other kinds of Cornish-themed drama might have existed during this phase. Events develop quickly from hereon. Captain Toplift falls in love with Lile's daughter Sukey, and she explains that Gammy, whom she cannot stand, has also tried to court her. Toplift and Sukey resolve to have some fun with him. Meanwhile, a very drunken Jan Drury has assumed the captain's role on the shipwrecked boat, swearing to take it into Porthleven harbour.[31] To add to the complexity of events, Dick's brother, Charles, falls in love with Polly Drury, with Jan wishing to know who is courting his 'huzzy' of a daughter. In another beautiful piece of local detail, Downing has Polly respond with: 'Why, the gentleman, who, who you was talking to on the road father! he promised to be my sweetheart, and to go to the Furry Dance with me.'[32] While this is occurring in the west, back at Hewas Superintendent Lile is angry and incredulous because he has received a letter from Mr Stirabout accusing him of 'running his son into expensive habits and foolery' in an 'endeavour to entrap his affections and cause him to marry my daughter'.[33]

One can see Downing layering the many complexities of the work. Whilst keeping the reality of established and known Cornwall, he excels himself in the final section of the play by integrating another aspect of Cornwall's culture: its spiritual 'otherness'. This theme had been established earlier on the drama, with Harry dressing up as a mystical Chinaman, but here Downing capitalises on pan-British knowledge of Cornwall by having a climactic scene take place at the Logging Rock (Logan Stone) at Treryn Dinas. Andrews is dressed up as 'an astrologer or magician'[34] though there is, as we shall see, perhaps more of the druid embodied in him. Harry, at this point, is pretending to be a spirit, and a stage direction appears where 'two trap doors open, at one of which, Harry, dressed as a spirit appears, and at the other a table is spread'.[35] Andrews invents the name of Brodago for Harry and, in a bizarre speech, Harry details the way in which he can soar above all of Cornwall. At this point he integrates druid lore:

Harry: Aye, dread sire, there perched on lofty elm, in likeness of an
          eagle bred in this country: twas so, – I scoured along to famed
          Ramehead, which serves as land mark to the Channel mariners,
          thence by Looe Island, and the Sister Towns, to where
          Pendennis by her lofty bastions secures wealthy Falmouth;

passing those buildings formed to give warning of the
outjutting rocks at Lizard's Point, – entered Mount's Bay, saw
Helstone's landmark, and the Pool for trout so formed, and
while seated, in form of a da[w] on St Austen's high turrets,
surveyed a scene, which only those beings gifted with poet's
keen eye and ready utterance could well describe... Whence
comes the change so manifest, for of yore, this was a temple of
the long-bearded druids, and this stone of weight and size
enormous, was consecrated to unravel mysteries by touch of
want enchanted.[36]

In an act of punishment for his actions in the play, Andrews and Harry then
bring Gammy before them. Gammy is stripped of his coat and waistcoat, while
Harry, drawing from his pocket the jacket and apron, puts them on. Then they
sit him on the Logging Rock, in indescribable terror, while several larger birds
come to annoy and peck at him.[37] In a way, this machismo and punishment-
orientated ending to the drama is quite a surprise to the audience, who surely
would have preferred the Londoner to have suffered less of a terrifying fate.
Located somewhere in this ending are some of the concepts of earlier
Renaissance revenge dramas. Having said that, Gammy becomes more disliked
as a character as the play progresses so, in a way, the ending is more than
justified. Downing was also reinforcing notions of Cornwall's peripherality.
Perhaps this was what happened in Cornwall? People still dressed up and
performed rituals upon rocks. The overall pagan message of this is undercut
however when, in Act V, we move to a scene on the eighth of May, for the Furry
Dance.[38] Dick Andrews confesses that in reality he is nothing more than a
showman who likes to dress up, but this showmanship is part of the overall
celebration of marriage, space and community. Although *The Great Hewas Mine*
is, as I have argued so far, clearly an important text, it is not entirely satisfactory.
The ending of the drama is somewhat rushed and, in his efforts to integrate
another known pan-British symbol of Cornwall (the Furry Dance at Helston),
other locations in Downing's drama (at Hewas, Mevagissey and
at the Logan Rock) are compromised. That said, such is the range and vivacity of
place and characterisation in the drama, it ought to have been performed not only
in London, but in Cornwall as well. Perhaps the sheer ambition of the work
forced managers and performers to avoid it. It is doubtful whether any of the
urban theatres of Cornwall of this period could have pulled off such an epic piece.

Having therefore examined one text which certainly placed Cornwall on
the London stage, let us next turn to this culture of urban theatre in Cornwall
during the early nineteenth century. I still define this theatre as urban since it

takes place in the most populous towns during the winter months. For the most part, this is touring theatre, or adaptations of established drama although, as we shall see, there are moments when urban, indigenous Anglo-Cornish drama also occurs, perhaps matching the development of the Anglo-Cornish novel. Undoubtedly, summer rural theatre is still taking place, and although somewhat less ambitious than in the centuries before, it is still highly community-orientated and probably created in a short, pithy Cornu-English style. For example, in the pages of *The Royal Cornwall Gazette* newspaper throughout the century, there are yearly advertisements for Helston's Flora (or Floral) Day, when we would expect the *Hal-an-Tow* drama to be taking place.[39] Theatrical events would also undoubtedly accompany the various fairs, 'feasten' days and markets that took place across the parishes (the cultural forerunners of many of Cornwall's twenty-first century community festivals).[40] During the century, we also witness both urban and rural entertainments (touring show-ground fairs, circuses and magicians), which perhaps in its broadest sense could also be labelled theatre. As technical changes occurred, and new phenomena occurred globally, we see these appear in Cornwall as well. Given Cornwall and Cornish culture's global activity during the century, we might expect innovation from 'outside' to occur here, rather than in other parts of the south-west peninsula of Britain, or even London itself. Cornish culture's inter-changeability and its success in a trans-national context would have implications for theatrical activity at home.[41]

Sources for nineteenth-century theatre in Cornwall are neither prolific nor as lengthy as accounts of work in London, and it is unusual to find descriptions of performances. Given the ephemeral nature of theatre, this is not surprising, though it can be frustrating when newspapers give accounts of intended per-formances but do not always follow them up with reviews. We are therefore often just given a tantalizing picture of what might have occurred, with a few notable exceptions. Another difficulty is that the two main newspapers of the period, *The Royal Cornwall Gazette* and *The West Briton* tend to concentrate only on Truro, Falmouth, Redruth and Penzance. Thus other centres such as Bodmin, Liskeard and the rest of east Cornwall (not to mention 'Cornish'-themed material in, for example, Great Torrington, Tavistock and Plymouth) are not as well documented. The newspapers also show a distinctive cultural gaze towards the apparently admirable cities of Plymouth, Bristol and Bath, which are obviously seen by some of the reporters and journalists as apt centres of culture for Cornwall to model. This bias comes across in the way in which drama is talked about and reviewed. London is seen as both the place where taste and values are formed and the innovator of good theatrical practice. This runs counter to the evidence we have that much contemporary theatrical work relied on Cornwall's trans-national status. The picture of drama about Cornwall, and Cornish dramatists operating elsewhere, would be even less complete were it not for the detailed records kept in George Clement Boase and William Prideaux Courtney's *Bibliotheca Cornubiensis* (1874)[42] which happily records many of the dramatists, texts and performance dates relating to Cornwall. Boase's later work, *Collectanea Cornubiensia: A Collection of Biographical and Topographical Notes relating to the County of Cornwall* (1890)[43] is also a useful record of theatrical activity. With a combination of these two sources and newspaper records, we can begin to map the history of the century.

The densely-packed columns of the forerunner of *The Royal Cornwall Gazette and Falmouth Packet* are a useful starting point for understanding the theatre of the opening years of the century. Sandwiched between advertisements for 'Godbold's Vegetable Balsam' and 'Welch's Female Pills' are found several advertisements for theatre in Cornwall, as well as the occasional review from inside Cornwall and further afield. A typical advertisement from this phase comes in the newspaper on 23 January 1802:

> Falmouth Theatre. On Monday next, the 25th. Will be performed the much-acclaimed comedy called *The Way to Get Married* with the favourite entertainment of *Blue-Beard*. Characters, and other Particulars will be given in the Bills. The doors open at six; and the curtain rises a quarter before seven. Boxes 3s. Pit 2s. Gallery 1s. Tickets to be had of Mr. Elliott, at Wynn's Hotel, and of Mr. Fisher, at Mr. Rowe's, Cooper, Falmouth; also of Mr. Brokenshire, at the Crown, Penryn. Nights of playing are Mondays, Wednesdays and Fridays.[44]

Although brief, this advertisement tells us a great deal about urban theatre. The venue is the Falmouth Theatre, run by the established Cornish-based 'comedian' Samuel Fisher. It initially seems that, during the opening years of the century, cosmopolitan Falmouth held theatrical dominance over Truro, Penzance and Redruth. James Whetter has shown the massive growth and central position of Falmouth in Cornish culture during this phase,[45] so this seems appropriate. Theatre, for the next few decades, would be advertised in this way. *The Cornwall Gazette and Falmouth Packet* was published on Saturday, when the run was announced for the next week. Similar advertisements are also found in the pages of *The West Briton and Cornwall Advertiser*. We note that there are three evenings of performances, though usually not on a Saturday. This may have been because of legislative restrictions. The bill is mixed, with a comedy initially, almost certainly containing songs, followed by the burletta of *Blue-Beard*. By 'characters, and other particulars' we are talking about the cast list, who is playing whom, and some details about the casting

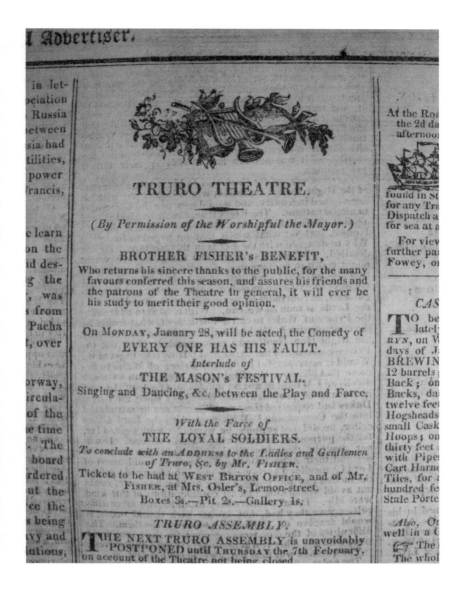

Fig. 63. An advertisement for the Truro Theatre, for Samuel Fisher's benefit, contained in *The Royal Cornwall Gazette and Falmouth Packet.*

453

and manager of the show. Theatres opened quite early in this time and the audience had three quarters of an hour to settle before the show started. Clearly, the performance was attracting all classes of people from Falmouth and its surrounds, with the price of the boxes, pit and gallery remaining fairly stable for the next few decades. The ticketing operation was quite advanced, having a couple of locations in Falmouth, and also one at that older centre of theatrical culture, Penryn, proving that people were willing to travel the distance into Falmouth to see the production.

The play being viewed, *The Way to Get Married*, was a comedy by a John Johnson (1706-1791), or at least an adaptation of it. Johnson's origins are not well recorded, but the play was published in Philadelphia in 1810. It has the subtitle of 'And the Advantages and Disadvantages of the Marriage State, represented under the similitude of a dream'.[46] The play is effectively an allegory of a woman's decision between men and other directions in life. Whilst maintaining the linguistic feel of the previous age (*The Way to/of…*),[47] the drama does seem to point towards a more liberated female experience, or at least to ask some pertinent questions. Thus, we have in operation in Falmouth an internationally-recognised text, which obviously appealed to the audience of the day. Considering other legal debates over marital issues in the pages of *The Cornwall Gazette and Falmouth Packet* and *The West Briton and Cornwall Advertiser*, the play entirely suits its moment of production, and is probably of a kind that had mass appeal across Britain.

Perhaps of more interest to us now, however, is the 'favourite entertainment of *Blue-Beard*'. The billing suggests that this text had been performed a number of times already and, because of the nature of the legend of Bluebeard, there is a Brythonic connection to Brittany. Bluebeard (so-called because of his supposedly ugly blue beard) is the title character in the famous fairy tale about a violent nobleman and his curious wife, appearing in Charles Perrault's *Les Contes de ma Mèr l'Oye*, first published in 1697.[48] The story is often told in connection with a fifteenth-century Breton nobleman and later self-confessed serial killer, Gilles de Rais.[49] Although the tale was very popular in late eighteenth- and nineteenth-century Britain, there may, of course, be a reason for its particular appeal in Cornwall: fellowship between Brittany and Cornwall and their similar language and folklore,[50] as well as Falmouth's seafaring links across the Channel, helped guarantee its success. The love of folklore and folk narrative is something we have seen in previous Ages, and which we shall see emerge again in the twentieth and twenty-first centuries within the theatrical context of Cornwall. Thus, in this one advertisement we can see much of the pattern of theatrical activity in this period. There is the one text, which has perhaps pan-British or maybe even international appeal, with another which is more locally and 'internally' sourced. Here, two texts are performed, but the usual model for early nineteenth-century urban theatre in Cornwall, as we shall see, features three texts. In this way the theatre managers could cater for as wide an audience as possible, so that even if one text did not appeal, others would. The repetition of successful texts, sometimes in the same season, was another way of bringing people into the theatre. Clearly there was also an economic benefit in moving certain texts and shows from, for example, Falmouth, to Penzance, or from Plymouth to Truro.

For the year 1802 in Falmouth, however, it was usually paired dramas that were the norm. It becomes clear from the following advertisements that Samuel Fisher was the actor-manager of the Falmouth Theatre; in all likelihood, it was his innovation and commitment that contributed to this very productive phase. In January 1802, Falmouth Theatre presented *Pizarro* and *The Horse and the Widow*.[51] Again, tickets were available from the locations above, and directly from Mr Fisher. The same weekly schedule of performances was also outlined in the advertisement. *Pizarro* was probably the tragedy adapted by Richard Brinsley Sheridan from the German play by August von Kotzebue (1761-1819).[52] It concerned Pizarro, the Spanish conqueror of Peru (1471-1541). It is interesting to contemplate Fisher's reasoning behind this production. Obviously, Sheridan had fame, and there was obviously a continuum of performance of Sheridan's works in Cornwall. Doubtless, its exotica also appealed – backed by the trans-nationalism of the Cornish, who were already exploring Central and South America.[53] The second piece, *The Horse and the Widow*, might have been given some local flavour, but it was more than likely an adaptation of a popular Scottish folktale.[54]

February 1802 saw what was advertised as 'a comedy (never acted here)' called *The Poor Gentleman*, in which the lead role of Dr. Ollapod was played by Samuel Fisher.[55] Added to this was 'a musical farce' titled *Of Age To-morrow*.[56] The season continued with 'the grand and popular pantomime' of *Perouse*, 'previous to which will be performed the comedy' of *The Heir at Law*.[57] The author of *Perouse* remains lost, but the pantomime is likely to have been based on the life of Jean François de Galaup, comte La Pérouse (1741-1788) who was a Breton-based French Navy officer and explorer whose expedition vanished in Oceania.[58] The choice of text is interesting, since events concerning La Pérouse were now far enough away historically to be shrouded in mystery. Again, there was the active Breton and maritime connection. *The Heir at Law* (first performed in 1797) was written by George Colman the Younger (1762-1836), and is an outstanding comic drama, concerning the life of an elderly pedant called Dr. Pangloss. Clearly, such doctors were ripe for satire, because *The Poor Gentleman* (concerning Dr. Ollapod) had another run in late February.[59] This time it was accompanied by a very popular piece of the period, *Ways and Means, or A Trip to Dover*, a text performed in numerous places and re-run over several venues in early nineteenth-century Cornwall. There was a further connection with *The Heir at Law*: George Colman the Younger was the son of George Colman the Elder, who had bought the Haymarket from Samuel Foote.

Clearly, Mr Fisher had an instinct for what other drama was being produced successfully across Britain, and this may have influenced his decision to bring a production of *The Jew* by Richard Cumberland (1732-1811) to Falmouth in March 1802.[60] Cumberland's dramatic presence in Falmouth was doubly significant: he had an eye for sentimentality and morality; he also had a talent for inventing characters of the British periphery and colonial experience. These included vindications of the good qualities of Scots, Irish and other other groups from the British Empire.[61] Whether Fisher saw comic potential in *The Jew* for adapting certain characters to Cornish types is interesting to speculate upon. Certainly Cumberland's method of writing allowed a highly patriotic exploration combining domesticity and moral humour. *The Jew* was drawing on a tradition of usually anti-semitic drama in Cornish, British and European theatre, though apparently the drama became very popular across Europe, when the great German actor Theodor Döring played the eponymous role of Sheva. Unfortunately, we have no record of how Jewish communities in Cornwall during this period responded to the protracted farce of this play.[62] Cumberland himself is now rarely mentioned in contemporary theatrical history,[63] but during this time he would have been at the height of his success.

Cumberland's drama was followed by what must have been an equally ambitious show to *Perouse*, which was that 'unequalled pantomime' of *The Death of Captain Cook (Our beloved and lamented countryman)*. The choice of the story of Captain Cook is significant because much of the costuming and scenery must have been in place for the similarly-styled *Perouse*. However, the advertisements for this drama suggest an enhanced performance since 'the scenery, machinery, dresses and decorations are in the first style of elegance, and according to the costume'.[64] Here, certainly, we have something of a taste of the operation of the theatre during this phase. The advertisement mentions machinery, suggesting technical sophistication backstage to enhance the performance. We also see that scenery is important in such productions, and even if it were just a backdrop, it shows some ambition here. Likewise, the theatre appears to be moving towards realism for the phrase 'according to the costume' is indicative of an awareness of achieving accuracy with the historical context and its costuming; Cook's first voyages were some thirty years earlier.[65]

'Decorations' is a more intriguing phrase, perhaps indicating properties or set dressing of some kind. Fashion again seemed to be dictating Mr Fisher's choice of production: early nineteenth-century audiences were fascinated by aboriginal cultures and since the location was Falmouth, the sea and maritime theme must have greatly appealed.

During this phase, the theatrical winter season continued well into March before performances ended. On March 15 1802, Falmouth presented 'for the benefit of Mr Wilson, by desire of the Right Worshipful Mayor and gentlemen of the Corporation of Falmouth', Frederick Reynolds' comedy *Life*.[66] Reynolds (1764-1841) was an incredibly prolific dramatist, writing nearly one hundred plays throughout his career. The fact that Mr Fisher could invoke such civic support for such an endeavour shows us that he himself had much respect in the town, but it also goes some way to telling us how significant theatre had become in the social culture of Cornwall. *Life*, if it is like other dramas by Reynolds,[67] satirises the modes and follies of people's lives during the late eighteenth century and early nineteenth century. This comedy was then to be followed by a 'celebrated farce' titled *Ghost*, then by *The Muffin Man*, 'by a person of the town'.[68] The season progressed into April, which saw an established dramatic liaison with 'the Ancient and Honourable Society of Free and Accepted Masons' for 'Mr Fisher's benefit'.[69] This was a new comedy called *Deaf and Dumb*. Though anathema to us now, disabilities such as these were of immense comic value for early nineteenth-century audiences. This comedy was to be accompanied by a new farce called *The Wags of Windsor* by the popular dramatist – in Cornwall at least – George Colman the Younger. There is no guarantee that it received its premiere in Cornwall, but the first edition of the text was not published until 1808, so it is at least an early performance. The play is set in an army camp near Windsor, and has the following characters: Grace Gaylove, Phoebe Whitethorn, Caleb Quotem and an Irish servant named Looney Mactwolter; Colman followed previous centuries' fashions for naming characters after their characteristics, alongside some received stage Irish racism.[70] Operating in rotation with these was a comedy entitled *The Wonder, or A Woman Keeps a Secret*, with the lead role of Don Felix played by a Mr Palmer (in his 'first appearance this season'). At this end of this drama, another 'serious pantomime' was presented, with the Cornu-centric title *The Shipwreck*, and the lead role of the Captain of the ship again being played by Mr Palmer. Following this came a 'musical farce' titled *The Padlock*.[71]

Of early nineteenth-century theatre in Falmouth, all of the above texts are significant, though for very different reasons. *The Wonder* is important to discuss since it was one of the few texts written by a woman that came to

Cornwall. The playwright was Susannah Centlivre (1669-1721).[72] Centlivre wrote some nineteen plays in her career, most of which were comedies. *The Wonder* is set in another Atlantic peripheral territory – Portugal – and this may be part of its appeal. The plot is effectively a study of frustrated lovers, thwarted from being with their real loves by tyrannical fathers – in essence, then, a study of arranged marriage. One might see a similarity to *The Rover* by Aphra Behn (1640-1689),[73] which follows a similar theme. However, it may be that Centlivre's popularity in Cornwall, and in Britain in general during this time, was because of her mockery of priests and Catholicism. It is perhaps incredible to think that such a text, satirising arranged marriages and by a woman, should be staged in what was perhaps quite conservative Falmouth; even more so, that such a text would be advertised in the predominantly Whig newspaper, *The Cornwall Gazette and Falmouth Packet*.

We have no evidence about *The Shipwreck*'s content, but this would appear to be part of the growing canon of writing about such dramatic events off the Cornish coast, which were to feature in many Anglo-Cornish dramas (and indeed in much Anglo-Cornish fiction during the century[74]). Given Mr Fisher's fondness for technical effects and machinery, a shipwreck seems an adequate opportunity to show these off to the public. *The Padlock*, meanwhile, is part of a continuum of writing and performance that was to develop markedly during the early half of the nineteenth century, and was based on black experience. Its popularity in Falmouth, of all places, was linked to its cosmopolitan nature,[75] as well as popular interest in figures such as Joseph Emidy, the black violinist, who made a highly successful career in Cornwall.[76] *The Padlock* is a comic opera written by Isaac Bickerstaffe and Charles Dibdin, premiering at the Drury Lane Theatre in 1768.[77] The play had immediate impact, primarily down to the portrayal of the central character, Mungo, a black servant from the West Indies,[78] though the title of the piece comes from the lock which an old miser keeps on his cottage door for fear that his wife will be unfaithful to him. One can see that in these three texts a whole range of geographies and cultural dynamics were portrayed in just one evening at the theatre in Falmouth. Certainly, based on the evidence of a season in 1802, the theatrical culture operating was highly sophisticated and progressive. There is evidence of this from not only the actual texts being performed, but also wider interest in theatrical matters. Occasionally, *The Cornwall Gazette and Falmouth Packet* would detail theatrical memorabilia, usually from London. Here, the writer recalls an unintentionally funny performance of *Hamlet*, which starred the famous eighteenth-century actor David Garrick (1717-1779). This gives us a feel of what conditions on stage still affected performers of this period:

During the time of Mr. Garrick's performance in Goodman's fields, the stage rose so much from the lamps to the back scenery, that it was very difficult for a performer to walk properly on it, and unfortunately it was then the custom to introduce their ghosts in a complete suit, not of leather, but of real armour. The dress for this august personage was one night, in honour of Mr Garrick's Hamlet, borrowed from the Tower, and was consequently too ponderous for the ghost of the Royal Dane. The moment, therefore, he was put up at the trap door, unable to keep his balance, he rolled down the stage to the lamps, which catching the feathers of his helmet, the ghost seemed in danger of being consumed by mortal fires, till a gentleman roared out from the pit, "Help! Help! the lamps have caught the casque of your spirits, and if the iron hoops fly, the house will be in a blaze!" The attendants ran on stage, carried off the ghost, and laid him in a tub of water.[79]

Two interesting things strike us about this piece of writing. The first is that the journalist is referring to a performance of the preceding century, and writing as if that era had better theatrical sensibilities. It seems that even by the opening years of the nineteenth century, the previous Age was looked upon with considerable pride and affection. It also gives us another impression of the theatre of the time, with the highly raked stage and, again, the quest for realism (with the suit of armour). The newspaper also sometimes contained a column titled 'Theatricals' in which reviews of other plays across Britain were given, thus informing theatrical sensibilities in Cornwall. A notable example comes from 14 August 1802, where the writer reviews a play called *The Voice of Nature* at the Haymarket Theatre, Covent Garden:

The dialogue, though not remarkable for particular spirit or elegance, was impressive; and the piece went off with considerable applause until the end, when the sensations of horror, excited by the feint to carry Alphonso's decree into effect, produced considerable and marked disapprobation. It was announced, however, for repetition; and, with a few curtailments, may probably have a tolerable run.[80]

The 'stringer' reviewer sounds fairly non-committal about the piece, and gives an indication of the kind of language in which theatrical reviews were couched. No doubt many melodramas in Cornwall also had 'tolerable' if not highly successful runs. Another indicator of theatrical Cornwall comes from the newspapers of the time. By 1803, *The Royal Cornwall Gazette and Falmouth Packet* contained regular advertisements for Bell's British Theatre pocket library,[81] each costing only sixpence. We are told that operas are available as well, proving that there was enough of an intellectual class in Cornwall to pursue home reading, as well as watching such dramas. This seems to ring true when we look at other urban centres across Cornwall, for although at this point Falmouth seems to be leading theatrical activity, other places also had their fair share of ambitious drama. The Assembly-Room Theatre at Truro (still run at this point by a Mr Hughes, the owner of several theatres in south-west Britain, stretching from Exeter to Penzance) had proven its importance in the previous decades, but seemed at this point to be developing performances in conjunction with touring companies. In July 1803, 'for the benefit of Mr and Mrs Clarke' we learn of a performance of *Alexander the Great, or The Rival Queens* with 'appropriate scenery, decorations, etc'.[82] This was to be performed by His Majesty's Servants from the Theatre Royal Weymouth, who appear to have been touring the peninsula, since the previous week they were in Exeter. Again, we notice that this is not really the playwright's theatre, since the author of the work – Nathaniel Lee (1649-1692) – is not even mentioned.[83] Perhaps the piece was so well known that his name did not need to be in the billing. Certainly, however, this was an ambitious production for Truro, given the casting and sheer number of performers:

Alexander, Mr Sandford.
Lysimachus, Mr Clarke.
Hephestion, Mr Farren.
Cassander, Mr Woodley.
Perdiecas, Mr Weston.
Polyperchon, Mr Wheatley.
Thessalus, Mr Miller;
and Clytus, Mr Emery.
Rozanna, Miss Logan.
Parasatis, Mrs Clarke.
Sysigambia, Mrs Emery.
and Stratira, Mrs Farren.[84]

The Rival Queens was clearly a spectacle, and one which drew on classical pan-European learning. However, the narrative itself still has impact in the twenty-first century,[85] so this justifies the one hundred year period previous to 1803 that Lee's text held the stage in Britain. The text also reflected Britain's colonial quest, in that by the time he was just twenty-seven years old, Alexander the Great had conquered some ninety per cent of the known world. The company would have known that, with such heroic subject matter, the tour was likely to be successful. If the 'appropriate scenery, decoration etc' matched this, then both the touring company and the home management at Truro would have been happy with the attendance. What remains unclear is whether the company itself brought the scenery and decoration with them on the tour, or whether stock materials were used from Truro. Either way, the picture we have is of sophisticated subject matter, and of complex touring procedures.

The owners at Truro, however, were not satisfied with the spectacle of *The Rival Queens*, and instead, appear to follow the format established elsewhere in Cornwall, where an 'external' drama was combined with one that was 'internal' to Cornwall. In Truro in July 1803, there was a 'play and a farce' titled *The Two Recruits* 'in which Mr Weston will deliver a humorous address in the character of a Cornish Miner, written expressly for this purpose by a gentleman of Truro'. This is an enormously significant piece of performance, which gives a tantalizing glimpse into Cornu-English drama during this phase. The likelihood is that the subject matter of the piece is similar to some of the Cornu-English monologues established in the works of writers such as Uncle Jan Trenoodle, W.B. Forfar and John Tabois Tregellas,[86] the major dialectician writers of the middle of the century, but here too is a flavour of industrial life, which is perhaps no better embodied than in John Opie's 1786 painting of 'Gentleman and a Miner'.[87] We should look to this for a visual cue to the performance, since it is quite close to this period. The immediacy of this piece is followed by a third event in the evening: this was 'the much admired entertainment of *The Sultan, or The Female Captive*, which steers the stage back towards the exotic and perhaps even fashionable titillation. The Sultan and his captive Roxalana were to be played by Mr Clarke and Mrs Clarke, probably the actor-managers of the Weymouth Company. As in Falmouth, doors were opened at six and the dramas began at seven o'clock, with the boxes, pit and gallery at 3*s*, 2*s* and 1*s* respectively. This event signalled the end of the season. In the same edition of *The Royal Cornwall Gazette and Falmouth Packet* we learn in 'Truro Theatricals' of the following:

> Our theatre closes next week. The veteran Manager, Mr Hughes, is deservedly a favourite in this neighbourhood. He has at great expense, got up and performed most of the popular new pieces during his short season here, in a manner truly creditable to his company, and we hope with profit to himself. The merits of the different performers have hitherto been rewarded with liberal benefits, which have increased, and are increasing, as the time of their departure approaches.[88]

Hughes obviously had respect in Truro, and clearly performed several pieces in the role of actor-manager there. Interestingly, however, it seems that there was a seasonal departure of the performers, thus suggesting that the company reformed for each new winter season, and that once this was complete, they scattered to different parts of Cornwall, into Devon and Dorset (Exeter and Weymouth) and indeed the rest of Britain. It may be that many of the performers returned to London, since there were fewer seasonal restrictions there. This seasonality of theatre is evidenced in Penzance in the winter of the same year, when Mr Fisher (of Falmouth) announced the opening of the season there. Cleverly, Fisher knew that the West Cornwall audience had not seen work previously performed in Falmouth, and therefore decided to open the season with two established favourites. Fisher, striving for fashion and dominance, may well have had control of both theatres at this point:

> Penzance Theatre. Mr. Fisher respectfully informs the ladies and gentlemen of Penzance, Marazion &c. The theatre will open in the course of the next week; and all the fashionable novelties of the London house will in regular succession be produced; and he humbly requests that sanction and support he has on former occasions so liberally experienced. The season will commence with Colman's celebrated comedy of *The Poor Gentleman* – singing and dancing between – with a new farce called *The Review, or The Wags of Windsor.*[89]

Fisher's season in Penzance appears to have been lucrative since in the January of 1804 we learn of 'the winter campaign of the theatrical corps at Penzance' being 'very successful' and that 'Mr Fisher deserves great credit for having so earnestly laboured in his vocation to fan the generous spirit of loyalty and patriotism, which nowhere burns with more fervour than on the shores of Mount's Bay'. Alongside this, the performances were apparently heightened by 'the effusions of several private gentlemen, happily adapted to the common feelings of Cornishmen'.[90] Again, this note suggests that Fisher benefited from the assistance of a number of patrons when, on 23 December, he had ventured to put on Sheridan's *The Rivals* 'to an elegant and crowded house'. The performance had been 'desired' by one Colonel Hitchens and the Officers of the Mount's Bay Volunteers. *The Rivals* – set in Bath, and first produced in 1775 – features the famous characters Captain Absolute and Mrs Malaprop.[91] Although over twenty-five years old, the piece had an enduring quality, and still appealed to the west Cornish audience, who must have identified many of their own experiences in the text of the drama. Between the Play and Farce (though the farce is not named), the following Song (written by a gentleman of Penzance) was sung by Mrs Fisher, in the first verse 'pointing to the boxes, pit and gallery':

I sing of Cornubia's fam'd loyal bands,
Whose valour recorded in history's sands;
I sing of her sons, brave, loyal and free,
Who in arms to protect her, surrounding you see.

Amidst all the factions that have harass'd the land,
In loyalty still they've been joined hand in hand:
To her King and her Country Old Cornwall was true,
To prove she remains so Volunteers, rests with you.

The Genius of Albion has oft with delight,
Seen her sons from Cornubia pour forth to the fight;
Inferior to none, this night shall survey
The Corps here united, the pride of Mount's Bay.[92]

This was a period in which war had again broken out between Britain and France, so the patriotic vigour of the song matched the 'British' feel of *The Rivals*. This 'old Cornwall' of 'Cornubia' was ready for the present fight after the Act of Union.[93] Although only a song, these lines give a feel of the 'internally'-crafted pieces of Cornu-centric drama during this phase. The newspaper account also explains that the previous week had seen a presentation of Shirley's *Tragedy of Edward the Black Prince*. The 'Black Prince' (1330-1376) was peculiarly apt subject matter. Edward was not only the first Duke of Cornwall in 1337,[94] but had been involved in several mid-fourteenth century campaigns against the French. Therefore, the drama reflected not only popular local Cornish pride, but a wider British negative perspective on the French. The review comments on how 'the patriotic sentiments of Edward were well given, and received with reiterated bursts of applause'. Apparently, this was 'brought forward in a very respectable style; the dresses in exact costume – the scenery appropriate'.[95] The author of the text is listed as Shirley and this is presumably John Shirley (1596-1666), though most modern editions and studies of his work fail to note this title.[96] An epilogue was written for the occasion, and this was delivered by a Mr Lowell. The convention of rewriting the ending, or negotiating an epilogue which would be more relevant to the contemporary context, was very popular during this phase[97] – notice his call to ancient Celticity with his images of 'Druid Britons', 'Saint Michael', and the patriotism of 'one and all'. At the time, the writing 'electrified the audience':

Yes, my dear country – still let's keep in view,
That all thy sons are sons of freedom too,
And lo, to guard thee, prodigal of blood,
As Druid Britons rushing in the flood,
Our King – his subject – son, all – "one and all",
Resolve to conquer, or like brothers fall.
Hail Britons! ever loyal, never slaves
Whom heaven ordains to grace and rule the waves!
Hail patriot squadrons! hail by whom Penzance
Breathes loud defiance to this scourge of France!
On his own Mount's high tower see Michael stand,
He waves your sacred banners in his hand,
Which he, as to the fanning breeze they fly,
Inscribes, To glory – death – or victory![98]

Throughout the opening decade of the nineteenth century then, we have a number of theatrical conventions established, which are repeated throughout Cornwall. The entertainment culture of the period is defined by winter theatricals and a summer culture of concerts and balls, the buildings still being adapted to purpose and need.[99] Adaptability of venue is still seen as very much a twentieth and twenty-first century phenomenon, but here we see it successfully employed once again in the Cornish theatrical continuum – essentially the multi-use strategy of the *plen-an-gwarries* of the medieval and Tudor periods.

During 1804, we see Falmouth seemingly gaining the upper hand in the dramas presented. In November, Thomas Morton's comedy *Speed the Plough* was combined with a farce, *The Agreeable Surprise*.[100] Morton (1764-1838) entered Lincoln's Inn in 1784 and his play was based on the traditional song, sung by ploughmen, 'God speed the plough', an agrarian wish for success or prosperity. Morton's play would perhaps have appealed to any Cornishmen or women in the audience with an agricultural background, though probably the text was most notorious for the name and character of Mrs Grundy; a 'Grundy-ism' being a conceptualisation of extreme moral rigidity.[101] *The Agreeable Surprise* is a lesser-known comic opera by John O'Keeffe (1747-1823),[102] the Irish actor and dramatist, which was first produced at the Haymarket back in 1791. In this, the characters Eugene and Laura are in love but her father, Sir Felix, insists that she must marry someone else. The surprise is that he has been teasing them. In the same month at Falmouth there is again 'the grand drama' of *Pizarro* followed by *The Romp*, a farce which has passed out of knowledge, but whose subject matter can be easily guessed. As the season progressed, it seems that more explicitly Cornish subject matter was the order of the day:

> The performances at our Theatre on Friday last were the new comedy of *John Bull*, and the farce of *Raising the Wind*. The scene of the play being laid at Penzance, and most of the characters our own countrymen, the audience seemed much interested in the representation. The blunt honesty of the Penzance Brazier, Job Thornberry, was well portrayed by Mr Drake; and Mr Clarke, by his impressive and animated delivery of the sentiments of Peregrine, drew forth repeated bursts of applause, while Mr Fisher's whimsical representation of Dennis Brulgruddery, afforded great entertainment to the good folks in the gallery. Mrs Clarke gave great interest to the betrayed daughter of the Brazier; and in short, the whole of the performance was respectable. The farce of *Raising the Wind*, tended to raise the hearty laugh, and the novelty of two new pieces did not fail of raising a fair wind for the manager.[103]

In the drama of *John Bull*, we have a notable – and perhaps strange – merging of Cornish and English culture. The figure of John Bull is usually seen as a personification of the United Kingdom, though more often of England in particular.[104] Its origins lie in the creation of a character by John Arbuthnot (1667-1735) in 1712,[105] and this was immediately taken up by British print-makers, to show the figure as a well-intentioned, portly man, probably of country stock. Obviously, in Scotland and Wales, Bull has never been accepted as a symbol, though given Cornwall's position in terms of wider British defence and maritime history, not to mention its accommodation into England in this phase, Bull was possibly more accepted. Perhaps there was even room to 'Corn-ify' the concept for the audiences. This would seem to be the case, given James Dawson's observations, as we shall see below. Although there were probably other dramas of John Bull, this play seems an exception to the usual fare at Falmouth. The drama was written by George Colman the Younger and 'the scene is laid in Cornwall, near Penzance'.[106] It was a comedy written in five acts, and sometimes subtitled 'An Englishman's Fireside'. Although *John Bull* was premiered at the Theatre Royal in Covent Garden, London in 1805,[107] Colman may well have had his eye on the Cornish market, for he was very popular there. The brazier (Mr Thornberry) draws on established Cornish archetypes from previous centuries,[108] while the character of Peregrine is chivalric and, therefore, has an Arthurian impetus. Fisher's development of Dennis Brulgruddery was perhaps rooted in other drama he had witnessed (for example, the Mrs Grundy figure) but probably given Cornish spin. In comparison, *Raising the Wind* is given less detail and appears not to be by a pan-British or Irish dramatist. Its maritime theme also gives the impression of it being a resolutely Cornish-focused piece of drama.

John Bull then is clearly worthy of a more detailed discussion, as one text that is fully focused on Cornish experience. The setting in Cornwall, near Penzance begins with the following piece of stage direction: '*A Public House on a Heath: over the Door the Sign of the Red Cow; – and the name of "Dennis Brulgruddery". Enter Dennis Brulgruddery and Dan from the House. Dan opening the outward Shutters of the House*'.[109] The character of Brulgruddery, who is central to the drama, we quickly learn has Irish-isms, and he and Dan, his servant (a more obvious Cornish character), comically mispronounce words and phrases. Their peripherality is emphasised linguistically, but also by their poverty and lack of sophistication. Whilst a public house called the Red Lion would sound grand and important, their tavern is comically labelled the Red Cow:

Dennis:	A pretty blustratious night we have had! and the sun peeps through the fog this morning, like the copper pot in my kitchen. - Devil a traveller do I see coming to the Red Cow.
Dan:	Na, master! – nowt do pass by here, I do think, but the carrion crows.
Dennis:	Dan; – think you, will I be ruin'd?
Dan:	Ees; past all consumption. We be the undonestest family in all Cornwall. Your ale be as dead as my grandmother; mistress do set by the fire and sputter like an apple a-roasting,; the pigs ha' hotten the measles; I be grown thinner nor an old sixpence; and thee hast drunk up all the spirity liquors.[110]

The 'undonestest-ness' is enhanced by our learning that Dennis has been married for some three months to Mrs Brulgruddery. He has moved her from more genteel Lostwithiel to the more barren surrounds of Penzance (presumably the Penwith hinterland). Dan makes a joke about the interfering nature of Mrs Brulgruddery, and Dennis responds in the following way:

Dennis:	Never you mind Mrs Brulgruddery's nose. Wasn't she fat widow to Mr. Skinnygauge, the lean exciseman of Lestwithiel? and didn't her uncle, who is fifteenth cousin to a Cornish Boronet, say he'd leave her no money, if he ever happen'd to have any, because she had disgraced her parentage by marrying herself to a taxman? Bathershan, man, and don't think he'll

help us out of the mud, now her second husband is an Irish jontleman, bread and born.[111]

Colman's talent as a writer is to keep the gags coming thick and fast here. The sentence 'fat widow to Mr. Skinnygauge, the lean exciseman of Lestwithiel' is a brilliant piece of comic writing. He also manages to incorporate a notion of all Cornishmen being cousins into the same sequence, while indicating the intrigue over the second marriage of Mrs Brulgruddery to Dennis, marriage being the theme of the rest of the play. The plot of *John Bull* is really started, however, with the arrival of Peregrine. He is a noble, chivalrous character who has been shipwrecked on the Cornish coast, and while Dennis and his wife are keen only for him to use their otherwise failing business, Peregrine is glad to be near to Penzance, for he knows of a friend there, named Mr Thornberry, who will be able to help him:

Peregrine:	So! – And I have wander'd upon the heath four hours, before day break.
Mrs Brul:	Mercy on us! cast away!
Peregrine:	On your coast, here.
Dennis:	Then, compliment apart, sir, you make a ducking as if you had been used to it.
Peregrine:	Life's a lottery, friend; and man should make up his mind to the blanks. On what part of Cornwall am I thrown?
Mrs Brul.	We are two miles from Penzance, sir.
Peregrine:	Ha! – from Penzance! – that's lucky!
Mrs Brul:	[*Aside to Dennis*] Lucky! Then he'll go on, without drinking at our house.[112]

Peregrine then asks after Mr Thornberry and reveals that he last saw him some thirty years ago when he was but a child. The on-stage characters then hear a scream. It is from a character named Mary Thornberry, who has been robbed. Peregrine saves her and asks why she is out on the heath. The audience learn that she has left home, without her parents knowing. She has run off to meet her lover, but in the long term intends to run off to London to forget her misery. This is because her lover Frank Rochdale is to marry a woman of high status: the snobby and Cornu-sceptic Lady Caroline Braymore. It is this premise that sets the whole of the rest of the drama in action. As yet though, there is no idea that Mary is actually Mr Thornberry's daughter. Mr and Mrs Brulgruddery will look after Mary, while Dan accompanies Peregrine to Penzance to find Mr Thornberry:

Dan:	I be ready, zur.
Peregrine:	For what, friend?
Dan:	My master says you be a-going to Penzance; if you will be agreeable, I'll keep you company.
Peregrine:	Oh – the guide. You belong to the house?
Dan:	Ees, zur; Ise enow to do: I be head waiter and hostler: – only we never have no horses, nor customers.
Peregrine:	The path, I fancy, is difficult to find. Do you never deviate?
Dan:	No, zur, – I always whistles.
Peregrine:	Come on, friend. – It seems a dreary rout: but how cheerly the eye glances over a sterile tract, when the habitation of a benefactor, who we are approaching to requite, likes in the perspective![113]

It was probably such imagery that caused the Anglo-Cornish poet Charles Valentine Le Grice to react to John Bull, for he argued that, in fact, the surrounds of Penzance were not quite the 'dreary routs' established in the drama.[114] For Colman, however, such a concept was serving his purpose for he wished to contrast the atmosphere on the heath with that of the sophistication of urban Penzance. Here we meet Sir Simon Rochdale and Tom Shuffleton. The latter has been 'posting all night, through Cornish roads, to obey the summons of friendship'.[115] Rochdale says that Shuffleton is 'one of the highest finish'd fellows of the present day'.[116] It is Shuffleton and Rochdale who will eventually help to create the solution, but for now, Sir Simon has plans for his son. The scene then moves to his son, Frank Rochdale, with Williams attending. Frank confesses his love for Mary and his objection to the arranged marriage:

Frank:	Must I marry this woman, whom my father has chosen for me; whom I expect here tomorrow? And must I, then, be told tis criminal to love my poor, deserted, Mary, because our hearts are illicitly attach'd? Illicit for the heart? fine phraseology! Nature disowns the restrictions; I cannot smother her dictates with the polity of governments, and fall in, or out of, love, as the law directs.[117]

The remainder of the play involves the resolution of events. We also meet Lady Caroline, who is English, and dislikes the arrangement as much as Frank Rochdale. She comments: 'Company in the house! – some Cornish squire, I suppose. [*Resumes her reading*]'[118] The prevention of the marriage happens only in the nick of time. It is here that Colman more directly addresses the title of the drama, and makes claim to a certain kind of 'English equity', which has been embodied in the play by the character of Peregrine. The equity is presumably constructed as the opposite of what he has seen abroad, but also in terms of the Act of Union. The imagery of the Englishman's fireside is connected back to their place at the Red Cow Inn:

Frank: May I sir? Oh, then, let the libertine now make reparation, and claim a wife. [*Running to Mary, and embracing her*]
Dennis: His wife? Och! what a big dinner we'll have at the Red Cow!
Peregrine: What am I to say, sir? [*To Sir Simon*]
Sir Simon: Oh, you are to say what you please.
Peregrine: Then bless you both! And, tho' I have pass'd so much of my life abroad, brother, English equity is dear to my heart. Respect the rights of honest John Bull, and our family's concerns may be easily arranged.
Job: That's upright. I forgive you, young man, for what has passed; but no one deserves forgiveness, who refuses to make amends, when he has disturb'd the happiness of an Englishman's fireside.[119]

Ironically, of course, this is happening in a peripheral territory, which throughout its history was having difficulty negotiating its arrangement with the imperialist drive of England. Colman, although foregrounding Cornish identity and ethnicity within the play, seems rather less keen on a final settlement in which Cornishness is respected. That said, for the audience at Falmouth during this phase, this issue would not have been important. In fact, their very incorporation into the conceptualisation of a wider England, or rather, 'united kingdom' of John Bull, would have been very much embraced. The character of Dennis Brulgruddery, 'an Irish jontleman', was going through the same process of cultural integration. No doubt at Falmouth, Fisher would have accentuated and developed the role, making it his own.

The rest of the season in Falmouth offers a considerable variety of theatre. Sheridan's *The Rivals* was presented in November, alongside the opera of *Inkle and Yarico* and another play titled *The Adopted Child*.[120] The former was a comic opera with libretto by the ever-popular George Colman, and music by Samuel Arnold, and concerns Inkle, an English trader, who becomes shipwrecked in the West Indies and falls in love with Yarico, a Negro maiden. The play is a moral study, since when Inkle returns to civilization he plans to sell Yarico into slavery. However, his sensibilities prevent him from doing so and, in the end, he chooses to marry Yarico. Again, this text explores the Atlantic's economics – very close to the pervading activity in the harbour. The latter text is probably the 'musical drama in two acts' by one Samuel Birch, published eventually by Samuel French in 1856.[121] The season continued with another Colman the Younger play titled *The Iron Chest*, to which was added a farce called *The Review*. This was followed the next week by *The Young Quaker* and *The Tale of Mystery*. Friday saw *Macbeth*, and the farce of *The Deaf Lover*.[122]

Two texts here are significant. Firstly, *The Iron Chest*. 'Iron chests', as Marjean D. Purinton has argued, were significant stage symbols in the eighteenth century.[123] They were quack curiosity cabinets which allowed for private, amateur collections to demonstrate their scientific or sensational powers. It seems Colman was using the 'iron chest' motif as a structuring and sensationalist device in the drama. Clearly in Cornwall, which had seen the birth of so much science and engineering,[124] alongside a special breed of industrialists and innovators, such a drama was bound to appeal. It was, after all, in this year that Trevithick built the first successful steam locomotive. Such 'iron chests' of power were probably of prime interest to Cornish audiences, who were witnessing a new spurt of industrial growth all around them. Secondly, John O' Keeffe's *The Young Quaker* (1794) would have been an interesting proposition for the stage in Cornwall. In 1655, George Fox had been imprisoned in Launceston Gaol for publishing a manifesto about his ideas on what would become the Religious Society of Friends.[125] As Rawe notes, this 'led to considerable interest in the Quaker faith, and the Society began to spread in Cornwall… [and] by 1700 there were twenty-seven meeting houses and four hundred members'.[126] Even by the beginning of the nineteenth century, there would still have been enough interest in the Society of Friends' commitment to peace (particularly in the context of the conflict with France), their plainness of dress and manners and the absence of clergy or ministers in their practice, to prompt what was probably still a controversial dialogue on stage. The youth of the central character suggests that his inexperience and idealism will be crushed. What better place to perform it than in one of the front-line harbours in the war on France? Also of note was the Quaker Fox family of nearby St Budock[127] who, although doing well in mining, also became better employers through their commitment to the Society of Friends. In this way, we see Cornish theatre working through the significant cultural and theological debates of the day. While audiences were perhaps challenged by O'Keeffe's work, light relief was probably found in the *The Tale of Mystery*, another very popular piece of the era. The version of *Macbeth* offered would almost certainly have been heavily edited, with possible exaggeration of the role of witches (Cornwall was a place where folk belief in witches stayed well into the modern era[128]), while the more obscure *The Deaf Lover* seems a light-hearted enough farce to follow up the tragedy. A similar balance of material comes in the week following with *The Stranger*, followed by 'an interlude' titled *The Scotch Ghost* (a follow-up, or adaptation of the Scottish play perhaps?), then another farce, *The Jew and the Doctor*.[129] This play, written by the favourite author Thomas Dibdin and published in 1800[130] was a much more contemporary drama than that which was normally performed in the theatres of Cornwall at this time.

The balance of non-Cornish and Cornish material was maintained during the month of December 1804, when the Falmouth Theatre decided to present George Lillo's version of the Bohelland Tragedy, *Fatal Curiosity*.[131] This text, as explained in the previous chapter, was a perennial favourite (at least after its revival in 1782 by George Colman the Elder), and had been in existence for some seventy-five years.[132] It was no doubt played in Falmouth in this period because of its close proximity to Penryn. As we have seen in the story of the theatre of Cornwall, Penryn was the centre-point of popular conceptualisations of drama in the territory.[133] Significantly, as we well know, it was the site of Glasney College, and was the literary heart of medieval Cornwall, with many of the writers from Glasney's surrounds and parishes focusing their learning at the College. It is therefore perhaps fitting that Lillo's embellishment of the narrative should be brought back to a theatre just down the road, at Falmouth. Penryn is the older town, and had for a long time been the centre not only of learning and drama in Cornwall, but also of the kind of exploration overseas explored in the original story, and in Lillo's drama. Whether Fisher was actively exploiting these linkages, or even if he knew of them is unclear. However, he appeared to understand the sensationalism and drama of the story, and knew that its local connections would ensure an audience. Lillo's synthesis of a style from the pan-British continuum of writing with an explicitly Cornish narrative is an important moment in the theatrical history of the territory. The fact that Lillo – in writing the play – had earlier drawn on motifs from pan-European folktale and also influenced other traditions in the process is significant and, again, highlights Cornwall's theatrical importance for Europe as a whole. Fisher had another trick up his sleeve in terms of marketing his product: this was the technique of employing a specific local artist to paint a spectacular backdrop to the piece, so that even if some of the audience had seen the piece performed before, here was something else to tempt them back again. In this case, the backdrop was by a promising young artist, Mr Whitfield: 'In Act the 1st a new scene incidental to the play painted by Mr Whitfield, being a view of the port and town of Penryn, the Behellen field and Behellen House, nearly as it stood, when the murder was actually committed.'[134] Clearly Fisher's vision for the piece paid off. Within a fortnight, the piece was mounted again, and was described as being 'well attended'. A reviewer described how the piece 'being laid so near to us at Penryn was an inducement for many to be present'.[135]

On this run, after *The Fatal Curiosity* was a farce titled *Fortune's Frolic*, in which Mr Drake starred as a character named Old Snarl, and Mr Fisher played a character called Robin Roughbeard, who apparently kept the audience 'in roar of laughter'.[136] Not surprisingly perhaps, Fisher negotiated the rights also to perform on 28 December, close to the end of the year, what was then known as *The History of George Barnwell*.[137] This was Lillo's most famous drama, first performed in 1731. Significantly, it is again a drama that specifically suited life in Penryn and Falmouth, since the subject matter was everyday commercial life. In this context, *The History of George Barnwell* is a peculiarly modern tragedy, and also one very fitting for the Cornish context. According to Drabble, it was 'frequently performed at holidays for apprentices as a moral warning'.[138] This seems fitting considering the seasonal timing of the piece, but Drabble's observation also gives us insight into some of the age-group attending: young men, and probably young (accompanied) women as well. The run across the New Year period included a commonly performed piece titled *The Tragedy of Douglas, or The Noble Shepherd*, which was based on a famous ballad included in Sir Walter Scott's *Minstrelsy of the Scottish Border*,[139] the story of the carrying off of Lady Margaret by Lord William Douglas. This was paired with a farce called *The Gay Deceivers*.[140] *The Tragedy of Douglas* continued on into January combined with the 'grand spectacle' of *Phantasmagoria*.[141] This latter performance was hardly theatre, but instead, a pre-cinematic projection ghost show. Such shows enjoyed enormous popularity throughout Europe in the early nineteenth century. We might even say that Fisher had seen the writing on the wall, anticipating later developments in cinema. The combination of tragedy and the magic lantern show would surely have been popular seasonal attractions.

The picture we have at Falmouth, then, is of a great range of texts and performances being offered. The remainder of the season included the following: the comedies *The Birth-Day, or Veteran Tar*, *The Soldier's Daughter*, *The West Indian*, and *The Point of Honour* as well as a number of farces titled *The Lyar* (probably Samuel's Foote's text), *Lock and Key* and *Rosina*.[142] *The Birth-Day, or Veteran Tar* would seem to have a maritime theme, while *The West Indian* draws on the interest in slave narratives and perhaps even events in Lillo's *The Fatal Curiosity*. The comedies were sometimes combined with 'Signior Saxoni exhibiting unrivalled feats of the tight rope' while in the middle of February there was 'a grand display of fire works'.[143] Within this period, there appears to have been a production of Shakespeare's *King Richard the Third*, though there were no prior advertisements for it.[144] February saw the comedies of *The Child of Nature*, and Shakspeare's *As You Like It*, combined with the farces *The King and Miller of Mansfield*, and *Miss in Her Teens*.[145]

The King and Miller of Mansfield is perhaps the strangest of these. It was a satire of court life by Robert Dodsley (1703-64), first produced at Drury Lane in 1737, and transports the court from London to the confines of Sherwood Forest.[146] However, it would appear to match other texts on offer for this month in Falmouth: *Robin Hood, or The Merry Foresters of Sherwood*, and *Columbus, or A New World Discovered*, where presumably any forest scenery could be used for Sherwood, the new world, and Arden in *As You Like It*. Although Dodsley's text was quite ancient, it drew on a continuing theatrical tradition in Cornwall for presenting Robin Hood and Sherwood Forest narratives.[147] *As You Like It*, meanwhile, seems to be a perennial favourite amongst Cornish audiences, perhaps because of its rural theme. On 23 February more Cornu-centric material appeared to be on offer in the form of an interlude titled *The Shipwrecked Sailor*,[148] with 'characters by Messrs. Lovel, Hayden, Coombs and Whaley – Mesdames Clarke, Lovel, Whaley and Hooper'. This latter piece of information may not tell us much about the text or its themes, but clearly these were theatrical families and marriages working together, probably doubling parts in many of the plays on offer, and of course, learning lines for the next play to be produced.

March 1805 proved equally ambitious, with productions of Shakespeare's *King Henry the Fourth* (it is unclear whether Part 1, 2 or both), and a version of *King Henry the Second*.[149] The latter's author is unknown, though it is usually a drama about Henry II's desire to kill Thomas Becket.[150] The month also brought about a revival of *The Padlock* alongside 'the grand melodrama' of *The Tale of Mystery* (another repeat). O' Keeffe's presence on the stage in Cornwall continued with a production of *Wild Oats*, as well as interludes titled *The Soldier's Glory* (reflecting the ongoing military situation), *The Honeymoon* and *Ways and Means, or A Trip to Dover* (a similar trope to earlier plays).[151] The season concluded with *The Marriage Proposal* and *The Maid of the Hill*, interspersed with the interludes *Quarter Day*, *The Village Lawyer*, *The Blind Bargain* and *The Irishman in London*.[152] The grand event of this month however, was Thomas Holcroft's *The Lady of the Rock*, which according to the advertisement was 'now performing at the Theatre Royal, Drury Lane, with unbounded applause'.[153] Holcroft (1745-1809) was instrumental in developing melodrama in Britain, and his plays *Deaf and Dumb* (1801) and *A Tale of Mystery* (1802) had already been staged in Cornwall. However, as Karr has argued, Holcroft was actually a radical figure,[154] supportive of the early ideals of the French Revolution. In the autumn of 1794 he was tried for high treason, but later acquitted. His post-arrest situation meant that his dramas were initially not successful, but by the beginning of the eighteenth century he managed to achieve considerable success with the above texts.

The theatrical culture of urban Cornwall in the early nineteenth century has been defined by the above texts and performances and it remains more or less unchanged throughout the first twenty years of the century. Under the guidance of Samuel Fisher at Falmouth, until his death in 1817, Falmouth continued to present lively and progressive theatre. Truro followed with a range of performances, but as the century progressed, and tastes changed, seems to have presented more balls, concerts and music festivals rather than drama.[155] Occasionally we see references to other urban centres such as Bodmin, Liskeard, Lostwithiel and Penzance. This period was a time of great uncertainty, with Cornwall and a wider Britain engaged in the Napoleonic Wars. It was not until 1815, when Napoleon was defeated at Waterloo, that some semblance of peace returned. Other world events were also having impact on theatre in Cornwall: in 1807 the slave trade was abolished in the British Empire; between 1812 and 1814 Britain and the United States of America were at war over shipping and territorial disputes, the effects of which were felt immediately in Cornwall.

During this phase there was, in essence, an overhang of the grand theatrical culture of the previous century, and by the 1840s, theatre in Cornwall reached a crisis. The crisis was threefold. First of all, the texts that had been in circulation for the previous fifty years simply did not reflect the manners, culture and interest of a by-now highly technical and 'modernised' Cornwall. Melodrama and sensationalism of the kind presented in Falmouth and Truro simply ran out of steam. Secondly, as I have argued above, legal changes in the nature of theatre also seemed to cause turbulence in the vision for theatre in Cornwall. Thirdly, given temporary industrial collapse in the early 1830s and 1840s (due to what Payton terms 'over-specialisation'[156]) and difficulties over crops and famine,[157] many Cornish people began to seek opportunities overseas. Therefore, advertisements for theatre in *The Royal Cornwall Gazette and Falmouth Packet* were displaced by ships offering passage to Canada, the United States of America and Australia. Given the somewhat unexpected cultural meltdown at home in the wake of this, theatre lost its audience. However, although records are scant, the Cornish also took their theatrical culture overseas. This, then, is the broad sweep of the period. We now need to look further at the detail.

In Falmouth, we see something of a revival of earlier successes occurring, as well as the useful pairing of internal and external drama. In November 1806, *Hamlet* (presumably in a truncated and much-altered form) was presented

Fig. 64. A playbill from the Truro Assembly-Room Theatre, featuring Mr James Dawson. Courtesy of the Royal Institution of Cornwall.

alongside *Blue-Beard*, with the comedies *The Deserted Daughter*, *The Blind Bargain*, *Fortune's Fool*, and *Don Juan*.[158] The same season featured *The English Fleet*, which had never before been acted in Cornwall.[159] The title suggests that it could be about events during the Spanish Armada (for dramas of this kind were popular during this period), but it may well have had allegorical elements related to Nelson's victory. Farces and burlettas of the period included *The Midnight Hour*, *The Gamester*, *Love at Cross Purposes* and *The Chapter of Accidents*. In December, *The Iron Chest* had a re-run, while a new comedy titled *The Belle's Stratagem* appeared; obviously a pun on *The Beaux' Stratagem* by George Farquhar (1678-1707).[160] The opening months of 1807 saw re-runs of the old favourites, *Deaf and Dumb*, *The Young Quaker*, and *Speed the Plough* which must have been easy enough to mount.[161] *As You Like It* was back in February, coupled with *The Scotch Lovers, or Gretna Green Blacksmith*.[162]

In March there is mention of a play at Penzance: *The Castle Spectre*,[163] while in the summer Truro re-engaged with theatre, producing a revived version of Colman's *The Heir at Law* and another popular drama *Raising the Wind*. This was followed in June by *The West Indian* (a retention of this long-standing theme), *Tekeli, or The Siege of Montgatz* (a popular melodrama based on the life of the Hungarian patriot, Emeric, Count Tekeli [1656-1703]), *Hamlet, Prince of Denmark* and a new play titled *The Curfew*.[164] In June, there was a production of Macbeth, though this was coupled with a very different kind of dance between the tragedy and the farce:

> *Macbeth, King of Scotland.* In the course of this piece, the nocturnal rites of the
> witches, with the original music and a procession of eight kings. Between the
> play and the farce, a Turkish dwarf dance by Mr. Bennett. *Town and Country.*
> Farce of *Edgar and Emmeline*.[165]

The witches, as we have already noted, are given due attention, and the 'procession of eight kings' suggests a display of interesting costumes. Less detail than this is given in the billing for the remaining shows of the summer at Truro, but among the performances are the following: *Stranger, Harlequin Highlander, Road to Ruin, The Fatal Curiosity, or The Penryn Tragedy, The Deaf Lover, Who's the Dupe?* and *The Soldier's Daughter*.[166] Much of this seems familiar territory, though in July there appears an interesting new comic duet titled *One and All*.[167] Bodmin Theatre, meanwhile, chose to mount productions of Oliver Goldsmith's *She Stoops to Conquer* and the perennially popular *Raising the Wind*,[168] though it seems this was something of a one off for August. For the winter season in Truro, *Adrian and Orrila* was the opening drama, followed by *The Curfew*.[169] The former play here was by a now obscure dramatist named William Diamond and concerned a mother's vengeance.

Falmouth returned for the 1810 season with familiar fare: *The Tragedy of the Rival Queens, The Foundling of the Forest, The Romance of Blue Beard* and *The Death of Captain Cook*.[170] During this phase there is evidently a decline in the number of Cornu-centric pieces being performed, with Samuel Fisher selecting more material from elsewhere in Britain. Certainly from 1810 to 1811, there is a dearth of 'internally'-conceived drama. Interest in colonial exotica remained though, for there were successful productions of *The Africans* and *Othello* in December 1810.[171] Newspaper evidence of the period, however, points to something of a decline in innovation at this point, with only popular favourites being turned out.[172] By 1813, the theatre in Falmouth was still operational, but the season appears shorter, and the plays less promoted and less progressive. There is perhaps one last hurrah in the form of Shakespeare's *The Tragedy of King Lear and His Three Daughters* (with its limited Cornu-centric subject matter).[173] It appears the theatre in Falmouth was still open in 1815, but the following couple of years are not well documented, and its subsequent decline is explained by evidence from March 1817:

Falmouth Theatre. To be sold by auction on Wednesday the 28th day of March next, by four o'clock at the Ship and Castle Inn, in the town of Falmouth, on such conditions as will be then produced, for the remainder of a term of 99 years, now held on the Lives of Two Persons, aged about 38 and 15 years, with a perpetual Right of Renewal, at a fixed fine, all that newly-erected Theatre and Premises, situate in Killigrew Street, close adjoining the said Town: Lately occupied by Samuel Fisher, comedian, deceased.[174]

Fisher's death marked a turning point for theatre in Cornwall in the nineteenth century, and yet he was essentially a comedian of the former age. When one considers his achievement within this period, then he is clearly a figure of major importance and a considerable loss. In the 1820s, it was Truro that assumed prominence, led there by the touring manager and later manager and impresario James Dawson. The type of entertainment had, however, to change greatly. Although still relatively young, Dawson invested in more lavish productions, but also brought more unusual touring acts to the city, cultivating patronage and support from the moneyed gentlemen of Truro. This ambition for the theatre is seen in an advertisement for the opening of an 1824 summer season:

Truro Theatre reopens for a short season. Mr J. Dawson will have the honour of opening the theatre, when from the great novelty he can produce, aided too, by the talents of a respectable Company, he trusts once again to experience that Approbation and Patronage he has on a former occasion been honoured with, and the which it has been his pride to acknowledge.[175]

Pretentious though this may have been, it was hard to doubt Dawson's expertise. In 1819 he had been battling against new touring entertainments in Cornwall. At the May fairs in Truro, Helston and Penzance, there was a circus, and among 'Mr Powell's Troop of Equestrians' was 'Mr Henning, clown to the whole performance'. For several years, Dawson went back to the safety of the winter season, promoting, in February 1821, a topical piece titled *The Slave*, which saw him playing the character Nicholas, with Mr Osbaldiston as Gambia (the slave) and Mrs Osbaldiston as Flora.[176] The Osbaldistons were significant performers for Dawson, and a couple he had worked with in the Exeter Company. Their names are repeated in many of the advertisements and bills of the era, and were obviously something of a draw. The farces and melodramas continued, however, in the form of texts like *The Midnight Hour*, *The Miller and His Men*, *The Blind Boy*, *The Sleeping Draught* and *The Manager in Distress*.[177] None of these texts were particularly progressive pieces of drama, but they were popular. Little seems to have taken place between the years 1822-3, and when the theatre returned again in 1824 for the winter season, Dawson elected for sensationalism: 'The Celebrated Burke. A Child only six years old! The musical and dramatic phenomenon, considered the wonder of the Age! Musical and Dramatic Entertainment'[178] Such a populist piece, however, was followed by more classic fare: *The Merchant of Venice* in November, with Shylock played by Mr Russell and Portia by a Miss Leigh. Dawson combined this with a farce about a character titled Tristram Sappy, whom he played.[179] Theatrical activity seems to be less advertised in 1826, but in the following year a number of productions were scheduled for the season. These included *The Wonder* (a comedy), *Charles the Second* (a farce), *The Stranger*, *Aladdin*, *The Mountaineers*, *The Norwegian Wreckers* (with maybe an undercurrent of parallel Cornish activity), *Cinderella*, *She Stoops to Conquer*, *The Lady and Devil*, *The Boy of Santillane*, *Robinson Crusoe*, and *Three-Fingered Jack*.[180]

We see here a move to more traditional pantomime fare, but there are some interesting exceptions. On 24 November 1827 Dawson claimed to be presenting *Shakespeare's Tragedy of Jane Shore*.[181] Elizabeth "Jane" Shore (c.1445-c.1527) was one of the many mistresses of King Edward IV. Although referred to in *Richard III*, there is actually no play about her by Shakespeare, even in lists of apocryphal texts. Dawson was obviously misinformed, or he thought he might be able to get away with promoting a piece which seemed 'Shakespearean'. In December, he tried a new comedy, performed in two acts, which went under the title *The Cornish Miners*.[182] Little other detail is given, and no reviews follow, so it is difficult for us to imagine how this drama would have been performed. The fact that it is in two acts suggests a piece of good length, probably developed by the small theatre company at Truro. The subject matter is probably industrial activity: there is a lasting tradition of humour associated with mining both in Cornwall,[183] and in other places where the Cornish emigrated.[184] In the latter, this came to full fruition in what I have elsewhere termed the 'industrial droll' of the Cousin Jack narratives.[185] As we have seen, dialecticians of the era also made good use of industrial narrative, so we might expect a performance with aspects of that kind of comedy. In traces too, we mark a continuum forwards to other more recent dramatic writings about 'Cornish miners' in plays shaped by Nick Darke, D.M. Thomas, and myself.[186]

In 1828 a full season continued at Truro, with *The Clandestine Marriage*, *Diamond Arrow*, *The Solway Mariner, or The Pirate's Drama*, *Heart of Mid-Lothian*, *Three Weeks after Marriage*, *All the World's a Stage*, *The Gamester*, *A Bold Stroke for a Husband*, *Love in Humble Life*, a revival of *Tekeli, or The Siege of Montgatz*, culminating at the end of February with 'the laughable Burlesque Tragedy of Tragedies' *Tom Thumb the Great* (probably an adaptation of Henry Fielding's work).[187] Scottish, maritime and marital themes remained popular. Although the theatre in Truro was back in season in 1829-30, there were few advertisements in the newspapers, and then in 1830-31, there appears a complete paucity of performance in the city. In the opening years of the 1830s, a shift occurs. Some dramas continued, but other forms of entertainment were trialled. In July 1832, there was a 'diorama of Shakespeare's Jubilee' on a tour of Britain,[188] but again little performance appeared to take place in 1834, 1835 and 1836. There are several possible reasons for this. The theatre itself might have been refurbished (it probably looked a little tired by now), but this is also an era of great social change and reform. The Factory Act in 1833 forbade employment of children under nine in factories; 1834 saw the rise of the Tolpuddle Martyrs, six Dorset labourers transported to Australia for attempting to form a trade union (much too radical a topic for the Weymouth troupe); in 1836 the Chartist movement began in Britain, demanding the vote for all adult males; and in 1837 Victoria became Queen of Britain.[189] These wider phenomena all had impact in Cornwall. Perhaps Dawson felt the theatre was too dangerous an institution and debate on stage might prompt unrest. Certainly this would seem the case by the opening months of 1838, when the safe 'Mr Jacobs, the celebrated illusionist, ventriloquist, and improvisatore' would be performing at the Assembly-Room Theatre.[190] We learn that as early as June 1832, Dawson had opened a fashionable dancing academy in Truro. This would appear to have been a more lucrative method of making money, and his academies continued throughout the 1830s as Dawson himself moved into his thirties.[191]

1838 brought a change. October that year featured a somewhat bizarrely-named ballet starring Monsieur Gouffe, titled *Jocko, The Brazilian Ape*. This fashionable piece had premiered in Stuttgart in 1826, and was a four act work with libretto by F. Taglioni and music by Peter von Lindpaintner. The ballet was based on a well-known French melodrama about a Brazilian woman who saves an ape, Jocko, from being bitten by a snake. The ape repays her kindness by later preventing her son from being kidnapped.[192] Clearly, the technicalities of presenting a ballet with an ape in it were part of the attraction to the audience, but also, as Callum G. Brown has noted,[193] this Age was one first beginning to question evolutionary links between man and apes, thus dismissing biblical notions of creation, and culminating in the publication of Charles Darwin's *On the Origin of Species by means of Natural Selection* in 1859. Despite such grand themes, the Assembly-Room Theatre of Truro still saw the benefit of presenting internal Cornu-centric work. A favourite, *The Wreck*

Ashore, was played in November;[194] this was advertised in *The Royal Cornwall Gazette and Falmouth Packet* amongst pages offering free passage to Australia. Just as, for example, the mid-nineteenth-century Anglo-Cornish poetry of John Harris (1820-84) reflected the immediate concerns over death and destruction in the mining world,[195] so dramas like this offered people dramatic simulations of possible disaster when travelling overseas. Such material was popular despite the bitter reality that this kind of catastrophe really happened. Meanwhile, the new trend for costume balls continued in Truro. Here then, was a kind of 'drama' (only without a script) that allowed the fashionable gentlemen and women of Truro to parade and court.[196] Competition, however, was intense. An opening up of venues in other urban centres in Cornwall (in particular in Liskeard, St Austell and Bodmin) reveals an intensive period of touring work. Although the actual drama is unclear, we learn in October 1839, that:

Master B. Grossmith and His Brother, who appeared to overflowing Houses in the above Towns, a few years since, will produce their New and Novel entertainment with splendid wardrobe, scenery &c making along 60 changes in all their Original and Popular characters for one night only, and the last time.[197]

Fig. 65. A playbill from the Truro Assembly-Room Theatre, featuring Master B. Grossmith. Courtesy of the Royal Institution of Cornwall.

This was to be toured at the Lecture Hall, Devonport, the Assembly Room, Lostwithiel (still significant as a Stannary town), the Market House, St Austell, and the Truro Theatre, where the venues would be 'fitted up with the new costly scenery, &c, constructed for Master G's Annual Performance in Windsor Castle'.[198] Quite what this 'new and novel entertainment' was is uncertain, but it was clearly touring on a grand scale, and perhaps more in line with public expectation. Given this, it is not surprising that we learn of a tour conducted in April 1841 by a Mr Bernardo Eagle, 'exhibiting his necromantic wonders' in Helston, Penzance and Falmouth. Apparently Mr Eagle offered 'extraordinary wonders, photographic phenomena, astounding changes, cabalistic conjurations, automaton wonders, Mephistophelian transmutations and magic in all branches'.[199] By then, urban Cornish theatrical culture seems to be somewhat dissipated compared to the previous forty years. We know that the Truro Assembly-Room Theatre was still owned by Mr Dawson in March 1842 (when there were performances of *Hamlet* and *Catching an Heiress*),[200] but there were few performances in 1843 or 1844, the central years of the 'hungry forties'.

July 1845 appeared to bring a change when a 'Mr Doel, Manager of Theatre Royal, Devonport, Plymouth and Exeter' started to promote drama in Cornwall. This was *My Wife's Second Floor*, but James Doel also seemed to have had an eye on local patronage because he allowed some 'gentleman amateurs from Helston' to perform a piece on the same night titled *The Village Lawyer*.[201] In this we may be witnessing a change in Dawson's reign in Truro, and certainly his name disappears from either promotion or performance. The quality of entertainment offered appears to decrease: there is Mrs Philips on 'entertainments on the Minstrelsy of Ireland comprising the antiquities, superstition, tradition and bardic history'; 'Herr Kitler's Hanoverian Band', and 'Mr Jacobs, the Great Original Wizard'.[202] The continuum of black minstrelsy continues with 'the Philadelphia and Mississippi Ethiopian Serenaders, consisting of Negro Melodies, Droll Sayings and Comicalities of Ethiopian Life' and 'Henry Russell, from America, giving his vocal entertainment, interspersed with anecdotes of Negro life and character'.[203] From this it seems clear that by 1850 urban theatre – in Falmouth and Truro at least – had partially collapsed. Particular low points appear to have been George Wrightwick of Plymouth agreeing to read Shakespeare's play of *As You Like It* (only a few years before, it had been performed regularly), and Miss Georgiana Eagle, 'who will illustrate clairvoyant visions of the mind in a magical soiree'.[204]

Although theatre reaches something of a low point in Falmouth and Truro, elsewhere in Cornwall it remains, at this point at least, vibrant and perhaps more Cornish than in the more fashionable urban centres. The best description of a theatre during the mid-nineteenth century is given by the novelist William Wilkie Collins (1824-89)[205] who made the by-then fashionable tour of Cornwall around 1850, and visited the Sans Pareil Theatre in Redruth.[206] In 1851, Collins – now regarded as one of the innovators of the detective story genre – published a journal of this tour in his classic account of pre-railway Cornwall titled *Rambles beyond Railways, or Notes in Cornwall taken a-foot*. Although he was only some four works into a long and distinguished writing career, Collins is, for the most part, an astute and creative observer of the cultural life of Cornwall. Inside the volume he carefully juxtaposes 'The Ancient Drama of Cornwall' (based on the visit he made to Perran Round)[207] with 'The Modern Drama of Cornwall'. In this latter chapter, he describes the by-then famous Sans Pareil theatre. The play was advertised 'by a public notice, printed on rainbow-coloured paper, and pasted up in the most conspicuous part of the marketplace [saying that] "the beautiful drama of *The Curate's Daughter*" was to be performed that night in the "unrivalled Sans Pareil Theatre," by "the most talented company in England," before "the most discerning audience in the world".'[208] Collins then begins with a powerful description of the architecture and atmosphere within the building:

> There was nothing "florid" about it; canvas, ropes, scaffolding poles, and old boards, threw an air of Saxon simplicity over the whole structure. Admitted within, we turned instinctively towards the stage. On each side of the proscenium boards was painted a knight in full armour, with powerful calves, weak knees and an immense spear. Tallow candles, stuck round two hoops, threw a mysterious light on the green curtain, in front of which sat an orchestra of four musicians, playing on a trombone, an ophicleide, a clarionet, and a fiddle, as loudly as they could – the artist on the trombone, especially, performing prodigies of blowing, though he had not room enough to develop the whole length of his instrument. Every now and then great excitement was created among the expectant audiences by the vehement ringing of a bell behind the scenes, and by the occasional appearance of a youth who gravely snuffed the candles all around.[209]

Two things strike the reader from this description. First of all, Collins takes a sarcastic attitude, and is at pains to note the 'simplicity' of the theatre. This sarcasm and simplicity appear to be an intentional follow-through of his imagining of the ancient drama of Cornwall, which in itself (and as this volume has demonstrated) was never 'simple'. Moreover, he makes this a 'Saxon simplicity' – something which might well grate in contemporary

Cornwall. In saying this, Collins tries to show how unpretentious the venue is. However, in high contrast to this there are the knights – possibly Arthurian in nature – which fitted the culture in which the theatre operated. The 'mysterious light on the green curtain' is perhaps a bit of dramatic licence, but it does create an impression of what it would be like to sit in the theatre in Redruth in the middle of the nineteenth century. The purpose of the bell ringing behind the scenes is unclear, though it might presumably inform actors backstage of the impending performance. The candles being snuffed show how a transformation was made between the audience settling and the beginning of the play. Such a process would inevitably signal the imminent start of the performance.

The playwright of *The Curate's Daughter* is not listed in any records or archive sources. Two possible origins of the play exist, one less Cornish than the other. Popular tropes in the early half of the nineteenth century were plays featuring all kinds of curates. Though this wider interest may be applicable, a more likely source would be an 1813 Cornish-themed novel by Elizabeth Isabella Spence. The original novel was called *The Curate and His Daughter, a Cornish Tale*, the narrative being set in a parsonage 'in a remote village, in Cornwall, called Boss Castle [Boscastle]' and concerning a clergyman named Mr Trevanion who dotes upon his daughter Matilda.[210] Other significant characters in the novel are the Countess Dowager Seyntaubyne at Pengwilly Hall, and Dr Martin Arundell. The Countess takes it upon herself to educate Matilda in London. In many ways, the novel sets up a conflict between the values and ideology of the periphery, and the manners and interests of the metropolitan world.[211] Spence's novel is a significant work in looking at class and manners; Matilda is effectively caught between the two worlds. It was also very popular and probably inspired the sub-genre of 'Curate drama'. As we shall see, there are moments where events in this novel seem to match action on stage. However, the names of the characters appear to have changed quite substantially, and although some characters are featured in the drama, others are new inventions. Given the thirty-seven years between the original text and the presentation at Redruth, this seems entirely possible. Although we have some notion of dramatic action from Falmouth and Truro, no account is perhaps as detailed as Collins's observations, which are clearly worth reproducing here, in order to demonstrate the depth and complexity of action, even if the play is seen through the filter of Collins's rather sarcastic eyes:

> At last the bell was rung furiously for the twentieth time; the curtain drew up, and the drama of *The Curate's Daughter* began.

Our sympathies were excited at the outset. We beheld a lady-like woman who answered to the name of "Grace"; and an old gentleman, dressed in dingy black, who personated her father, the Curate; and who was, on this occasion (I presume through unavoidable circumstances); neither more nor less than – drunk. There was no mistaking the cause of the fixed leer in the reverend gentleman's eye; of the slow swaying of his gait; of the gruff huskiness in his elocution. It appeared, from the opening dialogue that a pending law-suit, and the absence of his daughter Fanny in London, combined to make him uneasy in his mind just at present. But he was by no means so clear on this subject as could be desired – in fact, he spoke though his nose, put in and left out his *h*s in the wrong places, and involved his dialogue in a long labyrinth of parentheses whenever he expressed himself at any length. It was not until the entrance of his daughter Fanny (just arrived from London: nobody knew why or wherefore), that he grew more emphatic and intelligible. We now observed with pleasure that he gave his children his blessing and embraced them both at once; and we were additionally gratified by hearing from his own lips, that his "daughters were the h'all on which his h'all depended – that they would watch h'over his 'ale autumn; and that whatever happened the whole party must invariably trust in heabben's obdipotent power!"[212]

Maybe Collins is being deliberately amusing here by renaming Matilda 'Fanny' because he cannot be bothered to acknowledge her real name. He seems to indicate by both the 'huskiness in his elocution' and his dropping of *h*s (a well-documented aspect of Cornu-English dialect[213]) that the Curate (perhaps Trevanion) speaks with a strong Cornu-English voice ('heabben' seems particularly dialectical). Given the role, this would be entirely appropriate for the actor. However, it is a touch too 'local' for Collins's taste. The interplay between Cornwall and London would seem to have arisen from Spence's original, as does an interpretation of the lines of dialect at the end, which closely match the overall narrative of the original. Collins's narrative account continues with the following description of the action on stage:

Grateful for this clerical advice, Fanny retired into the garden to gather her parent some flowers: but immediately she was followed by a Highwayman with a cocked hat, mustachios, bandit's ringlets, a scarlet hunting coat, and buff boots. This gentleman had shown his extraordinary politeness – although a perfect stranger – by giving Miss Fanny a kiss in the garden; conduct for which the Curate very properly cursed him, in the strongest language. Apparently a quiet and orderly character, the Highwayman replied by beginning a handsome apology, when he was interrupted by the abrupt entrance of another personage, who ordered him (rather late in the day, as we ventured to think) to "let go his holt, and beware how he laid his brutal touch on the form of innocence!" This newcomer, the parson informed us, was "good h'Adam Marle, the teacher of the village school." We found "h'Adam," in respect of his outward appearance, to be a very short man, dressed in a high-crowned modern hat, with a fringed vandyck collar drooping over his back and shoulders, a modern frock-coat, buttoned tight at the waist, and a pair of jack-boots of the period of James the Second. Aided by his advantages of costume, this character naturally interested us; and we regretted seeing but little of him in the first scene, from which he retired, following the penitent Highwayman out, and lecturing him as he went. No sooner were their backs turned, than a waggoner, in a clean smock-frock and high-lows, entered with an offer of a situation in London for Fanny, which the unsuspicious Curate accepted immediately. As soon as he had committed himself, it was confided to the audience that the waggoner was a depraved villain, in the employ of that notorious profligate Colonel Chartress, who had commissioned a second myrmidion (of the female sex) to lure Fanny from virtue and the country, to vice and the metropolis. By the time the plot had "thickened" thus far, the scene changed, and we got to London at once.[214]

This is high melodrama of the kind advertised in the pages of *The Royal Cornwall Gazette and Falmouth Packet* and *The West Briton and Cornwall Advertiser* for the performances earlier in the century at Falmouth and Truro. Collins is critical of the costuming for its apparent lack of realism and 'mish-mash' of periods. It is hard to tell, for the period the play is set in is not clear to us, though the presence of the highwayman probably indicates the previous century. The play here deviates from the novel, however, since in that text there is no Adam Marle or highwayman. That said, when the plot apparently shifts to London, it is very similar to the original narrative. Judging by the following quote, it would appear that the original story may have been taken from Spence's work, but reshaped for the stage in a fast-paced melodramatic form. Highwaymen were exciting, highly melodramatic figures for the audience of the day; even better if they turned out to be uncertain figures. Part of the fun for the audience was deciding whether they were good or bad characters.

Curiously Collins is critical of the swift transition from Cornwall to London. Although this is acceptable in twenty-first century theatre – and even valued for moving the plot forward – here, it is seen as a weakness, with Collins anticipating some further adventures along the way. While Fanny is in London, the melodrama continues with a fight, showing another speedy transition:

We now behold the Curate, Chartress's female accomplice, Fanny, and the vicious waggoner, all standing in a row, across the stage. The Curate, in a burst of amiability, had just lifted up his hands to bless the company, when Colonel Chartress (dressed in an old naval uniform, with an opera hat of the year 1800), suddenly rushed in, followed by the Highwayman, who having relapsed from penitence to guilt, had, as a necessary consequence, determined to supplant Chartress in the favour of Miss Fanny. These two promptly seized each other by the throat; vehement shouting, scuffling, and screaming ensued; and the Curate, clasping his daughter round the waist, frantically elevated his walking-stick in the air. Was he about to inflict personal chastisement on his innocent child? Before there was time to ask the question, the curtain fell with a bang, on the crisis of the final act.[215]

The difficulty the actors obviously faced was that the stage of the Sans Pareil Theatre was not large (an observation also made by Dawson), and therefore the acting area was restrictive. However, while not acceptable in the early naturalism of this period, Brechtian principles of theatrical practice would fully embrace this.[216] It could be argued that the cast were using the space well and, in some ways, looking forward to what became acceptable practice in the next century. Brecht's theories on theatre, however, were a long way off.[217]

In Act Two, Collins focuses on both the set and the journey of Adam Marle. With regard to set, Collins is sometimes reluctant to make the imaginative leap that the audience are making, seeming not to realise that full realism is not necessary for theatre to work. The likelihood is that the actors were using techniques originally established in early theatre in Cornwall; that is, that set was not necessary if either the words or simple symbolism alone conveyed a sense of place. It is surprising that Collins does not note that the actions of someone like Marle are classic 'rescue' sequences from Victorian melodrama, and moments of what Russell Jackson has termed 'improvement works',[218] where the audience is to learn from the heartache of the characters' journeys through life, and where morality is expressed in a public forum ("Poor dear Marle!" is exactly the right response from the audience, if not said sarcastically). This was what a Cornish audience wanted. It understood Marle's heartache and search in an era of migration, poverty and uncertainty. We can see, though Collins apparently didn't, that Cornwall is personified in Marle. In this sense, the set and the exactitude of the costuming are the last things on the audience's minds. It is the choices and decisions made that are important, as can be witnessed in the observation of this sequence:

In act the second, the first scene was described in the bills as Temple Bar by moonlight. Neither Bar nor moonlight appeared when the curtain rose – so we took both for granted, and fixed our minds on the story. The first person who now confronted us, was "good h'Adam Marle." The paint was all washed off his face, his immense spread of collar looked grievously in want of washing; and he leaned languidly on an oaken stick. He had been walking – he informed us – through the streets of London for six consecutive days and nights, without sustenance, in search of Miss Fanny, who had disappeared since the skirmish at the end of act the first, and had never been heard of since. Poor dear Marle! how eloquent he was with his white handkerchief, when he fairly opened his heart, and confided to us that he was madly attached to Fanny; that he knew he "was nothink" to her; and that under existing circumstances, he felt inclined to rest himself on a door step![219]

What follows is the response to this scene. Although Collins sees unintentional humour in its execution, his writing does give us useful insight into theatrical practice in Cornwall during this time. There is the deft touch of using the musicians as his comrades in villainy, breaking the fourth wall in the process, multi-role-playing, the melodramatic cloak, and the convenient use of 'feinting' as another transition and to facilitate further capture. Clearly, the problem facing this performance was the need to move the plot forward, and to do so conveniently and quickly, hence Collins's criticism of Fanny 'recovered on a sudden':

The next scene disclosed Fanny, sitting conscience-stricken and inconsolable, in a red polka jacket and white muslin slip. Mr. Marle, having discovered her place of refuge, now stepped in to lecture and proclaim. Vain proceeding! The Curate's daughter looked at him with a scream, exclaimed, "Cuss me, h'Adam! cuss me!" and rushed out. "H'Adam," after a despondent soliloquy, followed with his eloquent handkerchief to his eyes; but, while he had been talking to himself, our old friend the Highwayman had been on the alert, and had picked Fanny up, feinting in the street. And what did he do with her after that? He handed her over to his "comrades in villany". And who were these comrades in villany? They were the trombone and ophicleide players from the orchestra, and the "Miss Grace" of act first, disguised as a bad character, in a cloak, with a red pocket-handkerchief over her head. And what happened next? A series of events happened next. Miss Fanny recovered on a sudden, perceived what sort of company she had about her, rushed out a second time into the street, fell feinting a second time on the pavement, and was picked up on this occasion by Colonel Chartress.[220]

All of Collins' observations on the play are made with the same 'sneer' over the quality of the production. He does criticise the actors for their apparent amateurism, and laughs at their delivery. It is uncertain whether the company itself was Cornish-based or English in origin, though obviously Collins was comparing the 'innocence' of the Redruth production with the standard of theatre in London. Whether his criticism was justified is hard to tell, for *The Curate's Daughter* was obviously a very popular mid nineteenth-century melodrama, intentionally acted in this way. Clearly however, the drama made some impression on Collins or he would not have devoted several pages of his volume to the performance. He finishes with:

> Marle – well-bred to the last – politely offered his arm to Grace; and pointing to the coffin, asked Chartress, reproachfully, whether that was not *his* work. The Colonel took off his opera-hat, raised his hand to his eyes, and doggedly answered, "Indeed, it is!" The Tableau thus formed, was completed by the Highwayman, the coffin, and the defunct Curate; and the curtain fell to slow music.
>
> Such was the plot of this remarkable dramatic work, exactly as I took it down in the theatre, between the acts; noting also in my pocket-book such scraps of dialogue as I have presented to the reader, while they fell from the actors' lips. There were plenty of comic scenes in the play which I leave unmentioned; for their humour was of the dreariest, and their morality of the lowest order that can possibly be conceived.[221]

This last comment is the most critical. It is unclear exactly what this 'low order morality' was, but perhaps it genuinely was the kind that appealed to the sensibilities of the Redruth theatre-going public. Needless to say, it probably did offend Collins's sensibilities. His ideological perspective on Cornwall was not very far removed from conceiving it still as 'West Barbary'.[222] Nevertheless, he concludes (as at the beginning of this chapter) by saying that as a result of his own experiences at Redruth he was still impressed with 'the locomotive stage of Cornwall' and hopes that theatrical reform will bring further benefits there. In some ways, the position Collins arrives at is predictable: that the centre should define what nineteenth-century drama was all about. It is curious, therefore, that in the volume he then goes on to provide his imaginative reconstruction of what it was like to watch a Cornish mystery play – clearly acknowledging that the periphery (in this instance Cornwall) – had actually been the genesis of theatre in the island of Britain. With or without Wilkie Collins, Redruth's theatrical cultural clearly continued throughout the second half of the century. The historian Frank Michell, writing in 1949, has reflected on the layers of theatrical culture that existed there, noting the continuum and atmosphere of the performance space:

> To music and drama Redruth has always been closely wed. The miracle plays, the "rude" theatres for Edmund Kean and James Dawson, the Sans Pareil theatre, the miners' and religious choirs, the "grand costume concerts" and "dramatic entertainments" which took place "before a fashionable audience" in the second half of the Victorian era and were "held in the Druids Hall illuminated by Chinese Lanterns", the formation of philharmonic debating and photographic societies, an Amateur Dramatic club in 1885 , which grew into a society in 1886 and was incorporated in 1909 into the Amateur Operatic and Dramatic Society – all these contribute to the stream of culture and entertainment in Redruth, now and in the days of greater self-amusement and larger dependence on local talent.[223]

In his very readable and witty *Autobiography* of 1865, written when he was sixty-six years old, James Dawson also comments on his experiences of playing Redruth. It would seems that the Sans Pareil Theatre was actually the Town Hall, described by Dawson as 'such a slip of a place, metaphorically there was not room to swing a *cat*, but we did not intend to be guilty of such a piece of cruelty, or to bring about any *cat*astrophe; we only wish to *coronat o-pus*'.[224] This would seem to support Collins's observations that the place was tiny. Dawson gives an impression of the cramped nature of the theatre when he humorously explains that 'the gentlemen's dressing room was a blacksmith's shop under the stage, where Vulcan might have forged the bolts of Jove… I and my partner dressed on the bellows, so we could play *Raising the Wind* on Saturday and blow up our Company'.[225] While in Redruth, Dawson descended one of the mines in the neighbourhood and wined and dined at Mr John Pearce's 'the jovial pleasant landlord of the Redruth Hotel'.[226] This would indicate that there was a regular arrangement, where touring actors would stay if they performed there. We know that Edmund Kean (1789-1833), the great tragic actor, also came to Redruth in 1828 to assist in the 'benefit' for James Dawson in 1828. Kean's party gave a performance of his by-then legendary interpretation of Shylock in the *The Merchant of Venice*. The Town Hall building (incorporating the theatre) was located in Penryn Street, south of the present Baptist Chapel. According to Frank Michell, drawing on manuscript records, when Shylock sharpened his knife, a butcher present is said to have remarked that he could not do it better himself, and tradition relates that Kean regarded this as one of the highest compliments he ever received.[227]

As can be seen, the Sans Pereil Theatre is quite well-recorded in the middle of the nineteenth century. It is to James Dawson's autobiography we should go, however, if we want to know more about the experiences of a touring actor in Cornwall during the first half of the century. Although Harvey Crane documents a number of touring actors in Devon, he is less comprehensive on Cornwall.[228] There is actually a wealth of material relating to different venues and locations in Dawson's writings. Dawson's life is something of an enigma, however. For example, we know that he was born into a theatrical family, and that later in life he chose to settle in Truro. In Truro, however, it seems his circumstances altered according to income and success on the stage. When times were good, he lived at the grander Paul's Terrace, but when his earnings dwindled, he set up his dance academy and moved to the less imposing St Clement's Street.[229] Despite this, Dawson continued to be enormously important in shaping theatre in Cornwall, but also, as we shall see from his writings, understanding the continuum and purpose of theatre. Dawson is also a very sharp writer, who fills his reflections with puns, theatrical in-jokes and a certain fondness for Cornwall. By the time he was in his later teenage years, it seems he was already well-established as an actor, and across his writings we encounter many of the commonly performed texts of the period. Wittily, he begins the work, by asking, 'Have I not made an ass of myself for the amusement of the public?'[230] He had, of course, for Dawson's primary skill as an actor was comedy. His first memory is of performing in pantomime:

> The first deep trace my memory wears, pictures me riding, or carrying, a pasteboard pig across a stage in a Christmas pantomime; when I, being too young to go the whole hog, turned the unpainted part to the spectators; and they, not being a kind and discerning audience, were unable, by any outward sign, to make out the nature or properties of the creature I was supposed to be riding, for, like an ill-roasted egg, it was done only on one side.[231]

It would appear that property construction has altered little. Such techniques are still used within theatre, film and television today. If this image of the paste-board pig is true, then it would seem Dawson was a child performer, indicating that companies could legally use children in their productions. We learn too, of his entrance into the world:

> I made my appearance in Scarborough, on the 16th October, 1799 *vide* our Family Bible... I beg most respectfully to announce to the ladies and gentlemen, and the public of Cornwall, that I made my first appearance in *The Birth Day*, It was not *Love's Labour's Lost*, though my father would have preferred *Much Ado*

About Nothing, and my mother *Midsummer Night's Dream*. But it cannot be always *As You Like It* in this eventful drama of life; nor are we permitted to select our own character; we must hold the world but as the world, where every man must play his part.[232]

Declared in the style of theatrical announcements of the period ('I beg most respectfully…') Dawson appears to have been born whilst on tour in Scarborough, though his family background is in the west of Britain. Since he knows Cornwall will be significant later in his life, Dawson chooses to poke fun at it early on: 'I remained Bonny until I came into Cornwall, where Bonny became *Bony*. They say, if you cling to a rock you will get fat on it; my experience will not bear out that assertion, for I have clung most tenaciously to the granite rocks of Cornwall, and I have got thin, and that is all I have got'.[233] Dawson then documents his apprenticeship into the theatre, noting Mr Hughes (the owner at Truro and Penzance in the eighteenth century) and how he went through a process of training (probably not the done thing in the south west until this period):

It was in Exeter that my histrionic powers were first evoked. My mentor was a Mr Hughes, a gentleman fully competent to teach the young ideas of how to shoot theatrically, for he had had great experience, and was noted for his dramatic acumen. He was the manager of the Theatres Royal Weymouth, Plymouth, Exeter, Guernsey, Devonport, Truro, Penzance and Sadler's Wells… An engagement was now made for me to perform at the Academical Theatre in London: it was under the immediate superintendence of Colonel Greville. This gentleman entertained an opinion that actors, like lawyers and doctors, should go through a regular course of studies, and be duly initiated in the arduous profession; as in the Elizabethan age, when plays were performed by choristers and singing boys, and by the children of Paul's…[234]

As well as clearly showing the sophistication of management over the south-western area of Britain (and the connection to Sadler's Wells), this also documents how well Dawson understood theatrical history. He became interested in what he terms 'sensation drama'[235] and it is this that allows him to travel far; there are performances occurring in London, Bristol and Cheltenham, but also in Ostend, Flanders and the Netherlands. Here then is a young man, who at a very young age is taking a vibrant theatre to the rest of Europe. It again demonstrates a network of not only Britain-wide theatrical connections and promotions, but one which was actively crossing the Channel. Sadly, Dawson does not record what texts were being performed, but it seems that after he had paid his dues, he discovered 'my parents having agreed to join, once again, the Exeter Company'.[236] This provides more information explaining that the Exeter Company of Players was well-established, and that this would be Dawson's introduction to Cornwall. The era under consideration here was obviously Dawson's first runs into Cornwall, probably during the years 1818-21.

As I have described above, *John Bull* was a very Cornu-centric and popular drama of the early nineteenth-century, and it is in this text that we first learn of Dawson recording the theatrical conditions of Cornwall. There is a sense that he knew it would be economically viable because there was money there ('we want tin more than the ancient Phoenicians'), but also his projected role of the Copper Captain seems tempting to him:

> When having lost the rubber and points, I observed to my partner, "we be the honestest family in Cornwall," a quotation from the play of *John Bull*, and one frequently used by actors in their distress, "their dolor." The incidents of this comedy are all supposed to have occurred near the Land's End and Penzance. "I should very much like to visit that *terra incognita*," said I, "it is very sterile country I have heard, but I hear the man who can travel from Dan to Beersheba and say 'tis all barren; besides, we want tin more than the ancient Phoenicians; we have plenty of Corinthian brass, ironically speaking, and I may play the Copper Captain, so we'll steal into the county and gain golden opinions from all sorts of men; and may our happiness be unalloyed by the baser metal.[237]

The Exeter Company obviously proceeded into Cornwall from the north east because their first engagement of the tour was at Great Torrington; a town not far across the border into Devon in England. Their appearance there proved to be unsuccessful, so they travelled the distance across Bodmin Moor to Liskeard. There are, of course, huge logistical decisions to be made in touring theatre, and during this period, the process cannot have been easy, especially given some of the terrain in Cornwall (the 'sterile country'). Dawson explains what happened:

> So we agreed to engage the Exeter Company and journey to the far West. There were to be four managers, "too many eggs in one basket". Our *coup d'essaie* was in Great Torrington, where we met with little success, for we were playing to a "beggarly account of empty boxes," and we soon found there was no "culling of simples" there; so to prevent sharp misery wearing us to the bone, we moved on to Liskeard "with over-whelming brows." This was our first appearance in

Cornwall, and it had very nearly been our last, for we made a most lame and impotent conclusion in that town.[238]

While on the tour, they visited the Well of St Keyne,[239] and probably before arriving at Liskeard, encountered the famous landmark of Dozmary Pool, though it was not then as famous as it would be later on in the century after Alfred Lord Tennyson's *Idylls of the King*.[240] Dawson notes that it was 'a deadly lively place. If a man be merry at Dozmerry he must be particularly merry, and long may he continue so, for it is a spot "Replete with vapour, and disposes much. All hearts to sadness, and none more than mine"'. To this he adds, 'even our Light Comedian became heavy, and our funny man serious'.[241] Although the initial visit to Liskeard's Barn Theatre was not as successful as he had hoped, later performances were better welcomed. That said, Dawson did not feel that Liskeard was a place that wholly welcomed theatrical activity – probably the reason why performances there during the nineteenth century are not well recorded:

> I was the manager in Liskeard, "our *chacun a son* tour," and I have a grateful rec-
> ollection that they filled the Barn-Theatre on the night of my benefit; I have
> many a time and oft visited Liskeard professionally since, and have ever been
> received with the most kind and hearty welcome. Still, as regards that town, in
> a theatrical sense, I do opine that the inhabitants are not dramatically given.[242]

The Exeter Company did not easily give up their ambitions for Cornwall though, and it is behind the lines of his *Autobiography* that one senses Dawson falling in love with the place. The Exeter Company brings to mind a military operation in terms of its desire to conquer the territory. Truro was clearly a target, with Mr Osbaldiston, one of Dawson's closest confidants:

> At length, in conjunction with Mr Osbaldiston, I resolved to muster all the
> forces I could make, and march a second time to Cornwall. We by spies had been
> well informed that, could we but surprise Truro, we might there "laugh a siege
> to scorn." So we summoned the town to surrender; and Governor Banallack,
> finding that we were irresistible, capitulated on honourable terms. There was "no
> cry of matrons in sacked towns," in fact, the ladies were all on our side, so there
> was no occasion to take them by storm. Our corps was certainly strong… We
> opened in Truro with *The Castle Spectre*… The patronage conferred on our
> efforts to amuse was very great during this, our first season in Truro. We seldom
> played to less than twenty pounds a night… This town has been my stronghold.
> Truro, your favours are registered where every day I turn the leaf to read them.[243]

Once the presence of the Company had been established in Truro, the Exeter group then targeted other theatrical centres. The metaphorical base of *John Bull* is sustained in Dawson's writings. As we know, Redruth became a regular venue, but the Company also wished to play in the far west:

> Our next attack was Penzance. This was not quite so profitable as Truro; still, as Dan in "John Bull" says, "they treated us in an hospital manner and shewed us a deal of contention". Our theatre was at that time in the Inn yard... We did not play under favourable auspices, for our stage was over the stable... The aroma made our ghosts sneeze.[244]

Penzance, so it seems, was successful for Dawson's company, but on the close of the seasons in the west, we learn that Mr Osbaldiston left, so Dawson ventured to take the Company to Bodmin on his own. From Dawson's observations, it seems as if Assize Week was a particularly apt moment in the year for theatre to be mounted (presumably because of the number of people in the town). However, their performances that week coincided with the memorable trial of Queen Caroline.[245] This was just after the Pains and Penalties Bill of 1820, which had been introduced in Parliament in order to strip Caroline of the title of queen consort and dissolve her marriage to George IV. Despite George IV's attempts to destroy Caroline's life, the Queen remained incredibly popular amongst the working classes of Britain, and hence Dawson's difficulties in Bodmin:

> We opened in the Assize week, and about the time of Queen Caroline's memorable trial... One part would call for "God save the King" and the other for "God save the Queen"; so to put an end to the nightly disturbance, I requested our leader not to play the national anthem when thus so vociferously and rudely demanded. On the ensuing night, the usual riot commenced, and when they found their wishes were not responded to, they became very violent... and threatened to pull down the Theatre.[246]

Despite these threats, according to Dawson, 'our first season in Bodmin was very good, and the inhabitants vied with each other to make our stay agreeable'. Alongside this, he notes that 'hospitality, with kind and polite attention to strangers, are the estimable characteristics of Cornwall'.[247] After success in Bodmin, Dawson, still working independently moved the company to St Austell, where they 'played in a Brewery'.[248] Although Dawson offers detailed accounts of such day-to-day life on the road with his Company, he is also more than aware of the continuum of drama in Britain. Consider this section, where he reflects on the origins of his profession. It has, of course, a very peculiar Cornish dimension because of the earlier dramas, and it is perhaps a pity he does not mention, for example, the *Ordinalia* by name. Nevertheless, he demonstrates some knowledge of the origin of his profession:

> It may, perhaps, be necessary to inform those who have not studied the matter, that our English stage originated from the Ecclesiastics, and that the first exhibition in this country was "The Miracle of St. Catherine," written by the Bishop of St. Albans. All our first dramatic pageants were called Miracle Plays, or Religious Mysteries; they were taken, without any alteration, from the Scriptures, and were acted for the most part in churches by the monks.[249]

Monks may not have acted these 'miracle plays' or 'religious mysteries' but in Cornwall, it is very possible that they may have written them. The date of Dawson's 1865 autobiography is significant, for it was composed only a few years after Edwin Norris's translation of the *Ordinalia* first became available,[250] and maybe Dawson was thinking along these lines, in a way comparable to Collins's view of ancient and modern drama in Cornwall. Dawson was writing slightly too early for the Cornish Revival proper,[251] though drama and its traditions were to feature so importantly within that future.[252] In these words then, we have a significant link to both the past and future of drama within Cornwall. Although Dawson almost seems to have thought through these connections, his heart was still with the practical day-to-day running of a theatre troupe. Significantly, in this phase, they move to perform at Lostwithiel, a town on the brink of losing its Stannary status,[253] but of significant status within living memory and tradition of the wider Cornish community. The very fact that Dawson mentions the 'old prison' shows the jurisdiction of the Stannary Court:

> Our next town was Lostwithiel… Many of my Company having been accused of injuring, maiming, and cutting several respectable characters, I thought it right to have them all put into the old prison at Lostwithiel, there to await their trial, and thus stop the babbling of such vain gainsayers. But I gratefully acknowledge that the elite of the town and neighbourhood, feeling assured that we were more sinned against that sinning, did all they could to encourage and support us, and make our incarceration endurable; to this end they would visit us in the morning, bringing the choicest flowers and fruits, and most kindly shared our captivity in the evening.[254]

The welcome they received in the town obviously touched Dawson's heart. It seems that at such locations, the players relied on this hospitality to survive. Lostwithiel is a very significant location. It may have been that the first tellings or even performances of Tristan narratives were conceived nearby, at Restormel Castle,[255] and even to the present there is a continuum of theatrical activity within the town.[256] A similar welcome greeted them at Falmouth, which by this phase had an expectation of theatre, thanks to the efforts of Samuel Fisher:

> Now, though last, not least, in our dear love, is Falmouth; for that has been a main stay to me in all weathers; a harbour of refuge; a port in a storm… It was a long time ere we found a place suited for our purpose, for the very pretty Theatre in the Moor, built by my worthy predecessor Mr. Fisher, had been converted into a Unitarian Chapel. At last we found a Brianite meeting house which was to be let or sold, so we took it, thinking with Hamlet, "Nay, an thou't mouth I'll rant as well as thou."[257]

It seems that shortly after this success in Falmouth Dawson temporarily moved to Mulberry Square there.[258] He was by then completely besotted with Cornwall, noting its magic and sense of drama, and understanding that it is 'certainly the stronghold of the Pixies…'[259] In Falmouth, Dawson was urged to reopen the Falmouth Theatre, but apparently chose instead to settle with Truro, and then the Devonport Theatre.[260] By the end of his autobiography, despite the ups and downs of touring theatre, he confidently resolved to 'make the tour of Cornwall once again'.[261] In this way, Dawson ends his account, perhaps before the real business of his time in Cornwall as an actor-manager begins. However, the account is the best source we have of the touring processes of the period.

Touring on the scale described by Dawson seems to subside in the middle of the nineteenth century, as the major venues of Cornwall declined. During the 1850s, advertisements for theatre – particularly at Falmouth and Truro – become scarcer, though this is not to say that performances did not occur in other locations. It would, however, be strange for companies not to visit these major venues, so one hypothesis is that the touring circuit, if not dead, was then much more intermittent. In this phase, although 'Cornwall' and Cornish subject matter were becoming popular on the wider British and European stage, there seems little indigenous theatre at home. Theatre is particularly thin on the ground through 1851, 1852, and 1853. 1865 brought a number of musical concerts to Truro, as well as an event described as 'Prout's Voyage to Australia and Visit to the Gold Fields: A most interesting and popular panorama followed by a descriptive lecture'.[262] This was nowhere near the kind of progressive drama available just a decade before. What had happened? For one thing, the theatre had altered immeasurably very quickly, in the light of new legislation. For another, Cornwall was temporarily suffering from the effects of emigrations. Finally, the major entrepreneurs of the early half of the century had either died or were approaching retirement. Lectures such as 'Prout's Voyage to Australia' probably required less initial outlay. The public also demanded a more sophisticated theatrical vision, which was not achievable in the confines of the old theatres. The locomotive theatre of Cornwall had suddenly modernised.

Little had changed by 1856 when the Assembly-Room Theatre of Truro presented the popular entertainment 'The Far West, or Every Day Life in America' performed by Henry Russell, who would 'sing most of his celebrated compositions, followed by a series of sketches on Negro Life'.[263] Clearly, audiences were attracted to hear about the lands to which the Cornish were emigrating, but the impression is of a tired venue, unsure of itself and its future. In this, we perhaps witness the beginnings of music hall in Cornwall.[264] An example of this is found in January 1857, when Charles Cotton, the celebrated dramatic vocalist, would present 'a new vocal and musical entertainment titled *Rose, Shamrock and Thistle*.[265] We also see the beginnings of decline, with more amateur performances, the first of these taking place at the end of the Winter 1857 season.[266]

Another important change was occurring. As Pawling, and Dixon note, the 1850s brought a dramatic rise in literacy levels across Britain,[267] resulting in more reading amongst previously less well-educated social groups. Therefore, there was less impetus to attend theatre, because audiences could find suitable narratives elsewhere: in serials, stories and novels. One sees the transition in the press of the period. There are advertisements for popular fictions and Cornu-English poetry offering 'mirth for long evenings'. A flavour of the narratives can be gleaned from the titles: *The Miner, John Treloar and Mal, Jan Knuckey and Gracey, Squab Pie, Visit to Lunnon, Carn Breh* [sic] and *The old Cornish Woman's Visit to the Great Exhibition*.[268] These were the kind of popular 'tales' which twenty years previously had formed the backbone of many of the indigenous farces and interludes, a fact perhaps captured by the fact that one story advertised is titled *Account of a Christmas Play*. Home entertainment seems more the fashion of the day towards the end of the decade, with the following Cornish ballads available: *The Cornish Farmer and Lunnon Sharper, The Miners' Children's Hymns, Penna's Van, A Cornish Mouse-trap* and *The Mare's Egg*.[269] In these, we have curious echoes of earlier performances. Early in 1859, J. Stephens Mitchell presented a 'A Cornish Village Glee and

Madrigal Class' at Truro.[270] The dearth of performances continued through the closing years of the decade, the best of a bad lot being Professor Whitworth's 'electro biology', also on tour in Redruth, St Austell, Falmouth, Penzance and Plymouth.[271] This new interest in scientific 'theatre' also brought 'Signor Blitz, the wonder working magician ventriloquist with all his learned canary birds' and 'Monsieur Zamoiski of Warsaw, Poland, offering Extraordinary entertainments, experiments in electro-biology and mesmerism'.[272] Only by the late 1860s was there a return to form, seemingly under the ownership of Mr Walter Shelley. The two plays mentioned appear to be not touring shows, but in-house productions. The audience was clearly different than in the previous decades, now an upper-class clientele:

> Very many years have elapsed since the Truro Theatre has been in such good hands as it is at present, and we sincerely hope the efforts which are being made by Mr Walter Shelley and his excellent staff, to afford amusement and instruction by the creditable production of plays by the best masters, will be fittingly rewarded. Thus far, the lessee has, we think no reason to complain, as during the past week he has been honoured by two bespeaks – one, on Monday, by the Hon. Capt. Vivian, M.P., when *The Corsican Brothers* was performed; the other, on Wednesday, by the officers of the Volunteer Corps, when *Othello* was performed.
>
> A large and fashionable audience assembled each evening, and unmistakable satisfaction was expressed with the entertainments. Mr Shelley, as Othello was first-class; he was at home in one of the most difficult characters that can fall to the lot of a tragedian, and in all respects he acquitted himself well. At the conclusion of the piece he was called before the curtain; so indeed was Miss Stammers, a young and very promising actress who put herself in Desdemona's place: Miss Stammers must persevere, and before she gets out of her teens she will attain a high position. Mr Edward Terry is an out and out comedian, and is a host in himself; he has long been a great favourite at Plymouth, and no wonder. Mrs Stammers and Miss Deutz are both good, and in fact, the company is altogether a capital selection. We must not extend our remarks beyond a word in just praise of Mr Ernest Siddons, who is not only an able actor, but a capital stage manager, and we need hardly say that without good stage management not much can be expected.[273]

This outpouring of praise is short-lived, however. During the 1870s and 1880s both indigenous and touring theatre appears to collapse completely. The newspapers contain no advertisements for performances, and no reviews are printed. Only a small story in January 1888 even expresses any interest in the theatre in Truro. By now, it is renamed the Concert Hall (indicating that it was only a place for musical events) and concern is raised over its safety after a fire in an Exeter theatre.[274] Although the talk of the column is about installing a sprinkler system to make the building safer, this debate seems to ensure that the hall would be used less and less in the closing decades of the century. With Falmouth already dispatched by the middle of the decade, and Redruth struggling to survive, the urban theatrical venues of Cornwall were about to hit a nadir. The seeming wish to make the building safer is offset by a dramatic story in February 1888 about a theatre in Madrid burning down.[275] Public mood had shifted, and although some wished for the locomotive's fire to reignite, others felt it best to just damp it down. If theatre would no longer come to Cornwall, then Cornwall would take theatre to the rest of the world. We thus enter the next phase of the theatrical history of Cornwall.

CHAPTER FOUR: NOTES AND REFERENCES

1.   Wilkie Collins, *Rambles beyond Railways, or Notes in Cornwall taken a-foot*, London: Westaway Books, 1948 [1851], p.128.

2.   Harvey Crane, *Playbill: A History of the Theatre in the West Country*, Plymouth: Macdonald and Evans, 1980, p.157.

3.   See John Rowe, *Cornwall in the Age of the Industrial Revolution*, St Austell: Cornish Hillside Publications, 1993 [1953].

4.   John Raithby, *The Statutes at Large of England and of Great Britain*, London: G. Agre and A. Strahan, 1806. See Vols. 5 and 9 for the 1737 and 1788 Acts respectively.

5.   R.A. Banks, *Drama and Theatre Arts*, London: Hodder and Stoughton, 1985, p.201.

6.   Philip Payton, *The Making of Modern Cornwall: Historical Experience and the Persistence of "Difference"*, Redruth: Dyllansow Truran, 1992, p.103.

7.   See Alan M. Kent and Gage McKinney (eds.), *The Busy Earth: A Reader in Global Cornish Literature 1700-2000*, St Austell: Cornish Hillside Publications, 2008; Philip Payton, *The Cornish Overseas*, Fowey: Alexander Associates, 1999.

8.   W.S. Gilbert and Arthur Sullivan, *The Complete Annotated Gilbert and Sullivan*, Oxford: Oxford University Press, 1996.

9.   See Barry Millington (ed.), *The Wagner Compendium: A Guide to Wagner's Life and Music*, London: Thames and Hudson, 2001. Wagner was influenced by Gottfried von Strassburg's version of the Cornish romance. See A.T. Hatto (ed. and tr.), *Gottfried von Strassburg: Tristan, with the Tristan of Thomas*, Harmondsworth: Penguin, 1967.

10. George William Downing, *The Great Hewas Mine, or The Humours of Cornwall: A Comedy in Five Acts and in Prose*, London: by C. Chapple, c.1816.

11. George Clement Boase and William Prideaux Courtney (eds.), *Bibliotheca Cornubiensis Vols. 1-3*, London: Longman, Green, Reader and Dyer, 1874, p.117.

12. See Downing, op.cit., p.i.

13. Ibid., p.9.

14. Ibid.

15. Ibid., p.15.

16. Ibid., pp.11-12. Are Snapps and Stamps the same thing here?

17. Ibid., p.12. This kind of witty, well-travelled and industrially aware figure is found in many of Nick Darke's historical dramas of Cornwall.

18. Ibid.

19. Ibid., p.20.

20. Ibid., pp.20-21.

21. Ibid., p.21.

22. Ibid., p.25.

23. Ibid., p.26.

24. See W.G. Orchard (ed.), *A Glossary of Mining Terms*, Redruth: Dyllansow Truran, 1991, p.9.

25. See Lynne Mayers, *Balmaidens*, Penzance: The Hypatia Trust, 2004.

26. Downing, op.cit., p.31.

27. Ibid., p.32.

28. Ibid., p.33.

29. Ibid., p.34.

30. Ibid., p.36.

31. Ibid., pp.43-4.

32. Ibid., p.59.

33. Ibid., p.60.

34. Ibid., p.83.

35. Ibid., p.84.

36. Ibid., p.88.

37. Ibid., p.92.

38. Ibid., p.107.

39. See Tony Deane and Tony Shaw, *Folklore of Cornwall*, Stroud: Tempus, 2003, p.156-8.

40. A useful compendium of these is found in Margaret A. Courtney (ed.), *Cornish Feasts and Folklore*, Exeter: Cornwall Books, 1989 [1890]. A more exhaustive list is found in George Clement Boase, *Collectanea Cornubiensia: A Collection of Biographical and Topographical Notes relating to the County of Cornwall*, Truro: Netherton and Worth, 1890, pp.1579-96.

41. For some of the possible narratives, see Kent and McKinney, op.cit. We also see this trans-national nature of Cornwall recorded in the twentieth century. See A.L. Rowse, *A Cornish Childhood*, London: Anthony Mott, 1982 [1942].

42. See Boase and Courtney (eds.), *Bibliotheca Cornubiensis Vols. 1-3*, London: Longman, Green, Reader and Dyer, 1874, 1878 and 1882.

43. Boase, op.cit.

44. *Cornwall Gazette and Falmouth Packet*, 23 January 1802, p.3.

45. James Whetter, *The History of Falmouth*, Gorran: Lyfrow Trelyspen, 2004 [1981], p.21.

46. John Johnson, *The Way to Get Married: And the Advantages and Disadvantages of the Marriage State, represented under the similitude of a dream*, Philadelphia: Johnson and Warner, 1810.

47. See, for example, William Congreve's *The Way of the World* in Robert G. Lawrence (ed.), *Restoration Plays*, London: J.M. Dent and Sons, 1976, pp.163-236.

48. Charles Perrault (1628-1703) was a French author who perhaps more than anyone else, created the literary genre of the fairy tale.

49. This narrative also influenced the writer Angela Carter (1940-1992) in her story *The Bloody Chamber*. See Angela Carter, *Burning your Boats: Collected Short Stories*, London: Vintage, 1996, pp.111-43.

50. See the observations of A.S.D Smith, *The Story of the Cornish Language: Its Extinction and Revival*, Camborne: Smith, 1947.

51. *Cornwall Gazette and Falmouth Packet*, 30 January 1802, p.3. The advertisements rarely give the author of the play.

52. Sheridan's most famous play was the 1775 production of *The Rivals*. Kotzebue's original title was *Die Spanier in Peru*.

53. Although slightly later, Richard Trevithick (1771-1833) left to work as a mining consultant in Peru in 1816. See Anthony Burton, *Richard Trevithick: Giant of Steam*, London: Aurum Press, 2000, pp.158-74.

54. Probably *The Tale of the Shifty Lad, the Widow's Son*.

55. *Cornwall Gazette and Falmouth Packet*, 6 February 1802, p.3 The motif of the 'poor gentleman' seems a common trope in early nineteenth-century drama, but the author remains slightly unclear. A possible candidate is George Colman, whose *The Poor Gentleman* was published by Longman in 1810. Clearly, this was a significant drama, for the role of Dr Ollapod was taken by the American comedian and actor John Sleeper Clarke (1833-1899).

56. This is most likely to be by Thomas Dibdin. It was published in New York in 1808.

57. *Cornwall Gazette and Falmouth Packet*, 13 February 1802, p.3.

58. The ships of the expedition were wrecked on reefs.

59. *Cornwall Gazette and Falmouth Packet*, 20 February 1802, p.3.

60. Ibid., 6 March 1802, p.3,

61. Something also seen in Shakespeare's histories.

62. For a context, see Keith Pearce and Helen Fry (eds.), *The Lost Jews of Cornwall*, Bristol: Redcliffe, 2000.

63. As in Banks, op.cit.

64. *Cornwall Gazette and Falmouth Packet*, 6 March 1802, op.cit.

65. Several famous artists of the era painted Cook's death.

66. *Cornwall Gazette and Falmouth Packet*, 13 March 1802, p.3

67. For comparison, see Frederick Reynolds, *Plays: A Collection of Thirty 18th-Century English plays, Principally Comedies*, London: n.p., 2008.

68. It is unclear what the plot of *Ghost* was. *The Muffin Man* was clearly based on the call and respond nursery rhyme of "Do you know the Muffin Man? The Muffin Man, the Muffin Man. Do you know the Muffin Man, Who lives on Drury Lane?"

69. *Cornwall Gazette and Falmouth Packet* 17 March 1802, p.3. For a Masonic history of Cornwall, see Cornwall Province of Freemasons, *Thread of Gold: Celebrating the Unbroken History of 250 Years of Freemasonry in the Province of Cornwall*, Cornwall: Cornwall Province of Freemasons, 2001.

70. George Colman, *The Review, or The Wags of Windsor: A Musical Farce in Two Acts*, London: J. Cawthorn and James Cawthorn, 1808.

71. *Cornwall Gazette and Falmouth Packet*, 27 March 1802, p.3.

72. Susannah Centlivre, *The Wonder, or A Woman Keeps a Secret*, Canada: Broadview Press, 2001.

73. W.R. Owens and Lizbeth Goodman (eds.), *Approaching Literature: Shakespeare, Aphra Behn and the Canon*, London: Routledge, 1996, pp.131-192 and pp.261-327.

74. James Francis Cobb, *The Watchers on the Longships*, Redhill: Wells, 1876; F. Frankfurt Moore, *Tre Pol and Pen*, London: Society for Promoting Christian Knowledge, 1887; Walter Besant, *Armorel of Lyonesse: A Romance of Today*, Felinfach: Llanerch, 1993 [1890]; Sabine Baring-Gould, *In the Roar of the Sea*, London: Methuen, 1892.

75. See Roger Jones (ed.), *John Skinner: Westcountry Tour, being the Diary of a Tour through the Counties of Somerset, Devon and Cornwall in 1797*, Bradford upon Avon: Ex Libris Press, 1985, pp.75-77; Whetter, op.cit.

76. See Richard McGrady, *Music and Musicians in Early Nineteenth-Century Cornwall: The World of Joseph Emidy – Slave, Violinist and Composer*, Exeter: University of Exeter Press, 1991. Evidence of Emidy playing at Wynn's Hotel is found in *Cornwall Gazette and Falmouth Packet*, 31 July 1802, p.4. See also Alan M. Kent, *The Tin Violin*, London: Francis Boutle Publishers, 2008.

77. For background, see Dale Cockrell, *Demons of Disorder: Early Blackface Minstrels and Their World*, Cambridge: Cambridge University Press, 1997. This has cultural implications in Cornwall. See Merv Davey, "Guizing': Ancient Traditions and Modern Sensitivities' in Philip Payton (ed.), *Cornish Studies: Fourteen*, Exeter: University of Exeter Press, 2006, pp.229-44.

78. It appears that while the role of Mungo was originally played by a blacked-up white actor, later performances employed black actors.

79. *Cornwall Gazette and Falmouth Packet*, 11 April 1801, p.4.

80. This was a melodrama with music by Victor Pelisser and a script by William Dunlap.

81. *Royal Cornwall Gazette and Falmouth Packet*, 2 July 1803, p.1. From 1803 onwards the 'Royal' prefix is added. A similar advertisement is found twelve years later in *The West Briton and Cornwall Advertiser*, 24 November 1815, p.3, where anthologies of plays and other dramatic texts are advertised, presumably for home reading. Many of the plays of the previous twenty-five years were on sale.

82. *Royal Cornwall Gazette and Falmouth Packet*, 2 July 1803, p.4.

83. Lee was educated at Trinity College, Cambridge, and after a failed career as an actor, turned to playwriting. Known for his tragedies, he was at one point confined to Bedlam and died after a drinking bout.

84. *Royal Cornwall Gazette and Falmouth Packet*, op.cit.. The play was based on the *Cassandre* of La Calprenede, produced in 1677. In short, the plot involves Stratira, the daughter of Dairus and wife of Alexander, learning that Alexander has fallen in love again with his first wife, Roxana. Alexander is poisoned by the conspirator Cassander.

85. See Oliver Stone (dir.), *Alexander*, Los Angeles: Warner, 2004. This version starred Colin Farrell and Angelina Jolie.

86. See for example, Uncle Jan Trenoodle, *Specimens of Provincial Cornish Dialect*, London: John Russell Smith, 1846; John Tabois Tregellas, *Cornish Tales*, Truro: Netherton and Worth, c.1863; W.B. Forfar, *The Exhibition and Other Cornish Poems*, Truro: Netherton and Worth, n.d.

87. This painting is held in the Royal Cornwall Musuem, Truro and is a portrait of Thomas Daniell of Truro and the miner Captain Morcom. For background on Opie, see Viv Hendra, *The Cornish Wonder: A Portrait of John Opie*, Mount Hawke: Truran, 2007.

88. *Royal Cornwall Gazette and Falmouth Packet*, op.cit.

89. Ibid., 12 November 1803, p.1.

90. *Royal Cornwall Gazette and Falmouth Packet*, 7 January 1804, p.3.

91. See Eric Rump (ed.), *Richard Brinsley Sheridan: The School for Scandal and Other Plays*, Harmondsworth: Penguin, 1988. Mrs Malaprop gave rise to the term malapropism.

92. *Royal Cornwall Gazette and Falmouth Packet*, op.cit..

93. For background on this, see Linda Colley, *Britons: Forging the Nation 1707-1837*, New Haven and London: Yale University Press, 1992.

94. For a perspective on the impact of the Black Prince in Cornwall, see John Angarrack, *Breaking the Chains: Censorship, Deception and the Manipulation of Public Opinion in Cornwall*, Camborne: Stannary Publications, 1999, p.33.

95. *Royal Cornwall Gazette and Falmouth Packet*, op.cit..

96. James Shirley, *The Dramatic Works and Poems: Now First Collected, Vols. 1-3*, Boston: Adamant Media Corporation, 2005. The text could have been lost.

97. See this operating in Timberlake Wertenbaker, *Our Country's Good*, London: Methuen, 1987.

98. *Royal Cornwall Gazette and Falmouth Packet*, op.cit..

99. Ibid., 2 June 1804, p.3. This is an example of an advertisement for a Concert and Ball: 'Mr Hempel respectfully informs the inhabitants of the town of Truro and its Environs, that his Concert and Ball will on Wednesday next at the Assembly Rooms. Doors to be opened at Half past Seven o'clock. Tickets 3s 6d each, to be had at the *Royal Cornwall Gazette* office, Truro'.

100. *Royal Cornwall Gazette and Falmouth Packet*, 17 November 1804, p.3.

101. See Barry Sutcliffe (ed.), *Plays by George Colman the Younger and Thomas Morton*, Cambridge: Cambridge University Press, 1983.

102. O'Keeffe was the most produced playwright in London in the last quarter of the eighteenth century. For background to O'Keeffe, see Christopher Morash, *A History of Irish Theatre 1601-2000*, Cambridge: Cambridge University Press, 2002, pp.71-4. A revival of his romp *Wild Oats* by the Royal Shakespeare Company in 1976 has introduced his work to a late twentieth-century audience.

103. *Royal Cornwall Gazette and Falmouth Packet*, 24 November 1804, p.3.

104. See Ben Rogers, *Beef and Liberty: Roast Beef, John Bull and the English Nation*, London: Vintage, 2004.

105. Arbuthnot is said to have helped inspire the satire of Jonathan Swift's *Gulliver's Travels* (1726).

106. See Boase and Courtney, op.cit., p.83. Some detail about the play is found in *The Cornish Telegraph*, 6 February 1867. George Bernard Shaw wrote a comedy about Ireland in 1904 titled *John Bull's Other Island*.

107. George Colman, *John Bull, as Performed at the Theatre Royal, Covent Garden*, London: Longman, Hurst, Rees and Orme, 1806. The original cast was as follows: Peregrine: Mr Cooke; Sir Simon Rochdale: Mr Blanchard; Frank Rochdale: Mr H, Johnstow; Williams: Mr Klanert; Lord Fitz-Balaam: Mr Waddy; Hon. Tom Shuffleton: Mr Lewis; Jon Thornberry: Mr Fawcett; John Bur: Mr Atkins; Dennis Brulgruddery: Mr Johnstone; Dan: Mr Emery; Mr Pennyman: Mr Davenport; John: Mr Abbot; Robert: Mr Truman; Simon: Mr

Beverly; Lady Caroline Braymore: Mrs H. Johnston; Mrs Brulgruddery: Mrs Davenport; Mary Thornberry: Mrs Gibbs. A rare revival was staged by the Bristol Old Company in 1987.

108. See the Smith in 'The Passion' of *Ordinalia*. See Alan M. Kent, *Ordinalia: The Cornish Mystery Play Cycle – A Verse Translation*, London: Francis Boutle Publishers, 2005, pp.192-3. See also Michael Joseph 'An Gof' [The Smith] of St Keverne in Maurice Smelt, *101 Cornish Lives*, Penzance: Alison Hodge, 2006, pp.141-3.

109. Colman, op.cit., p.1.

110. Ibid.

111. Ibid.

112. Ibid., p.13.

113. Ibid., p.23.

114. See P.A.S. Pool, *The History of the Town and Borough of Penzance*, Penzance: The Corporation of Penzance, 1974, pp.118-9. The letter is quoted in full in the Notes to Chapter Three.

115. Colman, op.cit., p.24.

116. Ibid., p.26.

117. Ibid., p.30.

118. Ibid., p.51.

119. Ibid., p.99.

120. *Royal Cornwall Gazette and Falmouth Packet*, op.cit..

121. I am indebted to the British Library for this information. He should not be confused with the Egyptologist Samuel Birch or the Cornish-based painter, Samuel John Lamorna Birch.

122. *Royal Cornwall Gazette and Falmouth Packet*, 8 December 1804, p.2.

123. See Marjean D. Purinton, 'George Colman's *The Iron Chest* and *Bluebeard* and the Pseudoscience of Curiosity Cabinets' in *Victorian Studies*, Vol. 49, No.2, 2007, pp.250-7. Purinton suggests that as well as scientific curiosity, some of the displays were on sexology.

124. Rowe, op.cit.

125. See Charles Thomas and Joanna Mattingly, *The History of Christianity in Cornwall: AD 500-2000*, Truro: Royal Institution of Cornwall, 2000, pp.29-31. The legacy of the Society of Friends in Cornwall is evident in the meeting houses found at Marazion and Come-to-Good, near Feock.

126. Donald R. Rawe, *A Prospect of Cornwall*, London: Robert Hale, 1986, p.145.

127. Smelt, op.cit., pp.90-92.

128. See Robert Hunt (ed.), *Popular Romances of the West of England: The Drolls, Traditions, and Superstitions of Old Cornwall (Second Series)*, London: John

Camden Hotten, 1865, pp.314-40; Kelvin Jones, *Witchcraft in Cornwall: An Account of Witchcraft, its Practice, its Customs and Condemnation*, St Just in Penwith: Sir Hugo Books, 1995. For a recent contemporary exploration, see Jason Semmens (ed.), *The Cornish Witch-finder: William Henry Paynter and the Witchery, Ghosts, Charms and Folklore of Cornwall*, Cornwall: The Federation of Old Cornwall Societies, 2008. The Cornwall Theatre Collective presented a 'Cornish-language-ized' version of *Macbeth*, titled *Mapbeth: Son of the Grave*, in 2001.

129. *Royal Cornwall Gazette and Falmouth Packet*, 15 December 1804, p.3.

130. Thomas Dibdin, *The Jew and the Doctor*, London: T.N. Longman and O. Rees, 1800. Dibdin appears to have often toured Cornwall. See *Sherbourne Mercury*, 9 July 1798. He took a tour to Land's End as "novel and rational entertainment, without any assistance".

131. *Royal Cornwall Gazette and Falmouth Packet*, 22 December 1804, p.3.

132. For the text, see Thomas Davies (ed.), *Lillo's Dramatic Works Vol. 2: Fatal Curiosity, Marina, Elmerick, or Justice Triumphant, Britannia and Batavia, Arden of Feversham*, Whitefish, Montana: Kessinger Publishing, 2008.

133. Roland J. Roddis, *Penryn: The History of an Ancient Cornish Borough*, Truro: D. Bradford Barton, 1964.

134. *Royal Cornwall Gazette and Falmouth Packet*, op.cit..

135. Ibid., 29 December 1804, p.3.

136. Ibid.

137. Ibid.

138. Margaret Drabble (ed.), *The Oxford Companion to English Literature*, Oxford: Oxford University Press, 1985, p.347.

139. See Thomas Henderson (ed.), *Sir Walter Scott: Minstrelsy of the Scottish Border*, London: George G. Harrap and Company Ltd, 1931.

140. Little is known about this text. A gay deceiver can refer to a 'rakehell' of the period, or it was also used as another term for a highwayman.

141. *Royal Cornwall Gazette and Falmouth Packet*, 12 January 1805, p.3.

142. Ibid., 19 January 1805, p.3, 26 January 1805, p.3, 2 February 1805, p.3 and 9 February 1805, p.3.

143. Ibid., 16 February 1805, p.3.

144. A short review is given in ibid., 2 February 1805, p.3.

145. Ibid., 16 February 1805, p.3 and 23 February 1805, p.3.

146. See Harry M. Solomon, *The Rise of Robert Dodsley: Creating the New Age of Print*, Illinois: Southern Illinois University Press, 1996.

147. See, for example, the so-called The Green Book of St. Columb Major: *St Columba the Virgin Churchwardens' Accounts* CRO: P/36/81. This continues in contemporary pantomime culture in Cornwall. The Minack Theatre at

Porthcurno has also presented numerous performances of Robin Hood.

148. *Royal Cornwall Gazette and Falmouth Packet*, 23 February 1805, p.3. Although almost two centuries apart, this would appear to have striking similarities to *The Bedlam Theatre Company's* 1999 production titled *The Governor of Sombrero Rock* (1999).

149. *Royal Cornwall Gazette and Falmouth Packet*, 2 March 2005, p.3.

150. Despite the continuum of texts on this theme, Henry II's intentions are now regarded as being misinterpreted.

151. *Royal Cornwall Gazette and Falmouth Packet*, 9 March 2005, p.2.

152. Ibid., 23 March 1805, p.3.

153. Ibid., 16 March 1805, p.3.

154. See David S. Karr, 'Thoughts That Flash like Lightning: Thomas Holcroft, Radical Theatre, and the Production of Meaning in 1790s' London' in *Journal of British Studies*, No. 40, 2001, pp.324-56.

155. *Royal Cornwall Gazette and Falmouth Packet*, 16 August 1806, p.1. The advertisement reads: 'Truro Grand Musical Festival September, 9, 10 and 12, under the direction of Messrs. Ashleys, managers of the Oratorios at the Theatre Royal, Covent Garden'.

156. Payton, 1992, op.cit., p.81.

157. Bernard Deacon, 'Proto-industrialization and Potatoes: A Revised Narrative for Nineteenth-Century Cornwall' in Philip Payton (ed.), *Cornish Studies: Five*, Exeter: University of Exeter Press, 1997, pp.60-84. See also Philip Payton, "Reforming Thirties' and 'Hungry Forties': The Genesis of Cornwall's Emigration Trade' in Philip Payton, (ed.), *Cornish Studies: Four*, Exeter: University of Exeter Press, 1996, pp.101-27.

158. *Royal Cornwall Gazette and Falmouth Packet*, 29 November 1806, p.3. There were several European dramas on Don Juan written before Byron's defining poetic version – still incomplete at his death in 1824.

159. *Royal Cornwall Gazette and Falmouth Packet*, 20 December 1806, p.3.

160. Ibid., 27 December 1806, p.3.

161. Ibid., 10 January 1807, p.3 and 21 February 1807, p.3.

162. Ibid., 28 February 1807, p.3.

163. Ibid., 7 March 1807, p.3.

164. Ibid., 30 May 1807, p.3 and 13 June 1807, p.2. The National Library of Scotland collection of the Theatre Royal, Edinburgh memorabilia lists *The Curfew* as being by Mr. Tobin. It was a 'much admired new play interspersed with glees'. See http://www.nls.uk/playbills.

165. Ibid., 27 June 1807, p.3.

166. Ibid., 4 July 1807, p.2 and 11 July 1807, p.3.

167. Ibid., 18 July 1807,p.3.

168. Ibid., 1 August 1807, p.2.

169. Ibid., 5 December 1807, p.2.

170. Ibid., 27 January 1810, p.3 and 3 February 1810, p.3. The years 1810-1811 appear to be a particularly productive phase. Among the texts at Truro were *The Jew, or A School for Christians*, *A Cure for the Heart Ache*, *Young Hussar*, *The Weathercock*, *The Village Lawyer*, *Laugh when you Can*, *Plot and Counterplot*, *The Merchant of Venice*, *Of Age Tomorrow*, *The Africans*, *The Rival Queens*, *The Prize*, *The Heir at Law*, *The Tragedy of Jane Shore*, *The Clandestine Marriage*, and *The Aukward [sic] Recruit*. Many of these had been performed at Falmouth first. See *The West Briton and Cornwall Advertiser*, 9 November 1810 p.3, 23 November 1810, p.3, 30 November 1810 p.3, 7 December 1810, p.3, 14 December 1810, p.3, 28 December 1810, p.3, 11 January 1811, p.3, 18 January 1811, p.3, 25 January 1811, p.3, and 1 February 1811, p.3.

171. *Royal Cornwall Gazette and Falmouth Packet*, 1 December 1810, p.3.

172. For the range of performances, see ibid., 17 March 1810, p.3, 17 November 1810, p.3, 24 November 1810, p.3, 5 January 1811, p.3, 12 January 1811, p.3 and 28 December 1811, p.3. In this period there were also several Masons' Festivals which included singing and dancing between the play and farce.

173. Ibid., 19 February 1813, p.3.

174. Ibid., 8 March 1817 p.1.

175. Ibid., 5 June 1824, p.3.

176. Ibid., 10 February 1821, p.3.

177. Ibid., 17 February 1821, p.3, 24 February 1821, p.3 and 3 March 1821, p.3.

178. Ibid., 20 October 1825, p.3.

179. Ibid., 19 November 1825, p.3.

180. Ibid., 6 October 1827, p.3, 13 October 1827, p.3, 20 October 1827, p.3, 27 October 1827. p.3, 3 November 1827, p.3 and 10 November 1827, p.3. Advertisements are few and far between in *The West Briton and Cornwall Advertiser* in this period. This list of texts is interesting. *The Boy of Santillane* is sometimes known as *Gil Blas and the Robbers of Asturia* and was a musical play. The story originated from the writings of the French novelist and playwright Alain-René Lesage (1668-1747) and was translated into English by Thomas Smollett in 1749. We see continuity here in the theatrical continuum of Cornwall – and especially Truro. A version of *Cinderella*, titled *The Ash Maid*, was presented by Truro-based Kneehigh Theatre in 1994. See Kneehigh Theatre, *The Ash Maid*, Truro: Kneehigh Theatre, 1994.

181. Ibid., 24 November 1827. p.3.

182. Ibid., 8 December 1827, p.3.

183. See Forfar, op.cit.; Tregellas, op.cit.; C.D. Pollard (ed.), *Joseph Henry Pearse: Cornish Drolls*, Felinfach: Llanerch, 1998, and various contributors in Alan M.

Kent (ed.), *Voices from West Barbary: An Anthology of Anglo-Cornish Poetry 1549-1928*, London: Francis Boutle Publishers, 2000.

184. See Oswald Pryor, *Australia's Little Cornwall*, Adelaide: Rigby, 1962, and *Cornish Pasty*, Adelaide: Rigby, 1966. For Pryor's significance see Philip Payton, *Making Moonta: The Invention of Australia's Little Cornwall*, Exeter: University of Exeter Press, 2007. See also Ian Glanville, *St Just's Point: Down Under Cornish Humour*, Bendigo, Victoria: Ian Glanville, n.d.

185. See Alan M. Kent, "Drill Cores': A Newly-Found Manuscript of Cousin Jack Narratives from the Upper Peninsula of Michigan, USA' in Philip Payton (ed.), *Cornish Studies: Twelve*, Exeter: University of Exeter Press, 2004. pp.106-43.

186. See Nick Darke, *Ting Tang Mine and Other Plays*, London: Methuen, 1987; Mundic Nation and Hall for Cornwall, *D.M. Thomas: Hell Fire Corner Programme*, Truro: Hall for Cornwall, 2004; D.M. Thomas, *Hell Fire Corner*, unpublished script, 2003; Kent, *The Tin Violin*, 2008, op.cit., and *Surfing Tommies*, London: Francis Boutle Publishers, 2009.

187. See *Royal Cornwall Gazette and Falmouth Packet*, 5 January 1828, p.3, 12 January 1828, p.3, 19 January 1828, p.3, 26 January 1828, p.3 and 2 February 1828, p.3. Prices for performance had altered slightly. The Pit was then 1*s* 6*d*.

188. Ibid., 30 June 1832, p.3.

189. For a useful survey of this, see Christopher Hampton (ed.), *A Radical Reader: The Struggle for Change in England 1381-1914*, Harmondsworth, Penguin, 1984, pp.339-504. For a Cornish context, see John Rule, *Cornish Cases: Essays in Eighteenth and Nineteenth Century Social History*, Southampton: Clio Publishing, 2006.

190. *Royal Cornwall Gazette and Falmouth Packet*, 2 February 1838 p.3.

191. Ibid., 30 June 1832, p.3. Balls and dances continue at Penryn and Truro during this phase.

192. For a copy of this text, see http://www.erbzine.com/mag18/jocko.htm

193. Callum G. Brown, *The Death of Christian Britain: Understanding Secularization 1800-2000*, London and New York: Routledge, 2001, pp.16-34.

194. *Royal Cornwall Gazette and Falmouth Packet*, 2 November 1838, p.3.

195. Kent (ed.), 2000, op.cit., pp.125-144.

196. *Royal Cornwall Gazette and Falmouth Packet*, 11 January 1838, p.3.

197. Ibid., 18 October 1839, p.3.

198. Ibid.

199. Ibid., 9 April 1841,p.3.

200. Ibid., 25 March 1842, p.3 and 9 December 1842, p.3. Dawson was also in competition with Plymouth. In December 1841, a New Zealand fete was at the Theatre Royal, Plymouth, with 'dioramas, quadrilles, waltzes, gallopades, and tableaux with appropriate music alternately'. Ibid., 10 December 1841, p.3.

201. Ibid., 11 July 1845, p.3. For more on James Doel, see Crane, op.cit., pp.87-88. Apparently, Doel had only to stroll across the stage and ask, "What are you looking at?" for the audience to fall about laughing. At this point, Doel might have had a peripheral interest in Cornwall, but he later toured extensively with Edmund Kean and William Macready and seems to have dropped his interest in Truro.

202. Ibid., 2 January 1846, p.3, 22 January 1847, p3 and 19 March 1847, p.3.

203. Ibid., 25 June 1847, p.3 and 6 August 1847, p.3.

204. Ibid., 5 January 1849, p.4 and 20 December 1850, p.5.

205. For background, see Norman Page, *Wilkie Collins: The Critical Heritage*, London and Boston: Routledge and Kegan Paul, 1974.

206. Tours of Cornwall were immensely fashionable between 1750 and 1870. For a selection, see Todd Gray (ed.), *The Travellers' Tales: Cornwall*, Exeter: The Mint Press, 2000, pp.42-142. See also Charles Thomas and Melissa Hardie (eds.), *Dinah Craik: An Unsentimental Journey Through Cornwall 1884*, Penzance: Jamieson Library, 1988.

207. Collins, op.cit., pp.129-41.

208. Ibid., pp.119-20.

209. Ibid., p.120. An ophicleide is a long brass bugle.

210. Elizabeth Isabella Spence, *The Curate and His Daughter, a Cornish Tale*, London: Longman, Hurst, Rees, Orme and Brown, 1813, p.1. Two authors link to the dramatisation here. Robert Stephen Hawker (1803-75), who lived at Morwenstow in north Cornwall, may well have appeared in the public eye as a kind of 'isolated clergyman' of the type imagined in the drama. See Patrick Hutton, *I would not be forgotten: The Life and Work of Robert Stephen Hawker*, Padstow: Tabb House, 2004. The work of Thomas Hardy gives another impression of the isolation of north Cornwall. See the observations in Chapter Six, and Thomas Hardy, *A Pair of Blue Eyes*, Harmondsworth: Penguin, 1986 [1873].

211. For similar debate over improvement and education away from Cornwall, see 'A Mere Interlude' [1885] in Thomas Hardy, *The Distracted Preacher and Other Tales*, Harmondsworth: Penguin, 1979, pp.99-133.

212. Collins, op.cit., p.121.

213. Best seen in the Cornish overseas. See "Andsome 'Arry with the H'auburn 'Air' by Walter F. Gries and Donald D. Kinsey, in Kent and McKinney, op.cit., p.214.

214. Collins, op.cit., p.121-2.

215. Ibid., p.123.

216. Bertolt Brecht (1898-1956) sat his actors on the side of the stage if they were not in a particular scene or imagined elsewhere. See John Willet, *The Theatre of Bertolt Brecht*, London: Methuen, 1959.

217. Ironically, many Brechtian techniques were used in the stage adaptation of Collins's *The Woman in White* in early twenty-first-century London.

218. Russell Jackson, *Victorian Theatre: The Theatre in Its Time*, New York: New Amsterdam, 1994, p.6.

219. Collins, op.cit., p.123.

220. Ibid., p.124.

221. Ibid., p.127.

222. For a definition of this term, see Bernard Deacon, "'The hollow jarring of the distant steam engines": images of Cornwall between West Barbary and the Delectable Duchy' in Ella Westland (ed.), *Cornwall: The Cultural Construction of Place*, Penzance: The Patten Press and the Institute of Cornish Studies, 1997, pp.7-24.

223. Frank Michell in *The Cornish Review: First Series*, No 3, 1949, p.81.

224. James Dawson, *The Autobiography*, Truro: J. R. Netherton, 1865, p.100. The Latin expression 'Finis Coronat Opus' literally means 'The end crowns the work' ('The last is best') and seems to have been a medieval proverb arising from a misquotation from Ovid's Heroides. The 19th century ascetic and Catholic poet Francis Thompson (1859-1907) used it as the title of a poetry book.

225. Ibid.

226. Ibid., pp.100-1.

227. Frank Michell, *Annals of an Ancient Cornish Town: Notes on the History of Redruth*, Redruth: Frank Michell, 1978 [1946] p.85. Robert Blee's manuscript book under the date 9 August 1828 enters "purchase of tickets for Keen's night of performance". Blee's manuscript also records that during the performance a young man fell out of the window and was killed.

228. Crane, op.cit.

229. I am indebted to Angela Broome for this information. For a sense of this time period, see June Palmer (ed.), *Truro in the Age of Reform: 1815-1837*, Truro: June Palmer, 1999.

230. Dawson, op.cit., p.5.

231. Ibid., p.3.

232. Ibid., p.11-13.

233. Ibid., p.15.

234. Ibid., p.18 and pp.28-9.

235. Ibid., p.75.

236. Ibid., p.83.

237. Ibid., p.85-8.

238. Ibid., pp.86-7.

239. It is said that whichever partner of a newly-married couple drinks from the well will dominate the other. The poet Robert Southey (1774-1843) also wrote a poem about it.

240. J.M. Gray (ed.), *Alfred, Lord Tennyson: Idylls of the King*, Harmondsworth: Penguin, 1983. Dawson is obviously aware of Tennyson's later impact.

241. Dawson, op.cit., p.88. The quote is from William Cowper's 1785 poem 'The Task, Book V, The Winter Morning Walk': 'Replete with vapors, and disposes much / All hearts to sadness, and none more than mine'.

242. Ibid., pp.91-2.

243. Ibid., p.92 and pp.93-4.

244. Ibid., p.95-6. While in Penzance, Dawson tried unsuccessfully to trace 'the original family of *John Bull*'. This is a curious idea and would seem to be a metaphor for him trying to trace the origins of Britishness. In the sense that the Cornish were the original Britons, it appears that Dawson knew more than he was letting on.

245. Caroline of Brunswick-Wolfenbüttel (1768-1821) was the queen consort of George IV from 1820 to her death.

246. Dawson, op.cit., p.111-2.

247. Ibid., p.114.

248. Ibid., p.121. The location of this is not clear. St Austell Brewery was established in 1851 by Walter Hicks. Its present location is at 63 Trevarthian Road, but this is probably not the site of this performance *c*.1820.

249. Ibid., p.123.

250. Edwin Norris (ed. and tr.), *The Ancient Cornish Drama*, New York: Blom, 1968 [1859].

251. See Amy Hale, 'Genesis of the Celto-Cornish Revival? L.C. Duncombe-Jewell and the Cowethas Kelto-Kernuak' in Philip Payton (ed.), *Cornish Studies: Five*, Exeter: University of Exeter Press, 1997, pp.100-11. See also Derek Williams (ed.), *Henry and Katharine Jenner: A Celebration of Cornwall's Culture, Language and Identity*, London: Francis Boutle Publishers, 2004. The precise moment of the Celto-Cornish Revival is still in dispute, but a number of factors and activists contribute during the last thirty years of the nineteenth century.

252. Much revivalist activity is connected to a concern with Cornwall's dramatic tradition. The plays formed the textual pool from which a revived language could be drawn.

253. See George Harrison, *Substance of a Report on the Laws and Jurisdiction of the Stannaries in Cornwall*, London: Longman, Rees, Orme, Brown, Green and Longman, 1835.

254. Dawson, op.cit., pp.134-5.

255. See Henry Jenner, 'The Tristan Romance and its Cornish Provenance' in *Journal of the Royal Institution of Cornwall*, No.14, 1914, pp.464-88.

256. Kneehigh Theatre performed a version of *Tristan and Yseult* in the grounds of

Restormel Castle in the early twenty-first century. Lostwithiel Community Centre is a regular touring venue for theatre companies in Cornwall.

257. Dawson, op.cit., pp.135-6.

258. Ibid., p.144.

259. Ibid., p.149.

260. Ibid., p.153 and p.156.

261. Ibid., p.166.

262. *Royal Cornwall Gazette and Falmouth Packet*, 20 August 1854, p.4.

263. Ibid., 9 May 1856, p.4.

264. For a context, see Richard Anthony Baker, *British Music Hall: An Illustrated History*, Stroud: Sutton Publishing, 2005.

265. *Royal Cornwall Gazette and Falmouth Packet*, 28 January 1857, p.4.

266. Ibid., 6 February 1857, p.4.

267. Christopher Pawling, *Popular Fiction and Social Change*, Basingstoke: Macmillan, 1984; John Dixon, *A Schooling in 'English': Critical Episodes in the Struggle to Shape Literary and Cultural Studies*, Milton Keynes: Open University Press, 1991.

268. *Royal Cornwall Gazette and Falmouth Packet.*, 25 December 1857. p.4.

269. Ibid., 6 May 1859, p.4.

270. Ibid., 28 January 1859, p.4.

271. Ibid., 9 December 1859, p.5.

272. Ibid., 21 March 1862, p.8 and 11 September 1863 p.5.

273. Ibid., 31 May 1866, p.8.

274. Ibid., 20 January 1888, p.4.

275. Ibid., 3 February 1888, p.2.

CHAPTER FIVE

Treading the Boards beyond West Barbary: The World Stage of Cornwall, 1850–1900

'I have devised in my mind a *Tristan und Isolde*, the simplest, yet most full-blooded musical conception imaginable.'

Letter to Franz Liszt from Richard Wagner, 16 December 1854, cited in Robert W. Gutman, *Wagner: The Man, His Mind and His Music*, 1968[1]

'Far away from toil and care,
Revelling in fresh sea-air,
Here we live and reign alone
In a world that's all our own.'

Kate, in Act I, from *The Pirates of Penzance* by W.S. Gilbert and Arthur Sullivan, 1879[2]

Although the post-1850 period witnessed something of decline in theatre at home, Cornish theatrical activity beyond the Tamar continued unabated, and perhaps to new heights of success. Certainly Cornwall was projecting imaginings of itself onto the world stage. Cornwall, as a place of mythology, of myth, of legend and of adventure, was being re-embedded, not only in the late nineteenth-century mindset in Britain, but across the world as well. Cornwall's industrial primacy and engineering lead had been somewhat shaken by events in the middle of the century, but in no way was this aspect of life and the economy in Cornwall thought to be in terminal decline. Industrial Cornishness was, however, crossing the globe, and took with it much of Cornwall's creative and theatrical energy as well. Communities were being broken up by time spent overseas, or by full emigration to other countries. However, new communities were forming, and old ones adapted to a theatri-cality that was trans-national. The base landscape of Cornwall was still intact, but during this phase outside groups looking in probably still associated it with mineral exploration, smuggling, wrecking and piracy. Indeed, it still remained 'West Barbary'. However, other groups predicted shifts in sensibilities, and saw that Cornwall's Celticity and Arthuriana would be reinvented and transformed in new ways at the end of the century. Certainly, folklorists collecting theatrical, para-theatrical and proto-theatrical work were completing a process of cultural realisation and proto-nationalism that would have huge impact in the next century. In Cornwall itself, working-class groups continued to respond to the ritual year in ways unaltered from the pre-modern period. However, they were also being asked to compromise those activities, according to establishment morals of the Age. Writing had shifted somewhat. Any imagining of Cornwall on the professional stage had to make it connect somehow with wider British experience, even though the territory, its history and its people still fascinated the British public. To an extent, misinterpretations about the Cornish were still being peddled. The accommodation of the difficult 'Celtic drama queen' that was Cornwall, and its more politically- and culturally-powerful neighbour, England, continued with the formation of the 'County Council' after the Local Government Act of 1888. Despite the Stannary's powers of jurisdiction seemingly disintegrating, and a new unclear 'Duchy' in place, there would still be room in the theatrical continuum for dissidence and revolt. For a few years, though, this response was hard to perceive.

Not only was a 'cultural broadening' of Cornwall happening with a number of texts, but also with actors. One of the most popular actors of the nineteenth century was Sir Henry Irving (1838-1905), who initially achieved stage success in his performance as the character Mathias in the melodrama *The Bells* (1871-2),[3] and afterwards in a large number of productions of Shakespeare. Irving had spent much of his early life in Cornwall at Halsetown, near St Ives. He was born John Henry Brodribb at Keinton near Glastonbury, but moved when his father married a Miss Behenna, one of six sisters belonging to an old Cornish family. One of the sisters, Sarah Behenna, took care of the young Irving after his parents moved to London. Irving, as Richards, and Holroyd detail, went on to have a spectacular stage career, his peak years being his partnership with Ellen Terry, when he took over the Lyceum Theatre.[4] His core roles included Hamlet, Shylock and Iago; but it was, perhaps, Irving's Celtic background that inspired him to mount a production of Comyn Carr's *King Arthur* in 1895 and to play Jachimo in Shakespeare's *Cymbeline: King of Britain*[5] the following year. Irving was the first actor to be awarded a knighthood, and was an important theatrical innovator. His performances were sometimes criticised – his voice and deportment dividing opinion – and yet he always brought an intellect and

Fig. 66. The actor Henry Irving (1838-1905).

individuality to the characters he portrayed, perhaps in more modern ways than some of his contemporaries. Irving's recollections of Cornwall were recorded in 1898 in Arthur Quiller-Couch's *The Cornish Magazine* and, as well as giving insight into perhaps the most famous actor of the century, they also give us considerable insight into the popular theatrical culture of Cornwall, which heavily influenced him, and must have been the antithesis of the Behenna family's Methodism. Here, Irving recalls Cornwall's theatricality and the ritual year:

> You are to know the character of this part of the Duchy before clashed in our minds with the Scriptural teachings which were our daily portion at home. These legends and fairy stories have remained with me but vaguely – I was too young – but I remember the "guise dancing", when the villagers went about in masks, entering houses and frightening the children. We imitated this once, in breaking in on old Granny Dixon's sleep, fashioned out in horns and tails, and trying to frighten her into repentance for telling us stories of hell-fire and brimstone.[6]

This is a perceptive account, with which we make many connections back and forwards. Guizing is clearly perceived as a theatrical activity, and the ritual and folklore of place seems to have influenced him greatly, perhaps even encouraging his eventual career. Although Irving confesses in his interview with Arthur Brasher that he has 'lost the half-tones, the subtle lights and shades of my early life',[7] there is detailed information about his family. Sarah Behenna had married one Captain Isaac Penberthy, who settled down as captain of the mines in Halsetown after a successful experience of mining in Mexico.[8] Irving, therefore, intimately understood the Cornish situation in this time period. He also knew intimately the Cornish psyche and imagination:

> My uncle [Isaac] was a big man, bearded, broad in the shoulders, perhaps a bit rough, and possessing the Celtic temper. He was a man born to command and to be loved. I can hardly describe to you how dominating was his personality, and yet how lovable. I remember that my aunt, my cousins, and myself went to meet him coming home from the mines every evening, that his greeting was boisterously affectionate, and that we knew no better task than to win his approval.[9]

Although his uncle was an influence on his young life in Cornwall, perhaps it was his aunt, Mrs Penberthy, who set him on the straight and narrow, and shaped him as an actor. Paradoxically, it would have been the type of Methodists like Mrs Penberthy who, in all likelihood, would have disapproved of some of the theatrical activity in Cornwall during Irving's childhood.[10] It was only in the latter half of the nineteenth century that the stage gained some credibility, as Temperance movements lost some of their ground. He speaks of his aunt in the following way:

> She was the union of two strong individualities. She was a woman of severe simplicity in dress – the straight lines of her gowns are before me now – and deeply religious in character. It was the time of the great religious revival in Cornwall. My aunt was a teetotaller and a Methodist, and her whole life was coloured by her convictions. Perhaps the stern asceticism of the daily routine imposed by my aunt may have jarred upon us youngsters; but it was tempered by strong affections. At any rate, the angles have worn off that recollection. My aunt inspired both respect and affection among us, and I have no doubt the discipline imposed upon us was good and healthful.[11]

When he was eleven years old, in 1849, Irving left Cornwall and joined Dr. Pinches' School in George Yard, Lombard Street, London. It was from there that he entered the theatre. Irving is, in some ways, one of Cornwall's most famous theatrical sons, though this heritage is perhaps not given the recognition it deserves. Writing in 1898, the journalist Brasher had, however, made the connection between the 'West-Briton' experience and his eventual calling. Brasher's view is perceptive, since it seems to encapsulate much about the theatrical verve in Cornwall:

> The life at Halsetown was well calculated to develop a sense of the poetic and dramatic aspect of life in young Irving. At home there were the Scriptual teachings and readings daily, and a Puritan simplicity of routine stimulating to the youthful imagination. For recreation Sir Henry recollects *Don Quixote* and an old volume of English ballads, and these inspired a longing for adventure and romance. Outside were a wild and desolate landscape and a rough mining population redeemed in the youngster's eyes by its eerie tales and legends.[12]

His view on the simplicity of routine, paradoxically stimulating the youthful imagination, is something we shall return to again. Yet also here, Irving understood that core force within theatre in Cornwall – romance and legends of place – as well as the distinctive sense of place that surrounded him. One might even argue that this was why Irving became a performer. In terms of our layering of theatre, perhaps it was these very industrial places that encouraged the individual to run as far away as possible into the world of theatre, thus escaping the harshness of the everyday: precisely what we do when we enter the theatre. Irving's observations therefore merit a constant rereading and reviewing in the context of the Cornish theatrical continuum.

So far we have mainly been exploring the story of theatre in Cornwall in the nineteenth century through venues and the cultural and social circumstances of those locations. It is perhaps now that we should turn our attention away from the theatres themselves, and look more closely at the texts and writers operating in them, and in other theatrical space across these islands. This kind of survey, initially at least, necessitates a broad brush approach, for we are exploring a wide range of writing: writers from and operating in Cornwall during the century, developing work for performance both inside and outside of Cornwall, as well as those writers and texts which are more focused on Cornu-centric themes. The picture will blend and melt into the physical theatrical activity already considered. A travel through the opening half of the century will give us a sketch of how material developed, and allow us to understand what happened in the final five decades, for the trend towards this wider stage actually began earlier.

In the early half of the century, we learn of several playwrights previously lost in the history of literature in Cornwall. One example is William Vone, whose play *Love's Systems* was 'acted by persons of fashion' on 22 December 1807 at Fobsey Magus, the later Cornish residence of the architect Sir James Knowles (1831-1908).[13] On the same night, another operatic drama was performed, titled *My Uncle's Parlour*, but there is no surviving record of the author's name. Considering the night of the performance, these pieces may well have displayed Christmas themes; we now understand the Cornish penchant for such seasonal drama. These Christmas themes in particular help to take Cornish dramatic material outside of the territory as the century progresses. Another tantalising glimpse into the playwright's world in Cornwall in the opening years of the nineteenth century is found in the work of Thomas Foster Barham who, though born in Bedford in 1766, died at Leskinnick, Penzance in 1844. Clearly a committed Christian, Barham wrote two significant works: *Abdallah, or The Arabian Martyr: A Christian Drama in Three Acts and in Verse* (1820) and *Colonial Gardiner: A Christian Drama in Three Acts* (1823).[14] The plays obviously have no Cornish material, and it is not known where they were performed. Nevertheless, it is intriguing to see Barham operating here in this period, with these texts probably used outside of Cornwall. Publication by a major London publisher of the period – Hatchard and Son – shows that his work had a major pan-British influence. Further to the east, in mid Cornwall, was the Reverend Archer Thompson Gurney who, born in Tregony in 1820, went on to translate the second part of the tragedy of *Faust*, also writing *King Charles the First: A Dramatic Poem in*

Five Acts (1846).[15] In a figure like Gurney, who obviously knew Cornwall well, it is perhaps a pity he did not write more Cornish material, choosing instead the more lucrative wider British and European material. As we shall see later in this chapter, however, there may even be a case for asserting a Cornish variant of the 'Faust' legend, so maybe Gurney was making a wider link to the rest of Europe.

In the 1830s a number of intriguing comedies were written by Charles Devonshire, who was born in Falmouth on 10 December 1783 and later died in Indiana, in the United States of America on 15 October 1851. His most famous play was *Kenilworth: A Tragedy in Five Acts*. This was founded on Sir Walter Scott's celebrated romance of *Kenilworth* (which has some Cornish characterisation, albeit limited). The play was produced around 1830, and this was followed by a number of works including *Clare, or The Marriage Feast: A Tragic Drama in Five Acts* (1836) and *The Sorceress of Saragossa: A Play in Five Acts*, which premiered in 1846. According to Boase and Courtney, at least two of Devonshire's plays were performed at the Falmouth Theatre.[16] These were *Eugene Aram: A Drama in Three Acts* and *The Love Chase, or The Magic Phials*. No publication or performance dates for these texts are given, but presumably they must be from the same time period. Around the same time, an interesting work (already considered in this volume) was also published by Robert Dyer, 'late of the Theatre Royal, Plymouth'. This is an account of *Nine Years of an Actor's Life* (1833), and the first and second years contain accounts of theatrical journeys into Cornwall, detailing the distinctive relationship that Plymouth had with Cornwall during this decade. Many of Dyer's observations could be applied to the end of the eighteenth century, but several were also applicable to the nineteenth century as well, as in these two recollections:

> Though on the whole, an excellent temper, Manager Dawson occasionally was very irritable. Once, when playing Hecate, the leader of the orchestra, by some means, offended him so much, that he belaboured the poor fiddler with his broom, until one birch in the bunch could not call another fellow, and when a critic in a crowded gallery expressed his contempt of Dawson's acting, by throwing an apple at him, Dawson deliberately took up the forbidden fruit and returned it with such force among the assembled gods that he knocked out the eye of an unoffending man!... The business of Launceston was worse than bad, yet the disgust attending the empty benches was lessened to me by the attention I received from those *bon-vivants* who give life to the otherwise dull town. The "world's wo" must be indeed heavy, which the society of such men, could fail to dispel.[17]

Another theatrical activist in the same period was James Sheridan Knowles, who was born in 1784 and died in Torquay in 1862. His most famous work was *The Daughter: A Play in Five Acts*, which was first produced at Drury Lane, on 29 November 1836. The scene of the play is 'laid out on the coast of Cornwall',[18] somewhere that Knowles could have known well if he lived at Torquay during its composition. In all these texts we notice the world stage of Cornwall emerging. While this text appears populist in feel, elsewhere more classical fare was being created. George Croker Fox (1784-1855), who was born in Falmouth, worked on translations of Greek tragedy and poetry that were more for reading than performance.[19] Fox seems to be one of the few classical scholars operating in Cornwall during this period. Other figures were writing too. Born in Penquite, near Fowey in 1813, was Anne Gibbons.[20] She is another intriguing figure in Anglo-Cornish theatrical history, for when aged just twenty-five, she completed a translation of the tragedy of *Mary Stuart*, from the German of Schiller, and in the following decade assembled a collection of poems titled *An Easter Offering*.[21] We then hear no more of her life or work, but she serves as an example of how these Anglo-Cornish writers embraced other European influences.

Outside of Cornwall, however, more playwrights became interested in directly Cornish subject-matter. John Westland Marston was born in Boston, Lincolnshire in 1820, and his notable play (written in conjunction with the prolific Bayle Bernard) *Trevanion, or The False Petition* was first presented at the Royal Surrey Theatre on Monday 22 October 1849, being published in the same year by C. Mitchell of London. According to Boase and Courtney, 'the hero of this play who gives his name to the piece, is represented as being a Cornishman'[22] though it is less clear what the setting was. Meanwhile, *The Dream at Sea: A Drama in Three Acts* by John Baldwin Buckstone (b.1802 in London), was published in New York in 1856.[23] Although editions of the play are rare, the drama is said to be set in Cornwall, proving the appeal of such subject matter in the United States of America, as well as in Britain and the rest of Europe. Similar interest came in Captain Henry Curling's 'petite comedy' titled *The Fractitious Man*, which was also produced in 1865 and featured three acts all set at 'Muddy Moat Hall, Cornwall'.[24] Judging from the entry in Boase's *Collectanea Cornubiensia*, Henry Curling may have produced this piece at the so-called 'Camp Club' during the Crimean War (1854-6) when Russia invaded Turkish territory in Europe. Curling's intentions with the piece may well have been to provide entertainment for the troops.[25]

Although not born in Cornwall, and not brought up there, one dramatist with Cornish family connections during the nineteenth century was the prolific Leicester Silk Buckingham. Leicester was the youngest son of the journalist, and Member of Parliament for Sheffield, James Silk Buckingham (1786-1855) who had been born in Flushing, then later became the incidental biographer of Joseph Emidy.[26] Leicester was born in 1825 at Cornwall Terrace, Regent's Park in London, and probably inherited a love of Cornwall and Cornish humour from his father. As a boy, he had travelled to America, France and the East, so had experienced many different cultures and communities. Between the early 1850s and 1870, Leicester Silk Buckingham wrote over 30 dramas, operettas and farces.[27] Clearly, he was a 'name' dramatist of the era, with many of his works performed at the Lyceum, St James' and the Strand Theatres, as well as around the rest of Britain. Buckingham was highly influenced by French drama, and several of his works were translations. Curiously, there are no records of his works being performed back home in Cornwall, but that certainly does not say that they never were. Buckingham has good claim to be one of most significant Cornish dramatists of the nineteenth century. His first success came in 1854 when on 6 December the Lyceum Theatre presented *Aggravating Sam: A Comic Drama, in 2 Acts [and in prose]*.[28] This was quickly followed in March 1855 by a translation from the French, titled *Take the Girl Away: A Comic Drama in Two Acts [and in prose]*,[29] which was also presented at the Lyceum. A number of farces followed,[30] then in 1856 he presented the incredibly-titled *Belphegor: A new and original, acrobatic, dramatic, epigrammatic and decidedly un-aristocratic burlesque*.[31] This was performed at the Strand Theatre in September that year, and sealed his reputation as a comic writer. Other burlesques and farces came in quick succession,[32] but by 1856 he had begun to write more pantomimes and operettas,[33] which were also highly successful. Between the years 1857 to 1867 he was the drama and music critic for *The Morning Star*. A number of plays followed,[34] right up until his death – aged just forty-two – in 1867. By this time, he had converted to Roman Catholicism. His name is much underrated in Cornish letters.

As the 1860s came to a close, other dramatists were using Cornish space within their work. One of them was Brownlow Hill (d. January 1872) who wrote the intriguing play *Kiddle-a-wink: A Cornish Drama*, first performed at the Victoria Theatre, London, 30 January 1864.[35] This is a beautiful sounding, and wholly Cornish, piece of theatre. A Kiddly-wink was an unlicensed cider or beer-shop, which makes the play sound quite a riot. Kiddly-winks continued into the late nineteenth century and probably also formed centres of popular entertainment for working-class Cornish people. The characters included Sir Anthony Trevillian (played by J. Howard), Evelyn Trevillian, his nephew (George Rose), Ivan Bone – Miner (Brownlow Hill), Mat of the Mine (Frederick Villiers), Hobbleton Huddlepate, Proprietor of the 'One and All'

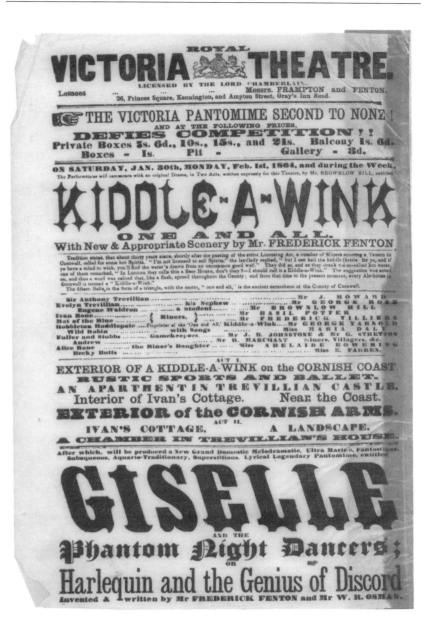

Fig. 67. A playbill advertising the Victoria Theatre's production of Brownlow Hill's *Kiddle-a-wink* in 1864. Courtesy of the University of Bristol Theatre Collection.

Kiddle-a-Wink (George Yarnold), Wild Robin (Maria Dally), Fuller (J.B. Johnstone), Stubbs (G. Stretton), Andrew (R. Marchant), Alice Bone (Adeline Bowering) and Becky Butts (K. Farren). Posters advertising the production tell potential audience members that it included 'new and appropriate scenery by Mr Frederick Fenton, while Act I contained the following scenes: *Exterior of a Kiddle-a Wink on the Cornish coast*, *Rustic sports and ballet*, *An apartment in Trevillian Castle*, *Interior of Ivan's Cottage*, *Near the Coast*, and *Exterior of the Cornish Arms*. Act II took place in the *Exterior of the Cornish Arms*, *Ivan's Cottage*, *A Landscape*, and *A Chamber in Trevillian's House*. It is a pity that there is no extant script.

As many as three plays presenting Cornwall on the British stage were seen within one year in 1867-68. Popular entertainment at Christmas also made use of Cornish space and place in performance, in the form of Edward Leman Blanchard's 'comic Christmas pantomime' tiled *Faw Fee Fo Fum, or Harlequin Jack, the Giant Killer*, which was first performed at Drury Lane on 26 December 1867.[36] Blanchard, born in London in 1820, was writing for one of the most successful theatres in London at this point, and it is significant that Cornwall forms part of the setting. Scene *iii*, was set in a 'fishing village on the Cornish coast', while scene *iv* is on the 'road to St Ives'. Although 'giants' are a pan-British motif in folklore, there is also substantial material on such figures in Cornwall, with Jack often featuring as the giant's adversary.[37] The 'road to St Ives' would also seem to be based on the traditional riddle.[38] Watis Phillips (1829-74), who was born in London, wrote a 'romantic drama in three acts' titled *Nobody's Child*, which was first produced at the Surrey Theatre on 14 September 1867.[39] We know that the scene (meaning the whole of the play) is 'laid on the coast of Cornwall' and that the text contained a 'ravine' (perhaps a cliff-side *zawn*?) scene as well. This text was produced just before prose writers such as Silas K. Hocking emerged, using a similar sentimental theme of children and the ocean.[40] Cornwall was, of course, the perfect location to set such plays and narratives.

Somewhat more obscure is a text titled *Old Salt: A Serio-Comic Drama in Two Acts*, which was produced at the Strand Theatre, London on 12 January 1868. The play was by one John Besemeres, whom Boase and Courtney record as a resident of Calcutta.[41] The title would indicate a sea-faring narrative. We know that the drama was set at 'Trefusis, Falmouth'. Beyond this, nothing more is known. A better-known text of the period was Alfred, Lord Tennyson's narrative poem, *Enoch Arden*, which was first published in 1864.[42] The hero of the poem is a fisherman turned merchant sailor, and it was this information that prompted Joseph Stirling Coyne (1805-68) to set his tragedy *The Home Wreck* (based on Tennyson's poem) in Cornwall.[43] The drama was first produced at the Surrey Theatre, London, on 8 February 1869; due to Coyne's death the previous year, the text was completed by his son, J. Denis Coyne. *The Cornish Telegraph* of the time confirms that the drama was based on *Enoch Arden*.[44] The basic plot is that Arden leaves his wife Annie and three children to go to sea with his old captain, who is offering him work. Enoch had lost his job when he was involved in an accident. The hero has a very masculine view of personal toil and hardship in order to support his family, so he left his family in order to better serve them as a husband and father. During his voyage away, he is shipwrecked and is missing for ten years. Eventually, he returns home to find that his wife, who believed him to be dead, is now married happily to another man, his childhood friend Philip (Annie has known both since her childhood; thus the rivalry), and has a child with him. Enoch's life remains unfulfilled, with one of his children now dead, and his wife and remaining children now being cared for by his onetime rival. He eventually dies of a broken heart. The text of *Enoch Arden* has had ramifications on long-term performance in Cornwall and has, in fact, had a remarkable continuity. For example, the esteemed baritone singer and actor Benjamin Luxon (b. Redruth, 1937) completed 'a melodrama for narrator and piano' based on *Enoch Arden* in 2002.[45] Alan Opie, another baritone singer (b. Redruth, 1945), also later starred in the Benjamin Britten opera *Peter Grimes* which, although based on an earlier poem by George Crabbe, shows some structural similarities to *Enoch Arden*.[46]

Clearly, these kind of quasi-Cornish coastal dramas were popular. The London-born dramatist James Albery (1838-89) combined with the musical talents of W.H. Birch in 1871 to produce 'an operetta in 3 Acts' titled *The Wreck of the Argosy*. The whole of the operetta is 'laid on the coast of Cornwall'. It made its debut at the Town Hall, Reading on 3 October.[47] Away from dramas of the coast, Albery also seemed to hit a particularly productive phase of Cornish-related work in 1871.[48] The comedy *Apple Blossoms*, first produced at the Vaudeville Theatre in London on 9 September 1871, was set in Cornwall, while his 'romantic English drama in three acts' titled *Watch and Wait* had its third act 'laid out in Cornwall'. This drama was first produced at the Surrey Theatre, on 23 September 1871. Clearly, Albery's dramas were very much in vogue in England at this point; a somewhat ironic situation given the collapse of Cornu-centric theatre back home in Cornwall. This latter text seems somewhat indicative of the way Cornwall is presented in many dramas of this period, when either the opening or final acts featured the territory. For example, Charles Smith Cheltnam's *The Shadow of a Crime*, a 'drama in three acts and prose' was first produced at the Theatre Royal, Belfast on 23 August 1869, and Act I is 'laid out at Greywood Hall, Cornwall'.[49] Though now consigned to obscurity, Cheltnam was, at this point, one of the more famous creators of what were termed drawing-room dramas or parlour pantomimes, a genre into which *The Shadow of a Crime* obviously fits. Cornwall's peripherality obviously suited this felon-based text. The peripheral nature of Cornwall also formed the context for Frank W. Green's 1875 pantomime *Jack the Giant Killer and Tom Thumb or Harlequin King Arthur and the Knights of the Round Table*.[50] Arthuriana, as Christine Poulson argues,[51] was very much back in fashion in the 1870s and so tying up the timeless theme of Arthur with Cornwall was inevitable. We know that the 'greater part of the plot is laid in Cornwall, more especially Scene 2 – St Michael's Mount' and that Scene 5 takes place in the 'village of Penlittle in Cornwall'. This again shows the giant theme, and Green was obviously aware of the symbolic value of St Michael's Mount, both for Arthuriana and folklore concerning giants in Cornwall.[52]

The European dimension of all this interest in Arthuriana came with Richard Wagner's *Tristan und Isolde* (1865).[53] There is not time nor the space here to fully document the significance of Wagner's text but, in our story, Wagner's new conceptualisation of the narrative thrusts a sense of Cornish drama back into the centre-ground of pan-European culture. Interpretation of the opera has varied. Kerman observes Wagner's opera as the ultimate 'symphonic poem', noting its 'mystic vision',[54] while Furness observes its 'decadence' relating its themes to the life of the composer.[55] Wagner (1813-83) was a German composer, conductor and theatre director, whose advanced use of chromaticism, orchestral colour and harmonic suspension have had an enormous influence on the direction of opera.[56] His three act drama was largely based on Gottfried von Strassbourg's version, which in itself was based on that of Thomas, who had based his telling on an original (or originals) closely connected to Cornwall. However, so it is said, Wagner's composition was also inspired by his love affair with Mathilde Wesendonck and the philosophy of Arthur Schopenhauer.[57] Events surrounding the development of the opera of *Tristan und Isolde* are somewhat legendary. In 1849 Wagner had been forced to leave his position as conductor at the Dresden opera, since there was a warrant out for his arrest after his participation in the May revolution. Wagner fled to Zurich, meeting there Mathilde, the wife of a silk trader, Otto Wesendonck. It was Wesendonck who bankrolled his work during this phase. At the same time Wagner, in line with much of the German Romantic movement of the middle of the nineteenth century, became interested in texts such as von Strassbourg's version of *Tristan*, the *Nibelunglied* and Wolfram von Eschenbach's *Parzival*.[58] According to *Mein Leben*, Wagner's autobiography, he decided to dramatise the legend of Tristan after his friend, Karl Ritter, attempted the same project. Wagner comments:

He had, in fact, made a point of giving prominence to the lighter phases of the romance, whereas it was its all-pervading tragedy that impressed me so deeply that I felt convinced it should stand out in bold relief, regardless of minor details.[59]

Schopenhauer's influence was significant. According to him, human beings are driven by continued unachievable desires, and the gulf between our desires and the possibility of achieving them leads to misery. He outlines this basic theory in his work titled *Die Welt als Wille und Vorstellung* [The World as Will and Representation].[60] This philosophical state has many repercussions in the Second and Third Acts of Wagner's opera. The opera was eventually premiered in Munich, with a run of bad luck,[61] and initially reviews of it were unfavourable. Interestingly, the Cornu-American writer Mark Twain later saw *Tristan and Isolde* at Bayreuth, and commented that he 'had heard of many who could not sleep after it, but cried the night away'.[62] However, in line with Twain, as the 1860s continued, more and more observers found the piece compelling. The premiere cast for the performance of June 10 1865 was conducted by Hans von Bülow, with the tenor Ludwig Schnorr von Carolsfeld as Tristan, and soprano Malvina Schnorr von Carolsfeld as Isolde. Baritone Ludwig Zottmayer played King Mark, while the mezzo-soprano Anna Possart-Deinet played Brangäne, Isolde's maid. Within his opera, Wagner enhances the roles of Kurwenal, Tristan's servant, and Merlot, Tristan's friend, while the difficult character of Isolde of the White Hands is absent.[63] Significantly, at the end of the opera, Tristan experiences the concept of 'liebestod' – or 'love death' – the driving force of the opera, and also a concept closely akin to the theories of Schopenhauer. This pervading concept affects not only Tristan, but all those within the tragedy – as in this sequence in Act Two, when King Mark reflects on events:

Mir dies?	This to me?
Dies, Tristan, mir?	To me, Tristan this?
Wohin nun Treue	Where now is loyalty
da Tristan mich bretrog?	if Tristan had betrayed me?
Wohin nun Ehr'	Where are honour
und echte	and true breeding
da aller Ehren Hort,	if Tristan, the defender
da Tristan sie verlor?	of all honour, has lost them?
Die Tristan sich	Where is virtue,
zum Schield erkor,	that Tristan chose as device
wohin ist Tugend	for his shield,

nun entflohn,	now flown
da meinen Freund sie flicht	if it has flown from my friend
da Tristan mich verriet?	and Tristan has betrayed me?[64]

Wagner continued the heroic theme with his opera *Parsifal*, which was based on the thirteenth-century epic poem of Wolfram von Eschenbach.[65] Von Eschenbach was already drawing on the pan-European Arthurian tradition, which Wagner was to reinvent during the middle of the nineteenth century. The poem and opera related events concerning the Arthurian knight Parzival and his quest for the Holy Grail. Wagner had conceived of this opera – or as he preferred to call it '*ein Bühnenwihfespiel* [a festival play for the consecration of the stage] – in April 1857, but it was not completed until some twenty-five years later, and not produced until the Bayreuth Festival in 1882, a year before Wagner's death. Although a transmutation has occurred which places the Arthurian knights in 'the castle of Monsalvat', the opera is still recognisably drawing on the romance of Cornu-Celtic ideology. Titurel – Amfortas's father – connects us to Tintagel, while Klingsor, a magician, draws on Merlin 'shamanistic' archetypes.[66] Critical interpretation of the play has noted its heavy use of Christian symbolism, as well as a certain anti-semitism.[67] The latter is perceived in Klingsor who, as well as being a Merlin figure, is also a Jewish stereotype because he opposes the Christian quest of the knights of the Grail. Other observers have considered the play a more refined version of Schopenhauerian philosophy.[68]

The desire for Cornish-themed work outside of Cornwall did not falter in the 1870s. Indeed, there might be a case for asserting that this was the decade when Cornwall asserted itself most convincingly on the pan-British and international stage. On Thursday 26 December 1872, the Royal Bijou Theatre in Paignton presented *The Cornish Brothers, or The Bride of Lisbon*.[69] This drama was by H. Pomeroy Gilbert, and sounds a grand adventure, obviously connecting Cornwall – across the Bay of Biscay – with the Iberian peninsula, though the text has not come down to us. A couple of years later on Saturday 21 March 1874, The Haymarket Theatre in London produced *Queen Mab: A Comedy in Three Acts*, written by G.W. Godfrey.[70] We know that many of the characters of the play are Cornish, and that the scene in the second half of the play is laid at Sir Grevile Carew's seat named Triermain in Cornwall. Several things strike us when we consider this drama: Godfrey was obviously aware of the significance of famous Cornish families, aligning the name Greville (Grenville?) with that of Carew, but also we note the name Triermain (a probable interpretation of Tremaine). Not only are these names significant; it is perhaps the title of the drama that is most interesting. Queen Mab is a folkloric figure, whose origins may lie with the name of a Celtic goddess who was worshipped in Ireland and Wales,[71] and potentially Cornwall. This strongly links to the discussion of worship of gods and goddesses in proto-theatrical activity considered in Chapter One. Mab is variously presented as a midwife and a queen of the fairies, and formed a popular imagining of fairy life in seventeenth-century poetry in particular.[72] Queen Mab plays might once have been presented in Cornwall since fairy lore is well-recorded,[73] and since Godfrey chose to set his text in Cornwall he reactivated that connection. Although not well known, another author writing Cornish-themed drama was Alfred Farthing Robbins (b.1856). On 13 December 1877 at the Theatre Royal, Lincoln, his play *Helps: A Comedietta in One Act* was presented. According to Boase, this was set in Cornwall, as was another Robbins-penned farce in one act, titled *A Pleasant Hour*, which premiered at Pullan's Theatre in Bradford on 6 September 1878.[74]

Cornwall had now been established as a construct for excitement and drama, as well as absurd comedy and humour. It was therefore no coincidence that William Schwenck Gilbert and Arthur Sullivan decided to set their 1879 project, *The Pirates of Penzance, or The Slave of Duty*, in Cornwall. As with Wagner's *Tristan und Isolde*, an entire chapter could be devoted to discussion of this major comic opera, but there is simply not the space to do so. By 1879 Gilbert and Sullivan were already established as a successful partnership. Gilbert (1836-1911), who wrote the libretto, was able to create particularly fanciful worlds, while Sullivan (1842-1900), the composer, developed melodies which conveyed both humour and pathos.[75] The libretto for the opera was begun in December 1878, just after the success of *H.M.S. Pinafore*.[76] Several origins for the opera have been suggested: Penzance was, by then, a tranquil seaside resort,[77] and not perhaps the place to set a pirate-themed opera. Despite this, Cornwall still had associations of being 'West Barbary' filled with wreckers, buccaneers and free-traders, and so theme and space still fitted into the popular imagination. However, some observers feel that the title was more a dig at the theatrical pirates who had staged unlicensed productions of *H.M.S. Pinafore*.[78] Characteristically, Gilbert and Sullivan chose to include a wide range of voices in the opera, ranging from Major-General Stanley's comic baritone, and the Pirate King's bass baritone, to the soprano and mezzo soprano of Mabel and Kate. The bass of the Sergeant of Police is also a significant role, though it is perhaps the effect of the Chorus of pirates, police and General Stanley's daughters who reinforce the power of the piece. The themes of the piece, as in many of Gilbert and Sullivan's works, are identity and law.

The opera is divided into two Acts, each with fourteen scenes. The main plot is driven by Frederic, a young man with a strong sense of duty. The initial scenes are set on the coast of Cornwall during Queen Victoria's reign. Frederic is celebrating his twenty-first year, yet is apprenticed to a *pirate*, instead of a ship's *pilot*. He is in love with Mabel, one of Major-General Stanley's daughters. In the drama, piracy is presented as being an honest profession, yet this is held in counterpoint to the wishes of the Major-General ('I am the very model of a modern Major-General'), who does not want the pirates to take his daughters. The opera culminates in a fight between the police and the pirates, although eventually we learn that the pirates are actually noblemen. Frederic and Mabel are reunited and the Major-General is happy for his daughter to marry the pirates after all. One reason why *The Pirates of Penzance* remains significant is for its dual opening. It was first produced at the Royal Bijou Theatre, Paignton, on 31 December 1879 and at the Fifth Avenue Theatre, New York on the same night.[79] The London premiere was four months later, at the Opera Comique, on 3 April 1880, where it ran for 363 performances, having already been successfully played in New York for three months. A revival occurred in 1888 at the Savoy Theatre, and again in 1900 and 1908. During the twentieth century it was often presented by the D'Oyly Carte Touring Company, and there have been numerous contemporary revivals as well.[80] *The Pirates of Penzance* has become an iconic opera, and has been frequently parodied in popular culture. All this said, its 'Cornishness' is, in fact, somewhat tangential, and although a sense of place is given in the opera, this is not reflected in the manners, dialect or actions of the characters, thus proving that – whilst the draw of a stage Cornwall was desirable at this point – real Cornwall was less well-embraced, perhaps because its belligerent Celticity (the very stuff of piracy and 'West Barbary') remained intact. Cornwall thus needed to be looked at through a softened lens if it were to survive on the major stages of the world.

This softened Cornwall comes across in several works of 1884. Alfred Farthing Robbins (b.1856) had his *Over the Cliff, or By Accident or Design*, 'a drama in four acts' presented at the Theatre Royal Grimsby on 11 February 1884.[81] The scenes of this piece were 'laid in Cornwall' perhaps showing the influence of Gilbert and Sullivan in using Cornwall as dramatic space. The 'barbaric' nature of Cornwall was also presented at Her Majesty's Theatre, Carlisle on 4 December 1884, where a company presented R. Dodson's *The Wreckers, or Martial Law*. The scene of the entire show was set 'on the coast of Cornwall'.[82] As can be seen from this text, and that of *The Pirates of Penzance*, there is a perennial context of legal issues within dramas about Cornwall, suggesting attempts by authority figures (like the Major-General, and others) to clamp-down on those 'Cornish' who break the law for personal and community gain. This notion is seen in Cornish drama down the centuries, and is ongoing.[83]

Gilbert and Sullivan returned to an imagining of Cornwall in 1887 with another comic opera titled *Ruddygore* (later *Ruddigore*[84]), *or The Witch's Curse*. It was first performed by the D'Oyly Carte Opera Company at the Savoy Theatre, London on 22 January 1887.[85] Having seen the success of *The Pirates of Penzance*, Cornwall was an obvious place to locate their next work, and so the first scene of the opera is set in the village of Rederring in Cornwall. Here, a chorus of professional bridesmaids fret that there have been no weddings for the past six months. In the village, all the young men would like to marry Rose Maybud, the prettiest girl there, but are too timid even to approach her. The audience then learn of an ancient curse, and that, centuries ago, Sir Rupert Murgatroyd, the first Baronet of Ruddigore, had persecuted witches there. Ancestral crime then forms the theme of the work as we encounter ghosts from the past. Robin Oakapple, the inheritor of this curse, must break the chains of his past in order to resume his engagement with Rose. Again, though the plot of Ruddigore moves increasingly away from its Cornish beginnings, the setting and theme remain important. Rederring is fictional, though it has enough of a feel of Cornwall[86] for it to seem genuinely Cornish – especially for audiences outside of Cornwall, and more particularly in London. Like piracy, witchcraft also fits the 'West Barbary' notion of Cornwall, and like the fairy lore of Queen Mab, there is a tie in to the established continuum of witchcraft and the supernatural in Cornwall,[87] which was also convincing for audiences of this period.

The success of Cornish subject matter in the United States of America was also proven in a work titled *Our Joan*. This was jointly written by Herman Merivale[88] and Cecil Dale, and originally produced by Rose Coghlan – probably in New York – on 6 February 1887.[89] We know that the story of this piece concerns Jane Trevenna, the daughter of a lighthouse keeper and the belle of a Cornish village. The production later transferred to the Prince of Wales Theatre, Birmingham, and opened on 22 August. We know that the character of Joan was played here by Amy Roselle and the character Arthur Meredith by Roselle's husband, Arthur Dacre.[90] The fashionability of Cornwall continued in the Theatre Royal, Bradford on 3 November 1887, when a three act comic opera titled *Gipsy Gabriel* was performed. This piece, written by William Park and William Hogarth, with music composed by Florian Pascal,[91] was set in Cornwall and almost certainly based on the stylings of Gilbert and Sullivan. The following year offered a similar drama by Frank Maryat. This was *Golden Goblin*, which was produced at the Theatre Royal, Croydon and was 'a story of wrecking in Cornwall'.[92] Whether it was coincidence or intention, the piece had its premiere on St Piran's Day, 5 March 1888.[93] Another significant drama of this phase was *The Loadstone: A Drama in 4 Acts* by T. Edgar Pemberton and W.H. Vernon. It was first produced at the Lyceum Theatre, London, on 7 April 1888.[94] The scene of this drama was laid in Cornwall and the heroine was Kate Trevenna. Kate Trevenna and the above named Jane Trevenna form the beginnings here of the typical strong Cornish female heroine, as encountered in later twentieth-century fiction and drama about Cornwall.[95] Although, for the most part, these dramas were performed outside of Cornwall, occasionally some did make it into the west. An example from the late 1880s is J. Carne Ross's *Forgery*. This 'drama in three acts' was originally produced on 10 April 1888, at Ladbroke Hall, London. However, it was also played twice by the London Comedy Company at St John's Hall in Penzance on 16 and 17 April 1888.[96]

In the background of all of this nineteenth-century theatrical tradition in Cornwall is Methodism, and Methodism's reaction to theatre. In the Thomas Shaw Collection at the Royal Institution of Cornwall,[97] there are, as we might expect, no references to theatrical activity in chapels in Cornwall, and – perhaps quite oddly – no explicit references to Methodist disapproval of theatre. Two senior Methodist scholars recollect that no drama was ever used to illustrate a sermon during the twentieth century,[98] and most likely this attitude persisted from the previous century. Attitudes towards theatre from Methodists during much of the nineteenth century are embodied in the observations of the Hocking siblings' parents. Writing in 1926, but reflecting on his time as a young adult, the novelist Silas Kitto Hocking recalls that:

> when I began to write, fiction was deliberately barred out of many homes, like theatre-going. My father, was distressed, that I, a minister should write "stories".[99]

The basic principle here is that 'stories' were not the direct word of God, and could lead people in the wrong direction. It was Hocking who transformed this idea – showing that moral fictions or 'pulp Methodisms' could be a useful preaching tool – although the position of Methodism during the nineteenth century was all the more ironic, given the fact that theatre had been used as a method of instruction in the Christian church in Cornwall for centuries previous. An over-hanging legacy, however, was probably Samuel Foote's satirical look at one of the major figures of eighteenth-century Methodism, George Whitefield; probably the leaders of the Methodist Churches had never quite reconciled that era with the present. H. Spencer Toy, in his history of Methodism in Launceston, notes that the Weslyan Methodist choir was not to take part in a local theatre production. On 5 March 1832, the trustees of the Church wrote: 'You must be aware of the inconsistency of one night taking part in the theatre and another in the House of God.' Toy notes that in the same period 'dramatic performances were viewed with horror by the local non-conformists, and when the Rev Childs Clarke, Headmaster of the Grammar School and Vicar of St Thomas, introduced them for the boys, prayers were offered in at least one Chapel to counteract the supposed evil'.[100] Although John C.C. Probert believes short sketches were sometimes performed in chapels in the 1920s, he does not believe this had been a regular occurrence.[101] Likewise, there are some references to lectures on Shakespeare within a Methodist context in 1888, but these are more likely to be academic rather than practical.[102] Newspaper reports of the century do not, as a whole, contain any reports of conflict between Methodist groups and theatre, and although this is not to say that they never occurred, perhaps some differences had already been worked through during the previous century. The exception to this academic silence upon the relationship between theatre and Methodism comes in a 1982 article by John Rule, in which he explored the relationship between Methodism, popular belief and village culture in the early nineteenth century.[103] Rule, an expert in social history, considers that 'the confrontation of religion with 'revelry' is not just part of the history of popular recreation: it is central to the understanding of the social history of religion in industrialising Britain'.[104] Drawing on the work of B. Harrison, Rule notes that the conflict was caused by attempts by the church to dominate the popular leisure activities of the working classes. As Harrison puts it:

> Nineteenth-century Christians deplored that recreational complex of behaviour which included gambling, adultery, drinking, cruel sports and sabbath breaking and blasphemy – all of which took place together at the race-course, the drinking-place, the theatre, the 'feast' and the fair.[105]

In effect, these were the patterns of ritual life that had been carrying on in Cornwall since the pre-1200 period, but were given new vigour in the nineteenth century. This was Bakhtin, and Barber's 'carnival' world,[106] which had so notably influenced theatrical activity in the past. The term 'recreational complex' is important here, since it suggests a covert alliance between these areas: for example, theatre and alcohol which, in Christian belief, was the polar opposite of the church and the popular Temperance movements from the 1830s onwards. The specific issue in Cornwall over these attempts at social control was the conservatism of the Methodist 'establishment' in each of the towns and villages – what Rule terms the 'town-chapel elites' who were concerned only with 'respectability'.[107] Methodism, he argues, had been so 'internalised' that it was difficult to escape.[108] This was particularly difficult where the mining management aligned itself to Methodism as well.[109] However, this internalised Methodism had been ingrained in the populace for some time. As Rule notes, John Wesley's *Journal* shows the extent to which, since its earliest days, Methodism had come into conflict with traditional uses of leisure time. There are numerous Cornish examples,[110] but in other parts of Britain, Wesley recorded his disgust at the 'savage ignorance and wickedness' of colliers in Newcastle in 1743, who assembled on Sundays to 'dance, fight, curse and swear, play at chuck ball, or whatever came next to hand'. In Ireland too, he faced up to a company of revellers and dancers who had taken over his usual preaching place.[111] There was, therefore, long-standing ideological opposition within Methodism to idle 'leisure time'. To an extent, by this phase, the surviving, vestigial 'tolerated anarchy' of the medieval period, was being slowly squeezed. In Cornwall, battles against drunkenness and over leisure time, were also about 'improvement' and 'modernisation' in the mining districts. Indeed, it was not only theatre itself that Methodists reacted against; it was also, as Rule argues, para-theatrical events such as hurling and wrestling. In 1849, the Reverend Thomas Collins, of the Camborne Wesleyan Sunday School, took his children on a seaside trip in order to avoid the influence of a 'noisy, revelling fair' – probably a fair related to the ritual year, and likely to have connected with the earlier performance of texts such *Bewnans Meriasek*. He had composed a special hymn for the occasion:

> We rejoice, and we have reason,
> Though we don't attend the fair;
> Better spend the happy season
> Breathing in the fresh sea air.
>   Happy Children!
> What a number will be there![112]

It is this connectivity which has meant that many activists within the Cornish-language movement have criticised the over-riding nature of this 'establishment' Methodist culture, in both further destroying the community-dramatic culture of the previous centuries, and also therefore covertly destroying the use of the Cornish language.[113] This conflict is no better embodied than in events in the year 1843, when a grand procession of Rechabites and teetotallers walked through Redruth, and then assembled for an open-air meeting at *Plain an Gwarry*, Redruth's theatre site, which had held popular amusements from time immemorial.[114] Another example comes, not surprisingly, from Padstow, where Thomas Trevaskis, a Bible Christian known as the 'Temperance Father of the West', spoke out in 1845 against the proto-theatrical May Day Obby

Oss as a celebration of 'riot, debauchery and general licentiousness – a perfect nuisance to the respectable inhabitants of the town'. He backed up his condemnation of the event by offering a substitution:

> To the Proprietors of the Hobby Horse of Padstow. This is to give notice that on or about the end of the month, I shall offer you the bullock, according to promise. It is for you to consult against that time, whether you will give up your vain practice of the Hobby for the more rational amusement of eating roast beef.[115]

Apparently, Trevaskis did drive his bullock into the town, but the people of Padstow drove him out with a hail of stones. The theatricality of the Obby Oss continued. One of the late nineteenth-century Cornish-language activists who also encountered Methodist opposition was the Reverend W. Lach-Szyrma (1841-1915). Lach-Szyrma was vicar at Carnmenellys near Newlyn, and a member of the progressive-thinking and revivalistic Newlyn Institute. In a letter to Henry Jenner, Lach-Szyrma had commented on how it might be a good idea to offer prizes for the study of Cornish (in a kind of proto-Gorsedd), but had encountered Methodists who felt it would be 'carnal and wicked' and, perhaps more interestingly, observed that it would 'not pay'.[116] Again, with this latter observation, Methodism during this phase was committed to modernisation and work. This chapter makes note of the term widely applied to Cornwall during the late eighteenth and nineteenth centuries: that it was ideologically viewed as 'West Barbary'.[117] Accordingly, a myth of Methodism's influence on Cornwall has grown up: that, as Rule observes, 'swearing, fornicating, drinking, fighting, wrecking, smuggling [and] profaning the Sabbath,' were reformed by the presence of Non-conformism. Rule regards this explanation as 'to say the least, partial'.[118] I have argued further, suggesting that the transformatory effect of Methodism was an 'artificial myth'.[119] Although Methodism may have tried its best to stop 'West Barbaric'-theatre, it failed in the end because, perhaps, theatre and the ritualised year in Cornwall were too well-embedded. Methodism may well have suppressed theatrical activity, but it could not have entirely stopped it. Outside of this, some of the major histories of wider pan-British Methodism,[120] and Methodism in Cornwall,[121] are paradoxically very quiet on the topic of Non-conformist reaction against theatre. It is clearly a topic which merits further investigation, though one that I do not have time to explore any further here.[122]

There was, however, in the late nineteenth century, a notable exception to this position. Joseph Hill, born at Manaccan on The Lizard, seems to have been as innovative in his exploration of Methodism as the Hocking siblings. Hill had a very active life within the Methodist movement, being the principal teacher in the Sunday School at St Hilary, near Penzance.[123] He later died on the Isle of Man, c.1869, perhaps travelling there to work with other emigrant Cornish on the Isle. On 25 September 1875 however, a piece of drama was performed at the St Stithians Methodist Free Church schoolroom, for the benefit of the St Stithians Church restoration fund. Not only was this event ecumenical, it also showed changing attitudes towards theatrical activity.[124] *The History of Joseph and His Brethren* may not have been a play in any convention-al sense of the word, since it is subtitled 'A Sacred Drama in Rhyme' and this may indicate a reading rather than performance. However, the very fact that it was performed in St Stithians, and apparently 'on other occasions', shows a more enlightened attitude towards theatre. Such was the success of the 'drama' that it was published by R. Woolcock of Helston, perhaps to be read and 'performed' at home. Nativities began to be performed on a regular basis in Cornish chapels in the twentieth century – and possibly at the end of the nineteenth century – perhaps reflecting a wider tradition of Christmas drama at this point in the ritual year. As Methodism moved into the twentieth century, however, there was a less hostile reaction to theatre, and perhaps even a sense of its age-old benefits in terms of direct Christian experience. Ironically, given the way the Pit has been used over the centuries, there may even be a case for stating that one of Methodism's greatest symbols in Cornwall – the several phases of Gwennap Pit, and its surviving incarnation – is, paradoxically, one of Cornwall's finest religious theatrical venues.[125] Shaw even describes the pit as 'John Wesley's amphitheatre'. Attendance at the original pit between 1762 and 1789, and then the remodelled version from 1807 onwards, must have been akin to an open-air theatrical experience.[126] Indeed, it may be that the Cornish imagination subconsciously completed the design according to tradition, since the venue resembles in so very many ways a *plen-an-gwarry*.[127]

Celto-Christian experience was also being revisited in the nineteenth century, as a succession of scholars began to examine and translate the repository of Cornish-language drama. The origins of this movement were in part antiquarian, but also revivalist in nature. Indeed, the antiquarianism was a necessary initial part of the process of revival. As I have argued elsewhere, the continuum of literature and drama in Cornish has been punctuated by a series of declines and revivals through all phases of its history.[128] The Revival from the 1850s onwards has been extensively studied by a number of scholars, and the interested reader should visit those texts. Spriggs convincingly argues that it was actually William Scawen (1600-1689) who was the 'Father of the

Cornish Language Revival',[129] and that his work eventually had a latent but lasting effect through the successive centuries. More conventional narratives such as those offered by Smith, and Stalmaszczyk have usually asserted the importance of the work of Henry Jenner,[130] while Kent and Saunders have noted the significance of the work of W.S. Lach-Szyrma in Cornwall.[131] Ellis, meanwhile, notes the wider importance to Cornwall of the work of the Indo-European-style Celticists Franz Bopp and Johann Casper Zeuss in Germany,[132] as being significant in initiating nineteenth-century revivalist activity. A useful overview of the process is found in Deacon,[133] while the major significant textual sources can be found in Kent and Saunders.[134] What all are agreed upon is that the 1878 meeting at Paul, near Newlyn, commemorating the centenary of Dolly Pentreath's projected death, activated popular interest in Cornish being a living language once again.

Here, we are perhaps less concerned with the micro-detail of the revivalist movement, but rather more with how this movement reconsidered dramatic texts of the past. Back in 1816, the clergyman Richard Polwhele (1760-1838) had considered some aspects of Cornish drama in his *History of Cornwall* (1803),[135] but his work contained several inaccuracies. Davies Gilbert (1767-1839),[136] the St Erth-born antiquarian, President of the Royal Society, MP for Helston and Bodmin and High Sheriff of Cornwall, took something of a lead in 1826 when he published John Keigwin's version of *Pascon Agan Arluth* (the text of which has many links to the 'Passion' of the *Ordinalia*), renaming it *Mount Calvary*,[137] yet clearly Gilbert had no knowledge of Cornish, for the text had many inaccuracies. Gilbert repeated this error in 1827, when he attempted another publication: Keigwin's translation of the drama *The Creacion of the World*.[138] According to Ellis, observers such as Edwin Norris and Zeuss were unimpressed.[139] Although Gilbert had attempted to place these texts before a modern audience, his only opinion on Cornish was paradoxically that its disappearance was helpful:

No one more sincerely rejoices than does the editor of this ancient mystery that the Cornish dialect of Celtic or Gaelic languages has ceased altogether from being used by the inhabitants of Cornwall; whatever may have been its degree of intrinsic excellence; experience amply demonstrating, that no infliction on a province is equally severe, or irremediable, as the separation by distinct speech from a great and enlightened Nation, of which it forms a part. A separation closing against it most of the avenues to knowledge, and wholly intercepting that course of rapid improvement which eminently distinguishes the present age from all other periods in the history of man…[140]

Davies's view was that the modern, world stage of Cornwall no longer required an antiquated language – despite publishing a place-name rhyming poem in Cornish.[141] Modern publishing of Cornish-language dramatic texts therefore got off to a shaky start.[142] The lack of a university in Cornwall during this period, or in wider south-west Britain, contributed to poor production values regarding the publication of Cornish drama, which are only just being rectified in the twenty-first century.[143] Thankfully, while other antiquarians were also seeking out 'living fossils' of Cornish in Cornwall (one of the most significant was Prince Louis Lucien Bonaparte, at the end of the 1850s),[144] by the middle of the century other enlightened scholars embarked on more professional work on Cornish-language drama. By 1859, the Taunton-born philologist Edwin Norris (1795-1872) had completed his *Ancient Cornish Drama*,[145] which contained the full text of the *Ordinalia*, alongside the *Old Cornish Vocabulary* and a grammar.

Another significant nineteenth-century Celtic philologist was Dr Whitley Stokes (1830-1909). Born in Ireland, and educated at Trinity College Dublin, Stokes was originally a lawyer, though later successfully turned his hand to Celtic studies. Cornish dramatic history has much to thank Stokes for, since in a very short space of time, he professionally presented much of the canon to the late-nineteenth-century world. By 1860, Stokes had edited, and then in 1861 published, his translation of *Pascon Agan Arluth*,[146] and in the following years, completed an edited version and translation of *Gwreans an Bys: The Creation of the World*.[147] These were major steps forward in reasserting the Cornish-language dramatic tradition for the modern age, despite other observers who were knocking the significance of the continuum. For example, in 1861, at a meeting of the Royal Cornwall Polytechnic Society, John Bellow read a paper which argued that '[Cornish] contains no literature of significance'.[148] In 1869, however, a remarkable discovery was made by W.W. E. Wynne of Peniarth Library, who found a new manuscript in the Hengwrt manuscripts.[149] This ninety-leaved manuscript was not a Welsh text but, in fact, a Cornish one. It was *Bewnans Meriasek* [*The Life of St Meriasek*]. Although the Reverend Robert Williams published thirty-six lines of the opening of the play in 1869,[150] it was Whitley Stokes who, in 1872, edited and translated the drama for the Philological Society, then published the completed text. Stokes's contribution is significant. He also knew of *The Prophecy of Merlin* manuscript by John of Cornwall, and was aware of the Cornish-language life of St Columba – probably from Nicholas Roscarrock's *Lives of the Saints*.[151] Considerable strides forward had therefore been made in disseminating the dramas of the past, although the real impact of any kind of revival of Cornish theatre in this tradition was quite a long way off, and greeted in the next century, as we shall see, with a certain degree of scepticism. It is also fascinating to note that although these texts were being considered by philologists – primarily for linguistic and quasi-literary purposes – none were actually being examined by the theatrical community of dramatists, directors or actors; a position that is not much altered in the twenty-first century.

While some degree of success was occurring in the publication of Cornish-language drama, folklorists also began to examine the origins of dramatic arts in Cornwall – and their successive impact on the continuum of folktale and folklore. Although folkloric elements have been considered from the outset of our story of theatre in Cornwall, it was during the middle decades of the nineteenth-century that much of the significant folklore of Cornwall was recorded and presented to the wider world in the form of published accounts and narratives. Importantly, not only was this folklore composed of material that had, in part, shaped the drama of the previous centuries, but also the folklore itself, as we shall see below, contained elements of drama and performance. Alongside this, the folklore collected during this period would form a crucial part of the future identity of Cornwall and significantly impact on the subject matter of drama in the twentieth and twenty-first centuries. Indeed, it is hard to imagine some theatre companies of the late twentieth century operating in a world without this corpus of material. Put another way, the storytelling origins of theatre in Cornwall were about to be collated, and once collated, they would be redistributed in new ways, often for remarkably different audiences than their original moments of production. Much of the same antiquarian impetus over the Cornish-language plays was applied to the Cornish folklore, the difference being that in many cases the folklore had actually survived into the modern, industrial era. However, amongst the folklorists of the period, there was already a notion that these narratives and anecdotes were passing out of memory, and in order for them to be preserved, they needed to be written down. Like the Cornish-language drama, we know that many narratives, legends, and 'origins' for drama (whether in English or in Cornish) were also lost.[152] Crucially, however, Cornwall was collectively highly successful in retaining a wide corpus of folklore (certainly considering its relatively small geographical area).[153] One could go further: in some senses, it might even be argued that the early twentieth-century and contemporary sense of cultural difference in Cornwall is a direct result of this period of cultural-geographic collection.[154]

Three important folklore collectors in the second half of the nineteenth century were Robert Hunt (1807-87), William Bottrell (1816-81) and Margaret Ann Courtney (1834-c.1904).[155] These writers were influenced by the dramatic continuum, and inadvertently contributed to it through their work. Paradoxically, they were recording 'tradition' at a time when Cornwall was at the zenith of its industrial progress. The three collectors had different backgrounds. Hunt's was scientific. Born in Devonport, he initially tried medicine, and then poetry, but later became interested in chemistry and physics, becoming Keeper of Mining Records at the Museum of Economic Geology.[156] Bottrell, meanwhile, was born at Raftra in the parish of St Levan,[157] and comparatively little is known of his life between 1837 and 1851 but, like many other Cornishmen of the period, he was probably working overseas. We know that he obtained a position as an English teacher in Quebec in the years 1847-51, before returning to Penzance. Bottrell then married, and travelled to Australia, but over there his wife died, and he returned to live at Hawke's Point, Lelant, as a virtual recluse. Bottrell's experiences on the world stage gave him intimate knowledge of the Cornish traditions of oral narrative. Although he was at first one of Hunt's informants, Bottrell gradually became aware of the qualities of his own work and was persuaded to collect it in anthologies. Less is known of the life and work of Courtney, even though she was a resident of Penzance for all of her adult life. Her folkloric focus was different from Hunt's and Bottrell's, in the sense that she recorded more of the feasts and festivals which, as we discussed in Chapter One, contributed heavily to the early origins of theatrical culture in Cornwall. It is not my purpose here to repeat discussion of many of the narratives and festivals collected by Hunt, Bottrell and Courtney, since that is available elsewhere, but rather to demonstrate specific theatrical material in their collections. Hunt's collections are better organised than Bottrell's, more narrative, and less dramatic. His telling of narrative often seems sharper than Bottrell's, though there is subsequently more of a loss of Cornu-English speech. Consequently, overall, Hunt's volumes are more comprehensive. This volume has already dealt with Hunt's work as a repository for matters concerned with the origins of theatre and drama, as well as its significance in imagining a 'greater Cornwall' or land of the west Britons beyond the strict confines of the River Tamar.

Hunt perceives theatre in other ways. For example, in the Introduction to the work, he spends much time recounting the life and work of 'Uncle' Anthony James, a wandering droll-teller operating from the parish of Cury, whom one of his informants describes as being an 'old blind man'. This was around the year 1829. James was an ex-soldier, who was accompanied by a boy and dog, and travelled widely in west Cornwall. His movements accorded with the ritual year, and he used to arrive in St Levan at the end of August (perhaps when the harvest had begun). As well as telling narratives (several of which concerned Luty of Cury, and the mermaid), James also played the fiddle and sang ballads. Clearly, Anthony James was a theatrical story- or droll-teller, though again he is embracing the tradition of single strolling players in south-west Britain. Hunt also informs us that James avoided Methodists (whom he labelled 'Conorums'), perhaps because many of his stories concerned the devil and supernatural deeds, and because the stories were told at unapproved gatherings. However, to other 'religious folks', apparently, he presented 'Babes in the Wood' (which again, may have had elements of Robin Hood).[158] Hunt's informant also knew of another old droll-teller, who went by the name of Billy Frost. Frost originated from St Just-in-Penwith, but used to travel to neigh-bouring parishes for the feast events.[159] Frost also entertained people in the public houses. It is significant that both James and Frost were then operating in the far west, when it would have taken a considerable time to travel the distance to Penzance. Thus James and Frost were working a circuit, where they were perhaps the only form of theatre available to these isolated west Cornish communities during this time. Their seasonal work would suggest operation during the summer, which is when many of the feast days took place. This would not be in opposition to other forms of urban theatre, which, as we have seen, tended to work from November to March.

Hunt also recognised the common origin of certain tales and motifs in his collections; hence perhaps the scientific grouping and classification they undergo. Through the whole of the Introduction – whether it be saints' lives or mermaids – Hunt understands the historical dimension. At one point, he comments that they 'may be regarded as true types of the ancient Cornish mythology'.[160] We recognise the Celtic dramatic continuum of Cornwall here, but Hunt indicates that the heroic narrative recorded elsewhere is also present. He alludes to the imagined oral culture of the past, observing that 'romances such as these have floated down to us as wreck upon the ocean'.[161] This is tinged with lament but, above and beyond that, it also indicates that this 'wreckage' may once have formed a more sustained, extant theatrical culture. This volume has already shown the significant of mythology in Cornish folklore and theatre works, and Hunt provides a number of narratives here. This naturally leads into further mythological creatures, among them the fairies; Hunt chooses early on in the collection to include a Cornish droll (of secular orality), which clearly had a proto-theatrical origin. He names it 'The Spriggan's Child' and its rhyming couplets allowed the teller an ability to recall the lines easily. Here, we see effectively a dramatic monologue, based on the theme of a changeling child:

I'll tell you a tale, an you've patience to hear an,
'Bout the Spriggans, that swarm round Partinney still –

You knew Janey Tregear, who lives in Brea Vean,
In the village just under the Chapel-Hill.
One arternoon she went out for to reap,
And left the child in the cradle asleep;
Janey took good care to cover the fire; –
Turn'd down the brasdis on the baking-ire,
Swept up the ashes on the hearthstone,
And so left the child in the house all alone –
The boys had all on 'em gone away,
Some to work and some to play.
Janey work'd in the field as gay as a lark,
And when she came home it was nearly dark;
The furst thing she saw when she open'd the door
Was the cradle upset – all the straw on the floor.
But no child in sight –
She search'd all round –
Still no child was found.[162]

Hunt is particularly good at creating a sense of complete belief in this other-worldly culture. That said, he was, of course, recording a world that still retained that belief in spite of rapid modernisation. Another of Hunt's achievements is his recording of the legends of Tregeagle.[163] We may assert a new paradigm for the mythology of Tregeagle: if it is considered a pan-European narrative, then it tells us something about the importance of Cornwall's position on the world stage. We may here be looking at a more localised telling of the generic 'Faust' narrative.[164] This signifies to us not only that Cornish dramatic themes can travel across the world, but that other thematic threads can arrive in Cornwall, and be given a particularly Cornish context. It is said that the real Faust existed in Germany around 1488-1541. Faust-type narratives spread widely across medieval Europe and, given that Christopher Marlowe developed his first version of *Dr Faustus* in 1602,[165] there is every reason to suggest that the narrative might have passed to Cornwall via Brittany (consider, for example, a similar transfer of the *Blue-Beard* narratives), or even from England. This may then have been applied to the local story. What is known is that Jan Tregeagle was a magistrate in the early seventeenth century, and a steward under the Duchy of Cornwall. As a lawyer he was said to have been particularly harsh, and as a landowner was cruel to his tenants. There were also rumours of him murdering his wife and making a pact with the devil. Certainly there are core similarities between the tales, but it may also be the case that material was added, dropped or simply redesignated according to local culture. Given the cultural-geographic context of Tregeagle (Bodmin Moor, Dozmary Pool, Roche Rock, Loe Bar, Gwenor Cove, and Porthcurno), perhaps one of the most intriguing questions in Cornish theatrical history is why the material was first presented on the stage as late as 1985 (by Kneehigh Theatre) as 'the Cornish Faust'. If a German Faust is the early origin, then we have a notable reversal of the general trend for Cornish drama, but also another demonstration of how far myths travelled across Europe.

Some of the material in the second of Hunt's volumes is important in our theatrical history of Cornwall. As noted in the first chapter, Hunt's recollections of the saints' narratives are not as comprehensive as, for example, those of Gilbert Hunter Doble; however, these still offer a strong link back to previous dramatic works. The best example is that of 'St. Kea's Boat',[166] which has at least a connection to *Bewnans Ke*, if not following the narrative of the play. Clearly, there is a certain continuity, however, and we must appreciate there may have been other versions of the narrative. When we consider the narratives of *Bewnans Ke* and *Bewnans Meriasek*, there is obvious interest in each saint opening holy wells. Hunt follows this tradition by devoting a substantial section of his work to holy wells and springs, demonstrating the link between saints and communities, and again asserting the celebratory aspect of community drama. Arthurian matter in Cornwall had sometimes been too tenuous for many early Celticists, but one can observe a direct link in what had come down to Hunt from the era of *Bewnans Ke*, since the play contained a proliferation of Arthurian material. Hunt appears to collate several disparate elements in his entry on 'Carlian in Kea' ('One of the most celebrated of Arthur's knights, Sir Tristam is said to have been born in this parish. A tradition of this is preserved in the parish…'[167]) but nevertheless, there is a very real link back to the dramas of centuries before. One senses that Hunt knew there was more Arthurian material somehow just out of reach. His view was justified, given the 2000 discovery of *Bewnans Ke*.

The rest of Hunt's second volume is devoted to the kind of material more favoured by Courtney, in that it concerns customs of the ritual year, and moments of para-theatre. However, there are some notable exceptions, where Hunt records examples of Christmas dramas from Cornwall. The first is a 'St George Play'. As indicated earlier, this may seem some kind of anathema from a present-day Cornish- nationalist position, in the sense that what may be expected is a play about St Piran. However, as this volume has shown, St George is, paradoxically, a highly celebrated figure within the Cornish continuum.[168] Hunt says something quite interesting before he introduces the play:

> The Christmas play is a very ancient institution in Cornwall. At one time religious subjects were chosen, but those gave way to romantic plays. The arrangements were tolerably complete, and sometimes a considerable amount of dramatic skill was displayed.[169]

What Hunt appears to say here is that he recognises the tradition (as seen in Chapter One, where the early origins of the Camborne mummers' play were considered, and in Chapter Three where the Truro or Mylor Cordwainers' Play was examined), but that religious plays as well as the usual mummers' tradition were presented at one time. This is a significant statement, which might indicate a lost tradition of Nativity or Christ's Childhood drama, for which there is some limited evidence.[170] Quite why these died out in favour of what he terms 'romantic plays' is not known. Here, Hunt would seem to indicate 'romances' rather than 'romantic', hence the further development of the mumming tradition. There are also obvious links to the *Hal-an-Tow* event at Helston, and Obby Oss at Padstow. Clearly there, the drama or para-drama was connected to the 'May' of the ritual year, whereas here the drama seems associated with the winter solstice, and rebirth for the next agricultural year. Much of the detail about the characters of the St George-style mumming plays is lost in locations elsewhere, but here Hunt offers considerable details about costuming and stylisation. Consider the following observations on St George:

> *St George*, and the other tragic performers, are dressed out somewhat in the style of morris-dancers, in their shirt sleeves and white trousers, much decorated with ribbons and handkerchiefs, each carrying a drawn sword in his hand, if they can be procured, otherwise a cudgel. They wear high caps of pasteboard, adorned with beads, small pieces of looking glass, coloured paper, &c.; several long strips of pith generally hang down from the top, with small pieces of different coloured cloth strung on them; the whole has a very smart effect.[171]

This appears similar to the classic 'tatters' of Morris in Britain.[172] Hunt then makes further observations about the other characters in the drama, as well as a link back to Bakhtin, and Barber's carnival world:

> *Father Christmas* is personified in a grotesque manner, as an ancient man, wearing a large mask and wig, and a huge club, wherewith he keeps bystanders in order.
>
> The *Doctor*, who is generally the merryandrew of the piece, is dressed in any ridiculous way, with a wig, three-cornered hat, and painted face.

The other comic characters are dressed according to fancy.

The *female*, where there is one, is usually in the dress worn half a century ago.

The *hobbyhorse*, which is a character sometimes introduced, wears a representation of a horse's hide.

Beside the regular drama of "St George," many parties of mummers go about in fancy dress of every sort, most commonly the males in female attire, and vice versa.[173]

Although there are similarities to other St George mumming plays considered throughout the story of theatre in Cornwall, this one is perhaps distinctive for two reasons: firstly, the detailed stage direction provided by Hunt that is absent in some of the other texts; secondly the integration of the minor characters Hub Bub and the Box Holder (roles suited to more minor players, who perhaps could not remember longer sections of text). Witness the following section at the end of the play, and how the Box Holder asks the audience for financial rewards for the performance:

Enter Hub-Bub

Here comes I, old Hub Bub Bub Bub;
Upon my shoulders I carries a club,
And in my hand a frying-pan,
So am I not a valiant man.

[*These characters serve as a sort of burlesque on St George and the other hero, and may be regarded in the light of an anti-masque.*]

Enter the Box Holder

Here comes I, great head and little wit;
Put your hands in your pockets, and give what you think fit.
Gentlemen and ladies, sitting down at your ease,
Put your hands in your pockets, and give me what you please.[174]

In this way, the brevity of the performance and the efficiency of the scripts suggest that such pieces would have been mobile, and that the mummers proceeded from house-to-house, or one area of a community to another. Frustratingly, Hunt fails to date the St George play, and does not tell us its location, nor who informed him. Presumably he was writing with a sense that this tradition was about to collapse, although he is much more detailed in his observations on 'guise-dancing',[175] which suggests that the event was still occurring with some degree of frequency. He finishes the section on Christmas drama with some rather dismissive observations on earlier drama and theatrical space:

> Of the Cornish mystery plays which were once acted in the famous "Rounds", it is not necessary, in this place, to say anything. The translation by Mr Norris preserves their characteristics, which indeed differ in few respects from the mystery plays of other parts. The "Perran Round" is fortunately preserved by the proprietor in its original state. Everyone must regret the indifference of the wealthy inhabitants of St Just to their "Round," which is now a wretched ruin.[176]

Reading between the lines of this, however, we begin to note something more significant. Although Hunt fails to note the distinctive dramatic nature of Cornish culture, he does note that it was the wealthier classes who were foregoing the protection of their indigenous Cornish culture at St Just-in-Penwith. This strongly matches the observations of Scawen in the seventeenth century, who argues that such classes gave up their Cornishness too easily, in favour of English culture. Indeed, for Carew, this was actually something to be welcomed. It was a debate that, in the light of this antiquarian activity, would have long-standing consequences in the opening decades of the next century.

After considering the Christmas drama, and dismissing the mystery plays, Hunt does look at three other dramatic pieces: 'Lady Lovell's Courtship', 'Madam Pender' and 'The Penryn Tragedy'. The former is another variant of the 'Duffy and the Devil' play (considered in more detail by Bottrell below), which Hunt prefaces with the following statement:

> By the especial kindness of one who had a more abundant store of old Cornish stories that any man whom I have ever met, I am enabled to give some portion of one of the old Cornish plays or guise dances. Many parts are omitted, as they would, in our refined days, be considered coarse; but as preserving a true picture of a peculiar people, as they were a century and a half or two centuries since I almost regret the omissions.[177]

The 'one' referred to is, of course, William Bottrell. It is something of a pity that Hunt chose to edit out the more 'coarse' material, for that bawdiness may have given a connection back to some of the components of the medieval dramas. There was clearly a similar primary source: comparison between the two versions shows that Bottrell's is the more comprehensive in its surviving form, but the piece is no more 'coarse', so quite what was so offensive to Hunt is unclear. 'Madam Pender' is preserved in what he terms 'doggerel verse' but there must have been a mumming origin for the piece. It is, in fact, another Christmas-themed drama, in which Madam Pender and Bet of the Mill, of Trevider House, choose to spend Christmas night spinning rather than with the other inmates, who have gone off to a guize dance. Although the piece is preserved in verse, Hunt's version is incomplete. It is not difficult to see a comparison with some of the thematic elements of 'Duffy and the Devil'; in previous ages this kind of drama must have been highly popular. The verses display a Cornu-centric awareness of place and were probably formalised sometime in the early nineteenth century. Again, the couplets spoken by Bet suggest easy recollection:

> We took the rushes up from the floor,
> From up the chimney down to the door:
> When we had the wool carded, ready to spin,
> It came into our heads, before we'd begin
> We'd have a jug of hot spiced beer,
> To put life in our heels, our hearts to cheer,
> So we drank to the healths of one and all,
> While the holly and bays
> Looked bright on the wall.[178]

The final text considered by Hunt is 'The Penryn Tragedy'. When writing, Hunt had not encountered the black letter pamphlet himself, so this 'does not appear to be in existence'.[179] The text had, however, survived elsewhere.[180] There follows a lengthy quotation from Davies Gilbert about the narrative, which Hunt connects with Lillo's *The Fatal Curiosity*. Here, we see that Lillo's work continued to be in the public eye, long after its performance had fallen out of fashion. Hunt is keen to assert the power of this piece and quotes from a Mr Harris of Salisbury, who comments on Lillo's version by saying that:

> it is no small praise to this affecting fable that it so much resembles the Oedipus Tyrannus of Sophocles. In both tragedies, that which apparently leads to joy, leads in its completion to misery; both tragedies concur in the horror of their discoveries, and both in those great outlines of a truly tragic revolution (according to the nervous sentiments of Lillo himself) –
> > 'The two extremes of life,
> > The highest happiness the deepest woe
> > With all the sharp and bitter aggravations
> > Of such a vast transition.'[181]

This is one of the last times that Lillo's work features in the Cornish literary continuum. Considering the high status of the work at the start of the nineteenth century, this in itself is quite a tragic fall. Although not performed since that time, the narrative of 'The Penryn Tragedy' was still to have a hold over playwrights in Cornwall, as we shall see more fully in the twentieth century. Hunt himself probably realised that changes in fashion would see the work no longer performed, hence perhaps this last hurrah. Despite its obvious folkloric and folk-tale intent, Hunt's collection does offer us much insight into popular theatrical culture, not only of his time of writing, but also from the previous centuries.

Bottrell presents the continuum of theatrical Cornwall in different ways. He begins his three-volume collection by explaining that the para-theatrical culture that he writes about evolved because of West Penwith's isolation, which allowed the neighbourhood to 'droll away', 'drolls' being the Cornu-English term for the narratives told. Bottrell notes the 'droll teller's fanciful invention',[182] showing that when these stories were first told there was a certain art to their performance. These 'semi-professional droll-tellers… were formerly welcomed at all firesides, fairs and feasts for their recitals of the old ballads and stories in which they abounded, and of which their audiences rarely tired'.[183] Thus what Bottrell observes is that the stories told had a theatrical presence to them, and were told at theatrical venues in west Cornwall. Although Bottrell confesses that he had altered the idiom they were told in (for fear that readers would not understand),[184] his versions have a remarkable sense of dialogue within them, suggesting a performance by the teller which necessitates swapping from idiom to idiom and character to character. In essence, then, these are composite one-man or one-woman shows. Even so, Bottrell still has a remarkable ear for dramatic dialogue, as in this sequence from the 'The Piskey-Led Commercial Traveller's Ride over the Hills':

Jan:	The Lord Bless 'e sir. I'll be down to 'e in a minute: you are one of the venturars I spose? How sorry I am that I didn't know 'e before; lev me put on a few rags and I'll be down in a crack: excuse me sir, please. I'll be down in a jiffey, quick as a wink, and put 'e in the road to the town or the bal.
Traveller:	No, my good man, don't come down by any means; besides I've nothing whatever to do with mines.
Jan:	Ha! arn't 'e a venturar sir, an? who or what are 'e, an? where ded 'e come from?
Traveller:	I'm a pin-maker from Birmingham.

Jan: A pin-maker! A pin-maker! Why a great man like you don't
                make the things the women fasten their rags with, do 'e? And
                you are come from the place we cale Brummagam, where the
                buttons come from...[185]

Bottrell's brilliance as a recorder of folk narrative is to emphasise the dialogue,
and thus the dramatic elements of it. Put another way, unlike Hunt, Bottrell is
more focused on showing rather than telling. One might go further, and argue
that many of Bottrell's tales operate as distinctive pieces of drama, in which an
editor might merely remove the description to end up with a compelling play.
An important point to make is that Bottrell here is no simple recorder of the
mumming tradition.[186] This is operating at a much more sophisticated level.
Such subtle dialogic interchanges are to be found in all of Bottrell's work: he
has uncanny ability to record how Cornish 'dramatic' speech exchanges
operate; perhaps this is the reason why later Cornish theatre companies have
found his work appropriate to adapt for the stage. Another feature of Bottrell's
writing is the sense of community, which is, of course, connected to the
medieval plays of each parish. Most of Bottrell's tales (in the first two
collections at least) are linked to a cultural-geographic area, just like the
medieval texts. Two early examples of this are 'Betty Toddy and Her Gown: A
St Just Droll', and 'Nancy Trenoweth: The Fair Daughter of the Miller of
Alsia'.[187] In such tales, there is something of a quasi-Chaucerian morality about
them (incidentally also found in the tale of *John of Chyanhor*), which indicates
that at one point they were perhaps tools of instruction for the audience on
how best to lead their lives.

One area of dramatic activity that Bottrell does record in detail is the
tradition of Christmas drama in Cornwall. In the 1870 volume, he notes in
'Joan's Trip to Penzance on Christmas Eve', the tale of 'Duffy and the Devil'
(a Cornish variant on the 'Rumplestiltskin' motif). Joan observes that: 'Little
more is known of these folks than what had been preserved by an old
Christmas play. This ancient form of mummery, or primitive drama (if one
may apply so grand a term to what was probably never known the other side
of Penzance)... [tells the story of old squire Lovel, of Trove]'.[188] Clearly
Bottrell knew more than he was letting on, because his lasting dramatic
achievement was to retell the story of 'Duffy and the Devil' as an admixture of
narrative and script in the second collection of his work. In this work, Bottrell
is able to refine the 'showing' approach of his storytelling, by incorporating
probable memories of how the Christmas play proceeded with interjections of
narrative to make the piece clearer for the reader. This is in direct contrast to
Hunt's version, where the text is fully narrative. Bottrell's twenty-six pages are

a considerable achievement for folk drama. Thus, in the first section of the drama, Bottrell's inventions are juxtaposed with what appears to be recorded folklore (the italicised section below indicating the recorded text):

Duffy:	I may as well tell 'e master that I shan't knit much more for 'e, because Huey Lenine and I have been courtan for a long time. We are thinkan' to get married before Winter, and then I shall have a man of my own to work for.
Squire:	What! Huey Levine! I'll break every bone in his carcase if he shows his face near the place. Why the devil is in it that a young skit like thee should have it in thy head to get married! Now I'll sit down a minute and talk reason with thee.

[*The Squire sits close beside Duffy. The Devil tickles them with his tail. Huey is seen peeping from the oven.*]

Squire:	*Give up thy courting with Huey Lenine,* *And I'll dress thee in silks an satin fine.*
Duffy:	*No, I'll never have an old man, an old man like you,* *Though you are Squire Lovell:* *To my sweetheart I'll be constant and true,* *Though he work all day with threshal and shovel.*[189]

This interpretation of the text appears appropriate, since the traditional oral version would, in all likelihood, have been in verse, because it would have made it easier for the actors to remember. Bottrell is then able to fill in any gaps with his own invented dialogue (as above) or ordinary narrative. This is the case in the second section of the story, where the traditional narrative is fragmentary and Bottrell has to invent more of the telling. Within his vision of Cornish experience, Bottrell also contests several notions. Very often, Cornish experience is seen as being narrow (perhaps allied with the issue of locality), although Bottrell subverts this considerably, proving that the canon of folk narrative is actually highly international, through Cornwall's maritime connections. This stands in a continuum of theatrical telling which stretches back to Lillo's *Fatal Curiosity*, but which in Bottrell's work is seen in 'The Last Cardew, of Boskenna, and the Story of Nelly Wearne'. Here, the narrative contains all the dramatic methods outlined above, but also moves the characters (including a wise woman of the East) through a number of locations, including St Loy, Burian Fair, Mount's Bay, and Madagascar.[190] Bottrell, perhaps because of his own personal experiences, understood that the nineteenth-century Cornish experience, though rooted in the locality, was very much trans-national; an ethos that clearly has continuum forwards in time, since it is also enshrined in Kneehigh Theatre's oft-quoted mantra of Joan Miró: 'To be universal, you must be truly local'.[191] Seemingly, Bottrell had also realised this in 1873.

Sense of place and space are crucial in his collections. Particular locations appear to have particular dramatic appeal for Bottrell. One of them is Sancreed. For example, he writes of a 'Modern Sancreed Witch',[192] and many of the tales operate there or nearby. There is also the more specific sequence of writing titled 'Miracle, Christmas Plays, &c' which was dealt with earlier in this story.[193] Although it is not explicitly explored in Bottrell's work, Sancreed is significant both for one of the surviving manuscript copies of *Pascon Agan Arluth* being found there,[194] and for its magical holy well.[195] We know also from the *Cornish Telegraph* of 1868 that there was an article exploring the performances of miracle plays there.[196] Bottrell knew well the layeredness of the place. In the third volume (1880), in notes about Cornish Christmas carols, he mentions the 'favourite carols', which 'for the most part contained such legends as are preserved in the Mysteries, or Old Miracle Plays, which continued to be performed in western parishes, on Sunday afternoons, down to Elizabeth's reign or later'.[197] Here, Bottrell may well have been thinking of Sancreed, or even St Just-in-Penwith. Not only was the canonised Bible considered, but also the apocryphal Gospels. Echoes of this past theatrical culture are found, according to Bottrell, in the surviving carols, such as the 'Cherry Tree Carol':

> Joseph was an old man, an old man was he,
> When he wedded Mary, in the land of Galilee,
> When Joseph and Mary walked in the garden good,
> There were cherries and berries as read as the blood.[198]

Another example is the 'Holy-well' which begins thus:

> As it fell out, one May morning,
>   And upon one bright holiday,
> Sweet Jesus asked of His dear Mother,
>   If he might go out to play.[199]

Here Christ is the 'player' – an actor, in the pretend world of childhood. To present him in this way is resolutely Cornish. Bottrell's theories on this have been subject to the scrutiny of Richard McGrady, who has found 'traces of ancient Mystery' in the ballad carols of Davies Gilbert and William Sandys.[200] It seems then, that these are the last vestiges of medieval theatricality. The argument is interesting because it also closely parallels what Andrew C.

Symons has noted in the work of John Harris. As Thomas, Newman, and Harding have discussed,[201] Harris is primarily presented as the Romantic poet of industrial Cornwall, though Symons notes a different thread: that Harris's poetry was slipping through a closing door of ancient Celtic bardism, seemingly straight out of Taliesin.[202] Put together with what Bottrell has recorded, and Gilbert and Sandys' writing, we have a picture of medieval theatrical culture still with a toe-hold in the nineteenth century. The apocryphal nature of possible past drama (particularly Christ in Cornwall legends) is seen reinvented in B.D. Vere's 1930 verse drama, *King Arthur: His Symbolic Story in Verse*, in my own *Nativitas Christi [The Nativity]* (2006), and Ken George's *Flogholeth Krist* (2006).[203] The playful humour of the above examples of verse is also seen in the poetry of Charles Causley, and even more specifically within his much-undervalued verse dramas.[204] Bottrell therefore not only notes the internationalism of drama in Cornwall, but also has a strong awareness of continuity from ancient sources. Other important spaces include Treen Castle (now facing the Minack Theatre), Porthcurno, fogous, Ballowal and Chapel Uny Well. For Bottrell, space intimately governed the narrative, and such narratives were constantly to form inspiration for new dramas, from this point onwards. A good example is a story right at the end of the second volume: 'The Mermaid of Zennor',[205] which undoubtedly had influence on Pearl Peirson's 1951 version, and the Bedlam Theatre Company of Cornwall's 1990 telling.

Bottrell's third volume shifts its focus to stories found in mid-Cornwall (Ladock, for example), and also explores ghosts and spectres. Again, festival culture is important in defining para- or proto-theatrical activity. Here, Bottrell explores working-class expression during Hallantide at St Just-in-Penwith, and indicates that although the festival was in full swing fifty years ago (making this around 1830), by 1880 it was in decline.[206] A final theatrical flourish in Bottrell's work is found in his duologues, where we witness various conversations between two individuals. These include 'Mal Treloare and Sandry Kemp Kiss and Become Good Friends Again, or Backbiting Crull Outwitted'[207] and 'Cornish Dialogue between Two Very Old Men'.[208] The most famous of these however was 'A Dialogue between Gracey Penrose and Mally Trevisky'. This form of writing was a popular genre for working-class audiences, and perhaps, like the two above, arose out of the dialogues between Cornish miners presented on the late eighteenth-century stage in Cornwall. Polwhele had actually collected them as early as 1803. The pieces work as 'living' drolls, which were presumably learnt and performed by local wags:

Gracey: Faith and trath then, I b'lieve, in ten parishes round,
           Sickey roage, sichey vellan, es nat to ba found.

Mally: Whot's the fussing, un Gracey! long wetha, cheel vean?
Gracey: A fussng aketha! od splot es ould bracane!
            Our Martin's cum'd hum, cheeled, so drunk as a beast,
            So cross as the gallish from Perranzan veast,
            A kicking, a tottering, a cussin, and swearing,
            So hard as the stomses a tarving and tearing.[209]

Gossiping, stagey women, who speak an unadultered Cornu-English about drunken men make great theatrical devices; this is about as non-English as its gets in Cornu-English writing. Bottrell does not record a source here, so it is hard to say whether this is his own invention, or something he has recorded. Cornu-English writer W.B. Forfar was also to record a similar version of the duologue,[210] but was presumably drawing on Polwhele, and even Bottrell. There is an echo of these types of pieces in the modern works of Brenda Wootton and Camborne's Mrs Rosewarne,[211] and maybe also a trace of earlier stage Cornishness. In this sense, in Bottrell, we again note continuity, backwards and forwards.

The sheer quantity of para-theatrical, carnival and ritual activity contained within Margaret Ann Courtney's 1890 volume *Cornish Feasts and Folklore* makes it impossible to summarise in a volume of this size. Courtney takes a different approach from Hunt, and Bottrell, favouring an initial section where she leads the reader through the Cornish ritual year.[212] This is highly useful from a theatrical point of view, since the section offers pointers to performance conditions. Like Hunt, and Bottrell, Courtney has much to say on guize-dancing in west Cornwall in particular, linking this to performances of what she terms 'St George and the Dragon', as well as 'Duffy and the Devil'. She also quotes from R. Edmonds' work *The Land's End District* about the hobby-horse which accompanied revellers in Penzance:

A well known character amongst them, about fifty years ago, was the hobby-horse, represented by a man carrying a piece of wood in the form of a horse's head and neck, with some contrivance for opening and shutting the mouth with a loud snapping noise, the performer being so covered with horse-cloth or hide of a horse as to resemble the animal, whose curvetings, bitings and other motions he imitated.[213]

Also noted was that 'some of these 'guise-dancers' occasionally masked themselves with the skins of the head of bullocks having the horns on'.[214] This is a striking image, with some similarities to the 'shaman' Jack the Tinkeard, as discussed in Chapter One. Clearly, Edmonds and Courtney are recording ritualised misrule, still occurring in modern west Cornwall, though it seems not everyone was happy with their behaviour:

> They often behaved in such an unruly manner that women and children were afraid to venture out. If the doors of the houses were not locked they enter uninvited and stay, playing all kinds of antics, until money was given them to go away.[215]

Indeed, it was this very fear over civil misrule that encouraged the authorities to ban such events; Courtney notes that 'in Penzance, the Corporation put them down about ten years since [making that around 1880], and every Christmas-eve a notice is posted in conspicuous places forbidding their appearance in the streets'.[216] In recent times there has been a move to revive the custom, as part of the so-called 'Montol' celebrations.[217] St. Ives, according to Courtney, was different however, and customs carried on there to at least 1890. There is a continuum of this celebratory and theatrical culture in St Ives, since for several years in the twentieth and twenty-first centuries, New Year's Eve has witnessed a massive fancy dress event in the town, accompanied by revellers parading the streets. Apparently such community theatre was highly popular at the end of the eighteenth century, giving rise to the phrase 'as good as a Christmas play'.[218]

There is a brief mention in Courtney's writings of Jack the Giant Killer, which was a common fairy story told to children and, as discussed above, a common theme for pantomimes in the second half of the century. Courtney repeats a rhyme which accompanied the tale: 'I am the valiant Cornishman, who slew the giant Cormoran',[219] but does not develop this further. Another piece of theatrical folklore is contained in her work: the moment when the news of Nelson's death was first heard at Penzance.[220] Lillo's *The Fatal Curiosity* also receives a brief note (its final mention in nineteenth-century Anglo-Cornish literature), as does some apocryphal history of the origins of *The Pirates of Penzance*. Apparently, a friend told Courtney that:

> The popular play of *The Pirates of Penzance* had not its origin in that town, but in the little fishing village of Penberth, near the Land's End; but that, alas, is its 'custom port'. The captain of the pirate vessel, and all his ship's crew, were wrestlers. They would go out to the small Spanish, Dutch, and other merchant ships, and would ask for provisions, or tender assistance, and on making sure that the ship was unarmed they would overpower the sailors and plunder it. This was before the time when the Trinity Corporation had begun its work on the Cornish coast.[221]

This is an interesting premise, but in reality it seems little more than a piece of urban legend. In such ways, though, Courtney helps us understand further the popular theatrical culture of Cornwall during the late nineteenth century. Related to the dramatic elements of folklore were, of course, the many fairs, feasts and markets which continued on from the previous centuries, offering here and there, 'tasters' of dramatic activity from the past.[222] Often rural and isolated, and certainly away from the urban touring and indigenous theatres of Truro, Falmouth, Penzance, St Austell and Bodmin, there were no doubt throwbacks of parish-formed performance, as well as novel entertainments that were brought in from over the Tamar. This story has already shown the significance of saints, local legends and community in shaping unique dramas of place in Cornwall. The picture becomes all the more astonishing when one considers the list of fairs, feasts and markets at the end of Boase's *Collectanea Cornubiensia*, which lists seventeen pages of parish activity from the Isles of Scilly to the River Tamar, operating in the period 1880-90.[223] If even the smallest remembrances or traces of folklore carried on from the medieval period, then we still have a striking picture of a community and culture still committed to celebration of the ritual year (whether pagan, Christian, or non-religious).

Inevitably, similar changes occurred to the fairs and feasts in the late nineteenth-century as came with the decline of the 'gwarry miracles' during the Tudor period. Theatre in its most populist sense came from a newly mechanised breed of showmen and travelling amusements. As Scrivers and Smith detail, owners such as William, Charles and Sophie Hancock brought their 'fairground' attractions to Cornwall on a regular basis.[224] These amusements were, in some ways, the modern end of a continuum which ran back to strolling players of previous ages, as well as the more 'modern' and exotic forms of entertainment being offered by the theatres in Truro and Falmouth, as working-class audiences sought fresh innovations. Among the attractions available in Cornwall during the Hancocks' classic years of touring, between 1861 and 1895, were an Anglo-American Marionette Show, a Steam Dobby Set, the Bio Tableaux Show (with Professor Henri), a Tunnel Railway, Rolling Gondolas, Magic Lantern Shows, a Helter Skelter and the subtly-named 'Harem Parading Costumes'. The Wash at Newlyn, Penzance Quay, Redruth Whitsun Fair and Tavistock Goose Fair all formed major stopping points on the Hancocks' touring pattern through Cornwall and West Devon, as well as numerous parishes in between. This was a theatre of participation and titillation, which paradoxically had its origins – particularly with steam and railways – in Cornwall and Cornish invention. As we move to the latter years of the century, it would appear that while these new forms of entertainment rose in popularity, indigenous theatre in Cornwall declined to virtually nothing. *The West Briton* and *Royal Cornwall Gazette* newspapers carry few advertisements even for popular entertainments, let alone theatre.

Theatrical activity originating in Cornwall was, at this point, making its way onto the world stage. Part of the collapse of both indigenous and touring drama around 1860 in Cornwall may well be put down to the disappearance of working- and middle-class audiences in Cornwall; from the 1840s onwards, they had migrated in mass numbers to other parts of the globe. Initially in Australia and South Africa, and then more fully in North, Central and South America, thousands of Cornish men and women left the homeland for a life elsewhere. Of course, Cousin Jack and Jenny culture was not just a transplant from back home: its trans-national ethos took several Cornish elements, but synchronised these both with the indigenous habits of the countries and continents they travelled to, and with other ethnic groups who worked there. Although ignored by most Anglo-centric histories, the emigration of the Cornish overseas was a phenomenal movement and displacement of people, with far-reaching consequences for the economies, communities and cultures to which they travelled. Fortunately, much Cornu-centric scholarship has recently been devoted to demonstrating the importance of this process,[225] with several more texts offering further insight into the Cornish emigration experience.[226] Certain aspects of Cornish culture did, however, cross the oceans to these new locations. In many cases, as Kent and McKinney have shown, this was folklore, superstition, and narrative,[227] but the period also shows traces of the theatrical leanings of the Cornish. As with some of the lost plays of Cornwall, sometimes we see only a glimpse into activity, but the glimpse is wide enough for us to see both para-theatrical and fully theatrical activity at work.

Thurner details the work and lives of many migrant Cornish who settled in the Keweenaw Peninsula of Northern Michigan.[228] An influential figure in the late 1850s was Justus H. Rathbone, who originated in upstate New York, but moved to the Keweenaw to work at Central Mine, where hundreds of Cornish worked. Fond of the theatre, Rathbone formed a drama group,[229] which featured migrant Cornish, and it was while working on a play titled *Damon and Pythias*, that he conceived of the fraternal order of the Knights of Pythias. Meanwhile, to the west of the Central Mine, grew the town of Calumet, which was incorporated as a town in 1867, and which by 1900 had a population of 26,991 people, making it one of the largest in the United States of America.[230] Most of Calumet's wealth was founded on copper mining, and many of its citizens were Cornish. It was thanks to a boom period in the copper-mining industry that the town corporation had an enormous surplus in its treasury, and so in the year 1898 began to construct a theatre and opera house. Known as the Calumet Theatre, the building was opened in 1900, and between then and

1918, hosted many of the major entertainers of the era, including Madam Helena Modjeska, Douglas Fairbanks Sr., Lillian Russell, Lon Chaney Sr., Sarah Bernhardt and Jason Philip Sousa.[231] Now a National Historic Landmark, the Calumet Theatre is perhaps the greatest surviving structure of Cornish overseas' theatrical culture. Though slightly later (built in 1914), the Opera House at Mineral Point, Wisconsin,[232] demonstrates much of this energy of Cornu-American theatrical endeavour, even if the plays presented there were by then more mainstream. In the early twentieth-century, the Opera House was famous for its promotion of vaudeville touring companies.

Another important area in the United States of America to which the Cornish travelled was Butte City, Montana, again to mine copper. Butte was an isolated community, filled with technologically-adept, Methodist Cornish, managing labouring Catholic Irish workers.[233] George D. Marsh and the Writers' Project of Montana have compiled a great deal of material concerning early performances in Butte, which must have been witnessed by at least some of the Cornish there. Possibly too, they would have contributed their own performances. The first recorded performance in the camp was in 1875, when a strolling Irish minstrel called John Maguire arrived. His act consisted of monologues and recitations, taking place in the King and Lowry Gambling Hall. A year later he was back again, this time in a room above the Brophy Grocery Company building, where 'planks resting upon empty nail kegs served as seats, and candles secured by nails driven in a scantling served as a light'.[234] This gives an indication of the kind of performances given and watched by the Cornish in Butte. In 1880, Owsley's Hall was opened as a regular theatre, and among the plays presented were *Camille*, *A Case for Divorce*, *Uncle Tom's Cabin* and *The Banker's Daughter*. By 1885, Butte had its own Grand Opera House, said to have been the finest one on the Pacific Coast, outside of San Francisco. Influential figures of America theatre, such as Richard 'Dick' Sutton often played Butte, though after the boom years and certainly by 1920, much of this theatrical energy had dissipated, as had much of the boom mining community. The pattern of 'boom-and-bust' mining therefore created a pattern of 'boom-and-bust' theatre across the United States of America: Dodgeville, Mineral Point and Galena in Wisconsin and Illinois succumbed to Calumet, Haughton and Hancock in Michigan, which then lost out to Boulder, Central City and Leadville. Todd has argued that travelling players probably accompanied the Cornish miners to where they travelled, though provides no further evidence of their activities, again because the activity was transitory.[235]

Leadville, in particular, had an active theatrical community for the Cornish there, perhaps because in its day it was known as one of the 'wickedest towns of the west'.[236] One of the most famous Cornishmen there was Charles

Fig. 68. Publicity leaflet for the Calumet Theatre, Calumet, 2004.

Algernon Sidney Vivian who, though born in Exeter in 1846, was the son of a Cornish clergyman. Vivian was one of the founders of the Benevolent Order of Elks and a famous entertainer, noted for his songs, skits and character sketches. An utter dandy, Vivian frittered away his money, but when playing Leadville or other mining towns in California, he found great success. He would bring the house down with a song titled 'Ten Thousand Miles Away', which reverberated emotionally with Cornish audiences, many thousands of miles away from Camborne and Redruth. Vivian even managed to produce a stage version of *Oliver Twist* in Leadville, though when aged only thirty-three he caught pneumonia and died in the severe winter of 1880. He perhaps stands as the most important Cornu-American theatrical entrepreneur and performer. His achievement would have been greater had he lived longer; we are left with a glimmer of an insight into theatre on the mining frontier. Another prime mover in the theatrical world of Leadville was Horace Austin Warner Tabor. Tabor was originally a stonemason, but became 'king' of the town, building both the Tabor Grand Hotel and the Opera House; the latter hosting entertainments by Oscar Wilde. By the middle of the 1890s, however, the price of silver collapsed and, yet again, people moved on. As mining travelled westwards, so did theatrical activity – to Deadwood,[237] Butte and Bingham and, in the south-west, Globe, Tombstone and Goldfield; finally on to Placerville, Virginia City and Grass Valley.

This latter centre of Cornish-Californian culture has been studied in detail by Shirley Ewart and Harold T. George. We know, for example, that in 1859 in Grass Valley, grand balls and suppers took place (perhaps similar to those in Truro, Falmouth and Penzance). In the following decades miners' picnics and fairs were popular, and conceivably there may have been vestiges of performance there, but the 'rules' of the Methodist church prevented people attending 'dancing and theatergoing'.[238] There were also the para-theatrical competitions in the form of drilling contests for Cornish miners, as well as 'wrassling' competitions which were sometimes held at theatres.[239] Most creative energy in Grass Valley, however, as in Cornu-Australian towns (see below), went towards the performance of Cornish carols, a tradition which, as McKinney has shown, continued into the twentieth and twenty-first centuries.[240] Sometimes abroad, it was the Cornish love of music and singing that triumphed rather than that other love of story and drama. There was, however, an interesting conjunction. As early as 1868, the Cornish brass band there turned out to serenade Alice Kingsbury, the star of a touring theatre company who that year visited the gold-mining town.[241] The show must have been highly respectable.

One individual who must have encountered Cornu-American theatre was Richard Jose. Born at Redruth in 1862, Jose was sent to Virginia City in

Nevada after his father died, searching for his uncle, only to find that he had disappeared. Jose later claimed a birth date of 1869, promoting his story as a child travelling alone across America. He also changed the pronunciation of his name, and hence his ethnicity. Jose, pronounced like 'Joe's' and rhyming with 'rose', is Cornish. Later in life, he added an accent, as in José (hoh-zay) to try to demonstrate an invented Hispanic heritage.[242] Initially, Jose had to fend for himself, but then headed for Carson City. Here he sang in saloons amongst other Cornish entertainers, and his incredible, high-pitched voice helped him claim he was younger than he actually was. While developing as an alto tenor and performer, he worked delivering bread to miners, and as a blacksmith in Reno. When in California in 1884, he joined a minstrel troupe, and by the 1890s he was appearing in New York, singing dozens of sentimental ballads, the most famous of which was *Silver Threads Among the Gold*.[243] Jose's reputation was as a singer, though through his travels across the United States of America (particularly in the mining frontier of the West) he would have encountered much Cornish theatre, ranging from burlettas like the ones at home in Redruth, to improvised sketches and comedies in the mining camps.[244] By the 1920s, Jose's voice was no longer in fashion, but after a period of readjustment (and becoming a Mason of the Ancient Arabic Order of the Mystic Shrine at San Francisco), he went on to become the Deputy Real Estate Commissioner of California. According to Todd, one ballad writer of the Sierras described Jose as follows:

Youthful minstrel of the Comstock,
Carson's barefoot ballad boy,
Who filled saloons with Cornish tunes
And miners' hearts with leaping joy.[245]

Clearly, Jose was operating in a tradition – well-established in Cornish life, during the eighteenth and nineteenth centuries – of the travelling entertainer. Although a singer rather than an actor, Jose shows many of the adaptable, trans-national qualities of Cornish performers, who, during this phase, had to ply their trade across a wider world stage. While the drama of previous centuries had moved towards 'high art' and was no longer performed, live theatre was still part of Cornish working-class experience in the late nineteenth century.

Theatre in Australia was less well-established, perhaps because of the highly-developed Methodist (and supposed anti-theatrical) culture of Cornish-dominated places such as South Australia's Moonta and Burra Burra. Cornish 'curls', midsummer bonfires and chapel anniversaries appear to be the

Fig. 69. 'St Meriadoc' at Norton's Park, Wantirna South, Melbourne, 1996. Courtesy of Bill and Gwen Phillips, and the Cornish Association of Victoria.

Fig. 70. 'Noah and the Ark' at Geelong, Australia, 1999 performed by the Cornish Association of Victoria. Courtesy of Bill and Gwen Phillips, and the Cornish Association of Victoria.

main events where ritual, performance and community interact and, certainly with the Methodist revivals of the mid-1870s, it was the chapels that were packed with audiences. Oswald Pryor, one of the leading historians of life in Moonta – 'Australia's Little Cornwall' – gives little indication that any theatrical culture occurred there at the end of the nineteenth century.[246] Payton, in his detailed observations on Moonta, notes that its Cornishness was singularly determined by the mining-Methodist heritage,[247] rather than any other significant cultural movements involving drama or theatre. This is still the case in Moonta and the rest of the 'Copper Triangle', where Cornishness is very much rooted in these twin threads of heritage, to the exclusion of anything else Cornish. Perhaps it was simply that the mechanics of theatre were too difficult in such locations.[248] There would also be difficulties in accessing scripts, properties and costumes. However, we do know that an Amateur Dramatic Club was formed in nearby Wallaroo in May 1872 and the group's debut was *The Smoked Miser, or The Benefit of Hanging*, with a supporting play called *My Wife's Out*. According to Wiltshire, these were performed 'in the local Assembly Rooms next to the Wallaroo Inn'.[249] Apparently 'special conveyances brought patrons from Kadina', which shows the significance of the event. Given the high number of Cornish in these towns, it seems likely they would have either watched or contributed. Certainly the format of these kind of burlettas was identical to what was occurring back home in Cornwall. While there is at least some detail of theatre operating in early Cornish communities in Australia, the evidence for performance in New Zealand is scant. Even first hand accounts, such as those now known as 'the Echunga Diaries' are devoid of theatrical references.[250]

The process of interaction between successive generations of those original emigrants and the Cornish at home has not stopped. At many of the Cornish gatherings across the world during the twentieth and twenty-first centuries, theatre and drama have formed part of the celebration of trans-national Cornishness. The sense of topsy-turvy 'Bakhtin/Barber'-carnival culture is a major feature of Australia's *Kernewek Lowender* festival,[251] while back home at the three *Dewhelans* [Homecoming] gatherings of 2002 (Falmouth), 2004 (Newquay) and 2008 (Looe), drama and theatre have formed part of the range of entertainment and activities for the returning overseas Cornish.[252] Meanwhile Sue Hill of Kneehigh Theatre was one of the presenters at the Eleventh Gathering of Cornish Cousins in Mineral Point in 2001,[253] while Sue Pellow, an accomplished actress in her own right, has performed her interpretation of Susanna Wesley at worldwide Cornish gatherings in the United States of America and Canada.[254] Perhaps more interestingly, in July 1992, the Centre for Celtic Studies at the University of Sydney staged *St Meriasek and King Tudor in*

Cornwall (composed of extracts from Myrna Combellack's English verse translation, and produced by Jonathan Wooding[255]), during the First Australian Conference of Celtic Studies, while in 1998 the Cornish Association of Victoria presented an extract of 'Noah and the Flood' from the *Ordinalia* at Geelong. The performance was interestingly presented in a mummers' play style, with characters' names on signs around their shoulders, and God on a step-ladder. The same Association had also presented an adaptation of *Bewnans Meriasek*, which they titled *St Meriadoc* with a cast of over twenty.[256] It was presented at Norton's Park, in Wantirna South, a suburb of Melbourne in 1996. Thus a text found a hundred years before in the late nineteenth century was still having contemporary relevance. Perhaps even more intriguing was the presentation at the 2002 Bendigo Cornish Festival of a quasi-political comic play written in Cornish by Peter Trevorah titled *She Doesn't Like Pasties*.[257] This is an intriguing move since, although there was little or no direct connection between the Cornish language and nineteenth-, let alone twenty-first century Cornwall, this was a Cornish community still defining themselves through Cornish-language, at the other side of the world. This is a prime example not only of the enduring nature of Celto-Cornish identity, but also of the continuum of Cornish-language drama. Intriguingly, although Trevorah's play contains elements of nineteenth-century Cornish stage farce, at the same time it consciously rejects the Methodist ethic that probably prevented more drama emerging in towns like Burra Burra and Moonta.

One of the most intriguing female faces of Cornish theatre during the late nineteenth century was Fanny Moody (1864-1945), a singer, known as the 'Cornish Nightingale'.[258] Her main connection is through that other main region to which the Cornish migrated: Southern Africa.[259] Moody came from Redruth, but spent much of her life touring Britain and the rest of the world, performing principal parts in *Mignon*, *The Bohemian Girl*, *Faust* and *Maritana*. At one concert in Redruth in 1884, while still only eighteen years old, she caused business at the Mining Exchange to come to a standstill; the performance was so successful that many people could not get in. She performed in over fifty operas (mainly with Carl Rosa) and in 1896 travelled to South Africa, performing there to great critical acclaim, singing songs such as *Trelawny*, *Tre, Pol and Pen* and *One and All* before audiences of Cornish miners of the Rand. In 1893 and 1895, Moody had toured Australia and North America respectively, meeting her Cornish supporters, in a world of trans-national Cornish theatre, yet it was in South Africa that her theatrical and musical success had the most impact:

I shall never forget the scene when I arrived at Johannesburg. A red carpet had been put down form the carriage door all the way along the platform which was crammed with Cornish people, all pressing forward to shake my hand. I was escorted by a prominent member of the large Cornish community in the city, and whole-hearted enthusiasm of the good, kind Cornish bodies made me feel like a queen. My hotel was near the famous Town Clock in Johannesburg where on Saturday nights all our dear 'Cousin Jackies' were wont to congregate to talk over the home news. Very soon the piano was pulled out on to the balcony and I was signing 'Home Sweet Home' to my fellow exiles far from home but still true Cornish people.[260]

Moody was certainly one of the closest people Cornwall had to the modern superstar. In 1898, she was interviewed by Laura Smith for Arthur Quiller-Couch's *Cornish Magazine*. A useful picture of theatrical 'touring' life for a woman is given, as Moody reflects on the response to her in Cornwall:

Our Cornish tour is the only one we undertake on our own responsibility. We are always sure of success there. Everywhere we meet with the most enthusiastic receptions, and friends seem to crop up at every corner. I often say that in all my travels I never come across any place to equal dear old Cornwall. Each time I come down I see the same friendly faces, the same familiar spots and I just long to be able to stay and sing for the pleasure of my friends.[261]

Though there is something of the star's language in this, it does offer a useful picture of the successful returning artiste. In the 1890s her husband, the impresario and singer Charles Manners, spent much of his time organising the Moody-Manner Opera Company, which evolved into one of the more popular operatic companies working in Britain at the end of the nineteenth century. Manners had previously been principal bass in the Carl Rosa Opera Company and at the Royal Italian Opera, and sang several songs alongside his wife in South Africa, adding this chorus to *One and All*:

Old Cornwall can boast of her daughters, too,
They're happy and gay and free.
There may be as good in other lands,
But better there cannot be.
So in that land I found my bride,
And thus I think you'll see
I've proved my taste to sing with pride,
A Cornish girl for me.[262]

At Moody's farewell concert in South Africa, she was presented with a gold and diamond tiara on behalf of the Cornish Association, inscribed with 'One and All'. A fan of Moody's at the time, one R. Arthur Thomas, summed up all the feelings of South Africa about the tour of this Cornish star of the day, by commenting how Moody's 'triumphant tour through South Africa has aroused all of us from our lethargy and it has done more to unite the Cornish people of this community than any other event in its history'.[263] The specific experience of Fanny Moody and the general thread of this chapter have given us an important picture of theatrical activity emanating from Cornwall and crossing the globe. Not only were Cornish stars of the theatre travelling across the world, but they also had superstar status. Meanwhile, the subject matter of Cornwall and Cornish identity had somehow transcended its origins to become significant on the global stage. At home, however, theatre had reached a turning point: in the beginning of the twentieth century, a very new kind of theatre was about to emerge. Cornwall was rapidly modernising, with some parties looking in the direction of tourism, and an even closer alignment with the old enemy: England.[264] Others were showing a theatrical interest as part of a wider revivalism of Cornish culture to replace the imminent collapse of hard-rock mining.[265] While the 'locomotive' impetus of the nineteenth century theatrical culture had been to look forward, suddenly there seemed a dramatic ethos that was looking closely in the rear-view mirror. This paradox was to shape the next fifty years of performance in ways unimagined only a few years before.

CHAPTER FIVE: NOTES AND REFERENCES

1. Robert W. Gutman, *Wagner: The Man, His Mind and His Music*, New York: Harcourt, Brace and World, 1968, p.163.

2. Ed Glinert (ed.), *The Savoy Operas: The Complete Gilbert and Sullivan*, London: Penguin, 2006, p.155.

3. Ronald Harwood, *All the World's a Stage*, London: Methuen, 1984, pp.207-9.

4. See Jeffrey Richards, *Sir Henry Irving: A Victorian Actor and His World*, London: Hambledon Continuum, 2006; Martin Holroyd, *A Strange and Eventful History: The Dramatic Lives of Ellen Terry, Henry Irving and Their Remarkable Families*, London: Chatto and Windus, 2008.

5. This is an interesting choice of text, considering its 'ancient Briton' theme. Kneehigh Theatre also chose to present *Cymbeline: King of Britain*, as their contribution to the Royal Shakespeare Company's staging of the full works of Shakespeare in 2006. See *The Times*, 25 September 2006.

6. Arthur Brasher, 'Sir Henry Irving's Childhood: The Great Actor's reminiscences of Cornwall' in *The Cornish Magazine*, Vol. I, 1898, pp.105-10. For detail on guizing in Cornwall, see Tony Deane and Tony Shaw, *Folklore of Cornwall*, Stroud: Tempus, 2003, pp.141-2 and pp.174-5.

7. Ibid., p.105.

8. For a context, see Arthur Cecil Todd, *The Search for Silver: Cornish Miners of Mexico 1824-1947*, St Austell: Cornish Hillside Publications, 2000 [1977].

9. Brasher, op.cit., p.106.

10. A similar attitude is found in the parents of the Anglo-Cornish novelists Silas, Joseph and Salome Hocking, and in the mother of Jack Clemo.

11. Brasher, op.cit., p.107.

12. Ibid., p.109. Interestingly, Irving apparently had a very distinctive way of both moving and talking, which divided his critics. Edward Gordon Craig (1872-1966), who was the son of Ellen Terry, apparently defended Irving. He would say, "Gud" for "God", "Cut-thrut dug" for "Cut throat dog" and "Tack the rup frum mey neck" for "Take the rope from my neck". Paul Edmundson therefore conjectures he would have said "Some are born great, some achieve greatness, and some have greatness thrust upon 'em" as "Sum arr boryrner greyt, sum arrcheever greytnesser, ond sum harver gretynesser thrubst uborn 'eym". Are Craig, and Edmundson actually commenting on Irving's residual Cornu-English here? For discussion of Irving's style of performance, see Paul Edmundson, *Twelfth Night: A Guide to the Text and its Theatrical Life*, Basingstoke: Palgrave Macmillan, 2005, pp.31-3.

13. George Clement Boase and William Prideaux Courtney (eds.), *Bibliotheca Cornubiensis*, London: Longman, Green, Reader and Dyer, 1874, 1878 and 1882, p.838. Knowles published *The Story of King Arthur* in 1860 and designed Tennyson's property 'Aldworth'.

14. Ibid., p.12. See Thomas Foster Barham, *Abdallah, or The Arabian Martyr: A Christian Drama in Three Acts and in Verse*, London: J. Hatchford and Son, 1820, and *Colonial Gardiner: A Christian Drama in Three Acts*, London: Hatchard and Son, 1823.

15. Ibid., p.1210.

16. Ibid., p.115.

17. See Robert Dyer, *Nine Years of an Actor's Life*, London: Rees, Orme, Brown, and Co., 1833, pp.41-2. For comparison to Cornwall, Dyer also writes about Devon and Wales. Of the Cullompton Theatre he writes that it was 'six weeks' unprofitable rustication'. Having passed some time in Carmarthen, he writes: 'We ... found much pleasure amongst our Welsh friends, who, like the natives of Cornwall, are emulous to show kindness to the stranger.' See p.89 and p.131 respectively.

18. Boase and Courtney. op.cit., p.302. This seems to have an echo of *The Curate's Daughter*. Could the drama have been retitled for its showing in Redruth?

19. Ibid., p.161. George Croker Fox (ed. and tr.), *The Prometheus of Aeschylus and the Electra of Sophocles, translated from the Greek, with notes intended to illustrate the typical character of the former*, London: Darton and Harvey, 1835, and *The Death of Demosthenes and other Original Poems, with the Prometheus and Agamemnon translated from the Greek*, London: John Bohn, 1839.

20. Ibid., p.170.

21. Anne Gibbons, *Mary Stuart: A Tragedy from the German of Schiller*, London: A. Schloss, 1838, and *An Easter Offering*, London: Edwards and Hughes, 1845.

22. Boase and Courtney, op.cit., p.337.

23. Ibid., p.49. The text was published by Samuel French.

24. George Clement Boase, *Collectanea Cornubiensia: A Collection of Biographical and Topographical Notes relating to the County of Cornwall*, Truro: Netherton and Worth, 1890, pp.1373-4.

25. Curling was the compiler of the famous 'Rifleman Harris' series of memoirs. These were the adventures of a soldier of the 95th Rifles during the Peninsular Campaign of the Napoleonic Wars. Entertainment for British troops on active service is a common theme in British culture. See the BBC's *It Ain't Half Hot Mum* – first broadcast between 1978 and 1981. For background on the Duke of Cornwall's Light Infantry in this campaign, see Hugo White, *One and All: A History of the Duke of Cornwall's Light Infantry, 1702-1959*, Padstow: Tabb House, 2006.

26. James Silk Buckingham, *Autobiography*, London: Longman, Brown, Green and Longmans, 1855.

27. Ibid., pp.48-9.

28. Leicester Silk Buckingham, *Aggravating Sam: A Comic Drama, in 2 Acts [and in prose]*, London: Thomas Hailes Lacy, 1854.

29. Leicester Silk Buckingham, *Take the Girl Away: A Comic Drama in Two Acts [and in prose]*, London: Thomas Hailes Lacy, 1855.

30. These were *For the Benefit of the Playful Crocodile* (1855), *An Impudent Puppy: A Comic Drama in 2 Acts* (Drury Lane, 7 November 1855), *So Very Obliging: A Farce* (Drury Lane, 6 December 1855) and *Two Precious Scoudrells: A Farce* (Strand Theatre, 21 August 1856). See Boase and Coutney, op.cit..

31. Leicester Silk Buckingham, *Belphegor: A new and original, acrobatic, dramatic, epigrammatic and decidedly un-aristocratic burlesque*, London: Thomas Hailes Lucy, 1856. This was presented at the Strand Theatre, 29 September 1856.

32. Boase and Courtney, op.cit. *Drat the Comet: A Farce* (1856), *Over the Way* (1856), *Don't Lend Your Umbrella: A Comic Drama* (1857), *The Gentleman Opposite: A Farce* (1857), *Do Shake Hands: A Farce* (1857) and *La Traviata: A Burlesque* (1857).

33. Ibid. *The Magic Mistletoe or a Harlequin Humbug and the Shams of London: A burlesque pantomime* (1856), *Jeannette's Wedding, An Operetta* (1857).

34. Ibid. These include *William Tell, An Original Burlesque* (1857), *Harlequin Novelty and the Princess who lost her heart* (1857), *A Woman in My Dust Hole* (1858), *Quixote Junior* (1859), *Virginus* (1859), *Cupid's Ladder* (1859), *A Pleasant Time of It* (1860), *You're Another* (1860), *The Phantom Wives* (1860), *The Forty Thieves* (1860), *Lucrezia Borgia* (1860), *Valentine and Orson* (1860), *Little Red Riding Hood and the Fairies of the Rose, Shamrock and Thistle* (1861), *Pizarro, or the Leotard of Peru* (1862), *The Merry Widow* (1863), *Silken Fetters* (1863), *The Silver Lining* (1864), *Love's Young Dream: A Comedietta* (1864), *Faces in the Fire* (1865) and *Love's Martyr* (1866).

35. Ibid., p.1155. For some definitions and a discussion of Kiddle-a-winks, or more properly, Kiddly-Winks, see K.C. Phillipps, *Westcountry Words and Ways*, Newton Abbot: David and Charles, 1976, pp.62-3. A reconstructed Cornu-American Kiddly-Wink is found at the Pendarvis Historic Site, Mineral Point, Wisconsin. See Mark H. Knipping and Korinne K. Oberle, *On the Shake Rag: Mineral Point's Pendarvis House, 1935-1970*, Mineral Point: The State Historical Society of Wisconsin and The Memorial Pendarvis Trust, 1990, pp.45-7.

36. Ibid., p.25. The pantomime was published as *Faw Fee Fo Fum, or Harlequin Jack the Giant Killer, A Comic Christmas Pantomime*, London: J. Tuck, 1867. I have been unable to track down a copy.

37 Robert Hunt (ed.), *Popular Romances of the West of England: The Drolls, Traditions, and Superstitions of Old Cornwall (First Series)*, London: John Camden Hotten, 1865, pp.35-77.

38. The rhyme is: 'As I was going to St Ives, I met a man with seven wives. And every wife had seven sacks, And every sack had seven cats, And every cat had seven kits. Kits, cats, sacks, wives, How many were going to St Ives?' The traditional answer is that only one person is going to St Ives: the narrator. The St Ives of the poem may or may not be the Cornish town.

39. Boase and Courtney, op.cit., p.483. A note on this is also found in *The Cornish Telegraph*, 25 September 1867.

40. The best examples are Silas K. Hocking, *Alec Green: A Tale of Sea Life*, London: Frederick Warne and Company, 1878, and *Sea Waif: A Tale of the Cornish Cliffs*, London: Frederick Warne and Company, 1882. See Alan M. Kent, *Pulp Methodism: The Lives and Literature of Silas, Joseph and Salome Hocking*, St Austell: Cornish Hillside Publications, 2002, pp.143-59.

41. Boase and Courtney, op.cit., p.21.

42. Alfred, Lord Tennyson, *Enoch Arden &c*, London: Dodo Press, 2008 [1864].

43. Ibid., p.97.

44. *The Cornish Telegraph*, 14 April 1869.

45. See Benjamin Luxon and Frederick Moyer, *Enoch Arden: Opus 38, Melodrama for Narrator and Piano. Poetry by Alfred, Lord Tennyson. Music by Richard Strauss,* Cornwall: JRI Recordings, 2002.

46. See Paul Banks (ed.), *The Making of Peter Grimes,* Cambridge: The Boydell Press, 2000. *Peter Grimes* was first performed in 1945. Opie sang in 1994 in a version by the English National Opera and in 1995 with the City of London Sinfonia and the London Symphony Orchestra. The text of *Peter Grimes* is based on the George Crabbe poem *The Borough* published in 1810. See Gavin Edwards (ed.), *George Crabbe: Selected Poems,* Harmondsworth: Penguin, 1991.

47. Boase and Courtney, op.cit., p.1018. The standard edition of his works is Wyndam Albery (ed.), *The Dramatic Works of James Albery, together with a Sketch of his Career, Correspondence Bearing Thereon, Press Notices, Casts, 2 Vols.*, London: Peter Davies, 1939.

48. Ibid.

49. Ibid., p.1004.

50. Ibid., p.1204. For background on this narrative, see Thomas Green, 'Tom Thumb and Jack the Giant Killer: Two Arthurian Fairytales?' in *Folklore,* Vol. 118, No. 2, 2007, pp.123-140.

51. Christine Poulson, *The Quest for the Grail: Arthurian Legend in British Art 1840-1920,* Manchester: Manchester University Press, 1999. Although this book's theme is art, Poulson makes a number of interesting remarks about phases of Arthurian revivalism in nineteenth-century Britain.

52. See Hunt, op.cit. There are long-standing connections between Arthuriana and St Michael's Mount in Cornwall. It is curious why Arthuriana has dropped out of pantomimes in Cornwall. There is one exception however. In 2000 Probus Parish Players presented *King Arthur.* See Alan M. Kent and Danny L.J. Merrifield, *The Book of Probus: Cornwall's Garden Parish,* Tiverton: Halsgrove, 2004, p.234.

53. Millington (ed.), op.cit., 2001 and Hatto (ed. and tr.), op.cit., 1967.

54. Joseph Kerman, 'Wagner's Tristan und Isolde: Opera as Symphonic Poem' in Joan Tasker Grimbert (ed.), *Tristan and Isolde: A Casebook,* New York and London: Garland, 1995, pp.357-76.

55. Raymond Furness, 'Wagner and Decadence' in Grimbert (ed.), op.cit., pp.377-424.

56. Chromaticism refers to a compositional technique which intersperses primary pitches and chords with other pitches of the chromatic scale. Harmonic suspension is when tension is created for the listeners by a series of prolonged and unfinished musical cadences. I am indebted to Simon Cartwright for this information.

57. Arthur Schopenhauer (1788-1860) was born in Danzig and is known for his gloomy philosophical writings.

58. *The Song of the Nibelungs* is an epic poem in Middle High German.

59. See Richard Wagner, *Mein Leben*, English translation at Project Gutenburg: http://www.gutenberg.org/dirs/etex04/wglf210.txt

60. E.F.J. Payne (ed. and tr.), *Arthur Schopenhauer: The World as Will and Representation*, Vols I and II, New York: Dover, 1967.

61. Malvina Schorr's hoarse throat prevented the planned premiere on 15 May. Three weeks after the actual premiere, Ludwig Schnorr von Carolsfeld died suddenly.

62. See Mark Twain, *Chicago Daily Tribune*, 6 December 1891. Available on-line at: http://www.twainquotes.com/Travel1891/Dec1891.html. Twain's original name was Clemens, and his mother's family came from Camborne.

63. This is in line with von Strassbourg.

64. Translation from Daniel Barenboim (cond.), *Tristan und Isolde*, Berlin: Teldec, 1995, p.28 of CD Insert. The Tristan theme has been given further attention in the musical canon of contemporary Cornwall. See Celtic Legend, *Tristan and Isolde*, France: Well Played Music, 2005, and Mike O'Connor, *Tristan and Iseult*, Wadebridge: Lyngham House, n.d.

65. A.T. Hatto (ed. and tr.), *Wolfram von Eschenbach: Parzival*, London: Penguin, 1980.

66. For examples of Merlin archetypes, see Michael Dames, *Merlin and Wales: A Magician's Landscape*, London: Thames and Hudson, 2002. See also Nikolai Tolstoy, *The Quest for Merlin*, London: Hamish Hamilton, 1985.

67. For the debate, see Dieter Borchmayer, *Drama and the World of Richard Wagner*, Princeton: Princeton University Press, 2003.

68. Bryan Magee, *The Tristan Chord*, New York: Owl Books, 2002.

69. Boase, op.cit., pp.1373-4.

70. Ibid.

71. Irish: *Medb*; Welsh: *Mabb*.

72. See Mercutio's speech in Romeo and Juliet, Act I, Scene iv. See also Ben Johnson's *The Entertainment at Althorp* and Michael Drayton's *Nymphidia*.

73. See Hunt, op.cit., pp.70-130.

74. Boase, op.cit., pp. 810-11.

75. See the observations of Mike Leigh, in Glinert, op.cit. pp.vii-xvi.

76. See Ian Bradley, *Oh Joy! Oh Rapture! The Enduring Phenomenon of Gilbert and Sullivan*, Oxford: Oxford University Press, 1986, and Michael Ainger, *Gilbert and Sullivan: A Dual Biography*, Oxford: Oxford University Press, 2002.

77. Cornwall was being marketed as a tourist destination by this time. See Peter Laws, 'The Cornish Riviera – Architects and Builders Provide the Necessary Ingredients' in Joanna Mattingly and June Palmer (eds.), *From Pilgrimage to*

Package Tour, Truro: Royal Institution of Cornwall, 1992. For a context, also see Philip Payton and Paul Thornton, 'The Great Western Railway and the Cornish-Celtic Revival' in Philip Payton (ed.), *Cornish Studies: Three*, Exeter: University of Exeter Press, 1995, pp. 83-103.

78   See Bradley, op.cit.

79.   See *The Daily News*, 29 December 1879, p.11; *The Figaro*, 17 January 1880, pp.12-13; *The Era*, 18 January 1880, p.15.

80.   The author saw a version at the Sydney Opera House in 2006, which was heavily influenced by Walt Disney's *The Pirates of the Caribbean* film trilogy. The Pirate King was dressed like Jack Sparrow.

81.   Boase, op.cit.

82.   *The Era*, 13 December 1884, p.15.

83.   Consider the legal arguments in *Bewnans Meriasek*. See also Simon Parker, *A Star on the Mizzen*, Liskeard: Giss' On Books, 1997; Nick Darke, *The Riot*, London: Methuen, 1999. Parker's two-man show – with himself and actor Jonathon Plunkett – was presented at the Acorn Theatre, Penzance in 1997.

84.   See Glinert, op.cit., pp.425-84. Ruddy was apparently too similar to 'bloody' and so was shortly changed.

85.   Boase, op.cit.

86.   Places such as Redruth and Rejerrah have a similar construction, though the intention here could be to pun on 'red herring'.

87.   See Semmens, op.cit., 2008; Hunt, op.cit., 1865; Kelvin Jones, *Witchcraft in Cornwall: An Account of Witchcraft, its Practice, its Customs and Condemnation*, St Just in Penwith: Sir Hugo Books, 1995. For a contemporary context, see Ronald Hutton, *The Triumph of the Moon: A History of Modern Pagan Witchcraft*, Oxford: Oxford University Press, 1999.

88.   Not to be confused with Herman Melville, the author of *Moby Dick*.

89.   See *The Era*, 6 February 1887, p.7. Although this report says the production occurred in the United States of America, it fails to inform the reader in exactly which city.

90.   Ibid., 27 August 1887, p.7 and p.11. The report appears to conflate Joan and Jane.

91.   Ibid., 22 November 1887, p.8.

92.   Boase, op.cit.

93.   Given the decline in celebration of St Piran's Day since the Middle Ages, it is most likely that this was unintentional.

94.   *The Times*, 9 April 1888, p.8; *The Era*, 14 April 1888, p.9.

95.   See, for example, Janna Roslyn in Susan Howatch, *Penmarric*, London: Hamish Hamilton, 1971; Anne Trevenna in Elizabeth Ann Hill, *The Driftwood Fire*, London: Heinemann, 1996; and Alice Tregowan in Anita Burgh, *Daughters of a*

Granite Land 1: The Azure Bowl, London: Chatto and Windus, 1989. See also Mary Yellan in Daphne du Maurier, *Jamaica Inn*, London: Arrow Books, 1992 [1936].

96. See *The Cornish Telegraph* 19 April 1888, p.8. J. Carne Ross was a medical doctor.

97. Thomas Shaw Methodism Collection, Courtney Library, Royal Institution of Cornwall.

98. I am indebted to John C.C. Probert and Cedric Appleby for their correspondence and comments here.

99. *The Cornish Guardian*, 18 June 1926, p.7. A similarity to the Hockings can be observed in the works of the Welsh novelist Daniel Owen (1836-1835) who reacted to similar nonconformist prejudice to fiction.

100. H. Spencer Toy, *The Methodist Church at Launceston*, Launceston: Launceston Wesleyan Methodist Church, p.45.

101. Letter to the author, 13 September 2008.

102. John C.C. Probert, *Worship and Devotion of Cornish Methodism*, Redruth: John C.C. Probert, 1979, p.110.

103. John Rule, 'Methodism, Popular Beliefs and Village Culture in Cornwall 1800-50' in Robert Storch (ed.), *Popular Culture and Custom in Nineteenth-Century England*, London and Canberra: Croom Helm, 1982, pp.48-70. This article also appears in John Rule (ed.), *Cornish Cases: Essays in Eighteenth and Nineteenth Century Social History*, Southampton: Clio Publishing, 2006, pp.162-89.

104. Ibid., p.50. For an additional perspective, see John Rule, 'Idle Hands? Controlling non-Work Time in England c.1750-1815' in *Il Tempo Libero Economia E Società*, No. 26, 1995, pp.689-703.

105. B. Harrison, 'Religion and Recreation in Nineteenth-century England' in *Papers Presented to the Past and Present Conference on Popular Religion*, July, 1966, p.6.

106. See David Shepherd, *Bakhtin: Carnival and Other Subjects*, Amsterdam, Georgia: Rodophi B. V. Editions, 1993; C.L. Barber, *Shakespeare's Festive Comedy: A Study of Dramatic Form and its relation to Social Custom*, Oxford: Oxford University Press, 1959. See also Ronald Hutton, *The Rise and Fall of Merry England: The Ritual Year 1400-1700*, Oxford: Oxford University Press, 1994.

107. Rule, op.cit.

108. Ibid.

109. There are numerous examples in Cornish mining history, but it was particularly so in South-Australian Cornish communities, and embodied in figures such as Captain Henry Richard Hancock. See Philip Payton, *Making Moonta: The Invention of Australia's Little Cornwall*, Exeter: University of Exeter Press, 2007.

110. Many of these are fictionalised in the work of Silas Kitto and Joseph Hocking. See Kent, op.cit., 2002.

111. See John Wesley, *Journal*, London: Everyman, 1906, Vol. 1, p.420, p.425; Vol. 2, p. 99, p.265.

112. S. Colley, *Life of the Rev. Thomas Collins*, London: Privately published, 1871, pp.297-9.

113. There are threads of this in A.S.D. Smith, *The Story of the Cornish Language: Its Extinction and Revival*, Camborne: Smith, 1947; P.A.S. Pool, *The Death of Cornish*, Cornwall: Cornish Language Board, 1982, but perhaps not as vitriolic as one might expect. The point may be that much of the damage was already done. See also 'A Meditation upon John Wesley's Short English Grammar' in Alan M. Kent, *Love and Seaweed*, St Austell: Lyonesse Press, 2002, pp.38-9.

114. *Diary of Thomas Nicholl*, MSS. Entry 5 June 1843, CRO. See Rule, op.cit., p.58.

115. See *West Briton*, 31 May 1844. This incident is also recorded in Lawrence Maker, *Cob and Moorstone: The Curious History of some Methodist Churches*, London: Epworth Press, 1935.

116. Letter dated 5 February 1875. See the *Jenner Papers*, Box 8, Royal Institution of Cornwall.

117. For comment on this, see Bernard Deacon, "The hollow jarring of the distant steam engines': images of Cornwall between West Barbary and the Delectable Duchy', in Ella Westland (ed.), *Cornwall: The Cultural Construction of Place*, Penzance: The Patten Press and the Institute of Cornish Studies, 1997, pp.7-24. See also Deacon, in Kent (ed.), *Voices from West Barbary: An Anthology of Anglo-Cornish Poetry*, London: Francis Boutle Publishers, 2000, pp.13-14.

118. Rule, op.cit., p.61.

119. Alan M. Kent, *The Literature of Cornwall: Continuity, Identity, Difference 1000-2000*, Bristol: Redcliffe, 2000, p.137.

120. Rupert Davies, *Methodism*, Peterborough: Epworth Press, 1985 [1963]; Frederick C. Gill, *The Romantic Movement and Methodism: A Study of English Romanticism and the Evangelical Revival*, London: The Epworth Press, 1937.

121. See Thomas Shaw, *The Bible Christians*, London: Epworth Press, 1965, and *A History of Cornish Methodism*, Truro: D. Bradford Barton, 1967; John C.C. Probert, *A Sociology of Cornish Methodism*, Truro: Cornwall Methodist Historical Association, 1971; Peter Isaac, *A History of Evangelical Christianity in Cornwall*, Gerrards Cross: WEC Press, 2000. Individual communities also remain quiet on this issue. See, for example, Thomas Shaw (ed.), *Book of Memories of Cornish Methodism: Parts One and Two*, Truro: Cornwall Methodist Historical Association, 1992 and 1994.

122. There is little on this issue in *Proceedings of the Weslyan Historical Society*'s fifty volumes. The ten volumes of the regular *The Journal of the Cornish Methodist Historical Association* also suffers from a paucity of articles on this topic.

123. This has considerable continuity when one also thinks of the controversial dramas of Bernard Walke at St Hilary. See Bernard Walke, *Twenty Years at St Hilary*, London: Anthony Mott, 1982 [1935]. See also Chapter 6.

124. Boase and Courtney, op.cit., p.1230.

125. Many preaching pits in Cornish communities have been used as theatrical venues in the twentieth and twenty-first centuries. A good example is Indian Queens Pit, where *Peer Gynt* (1991) and *Ship of Fools* (1992) were presented by Kneehigh Theatre. Preaching pits are given surprisingly scant attention in Jeremy Lake, Jo Cox and Eric Berry, *Diversity and Vitality: The Methodist and Nonconformist Chapels of Cornwall*, Truro: Cornwall Archaeological Unit, 2001.

126. For a history, see Thomas Shaw, *Gwennap Pit: John Wesley's Amphitheatre, a Cornish Pardon*, Busveal: Busveal Methodist Church Council, 1992.

127. Gwennap Pit has featured recent performances such as *A Wesley Tableau*. In 1999, the Ordinalia Trust considered putting on a performance of *Ordinalia* at the location, in an interesting merging of Catholic and Protestant Cornwall.

128. Kent, op.cit., 2000, pp.276-84.

129. Matthew Spriggs, 'William Scawen (1600-1689) – A Neglected Cornish Patriot and Father of the Cornish Language Revival' in Philip Payton (ed.), *Cornish Studies: Thirteen*, Exeter: University of Exeter Press, 2005, pp.99-125.

130. Smith, op.cit., pp.12-13; Piotr Stalmaszczyk, *Celtic Presence: Studies in Celtic Languages and Literatures: Irish, Scottish Gaelic and Cornish*, Łódê: Łódê University Press, 2005, pp.126-7.

131. Alan M. Kent and Tim Saunders (eds. and trs.), *Looking at the Mermaid: A Reader in Cornish Literature 900-1990*, London: Francis Boutle Publishers, 2000, pp.357-8.

132. Peter Berresford Ellis, *The Cornish Language and its Literature*, London and Boston: Routledge and Kegan Paul, 1974, pp.125-46.

133. Bernard Deacon, *Cornwall: A Concise History*, Cardiff: University of Wales Press, 2007, pp.186-90.

134. See Kent and Saunders, op.cit., pp.310-7.

135. See Richard Polwhele, *The History of Cornwall*, London: Cadell and Davies, 1803, pp.3-108. This section contains substantial material on drama in Devon and Somerset. Polwhele was educated at Truro Grammar School and became Vicar at Manaccan. He contributed to *The Gentleman's Magazine* and to *The Anti-Jacobin Review*.

136. For a life, see Arthur Cecil Todd, *Beyond the Blaze: A Biography of Davies Gilbert*, Truro: D. Bradford Barton, 1967.

137. Davies Gilbert, *Mount Calvary... Interpreted in the English Tongue... by John Keigwin*, London: J.B. Nichols, 1826.

138. Davies Gilbert, *The Creation of the World with Noah's Flood, written in Cornish in the Year 1611 by Wm. Jordan, with an English Translation by John Keigwin*, London, J.B. Nichols, 1827.

139. Ellis, op.cit., 1974, p.132.

140. Gilbert, op.cit., 1826, p.10.

141. See Kent and Saunders, op.cit., pp.315. This was published under the pseudonym of Edward Collins Giddy. Davies took his wife's name (Gilbert).

142. This is a trend that some observers might argue has continued until the present. Many twentieth-century Cornish-language texts were shoddily presented, perhaps because of the low print-runs.

143. See the design of Graham Thomas and Nicholas Williams (eds. and trs.), *Bewnans Ke: The Life of St Kea – A Critical Edition with Translation*, Exeter: University of Exeter Press, 2007, and Kent and Saunders (ed.), op.cit.

144. For impressions of this period of cultural history in Cornwall, see P.A.S. Pool, *The Death of Cornish*, Cornwall: The Cornish Language Board, 1982; Craig Weatherhill, *Cornish Place Names and Language*, Wilmslow: Sigma, 1995, pp.147-9; Rod Lyon, *Cornish: The Struggle for Survival*, Nancegollan: Tavas an Weryn, 2001.

145. Edwin Norris (ed. and tr.), *The Ancient Cornish Drama*, London and New York: Blom, 1968 [1859]. This was originally published by Oxford University Press.

146. Whitley Stokes, 'The Passion: A Middle Cornish Poem' in *Transactions of the Philological Society*, 1860-1, Appendix, pp.1-100.

147. Whitley Stokes (ed. and tr.), *Gwreans an Bys: The Creation of the World*, London and Edinburgh: Williams and Norgate, 1864.

148. John Bellow, 'On the Cornish Language' in *Report of the Royal Cornwall Polytechnic Society*, 1861. Bellows offers negative comments about Cornish literature. However, he does comment that the 'Cornish language lies like a buried city under our feet', implying that the Cornish do not have to look far to find it.

149. This was one of the numerous manuscripts amassed at the mansion of Hengwrt, near Dolgellau, Gwynedd by the Welsh antiquarian Robert Vaughan (c.1592-1667), which later passed to the newly-established National Library of Wales as the Peniarth Manuscripts. See Whitley Stokes (ed. and tr.), *The Life of Saint Meriasek, Bishop and Confessor: A Cornish Drama*, London: Trübner and Co., 1872, p.1.

150. See *Archaeologia Cambrensis*, 1869, p.409. Robert Williams published his *Lexicon Cornu-Britannicum* in 1865.

151. See *Revue Celtique*, Vol. 3, p.85 and p.224. See also Nicholas Orme (ed.), *Nicholas Roscarrock's Lives of the Saints of Cornwall and Devon*, Exeter: Devon and Cornwall Record Society, 1992, p.68.

152. Hunt, op.cit., p.21. Hunt notes that he vaguely recalls a story titled Hender the Huntsman of Lanhydrock he was told in Bodmin, but failed to note the full narrative. The full narrative of a Cornish story about monks poisoning a stream, and of a devil (connected with a local tower) who played strange pranks on people, were also unrecorded. These failings were the impetus for his work.

153. Cf. Ellis Owen, *Welsh Folk-Lore: A Collection of the Folk-Tales and Legends of North Wales*, Felinfach: Llanerch, 1996 [1887], and F.M. Luzel, *Folktales from Armorica*, Felinfach: Llanerch, 1992 [c.1870]. Both of these volumes contain many narratives, but are neither as comprehensive nor detailed as the Cornish collections.

154. Numerous texts could be held up as examples here, but see Great Western Railway, *Cornwall's Legend Land*, Vols. 1 and 2, Penzance: Oakmagic Publications, 1997 [1922]; Craig Weatherhill, *The Lyonesse Stone*, Padstow: Tabb House, 1991; Jack Trelawny, *Kernowland: The Crystal Pool*, Waltham Abbey: Campion Books, 2005.

155. The Reverend H.J. Whitfield completed similar work on the Isles of Scilly, but there are relatively few theatrical or para-theatrical concepts within his collection. See H.J. Whitfield, *Scilly and its Legends*, London: Timpkin, Marshall and Co.,1852.

156. A. Pearson, *Robert Hunt, F.R.S. (1807-1887)*, Cornwall: Federation of Old Cornwall Societies, 1976. Hunt's interests in poetry and science have other parallels in Cornwall, with the work of Humphry Davy (1779-1829). For both writers' poetry, see Kent (ed.), op.cit., 2000, pp. 45-57 and p.114-5.

157. See Boase and Courtney, p.1090.

158. Hunt, op.cit., pp. 26-7.

159. Ibid. This informant was probably Bottrell.

160. Ibid., p.32.

161. Ibid.

162. Ibid., pp.91-5.

163. Ibid., pp.130-46. Lots of folklore collections also consider Tregeagle. See the following for some examples: J. Henry Harris, *Cornish Saints and Sinners*, London: Jane Lane The Bodley Head Limited, 1906, pp. 244-6; Donald R. Rawe, *Traditional Cornish Stories and Rhymes*, Padstow: Lodenek Press, 1992 [1971], pp.36-8.

164. John Clifford (ed. and tr.), *Johann Wolfgang von Goethe: Faust*, London: Nick Hern Books, 2006. See also Paul Bishop, *A Companion to Goethe's Faust, Parts 1 and 2*, New York: Camden House, 2006. For a study on the pan-European dimension of Faust, see Ian Watts, *Myths of Modern Individualism: Faust, Don Quixote, Don Juan, Robinson Crusoe*, Cambridge: Cambridge University Press, 1996.

165. See Linda Cookson (ed.), *Christopher Marlowe: Doctor Faustus*, Harlow: Longman, 1984.

166. Robert Hunt, *Popular Romances of the West of England: The Drolls, Traditions and Superstitions of Old Cornwall (Second Series)*, London: John Camden Hotten, 1865, pp.270-1.

167. Ibid., p.312.

168. For more on this paradox, see Alan M. Kent, "Some ancientry that lingers': Dissent, difference and dialect in the Cornish and Cornu-English Literature of Robert Morton Nance' in Peter W. Thomas and Derek Williams (eds.), *Setting Cornwall on its Feet: Robert Morton Nance 1873-1959*, London: Francis Boutle Publishers, 2007, pp.96-152. There have been various attempts to expurgate St George material from traditional Cornish festival and drama, and replace it with St Piran.

169. Hunt, *(Second Series)*, op.cit., p.389.

170. The final lines of 'Origo Mundi' contain the word *flogholeth* [childhood] above the word *passyon* [Passion] in MS. Bodl. 791, Oxford.

171. Hunt, *(Second Series)*, op.cit.

172. For exploration of this, see Georgina Boyes (ed.), *Step Change: New Views on Traditional Dance*, London: Francis Boutle Publishers, 2001.

173. Hunt, *(Second Series)*, op.cit., pp.389-90.

174. Ibid., p.391. Hub-Bub is often a devil figure (Beelzebub).

175. Ibid., pp.392-5.

176. Ibid., p.392.

177. Ibid., p.395.

178. Ibid., pp.398-9.

179. Ibid., p.442.

180. See *Black Letter Pamphlet: News from Pe[n]rin in Cornwall of a most Bloody and un-exampled Murder*, Quarto, Bodley, 4 M G29 (2), Oxford.

181. Hunt, *(Second Series)*, op.cit., p.444. This quotation, cited in Hunt, is from *Philological Inquiries*.

182. William Bottrell (ed.), *Traditions and Hearthside Stories of West Cornwall: First Series*, Penzance: W. Cornish, 1870, p.iv. For origins on the word 'droll' in Cornwall, see Henry Jenner, 'Some Possible Arthurian Place-Names in West Penwith' in *Journal of the Royal Institution of Cornwall*, 1912, p.87.

183. Ibid., p.v-vi.

184. Ibid., p.v.

185. Ibid., p.51.

186. Cf. The Camborne mummers' play. See Chapter One.

187. Bottrell, op.cit., pp.141-51, and pp. 189-212.

188. Ibid., p.212.

189. William Bottrell (ed.), *Traditions and Hearthside Stories of West Cornwall: Second Series*, Penzance: Beare and Son, 1873, p.8.

190. Ibid., pp.36-59.

191. Bill Mitchell, Mike Shepherd, Emma Rice, and Victoria Moore, *Kneehigh Theatre*, Truro: Kneehigh Theatre, c.2005, p.1. Joan Miró (1893-1983) was an ethnic Catalan, famous for his sculpture, paintings and ceramics.

192. Bottrell, op.cit., 1873, pp.65-6.

193. Ibid., pp.268-70.

194. This is BL. MS. Harley 1782. A facsimile copy is found in Harry Woodhouse (ed.), *The Cornish Passion Poem*, Cornwall: Gorseth Kernow, 2007.

195. See Paul Broadhurst, *Sacred Shrines: In Search of the Holy Wells of Cornwall*, Launceston: Pendragon Press, 1991; Cheryl Straffon, *Fentynyow Kernow: In Search of Cornwall's Ancient Wells*, St Just-in-Penwith: Meyn Mamvro, 1998.

196. See *Cornish Telegraph*, 29 January 1896, and Boase and Courtney, op.cit., p.983.

197. William Bottrell (ed.), *Traditions and Hearthside Stories of West Cornwall: Third Series*, Penzance: F. Rodda, 1880, p.177.

198. Ibid.

199. Ibid.

200. See Richard McGrady, *Traces of Ancient Mystery: The Ballad Carols of Davies Gilbert and William Sandys*, Redruth: Institute of Cornish Studies, 1993.

201 See D.M. Thomas (ed.), *Songs from the Earth: Selected Poems of John Harris*, Padstow: Lodenek Press, 1977; Paul Newman, *The Meads of Love: The Life and Poetry of John Harris (1820-84)*, Redruth: Dyllansow Truran, 1994; Jacqueline Anne Harding, *John Harris (1820-1884), 'The Cornish Miner Poet': An Exploration of the Cultural Construction of Place and the Creation of Cornish Identity*, Open University MA Dissertation, 2008.

202. Andrew C. Symons, 'John Harris – A Weaving of Traditions' in *An Baner Kernewek / The Cornish Banner*, No.82, 1995, pp.11-12.

203. B.D. Vere's *King Arthur: His Symbolic Story in Verse*, 1930, cited in Amy Hale, Alan M. Kent and Tim Saunders (eds. and trs.), *Inside Merlin's Cave: A Cornish Arthurian Reader 1000-2000*, London: Francis Boutle Publishers, 2000, pp.193-8; Alan M. Kent, *Nativitas Christi / The Nativity: A New Cornish Mystery Play*, London: Francis Boutle Publishers, 2006; Ken George, *Flogholeth Krist / The Cornish Ordinalia – the missing play: The Childhood of Christ*, Cornwall: Kesva an Taves Kernewek, 2006.

204. See, for example, 'Ballad of the Bread Man' in Charles Causley, *Collected Poems 1951-1975*, London: Macmillan, 1975, pp.165-7. See also Papers of Charles Causley EUL MS. 50a, Exeter.

205. Bottrell, op.cit., 1873, pp.288-9.

206. Bottrell, op.cit., 1880, pp.48-59.

207. Ibid., pp.97-9. Bottrell notes that 'the guest, for whose entertainment the old men had furbished up their memories, said, 'that piece is a capital one, and it seems all the better for the way you have told it. Your dialect is pleasant to the ear...' Bottrell also comments that many Cornish drolls remind him of Irish stories.

208. Ibid., p.173-4. The old men are Job Munglar and Jan Trudle, who are established fictional characters from 1803 onwards. See Polwhele, op.cit.

209. Ibid., p.175-6.

210. W.B. Forfar, *The Exhibition and Other Cornish Poems*, Truro: Netherton and Worth, n.d., pp.80-3.

211. See Brenda Wootton, *Pantomime Stew*, Hayle: Sue Luscombe, 1994. Brenda Wootton (1928-1994) was a famous Cornish folk-singer and radio presenter. Mrs Rosewarne was known as the 'Queen of Camborne' and often featured on BBC Radio Cornwall in the late 1990s/early 2000s.

212. Margaret A. Courtney (ed.), *Cornish Feasts and Folklore*, Exeter: Cornwall Books, 1989 [1890], pp.1-55.

213. Ibid., p.10. This creature has come to be embodied as 'Penglaz' or 'Pengwyn'. Pengwyn was used as a symbol by the Cornish dance group *Cam Kernewek*, from the 1980s onwards, and has more recently been incorporated into Penzance's Golowan Festival. The device is sometimes called the 'mast horse'. For context on this kind of activity, see E.C. Cawte, *Ritual Animal Disguise: A Historical and Geographical Study of Animal Disguise in the British Isles*, Cambridge: D.S. Brewer, 1978, pp.157-77; Violet Alford, *The Hobby Horse and other Animal Masks*, London: The Merlin Press, 1978, pp.35-44. Historically, there was an 'oss at Combe Martin, and a tradition continues at Minehead.

214. Ibid.

215. Ibid.

216. Ibid., p.11.

217. Montol occurs between 14 and 22 December. The festival was 'revived' in 2007.

218. Ibid.

219. Ibid., p.57.

220. Ibid., pp.81-2.

221. Ibid., pp.100-1.

222. For a context for this, see Brian Day, *A Chronicle of Celtic Folk Custom: A Day-to-Day Guide to Folk Traditions*, London: Hamlyn, 2000.

223. Boase, op.cit., pp.1579-96.

224. Kevin Scrivers and Stephen Smith, *Showmen of the Past: Hancocks of the West*, Telford: New Era Publications, 2006, p.4.

225. See Arthur Cecil Todd, *The Cornish Miner in America*, Spokane, Washington: Arthur H. Clark Co., 1995 [1967]; A.L. Rowse, *The Cornish in America*, Redruth: Dyllansow Truran, 1991 [1969]; John Rowe, *The Hard Rock Men:*

Cornish Immigrants and the North American Mining Frontier, Liverpool: Liverpool University Press, 1974; Jim Faull, *The Cornish in Australia*, Melbourne: A.E. Press, 1983; Philip Payton, *The Cornish Miner in Australia: Cousin Jack Down Under*, Redruth: Dyllansow Truran, 1984.

226. Richard Dawe, *Cornish Pioneers in South Africa: Gold and Diamonds, Copper and Blood*, St Austell: Cornish Hillside Publications, 1998; Philip Payton, *The Cornish Overseas*, Fowey: Alexander Associates, 1999; Sharon P. Schwartz, *Voices of the Cornish Mining Landscape*, Truro: Cornwall County Council, 2008; Alan M. Kent and Gage McKinney (eds.), *The Busy Earth: A Reader in Global Cornish Literature 1700-2000*, St Austell: Cornish Hillside Publications, 2008.

227. Ibid.

228. Arthur W. Thurner, *Strangers and Sojourners: A History of Michigan's Keweenaw Peninsula*, Detroit: Wayne State University Press, 1994.

229. Ibid., pp.69-9.

230. See Arthur W. Thurner, *Calumet Copper and People: History of a Michigan Mining Community, 1864-1970*, Hancock, Michigan: Turner, 1974.

231. Calumet Theatre, *Discover the Calumet Theatre in Historic Calumet, Michigan*, leaflet, 2002.

232. See George Fielder, *Mineral Point: A History*, Madison: The State Historical Society of Wisconsin, 1997 [1962]. In the twenty-first century, Mineral Point has a local amateur dramatic group called the Shake Rag Players. This group is named after a phenomenon in Mineral Point, when the wives of miners at Christmas Mine would come out into the street and wave rags when their pasties were ready to eat.

233. This ethnic tension is explored in Michael P. Malone, *The Battle for Butte: Mining and Politics on the Northern Frontier 1864-1906*, Helena: Montana Historical Society Press, 1981.

234. George D. Marsh and the Writers' Project of Montana, *Copper Camp: The Lusty Story of Butte, Montana, The Richest Hill on Earth*, Helena: Riverbend Publishing, 2002 [1943], pp.285-6.

235. See Todd, op.cit., p.101.

236. See Alan M. Kent, *Cousin Jack's Mouth-Organ: Travels in Cornish America*, St Austell: Cornish Hillside Publications, 2004, pp.84-105.

237. This was the site of the legendary Deadwood Dick stories – in part inspired by the Ruthvoes [Ruthers]-born bullion guard Richard Bullock. He is sometimes known as the 'china-clay cowboy'.

238. Shirley Ewart and Harold T. George, *Highly Respectable Families: The Cornish of Grass Valley, California 1854-1954*, Grass Valley: Comstock Bonanza Press, 1998, p.50.

239. See Rowe, op.cit., p.274. At the Alhambra Theatre in Virginia City, a prize of two hundred and fifty dollars was on offer for the winner of a wrestling match.

240. Gage McKinney, *When Miners Sang: The Grass Valley Carol Choir*, Grass Valley: Comstock Bonanza Press, 2001.

241. See *Grass Valley Union*, 3 January 1868.

242. For some observations on Cornish and Hispanic heritage, see Alan M. Kent, "'Mozeying on down…'": The Cornish Language in America' in Hildegard L.C. Tristram (ed.), *The Celtic Languages in Contact*, Potsdam: Potsdam University Press, 2007, pp.193-217.

243. See Todd, op.cit., p.104-5.

244. For the para-theatrical feel of these camps, see Reuben H. Margolin (ed.), *Bret Harte's Goldrush*, Berkeley: Heyday Books, 1997; Barbara Braasch, *California's Gold Rush Country*, Medina, Washington: Johnston Associates International, 1996; Rodman W. Paul (ed.), *A Victorian Gentlewoman: The Reminiscences of Mary Hallock Foote*, San Marino: Huntington Library, 2000 [1972].

245. Todd, op.cit., p.6.

246. Oswald Pryor, *Australia's Little Cornwall*, Adelaide: Rigby, 1962.

247. Payton, op.cit., 2007.

248. This did not stop a performance of George Farquhar's *The Recruiting Officer* in Botany Bay in 1789 by an all-convict cast. See Robert Hughes, *The Fatal Shore: A History of the Transportation of Convicts to Australia, 1787-1868*, London: Vintage, 2003 [1986], p.340. One of the performers is thought to have been the Fowey-born Mary Bryant.

249. See Rex Wiltshire, *Copper to Gold: A History of Wallaroo – South Australia – 1860-1923*, Wallaroo: Corporation of the Town of Wallaroo, 1983, p.139. By 1869 nationally touring circuses arrived in Wallaroo, as well as the Bert Bailey Dramatic Company, performing Steele Rudd's four-act drama *On Our Selection* in 1913.

250. See James M. Groves (ed.), *The Echunga Diaries: London to New Zealand by Sailing Ship, 1862*, Gormley, Ontario: Preston Lake Publishing, 2003.

251. For carnival, see Mikhail Bakhtin, *Rabelais and His World*, Cambridge, Massachusetts: MIT Press, 1968 [1965]. For Kernewek Lowender, see Payton, op.cit, 2007, pp.192-221.

252. See for example, Cornwall Youth Theatre, *Hotel!* and Angie Butler, *Storytelling*, and Scavel an Gow in Dehwelans, *Dehwelans 2004: Festival of Cornwall, Souvenir Guide*, 2004, pp.10-18.

253. Although this talk was mainly about Sue Hill's work at the Eden Project, her theatrical experiences also formed part of her account. See Mineral Point,

Eleventh Gathering of Cornish Cousins, September 27-30, 2001, Mineral Point, Wisconsin, Souvenir Programme, 2001, p.19.

254. See Sue Pellow, *A Wesley Family Book of Days*, Aurora: River Street Press, 1994. Pellow's performance is based on this text.

255. See Myrna Combellack (ed. and tr.), *The Camborne Play: A verse translation of Beunans Meriasek*, Redruth: Dyllansow Truran, 1988. See also Jonathan Wooding, *St Meriasek and King Tudor in Cornwall*, Sydney: n.p., 1992. I am indebted to Philip Payton for this information.

256. *Cornish World / Bys Kernowyon*, No.19, 1998, p.11. The Association also performed extracts of 'Noah and the Flood' at Christmas events. *Meriadoc* was repeated in 1997. The role of Meriadoc has been performed by both Bill Phillips (1996) and Richard Snedden (1997).

257. See http://home.vicnet.net.au~caov/language/pasties.htm. This drama also holds some similarities to *An Balores / The Chough* by Robert Morton Nance.

258. See Maurice Smelt, *101 Cornish Lives*, Penzance: Alison Hodge, 2006, pp.175-6. See also Donald Bray, 'The Cornish Nightingale' in *Cornish Life*, Vol 5, No.1, 1978. Moody's later years are shrouded in mystery. All that is known is that she died aged 70 in Dublin.

259. For background to the Cornish in South Africa, see Dawe, op.cit. For an Anglo-centric history of the Cornish in South Africa, see also John Hall, *That Bloody Woman: The Turbulent Life of Emily Hobhouse*, Mount Hawke: Truran, 2008.

260. *The Cornishman*, 7 November 1923.

261. See Laura Smith, 'Madame Fanny Moody at Home: A Talk with the Cornish Nightingale' in Arthur Quiller-Couch (ed.), *The Cornish Magazine*, Vol 1, 1898, pp.29-36.

262. Ibid., p.35.

263. *The Cornubian*, 2 April 1897.

264. See Ronald Perry, 'The Making of Modern Cornwall: A Geo-Economic Perspective' in Philip Payton (ed.), *Cornish Studies: Ten*, Exeter: University of Exeter Press, 2002, pp.166-89. See also the tourism efforts of Silvanus Trevail in Ronald Perry and Hazel Harradence, *Silvanus Trevail: Cornish Architect and Entrepreneur*, London: Francis Boutle Publishers, 2008.

265. See for example, David Everett, 'Celtic Revival and the Anglican Church in Cornwall 1870-1930' in Philip Payton (ed.), *Cornish Studies: Eleven*, Exeter: University of Exeter Press, 2003, pp.192-219, and various contributors to Derek Williams (ed.), *Henry and Katharine Jenner: A Celebration of Cornwall's Culture, Language and Identity*, London: Francis Boutle Publishers, 2004; Peter W. Thomas, and Derek Williams (eds.), *Setting Cornwall on its Feet: Robert Morton Nance 1873-1959*, London: Francis Boutle Publishers, 2007.

CHAPTER SIX

'The Protagonist St George and the Antagonist St Piran': Dramaturgy, Revival and Nationalism, 1900-1950

'Enthusiasts beg us to make the experiment of 'reviving' these old plays in their surroundings... but one does not want an audience to be acting, and this audience would be making-believe even more heroically than the actors – that is, if it took the trouble to be in earnest at all. '

From *From a Cornish Window* by Arthur Quiller-Couch, 1906[1]

'But they were Cornish people and the Cornish are true Celts in their love of dressing up and playing 'make believe'.'

From *Twenty Years at St Hilary* by Bernard Walke, 1935[2]

Like the Cornish economy of the early twentieth century, theatre in Cornwall had to change. As witnessed in many areas of Cornish life, the opening decades of the new century brought about industrial decline, but also a parallel growth in tourism.[3] While many thousands of Cornish people were still leaving Cornwall for opportunities elsewhere across the globe,[4] there were also some who felt that the decline in Cornish culture had somehow to be stopped, or else Cornwall would end up like everywhere else in England – a fate to which the people had seemingly resigned themselves. Thus began a small but important revivalist movement (having roots in the previous decades), with an eye on using drama as just one method within the revitalization project. There were also those who saw Cornwall's space and place as an important and different place on the periphery, which drama and theatre seemed to suit. This group were starting to become attracted to Cornwall because of its 'romance' and 'otherness' – perhaps even its Celticity – and its connection to ritual, landscape and community. They were certainly rejecting the mores and values of metropolitan England.[5] The comments of the playwright Bernard Walke appear to emphasis the continuity of Cornish passion for drama from previous Ages, while Arthur Quiller-Couch, always more of a sceptical supporter of the Revival in Cornwall, alluded to the fact that it would be supremely difficult to conduct any kind of dramatic revival, because Cornish culture had progressed and moved on.[6] It was Quiller-Couch, in his *Cornish Magazine* (1898-99), who had first asked his readers to conduct debate on the future economic direction of Cornwall. Views were mixed. Some felt industrial decline could be stopped.[7] Others felt the way forward was to develop shipping and 'Cornwall as a holiday resort'.[8] Given the way Cornwall developed during the twentieth century, it is quite obvious which group won the debate, but at this point the kind of mass tourism and in-migration experienced in the post-war period could not have been predicted.[9]

The period was also characterised by two world wars, which had a devastating effect on communities, but also up-ended much traditional practice and beliefs. The millions killed in the First World War challenged established Christian belief.[10] The Second World War also forced a renegotiation of all received ideology, resulting in massive social and cultural changes in the post-war period.[11] Those small groups of Cornish activists in the period who had commitments to developing language and a new form of cultural nationalism for Cornwall[12] sometimes had to be closeted about their approach. Internal conflict and dissent was inappropriate when the island of Britain had to pull together to fight greater foes. That said, residual Cornu-English Cornishness appeared to carry on without major change, but in the light of the decline of the industrial infrastructure, there seemed little for Cornish people to celebrate. Indeed, amongst the bulk of the population, a sense of proud 'Cornishness' seemed to have dissipated. While, as we have seen, Cornwall was back on the world stage of theatre, at home it almost seemed content enough to absorb whatever Anglo-centric theatre came its way. What we witness in the period is, in effect, a kind of 'theatrical wrasslin' match', between the antagonist St George and the protagonist St Piran. It was a match conducted on both a cultural and political level: the giant culture of St George and England was dominant; although smaller and badly bruised, a St Piran-themed resistance movement was determined to take on the giant. This appears to indicate the age-old battle between Cornwall and England although, as we shall see, the boundaries and barriers – both physical and metaphorical – are a good deal more complex. Although events in Cornwall during this phase were not quite as dramatic or violent as those occurring in Ireland,[13] there are a good many parallels between the two territories, in terms of what cultural revivalists were seeking to achieve, and those resisting that revival. When examined in detail, the drama produced in Cornwall in the first half of the twentieth century forms some of the most hidden, yet controversial and progressive developments of Celtic nationalism in the history of these islands.[14] It was to set the agenda for even greater change and resistance in the post-war period.

There is not the time or the space in this volume to consider the full range of developments in this phase. Besides, detailed histories of the period's industrial and cultural development have already been made.[15] Indeed, this period of Cornish history has, over the past few years, seen a remarkable amount of attention in the works of various scholars.[16] The fundamental debate that is reflected in the drama of this period is concerned with a notion that the revivalist group were too backward-looking in their ideological concerns, which were primarily medieval, Catholic, Welsh-and-Breton-gazing, and linguistic. Some particularly viewed the linguistic energy of leading activist, poet, translator and dramatist Robert Morton Nance (1873-1959) as flawed, because he was trying, in his Unified Cornish project, to synthesise too many disparate phases of the language.[17] The medieval and Catholic impetus was to understand past Cornwall as a place of happy union between community and drama, and the *plen-an-gwarry* culture of this period as symbolising a unity somehow absent in modern Cornwall – hence the cod medievalism of many Cornish-language texts and publications in this period and its aftermath.[18] Thus, not only did the revivalists of the Age fail to connect with most of the working-class, modern, Methodist and Cornu-English-speaking population of Cornwall, but – because of the perceived flaws in revived Cornish – they also failed to be appreciated on the wider field of Celtic studies. What Saunders terms 'the Nancean synthesis'[19] could not be sustained. In essence, this is a further development of the kind of double jeopardy (alluded to in the Introduction to this book) that Cornwall was in during this phase. However, we might argue that this imagining of Cornish activity is far too simplistic a model of what actually occurred, and the revivalists and the revivalist dramatists were merely trying to assert the best way forward, given a difficult set of circumstances on which to build their work. All of that said, this unique set of constructs has prompted a unique dramaturgy that distinguishes dramatic activity in Cornwall between 1900 and 1950 from anywhere else in Britain. For such a small territory as Cornwall to conduct this reawakening in theatrical culture is perhaps one of the most interesting cultural developments in Britain in the past century.

Magnus Maclean's influential volume, *The Literature of the Celts*, appeared in 1902, with its dismissive views of Cornish drama,[20] but this did not stop Henry Jenner (1849-1934) reasserting the importance of this heritage in his groundbreaking volume *A Handbook of the Cornish Language: Chiefly in its Latest Stages with some account of its History and Literature* in 1904.[21] Jenner, who worked for much of his life as librarian in the British Museum, was born at St Columb Major. Uniquely, he was able to consider the surviving oral tradition in west Cornwall, but also brought to his work knowledge of the traditional texts. Jenner's wider contribution to the Cornish Revival has been documented by contributors to Derek Williams's recent collection,[22] but here, Jenner's significance was not only to reintroduce the dramatic history and linguistic heritage of Cornwall, to those both inside and outside of it, but also to assert its individuality. In chapters such as 'On Prosody', Jenner was able to argue for the distinctiveness of Cornish verse drama, as well as demonstrating to the reader how the major dramas were constructed.[23] This was an important step forward, because although previous scholars had made similar attempts at cataloguing and organising material in Cornish, Jenner completed it not only with an eye on modern linguistic methods, but also with the explicit aim of getting the people of Cornwall to relearn their language, and write and speak in it. Effectively, Jenner had moved from a purely antiquarian interest in the Cornish language to a more active cultural nationalism. In part, Jenner had been gathering and combining many of the ideas of earlier revivalists (such as L.C. Duncombe-Jewell and W.S. Lach-Syzrma[24]) and had produced the book at their request. Although perhaps the true ignition point of the revival of Cornish in the modern era was the centenary in 1877 of the death of Dolly Pentreath,[25] this text was able to present the language to a new generation. Jenner's lead would have major ramifications throughout the century.

Arthur Quiller-Couch (1863-1944) was working in a different sphere from the revivalists but had known of Jenner's work, and that of the other revivalists during the latter decades of the nineteenth century and the early half of the twentieth century.[26] In 1912 he gained the Professorial Chair of English at the University of Cambridge and by 1917, in a considerable breakthrough, he had established the Final Honours School in that subject. However, Quiller-Couch retained his Cornish connections, and had already had Robert Morton Nance contribute illustrations and poems to his *Cornish Magazine*.[27] He had also read Norris's translation of the *Ordinalia*, and was aware of the continuum, notably from the writings of Richard Carew.[28] Therefore, he was intimately aware of the revivalists' desire to put on the mystery plays again, as symbols of Cornwall's once great theatrical culture. Quiller-Couch has a mixed reaction to their literariness, for despite describing them as 'by no means masterpieces of literature' he also finds that 'they reveal here and there perceptions of beauty such as go with sincerity even though it be artless'.[29] To reinforce this, Quiller-Couch quotes the moment when Adam, bowed by years, sends his son Seth to the gate of Paradise. He also praises the local nature of the rewards from Pilate to the Jailor (Fekenal, Carvenow and Methyn).[30] Although Q admits the 'temptation' of revival, he also sees what he terms 'the terrible unreality which would infect the whole business.' After reflection, he concludes:

> For the success of the experiment would depend on our reconstructing the whole scene – the ring of entranced spectators as well as the primitive show; and the country-people would probably, and not entirely without reason, regard the business as 'a stupid old May game.' The only spectators properly impressed would be a handful of visitors and solemn antiquarians. I can see those visitors. If it has ever been your lot to witness the performance of a 'literary' play in London and cast an eye over the audience it attracts, you too will know them and their stigmata– – their ineffectable attire, their strange hirsuteness, their air of combining instruction with amusement, their soft felt hats indented along the crown. No! We may perhaps, produce new religious dramas in these ancient Rounds: decidedly we cannot revive the old ones.[31]

Quiller-Couch was proved wrong by the 1969 and millennial revivals of the *Ordinalia*.[32] We may wonder why he adopted this position. Perhaps Q, as a 'modernist' literary scholar, failed to recognise the power of the medieval and late medieval works. He does not, for example, write very often on any literature earlier than Shakespeare,[33] with the exception of Chaucer. This attitude may also be derived from the mantle of fashionable professorial judgement from this era; the text did not have the appropriate conditions of greatness as defined by this generation of literary scholarship.[34] We find ourselves questioning how familiar Q was with the full aspects of the Cornish literary continuum, However, he does offer the revivalists hope that new dramas might be created – a call taken up later, as we shall see, by Peggy Pollard, Donald R. Rawe, Ken George and myself. Part of this cynicism may have come less from his dismissal of the Revival, but perhaps more from his own understanding of the needs and function of drama. It is curious, for example, that Quiller-Couch remains well-known for his prose, poetry and criticism,[35] but less so for his dramatic works. In the Arthur Quiller-Couch archive at Trinity College, Oxford, are some ten dramas, alongside some fragments of others. The problem is that although much of Quiller-Couch's prose was heavily influenced by Cornwall, its seems that for drama he chose more Anglo-centric subject matter; perhaps the reason for their lack of publication was that they were, in essence, period pieces, and have dated badly.

Among the complete plays are his first work, *The Bishop of Eucalyptus*, dating from 1895, *It's Hard To be Toogood* (1914) and *This Sceptred Isle*.[36] This last play was a pageant in the form of a children's masque. It was performed at Place, Fowey on the Coronation Day of King George VI in 1937, and documented the history of Britain. Among the characters the children had to play were the ancient Britons and Druids.[37] Other complete Q dramas are more difficult to date, though are presumably mainly from the period 1914 to 1937. These are *Next Door To Toogood* (only Acts I and III have survived), *Home*, *The Regens*, *Parkinson, Hocken and Hunken or What the Parrot Said* (only Act I surviving), *The Great Panjandrum* and *The Two Householders*.[38] The archive contains no records of where and when these pieces were performed. The fragments include *Miss Limpenny's Party* (this was an adaptation of a scene from *The Astonishing History of Troy Town*[39]), *Westminster School* (only Act I, Scene i surviving), *Ye Sexes Give Ear* (two pages surviving), *Soria-Moria-Blitzen* (two pages surviving) and some other pages from an untitled pastoral myth.[40] We also know that Dennis Arundell completed a stage version of *Hetty Wesley*,[41] and that Arundell collaborated with John Carol on an adaptation of *Home is the Sailor*.[42] Again, these pieces have proven difficult to date, and no details are given of their performance. As an academic, Q (in a way, pre-dating A.L. Rowe) also had a wider interest in pan-British drama. In 1899, he completed a set of adaptations from the major history plays of Shakespeare, which he titled *Historical Tales from Shakespeare*.[43] In *Shakespeare's Workmanship* (1918),[44] he offered analysis of some of the major plays, while in 1924 he offered a lecture on W.S. Gilbert.[45] In *Studies in Literature Series III* (1929) he considered Shakespeare's Comedies,[46] as well as giving a continuing series of lectures on the bard.[47] Interestingly, he rarely looked at any other dramatists within his lectures.[48] In the mid-1940s, Quiller-Couch had been reconsidering the story of Tristan and Yseult in a manuscript he titled *Castle Dor* (based on the earthwork close to Fowey, and perhaps connected to historical events). The manuscript was left incomplete upon his death in 1944, and was then completed by Daphne du Maurier, for eventual publication in 1962.[49] It is curious that Quiller-Couch, who rarely acknowledges the significance of Cornish narratives, saw the dramatic potential of this most ancient example. This encourages us to see him in terms of an individual balancing the culture of St George and St Piran in his life and his work. This was geographic, as well as cultural, since he spent his time between the University of Cambridge and The Haven, in Fowey. A similar cultural dichotomy is found in the writings of A.L. Rowse and J.C. Trewin.[50]

The cultural dichotomy found in writers such as Quiller-Couch, Rowse and Trewin could also be detected in an earlier Anglo-Cornish dramatist and poet. This was James Dryden Hosken (1861-1953). Hosken lived a long life and noticed many cultural changes in Cornwall. Although perhaps now better known as a compelling and powerful poet, lamenting the life and culture of late nineteenth-century Cornwall in particular,[51] Hosken was perhaps best known in his lifetime for his verse drama, not only in Cornwall, but elsewhere in Britain. In some other ways, Hosken was a proto-nationalist poet, forced to operate within the split literary personality of Anglo-Cornish and Cornish writing during this period. While being resolutely a Cornish poet, he also saw the need to manoeuvre within wider European literature. To this end, Hosken's ambitious start to his dramatic career came with *Phaon and Sappho: A play (in five acts and song)*, which was published in Penzance by F. Rodda in 1891.[52] This tragedy considered events concerning the life of Phaon who, in Greek mythology, was a old and ugly boatman, made young and handsome by ointment from Aphrodite. Sappho fell in love with him but Phaon rejected her, so she threw herself into the seas to drown. Although obviously a pan-European narrative, one can see why it appealed to the Anglo-Cornish writer. Hosken saws parallels from mythological Greece to the Cornish world of boats, islands and cliffs (something we shall also see in the ideology of the Minack Theatre). It remains unclear whether the tragedy was actually performed.

Two volumes of verse followed: *Verses by the way* with a preface from Arthur Quiller-Couch, who clearly saw Hosken's potential, and *A Monk's Love and Other Poems*.[53] His most famous work, however, came from 1896. This was a dramatisation of the life and death of Christopher Marlowe.[54] Another ambitious drama, this saw Hosken grappling with one of the great English Renaissance dramatists. The resultant drama, although popular in its day (judging from its reprints[55]) suffers from a pretence and artifice that would make it difficult to perform now. This may be the reason why Hosken himself steered his later work to more Cornu-centric poetry,[56] but it is perhaps a pity he did not see fit to apply his dramatic abilities to Cornish subject matter, for clearly he was a talented dramatist. Curiously, the original edition of *Christopher Marlowe: A Tragedy in Three Acts in Prose and Verse* (1896), is accompanied by what he terms 'a Harlequinade in Doggerel' which he titled *Belphegor*,[57] which would also be performed. Although perhaps not as significant a figure as he might have been, clearly the wider public in Cornwall knew of his work; alongside Quiller-Couch, the dramatist was among the first to be barded at the 1928 Cornish Gorsedd ceremony, taking the bardic name, *Caner Helles* [Poet of Helston].[58] There may even be a para-theatrical connection here, since Hosken also published a volume on Helston Furry Day.[59] In Hosken, we perhaps see the embryonic writing of a dramatist with the potential to achieve on a pan-British or even European scale. This ambition was, however, never quite reached.

Other ambitious drama did emerge in the period. One example was Thomas Hardy's *The Famous Tragedy of the Queen of Cornwall at Tintagel in Lyonesse*, which emerged in 1923.[60] The development of this drama has complex origins, which in part support this chapter's paradigm of a cultural conflict between the protagonist St George and the antagonist St Piran. The text also actively demonstrates the shift between Hardy's own concerns as a writer and his relationship with Cornwall. Hardy (1840-1928) first came to Cornwall as a young architect in March 1870 to supervise the restoration of St Juliot's Church near Boscastle. Upon his arrival, he met and fell in love with the rector's sister-in-law Emma Lavinia Gifford.[61] Financial and critical success in his fiction enabled him in 1874 to give up architecture for writing, and to marry Gifford.[62] His time spent with Gifford in north Cornwall would have major ramifications on his writing at the end of his life. Hardy's marriage was under intolerable strain for much of his life,[63] but it was Emma's death in 1912 that seemed to prompt some of his most famous poetry, as well as the above drama.

Two earlier prose texts did emerge. These were the north-Cornish novel *A Pair of Blue Eyes* (1873) and the Scillionian-themed short story 'A Mere Interlude' (1885).[64] In the development of Hardy's Tristan-themed drama, some points are worth noting from these non-theatrical works, to which Kent, and Trezise, amongst others,[65] have given considerable critical attention. When Hardy arrived in Cornwall in 1870, Boscastle was, by English standards at least, a very remote part of Britain. Throughout his career, Hardy had developed a conceptualisation of Lyonesse that was wider than its original bounds. In Cornish folklore, Lyonesse was the Atlantic-like submerged region between west Cornwall and the Isles of Scilly. However, Hardy chooses the mythical concept of Lyonesse to stand for the whole of the territory of Cornwall. This was embodied early on in his proto-dramatic and iconic poem from 1870 'When I Set Out for Lyonnesse':

What could bechance at Lyonnesse
　　While I should sojourn there
　　No prophet durst declare,
Nor did the wisest wizard guess
What would bechance at Lyonesse
　　While I should sojourn there.[66]

Already then, Hardy knew of Cornwall's folkloric and para-theatrical heritage, since he was already imagining wizards (in the shape of the shaman Merlin) and magic there. According to Trezise, this vision of Cornwall played a vital role in the life of Hardy.[67] This can be seen in the 1895 preface to *A Pair of Blue Eyes*, where Hardy refers to the 'vague border of the Wessex Kingdom… which like the westering edge of modern American settlements, was progressive and uncertain'.[68] The terms 'progressive and uncertain' seem to represent the antagonist St Piran, in that for Hardy (and perhaps the rest of England) the Celtic world is less understood, still marginal and dangerous. The border of St George's England is also conceived of here, but again, there seems a blending and merging between territories. In some ways, this draws us back to Robert Hunt's concept of a 'Greater Cornwall' – but for Hardy (as for many other writers of the period, such as Virginia Woolf and D.H. Lawrence) the delineation is difficult. Thus two elements emerge in Hardy's understanding of Cornwall – the marginal, to use Trezise's useful term 'Off Wessex',[69] but also the concept of a 'far-off land' – equated with Lyonesse. Hardy's Cornwall is therefore both mythic and real: in the two fictional works Plymouth and London retain their real names, but Cornish places have been renamed, recombined or relocated, which has the effect of shifting the action from a real to an unreal place. For example, in *A Pair of Blue Eyes*, Bude becomes Stratleigh, and Camelford, Camelton.[70] This cultural geography helped to shape Hardy's drama.

The composition of *The Famous Tragedy of the Queen of Cornwall at Tintagel in Lyonesse* comes at the high watermark of Arthurian fever in Cornwall – the period 1920-1930. In this respect, Hardy's play's 'moment of production' in 1923 completely matches the materialist context around it. In some senses, Hardy's text also predicted events later on in the decade, and in part contributed to them. Charles Thomas neatly summarizes events of the era:

> Papers on Arthurian topics for all the issues of the Cornish journals, and an Arthurian congress was held in Truro in 1930, organized by the Revivalist J. Hambly Rowe. Pamphlets like Dickinson's *The Story of King Arthur in Cornwall*, started endless reprinting.[71]

At this point, it is worth noting how Arthuriana comes to exemplify specific ideological differences between Cornwall and England. For Victorian and Edwardian England, King Arthur (and to an extent Tristan) had come to symbolise everything that was powerful and majestic about the age –in painting and in literature, Arthur had been transformed into a champion of Englishness – a kind of contemporary St George 'with attitude'.[72] Yet the same was not true in Cornwall, where an alternative reading of Arthur still persisted, which was reasserted by the emergent ethos of Celtic revivalism (perhaps even more so, if the 'genuine' medieval Arthuriana of *Bewnans Ke* had been discovered earlier[73]). Here, for revivalists, Arthur was the bastion of resistance against Anglo-Saxon (and by extension, 'English') invasion; he was a Celtic Warrior King who both stood for the identity of past Cornwall and offered hope for a revived Celtic nation in the future. Indeed, for them, Cornwall had been the genesis of the Arthurian and the Tristan legend, and thus all other pan-European versions. There was also the fact that Wagner had reasserted the story in the nineteenth century, which may well have appealed to Hardy's understanding of the romance of place.

The Famous Tragedy of the Queen of Cornwall at Tintagel in Lyonesse is a very important text in Cornwall's theatrical history for it synthesises a number of established elements; at the same time it is quite eclectic in its dramaturgy. Clearly, Hardy assembled elements of a classical Greek tragedy (a component not surprising given the themes of his major fiction). Wider British folk drama is also recalled by the piece's structure and by its subtitle: 'Arranged as a play for mummers… in one act, requiring no theatre or scenery'.[74] We know from his fiction that he found such folk drama interesting,[75] so it is perhaps not surprising to see him employ the technique in a play. Thus, we see four central components of Cornish theatre come together: Tristan, Merlin lore, the wider

Fig. 71. Hardy's imaginary view of Tintagel Castle at the time of the tragedy of the Queen of Cornwall. Frontispiece to Thomas Hardy, *The Famous Tragedy of the Queen of Cornwall at Tintagel in Lyonesse*, 1923.

classical dramatic heritage and folk drama. Hardy also seems to imagine the piece being written for a local community, celebrating their most famous narrative in a ritualistic form. Although this is the broader cultural context of the piece, certain observers, such as Phelps, and Millgate,[76] have also noted that the drama was curiously personal to Hardy since the two Iseults (which have caused problems for other dramatists) may here represent Hardy's two wives, Emma Gifford and Florence Dugdale. Although we must be sceptical of such an autobiographical reading, it is nevertheless a convincing argument when one holds in mind the structural positioning of Iseult and Iseult of the White Hands. The core value of Hardy's version of Tristan and Yseult, however, is its simplicity and imagined rusticity. In the stage directions, this simplicity is central: Hardy does wish for the audience to imagine that 'the Atlantic is Visible', but 'the Stage is any large room, round the end of which the audience sits'.[77] Merlin operates initially as the narrator, with Hardy cautious in his use of effects ('a blue light *may* be thrown on Merlin'[78]). Hardy understood the pan-European dimension of the story, but seemed to want to bring the tale back to its roots (perhaps even imagining a presentation in an early medieval Cornish setting). The verse is not quite that of the *Ordinalia*, but we see in its construction an attempt to create a rude and unrefined poetic, which at the same time carries Quiller-Couch's view of 'perceptions of beauty such as go with sincerity, even though it be artless':

Merlin: The tale has travelled far and wide:-
            Yea, that King Mark to fetch his bride,
            Sent Tristram [sic], then that he and she
            Quaffed a love potion witlessly
            While homeward bound. Hence that the King
                Wedded one heart aflame
            For Tristram! He in dark despair,
            Roved recklessly, and wived elsewhere
                One of his mistress' name.[79]

Artless, this text is not. Hardy retains the poetic quality throughout, and uses some deft sequences to concentrate the power of the drama. These include the recitative use of the so-called 'Shades of Dead Old Cornishmen and Women',[80] who operate chorally, and are the voice of public and Celtic reasoning within the drama. Unlike some other versions (Wagner included), Hardy chooses to accentuate the stage time of Brangwain and Iseult, since he understands the dramatic need for their debate and discussion behind the backs of the male characters. In this way too, the tragedy of the Queen of

Cornwall can be enhanced. Tristram himself has a more functional role within the piece, though he has action sequences against the Baron Andret. The conflict with Ireland at the start, over the Cornish tribute, is given little weighting, again so that the tragedy in Cornwall and Brittany is emphasised. Less critical energy has been expended on this drama than Hardy's other work, though Phelps has studied the play in considerable depth. In his 1975 work, he notes two important letters, which explain much about Hardy's development of the piece. On 20 September 1916, in a letter to Sir Sidney Cockerell, Hardy confessed that Cockerell's 'hopes of a poem on Iseult – the English, or British Helen – will be disappointed'.[81] This is interesting since it suggests the writer was already making a classical tragic connection between Iseult and King Menelaus's wife, and the beginnings of the Trojan War. His correction of 'English Helen' to 'British Helen', also suggests a tension in his thoughts, but an awareness of the ethnic difference (of course, we might well argue that Iseult was Irish, but at least he was reading her within an ancient British context).[82] It does seem that the project had been on Hardy's mind for much of his life, since he confessed in a letter to the poet and playwright Alfred Noyes on 17 November 1923, that his 'little play had been 53 years in contemplation'.[83] As mentioned, Phelps offers much debate over the inspiration for the female characters of the drama, but in the end concludes that she was Hardy's 'composite, well-beloved dream woman'.[84] However, the lasting presence of Yseult in Cornish theatre may symbolise something greater still, not only Hardy's 'composite well-beloved' but a nation's dramatic symbol too.

Other dramas followed in the wake of Hardy's effort. Among these was John Baragwanath King's 1925 epic, *The Coming of Arthur*.[85] King (1864-1939) was born in Penzance, and worked as a painter, satirist and poet. His drama appears to draw heavily on William Hals' eighteenth-century version of Uther and Arthur's story.[86] The piece is perhaps overblown in places, but the verse is nevertheless beautifully rendered, incorporating figures such as Jubelin (a disciple of St Piran), and pagan elements, such as the witches and the good spirits, the latter drawn from what was then a fashionable esoteric study in Cornwall.[87] The important figure is the disciple of St Piran, for this suggests not only a connection, in King's mind, to the disciple characters of the *Ordinalia* (which King appears to know of), but also a continuity of spirituality from the original patron saint. Here, Ursan, one of Uther Pendragon's men, calls for him to fight once again against the Anglo-Saxons, invoking St Piran:

Ursan: Then arouse thee Pendragon, thy dolour confess
                    To the presbyter Piran who passed hence to-day,

<blockquote>
And will yet anon,
Ere night well is gone.
</blockquote>

Jubelin: Who calleth on Piran? be it it Ursan the bear:
Cries a voice from the gloom of the hastening day:-
I, Jubelin, from that sainted isle fair,
Am changing for Piran this joy-bearing lay.[88]

As can be seen, King's achievement is a much more symbolic piece of drama, which relies on movement, choral work and ritual – and uses archaic language. It is highly patterned, with characters speaking in regular blocks of text. The piece does not carry the simple rusticity of Hardy's work. Neither does it suffer from a split personality. King's aim is clear: he wishes to retell the Cornu-centric Arthurian drama. While other texts appeared to dismiss or forget the centrality of the battle at Demeliock in mid-Cornwall, King reasserts it, thus widening the sphere of Arthurian influence across Cornwall, and lessening the overall status of iconic space such as Tintagel (perhaps something that Jenner would favour). This time then, King asserts a profoundly and openly more nationalistic text, which was correcting received views of an English-conceived Arthur. Although virtually ignored by historians of the Revival, King's drama deserves to be better known. In his day, people were aware of this and other work, for he was made a Bard of the Cornish Gorseth in 1930. Away from King, however, it was perhaps all the wider dramatic and romantic activity about Tintagel that seemed to cause Jenner concern during this decade. As a response to what he saw as the worrying 'romanticisation' of Tintagel, he wrote his influential paper, 'Tintagel Castle in History and Romance' (1927), which looked at the wider cultural pedigree of the Arthurian matter in Cornwall.[89] Likewise, J. Hambley Rowe developed Jenner's cultural-geographic ideas in a paper called 'King Arthur's Territory' (1929).[90] Both Jenner and Rowe were at pains to deny the dramatic imperative established by Hardy (probably in their view, a well-intentioned, but uninformed outsider) but assert King's patriotic, and somewhat more realistic, view of the past. The efforts of Jenner and Rowe appeared to have little effect. Arthuriana, according to Thomas, had reached its zenith:

> with the arrival from the north of Frederick Glasscock, custard millionaire and philanthropist… and the construction of King Arthur's Hall [in 1933] in the village. It is still there, the size of a small abbey with some of Britain's finest 20th-century stained glass windows by Veronica Whall, and William Hatherell's ten oil paintings of Arthurian scenes.[91]

In 1930, the chivalric-named B.D. Vere published *King Arthur: His Symbolic Story in Verse*,[92] which was a very actable verse drama, crafted for performance at King Arthur's Halls of Chivalry in Tintagel. The piece drew upon Christ-lore in Cornwall, with the opening sequence showing the boy Jesus completing a wood-carving on Tintagel Island. It not only conceives Christ as having a presence in Cornwall (perhaps a major mythological construct not surviving in the extant texts) but also sets the eventual Grail quest in motion. Joseph of Arimathea, is central – a character also found in the 'Passio Christi' and 'Resurrexio Domini' of the *Ordinalia*. Important dramatic connections were being made to consciously reassert an ancient spiritual pedigree. Despite efforts to trace Vere's real name, none has come into the frame. However, Vere's dramatic purpose should not be underestimated, because within the text we find a lively synergy between Cornish space and Celtic Christianity, and a neat allegory in Jesus' answer to Joseph of Arimathea about whether he has finished all his work:

Jesus: The simplest part is finished (*he turns to the west*) but the sea
          Means peace and quiet and rest. It is so smooth
          And even that the plan is e'er the same.
          (*He points to the east*)
          That of the land, with all its rugged rocks,
          Its mountains steep, its hidden vales, its moors,
          Which windswept, hold the slimy bog like traps,
          And soft, enticingly, attract, and draw
          The wanderer from the path where safety lies,
          Is like the twistings of the minds of men.
          'Tis hard to make a pleasing curve of these,
          They will not with the sea make harmony.

Joseph: I heard Thee speak as I came up. Thou'rt full
          Of Knowledge for Thine age... but Thou art sad.

Jesus: Those who can see the end and who can read
          The hearts of men, have much to make them sad.[93]

Although the trend temporarily ends with Vere's imagining, the next few decades would see other writers and dramatists take up the baton of Tristan once again, notably A.S.D. Smith's 1951 epic Cornish-language poetic rendering of *Trystan hag Ysolt* (finally completed by D.H. Watkins in 1962), and also Nora Ratcliff's *Tristan of Cornwall* (1951).[94] The former is an

Fig. 72. Robert Morton Nance (1873-1959) in Cornish Gorsedd regalia. Courtesy of Audrey Randle Pool.

imagining of a version composed by the 'original' Tristan poet, while Ratcliff's version encompasses a more realistic take on the tale. It seems that for Cornwall's theatrical continuum, Arthuriana and Tristana are never very far away. In the assertion of a new awareness of Cornwall's Celticity, they were hugely important mythological figures. Other dramatists were also to follow this pattern of emergent ethno-nationalistic theatre. One of these was one of the founding fathers of the Cornish movement of the twentieth century: Robert Morton Nance. Nance (1873-1959) had originally trained as an artist under Sir Hubert von Herkomer, who designed the regalia of the Welsh Gorsedd. His Cornish-born parents belonged to a Cornish community in Cardiff and instilled in him an interest in Cornish culture and language. By 1906, Nance had settled in Cornwall in Nancledra. While there he continued his study of Cornish, and additionally developed drama in Cornu-English and in Cornish. As a recent study has shown, Nance's contribution to Cornish culture has been enormously important.[95] Perhaps no figure has been so celebrated or vilified in Cornish culture as he has. Celebrated for not only acting as the true ignition point of the twentieth-century Cornish language revival and the invention of the Cornish Gorseth,[96] but also for rediscovering and recording much 'lost' folklore of western Britain,[97] Nance has also been fiercely attacked for his apparently 'synthetic' construction of Unified Cornish[98] (untouched and ignored for many years by the mainstream Celtic academic establishment[99]) and his 'reconstructionist' approach to culture, merging the 'found' and newly-created, so that they became fused. To his supporters, Nance offers a productive collision between past and present. To his detractors, the supposition is that his collusion of past and present offers un-historic 'invention'. These twin poles of his work have important impact on his drama. Also influential on his work are the twin figures of St George and St Piran; of all the playwrights of the era, it is he who most resolves their conflict.

The middle phase of Nance's writing in English is dominated by his interest in the mummers' plays and the Christmas and folk drama of these islands. Although there is no record of how he came to be aware of the Cornish dimension of this tradition, it is perhaps through his interest in Cornish language drama that he first encountered the extant and documented (but lost) mummers' plays of Cornwall. Mummers' plays, as R.J.E. Tiddy, and E.K. Chambers argue in their classic studies *The Mummers' Play* (1923), and *The English Folk Play* (1933),[100] have been performed for hundreds of years. As this volume has shown, they are usually folk dramas based on the legend of St George and the Seven Champions of Christendom; the principal characters are St George (sometimes Sir George, King George, or Prince George), Captain Slasher, the Turkish Knight, the King of Egypt, a Doctor and several men-at-arms. Minor personages bear a great variety of names, normally locally determined. After a brief prologue, the fighting characters advance and introduce themselves, or are introduced, in basic and vaunting rhymes. A duel or several duels follow, and one or other of the combatants is killed. The Doctor then enters and demonstrates his boastful skills as a medical practitioner by resuscitating the dead knight. Supernumerary grotesque characters are then presented, and a collection is made.

Performed usually at Christmas or at the end of the year, the plays are connected with a celebration of the death of the year, and its resurrection in the spring, and are, as we have seen, a crucial theatrical component of the 'ritual year' in Britain. All the characters were played by men who kept the same part for many years. Eventually dialogue was added, and was passed on by word-of-mouth through generations of performers. A useful celebrated depiction of mumming is to be found in Book 2, Chapters 4-6 of Thomas Hardy's *The Return of the Native* (1878), in which the heroine Eusticia Vye disguises herself as the Turkish knight, in the place of the young lad Charley, in order to engineer a meeting with Clym Yeobright.[101] As shown above, Hardy also incorporated elements of mumming and folk drama into his play

The Famous Tragedy of the Queen of Cornwall at Tintagel in Lyonesse.[102] As a scholar Nance had already been drawn to the surviving medieval plays (most located in libraries and institutions outside of Cornwall), but in his search for things Cornish, we can say with some certainty he also tackled other manuscripts – hoping for threads of Cornish, Cornu-English dialect or pieces of recorded folklore. Nance used his rediscovery of texts such as the '"Truro" Mummers' Play', 'The Truro Cordwainers' Play' and 'The Mylor Christmas Play'[103] to support his developing notion that Cornwall had a complex and sustained folk drama tradition, which enhanced both the discoveries he was making about medieval Cornish drama and the separate continuum of work written in English. The acceptance of a separate English-language continuum of drama within Cornwall inevitably led Nance to make a connection between the working-class populace (who he imagined spoke Cornu-English) and the drama that therefore most suited them. He hoped that his separate project of encouraging interest in Cornu-English would eventually lead performers and their audience into a re-engagement with Cornish itself, a position that Jenner (Nance's mentor) had championed earlier, but which was broadly rejected later on in the revivalist movement, within which Cornu-English was most often side-lined, and considered second best.

Possibly, over time, the Cornish revivalist movement, and indeed the Gorseth in particular has, until now, been reticent about promoting Nance's engagement with folk drama, especially mummers' plays, since they appear to champion many problematical aspects of English culture, which observers felt did not fit comfortably with Nance's development of Unified Cornish, or with his crucial role within the early years of the Cornish Gorseth. Put simply, Nance's fascination with Cornu-English did not sit well with a revivalist culture seemingly hell-bent on a Cornish-language future, and hostile to all things English. Looking back from our twenty-first century perspective, it is easy to see how this happened, but also how naïve the view was. The subject of St George was actually pan-British and not restricted only to English culture, and despite several recent attempts to 'erase' perceived English material, St George and his narrative always formed a crucial part of the pictorial and lyrical backdrop. Nance knew that the legend has been integrated into Cornish folk culture and was therefore unafraid to address and rework the material. It was a brave move, and has yet to be bettered.

Historical interest in St George paradoxically features in two of Cornwall's most 'Cornish' of festivals: the Helston 'Furry' or 'Flora Day' and Padstow May Day.[104] Quite early on in his folkloric studies of Cornwall, Nance identified the importance of these days in the Cornish ritual year, and became intensely interested in their origins and development. Both had elements of mumming within their festivals. However, Nance's major interest in the May celebrations at Helston was in the so-called *Hal-an-Tow*. The ceremony of the *Hal-an-Tow* was revived by the Old Cornwall Society of Helston in 1930, with much input from Nance,[105] so that it has become associated with 'The Furry', though, as we know, the ceremony and song of *Hal-an-Tow* seem a good deal older, with its roots in May ritual and mumming. The characters are standard mumming characters from the rest of these islands. Despite the obscurity of its origins, this has not stopped many observers wishing for 'Cornish-ised' versions of the song. Sowena, a contemporary Cornish folk-group, who fuse traditional and contemporary instrumentation, have recorded a version of the song rewritten to incorporate St Piran.[106] This may be a step too far – even for Nance – considering that a similar section on St George was originally found in obsolete versions of the Day Song at Padstow:

Awake St. George, our English knight O,
For summer is acome O, and winter is ago,
And every day God gives us his grace,
By day and by night O.

Where is St. George, where is he O,
He is out in his long boat all on the salt sea O,
And in every land O, the land that ere we go.

And for to fetch the summer home, the summer and the May O,
For summer is acome O, and winter is ago.[107]

Nance therefore legitimately uses St George for cultural-revivalist purposes in Cornwall. If Helston and Padstow could use it in May, then there was good reason for him to use it at Christmas. This he did in one of Cornwall's finest modern mumming plays: 'The Christmas Play of Saint George and the Turkish Knight'. In Box 9 of the Courtney Library, Royal Institution of Cornwall, there are several drafts of the play. I have selected the prompter's copy, for accuracy, not only in the additional marks made on the stage directions, but also for the additional lines (added in Nance's hand). The interested reader can seek out the minor variations of the texts. This would appear to be the version of the play that was successfully produced at a Christmas meeting of St Ives Old Cornwall Society. Box 9 is also filled with much correspondence, together with notes, articles and theories on mumming traditions elsewhere in Britain. Here, the characters broadly pattern those found elsewhere: these were Saint George (played originally by

Fig. 73. A performance of *The Christmas Play of St George and the Turkish Knight* by Robert Morton Nance, in St Ives, c.1924.

Robert Morton Nance), The Turkish Knight (played by A.K. Hamilton Jenkin), The King of Egypt and The Doctor (Bernard Leach). However, Nance also adds Father Christmas (R.J. Noall), Princess Sabre (Phoebe Nance), Slasha and The Dragon. Michael Cardew also performed in the original version, but it is unclear which part he played. The parts appear to have been in draft for some time, in a continuous state of evolution. Indeed, there is, in Box 9, a shorter draft from 1911, which appears to have been acted in Nancledra in that year, a good deal earlier than traditional scholarship of the Revival suggests.

The play begins with a Prologue, written in rhyming couplets and spoken by one of the players outside of the main performance area. He asks 'Who comes here, this time of night, / Neither by day nor by candle-light?' and in response, enters Father Christmas, who pleads for 'room' for the actors who follow.[108] The stage directions inform us that 'no scenery is required',[109] making the performance characteristically mobile. Father Christmas is a useful seasonal touch, but also acts as narrator for the start of the main action: the entrance of the King of Egypt, and his daughter Princess Sabra. The King and the Princess speak in verse, with their speeches ending in couplets. The Turkish knight Salaams arrives to inform them that 'a dragon vile / Has left the water of the Nile'[110] and has been terrorising the locality. The King

Fig. 74. Nance's unpublished illustration for *The Christmas Play of St George and the Turkish Knight.* Courtesy of the Royal Institution of Cornwall.

demands that Salaams should provide food for the dragon, but the audience soon learns that the creature wants younger meat. Lots are drawn and it is Sabra who is to be fed to the dragon; yet Salaams is too cowardly to fight for her. So ends Act I of the drama. The Princess decries the pathetic nature of the Turkish Knight, with Nance using the language of mining and metallurgy to hammer home the point in controlled and powerful couplets:

> Where's now they heart of gold, base-metalled suitor?
> Thy silver-seeming tongue turns out but pewter.
> Whose tinkling tin with lumpish lead alloyed
> Thy paltry heart proves pinchbeck, false and void—
> A tinselled spangle glittering in thy breast,
> That turns to dross when put beneath the test!
> Farewell for ever, coward! Quit my sight!
> Rather I'd die than wed thee, Turkish Knight.[111]

Act II begins with an image of Sabra in chains. Nance's touches are both apt and amusing. The stage directions say that 'her chain may be made of twisted paper or cardboard. Links painted with gold paint'.[112] This suits the seasonal popularity of such home-made decorations. At the same time, Sabra's triplet plea carries the real sense of horror she faces:

> I hear his horrid jaws go snap;
> I hear his leathern pinions flap;
> I hear his claws that beat the ground —[113]

It is at this point that St George enters 'on Hobby Horse'[114] to a flourish of trumpets. Nance, being an artist, cleverly imagined exactly how he wanted the Hobby Horse to work in the production: in Box 9 of the Courtney Library collection are several detailed drawings of the costume design. It conceptually fits that he had in mind the Padstow Obby Oss, though the eventual design perhaps owes more to children's toys than to the ritualised dance from north Cornwall. The St George imagined here is identical to that of the *Hal-an-Tow* of Helston and the Day Song of Padstow. Nance gives him 'corny' lines, but they are essential to the character, if the overall mumming is to work. St George is a kind of everyman, with whom the Cornish audience needed to empathise. Though he does not speak in Cornu-English, he is at least straight-talking and honest:

Fair maid, I cannot leave thee so –
Alone, alarmed, and full of woe–
I've vowed a vow, O fair Princess,
To aid all damsels in distress!
I prithee then make known thy grief–
This sword is sworn to thy relief![115]

The conflict with the dragon is comic. As we might expect, there are touches of the Mechanicals performing 'Pyramus and Thisbe' in Shakespeare's *A Midsummer Night's Dream*. Nance also designed the dragon's costume in some detail, allowing it to be mobile and to be chased by St George. The dragon has melodramatic rhyming couplets, filled with puns and 'bad' rhymes ('Ho! Ho! Here's something like a dinner! / I'll snap her nose off, to begin her!'[116]) that intentionally enhance the rusticity of the production. However, there is a complexity to the blocking of this conflict. Witness this stage direction, which is enhanced on the Prompter's copy by a spiral diagram showing the exact moves the dragon and St George are to make in their choreography. The effect is to make the piece seem 'amateur' when actually the performance is highly stylised and non-naturalistic, classic components of 'poor theatre':

> They fight up and down the stage to Brian Boru's *Lament*. The Dragon falls. All the fights in this play are done to music, each movement being arranged and rehearsed. St George then frees Princess Sabra from her chain which he throws over the Dragon's back with "strong man" actions. Trumpets as St. George bows before her and she curtsies.[117]

Once defeated, the dragon is carted off to market, with Sabra riding pillion on St George's hobby horse. Symbolically, she carries with her a lamb. Eventually, St George kills the dragon in front of the King of Egypt. This is cleverly staged by the use of 'red flannel tatters' which 'hang from the severed neck',[118] an image strikingly medieval in nature, and perhaps used in earlier Cornish-language drama. Simultaneously artful and sophisticated, Nance reverts whenever possible to 'folk-drama' techniques to enhance the 'ancientness'. Act III tends to have more similarities with other English mumming dramas, for it is the conflict section, and shows the response of the 'Quack' Doctor to the injuries on stage. Learning that Sabra has been stolen from him, the Turkish Knight swears to kill St George. He is also fitted into a Hobby Horse. Comically, they fight or joust at each other with 'artichoke or other brittle stems'[119] until the Turkish Knight falls. At the Knight's death, the music is 'Helston Furry', cleverly creating a link between this text and St George and

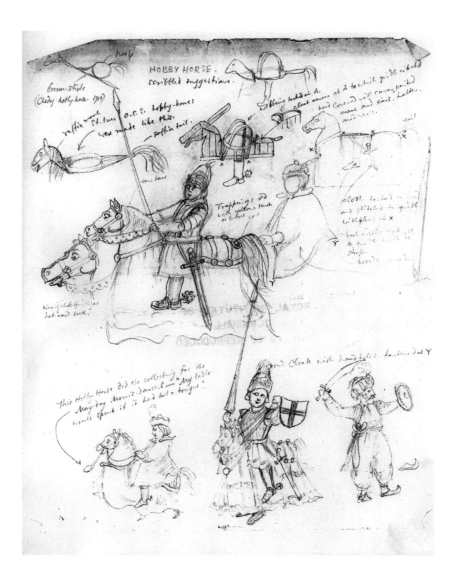

Fig. 75. Nance's sketches for costumes of St George in the St George mummers' play. Courtesy of the Royal Institution of Cornwall.

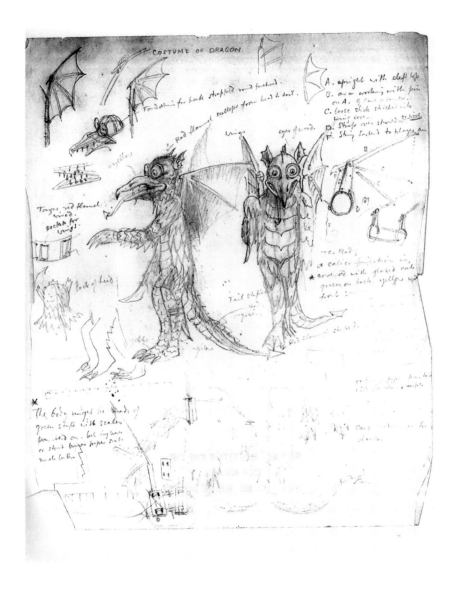

Fig. 76. Nance's sketches for the costumes of the Dragon in the St George mummers' play. Courtesy of the Royal Institution of Cornwall.

the dragon in the *Hal-an-Tow*. Many of the audience would have recognised the connection. Father Christmas calls for the Doctor (a practitioner of folk medicine), who arrives with 'a huge bottle under his arm, and has a blacksmith's pincers in his girdle'.[120] The Doctor's opening speech is a litany of travel both in west Cornwall and elsewhere in Europe:

> I've climbed the mountain tops of Cripple's Ease
> Crossed from Leland [sic] to Hayle, the raging seas;
> I've travelled far that Light to gain–
> In Italy, France and Spain;
> Three times round the world and back again.
> And tramped, mid bleaching bones, on desert sands,
> In parching thirst, o'er Gwithian's barren lands!
> Till with these eyes I've caught the glorious sight,
> The far-flung radiance of Godrevy Light!
> And still undaunted kept on – only think!
> Till Hell's Mouth yawned, and I, upon its brink.[121]

This would clearly have delighted the original St Ives audience. The Turkish Knight temporarily revives at the Doctor's presence, but once again St George dispatches him. Finally, the English Knight must deal with one Slasha, who arrives to be 'avenged of my master's son'.[122] Slasha's purpose is quite clear. He is there to test St George again, but also to represent the dying of the ritual year. It is Father Christmas who asks them to 'Lay down those swords, and be at rest, / For peace and quietness are the best'.[123] At the end of Act III, St George and Princess Sabra exit to the sound of wedding bells, while Father Christmas offers an epilogue. In the prompter's copy this is followed by the singing of a patriotic 'Trelawny', 'The Grand Old Duke of York', then a mumming song. The ritual nature of the piece is accentuated at the end with all the cast shouting 'May every field fine harvest yield, full crops each garden grow! / And a Merry Christmas may you have, and a good New Year also!'[124] Clearly, the piece has considerable dramatic power, though the audience who first witnessed it probably knew little of its significance in terms of what Nance was trying to achieve with Cornish culture. As a reconstruction of what a mumming play in west Cornwall might have been like during the previous centuries, Nance had created a remarkable piece of work. Thanks to careful research, whilst each 'rustic' delivery had an air of realism, it had been carefully choreographed and developed to demonstrate Cornish difference. It was a piece of Yuletide dissent, aimed at asserting a very Cornish new year and era. Constructed this way, St George did not need to be an aggrandising and imperialist symbol. He was purely a pan-British character, who happened to speak 'broad'.

The success of the Christmas play inspired Nance to continue writing drama during the late 1920s and the early 1930s. A number of plays were drafted but not all of the pieces were published and these (alongside drafts of the published texts) remain in Box 9 in the Nance Collection. In 1956, however, three plays were selected for publication by Nance, and published by the Federation of Old Cornwall Societies in a volume titled *The Cledry Plays: Drolls of Old Cornwall for Village Acting and Home Reading*.[125] The title of the collection comes from Nance's fondness for the west Cornwall village of Nancledra,[126] known locally by the familiar name of Cledry. According to Henry Jenner,[127] the Cornu-English term 'droll' is derived from the word *'Daralla'* (Cornish: a tale). Using the word 'droll' was an act of homage to older tellers, while the 'Village Acting' and 'Home Reading' referred jointly to the folk-play heritage of Cornwall,[128] alongside the pre-radio and pre-television age of early-twentieth-century home entertainment. Nance suggests in his Preface to the collection that the plays were firstly conceived for children. In Box 9, I have found no evidence of drafts purely intended for children (though this is not to say they did not exist). They may have originally been conceived in this way, but perhaps even the most literate child of the 1920s would have struggled with the sheer detail of the language. In the Preface, Nance explains their assembly and development, from the perspective of the late 1950s:

> Written nearly fifty years ago for acting by the children of a village school, these plays aimed at carrying on the West Penwith tradition of turning local folk-tales into plays for Christmas acting. What they took over from these guise-dance drolls as they were called, was their love of the local speech and their readiness to break here and there into rhyme or song; what they left was what in them seemed to stress the farcical at the expense of the tale being told. From their native village they were taken round to many others as Christmas or feastentide entertainment.[129]

The evidence for the touring nature of such dramas is actually fairly scarce within both the folkloric and dramatic canon of Cornwall,[130] though it may be to oral recollection that Nance is referring. He is more correct, however, with the Cornish tradition of breaking into song or poetry within the middle of a droll. Many of the tales in Bottrell and Hunt incorporate this technique,[131] very often used to accentuate the mood or emotions of a particular scene, and this method continues in all of *The Cledry Plays* and remaining unpublished plays. Clearly the plays went though several phases of drafting, as can be seen in the contents of Box 9; it seems likely that for the transition into urban environments and for larger occasions, minor changes in both staging and dialogue were made. Nance reflects upon this, and the crucial performance of 'Duffy' that helped to create the first Old Cornwall Society[132]:

> Later, grown to their present form and interpreted by mature actors, they found their town audiences too. It was a performance of "Duffy" at St. Ives that led to the formation there in 1920 of the first Old Cornwall Society – and so in time to the Federation of Old Cornwall Societies and to the Cornish Gorsedd. Apart from public performances there have been many readings of these plays to small audiences of lovers of dialect.[133]

Nance is also keen to accentuate the primitive nature of the dramas, in a way that we imagine Thomas Hardy would have approved. The audiences were never large, but Nance realised early on what the theatrical historian Baz Kershaw has more recently termed 'a theory of performance as ideological transaction, cultural intervention and community action... used to illuminate the potential social and political effects of radical performance practice'.[134] Put another way, Nance knew that his reconfiguration of folk drama in Cornwall could influence socio-political history, and this radicalised 'mumming' could help prevent incorporation into the *status quo* of early twentieth-century England. The fact that the text was written in extreme Cornu-English was only one part of this act of cultural intervention. There were other strands to Nance's drama: the clever and sustained incorporation of phrases in Cornish; the fact that there was a 'punk' ethos of home-produced, low-tech entertainment; and the view that local people were certainly good enough to act the pieces. As Nance comments:

> The simple airs do not ask for accompaniment or for trained voices to do them justice. They are only a slight extension of the music that West-Penwith voices will put into the dialogue. The plays have few characters and very little change of scene; the furniture and properties should be carefully chosen, however, and the costumes and accessories convincing, if they are to have the right effect.[135]

This is an interesting statement. 'Trained voices' suggests that by now Nance rejected the imposition of Standard English, and was fully committed to a linguistically-devolved drama that did not require a perceived English sophistication. Likewise, the statement was also supportive of the transformation of the working-class Cornish, as an ideological recovery process. Three plays made this collection: 'Duffy: A Tale of Trove', 'Sally's Shiners: A Droll of Smuggling

Days' and 'The Kite in the Castle: A Legend of Lamorna'. It is hard to say why these three made publication while other texts did not. Possibly, they were Nance's favourites, although judging the pieces now, there seems little difference in their quality from the texts that are unpublished and considered below. However, 'Duffy' and 'The Kite in the Castle' have character linkages (in the form of Duffy herself and Squire Lovell), so the latter makes for an interesting continuation of the first play. Remarkably, these texts have been more or less ignored by Cornish Studies for many years now.[136] I would like to posit that they are potentially the finest depiction of Cornu-English in print that is extant. The plays are filled with archaism (as elsewhere in Nance's writing), but in their sustained ideology, language and characterisation, there has been little to touch them in terms of their achievement. Criticism of the texts now comes partly from the fact that Cornu-English itself has altered remarkably,[137] and that many terms and concepts have dropped from usage, while, as I have argued elsewhere, others have entered.[138] Alas, the scripts in their published form remain near un-actable for any modern actor, even one consummate in the delivery of Cornu-English.[139] Not many plays or even fragments have survived,[140] and those crucial to the canon radically diverge from what Nance was thinking. By the time Nance was writing, many of the old dialecticians of the nineteenth century – such as John Tabois Tregellas, William Sandys and William Bentinck Forfar – had been forgotten.[141] Nance wanted his folk-plays to be performed in Cornu-English and wrote the scripts accordingly.

As a folk-tale, what is broadly called 'Duffy and the Devil' is an interesting narrative, and its reception and popularity appear to have waned during the twentieth century, in favour of more fashionable folklore such as, in particular, Madge Figgy and her Pig, Tom and the Giant, and the Mermaid of Zennor.[142] In the late twentieth century the truncated tale is contained in Eileen Molony's *Folk Tales of the West* (1971)[143] but not in Donald R. Rawe's influential *Traditional Cornish Stories and Rhymes* (1972).[144] It was briefly revived for Eric Quayle and Michael Foreman's *The Magic Ointment and Other Cornish Legends* (1986)[145] and Shirley Climo and Anthony Bacon Venti's *Magic and Mischief: Tales from Cornwall* (1999),[146] yet always occurs as a lesser tale. Often considered to be the Cornish variant of the international 'Rumpelstiltskin'[147] (and with some similarities to the St Agnes-based narrative of 'Skillywhidden'), the tale was clearly more popular and better known in the nineteenth century. Indeed, it is the lead tale in William Bottrell's *Second Series of Traditions and Hearthside Stories of West Cornwall*,[148] first published in 1873, and in that collection it is nearly double the length of the rest of the narratives. It also features in the *First Series* of Robert Hunt's *Popular Romances of the West*

Fig. 77. A performance of *Duffy and the Devil*. Nance is standing stage right, with A.K. Hamilton Jenkin on the left of the picture. Seated are Miss R. Frazier and Mrs Stanley R. James. Courtesy of the Carola Nance Sculpham/Gorseth Kernow archive.

of England (1865)[149] where it is somewhat truncated compared to Bottrell's version. Clearly the tale was known in an oral capacity as well, though it certainly must have been Bottrell's subtitle of his 'Duffy and the Devil' that most interested Nance, since he calls it 'An Old Christmas Play'[150] and this must have made him reconsider it and scrutinise the tale very closely.

The Cledry Plays themselves are prefaced with a single Nance poem, titled 'Little Cledry', which sets the cultural-geographic context for the dramas that follow. Written in five verses, each composed of sixteen lines, alternating between broadly eight and six syllabic lines, the poem harks back to an earlier phase of Nance's writing for Arthur Quiller-Couch's *Cornish Magazine*, although the rhyming and rhythm appear more sophisticated and controlled. The poem is not a lament, but rather a Betjeman-esque tribute to an area of Britain which remains undisturbed, peaceful, and therefore culturally genuine ('It's quiet down in Cledry, / We're out of all the fuss. / Winds roar right over Cledry / And never trouble us'[151]). Isolation, and a lack of modern conveniences are, according to Nance, both desirable and fitting for the world of the drama about to unfold – 'We've got no trains, no gas, no drains, / No telegraph nor 'phone' –though in some ways this is contradicted by an earlier line referring to 'the stamps that's working still'.[152] Nance clearly approves of resolutely Cornish technology; Cornu-English discourse was integral to the tin industry.

'Duffy: A Tale of Trove' establishes the textual layout for the rest of the volume. On the verso page is a Nance illustration of Duffy at her spinning wheel, watched by Squire Lovel.[153] The picture is in a similar style to those contained in *'The Cornish Magazine'*. Opposite this is the cast of characters, there tending to be no more than four to each play, which suited both small-scale performance and home-reading. Dramatically, this also makes for equal stage-time for each of the four actors. Here they are described in considerable detail. For example, with 'Squire Lovel, an old-fashioned gentleman', we are told that:

> He wears a red, skirted coat; flowered waistcoat, and stockings drawn up over the knee, grey or brown with darns of divers colours in the first act; in the second, white with green clocks [sic]; in the third act his legs are bare and mudstained, and his shoes muddy.[154]

Similar detail is given to Terrytop ('a deluding imp'), Duffy ('a giddy giglet, later Lady Duffy'), and Joan ('housekeeper to Squire Lovel'). This is very typical of Nance's Cornu-English drama – he often indicates the dramatic function of the character, so that the actors clearly know their purpose; a technique found in most other folk drama. Nance also appears to prefer the tripartite model of folk drama, retaining Acts I, II and III as exposition, expansion and conclusion; 'Sally's Shiners' is the one exception to this pattern, having just two Acts. In wider 'modernist' early twentieth-century drama, Prologues were falling out of fashion, seen as unnecessary hindrances to the opening of the play, but the Prologue here is of interest, since it is explicitly concerned with linguistic shift, and crucially Nance's fascination with 'some ancientry that lingers':

> Old Cornwall, too, is changing,
> As surely is as slowly –
> New words and ways estranging
> With time transform us wholly –
> The tongue our forebears cherished
> Is lost from living speeches;
> Yet, as of vessels perished
> The boards drift up on beaches,
> So here and there, time still may spare
> Some ancientry that lingers –
> Let's, as each goes, its eyelids close
> At least with loving fingers.[155]

This verse has never quite been equalled in terms of an English-language lament for the loss of Cornish, as well as a more positive exploration of the Cornish language entering Cornu-English.[156] It is after this that the drama begins properly at Trove Manor House, with the thoughts of Joan the housekeeper, who, aged seventy-seven and near-blind, is having difficulty knitting as she used to. Joan is the physical manifestation of this lament. She is Dolly Pentreath-like in Nance's construction, but also highly practical, and shows understanding of the lot of the Cornish underclass in the period the tale is set (the late eighteenth century). In William Bottrell's version of 'Duffy and the Devil', Joan (there Jone[157]) is a minor character, but Nance cleverly enhances her role as the narrator and the comic interest by making her critical of both Duffy and Lovel. The multi-functional role is important and, as in the other plays, Nance allows the character to enter in a burst of language, seemingly pulling out every 'dialect trick in the book', in one speech that lasts for nearly two pages; a small sample of which is given here:

> Aw! 'Tes a wisht poor ould piliack I've comed to be, sure 'nough – what weth the wan eye clain gone, and t'other jist upon, my woorkin' days es most awver! – Why, I caen't sa mooch as knitty like I da belong – this'll maake the fower times, now. I've been an' took back the turnin' o' this wan heel, and nothen the better of et! – A edn' for me aege, ne'ther! – no aege at all I aren't – tedn' like as ef I was gittin' up in 'eears, 't all – I shaen't *be* but sibmty sibm o'me nixt birthday, ef I shud lev to see it; and sa hearty to me mait as iver I were![158]

This is powerful Cornu-English dramaturgy. Not only is the Cornu-English very developed and therefore difficult for most modern readers both inside and outside of Cornwall, the grammar is also vastly different from Standard English, and acutely manipulated for effect. Few scholars have sought to understand the grammar of Cornu-English,[159] but on the strength of Joan's speech here, Nance has considerable comprehension of the major trends as well as the tiny nuances of difference. There is not the space here to enter into a full discussion, but the word 'she' is used to good effect here: 'But, law! that'd be too swait for *she*, I reckon; for nothin' edn; to her mind, seemin', but what da look ill and smill woorse!' as well as the use of the adverb 'some' to indicate degree: 'Well, some proud I'll be ef he don't breng me back a click-handed edjack'.[160] The finest contemporary essay on Cornu-English grammar is by K.C. Phillipps,[161] and several of the features that he mentions are to be found in Joan's opening speech. A number of the words are explicitly drawn from Cornish, in order to demonstrate the linkages and the sound systems in operation, thus exposing the audience to their indigenous language and counteracting the sentiments of the lamenting Prologue. In Box 9 of the Nance Collection, one parcel has an early list of 'Keltic [sic] Words' entering Cornu-English, and this is expanded in the Glossary at the end of *The Cledry Plays*.[162] An example comes early on when Joan mentions 'pajerpaws' [English: newt] and 'grammarsows' [English: woodlouse] in this statement: 'And now, time she da come to saay as a pultice o'pounded up pajerpaws and grinded-up grammarsows es like to be the theng.'[163]

Despite the compromises (perhaps even gibberish?) – and they are compromises which all writers of dialect have to face – the Cornu-English of this opening play is as striking and as 'exotic' as any script in other British dialects over the course of the twentieth-century,[164] and an equally valid and perhaps more acceptable (to the working classes at least) depiction of Cornish difference. As the twenty-first century has unfurled, more scholars, writers and activists have subscribed to this point of view.[165] The burning question is perhaps how accurate Nance's transcription and depiction of the dialect is. It is a question that is impossible to answer fully within the realms of this chapter. If, however, it is a genuine attempt to equate the text with the living Cornu-English of Nancledra and west Cornwall during the late 1920s and early 1930s, then we have a compelling picture of this difference. However, despite the tendency to gaze at this sound-scape – and not least to wonder at what late twentieth-century and early twenty-first Cornwall might have been like linguistically if this kind of Cornu-English had continued – the evidence points perhaps more to historical invention of 'what people spoke like' in the period in which the play is set – a world in which the Cornish language is seemingly touchable, reachable and indeed recoverable. It might even still be spoken elsewhere in the Trove community.

Nance does not see Cornu-English as one-dimensional and invariably associated with lower-class or humorous characters. Lovel speaks 'posh' Cornu-English ('But as for who she es, I don't know, no more than thee; for I never thoft to ax it'[166]), which demonstrates class difference within Cornu-English. This was rarely found in Cornu-English dialecticians and novelists of the nineteenth-century, who usually employed a straightforward black and white division of English for upper-class characters and Cornu-English for lower-class characters. Although Nance does not explicitly mention this awareness in any of the plays or in his notes, it seems that he was intensely aware of not applying simple linguistic rules to dialect studies (be they creative or academic), a view that has found growing support in late twentieth century studies of dialect, by scholars such as Penhallurick, and Mufwene, which have moved away from a modernist, empirical view, to a more sympathetic under-standing of just how dialects affect the identity of people.[167] This present reassessment patterns and reconfigures the arguments that Nance had advanced much earlier. Nance's 'reconstruction' therefore becomes less problematical when viewed in the light of Kershaw's argument on the politicality of theatre, Penhallurick's alignment of deconstruction with dialectology and Nance's desire to preserve and nourish what Mufwene terms the 'ecology' of language systems, which are always complex.

All of these issues come to the fore within 'Duffy: A Tale of Trove', and although it is important to emphasise Nance's linguistic achievement with the play, we should not forget his narrative skill. His main accomplishment was to hone down the rather circuitous telling offered by Bottrell, and to concentrate on the core components of the folktale's narrative. Bottrell shifts his telling between narrative and drama, filling in with narrative those parts of the story unrecorded or unclear for the reader. Bottrell uses the Christmas frame explicitly throughout, but Nance offers this only at the end, and in the epilogue in particular, when Squire Lovel and Duffy are married ('But 'tis good to have things righted / With a husband and his bride- / And, if not when troth is plighted, Next best time is Christmastide'[168]). At the same time, there is much correlation between the two versions, which may in itself be worthy of separate study in the future. In short, the narrative is concerned with the arrival of Duffy at Trove, in part-replacement for the elderly Joan. Duffy is to work for Squire Lovel, but he clearly has his eye on her for marriage. She is pretty, but idle, and when challenged to spin and knit, she makes a bargain with Terrytop the imp, who will magically provide both the spinning and knitting. Such a deal comes with a price, and although she can wish for whatever she wants (to be found under the black ram's fleece), Terrytop explains the rules of the game:

> Your spinning all I'll do, Duffy,
> And all your knitting too, Duffy,
> I give my promise true, Duffy:
>   A lady you shall be.

> Three years I'll play your game, Duffy-
> Three years – and all I claim, Duffy,
> Is that you guess my name, Duffy;
>   Or then come off with me![169]

Although Duffy is keen to accept his services, she responds by thinking his words are a 'g'eat yafful o' yarn'.[170] However, Nance never makes Terrytop innately evil; he is more an 'imp at work' completing his daily business to

THE . . .
ꞒORNISH
GꝊRSEDD

AT BOSCAWEN-UN STONE CIRCLE, NEAR ST. BURYAN.

(SEPTEMBER 21st, 1928.)

From "The Cornishman" Group of Amalgamated Newspapers, Penzance.

PHOTO BY GIBSON and SON PENZANCE.

The Arch-Druid (Pedrog Rev. J. O. Williams), and Grand Bard of Cornwall, Gwas Myhal, (Mr. Henry Jenner).

[PRICE THREE PENCE.

Fig. 78. An insert that came with *The Cornishman* newspaper, celebrating the first modern Cornish Gorsedd.

survive in the harsh landscape of west Cornwall. At the same time though, Terrytop is a grotesquely imagined character – always hunched, limping with 'elbows jauntily crooked'[171] – melodramatic and goblin-like, with personality and morality linked to appearance in the manner of fiction and pan-European constructions of fairy creatures from the nineteenth century.[172] Act I of the drama concludes with Duffy accepting Terrytop's offer, thinking that nothing will come of the threat. Meanwhile, Squire Lovel decides that Duffy is a miracle, and that despite Joan having the measure of her idleness, she proves herself to be 'the best spinner on earth'.

The musical interludes are another reason why 'Duffy: A Tale of Trove' may be viewed as a typical Nance drama. They are not operatic, nor even similar to songs in a musical, but instead are reflective monologue sequences, offering the audience an insight into the characters' motivation, as well as a cultural-materialist reflection on class, marriage and opportunity for women in the early twentieth-century. Lovel's song at the start of Act II is a reflection on the benefit of spinning and knitting clothing, but comes to reflect on Duffy herself.[173] There is a darker and perhaps even salacious and materialist edge to the narrative here, in which Lovel asks her 'Aren't 'ee finely set up?',[174] then asks Duffy if she will marry him. There are benefits, Squire Lovel argues, to marrying the more mature man. When she accepts, understanding the 'betterment' of her class, it is Joan who offers the Cornu-English rebuke to the time they are spending together: 'What are 'ee tellin' of 'en che'l-vean? Kaipin' comp'ny? Thee and Squire?'.[175] It is interesting that at this crucial point in the narrative, Nance reverts to Cornish [*vean*, meaning 'little'].

A second visit by Terrytop allows him to taunt Duffy, but now that she has risen through the classes, and is about to become Lady Lovel, she confidently ignores his threat. In Act III, in returning late home from hunting, one of Squire Lovel's hounds happens to go down a fugo,[176] and he follows the dog into the dark, finding a gathering of 'buccas'[177] led by Terrytop. When Duffy realises it is the bucca who has been helping her, and who is about to take her away, she quickly questions Lovel about his name. When Terrytop returns on Christmas Eve to take her away, he is filled with confidence: 'Have you finished your packing Duffy?'.[178] On her third guess however, she names him correctly. Now revealed, Terrytop is devastated and leaves dejected, as carol singers arrive to demonstrate it is Christmas Day; evil and greed are defeated at the celebration of Christ's arrival. Here, the drama works as a morality play, exposing sins that we, as audience, should not commit. Duffy herself has been lucky, fitting into a group of characters in Cornish folklore who despite making bargains with ne'er-do-wells and 'devils' still come out on top. Duffy's victory over sex, class and materialism (in the form of the greedy bucca) makes her a potent symbol of Cornish feminism, which Nance recognises and celebrates in the drama. Interestingly, an innovative radio version of the drama of 'Duffy' was broadcast by the BBC on Friday 4 May 1928, with Kathleen Frazier voicing Duffy, Mrs Stanley James playing Joan, A.K. Hamilton Jenkin as Terrytop and Nance himself as Squire Lovel. The piece was recorded in Plymouth, but broadcast across the whole of the United Kingdom, the setting being 'a room at Trove Manor house in ancient times'.[179]

Chronologically, the next drama in *The Cledry Plays* is 'Sally's Shiners: A Droll of Smuggling Days', but perhaps it is more logical to deconstruct the final play *The Kite in the Castle: A Legend of Lamorna*; in several ways, this is a direct sequel to 'Duffy', and forms the second part of the narrative in Bottrell's version. Set soon after Duffy has married Squire Lovel to become Lady Duffy, she is a background character in the play, which examines the fortunes of one Ezekiel Lanine, a poor cobbler, whose family lost the mansion of Trove, and is now forced to live in poverty. He discovers this through his meeting with a strange gentleman customer – the Demon Mason – who arrives at Lanine's cobbler's shop to have a pair of shoes made. The Demon Mason has one hoof, so Lanine's task will be difficult. If, however, he makes the shoes so they are comfortable, the cobbler will be placed into a mansion (built by the Mason) with all the riches he requires. The comedy in the early part of this play is clever. Lanine understands the Demon Mason as 'exotic other' and is trying to banter with him, aiming to find out where he is from. Confusion reigns as Lanine believes he might be a Frenchman, which allows Nance to make a Breton-Cornish connection: 'I mind my gran'f'er tellin' o' much about the saame thing, time he were in the smooglin' sarvice, gooin' awver to Roscoff and they Frinch plaaces. Thoft as how he were spaikin' the ould Cornish to em, he ded.'[180] We soon find out the Demon's origin: 'You see, with us, it's all down-down, down, down, down- and never a bottom'.[181] There is also an intriguing reference to Lanine thinking that the Demon Mason is a Saracen, which has parallels with the Tudor Cornish drama *Bewnans Meriasek* (which Nance would have known well from Whitley Stokes's edition), in which evil Teudar is conceived as 'other' and presented as Islamic.[182] This may also be compared with the standard Turkish Knight of Nance's *Christmas Play*.

Lanine's speeches are fascinating pieces of Cornu-English, which would be enormously difficult for a contemporary actor to deliver, not least in their length, but also in their complexity of ideas and, as noted above, their grammar. One of Nance's methods of working up the speeches was clearly to incorporate core dialect phrases or sayings into them, so that this phrase might then form the subject matter. A good example is to be found early on in Act II, when the term 'They as caen't schemey as ha' got to louster'[183] allows him to explain his family history. This comes with considerable irony since, as Duffy has already proved in the volume, she is certainly a Cornish character who can 'schemey'. This comes out in their conversation about Lanine's heritage, in which he draws on the heraldic symbols of a 'kite in a castle' to explain how his heritage has been stolen from him:

> Why, there's market-town awver to France to we, by rights. Et da goo by aour name, yit, Lanine; and, to prove iet, that very saame coat-an-arms, theer, es cut upon the market-house. My gran'f'er seed'n to one time, when he were awver 'pon smugglin' – a Kite in a Castle![184]

The relationship between Lanine and the Demon Mason is one of Nance's greatest dramatic achievements, filled with deft linguistic touches and puns. When the Demon Mason returns to remind Lanine of his promises, he neatly calls the Demon 'Cap'm!'.[185] The Demon Mason chillingly asks for 'the best *sole* you have to give me'.[186] The Demon's hoof is labelled a 'trifling malformation'[187] while Lanine advises him to perhaps visit a blacksmith and have a shoe fitted ('That would do for you-party, fine!'[188]). However, the castle awarded to Lanine makes him miserly, and when he is visited by Polly, his grand-niece, he will not lend her any money. Importantly, she is told to visit him by 'a straange, ugly-looking man'[189] who is the Demon Mason. Not only this, but Lanine refuses to repair the Demon's shoes. In the end, he loses everything. Again, the text works as a morality play, which argues that the audience should be happy with their lot and certainly never to have 'sawld your sawl for a house'.[190] The Demon Mason as devil in disguise has the same function as Terrytop, but here the bargain made is more serious, and unlike Duffy, who comes up roses, Lanine's future is bleak. This is emphasised in the epilogue:

> Grasping, yet empty, he,
> She, giving, rich in love,
> Lanine a kite would be,
> While Polly stayed a dove.
> Despite our curtain's fall,
> Perhaps, some later day,
> The moral you'll recall,
> Though you forget the play.[191]

This is not the summation of Nance's work in Cornu-English. There remain other important unpublished works. There is, in Box 9, an undated draft of another Christmas-themed play titled *Change-about is Fair Play: A Christmas*

Droll, concerning the characters of Squire Roseveor (an old-fashioned country squire), Jeremy Bawse (a bellows maker), an Astrologer (reflecting arcane Cornishness), Lady Bezantia Roseveor, Tamsin Hawking[192] and Moll, the bellow-maker's wife. A longer drama than the published works, the play presents a strange clamour, focused on Lady Bezantia's cynicism over Christmas; Tamsin describes her as 'a kill-joy, that's what she 'es – with her fancy notions'.[193] Characteristically, in a Nance drama, the lead character, Jeremy, sings two songs, which are summarised in one line of the second song, 'I must work that others play'.[194] Eventually, it is Tamsin and Jeremy who convince Bezantia to enjoy the season. Nance's Cornu-English in this text is as vibrant as the published pieces, but although it is an interesting surviving text, it seems unlikely it will ever reach publication. The same might be said for *The Tragedy of the Chrononhotonthologos: being the most Tragical Tragedy that was ever Tragedied by any Company of Tragedians*.[195] Purported to have been written by Benjamin Bounce, Esq. and printed by Henry Carey, 1734, the work is a learned, cryptic, Latinate satire on early eighteenth-century drama; the stage business is full of archaisms, billowing rhetoric and over-inflated acting. It seems doubtful that it was ever performed, and remains a curious remnant of Nance's knowledge of this genre and period, perhaps to share amongst educated friends. A more accessible and congenial unpublished play is *Tom and the Giant: A Christmas Play* – a retelling of the folktale alluded to above. The characters are Tom of Boujyheer, Giant Blunderbore, Jack the Tinkard, and Joan, the giant's wife. This is a more complete draft than *Change-about is Fair Play: A Christmas Droll*, but it is much shorter –only five pages. It takes a similar mumming approach to the other Christmas dramas, as can be seen from Tom's opening lines:

Here comes I, Tom-Long, Tom of Boujyheer,
From Market-jew, bound for St Ives, with beer.[196]

The story develops in much the same way as in other published versions. Joan and Tom outwit the Giant Blunderbore, although the Giant's supple death speech is more interesting since it incorporates a traditional Cornish language motto:

Fortune must favour such a pious pair! –
Farewell! – Write on my tomb, "He could play fair."
Though all my life, false-play has been my plague
I've learnt now, *Gwary whêg yu gwary têg*.[197]

This play would be of greater interest to modern readers and is perhaps, one day, worth publishing. As Nance progressed, his Cornu-English plays subsequently became more ambitious. *John Knill* (n.d.) is a more epic and ambitious prose drama, which merits much further study.[198] The threnody is a life of Knill, the one-time mayor of St Ives, who was greatly admired by the people of the town, and who is said to have also been a smuggler. Knill decreed that every fifth year on St James' Day (25 July), the town should honour him by a parade of ten local girls, all dressed in white who would dance through the town up to his pyramid-shaped mausoleum on Worvas Hill. At the mausoleum, the girls would dance around it, and be met by the town's mayor and two widows. People watching would sing 'The Hundredth Psalm'. The topic for the play is inspired, pre-figuring the subject-matter of later twentieth- and twenty-first century Anglo-Cornish drama, and again, it is a curious marshalling of folklore and drama, filled with historical allusions. Part-versions of this are found in Box 9. It is one Nance play that really deserves to be much better known, and possibly revived. As can be seen from the above, there is much similarity between what Nance was trying to do in Cornwall, and what W.B. Yeats was achieving in Ireland. As in Yeats, the intimacy of the staging of Nance's plays, coupled with their formal ritual in verse, dance, music and mumming, created a drama of extraordinary intensity.[199] In many ways, Nance repudiated realism in the same way that the Irish scholar had and, like Yeats, Nance was also heavily influenced by his land's folkloric traditions.[200]

The 1920s had been a busy decade for Nance. Not only had he developed a body of work in Cornu-English that would stand unrivalled for the rest of the twentieth-century, but he had founded the first Old Cornwall Society in 1920 at St Ives, igniting other Societies in other Cornish towns to grow into a Federation. The unique development and structure of the Old Cornwall Societies has been given considerable academic energy, and it is ground I do not wish to cover again here. The same may also be said for the establishment of the Gorseth of the Bards of Cornwall, which is given coverage in many scholars' works, ranging from Ellis, and Miles, to Carr-Gomm, and Lyon.[201] The para-theatrical inauguration ceremony, conducted by Pedrog, Archdruid of Wales, took place at Boscawen Ûn on 21 September 1928. Nance's writing was to have considerable influence on the invented ritual of the Gorseth, which will be examined in the context of his Cornish language work below. In the following year, Nance published his influential textbook *Cornish for All*.[202] Henry Jenner, and other activists such as L.C. Duncombe-Jewell, had long been working towards Cornwall being accepted into the Celtic Congress. As Ellis details, Cornwall had been consistently rejected by the

Celtic Congress in the opening years of the twentieth century, failing because of the 'linguistic criterion'.[203] In particular, when the Congress first met in Dublin in 1900, other Celtic territories appeared to pull Celtic weight on the smaller and university-less Cornwall. However, after a convincing address by Jenner on 31 August 1904,[204] Cornwall was admitted, yet it was almost thirty years before the Celtic Congress was held in Truro for the first time, in 1932. According to Smith, 'eight among those present delivered short addresses in Cornish'.[205]

The timing was, however, perfect for the foregrounding of Nance's work, but this time, in the drama conceived, he decided to exchange Cornu-English for Cornish. The reasons behind this are two-fold. First of all, Nance's own Cornish had, over the past decade, become highly sophisticated: he aimed to match earlier writings from the Cornish literary canon. Secondly, with the eyes of the contemporary Celtic world watching, he could not only prove the viability of his Unified project, but also demonstrate that the language was alive and kicking – not least in the most potent symbol of Cornish identity and the title of the allegorical play – *An Balores* [The Chough].[206] It was a meditation on nationalism which was to awaken hope in Cornwall. One of the most important strands of Cornish identity, as Nance perceived it, was King Arthur and the ongoing imagination of his presence in the form of a chough.[207] If Arthur and choughs might one day return and lead a reconstructed Cornwall, then there was at least hope for a Cornwall in industrial, economic and cultural turmoil. In the drama, Nance promotes a vision of a Cornish-speaking Arthur – something rarely conceived of outside Cornwall, while the play's structure appears to incorporate elements of mumming as well as Cornish liturgical and medieval drama. The drama is comparatively short, having on the cover – '*owtheswonvos gweres* Syr Thomas More' – a short apology to the judge and writer Sir Thomas More (1477-1535),[208] since the central character of Nance's drama is also 'The Justice'; clearly Nance had in mind his famous story of imprisonment and high treason over Henry VIII's divorce from Queen Catherine. There also appear to be veiled references to other dramas on More. The first stage direction tells us that '*An bobel, peswar den ha dyw venen, a-sef adro dhe un vasken vyghan, warnedhy palores varow, yn-dan elerlen.* [The folk, four men and two women, stand round a little bier with a dead chough on it under a pall]'.[209] The two male characters, who we later learn are called Peter Grief and Bartholomew Battler (a naming technique already established in Nance's Cornu-English drama), debate the reasons behind the death of the chough – or rather, allegorically, the Cornish language. Battler believes it was the Saxons who drove his forefathers out of their country [Britain] and into the peninsula of Cornwall, though Grief believes it was the Cornish themselves:

My a-bref bos henna gow – Ny agan-honen yu dhe vlamya! Ny, an dus Kernow, yu, re-s-ladhas! Hy res-ombrederas, "Pandr' a-dal dhem bewa, ynnof ow-quytha yn-few spyrys Myghtern Arthur, aban na-vyn tus Kernow kewsel Kernewek na-moy? – Pandr' a-dal bos Arthur bew, marow mar pe y davas?" Ena, hep mar, hy a-wrowedhas a-hes, has dascor an spyrys-na, ha merwel, terrys hy holon-hy!

[I will prove that to be false. We ourselves are to blame! We, the people of Cornwall, it is, who have killed it! It thought within itself, "What good is it for me to live, keeping the spirit of King Arthur alive in me, since the folk of Cornwall won't speak Cornish any more? What is the use of Arthur being alive, if his tongue is dead?" Then, doubtless, it lay down and gave up this spirit, and died, broken-hearted!][210]

Further debate is caused by the discussions of Jack Smart, Tom Hardhead and Aunt Molly Thickhead. The Justice, meanwhile, tries to find out the truth of the matter. The truth status of each of the characters is tested in the play, generally through further absurdist allegories of hens, eggs and clothes. Aunt Molly Thickhead seems to believe that the chough was killed by an old wise woman, who perhaps had the Devil to help her (a motif that reminds us of the Demon Mason). She is also termed a gypsy – invoking a reference to Egypt (a recollection of the King in Nance's 'Christmas Play'). At the very moment of the discovery of this mysterious woman however, the dead chough comes to life. In this construction Nance invokes one of the most powerful symbols of 'revivalism' in Cornwall in the twentieth century, inspiring countless other poets to continue to use the chough as an icon.[211] The short, stichomythic-style lines at the end of the piece offer a vigorous new energy to the language (later termed *Dasserghyn* [Resurgence]), newly 'flying' above Cornwall:

AN KENSA DEN: Otomma marthus! Ass-yu hemma da!
AN NESSA DEN: Hy a-agor hy deulagas!
AN KENSA DEN: Yma-hy ow-lesa hy dywaskel!
AN TRESSA DEN: Hy a-nyj!
AN PESWARA DEN: Hy a-vew!
AN NESSA BENEN: Nyns-yu marow an balores!

[1ST MAN: Here's a miracle! How good this is!
2ND MAN: It opens its eyes!

1ST WOMAN: It's spreading its wings!
3RD MAN: It flies!
4TH MAN: It's alive! Hurrah!
2ND WOMAN: The chough's not dead!][212]

In the rampant stupidity of the comic characters, there are traces of Nance's mumming folk drama, but in the Justice figure, we see echoes of the arrest of Jesus from 'Passio Christi' and the Emperor's Doctors from *Bewnans Meriasek*. While the Cornish of the play is comparatively basic (the prose tends to stumble rather than flow), *An Balores* is still something of an achievement. What the piece loses in dramatic complexity, it gains in radicalised theatre. There are relatively few other pieces of drama in Cornish during this phase, and Nance's imagining was to have a lasting effect. The culmination of the drama is a song – epilogue-like in its structure – that celebrates Arthur's spirit within the chough, as well as a new phase for the Cornish language.[213] Arthur therefore is neatly and ideologically connected with the language:

Yeth Kernow, re-be hyrneth
    A'y groweth yn enewores,
Ena a-dhassergh ynweth
    Maga few avel palores.

Nyns-yu marow Myghtern Arthur!

[So again our Cornish tongue
    That has lain so long a-dying,
Shall rise up as strong and young
    As is e'er a chough that's flying.

King Arthur is not dead!][214]

The Cornish Gorseth has, until now, been remarkably reluctant to release the author(s) and inspiration for much of the Gorseth ceremony's text (perhaps to enhance its 'ancientry'). However, the Arthur and Chough theme would find further integration into Cornish culture in general, and as the Gorseth developed in this early phase, it was in all likelihood Nance who added these lines to Part XIII of the Gorseth ceremony – *Cledha Myghtern Arthur* [The Sword of King Arthur], in itself a powerful piece of experimental dramatic ritual, based on call and response, and deeply connected to the later *An Balores*:

CANNAS BARTH MUR:	*An als whath Arthur a wyth,*
	Yn corf Palores yn few;
	Y Wlas whath Arthur a bew,
	Myghtern a ve hag a vyth,
AN VYRTH OLL:	*Nyns yu marow Myghtern Arthur!*
BARTH MUR:	*Otomma Cledha us yn le Calespulgh, Cledha*
	Myghtern Arthur, a dhuth dyworth an Logh, ha
	dhe'n Logh eth arta. A vynnough-why ty
	warnodho bynytha bos lel dhe Gernow, agan
	Mamvro?
AN VYRTH OLL:	*Ny a'n te!*
[DEPUTY GRAND BARD:	Still Arthur watches our shore,
	In guise of a Chough there flown;
	His Kingdom he keeps his own,
	Once King, to be King once more.
ALL THE BARDS:	King Arthur is not dead!
GRAND BARD:	Behold a Sword which represents Excalibur,
	the Sword of King Arthur, which came from
	the Lake, and went to the Lake again. Will
	you swear upon it to be ever loyal to Cornwall,
	our Motherland!
ALL THE BARDS:	We swear it!][215]

Not only was Nance sanctifying the chough, he was reactivating it as myth. Here, theatre, ritual, reconstruction, poetry and patriotism merge. Not only was *An Balores* to be indicative of Nance's achievement, it was also to be the launch-pad for the final phases of his literary career. Nance's range was extensive and various; his theatre had levelling techniques and was a synaesthetic experience of Cornwall for the audience. There was a large amount of ceremony and ritual about Nance's theatre, reflected in his conceptualisation of a Cornish Gorseth. It was, like the Gorseth, a place of enchantment, with Nance as a glorious assimilator. While Nance was completing this work, he had also been translating and exploring the major canonical dramatic texts within Cornish literature. In the summer of 1931 he completed what he terms a 'unified rendering' of 'If Cornish folk would but listen'[216] and in 'A Cornish Poem Restored' reflected on the integration of the Passion Poem into the *Ordinalia*.[217] He and A.S.D. Smith (1883-1950) had worked on both the *Ordinalia* and *Bewnans Meriasek* making core sections of the plays available in Unified Cornish for the first time: 'Extracts from the Cornish Texts in Unified Spelling with amended translation'. These were published as a series of pamphlets produced by the Federation of Old Cornwall Societies. From 1966, they were reproduced by the Cornish Language Board.[218]

The culmination of this work came much later, however, after Nance and Smith's deaths. The Cornish Language Board published Nance and Smith's translation of 'Christ's Passion' and 'The Resurrection' in 1982 and 1984 respectively.[219] 'Origo Mundi [The Beginning of the World]' remained available only in manuscript form until 2001, when it was published by Agan Tavas,[220] almost twenty years after the first titles. This had been a huge project for Nance and Smith to complete and was, in very many ways, the culmination of their lives' work. Nance and Smith had put the status of Cornish theatre back on the European cultural map. Nance had drawn imaginatively on the Brythonic tradition, in much the same way as other activists such as J.R.R. Tolkien and W.B Yeats had respectively with Anglo-Saxon and Gaelic culture.[221] His poetic legacy in Cornish, though not large, contained pointers towards the future development of poetry in Cornish, and at the same time his interest in the 'magical Celtic' pre-figured the concerns of many interested observers, from as diverse groups as neo-pagans to minority language enthusiasts.[222] Nance's translations allowed a new generation of readers and performers access to dramas crucial in understanding the theatrical history of these islands. His dramatic works are equally important, because in Nance we see, for the first time, someone activating a new culture of Cornish theatre.

As Nance knew well, culture can take bizarre twists and turns. On 23 December 2004, this writer attended the para-theatrical celebrations at Mousehole in west Cornwall commemorating the famous mission of Tom Bawcock to end the famine in the village. Now known as 'Tom Bawcock's Eve', the event has not only developed Mousehole's own tradition of Star Gazy Pie and Christmas lights, but has integrated 'exterior' texts such as one of the most lasting children's picture books of recent years, *The Mousehole Cat* by Antonia Barber and Nicola Bayley.[223] As a torchlight procession (complete with bombards and drums) headed through the streets of the village, complete with willow and paper recreations of Star Gazy Pie and Bawcock's boat, the children of the village sang a song, not too different from that which follows:

A merry plaace, you may believe,
Was Mouzel 'pon Tom Bawcock's Eve.
To be there then who wudn' wesh,
To sup o' sibm sorts o' fish.

When morgy brath
Had cleared the path,
Comed lances for a fry,
And then us had
A bit of scad
An' starry-gazy pie![224]

Nance 'reconstructed' this song early on, in the Cornu-English phase of his poetic career. In the April 1927 edition of *Old Cornwall* he writes how he found this 'little verse, written years ago, that I turned out of a drawer'. He also comments: 'At Mousehole this is the eve before Christmas Eve, which was formerly kept as a feast among the fisher-folk there. Its particular feature was the eating... of seven different sorts of fish... with (if possible) plenty of moonshine to wash it down.'[225] In the eyes of Nance then, the above song was a 'conjectural description' of what might have once been sung at this feast in former times.[226] That conjectural description, like much of Nance's dramatic work, is now fully embedded in Cornish culture. The children of Mousehole seem unlikely to stop singing it. This one small song is perhaps symbolic of Nance's literary achievement in Cornwall. Although his methodology may now seem questionable, its result has been increased 'Cornishness'. That mantra exudes from all his work. When Nance died on 27 May 1959, aged 86, an observer of the time commented:

> Realistically, not metaphorically, Nance saw the Cornish language of our ancestors permanently revived and produced meticulously in volume form. Thus today the Cornish language and dictionaries remain safely with global literature, often prized in the libraries of universities and in the loving care of scholars.[227]

The same might be said for his achievements in Cornu-English and folklore. Nance's grave in Zennor churchyard is still visited by admirers and pilgrims, who understand his need for 'conjectural description'. There are, therefore, many descriptions of Nance we might apply with regard to his theatre, above and beyond 'some ancientry that lingers'. He was an arch-reconstructionist, yet so were J.R.R. Tolkien and W.B. Yeats; his work prefigures and predates the work of respected folklorists and para-theatrical observers such as Georgina

Boyes, and Ronald Hutton.[228] However, his assimilation of Breton and Welsh vocabulary may be a borrowing too far;[229] his work in English was filled with archaisms of language; his dramatic interpretation of the folk-play in Cornwall may itself be labelled 'conjectural' at best, and 'invented' at its worst. However, as we have observed, given his 'moment of production', and in response to his detractors, Nance actually copes supremely well with the promise and problems of literary and theatrical revival in Cornwall. Nance was a harbinger of a new kind of Cornish writer – practical, pragmatic and politically active – who made Cornwall culturally respectable again. His linguistic dissent, his realisation of Cornish difference, and his interest in the twin 'dialects' of Cornish and English (as well as their interaction) confirm his core position in the modern theatrical culture of Cornwall.

Possibly one of the most important, if underestimated, figures in early twentieth-century drama in Cornwall is Bernard Walke. Walke was born in Wiltshire, but came to Cornwall after being ordained into the Church of England, first at St Ives, and then at Polruan. He had previously worked in the East End of London. However, in 1912, he was offered the position of Vicar of St Hilary, in west Cornwall, and was involved with the church and parish there until his death from tuberculosis in 1940.[230] His ministry itself lasted for twenty years. At St Hilary, his tenure there was notable for two reasons. First of all, 'Ber' Walke (known there as 'Passon [Parson] Walke') tried to bring his fiercely independent parishioners back to the faith of their pre-Reformation forefathers. He had a strong sense of ritual, drama and art, connected to his Anglo-Catholic sensibilities. This activity ensured a good deal of anxiety amongst certain observers, and in 1932, the church was broken into by extremist Protestant agitators of Kensitite persuasion. The *Daily Mirror* wrote of a 'Raid on a Church. Bellringer overpowered and 'illegal' ornaments seized' and 'Preachers Storm Village: Vicar held Prisoner'.[231] The agitators (many of them from outside of Cornwall) removed and destroyed many of the fittings, art and furnishings installed by Walke, and held him captive. Such events prompted much national media coverage. Although their anger was directed at Walke, he was part of a small but significant trend in Cornwall during this phase, which was embracing the Anglo-Catholic component of the Cornish Revival.[232] This was seen elsewhere in the Anglican Church in Cornwall, which had started to observe the importance of the major Cornish saints, and looked to both Brittany and Ireland as centres of this older style of liturgy.[233] This was further embodied in the Breton-style architecture of Truro Cathedral, built between 1880 and 1910.

The second reason for Walke's fame is related to the first. In the 1920s and 1930s, Walke wrote a series of dramas exploring a Celto-Catholic Cornish experience,[234] beginning in December 1926 with a radio broadcast version of a Christmas-themed play titled *Bethlehem*. This drama was broadcast and re-recorded annually for some nine years after its first airing, and such was its impact that for many years people travelled to St Hilary to see where the event was staged. It became an early example of a media pilgrimage site. A major contributor to the success of this radio drama was Filson Young (1876-1938) who produced the show.[235] Walke had met Young when he came to St Hilary to play the organ, Young sharing Walke's Anglo-Catholic views. Initially, Walke had been reluctant to allow the drama to be broadcast, but relented when Young agreed to combine the broadcast with an appeal for donations for a home for abandoned London children.

With the success of *Bethlehem*, Walke wrote a series of plays, some of which were staged in the church, with a number also broadcast by the BBC. No doubt the success of Walke's dramatic endeavours also helped cause the agitation of the Protestant Truth Society in 1932.[236] Although Walke's dramas were not overtly nationalist in the sense of other Cornish drama of the early twentieth century (such as Nance's *An Balores / The Chough*[237]) – and neither did they involve the Cornish language – Walke, as we shall see, was clearly aware of working within a Cornish dramatic continuum, and felt this would be an apt vehicle to foreground his Anglo-Catholic ideology. Curiously, Walke seems to have been neatly side-stepped by the broader revivalist movement (perhaps his views, post-1932, were too extreme, even for the mainly Anglican-led revivalists),[238] as well as most observers of the period.[239] His drama too, has barely been considered by the academy.[240] A reappraisal is long overdue.

In some respects, Walke fits into a tradition of ecclesiastical eccentrics which goes back to figures such as the poet Robert Stephen Hawker, who also embraced Anglo-Catholicism (fully committing to Catholicism on his death bed),[241] but in other senses, Walke was extremely progressive in understanding the power, for example, of liturgical drama and its impact upon a community, but even more so, for his early embracing of the power of pan-British media. In his autobiography, *Twenty Years at St Hilary*, first published in 1935, it is clear that the violent events of 1932, haunted and disturbed him greatly, although we also note that he understood very well indeed the connections between space, place and performance in St Hilary, and had a deep knowledge of the purpose of ritual, community and landscape in theatre. In a 1939 anthology of his plays, Walke explains his influences:

In the Parish of St Hilary, within sight of the Church, there is a field called 'Plain-an-Gwarry' – the Field of the Play. Here, in the Middle Ages, from a farm wagon or rough staging, the men and boys of the parish paraded and gestured in scenes from the Old and the New Testament representing man's fall from grace and God's redeeming love in the death and resurrection of His Son. It was the thought of this field, still known to the people as 'Plain-an-gwarry', that led me to write these plays for St. Hilary.[242]

As Lyon, and Spriggs note, there is considerable evidence for theatre space at St Hilary,[243] the *plen-an-gwarry* lying just off Gear Lane. Lyon theorises that Gear is Cornish for 'Camp' and that the playing place may well have been an adaptation of that original earthwork.[244] If this is the case, then Walke's writing at the start of the twentieth century shows considerable correlation with what may well have occurred there some four or five hundred years before. In addition, Walke, as we later observe with Charles Causley in this chapter, had a profound understanding of Cornwall and the Cornish, alongside a remarkable ear for their Cornu-English speech rhythms and intonation. Walke's view of 'country' people was essential in his dramaturgy. It was the antithesis of Arthur Quiller-Couch's views on reviving native Cornish drama:

My aim was to produce plays that could be spoken easily and naturally by country people, making use of that rhythmic mode of speech, which, distinct from dialect, is common to all people who live on the land. Further, I hoped, as in the old miracle plays, to represent the conflict between good and evil in a setting familiar to the people.[245]

There were echoes of this 'culture' in modern Cornwall. Frank Baker, who worked as the organist at St Hilary Church during Walke's time there, observes traces of the past still present there, which had completely died out elsewhere in Cornwall. While there are, in Baker's view, elements of medieval, Celto-Catholic Cornwall, Walke's spirituality can almost be traced back further − in the ritual origins of drama. Indeed, Baker's description offers a sense of Walke's 'druidic' power:

There were the processions at Corpus Christi and the Assumption, through the lanes and across the glebe fields, when all the clergy in Penwith seemed to present, pleased as proud children in the gorgeous copes. On the Corpus Christi when I first met him... I saw in the austere gold-vested figure under the canopy who held high to the sun the gleaming monstrance with its precious Charge, the timeless figure of the Priest, detached from all human affairs so long as this ancient ceremony of the Revelation of the Body of God continued.[246]

Walke, too, was obviously very aware of the ritualistic origins of theatre, as he explains in this sequence of his autobiography:

> There is Corpus Christi Fair at Penzance, to which people flock from the neighbouring villages; there is the Feast of the patron saint, known in St Hilary as Feast Monday, and best of all Roguery Tuesday, a delightful substitute for carnival, when all the young men of St. Hilary go about unhinging gates and engaging in other rogueries.[247]

Such 'topsy-turvy' events were connected with Walke's imagining of a dramatic past and present. It appears that he wrote a number of plays during his time at St Hilary, some of which ended up in his anthology of drama; some of which did not. For example, *The Little Ass*, which is mentioned in his autobiography, was written some time between 1926 and 1935, but has not been traceable. There was also another radio drama, *The Western Land*, which has been described by Walke as 'a dialogue between a farmer (played by a real farmer called Hocking, from Penberthy), fisherman, flower-grower and miner'.[248] It sounds more secular than the other early pieces, which were generally more focused on Christmas. Walke was particularly interested in this part of the year and its Christian message. For him, the statement of the rebels in 1549 concerning how the 'Mass... was like to them a Christmas Play' had a particular irony.[249] Several of the plays follow re-examinations of this part of the ritual year. Although Walke confesses to the influence of the 'mystery and miracle play' Age, the reality is that he is following the long-surviving Cornish tradition of Christmas drama, which was going through a concurrent revival (in the form of mummers' plays) in the Old Cornwall Societies. Walke may have believed that the playing place could have been used at this time of year as well, but this is perhaps unlikely, given weather conditions.

Three plays are contained in the 1939 anthology of his work. The first in the collection is actually a non-Christmas-themed work: a 'Passion play' called *The Upper Chamber*. In terms of style, this is the text which draws more fully on the mystery play tradition, featuring the time before Judas' betrayal, the locations being 'The Crossroads', 'The Place of Caiaphas' and the upper room both 'before' and 'after the last supper'. It is not clear whether Walke read and studied earlier Cornish-language texts, but the cast of characters could easily have come from the 'Passion' of the *Ordinalia*: Peter, John, Judas, a Boy, a Man, Caiaphas, Annas, Servant, Our Lady, Mary Magdalene, the Other Mary, and Andrew. Although Walke thinks of his text as 'countrified' English, the characters speak in beautifully-observed Cornu-English, as in this speech by John:

Judas, my dear, you're strange to-day. I can't make 'e out at all. It never were Peter
nor James nor John. The Master d'love us all. 'Tis His love that we care for more
than His Kingdom. I ain't sure whether love ain't His Kingdom, and His
Kingdom His love, if a man can put it that way.[250]

A Cornish 'sense of logic' comes across strongly in such dialogue. Walke had
clearly listened to his parishioners, but he also had an eye on the industrial
aspect of Cornwall. For example, in the 1920s, Walke and his colleagues had
tried in earnest to set up a political and social movement committed to relieve
mining communities from the unemployment caused by the decline in tin
production.[251] He therefore understood their passions, as well as their socio-
linguistics. There is an intimacy of place projected onto the biblical narrative;
just as in the medieval texts, Walke almost seamlessly merging Cornu-English
with biblical language. In the same play, the Other Mary says, 'Everything
now is all fittie as it belong. There are places for all, Simon, Andrew, and
John...'.[252] Later, Walke builds in the legend of the Cuckoo Feast from
Towednack, incorporating a local motif, just as the earlier playwrights had
done with the mermaid; the tradition of the cuckoo had been noted by Deane
and Shaw as being pan-Cornish.[253] Here, the words of the song are uttered by
the 'half-witted' boy and pre-figure the moment of betrayal.[254] Because of the
way the drama is constructed, the piece would be peculiarly apt to perform in
front of a congregation, because it requires only simple staging; it also lends
itself well to radio. We may note that the Cornu-English is not the 'extreme'
style of Nance,[255] but a more blended, softer approach, which may well have
been closer to the kind of Cornu-English spoken in the parish.[256] In his plays,
Nance was already reconstructing bygone phrases and rhythms. In Walke's
drama, there is not this sense of folkloric preservation.

The Eve of All Souls is another non-Christmas-themed play in the canon of
Walke's work. Of all Walke's drama, this text is the most disturbing, and
perhaps the most alarming in the entire Cornish and Anglo-Cornish
continuum. It features a complex metaphorical examination of death as the last
enemy to be overcome, and tells the story of a bride, Mary Tregenza, whose
marriage that day in the Parish Church the whole of the village has attended.
She is distraught with fear on her wedding night, concerned that death will
bring their love to a close. Walke tries to offer a corrective: that there is hope
that it will not, although the play is not an easy journey. The construction of
the scenes at the 'Church at Night' are unsettling, with Walke making the
'voices of the dead' eerie and unrelenting. Mary's husband, John, comments 'I
can't say I feel happy at all with the thoughts of the dead all around us as they
be'.[257] Sometimes, Walke's overt high-church Anglo-Catholicism intrudes too

far into the text, so there is an artificial religiosity, in what might actually seem like a more standard Cornish-Methodist marriage: 'There he is on the chest-of-drawers; give en to me Mother, for I know where the Solemnization of Matrimony do come. Here 'tis next to the Cathechism and Confirmation.'[258] The build-up to the marriage is well-observed, with Mary's father an old-school Cornishman ('God bless 'e and make 'e as good a wife to John as your mother has been to me'[259]). There are also some well-drawn cameos in the form of the villagers William Henry and Silas Penberthy (who, Walke indicates in his autobiography, were based on real parishioners). It is not clear whether Walke intended the play to be performed around Halloween, but the text's premise makes it particularly appropriate for this part of the ritual year. Indeed, maybe Walke intended it as a corrective to other 'pagan' activity. Though ambitious in its themes, the play is perhaps too overtly concerned with Anglo-Catholic doctrine to transcend any further.

Returning to Walke's preoccupation with Christmas-themed work, *The Stranger at St Hilary* is a more celebratory drama from Walke's later period of writing. This text builds upon the tradition of seasonal drama at the church by self-consciously having a stranger arrive there in order to see a production: 'Is this St Hilary Church town where they belong to do the Christmas Play?'.[260] Here, the stranger is a man from Bodmin Moor who, haunted by spirits of the moors, comes to St Hilary and is granted a vision of the Nativity. Initially, however, he is told by the Sexton that no play will be performed this year:

No play, you d'say? That can't be. Think where I have come from. You'm gaming me. Hearken, and when I tell 'e the craving I have to see this play you won't want to play no games on me. I live, as I told 'e on Bodmin Moor. It may be you have heard of Rough Tor and Dozmary Pool. Well, Warleggan, where I d'live, is half-way between they. The moor is a terrible place in winter time; the ponies can scarcely live and don't carry more flesh than lichen on the stones.[261]

When the sexton leaves, the space and performance place merge, since the audience watch the stranger in the real confines of the church, where the Nativity then unfolds. The inn is revealed as a kind of old-fashioned Cornish kiddlywink, and the men sat in it – as travellers, and then later, shepherds – almost representations of Cornish miners relaxing after a day's work. The play is presented as a close fusion of biblical and Cornish landscape, which is redolent of the paintings of Walke's wife, Annie Walke, and also of the other artists whom he commissioned to decorate the church,[262] painters now established amongst the finest in modern Cornish art: Ernest Proctor, Harold Harvey, Norman Garstin, Harold Knight, Alathea Garstin, and Gladys

Hynes.[263] Very often, such paintings also looked at the lives of Cornish saints. Walke was keen to imitate the surviving colour and energy of the churches where pictures and images had survived – for example, at nearby Breage, and at St Just-in-Penwith. In this drama, though, Walke relaxes the medieval hold over his writing, to express the genuine experience of the Cornish during this period, merging the liturgical narrative with emigration overseas, an experience which was embedded in Cornish ideology during this phase, as we know from the writings about A.L. Rowse's childhood.[264] In the Second Traveller, international Cornish wit and wiles are foregrounded:

> But what was I saying when the shepherds come in? I remember now. About that old mine at Retallack that was worked out years ago. The man from London thought he'd make a deal, but Cousin Jack was too sharp for en. They can't get round a Cornishman.[265]

The mixture of religiosity and Cornish identity in Walke's work is a fascinating modern recreation of what was created in the playing places of medieval Cornwall. Clearly, he believed in the comments about the Celtic people's love of dressing up,[266] made at the start of this chapter. As in the final play of the *Ordinalia* ('Resurrexio Domini'), the ending is celebratory,[267] with a notion of thanks to God, as well as a community celebration, embodied here in the Choir singing and the Stranger's lines, when he comments, 'If you 'ed looked on what I have you'd never doubt no more'[268] – a message which would have had profound relevance five hundred years earlier – and which Walke was hopeful of achieving in the present as well. Of Walke's battles, there is an interesting section in his autobiography where he reflects on the controversy caused when he attempted to mount a play on Feast Day instead of the usual concert. In Walke's view, the drama would have been the tradition, but in more recent times this had been supplanted by the concert. Nicholas Peters, the sexton at St Hilary, remarked: 'It's a pity that you have gone and done a thing like that, Parson. They'm all talking down Relubbus that Feast is not going to be same as it belongs'.[269] One response from the parish was 'Wonder 'tis allowed. 'Tis all of a piece with the games that do go on up the church. Nothing but play-acting I do say'.[270] Of course, for Walke, his dramas were not just 'play-acting' but a very real way of promoting the Christian message. Unlike some observers in 'modern' Cornwall, Walke was convinced that drama would still operate as a powerful medium, particularly if it were written in a politically-committed Cornu-English, and was not versified. Walke's initial energies had come from the Anglican church itself – representing our protagonist St George – though as his career progressed in Cornwall, much the same as Daphne du Maurier,[271] he appears to have more fully embraced the antagonist St Piran, once he gained understanding of his community and, in his view, its 'original' pre-Reformation spirituality. Although his commitment to nationalism is more ambivalent, compared to the efforts of organisations such as *Tyr ha Tavas*,[272] his dramaturgy certainly matches the wider revivalism in all things Cornish during this period. Walke has a great deal in common with the revivalists' wish for a pre-Reformation Cornwall, where 'apparently' Cornish language, culture and custom were fully operational. His drama would also come to be seen as a developmental phase of a response to indigenous Cornish drama, which would result in the work of later writers who were drawing on similar dramaturgy.[273]

The response to older forms of drama and theatre would also find expression at Porthcurno in the 1930s, with the development of a Greek-style amphitheatre on the cliffs at Minack. There is, in the public imagination, perhaps no greater symbol of theatre in Cornwall than the Minack Theatre.[274] It is a space and place that captures the public's imagination. On the face of it, the venue would appear to encompass many elements of the Cornish theatrical continuum: an organic, community-driven project, with a grass-roots base, its season consistent with the older period of summer festival. The Minack Theatre is also an open-air venue, and would appear to be intrinsically Cornish, located on a Cornish-language named cliffside [*Minack* means 'stony or rocky place'], facing the ocean in west Cornwall. The Minack Theatre also has a famous 'origin' story, embodied in an image of its pioneer Rowena Cade (1893-1983) sat in an upturned wheelbarrow. The Minack's current wording and iconography – 'a dream or a vision?' and 'an enduring fiction' – extols the mystical creative vision (a Celtic trait?) of the creator.[275] This origin story, however, does provide us with difficulties. Although one might expect the Minack to fit within a non-metropolitan and thus antagonistically St Piran-themed response to developing theatre on the periphery of Britain, the origins and development of the theatre have actually been much more along the lines of the protagonist figure, St George. A second difficulty is also worth debate: what the theatre has become is probably a much different project from its original intentions, certainly in terms of productions. Finally, there is a cultural-imperialist difficulty with the Minack Theatre. For all its original, community-driven fervour, building a theatre in that location would not have been allowed in the twenty-first century, because it has altered beyond recognition the indigenous and now protected coastal landscape. In an environmentally-sensitive spatial sense, its construction has been imperialist, and the imperative behind it has come from an English cultural perspective.

Cade's family originated from Spondon in Derbyshire, where her father owned a cotton mill, but the family later moved to Cheltenham. Her childhood was quite idyllic and middle-class. When the First World War began, the family was scattered, and so Rowena and her mother moved to the by-then fashionable Lamorna, renting a house there. Discovering that the Minack headland was for sale for some £100, Rowena bought it and began the process of constructing a house there, built from granite from St Levan quarry.[276] Aged eight, Rowena had taken the lead role in a production of *Alice Through the Looking Glass*, and discovered she had a talent for costume-making. She brought this skill to a 1929 project of *A Midsummer Night's Dream*, directed by Dorothea Valentine and augmented by music from the Penzance Orchestral Society. The performance took place a mile inland at Crean, where there was a tree-lined meadow, suitable for the forest to where the Athenian lovers abscond. Rowena designed the costumes and properties. So successful was the production that it was repeated again in 1930. This open-air method of performance and environmental theatre was, as we know, established in the Cornish theatrical continuum, but whether Valentine and Cade knew they were continuing something much older is unknown. The success of *A Midsummer Night's Dream* prompted Cade to offer her garden as a venue to stage the 'Minack lot's'[277] next performance of *The Tempest*. The most obvious location was the gully above the Minack Rock. Cade, her gardener Billy Rawlings, and later his mate Charles Thomas Angove then began the process of converting the gully into a simple stage with some rough-hewed seating for the audience. This took most of the winter of 1931-1932, and in the summer of 1932 the first performance, of *The Tempest*, took place on the rudimentary first Minack Theatre. The production was lit by batteries, car headlights and power from the house.[278] Set upon Caliban's Island, *The Tempest* was quite a wise choice of play; this early production must have given Cade an idea of the potential of the site, not least in the wonderful natural backdrop of ocean and the headland hill fort of Treryn Dinas.

During the remainder of the 1930s, Cade, Rawlings and Angove laboured at the site, infilling the terraces, moving boulders, constructing further seating and hauling materials down from the house, or up from the beach below. The work was sometimes dangerous: the stage quickly falls away to a 70-foot *zawn* (cliffside chasm). However, the busy production schedule continued. In August 1933, local players performed *Twelfth Night* (augmented by two pro-fessional actors, Stephen Jack and Neil Porter, who played Orsino and Antonio respectively). In 1935 *Gringorie* (an adaptation of *The Hunchback of Notre Dame*) was followed by John Heywood's *The Play of the Weather*, and Richard H. Barnon's *The Jackdaw of Rheims* – three plays that established the

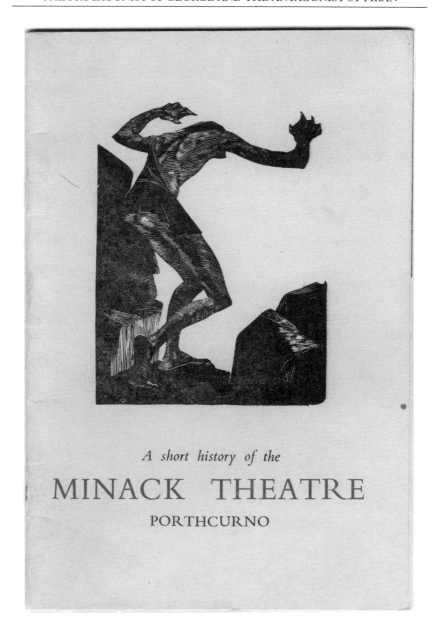

Fig. 79. 'Enter Caliban' from a woodcut, 1932, by Hilda M. Quick illustrating *A Short History of the Minack Theatre*, Porthcurno.

seasonal model for the theatre.[279] Another Shakespeare, *Anthony and Cleopatra*, was presented in 1937. The theatre's potential was perhaps best shown in July 1939, when the Warwick Players presented John Masefield's little-known version of *Tristan and Isolt*; Masefield was perhaps chosen because of his fame as a poet and writer of the sea.[280] Suddenly the Minack, despite presenting mainly imported English drama, was linking itself to the wider Celtic revivalism of the period, and connecting with a narrative that has a long-standing connection with Cornwall. This showed the venue's potential for organic Cornu-centric drama, but it was shortly curtailed by the Second World War, when the theatre was closed and various coastal defences were built, including a gun emplacement and barbed wire. The final pre-war show was *The Count of Monte Cristo*, presented in August 1939.

Part of Cade's early design ethic for the theatre was to combine a classical feel with a representation of its Celtic situation. Cement surfaces were decorated with lettering and intricate pseudo-Celtic designs, which Cade etched in, using the tip of an old screwdriver. It seems that Cade herself recognised the inherent Celticity of the space, but was less able to engender productions that matched

Fig. 80. The Minack Theatre, Porthcurno at the start of the twenty-first century. Courtesy of Paul Watts Photography.

this Celticity – as a middle-class Englishwoman of the 1930s,[281] she predictably drew on canonical English texts. The intention seems to have been that Celtic space and place would merge with performance, but since its construction, this convergence has occurred in a much more piecemeal way. Work was ongoing during the war years, but there was uncertainty about when new theatre would be presented again. Meanwhile, Cade also worked as a local billeting officer for evacuees to Cornwall. Some hope came in 1944, when the theatre was used for the Gainsborough Studio's film *Love Story*, which starred Stewart Granger and Margaret Lockwood, but inclement weather forced them to move to a studio mock-up. Productions did not properly begin until 1949, when the coastal defences were cleared (a pill-box remained as the box-office for a number of years). The first post-war production was Euripedes' *The Trojan Women*, which was presented by a collective of Penzance Grammar Schools. Two years later, in 1951, Nora Ratcliff's *Tristan of Cornwall* was presented as part of that year's Cornwall Drama Festival. This play was commissioned especially for presentation at the Minack.[282]

In the post-war period, some of the impetus of this Celticity was kept. For example, some local players presented a follow-up to *Tristan of Cornwall*, titled *Arthur of Britain* (1953), again by Ratcliff, but thereafter, especially in the

Fig. 81. T.Q. Couch's sketch of an incomplete image which he posits might be of St Ursula, from Lanivet Church. St Ursula was the subject of a drama by the Cornish Religious Drama Fellowship, in 1955. Courtesy of the Royal Institution of Cornwall.

1950s and 1960s, Cornish subject-matter is very sparse. In 1953, Ardingly College Drama Club presented *King Lear*, with its tangential Cornish material, while in August 1955, the Cornish Religious Drama Fellowship presented a version of the lost Cornish narrative of *St Ursula* (probably a narrative that was once staged in the medieval period).[283] Inglis Gundry's *The Logan Rock* was presented by Cornwall Opera Group in August 1956, but when Cornwall Religious Drama Fellowship returned in 1958 with a saint's play, *The Marvellous History of St Bernard*, it was a non-Cornish narrative, and their *Noah* in June 1960 was a non-Cornish version, though its subject-matter related to the continuum. Thereafter, it appears the original vision was dropped. The 1960s, despite establishing the Minack season, is especially sparse for Cornu-centric work, which fares slightly better in the early 1970s, when politicised pan-Celticism became more popular. Among the plays presented then were Nora Ratcliff's *The Net* (August 1971) by the West Cornwall Theatre Group, *The Pirates of Penzance* (August 1974) by Cambridge University Gilbert and Sullivan Society, and *The Legends of King Arthur* (June 1974) by Exeter University Drama Department. The pieces were still ideologically 'safe' investigations of Cornish Celticity, however. In the late 1970s, it was again more English-canonical texts that dominated, changes coming only in the 1980s with Shiva Theatre presenting *King Arthur* (June 1982) and *Meryasek* (September 1983) and the West Cornwall Theatre Group reviving Ratcliff's *Tristan of Cornwall* (July 1982). It was the mid-1990s before Kneehigh Theatre began any sustained work at the theatre.

Tradition has been important at the Minack Theatre. As the site has developed, the titles of previous productions have been scratched into the concrete seats. When Rawlings died in 1966, the one granite seat remaining in the whole auditorium was inscribed in his memory. Cade herself was still active on the site well into her mid-eighties, and Rawlings' builder's mate, Thomas Angove, carried on working until 1993. The theatre (like many others) has often found it difficult to balance the books, especially in the 1950s, and over the years it has not been especially well-supported by pan-British arts organisations. In many ways, it has relied upon the links and associations made with university companies and other semi-professional companies to help fund a week's run at the Minack. Of course, for those companies, a week spent in west Cornwall during the summer is highly desirable, so it would seem there is never a shortage of companies available to play there. Contributors to Demuth's symposium anthology on working at the Minack provide interesting perspectives on operating in the theatre in the twentieth century;[284] despite the difficulties caused by inclement weather, the Minack very rarely cancels performances.

In 1976, Cade gave the Minack Theatre to a charitable Trust which strengthened its operation well into the twenty-first century and, as we shall see later, the Minack continues to be an important component of theatrical life in Cornwall. By the early 1950s, the Minack Theatre was fully established as a theatrical venue but, as we have seen, its Celtic credentials were always somewhat superficial; this perhaps continued through the post-war period, and into the twenty-first century. Although Philip Payton has argued that the Minack Theatre is another representation of a wider revived Celticty in pre-war Cornwall – what he terms 'somehow outlandish, and exotic, thoroughly un-English in conception and form'[285] – on reflection, the basis for this argument is rather limited. The Celtic knotwork on the concrete of the theatre symbolises Celticity, but a real response to Cornish Celticity has been much more limited in terms of performance. Indeed, one could go further and argue that, with a few exceptions, the theatre presented at the Minack over successive decades has usually been imported, English, and canonical. With the exception of some later companies, such as Kneehigh Theatre, even Cornish companies (both amateur and professional) have tended not to present Cornish-themed material. The inherent Celticity of the theatrical experience at the Minack is perhaps more environmental, related to the cliff-side itself, Porthcurno, the ocean, the Logan Stone and Treryn Dinas – in a way, utterly incidental to the theatre being staged. As the Minack quietly developed in the 1940s, taking place elsewhere were other theatrical performances of Celticity, which were far removed from the predominantly English, and actually quite conservative, canon at the Minack Theatre.

In 1942, Canon Gilbert Hunter Doble (1880-1945) presented an English language version of *Bewnans Meriasek* in Redruth, in order to demonstrate the territory's theatrical continuum to people in Cornwall.[286] This was a ground-breaking idea. It is unclear whether Doble presented the full two days of the play, or selections from it, or whether he adapted Stokes' translation.[287] Even so, this was probably the first time *Bewnans Meriasek* had been performed since its original run. As Cornwall's premier hagiographer during this phase, Doble had an interest in such works, because they theatricalised the *vitae* (or lives) he studied.[288] Doble, like Walke, had Anglo-Catholic leanings: he had controversially spoken in 1924 on 're-Catholicising Cornwall'. Having served as curate in the parish of Redruth from 1919 to 1925, and then served as Vicar of Wendron until his death, Doble knew intimately the landscape of the Camborne-based *Bewnans Meriasek*. He reignited interest in the heritage of saints' plays in Cornwall, which prompted, as we shall see shortly, new dramatic imaginings of saints' lives. Doble himself had also committed to the para-theatrical stylings of the Cornish Gorsedd, taking the name of *Gwas Gwendron* [Servant of Wendron] at the 1928 ceremony.[289]

Taking up this influence and energy was Margaret 'Peggy' Pollard (1903-96). Pollard was a relative of W.E. Gladstone, and was widely read in the classics and a scholar of ancient Indian languages.[290] She was working concurrently with Doble, and Nance. In 1940 she responded to the continuum of drama written during the medieval period, and completed a work titled *Beunans Alysaryn / The Life of Alysaryn,* which won the Gorseth annual literary prize that year. The work took its cues from the earlier dramas but, perhaps reflecting British-wide feeling during the Second World War, is a stark study of 'agnosticism' in the Middle Ages, retaining the established structure and form of the Cornish mystery play continuum, but re-evaluating and reinventing the subject-matter. In major ways, the play may be seen as a breakthrough piece. First of all, it was one of the first modern Cornish dramas to be written by a woman, and in boldly taking on such subject matter, Pollard was opening herself up not only to the critique of the small group of language revivalists, but potentially of the wider Christian base of British society, though this never really occurred because of its limited linguistic accessibility. There was already a growing consensus that if

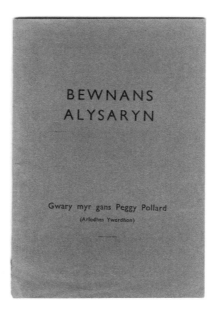

Fig. 82. The stark cover of Peggy Pollard's 1940 play *Bewnans Alysaryn.*

literature were going to succeed in Cornish, it needed to move away from the religious themes of the early revivalists – a view on this period also held by the scholar Brian Murdoch.[291] Perhaps rather unsubtly Pollard uses archaism in her English-language stage directions: 'The first day of ye playe. Rubia Peregrina be in a fine chamber with a table and thereon a greate basket of herbys and flowerys. A serving maid sweeping with a besom'.[292] However, this was purely to give the piece a kind of anti-modernist approach. The Cornish is not sophisticated, but is inventive in offering a new imagining of the older format for drama in Cornish:

Rubia: *Otomma gaya canstel!*
Ow map a'n jeves skyans
hag a wonys gans mur nell
ow tyndyl dhyn mur arghans.
Jentyl yu ha whek y gnas,
hep dowt a'n eas.

Alysaryn: *Prag y whreta crothvolas?*
Ty a 'fyth gober certan:
nyns yu dhe gana ellas,
del welyth splan.
A dhama, myr y'n canstel
mayth us dek sols hep fyllel
o res dhyso genef-vy.

[Rubia: Here is a splendid basket!
My son has knowledge
which will work with great strength
earning for us much silver.
He is gentle and of sweet nature
without any doubt in the case.

Alysaryn: Why do you complain?
You will certainly have a reward:
there is no reason to sing alas,
as you will see clearly.
O mother, look in the basket
where there are ten shillings without fail
that were given to you by me.][293]

More plays of this kind followed in the early 1940s: *Synt Avaldor* (winning first prize again in 1941) and later *Synta Acherontia* and *Synt Tanbellan*. *Synt Avaldor* appears to have been lost, but the other two texts survive in manuscript copy in Box 10 of the Robert Morton Nance Collection in the Courtney Library, Royal Institution of Cornwall. *Synta Acherontia*, written around 1943, has the subtitle of *Gwary-myr* [Miracle Play]. The six days ascribed to this play is an imitation of the structure of medieval Cornish drama. The total performance time would be around one hour and a half. The play combines the life of Acherontia with the life of Nonna. Another important character is Sister Budy, who works on illuminated manuscripts. Again, archaic English language is used to set the scene, alongside archaic Cornish:

> *1st daie of ye plaie. A typicall dwelling of ye Anthracenes. A larger chambour with one window entirely filling one wall, draped across with lines whereon washing is hung. A verie large dirtie bed filled with horse blankets, grubbie pillows, old shawlys and rugges. A large broken table with chairs in ill repair, likewise a smalle table at ye window. Acherontia sitting here, making of lace.*

Acherontia:	*Hemma yu agan fyth*
	ha'gan crysyans:
	whylas yn pup tra-oll
	form ha shapyans.
	Pup tra a's teves form,
	patron shapys:
	Wheryth Du Acheron
	hemma a grys.
	Ny dal dhyn fals gober;
	ny dal strevyans.
	Kemyskeugh cartennow...
	perthyans, perthyans!
	Golyeugh ha gothvedheugh,
	pertheugh yn fas.
	Patron a vyth shapys,
	kepar ha las.

[Acherontia:	This is our faith
	and our belief:
	to seek in everything
	form and shape.

Everything has form,
a shaped pattern:
The Black Sisters of Acheron
believe this.

False reward is worth nothing to us
struggle avails nothing
Shuffle cards...
patience, patience!
Watch and know,
endure well.
A pattern will be shaped,
like lace.][294]

Synt Tanbellan: A tryfle in one Scene [Saint Tanbellan: A trifle in one Scene], from around the same time period, is a skit and satire on revived bardic culture in Cornwall. Compared to her other two works, which were directly influenced by Catholic Celtic Cornwall and wholly epic in form, this play shows her ability in another genre. The piece is set in Falmouth, which is an unusual choice, because no Gorsedd ceremony took place there until 2000. However, the drama is important since it is the first piece of drama to comment directly on the development of the ceremony:

Ye Moor at Falmouth. A wilde desolate space with plane trees, a fountain, a Poste Office, a Wesleyan Chapel, a Garage, shops, and a Publick Librarie. Buses wandering to and fro in ye distance moaning dismallie. Let a Procession of Bardys enter, led by ye Grand Bard Gorowrys Y Gernygow. They take up positions in a circle with ye Grand Bard in ye centre. Ye Bard Newlak y Vrys, who is very ancient, supporteth himself on a shooting stick, which is somewhat liable to capsize in moments of emotion. Gorowrys Y Gernygow beginneth to bustle through ye ritual, skipping out of ye path of ye traffic from time to time.

Carer Usadow (to hys neighbour in a penetrating whisper):
   Ty a wor, ow har Glujek,
   synsy Gorseth ny dal man
   yn termyn bresel, certan.
   Hem yu camwyth pur dhyveth;
   whath yma 'gan Barth Mur whek
   den coth ha nebes sempel,
   dhym del hevel.

645

Bodhar Y Scovarn: *Lavar ughel, coweth da,*
ny yllyn clewes henna.

Gorowrys Y Gernygow: *Dhe'n negys, kescowetha!*
Carer Onyon, gwra redya
record dhyn-ny, del dhegoth,
a'n cuntellyans dewetha.

[Habit's Friend (*to his neighbour in a penetrating whisper*):
You know, my friend Sticky,
it is not worth holding a Gorseth
in time of war, certainly.
This is a very shameless offence;
but still is our sweet Grand Bard
an old man and a little simple,
as it seems to me.

Deafboy: Speak loudly, good friend,
we cannot hear that.

Goldyhorns: To business, comrades!
Lover of Onions, do you read
the record to us, as is fitting,
of the last gathering.][295]

Perhaps because of the impact of this satirical piece, Pollard chose not to write any further drama, which is a tremendous pity, since she stands as the first serious female writer in Cornish. As well as drama, she also wrote a number of poems, but in the late 1940s she turned her skill to history, writing for children one of the first important school text book histories of Cornwall,[296] a staple of many primary schools in the post-war period. As Riche details, she also retained an interest in Celto-Catholic Cornwall, researching the ancient Marian shrine of Liskeard.[297] The significance of Pollard's work should not be underestimated. Not only was she offering an antagonistically radicalised new drama of Cornwall in the Cornish language, she was also a woman, a rarity within Cornish-language writing.[298]

A separate study is very much needed on the development of Cornish opera through recent centuries. I am not the author to write it, but it would be bizarre in a book of this kind to ignore completely the contribution made to Cornish theatrical culture by opera. In many ways, as Maisie Radford notes in her 1966 review of the corpus, Cornwall has the grand scenery, subject-matter and culture to lend itself well to opera.[299] In 1909, Ethel Smyth and the librettist Henry Brewster had written *The Wreckers*, an obvious Cornish story, though it is unclear whether it was ever performed in this period. Even so, such a work seems a direct continuation of much of the 'mythical' subject-matter of Cornwall, which had formed the core ingredients of other melodramas and musicals of the late nineteenth century.[300] In fact, it would seem *The Wreckers* was probably the climax of that phase. Future material produced on that theme would be seen as unfashionable. Interests were changing and as the 'Celtic twilight' and indeed Celtic revivalism in general began to shift more to the centre, other operas began to see Cornwall in a new light. In the early twentieth century it was perhaps Rutland Boughton (1878-1960) who did more than anyone else to focus operatic energies on a more self-consciously 'Celtic' Cornwall. He sought initially to create a centre for English opera at Glastonbury with a series of librettos based on Arthurian legend. For one of these, Boughton took Hardy's text *The Famous Tragedy of the Queen of Cornwall* and produced it at Tintagel in 1924 in tandem with the other Arthurian theatrical revivals there over that decade and the ones to follow. Before Hardy's work he also completed *The Birth of Arthur* (1913), *The Round Table* (1916), and later *The Lily Maid* (1934), and *Avalon* and *Galahad* (both 1945) at Glastonbury.[301]

However, the finest opera to emerge in this phase written by a Cornishman was the wonderfully innovative *Iernin* (1934) written by the Zennor-based George Lloyd (1913-98) with a libretto by his father, William Lloyd, the poet and amateur flautist.[302] Paralleling the rise of cultural nationalism in Cornwall – the explicit symbols of this being the Cornish Gorsedd and the revival of Cornish – Lloyd made sure that *Iernin* was effectively a nationalist statement of intent. The story takes place in post-Roman Cornwall, when the Saxon Kings were beginning to enforce their control on the territory, and when Christianity and paganism were still jostling for position. It is based on the legend of the Nine Maidens – not the non-conformist version where they are turned to stone for dancing on the Sabbath, but a version in which a priest turns them into stone for seducing young men. The plot of the opera then considers the plight of Iernin, the most beautiful of the maidens, who falls in love with a mortal who returns her love. His seduction from his Anglo-Saxon bride-to-be forms the main theme of the text. At the end Iernin renounces him and turns back to stone, as the old Celtic gods of Cornwall might have wished. Lloyd was only twenty-one when the opera was produced in Penzance with him conducting. At the time the opera was acclaimed. A critic from *The Times* suggested that Lloyd 'showed an unerring sense of what the stage requires and in which the balance of interest is fairly held between voices, stage situations and orchestra'.[303] However, this initial promise seems not to have developed. In this period, with *Iernin*, we have a tantalising glimpse of the power of Cornish opera, on fundamentally Cornish themes.

Another playwright was also considering the same issues as Lloyd, Nance and Walke during this period. Operating independently from the revivalist movement in Cornwall is one writer who tends to be ignored as a playwright, but foregrounded as a poet. That writer is the Launceston-born Charles Causley (1917-2003). Certainly, popular opinion would be that Causley wrote almost exclusively poetry in the post-war period, even though this is, in fact, wildly inaccurate. Although Causley became famous for his folkloric, ballad-like verse, which drew on a tradition often keenly out of step with other modernist and post-modernist poetry of the twentieth century,[304] he began his writing career as a dramatist, and the dramatic impetus in his work never left him. One could argue that although his poetry has been placed over and above his dramatic work, in some ways his verse drama is superior. Furthermore, in Causley's dramas, one might note more consciously the threads of Cornish theatrical continuity from previous Ages, which are often ignored. Harry Chambers' 1987 *festschrift* on the writer, *Causley at 70*, is indicative of the problem. Almost all the observers considering Causley's work examine his poetic contribution, with only one – Ronald Tamplin – venturing to consider his impact on the theatre.[305] Causley, especially in his later life, rarely talked about his dramatic work,[306] much of which (especially before his working relationship with Kneehigh Theatre in the early 1990s) was performed outside of Cornwall. Thus, ironically, Cornish audiences rarely got to see his theatrical work.

The general pattern of Causley's dramatic work is in three phases. Initially, before the Second World War, he wrote straightforward contemporary prose dramas, for the stage and for radio. These were the first efforts of his career, and although some achieved success by being broadcast by the BBC, others were not broadcast or performed live. As we might expect, this work resulted in him beginning to work more adeptly with verse-drama. Such verse-drama was, either consciously or unconsciously, drawing on a Cornish tradition, but it was still composed much less self-consciously – and in English – compared with the overtly Cornish and Cornish-language stylings of the revivalists.[307] There was a pause in Causley's theatre works in the post-war period, when his poetry became better known,[308] though he was to return to it again in the 1970s, and continued to write drama until his death in 2003. Unlike his poetry, many of Causley's dramatic works have not been published. Fortunately, many of these texts are preserved in the Exeter University Library's Special Collection of Modern Literary Papers.[309]

Fig. 83. A signed photograph of a young Charles Causley. Courtesy of the University of Exeter Library Modern Literary Papers Special Collection.

Causley was the only son of Charles Causley and Laura Barlett, and he attended Launceston National School, Horwell Grammar School, Launceston College and Peterborough Teacher-Training College. His wartime experiences in the Communications Branch of the Royal Navy continued to inspire his work; this period, and his time training as a teacher, were the only times that he lived away from Launceston.[310] He returned to the town to work as a teacher at the primary school where he had been a pupil. His work, though intensely Cornish, is much influenced by his border experiences, with the cultural geography of Launceston lying between Cornwall and England;[311] indeed, there is perhaps even an understanding of the wider Dumnonian experience. Throughout Causley's work there is an enormous awareness of the ritual year, deriving from both the Church and the community in which he lived and worked. This is accompanied by a strong sense of storytelling and narrative. There is a notable biblical dimension to his writing as well; one might argue that he represents the modern end of a process shaped in the medieval period. In the papers at Exeter, it is often hard to find Causley reflecting on his work as a dramatist, but one or two clues do emerge. For example, in some papers relating to a new introduction to a reprint of Arthur Quiller-Couch's *The Splendid Spur*, Causley confesses the influence of that book on his development as a writer, and also the significance of the other major Cornish dramatist of this phase, Bernard Walke:

> My earliest and only ambition was to be a writer, and two events of my boyhood in Cornwall declare themselves in the memory as sharply as the sight of Brown Willy and Rough Tor on a clear day. One was the first time I met an author. This was Father Bernard Walke, who had just published *Twenty Years at St Hilary*, an autobiography still also remaining for good measure, one of the most perceptive books ever written on the elusive subject of Cornwall and the Cornish.[312]

Walke did indeed understand the Cornish,[313] and also directly drew upon the *plen-an-gwarry* tradition of liturgical, community drama, which would also come to influence Causley. Another comment, however, also proves insightful. In a document which has the working title of *Donkey* (based on notions of school nativity plays), while describing himself as 'a cautious and superstitious Celt', Causley also explains the importance of Shakespeare in his life, even when away at war:

> A production of *Twelfth Night* in my last year of school had implanted in me what was to become a life-long love of Shakespeare. Adding even more weight

to my sadly stuffed kitbag was always a Shakespeare play; something quite indispensable.[314]

These twin influences probably prompted Causley to write his first pieces of drama, which were shaped in the mid- to late-1930s. Causley was then only in his late teens, so they were a considerable achievement for such a young man. The plays were short, contemporary pieces, usually domestic in theme, which although sometimes having Cornish-named characters were not always set in an overtly Cornish context. The first published text was *Runaway* in 1936, then came *The Conquering Hero* in 1937 – both broadcast as radio dramas;[315] but the most significant of these early plays is *Benedict: A Play in One Act*, published in 1938. The characters of the piece are Benedict Jones (described as a 'nice, earnest-looking young man of twenty five'[316]), Freda, David, Mrs. Carroll, and Stanley Carroll. In the play, Benedict is a jazz-loving pianist, and the action is set somewhere near Norwich. Tension is created in the play over the marriage between Freda and David. Freda is unsure about David, so Benedict disrupts events by asking, 'Then why the hell don't you marry me?'.[317] There are moments in this play which seem to look forward to the kind of angst-driven individuals who would emerge in post-war plays by writers such as John Osborne and Harold Pinter.[318] Despite his feelings, Benedict is 'holding himself in check',[319] which perhaps Osborne's and Pinter's individuals would not have done. This is perhaps, therefore, a direction that Causley's writing may have taken, had he pursued this form of drama. Even though the piece is set outside of Cornwall, some Cornish elements remain: one of the songs Mrs Carroll wishes to hear is titled 'The Pixies' Patrol'.[320]

These were not the only dramas of this phase, however. Around the same period, he also wrote *The Music Box: A Play in One Act*, *Family Ballet*, and *Arms and the Maid*. These plays were very similar in structure and feel to the ones that were published, so it remains unclear why some emerged and the others languished in Causley's files. Of these, *The Music Box* is the most Cornish, and appears to have been written between *The Conquering Hero* and *Benedict*. This was when Causley still lived at 23 Tredydan Road in Launceston, and the play was surely inspired by events and people in the town. The characters are Grandma Treloar, Maggie Treloar, Letitia Treloar, Mrs Spooner and Miss Spooner. The scene is 'The Living room at the Treloar's'.[321] The plot here is based around the music box itself, which belongs to Grandma Treloar. The Treloar family are about to be evicted from their family house because they cannot afford to pay their rent. A chance visit from the Spooners causes Letitia to drop and break the music box, out of which comes a piece of paper, with a message from Grandfather Treloar telling them where he buried his money:

'beneath the third apple tree in the orchard. Eight hundred pounds'.[322] The find means they can pay the landlord and carrying on living in the same house. Perhaps the subject-matter of such a drama does not sound world-beating, but as vignettes of Cornish life during the 1930s, such pieces have an important function. Community and identity remain important. Judging from the way the stage directions are written, clearly Causley imagined the piece for stage performance rather than as a broadcast. In 1937, Causley returned to the theme of elopement (a concept which would be later powerfully expressed in his poetry[323]) with *Family Ballet*. This time, the piece is set in the South Kensington home of a Mr Tolley. Although the play is long – and therefore perhaps not suitable as a radio drama – it is set in a very tight time frame, around box-set dramaturgy.[324] One senses Causley testing the water with a piece geographically outside of what would become his usual area for setting drama. *Arms and the Maid* – obviously a pun on George Bernard Shaw's *Arms and the Man*[325] – was another of these early plays. The theme of the play is Cornish – specifically, on the idea of the press-ganging, a notable theme in earlier folkloric writings in Cornwall.[326] There is some suggestion that this may well have been written for radio, but the overall impression is of a drama with mummers' play elements contained within it. The significance of this text is that it is the first to feature verse, as in the speeches by the Doctor and David:

Doctor
    The recipe for this dramatic salad,
    Is there from an ancient country ballad,
    A simple tale not too sublime or sordid,
    Where rogues are foiled and honest worth rewarded.
    And so adroitly has the author planned it,
    That even the highest brow can understand it.
    It mayn't be pleasing, and it mayn't be funny,
    But anyhow, you won't get back your money.....

David
    After long years of piracy and pillage
    On the high seas, I'm back here in the village,
    Why, there she sits all pensive like and dreamy,
    Amy, my love! my angel! Don't you see me?[327]

Although these are comparatively simple couplets, the text features the same kind of purposely 'naïve' rhyming that we associate with Causley's non-dramatic poetic work. This is not to deny its careful construction. Another dramatist and poet, D.M. Thomas, has commented on Causley's poetic vision, albeit with equal relevance to his verse drama:

Economy is one of the most striking features of his style. Every adjective, every verb, conveys a complexity of emotion, and no word is ever used just for the sake of the metre or rhyme... He is one of our finest poets because his imagination is both immensely sophisticated and childlike: childlike in its wonderment and generosity.[328]

Thomas clearly understands how Causley operates as a writer. We gain further insight into Causley's development as a dramatist when we see his response to Andrew Drewe, the Education Officer of the Poetry Society sometime in April 1995. Drewe had asked Causley about his influences, and this is Causley's response:

I was an only child. My soldier father returned from the First World War an invalid and died when I was seven. Books were my closest companions and as soon as I learned to read I became totally addicted to them. Imaginative writing seemed to me an act of pure magic. There wasn't much poetry on offer in my Cornish primary school, but there was plenty of singing: chiefly of folk-songs collected by such as Cecil Sharp, which we learned by the dozen. The simple words of those beautiful songs, and the truths they told of life and love, I now see, were my introduction to true poetry.[329]

What Causley offers here is an insight into how he operates as a dramatist. The folk-songs, and therefore ritualised aspects of life, are significant in his development, as is his desire for 'the truths they told of life and love'. This latter statement could be applicable to many of the medieval dramas of Cornwall, and so it is perhaps not surprising that Causley's first piece of epic verse drama had a biblical theme, interwoven with the voices and dialect of local people from Launceston, recalling the way Walke had imagined his dramas. This was 1939's *Journey of the Magi*. It is certainly not clear from Causley's correspondence that he was ever aware of texts such as the *Ordinalia* in any detailed way. Clearly he knew of the wider dramatic tradition in Cornwall, but it is curious here why his first large-scale dramatic exploration should be in one of the areas which is missing from the *Ordinalia*: the Nativity sequence. One sees here, too, another echo of the work of Bernard Walke, in that Walke also remained committed to the power of the Christmas message in his writings.[330] Christmas, and the folklore of Christmas, remained a thread in Causley's work until his death. *Journey of the Magi* was certainly an ambitious project for the time. It was written specifically for the players of St Stephen's Church at Launceston, and was performed with a large cast, from 15 to 19 January 1940. The director was Reg Allen; from the manuscript copy of the text, he and Causley clearly collaborated on the look of the play. There are many comments upon staging and design of the piece, with the costumes being particularly spectacular. Echoes of later poems of Causley, such as the famous 'Ballad of the Bread Man'[331] are found in the opening of the work, when the Wise Men speak together as a chorus:

> We are the Wise Men, we
> Have travelled the cold mountains and the ancient sea
> Crossed the pale deserts and the bitter snow,
> Blown by the hungry wind, burnt by the heat
> Of strange suns that are but of the sun we know.
> We are the tired men of the stars, the thin moon,
> The glitter of other worlds in the tall sky.
> We are the Wise Men.[332]

The vicar at the time was Reverend W.W. Bickford, and he was clearly supportive of the endeavour. Obviously we note how different Launceston is now, from the period of Methodist and other Church resistance against theatre there in the previous century. Nativity plays were, of course, a somewhat safer option. Although presented just after Christmas (though seasonally near to twelfth night[333]), this play represents an early twentieth-century example of the continuum of community, space and place in Cornwall. It also establishes Causley as a serious creator of verse-drama. Unfortunately, in 1939, events on the world stage would mean that Causley had to put such theatrical ambitions on hold. He packed his copies of Shakespeare into his kit bag, but by the end of the conflict and its aftermath, Causley had developed his first notable poetry collection, *Farewell, Aggie Weston!* (1951), referencing his experiences in Devonport, and in the Royal Navy.[334] He would also make a transition to prose, with his collection of Naval and Cornish short stories, *Hands to Dance and Skylark* (1951).[335] The imperative to write drama was deeply ingrained in Causley. As we shall see in Chapter Seven, once he had established himself as a serious poet in the post-war period, he was to return to drama reinvigorated, and still closely concerned with medieval, biblical and classical themes.

A point of puzzlement during this phase is why the revivalist movement did not see potential in Causley's dramas for conversion into Cornish. One senses a distance between Causley and the cultural-nationalist groups in Cornwall. Perhaps if Causley had collaborated with a writer such as A.S.D. Smith, or even Nance himself, on a translation of *Journey of the Magi* in this period,[336] we might have an altogether different understanding of drama. This cultural

Fig. 84. A sheep, donkey and bull from the 1939 performance of Charles Causley's *Journey of the Magi* at St Stephen's Church, Launceston. Courtesy of the University of Exeter Library Modern Literary Papers Special Collection.

tension appears to have continued in the post-war period: although predominantly a Cornish writer, he seems rather less committed to the nationalist project elsewhere. Perhaps some of Causley's more 'English'-themed work alienated aspects of the revivalist movement.[337] Sometimes his poetry examined clearly non-Cornish subjects, though an alternative reading might see Causley as a champion of wider 'Britishness'.[338] Causley had also confessed that it was 'merely a matter of chance that he was born a Cornishman rather than a Devonian'.[339] That said, there is a parallel in the work of Causley's friend Jack Clemo, who also viewed the revivalist movement with some degree of scepticism.[340] In Causley's work, we again see embodied the full tension of the protagonist St George, and an antagonistic St Piran.

While Nance and others were looking at a 'performance' of cultural nationalism in Cornwall, other groups were looking at how drama might be performed in a modern Cornwall, rapidly becoming a centre for tourism. At the heart of moves to develop tourism in the territory was Newquay, so it is perhaps not surprising that in the early twentieth-century, moves towards an 'end of promenade'-style theatre were being mooted in the town. Recollection of its exact emergence remains sketchy, but the first version of Newquay's Cosy Nook Theatre was in place just after the end of the First World War.[341] This theatre was constructed for the summer season, and consisted of a raised area

Fig. 85. The Newquay lifeboat passes by the first Cosy Nook Theatre (middle right), c.1920. Courtesy of Peter Hicks and Newquay Old Cornwall Society.

for the stage (still present today), which was screened and roped off. It was a temporary structure, with the audience covered by canvas, and deckchairs forming the stalls. The box office has been described as being like a 'garden shed'.[342] In the post-World War One period, it was apparently well-attended, offering revues and sketches for audiences striving to escape urban Britain, and the European theatre of war. The Cosy Nook proved so successful an endeavour in the 1920s that in 1928, Newquay Urban District Council decided to commit to building a permanent structure on the promenade; this second Cosy Nook was completed in 1929. Over the next few decades, it was let out to various management groups for summer seasons between May and September, and was also used by local drama groups (for more serious one-act plays) and the local operatic society in the winter.

The summer shows were standard variety shows, with a range of different performers contributing set pieces, as well as ensemble works. For its time, the Cosy Nook was quite a well-designed piece of theatrical architecture, though it was not flawless. For one thing, there was no way of crossing from one side of the stage to the other without having to walk around the building; this could be a problem for actors in costume in windy weather. For another, the theatre relied on the promenade toilets, rather than having some inside the theatre

Fig. 86. The cast of *Out of the Blue*, performed at the Cosy Nook Theatre in Newquay, 1946. Courtesy of John Trembath.

itself. The design of the theatre also meant that during stormy winter weather, the walls of the building were subject to the power of the Atlantic's swell. Sometimes, audiences could hear the waves breaking on the outside of the building. However, this did not stop both local people and tourists attending shows there, and it was well-supported. Shows by companies such as the Summer Revellers showcased local talent for charities, often putting on productions at midnight for especial effect. This was the case on 25 August 1939.[343] However, with the outbreak of the Second World War, the Cosy Nook was requisitioned as a lecture theatre for the Forces. When it reopened in 1945, two core producers of this phase, Ronald Brandon and his wife Dickie Pounds, began a run of work in Newquay that lasted until the 1970s. A typical early show was *Out of the Blue* (1946 and 1947) which made much of the local RAF connections, and in 1946 contained an opening number featuring a spectacular aeroplane on a backdrop through which the cast entered.[344] In 1947, part of the show was a Dickie Pounds' number called 'This Battling Peace' described in the programme as 'a ballet of the Times'.[345] These shows were formulaic but popular: they usually featured two comics, a female singer, dancers, and 'an odd man to fill in'. The humour was clean, and each performer showcased their particular talent. Around this time, the Cosy Nook suffered a serious fire in the stage area, which fortunately did not reach the auditorium. Such a fire demonstrates how unsafe the theatre was: lighting was primitive, with coloured lamp bulbs and a few spotlights and floods. The fire cut the run completely, but Brandon and Pounds persevered; they took the scenery to St Michael's Church Hall, and performed the revue there. According to folklore, no dancing girls were allowed. Newquay Urban District Council quickly refurbished the theatre, and this time installed fly towers. The Cosy Nook was up and running again in the same season. Like most producers of their type, operating the pan-British circuit, Brandon and Pounds were to move elsewhere for the season after 1948, but they would return to Newquay again. Newquay resident John Trembath recalls the excitement over the Cosy Nook summer seasons:

> It was wildly exciting. You had to book well in advance – by midday on a Monday. If they weren't booked up solid for the week, it would have been really surprising, because everybody went. For the final performance of the season you would have to book weeks in advance.[346]

The development of the Cosy Nook was not the only dramatic force operating in the town in the first half of the twentieth-century. During the late 1920s, the Newquay Theatre was built on St Michael's Road. This very 'modernist' structure was composed of two separate units. Above the theatre was a

Masonic Temple.[347] Like the Cosy Nook, the Newquay Theatre was also req-
uisitioned, this time by the NAAFI [The Navy, Army and Air-force
Institutes]; its maple sprung dance floor was often used for dances. After 1946,
Ronald Brandon obtained the lease for shows there, later followed by Geoffrey
Hastings, an impresario for repertory companies. The New Theatre (later the
Astor) at Narrowcliff provided Newquay with a third theatre space. This was
opened in 1937, to operate as both a cinema and a theatre. Compared to the
Newquay Theatre and the Cosy Nook, this was a better space to work in:
although not deep, the stage was wide, and one could move from one side to
the other without encountering Atlantic gales. Its dressing rooms were located
under the stage, and it had large doors at the rear to facilitate the setting and
striking of scenery – again unlike the Cosy Nook, where material had to be
loaded through the auditorium. For theatre and operatic productions, the
cinema screen could be moved back. The venue often housed the Newquay
Operatic Society's productions. The New Theatre was built by a local family,
the Hockings, who sold the premises to a cinema consortium in the 1970s.

At the turn of the 1930s, another group of activists also decided to develop
theatre in the town and its surrounds. Newquay Amateur Dramatic Society
was formed on Tuesday 19 May 1931 at an inaugural meeting held at Cheriton
House in the home of Dr D.R. Mitchell. According to a booklet produced
after twenty-one years of the Society, published in 1952, this group was glad
that 'those strong traces of super-puritanism which at times were actively
hostile [to theatre] in the nineteenth century, practically disappeared'.[348] We
know that 'certain citizens of the town… from time to time, seeking to further
dramatic taste, occasionally provided a play',[349] but this Society had ambitious
plans. The original officers were James Knight (President), Mr. R.A. Bury
(Honorary Secretary), Mr. C.W. Davies (Assistant Honorary Secretary), Mr.
E.W. Hewish (Honorary Treasurer) with a committee including Dr Mitchell,
Mr. E.A. Pope, Mrs. E.A. Pope, Captain H.P. Peters and Captain Fairfax
Ivimey. The objective of the society was to provide assistance in concerts and
entertainments, in aid of local charities, by giving short plays. Thus, with the
support of over forty members, the group planned its first production in 1932:
a light comedy titled *Nothing but the Truth* by James Montgomery, under the
directorship of Mr. E.A. Pope. *The West Briton* wrote of the first night: 'A fairly
large audience showed every sign of appreciation'.[350]

There followed a production of P.G. Wodehouse's farce *A Damsel in
Distress*, again in the hands of E.A. Pope. The more ambitious *The Sea Urchin*
by John Hastings Turner was produced in December, but does not seem to
have been as successful as the previous two. Given its more 'sea' and Cornish-
themed content, one might have expected it to fare better, which was no doubt

the Society's intention as well. According to the *Newquay Express*, it was a play that dealt 'with the feud between two old Cornish families... [but] the washing up of a sea urchin on the shingle leads to a quaint little love story which ends in the uniting of the two families'. The central characters were Sir Trevor Trebarrow, Guy Trebarrow, the urchin herself (Fay Wynchebek) and the Reverend Richard Penny – said to have been a 'character sketch of a manly clergyman whom one would expect to find in Cornwall'.[351] Nevertheless, a sum of some forty-seven pounds was presented to Newquay Hospital. Throughout the 1930s many plays were performed, raising money for other charities including the Rotary Unemployment Fund. During this phase, the Society did not have a permanent venue. Some productions were performed in the various hotels around Newquay, while others took place in a local shop. During the early 1930s, it was the responsibility of members themselves to take tickets and sell them to their friends, but as the decade wore on, this became increasingly difficult to do.

By the late 1930s, more sophisticated dramas were being attempted, including A. Armstrong's *Ten Minute Alibi* and Ivor Novello's *Full House*. In Easter 1939, the Society made a major step forward in presenting a Cornish-themed psychological thriller called *Suspect*, written by E. Percy and R. Denham. Had the Second World War not intervened, then perhaps the Society might have developed more material of this type, instead of the more comfortable comedies and thrillers of the early and middle years of the decade. From the outset, the Society had wanted to find its own venue, and so some monies were retained for this purpose, though it certainly would not be possible until the post-war period. During the war years, the Society was forced to spend time between the Newquay Theatre (by then a standard repertory venue) and the Cosy Nook Theatre, as well as other venues. The war brought a halt to development again, but the Society still found time to produce performances at RAF St Eval, Trerew, and St Mawgan, as well as Penhale Camp.[352] The lack of male performers meant that sometimes all female cast plays were developed, such as *Nine till Six* in 1945. In the immediate aftermath of the war, it was difficult to produce full length plays, so in May 1946, a set of One Act Plays was performed: *On Dartmoor* (a tale involving prison escapees), *Elizabeth Refuses*, *Fumed Oak* and *Puck's Good Deed* (a modern adaptation of *A Midsummer Night's Dream*). When men started to return home from the conflict, an ambitious full-length play was developed. Interestingly, this was *The Corn is Green*, an Emlyn Williams drama about Welsh mining, set in the village of Glansarno, but with plenty of Cornish parallels. Local choral societies contributed by rehearsing and performing Welsh-language songs to augment the piece.

Perhaps the highlight of the immediate post-war years was a production of the play version of Daphne du Maurier's *Rebecca* in 1948. The novel *Rebecca* had been published only ten years earlier, and the stage adaptation, by du Maurier herself, appeared in 1939. This production was directed by Miss E. Bryan Stevens, and apparently 'a real success was scored with the play and its Cornish settings'.[353] The cast included Margaret Davies (Mrs Danvers), Clare Linton (Mrs de Winter), Joan Polglaze (maid), Marie Bonet (maid), John Murray (Maxim de Winter), William Bryant (Robert), Jack Gould (Giles Lacy), Billy Knight (William Tabb), Leslie Lee (Colonel Julyan), Cyril Luke (Frith), Emrys Roberts (Frank Crawley) and Warwick Ruskin (Jack Favell) – many of whom had been staple performers over the previous decade.[354] Building on the success of *Rebecca*, 1949 saw them present du Maurier's *The Years Between*. This war-themed piece had emerged as recently as 1945, so it was quite a coup that the Society produced it this early.[355] It starred Brian Collins (Robin), John Murray (Richard Llewylyn), William Northey (The Vicar), Clare Lane (The Vicar's Wife), Griffith Sandy (Michael Wentworth), Phyllis Woolf (Nanny), Pamela Chirgwin (Diana Wentworth), Leslie Lee (Sir Ernest Foster), Cyril Luke (Venning), and Pat Lyne (Mrs Jameson), and was directed by Reg. C. L. Harris. By this phase, several of the plays were again being performed at the Cosy Nook Theatre. Liaison with Mrs Collingwood-Selby, Cornwall's education department's drama advisor was also taking place, with the advisor attending performances in the 1949-50 season, and the Society making a donation of three pounds to the Cornwall Drama Fund of the Festival of Britain.[356] Such works and performances continued in the 1950s but, as we shall see in the next chapter, the Society was about to move into an interesting new phase.

The Second World War put a stop to much of the development of theatre within the Cornish Revival. For a while, the antagonist St Piran had to step back from the spotlight. Part of the reason was that any emergent Cornish nationalism (still, one has to remember, being conducted on a very small scale) needed to be submerged within the wider British war effort.[357] Likewise, as Hechter has shown, other emergent nationalisms within the Celtic territories also needed to be careful.[358] Indeed, due to Hitler's rise in Germany, any kind of nationalism – cultural or otherwise – was bound to receive poor support. There were also some concerns over Irish and Breton support for Nazi Germany.[359] Although public entertainment continued, it took most of its form in dances, balls and the cinema[360] rather than in the theatre. Only after the war did drama groups start to coalesce and re-emerge. In 1948-9, the Merlin theatre opened in Mousehole. It was a small theatre, seating around 180 people, and clearly named after the Merlin rock to the west of Mousehole

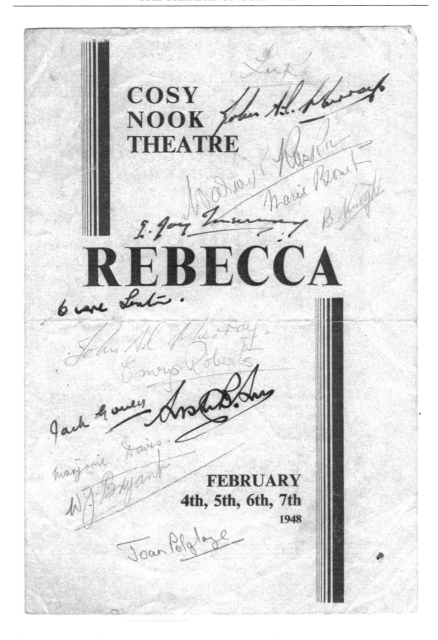

Fig. 87. A signed programme of a stage version of Daphne du Maurier's *Rebecca*, performed at the Cosy Nook Theatre in Newquay in 1948. Courtesy of the Reg Harris Archive.

harbour.[361] Developed by the painter George Lambourne (1900-77), it was a conversion from a schoolroom that had been abandoned when new premises were built.[362] An apron stage was constructed, while the back wall of the stage was whitewashed to act as a colour reflector. Acoustically, the theatre was very good; it was used for a number of years by the Mousehole Male Voice Choir for BBC broadcasts. At the time, an observer named Lambourne described the theatre as aspiring 'to be a home of communal activity for the dramatic arts, creative and imaginative, with no political axe to grind'.[363] In 1948 they presented four plays: Shakespeare's *The Merchant of Venice* and *The Taming of the Shrew*, Clemence Dane's *Will Shakespeare* and Charles Dickens' *A Christmas Carol*.

Elsewhere in Cornwall, similar small-scale 'repertory' companies were forming. In 1948, another company began in Newquay. Called The Dolphin Players, they hoped 'to give hearing to the new play, the costume play and to the foreign translation'.[364] Their model was the Dublin Gate Theatre, though clearly Cornish drama of this period was not able to develop in the same way that Irish drama was progressing.[365] In Penzance, the perhaps problematically-named 'English Ring Actors' produced plays at the Pavilion there, managed by the impresarios Frank Barnes and Elizabeth Gilbert.[366] Interestingly, this company did, however, have progressive views on theatre-in-education and was already assembling an elementary schools' programme. Falmouth benefited from performances at the Princess Pavilion by both a local company and, in summer rep, a visiting Bristol Old Vic Theatre School troupe.[367] From 1946-9, the Studio Theatre operated in Camborne, though with the explicit aim of putting on non-Cornish plays, presenting only Shaw, Ibsen, Noël Coward and Ian Hay dramas. The Studio could seat 200 but, as David Eames wrote in a retrospective article in 1969, the theatre had difficulty flourishing in the changing social mores of the 1950s and closed shortly afterwards.[368] In the period 1948-50, The Contemporary Players also formed in Truro, housed in a church hall under the viaduct, presenting *Murder in the Cathedral*, *Everyman*, and plays by Shakespeare and Shaw.[369] Similarly non-Cornish material was presented at the Perranporth Little Theatre,[370] run by Peter Bull and Robert Morley – perhaps ironic in the light of Perran Round's location, some two miles to the east.

As we can see, although each major Cornish town had its own company, the drama itself was usually 'imported' from elsewhere in Britain, appealing mainly to middle-class sensibilities and rarely imagining the world from a Cornu-centric point of view. However, elsewhere in Cornwall, there was a project to get Cornwall noticed in the West End. In 1949 the very successful (on home ground, at least) Redruth Amateur Operatic Society travelled to the

Fig. 88. A publicity photograph from the production of Newquay Amateur Dramatic Society's *Rebecca*. Courtesy of the Reg Harris Archive.

Fig. 89. A playbill advertising a production of Daphne du Maurier's *The Years Between* in 1949. Courtesy of the Reg Harris Archive.

664

Fortune Theatre in the West End to mount a production of A.G. Davey's *Tears from their Eyes*. Davey was the company's secretary at the time and was evidently a visionary character, wanting Cornish theatre to succeed outside Cornwall. Unfortunately, the company's London run resulted in heavy losses, despite the acting talents of major Cornish-circuit players such as Gerald Curtis, William Ninnis, Hilary Heard and Jon Davey. Commenting on the venture, M. Daniels said that it was 'reminiscent of the Cornish spirit in days gone by – an assault on the capital!' thereby connecting the Redruth Amateur Operatic Society with events of the 1497 rebellion.[371] However, the losses did not deter the company; their future aim was to make 'a Cornish-for-the-Cornish theatre season in London'.[372] Sadly this never came to pass, although it was a noble and important endeavour. By 1949, the Society was forty years old, and it claimed that it never had an empty seat in the house since 1946. Its immediate 'home' post-war productions included *The Vagabond King*, *Desert Song*, *New Moon* and *Balalaika*. As Frank Michell noted in 1949, Redruth had a distinguished theatrical past. The Redruth Amateur Operatic Society was the latest in a long line of theatrical ventures in the town – stretching back to its *plen-an-gwarry*, the Sans Pereil Theatre, then the dramatic entertainments which were 'held in the Druid's Hall illuminated by Chinese lanterns' at the end of the nineteenth century.[373] Connected to the Redruth Amateur Operatic Society were the Town Band and Choral Society, the Redruth Musical Festivals, the Cornwall Symphony Orchestra, the Madrigal Society and another theatrical group called the Players' Club. Redruth Amateur Operatic Society would continue to be successful in the post-war period, and into the twenty-first century.

While the Redruth Company was trying to make headway in London, in the periphery the popular Cornish Shakespearean Festival was again staged, presenting the usual favourites from the Shakespearean canon.[374] The festival had its origins in the middle of the 1930s under the patronage of The Right Reverend Lord Bishop of Truro, Brigadier General Lord St Levan, Sir Arthur Quiller-Couch, the Right Honorable Walter Runciman, and the Right Honorable Sir Francis Dyke Acland. During the 1930s and 1940s, productions at the festival were co-ordinated by Ernest Peirce and Alexander Marsh, who were major innovators during this period.[375] Peirce was the founder of the Cornish Shakespeare Festival, the very first of which was opened at Falmouth by Sir Arthur Quiller-Couch in 1934.[376] Peirce, in particular, realised the possibilities of environmental theatre (which, since the days of *plen-an-gwarries*, was a staple of the Cornish continuum – and would have more impact in the post-war period). Texts such as *The Merry Wives of Windsor*, *The Merchant of Venice*, *Much Ado About Nothing*, *Twelfth Night*, *The*

Taming of the Shrew and *A Midsummer Night's Dream* were presented in summer 1935 in venues such as Tremorvah (Truro), Kimberley Park (Truro), Lewinnick at Pentire (Newquay), Ponsadene (Penzance), Treloyhan Manor (St Ives), Roswarne (Camborne), Place (Fowey), Lismore (Helston) and Trevarrick (St Austell). These venues had remarkable similarities to the older 'playing-place' culture.[377] In such events, we begin to see the emergence of the later twentieth and twenty-first-century festivals that now dominate Cornish culture. They are not part of the Cornish ritual year, but rather newly-created festivals, providing not only forums for drama and artistic expression, but also a method of generating tourist income. The festival ran until the end of the 1940s. with an apparent break during the war years. 1949 saw an International Youth Drama course held at Lostwithiel, using Restormel castle as a 'theatre' (an interesting venue in the light of both previous and future activity there). On 21 August, 304 years earlier, Sir Richard Grenville had stormed and captured the castle from the Roundhead army.[378] At the 1949 course, according to the influential county [sic] drama advisor, Frances Collingwood Selby, a play was developed around the relationship between Grenville and a young Roundhead boy captured by Cornish Royalist soldiers. Alongside a storyline featuring the boy's widowed mother being suspected of witchcraft, there was also a presentation of the mummers' play *St George and the Dragon*, followed by folk dancing.[379] Ultimately the present intervened, in the form of a woman from the audience. By all accounts, this was progressive theatre-in-education for its time – also developing resoundingly Cornish-themed subject matter.

This period also witnessed the development of one of the most important theatrical critics in the twentieth century: a Cornishman, named John Courtenay Trewin (1908-90). More famously known as J.C. Trewin, he was born in Plymouth, but both of his parents were Cornish, and had family on the Lizard peninsula in south Cornwall. Before his secondary education, he spent much of his childhood there. Trewin is best known as a drama critic, but was also a considerable writer and theatrical historian in his own right. In a way, Trewin curiously represents both threads of theatrical experience during this phase. His theatrical input stands as that of the protagonist St George, in that he embraced the specifically English theatrical tradition, as an observer, commentator and historian. However, Trewin was also profoundly aware of his Cornish identity and history, not least his theatrical and cultural origins. As a figure therefore, he is something of a paradox, akin in many ways to others of the period, such as Arthur Quiller-Couch and A.L. Rowse, both of whom he knew well.[380] As a theatre critic, Trewin profoundly shaped public opinion on London and Stratford theatre during the Second World War, and the immediate post-war period, having as much significance then as those following in his footsteps, notably Michael Billington, Kenneth Hurren, Charles Spencer, Nicholas de Jongh and Michael Coveney. His reviews of Shakespearean productions during this period are particularly well-remembered. Educated at Plymouth College, in 1926, Trewin joined *The Western Independent* newspaper as a cub reporter, transferring to London in 1932 to work at *The Morning Post*. When *The Morning Post* folded in 1937, he transferred to *The Observer*, serving as that newspaper's drama critic for some sixty years.

Although Trewin is known elsewhere in Britain for his theatrical studies,[381] in Cornwall he is primarily known for his autobiographical works, *Up from The Lizard*, which emerged in 1948, and its sequel *Down to the Lion* (1952).[382] Both chart the experiences of a young Cornishman growing up in the territory, but are inter-cut with material from his experiences in the theatrical world. In *Up from The Lizard*, we learn of his literary and dramatic influences, including para-theatrical customs and events, and his understanding of the wider 'drama' of Cornwall – for example, not only his father's life on the ocean, but also drownings from shipwrecks. Perhaps predictably, Trewin makes connections between Cornwall and theatre. In 1952, but reflecting on the pre-war period, he described the Lizard as being 'perched on the furthest spur of England: on a prow thrust out, as an Elizabethan platform stage, into a waste of waters where the lighthouse nightly mouthed its gorgeous soliloquy to the tide'.[383] We may question his views of political and cultural geography but, as a piece of poetry, this is quite beautiful, and if our model of 'peninsularity' from Chapter One is followed, then he is also quite correct. In an interesting section of *Down to the Lion*, he also recalls a version of a play much discussed in this book: *Blue-beard*. It appears he saw the play performed in early twentieth-century Cornwall (but does not indicate where), yet also saw a revival 'not that long ago' in the Bedford Theatre in Camden Town.[384] The Cornish reference again shows a continuity backwards to an earlier time, and shows the lasting impact of this text. He also explains, perhaps echoing the comment of Bernard Walke at the start of this chapter, how he and his sisters, when staying at Kynance Bay Hotel, liked nothing better than to 'dress up'.[385] Curiously too, Trewin appears to be a fan of *Cymbeline*, which he terms the 'odd and lovely collision of the Renaissance with Snow White and Lear's Britain'.[386] All this somehow shows that Trewin had an intimate knowledge of how and where the Cornish theatrical tradition intersected with that of the rest of Britain. He is, for example, particularly adept at criticising the way dramatists portray Cornwall. In what he terms a 'feeble piece' (frustratingly unnamed) we learn his criticism of:

a burlesque of a young Cornish police constable, the kind of thing once thought to be funny in the P.C. Bullock vein of *East Lynne*. Novelists and dramatists have believed oddly that Cornwall is inhabited by Character Parts, with a bottom layer of earnest, simple souls, and a top layer of March-of-Intellect Boys who see themselves collectively as a civilising influence among a savage tribe.[387]

This indeed is Trewin commenting on the dramaturgy of St George versus St Piran. In another review, he notes in London club theatre 'an extraordinary business set in West Penwith'.[388] His observations detail the problems with how wider Britain sometimes perceived a 'stage' Cornwall during this phase. In a perceptive piece of observation, Trewin notes how he would 'almost have preferred *John Bull*' (1803) by George Colman the Younger, a Cornish-themed play discussed earlier in this volume. In the same section he recalls a long-forgotten eighteenth-century comedy by Mrs Cowley, titled *White Is the Man?* in which a 'rustic pair' named Bobby and Sophie Pendragon travel up from Cornwall to fashionable London. It is not clear whether Trewin is reproducing that text, or merely imitating it, but the dialogue is presented as such and, according to Trewin, this is the problem of how Cornish people are presented in pan-British theatre:

Sophie: Brother Bobby, Brother Bobby!

Bobby: I desire, Miss Pendragon, you won't brother me at this rate; making one look as if one didn't know life. How often shall I tell you that it is the most ungenteel thing in the word for relations to brother, father, and cousin one another, and all that sort of thing. I did not get the better of my shame for three days, when you bawled out to Mrs. Dobson at Launceston concert, 'Aunt, aunt! here's room between brother and I, if cousin Dick will sit closer to father!'[389]

It is a striking piece of observation (on how the Cornish have pretensions above themselves but cannot help but call each other 'cousin'[390]), and there is almost a Cornu-English undertone to the dialogue. Trewin, however, is also aware of another Cornish-themed comedy called *The Wheel of Fortune*, by Richard Cumberland (1732-1811). Trewin describes this as 'stilted' and explains how the audience wait for the voice of Timothy Weazel as he calls to the solitary, Roderick Penruddock: 'I bring you news out of Cornwall; news of great consequence... Timothy Weazel, of Lostwithiel, attorney-at-law, and agent to Sir George Penruddock. Let me into your house'.[391] The indication here is that writers like Cumberland saw the Cornish as legalistically-minded.

It is significant that he presents Weazel as hailing from Lostwithiel, which was the site of the Duchy Palace. Clearly, in citing it in 1952, Trewin knew of its significance. Interestingly, he also greatly praises Lillo's *Fatal Curiosity*, applying the observations of a Manaccan man on the weather: 'Sometimes it streams, sometimes it teems, but the gaps is good';[392] although it is an imperfect text, the play's overall impact is successful. Trewin is not much mentioned in Cornish letters at the start of the twenty-first-century, but the reality is that he had an astute understanding of modern theatrical tradition. It is perhaps a pity that nowhere else in his writing does he connect with a longer continuum of performance in Cornwall. Trewin's impact as a critic was wider in pan-British theatre, because conditions at home were not yet fully conducive for the kind of theatre of Cornwall for which he hoped. By the time of his death in 1990,[393] a contemporary theatre of Cornwall had more fully emerged, though Trewin, by then retired, and less active on the wider cultural stage of Britain, was not in a position to champion it.

Though, like Trewin, not a dramatist himself, one writer who explores the problems of being split between Cornwall and England during both this phase, and the period after 1950, is A.L. Rowse (1903-97). Since his death Rowse has been the subject of much biographical assessment, with Ollard labelling him 'a man of contradictions', and Payton naming him 'a paradoxical patriot'.[394] Both observers comment on Rowse's difficulty operating as an academic in the very English world of Oxford, while also dealing with his Cornish heritage and identity. As a homosexual Rowse was challenged by the need to conform to society's expectations, and never quite dealt with his sexuality.[395] Similar observations about his irascibility and mixed feelings about Cornwall are made by Jacobs, and Whetter.[396] He has also been the subject of much critical reassessment, with some scholars feeling that his historical work pre-figures much of the so-called 'new British historiography', which explores the differences rather than the similarities between parts of the Atlantic archipelago.[397] Although some reappraisal has been made of his poetry and short stories,[398] more needs to be undertaken. Throughout his life it seems Rowse did not write any drama. However, his significance in the field of theatre comes from his studies of Elizabethan and Renaissance drama, in particular, the life and works of William Shakespeare. Thus, though not con-tributing specifically to the Cornish theatrical continuum, his enquiries have had, as we shall see, a wider pan-British significance.

Rowse's career has garnered a kind of mythos of its own. Born at Tregonissey in mid-Cornwall, the son of Richard Rowse (a china clay worker) and Annie Vanson, he won a place at St Austell Grammar School, eventually winning a scholarship to Christ Church, Oxford in 1922. His abilities were noted and supported by Quiller-Couch. After graduating in History he was elected a Fellow of All Souls College, and after a brief political career (twice contesting the parliamentary seat of Penryn and Falmouth for the Labour Party) returned to academia, lecturing at the London School of Economics, then becoming Sub-Warden at All Souls College, and making regular trips to the Huntingdon Library in California, eventually becoming Senior Research Fellow there. Throughout this period, Rowse continued to promote and explore his Cornish identity and history, eventually retiring from Oxford to Trenarren House, near Blackhead in 1973, from where he continued to write until his death. Although Rowse was obviously aware of the miracle plays of Cornwall, he only ever dealt with this continuum in a limited way in his career.[399] The title that has most relevance to the theatricality of Cornwall is his 1941 work, *Tudor Cornwall*, which documents the political and religious upheavals of the period, directly influencing Cornish dramaturgy.[400] There is, however, a sense with Rowse that, although he looked at the tradition in Cornwall, there simply was not enough material for him to explore further. Despite coming at the texts from a broadly 'English' literary culture, he matched many of the observations of the Celtic Studies academic community.[401] Although becoming a bard of the Cornish Gorsedd, like his predecessor, Quiller-Couch, Rowse was sceptical of what could be achieved in the Cornish Revival.[402] Even some of the theatrical texts and figures operating in eighteenth and nineteenth-century Cornwall were off the radar for Rowse; generally, he preferred to concentrate on more tangible aspects of Cornish culture.[403] Rowse's other significant history, *The Cornish in America* (1969) perhaps also had the potential to have considered trans-national Anglo-Cornish theatre, but aside from some brief observations on entertainments, a fuller picture is not given.[404] Likewise, given Rowse's friendship with the Cornish historian Charles Henderson, their passion for exploring Cornish churches, and Henderson's specific interest in medieval Cornwall,[405] one might have expected more studies on the culture of the medieval period.

The impetus and success of *Tudor Cornwall*, however, gave Rowse the confidence to explore more fully the Elizabethan Age, which he felt was one of the most important phases of British history. This was indicated in his general history of 'England', *The Spirit of English History* (1943) and *The English Spirit: Essays in History and Literature* (1944),[406] but developed more in a trilogy of works titled *The England of Elizabeth: The Structure of Society* (1950), *The Expansion of Elizabethan England* (1955), and *The Elizabethan Renaissance* (1971-1972).[407] Although all of these works examined constructions of Englishness during this period, there was always an eye on the position of Cornwall, and sometimes Devon. Rowse's interest in this Age prompted his 1963 enquiry into that symbol of English drama: William Shakespeare.[408] His examination of Shakespeare's work related the plays and sonnets directly to biographical moments in the playwright's life, and was in many ways averse to what later emerged as cultural materialism. This first biography claimed to date all of the sonnets and identify Christopher Marlowe as the suitor's rival. Enquiry here led to one of Rowse's most controversial books, *Shakespeare the Man* (1973), in which he claimed to have identified the so-called 'Dark Lady' from a close reading of the sonnets.[409] This, he posited, was Emilia Lanier. The volume also unravelled a number of other intriguing aspects of Shakespeare's life,[410] but his views were rejected by others, notably the English literati of the period. In part, this was because Shakespearean criticism, like other literary criticism of the era, was absorbing new critical theory,[411] something to which Rowse gave little attention. Interest in the Elizabethan Age and the wider Renaissance continued in Rowse's work, however. He felt this was the true blossoming of theatrical culture in Britain, and continued to write and publish works on Shakespeare until his death.[412] In 1965, the work on Shakespeare had naturally led him to produce a biography of Christopher Marlowe.[413] Rowse was not the first Cornishman to look at the life of the playwright, since James Dryden Hosken had already imagined his experiences in the form of a drama.[414]

Rowse is significant for his investigation of drama in the Elizabethan period. Whilst it may not be directly part of the Cornish continuum, it certainly fits within the wider crisis of identity and academia that was shaped during this phase. It is unclear why Rowse himself never wrote for the stage.[415] Certainly, many of his poems have a dramatic voice behind them; some are deft soliloquies that would have worked well coming from characters on stage. 'I was before my time, caught betwixt and between,' he famously commented about his career.[416] To an extent, this is exactly what might have made him interesting as a dramatist. When, in his poetry, he comments on the difficulty of coping with being Cornish in an English system, as well as his covert homosexuality, Rowse was exploring something very modern and contemporary. There is even an implicit dramaturgy in his poetry of Cornwall, which suggests a reflective Shakespearean mood, as in 'The Old Cemetery at St Austell':

I see them: so many insects on the heave of hill
Scurrying about, burrowing underground;
If you listen closely you may hear the sound
Of the rumour of their toil, the dead men sing
Along their levels and hidden galleries,
A remote murmur like a hive of bees.[417]

To see such work 'theatricalised' would have made Rowse the link between the Cornish continuum and the wider academic and theatrical world of the period, as well as exploring the feelings of a generation of Cornish people who, whilst not fully embracing the concerns of either the revivalists or, indeed, nationalists in Cornwall, knew and felt their cultural 'difference'. Speculating on this is fine, but it did not happen. Rowse had, however, explored the tensions between England and Cornwall, and had shaped the new awareness of British historiography that would help facilitate devolutionary calls in the next phase; furthermore, his poetry made it legitimate to explore the contradictions and paradoxes of Cornish identity in the modern era – something that would be crucial in the next phase. By the dawn of the early 1950s, the tension between England and Cornwall was still unresolved, but not only was Cornish and Anglo-Cornish theatre asserting its difference, it was doing so in ways that not only continued the theatrical traditions of the territory, but also broke radically new ground. The social, political and academic framework made it difficult for many of the dramatists and commentators on drama to decide their allegiances – notably Thomas Hardy (who was coming from an English position), Arthur Quiller-Couch and James Dryden Hosken, and later J.C. Trewin and A.L. Rowse. They were caught between a rock and a hard place. Nance, Walke and Pollard had directly picked up the baton almost from where it was dropped in the seventeenth century, with Causley (after an attempt at modernist writing) following suit.

In the post-war period there would be a generation of new scholars, dramatists, directors and performers directly re-engaging with the dramatic continuum in Cornwall, but they would also be making a direct assault on the incorporation of Cornwall within England. There was also the issue of industrial decline, and a growing sense that tourism was encroaching too much, and about to ruin the very ritual, landscape and community that had been the backbone of Cornish life.[418] Not surprisingly though, many threads continued into the modern era, but notions of ritual, landscape and community would also be radically altered, again in line with social, economic, political and cultural change on an unexpected scale. New scholars were starting to put Cornwall on the map of Celtic literary studies,[419] and asserting that Cornwall had something distinctive to offer: theatre. This was not something second-rate or inferior. It was just different. Political changes across the European Union (from the 1970s onwards) and also in the United Kingdom itself (in the 1990s) were prompting a renewed look at the experience of Cornwall.[420] Although the kind of political devolution achieved by other territories during this next period would not happen to Cornwall, it was not going to stop a new generation 'performing' an imagined devolution. Likewise, the kind of theatre that developed in Cornwall during this phase has set the blueprint for all kinds of pan-British theatrical activity. Not only was the environment and a sense of place back on the agenda, so were moves towards an alternative, 'green', and highly non-metropolitan theatre. Cornwall was to reinvent itself once again, and theatre was going to offer its people a new sense of belonging. It is to this new theatre of Cornwall that we next turn.

CHAPTER SIX: NOTES AND REFERENCES

1.   Arthur Quiller-Couch, *From a Cornish Window*, Cambridge: Cambridge University Press, 1906, p.267-8.

2.   Bernard Walke, *Twenty Years at St Hilary*, London: Anthony Mott Ltd, 1982 [1935], p.167.

3.   For a general overview, see Bernard Deacon, *Cornwall: A Concise History*, Cardiff: University of Wales Press, 2007, pp.180-206.

4.   See Philip Payton, *The Cornish Overseas*, Fowey: Alexander Associates, 1999; Alan M. Kent and Gage McKinney (eds.), *The Busy Earth: A Reader in Global Cornish Literature 1700-2000*, St Austell: Cornish Hillside Publications, 2008.

5.   Typified in literary visitors such as D.H. Lawrence, Virginia Woolf, and Leo Walmsley. See Alan M. Kent, *The Literature of Cornwall: Continuity, Identity, Difference 1000-2000*, Bristol: Redcliffe, 2000, pp.147-94. See also the artistic visitors mentioned in Denys Val Baker, *Britain's Art Colony by the Sea*, Bristol: Sansom and Company, 2000 [1959]; Michael Tooby, *Tate St Ives: An Illustrated Companion*, London: Tate Gallery, 1993.

6.   This did not prevent Quiller-Couch being made a bard at the first Cornish Gorsedd in 1928. See Hugh Miners, *Gorseth Kernow: The First 50 Years*, Cornwall: Gorseth Kernow, 1978, p.55. Quiller-Couch's bardic name was *Marghak Cough* [Red Knight].

7.   *Cornish Magazine*, 1899, pp.77-9 and pp.153-6.

8.   Ibid., 1898, pp.157-9.

9.   See chapters on these issues in Philip Payton (ed.), *Cornwall Since the War: The Contemporary History of a European Region*, Redruth: Institute of Cornish Studies and Dyllansow Truran, 1993.

10.   For Cornwall's direct involvement, see Everard Wyrall, *The History of the Duke of Cornwall's Light Infantry 1914-1919*, London: Methuen, 1939. See also Stuart Dalley, 'The Response in Cornwall to the Outbreak of the First World War' in Philip Payton (ed.), *Cornish Studies: Eleven*, Exeter: University of Exeter Press, 2003, pp.85-109. For a response, see Callum G. Brown, *The Death of Christian Britain: Understanding Secularization 1800-2000*, London and New York: Routledge, 2001.

11. See Viv Acton and Derek Carter, *Cornish War and Peace: The Road to Victory and Beyond*, Devoran: Landfall, 1995; Peter Hancock, *Cornwall at War, 1939-1945*, Tiverton: Halsgrove, 2006. For changes, see Alan Sinfield (ed.), *Society and Literature 1945-1970*, London: Methuen, 1983.

12. For understanding of the complexity of such processes, see Athena S. Leoussi, and Steven Grosby (eds.), *Nationalism and Ethnosymbolism: History, Culture and Ethnicity in the Formation of Nations*, Edinburgh: Edinburgh University Press, 2007.

13. For a context, see Christopher Morash, *A History of Irish Theatre 1601-2000*, Cambridge: Cambridge University Press, 2002.

14. See Peter Berresford Ellis, *The Celtic Revolution: A Study in Anti-Imperialism*, Talybont: Y Lolfra, 1988 [1985], pp.134-48.

15. See for example, Ronald Perry, 'Celtic Revival and Economic Development in Edwardian Cornwall' in Philip Payton (ed.), *Cornish Studies: Five*, Exeter: University of Exeter Press, 1997, pp. 112-24; Ronald Perry and Charles Thurlow, 'The 1913 China Clay Dispute: 'One and All or 'One – That's All'?" in Philip Payton (ed.), *Cornish Studies: Fourteen*, Exeter: University of Exeter Press, 2006, pp187-203.

16. David Everett, 'Celtic Revival and the Anglican Church in Cornwall' in Philip Payton (ed.), *Cornish Studies: Eleven*, Exeter: University of Exeter Press, 2003, pp.192-219; Ronald Perry, 'The Changing Face of Celtic Tourism in Cornwall 1875-1975' in Philip Payton (ed.), *Cornish Studies: Seven*, Exeter: University of Exeter Press, 1999, pp.94-106; Garry Tregidga, 'The Politics of the Celto-Cornish Revival, 1886-1939' in Philip Payton (ed.), *Cornish Studies: Five*, Exeter: University of Exeter Press, 1997, pp.125-50.

17. See Peter W. Thomas, and Derek Williams (eds.), *Setting Cornwall on its Feet: Robert Morton Nance 1873-1959*, London: Francis Boutle Publishers, 2007. This is a comprehensive guide to Nance's life and work.

18. For a commentary on this, see Brian Murdoch, *Cornish Literature*, Cambridge: D.S. Brewer, 1993, pp.144-50; Kent, op.cit., pp.270-84.

19. Tim Saunders, 'Cornish – Symbol and Substance' in Cathal Ó Luain (ed.), *For a Celtic Future: A Tribute to Alan Heusaff*, Dublin: The Celtic League, 1983, p.257.

20. Magnus Maclean, *The Literature of the Celts*, London: Blackie and Son, 1908, p.248.

21. Henry Jenner, *A Handbook of the Cornish Language: Chiefly in its Latest Stages with some account of its History and Literature*, London: David Nutt, 1904. For the influence of Jenner's work, see Richard Jenkin, 'Modern Cornish Literature in the 20th Century' in *The Celtic Pen*, Vol. 1, No. 3, 1994, and Tim Saunders (ed. and tr.), *The Wheel: An Anthology of Modern Poetry in Cornish 1850-1980*, London: Francis Boutle Publishers, 1999.

22. Derek Williams (ed.), *Henry and Katharine Jenner: A Celebration of Cornwall's Culture, Language and Identity*, London: Francis Boutle Publishers, 2004.

23. Jenner, op.cit.

24. See Amy Hale, 'Genesis of the Celto-Cornish Revival? L.C. Duncombe-Jewell and the Cowethas Kelto-Kernuak' in Philip Payton (ed.), *Cornish Studies: Five*, Exeter: University of Exeter Press, 1997, pp.100-111. For Lach-Szyrma, see Margaret Perry, 'Eminent Westcountryman, Honorary Cornishman' in *Journal of the Royal Institution of Cornwall*, 2000, pp154-67.

25. See Peter Berresford Ellis, *The Cornish Language and its Literature*, London and Boston: Routledge and Kegan Paul, 1974, p.135-6.

26. For biographies, see F. Brittain, *Arthur Quiller-Couch: A Biographical Study of Q*, Cambridge: Cambridge University Press, 1948; A.L. Rowse, *Quiller-Couch: A Portrait of 'Q'*, London: Methuen, 1988. For a useful survey of Quiller-Couch's work, see F. Brittain (ed.), *Q Anthology: A Selection from the Prose and Verse of Sir Arthur Quiller-Couch*, London: J.M. Dent, 1948.

27. See, for example, *Cornish Magazine*, op.cit., pp.48-50.

28. See Edwin Norris (ed. and tr.), *The Ancient Cornish Drama*, London and New York: Blom, 1968 [1859]; F.E. Halliday (ed.), *Richard Carew: The Survey of Cornwall*, London: Melrose, 1953.

29. Quiller-Couch, op.cit., p.266.

30. Ibid., pp.266-7.

31. Ibid., p.268.

32. K. G. Foster (ed.), *Piran Round, Perranporth: Souvenir Programme*, Cornwall: Cornwall County Council, 1969; Ordinalia Company, *Ordinalia: The Full Cycle*, Penzance: Three S Films, 2004.

33. Arthur Quiller-Couch Archive, Trinity College, Oxford. See C. Mellors, *Sir Arthur Quiller-Couch 1863-1944: A List of Archive Material held at Trinity College*, Oxford, 1991. I am indebted to Gerry Hones for bringing this material to my attention.

34. Useful background here is found in John Dixon, *A Schooling in 'English': Critical Episodes in the Struggle to Shape Literary and Cultural Studies*, Milton Keynes: Open University Press, 1991. Q was nowhere near the position of F.R. Leavis however. See F.R. Leavis, *The Great Tradition*, London: Chatto and Windus, 1948. Quiller-Couch's notion of literary studies was, in essence, populist. See, for example, Arthur Quiller-Couch (ed.), *The Oxford Book of English Verse*, Oxford: Oxford University Press, 1900.

35. For a survey, see Kent, op.cit., pp.164-8. Quiller-Couch deserves a wider reappraisal.

36. Arthur Quiller-Couch Archive, op.cit.

37. Video footage of this is contained in Sir Arthur Quiller-Couch Memorial Fund

Committee, *Q: A Great Cornishman*, Truro: Sir Arthur Quiller-Couch Memorial Fund Committee, 2008.

38. Arthur Quiller-Couch Archive, op.cit.

39. See Arthur Quiller-Couch, *The Astonishing History of Troy Town*, London: Anthony Mott, 1983 [1888]. It is perhaps surprising that this story has not been dramatised more often.

40. Arthur Quiller-Couch Archive, op.cit.

41. Ibid. For original novel, see Arthur Quiller-Couch, *Hetty Wesley*, London: Harper and Brothers, 1903.

42. Arthur Quiller-Couch Archive, op.cit. Mellors believes that this is one of Quiller-Couch's short stories.

43. See Arthur Quiller-Couch, *Historical Tales from Shakespeare*, London: Edward Arnold, 1910. Quiller-Couch edited many editions of Shakespeare's plays.

44. Arthur Quiller-Couch, *Shakespeare's Workmanship*, London: Henry Holt and Company, 1918.

45. Arthur Quiller-Couch Archive, op.cit.

46. Arthur Quiller-Couch, *Studies in Literature Series III*, Cambridge: Cambridge University Press, 1929.

47. Arthur Quiller-Couch Archive, op.cit.

48. This was akin to many other lecturers at this point in time. English Literature was still a relatively young subject. See Dixon, op.cit.

49. Arthur Quiller-Couch and Daphne du Maurier, *Castle Dor*, London: Dent, 1962.

50. A. L. Rowse, *A Cornishman at Oxford: The Education of a Cornishman*, London: Jonathan Cape, 1965; J.C. Trewin, *Down to the Lion*, London: Carroll and Nicholson, 1952.

51. A substantial selection of his verse is found in Alan M. Kent (ed.), *Voices from West Barbary: An Anthology of Anglo-Cornish Poetry 1548-1928*, London: Francis Boutle Publishers, 2000, pp.171-85.

52. James Dryden Hosken, *Phaon and Sappho: A play (in five acts and song)*, Penzance: F. Rodda, 1891.

53. James Dryden Hosken, *Verses by the way*, London: Methuen, 1893, and *A Monk's Love and Other Poems*, London: James Dryden Hosken, 1895.

54. James Dryden Hosken, *Christopher Marlowe: A Tragedy in Three Acts in Prose and Verse, and Belphegor: A Harlequinade in Doggerel*, London: Henry and Co., 1896.

55. It was also included in James Dryden Hosken, *Shores of Lyonesse Poems: Dramatic Narrative and Lyrical*, London: J.M. Dent and Sons Ltd. c.1928. This volume seemed to celebrate Hosken's bardship in 1928.

56. See James Dryden Hosken, *Poems and Songs of Cornwall*, Plymouth: Mitchell, Burt and Co., 1906.

57. Hosken, op.cit., 1896.

58. Miners, op.cit.

59. James Dryden Hosken, *Helston Furry Day*, Helston: Helston Old Cornwall Society, 1931.

60. Thomas Hardy, *The Famous Tragedy of the Queen of Cornwall*, London: Macmillan, 1923.

61. See Denys Kay-Robinson, *The First Mrs Thomas Hardy*, London: Macmillan, 1979.

62. Michael Millgate, *Thomas Hardy: His Career as a Novelist*, London: Bodley Head, 1971.

63. For a recent reassessment, see Ralph Pite, *Thomas Hardy: The Guarded Life*, London: Picador, 2006.

64. See Thomas Hardy, *A Pair of Blue Eyes*, Oxford: Oxford University Press, 1983 [1873]. For 'A Mere Interlude', see Thomas Hardy, *The Distracted Preacher and Other Tales*, Harmondsworth: Penguin, 1979, pp.99-133. In July 1991, Theatre Rotto presented a stage version of *A Mere Interlude* in Penzance. Publicity photographs saw performers standing before St Michael's Mount.

65. See Kent, op.cit., 2000, pp.170-2; Simon Trezise, "Off Wessex' or a Place in the Mind' in Melissa Hardie (ed.), *A Mere Interlude: Some Literary Visitors to Lyonesse*, Penzance: The Patten Press, 1992, pp.27-36; Trevor Johnson, "Time was Away': *A Pair of Blue Eyes* and the Poems of 1912-13' in ibid., pp.37-56; George Wootton, *Thomas Hardy: Towards a Materialist Criticism*, Lanham: Rowan and Littlefield, 1985.

66. See James Gibson (ed.), *Chosen Poems of Thomas Hardy*, Basingstoke: Macmillan, 1975, p.46. Hardy spells Lyonesse with a double n here.

67. Trezise, op.cit.. This point is also made in Simon Trezise, *The West Country as a Literary Invention: Putting Fiction in its Place*, Exeter: University of Exeter Press, 2000.

68. In Hardy, op.cit., 1983 [1973], p.3.

69. Trezise, op.cit., 1992.

70. A detailed map is offered in Thomas Hardy, *A Pair of Blue Eyes*, Harmondsworth: Penguin, 1983 [1873], pp.42-3.

71. Charles Thomas, 'Hardy and Lyonesse: Parallel Mythologies' in Hardie (ed.), op.cit., p.16.

72. See the discussion in Christine Poulson, *The Quest for the Grail: Arthurian Legend in British Art 1840-1920*, Manchester: Manchester University Press, 1999; Alan Lupack (ed.), *Modern Arthurian Literature: An Anthology of English and American Arthuriana from the Renaissance to the Present*, London and New York: Garland, 1992.

73. An exploration of both the lack, and potential, of a medieval Cornish Arthurian text is discussed in Hale, Kent and Saunders, op.cit. Their prediction came to

pass with the discovery of *Bewnans Ke*. See Graham Thomas and Nicholas Williams (eds. and trs.), *Bewnans Ke: The Life of St Kea – A Critical Edition with Translation*, Exeter: University of Exeter Press, 2007. *Bewnans Ke* contains substantial Arthurian matter.

74. Hardy, op.cit., 1925, p.i.
75. See Thomas Hardy *The Return of the Native*, Harmondsworth: Penguin, 1994 [1878], pp.141-172.
76. Kenneth Phelps, *The Wormwood Cup – Thomas Hardy in Cornwall: A Study in Temperament, Topography and Timing*, Padstow: Lodenek Press, 1975, pp.99-114; Michael Millgate, *Thomas Hardy: A Biography*, Oxford: Oxford University Press, 1985, pp.550-55.
77. Hardy, op.cit., p.1.
78. Ibid.
79. Ibid., p.2.
80. Ibid.
81. Cited in Phelps, op.cit., p.99.
82. For perspective on this wider debate, see Robert J. C. Young, *The Idea of English Ethnicity*, Oxford: Blackwell, 2008.
83. Phelps, op.cit.
84. Ibid., p.114.
85. John Baragwanath King, *The Coming of Arthur*, London: Erskine Macdonald, 1925.
86. William Hals (1666-c.1737) was a scholar and historian. He claimed one of the sources of his History was John Trevisa's now lost *Book of the Acts of Arthur*. For more, see Hale, Kent and Saunders, op.cit., pp.73-80.
87. See, for example, Paul Newman, *The Tregerthen Horror: Aleister Crowley, D.H. Lawrence and Peter Warlock in Cornwall*, St Austell: Abraxas, 2005; Jason Semmens (ed.), *The Cornish Witch-finder: William Henry Paynter and the Witchery, Ghosts, Charms and Folklore of Cornwall*, Cornwall: The Federation of Old Cornwall Societies, 2008.
88. King, op.cit., p.2.
89. Henry Jenner, 'Tintagel Castle in History and Romance' in *Journal of the Royal Institution of Cornwall*, No.74, 1927.
90. J. Hambley Rowe, 'King Arthur's Territory' in *Journal of the Royal Institution of Cornwall*, No.76, 1929. For background, see Hugh Miners and Treve Crago, *Tolzethan: The Life and Times of Joseph Hambley Rowe*, Cornwall: Gorseth Kernow, 2002.
91. Thomas, op.cit., pp.19-20. The upstairs area of the Halls is a Masonic Lodge. Cf. the Newquay Theatre. Another iconic building with an Arthurian theme was King Arthur's Castle Hotel, designed by Silvanus Trevail and opened in 1899. See Ronald Perry and Hazel Harradence, *Silvanus Trevail:*

Cornish Architect and Entrepreneur, London: Francis Boutle Publishers, 2008, pp.138-9.

92. B.D. Vere, *King Arthur: His Symbolic Story in Verse*, Tintagel: King Arthur's Hall, 1930.

93. Ibid., pp.3-4.

94. A.S.D. Smith, *Trystan hag Ysolt*, Redruth: J. & M. Roberts, 1951; D.H. Watkins, *Trystan hag Ysolt*, Camborne, An Lef Kernewek, 1973. For translations of selected sequences, see Hale, Kent and Saunders, op.cit., pp.203-13. For Ratcliff, see Francis Collingwood Selby, *Cornwall Drama Festival 1951 Programme*, Cornwall: Cornwall County Council, 1951, p.2.

95. Thomas and Williams, op.cit.

96. See Miners, 1978, pp.7-34; Dillwyn Miles, *The Secret of the Bards of the Isle of Britain*, Llandybie: Gwasg Dinefwr Press, 1992, pp.226-31.

97. Tony Deane and Tony Shaw, *Folklore of Cornwall*, Stroud: Tempus, 2003. See also Robert Morton Nance 'What we stand for' in *Old Cornwall*, April, 1925, pp.3-6, and *When was Cornish Last Spoken Traditionally?* Truro: Royal Institution of Cornwall, 1973.

98. See Saunders, op.cit., 1983, pp.253-9; Piotr Stalmaszczyk, *Celtic Presence: Studies in Celtic Languages and Literatures – Irish, Scottish Gaelic and Cornish*, Lódê: Lódê University Press, 2005, pp.126-31. Nance was also satirised in the progressive and comic Cornish language magazine *Eythen*, running between 1976 and 1980. Nance's main principles are outlined in Robert Morton Nance, *Cornish for All: A Guide to Unified Cornish*, Cornwall: Federation of Old Cornwall Societies, 1958 [1929].

99. A representative sample includes J.E. Caerwyn Williams (ed.), *Literature in Celtic Countries*, Cardiff: University of Wales Press, 1971; Victor Edward Durkacz, *The Decline of the Celtic Languages*, Edinburgh: John Donald Publishers Ltd, 1983; Paul Russell, *An Introduction to the Celtic Languages*, Harlow: Longman, 1995. There are many others.

100. R.J.E. Tiddy, *The Mummers' Play*, Oxford: Clarendon Press, 1923; E.K. Chambers, *The English Folk Play*, Oxford: Oxford University Press, 1969 [1933]. For a Cornish perspective, see Tom Miners, 'The Mummers' Play in West Cornwall' in *Old Cornwall*, Vol. 1, 1925-1930, pp.4-16.

101. Hardy, op.cit., 1994 [1878].

102. Hardy, op.cit., 1923.

103. For modern scholarly views on these texts, see Peter Millington, 'The Truro Cordwainers' Play: A "New" Eighteenth-Century Christmas Play' in *Folklore*, Vol. 114, No. 1, 2003, pp.53-73; Tom Pettitt, 'From Stage to Folk: A Note on the Passages from Addison's Rosamond in the "Truro" Mummers' Play' in *Folklore*, Vol. 114, No. 2, 2003, pp.262-70. In Box 9, the Nance Collection, Courtney

Library, Royal Institution of Cornwall, there is a version of 'The Mylor Play' in Nance's hand, alongside a copy of 'The Tenby Christmas Play'. There is also a paper titled 'Folk-Plays of Cornwall' which was read to the Village Drama Society, Exeter in 1921, and to the Cambridge Antiquarian Society in November 1929. See also Robert Morton Nance, 'A Redruth Christmas Play' in *Old Cornwall*, April, 1925, pp. 29-31. This was communicated by Miss L. Eddy to Mr A.K. Hamilton Jenkin, a witness of its performance. The characters are King George, Jack, Doctor Brown and Jacky Sweep. This drama seems to have been originally written in the light of Nelson's victory at Trafalgar. See in addition, Robert Morton Nance, 'A Guise-Dance play, St Keverne' in ibid., pp.31-32. This was communicated by Capt. F.J. Roskruge, R.N. and written after Mr William Mitchell's memory of a performance over seventy years earlier (c.1850). The characters were Father Christmas, Turkish knight, King George (St George), Doctor and Little Man Jack.

104. For pictorial representation, see Douglas Williams, *Festivals of Cornwall*, St Teath: Bossiney Books, 1987.

105. See Deane and Shaw, op.cit., p.156 and p.158. Nance apparently added another verse: 'But to a greater than St George our Helston has a right-O, / St Michael with his wings outspread; the Archangel so bright-O, / Who fought the fiend-O, of all mankind the foe'. Deane and Shaw rightly argue this 'totally misses the point of its original meaning'.

106. Sowena, *A Month of Sundays*, St. Agnes: Sowena, 1999.

107. Cited in Donald R. Rawe, *Padstow's Obby Oss and May Day Festivities: A Study in Folklore and Tradition*, Padstow: Lodenek Press, 1990 [1971], p.7. There are noticeable similarities here to the Helston *Hal-an-Tow* song. Nance makes comprehensive notes on Padstow's folkloric heritage, and these are contained in Box 9. For contemporary scholarship on this, see Jason Semmens, 'Guising, Ritual and Revival: The Hobby Horse in Cornwall' in *Old Cornwall*, Volume 13, No.5, 2005, pp.39-46. For a consideration of the St George motif, see Bob Steward, *Where is St George?: Pagan Imagery in English Folk Song*, London: Blandford, 1988; Paul Broadhurst and Gabriele Trso, *The Green Man and the Dragon: The Mystery Behind the Myth of St George and the Dragon Power of Nature*, Launceston: Mythos, 2006.

108. 'The Christmas Play of Saint George and the Turkish Knight' in Nance Collection, Box 9, op.cit., p.1. A full version of this is found in Thomas and Williams, op.cit.

109. Ibid.

110. Ibid., p.2.

111. Ibid., p.5.

112. Ibid.

113. Ibid.

114. Ibid.
115. Ibid., p.6.
116. Ibid., p.7.
117. Ibid., p.8. Nance is very specific about the musical motifs used in the production.
118. Ibid., p.10.
119. Ibid., p.12.
120. Ibid.
121. Ibid., p.13.
122. Ibid., p.16.
123. Ibid., p.17.
124. Ibid., p.19.
125. Robert Morton Nance, *The Cledry Plays: Drolls of Old Cornwall For Village Acting and Home Reading*, Penzance: The Federation of Old Cornwall Societies, 1956. After Nance's name comes the phrase: *Dun yn – tak gans an gawry!* [Let's get on with the play!]. Cornish phrases introduce all three plays.
126. See O.J. Padel, *A Popular Dictionary of Cornish Place-Names*, Penzance: Alison Hodge, 1988, p.127. Padel indicates that this was once 'valley of Clodri'. The local pronunciation is Nan*cledry* or *Cledry*.
127. Henry Jenner 'Some Possible Arthurian Place-Names in West Penwith' in *Journal of the Royal Institution of Cornwall*, 1912, p.87.
128. This is given considerable discussion in Rosalind Conklin Hays, C.E. McGee, Sally L. Joyce and Evelyn S. Newlyn (eds.), *Records of Early English Drama: Dorset / Cornwall*, Toronto: University of Toronto and Brepols, 1999, pp. 397-438.
129. Nance, op.cit., 1956, p.3. Nance collected fragments of Folk-Play scholarship from all over Britain. See, in particular, Arthur Beckett (ed.), *The Sussex County Magazine*, Brighton: T.P. Beckett, 1927, pp.545-52; and 'The Plough Boy's Play: A Version Recorded' in the *Yorkshire Post*, 11 January 1937. See also the bundle marked 'Mumming Plays'. Various events are mentioned including the Stithians Play, a St Keverne Guize Dance and other fragments.
130. Joyce and Newlyn indicate some limited touring activity, but only to the next village. Jane A. Bakere, *The Cornish Ordinalia: A Critical Study*, Cardiff: University of Wales Press, 1980, p.17 offers that sometimes players did move to alternate venues in medieval Cornwall. Touring medieval folk-theatre is given an interesting fictional treatment in Barry Unsworth, *Morality Play*, London: Hamish Hamilton, 1995, where Cornwall is mentioned. In later centuries, there is less evidence of the kind of mobile drama to which Nance alludes.
131. See William Bottrell (ed.), *Traditions and Hearthside Stories of West Cornwall: First Series*, Penzance: W. Cornish, 1870, and (ed.), *Traditions and Hearthside Stories of West Cornwall: Second Series*, Penzance: Beare and Son, 1873, and (ed.), *Traditions and Hearthside Stories of West Cornwall: Third Series*, Penzance: F.

Rodda, 1880; Robert Hunt (ed.), *Popular Romances of the West of England: The Drolls, Traditions, and Superstitions of Old Cornwall (First and Second Series)*, London: John Camden Hotton, 1865.

132. For a useful introduction to this, see Philip Payton, *Cornwall*, Fowey: Alexander Associates, 1996, p.268. See also Derek Williams, 'Robert Morton Nance' in *An Baner Kernewek / The Cornish Banner*, No. 88, 1997, pp.14-18.

133. Nance, op.cit., p.3. It appears that 'Duffy' was in draft for several years. *The Times* 23 June 1919 has an intriguing reference to a Cornish play by Nance being performed in the Pavilion Theatre. This was part of the centenary celebrations of the Penzance subscription library. The likely candidate is 'Duffy'.

134. Baz Kershaw, *The Politics of Performance: Radical Theatre as Cultural Intervention*, London and New York: Routledge, 1992, p.1. See also Sandy Craig (ed.), *Dreams and Deconstructions: Alternative Theatre in Britain*, Ambersgate: Amber Lane Press, 1980.

135. Nance, op.cit., p.3.

136. Exceptions are Williams, op.cit., and Kent, op.cit., p.158 and p.173.

137. Compare two recent 'dialect' glossaries – K.C. Phillipps, *A Glossary of Cornish Dialect*, Padstow: Tabb House, 1993; Les Merton, *Oall Rite Me Ansum! A Salute to Cornish Dialect*, Newbury: Countryside Books, 2003 – with earlier glossaries such as Nance, op.cit., pp.103-9 and even W.F. Ivey (ed.), *A Dictionary of Cornish Dialect Words*, Helston: Helston Printers, 1976. The difference is greater still with F.W.P. Jago (ed.), *The Ancient Language, and the Dialect of Cornwall, with an enlarged Glossary of Cornish Provincial Words*, Truro: Netherton and Worth, 1882. The bundle in Box 9 marked 'Cornish Dialect' is an excellent collection and merits further study.

138 Alan M. Kent, '"Bringin' the Dunkey Down from the Carn": Cornu-English in Context 1549-2005 – A Provisional Analysis' in Hildegard L.C. Tristram (ed.), *The Celtic Englishes IV: The Interface between English and the Celtic Languages*, Potsdam: Potsdam University Press,, 2006, pp.6-33.

139. Such an actor might be David Shaw of Penzance – famed for a recent stage interpretation of William Bottrell.

140. See Joyce and Newlyn, op.cit.

141. See Kent (ed.), op.cit., 2000, pp.85-89, pp.90-92 and pp.121-24.

142. For the former, see Will Coleman, *Madgy Figgy's Pig*, Cornwall: Brave Tales, 2005, and *Tom and the Giant*, Cornwall: Brave Tales, 2005. For the latter, see Charles Causley and Michael Foreman, *The Merrymaid of Zennor*, London: Orchard Books, 1999.

143. Eileen Molony, *Folk Tales of the West*, London: Kaye and Ward, 1971.

144. Donald R. Rawe, *Traditional Cornish Stories and Rhymes*, Padstow: Lodenek Press, 1992 [1971].

145. Eric Quayle and Michael Foreman, *The Magic Ointment and Other Cornish Legends*, London: Anderson Press, 1986.

146. Shirley Climo and Anthony Bacon Venti, *Magic and Mischief: Tales from Cornwall*, New York: Clarion Books, 1999.

147. See Jacob Grimm, Wilhelm Grimm, Carol Ann Duffy and Marketa Prachaticka, *Rumpelstiltskin and other Grimm Tales*, London: Faber and Faber, 1999.

148. Bottrell, op.cit., 1873, pp.1-26.

149. Hunt, op.cit., *(First Series)*, pp.239-47.

150. Bottrell, op.cit., p.1.

151. Nance, op.cit., p.4.

152. Ibid.

153. Ibid., p.6.

154. Ibid., p.7.

155. Ibid., p.8.

156. Similar sentiment in Cornish is offered in the rhyme given to Edward Lhuyd in 1700 by the parish clerk of St Just-in-Penwith, and later recorded by William Pryce: 'An Lavor gôth ewe laver gwîr. / Ne vedn nevera doas vâs a tavaz re hîr; / Bez dên heb tavaz a gollas e dîr' [The old saying is a true saying, No good will be counted to come from too long a tongue; But a man without a tongue lost his land]. Nance knew this triplet well. See Alan M. Kent and Tim Saunders (eds.), *Looking at the Mermaid: A Reader in Cornish Literature 900-1900*, London: Francis Boutle Publishers, 2000, pp.246-7. In a letter to Jenner, dated 29 May 1918, Nance refers in passing to "my salvage work on the flotsam and jetsam of Old Cornish" (meaning the words of the Cornish language still to be found in Cornu-English). See Box 1 of the Nance Collection.

157. Bottrell, op.cit., p.4.

158. Nance, op.cit., p.9.

159. The exception is Phillipps, op.cit., pp.9-13.

160. Nance, op.cit.

161. Phillipps, op.cit.

162. Nance, op.cit., pp.103-9.

163. Ibid., p.9.

164. See, for example, James Kelman, *How Late it Was, How Late*, London: Secker and Warburg, 1994.

165. See Kent, op.cit., 2000, pp.269-71, *Proper Job, Charlie Curnow!* Tiverton: Halsgrove, 2005; K.C. Phillipps (ed.), *The Cornish Journal of Charles Lee*, Padstow: Tabb House, 1995; Payton, op.cit., 1996, pp.252-3; Nick Darke, *The Riot*, London: Methuen, 1999; N.R. Phillips, *Apocalypse Dreckly*, Tiverton: Halsgrove, 2005.

166. Nance, op.cit., p.11.

167. See Rob Penhallurick (ed.), *Debating Dialect: Essays on the Philosophy of Dialect Study*, Cardiff: University of Wales Press, 2000, and *Studying the English Language*, Basingstoke: Palgrave Macmillan, 2003, pp143-55; Salikoko S. Mufwene, *The Ecology of Language Evolution*, Cambridge: Cambridge University Press, 2001.
168. Nance, op.cit., p.35.
169. Ibid., p.14.
170. Ibid.
171. Ibid., p.13.
172. See Christina Rossetti (1830-1894) 'Goblin Market' cited in Liz Goodman (ed.), *Approaching Literature: Literature and Gender*, London: Routledge, 1996, pp.272-6.
173. Nance, op.cit., p.17.
174. Ibid., p.18.
175. Ibid., p.20.
176. *Fugo* is the Cornish word for a cave. The modern term *fogou* is generally applied to the stone-lined and roofed passages found west of the Fal estuary in Cornwall. Their function is still unclear.
177. *Bucca* is the Cornish word for a mischievous sprite or goblin.
178. Nance, op.cit., p.33.
179. See *BBC Drama 1922-1928* at www.kent.ac.uk/sffva/invisible. This web database, created by Alan Beck, is highly useful. *The Times* 4 May 1928 says 'This symphony concert will be preceded by a performance of 'Duffy' in three acts by Mr. Morton Nance, with Miss Katharine Frazier, Mrs Stanley Jones, Mr Robert Morton Nance and Mr A. K. Hamilton Jenkin in the cast.' The performance was scheduled for broadcasting at 9.35pm from 2LO [?] and other stations.
180. Nance, op.cit., p.79.
181. Ibid.
182. See Kent and Saunders, op.cit., pp.127-43.
183. Ibid., p.86. To *louster* means to do hard, labouring work.
184. Ibid., p.87.
185. Ibid., p.90.
186. Ibid.
187. Ibid., p.89.
188. Ibid.
189. Ibid., p.90.
190. Ibid., p.91.
191. Ibid., p.100.
192. *Change-about is Fair Play: A Christmas Droll* in Box 9, op.cit. The character was originally called Becky.
193. Ibid., p.3.

194. Ibid., p.14.

195. *The Tragedy of the Chrononhotonthologos: being the most Tragical Tragedy that was ever Tragedied by any Company of Tragedians* in Box 9, op.cit.. Nance was clearly following a tradition. There is a seventeenth-century German play by Gryphius, titled *Horribilicribrifax*, which features a character called Daradiridatumtarides.

196. *Tom and the Giant: A Christmas Play* in ibid. All of these dramas, and several drafts of the published plays, are hand-written in 'The Clincher' style writing pad. For the most part, Nance is chaotic in his scholarship. Notes and ideas are recorded on scraps of paper, undated and unreferenced.

197. Ibid. This means 'Fair play is good play'.

198. See *John Knill* in ibid. There is also a drama titled 'Honest Folk' concerning exploits of the Rosevear family, but this is not in Nance's hand, and appears a later composition.

199. Cf. W.B. Yeats, *Selected Plays*, London: Penguin, 1997.

200. Cf. W.B. Yeats, *Writings on Irish Folklore, Legend and Myth*, London: Penguin, 1993.

201. Peter Berresford Ellis, *The Cornish Language and its Literature*, London and Boston: Routledge and Kegan Paul, 1974; Miles, op.cit.; Philip Carr-Gomm (ed.), *The Rebirth of Druidry: Ancient Wisdom for Today*, London: Harper Collins, 2003; Rod Lyon, *Gorseth Kernow: The Cornish Gorsedd – what it is and what it does*, Cornwall: Gorseth Kernow, 2008.

202. See Nance (1958 [1929]), op.cit.

203. Peter Berresford Ellis, *The Celtic Dawn: A history of Pan-Celticism*, London: Constable, 1993, p.78.

204. See Henry Jenner, 'Cornwall: A Celtic Nation' in Williams, op.cit., 2004, pp.56-69. This paper was originally read before the Pan-Celtic Congress in Caernarfon in August 1904 and then published in the *Celtic Review* in January 1905. See also Derek Williams, 'Henry Jenner: The Years of Fulfilment' in *An Baner Kernewek / The Cornish Banner*, No.85, 1996, pp.15-18.

205. A.S.D. Smith, *The Story of the Cornish Language: Its Extinction and Revival*, Camborne: Smith, 1947, p.16.

206. Robert Morton Nance, *An Balores*, St Ives: James Lanham, 1932. There are some parallels in *An Balores* to an earlier skit by Nance involving a jury. See Robert Morton Nance, *The Cornish Jury: A Dialect Dialogue for XII Characters*, St Ives: St Ives Old Cornwall Society, 1926. The twelve are Foreman, Trebilcock, Angwin, Chegwidden, Mennear, Trenerry, Spargo, Pengelly, Quinterell, Polglaze, Trevaskis and Bosence, and the play investigates the guilt of an old woman.

207. The link is made explicit in numerous sources, but one of the most famous is in Cervantes' *The Ingenious Hidalgo Don Quixote de la Mancha* (1604-5 and 1625). The translation reads: "'Have you not read," cried Don Quixote, "the Annals and

History of Britain, where are recorded the famous deeds of King Arthur who according to an ancient tradition in that Kingdom never died but was turned into a crow (chough) by enchantment and shall one day resume his former shape and recover his Kingdom again? For which reason, since that time the people of Great Britain dare not kill a crow. In this good king's time the most noble order of the Knights of the Round Table was first instituted.'" Cited in Jas. L. Palmer, *The Cornish Chough through the Ages*, Cornwall: Federation of Old Cornwall Societies, n.d., p.4.

208. For a life, see Peter Ackroyd, *The Life of Thomas More*, London: Chatto and Windus, 1998.

209. Nance, op.cit., p.2.

210. Ibid., pp.2-3.

211. The iconography and imagery is continued in the Richard Jenkin-edited magazine *Delyow Derow*, 1989-96. There is a contemporary publishing house called Palores Publications. See also the concerns of the poets in Tim Saunders (ed. and tr.), *An Anthology of Modern Poetry in Cornish 1850-1980*, London: Francis Boutle Publishers, 1999.

212. Nance, op.cit., pp.8-9.

213. No doubt the early twentieth-century poets would be genuinely impressed with the real chough's return to Cornish cliffs, as well as the official status now afforded to the Cornish language.

214. Nance, op.cit., p.10-11.

215. Gorseth Kernow, *Ceremonies of the Gorsedd of the Bards of Cornwall*, n.d., pp.10-11. For a useful perspective on the imagining of a past 'Celtic world' see contributors to Gerard Carruthers and Alan Rawes (eds.), *English Romanticism and the Celtic World*, Cambridge: Cambridge University Press, 2003. For an interesting examination of Nance's spirituality, see Peter W. Thomas, 'R.M. Nance's Spirituality and the Cornish Gorsedd' in *Journal of the Royal Institution of Cornwall*, 2008, pp.61-70.

216. *Old Cornwall*, Summer, 1931, pp.24-5.

217. *Old Cornwall*, Volume 4, pp.368-9.

218. See, for example, Robert Morton Nance and A.S.D Smith (tr.), *Sylvester ha'n Dhragon*, Marazion: Worden, n.d., and (tr.), *Abram hag Ysak*, Marazion: Worden, n.d., and (tr.), *An Veven ha'y Map*, Cornwall: The Cornish Language Board, 1969, and (tr.), *An Tyr Marya* (R.D., lines 579-834), Cornwall: The Cornish Language Board, 1973 [1951].

219. Robert Morton Nance, A.S.D. Smith and Graham Sandercock, (eds. and trs.), *The Cornish Ordinalia, Second Play: Christ's Passion*, Cornwall: The Cornish Language Board, 1982, and (eds. and trs.), *The Cornish Ordinalia, Third Play: Resurrection*, Cornwall: The Cornish Language Board, 1984. See also Robert

Morton Nance, 'The Plen an Gwary or Cornish Playing-Place' in *Journal of the Royal Institution of Cornwall*, 24, 1935.

220. Robert Morton Nance, A.S.D. Smith, Ray Chubb, Richard Jenkin, and Graham Sandercock (eds. and trs.), *The Cornish Ordinalia, First Play: Origo Mundi*, Cornwall: Agan Tavas, 2001.

221. For a perspective on Tolkien, see Brian Bates, *The Real Middle Earth: Magic and Mystery in the Dark Ages*, London: Sidgwick and Jackson, 2002; Clive Tolley, 'Old English Influence on *The Lord of the Rings*' in Richard North and Joe Allard (eds.), *Beowulf and Other Stories: A New Introduction to Old English, Old Icelandic and Anglo-Norman Literatures*, Harlow: Pearson Longman, 2007, pp.38-62. See Yeats, op.cit.

222. See Carr-Gomm (ed.), op.cit.; Nigel Pennick, *Celtic Sacred Landscape*, London: Thames and Hudson, 2000 [1996]; Mark Ably, *Spoken Here: Travels Among Threatened Languages*, London: William Heinemann, 2003; Marcus Tanner, *The Last of the Celts*, New Haven and London: Yale University Press, 2004.

223. Antonia Barber and Nicola Bayley, *The Mousehole Cat*, London: Walker Books, 1990.

224. Robert Morton Nance, 'Tom Bawcock's Eve' in *Old Cornwall*, April 1927, pp.20-22. Older residents of Mousehole critique the 'festival' as inauthentic invention developed through 'Kneehigh [Theatre] and people like that'. Interview conducted by Alan M. Kent at Mousehole Old Cornwall Society, January 2009.

225. Ibid.

226. Ibid. See also Ralph Dunstan (ed.), *Cornish Dialect and Folk Songs*, Truro: W. Jordan, 1932, p.7. A separate study is needed of Nance's song-lyrics and contribution to the musical heritage of Cornwall.

227. 'Nyns-yu marow Mordon' in *Old Cornwall*, op.cit., 1951-1961, pp.450-1.

228. See Georgina Boyes, *The Imagined Village: Culture, Ideology and the English Folk Revival*, Manchester: Manchester University Press, 1993; Hutton, op.cit.

229. Robert Morton Nance (ed.), *A New Cornish Dictionary / Gerlyver Noweth Kernewek*, Redruth: Dyllansow Truran, 1994 [1955].

230. For an image of Reverend Bernard Walke and his mother, painted by Annie Walke, see Charles Thomas and Joanna Mattingly, *The History of Christianity in Cornwall: AD 500-2000*, Truro: Royal Institution of Cornwall, 2000, p.37.

231. Walke, op.cit., p.2.

232. Horace Keast, *The Catholic Revival in Cornwall 1833 to 1983*, Cornwall: The Catholic Advisory Council for Cornwall, 1983.

233. For context, see H. Miles Brown, *A Century for Cornwall: The Diocese of Truro 1877-1977*, Truro: Oscar Blackford, 1976; G.H. Doble, *The Saints of Cornwall: Parts 1-5*, Felinfach: Llanerch, 1997 [1960-1970]. For a contemporary view, see Andy Phillips, *Reclaiming Cornwall's Celtic Christian Heritage: A Study Guide*, Portreath: Spyrys a Gernow, 2006.

234. Walke observes that: 'I was also persuaded that the religious instinct of the Cornish people would never find satisfaction apart from the teaching and worship of the Catholic Faith; as the last of the English [sic] people to forsake the old religion they would be the first to return to the old ways.' See Walke, op.cit., p.30.

235. Ibid., pp.241-55.

236. An Anglo-Cornish writer with extreme Protestant views was Joseph Hocking (1860-1937), though his views softened during the First World War, when Catholic countries fought against what he considered to be the greater evil of Germany. In his retirement in Cornwall, he would surely have known of this incident. For his early position, see Joseph Hocking and R.E. Horton, *Shall Rome Reconquer England?* London: National Council of Evangelical Free Churches, 1910.

237. Nance, op.cit.

238. Few leading figures seem to have relations with him. See Williams, op.cit.; Thomas and Williams, op.cit.

239. Walke is only given cursory attention in Philip Payton, *The Making of Modern Cornwall: Historical Experience and the Persistence of "Difference"*, Redruth: Dyllansow Truran, 1992 and not mentioned in Deacon, op.cit. For an interesting Cornu-historical perspective of Walke, see James Whetter, 'The Life and Work of Bernard Walke' in *An Baner Kernewek / The Cornish Banner*, No. 123, 2006.

240. There have been no published studies of Walke's drama.

241. See Piers Brendon, *Hawker of Morwenstow*, London: Anthony Mott, 1983 [1975].

242. Bernard Walke, *Plays from St Hilary*, London: Faber and Faber, 1939, p.vii.

243. Rod Lyon, *Cornwall's Playing Places*, Nancegollan: Tavas an Weryn, 2001, pp.61-2; Matthew Spriggs, 'The Cornish Language, Archaeology and the Origins of English Theatre' in M. Jones (ed.), *Traces of Ancestry: Studies in Honour of Colin Renfrew*, Vol. 2, Cambridge: McDonald Institute Monograph Series, 2004, p.160.

244. Ibid.

245. Walke, op.cit.

246. Walke, op.cit., 1982 [1935], p.v.

247. Ibid., p.27. Walke also reflects on being held up in Marazion by 'a long cavalcade of shows and roundabouts that was on the road after Corpus Christi Fair'. This fairground tradition was examined in Chapter Five. See ibid., p.215.

248. Ibid., p.37.

249. Ibid., p.35. For the full statement, see Kent and Saunders, op.cit., p.267.

250. Walke, op.cit., 1939, p.7.

251. See Walke, op.cit., 1982 [1935], pp.202-13.

252. Walke, op.cit., 1939, p.22.

253. Deane and Shaw, op.cit., p.102.

254. Walke, op.cit., p.25.

255. Nance, op.cit., 1956.

256   For insight on this, see David J. North, *Studies in the Phonology of West Penwith English*, Redruth: Institute of Cornish Studies, 1991; David J. North and Adam Sharpe, *A Word-Geography of Cornwall*, Redruth: Institute of Cornish Studies, 1980.

257. Walke, op.cit., p.33. *The Eve of all Souls* was broadcast.

258. Ibid., p.7.

259. Ibid., p.9.

260. Ibid., p.5.

261. Ibid., p.6.

262. Walke, op.cit., 1982 [1935], p.24.

263. For context of this group, see Kenneth McConkey, Peter Risdon and Pauline Sheppard, *Harold Harvey: Painter of Cornwall*, Bristol: Sansom and Company, 2001; Richard Pryke, *Norman Garstin: Irishman and Newlyn Artist*, Reading: Spire Books, 2005.

264. See A.L. Rowse, *A Cornish Childhood*, London: Anthony Mott, 1982 [1942]. Rowse has numerous comments about the linkages back home from Cousin Jacks and Jennies overseas.

265. Walke, op.cit., p.23.

266. There may be something in this. See Marion Löffler (ed.), *A Book of Mad Celts: John Wickens and the Celtic Congress of Caernarfon 1904*, Llandysul: Gomer, 2000.

267. See Nance, Smith and Sandercock, op.cit., 1984, p.156-61.

268. Walke, op.cit., p.34.

269. Walke, op.cit., 1982 [1935], pp.54-5. Walke's work appealed beyond his Anglo-Catholic interests. He notes hearing someone saying, 'Whether you be Church or Chapel you belong to go to see the play up to St Hilary'. See p.199. One visitor was George Bernard Shaw. See p.200.

270. Ibid., p.56.

271. See Daphne du Maurier, *Vanishing Cornwall*, Harmondsworth: Penguin 1972 [1967], and *Rule Britannia*, London: Arrow Books, 1992 [1972]. Kent and Westland have both explored du Maurier's changing sympathies. See Kent, op.cit., 2000, pp.178-87; Ella Westland, 'Rule Britannia' in Helen Taylor (ed.), *The Daphne du Maurier Companion*, London: Virago Press, 2007, pp.217-25.

272. See *Tyr ha Tavas* membership leaflet, c.1930. One of the aims of *Tyr ha Tavas* [Land and Language] was to 'encourage an expression in Music, Drama, Literature, Art and other cultural forms of the innate Cornish instinct'. For a general history, see Bernard Deacon, Dick Cole and Garry Tregidga, *Mebyon Kernow and Cornish Nationalism*, Cardiff: Welsh Academic Press, 2003 pp.36-7. See also Garry Tregidga and Treve Crago, *Map Kenwyn: The Life and Times of Cecil Beer*, Cornwall: Gorseth Kernow, 2000.

273. See Donald R. Rawe, *Petroc of Cornwall*, Padstow: Lodenek Press, 1970; Ken

George, *Flogholeth Krist / The Cornish Ordinalia – the missing play: The Childhood of Christ*, Cornwall: Kesva an Taves Kernewek, 2006; Alan M. Kent, *Nativitas Christi / The Nativity: A New Cornish Mystery Play*, London: Francis Boutle Publishers, 2006.

274. Images of the Minack Theatre can be found on many postcards and DVD productions featuring Cornwall. For a live feed, see http://www.minack.com.

275. Ibid.

276. For background on this, see Denys Val Baker, *The Minack Theatre*, Cornwall: G. Ronald, 1960, and Rowena Cade and Darrell Bates, *A Short History of the Minack Theatre*, Porthcurno: The Minack Theatre, 1971.

277. A phrase from Dorothea Valentine. See Avril Demuth, *The Minack Open-Air Theatre: A Symposium*, Newton Abbot; David and Charles, 1968, p.13. Valentine had been a schoolteacher, who was then looking after her elderly parents at St Levan Rectory. On p.13 she writes that while at events in the Eastern Telegraph Company's Hall in Porthcurno, she recognised the 'acting potential of the Cornish'.

278. Ibid., p.15.

279. A detailed listing of all performances since 1932 to the present is given on http://www.minack.com.

280. John Masefield (1878-1967) wrote some 21 novels and many memorable sea-themed poems. He was Poet Laureate from 1930 until his death.

281. For some definitions of this, see Alison Light, *Forever England: Femininity, Literature and Conservatism between the Wars*, London: Routledge, 1991, and Judy Giles and Tim Middleton (eds.), *Writing Englishness 1900-1950*, London: Routledge, 1995.

282. For Ratcliff's detailed comments on the development of this work, see Denys Val Baker, *The Timeless Land: The Creative Spirit in Cornwall*, Bath: Adams and Dart, 1973, pp.58-9.

283. This appears to be a very common narrative and likely drama in Cornwall in previous centuries, concerning St Ursula and the Ten Thousand Cornish Virgins, and their tragic journey to Cologne. See Alan M. Kent, *Stannary Parliament*, St Austell: Lyonesse, 2006, pp.91-3.

284. See Demuth, op.cit. The volume covers direction, acting, lighting, sound and company management. Another important contributor is Frank Ruhrmund (b.1928), who has been a regular reviewer of theatre in Cornwall since the late 1960s. Ruhrmund has written an impressive poem about the Minack. See Frank Ruhrmund, *Penwith Poems*, Padstow: Lodenek, 1976, p.13.

285. Payton, op.cit., 1996, p.263.

286. See Robert Mason Catling and J. Percival Rogers, *G.H. Doble: A Brief Memoir and Bibliography*, Exeter: Sidney Lee, 1949; Charles Thomas, *Canon Doble: An Appreciation Fifty Years On: Address in Wendron Church April 30, 1995* – typescript

copy in the Courtney Library, Royal Institution of Cornwall, 1995.

287. Whitley Stokes (ed. and tr.), *The Life of Saint Meriasek, Bishop and Confessor: A Cornish Drama*, London: Trübner and Co., 1872.

288. G.H. Doble, *The Saints of Cornwall: Parts 1-5*, Felinfach: Llanerch, 1997 [1960-1970].

289. Miners, op.cit.

290. See notes in Saunders, op.cit., 1999, p.219. Her bardic name was *Arlodhes Ywerdhon* [Lady of Ireland].

291. See Murdoch, op. cit., pp.146-50.

292. Peggy Pollard, *Beunans Alysaryn*, St Ives: James Lanham, 1941, p.1. For a critical commentary, see Jerome Wilson, 'A Modern Cornish Miracle Play' in *The Celtic Pen*, Vol. 2, No. 2, 1994, p.24.

293. Ibid. I am indebted to Tim Saunders for the translations of this play, and the others which follow. Saunders also feels that Pollard was influenced by the writings of the Swiss psychiatrist and philosopher Carl Jung (1874-1961), who took walking tours in Cornwall during this period, giving lectures at hotels where he stayed.

294. Peggy Pollard, *Synta Acherontia: Gwary-myr* in Nance Collection, Box 10, Royal Institution of Cornwall, n.d.

295. Peggy Pollard, *Synt Tanbellan: A tryfle in one Scene* in Nance Collection, Box 10, Royal Institution of Cornwall, n.d. A version of *Synt Tanbellen* was broadcast on the internet-based, Cornish-language radio station *Radyo an Gernewegva* in 2008.

296. Peggy Pollard, *Cornwall: Vision of England*, London: Paul Elek, 1947. Despite the problematical title, this work is actually a careful study of Cornish history.

297. Claire Riche, *The Lost Shrine of Liskeard / An Greva Gellys a Lyskerrys*, Liskeard: Saint Austin Press, 2002.

298. For a context, see Alan M. Kent, *Wives, Mothers and Sisters: Feminism, Literature and Women Writers of Cornwall*, Penzance: The Jamieson Library, 1998, pp.33-35.

299. See Maisie Radford, 'Cornwall in Opera' in *The Cornish Review*, No. 2, 1966, pp.33-8.

300. See Kent, op.cit., 2000, pp.134-41.

301. For an overview, see Richard Barber, *King Arthur in Music*, Cambridge: D.S. Brewer, 1993. For the Glastonbury context, with some links to Tintagel, see Patrick Benham, *The Avalonians*, Glastonbury: Gothic Image, 1993. There is a further link here to the work of John Cowper Powys, *A Glastonbury Romance*, London: Penguin, 1999 [1932]. Powys' novel details the scene in Glastonbury during the 1930s. One of the characters, John Geard, wishes to mount a Passion Play.

302. See *The Times*, 6 July 1998. For background, see Radford, op.cit.

303 Radford, op.cit., p.34.

304. For an overview, see John Hurst, 'Literature in Cornwall' in Payton, op.cit., 1993, pp. 291-308; Peter Stanier, *Cornwall's Literary Heritage*, Twelveheads: Twelveheads Press, 1992, p.19; Alan M. Kent (ed.), *The Dreamt Sea: An Anthology of Anglo-Cornish Poetry 1928-2004*, London: Francis Boutle Publishers, 2004, pp.98-106.

305. See Ronald Tamplin, 'As New as it is Old' in Harry Chambers (ed.), *Causley at 70*, Calstock: Peterloo Poets, 1987, pp.46-54. Even then, this deals only with his post-war drama.

306. Interview with Alan M. Kent, Liskeard Community School reading, November 1991. Causley only occasionally reflects on his dramatic work, compared to much material on his poetry in the Exeter University Library Special Collections: Charles Causley.

307. See, for example, Nance, op.cit., 1932; Peggy Pollard, op.cit., 1941.

308. In particular, Charles Causley, *Farewell, Aggie Weston!* Aldington: Hand and Flower Press, 1951, and *Survivor's Leave*, Aldington: Hand and Flower Press, 1952, and *Union Street*, London: Hart Davis, 1957, and *Figgie Hobbin*, Harmondsworth: Penguin, 1985 [1970].

309. See Jessica Gardner and Ian Mortimer, *Modern Literary Papers in the University of Exeter Library: A Guide*, Exeter: University of Exeter Library, 2003, pp.15-18. See also John Hurst, 'A Poetry of Dark Sounds: The Manuscripts of Charles Causley' in Philip Payton (ed.), *Cornish Studies: Seven*, Exeter: University of Exeter Press, 1999, pp.147-64.

310. See Charles Causley, *The Spirit of Launceston: A Celebration of Charles Causley's Poetry*, Launceston: Launceston Calligraphers, 1994.

311. For an example of this, see 'On the Border' in Charles Causley, *Collected Poems 1951-1975*, London: Macmillan, 1975, p.258, where he writes: 'Is it Cornwall? Is it Devon? Those promised fields, blue as the vine, Wavering under new-grown hills; Are they yours, or mine?'

312. This is in Exeter University Library Special Collections: Charles Causley, EUL MS. 50a LIT/3/24 – Papers relating to *The Splendid Spur*.

313. See Walke, op.cit., 1982 [1935].

314. EUL MS. 50a LIT/3/11, p.5.

315. Charles Causley, *Runaway*, London: Curwen, 1936, and *The Conquering Hero*, London: Curwen, 1937.

316. Charles Causley, *Benedict: A Play in One Act*, London: Muller, 1938, p.107.

317. Ibid., p.115.

318. John Osborne, *Look Back in Anger*, London: Faber and Faber, 1957; Harold Pinter, *Plays: One*, London: Methuen, 1977.

319. Causley, op.cit., p.119.

320. Ibid., p.108.

321. EUL MS. 50a LIT/3/47.
322. Ibid.
323 See Causley, op.cit., 1975, pp.120-3, and p.226.
324. EUL MS. 50a/LIT/1/22.
325. See George Bernard Shaw, *Plays Pleasant*, Harmondsworth: Penguin, 1985 [1898].
326. See Ralph Dunstan (ed.), *Cornish Dialect and Folk Songs*, Truro: W. Jordan, 1932, pp.38-9.
327. EUL MS. 50a/Lit/1/5. David's speech is from later in the play.
328. D.M. Thomas, 'Faithful Travelling' in Chambers, 1987, op.cit., pp.10-11.
329. EUL MS. 50a LIT/3/49. Drew's letter is from April. Causley replies swiftly afterwards. The drafts of this reply are contained in the Papers.
330. Walke, op.cit.
331. Causley, op.cit., 1975, pp.165-8.
332. EUL MS 50a/LIT/1/38.
333. Part of Causley's awareness of the ritual year. See also, Charles Causley, *The Young Man of Cury*, London: Macmillan, 1991, pp. 90-1 and p.95.
334. Causley, op.cit., 1951.
335. See Charles Causley, *Hands to Dance and Skylark*, London: Anthony Mott, 1983 [1951].
336. Smith (1883-1950) would have been capable of the task. See his version of *Trystan hag Ysolt*; A.S.D. Smith, op.cit., 1951.
337. See many of the poems in Causley, op.cit., 1975.
338. Cf. Geraldine McCaughran and Richard Brassey, *Britannia: 100 Great Stories from British History*, London: Orion, 1999. Causley is also particularly adept at poetic retellings of great moments in Cornish history. See Causley, op.cit., 1975, pp.72-4, pp.145-6 and pp.186-8.
339. Jan Beart-Albrecht, 'Charles Causley' in *Artswest*, October, 1989, pp.22-5.
340 Jack Clemo, *Confession of a Rebel*, London: Chatto and Windus, 1949, p.121.
341. I am indebted to the knowledge of John Trembath, Chris Blount and Peter Hicks here.
342. Ibid.
343. See Summer Revellers, *Midnight Charity Matinee: Friday 25th August*, Newquay: Cosy Nook Theatre, 1939, in John Trembath Theatrical Archive, Newquay.
344. Ronald Brandon and Dickie Pounds, *Out of the Blue* Poster, Newquay: Cosy Nook Theatre, 1946, in ibid.
345. Ronald Brandon and Dickie Pounds, *Out of the Blue*, Newquay: Cosy Nook Theatre, 1947, in ibid.
346. Interview with John Trembath conducted on 27 October 2008.

347. There are other examples of this kind of arrangement in Cornwall. See King Arthur's Halls of Chivalry, in Tintagel.

348. *Newquay Amateur Drama Society, Its First 21 Years*, Newquay: Newquay Amateur Dramatic Society, 1952, p.4.

349. Ibid.

350. Ibid.

351. *Newquay Express*, 1 December 1932. Cutting in Reg Harris Archive, Lane Theatre, Newquay.

352. For background on Cornwall during this period, see Hancock, op.cit. See also Viv Acton and Derek Carter, *Operation Cornwall 1940-1944*, Devoran: Landfall, 1994, and op.cit., 1995.

353. Newquay Amateur Drama Society, op.cit., p.19.

354. See *Rebecca* Programme, Reg Harris Archive, op.cit. For background on du Maurier's drama, see Stanley Vickers and Diana King, (eds.), *The du Maurier Companion*, Fowey: Fowey Rare Books, 1997, p.38. As a whole, du Maurier's drama tends to be ignored in favour of her fiction and non-fiction. There is little discussion of it in Helen Taylor, *The Daphne du Maurier Companion*, London: Virago Press, 2007.

355. In a letter from Menabilly, dated 14 April 1948, du Maurier wrote to the Society saying: 'Thank you for your letter and invitation. I am so sorry neither my husband nor myself will be able to get over to Newquay to see the performance, but may I send you and the company my very best wishes for a big success'. Reg Harris Archive, op.cit.

356. A flavour of the relationship between the advisor and the Society is found in the Reg Harris Archive, where Newquay Amateur Dramatic Society contributed to 'The County [sic] Performance' in 1953 and the 'County [sic] Drama Festival' the same year.

357. See the observations in Deacon, Cole, and Tregidga, op.cit., pp.26-31. The wider problem is considered in Murray G.H. Pittock, *Celtic Identity and the British Image*, Manchester and New York: Manchester University Press, 1999.

358. See Michael Hechter, *Internal Colonialism: The Celtic Fringe in British National Development, 1536-1966*, London: Routledge and Kegan Paul, 1975. In essence the Celtic periphery having to help the centre was nothing new. See the observations by contributors to Brendan Bradshaw and John Morrill (ed.), *The British Problem c.1534-1707: State Formation in the Atlantic Archipelago*, Basingstoke: Macmillan, 1996.

359. See Gerry Mullins and Sean O'Keefe, *Dublin Nazi No.1: The Life of Adolf Mahr*, Dublin: Liberties Press, 2007. In the 1930s Mahr was head of the National Library Museum of Ireland and also Head of the Nazi Party in Ireland. See also Julian Jackson, *The Fall of France: The Nazi Invasion of 1940*, Oxford: Oxford

University Press, 2003. There is some indication that Breton Nationalists would welcome the German troops as allies against the French. For the most part, this is unfounded.

360. For exploration of this, see contributors to Bernard Waites, Tony Bennett and Graham Martin (eds.), *Popular Culture: Past and Present*, London: Croom Helm, 1982; Justine Ashby and Andrew Higson (eds.), *British Cinema: Past and Present*, London and New York: Routledge, 2000.

361. *The Cornish Review*, No.1, 1949, pp.76-7.

362. This is probably St Clement's Hall, originally built in 1880.

363. *The Cornish Review*, op.cit.

364. Ibid., pp.78-9.

365. Cf. Morash, op.cit., pp.178-89.

366. *The Cornish Review*, op.cit.

367. Ibid.

368. David Eames, 'Camborne's Repertory Theatre' in *The Cornish Review*, No.12, 1969, pp.36-9.

369. Ibid.

370. Ibid.

371. See *The Cornish Review*, No.2, 1949, pp.89-92.

372. Ibid.

373. Frank Michell, 'Redruth's Theatrical Past' in *The Cornish Review*, No.3, 1949, p.81.

374. Cornish Shakespeare Festival, *Cornish Shakespeare Festival Programme: Season 1935*, Cornwall: Cornish Shakespeare Festival, 1935.

375. At the age of 21, Peirce joined a theatrical touring company under the management of Sir Seymour Hicks. He had a long and varied career on the stage in character parts in Shakespeare and old English comedies, and in light opera. He also designed scenery for several London productions and had a one man show of pictures painted in Cornwall at the Greatorex Galleries, London.

376. I have been unable to trace the 1934 programme. Major performers of this era were Stephen Jack, Richard Kerr Carey, W. Lyon Brown, Thomas Mercer, Alexander Marsh, Stanley Van Beers, Donald Layne Smith, Dennis Barry, Lawrence Ray, C.B. Crofts, P.M.B. Parsons, Leslie Johns, Elizabeth Mees, Margaret Jacobs, Peggy Blazele, Marjorie Clayton, Mildred Howard, Christine, Powell, Alma Kenyon, Fay Scott.

377. In the immediate years afterwards, tours followed a similar format. See, for example, Cornish Shakespeare Festival, *Cornish Shakespeare Festival Programme: Season 1937*, Cornwall: Cornish Shakespeare Festival, 1937. This featured *Henry V*, *The Merchant of Venice*, *A Midsummer Night's Dream*, *Macbeth*, *Much Ado About Nothing* and *Two Gentlemen of Verona*, appearing at the Castle Green

(Launceston), Lewinnick, at Pentire (Newquay), Kimberley Park (Falmouth), Kilmarth (Par), Roswarne (Camborne), Trenoweth (St Ives) and St Erbyn's School (Penzance).

378. For the historical context, see Mary Coate, *Cornwall in the Great Civil War and Interregnum 1642-1660*, Truro: D. Bradford Barton, 1963 [1933].

379. Despite my investigations, I cannot discover who the author of this drama was, or the mummers' play mentioned.

380. See Rowse, op.cit.,1998; Philip Payton, *A.L. Rowse and Cornwall: A Paradoxical Patriot*, Exeter: University of Exeter Press, 2005. An interview with J.C. Trewin is found on Sir Arthur Quiller-Couch Memorial Fund Committee, op.cit.

381. See, for example, J.C. Trewin, *The Birmingham Repertory Theatre 1913-1963*, London: Barrie and Rockliff, 1963, and (ed.), *The Journal of William Charles Macready*, London: Longman, 1967, and (ed.), *Theatre Bedside Book: An Anthology of the Stage*, Newton Abbot: David and Charles, 1974.

382. J.C. Trewin, *Up from The Lizard*, London: Anthony Mott, 1982 [1948], and op.cit., 1952.

383. Ibid., p.31.

384. Ibid., p.34-5.

385. Ibid.

386. Ibid., p.90.

387. Ibid., p.170.

388. Ibid.

389. Ibid., p.171. This is probably Hannah Cowley (1743-1809). She wrote both comedies and tragedies. Her dramas embrace marriage and domestic virtue.

390. For the theory on 'cousins' see Halliday (ed.), op.cit., p.136. See also 'Cousin Jack' lore in Kent and McKinney (eds.), op.cit.

391. Trewin, op.cit. Cumberland was educated at Cambridge and the author of a number of sentimental comedies. He also wrote novels, one of which was titled *Arundel* (1789).

392. Ibid.

393. Trewin married Wendy Monk (1815-1915) and was awarded Order of the British Empire (OBE) in 1981. Since 2000 an award has been given by the Critics' Circle for the Best Shakespearean Performance of the Year: 'The John and Wendy Trewin Award for Best Shakespeare Performance'. His son Ion Trewin is currently the Administrator of the Man Booker Prize.

394. Richard Ollard, *A Man of Contradictions: A Life of A.L. Rowse*, London: Allen Lane, 1999; Payton, op.cit. Ollard's biography deals with Cornwall only in a cursory way.

395. This comes across in Richard Ollard (ed.), *The Diaries of A.L. Rowse*, London: Allen Lane, 2003.

396. Valerie Jacob, *Tregonissey to Trenarren: The Cornish Years of A.L. Rowse*, St Austell: Valerie Jacob, 2001; James Whetter, *Dr A.L. Rowse: Poet, Historian, Lover of Cornwall*, Gorran: Lyfrow Trelyspen, 2003. Jacob worked as Rowse's house-keeper. Whetter and Rowse had a long-standing friendship after his return to Cornwall.

397. See Philip Payton, 'I was before my time, caught betwixt and between': A L. Rowse and the Writing of British and Cornish History' in Payton, Philip (ed.), op.cit., 2003, pp.11-39; Mark Stoyle, *West Britons: Cornish Identities and the Early Modern British State*, Exeter: University of Exeter Press, 2002.

398. See Kent, op.cit., 2000, pp.200-8; Hurst, op.cit., 1993, p.294. In an examination of Rowse's poetry, Kent concludes that 'the love-hate relationship with Cornwall could not be solved, because for much of his life he was drawn between the two cultures'. Hurst acknowledges that Rowse, in the closing pages of *The Little Land of Cornwall*, extols 'the attractions of the notion of Cornish political autonomy'. See A. L. Rowse, *The Little Land of Cornwall*, Gloucester: Alan Sutton, 1987.

399. See, for example, A.L. Rowse (ed.), *A Cornish Anthology*, Penzance: Alison Hodge, 1990 [1968], p.259. Here, he quotes Richard Carew's observations on 'The Miracle Plays'. Rowse clearly approves of Carew.

400. A.L. Rowse, *Tudor Cornwall*, Redruth: Dyllansow Truran, 1990 [1941].

401. See Maclean, op.cit.; Williams, op.cit., 1971.

402. Letter to the author, 15 March, 1988.

403. This is embodied in the architectural commentary in A. L. Rowse, *A.L. Rowse's Cornwall: A Journey through Cornwall's Past and Present*, London: Weidenfeld and Nicholson, 1988.

404. See A.L. Rowse, *The Cornish in America*, Redruth: Dyllansow Truran, 1991 [1969].

405. See A.L. Rowse and M. I. Henderson (eds.), *Charles Henderson: Essays in Cornish History*, Oxford: Clarendon, 1935; Charles Henderson, *Cornish Church Guide*, Truro: D. Bradford Barton, 1964 [1925]. See also Charles Henderson Collection, Courtney Library, Royal Institution of Cornwall, Truro.

406. A.L. Rowse, *The Spirit of English History*, London: Jonathan Cape, 1943, and *The English Spirit: Essays in History and Literature*, London: Macmillan, 1944. Another text from this early period of Rowse's work is A.L. Rowse and G.B. Harrison, *Queen Elizabeth and Her Subjects*, London: Allen and Unwin, 1935. For a complete list of Rowse's works, see Sydney Cauveren, *A.L. Rowse: A Bibliophile's Extensive Bibliography*, Maryland: The Scarecrow Press, 2000.

407. A.L. Rowse, *The England of Elizabeth: The Structure of Society*, London: Macmillan, 1950, and *The Expansion of Elizabethan England*, London: Macmillan, 1955, and *The Elizabethan Renaissance: The Life of Society*, London: Macmillan, 1971, and *The Elizabethan Renaissance: The Cultural Achievement*, London: Macmillan, 1972.

408. A.L. Rowse, *William Shakespeare: A Biography*, London: Macmillan, 1963.

409. A.L. Rowse, *Shakespeare the Man*, London: Macmillan, 1973.

410. This included ideas that the 'Fair Youth' was the bisexual Henry Wriothseley, Third Earl of Southampton, that the 'rival poet' was the homosexual Christopher Marlowe, and that Shakespeare was heterosexual and put in a difficult situation when Wriothseley fell in love with him.

411. Embodied in later work such as John Drakakis (ed.), *Alternative Shakespeares*, London and New York: Methuen, 1985. Rowse seems out of favour in the present-day climate of Shakespearean scholarship.

412. A.L. Rowse, *Shakespeare the Elizabethan*, London: Weidenfeld and Nicholson, 1977, and *Shakespeare's Globe: His Intellectual and Moral Outlook*, London: Weidenfeld and Nicholson, 1981, and *Shakespeare's Characters: A Complete Guide*, London: Methuen, 1984, and *Discovering Shakespeare: A Chapter in Literary History*, London: Weidenfeld and Nicholson, 1989, and *My View of Shakespeare*, London: Duckworth, 1996.

413. A.L. Rowse, *Christopher Marlowe: A Biography*, London: Macmillan, 1965.

414. See Hosken, op.cit., 1896.

415. In March 2007, BBC Radio 4 re-broadcast Christopher William Hill's play *Accolades*. It starred Ian Richardson, and was about the period leading up to the publication of *Shakespeare the Man*, and Rowse's belief that he had discovered the identity of the 'Dark Lady' of the Sonnets. It is curious why Rowse's *A Cornish Childhood* has not received more media adaptation, although a 'play-for-voices' style adaptation of the text was made by Judith Cook, sometime in the 1980s.

416. A.L. Rowse, *A Man of the Thirties*, London: Weidenfeld and Nicolson, 1979, p.181.

417. A. L. Rowse, *A Life: Collected Poems*, Edinburgh: William Blackwood, 1981, p.95.

418. A flavour of this change, as well as a lament for the past is found in the following texts: Daphne du Maurier, *Vanishing Cornwall*, Harmondsworth: Penguin, 1972 [1967]; Jack Gillespie (ed.), *Our Cornwall: The Stories of Cornish Men and Women*, Padstow: Tabb House, 1988; Colin Robins and Bernard Deacon, *Merlin's Diner*, Tiverton: Cornwall Books, 1992; Patricia Moyer and Brenda Hull (eds.), *Anne Treneer: School House in the Wind*, Exeter: University of Exeter Press, 1998. *School House in the Wind* and *Cornish Years* were first published in 1944 and 1949 respectively.

419. See Murdoch, op.cit.; Hurst, op.cit.; Kent, op.cit.; Saunders, op.cit.

420. See, for example, James Whetter, *Scryow Kernewek / Cornish Essays 1971-76*, Gorran: CNP Publications, 1977; Arthur Aughey, *Nationalism, Devolution and the Challenge to the United Kingdom State*, London: Pluto Press, 2001.

CHAPTER SEVEN

——

Performing Devolution: Dramatic Re-invention, New Theatre and New Belonging in Cornwall, 1950-2010

'We meet at this Round, this *Plen-an-Gwarry*,
This gathering place of Cornish men in times
Past, present and future: an amphitheatre
Where all their hopes of grace and fears of death,
Hell's torments and the shining joys of heaven
Are made apparent, by the actor's skill.'

'St Petrock' in *The Trials of St Piran* by Donald R. Rawe, 1971[1]

'Do you know that feeling jowsters? Do you have that in your land? Losing your identity is worse than losing a limb. It keeps me awake. It stops me eating.'

'Joseph Emidy' in *The Tin Violin* by Alan M. Kent, 2008[2]

While the first half of the twentieth century effectively saw theatre in Cornwall renegotiate its position with the 'English' centre, the post-war period saw a gradual reinvention of theatrical space and place, so that a distinctly new kind of theatre began to be performed. Although initially small in scale in the immediate aftermath of the Second World War, some theatrical activity was asserting a reinvigorated cultural nationalism, in what was then a Cornwall that had, in general (though there were exceptions), little sense of its 'devolved' identity in a wider Britain. Gradually, however, and in reaction to many social, political and global trends (governed more specifically by in-migration, further challenges to Cornishness, mass tourism and a mass media seemingly resistant to the Cornish viewpoint), Cornwall has slowly but surely reasserted its historical difference. This geo-political pattern has been matched by changes on the stage in Cornwall. In many ways, theatre can be seen to be predicting trends and, later, moves towards devolution. In some sense, Cornish theatre's understanding of what I term in this chapter 'performing devolution', had always been there: it was just that in this period, it was going to be asserted in a more sophisticated way, and with a greater understanding of self. The new theatre in Cornwall would additionally help shape a new sense of belonging. As Donald R. Rawe understood in his 1971 play, the culture of the *plen-an-gwarry* still had a remarkable impact on the shaping of contemporary Cornwall, still 'made apparent, by the actor's skill'. There was also a sense that Cornwall could not lose its identity any further. As the character of Joseph Emidy asserts in *The Tin Violin*, it was seemingly worse than losing a limb – and might still be if Cornwall did not react and dissent against further incorporation. In fact, in a move with parallels to many oppressed groups and territories in the late twentieth century, Cornwall was going to reclaim and reassert its identity again on a hitherto unexpected scale.

The centrality of Cornwall within British and European culture was also to come full circle. This had been the case in the early medieval and medieval periods, but subsequent integration into England had neatly brushed over Cornwall's unique historicity – and its culturally specific dramatic continuum. A European Union of 'regions' and small 'territories' appeared to benefit the peripheral parts of the Community, culminating in Cornwall recently receiving funding from the Objective One scheme. The road to this kind of funding has, however, been painful, with traditional industries such as fishing finding the legalistic and environmental requirements of incorporation problematical. Matching these economic and environmental developments, we note that many of the styles, techniques and innovative uses of performance space in contemporary British theatre have their origins in post-war theatre in Cornwall. Due to a lack of theatrical institutions and modern spaces, sheer necessity had bred invention. While theatrical culture elsewhere in Britain was stuck in a London-governed, Arts Council-funded, untouchable 'garden' of non-achievement,[3] Cornwall had again gone its own way – with a series of companies, writers, designers and performers making innovative theatre without kowtowing to the 'centre'. By the turn of the twenty-first century, it appears that the 'centre' was even recognising this, and coming to Cornwall to see how it was done.[4] Gradually, too, cultural activity in Cornwall has become interesting to academics[5] and, perhaps more interestingly, also to popular culture in the decades after the Second World War.[6]

Although industry continued to decline in the post-war period, as did the traditional seaside holiday, Cornwall has slowly reinvented itself, so that there is now a curious merging of green ethics (embodied initially in wind farms and geo-thermal energy, but more recently in the Eden Project and wave hubs), art (The Tate St Ives), neo-pagan reconsideration of an ancient landscape, and a United Nations Educational, Scientific and Cultural Organization World Heritage Site, based on Cornwall's mining past.[7] Other changes – such as the Combined Universities of Cornwall (campaigned for, for much of the twentieth century),[8] the development of the Internet (allowing on-line Cornish communities around the world to communicate[9]) and the eventual government funding of development work in the Cornish language (as opposed to the small scale, often quasi-amateur works of the post-war revivalists)[10] – were shaping a brand new Cornwall, and a brand new theatre. In the early texts of this period (in the 1950s and 1960s especially), one can notice the realisation and even prediction of all of these, but it would take the 1970s and 1980s to develop the concepts and the 1990s and the 2000s to realise them more fully. Put another way, the intent had always been there: it was a matter of finding the right way to make it a reality.

There is not the space here to enter into a decade-by-decade analysis of the historical context of Cornwall in the post-war period. The interested reader can find a general examination of the major trends in many aspects of post-war Cornwall in contributions to the volume *Cornwall Since the War* (1993).[11] This collection reviews the immediate aftermath of the Second World War, economic change, mass tourism, the extractive industries, demographics, housing, language change and politics. This volume can be viewed as a direct continuation of the ground-breaking *Cornwall at the Crossroads: Living Communities or Leisure Zone?* (1988),[12] which explored the 'angst' over Cornwall's direction. Such volumes have recently been challenged by the various contributions of John Angarrack, who forcibly argues that Cornwall has been subjected to much propaganda, censorship and deception, not only in the post-war period, but over a longer period of its history.[13] Some of Cornwall's contemporary 'angst' over its identity was in part driven by the changes to the make-up of the United Kingdom's political structure after the 'New Labour' government came to power in 1997.[14] Realising that the peripheries of Britain required democratic and devolved reform, Tony Blair's government facilitated an Assembly for Wales, a Parliament for Scotland, and widespread changes in power-sharing in Northern Ireland. Watching this was a Cornwall that knew its historical status, but appeared not to be benefiting from the shake-up in the United Kingdom's constitutional structure. Despite some 50,000 individual declarations calling for a Cornish Assembly, Cornwall would remain an 'English county'.

The political desire for self-determination in Cornwall began in earnest in the pre-war period, with organisations such as *Tyr ha Tavas*. However, it was in the post-war period that political and cultural nationalism in Cornwall truly progressed. As Deacon, Tregidga and Cole demonstrate, *Mebyon Kernow* was initially formed in 1951 as a cultural pressure group, but quickly transformed itself into a political party.[15] Although electoral success has, for the most part, eluded the party, its very existence and lobbying force meant that other political parties (both mainstream and additional nationalist, such as the breakaway Cornish Nationalist Party[16]) have had to deal with the difficult 'Celtic drama queen' that is Cornwall. Theatre in Cornwall in the post-war period has matched this awareness-building process. As we shall see, although the initial dramatic texts took a softly, softly approach to asserting (to use Anderson's term[17]) the 'imagined community' of Cornwall, later writers engaged more directly with the issues. The complexities of mass tourism, in-migration, and ignorance over Cornish history and language within the education system, would all start to be explored within the theatre, notably in the work of companies such as Kneehigh Theatre, with their nationalist exposé *Blast!* The changing context can also be seen in the fate of the Cosy Nook in Newquay, where theatre has been supplanted by the urban-escapee sport of surfing. I would certainly argue that Cornwall's angst during this period would help develop some highly interesting theatre.

Having considered some aspects of the post-war context, it is also necessary here to consider some theoretical positions. As I have argued earlier in this book, the work of Sandy Craig, and Baz Kershaw forms an important framework around which we may explore the theatre of Cornwall during this phase.[18] Craig positions theatre in Cornwall during the 1960s and 1970s as being distinctly 'alternative' within the wider British theatrical landscape, arguing that practice in Cornwall was showing the way for other spaces and places. In short, Craig was making a longer term examination of the way Cornish theatre had always operated – that it was uniquely connected to ritual, landscape and community; anything else was pretension and irrelevant. In 1980, this was a controversial and marginal view that the mainstream and centre theatrical establishment could afford to ignore. Changes in lifestyle, environment, and success criteria have meant that Craig's view now represents much more of the centre ground. If this is the case, then the kind of theatrical practice occurring in Cornwall in the 1960s and 1970s was ground-breaking. That ethic has continued in Cornwall but, as we shall note, this has had impli-cations elsewhere in the development of theatre – 'the world stage of Cornwall' returning under new auspices. Kershaw's work, though written in 1992, argues that theatre can influence socio-political history and initiate change – partic-ularly in alternative and community theatre. In this chapter, the influence of Kershaw's theory on radical performance practice can be seen again and again.

Thus the process of ideological transaction in both modern and contemporary theatre in Cornwall is highly important in determining identity, community and politicality. This is not a sudden change, but one that has been growing, continuing to promote Cornish 'difference' and challenging Cornish 'integration'.[19] Theatre is the perfect medium to do this because it encourages self-reflection in the community. Whether this community is indigenous or in-migrant, the net effect is important, because both groups have to deal with the other.

Many of the theories and concepts of Craig, and Kershaw have been extended and developed by the work of more recent theatrical theorists. An important observer is Helen Gilbert. Gilbert is perhaps best known for her editorship of the 1999 volume *(Post) Colonial Stages: Critical and Creative Views on Drama, Theatre and Performance.*[20] Here, Gilbert considers that the most interesting drama being developed across the globe occurs where 'colonial' territories are writing back at and against their imperial masters. There are, she argues, 'stages' to this process, and to achieving eventual post-colonial theatre. Gilbert draws on a range of global examples, but she may as well have been writing about the position of Cornwall during the post-war period. In essence, the awareness-building of early twentieth-century theatre is one important stage in this process. Another is ensuring the critical reflection and renewed understanding in the colonised group. After this, it is the colonised group taking their 'stages and theatre' to the imperial oppressor, and renegotiating their relationship for the new era. It is these two stages that we witness in Cornwall during the post-war period. In a combined work, Gilbert and Joanne Tompkins again explored what they term the 'traditional enactments' of a community in kick-starting this process.[21] If this awareness of traditional enactments is essential to the consciousness-raising of a community, and as a precursor to more theatrical drama, then surely Cornwall – given both its traditional and invented festival culture – has good claim to be significant.

In 2000, Roger Bromley also argued for the profound impact of 'diasporic cultural fictions' in creating new belonging.[22] Applied to Cornwall, Bromley's theories would take into account the huge Cornish diaspora around the world, and how it helped to shape a new understanding of their belonging to both the 'host' country and the 'home' country. This trans-global identity would certainly have an impact on the creation and reception of theatre texts related to Cornwall. The specific sense of 'belonging' would also create a specific and perhaps innovative dramaturgy not encountered in places that did not have this diasporic culture. We witness this in, for example, the important play scripts of Nick Darke and D.M. Thomas during this phase. Finally, and perhaps most importantly, Marc Maufort gives dramatic theory a useful understanding of what he terms 'postcolonial hybridizations of dramatic realism'. Put simply, Maufort notes that what is needed for small territories like Cornwall is 'dramatic reinvention of the ethnic minority order'.[23] However, as we shall discover, this is never simple, and, as I have argued elsewhere, Cornish identity is much more complex and much more hybrid than many observers think.[24] Therefore, in order to truly overcome overt and sometimes misleading cultural itineraries, writers, directors, designers and actors must take note of this hybridization and – more importantly – employ it in their dramaturgy. In Maufort's considered view, once this is done, then we move through dramatic reinvention to a new theatre. My feeling is that this is perhaps a work in progress for Cornwall, and that as yet (with a few exceptions), a sustainable hybridization is not quite yet part of performing devolution. That said, some of those starting to explore the political and cultural implications of devolution (in its wider sense) realise the need to transgress.

So, with an understanding of the distinctive social, cultural, economic and political situation in the second half of the twentieth century,[25] and the first ten years of the twenty-first century, let us now consider where the story of theatre in Cornwall now leads us in the immediate decade after the Second World War. As we shall see, it was a decade with considerable continuity from the past, but also perceiving the direction of the future. Paradoxically, alongside the manifestation of Cornish nationalism discussed above, came the Festival of Britain, which sought to celebrate the glories of Britain past and present, and to demonstrate to the public how great a country Britain was. It was a new era. The Second World War was over, and a mood of optimism pervaded. Part of the Festival of Britain celebrations in Cornwall was a Cornish Summer Festival of Amateur Drama, at which two things happened. First of all, although the aim of the Festival of Britain was to reinforce 'British-ness' (or in actuality 'Englishness'),[26] the result was that the festival ironically gave new force to Cornish identity, since the plays celebrated the difference of Cornish cultural history. Secondly, though it was perhaps unrecognised in the immediate aftermath, we can now look back on that festival as a landmark in modern Cornish theatrical work since it not only set the blueprint for the kind of drama that was to be written about Cornwall in the late twentieth century, but also established many working practices and theatrical spaces and techniques that would be employed for the next fifty years. In essence, a new tradition was born out of it.

As we review the productions of that year, much of the established subject matter of Cornish theatre is outlined. There are obvious parallels with aspects of the wider literary culture of the same period, with particular themes deemed 'appropriately Cornish'. A small group of Cornish-language enthusiasts and writers were also imagining a Cornish-speaking community both past and present. In effect, quite an arsenal of Cornish-themed drama was organised for the festival, down to the efforts of the county [sic] drama advisor, Frances Collingwood Selby.[27] Nora Ratcliff created a new telling of the Tristan and Yseult story by presenting her *Tristan of Cornwall* at the Liskeard Public Rooms, the Minack Theatre and the Halls of Chivalry at Tintagel.[28] The latter locations emphasise the continuous performance of Arthuriana from the early half of the twentieth century, where Tintagel became a focus for new drama, after Hardy's imagining of the same narrative.[29] In the production Ratcliff was at pains to remove the tale from 'the trappings of medieval romance' and 'to return them to the more primitive period to which they belong'.[30] This objective comes out in some of the dialogue of this version, which certainly shows the reality of Iseut's [sic] position:

> Iseut: It is not a small thing to leave my land;
> Not an easy thing, for a girl
> To give herself into a man's keeping.
> I will try to merit this gift you have offered.
> Your country is now my country, King Mark, henceforth.
> I am of Cornwall, King Mark, my King.[31]

In this sense, Ratcliff was striving for greater realism, though it is perhaps hard to imagine that realism being effective in the locations in which it was performed. Certainly however, within the history of theatre, the tale of Tristan and Yseult is Cornwall's greatest ongoing 'tragedy' so it was fitting that it was revived during this period.

Related to the Arthurian matter and to the mystery plays continuum was Wallace Nichols' *The Boy from Egypt*. This was a dramatic morality play presented in five scenes and produced by the Cornwall Religious Drama Fellowship at St Ives. It was designed for 'possible performance in churches and chapels as well as on the ordinary stage and in village halls'.[32] The plot is based on the legend that, as a boy, Christ came to Cornwall with his supposed uncle, Joseph of Arimathea, again, a continuing theme throughout the history of Cornish drama. Like the *Ordinalia*, Nichols' play was conceived as a dramatic poem, and though it may now seem a rather too overtly 'Christian' piece, its significance in its day is perhaps emphasised by its eventual publication in Denys Val Baker's *The Cornish Review*.[33] During this phase, Cornwall was also able to bring in more experienced producers and directors from outside. In this case, *The Boy from Egypt* was produced by Christopher Casson, from the Gate Theatre in Dublin. In such examples, we begin to see materialising the idea of limited pan-Celtic activity in the post-war period.

Religion was also to the fore in Cornish dramatist Christian Michell's play *The Wesley Tapestry*.[34] This biographical play was presented in Gwennap Pit, near Redruth, by the Methodist Church in Cornwall. A play at Gwennap itself was quite a bold move. Prior to this period, the pit had not been used in quite this way, and interestingly there were many similarities between it and the earlier 'playing places', despite the ideological and theological differences. The difficulty facing the producers – and those who later sought to mount the late twentieth-century solar eclipse *Ordinalia* production there – was that the pit was ideologically Protestant, whereas the *plen-an-gwarry* was originally Catholic.[35] Wesley was also not known for his tolerance of Celtic languages. Such a play – presenting a religious life about a man who supported the 'method' of Christianity rather than the performance – was still, in 1951, a progressive piece of theatre. Again, the drama's location here opened up new trends in theatrical production in the post-war period. Later companies were to produce their events in other pits and preaching places, the one at Indian Queens being a good example.[36] Even so, *The Wesley Tapestry* seemed to carry forward at least some of the themes of the earlier medieval religious dramas. As the programme notes to the production reveal, the parallel with the Jesus Christ of the *Ordinalia* is obvious: 'He bore the brunt of their anger, they stoned and persecuted him, there was riot and rebellion, but eventually they grew to respect and need him'.[37] Interestingly, it is in the post-war period that Methodism itself experienced further decline. This play might be read as the Methodist Church in Cornwall trying to regain lost ground in an era that viewed belief in God more cynically than any previous generation.[38]

These pieces were still at the more conservative end of the festival. Phyllida Garth chose to locate her musical drama *The Work of Our Hands* in Truro's Anglican Cathedral.[39] Here, the six singers in the work represented Cornish saints, each one a patron of the local industries that have developed from the natural resources of Cornwall. John Tallack, a Cornishman newly returned from abroad (like many of those returning home from service and from work overseas) is granted, because of his love for Cornwall, the power to share the vision of the saints; he and they see groups of tinners, china clay, granite and slate workers, fishermen, market gardeners and housewives perform their respective tasks in dumb-show. The play is divided into three sections – Rock, Sea and Land – and between each St Michael appears and exhorts the people to work together in harmony for the prosperity of the world, for the dignity of the human spirit and to the glory of God, ending with a prayer: 'Establish

Thou the work of our hands upon us'.[40] Again, within this production can be seen vestigial remains of the mystery plays, though notably this interacts with modern Cornwall.

Patricia Donahue's *Women of Cornwall* brought a more pageant-style drama to Penzance, Falmouth and Liskeard.[41] Performed by the Cornwall Federation of Women's Institutes, this play worked as a chronicle, attempting to portray, in dramatised incident, the part women have played in the history of Cornwall by focusing on some central female characters.[42] The first episode concerned itself with one of the many Cornish female saints, St Endellion, on the way to watch a miracle play on her feast day. The second took the audience to troubled Calais, still under 'English' rule in 1539. Here, Donahue constructed a picture of Lady Lisle, a Cornishwoman presiding as the wife of the Lord Deputy of Calais. The story intersected with the reception of Anne of Cleves, who broke her journey at Calais on her way to marry Henry VIII. The third episode was set on the quayside at St Michael's Mount during the War of Five Nations (Civil War). Mistress Anne Basset, in charge of the castle while her husband, the Sheriff of Cornwall, was with the King, awaited news of the battle raging near Launceston. Friction arose between the local fisher folk, followers of the Basset fortunes, and an old fish-wife from St Ives in sympathy with the Parliamentarians. Representing the eighteenth century, Dolly Pentreath – one of the last speakers of the Cornish language – was presented, followed by a ball at the Truro Assembly Rooms, home of eighteenth- and early nineteenth-century theatre in Cornwall.[43] This was followed by a depiction of Jane, Richard Trevithick's wife on the eve of his departure to seek his fortune in Peru.[44] The fifth episode moved on to 1840, and was lit by the furnace fires of the foundry at Perran-ar-worthal. The brilliant Fox sisters of Falmouth visited their uncle's foundry on a special occasion. The final episode crossed the sea to witness Dame Fanny Moody being presented with her diamond tiara in Johannesburg by wildly enthusiastic Cornish miners,[45] and then followed Mary Kelynack who, at the age of 84, walked from Penzance to London to visit the Great Exhibition of 1851. In the Epilogue the various strands of the play were brought together. Even in simple summary, one can see that this was quite an epic production and one that was beginning, in the light of increasing women's rights, to portray their achievements and stories on the Cornish stage.

More residual cultural material (in effect pre-dating the Second World War) was offered by Robert Morton Nance in the shape of productions of *Two Cornish Drolls*, including the traditional Christmas play of *St George and the Dragon*.[46] Dorothy Miles and Patricia Dedman also presented a new *St Petroc's Festival Play* in Bodmin Church, but details of this are sketchy. Even less detail

Fig. 90. Gwen Wood's distinctive cover design for the 1951 Cornish Drama Festival souvenir programme.

is available about the other crucial events of the festival. Six one-act plays were presented at the Public Rooms in St Austell.[47] A competition for the best play had been organised by *The Western Morning News* newspaper, the winner being Patricia Donahue's *The Cliff Edge*. Other plays produced included *The Carn Remembers* by Eileen R. Speck, *The Pilgrim Stone* by Michael Toms, *Aunt Saul's Recipe* by Constance Cleminson, *The Mermaid of Zennor* by Pearl Peirson and *The Stranger* by Edith M. Jolly. Meanwhile in the wonderful location of Holman's Works Canteen, Helena Jones mounted a production of her play, *Richard Trevithick*. Unfortunately, I have been unable to track down any of these dramas. They are either hidden or lost, which is unfortunate because they may well represent some of the most dynamic theatrical writing in post-war Cornwall.

By 1950, part of the saint's play *Bewnans Meriasek* had been produced in Cornish by a Camborne-Redruth theatre group formed by leading *Mebyon Kernow* activist Helena Charles. According to Peter Berresford Ellis, performances were held in Truro, St Day, Redruth and Camborne, and Collingwood Selby also assisted when it was submitted as an associate production to the Cornwall Amateur Drama Festival.[48] It was performed at Perran Round and then became Cornwall's contribution to the Festival of Britain in 1951. While the wider British stage began to take notice of Cornish-language drama, the Old Cornwall Societies at home initiated a publishing programme to allow a new generation access to the earlier dramas. They did this by breaking the *Ordinalia* and *Bewnans Meriasek* into what we might term 'bite-sized' chunks. Among the texts produced were *Bewnans Meryasek, An Tyr Marya / The Three Marys, Sylvester Ha'm Dhragon / Silvester and the Dragon, Abram hag Ysak / Abraham and Isaac, Adam ha Seth / Adam and Seth, Davydd hag Urry / David and Uriah* and *An Venen ha'y Map / The Woman and the Son*.[49] However, even those unfamiliar with the Cornish language can see the problem here. The texts, though short, were still indigestible not only for the bulk of the Cornish population, but also for those concerned with the revival of Cornish on the stage. They were too overtly religious for an Age that had eschewed traditional Christianity, as a result of the Second World War and the upheavals, as Sinfield details, associated with 'liberal' and 'permissive' 1950s' and 1960s' society.[50] Continuity persisted in other ways. For example, a Christmas play was performed at St Mawgan Church in 1959, which featured a Modern Christmas, an Ancient Christmas (featuring St Mawgan) and the Birth of Christ.[51] This was maintaining the traditions of saintly-themed and Christmas-themed drama in Cornwall. Religious themes remained prevalent in the culture of the Gorsedd. One of the younger writers of this period was N.J.A. Williams (b.1942) whose play *Trelyans Sen Powl / The Conversion of St*

Fig. 91. A Christmas Play being performed at St Mawgan Church in 1959.

Paul won the Gorsedd award in 1961.[52] Williams closely follows the style and form of texts such as the *Ordinalia* and *Bewnans Meriasek*, as can be seen by the opening of the verse-drama:

> *Hic pompabit Saul et postea dicit*

> *Ym gylwyr Saul yredy*
> *aswonys dres oll Judy*
> *avel compyer an lagha*
> *ow punsya an Grystoryon*
> *Cryst bos myghtern Yedhewon*
>   *mara ny vynnons nagha. . .*

>   *[Here Saul shall parade and afterwards he shall say*

> Saul, I am called,
> known through Judea
> as champion of the law,
> punishing the Christians
> if they will not deny
>   that Christ is the king of the Jews. . .][53]

A study of opera in Cornwall has yet to be written, but it is important to mention some operatic theatre here. Opera had a generous cross-fertilisation with theatre during the late nineteenth century, and in this phase matched the epic ambitions of other theatrical writing. One of the most important scholars and composers in the 1960s was Inglis Gundry. His first opera *The Tinners of Cornwall* was performed by amateurs at the Steiner Hall in London, its theme being the closing of the tin industry (a constant theme of post-war Cornish theatre).[54] Musically, the best parts of the opera were the rousing choruses of the miners and the melodramatic moment when the young hero was trapped by a fall of rock. If ever there was a subject for composers to consider, then this is it. It is a pity that Gundry's opera is not better known. His second work was *The Logan Rock*, an opera written especially for the Minack Theatre.[55] Here, the subject-matter was more explicitly folkloric, developing the interest shown by Nance and a previous generation of scholars. At the time, the opera was criticised for being 'forced'; reviewers commented that Cornu-English dialect and opera do work well together. It may well be that what Gundry was attempting to achieve with *The Logan Rock* was too progressive for the time, and its middle-class audience would have found the Cornu-Engish hard to bear. However, the text may be seen as an important progression, in its way a continuation from the proud nineteenth-century use of Cornu-English. Another Cornish-themed opera emerged in 1964, more successfully matching Cornu-English voices with music. This was *Morvoren*, written by Philip Cannon and produced first at the Royal College of Music in London, then at the Princess Pavilion in Falmouth. Here, the theme is broadly based on the tale of the Mermaid of Zennor, Cannon commenting at the time:

> Opera has been in my mind ever since I was a boy in Cornwall... The Cornish half of me wanted to reveal in musical terms the fascinating hinterland where truth and legend meet, where the ancient cults and superstitions of Cornwall would appear against their true background of ruggedly beautiful coastline and wilder sea... I felt I could set it to music.[56]

Cornish opera seems to have suffered a similar fate to the Anglo-Cornish novel.[57] There are individual marks of brilliance over the past two centuries but, as I have observed elsewhere,[58] the infrastructural limitations mean that there is only a relatively small audience to sustain such a genre. In order to develop further, it would seem that Cornu-centric opera would have to embrace the concerns of the wider period, making more of an effort to develop a performance of devolution. This is not easy, especially as the perceived audience for opera in Cornwall is middle-class and often ethnically English.

Fig. 92. Publicity leaflet for the Cornish Mystery Play Cycle (*Ordinalia*) at Perran Round, July 7-20, 1969.

The high watermark of this period of Cornish theatrical activity was the July 1969 production of the three plays of the *Ordinalia*, which were staged in English translation at Perran Round near Perranporth.[59] The plays were performed by students of the University of Bristol's drama department, directed and adapted by Neville Denny (based mostly on the text of Professor Markham Harris,[60] but also using elements of Norris, Nance, and Halliday[61]). Denny was Lecturer in Medieval and Renaissance Drama at Bristol, and had always been interested in the Cornish cycle. Although there were to be a variety of 'stabs' at mounting the *Ordinalia*, this remains one of the more iconic ones. Part of its status was the timing: the production, in the summer of 1969, came not only at the very end of the 1960s, a decade of enormous change globally, but also on the brink of the 1970s, when the old values would be upended and overthrown.[62] Theatre, in a pan-British sense, was taking a renewed interest in such community-driven projects, and medieval drama, after centuries of being ignored, was once again fashionable.[63] Some of this new enthusiasm was driven by the opportunity for spectacle and festival. Here was a text that somehow encapsulated the wider festival culture of the era. Celticity too, was back in fashion, as were pan-Celtic politics.[64]

Fig. 93. A sketch of a devil on the rear of the programme for the 1969 production of the Cornish Mystery Play Cycle (*Ordinalia*).

The 1969 production also demonstrated to the world the sheer scale of Cornish drama. A look at the programme confirms this.[65] There were some twenty-six actors playing lead roles in the cycle, with twenty devils, thirteen disciples, and twenty-five actors playing the roles of the angels, courtiers, Israelites and soldiers. In order to achieve his ambition Denny also had three assistant directors: Sara Yeomans, J. Kevin Robinson and, perhaps most importantly, Sidney Higgins. Higgins's input was invaluable: as we have seen earlier, it was in this production that Higgins first began to work at his ideas of how Cornish drama was staged.[66] Jenny Bolt's design for the production was notable for her idea of utilising the northern entrance as the mouth of Hell, and for her easily constructed ark. Glynis Davies's design for the costumes was a phased combination of medieval and biblical wear. Michael Cooper's musical arrangements were integral to the performance. Chris Warner (who was to make an impact with his company Warner's Corner, and later the Hall for Cornwall) co-ordinated the Cornish end of the production. If there is any criticism of the production, it was perhaps that the piece was an 'imposed' development from outside; but then again, there seemed no other group who could even attempt the scale of production offered. Secondly, although Perran Round seemed an obvious choice as a location, many scholars have argued that there is actually very little evidence of a connection between the *Ordinalia* and that *plen-an-gwarry*.[67] Nevertheless, such venues and texts were being connected in the popular imagination. Indeed, Denny was to make much use of archaeological features of the Round, such as the banks and the so-called 'Devil's Spoon' indentation. In his correspondence about the translation and dramaturgy of the *Ordinalia*, Denny remains concerned about achieving its 'act-ablity'. In a letter to H.L. Douch, Librarian at the Courtney Library in the Royal Institution of Cornwall, Denny notes:

> It should be a verse translation. But while the original verse structures are all very well, perhaps essential in a literary translation, they represent insuperable obstacles to the actor, and are moreover, fatally soporific in their effect on a modern British audience. Ordinary English speech rhythms are essential in any verse script intended for the stage: the ideal is a verse form that obtrudes so minimally as to go unnoticed.[68]

Denny was fully aware that his own adaptation had limitations. He also acknowledges the fact that he 'tinkered quite a bit' with the crowd passages, and the lengthy speeches of the Jews, Devils and Torturers in order to make the dramaturgy more fluid. Interestingly, Denny believed that 'improvisation played a much greater part than anyone had yet appreciated',[69] suggesting that although there were base texts for such productions, they were adapted and improvised upon, in much the same way as Denny's 1969 version. His wish for a verse translation would be realised some thirty years later.[70] Perhaps because of his wish for ordinary English speech rhythms, the 1969 version was vocally not very Cornu-English, but this was to be expected because those involved in the project, though sharing a connection with Bristol university, were drawn from all over Britain. This mounting of the *Ordinalia* was a central component of Cornu-centric drama in the post-war period, an ignition point for much future development.

In the wake of this production came the major dramatic phase of the writer Donald R. Rawe. Rawe's reputation as a novelist, poet and dramatist had been growing throughout the post-war period, but it was the early 1970s that witnessed an important development of his work. Paradoxically, Rawe never actually saw the production of the *Ordinalia* at Perran Round, but there is a sense of a shared literary moment in his writing. Rawe's reputation and contribution to literature in Cornwall is only just beginning to be recognised.[71] In a career spanning several decades, he had single-mindedly asserted a new literature of Cornwall, and also worked in a number of other significant areas, among them folkloristics, history and publishing.[72] Over time, Rawe's dramatic work has influenced a range of other practitioners in Cornwall, and an anthology of his theatre works is very much needed. Rawe was born in Padstow in 1930 and, after time spent teaching in Australia, has lived back in Cornwall since 1960. He had begun to work as a novelist, publishing *Looking for Love in a Great City* (1956) under the pseudonym of Daniel Trevose.[73] This novel is one of the most underrated texts of modern Cornwall, but a second novel, *The Mind has Its Mountains*, was not published. In Australia, ABC had broadcast a number of his radio plays, including *A Surge of Eucalyptus*.[74]

When Rawe returned to Cornwall, he took over his father's outfitting business in Padstow, and began to write for the theatre, first producing smaller dramas on the life of St Petroc, performed by the Kernow Players of Padstow at parish churches in both Padstow and Bodmin between 1964 and 1965.[75] An earlier drama on the life of St Petroc had been produced at Bodmin in the 1951 Cornish Drama Festival,[76] so clearly there was a continuity of practice. As Doble documents, St Petroc was the son of a Cambrian monarch, who after his father's death in 485 CE devoted himself to a religious life, renouncing his throne and travelling first to Ireland, then landing twenty years later at Trebetherick in Cornwall.[77] In 518, St Guron, the Cornish Anchorite who occupied a hut on the site of Bodmin Church, resigned it to St Petroc, who then established a small Benedictine monastery there. St Petroc died in 540 and after many vicissitudes his bones were restored to the parish church,

Fig. 94. The front cover of Donald R. Rawe's published version of *Petroc of Cornwall* (1970). Courtesy of Donald R. Rawe.

where they now rest in an ancient ivory casket.[78] This narrative was Rawe's starting point for the assembly of his dramas, which were eventually performed as a whole at Perran Round on 4 to 8 August 1970. In a Foreword to the publication of the play *Petroc of Cornwall*, Rawe writes that it was 'a condensation of the trilogy comprising The Coming of Petroc, The Fruitful Years of Petroc, and The Final Glory of Petroc'.[79] Although new mysteries had been imagined before (particularly in the work of Peggy Pollard), Rawe's play was a much more sophisticated affair, prompting the critic Paul Newman to write that he 'showed an instinctive flair for using the Round' and that the poetry would be 'difficult to better'. Newman particularly praises the description of Petroc in the wooded vale near Lanwethinoc:

> At dawn each day his matin psalms would rise
> As he stood naked on the river bed
> Unconscious of the icy torrent round
> His frail body, warmly praising God.
> Then hours of meditation and of prayer
> So still the woods that squirrels stared at him
> And robins lighted on him as he sat.[80]

The imagining of Petroc's world was epic, featuring characters such as Samson, Guron, Dator, Minifreda, Piran, Issey and Cadoc, and perhaps also paralleling the wider renewed interest in Celtic Christianity of a range of writers and observers.[81] Newman also realised that by writing from a 'defiantly nationalistic standpoint' Rawe was 'perpetuating the very tradition from which poetic inspiration was originally drawn'.[82] The nationalist standpoint was never so overt that it felt like a party political broadcast; it was in Rawe's imagining of a geo-political world with Cornwall at the centre. Here then was a dramatist self-consciously absorbing the continuity of theatre in Cornwall, but also repackaging it, by choosing a new saint to write about – although the narrative of St Petroc was likely to have been dramatised in the medieval period, no texts have survived. Rawe was also seeking and defining a new kind of 'performing devolution' of Cornwall. It is with this text that Cornwall begins its sense of new theatre and new belonging.

The nationalistic imperative in Rawe's work was given greater emphasis in his 1971 play, *The Trials of St Piran*.[83] Here the dramatist was imagining what possible narrative of the patron saint of Cornwall might once have been told, and bringing about a complete merging of space, place and performance: Perran Round presenting a drama about St Piran, performed by Cornish actors. Compared with the 1969 *Ordinalia*, this play had more comedy and featured more Cornu-English language, giving it what Newman describes as a 'crunch directness'.[84] However, Rawe carefully balances the Cornu-English with standard English, so that it does not inhibit understanding for some members of the audience.[85] This time the plot concerns a Cornish chieftain who abducts a nun from a convent. Piran undertakes the task of getting her back. The play is less formal than *Petroc of Cornwall*, with Rawe confidently moving between sections of blank verse and prose, depending on the status of the character. As in the drama from the previous year, throughout this play Rawe cleverly balances the events of Piran's recorded and folkloric life with the need for fast-paced dramaturgy. In devising revolutionary work that explored a national symbol at a time when it was still a radical move to display a St Piran's car sticker or fly a Cornish flag, Rawe was championing a growing symbol of Cornishness, and developing an accomplished vision of 'performing devolution'.

His next project was to develop the dramaturgy even further by positioning an Arthurian text in traditional Cornish theatre space. Up until the discovery of *Bewnans Ke*, there had been no medieval theatrical depiction of Cornish Arthuriana. This seemed a strange anomaly, given the status of the Arthurian matter in Cornwall. Rawe therefore offered a corrective in *Geraint: Last of the Arthurians* (1972).[86] Geraint is imagined as the former lieutenant of King Arthur; in the play, this defender of the Christian and Druidic faith, is dying. The action of the drama therefore concerns those who wish to succeed to his throne. One of the most spectacular moments occurred after the King had died, when a golden boat with silver oars was moved across the stage, bearing his body. This Arthurian 'set piece' was perhaps also suggesting a lament for a lost culture, demonstrating the more overtly political ambition of the drama. In the opening scene we learn of 'the Saxons heading westwards':[87] this was a metaphor both for resistance in Cornwall, and for how Cornwall was feeling about its immediate neighbour. Rawe's text was truly what Maufort describes as the 'dramatic reinvention of the ethnic minority order'.[88] Much of Rawe's work draws on elements I have discussed in Chapter One of this book. For example, he is acutely aware of the wider geo-political concept of Dumnonia,[89] as well as the interface between pagan and Christian Cornwall. One may go further: the roots of Rawe's dramatic awareness may have been strongly shaped by his childhood in Padstow – a place intensely connected to its own para-theatrical tradition. This is borne out in Rawe's detailed study of Obby Oss, which has become the standard text on the festivities.[90]

Newman was famously to conclude in 1973 that Rawe was 'becoming synonymous with a Cornish National Theatre'.[91] Rawe's own dramatic work took a different direction in the remainder of the 1970s. The 1972 production

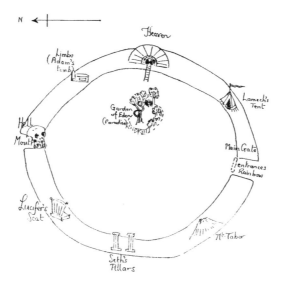

Fig. 95. Sketch for the design of the 1973 production of Donald R. Rawe's version of *The Creation of the World.* Courtesy of Donald R. Rawe.

of *Geraint: Last of the Arthurians* prompted him to investigate once again the established continuum of drama in Cornwall. He translated the 1611 text, *The Creation of the World*,[92] presenting this at Perran Round in 1973, using the three modern dramas that had already been completed as a model of production. In an anthology that year he published five play scripts, including two of his own: 'A Skeleton in the Cupboard'[93] and 'The Happening at Botathen'.[94] Set in 1665, the latter explored a famous north Cornwall ghost story recorded by Robert Stephen Hawker.[95] Rawe's ongoing interest in Cornish history led him to develop a 1975 play based on Hawker, which he titled *Hawker of Morwenstow*[96] – an interesting example of continuity, with a modern north-Cornish writer examining his forebear. Rawe had revolutionised what was possible in theatre in Cornwall, but as the 1980s dawned and new companies began to explore theatrical possibilities, his own dramatic output declined and he turned towards other literary projects.[97] In the 1990s two new plays emerged, *Murder at Bohelland* (based on the Penryn murder[98]) in 1991,[99] and the beautiful lament, *The Last Voyage of Alfred Wallis* (1994).[100] Like Rawe's previous pieces, it was ambitious: a docu-drama of Wallis's life with over forty separate characters. When performed at Falmouth Arts Centre, from 14 to 17 September 1994, it was directed by Angela Thomas, with Anthony Richards as Alfred, and Mary Stevens as Susan Wallis.[101] Rawe stands as a major figure in the development of contemporary drama in Cornwall, and has continuing influence.

As Rawe had discovered when he wished to move to other forms of theatre, one of the constant problems facing touring companies in Cornwall during the post-war period was finding appropriate theatre space. Historically, Cornwall's settlement pattern had led against the development of one central city, though this changed towards the end of the century, with Truro gaining more of the once dispersed institutions; therefore, there were many similar sized towns, the population more or less evenly distributed across the territory.[102] Three separate factors contributed towards solving this problem. First of all, Cornwall already had its long-standing tradition of community-based popular drama, so it seemed logical to reinvent it for the late twentieth-century. In the previous decades, revivalists like Robert Morton Nance and Helena Charles had promoted the community-theatre tradition on a smaller scale, but it took some time for it to be fully embraced again. Secondly, the arts climate in Britain during the early 1970s inclined towards dissipating the association of theatre, opera and other arts with 'high culture' and the middle and upper classes, attempting to hand it back again to the people.[103] Finally, new imaginings of Cornwall perceived the territory in its own right. Complementing the political gains made by Cornish nationalism, it suddenly became reasonable for theatre companies to complete a tour of Cornwall alone, without the need to take the work elsewhere. At the same time, there were initiatives towards theatre in Cornwall being respected and revered elsewhere. Donald R. Rawe's outdoor staging of new epic drama had encouraged people to rethink the confines of traditional theatre, certainly that then offered in the nearest large urban centres, in Plymouth, Exeter and Bristol.[104] Thus, as well as being a ground-breaking period for Cornish nationalism – and indeed pan-Celticism – across these islands, it was also an important point of change and development for Cornish theatre. In essence, though the standard of production was professional, space and performance were being reclaimed by the community. In addition, this 'alternative' new tradition of Cornish drama was able to operate without the normal confines of the world of theatre. Cornwall was once again leading this alternative method of theatre, using village halls, local spaces, quarries, old rounds, and even wildly new places where theatre had never been performed before.

As Craig notes, one of the ground-breaking companies during this phase was Footsbarn Theatre.[105] The company began life at the Drama Centre in London, where the actors and theatre workers Oliver Foot and Jon Paul Cook met. At the time, there was no professional theatre company in Cornwall. However, grants from the Arts Council were available, so the pair relocated to Cornwall in March

1971, with the specific intention of serving 'as a focal point for the community in much the same way as the church, the town fair, and the pageant of old'.[106] The project was not only an old-style revivalist one. Early work saw the group synthesising the pan-European theatrical continuum with that of Cornwall, so that early productions ranged from Samuel Beckett's *Endgame* and Eugène Ionesco's *The Bald Prima Donna* to mime plays on Cornish themes like *Perran Cherrybeam*. The origins of the company lay in the Foot family's barn – hence the name of the company – and key personnel during its initial development were Foot, Cook, Nancy Foot, Maggie Watkiss, Dave Johnston and Rick Worthy.[107] Their base was at Trewen, St Keyne, near Liskeard. *Perran Cherrybeam* was certainly an interesting work; the text was based on a nineteenth-century Cornu-English narrative, recorded and retold by writers such as John Tabois Tregellas.[108] The plot, in which two Cornishmen mistakenly shoot dead an owl was presented in Footsbarn's way as a Beckett-style absurdist comedy. Works such as this and another piece, *Woodcut*, were important because they were initially improvised, and then developed into performance pieces. One can here see a connection to the work of Kneehigh Theatre later in the century.

Falmouth Arts Centre was supportive of the company, allowing it to operate as a repertory company there.[109] In 1972 Footsbarn completed a month's run at Falmouth Arts Centre, culminating in a breakthrough play titled *Giant*, written by Dave Johnston. The play was based on Cornish Giant legends,[110] and involved progressive use of huge rod puppets, a 10 foot giant, masks, dancing and guize dancers. The company were among the first to reintegrate para-theatrical practice into the mainstream of Cornish theatre. In many ways *Giant* set the blueprint for much of the indigenous Cornish drama to follow. *Giant* became part of Footsbarn's annual May tour, from which an alternative theatrical touring circuit later developed in Cornwall. An early summer tour allows Cornish theatre companies to visit the provinces of Cornwall, and may also be linked to the medieval continuum when community theatre was enacted on Feast days, most of which occur during this time of the year. A pattern based on this model has built up among current Cornish theatre companies: a summer outdoor tour, followed by a period of rehearsal into the autumn, then a winter indoor tour, then rehearsing the summer show in the spring.

Taking a further lead, Footsbarn were also the first Cornish-based theatre company to develop theatre-in-education. Foot and Cook staged workshops in Cornwall and in Plymouth and developed courses in mask-making and mime.[111] It took a while for the rest of Britain to catch up with this kind of work, but Cornish theatre during this period is indicative of the ways in which later twentieth-century drama companies predominantly organised and sold themselves to schools and colleges. The company was also keen to integrate older ingredients of theatre and circus, such as juggling, riding unicycles, fire-eating, masks and live music. The European influence on their work was to prove crucial in their progression. For example, in 1974, the company toured *Master Patalan*, a medieval French farce, with connections – in style, at least – to the old mystery plays. By this phase, the company were living a commedia dell'arte lifestyle, prompting one reviewer to note 'how they were travelling with the play and performing in a different place every day'.[112] Footsbarn's touring productions in the early 1970s also included a retelling of the long-established continuum of Tristan and Yseult, put on in village halls and allowing the company to work 'their own brand of medieval magic; plots, dragons, love potions and all, to a capacity audience'.[113] Another innovative production mounted during this period was *John Tom*, a play based on the life of a Cornishman born in St Columb in 1799. His story – of a man who was a politician, world traveller, lunatic, revolutionary and would-be Messiah – is told as enacted by a Victorian travelling theatre family, the Grundleys. This distinctive method of touring plays was first developed in Cornwall, and has since become established for this kind of theatre elsewhere.

By the mid 1970s Footsbarn had effectively established a new Cornish theatrical tradition. Suddenly, Cornwall was on the brink of a major and exciting new trend in contemporary drama. Given the conditions, it seemed that Footsbarn would become the major theatrical company to emerge from Cornwall in the modern era. However, events did not quite turn out as expected. Despite attracting significant local audiences (in the mid-1970s, over 17,000 a year), Footsbarn found that its work was increasingly being recognised overseas, and that given the economic circumstances of the period, Cornwall simply did not have a big enough audience to keep them there. As Slater documents, funds expected from arts organisations and councils in Cornwall were not forthcoming.[114] Further Cornu-centric work was thus curtailed and, having found major success in mainland Europe, the company eventually left Britain in 1984 to tour internationally. Footsbarn remained without a base until 1991, when they settled in a farmhouse at La Chaussée in central France.[115] In November 2008, the company gave their first performance in Great Britain for twenty-five years, presenting *A Midsummer Night's Dream* in London.[116] The company is now well-known for setting-up circus-style 'big top' tents in order to present its show – in essence, a kind of mobile *plen-an-gwarry*. Although the company has moved on from its Cornish theatrical roots, its progress and present-day international reputation is perhaps proof of how theatre from Cornwall has had an impact on wider European culture. Footsbarn's work ethic and ideas of community theatre were an important shaping force in the way the theatre of Cornwall would develop in the rest of the century.

The 1970s also saw the re-emergence of Charles Causley as a dramatist. Before the Second World War, Causley had begun to develop epic verse drama, in a style reminiscent of works from the medieval period, but that development had been cut short by the start of the war. Following the success of his immediate post-war poetry collections, he had concentrated on poetry through the 1950s and 1960s. In the meantime, Rawe had taken up the baton with his intensely Cornish dramas, explicitly building on the Cornish populist and community-style of performance.[117] Causley almost picked up where he had left off, choosing another Nativity theme with *The Gift of a Lamb: A Shepherd's Tale of the first Christmas, told as a verse play* (1978).[118] Certainly the play was styled in the same way as his 1940 drama *Journey of the Magi*, but if the earlier emphasis had been on dramaturgy, here it was on verse. The play had been conceived not for a particular geographic community, either in Cornwall or elsewhere, but perhaps intended specifically for children. Its conceptualisation was remarkably similar to other kinds of narrative verse written especially for children, at which Causley had by then become a master. Indeed, it is almost possible to identify the individual poems contained within *The Gift of a Lamb* while reading it. 1978 also saw the publication of a long, narrative poem for children, *Three Heads made of Gold*,[119] which retold the traditional English folk-tale of the daughter of the King of Colchester. Though styled as a narrative, it contained many of the techniques used by Causley in his verse drama. Despite the 'English' themes, he was not averse to including moments of Cornu-English, so that, although notionally English, such works came across as being *told* in a Cornish way. This ethos would continue throughout his late dramatic work, and be embraced by companies like Kneehigh Theatre.

The zenith of this style of writing came with *The Ballad of Aucassin and Nicolette* which, though often ignored in the wider Causley canon, may stand as the high-water mark of his work, simply in terms of its scope and ambition.[120] First composed in 1974, it was premiered by Britain's South West Music Theatre at the Exeter Festival in 1978 with Robert Kareas as Aucassin and Paula Bent playing Nicolette.[121] Causley had been approached by Stephen McNeff, who invited him to prepare a libretto; their partnership would be of enormous importance over the next few years. The production was large, with fourteen people in the Chorus, and a fifteen-piece orchestra. The story of Aucassin and Nicolette is an interesting choice, bearing in mind what we have said about the European dimension of theatre in Cornwall. In it, we see some similarities to Tristan and Yseult, and certainly the courtly-love traditions upon which Arthuriana had such an influence. The narrative is one of the

Fig. 96. British Drama League Festival of Community Theatre Programme, 1971. There were always several entries from Cornwall and the south-west of Britain. This year had Donald R. Rawe's 'A Skeleton in the Cupboard' as an entry.

oldest extant epics of European literature, coming down to us in the form of an anonymous thirteenth-century Picardian manuscript, though some scholars suggest the sources are Arabic or even Greek. Like some medieval drama in Cornwall, it is an unusual mixture of courtly love and low, bawdy humour. It tells of the passion of Aucassin, son of a count, for Nicolette, a Saracen captive, their separation, and eventual reunion. Thrown into this narrative is a ridiculous war, in Torelore, which is fought with rotten crab apples, cheese, eggs and mushrooms. Causley outlined his ideas for the work in the published version: 'In this present form, the text will be seen to consist of a series of poems and ballads, linked by passages of prose dialogue, and with an absolute minimum of stage direction'.[122] This approach is the essence of Causley's dramaturgy. In one section of the drama, when Nicolette is locked in her tower cell, accompanied by an Old Woman, one sees not only flashes of Causley's narrative verse, but also the techniques established in his drama some forty years previously:

Nicolette   Would that I could fly as free
                    As the bird upon the tree.

In a painted cage of clay
I am locked for love away.

Old Woman   Turn the wheel and foot the tread;
Spin me strong a lovers' thread.
Turn the wheel and foot the tread;
Spin a heart to rule a head.

Nicolette   Yet as strong as is the sea
Do I know my love loves me.
Son of Mary, hear me say –
From this cell I must away
with least delay.[123]

Elements from the *Ordinalia* also seem to echo through this piece of text, in terms of the structural repetitions and the overt simplicity of the verse. The play was given a revival in 1980, when the BBC broadcast a radio version. This time, Aucassin was played by David Firth, with Nicolette voiced by Imelda Staunton.[124] Radio was certainly proving a fruitful area for Causley to work in: between the stage version of *The Ballad of Aucassin and Nicolette* and the radio version, he also found time in 1979 to develop *The Three Kings*, another children's nativity play.[125] Tamplin, one of the few observers to comment on Causley's drama, says of this phase that Causley had 'reinvigorated strictly medieval forms'.[126] There is something in this, and perhaps something about the continuum of Cornish drama here as well. Chapter One discussed the 'layeredness' of Cornish experience; in such drama, Causley's reinvigoration seems to have added another layer. Likewise, it is apt that Causley wrote the poem 'St Martha and the Dragon'[127] and *The Gift of a Lamb* during the same phase: one is a saints' legend; the other a mystery play. The medieval romance of *The Ballad of Aucassin and Nicolette* is the third strand we see in the continuum; again, it seems entirely appropriate for Causley to be writing this. His understanding of the origins of dramaturgy in Cornwall is given further approbation in Tamplin's conclusions on his drama:

> The unusual mixture of prose and verse in the original gives full rein to his own metrical skills and love of variety. The episodic manner of medieval romance fits well with Causley's inventiveness and feeling for larger-than-life characters. The topsy-turvy kingdom of Torelore lends itself to surreal comedy. Above all the quest of the lovers in search of each other fits in with Causley's own questing approach to the world as well as his celebration of the need for human love.[128]

We note here the 'episodic' approach (as seen in the structure of all medieval Cornish drama), the sense of the tradition of 'topsy-turvy' (found in mumming and other festivals in Cornwall), and the concern with 'surreal comedy' (something that perhaps prefigures the work of Kneehigh in its approach to storytelling). Again then, in Causley, we see continuities backwards and forwards. The sense of 'surreal comedy' is also found in Causley's next major dramatic project: an adaptation of a Dylan Thomas script, *The Doctor and the Devils*,[129] which emerged as a musical theatre project for Causley in 1980.[130] Thomas's story was about the famous body-snatchers Burke and Hare (renamed Broom and Fallon); with this project, Causley renewed his collaboration with the musical director Stephen McNeff.[131] Although the project combined the work of two Anglo-Celtic poets, the storyline and verse are wholly non-Celtic. Nevertheless, the original production – by Contact Theatre (Manchester's Young People's Theatre) at the University Theatre in Manchester – was highly successful.[132] This was Causley's first true effort at musical theatre. Significantly, the play may have drawn on the Cornish tradition of dramaturgy, for it was presented 'in the round'. The play then toured internationally, appearing at the Banff Centre School of Fine Arts in Calgary, in March 1984. The *Calgary Herald* newspaper showed great awareness of Causley as a dramatist:

> Charles Causley has been interested in the theatre for as long as he can remember. Although a prolific poet first, with many volumes of verse to his credit, the British writer has been creating a variety of theatre pieces (radio dramas for the BBC, dramatic documentaries and librettos for music theatre) for years.[133]

In the same article, Causley comments that '[I have] always loved Britten's church parables and have wanted to do something in that vein, and when I was least expecting it this subject just dropped into my lap.' The writer understands how Causley operates dramatically, noting that he 'inserts ballads, songs and oratorical passages... [with] never a pause for a number'.[134] This astute analysis supports the views of Tamplin.[135] Causley was perhaps thinking back home to Cornwall, for in between the two performances of *The Doctor and the Devils*, he had been working on what he termed 'a miracle play for musical theatre', titled *The Burning Boy*.[136] This was another project with Stephen McNeff, and surviving copies of the script date from 1982. To my knowledge, it has not been published, nor has it been performed. The text is based on the biblical story in the Second Book of Kings, about a Shunammite boy who dies of sunstroke in the harvest field and is subsequently raised from the dead by the prophet Elisha. According to Causley's notes, 'The action is continuous and takes place in a harvest field, a farm-house, and on a mountain-side'.[137] Clearly this can be traced in a direct line forwards from the *Ordinalia*, where similar miraculous events take place. The dramaturgy too, in its notion of 'continuous action', takes its cue from the medieval texts. The play is designed as a parable of birth, life, death and resurrection, and includes as an integral part of the text – as one of about twenty episodic scenes and incidents (very much like 'Origo Mundi') – a version of the ancient harvest ceremony of 'Crying the Neck', which is still practised in Cornwall:

Harvesters 2 and Harvesters 3:	What have you?
	What have you?
	What have you?

Oldest Harvester holds the Corn Boy in both hands near the ground. All bend down similarly, the men removing their hats and holding them in both hands towards the ground. During the following, all raise themselves three times, holding arms and hats high in the air. Oldest Harvester raises Corn Boy similarly three times.

All (*prolonged cry, harmonious*):	A neck!
	A neck!
	A neck!

Farmer:	Well cut.[138]

Here, Causley is doing something that the authors of the Cornish mystery and saints' plays were doing: expressly welding on a piece of local folklore to enhance the text's meaning. It is age-old, but an important technique nevertheless. In *The Burning Boy*, we have a fine example of a modern Cornish mystery play, which deserves greater recognition. Causley's lack of success with this text may have discouraged him from trying similar work; certainly during the late 1980s, he chose once again to concentrate on children's verse.[139] Causley returned to theatre in 1990, working in collaboration with Kneehigh Theatre (by then ten years old) and the Theatre Royal in Plymouth, to mount a promenade-style production of *The Tinderbox*, an adaptation of the story by Hans Christian Andersen.[140] McNeff again scored the music. The plot of this fairy tale is based on a soldier who acquires a magic tinderbox capable of summoning three magic dogs to do his bidding. When the soldier uses the tinderbox to bring a sleeping princess to his chamber, he is arrested, but escapes execution through the intervention of the three dogs. This narrative fits a post-modernist vision of 'magical realist' theatre (adeptly realised by

Kneehigh, and Miracle Theatre Companies),[141] but there are also some elements of the fairy-tale ethos of early nineteenth-century theatre in Cornwall.[142]

The company performing Causley's text included many mainstays of Kneehigh Theatre's early phase: Mike Shepherd, Janys Chambers, Nicola Rosewarne, Tristan Sturrock, Giles King, Charlie Barnecut, Jim Carey, Bill Mitchell, Sue Hill, Allan Drake, Alice King, and Amanda Harris. As well as a run at the Theatre Royal, Plymouth (a significant coup for the Cornish company, in view of the Plymouth venue's usual reluctance to mount Cornish-themed work), it also toured Cornwall in the autumn of 1990, visiting Launceston College, Poltair School, Newquay Treviglas School, The City Hall in Truro, and The Acorn at Penzance. *The Guardian* theatre critic, Allen Saddler, reviewed the work at Plymouth's Theatre Royal:

> This is the theatre of the imagination, with startling effects, quick changes of mood, some goonery, but disciplined and self-assured. The Cornish Style of theatre, physically active, broad and basic, has taken a long time to mature. With this production we see the results of years of experiments. There are huge, crude props, fantastic costumes, audience involvement, small shocks and surprises from a team of actors well versed in the epic style.[143]

Fig. 97. A poster advertising Charles Causley and Kneehigh Theatre's production of *Figgie Hobbin*, 1994.

Although Saddler's review is somewhat grudging in its praise, he does identify a 'Cornish Style of theatre', which was partly attributable to the ethos of Kneehigh Theatre itself, but also embraced a wider dramatic tradition 'alien' to that of the metropolitan and 'English' centre. We shall examine this issue further in a fuller consideration of Kneehigh Theatre later in this chapter. The success of *The Tinderbox* took Causley in two important directions. The Hans Christian Andersen connection led him to adapt the tale of *The Emperor's New Clothes* for a touring version (1990-1991) of Andersen's tales, featuring several different writers' adaptations of classic Andersen stories.[144] Additionally, however, it would see Kneehigh Theatre work on a theatrical version of his 1991 children's text, *The Young Man of Cury* (touring in 1992)[145] and then, even more successfully, an adaptation in 1994, of his classic 1970 collection of children's verse *Figgie Hobbin*,[146] performed by Mike Shepherd, Anna Maria Murphy and Will Coleman. The latter used 'ingenious devices, shadow puppets and enchanting effects' and toured venues including St Ives, Mevagissey, St Issey, Penzance, Falmouth and Coads Green.[147]

Causley's final large-scale theatrical work is one that is virtually unknown in Cornwall, but came during the same phase of work. This was the libretto of 1991's *Aesop: A New Opera*, presented by the National Youth Music Theatre at Blackheath Concert Halls, Tuesday 2 to 3 July, with a later run at the George Square Theatre, Edinburgh Fringe Festival between 26 and 31 August.[148] Again, the work was developed with Stephen McNeff. It was directed by John Wright and Jerome James Taylor. Freely based on *The Life and Fables of Aesop* by Sir Roger L'Estrange (1692), the narrative tells how Aesop, the Ethiopian, grew to fame in sixth-century BCE Greece as a teller of tales and also as a diplomat and adviser to kings and politicians, only to suffer assassination at the hands of his enemies. The style of the piece is almost a 'classical' mystery play; given Causley's often anthropomorphic children's poetry, it was a short step to imagining a key writer of fables. Causley possibly based his ideas on a Cornwall fully aware of the need to market material culture for the tourist industry, and a review in *The Independent* newspaper made the following observation:

A hare and a tortoise come and go in the guise of two time-travelling tourists, he vague and laden with backpack, she younger and bounding ahead with camera. Their reflections take on the Greek chorus role. The general tone is amusing and wry rather than direct, oddly middle-aged for a young people's show.[149]

Although such a review might suggest some decline in Causley's dramatic ability (and perhaps even his ability to shape text for young people), this seems not to be the case, as can be evidenced from the sharpness of his verse, which has almost the staccato of rap:

Chorus: In the kingdom of the animal
No story can compare
With the story of the tortoise,
The story of the hare...

But Aesop, Aesop
Was born a high-stepper.
When he told his stories
There was no-one better.[150]

With Aesop played by Vernon Henry Jr., Tortoise by Mike Bowden and Hare by Sarah Moore, the narrative begins after a prologue by a group of Aesopic animals. A group of slaves are on the road to the slave-market at Ephesus under the watchful eye of a group of bully boys who work for the slave-master Critias. Aesop then makes his presence known to the audience. He is unwanted, and still unsold, and so is given to Xanthus the Philosopher and teacher. A crucial moment of dramatic action in the play comes when Xanthus, in a drunken moment, makes a bet with Pasion the Poet that he can drink the salt sea dry. Of course, he fails. In such moments, we see adapted themes from the Cornish theatrical continuum: issues of masters and slaves (England and Cornwall), fable, parable and rebellion. There is certainly here, too, a Greek dramatic influence, especially in the final fable, when Aesop secretly visits King Croesus and dissuades him from his plan of war. At the end he is tried and found guilty of a crime he did not commit. With a final fable reflecting on the asinine behaviour of mankind, Aesop is flung to his death from a high rock. Causley comes full circle with this work. In him, we see a contemporary dramatist profoundly influenced by pan-European theatricality, but with an awareness of how localised colour can impact on universal and sometimes liturgical themes. Although Causley is never as explicit in his 'dramatic' Cornishness as, for example, Donald R. Rawe or Nick Darke, there is also something in his theatre that lurks just beneath the surface, and which is wholly Cornish. Causley is one of Cornwall's finest exponents of verse drama, and there is much room for his dramas to be studied further.[151] When we consider that Causley was developing as a dramatist for half a century, we must acknowledge him as another major figure in contemporary Cornish theatre.

Comedy – a central component in the work of Causley – is a long-established part of theatre in Cornwall. There are major comic sequences in the *Ordinalia*, as well as near slapstick sections of *Bewnans Meriasek* and *Bewnans Ke*. The tradition continued through the seventeenth and eighteenth centuries, nurturing figures such as Samuel Fisher, who was described upon his death as simply 'a comedian'. Compared with much of the intellectual end of Cornish theatrical experience, the Cornish stand-up comedian Jethro represents a very different response to Cornish community, space and place, but it is one that is equally valid in our story. Jethro's considerable ability as a storyteller makes him the latest incarnation of a long line of comic 'droll-tellers'. His earthy, bawdy and self-deprecating comedy is not too far away from similar innuendo-driven humour found in the mystery and saints' plays. Stand-up is para-theatrical in the sense that it is not a 'true' piece of theatre, but Jethro's comedy is driven by a highly theatrical understanding of popular Cornish sentiment.

Jethro's full name is Geoff Rowe, and he was born in 1948 in St Buryan in west Cornwall, where he undoubtedly, inherited a gift for narrative and a sense of the absurd. When just eighteen (and working as a timber man in a local tin mine), he joined the St Just and District Operatic Society, finding that he had a talent as a comedian. He began touring clubs and pubs and then, in the 1970s, joined Westward Television's *Treasure Hunt* as a co-host, dressed as a pirate, and capitalising on Cornu-English linguistic credentials. Further television appearances on mainstream variety shows have enhanced his pan-British image as a media and theatrical representation of Cornwall.[152] His successful video and DVD releases indicate a popular market, both in Cornwall and elsewhere in Britain.[153] Jethro has toured extensively in Britain at the end of the late twentieth and early twenty-first centuries. Until 2008, when his Club at Lewdown (on the English side of the border) closed, he also appeared there regularly.[154] As a commentator on contemporary Cornish experience, Jethro's response to the world is profoundly non-metropolitan, and often anti-European Union – a position antithetical to a Cornwall 'proudly' a European 'small nation-state' and benefiting from Objective One funding.[155] The humour is couched in a performance that puts Cornu-English expression, delivered in his bass voice, at the heart of the show: "What happened was…", "Go You Ahead Hmmm…!" and "Before we bleddy start…". His jokes often present the Cornish as underdogs, but underdogs who tend to come out on top, characterisation often pitting Cornish rurality against city sophistication and pretensions. His most important character is his 'imagined' friend Denzil Penberthy, whilst one of his famous routines involves the story of how the 'train don't stop Camborne Wednesdays' – a narrative that observes cut-backs on transportation links to Cornwall.[156] Jethro's stance is not explicitly nationalist, although by implication his humour makes the individuality and identity of the Cornish very strong. His representation is not to everyone's taste however: certainly, his lack of bardic status in the Cornish Gorsedd would indicate disapproval; his Cornishness does not fit a Gorsedd-approved cultural-nationalist response. Arguing that the Gorsedd is out of touch with popular opinion in Cornwall, Jethro founded his own 'Hall of Fame' in one Cornish magazine in the late 1990s.[157] Jethro may not appeal to intellectual Cornwall, but his creation and representation of para-theatrical Cornishness should not be underestimated. It is perhaps a pity that he has not moved into more theatre, because such pan-British theatrical imaginings of comic Cornishness are, at this point in time, very rare. Johnny Cowling aside (a younger Cornish comedian, with much para-theatrical Cornishness[158]), there seem few new comedians who might replace him.

Meanwhile, the amateur operatic and dramatic societies of Cornwall continued to make progress. In the post-war period, the Truro Amateur Operatic and Dramatic Society, which was founded in 1912, had been rehearsing in rooms in Pydar Street, but these were compulsorily purchased as part of a slum clearance programme in the town. The Society then took a major step forward by purchasing its own premises in 1968. Their building, originally an egg-packing station in Truro, was converted into a small theatre, with an auditorium seating 140 people, a fully-equipped stage, dressing rooms and a foyer. The new theatre, opened by the Mayor of Truro in 1973, was named the Redannick Theatre.[159] Performances of dramas began in 1975, with *Black Comedy*, followed intermittently in 1976 and 1979 by *Signs of the Times* and *Say Who You Are* respectively. Productions have followed more or less every year since, and in 2008 *The Beaux' Stratagem* made a direct link to Truro's theatrical past. Many of the plays in the 1970s and 1980s were directed by Brian Edwards of Truro School. Musical theatre has also been a speciality of the Redannick Theatre, with Truro Amateur Operatic Society first playing *Salad Days* there in 1980. 1993 saw a revival of Gilbert and Sullivan's *Ruddigore*; following the success of this, the Society decided to perform *The Pirates of Penzance* in 1995. These operettas were directed by Brian Odgers, who would later help shape the St Piran drama at Perranporth.[160] In recent years, the stage area of the Redannick Theatre has been reconstructed, and the foyer remodelled to incorporate a bar. The building is currently the headquarters of the Truro Amateur Operatic and Dramatic Society, where committee meetings are held, where scenery is built and where costumes are stored. The Redannick Theatre is also the Society's rehearsal venue for its productions in other theatre space such as the Hall for Cornwall, the Minack Theatre and

Trelissick Gardens. Other groups in Cornwall also use the theatre, such as Cornwall Dance and Drama, and New Cornwall Opera. In the 1980s, the space was also used by the professional company, Shiva Theatre. It is not the best known theatrical venue in contemporary Cornwall, but may be viewed as something of a hidden gem.

Other amateur dramatic organisations were also flourishing. Newquay Amateur Dramatic Society had continued to promote interesting theatre throughout the 1950s. Back in the 1930s, they had wanted to find their own venue, and created a fund to find a home of their own. The 1960s saw them put money into a building, the old Church Hall at Crantock, which acted a venue for the Society to meet, and as a scenery store. However, by the late 1970s, the Church Hall building was in a bad state, and the committee voted to sell it. The Society needed to find an alternative venue that had car-parking facilities. Several venues were considered, but the best one was felt to be the old village hall (built in 1948) in the hamlet of Lane, near Tredinnick on the eastern side of Newquay. Meanwhile the Society performed other 'canonical' plays elsewhere in the 1970s, among them *Billy Liar* in 1972, *A Streetcar named Desire* in 1973, *Treasure Island* (with tangential Cornish material) and *Tom Jones* in 1975, *Habeas Corpus* in 1977 and *Fringe Benefits* in 1979 – the latter

Fig. 98. The Second Cosy Nook Theatre on the promenade in Newquay, from a postcard from the 1950s. Courtesy of Peter Hicks and Newquay Old Cornwall Society.

Fig. 99. An aerial view of the Second Cosy Nook Theatre in Newquay during the 1970s. Courtesy of Peter Hicks and Newquay Old Cornwall Society.

featuring future BBC Radio Cornwall presenter Tim Hubbard. The venue at Lane had been found by society stalwart Eileen Pollard, and was converted into a theatre in 1979-80 under the supervision of the architect Charles Pickering. The aim was to 'provide a multipurpose theatre of moderate initial cost... [with] seating capacity of 140'.[161] The conversion of the existing village hall added a foyer, two ambulatories on the sides of the auditorium, dressing rooms and toilets. The new Lane Theatre was opened in 1981, and has since then been the home of the renamed Newquay Dramatic Society. A National Lottery Grant of £100,000 in 2000 allowed the theatre to update its facilities further.

Touring shows do not visit the Lane Theatre, which focuses on home-grown productions. There is presently a small but devoted band of enthusiasts who work to maintain and develop the theatre. Usually, four shows are produced a year: comedies in the twenty-week long summer season, catering for the tourist market; more serious drama in the winter.[162] However, the Lane Theatre does face difficulties. As several observers have noted, Newquay's construction of place altered remarkably in the late twentieth-century, when it became associated with surfing, hen and stag nights and clubbing,[163] rather than its family-orientated, bucket-and-spade culture of yesteryear. Newquay has had to adapt in response to the trend towards cheaper package holidays to

Fig. 100. The Lane Theatre, Newquay, being built in 1980. Courtesy of the Reg Harris Archive.

Fig. 101. The Lane Theatre, Newquay in 2008.

countries guaranteeing sun, and the Lane Theatre perhaps needs to find ways to embrace the new, younger 'audience' of Newquay if it is to survive. Certainly, this may require a progression away from domestic comedies and farce towards the edgier contemporary theatre of recent productions such as Robert Harling's *Steel Magnolias* (2007), and *Girls' Night* (2008) – the latter play, by Louise Roche, reflecting the karaoke machines and hen parties of Newquay now.[164] Meanwhile, the Cosy Nook Theatre had staggered on into the early 1980s, but there were logistical difficulties – some of a kind faced by all end-of-promenade style theatres across Britain, but others more specific: coaches found it enormously difficult to make their way down Beach Road to the venue; the building also required a massive technical, and health and safety overhaul to make it compatible with other theatres. The Friends of the Cosy Nook laboured hard to keep the venue open, but the writing was on the wall. A £9,000 fighting fund had been collected, but when the theatre eventually closed, this was given to help the Lane Theatre.

With a few notable exceptions, Newquay Dramatic Society has maintained a generally 'English'-focused programme of drama through the years. Anglo-Cornish writing rarely received an airing. The format of box-set, 'well-made' plays was maintained throughout the 1950s and early 1960s, with some productions, such as *Breath of Spring* (1960) suffering from low audience numbers, due to the counter-attractions of 'fine weather, Royal Wedding and the Cup Final'.[165] Nevertheless there were some progressive moments. *And a Size Larger* (1962) was a revue staged at the Cosy Nook Theatre, clearly taking its cues from television and radio, and in line with the development of programmes such as *The Goon Show* (1951-1960) and *Beyond our Ken* (1958-1964).[166] This styling comes across not only in the format but in aspects like the programme design as well. As Sinfield has noted, theatre was having to catch up quickly with television and radio, allowing what he terms a working-class 'break out', which was redefining the theatre audience.[167] Those behind *And a Size Larger* were fully aware of the need for this in Cornwall. One of a series of witty set pieces that were presented was the Malcolm Lloyd-written satire, 'Bards of a Feather', which presented eight Cornish bards on stage, saluting a Grand Bard, while a horner plays a horn. Judging from the photographic evidence of this performance, the bardic costuming used looks very authentic, while the blocks on the stage appear to make reference to one of Cornwall's ancient sites. It is quite telling that the Society saw fit to satirise the bardic culture of Cornwall, since before this time, the Gorsedd was still given a kind of reverence. The Gorsedd's 'pretence' at Celticity was perhaps met by the wider, working-class population of Cornwall with a degree of scepticism and bemusement. At the time E.G. Retallack Hooper was the real Grand Bard

Fig. 102. Programme for *And a Size Larger*, 1962. Courtesy of the Reg Harris Archive.

Fig. 103. 'Bards of a Feather' from Newquay Amateur Dramatic Society's *And a Size Larger*, 1962. Courtesy of the Reg Harris Archive.

737

of the Gorsedd.[168] Despite his commitment to raising enthusiasm for Cornish language among the working-class, the nature of the ceremony that year – ironically held at the Celtic centre of Tintagel – remained middle-class and in some ways, 'non-Cornish', at least for the non-intellectual population. The satire was more likely inspired by the 1962 Gorsedd, which had been held at the Barrowfields, Newquay.[169] Those taking part in the performance included Mary Cole, Jane Drake (wife of Society photographer Paul Drake), David Eyles, John Gould, Rocky Macleod, Nola Round, Gerry Shipp and Helen Tremain.[170]

1964 saw the Newquay Society promoting their own Shakespeare Festival (the quatercentenary of his birth).[171] However, like other amateur dramatic societies in Britain as a whole, the Society generally remained unaffected by the kind of sea-change in subject-matter affecting drama elsewhere in Britain, especially on the professional stage. One possible exception was Harold Brighouse's *Hobson's Choice* (1916), which was a precursor of the kind of questioning, radical drama then being written.[172] Other plays tended either to have historical subject-matter, or to be new looks at events of the Second World War. Despite the wider radicalism of the late 1960s, the Society's dramas tended to be conservative, middle-class and Anglo-philic in nature. A notable exception was 1967's *My Three Angels: A French Comedy*, by Sam and Bella Spewack, which was set in Cayenne, French Guiana, South America, in the year 1910. Perhaps predictably, reviews were not positive, with one describing it as a 'play which dragged on and on'.[173] The Society was still, however, engaging with the burgeoning folk scene of the period: what appears to be a fund-raising event for the Society featured John the Fish and Brenda Wootton, and The Great Western Jug Band.[174]

The Society also contributed to the more Cornish-focused performances of 'The British Drama League National Festival of Community Theatre: Western Divisional Final' which took place at the Cosy Nook, Theatre on 3 April 1971.[175] The radicalism of this period of theatre comes out in two ways: in the radical 'external' playwrights considered by Cornish theatre companies; and in the new Cornish playwrights given an airing. The Kernow Players of Padstow presented Donald R. Rawe's *A Skeleton in the Cupboard*, set in 'The Living Room of a Cornish Cottage' and starring Nicholas Haynes as Terence, Jenny Dawe as Hilda (his wife), Margaret Brenton as Jenny Tresize (a neighbour), and Maurice Coville as Mr Menhennitt (an estate agent).[176] The St Austell Drama Group chose to present *Wheal Judas*, by Burness Burn. It is set in the mining district of west Cornwall about 1890, the characters being Mathew Bawden, Mary Bawden (his wife), Daniel Trenoweth, Loveday Trenoweth (his wife), Dorcas Oliver, landlady of the Tinners' Arms, and three tinners.[177] St Austell embraced the new British and European theatre, with its Society of Arts Drama Group's production of Harold Pinter's *Night School*, and Arts Theatre's presentation of Eugene Ionesco's *The Lesson*. Meneage Arts Players produced *George: A Nonsense Play* by Glynne Davies. Newquay Dramatic Society presented Peter Shaffer's *Private Ear*. This appears to have been a radical period for these companies, who were not only absorbing 'absurdist' influences from elsewhere but also, in a small but important way, allowing an elementary 'national theatre of Cornwall' to emerge.

The work of du Maurier has continued to be part of the Newquay Dramatic Society's repertoire. In 1996, under the direction of Sheila Lines, they presented du Maurier's 1949 play *September Tide*.[178] Of all du Maurier's dramas, this text is perhaps the one that has the closest narrative similarities to her fictional writing. In summary, the play concerns the life of the widowed Stella, who lives in a comfortable house on a Cornish estuary. She is a woman of considerable gifts and beauty, who regularly rejects proposals of marriage from her neighbour Robert Hanson. Cherry, who is Stella's daughter, returns to Cornwall, bringing home for the first time her artist husband Evan, and Stella is shocked by the bohemian incompleteness of their marriage. She finds

Fig. 104. A view inside the auditorium of the Lane Theatre, set for Daphne du Maurier's *September Tide*, in 1996. Courtesy of Sheila Lines and the Reg Harris Archive.

herself attracted to Evan, and soon they are passionately in love. The play's conflict is over duty and desire, and this is only resolved when Evan accepts a job in New York. This du Maurier play seems to have a lasting appeal, as the text has been revived both in Cornwall and elsewhere.[179] Lines' revival of the text was timely, for interest in du Maurier's work was gaining momentum: in the canonisation of her fiction, alongside other notables such as Austen and the Brontës;[180] and in the newly-created Daphne du Maurier Festival of Literature and the Arts at Fowey.[181] Although *September Tide* does not display the sense of 'devolved' Cornwall that du Maurier seemed to embrace in her later work, the Cornishness is presented as exotic, peripheral and different, thus emphasising its Celticity for Evan. Considering the number of plays written by playwrights embracing more Cornu-centric work, one might have expected the Lane Theatre to subscribe to this agenda, but they have not. It seems that Newquay Dramatic Society no longer fields a 'Cornish' theatre team, and that socio-economic circumstances in the area have moved towards a more affluent and English-gazing production group and audience. What is clear is that, despite a confidently progressing contemporary Cornish identity, no explicitly Cornish-themed play has been presented at the theatre since 1996.

The Cosy Nook Theatre continued to have a keen presence in the post-war period. By the early 1950s, Hedley Claxton had taken over the promotion of shows during the summer season. These included 1952's *Gaytime*,[182] and sets of shows that promised similar 'sparkling summer fun'. Meanwhile, the New Theatre also offered revues based on the theme of *Into the Sun* in 1954 and 1955.[183] These featured early work by performers such as Terry Scott, Hugh Lloyd and Cyril Smith. The late 1950s saw the John Berryman-produced *Top o' the Town*,[184] featuring Bill Pertwee (later of *Dad's Army* fame). This was the era when such stars worked the summer seasons around the islands of Britain. Annual pantomimes continued at the Cosy Nook in the winter months: the last of the noted Triniman Group's efforts was *Robinson Crusoe* in 1958. According to observers at the time, such revues and pantomimes in the 1950s did look at Cornish culture; although 'national' material was provided by the comics or the management, it was always adapted. Likewise, the performers involved themselves in Newquay's cultural life during the long season from May to September. Brandon and Pounds were back in Newquay in 1964, offering repertory theatre for the summer season. By this phase, the revues had transformed into a new, popular format: *Olde Tyme Musical Hall*. This was in part inspired and influenced by the BBC light entertainment programme *The Good Old Days*, which ran from 1953 to 1983. The basic concept was to recreate an authentic atmosphere of the Victorian/Edwardian music hall era, with songs

Fig. 105. Programme cover for Hedley Claxton's *Gaytime* at the Cosy Nook Theatre Newquay, 1952. Courtesy of John Trembath.

Fig. 106. Programme cover for *Into the Sun* at the New Theatre, Newquay, 1954. Courtesy of John Trembath.

and sketches of that period performed by present-day artists. Here, Brandon acted as the chairman (behind a dais, of course), while Pounds looked after the costuming and dancing. Usually the company auditioned in London, but the stage management, musical director, and crew for the productions were always local. Newquay was entertained in this way from the mid-1960s until 1975.

The run ended when Brandon was knocked down and killed by a bus in London. Concurrently, there were still shows at the Cosy Nook, following a familiar seasonal format, with the 'national' summer shows continuing into the early 1970s. One group, composed of Barby Reeve, Vim Reeve and John Trembarth began a set of revues in 1971, which they titled *Funsapoppin'*. These shows aimed to take the best elements of the older revues and make them accessible to a new audience, and took place in one week before and after the summer season, thus extending theatrical entertainment in Newquay by a fortnight. The 1970s, however, witnessed different theatrical tastes emerging, and made it necessary for the summer shows to tie in with a television star. In effect, performances at the Cosy Nook were no longer revues, but elongated cabaret that showcased a lead star of the day, with no coherence and no sketches. The larger hotels in Newquay (now catering for mass bus tours from the rest of Britain) put on their own shows. By the mid-1980s, this form of

Fig. 107. Playbill advertising *A Night at the Music Hall* at the Newquay Theatre, 1982. Courtesy of John Trembath.

'end-of-promenade' theatre was dead in the water.[185] It was considered outmoded and faced competition in Newquay – specifically from nightclubs, designer pubs and the surfing scene. The Nook's days were numbered. The Theatre declined and, despite efforts to save it, by the turn of the 1990s it had been demolished, and replaced with a *Sea Life* Centre. Certainly, given the health and safety problems of the Cosy Nook, closure was the only option. In 1977, the Jimmy Jacobs Company had picked up the baton at the Newquay Theatre, with Paul Daniels operating there between 1979 and 1981. A music hall-style revival was again attempted between 1981 and 1984, but like the Cosy Nook, the Newquay Theatre's days were over. It has since been converted into a tourist attraction: *Tunnels through Time*. Theatre, so it seemed, was going the way of everything else in post-war Cornwall: gearing up for tourism on an unprecedented scale.

Meanwhile on the southern coast of Cornwall, another important amateur dramatic group emerged in the post-war period. This was the St Austell Players.[186] Founded in 1945 as part of the St Austell Society of Arts, the Players have presented almost 300 shows during the past half a century.[187] The St Austell Players developed as a celebratory response to the end of the Second World War, and were able within a year to present their first full-length play,

Fig. 108. The former Newquay Theatre in 2008; since converted into *Tunnels Through Time*.

Ivor Novello's *Fresh Fields*, at the County School hall (now Poltair School).[188] The director was the musical comedy star Norah Blaney, who continued to direct for the society in the late 1940s. Her name certainly helped the St Austell group to develop. The later 1940s also saw the emergence of Norman Lawrence as an important director for the Players, as well as E. Llewellyn Trudgeon and Gwilym Humphreys. With these enthusiastic members at the helm, the Society generally produced around five or six plays per year. By 1951, after St Austell District Council loaned them £200 towards a stage set-up they were using the town's Public Rooms as their theatre. Outside performances were also trialled at Tregarne Lodge, off Trevarthian Road. This period saw them tackle work by, among others, George Bernard Shaw, Anton Chekhov, Shakespeare and J.M Synge. In this sense, the St Austell Players' collective gaze was on what was 'rated' important drama in the eyes of the English establishment, which was in tune with the wider social and cultural trend of the period. To this end, most of the work entered into the County [sic] One-Act Play Festivals was also fairly mainstream. We should therefore not be surprised that no Cornish-themed drama was ever staged in the whole of the 1940s, '50s and '60s, although works by cutting-edge dramatists of the latter decade were aired in the 1970s. Among these were *Night School* by Harold Pinter, *I'm Talking About Jerusalem* by Arnold Wesker, and *In Camera* by Jean-Paul Sartre.[189] Indigenous drama came by way of *Something to Talk about* by Eden Philpotts (who hailed from Devon) in 1966, and a Christmas revue in 1970 titled *Up Brown Willie*. Spatially, in the 1950s the group temporarily moved to Roche Victory Hall to perform four productions, but moved back to St Austell, then at the new school at Penrice. By 1956, the Society of Arts had helped the group to purchase Tregarden, which was opened as a new theatre for St Austell in 1961.[190] Gradual expansion of this site formed the St Austell Arts Centre. The 1970s and 1980s saw the group again produce standard 'am-dram' material – mainly from Alan Ayckborn and Tom Stoppard. It seemed that the Society, like the one at Newquay, tended to attract a certain type of individual who had little interest in presenting Cornish or Anglo-Cornish work; many of its members were in-migrants to the area. Although the range and diversity of material did increase, Cornish-related material seemed to be restricted to Daphne du Maurier: *My Cousin Rachel* in 1995 and *Jamaica Inn* in 1998.[191] One exception was Nick Darke's adaptation of Laurie Lee's *Cider with Rosie*, performed in 1996. The St Austell Arts Centre has remained significant in the theatrical life of mid-Cornwall. Not only has it continued to mount productions, but also, between the late 1980s and the mid-1990s, hosted the Hub Theatre School.[192] Related to the St Austell Players was St Blazey Amateur Operatic Society, who for some sixty years had presented

Fig. 109. Programme cover for St Austell Players' production of *Murder at the Vicarage* by Agatha Christie, 1954. Courtesy of Agnes Thurlow and Charles Thurlow.

pantomimes in the mid-Cornwall area, sometimes rivalling those in Plymouth for ambition and success. Mainstays of the company included the comedians Wally Harrison, Nobby Clarke and Jim Peirce. Only with a revived tradition of pantomimes at the newly-opened Hall for Cornwall in 1997 was St Blazey Amateur Operatic Society's dominance of the genre tested.

Although the 1980s hammered the final nail in the coffin lid of some forms of theatre in Cornwall – such as those at Newquay and, to an extent, the St Austell Players' run of 'middle-class' plays – other forms of drama began to flourish. It is notable that the roots of these new forms of drama initially had at their heart the community, landscape and ritualistic elements of early incarnations of theatre. Kneehigh Theatre, which had its origins in 1980, was one of the theatre companies initiating this kind of work in this period.[193] It is hard to imagine the theatrical landscape of Cornwall without Kneehigh, such has been their importance in redefining post-war Cornish theatre. For some thirty years, the company has grown and developed beyond their initial Cornish roots to become a truly international company, yet despite this progression to the London and world stages, Kneehigh Theatre has maintained consistent promotion of highly Cornish-themed work. As well as this, the company continued in the late twentieth century to have a long and fruitful association with the Cornish playwright Nick Darke (1948-2005) and, more recently, with the writers Anna Maria Murphy and Carl Grose.

Kneehigh Theatre has grown through three phases of work. Mike Shepherd (b.1953), who founded the company, grew up in St Austell, and initially followed a career teaching drama in north London but began to spend more energy creating theatre, auditioning for parts and roles there. In an 'English' theatrical system that was based on working one's way up through companies to lead parts, Shepherd found metropolitan resistance to both his accent and attitude to theatre.[194] Good roles went only to those performers who had attended the 'right' colleges and drama schools – a form of theatre alien to the continuum in Cornwall, which had for the most part drawn its performers direct from the community. Working practice in Britain was still far removed from the principles of 'Brechtian' theatre, and Shepherd describes himself as 'the antithesis of the black box studio actor who comes straight out of RADA'.[195] So he chose to return to Cornwall, first forming the company to develop work for children – hence the name, Kneehigh. The emphasis would be on ensemble work, where performers would multi-role and have multiple talents. Touring initially would be to village halls, community centres and arts centres, as well as almost anywhere where performance could be mounted in Cornwall. Shepherd also developed a belief in an assembly of actors who lived, worked and ate together in a communal way, making energised creative space. Pieces of theatre would be developed organically and through 'communion' in the art of theatre: in an interview, lead member of Kneehigh Bill Mitchell (b.1951) talks about how 'actors have ownership as they tour'.[196] However, this view should also be tempered with the fact that underlying the organic development are research, experiment and an emphasis on crafting work. This aspect of Kneehigh Theatre's work is embodied in their rehearsal and development space at Lamledra Barns at Gorran Haven on the south coast of Cornwall.[197] Here was a venue far removed from the rehearsal space of other theatre organisations, where mutual trust and understanding could be developed. The performance would also be based on a high level of physicality and spectacle. Something of this early, and ongoing, ethos comes across in a 1990 programme, where Shepherd writes that he spent his 'Cornish childhood clambering on cliff tops, crawling around caves, climbing trees, throwing stones, lighting fires and now does it professionally'.[199]

Kneehigh's first production was the children's show *Awful Knawful* (1980) – a pun on motorcycling legend Evel Knievel. *The Mystery Machine,* based on the children's book *The Phantom Tollbooth* by Norton Juster, followed in 1981. Adapted, devised and directed by Mike Shepherd, this played school halls, village halls and outdoor spaces such as Penlee Park in Penzance, with a cast including Chris Humphries, John Mergler, Lisa North and Allan Drake.[200] In the same year, *Mrs Corbett's Ghost*, based on the Leon Garfield novel, also featured John Mergler, Allan Drake and Shepherd, with music by Pete Berryman. A more experimental piece came in 1982. This was *The Labyrinth* by Arabel. Again directed by Shepherd, it featured piano playing by Steve Betts, but played to only a few venues. It was booed by the audience at Elephant Fayre, and was perhaps a progression too far at this stage. In the same year, *Around the World in Eighty Days (Minutes)* was an important step forward. The play was written by Steve Betts and Shepherd, and rehearsed above a shop in St Blazey. The performance lasted for eighty minutes, with the audience counting down the end sequence. Dave Mynne took charge of making and production design, having the sets built by Tom Dudley, a traditional boat builder, at Percy Mitchell's boatyard in Portmellon. This show featured sumo wrestlers, the Old Bore's Club, and a talking brain floating in a fish tank.[201] In 1983, the company presented *The Golden Pathway Annual*,[202] directed by Maggie Hutton, with Hutton, Shepherd and Charlie Barnecut as its performers. In the same year, *Skungpoomery*, written by Ken Campbell and directed by Shepherd, began the Kneehigh Theatre tradition of warming up the audience before the show commenced.[203] 1984 saw them attempt a version of *Jungle Book*,[204] then in 1985 the company developed *The Further Adventures of the Three Musketeers*.[205] The shows were still being played to schools, village halls and community centres.

While this kind of material had been the mainstay of the company's earliest developments, it was *Tregeagle* in 1985 that set Kneehigh Theatre in a new direction. Although conceived originally by Shepherd, the director was Jon Oram – fresh from his work on the Restormel Borough Community play, *The Earth Turned Inside Out* – who brought new influences to the company, including masks and the concept of 'theatre sports' (high-energy physical theatre techniques). This show was important because the company toured out of Cornwall for the first time, and also began to perform outdoors as well as inside, using music and song as part of the narrative, thus merging the boundaries between musicians and actors.[206] Such was the success of this show that Jon Oram also devised the next piece, the ambitious and mime-driven *Fool's Paradise*, also in 1985.[207] This show played in venues from London to the Channel Islands. In 1988 Shepherd directed *Sun and Shadow*, a play by Bristol-based Stuart Delves about a couple, Reg and Gloria, who have retired to Cornwall.[208] It was at this point that Sue Hill joined the company as a designer and maker. *Stig*, an adaptation of Clive King's children's novel *Stig of the Dump*, was also toured around this time; in this, we see some development of the site-specific work of the company, who constructed a dump wherever they performed.[209] Liaison with the writer and director John Downie brought about *Cyborg: A Folktale of the Future* in 1987. Although well received at the Edinburgh Fringe Festival, it was considered too strange for mainstream Cornish audiences. However, again it demonstrated to the company the need for change, development and experimentation.

A third incarnation of *Tregeagle* was to prove highly important for the company. This was 1989's version, the company's first show built for touring outdoors, and the first to involve Bill Mitchell as a designer. Perhaps the most striking performances of this show were presented at the Minack Theatre, with the cast featuring Sturrock, King, Rosewarne, Hill, Mynne, Carey and Will Coleman. Success with this show encouraged the company to produce Boris Howarth's *Last Voyage of Long John Silver* in 1990, but Shepherd felt at the time that this was, perhaps, a step too far.[210] The company was keen to invite participation from members of Shepherd's community, whom he felt offered genuine 'voices'. In practice there would be a core group of individuals who could be drawn upon for each project. Core workers in the middle phase of the company were Janys Chambers, Nicola Rosewarne, Tristan Sturrock, Bec Applebee, Giles King, Charlie Barnecut, Jim Carey, Bill Mitchell, Sue Hill, Allan Drake, Alice King and Amanda Harris.

Fig. 110. The para-theatrical return of the Mermaid at Mevagissey harbour, during Mevagissey Feast Week, designed and constructed by Sue Hill, c.1995.

Of these, Bill Mitchell and Sue Hill were particularly important. Mitchell brought to Kneehigh Theatre both a design and directorial vision that has established the blueprint for much contemporary theatre, not only in Cornwall, but elsewhere in Britain. Sue Hill worked in the company as an actress, taking numerous lead roles,[211] but she also established a design, lettering and promotional ethic that was smart and contemporary. Initially, the company's promotional materials were very much influenced by children's books, particularly woodcuts, which matched the 'storytelling' element of the company's performances.[212] Indeed, 'story' in its widest sense remains crucial to the work of the company. According to Davey and Lewis, Kneehigh often show 'the aspects of the story which appeal very strongly to the deeper parts of human nature'.[213] Thus, it is not surprising that much of Kneehigh's work is concerned with fairy tales, folk tales, myths and legends. We may go further, and suggest that Kneehigh have chosen this emphasis because such elements are so important in defining identity in Cornwall – as I have argued in Chapter One.[214]

In the second phase of the company, Kneehigh Theatre quickly defined a new kind of theatre for Cornwall. Although the format for touring communities had been shaped in the early 1970s by Footsbarn, the company knew that a 'grass-roots' theatre could build audiences. Therefore, Kneehigh shows guaranteed a certain kind of dramatic experience, epitomised in the observations of Allen Saddler in his review of Causley's *The Tinderbox*.[215] While the 1985 version of *Tregeagle* established the blueprint for much of Kneehigh's later work – anarchic, ensemble-style performance that was highly visual and heavily stylised – it was in the 1990s that the company began to move fully beyond its early roots within children's theatre, and start to experiment with narratives from both inside and outside of Cornwall. *Tregeagle* and *The Tinderbox* almost represent the twin elements of the company: one highly Cornish; the other European. Having worked with Charles Causley,[216] the company also initiated a collaboration with Nick Darke, sealing their relationship with texts such as *Ting Tang Mine* (1990), *The Bogus* (1992) and *The King of Prussia* (1996).[217] Darke had been established as a playwright for a number of years previously, but it was with Kneehigh that he began to develop more explicitly Cornish-themed work. A new version of *Hell's Mouth* (2000)[218] – set in a post-apocalyptic dystopia with Cornish nationalists fighting for independence from England – was also assembled, culminating in Kneehigh working at the National Theatre with Darke's *The Riot* (2002).[219] Set in Newlyn in 1896, this focused on the so-called 'Sabbath riots', when the devout Methodist Cornish fishermen refused to fish on Sundays, demonstrating against the Sunday fishing fleet from Lowestoft.[220]

Such works saw Kneehigh moving in a more politically nationalist direction. Darke's plays seemed to fit well within Kneehigh's established methods of working. The dramas were also highly physical, and demanded actors who had been nourished by several years of ensemble work. It was a most effective collaboration. Tristan Sturrock, Giles King, Bec Applebee, Mary Woodvine, Dave Mynne, Sue Hill, Charlie Barnecut and Carl Grose remained core performers during this phase, with musical contributions from Jim Carey.[221] Productions were often stage managed by Allan Drake. Another central performer was Anna Maria Murphy who, like Grose, would later become an important writer. Shepherd continued to both direct and perform, while Mitchell directed and designed for the company.

A golden age for Kneehigh began in the early 1990s, with the outdoor shows *Peer Gynt* (1991), which toured nationally and internationally, and *Ship of Fools* (1992), a cross between a fairy tale and the Mexican Day of the Dead. *Windfall* (1993), devised by Mike Shepherd and Bill Mitchell, took as its inspiration the Gabriel García Márquez story 'The Very Old Man with Enormous Wings' and was not only successful at Trelissick Gardens, but also toured across Britain, and internationally. Also produced in this year were *Danger My Ally* (1993, a Nick Darke script), and a pan-British touring

Fig. 111. Kneehigh Theatre performing *Windfall* at Carn Marth Quarry in 1993. Courtesy of Paul Watts Photography.

adaptation of Charles Dickens' *Scrooge*. *The Bogus* (1994) – a consideration of contemporary Cornish politics, also by Darke – was another ambitious work, which somewhat overstretched itself. Other significant productions during this phase were *Don Quixote* (with a script written by Paul Farmer), *Ravenheart* (an interesting adaptation of the musical *Carmen)* and *The Ash Maid* (1994).[222] Although not Cornu-centric, this latter production was important because it signalled a new awareness of elements of European dramatic traditions, notably Italian commedia dell'arte.[223] In this version of Cinderella, all the characters (bar the ash maid) are grotesques, with Hill as the stepmother in a Medusa-style wig and the step sisters (played by Mike Shepherd and Giles King) also in exaggerated wigs and dresses. The commedia dell'arte influence was significant because in that tradition (from the sixteenth and seventeenth centuries) plays are developed from improvisations of standard plots. Like Kneehigh, troupes tended to work from temporary stages, and toured intensively. There was an emphasis on dance, mask, witty dialogue and all kinds of chicanery – also found in the work of Footsbarn. One can see how this development appealed to Kneehigh, since it was a natural development of the work they had begun back in 1980. Again, the text was developed by the company, but organised by Anna Maria Murphy (b.1957), who was now a writer for the collective. Alice King and John Voogd, who were later to work with other companies in Cornwall, contributed to the design. Darke's *The King of Prussia* was produced in 1995, with a fourth version of *Tregeagle* in 1996. The same year saw an adaptation of *Arabian Nights*, by Geoff Young. 1998 brought *Strange Cargo*, written and devised by Mike Shepherd and John Lee, while Darke's *The Riot* was played in 1999. The following few years marked something of a transition in the company's work, taking on different subjects, working methods and collaborations. *The Itch*, premiered in 1999, was written by Emma Rice, as a free adaptation from *The Changeling* (1622) by Thomas Middleton and William Rowley. Shepherd worked on *Cry Wolf* with the Baghdaddies, who played Balkan music with Middle Eastern influences. Rice also directed *Pandora's Box* in 2002, in a joint project with Northern Stage from Newcastle. At this point, Stu Barker was making an important musical contribution to the shows.

In tandem with these developments, some of the most progressive theatre Kneehigh Theatre has produced has been their 'environmental' work, where they have presented drama in highly imaginative ways in real landscape of village greens, harbours, estates, abandoned quarries, old mines and the seaside. Again, this is a direct link backwards to the community dramas of medieval Cornwall, although Kneehigh has worked hard to reinvent this form of representation. A notable collaboration was made between the

Fig. 112. Alice King as a member of a post-Holocaust tribe, in a Kneehigh Theatre Wild Walks production, 1994. Courtesy of Steve Tanner Photography.

752

designer/director Bill Mitchell and the artist and sculptor David Kemp,[224] who specialises in recycling industrial debris to make new civilisations and communities. His work turns the discarded into something else, for example, transforming Wellington boots into the 'hounds of Geevor'.[225] Kneehigh have utilised Kemp's creations in a number of their 'Wild Walks' projects – a form of exterior promenade theatre – in which an audience is led through a number of locales to experience episodic moments of theatre. Most famously this has occurred at locations such as Botallack, the gunpowder works at Kennal Vale, Geevor, Pendeen, and Gunnislake, but also in the Hayle Estuary and on Gwithian Sands. In one event, Mike Shepherd played an entrepreneur, able to offer the audience the first ever commercial time travel facility, named 'Time Link'.[226] This facilitated all kinds of dramatic possibilities and mayhem. 1996's version of *Tregeagle* drew upon this form of theatre, using rough sculptural scaffolding (not too far removed from the 'stations' of medieval theatre), presenting Shepherd as the evil master or devil ('I am the black hunter, I capture souls'), Hill as a white witch, King as a bumpkin and Rosewarne as a demon. Meanwhile, other members of the cast (carrying the energy of the Wild Walks-style performances) played the chorus: figures in bald pate wigs and black coats who tortured the 'Faustian' Tregeagle. Such work has raised the profile of Kneehigh Theatre's work within the communities of Cornwall, and associated artists with the company often produce 'solo' creations as part of Cornwall's contemporary festival culture – a link to the topsy-turvy world of past theatre. Part of this drive towards festival culture had been shaped by Bill Mitchell but, as we shall see, it was to have even greater potential in the future.

The twenty-first century has brought about a new incarnation of Kneehigh Theatre. This has occurred in various ways. While remaining an actor and director in the company, Shepherd stepped back from being artistic director, a role taken by Emma Rice (b.1967).[227] Rice created a further adaptation from Hans Christian Andersen, *The Red Shoes* in 2000, *The Wooden Frock* (2004, in a co-production with the West Yorkshire Playhouse in Leeds) and, in 2006, Annie Siddons' *Rapunzel* (with design input by Michael Vale). Rice was to win the Best Director award at the 2002 Barclay Theatre Awards, while Kneehigh's version of *The Bacchae* (adapted by Carl Grose from Euripedes)[228] won the TMA Theatre Award for best touring production of 2004. Kneehigh Theatre's work was at last appreciated by the very metropolitan, 'English'-based theatrical community from which Shepherd had initially been rejected – a testament to Shepherd's remarkable theatrical vision. The company was achieving wider acclaim for an approach to theatre that was deservedly recognised as historically and culturally significant not only in Cornwall but across Europe. Following successful co-productions with leading British theatrical institutions in the 1990s, the company also developed a further series of co-productions. For example, *Tristan & Yseult* (2004) toured internally and externally (in locations such as Syria and Australia) in conjunction with the National Theatre. *Nights at the Circus* (2006), an adaptation by Tom Morris and Emma Rice of the 'magical realist' novel by Angela Carter,[229] toured Britain and was co-produced with the Lyric Hammersmith and Bristol Old Vic. *Cymbeline* (directed by Rice and with music by Barker) was developed in conjunction with Nottingham County Council Stages and the Royal Shakespeare Company in their year of 'Festival of Complete Works', producing all of Shakespeare's works between April 2006 and March 2007. Another adaptation by Tom Morris and Emma Rice, *A Matter of Life and Death*, based on the film of the same name by Michael Powell and Emeric Pressburger, premiered at the National Theatre in May 2007.[230] This combination of work from the cinematic and theatrical tradition reached new heights with an adaptation of *Brief Encounter*, which toured Britain in 2008 before opening at the Haymarket in London. Of these, one of the most interesting recent projects during this phase was their version of *Cymbeline*. It is perhaps fitting that a 'West-Briton' company should create this project, for the tale – subtitled 'King of Britain' in one of the few surviving Shakespearean texts to consider this phase of history – is set in early, Celtic Britain. The company took the text and freely adapted it, with Carl Grose (b.1975) writing the script, and Emma Rice directing. Such an approach facilitated a much more wild and racy version than the original, with the company not only heightening the comic possibilities of the play, but also combining this with a new awareness of its tragic potential. *Cymbeline* is considered a difficult text by most actors and scholars,[231] but this version confounded such views.

Rice's current work has built upon and developed the kind of ethos established by Shepherd and Mitchell in the earlier period of the company's career. For example, Rice believes in approaching themes in a 'child-like way'[232] so that audiences have that sense of childhood wonder as they watch. She has also maintained the use of physical theatre and comedy, but this is sometimes positioned very purposefully alongside tragic themes. On this, Davey and Lewis observe that 'Kneehigh has developed the capacity to create truly populist productions, which don't compromise the nature of serious theatre; it is a theatre which explores areas of human nature and experience'.[233] *Nights at the Circus* is a good example of latter-day Kneehigh Theatre, with a cast who all sing, dance and have physical theatre skills, combined with inventive staging, acrobatics and slapstick comedy. This inventiveness continues in an

Fig. 113. Blast! promotional leaflet, Kneehigh Theatre, 2007. Courtesy of Kneehigh Theatre.

adaptation of *Don John* (2008-9), developed in association with the Royal Shakespeare Company and Bristol Old Vic. Here, the story is set in Britain in 1978, during the so-called 'winter of discontent', with Don John representative of incoming Thatcherism.[234] For Christmas 2009, Kneehigh presented *Hansel & Gretel, a wonder tale* as a co-production with the Bristol Old Vic.

Some observers might have felt that the company was transcending its Cornish roots, and leaving behind its original ideology. However, this was not the case. In 2007, for example, Kneehigh Theatre presented *Blast!* Described as 'A Cornish Exposé Performed by 3 Complete Idiots',[235] this show examined both cultural and political nationalism more than any other Kneehigh Theatre production. In part, the show was a response to world fears about suicide bombings and terrorism in the aftermath of 9/11, but it was also a reaction to wider feelings in Cornwall that its political and linguistic claim for independence and/or devolution was growing, and had never been more confident. Shepherd has spoken of the importance of texts by observers such as John Angarrack on the Cornish claim,[236] and so the show is also a response to the impact of works like *Breaking the Chains*.[237] Directed by Shepherd, and devised and performed by Carl Grose, Craig Johnson and Kirsty Woodward, the show was promoted along the following lines:

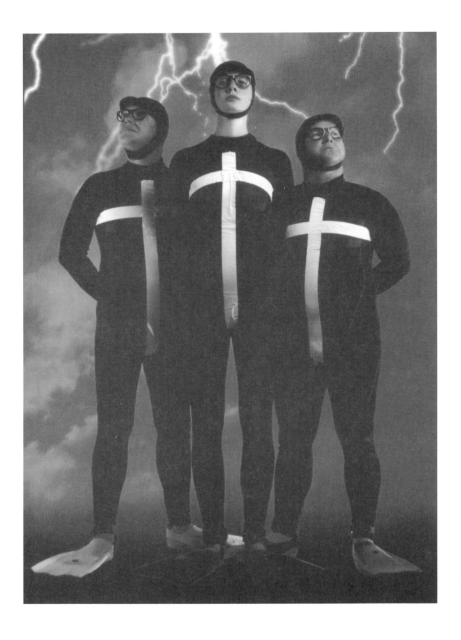

Fig. 114. Blast! promotional photograph, 2007. Courtesy of Kneehigh Theatre.

Trevor Stuggs, direct descendant of Cornish blacksmith An Gof, has had enough. His goat has been got. So Trevor and fellow Druid and failed surfer Chough embark on a course of direct action. Featuring the dance of the beach inflatables, live sea shanties, a small goat, the massacre of several saffron buns and interesting facts about Cornish hedges. Coming to a village hall near you with Apocalyptic results.[238]

The 'Cornish apocalypse' (in the face of mass immigration, Cornu-English linguistic destruction, unaffordable housing) was being considered in other work from this period, but the absurdist styling of this piece made it one of the most important pieces of recent years. The dramaturgy is imagined through a village hall audience attending a lecture on 'The Complete History of the Cornish Hedges of West Penwith'. While the lecture begins, Stuggs and Chuff enter with a bomb strapped to Stuggs, in a parody of the suicide bomber's last video. The problem is that the bomb does not go off. This premise allows an investigation into Cornish history and how Cornwall has been exploited and manipulated over time. In one sequence, a hand puppet is used to symbolise Edward IV, the son of Henry VIII. There follows a depiction of events at Glasney College, with direct association to the mythos of Glasney as the centre of literary and dramatic production in Cornwall:

Chough: What's that your majesty? You wish to raze Glasney College to the ground? One of the oldest universities in the country? You wish to destroy all the books housed there – some of the oldest, most ornate Celtic texts…? You want them all burned! Very good your majesty.

Stuggs: History. Literature. Language. All sentenced to death.

Books are burnt as "Jerusalem" is sung.

Stuggs: *An lavar koth yw lavar gwir,*
Na boz nevra doz vaz an tavaz re hir;
Bez den heb davas a glooaz i dir

Chough: A tongue too long never did good;
But the man without a tongue is without a land…

Stuggs: An old saying, but a true one… I think I need a moment alone wimme goat.[239]

757

The characters then decide to burn a *Poldark* novel, *Bewnans Meriasek*, and a copy of John Angarrack's *Breaking the Chains*. Although probably not understood by all the audience, this is extremely clever dramaturgy. The choice of 'Jerusalem' is also significant, not only because there are many stories concerning Christ's visitation to Cornwall,[240] but in the way 'revivalist' notions of lament and linguistic revival are comically undercut by Stuggs relationship with his goat.[241] Although Kneehigh were, in essence, performing devolution with works such as the plays of Nick Darke and *Tregeagle*, this text took audience understanding to new levels of perception. Perhaps curiously, Kneehigh Theatre have not as yet produced a version of the *Ordinalia*, or any of the late-medieval canon of plays from Cornwall; it would be interesting to see the practice used on *Cymbeline* applied to such texts. However, it may be the case that the company was directly avoiding such a 'revivalist'-linked text in its re-energising of the theatrical continuum. In their eschewing of the typical Cornu- and Celto-centric, Kneehigh Theatre has also created distance between itself and other nationalist groups in Cornwall, which makes for a highly independent and innovative take on contemporary Cornish experience. The flip side of this is that, despite their celebration of Celticity, Kneehigh (and to a greater extent all contemporary Anglo-Cornish drama) is undervalued by self-appointed cultural organisations, such as the Cornish Gorsedd.[242] Very few of the associates of Kneehigh Theatre are bards of the Cornish Gorsedd – but that is not uncommon among theatrical practitioners in Cornwall. Perhaps it could even be argued that the Gorsedd was running to 'Celtic type' and devaluing drama.

Kneehigh's version of *Tristan & Yseult* has been discussed already in this volume, although it is worth drawing attention to the text and its performance again here, as this 2003 production is the one for which they are best known in Cornwall. The script was developed by Carl Grose and Anna Maria Murphy, two writers from Cornwall who now deserve greater acclaim, and anthologies of their work. Several writers and companies in the past had tried to depict this most Cornish of legendary tales dramatically. Given the breadth and the scale of the narrative,[243] two of the hardest things to resolve with this story are the movement between multiple locations, and the perennial difficulty of the figure of Yseult of the White Hands. In essence, the breadth of the piece is resolved by limitations on casting and doubling (for example, in the original production at Restormel Castle, Lostwithiel, Craig Johnson doubled Morholt and Brangien), while White Hands is reconceived as a kind of narrator. The piece begins creatively with the 'unloved' Love Spotters, presented as geeky bird spotters looking for love, searching with binoculars and handing out 'Lovehearts' sweets. As the play begins, Wagner's 'Prelude to

Tristan' is heard, juxtaposing the grand opera with the reality of love. The piece is certainly Cornu-centric, with Mark's opening speech containing the following lines, while Frocin shows him a map:

Now picture this country etched on a map.
Then regard what you see as nothing but crap.
Forget what you've been taught or think you know:
The centre of everything's here – Kernow.[244]

Much of the script is conceived in rhyming couplets, a mechanism similar to some sequences in the medieval corpus. Interestingly, Tristan is conceived of as being French and French-speaking, a device that enables the translation difficulties between him and Yseult. The Morholt is brilliantly conceived, observing that 'If there is anyone I hate more than the Cornish, it's the French'.[245] All this is important because the text asserts the importance of Cornwall as having a separate territorial identity. Yseult's 'separateness' is viewed through her use of an Eastern European language, while the love potion's effect gives rise to a highly visual sequence called 'The Dance of Intoxication'.[246] Frocin is meanwhile written as a comic character, confessing how much he loves King Mark, and asking in Scene 8 for the 'freaky harp music' to be cut.[247] This is successful for it undercuts all of our preconceived ideas about the narrative. The piece is also inter-textual, incorporating a snippet of one of Emily Dickinson's poems ('Wild Nights').[248] The baron's jealousy of Tristan is dispensed with, as are most of the cultural-geographic components: Whitelands, Maplas, Roche Rock, and the Tristan stone itself. Instead, impressive dramaturgy is achieved in the punning simplicity and honesty of the writing, as in this sequence, when Whitehands reflects on the lovers:

Tristan and Yseult
Yseult and Tristan
Triseult
Love is blind to blemishes:
A red skin is rose coloured,
Dull hair a river to swim in:
And Christ, did they swim![249]

In a Foreword to the published edition of the play, Emma Rice comments on the process of devising the script, a process which is now very natural for Kneehigh, but which for many theatre companies would still be problematic.

Murphy and Grose shared out the writing of the piece. Thus: 'I asked Carl [Grose] with his technical and verbal genius to write for the court: King Mark and Frocin. I asked him to write in iambic pentameter as a reference to the great epic courts in literature. Anna [Maria Murphy] I asked to look at the heart-broken – Brangian, Tristan and Yseult – with her direct and emotional voice lending itself to the poetry of the desperate'.[250] Whatever the writing and devising process, in this piece Kneehigh not only managed to present anew one of Cornish literature's most enduring classics, but also to demonstrate a supreme awareness of cultural nationalism alongside a universal emotion – love – something this observer had called for in an article written a year before the play:

> Creatively the crucial task for Cornwall will be to see if its literature can truly transcend the Tamar; it must in effect make the 'local' become international, but in so doing it must not compromise its identity and history.[251]

It seems to me that Kneehigh Theatre achieve this balance completely in their version of *Tristan & Yseult*. Kneehigh Theatre's mantra of quoting Miró's statement 'to be truly universal, you must be truly local' is also profoundly relevant.[252] Crucially, given, for example, the lines of Morholt and Mark in this drama, there is no compromise of identity and history and thus 'performing devolution' is achieved. This play thus becomes the benchmark of new, twenty-first century Anglo-Cornish drama.

Alongside texts such as *Cymbeline, Blast!* and *Tristan & Yseult*, the post-millennial incarnation of Kneehigh Theatre has brought about some changes. Sue Hill, one of the important mid-period members of the company (joining in 1988), is now one of the artistic directors at the Eden Project (continuing there many of the strands and themes of her work established in Kneehigh), while Bill Mitchell has worked in new ways with 'environmental', landscape, and site-specific theatre, forming the company Wildworks.[253] While Kneehigh Theatre had moved in the direction of mainstream theatre, Bill Mitchell was keen to retain the values embodied in 'community arts'. Here, Mitchell reflects on his earlier work with Kneehigh, showing how this informed the principles of Wildworks:

> When we started this journey there were no purpose-built theatres in Cornwall. We worked in schools, village halls and tents. We turned to the extraordinary wild landscapes and industrial sites of Cornwall. We started to explore their potential for narrative and made some startling discoveries. Initially, we simply did the shows we were doing indoors outside. They didn't work well. The spoken

word behaves differently outside. It doesn't carry narrative well and it's better used for lyric effect or as texture. The story had to be carried by physical action, visual effect and music. Sets that were designed for studio theatres looked puny against landscapes and blew over. So a whole new thread of work was born.[254]

The statement Mitchell makes here is core to our understanding of contemporary theatre in Cornwall, in that it argues for alternative theatre space being just as important, if not better, than traditional space. Mitchell is also clearly aware of the continuum of theatre in Cornwall, and this too informed much of his work with both Kneehigh Theatre and with Wildworks. Also however, he had a keen eye on European festival traditions:

We were standing on giants' shoulders, following the traditions of the Cornish *Ordinalia*, ancient community feasts and our immediate ancestors, Foots Barn and Welfare State International. Touring in European festivals every summer we were heavily influenced by Spanish, Dutch and French companies who were creating very physical, visual work with less emphasis on text.[255]

Mitchell had already been the powerful driving force behind outside theatre at Carn Marth quarry, midsummer bonfires, events celebrating the beast of Bodmin Moor, Mazey Day, Golowan, Tom Bawcock's Eve, and Bodmin Riding – many of these festivals were begun 'anew'; others were reinvented along more contemporary lines, but so successfully that many people now regard them as utterly traditional.[256] A core component in this renewed link between carnival, festival and theatre was how banners, kites, and lanterns were used to reinvigorate old festivals – some of them, of course, the direct modern descendants of saint's feast days. Here then, was a renewed link between theatre, ritual and seasonality that had once informed *Bewnans Meriasek* and *Bewnans Ke*. One of Mitchell's shows with Kneehigh had been *Ghostnets*,[257] a piece that linked the concerns of mass tourism (also being explored at the same time in the academy in Cornwall[258]) with dreams of refugees (thus combining world-scale concerns with those closer to home). Mitchell has reflected on the interesting theatrical moment that occurred when the audience helped the performers to pull in the nets (thus breaking the traditional gap between them), and also how theatre could be presented to an audience who were walking, riding their bikes, hiding, escaping and playing.

While still under the auspices of Kneehigh Theatre, one of his most important pieces was an adaptation of the story of *Antigone*, described in posters of the time as 'spectacular landscape theatre'.[259] This show was titled *Hell's Mouth* (2002), and was a site specific work developed around Hendra

Pit, near Nanpean, at the heart of the china-clay mining industry – possibly one of the most untheatrical locations in Cornwall. Although the landscape and community had already been celebrated in works by other writers,[260] this was another Cornish industry actually in decline, for Hendra Pit had been 'worked out', and was then flooded and used as a reservoir. Mitchell noted that the area had been claimed by local youngsters on trial motorbikes, who used the landscape to practise jumps and turns. The bikers were integrated into the performance as warring armies, carrying samurai-style flags. Again, Mitchell's vision for theatre in Cornwall is highly progressive and innovative – taking one of the earliest classical texts and adapting it for a post-industrial landscape.[261] Such work led Mitchell, David Kemp and Mercedes Kemp to create a joint '3-island' project, *A Very Old Man With Enormous Wings*, initially with Malta, and then later with Cornwall, Malta and Cyprus, performing the latter piece at the green line in Nicosia, next to a United Nations border post in a derelict taverna, closed because of sniper fire. In this way Mitchell has not only opened up the internationalism of theatre from Cornwall, but also chosen to locate his theatre on cultural boundaries; exactly the kind of demanding and politically-active theatre demanded by observers such as Craig, and Kershaw.[262] Another important piece was *Souterrain* (2006-7), a pan-European project retelling the life of Orpheus. This site-specific promenade piece was performed in seven different underworlds including communities in Brighton, Hastings, Gosnay, Amiens, Colchester, Sotteville-les-Rouen and Cornwall. The sites included a village, a seventeenth-century French convent, a Napoleonic citadel, a department store, an Alzheimer's hospital and a disused mine (Dolcoath and South Crofty[263]). The Wildworks website explains the idea of the project:

> *Souterrain* explores themes of love, loss and regeneration. These themes resonated with our host communities who had said goodbye to their traditional industries, their countries of birth, their memory. We asked the audience to leave their most precious memories in the care of the angels of death during their journey through the underworld.[264]

Nowhere did this idea have more impact than at the much-lamented Dolcoath, and at South Crofty, where mining at Cornwall's last large-scale mine had stopped in 1998, just before the turn of the millennium. This engendered debate on how a post-tin-mining Cornwall would operate – it was later given the status of a UNESCO World Heritage site – but also how immediate communities in locations such as Camborne and Redruth would regenerate. The connection between this aspect of community and ritual was picked up in a preview of the event:

Fig. 115. The audience waits at the gateway to the Underworld in Wildworks' 'Souterrain', on their descent into the Red River valley at Dolcoath. The South Crofty headgear is visible on the skyline. Photo by Steve Tanner. Courtesy of Sue Hill and Wildworks.

> Wild Works shows are always grounded in the community in which it is made and these shows on a disused mining site should be a moving reminder of a disappeared way of life that cannot be brought back from the dead and the importance of rituals in learning to say goodbye.[265]

Thus in the work of both Kneehigh and Wildworks we see new imaginings of the linkage between space, place and performance. Their influence has been profound, and felt not only in Cornwall, but also across the rest of Europe.[266] From early and small beginnings in Cornwall, Kneehigh Theatre have transcended on home ground and beyond the Tamar to become a shaping force in contemporary theatre, which both reasserts the popular, community thread of theatre in Cornwall, and also shows how Cornish theatre can be viewed as significant on a global scale. Kneehigh's power as a company has informed the practice of a number of other important companies to emerge during this period, who were also seeking non-metropolitan and resolutely 'non-English' methods of theatrical exploration.

One of the more important of these contemporary theatre companies of Cornwall was founded and named on the basis of a link to Cornwall's theatrical past. That company is the Miracle Theatre Company,[267] who first came together in 1979, when three friends (the founding members of the company) decided to put on an adaptation of 'Origo Mundi [The Beginning of the World]'. Viewing this as a 'miracle play', it was therefore natural to name the company Miracle Theatre. One of the founders was Bill Scott, who was still running the company in 2010. In a recent interview with BBC Radio Cornwall's Matt Shepherd, Bill Scott commented:

> We fished around and found an old Victorian translation of *The Ordinalia*, and did just the first part, 'The Creation'. We put together a one hour show which was full of laughs, and toured it around parks and gardens of Cornwall in a glorious summer, and that's how we began.[268]

This shows explicitly the link between Cornwall's theatrical past and present, and suggests a format for theatre that again is based on humour, and the ritual year. It is perhaps not surprising, therefore, to learn that Miracle has created an outdoor production every summer, usually followed by a winter national indoor tour. The company has built its reputation on popular and interesting adaptations of the 'classics',[269] the ethos of the live work being 'witty, highly physical and entertaining'.[270] Early shows in the 1980s are less well recorded, but an important developmental period came in works such as *A Grand Catastrophe* (1992), *A Parcel of Rogues* (1993), and *The Scapegoat* (1995). In the summer of 2001, the company performed *The Beggar's Opera* by Barnstaple-born John Gay (1685-1732).[271] This ballad opera is indicative of the kind of material on which Miracle Theatre work well. Although Gay's opera has been much revived of late, no doubt the south-western local connection was also important to the company. Like Kneehigh Theatre, their focus is very often on collaborative work with other practitioners such as artists and musicians, which makes the work highly visual, and aurally dynamic. The company has come to specialise in pieces that satirise or imitate 'periods' of theatrical history – Restoration, Victoriana, or Music Hall – with an ensemble approach drawing on popular culture of the particular era. There is perhaps also a thread of the old-style touring company of the late nineteenth-century. Indeed, a figure such as James Dawson would recognise much of their practice.

Although Miracle have consistently toured both Cornwall and elsewhere over the past thirty years, the company has been less keen to embrace its Cornish identity, choosing instead adaptations and performances of better-known pan-British and European texts. Cornish is rarely used. Although the company sometimes makes use of Cornu-English culture, it does not display an overtly nationalist agenda. In some ways, this is curious, since it is at odds with Bill Scott's work elsewhere as an innovator in film – in works such as *An*

Dewetha Gweryow Dolly Pentreath / The Last Words of Dolly Pentreath (1994), *The Saffron Threads* (1995) and *Splatt Dhe Wertha / Plot for Sale* (1997)[272] – because in his cinematic projects he has consistently considered such issues as language and identity.[273] However, Miracle Theatre often presents texts from a post-colonial studies perspective 'reading against the grain', which shows an understanding of the colonised/coloniser relationship.[274] This was particularly well done in 1994's *The Tempest* and 1996's *Dr Livingstone I Presume*. For example, performing *The Tempest* at venues such as the ruined mining landscape of Kit Hill, near Callington, has a particular relevance to Cornish experience. Close by, to the north-east, sits Hingston Down, site of the 838 victory of the Anglo-Saxons over a combined Cornish-Viking army, while below sits the River Tamar, defined as the national border by King Athelstan in 926. It is here that Miracle invited us to watch the metaphor of Prospero's colonisation of Caliban's island. Miracle Theatre also regularly revamp other Shakespearean pieces to give them contemporary relevance, most recently *A Midsummer Night's Dream* (1997), *Twelfth Night* (2002), *Hamlet* (2004) and *The Taming of the Shrew* (2007). While their skill in theatrical adaptation (from novels and from film) has always been significant, the company has focused less on presenting original pieces by new writers. Particularly strong work has emerged in their period pantomimes: *Aladdin* (1993, and a revival in 2005), *The Revenge of Rumpelstiltskin* (1994) and *Sleeping Beauty* (1998).[275] The company is often found performing at venues such as the Minack, but still undertake regular tours of the village hall and community centre circuit of Cornwall – in a way, directly paralleling the community plays of the medieval period). Scott neatly summarises this scene in Cornwall:

> When we were in a village hall once, the only way to get on to the stage was through the tea hatch in the kitchen. The same hall had an electric meter that took 20 pence coins. It had to be filled up every 20 minutes during the shows![276]

As well as being comical, this demonstrates how relevant theatre is to Cornish audiences, and its lack of pretension. Space, place and performance work in happy union for community enjoyment. Miracle have come to typify much that is excellent about touring theatre in Cornwall in the late twentieth and early twenty-first century. Initially based in Falmouth, they have now moved to workshop and rehearsal space at the Krowji Centre in Redruth. Most recently, the Miracle Theatre Company has been comprised of Alan Munden, Kyla Goodey, Sally Crooks, Ben Dyson, Fay Powell Thomas, Jim Carey, Rosie Hughes, Jude Munden, Jo Bowis and Keri Jessiman (a long-standing actress with the company). Their most recent shows have included *The Time Machine*

(2006), *Jason* (2007) and an adaptation of the Kurt Vonnegut novel *Cat's Cradle* (2008).[277]

Another leading company in late twentieth and early twenty-first century drama in Cornwall was The Bedlam Theatre Company of Cornwall.[278] Like Kneehigh, Bedlam Theatre were keen to explore ensemble work, and toured unconventional settings: although the village halls and community centres provided much of the space for their performances, particularly for winter touring, in summer tours, they also presented material in outdoor venues. This author remembers particularly inspired versions of *The Good Dog Devil* at Charlestown harbour and *Duffy and the Devil* (in effect, the Cornish *Rumplestiltskin*) at Leedstown Village Hall. Initially, Bedlam were highly influenced by folklore (especially Cornish-Celtic folklore[279]), though by the beginning of the twenty-first century, the company appeared to take a new direction, producing what appear to be more Chekhov/Ibsen-inspired pieces, and choosing to be involved with both theatre in education and more community-based work.[280] Their logo is a Celtic triscal with three figures circling. The innovators behind the company were Rory Wilton and Emma Spurgin Hussey, who regularly either direct or appear in Bedlam's productions, assisted by other associate cast.[281] Bedlam were established in 1987, when they mounted an outdoor production titled *Scabriella and the King;*[282] by 1988, they had become a professional touring company, presenting a winter tour based around *Little Red Riding Hood.*[283] Another winter tour, *The Snow Queen* (directed by Hilary Coleman) came in 1989,[284] though they really began to hit a productive phase in 1990 and 1991 when they toured with *The Mermaid*[285] and *The Cornish Giant*[286] (a show which took a similar theme to the 1972 work by Footsbarn). Core performers at this point included Bec Applebee (a mainstay of Kneehigh for a number of years[287]), Will Coleman (teacher, storyteller and later author of a Cornu-centric children's literature[288]), Jo Tagney (musician and Cornish-dance teacher[289]), Jo Kessell, Anita King and Nick Ryall. Though inspired by the folklore of Cornwall, the pieces were all devised by the company.

Like Kneehigh, Bedlam also drew on the legend of Tristan for their inspiration, and in 1992 toured their version of *Trystan and Yseult* (directed by Hilary Coleman),[290] showing the long-standing influence of this tale on the theatrical continuum. Bedlam had by then reached a remarkable level of success and began a charged reinterpretation of several folk-tales. Summer 1993 saw a take on *The Good Dog Devil* (directed by the company),[291] followed by a winter tour of *Pengersick the Enchanter* (directed by Dee Evans),[292] then in 1994 came *Punch 'n' Judy's Changeling* (there are many changeling motifs in Cornish folklore[293]), followed by *Smuggler's Moon.*[294] 1995 brought *Punch 'n' Judy's Changeling II*, and *Duffy and the Devil* (both directed by Matthew

Smith). This latter text is of interest because it was picking up on a much older dramatic text, certainly performed (as Bottrell notes) in eighteenth and nineteenth-century Cornwall, and then more recently reconceived by Nance as one of his *Cledry Plays*.[295] In essence, this was the classic early phase of Bedlam as a touring company, with shows such as *Duffy and the Devil* defining these tales for a new generation. Their work on the stage was patterning re-interest and several retellings of these narratives elsewhere.[296] Similar success came with *Cherry of Zennor* in 1996,[297] the more political *Tin*[298] (Rory Wilton's first play) and a storytelling show, *Polperro Tales*, in 1997. In 1998, Bedlam produced *One and All:* directed by Becca Kaye and Donna Goddard with a text by Emma Spurgin Hussey, this was a significant show because its primary source was the tale of John of Chyanhor, one of the few Cornish-language prose texts.[299] Although 'John of Chyanhor' is explicitly set in west Cornwall, the company felt an obvious association with the space and place of Polperro in particular.[300] The expressly Cornish material was maintained with *The Governor of Sombrero Rock* (1999). This was a highly progressive show telling the story of the early nineteenth-century life of Polperro-based Robert Jeffery.[301] Accused of a crime, Jeffery is abandoned on a 30 foot wide rock away from shipping lanes. His story is told from the perspective of the bawdy and farcical Victorian stage. This piece alone displays a remarkable continuity with the kind of theatre presented in Cornwall in the late eighteenth and early nineteenth century and, given Bedlam's choice of material, it is easy to see how the company has drawn on some of the major narratives of Cornwall. The year also brought a new storytelling show, *Smuggling Skullduggery*, followed by a third in 2000, *Bodmin Beasts*, a collection based on the by then long-term folklore of the Beast of Bodmin Moor.

The Watched (2000) perhaps signalled a change of direction. Written by Christopher William Hill, this was a more serious piece, with music by Cornish composer Russell Pascoe.[302] Presented in the round (much like the medieval drama of Cornwall) this tense drama kept some of the folkloric elements ('The Gathering', 'The Coming of Frosts', 'Winter') but combined them with a Francis Ford Coppola-esque narrative. Set in a manor house kitchen and upon the moors, the production was a dark fairy tale, drawing on the tradition of Cornish folklore, but infusing it with a more Angela Carter-like disturbing magical realism.[303] The step away from Cornwall was completed by *Axe for the Frozen Sea* (2003), which was inspired by the life of the Czech writer Franz Kafka.[304] Described as a 'very serious comedy' the piece examined a moment in Kafka's life on an overnight train between Prague and Berlin. Eastern Europe also provided the inspiration for *Dark Woods Beyond* (2005): set in an apartment, the action moves between the 1930s and 1950s and focuses on two squabbling sisters. Such plays exemplify the more Chekhov/Ibsen-like qualities of Bedlam's work. Both pieces have often frightening parallels to the experience of Cornish communities, and were drawing on a similar continuity. A further storytelling show, *Ghosts*, followed in 2006. By this time, Bedlam were also devising work with the Barbican Theatre in Plymouth, and the Acorn in Penzance, as well as working with the Cornish Theatre Collective.

The Cornish Theatre Collective is a pool of creative artists who since 1997 have come together to work on a variety of theatre projects.[305] The founder of the Collective (and a central member of the Penryn Community Theatre) was Dominic Knutton. It was his development of Penryn Community Theatre – centred on the Seven Stars Pub in the town – that led to the formation of the larger company. Knutton, who died in 2007, was the Collective's artistic director, and developed a number of works over a ten-year period. Knutton's vision to organise the sometimes disparate theatrical activity in Cornwall culminated in his work on the *Ordinalia* (with writer Pauline Sheppard) at St Just-in-Penwith. The Collective takes its Celtic roots very seriously, indicating a concern with Cornish identity not only through its triscal logo but also in its development of text and performance. The first play written for the company was *Bohelland,* an adaptation of the Bohelland Tragedy, based on the 1618 *Black Letter Pamphlet: News from Pe[n]rin in Cornwall of a most Bloody and unexampled Murder.*[306] This story is proof of the remarkable continuity of some narratives in Cornish theatre: it had already been adapted into a drama by George Lillo (whose *Fatal Curiosity* had been very popular in both eighteenth- and nineteenth-century Cornwall) and by Donald R. Rawe.[307] This time the adaptation was by Justin Chubb.[308] It was performed at Penryn's Lady Killigrew Festival, toured Cornwall and also played at the Finborough Theatre in London. In 1998, Justin Chubb wrote an original drama called *Judas Worm*, which was toured by the Collective in Cornwall, and also played at the Finborough Theatre. Set in the context of nineteenth-century Cornish mining, the play told the story of the miner and artist Judas, who becomes famous overnight when a London art critic spots his work. However, back home in his Cornish village, a terrible disaster has occurred, and Judas, with his new found wealth and success, must decide whether to assist the villagers who once completely rejected him.

Clever as Paint, by Canadian playwright Kim Morrisey, was toured by the Collective in 1999. This was an examination of the world of the Pre-Raphaelite painters, and saw the Collective move in a less Cornu-centric direction. The same was true of *Possession*, in the same year – a 'talking heads' piece, authored again by Chubb. *Southern Comfort* was an important departure and development. Devised by female members of the Collective, and then 'written' by Chubb, this was a four-handed contemporary comedy about life in Cornwall, which perhaps deserves wider recognition, as one of the few contemporary feminist dramas about the territory.[309] *Mapbeth – Son of the Grave*, was another important innovation, which reset Shakespeare's *Macbeth* in early Cornwall. The show, which featured witches' chants in Cornish, was very successful.[310] It certainly gave audiences a taste of what a Cornu-centric Shakespeare drama might have looked like. The *Mapbeth* influence also tinged their revival of *Bohelland* at the Minack Theatre in 2003, for in some ways the two plays are about the same vices: greed, over-ambition and foul deeds. This was a busy time for the Collective: as we shall see, it was Knutton and Sheppard who eventually adapted and directed the truncated version of the *Ordinalia* at St Just-in-Penwith (2000-2004),[311] which is dealt with specifically below, when I consider the work of Sheppard. Other work in the Collective around this time included *The Grand Theatre of Action (The Life and Loves of Admiral Nelson)* for the 2005 Sea Britain Festival,[312] *Oral Fixation* (a drama about karaoke nights) and *The Alchemist*, an adaptation of Paulo Coelho's novel. Following a move to a base at the Krowji Centre in Redruth and Knutton's death, writer Pauline Sheppard appears to have steered development of the Collective. Her recent work includes *The Zig Zag Way*, an adaptation of Anita Desai's novel, telling the 'time-travelling' story of a young Cornish couple who travel to Mexico to find their fortune.[313] Initially set in 1910, the play then moves forward a century to focus on an American named Eric who is in Mexico seeking his Cornish roots in an old mining town. This production toured in 2007 to spaces such as the Tolmen Centre in Constantine, Cape Cornwall School in St Just-in-Penwith, and Calstock Village Hall.

A number of theatrical spaces were significant during the post-war period, and it is hard to summarise the vast range and variety of performances in each venue. Some had carried on as before. The two extant *plen-an-gwarries* at St Just-in-Penwith and at Perran Round continued to host small-scale theatre events. For example, in July 1996, Lowender Peran (the Celtic musical festival organisation) presented a so-called *Medieval Mystery Play* (which was actually 'Resurrexio Domini') at Perran Round. It promised 'players, minstrels, dancers, wrestlers, jugglers, saints, and even God, together with a few tinners' and 'a never to be forgotten experience of the festival atmosphere of these ancient plays'.[314] The Minack Theatre was well established before the Second World War, but in the post-war period, the venue witnessed several phases of expansion. Seating was improved and expanded, and more car parking space provided for visitors. Several improvements in the lighting and technology available to companies were complemented in the mid 1990s with a considerable revision of the box office area to accommodate a museum and a restaurant.[315] For a brief time in the early twenty-first-century, such was the iconic status of the Theatre, in both Cornish and British culture, that it was used as a BBC1 ident.[316]

Arts Centres in Cornwall continued to provide space and places for performance in the 1960s and 1970s. Some of the more successful were in St Austell and Penzance. In 1987, the trustees of the Cornwall Theatre Company took over the assets and liabilities of Penzance Arts Centre, with the explicit aim of increasing and expanding the audiences by widening the spectrum of arts available. This group then developed the Acorn Arts Centre in the town.[317] Major conversion work was started in 1996, and the new venue – with an auditorium for small-scale theatre – opened in 1998, and remains one of the most relevant and dynamic venues, known for being intimate and friendly. Most of the significant touring and Cornu-centric theatre in the contemporary period has been performed there.[318] As a centre-point for arts activity in Penzance, it has been highly influential in the revived Golowan Festival,[319] but has also ignited much artistic and theatrical endeavour in west Cornwall, matching the exterior Minack as west Cornwall's indoor venue.

Fig. 116. Adam and Eve in the performance of *Medieval Mystery Play* at Perran Round, 1996.

Another significant late twentieth and early twenty-first century venue was Falmouth Arts Centre, first formed in 1954,[320] with a theatre seating capacity of 200. Located in part of the building of the Cornwall Polytechnic Society of Cornwall, this was a well-used theatre space in the 1980s and 1990s, but was overshadowed in the following decade by the successful reopening of Falmouth's Princess Pavilions as a partial, if smaller, replacement for St Austell's Cornwall Coliseum – mainly a significant popular music venue, but also offering theatrical events.[321] At the other end of Cornwall, the Sterts Centre has provided a similar theatre touring venue to Falmouth Arts Centre and the Acorn. Sterts is a multi-use performance and arts space, founded in 1982 at Upton Cross, near Liskeard,[322] in a triangle between Launceston, Liskeard and Callington. In many ways, the Sterts venue takes the best ingredients of the continuum of theatre in Cornwall: it is integrated in the local community and offers a sizable, multi-purpose 'open-air' amphitheatre in which to perform. Usefully, this performance space has a canopy above it to counteract adverse weather conditions on Bodmin Moor. Although Sterts has suffered financial difficulties, the venue is still operating and is culturally significant in the present-day theatrical landscape in east Cornwall, resisting and reacting against the domineering theatrical institutions found in Plymouth: the Theatre Royal, and the Barbican Theatre.

The late 1970s and 1980s had seen the City Hall in Truro used for a variety of events, including popular music concerts, theatre and flea markets. By the turn of the 1990s, plans were in place to convert the building into a new hall. Originally the Truro Town Hall and Corn Exchange, it was first built in 1847, and successive years brought further development of the site. In 1909, the building was leased as a public skating rink, and an occasional picture house. Much of the original structure was destroyed when a fire gutted most of the building in 1914. However, by 1925 it had been remodelled to facilitate performances of plays (a continuity of the Assembly-Room Theatre of High Cross). These continued into the immediate post-war period, used mainly by the community rather than by professional companies. By the 1980s, the Hall was in a severe state of dilapidation, and Carrick Council wanted to sell it for development. A performance by Duchy Opera in Carn Brea Leisure Centre starring Benjamin Luxon highlighted the need for a middle-scale venue in Cornwall. A core group, including Benjamin Luxon, Chris Warner and some Carrick councillors met to discuss the future.[323] When Carrick offered them a 125-year lease on the Hall at £1 a year and £500,000, they accepted and initiated the campaign for a New City Hall. The Hall for Cornwall Trust began ambitious fund-raising and planning during the middle years of the 1990s in order to develop a multi-functional venue. The conversion of the building would preserve the Carn Brea granite façades, the clock tower and all the city council accommodation, but provide an auditorium, a foyer and restaurant, reception, dressing rooms, a board room and a green room. The Trust took over the running of the Hall in 1991. The original vision for the Hall for Cornwall was not only to provide a world-class venue for touring productions, but also to develop indigenous Cornish theatre and drama.

An important part of the driving force behind this project was the vision of Chris Warner. Born in Norwich in 1944, Warner was the son of a Spitfire pilot. He studied at Bristol University's drama department, and has been involved in drama in Cornwall since the late 1960s. He helped to co-ordinate the University's 1969 production of the *Ordinalia*, and was active in developing theatre in Cornwall in the 1970s, as well as being instrumental in the development of Duchy Opera and the setting up of Cornwall Arts Centre Trust, an advocacy organisation devoted to finding more arts space. Warner also successfully operated his own theatre company – Warner's Corner – touring both in and outside of Cornwall. His idea was to improve the possibilities for theatrical culture in Cornwall, and he saw the potential for the hall at Truro. The inaugural performance at the new Hall for Cornwall took place on 15 November 1997, with Chris Warner as the venue's manager. In just over a decade since then, the Hall attracted around 180,000 theatre-goers. It has

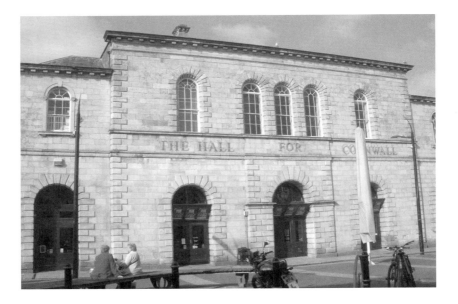

Fig. 117. The Hall for Cornwall, Truro, in 2008.

hosted many major pan-British companies such as the Royal Shakespeare Company, Method & Madness, the English Touring Opera, the Royal Ballet and the Rambert Dance Company, though its progression and development has not been easy. Due to various financial crises, first Warner, and then a second manager, Tim German, were both side-lined. The current manager is Tim Brinkman. There has also been criticism that the Hall for Cornwall promoted mainly tribute bands and second-rate theatre, rarely offering any truly Cornu-centric drama. Warner had anticipated staging the Cornish corpus of drama, and developing new playwrights. Given a few exceptions (such as D.M. Thomas's *Hell Fire Corner*, Duchy Opera and work by Kneehigh Theatre), the venue has failed to live up to the original vision. In certain respects, it continues to promote culturally safe theatre, which is imported rather than home-grown. Certainly the present venue encourages few of Cornwall's established or new playwrights in any capacity, though this is perhaps more to do with economics than lack of intention.[324]

One of the most modern venues in Cornwall is a development in St Austell. This is The Keay Theatre, located at John Keay House, formerly the headquarters of china clay mining company ECC International, but now a new campus of Cornwall College.[325] During the day, college students can take theatre courses (first developed in the town at The Hub training institution,[326] where several generations of Cornish actors had been trained). In the evenings, the venue also hosts small-scale touring companies. Cornwall's diffuse and diverse festival culture also provides an outlet for theatre. Most of the major festivals – whether ongoing, revived, invented or reinvented – contain theatrical elements, many drawing on the themes and concepts discussed in Chapter One. For example, significant performances of adaptations of Daphne du Maurier's novels are part of the annual Daphne du Maurier Festival in and around Fowey.[327] The Eden Project also hosts occasional theatre work, sometimes supporting the green ethics of its ideology. Village halls and community centres (the new *plen-an-gwarries*?) continue to have a place in the continuity of theatre in Cornwall, gathering the community in the time-honoured way for new performances. The Kidz R Us Theatre at St Ives (primarily intended for performances by local youngsters) also hosts a range of touring and Cornu-centric theatre.[328] Other significant venues are Port Isaac Village Hall (recently given a media make-over by BBC's *DIY SOS*), the Tolmen Centre at Constantine,[329] the Shire Hall at Bodmin, and Perranporth Memorial Hall, as well as a host of school, college and university buildings (among them, the Helford Theatre at Truro College). Paradoxically, English Heritage were also offering theatrical and para-theatrical activity at some of their locations in Cornwall – perhaps in an effort to 'write' and 'perform back' at those they were oppressing, with seemingly very little under-standing of the sustained continuum of theatre in Cornwall.[330] This was coupled with high-level ignorance of Cornish identity, language and experience. Publications from the Cornwall Heritage Trust showed better awareness of the theatrical continuum.[331] Yet elsewhere, despite all the dramatic activity, both historically and in contemporary Cornwall, tourist pub-lications displayed little awareness of playwrights, venues, space and place, or their significance.[332]

Having considered some of the important companies, and spaces and places where performance has taken place in Cornwall in the post-war period, I now turn to some of the more important dramatists of the end of the twentieth and beginning of the twenty-first centuries. James Stock is not a well-known name, and his Cornish credentials are based on just one play: *Star-Gazy Pie and Sauerkraut* (1995).[333] However, this play is a very important text. Stock was born in Padstow, the son of a teacher, and for the past twenty years has been a Lecturer in Drama in higher education. He is presently Programme Leader for Drama at Edge Hill University at Ormskirk in Lancashire. Stock had established his reputation with an American-themed work, *Blue Night in the Heart of the West*, which premiered at the Bush Theatre in London in 1991.[334] However, he really wanted to celebrate his Cornish background with his next work. His choice of topic was ambitious, and he employed a triple time frame to construct the work. Although star gazy pie is most associated with the village of Mousehole in west Cornwall, Stock chose a north Cornish coastal community in which to set the play. Fisherman Frank (no surname is given) faces the dual pressures of a failing business and his inability to communicate with Billy, his autistic son. He catches fish that will be used in the pie – named because the heads of the fish (normally mackerel) point skywards out of the top of the crust. This metaphor is used to unite the play: where dreams look skywards and to the future, but underneath is a disturbing past. The central character is Kathleen, a rebellious teenager, who is the only one who can speak to Billy. Kathleen's angst is derived from her mother's disturbing dreams about the treatment given to an early nineteenth-century folk figure, Bright Millar.[335] Millar comes back from a war (probably the Napoleonic Wars) with 'some madness germ inside' but after his death they 'put him out there on the headland [at] Stepper Point'. George then notes that:

> People round here believe the touch of a dead boy's hand is virtue. So the town fetch out every sick man and woman. There's a line of 'em from the head to the harbour. And while the children dance round the post, Bright's hand is curing every illness in the town.[336]

Here, Stock was drawing on the sometimes dark and disturbing folkloric heritage of charms and superstitions in Cornwall.[337] Frank wittily comments: 'Folklore's the only industry we got left. Idn it?',[338] an observation that matched the new reasons for tourists to travel to Cornwall during this period.[339] The play's ambition derives from this dark and disturbing folklore and the way in which Kathleen's German-born grandmother relives her starring role in a Nazi propaganda film glorifying eugenic extermination and sterilisation. Hitler is then featured as a character. This interplay between Cornwall and Germany is explicit in the concept of 'trepanning' (the medical process of drilling a hole in the skull to ease inter-cranial diseases, especially of mental illness[340]), which sounds frighteningly like the name of a Cornish village. The drama works by undercutting the horror of major twentieth-century historical events with humour and an exploration of the absurdity and banality of evil. This is often prefaced by the singing of Methodist hymns, which evoke not only a feeling of starkness, but also the wonder of redemption and forgiveness. With this play, Stock was one of the first figures to realise the dramatic potential of such hymns for promoting a self-questioning about the Cornish condition; virtually all the modern writers of Anglo-Cornish drama use this technique. In the final sequence of the play, Frank enters carrying the lifeless body of Billy, the play here drawing on Athenian notions of tragedy. Frank wonders what he should do, and decides to visit a mystical site in north Cornwall: St Nectan's Glen. At this point, the play appears to integrate several cultural references. There are many legends associated with the *Kieve* [English: bowl] and waterfall that lies between Tintagel and Boscastle, and many figures have also imagined an Arthurian link.[341] Frank's need for a place to escape is worked through in his final dialogue:

> I said – I know a place, Billy. There's this woman I knew in school, see. She's got this caff. Up in St Nectan's Glen. 'Tis above the waterfall. 'Tis desolate. I said – we could go there. The three of us. Maybe they'd never find us.[342]

Here, Frank is not only escaping the changing nature of Cornwall, but also the wider horror of the twentieth-century. Stock's play is not an easy ride, but perhaps – as in D.M. Thomas's fiction exploring the holocaust, dreams and psychology – we see something of the wider subject-matter that Cornu-centric drama could explore.[343] Unfortunately, Stock has developed no further Cornish work, but in this one play, we see a clever fusion of many strands of historical experience.

Nick Darke (1948-2005) has already been discussed in this chapter in the context of his work with Kneehigh Theatre, but deserves separate treatment as well. Like Stock, Darke grew up in north Cornwall. He was born at St Eval, near Padstow, the son of a chicken farmer and fisherman, and lived most of his later life at Porthcothan, where his family had lived for generations. His mother was the actress Betty Cowan. After attending Truro Cathedral School and then Newquay Grammar School, Darke trained as an actor at Rose Bruford College in Kent, learning his craft at the Victoria Theatre in Stoke-on-Trent throughout the 1970s. There, he acted in over eight plays and directed some five pieces between 1977 and 1979.[344] During this phase he also began to write stage drama; his first full length play was *Never Say Rabbit in a Boat* (1977), which was produced at the Victoria Theatre. This play established the major thematic and spatial concerns of Darke's drama. Set in Cornwall, it is about an ageing rabbit catcher and a beach seine net company. The play drew on Cornish folklore, in which it is supposedly unlucky to mention rabbits when at sea. Darke's concern with maritime, boat and Cornish themes continued in the earliest period of his work. *Low Tide* (1977), produced by the Plymouth Theatre Company, was set on a beach, exploring issues concerned with mass tourism. 1979's *Summer Trade* takes place in a pub in north Cornwall on the day after a landlord's last night, when a new landlord has plans to modernise. Such themes were striking in a Cornwall that was facing these very issues. Although not set in Cornwall, his other plays of this phase – *Landmarks* (1979, set in the 1930s in rural England during the transition of heavy horses to tractor-powered ploughing) and *A Trickle On the River's Back* (1979, about a family of lightermen on the River Thames and that industry's decline) – show a strong concern for specific communities and the changes they must face in the light of modernisation. This is a theme also found in *High Water* (produced by the Royal Shakespeare Company in 1980) where two men meet to go wrecking and discover that they are, in fact, father and son.

The 1980s saw further development of Darke's writing, in *Say Your Prayers* (1981) with the Joint Stock Theatre Company. A musical, this was a diversion from his normal concerns, featuring an atheist's interpretation of St Paul with the help of an Anglican priest and an American born-again evangelist. The interest in America, however, would stay within his work. More common thematic concerns are found in *The Catch*, also from 1981, produced for The Royal Court Upstairs. This concerns two fishermen who face difficulties in the light of European Union legislation, and come to catch not just fish, but cocaine. Again, this was a direct parallel to the economic situation in Cornwall, as outlined by academics and observers of this phase.[345] In 1982, Orchard Theatre Company produced a sequel to *The Catch* titled *The Lowestoft Man*, in which a mysterious American arrives to claim back his cocaine. 1983 was a significant year, for in his play *The Body*, we begin to see a more concrete realisation of the kind of drama that Darke was to create for the rest of his career. *The Body* is a black comedy, with a quite crazy narrative. The basic premise of the play is the story of a Cornish village that has an American weapons base as a neighbour (Darke was obviously thinking of RAF St Mawgan during this phase, and the concern with the iron bridge would seem to indicate an imagining of the old railway line from Bodmin to Padstow). One of the American soldiers drops dead of boredom (this itself a satirical comment on what Cornwall was offering), and the body is then discovered by the community. The play is structured as a combination of episodic moments from the village community and a chorus of farmers, who narrate and comment upon events. Lots of ingredients of past Cornish drama are found in the text. Much of the chorus is versified, while the lead characters often self-introduce in the style of the mummers' plays. This is exemplified in the Cornu-English reflections of the lead character, Archie Gross:

> Archie Gross, you'm a lucky man. You set out this mornin' with nothin' more in mind 'n' a handsome bucket fulla cockles, and here y'are returnin' 'ome with a cartload a dead body! Hero a the parish! I'll have 'em all yakkin'. An' Mrs May steamin' like a silage pit for lettin' a dead body through her toes while jabbin' for a cockle beneath the iron bridge. She think she'm the big I am, but who found the body?[346]

If Darke's imagining of Cornwall is based on the iron bridge near Padstow, then in him, and in the voices of Stock, and Rawe we witness a proliferation of drama growing out of this community. Padstow has always been a centre-point of festival, but during this phase was going through some of the most extreme socio-economic changes in Cornwall. If drama comes from turmoil and change, then Padstow might well be predicted as the place where a cultural-geographic drama of Cornwall would arise. In Darke's work then, that prediction has come true. Also, Darke's imitation of Cornu-English seems very accurate. It is not the 'preserved' dialect of previous generations, but the lived voice of working-class Cornwall. This marks Darke's work as important. Likewise, in this drama, we witness a combination of several dramatic trends and continuities. The chorus of farmers is derived directly from the Athenian influence on pan-European drama, while the focus on parish, community and landscape draws down a theatrical energy that is quasi-medieval. The piece also demonstrated that a Cornish community could have a direct engagement with the wider concerns of the cold war.

Echoes of this drama are also found in Darke's first large-scale community project in Cornwall. This was *The Earth Turned Inside Out*, from 1984.[347] The piece was commissioned by Restormel Borough Council as an attempt to involve professional, amateur and educational theatre groups from the area in one large-scale project. Again, this was drawing on older notions of community drama in Cornwall. The piece eventually developed was performed at Penrice School, and demonstrates the rivalries of two Cornish copper-mining communities in 1815. Other work in the 1980s included *Bud* (1985, Royal Shakespeare Company), a play that considered the relationship between Bud and his wife on a farm, drawing on Darke's own childhood on a farm. *The Oven Glove Murders* in 1986 was, according to some critics, an acerbic attack on British cinema. In *The Dead Monkey* (1986, Royal Shakespeare Company), the interest in American themes comes to the fore in a drama about a childless Californian couple.[348]

Described by Darke as 'a parable of capitalism', and how in past Cornwall 'fortunes were made and lost at the swing of a pick',[349] *Ting Tang Mine* (1987, for the National Theatre) was effectively a reworking of the earlier commission of *The Earth Turned Inside Out*. Darke simplified the numbers of the cast, but kept the rivalry. The play stands as one of the best dramatic depictions of the mining industry in Cornwall. This drama also defined Darke's approach as a dramatist. He tends to eschew use of the monologue, but favours fast-paced stichomythic dialogue, which runs from voice to voice and character to character, so that the audience listen to the whole as a chorus, rather than individual dialogue. Given the numbers involved in the original production, this seems entirely logical. Such a cast also allowed Darke to bring out the various voices of the community, and to show that mining is not the rosy-tinted spectacle that tourism preferred to present. Fast-paced transitions, interjections of song, and often a concern with Methodism (through hard-line Cornu-English) are core ingredients of the drama:

Trefusis: Christ in hell thass some oath Tom. Thass an oath not to be broke Tom. Ezekiel woulda sent em off, or the Booka Job. Revelation? Thass a desperate oath Tom. Christ in hell Tom, thass some oath.

Tom *goes*.

Trefusis (sings)

Thomas May and his son Arthur
Dig cathedrals underground,
They wield their cross and mitre
Where copper can be found.
Their reward is not in heaven,
But closer down to hell,

Where night is everlasting
And the devil rings the bell.[350]

As well as the fluctuating conditions of the market, the drama also notes the trans-national aspect of Cornish life (a theme also considered later in the work of Thomas, and Kent). Darke realised that this aspect of Cornwall's history needed showing on the stage. Interestingly, this also matched the concerns during this phase of young people in Cornwall who, without economic prospects, or a university in Cornwall, were forced to cross the River Tamar in order to study or work. Darke's central characters debate the possibilities, with echoes of the economic situation in real twentieth-century Cornwall, dominated by Thatcherite political decisions and further industrial decline:

Tom:	I'm too old for that.
Gran:	Too old? You're forty-four! You're a captain now, you'd make a damn fortune. They're cryin out for mine captains in the Americas.
Arthur:	If Jan can do it so can we. Think what he was like before e left…[351]

Ting Tang Mine was also produced by Kneehigh Theatre in 1990, directed and designed by Bill Mitchell. This was, in effect, the starting point of their liaison and work together throughout the 1990s; Darke's drama neatly fitted into Mike Shepherd's vision of Cornish international theatre. In the established performers of Kneehigh at this time (Giles King, Sue Hill, Anna Maria Murphy, Jim Carey, Charles Barnecut, Dave Mynne and Mary Woodvine), Darke found an established ensemble who would breath Cornu-English life and physicality into his work. By the end of the 1980s, Darke had initially steered his work away from Cornish themes. We see this in dramas such as *A Place called Mars* (1988, Colway Theatre Trust), *The Campesinos* (1989, the Royal Shakespeare Company), and *Kissing the Pope* (1989, the Royal Shakespeare Company). The latter play was set in revolutionary South America. Revolution also formed the theme of his reworking of Sophocles' *Antigone*, *Hell's Mouth* (1992, Royal Shakespeare Company), featuring a dystopic world in which Cornish nationalist revolutionaries fight for independence from England. Here, Darke's 'performing devolution' became part of his wider project, combined with a growing politicality within his work. The 1990s saw the collaboration with Kneehigh Theatre expand, in such productions as *Hell's Mouth*, *Danger My Ally* (an eco-themed play that they toured in 1993) and *The Bogus* (1994). In 1997 Darke retold the notorious aluminium sulphate water-poisoning incident at Camelford, in north Cornwall as *The Man with Green Hair* (1997, Bristol Old Vic). Darke will forever be remembered in Cornwall for two dramas that demonstrated how far Anglo-Cornish drama had come during this phase: *The King of Prussia* (1996), a combined work with the Theatre Royal Plymouth and Kneehigh Theatre; and *The Riot* (2000), a Kneehigh Theatre production at the National Theatre.

In *The King of Prussia*, Darke chose to examine traditional Cornish subject matter that had been depicted on stage as far back as the eighteenth century, retelling the story of the famous Cornish free-traders and smugglers, John Carter (1736-1807) and Harry Carter (1749-1809). 'Survival on the periphery' was an issue not only for the Carter brothers, but also for the contemporary audience watching the production. In John Carter, to use Smelt's term, we see a 'moral paradox'[352] for while he was a smuggler, he was also a God-fearing man. This gave Darke a complex character to explore. Harry Carter's autobiography also proved inspiring for Darke,[353] detailing the language, concerns and wiles of the era, which the playwright successfully uses in the dramaturgy. Here, the 'Robin Hood' figure of John Carter is contrasted with the by-the-book leanings of the Revenue in the shape of John Knill. The high energy of Darke's writing has no better example than the following sequence:

Carter:	How many ports?
Captain:	Eight.
Carter:	'Colour's is bulwarks?
Captain;	Yellow and black.
Carter:	Dark gaff tops'l?
Captain:	Yes,
Carter:	Jib?
Captain:	White.
Carter:	Tis the Revenue.
Captain:	Bearing down fast.
Carter:	I gotta brother imprisoned in France, a two undred tonner in pound and to cap it all ere come that bastard John Knill.
Knill:	God dammit John Carter!
Carter:	E dun't patrol Mount's Bay whass the bastard doin ere?[354]

Directed by Mike Shepherd, and with a set featuring ship paraphernalia and a moving yard-arm, the production brought a breathless charm to its imagining of this period of Cornish history. John Carter was played by another mainstay of Kneehigh Theatre during this phase – Tristan Sturrock, who was to front

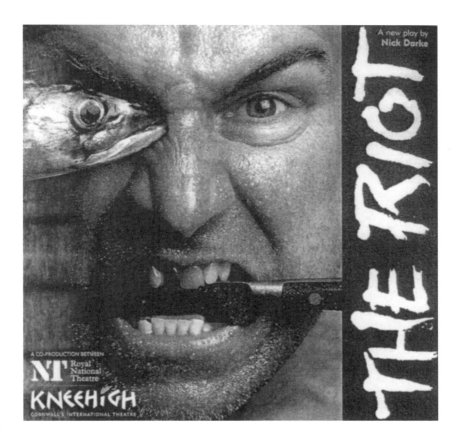

Fig. 118. Programme cover for Kneehigh Theatre's production of Nick Darke's *The Riot* at the National Theatre, in 1999. Courtesy of the National Theatre.

many of the productions in the late 1990s and the early twenty-first century (notably taking the lead in *Brief Encounter*). Bessie Bussoe (played by Bec Applebee) is another extremely well-drawn character, a kind of archetypal Cornish woman who takes no prisoners, and whom Darke is particularly good at imagining. The marine biologist John Stackhouse provides a scientific foil to the Methodist apocalyptic visions mentioned elsewhere. In *The King of Prussia*, we witness a fusion of writing and performance that is perhaps hard to match in contemporary Cornish theatre.

The Riot also drew upon this method of working, and Kneehigh Theatre's strong ensemble work. The riots at Newlyn over Sunday observance had already been examined in the work of Simon Parker (see below), but Darke's version tells events from the perspective of Thomas Bolitho, a merchant, magistrate, mine owner and mayor. In essence, this is typical Darke character-isation, where one individual has conflicting interests in the community and must try to take the right course of action. In this, Darke appears to see something of the peculiar nature of Cornish lives, where individuals must multi-role in order to survive. For example, at the end of the play, we see Bolitho contemplating an economic future: 'Broccoli's took a dive in this heat, plant mangles! Tin drops, invest in pilchards'.[355] The millennial moment of its production also comes to the fore in the observations of Mrs Triggs, who notes: 'I held me own in this kitchen. But with a fresh century comin on there's no better time to flee the nest'.[356] Again stichomythic one-liner dialogue is the main-stay of the work; the Cornu-English again not of the 'preservative' kind, but matching the way Cornish people spoke at the end of the twentieth-century. All told, *The Riot* is the natural climax of Darke's career, in that it combines several of his most lasting themes and concerns: community, the maritime world and the lives of ordinary people trying to get by. In texts like this, and *The King of Prussia*, Darke was able to show that Cornish-themed drama could not only have an impact in Cornwall itself, but could also appeal to wider audiences. This was nothing new in Cornish theatre, but Darke was able to transcend the Tamar in the modern era.

Throughout his career, many of Darke's plays were also converted for radio broadcast, but separate dramas were also developed for the specific medium of radio. Among these were *Gone Fishing* (1998), *Bawcock's Eve* (1999, a mystery story set in Mousehole in late December), *Flotsam and Jetsam* (1999, the story of family in Porthnant Bay), *Underground* (2000, a docu-drama featuring the voices of Cornish tin miners and their families), *The Fisherman's Tale* (2000, part of a radio celebration of the 600th anniversary of Chaucer's death, and featuring a group of travellers stuck in a motorway service station) and *Hooked* (2005, about a Cornish couple who are asked for advice by a Londoner on how to catch a sea bass). As well as being a playwright, Darke was also a writer, poet, lobster fisherman, environmentalist, beachcomber and film-maker. One of his last works was the documentary *The Wrecking Season* (2004),[357] which documented the lives of Cornish beachcombers, while his legacy as a writer has been considered by his wife, the painter Jane Spurway, in her film *The Art of Catching Lobsters* (2007).[358] In a moving audio diary, *Dumbstruck* (2003), Darke explored with brave humour how his speech was impaired after suffering a stroke.

Darke's final play, *Laughing Gas* (2005) – concerning the life of scientist and poet Sir Humphry Davy – was left unfinished at the time of his death. Completed posthumously by the Cornish actor and playwright Carl Grose, it was eventually toured by the Truro-based production company o-region.[359] This text followed the trend in Anglo-Cornish drama for exploring historical figures. Davy was also a remarkable figure, perhaps representative of the two faces of Cornwall: as a poet, he embodied the romantic, peripheral nature of Cornwall; as a scientist, he symbolised the practical, down-to-earth aspect of Cornish life, and the centuries of success in the fields of mining, engineering and research. This tension is explored in the drama, and also found in the wider work of Darke. In this latter part of his career, Darke was also considering a stage adaptation of John Angarrack's revelatory book *Breaking the Chains*.[360] This could perhaps have been one of the most successful expressions of 'performing devolution' in this phase; Angarrack alluded to his regret that this drama did not happen.[361] Such was Darke's impact on modern theatre in Cornwall, that it is hard to imagine the landscape without his work. No doubt the legacy of his dramatic work will continue to grow. We have yet to see a full volume of his collected works.

Indeed, the late 1990s, when Darke was active in Cornwall, appeared to be a particularly creative time for Anglo-Cornish drama. A significant text was *Where Are You Gone, Jimmy Trevenna?* (1996) by Simon Turley.[362] Turley is not Cornish by birth, but has an affinity with the territory. He was born in Bristol in 1958, and grew up in Somerset, eventually reading English at the University of Cambridge. In the 1980s, hoping to work in Cornwall, he took up a teaching post at Eggbuckland School in Plymouth, and worked there for some twenty years, leaving to write professionally, and teach part-time at Plymouth's Ridgeway School. Liaison with the Barbican Theatre in Plymouth allowed Turley to develop many theatre-in-education projects, while more recently he has become a pioneer of work linking drama to developments in science and bio-technology.[363] *Where Are You Gone, Jimmy Trevenna?* was premiered at Eggbuckland School (in itself interesting, since it is rare for a Cornu-centric text to be performed in Plymouth, especially in a school), and was later revived in 2001 by the Young Company at the Theatre Royal in Plymouth – subsequently also being produced at the 2003 Edinburgh Festival by the Trevenna Theatre Company and, in 2008, at the Ridgeway School. Turley's text has not been published, and this may be one reason why the work is not very well known in Cornwall. Set during the First World War, the play considers the impact of the conflict on a small fishing community in Cornwall called St Nevin. Turley well understands aspects of Cornish difference. In a very telling scene at the beginning of the play, the character David encounters Kitty Trevenna in the 'horn of strangers':

Lucy:	They aren't strangers to us.
David:	And, to be sure, I think I never saw a more handsome couple than your brother and that striking girl.
Tim:	Now, now.
Lucy:	Kitty Trevenna.
David:	Trevenna! Even the names here are spiky with poetry![364]

This is exquisite and adept writing, demonstrating Turley's concern with the insider/outsider theme familiar in much post-war Anglo-Cornish writing, and also a sensitivity and understanding of space and place – somewhat ironic, as the play has yet to be performed in Cornwall itself. Turley is perhaps less comfortable imagining a Cornu-English linguistic world: the characters tend to speak in Standard English. However, issues of identity are at the forefront of the thematic concerns of the play, as seen in this sequence:

David:	But what an extraordinary thing to say.
Maria:	What?
David:	He said that he couldn't claim to be Cornish.
Tim:	That's right.
David:	You were born here, weren't you?
Lucy:	And our father was born here too.
David:	What more do they want![365]

The 'they' here is the Cornish. Just as it was being dramatised, such a debate over Cornish identity was then entering the academy.[366] As can be seen from these sequences, Turley's style is very fast-paced; characters rarely give monologues. As in Darke's work, we are 'shown' rather than 'told' in his work. Inevitably, the opening scenes look at life in the village before the war (exploring the bizarre sport of 'cow-tipping'), while the later scenes look at events after the conflict has begun, contrasting innocence and experience.[367] The concept of 'tipping' also facilitates the Cornish characters use of this as a metaphor for getting their own back on imperial oppression: it is the empire writing back at the English. Jimmy's encounter with an angel ordains him as special: and following a kiss from the angel, he is set on the tragic trajectory of his life's course.

Turley integrates moments of Cornish language. Despite it being historically inaccurate, the teacher Nancy has a dispute over her wish to teach the children Cornish.[368] The cultural-nationalist position is embodied in the character of Albert, who while out fishing with Jimmy swears that he hears 'the ghost of An Gof I warrant... An Gof come agathering us up to go and tip the English...'[369] Such imaginings of Cornwall may well be unrealistic, but this perhaps does not matter: Turley is reinventing a Cornwall where cultural nationalism is realisable, or at least felt. The transitional device of the village hall dance allows Turley to have a large ensemble on stage, while the conflict ('You know as well as I it *is* an English war.'[370]) is created with tableaux and sound effects. Ironically – given this environment of the village hall – Turley's piece would completely suit the kind of touring theatre that had been established in Cornwall in the post-war period. Turley's text is, however, ambitious. At its best, one sees the true possibilities of contemporary theatre about Cornwall. For example, at Jimmy's death, when the Angel and Jimmy talk in Cornish and in English:

Jimmy:	Thought I might get away with Cornish. But you swims like a seal in every language.
Angel:	*Pengevig osta* [You're a prince], Jimmy Trevanna.[371])

Turley's writing is not well known but his voice is as significant as any from this period.

1997 – the 500th anniversary of the 1497 Cornish Rebellion – proved a very important year in 'performing devolution', commemorated by a walk and re-enactment from St Kerverne to Blackheath in London.[372] Emerging as a dramatist in this period was Simon Parker. Parker has great importance as a writer in the late twentieth and early twenty-first centuries: he worked as journalist for *The Western Morning News* newspaper, more recently editing its specific Cornish section, titled 'Living Cornwall', which enabled him to feature articles about Cornu-centric theatre and drama. Before his career as a journalist, Parker was the lead singer with late 1970s' Penzance punk band The Vendettas. In addition to these musical and journalistic careers, Parker was also operating as an important dramatist in the period. His first major endeavour was the duologue *A Star on the Mizzen*, which emerged in 1997. Conceived as a drama, and performed by Parker and his friend Jonathan Plunkett,[373] the piece (as I have argued elsewhere) set 'a new agenda and standard for Cornu-English dialect literature'.[374] Like Darke's *The Riot*, Parker was inspired by the thoughts of one of the imagined ringleaders of Newlyn fishermen, who in 1896 refused to go to sea on Sundays. Their livelihoods were threatened by Sabbath-breaking English crews from the East Coast, and in May of that year, more than 300 armed troops of the Royal Berkshire Regiment were stationed on the streets on Newlyn, while three navy gunboats patrolled Mount's Bay. Events culminated in pitched battles being fought on the promenade. Given the historic significance of 1997, it is perhaps not surprising that Parker chose to depict on stage a battle between Cornwall and England. Parker's duologue required only a stark stage set with very few properties; language alone created the atmosphere:

> We should ha' just stanked on over the top of 'en but instead we hesitated and squared up. Some of the boys starting linging stones and ellins and when one well aimed bully caught Nicholas on the chacks and scat 'en over, that was it… We soon scattered and retreated to the Esplanade. There were whacks injured.[375]

Parker's work has been influenced by his promotion and celebration of the Anglo-Cornish writings of Charles Lee, considered by him and K.C. Phillipps as one of the best literary imitators of Cornu-English.[376] Parker has continued to be a significant literary force in Cornwall, working as one of the storytellers from the group *Scavel an Gow*, and also helping to publish an anthology of their writings. *Scavel an Gow* means a 'Bench of Lies' and the collective show a 'strong sense of place and a diversity of styles'.[377] Interestingly, this project saw a combination of work from some of the leading theatrical writers and practitioners of the phase, including Anna Maria Murphy, Mercedes Kemp and Amanda Harris (all connected to Kneehigh Theatre), Pauline Sheppard (an experienced performer and writer in her own right), Stephen Hall (a musician, actor and arts activist), and Paul Farmer (a film-maker and writer). Many of the narratives and monologues from this group embody a style of writing, which was perhaps established by Charles Lee, and developed by Parker in this phase. Parker's work was to come to fuller fruition in the new millennium with his editorship of a literary journal, *Scryfa* [*Writing*],[378] carrying both Anglo-Cornish and Cornish writing (though, perhaps due to space, not much drama), as well as his anthology of twenty-five short stories, *Full as an Egg* (2006),[379] and his longer drama from the same year, *Seven Stars: A Cornish Christmas Play for Voices*.[380] This drama saw Parker apply the Cornu-English writing of the previous years to a longer and more ambitious piece of work, which stands solidly as a kind of Cornish *Under Milk Wood*. Here, Parker was perhaps extending and developing the continuum of the Cornish Christmas play in new ways. The play is about 'Christmas backalong' where 'allegiances were not built along blood lines but guided and steered by far deeper motives, such as quality of gifts, unwavering kindness and the ability to pass on a good yarn – the weirder the better'.[381] A strong sense of place and time is created, drawing on Parker's own childhood Christmas experiences some thirty years earlier. The text is divided into thematic sections titled Mizzle, Chuffa, Pop, Aunt Sophe, A Geek, Praze, Grunt, In Turd, Uggie, and Tissue Paper. Within these sections walk characters such as Little Eli, First Voice, Billy Ough, Granfer, Jimmy Jampot, Dicky Dido, Johnny Bash, Hedley and Bazooka Joe. In this vignette of Cornish life, Bill Ough and Little Eli discuss Chuffa:

Billy Ough:	Chuffa was Aunt Porthia's little boy. Chuffa shunned toys, preferring to play with a large cardboard box, where he spent all his days…
Chuffa:	Imagining…
Little Eli:	There was a hole in the side of the box, into which Aunt Porthia would insert a straw so he could drink…[382]

In this way, Parker is able to link the voices of the characters, but also time-travel between sequences, as the memories and events collate and collide with each other. The overlapping and continuity of expression make for a dramaturgy which imagines the busy atmosphere of a Cornish Christmas. The narratives also steer in different directions, as in this commentary on the life of Uncle Hank:

First Voice:	And here comes Uncle Hank.
Little Eli:	Real name Gary.
First Voice:	Who had thick, hairy sideboards almost to his chin and ran a second-hand shop in Redruth called
Davy Isaacs:	Zephyr
First Voice:	Which sold items he deemed to be…
Uncle Hank:	Cool.
First Voice:	Such as…
Jacey Blimmer:	Formica furniture
Jimmy Jampot:	Astro lamps.
Davy Isaacs:	78rpm records that played from the inside out.
Jack Tussey:	And old, well-thumbed copies of *Parade* magazine.[383]

This is great writing, which, though intrinsically Cornish, is able to consider wider issues in society. Clearly, although these thematic concerns had markedly altered, the notion and concept of Christmas drama in Cornwall was still alive and well in Parker's work. The conceptual application of Parker's drama 'performing devolution' was then realised more fully when the community of Perranporth commissioned him to rewrite the annual performance of a drama based on the life of St Piran, which took place on the Sunday closest to St Piran's Day. Although a drama had already been shaped by the community since 2000, Parker was able to develop a new, more focused approach to the saint's life, simply titled *Piran* – the latest retelling in a continuum that probably started with a now lost medieval drama, and continued with Donald R. Rawe's *The Trials of St Piran*, some thirty-five years earlier in 1971. Parker's text of the play has yet to be published, but given the rise in national consciousness in Cornwall – in particular since events of 1997 – it is peculiarly apt that he should have written this drama at this moment in Cornish history. Parker had also written the documentary book of the 1497-1997 celebrations.[384] One senses that Parker has more stories to tell, and his place in the front-rank of contemporary dramatists in Cornwall is guaranteed.

A sometime collaborator with Parker was Jonathon Plunkett, an actor, writer and Head of Drama at Callington Community College. Born in 1963, he had grown up with Parker in Penzance, then studied at Lancaster University and Bretton Hall. Although not as prolific as Parker, Plunkett had understood the need to present a dramatic imagining of the events of 1497, and produced a script telling the lives of Michael Joseph 'An Gof' and Thomas Flamank. Like Parker, Plunkett was embracing the need to perform devolution to new audiences in Cornwall; such was the nation-shaping significance of the blacksmith's story. Perhaps obviously, there was only one title that was apt for this work: *A Name Perpetual.*[385] The work was conceived at a time when many publications were reconsidering the narrative.[386] Plunkett's difficulty was not only trying to tell such an epic story in a couple of hours of stage time, but also being able to offer detailed enough characterisation of the central roles. The solution the dramatist employed was to offer Choral voices to accelerate the narrative and guarantee the neccesary changes in locale:

Chorus One: Days and weeks passed and those left behind in Cornwall heard nothing from those who had left them.

Chorus Two: Unknown to them, the march was moving ever eastwards, through Devon into Somerset.

Chorus Three: In every town Joseph and Flamank spoke to the ordinary men and women, and in very town and village more and more marchers joined the peaceful throng.

Chorus One: By the time the march reached the Wiltshire town of Salisbury their number had risen to as many as six thousand...

Chorus Two: Who knows what thoughts went through the minds of the men of Lannaghaveran?[387]

Unlike Parker, Plunkett used little Cornu-English (perhaps feeling the need to compromise realism in favour of clarity of narrative – especially working with younger actors). However, the political intent of the play is kept; Plunkett was uncompromising in terms of identity-raising back home in Cornwall. In the battle at Blackheath, a soldier steps forward to describe what he saw, using language to explore difference in a way that would perhaps have been inconceivable a few years earlier:

At first all I could see were the arrows from our archers like a hard rain falling on the English. Wave after wave of them. It seemed as if they were doing well, they were holding the English back at least. We were high up on the Black Heath. It was difficult to see what we were supposed to be doing, we knew we were waiting for that Lord Audley to give us a signal, but no-one knew what the signal was. Michael told us in advance, and then the Lawyer told us to stay. No-one seemed to know anything. A little group of us Helston men took it into our heads to move down the hill 'cos it looked like a lot of our archers were getting cut down. By the time we did set off there was a huge army of English coming up the hill towards us with the King's colours right in the middle of it. I saw an Englishman on horse bear down on me, he raised his sword, brought it down and everything went black.[388]

Politically, Cornwall's consciousness had been raised, and such plays were reflecting a wider realisation of the 'cheating', 'lies' and 'propaganda' that had seemingly been force-fed to a generation of dramatists who were more than willing to challenge them. By now, drama in Cornwall had developed a political edge that had been bubbling under in the pre-war period, but could now exhort writers to express their dissent. Plunkett, Parker and, as we shall see later, Kent, began mounting a direct challenge to the establishment and using drama to promote their dissatisfaction. Collusion with the model of Britain as promoted by the 'county' system was no longer appropriate for a Cornwall that was rattling its cage for devolved power. Although *A Name Perpetual* has not been performed professionally, it did form one of the many

Fig. 119. Programme cover of Shiva Theatre's *Meryasek*, 1980.

dramas and reenactments along the route and time period of the march.[389] In many ways, it deserves publication and wider incorporation into the modern canon – perhaps especially as a text to be performed within schools and colleges, institutions that often eschew Cornu-centric work.

Also significant during this phase is the work of Pauline Sheppard. Sheppard had worked in the field of the arts in Cornwall for a number of years, living and working there since 1972. From 1997 to 2003, she was the arts development officer for Penwith District Council. She later went on to found and run the Penzance-based Bash Street Theatre Company – a group specialising in educational work and physical theatre – and has also worked as the director of the Cornish Theatre Company.[390] Sheppard is a consummate writer and the author of a number of theatrical and radio works. One of the first companies that she was involved in was Shiva Theatre, who in 1980 toured a play titled *Meryasek*.[391] The company had been asked to participate in the International Berlin Festival, and wished to present a Cornish mystery play. Although *Meryasek* is credited to the company, Sheppard's input into its construction was important. The play was an interesting adaptation of two of Cornwall's historical texts: *Bewnans Meriasek* and the *Ordinalia*. Here, the company took elements of the Meriasek narrative (Sylvester and the Dragon, and Teudar of Cornwall), but combined them with some of the episodes from 'Origo Mundi'. These were Adam and Seth, Abraham and Isaac, and David and Uriah. 'Meryasek' operates as a storyteller, linking the whole narrative. Sheppard herself performed in this piece, taking the roles of the Duke of Cornwall, the Angel, Bathsheba and the Messenger to Teudar. The company was completed by David Shaw, Simon Uren, Philip Jacobs and Mike Shepherd (who was by then in the process of forming Kneehigh Theatre). *Meryasek* was directed by David Gilpin. Considering that the last major revival of the traditional canon (bar Rawe's *The Creation of the World*) was in 1969, Shiva's vision of *Meryasek* was important. The 'mining' of older texts for new imaginings of Cornish experience was pioneered in this kind of work, which was to become a staple of both Kneehigh Theatre and Sheppard's writing over the next few decades. The printed programme that accompanied Shiva Theatre's *Meryasek* draws heavily on Celtic ideology, showing a wheel headed cross and Celtic knotwork, which was, in essence, highly 'revivalist' in feel.[392] Although this iconography was apt for this work, both Pauline Sheppard and Mike Shepherd, ever looking forward, realised that this would not do for the future world of theatre in Cornwall. Hence, these practitioners have made no attempt to match this image with their theatrical vision. This is significant, for it suggests that contemporary Cornish and Anglo-Cornish theatre was strong enough to survive without the need to pander to revivalism, or outmoded pan-Celticism.

Among Sheppard's theatre works are another adaptation of *The Life of St Meriaesk* (1983, this time retitled *Meriasek* and presumably developing the earlier version), *Alice in Wonderland* (1987, for the Minack Theatre), *Alice Through the Looking Glass* (1988. for the Acorn Theatre, Penzance), *The Three Musketeers* (1997, Minack), *Badger's Cross* (1990, Acorn), *Heads* (1991, Cornwall Theatre Company), *Dogs* (1992, Cornwall Theatre Company), *Off the Rails* (1994, Kneehigh Theatre and Trust New Writing), *The Round Seat* (1998, Cornwall Promoters' Consortium), *Jonathan* (2005), and the aforementioned *The Zig Zag Way* (2007).[393] Sheppard has been able to balance work as an adapter of 'universally appealing narratives' with more Cornu-centric work. In her work, we see a close parallel to the themes and ways of working of the medieval period: universal issues with a Cornish context. For example, she has completed adaptations of texts such as *The Wind in the Willows* (1985, Minack), *Tom Sawyer* (1988, Minack),[394] and a highly Cornu-centric adaptation of Edward Bosanketh's 1888 novel, *Tin*[395] (1993, for Verbal Arts Cornwall). The mining theme continued in later work, with the drama *Tin & Fishes*, part of a 2005 St Just Regeneration and World Heritage Site project. Meanwhile, Bash Street Theatre continued to contribute to community events and educational projects, presenting *The Hunchback* in 1987. Her version of *The Railway Children* was also presented at the Palace Theatre, Redditch in 1996. Sheppard's significance is that she is one of the few female playwrights and theatre animateurs of Cornwall. Her breakthrough and most critically-acclaimed work was the 1996 play *Dressing Granite* (starring David Shaw),[396] which explored the theme of Alzheimer's, and went on to win the Meyer-Whitworth Award. The plot concerns a stonemason called Ben, who works in a Cornish quarry. He is awkward and forgetful, and soon the truth is revealed about his condition. Ben remembers previous times in his life, when Cornwall was a more innocent place, but his son is more ambitious, and must balance caring for his father and making a life for himself. Sheppard's script offers off-beat brilliance in its evocation of both contemporary and past Cornwall.

In the autumn of 1997, she also adapted a version of the Charles Lee story, *Our Little Town*,[397] which toured venues in St Ives, Phillack, Penzance, St Just, Zennor, Newlyn and Wadebridge. According to Parker: 'it was presented as a play for voices with a few hand props'.[398] This brought to the work the kind of dramatic effect that Nance had intended for Cornish audiences. The cast included Sheppard herself, David Shaw, Grevis Williams, Rik Williams, Dawn Barnes, Dave Trahair, Julia Twomlow, Stephen Hall, Stephanie Hayward and Anna Maria Murphy, with music by John Bickersteth, Neil McPhail and Mick McLeod. The work was revived again in 1999. Shaw's contribution to Sheppard's work has been considerable, and he is a major

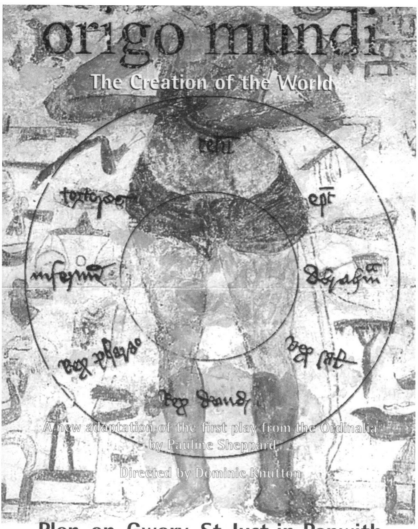

Plen-an-Gwary, St Just in Penwith
Thursday 14th - Sunday 17th September

Fig. 120. Flyer for *Origo Mundi: The Creation [sic] of the World*, at St Just in Penwith, 2000.

presence in the acting community in Cornwall, notably playing the role of the 'mock mayor' on Mazey Day in Penzance which truly connects Bakhtin-Barber 'carnival theory' with present day festival-theatrical culture in Cornwall. After Kent moved his millennial verse translation of the *Ordinalia* away from The Ordinalia Trust (working instead with Benjamin Luxon and Lyn Le Grice), Sheppard then assumed the task of adapting Nance's translation of the *Ordinalia* for production in St Just-in-Penwith. These were 'Origo Mundi' in 2000, 'The Passion' in 2001, 'The Resurrection' in 2002 and the full cycle of the *Ordinalia* in 2004.[399] In 2008, the Arthur Quiller-Couch Fund announced that Sheppard had gained funding from them for a new drama, provisionally titled *Hedge*.[400] Pauline Sheppard and Anna Maria Murphy are Cornwall's most significant female playwrights of the modern era.

In 2004, in an unusual departure from his established choices of writing (poetry and fiction), the Redruth-born Anglo-Cornish poet and novelist D.M. Thomas (b.1935) developed his first piece of stage drama, based on the life of the Cornish rugby player Bert Solomon. This play was titled *Hell Fire Corner*.[401] Thomas attended Trewirgie Primary School and Redruth School, and then graduated with First Class Honours from New College, Oxford in 1959.[402] He has encountered the culture of being a 'Cornishman abroad', having worked in Australia and the United States before returning to Cornwall to live in Truro. Thomas began his career with poetry, but established his reputation by writing the psycho-analytical-themed novel *The White Hotel*, which was published in 1981.[403] He has also continued to translate Russian poetry, and has remained fascinated with Russian culture.[404] Thomas's style of fiction is, in some ways, an extension of the post-modern narrative poetry he has written, presenting literary texts as collaborations and improvisations on established themes. Most of his fiction is set outside of Cornwall, and follows the themes established by *The White Hotel*. An exception is *Birthstone* (1980) which has a highly Cornu-centric storyline, being a narrative based around the Men-an-tol holed stone.[405] Thomas' poetry, meanwhile, often integrates Cornish themes and issues of identity.[406] Both Kent, and Nicol have offered critical studies of Thomas's importance in the Anglo-Cornish canon, and in the wider canon of post-modernist literature.[407] By the turn of the millennium, Thomas had returned to more Cornu-centric work, with his novel *Charlotte*[408] (having a connection to the Brontës' Penzance heritage[409]), while his acclaimed volume of verse, *Dear Shadows* (2004, his first since 1992[410]) was a study of his Cornish family and community. The volume also contains a poem based on the life of Solomon:

> How for example,
> Bert Solomon, in the Edwardian twilight,
> climbed up the interminable ladders
> of Crofty, saw to his carrier pigeons,
> which were more to him than rugby,
> took the Friday night milk-train
> to London, then with his mercurial grace
> phantomed through the Welsh
> to win the match for England...[411]

Thomas had expressed to the author some ten years earlier his wish to document the life of Bert Solomon,[412] but it was perhaps not expected to be a drama. Bert Solomon (1885-1961) was a Cornish rugby union player who competed in the 1908 Summer Olympics at the White City Stadium, London, and played for Redruth Rugby Football Club.[413] He also played some twenty-six times for Cornwall. Having been capped for England against Wales in 1910, Solomon, being a solitary, unconventional character, declined further selections, as well as a tour with the British and Irish Lions to Australia and New Zealand. Thomas's play indicates that several factors caused him to decline the invitation to play at this level. At that time in England, rugby was still the sport of the upper classes, and Solomon did not fit the set of values, nor their accent: what Thomas poetically describes as 'left the toffs – public school, Oxbridge – panting far behind, gasping'.[414] But Solomon's story is conceived not only in terms of class but also along more quasi-nationalistic lines. He felt uncomfortable playing outside of Cornwall, and for an English side with whom he had little in common, hence his rejection of the caps. Solomon was also known to be devoted to his pigeons, sometimes missing matches if they did not return. He was certainly an intriguing figure; Thomas rightly saw his dramatic potential as a representation of the Cornish condition.

Several events collided to ensure the moment of production for this text. First of all, although there was a strong rugby playing and watching tradition in the Redruth-Camborne conurbation, this aspect of Cornish cultural life had been given renewed vigour in the early 1990s by Cornwall's win over Yorkshire at Twickenham in 1991.[415] Not only was this a spectacular success for Cornish rugby football, but in the thousands of Cornish people crammed into Twickenham for the 'County' [sic] championship, this was also a display of national pride. With rugby so topical, Solomon was the quintessential figure to imagine in a new Cornish drama. The 2004 *Dehwelans / Homecoming* event would also ensure a ready and Cornu-centric audience who might relish the prospect of a new kind of sophisticated drama which explored narratives from a Cornish point of view. Thomas himself had been a highly successful international writer, but there had been critical calls for him to celebrate his Cornishness more explicitly in his writing.[416] The story of Solomon was the perfect vehicle for this, with Thomas employing his deft characterisation to new effect on the stage. A unique collaboration emerged between the Hall for Cornwall in Truro, and Mundic Nation, a production company formed by Marie and John Macneill.[417] Promoted by a tag-line that 'Inspiration can be found in the most unlikely places', the drama opened on Thursday 24 April, and ran until Saturday 8 May 2004. It was directed by Marie Macneill.[418] Most of the cast assembled for the production had Cornish origins or connections but were working in pan-British theatre and television. A notable exception was Stephen Hall, who played Dr Lawry. Hall was an important choice for this role because he had toured in many village-hall productions in Cornwall, and had also been a leading architect of the revived Golowan Festival in Penzance.[419] Hall gave his role a Cornu-English gravitas rarely experienced on the mainstream stage in Cornwall. The other performers also worked hard to establish convincing Cornu-English voices. Designers Alan Munden and Jude Munden were able to realise Thomas's ambitious ideas – a wooden derrick, and a rugby pitch – into a workable set.[420] The involvement of Redruth-born musician Al Hodge (1951-2006), one of Cornwall's most iconic and most successful professional musicians,[421] lent a populist credibility to the production.

The play begins at the surface of a mine, where a visitor to Cornwall, Sir Richard Hargreave, struggles out of the cold shaft. This allows Thomas to contrast the Cornu-English of the community of mine-workers with the observing 'English' character, a 'London toff',[422] predicting later events. Solomon is on-stage, but a silent character, who does not engage in the banter of the others. This marks his difference and importance, but Thomas neatly begins to merge the world of the mine (croustbag) with the sport of rugby, as can be observed in this stage direction:

Alfred *trudges down the ramp.* Solomon *runs behind him; seeing* Alfred, *he holds his croustbag like a rugby ball, runs at him from behind, swerves; and, as he draws level, he dummies to pass the croustbag to him, before running on with it.* Alfred *is so sure the bag has been hurried sideways at him that he lifts his hands to protect himself, stumbles and falls.*[423]

Such detail regarding the technique of playing rugby, as well as its precise physicality, is maintained in the performance. The slow-motion sequences of rugby tackles and runs allow for a graceful and near cinematic depiction of the

Fig. 121. Flyer for D.M. Thomas's *Hell Fire Corner* at the Hall for Cornwall, Truro, 2004.

game. Sound is important in the piece, with incidental music facilitating the segueing of scenes. However, wider identity is reinforced by Thomas incorporating Methodist hymns ('Lead Kindly Light', 'Hark the Glad Sound', and 'When I survey the Wondrous Cross'[424]) and other Anglo-Cornish songs ('Trelawny', 'The White Rose', 'Little Lize' and 'Goin' Up Camborne Hill'), matching the mining-Methodist construct of the play.[425] The play acknowledges the significance of the Cornish overseas: when the text incorporates iconic statements such as 'Johannesburg, that's the capital of Cornwall',[426] it perhaps reflects the new mobilisation of the early twenty-first century Cornish overseas – finding their identity in multi-cultural societies – as much as it evokes this period of Cornish history. This is also brought out in recollections of the 'Cornish nightingale' Fanny Moody singing to Cornish miners in 1896. Jack comments: 'Some crowd there was, you!'[427] It is precisely this kind of dialogue that makes *Hell Fire Corner* important, because it is a script genuinely reflecting the Cornu-English speech of contemporary Cornwall (yet also an imagined and non-romanticised past). Here we see the characteristically high level of realism in Thomas's writing. Amy informs Florrie about an unwanted pregnancy: 'That's what Lizzie's old boyfriend told she! – 'night he got her up the spout behind Carnkie chapel'.[428] In this way, Thomas is able explore taboo subjects in Anglo-Cornish drama – a process also happening in Anglo-Cornish fiction.[429] The device of a rock-fall (a continual motif in Anglo-Cornish writing) allows an investigation 'underground' into the psychology and lives of Jack, Sam and Alfred, the intensity of which contrasts markedly with the fluidity of Solomon's movements and freedom 'above ground'. All of the mining sequences display an implicit lament for a 'dead' industry.

Although the play's focus is on Solomon, other narratives mingle with considerable ease at Redruth Rugby Ground, where 'Hell Fire Corner' itself is to be found.[430] Thus, we witness Dr Lawry, Sam and Jack about to watch a game. This is useful dramaturgy, since it allows commentary on the actions of Solomon on the pitch, whilst allowing the individual characters to reveal their own narratives. Thomas combines this with lewd and hilarious observations about the opposing teams, their fans and the referees. The women in the play are very well drawn, and Thomas's skills as a comic dramatist are foregrounded when Jack and Amy's love-making is likened to making a try. Here, the dialogue captures much about 'Cornishness' and Cornish people's propensity towards humour in any situation, for example segueing from love-making into a rendering of 'Goin' Up Camborne Hill' – a perfect synthesis of contemporary, fast-paced dramaturgy and traditional notions of space and place:

Amy:	What are you thinking about?
Jack:	To be honest, I was wonderin' whether we'd beat Camborne on Saturday.
Amy:	Oh, Jack Trebilcock! For Christsake.
Jack:	Don't swear!
	Kisses her. Strokes her stockings.
Jack:	(*singing*) White Stockings, White Stockings she wore...[431]

The song then merges into it being sung at the rugby ground, thus acting as a choral soundscape for the rest of the play. Interestingly, Thomas realised that Solomon himself would not make a sufficient drama on his own, so the other characters' function is to reinforce the play's central themes. Although the drama is set in the early twentieth century, its depiction of the concerns of the Cornish is very much drawn from the third millennium. By highlighting the wider conflict in South Africa at the start of the twentieth century, Thomas indicates a global awareness that matches international events at the beginning of the twenty-first, thus harmonising 'domestic' Cornwall with its place on a world-wide scale, in both the fictional setting and the real world. This neatly encapsulates what Anglo-Cornish drama needs to do in the future. Although Thomas's depiction never quite moves to a full picture of 'performed devolution' (in the way that Kneehigh Theatre's *Blast!* does), the text is a good example of distinctive Cornish dramaturgy creating a strong theatricality of place. To use Kershaw's term, as a piece of 'cultural intervention'[432] *Hell Fire Corner* does exactly what it is meant to. The climax of the play comes in Act II, when Solomon does not bother to turn up for a game, and Dr Lawry and Florrie go to visit him. Solomon's solitude and care for his pigeons have earlier been juxtaposed with the carnival atmosphere of the May Dance. When the call up for the England squad comes, it is Lawry who encourages him to go. Thomas contrasts Solomon's awkwardness at Twickenham with the confidence of Stoop, the England captain. Despite Solomon's unwillingness to participate further, his achievement is noted with his line, 'I done it'[433] – three words which, put in this context, are highly realistic, and just what such a Cornishman would say.

As it stands, Thomas's drama was something of a one off. Since 2004, he has not developed any further dramas for public view and the Hall for Cornwall has not seen fit to develop any further new writing on the scale of Thomas's and Macneill's ambition. This is one of the failures of the Hall for Cornwall for a generation of Anglo-Cornish and Cornish dramatists. *Hell Fire Corner* demonstrated that audiences craved Cornu-centric work, and the Hall itself stood in a position where it might have truly developed into a theatre for Cornwall equivalent to the Abbey in Dublin or the Sherman in Cardiff.

Lukewarm reviews of the play[434] may perhaps explain why Thomas has not written further drama, and returned to fiction and poetry. This is a pity, because Thomas has an ear for the natural rhythms of Cornu-English speech. *Hell Fire Corner* brought Anglo-Cornish drama to the brink of brilliance, but it was prevented from progressing because the Hall's management apparently preferred to focus on substandard and un-progressive middle-class 'box set' touring plays and tribute bands rather than to develop an audience for indigenous drama. Thomas's vision of Solomon had established the blueprint of historical figures being of supreme interest to contemporary Cornish audiences, and this was to have an influence on later work in the decade. In Thomas himself, we see an undeveloped Anglo-Cornish voice for the theatre. As a text, *Hell Fire Corner* remains enormously important.

I now write as a participant observer, since the dramatic impetus in my own work had been there for a while. My Charles Lee Prize-winning narrative, *Dreaming in Cornish* (1998), was effectively a dramatic monologue written about Edward Lhuyd's visit to Cornwall from the perspective of John Keigwin.[435] My narrative poem *Out of the Ordinalia* (1995) included a conversation with a ghost whom I named 'Glasney', and drew on much of the theatrical continuum of Cornwall. The poem was bi-lingual, with some 500 couplets documenting the years 1497 to 1997:

> 1514 In Latin, Ordinali means 'Prompt Book'
> and this word, into action, has me shook,
> 1515 penning poem on Corpus Christi holiday,
> same time of year then, as play's first display.
> 1516 In this Poem of Days, sky light and sea dark
> cause me to mine deep down into my art.
> 1517 Create in mind's eye, new star-gazy verse.
> With family, friends, and our futures converse.[436]

I was then asked by The Ordinalia Trust to complete a new verse translation of the three plays of *Ordinalia* for performance initially around the time of the solar eclipse in August 1999.[437] Delays in the working practices of the Trust, however, led me to seek other partners with whom to develop the project. The aim in my verse translation of *Ordinalia* was to give the play a true Cornu-English voice, so that a contemporary audience could effectively hear the rhythms and power of the original, yet not have to struggle through the Cornish. This was what Denny had actually wanted in 1969. That said, it was planned that many sections would be delivered initially in Cornish, and then spoken again in translation. The translation process was a massive task, in which I imitated, as far as was feasibly possible, the rhyme schemes of the Cornish text. One of the difficulties of such a translation was finding the right register for a Cornu-centric Jesus. It is perhaps easier to make the Devil sound Cornish:

Eve maid, why dun't 'ee come near
an' speak with me all s'pure?
I do knaw somethin' - 'tis clear
it would delight 'ee for sure.
If you knew 'un, you'd laugh loud
full a' deep mirth I contend;
'zactly like a goddess proud,
and up to Heaven, you'd ascend.[438]

Although this version of the *Ordinalia* has not yet been performed in Cornwall, I have a hope that its full power might one day be realised. In my vision of the project it would move beyond the *plen-an-gwarries* of old (and in the productions at St Just-in-Penwith), and be realised in a new kind of venue, ambitious enough for twenty-first century Cornwall. Imagine, for example, the cycle being performed at the Eden Project, with hexagonal panels forming the structure of Solomon's Temple. Therein, Cornwall might well have a special theatrical event (equivalent maybe to the cycles at York, or at Oberammergau[439]), uniquely connecting space, place and performance: 'Origo Mundi's Eden at Eden', so to speak.

My work as a practitioner in theatre has taken new impetus with the formation of a company with the actor and producer Dean Nolan. Nolan (b.1982) had grown up in Probus, and studied at the Hub Theatre School in St Austell, quickly entering the profession, and touring across Britain and internationally.[440] Like myself, he wanted to develop a more Cornu-centric drama. Our company, BishBashBosh Productions, was assembled in 2006 to deliver a new kind of theatre for Cornwall and elsewhere, which would take Cornu-centric stories as its base, but only select stories that were novel, intriguing and not clichéd.[441] The overt project was to find, in a newly politically-aware Cornwall, a voice for left-field and unusual narratives, often from characters on the fringes of society or who did not fit to type. The company quickly found that figures in Cornish history were worthy of exploration, often offering unique parallels to twenty-first century Cornish experience, but also importantly projecting those figures onto a pan-British and London stage as well. This kind of exploration had, in part, been shaped by companies such as Bedlam and Kneehigh and the work of D.M. Thomas, but there was a new impetus in the developing theatre which was drawing on a shared consciousness of a 'national theatre society of Cornwall'. The initial project developed with Dean Nolan was a one-man show based on the life of Anthony Payne (c.1612-1691), the so-called 'Cornish giant'. Payne had served on the side of the Royalists during the War of Five Nations, assisting Sir Bevil Grenville. Nolan himself matched Payne's build, and the project was developed to allow educationalists and the company to offer workshops in schools and colleges, reconsidering Cornish and 'extreme' identities. The play was titled *Oogly es Sin: The Lamentable Ballad of Anthony Payne, Cornish Giant*.[442] Using breathless vocalisation, ventriloquism, physical theatre and dance, Nolan quickly established the role, so successfully that the company were invited to serialise the show on BBC Radio Cornwall. This was a brave move by the radio station, who were not well known for featuring drama, let alone work that blended Cornu-English ('I didn' worry nothun' 'bout 'un') with anarchic surfing lingo ('No-est way').[443]

BishBashBosh Production's breakthrough text came in 2008 with my exploration of the life of the slave, violinist and composer, Joseph Emidy,[444] in the form of a three-hander titled *The Tin Violin*. The success of this play both in Cornwall and in London was, I feel, down to several factors. The writing allowed me to explore how Emidy's concerns are shared with contemporary Cornwall. Thus 'Black' and 'Celtic' were fused, and spoke with the same voice, as at the head of this chapter, where Emidy's concern over identity was freely used as a metaphor for the identity of modern Cornwall.[445] This fusion was matched in the ambitions of Emidy himself who wanted to blend the music of Africa with that of Cornwall. Thus, for one of the few times in living memory, audiences witnessed a black actor as part of a Cornish ideological investigation. The play demonstrates Cornwall's internationalism with its heady mix of languages: African, Cornish, English and Portuguese. The company was also fortunate to find the actor Mbuguah Goro to play the role of Emidy,[446] in which he brought a new presence and dignity to the Cornish stage. Humour, too, is an important part of the work. Sir Edward Pellew, who organises the press-ganging of Emidy, reflects on his own identity:

Yes, I'm a Cornishman, but I don't like to think about it too much. It gives me palpitations, you know… I've left all that behind me. Well, one has to speak properly. One has to, to get on. [*Pause*] Why speak with the ugly dialectical intonations of some dung-encrusted farmer from Penwith when one can use the King's English. I make a point of it, running 'The Indefatigable'. I'll have no swearing and no proper-job cakey-head, dabbered-up, emmety, figgy-hobbin, tiddy-hoggan alright-my-handsome-beauty-wozon-my-lover-type shenanigans

BishBashBosh Productions and Second Wave Dance presents

a new play by Alan M. Kent

the tin violiŋ

The adventures of Joseph Emidy:
A true Cornish tale

*"Rich with dialect, dance and decadence,
this play will make you jig your heart out"*

Fig. 122. Flyer for Alan M. Kent's *The Tin Violin*, 2008. Courtesy of Bish Bash Bosh Productions.

on my watch. Let's have the prepositions and the past participles in all the right places. I am a veritable precision for it. And any member of the crew who even tries speaking Cornish, I'll have them clapped in irons and flogged round the fleet, and fed on mouldy bread and dripping for a week. We've no place for that stupid tongue in the modern era.[447]

In performance, this became a central section of the show, which allowed Cornish audiences to laugh at themselves, and also to satirise those Cornish who neglected and resented their own heritage.[448] In so doing, the play was able to assert a cultural nationalist position, without preaching. This was also borne out in the bastardised Cornish language and Cornu-English of the guardian of the tin violin, the blinded tinner Jabez Pender (performed by Trevor Cutherbertson[449]). The company was saying things that needed to be said on the stage in Cornwall, but which had previously been deemed too controversial:

Jabez:	Where you from, soas? You sound like you'm from Devon... Or Ireland? From there are '? You sound like you'm from there, yes...
Josh:	No. I'm from... [*thinks*] Well... I'm from all over the place.
Jabez:	English, are 'ee? Silly buggers they are... They'm usually all over the place. Dun't knaw their ass from their elbow.[450]

The success of *The Tin Violin* (also serialised on BBC Radio Cornwall) allowed BishBashBosh Productions to develop a new play for 2009. Titled *Surfing Tommies*,[451] it told the story of Cornish miners who fought in the First World War. In the trenches, the main characters, Jimmy Tamblyn, John Henry Pascoe, and William Tresawna hear about the sport of surfing and decide to try the sport back home in Cornwall after the war. The early surfboards included coffin lids. Sequences of the play also featured contemporary Cornwall, shaped by modern surfing, post-industrialism and tourist culture. This formed the background of a tragic plot, featuring class conflict, desertion and shattered love. Again, in marshalling a plot that self-consciously told a different kind of story, BishBashBosh Productions appear to have found a new formula for 'performing devolution'. As with *The Tin Violin*, the company developed innovative staging for touring both indoors and outdoors in Cornwall. In some ways, this thread of historical interest seems to be the way forward for much theatre in Cornwall: it was reconnecting to the romance of

Fig. 123. Jimmy Tamblyn (Dean Nolan), Robert Walling (Ed Williams) and William Tresawna (Trevor Cuthbertson) in *Surfing Tommies*, 2009. Courtesy of Stewart Girvan.

Cornwall's past (in a way that much historical-romantic fiction had previously done), but was telling this romance with a firm eye on cultural nationalism.

2006 was an important year for Christmas drama related to Cornwall, when three important texts emerged, all of which had cultural nationalist leanings. Parker's *Seven Stars* 'play for voices' has been considered above, but the two other dramas took their direct inspiration from the manuscript of 'Origo Mundi'. These were Ken George's *Flogholeth Krist / The Childhood of Christ*,[452] and my own *Nativitas Christi / The Nativity*.[453] Entirely independently, both George and myself had revisited the earlier text, where an intriguing reference in the form of the word '*flogholeth* [childhood]', was made to a possible fourth text of the *Ordinalia*, located between 'Origo Mundi' and 'Passio Christi'. Unlike most other medieval cycles, the *Ordinalia* appeared to have no nativity sequence. The play might, however, have an alternative ending alluding to a second play, now lost. George – born in 1947, and already a leading scholar in the revival of Cornish, promoting his system of Kernewek Kemmyn [Common Cornish][454] – decided to construct his vision based on the four Gospels, with events in the play focusing on Christ's birth, Christ growing up and Christ's encounter with John the Baptist. He follows the metrical devices of the Cornish in the surviving dramas. Intriguingly, both George and myself decided to embed, within the text, elements of nineteenth-century Cornish carols and hymns, principally because these often referred to concepts from the medieval period, and because they were uniquely connected to the Christmas experience in Cornwall.[455] Also, both writers included the legendary journey of Jesus to Cornwall: George had Christ travel to west and east Cornwall, while I had him encounter tinners, and make allusions forward in time to saints and to King Arthur. Joseph of Arimathea therefore becomes a central character in this construction. George creates performing devolution by sequences such as the following, when Joseph and Christ arrive at Glasney:

Joseph:
Unn dyffrans yw dhymmo kler:
  a'n Emproureth ni yw rann,
war an tenewenn konter
  Kernow yw gwlas hy honan,
mes piw a's rewl?
  Wosa dones lies gweyth,
  ny gonvedhav py par reyth
eus omma; puptra yw tewl.

[One difference is clear to me:
  we are a plan of the Empire,
on the other hand
  Cornwall is a country in her own right,
but who rules her?
  After coming many times,
  I do not understand what kind of law
there is here; all is obscure.][456]

George's work is one of the most sophisticated pieces of contemporary drama in Cornish. To a certain extent, such writing was a development of the drama developed by Bernard Walke, Peggy Pollard, and later Charles Causley, and Donald R. Rawe in the early 1970s – a 'model' to which Cornish and Anglo-Cornish writing could aspire. My own text fitted the pattern and design of the verse translation of the *Ordinalia*, picking up where 'Origo Mundi' had ended, and leading up to John the Baptist. Thus, a complete verse version of the full story was achieved. Featuring puns and numerous cultural references, *Nativitas Christi* is perhaps more anarchic and comic than George's imagining, which adheres more closely to the formula established in the medieval period. A diversion from the tax collection occurs when two Roman soldiers, named Gogius and Magogius, have a wrasslin' match. Bethlehem also has a Mock Mayor, paraded around by two constables. Parallels to the original *Ordinalia* are made through the handing out of land charters, while the Devils are seen moving through a subterranean landscape of fogous, mines, adits and levels, at once merging with established folklore:

Lucifer: Like dogs we creep 'round this mine.
Wagons I turn upside-down
Candles I make sure they don't shine
With pick and shovel I can clown.
In truth, the boy stopped a tempest,
but from cursing I took a rest.
Sire, I went to Linkinhorne,
for they say that's where we were born.[457]

The Three Magi feature as Druid, Alchemist and Astronomer. Similarly to George, the endeavour is to perform a devolved vision of Cornwall, which moves betwixt and between the biblical and the Cornish landscape. It is fair to say that the ambition in these two texts matches that of the original works. Both are yet to be staged. It would be interesting to see them performed on the streets of Truro, during the City of Lights festival in November, combined with 'stations' before the Cathedral, or in the various squares and the plaza of the city. With such imagination, the history of theatre in Cornwall comes full circle; and yet, in very many ways, all the authors who took inspiration from the medieval canon were, in fact, doing very little different than their forebears – welding universal narrative onto local legend. Perhaps Cornish and Anglo-Cornish drama is predestined for this kind of approach. What is left, perhaps, is to disengage with saints' lives and biblical narrative and to write more secular plays in this style.

Such work almost brings us full circle in an imagined performance of devolution. Two other performers and writers also merit consideration at the end of our story. Both Carl Grose and Anna Maria Murphy have been mentioned before in the light of their work with Kneehigh Theatre, but require separate study as well, since they form an important part of the future of theatre in Cornwall.[458] Grose began his career as an actor/director, forming the Grinning Gargoyle Theatre Company (1994-99).[459] Over its short development, the company presented a number of dynamic touring pieces, including Darke's *The Catch* (in 1999) and *The Eclipse Play* (1999).[460] Around 2000, Grose began to work more regularly with Kneehigh Theatre as a writer, prompting the 'Cornish Western Pantomime' *Quick Silver*, which was premiered at Mevagissey Jubilee Hall in 2002.[461] Set in the frontier town of Quicksilver, the show was dedicated 'to all those nameless Cornish men and

Fig. 124. Promo Pack for *Quick Silver* by Carl Grose, 2002. Courtesy of Kneehigh Theatre.

women who left their homeland and made something happen'.[462] The cast was composed of Grose himself playing Rob Ragg, Craig Johnson as Jack and Governor Gutlick, and Lucy Fontaine as Gwen and Obuke. This three-hander demonstrated Grose's power as a dramatist, and since then he has gone on to contribute to a number of Kneehigh Theatre's projects, including a skilful adaptation of *Cymbeline*.[463] Alongside his work with Kneehigh Theatre and as an independent writer in the past decade, Grose's Grinning Gargoyle Theatre Company mutated in 2002 into o-region, a theatrical and media production company, who produce Mark Jenkin and Brett Harvey's film work as well as theatre.[464] Co-founded by Grose, Simon Harvey and Oliver Berry, o-region has allowed Grose to develop his work in a number of new directions. His most recent projects have been *49 Donkeys Hanged* and *Superstition Mountain*. The former was broadcast as part of BBC Radio 3's series of cutting edge drama, titled 'The Wire'. The conceptualisation of *49 Donkeys Hanged* came from a headline observed in South Africa when Kneehigh Theatre were travelling from Soweto to central Johannesburg. As in most of Grose's work, there is a surreal comedy to the story, with him choosing to reinvent the narrative by having a Cornish farmer named Stanley Bray complete the donkey hangings. Stanley has a wife, Joy who, though a wheelchair user, is desperate to get out of the house, yet she is unable to, because Stanley has boarded up all the windows. The piece is set in Ventongimps, with the additional characters of Solomon Singo, Randy Tregersick and Sally Tregersick.

Such anarcho-gothic humour forms the basis of much of Grose's work, which represents an important breakthrough in the theatrical continuum, showing us what the future of Anglo-Cornish dramatic writing may look like. Similar dramaturgy is found in o-region's production of *Superstition Mountain*. Framed around the tag-line 'The Gunwallow brothers are in deep trouble',[465] this piece explores the lives of three scrapyard dealers from St Day (Slim, Dwayne and Mark). Broken and in debt, their lives are turned upside-down with the memory of a story told by their deceased father about a legendary lost gold mine in Arizona. Typically, Grose uses stichomythic, fast-paced Cornu-English dialogue, which has a certain directness and enormously Cornish dry wit:

Slim:	What you doin' up there?
Mark:	Sortin' through dad's stuff.
Slim:	Didn't chuck anything, did ya?
Mark:	No. Just lookin' through 'is things.
Slim:	Didn' take anything did ya?

Mark: No. (beat) Look at this coat of 'is.

Mark pulls out a coat from the box- a big worn leather job.

Slim: Thass' 'is horse-ridin coat.

Mark: E didn' ride 'orses.

Slim: E wore it watchin' John Wayne on telly ride 'em. Thass as close to 'orse as e'd like to get.

Slim puts it on.

Mark: Ere y'are look.

He takes a battered cowboy hat from the box, and throws it to Slim.

Slim: E ad all the gear, o'right.

Slim dons the hat. Enter Dwayne in a panic.

Dwayne: Dad?[466]

Paralleling in some ways Grose's earlier work, *Quick Silver*, the brothers decide to travel to America and find Superstition Mountain. Here, Grose was also recalling a century-long piece of Cornish emigration ideology – that fortune could be found elsewhere, outside of Cornwall, if one looked hard enough and worked hard enough. In its depiction of loss, there was the usual lament for past Cornish success, but this differed from the pre-war pieces by using self-deprecating humour and comedy, satirising Cornish propensity for such lamentation. What also makes this text so important is its almost anti-theatrical ethos. St Day is perhaps the last place in the world one would expect to set a drama. Grose deliberately chose this location in order to show that all experience in Cornwall is worthy of scrutiny, matching much of the direction of the Anglo-Cornish novel in its quest for realism and anti-romance.[467] *Superstition Mountain* also incorporated other elements of contemporary theatre: mixing live action with film and projection.

Anna Maria Murphy, meanwhile, has written in tandem with Grose, and separately. In many ways, she represents the future of female playwriting in Cornwall. Confessing in 2002 that she was a 'secret writer for a number of years' and that she first 'wrote a part for herself to avoid playing a dog',[468] Murphy has had an eclectic writing career in contemporary Anglo-Cornish theatre, choosing unusual but interesting projects. Her published pieces include *The Red Shoes* (premiered at the Sterts Theatre in 2000), *The Bacchae* (jointly written with Grose, and first presented in the West Yorkshire Playhouse, Leeds in 2002), and Kneehigh's *Tristan and Yseult*. Other work has included *Doubtful Island*, *Skulduggery*, *Ghost Nets*, *Wild Bride (The Shamans)* and *Women Who Threw The Day Away*.[469] Poetry and text by Murphy also formed the basis of a show performed by Rogue Theatre in 2007 titled *Madame Lucinda's Wonder Show*. Although Cornish-based, Rogue Theatre do

Fig. 125. Publicity poster for the St Piran Celebrations in 2005, including the play *Piran*. Courtesy of Tom and Barbara Tremewan.

not present Cornu-centric material; their style of inventive, illusionist physical theatre forms the perfect foil for Murphy's writing.[470] 2008 saw Murphy writing alongside the Cornish dance company C-Scape, to develop an exploration of Cornish mining culture, called *Below*.[471] Originally a short story by Murphy, the piece was adapted to dance by C-Scape members Helen Tiplady, Sally Williams and T.C. Howard. In late 2009, Murphy developed a one-woman show for the actress Bec Applebee titled *"Oh Mary"*. Directed by Simon Harvey and with music by Cornish bands Dalla and Radjel, the show looked at the life of Cornish highwaywoman and transportation victim Mary Bryant.[472] Murphy is a prolific writer, and considering the ground covered by Pauline Sheppard in the previous three decades, it will be interesting to see how her career develops. Although perhaps not as politically-conscious as Grose or Kent, Murphy's work offers a glimmer of feminist hope within what is still too broadly a male-dominated world of playwriting.[472] Put together, however, works such as *Below, Hell Fire Corner, Blast!, Laughing Gas, Superstition Mountain, 49 Donkeys Hanged, "Oh Mary", Oogly es Sin, The Tin Violin* and *Surfing Tommies* show the enormous variety and complexity of contemporary Anglo-Cornish theatre. The pieces being devised and written are as creative, witty and ground-breaking as contemporary theatre in any other European territory. The devolution being performed is at once bold and visionary; the new theatre of Cornwall has striking links to its past, but is also able to look to the future.

This chapter begins and ends with a play about St Piran. Donald R Rawe's 1971 drama *The Trials of St Piran* expressed much about ritual, landscape and community, redefining the patron saint of Cornwall – and therefore Cornish identity itself – for the post-war era. Since the early 1990s, when successive political campaigns for Cornish self-determination and devolution have markedly increased, a parallel theatrical activity was occurring, paradoxically only a stone's throw away from the oldest continually used theatre in Britain: Perran Round. The people of the town of Perranporth and the parish of Perranzabuloe began to mount a community play about the life of St Piran that would be performed every year on the closest Sunday to Perrantide (the week prior to the patron saint's day, 5 March).[473] In its initial format, performed in 2000, the cast – mainly drawn from the local community, and supported by singers and musicians from the Perraners and the Bolingey Troyl Band[474] – presented St Piran's life in a promenade-style performance over the vast sand dunes. A large audience of Cornish people turned out to watch: some dressed in Cornish tartan; some in surfing clothes; others proudly wearing Cornish colours or rugby shirts.[475] Many were waving the white cross and black background of the St Piran's cross flag, declaring their ethnicity, independence and Celticity for the world to see. The play depicted the evil Irish Kings, who shoved St Piran off the top of a high cliff in Ireland, strapped to a millstone,[476] and his subsequent journey across the Irish sea, arriving at the beach at Perranporth and inadvertently becoming, in the modern Cornish imagination, the first surfer.[477] There, he built a cell and converted to Christianity his first disciples: a fox, a badger and a bear. All this was part of the dramaturgy, as was a beautiful sequence (completed by local schoolchildren, with lengths of tin foil) where all the major mines of Cornwall gathered around the wheel-headed cross, and exuded forth streams of tin. Such ritual, in such a landscape, with such a community was unheard of a few decades earlier. There were few other communities doing anything like it in the rest of Britain. As I write, these past few years, the St Piran drama has grown exponentially, with more and more 'pilgrims' arriving to watch and celebrate each year. As conceived by Simon Parker, the play of St Piran is nowadays less a celebration of the Celtic spirituality of the distant past, and more a bold statement of nationalist intent; as this imagined devolution for Cornwall is enacted, the threads of space, place and performance are still there. They will surely be there for some time yet. In that, there is something for Cornwall to celebrate. In the words of an earlier Cornish drama:

Orth an jawl ha'y gompany
re'gas gwytho yn pup le,
ha'y vannath dheugh pup huny!
Lemmyn ens pop worth tre.
Now, menstrals, pybeugh bysy
may hellyn mos dhe dhonsya.

[Against the devil and his minions
may He preserve you everywhere
and His blessing be upon you every one.
Let all anon go homewards.
Now, minstrels, pipe up briskly
that we may go and dance.][478]

The theatre of Cornwall has been anarchic, chaotic and independent, yet a wholly entertaining epic. Long may it continue.

CHAPTER SEVEN: NOTES AND REFERENCES

1. Donald R. Rawe, *The Trials of St Piran*, Padstow: Lodenek, 1971, p.3.
2. Alan M. Kent, *The Tin Violin*, London: Francis Boutle Publishers, 2008, p.10.
3. Michael Billington, *State of the Nation: British Theatre Since 1945*, London: Faber and Faber, 2007.
4. See *The Guardian*, 2 December 2008, p.19-21.
5. The Institute of Cornish Studies, University of Exeter, facilitated Cornu-centric study in Cornwall. It opened in 1970 under the directorship of Charles Thomas. The present director is Philip Payton. Other scholars in Britain, Europe and America appear to be finding Cornwall an interesting case for academic treatment.
6. In the 1970s, *Poldark* and *Penmarric* were highly popular television shows. Recently television series have featured Padstow-based chef Rick Stein, the Isles of Scilly (*An Island Parish*, BBC) and north Cornwall (*Echo Beach*, ITV). See South West Tourism, *The Film and TV Map*, Exeter: South West Tourism, n.d.
7. For examples here, see Tim Smit, *Eden*, London: Chartered Institute of Personnel and Development, 2005; *Meyn Mamvro*; Michael Tooby, *Tate St Ives: An Illustrated Companion*, London: Tate Gallery, 1993; Sharon P. Schwartz, *Voices of the Cornish Mining Landscape*, Cornwall: Cornwall County Council, 2008. For the complex issues surrounding the industrial landscape of Cornwall, see Hilary Orange, 'Industrial Archaeology: Its Place within the Academic Discipline, the Public Realm and the Heritage Industry' in *Industrial Archaeology Review*, 30, 2, 2008, pp.83-95.
8. Combined Universities in Cornwall, *Higher Education Opportunities in Cornwall: Full and Part-time Courses 2003-2004*, Penryn: Combined Universities in Cornwall, 2003.
9. See, for example, http://www.cornwall24.co.uk. See also http://www.kernewek.org. There are countless others.
10. See *Maga*, 10/08. This is the newsletter of the Cornish Language Partnership. For comment on literature and studies by revivalists, see Brian Murdoch, *Cornish Literature*, Cambridge: D.S. Brewer, 1993, pp.143-50.
11. Philip Payton (ed.), *Cornwall Since the War: The Contemporary History of a European Region*, Redruth: Institute of Cornish Studies and Dyllansow Truran, 1993. Another useful modern history is Donald R. Rawe, *A Prospect of Cornwall*, London: Robert Hale, 1986.
12. Bernard Deacon, Andrew George, and Ronald Perry, *Cornwall at the Crossroads: Living Communities or Leisure Zone?* Redruth: Cornish Social and Economic Research Group, 1988. See also Andrew Lanyon, *The First and Last Straw*, Cornwall: Andrew Lanyon, n.d.; N.R. Phillips, *Apocalypse Dreckly*, Tiverton: Halsgrove, 2005.

13. John Angarrack, *Breaking the Chains: Censorship, Deception and the Manipulation of Public Opinion in Cornwall*, Camborne: Stannary Publications, 1999, and *Our Future is History: Identity, Law and the Cornish Question*, Bodmin: Independent Academic Press, 2002, and *Scat t'Larraps: Resist and Survive*, Bodmin: Independent Academic Press, 2008. Writing in Cornish matched many of these concerns. See Tim Saunders (ed. and tr.), *Nothing Broken: Recent Poetry in Cornish*, London: Francis Boutle Publishers, 2006.

14. For a review of this process, see Arthur Aughey, *Nationalism, Devolution and the Challenge to the United Kingdom State*, London: Pluto Press, 2001.

15. Bernard Deacon, Dick Cole, and Garry Tregidga, *Mebyon Kernow and Cornish Nationalism*, Cardiff: Welsh Academic Press, 2003. See also Joanie Willett, *Liberal Ethnic Nationalism, Universality and Cornish Identity*, unpublished paper, 2008.

16. See *An Baner Kernewek / The Cornish Banner*; James Whetter, *Scryow Kernewek / Cornish Essays 1971-76*, Gorran: CNP Publications, 1977.

17. Benedict Anderson, *Imagined Communities: Reflections on the Origin and Spread of Nationalism*, London and New York: Verso, 2006 [1983].

18. Sandy Craig (ed.), *Dreams and Deconstructions: Alternative Theatre in Britain*, Ambersgate: Amber Lane Press, 1980; Baz Kershaw, *The Politics of Performance: Radical Theatre as Cultural Intervention*, London and New York: Routledge, 1992.

19. This unresolved polarity forms the heart of the argument in Bernard Deacon, *Cornwall: A Concise History*, Cardiff: University of Wales Press, 2007.

20. Helen Gilbert (ed.), *(Post) Colonial Stages: Critical and Creative Views on Drama, Theatre and Performance*, Hebden Bridge: Dangaroo Press, 1999.

21. See Helen Gilbert and Joanne Tompkins, *Post-Colonial Drama: Theory, Practice, Politics*, London and New York: Routledge, 1996, pp.53-55.

22. Roger Bromley, *Narratives for a New Belonging: Diasporic Cultural Fictions*, Edinburgh: Edinburgh University Press, 2000.

23. Marc Maufort, *Transgressive Itineraries: Postcolonial Hybridizations of Dramatic Realism*, Brussels: Peter Lang, 2004, p.9.

24. Alan M. Kent, *The Literature of Cornwall: Continuity, Identity, Difference 1000-2000*, Bristol: Redcliffe, 2000, p.17.

25. The following is a useful wider consideration of the changes immediately after the Second World War: Alan Sinfield (ed.), *Society and Literature 1945-1970*, London: Methuen, 1983. For the period after 1970, see Mike Storry and Peter Childs (eds.), *British Cultural Identities*, London and New York: Routledge, 1997. For the complexity of national identity in Britain in the post-war period, see Richard Weight, *Patriots: National Identity in Britain 1940-2000*, London: Macmillan, 2002.

26. This is perhaps scarily similar to post-2000 attempts by the Labour government to develop concepts of Britishness for immigrants and children in mainstream education. See, for example, Tony Thorpe and Richard Jarvis, *Inside Britain*, London: The Citizenship Foundation and Hodder Murray, 2007.

27. See Francis Collingwood Selby, *Cornwall Drama Festival 1951 Programme*, Cornwall: Cornwall County Council, 1951, p.1. Selby had been appointed in October 1947 to the Cornwall Music and Drama committee in conjunction with Cornwall Education Authorities, to develop adult and youth drama groups. Prior to this she had worked with Frances Mackenzie in the training department of the British Drama League.

28. Ibid., p.2.

29. See Thomas Hardy, 'The Famous Tragedy of the Queen of Cornwall at Tintagel in Lyonesse' in Amy Hale, Alan M. Kent, and Tim Saunders (eds. and trs.), *Inside Merlin's Cave: A Cornish Arthurian Reader 1000-2000*, London: Francis Boutle Publications, 2000, pp.144-72.

30. Collingwood Selby, op.cit.

31. Nora Ratcliff, *Tristan of Cornwall: An Old Story Re-told*, unpublished manuscript, University of Bristol Theatre Collection, c.1951. p.23. This appears to be the only surviving copy of this text.

32. Collingwood Selby, op.cit., p.8.

33. *The Cornish Review*, No.7, 1951, pp.33-40.

34. Collingwood Selby, op.cit., p.9.

35. On this, however, see the observations in Thomas Shaw, *Saint Petroc and John Wesley: Apostles in Cornwall – An Examination of the Celtic Background of Cornish Methodism*, Cornwall: Cornish Methodist Historical Association, 1962.

36. Kneehigh Theatre presented *Ship of Fools* there in 1992. See also Joan Rendall, 'Cornwall's Preaching Pits' in *Cornish Scene*, No.4, 1997.

37. Collingwood Selby, op.cit.

38. Cf. Callum G. Brown, *The Death of Christian Britain: Understanding Secularization 1800-2000*, London and New York: Routledge, 2001.

39. Collingwood Selby, op.cit., p.4.

40. Ibid.

41. Ibid., p.5.

42. For a context, see Alan M. Kent, *Wives, Mothers and Sisters: Feminism, Literature and Women Writers of Cornwall*, Penzance: The Jamieson Library, 1998. See also Briar Wood, "The Words Are There Before Us': A Reading of Twentieth-Century Anglo-Cornish Poems Written by Women' in Philip Payton (ed.), *Cornish Studies: Fourteen*, Exeter: University of Exeter Press, 2006, pp.89-143.

43. See Christopher Ebden, *Plan of the Assembly Rooms (High Cross, Truro): 14 designs*

submitted for the erection of the Old Assembly Rooms at Truro, Royal Institution of Cornwall, Truro.

44. For detail of this, see Anthony Burton, *Richard Trevithick: Giant of Steam*, London: Aurum Press, 2000.

45. For a contemporary account, see Laura Smith, 'Madame Fanny Moody at Home: A Talk with the Cornish Nightingale' in *The Cornish Magazine*, Vol. 1, 1898.

46. Collingwood Selby, op.cit., p.8. It is unclear what the other droll was. Nance also contributes 'Cornwall and the Drama' to the programme. Ibid., pp.6-7.

47. Ibid., p.10.

48. See Peter Berresford Ellis, *The Cornish Language and its Literature*, London and Boston: Routledge and Kegan Paul, 1974, p.172.

49. Ibid., p.175.

50. Sinfield, op.cit.

51. See Reg Harris Archive, Lane Theatre, Newquay.

52. Williams would go on to become Associate Professor in Irish and Celtic Studies at the Department of Celtic Studies at University College Dublin. In the mid-1990s he prompted much debate over the spelling and pronunciation of Cornish. See N.J.A. Williams, *Cornish Today: An Examination of the Revived Language*, Sutton Coldfield: Kernewek dre Lyther, 1995. Williams has since been very active, completing, with Graham Thomas, a translation of *Bewnans Ke*. See Graham Thomas and Nicholas Williams (eds. and trs.), *Bewnans Ke: The Life of St Kea – A Critical Edition with Translation*, Exeter: University of Exeter Press, 2007.

53. Ellis, op.cit., pp.188.

54. See Maisie Redford, 'Cornwall in Opera' in *The Cornish Review*, No.2, 1966, pp.33-8.

55. Ibid. For another Gundry contribution, see Inglis Gundry, *Canow Kernow: Songs and Dances from Cornwall*, Cornwall: The Federation of Old Cornwall Societies, 1972.

56. Redford, op.cit., p.36.

57. See the observations of Deacon, op.cit., p.217.

58. See Alan M. Kent, "In Some State...': A Decade of the Literature and Literary Studies of Cornwall' in Payton, Philip (ed.), *Cornish Studies: Ten*, Exeter: University of Exeter Press, 2002, pp.212-39.

59. See Neville Denny (dir.), *Performance Texts for the Cornish Ordinalia*, 1969. This is presently in the archive collection of Alan M. Kent. There is also much material contained in the University of Bristol Theatre Collection. This includes BDD/00040 [Production photographs], BDD/000274 [press cuttings and ephemera relating to the production at Perran Round], BDD/C/000001 [Publicity File], BDD/C/000002 [Correspondence between David Machin, Bristol University Drama Department and Pains-Wessex Ltd, ref. fire and

smoke effects], BDD/D/000009 [Set and Costume Designs] and BDD/GW/081 [Papers of Glynne Wickham on the Cornish Cycle].

60. See Markham Harris (ed. and tr.), *The Cornish Ordinalia: A Medieval Dramatic Trilogy*. Washington D.C.: Catholic University of America Press, 1969.

61. Edwin Norris (ed. and tr.), *The Ancient Cornish Drama*, London and New York: Blom, 1968 [1859]; Robert Morton Nance, A.S.D. Smith and Graham Sandercock (eds. and trs.), *The Cornish Ordinalia, Second Play: Christ's Passion*, Cornwall: The Cornish Language Board, 1982, and (eds. and trs.), *The Cornish Ordinalia, Third Play: Resurrection*, Cornwall: The Cornish Language Board, 1984; Robert Morton Nance, A.S.D. Smith, Ray Chubb, Richard Jenkin and Graham Sandercock (eds. and trs.), *The Cornish Ordinalia, First Play: Origo Mundi*, Cornwall: Agan Tavas, 2001; F.E. Halliday, *The Legend of the Rood*, London: Gerald Duckworth, 1955. Although Nance and Smith's version of *Ordinalia* was not published until later, manuscript copies were clearly available to Denny.

62. See, for example, Miriam Akhtar, and Steve Humphries, *Far Out: The Dawning of New Age Britain*, Bristol: Sansom and Company, and Channel Four, 1999; Sinfield, op.cit. In an interview with the present author, promoter Chris Warner commented on how he nearly got The Rolling Stones to play at Perran Round.

63. A period culminating in *The Passion* on Easter Sunday on the terraces of the National Theatre in 1977. See Tony Harrison, *The Mysteries*, London: Faber and Faber, 1985.

64. See the observations in Peter Berresford Ellis, *The Celtic Dawn: A history of Pan-Celticism*, London: Constable, 1993 and also the ambition contained in works such as Cathal Ó Luain (ed.), *For a Celtic Future: A Tribute to Alan Heussaff*, Dublin: The Celtic League, 1983. This was also witnessed in a religious context. See for example, Shirley Toulson, *The Celtic Alternative: A Reminder of the Christianity We Lost*, London: Century, 1987, and Andy Phillips, *Lan Kernow: A Theology of Place for Cornwall*, Portreath: Spyrys a Gernow, 2006.

65. K.G. Foster, (ed.), *Piran Round, Perranporth: Souvenir Programme*, Cornwall: Cornwall County Council, 1969.

66. This was fully realised in Sydney Higgins, *Medieval Theatre in the Round: The Multiple Staging of Religious Drama in England*, Camerino, Italy: Laboratorio degli studi Linguistici, 1995. Higgins' contribution to the 1969 production is perhaps undervalued.

67. Jane A. Bakere, *The Cornish Ordinalia: A Critical Study*, Cardiff: University of Wales Press, 1980; Murdoch, op.cit., See also Ian Love, *Hic Descendit Deus Pater: Miracle Play Performance in Late Mediaeval Cornwall*, University of Cambridge, BA Dissertation, 2002.

68. Letter from Neville Denny to H.L. Douch, 25 July 1969 in Denny, op.cit., 1969, contained in Kent archive.

69. Ibid.

70. Alan M. Kent, *Ordinalia: The Cornish Mystery Play Cycle – A Verse Translation*, London: Francis Boutle Publishers, 2005.

71. He was recently presented with the first ever Lifetime Achievement Award given by the committee of the *Holyer an Gof* Literary Award. Rawe is also Chairman of the Cornish Literary Guild.

72. Rawe runs Lodenek Press, which has published a wide range of titles since its foundation in 1970.

73. Daniel Trevose, *Looking for Love in a Great City*, London: Cape, 1956.

74. See Paul Newman, 'Soldiers, Saints and Kings: The Plays of Donald R. Rawe' in *The Cornish Review*, No.24, 1973, pp.19-32. This can also be seen on http://abrax7.stormloader.com/donrawe.htm. This is one of the few pieces of genuine dramatic criticism written in modern Cornwall.

75. Donald R. Rawe, *Petroc of Cornwall*, Padstow: Lodenek Press, 1970, p.1. The story of Petroc is also considered in Rawe's highly influential children's collection. See Donald R. Rawe, *Traditional Cornish Stories and Rhymes*, Padstow: Lodenek Press, 1992 [1971], pp.28-9.

76. See Collingwood Selby, op.cit., p.10.

77. G.H Doble, *The Saints of Cornwall: Parts 4*, Felinfach: Llanerch, 1997 [1960-1970], p.132-66.

78. See Catherine Rachel John, *The Saints of Cornwall: 1500 Years of Christian Landscape*, Padstow: Tabb House, 2001 [1981], p.65-8. This book was originally published by Lodenek Press.

79. Rawe, op.cit.

80. Newman, op.cit.

81. See, for example, John Betjeman, *Collected Poems*, London: John Murray, 1988.

82. Newman, op.cit.

83. Rawe, op.cit., 1971.

84. Newman, op.cit.

85. The play-script included a Cornu-English glossary. See Rawe, op.cit., pp.56-7.

86. Donald R. Rawe, *Geraint: Last of the Arthurians*, Padstow: Lodenek Press, 1972.

87. Ibid., p.1.

88. Maufort, op.cit.

89. Rawe published the following text: Susan M. Pearce, *The Kingdom of Dumnonia: Studies in History and Tradition in South West Britain AD 350-1150*, Padstow: Lodenek Press, 1978.

90. Donald R. Rawe, *Padstow's Obby Oss and May Day Festivities: A Study in Folklore and Tradition*, Padstow: Lodenek Press, 1990 [1971].

91. Newman, op.cit.

92. Donald R. Rawe, *The Creation of the World*, Padstow: Lodenek Press, 1978.

93. Donald R. Rawe, 'A Skeleton in the Cupboard' in Donald R. Rawe (ed.), *A Cornish Quintette: Five Original One Act Plays*, Padstow: Lodenek Press, 1973, pp.5-16. Other texts in this volume include Burness Bunn's 'Wheal Judas' and 'The Christmas Widow', and Gwen Powell-Jones' 'Shadows of Men'.

94. Donald R. Rawe, 'The Happening at Botathen' in ibid., pp.17-27. This had been performed in 1970.

95. See J.C. Trewin (ed.), *Robert Stephen Hawker: Footprints of Former Men in Far Cornwall*, London: Westaway Books, 1948, pp.64-76. Hawker makes an interesting aside in this narrative, talking of 'the merry minister of the mines, whose cure was honeycombed by the underground men. He must needs have been artist and poet in his way, for he had to enliven his people, three or four times a year, by mastering the arrangements of a guary, or religious mystery, which was duly performed in the topmost hollow of a green barrow or hill, of which many survive, scooped out into vast amphitheatres and surrounded by two thousand spectators. Such were the historic plays. The Creation and Noe's Flood, which still exist in the Celtic as well as the English text, and suggest what critics and antiquaries Cornish curates, masters of such revels, must have been.'

96. Donald R. Rawe, *Hawker of Morwenstow*, 1975. This text has yet to be published. Rawe also wrote a film-script around the same period. This was *The Vicar in Seaboots (Revd. R.S. Hawker)* filmed by Truro School Film Unit. It was winner of the Westward Trophy at the Plymouth Film Festival.

97. These included poetry in Cornish and in English. For a selection see Saunders, op.cit., pp. 34-40; Alan M. Kent (ed.), *The Dreamt Sea: An Anthology of Anglo-Cornish Poetry 1928-2004*, London: Francis Boutle Publishers, 2004, pp.138-47. See also Donald R. Rawe, *The Mermaid of Padstow: Stories and Poems*, Padstow: Lodenek Press, 1983, and op.cit., 1986.

98. See *Black Letter Pamphlet: News from Pe[n]rin in Cornwall of a most Bloody and un-exampled Murder*, Quarto, Bodley, 4 M G29 (2), Oxford; Thomas Davies (ed.), *Lillo's Dramatic Works Vol. 2: Fatal Curiosity, Marina, Elmerick, or Justice Triumphant, Britannia and Batavia, Arden of Feversham*, Whitefish, Montana: Kessinger Publishing, 2008.

99. Donald R. Rawe, *Murder at Bohelland*, 1991. This text has yet to be published.

100. Donald R. Rawe, *The Last Voyage of Alfred Wallis*, 1994. For background on Wallis, see Edwin Mullins, *Alfred Wallis: Cornish Primitive*, London: Pavilion Books, 1994.

101. Kernow Productions, *The Last Voyage of Alfred Wallis*, programme, Falmouth: Falmouth Arts Centre, 1994.

102. See Buck, M., Williams, M and Bryant, L., 'Housing the Cornish: Containing the crisis' in Payton, Philip (ed.), *Cornish Studies: One*, Exeter: University of Exeter Press,1993b, pp.157-80.

103. Billington, op.cit., pp.205-82.

104. For urban theatre in south-west Britain, see Harvey Crane, *Playbill: A History of the Theatre in the West Country*, Plymouth: Macdonald and Evans, 1980. For Plymouth, see R.A.J. Walling, *The Story of Plymouth*, London: Westaway Books, 1950.

105. Craig, op.cit., pp.90-91.

106. For an early history, see Cathy Slater, 'Foots Barn Theatre' in *Cornish Review*, No.26, 1974, pp.73-8.

107. My thanks to Rick Worthy for his generous help documenting Footsbarn. Oliver Isaac Foot (1946-2008) was an actor, philanthropist, charity worker and Christian. He was the son of Hugh Foot (Jamaica's last British Colonial Secretary), descendent of Isaac Foot (1880-1960), Member of Parliament for Bodmin in 1922, and nephew of the former leader of the British Labour Party, Michael Foot. Jon Paul Cook studied at Goddard College, Vermont, and also at l'École Internationale de Théâtre Jacques Lecoq. Maggie Watkiss was born in 1948 in Canada. In Worthy's view, she was important in 'setting the style' of Footsbarn's work. Dave Johnston was an important member of the troupe: a talented writer and gifted clown. He left Footsbarn at the end of the 1990s, moving to work in theatre in Berlin. Rick Worthy, who helped organise Elephant Fayre for a number of years, worked with the early company. He trained at East 15, under Joan Littlewood, leaving in 1973 to work in music.

108. See John Tabois Tregellas, *Cornish Tales*, Truro: Netherton and Worth, 1863, pp.38-43.

109. Early non-Cornish-themed shows included Anton Chekhov's *The Bear*, Edward Albee's *Zoo Story* and N.F. Simpson's *A Resounding Tinkle*.

110. Clearly based on the narratives contained in Hunt. See Robert Hunt (ed.), *Popular Romances of the West of England: The Drolls, Traditions, and Superstitions of Old Cornwall (First Series)*, London: John Camden Hotten, 1865, pp.35-77.

111. Detailed in Slater, op.cit. Such work is now commonplace in education.

112. Cited in ibid., p.74.

113. Ibid., p.75.

114. Ibid., p.77.

115. See http://www.footsbarn.com. The company's original name 'Foot's Barn' changed to 'Foots Barn', then 'Footsbarn'.

116. For a review, see http://www.curtainup.com/midsummerfootsbarn.html.

117. See Rawe, op.cit., 1970, 1971, 1972.

118. Charles Causley, *The Gift of a Lamb: A Shepherd's Tale of the first Christmas, told as a verse play*, London: Robson Books, 1978.

119. Charles Causley, *Three Heads made of Gold*, London: Robson Books, 1978.

120. Charles Causley, *The Ballad of Aucassin and Nicolette: A Play in Three Acts*, London: Viking, 1981. See Papers of Charles Causley, EUL. MS. 50a/LIT/1/8.

121. See South West Music Theatre, *The Ballad of Aucassin and Nicolette*, programme, Exeter: South West Music Theatre, 1978.

122. Causley, op.cit., 1981, p.15.

123. Ibid., p.27.

124. See *Radio Times*, 12 May 1980, p.45. A review of the radio version is in *The Financial Times*, 17 May 1980.

125. See Papers of Charles Causley, EUL. MS. 50a/LIT/1/66. The play was for BBC Schools' Radio. This was also performed at Trebullett Methodist Sunday School, produced by Neil Burden in 1986.

126. Ronald Tamplin, 'As New as it is Old' in Harry Chambers, *Causley at 70*, Calstock: Peterloo Poets, 1987, p.50.

127. For 'St Martha and the Dragon', see Charles Causley, *Collected Poems 1951-1975*, London: Macmillan, 1975, pp. 208-221. It was also set to music in 1977.

128. Tamplin, op.cit., p.52.

129. See Dylan Thomas, *The Doctor and the Devils, and Other Scripts*, London: New Directions, 1970. This script was written in 1953.

130. For Causley's adaptation, see Papers of Charles Causley, EUL. MS. 50a/LIT/1/19.

131. Stephen McNeff studied composition at the Royal Academy of Music, and completed post-graduate research at the University of Exeter. He has composed for opera, music theatre and drama in the UK, the USA and Canada, was Composer in Residence at the Banff Centre, and worked with Comus Music Theatre and the Canadian Opera Company. In 2005, McNeff was appointed to the Bournemouth Symphony Orchestra as their Composer in the House.

132. See *The Times Literary Supplement*, 14 April 1980.

133. See *The Calgary Herald*, 22 March 1984.

134. Ibid.

135. Tamplin, op.cit.

136. See Papers of Charles Causley, EUL. MS. 50a/LIT/1/12.

137. Ibid.

138 Ibid., p.10. For discussion of the ceremony, see Old Cornwall Societies, *Crying the Neck: A Harvest Celebration*, St Agnes: Federation of Old Cornwall Societies, n.d.

139. See, for example, Charles Causley, *Early in the Morning*, London: Viking Kestral, 1986. Much of Causley's children's verse has para-theatrical motifs. See Charles Causley, *Collected Poems for Children*, London: Macmillan, 1996. Causley did, however, write the libretto for *Jonah: A Musical Morality* between 1987 and 1988.

This was first performed at Guildford Cathedral for the Guildford High School for Girls Centenary Concert on 6 July 1988. See Papers of Charles Causley, EUL. MS. 50a/LIT/1/37.

140. In Kneehigh Theatre and Theatre Royal, Plymouth, *Hans Christian Andersen's The Tinderbox*, programme, Truro and Plymouth, 1990, Causley comments, 'I have long thought of writing a stage adaptation of *The Tinderbox*.' *The Tinderbox* was later performed by the Unicorn Theatre and the Arts Centre University of Warwick, in 1992.

141. This was to expand in Kneehigh Theatre, post-2000.

142. See Chapter Four.

143 *The Guardian*, 13 April 1990.

144. See Papers of Charles Causley, EUL. MS. 50a/LIT/1/21. This was first performed by the Unicorn Theatre at the Arts Centre, University of Warwick in spring 1992. The show was named *Hans Christian Anderstories*.

145. Charles Causley, *The Young Man of Cury*, London: Macmillan, 1991. This title is a pun on the traditional story of 'The Old Man of Cury'.

146. Charles Causley, *Figgie Hobbin*, Harmondsworth: Puffin, 1985 [1970].

147. See Kneehigh Theatre, *Figgie Hobbin*, Truro: Kneehigh Theatre, 1994. This leaflet promised 'Figgie Hobbin: Charles Causley's choice of his own poems, illuminated by Kneehigh Theatre for children and their families'.

148. See Papers of Charles Causley, EUL. MS. 50a/LIT/1/1, and Blackheath Concert Halls, *Aesop*, flyer, Blackheath: Blackheath Concert Halls, 1991; George Square Theatre, *Aesop*, programme, Edinburgh: George Square Theatre, 1991.

149. *The Independent*, 5 July 1991. See also *Time Out*, 26/6-3/7 1991; *Evening Standard*, 2 July 1991.

150. Papers of Charles Causley, EUL. MS. 50a/LIT/1/1.

151. Another opera was planned: *St Jerome and the Lion: A Church Opera* (1995). See Papers of Charles Causley, EUL. MS. 50a/LIT/1/56.

152. Jethro has appeared on *Des O'Connor Tonight*, *The Generation Game*, *Jethro Junction*, and *The Royal Variety Show*.

153. See for example, Jethro, *From Behind the Bushes – Live!*, London: Universal Pictures UK, 1994, and *Live! What Happened Was...*, London: Universal Pictures UK, 1995, and *The Beast of Bodmin Moor*, London: Universal Pictures UK, 1997, and *Live at Jethro's: Back of Beyond*, London: Universal Pictures UK, 2007.

154. This was announced in October 2008.

155. See Jethro, *Says Bull'cks to Europe!*, London: Universal Pictures UK 2000, and *Rule Britannia!* London: Universal Pictures UK, 2001.

156. For a context, see Deacon, George and Perry, op.cit..

157. See, for example, *Cornwall Today, Yesterday and Dreckly*, Vol 2, No.3, 1995, p.43. Jethro also had a column in the same magazine.

158. Johnny Cowling, *Off the Back of a Lorry – Live at Carnglaze Caverns*, Cornwall: Turn it Around Records, 2007. In 2008, Cowling completed a lengthy national tour of Britain with the comedian Paddy McGuinness. See http://www.johnny-cowling.com/biog.htm.

159. Redannick means 'fern brake' in Cornish.

160. I am indebted to David E. Ivall for this information. The Truro Amateur Operatic and Drama celebrates its centenary in 2012.

161. Newquay Dramatic Society, *Lane Theatre Project, Newquay*, Newquay Dramatic Society, 1979, p.2. A letter to the West Country Tourist Board dated 17 September 1979 was also offered in support of the project by the county [sic] drama advisor, John D. Trelease. Letter held at Lane Theatre, Newquay.

162. See Lane Theatre, *Lane Theatre Newquay: 2008*, Newquay: Lane Theatre, 2008.

163 See the fictional creation of Newquay in Alan M. Kent, *Proper Job, Charlie Curnow!* Tiverton: Halsgrove, 2005. For a consideration of the changes, see Philip Payton, *A Vision of Cornwall*, Fowey: Alexander Associates, 2002; Robert Andrews, *The Rough Guide to Devon and Cornwall*, London: Rough Guides Ltd, 2007.

164. See Lane Theatre, op.cit.

165. See Reg Harris Archive, Lane Theatre, Newquay.

166. See Newquay Amateur Dramatic Society, *And A Size Larger*, publicity pamphlet, 1962.

167. Alan Sinfield, 'The Theatre and its Audiences' in Sinfield (ed.), op.cit., pp.173-98.

168. See Rod Lyon, *Gorseth Kernow: The Cornish Gorsedd – what it is and what it does*, Cornwall: Gorseth Kernow, 2008, p.47.

169. Ibid., p.52.

170. The iconography is worth comparing with the photographs in Marion Löffler, *A Book of Mad Celts: John Wickens and the Celtic Congress of Caenarfon, 1904*, Llandysul: Gomer, 2000.

171. See Harris, op.cit.

172. See Billington, op.cit.

173 See Harris, op.cit.

174. John the Fish and Brenda Wootton (1928-1994) were instrumental in the development of the contemporary folk scene in Cornwall, and performed together at the first Lorient Festival in Brittany.

175. See British Drama League National Festival of Community Theatre booklet, 1971.

176. See Rawe, op.cit., 1973.

177. Bunn, op.cit., 1973.

178. Daphne du Maurier, *September Tide*, London: Samuel French, 1994 [1949].

179. On 26 January 2008, BBC Radio 4 broadcast an adaptation by Moya O'Shea, starring Paula Wilcox and Jonathan Firth. The Theatre Royal, Windsor and the Chevy Chase Community Centre, Washington DC have also produced the play.

180. This process had begun in works such as Alison Light, *Forever England: Femininity, Literature and Conservatism between the Wars*, London: Routledge, 1991, pp.156-207 and Avril Horner and Sue Zlosnik, *Daphne du Maurier: Writing, Identity and the Gothic Imagination*, London: Palgrave Macmillan, 1998, but reached a new level in Helen Taylor (ed.), *The Daphne du Maurier Companion*, London: Virago Press, 2007. For a Cornish perspective on du Maurier, see Kent, op.cit., 2000, pp.178-87.

181. See Restormel Borough Council, *The Daphne du Maurier Festival of Arts and Literature*, Cornwall: Restormel Borough Council, 1999, 2000, 2002, 2003 and 2007. See also Graham Busby and Zoë Hambly, 'Literary Tourism and the Daphne du Maurier Festival' in Philip Payton (ed.), *Cornish Studies: Eight*, Exeter: University of Exeter Press, 2000, pp.197-212.

182. Hedley Claxton, *Gaytime*, Newquay: Cosy Nook Theatre, 1952, in John Trembath Theatrical Archive, Newquay.

183. *Into the Sun: A Revue in Four Editions*, souvenir programme, Newquay: New Theatre, 1954; *Into the Sun: A Revue in Three Editions*, souvenir programme, Newquay: New Theatre, 1955. Cf. *Run to the Sun*.

184. John Berryman, *Top o' the Town*, Newquay: Astor Theatre, *c*.1957.

185. See Cosy Nook Theatre by the Sea, *Showtime86, featuring Bernie Clifton*, Newquay: Cosy Nook, 1986, in Ibid.

186. See http://www.staps.co.uk.

187. An archive of programmes may be found at St Austell Arts Centre.

188. Other early core activists in the Society included William Robinson, David Michael, Jean Michael, Frederick Rowe, Sylvia Hocking, Agnes Thurlow, Barbara Ennor, Freda Lawrence, Leslie Lang, Edward Turner, Geoffrey Ennor, Edward Dorman, T. Ronald Trenerry, E.H.H. Dorman, E.A. Turner, J. Adam. H. Donnelly, D. Brown, M. Hocking, E. Dorman, P. Mobbs, P.C. Bays, M. Blackie, H. Hocking, G. Phillips and L. Lang. Of these, Frederick Rowe has been active in the society for a large number of years. I am grateful to Charles Thurlow for this information.

189. A full list is found on http://www.staps.co.uk.

190. Ibid. This process is detailed by Geoffrey Cooper. Cooper is a long-term supporter of St Austell Players. See this website also, for memories of St Austell Players in the Sixties by Ray Lincoln.

191. The production of these titles was matched by the development of the Daphne du Maurier Festival of Arts and Literature at Fowey.

192. It has also been much promoted by Restormel Arts. Keen supporters of the Centre have been Jonathan Aberdeen (a local arts activist and now a director of the Daphne du Maurier Festival) and Phil Webb (Arts Promotion Officer and, more recently, DJ). The Hub Theatre School later moved to St Austell College.

193. For an overview, see http://www.kneehigh.co.uk. See also Phil Hosking, 'Kneehigh Theatre' in *Cornish World / Bys Kernowyon*, No. 11, 1996, pp. 20-21. This article includes a quotation from John Le Carré who comments that 'Kneehigh is exactly what it should be: adventurous, outrageous, disciplined, magical and dedicated'.

194. Interview with Mike Shepherd by Alan M. Kent on 23 October 2008.

195. See John Adams (dir.), *Kneehigh Theatre: Imagination Burning*, Penzance: Three S Films, 1997.

196. Ibid.

197. See Bill Mitchell, Mike Shepherd, Emma Rice, and Victoria Moore, *Kneehigh Theatre*, Truro: Kneehigh Theatre, c.2005, p.5.

199. See Kneehigh Theatre and Theatre Royal, Plymouth, *Hans Christian Andersen's The Tinderbox*, programme, Truro and Plymouth, 1990.

200. The information here and following was kindly given to the author by Mike Shepherd.

201. Fog was provided by Allan Drake smoking a cigarette and blowing it down a tube. The cast here was Charlie Barnecut, Dave Mynne, Allan Drake, Tim Dalling, Jim Carey and Mike Shepherd.

202. Written by John Burrows and John Harding, this was what Shepherd describes as 'off the shelf', that is, not devised by the company.

203. According to Shepherd this was, in part, because of two musicians Tim Dalling and Jim Carey: it was 'hard to get them off to start the show'.

204. Here the cast featured Allan Drake, Jon Oram, Leslie Moss, Jackie McDoughall, Mike Shepherd, Dave Mynne, Tim Dalling and Jim Carey. This featured the company's first use of springing entrances via trampettes (small trampolines).

205. The cast included Arland Wrigley, Tim Dalling, Dave Mynne, Mike Shepherd, Gavin Hutton, and Annabelle McFadden. The show featured impressive sword-fighting for which the company was trained by Gerry Finch, an ex-Cornwall fencing captain.

206. The performers here included Will Coleman, Hilary Coleman, Mike Shepherd, Jim Carey, Tim Dalling and Dave Mynne. Oram's influence on Kneehigh Theatre was important. He eventually joined Ann Jellicoe's Colway Theatre Trust.

207. This was a difficult tour. There were a number of accidents and problems along the way.

208. At this point, the company benefited from a South West Arts initiative whereby theatre companies worked with Tony Robinson and John Downie. Boris

Howarth from Welfare State International also assisted. The cast here were Dave Mynne, Mike Shepherd, Sarah Jewell and Jim Carey. Another show during this phase was the spontaneous *Cabaret* (not the 1966 Broadway show), which toured in a variety of venues. A variety of other schools' shows were also performed in the 1980s. These were *We Stole the Sun, Trelumpkin and Trebumpkin, Rare Earth, Rubbish, Footprints I, Footprints II*, and *Poetry in Action*. The latter four shows featured the work of Anna Maria Murphy.

209. The cast included Tristan Sturrock, Giles King, Dave Mynne, Sarah Jewell and Mike Shepherd. This was the first time the company tried duplicate casting.

210. Shepherd labels this the 'most stressful' show and a 'low point'. The script was ambitious, and less accomplished performers had to be brought in because many of the company were committed to other projects. A second version was developed with the usual ensemble, performing at the Minack and Sterts Centre.

211. See Phil Hosking, 'Sue Hill: Gifted Lady of Cornish Theatre' in *Cornish World / Bys Kernowyon*, op.cit., p.18.

212. For example, Kneehigh Theatre, *The Ash Maid*, Truro: Kneehigh Theatre, 1994, and *Figgie Hobbin*, Truro: Kneehigh Theatre, 1994. Hill is also rumoured to have written the c.1998 politically-charged and famous piece of graffiti on the wall outside South Crofty tin mine, which reads 'Cornish lads are fishermen and Cornish lads are miners too. But when the fish and tin are gone, what are the Cornish boys to do?' In subsequent debate on http://www.cornwall24.co.uk, a connection was made between the lettering of Hill's other work and the lettering on the wall.

213. John Davey and Steve Lewis, *Edexcel AS Drama and Theatre Studies*, Harlow: Pearson, 2008, p.155.

214. For a perspective on this, see Craig Weatherhill, and Paul Devereux, *Myths and Legends of Cornwall*, Wilmslow: Sigma, 1998 [1994].

215. See *The Guardian*, op.cit.

216. Causley commented that 'Kneehigh is truly Cornwall's National Theatre: the admiration of many far beyond the county [sic] boundary. One of the brightest jewels in Cornwall's crown – no doubt about it – is Kneehigh.' No date is given for this observation, but it is found in Mitchell, Shepherd, Rice and Moore, op.cit., p.28.

217. Nick Darke, *Ting Tang Mine and Other Plays*, London: Methuen, 1987, and *Plays: One*, London: Methuen, 1999. Darke offers an interesting reflection here on the character of the Cornish and Cornu-English in theatre: 'The Cornish are a Celtic race, in character more canny that the Scots, less lyrical than the Welsh, closer to the Irish but most akin to the people of Brittany. They speak fast with a hard, unmusical accent. Their soft consonants are voiced so the word butter would be pronounced 'budder' and not 'bu'er' as Captain Birdseye might say it –

this is the most important feature to consider when speaking the language of this play. A native of Cornwall, when heard for the first time is frequently mistaken for an American, but he or she is *never* asked if they come from Somerset'. See Darke, op.cit.,1987 p.6.

218. This was originally from 1992, with the RSC.

219. Nick Darke, *The Riot*, London: Methuen, 1999.

220. Another retelling of this is found in Simon Parker, *A Star on the Mizzen*, Liskeard: Giss' On Books, 1997.

221. For a selection of music from productions, listen to Kneehigh Theatre, *Scat t'Larraps*, Truro: Kneehigh Theatre, 1999.

222. See Kneehigh Theatre, op.cit., 1994.

223. For background, see John Rudlin, *Commedia dell'Arte in the Twentieth Century: An Actor's Handbook*, London and New York: Routledge, 1994.

224. For an example of his work, see David Kemp, *Art of Darkness Museum Guide*, St Ives: David Kemp, 1996. Mercedes Kemp was also an influential designer during this phase.

225 Several of these sculptures are now found in Redruth, and renamed 'Tinners' Hounds'.

226. See Adams, op.cit.

227. See Kneehigh Theatre, *Peep Show*, Truro: Kneehigh Theatre, n.d., and *The Reviews*, Truro: Kneehigh Theatre, n.d.

228. Kneehigh Theatre, *Tristan and Yseult, The Bacchae, The Wooden Frock, The Red Shoes*, London: Oberon Books, 2005, pp. 65-120. Carl Grose was the writer.

229. See Angela Carter, *Nights at the Circus*, London: Chatto and Windus, 1984. There is an intriguing link here to the Bluebeard character of early nineteenth-century Anglo-Cornish theatre, through Carter's work in 'The Bloody Chamber'. See Angela Carter, *Burning your Boats: Collected Short Stories*, London: Vintage, 1996.

230. This film was originally released in 1946 and starred David Niven and Kim Hunter. It was released in the USA under the title *Stairway to Heaven*. The principle cinematic effect is an escalator running between the 'other world' and Earth.

231. See observers in John Pitcher (ed.), *William Shakespeare: Cymbeline*, London: Penguin, 2005.

232. A comment in Davey and Lewis, op.cit.

233. Ibid.

234. See http://www.kneehigh.co.uk. See also Kneehigh Theatre, *Don John*, programme, Truro: Kneehigh Theatre, 2008.

235. Kneehigh Theatre, *Blast! Publicity Leaflet*, Truro: Kneehigh Theatre, 2007.

236. Interview with Mike Shepherd by Alan M. Kent on 23 October 2008.

237. See Angarrack, op.cit, 1999.

238. Kneehigh Theatre, op.cit, 2007.

239. Mike Shepherd and Carl Grose, *Blast!*, 2007, p.16.

240. See Tony Deane and Tony Shaw, *Folklore of Cornwall*, Stroud: Tempus, 2003, p.35.

241. Goats feature in much Cornu-English literature from Cornwall and, most specifically, South Australia.

242. There is no award in the annual Gorsedd competitions for drama. The *Holyer an Gof* literary salver has not yet been awarded to a work of drama, but see note on Rawe above (71). This is quite a paradox considering Robert Morton Nance's work as a dramatist and translator of medieval drama.

243. See Joan Tasker Grimbert (ed.), *Tristan and Isolde: A Casebook*, New York and London: Garland, 1995.

244. Kneehigh Theatre, op.cit., 2005, p.25.

245. Ibid., p.29.

246. Ibid., p.39.

247. Ibid., p.41. Harp music forms a crucial part of most versions.

248. Ibid., p.48.

249. Ibid., p.56.

250. Ibid., p.18.

251. Kent, op.cit., 2002, p.231.

252. Mitchell, Shepherd, Rice, and Moore, op.cit., c.2005, p.1.

253. See http://www.wildworks.biz. Sue Hill and Bill Mitchell reflected on their achievement in the Annual Governors' Lecture, University College Falmouth, 2007. I am indebted to Sue Hill for drawing my attention to this.

254. Ibid.

255. Ibid.

256. For a perspective on this, see Eric Hobsbawm and Terence Ranger (eds.), *The Invention of Tradition*, Cambridge: Cambridge University Press, 1992.

257. See Adams (dir.), op.cit.

258. See, for example, Peter E. Murphy, *Tourism: A Community Approach*, New York and London: Routledge, 1985. This book has several Cornish examples. See also John Lowerson, 'Celtic Tourism – Some Recent Magnets' in Philip Payton (ed.), *Cornish Studies: Two*, Exeter: University of Exeter Press, 1994, pp.128-37.

259. A copy of the poster is on http://www.wildworks.biz

260. See A. W. Holmes, *Out of this Fury*, London: Hutchinson, 1944; Jack Clemo, *The Shadowed Bed*, Tring: Lion, 1986; Alan M. Kent, *Clay*, Launceston: Amigo, 1991.

261. There are some parallels here with the dramatist Tony Harrison. Cf. Tony Harrison, *Theatre Works 1973-1985*, Harmondsworth: Penguin, 1986.

262. See Craig, op.cit., Kershaw, op.cit. Mitchell collaborates with a wide range of practitioners – among them, Neil Davey, Roger Delves, Heidi Dorschler,

Benjamin Dunks, Adrian Freedman, Samuel Gardès, Sue Hill, Claire Inglehart, Steve Jacobs, Rebecca Jackson, Mercedes Kemp, Anna Lindgren, Paul Portelli, Nicola Rosewarne, Myriddin Wannell, Colin Seddon, Bec Applebee, Jessica Rainey, Paul Jarvis, Alhoucin Djahra, Agnieszka Blonska, Pigsy (Simon Hayward), Gabriella Nonino, Lucy Gaskell and Steve Tanner.

263. These two mines are in close proximity. For background, see Allen Buckley, *South Crofty Mine: A History*, Mount Hawke: Truran, 1997.

264. http://wildworks.biz.

265. http://wildworks.biz. See also Lyn Gardner, *The Guardian*, 15 May 2006.

266. Kneehigh Theatre has garnered much praise from *The Guardian* newspaper's theatre critic, Michael Billington. For a context, see Billington, op.cit. For reviews, see Kneehigh Theatre, op.cit., n.d. In Davey and Lewis, op.cit., as practitioners, Kneehigh are given the same status as Antonin Artaud, Bertolt Brecht, Konstantin Stanislavski, DV8 and Complicité.

267. See http://www.miracletheatre.co.uk.

268. See http://www.bbc.co.uk/cornwall/content/articles/2008/07/22/people_billscott_miracle_feature.shtml. The old Victorian translation was probably Norris, op.cit., 1968 [1859].

269. For example, *Cleopatra* (1998), *20,000 Leagues under the Sea* (2004), and *The Government Inspector* (2006).

270. http://www.miracletheatre.co.uk

271. The opera apparently arose from Jonathan Swift's suggestion that a Newgate pastoral 'might make an odd pretty sort of thing'.

272. See Bill Scott (dir.), *An Dewetha Gweryow Dolly Pentreath / The Last Words of Dolly Pentreath*, Cornwall: Wild West Films, 1994, and (dir.), *The Saffron Threads*, Cornwall: Wild West Films, 1995, and (dir.), *Splatt Dhe Wertha / Plot for Sale*, Cornwall: Wild West Films, 1997. In 2007 Bill Scott directed a film version of Pauline Sheppard's drama *Dressing Granite*.

273. For a context, see Alan M. Kent, 'Screening Kernow: Authenticity, Heritage and the Representation of Cornwall in Film and Television' in Philip Payton (ed.), *Cornish Studies: Eleven*, Exeter: University of Exeter Press, 2003, pp.110-43.

274. See arguments in Gilbert (ed.), op.cit., who argues that this approach can be taken with Shakespeare.

275. *Rumpelstiltskin* has many parallels with the Cornu-English narrative of *Duffy and the Devil*.

276. See note 268.

277. Other shows have included *Beauty and the Beast from Mars* (1995), *Knight of Passion* (1996), *The Fall of Robin Hood* (1997), *The Chairs* (2002), *Quasimodo* (2003), *The Great Silence* (2003), and *The Case of the Frightened Lady* (2005).

278. See http://www.bedlamtc.co.uk.

279. Deane and Shaw, op.cit.. For full background, see Hunt (ed.), and op.cit., (ed.), *Popular Romances of the West of England: The Drolls, Traditions, and Superstitions of Old Cornwall (Second Series)*, London: John Camden Hotten, 1865; William Bottrell (ed.), *Traditions and Hearthside Stories of West Cornwall: First Series*, Penzance: W. Cornish, 1870, and (ed.), *Traditions and Hearthside Stories of West Cornwall: Second Series*, Penzance: Beare and Son, 1873, and (ed.), *Traditions and Hearthside Stories of West Cornwall: Third Series*, Penzance: F. Rodda, 1880.

280. The company contributed to the Torbay Millennium Pageant and Rory Wilton was production manager for the St Just-in-Penwith productions of *Ordinalia*.

281. These presently include Tori Cannell, Andrew Crabb, Cordelia Chisholm, Christopher William Hill, T.J. Holmes, Liane Jose, Dominic Sewell and Kirsty Smeeth.

282. A devised piece.

283. This is number 333 in the Aarne-Thompson classification system of folktales. Most people are acquainted with Grimms' version but its origins are in French folklore.

284. This was based on the traditional tale by Hans Christian Andersen (1805-75). Hilary Coleman is now more famous for her musicianship in Cornwall. She is a leading member of the Cornish group *Dalla*. See Alan M. Kent, 'Alex Parks, Punks and Pipers: Toward a History of Popular Music in Cornwall 1967-2007' in Philip Payton (ed.), *Cornish Studies: Fifteen*, Exeter: University of Exeter Press, 2007, p.209-47.

285. This was based on the Mermaid of Zennor. A useful comparative text is Charles Causley and Michael Foreman, *The Merrymaid of Zennor*, London: Orchard Books, 1999.

286. There are numerous Cornish giant folk narratives.

287. Applebee operates as a member of *Dalla*, and as a solo performer.

288. See Will Coleman, *Tom and the Giant*, Cornwall: Brave Tales, 2005, and *Lutey and the Mermaid*, Cornwall: Brave Tales, 2005, and *Madgy Figgy's Pig*, Cornwall: Brave Tales, 2005, and *Tales from Porth: The Box Set*, Cornwall: Maga, 2008. Notice the continuity from the drama. Coleman had also worked with Kneehigh Theatre.

289. Tagney played with Hilary Coleman in Gwaryoryon. See Gwaryoryon, *Three Drunken Maidens*, Cornwall: Gwaryoryon, 1996.

290. This production very much patterns the imagining in Rosemary Sutcliffe, *Tristan and Iseult*, London: The Bodley Head, 1971.

291. A useful version of this narrative is found in Eric Quayle and Michael Foreman, *The Magic Ointment and Other Cornish Legends*, London: Anderson Press, 1986, pp.37-44.

292. See Hunt, *(Second Series)*, op.cit., pp.322-6.

293. See Quayle and Foreman, op.cit., pp.29-36; Shirley Climo and Anthony Bacon Venti, *Magic and Mischief: Tales from Cornwall*, New York: Clarion Books, 1999, pp.59-69.

294. This was actually based on a non-Cornish folktale: *The Buried Moon*.

295. See Bottrell, 1873, op.cit., pp.1-26; Robert Morton Nance, *The Cledry Plays: Drolls of Old Cornwall for Village Acting and Home Reading*, Penzance: The Federation of Old Cornwall Societies, 1956, pp. 6-35. Nance names his version, 'Duffy: A Tale of Trove'.

296. See Quayle and Foreman, op.cit.; Climo, op.cit.; and several in Neil Philip (ed.), *The Book of English Folktales*, Harmondsworth: Penguin, 1992, and Philip Wilson, *Celtic Fairy Tales for Children*, Bath: Parragon, 1999.

297. See Hunt, *(First Series)*, op.cit., pp. 120-6.

298. This is not based on the 1888 Edward Bosanketh novel of the same name.

299. See Alan M. Kent and Tim Saunders (eds. and trs.), *Looking at the Mermaid: A Reader in Cornish Literature 900-1900*, London: Francis Boutle Publishers, 2000, pp.212-19; Oliver J. Padel (ed. and tr.), *The Cornish Writings of the Boson Family*, Redruth: Institute of Cornish Studies, 1975. For a perspective on the continental and other Celtic origins of the folk-tale, see Brian Murdoch, 'Is *John of Chyanhor* Really a 'Cornish Ruodlieb'? in Philip Payton (ed.), *Cornish Studies: Four*, Exeter: University of Exeter Press, 1996, pp.45-64.

300. The imagining of Polperro is important in Bedlam's work. For a history, see Jonathan Couch, *The History of Polperro*, Clifton-upon-Teme: Polperro Heritage Press, 2004 [1871].

301. Ibid., p.93.

302. Pascoe is Head of Music at Richard Lander School, Truro. He is a Cornu-centric composer.

303. See, for example, Angela Carter, *The Magic Toyshop*, London: Virago Press, 1981.

304. See Franz Kafka, *The Collected Novels*, Harmondsworth: Penguin, 1988.

305. http://www.cornish-theatre-collective.co.uk.

306. See *Black Letter Pamphlet*, op.cit.

307. Davies (ed.), op.cit., Rawe, op.cit., 1991.

308. The show starred Jayne Denny and Pal Kelman.

309. It starred Darcy Green.

310. The cast included David Kershaw, Jason Squibb, Jayne Denny, Pat Kelman, Peter Cadewell and T.J. Holmes, and toured Cornwall, England and Wales.

311. See Ordinalia Company, *Ordinalia: The Full Cycle*, Penzance: Three S Films, 2004. The company was organised by the Cornish Theatre Collective. See also the observations in Derek Williams, 'The Ordinalia Company's production of *The Passion* at St Just-in-Penwith' in *An Baner Kernewek / The Cornish Banner*, No. 106, 2001.

312. The life of Nelson was undergoing much reassessment during this phase. See, for example, Barry Unsworth, *Losing Nelson*, London: Hamish Hamilton, 1999.

313. For background on the Cornish in Mexico, see Arthur Cecil Todd, *The Search for Silver: Cornish Miners of Mexico 1824-1947*, St Austell: Cornish Hillside Publications, 2000 [1977].

314. Lowender Peran, *Medieval Mystery Play*, poster, 7 July 1996. For background, see Lowender Peran, *Lowender Peran: Festival of Celtic Culture*, Perranporth: Lowender Peran, 1994. The performance used the following text: Nance, Smith and Sandercock, op.cit., 1984. Other companies outside Cornwall were also resurrecting the dramas. See James Whetter, 'Charterhouse Theatre Company is performing a cycle of Mystery Plays' in *An Baner Kernewek / The Cornish Banner*, No. 104, 2001; Ben Batten, 'The Cornish Ordinalia at Amersham' in *An Baner Kernewek / The Cornish Banner*, No. 110, 2002.

315. http://www.minack.com.

316. This was between 2003 and 2006. The Minack Theatre ident, showing a set of red-clad dancers on the main Minack stage, is the last piece featured on http://www.youtube.com/watch?v=pjhNhEwzKt0.

317. See http://www.acornartscentre.co.uk.

318. For examples of the range of arts activity available at The Acorn, see Acorn Theatre, *Acorn October-December 2000*, Penzance: Acorn Theatre, 2000; *Acorn Autumn Season 2001*, Penzance: Acorn Theatre, 2001; *Acorn January-March 2003*, Penzance: Acorn Theatre, 2003; *Events Guide September-December*, Penzance: Acorn Theatre, 2008.

319. See *Cornish World / Bys Kernowyon*, No.6, 1995, pp.20-21.

320. Ibid., No.13, 1997, pp.16-17.

321. http://www.carrickleisureservices.org.uk.

322. http://www.sterts.co.uk. See also Sterts Theatre, *The Theatre on the Moor: Summer 2008*, Liskeard: Sterts Theatre, 2008. For some of the financial difficulties affecting the theatre, see 'Troubled moorland theatre rises like a Phoenix with ambitious programme' in *Western Morning News*, 16 December 2008.

323. For a history, see http://www.hallforcornwall.co.uk. See also 'Cornwall Needs a New Hall' in *Cornish World / Bys Kernowyon*, No.5, 1995, p.39; Patrick Schama, 'A Hall for Cornwall: The Campaign to Provide a Cultural Centre for Cornwall and the Man Behind It' in *Cornish Scene*, No.15, n.d. (but c.1995). Warner also usefully provided the author with a document by Sarah Smith, titled *Hall for Cornwall: Some Memories*, 2007. Warner has been involved in a large number of new building projects in his career including the Northcott Theatre, Exeter, and The Globe Playhouse, Southwark. He was also an assistant director at the Royal Court in the last days of Lindsay Anderson, Bill Gaskill and Peter Gill. Warner is presently director of Suffolk Artlink. Other influential figures in the

development of the Hall for Cornwall included Sarah Smith, Arthur Pickering, Tina Evans, Tim Guy and Pete Boyden. Support also came from Roger Taylor, Suzanne Manuell, and The Levellers. For Warner, also see K. G. Foster (ed.), *Piran Round, Perranporth: Souvenir Programme*, Cornwall: Cornwall County Council, 1969.

324. For example, in 2008 the Hall for Cornwall mounted an ambitious in-house production titled *Barabas*, an adaptation of Christopher Marlowe's *The Jew of Malta*. A successful Cornu-centric piece during the Hall's development was Duchy Opera's *The Wreckers*, directed by David Sulkin, in 2006.

325. See http://www.cornwall.ac.uk/thekeay. See also Keay Theatre, *The Keay Events: September–December 2008*, St Austell: Keay Theatre, 2008.

326. The Hub was initially developed as a Mid-Cornwall College course at St Austell Arts Centre in the late 1980s.

327. For a range, see Restormel Borough Council, *The Daphne du Maurier Festival of Arts and Literature*, op.cit. Although initially focusing on 'local' literature and arts, this festival has increasingly embraced Anglo-centric presenters. It has shown poor understanding of theatre and literature from Cornwall.

328. See http://www.kidzrus.net.

329. See Tolmen Centre, *Constantine's Arts and Community Centre: September 2008–January 2009*, Constantine: Tolmen Centre, 2008.

330. See for example, English Heritage, *English Heritage Events 1999*, London: English Heritage, 1999. Similar ignorance was displayed in Cornwall County Council, *Historic Cornwall*, Truro: Cornwall County Council, 1997, which lists a plethora of industrial sites, but no theatrical venues for visitors.

331. Cornwall Heritage Trust, *To Safeguard Cornwall's Heritage*, Mevagissey: Cornwall Heritage Trust, n.d.

332. See West Country Tourist Board, *West Country Writers*, Exeter: West Country Tourist Board, n.d.; Kirsten Whiting, *Falmouth Festival of Literature and Arts*, Falmouth: Falmouth Festival of Literature and Arts, 2003. Neither featured dramatists.

333. 'Star-Gazy Pie and Sauerkraut' in James Stock, *Star-Gazy Pie: Two Plays*, London: Nick Hern Books, 1995, pp.81-160.

334. 'Blue Night in the Heart of the West' in ibid., pp.5-78.

335. This narrative formed the theme of a 1991 play, *The Shaming of Bright Millar*, which was produced by Contact Theatre in Manchester. Stock returned to the script again to develop the piece further into *Star-Gazy Pie and Sauerkraut*, Ibid., p.81.

336. Ibid., p.104.

337. See Hunt, *(Second Series)*, op.cit., pp.407-35.

338. Stock, op.cit.

339. Lowerson, op.cit.

340. The process has been undertaken since the Iron Age, but has had periods of revival, notably in the eighteenth century.

341. See, for example, Paul Broadhurst, *Tintagel and the Arthurian Mythos*, Launceston: Pendragon Press, 1992; Hale, Kent and Saunders, op.cit. Robert Stephen Hawker wrote a poem about the Kieve titled 'The Sisters of Glen Nectan' (*c*.1831). The waterfall descends to a bowl-like undercut, before passing down the valley.

342. Stock, op.cit., p.159.

343. See Bran Nicol, *D.M. Thomas: Writers and Their Work*, Tavistock: Northcote House Publishers Ltd, 2002.

344. See Nick Darke, *Plays: One*, London: Methuen, 1999, pp.vii-viii.

345. See Deacon, George and Perry, op.cit.

346. Nick Darke, 'The Body' (1983) in Andy Kempe, *The Script Sampler*, Cheltenham: Nelson Thornes Ltd, 2002, p.133.

347. For background, see Darke, op.cit., 1987. The play had a cast of 100 speaking parts and 1,500 local people were involved in the production.

348. Darkle, op.cit., 1999, pp.1-67.

349. Ibid., p.xii.

350. Ibid., pp.269-70.

351. Ibid., p.318.

352. Maurice Smelt, *101 Cornish Lives*, Penzance: Alison Hodge, 2006, pp.59-61.

353. John B. Cornish (ed.), *The Autobiography of a Cornish Smuggler: Captain Harry Carter of Prussia Cove 1749-1809*, Truro: D. Bradford Barton, 1971 [1894].

354. Darke, op.cit., p.74.

355. Nick Darke, *The Riot*, London: Methuen, 1999, p.88.

356. Ibid., p.86.

357. Nick Darke and Jane Darke, *The Wrecking Season*, Porthcothan: Boatshed Films, 2004. This was broadcast on BBC4 22 July 2005. See also http://www.thewreckingseason.com.

358. Nick Darke and Jane Darke, *The Art of Catching Lobsters*, Porthcothan: Boatshed Films, 2005. This was first broadcast on BBC4 27 September 2007. See also http://www.theartofcatchinglobsters.com. A festival of Darke's work began in 2009, titled 'Darke Visions': Rough Coast Theatre Company presented *The King of Prussia* at the Minack Theatre; *Ting Tang Mine* was also toured.

359. See http://www.o-region.co.uk. This text has not been published.

360. Angarrack, op.cit.

361. Angarrack, op.cit., 2008, p.iii.

362. Simon Turley, *Where Are You Gone, Jimmy Trevenna?* 1996. I am indebted to the playwright for supplying a copy of this text, which was revised for its performance in 2008.

363. See, for example, Simon Turley, *Seeing Without Light*, Cardigan: Parthian, 2005. This play explores the issue of immunity to HIV. It was produced at the Drum, Theatre Royal Plymouth as part of a 'Theatre of Science' project.

364. Turley, op.cit., 1996, p.6.

365. Ibid., pp.8-9.

366. See, for example, Rob Burton, 'A Passion to Exist: Cultural Hegemony and the Roots of Cornish Identity' in Philip Payton (ed.), *Cornish Studies: Five*, Exeter: University of Exeter Press, 1997, pp.151-63.

367. These are themes regularly found in the poetry and drama of Charles Causley.

368. Such teaching was extremely rare within the school system during this phase. Jenner's *Handbook* was only ten years old. An exception was E.G. Retallack Hooper, who did teach Cornish to children at Mount Pleasant House School, Camborne. See Peter Berresford Ellis, *The Cornish Language and its Literature*, London and Boston: Routledge and Kegan Paul, 1974, pp.150-1.

369. Turley, op.cit., 1996, p.34.

370. Ibid., p.37.

371. Ibid., p.55.

372. See Keskerdh Kernow / Cornwall Marches On, *Keskerdh Kernow / Cornwall Marches On Souvenir Programme*, Truro: Keskerdh Kernow, 1997.

373. This was downstairs at the Acorn Theatre, Penzance. The piece also played Coads Green, Bodmin and Polperro.

374. Kent, op.cit., p.269.

375. Simon Parker, *A Star on the Mizzen*, Liskeard: Giss' On Books, 1997, pp.21-2.

376. See K.C. Phillipps (ed.), *The Cornish Journal of Charles Lee*, Padstow: Tabb House, 1995; Simon Parker (ed.), *Chasing Tales: The Lost Stories of Charles Lee*, Linkinhorne: Giss' On Books, 2002.

377. Scavel an Gow, *Dream Atlas*, Linkinhorne: Giss 'On Books, 2002, p.5. For a consideration of the performance work of Scavel an Gow, see Patrick Laviolette, 'Where Difference Lies: Performative Metaphors of Truth, Deception and Placelessness in the Cornish Peninsula' in Leslie Howard and Helen Paris (eds.), *Performance and Place*, Basingstoke: Palgrave, 2006, pp.139-47. Laviolette also considers Kneehigh Theatre in this chapter.

378. See *Scryfa*, Vol 1, 2003.

379. Simon Parker, *Full as an Egg*, Mount Hawke: Truran, 2006.

380. Simon Parker, *Seven Stars: A Cornish Christmas Play for Voices*, Linkinhorne: Hairy Bear Books, 2006.

381. Ibid., p.196.

382. Ibid., pp.16-17.

383. Ibid., pp.36-7. For more traditional material on Christmas in Cornwall, see Tony Deane and Deane Shaw, *A Cornish Christmas*, Stroud: The History Press, 2008.

384. Simon Parker (ed.), *Cornwall Marches On! / Keskerdh Kernow*, Truro: Keskerdh Kernow, 1998.

385. Jonathon Plunkett, *A Name Perpetual*, 1997. Joseph is purported to have said that he would have 'a name perpetual and a fame permanent and immortal'. For a full context, see Mark Stoyle, *West Britons: Cornish Identities and the Early Modern British State*, Exeter: University of Exeter Press, 2002.

386. See, for example, J.P. Mustill, *Summer needs no brightening: An gof and the 1497 Cornish Rebellion*, Newmill: Blue Elvan Press, 1997; Ian Arthurson, *The Perkin Warbeck Conspiracy 1491-1499*, Stroud: Sutton, 1997.

387. Plunkett, op.cit., p.9.

388. Ibid., p.21-22. Plunkett and Parker also collaborated with Janine Southern and S. Vince on a play titled *To Catch a Tale*. See Jonathon Plunkett, Janine Southern, Simon Parker and S. Vince, *To Catch a Tale*, Callington Writers' Group, 2001. In this drama, the main characters interact with a storyteller.

389. The play was performed at Callington Community College. A radio version was broadcast on BBC Radio Cornwall. For other theatre along the way, see Parker, op.cit. 390. See http://www.creativeskills.org.uk/CaseStudies/PaulineSheppard.

391. See Shiva Theatre, *Meryasek*, programme, Cornwall: Shiva Theatre, 1980.

392. Cf. the Richard Jenkin-edited literary magazine, *Delyow Derow*. For an anti-Revivalist magazine during this phase, see *Eythen*, edited by Tim Saunders and Tony Snell.

393. For a full list of Sheppard's plays and the companies that produced the work, see http://www.doollee.com/PlaywrightsS/SheppardPauline.htm.

394. These two texts have Cornish connections. Graham was inspired to write his book from his time spent at Fowey, while Mark Twain was Cornish on his mother's side.

395. See Edward Bosanketh, *Tin*, Marazion: Justin Brooke, 1988 [1888].

396. See http://www.dressinggranite.net/background. This is the site related to the film version of the play.

397. For the story, see Arthur Quiller-Couch (ed.), *Charles Lee: Cornish Tales*, London: Dent, 1941, pp.109-216.

398. Parker, op.cit., 2002, pp.227-8.

399. See http://www.cornish-theatre-collective.co.uk.

400. See Sir Arthur Quiller-Couch Memorial Fund Committee, *Q: A Great Cornishman*, Truro: Sir Arthur Quiller-Couch Memorial Fund Committee, 2008.

401. D.M. Thomas, *Hell Fire Corner*, 2003. The script has not yet been published. I am grateful to the author for supplying me with a copy.

402. See D.M. Thomas, *Memories and Hallucinations*, Victor Gollancz, 1988. For current work, see http://www.dmthomasonline.com.

403. D.M. Thomas, *The White Hotel*, London: Viking, 1981, *Bleak Hotel: The Hollywood Saga of the White Hotel*, London: Quartet Books, 2008.

404. See, for example, D.M. Thomas (ed. and trs.), *Alexander Pushkin: 'The Bronze Horseman' and Other Poems*, Harmondsworth: Penguin, 1982, and *Alexander Solzhenitsyn: A Century in His Life*, London: Little, Brown and Company, 1998.

405. D.M. Thomas, *Birthstone*, London: Gollancz, 1980.

406. For a selection, see D.M. Thomas, *Selected Poems*, Harmondsworth: Penguin, 1983.

407. See Kent, op.cit., 2000, pp.221-3; Nicol, op.cit.

408. D.M. Thomas, *Charlotte*, London: Duckworth, 2000.

409. See Kerrow Hill, *The Brontë Sisters and Sir Humphry Davy: A Sharing of Visions*, Penzance: Patten Press, 1994. For more on this, see Kent, 2002, p.214.

410. D.M. Thomas, *The Puberty Tree*, Newcastle upon Tyne: Bloodaxe, 1992.

411. D.M. Thomas, *Dear Shadows*, Truro: Fal Publications, 2004, p.17.

412. Conversation between D.M. Thomas and the author of this volume in 1996.

413. A subsequent life has been published. See Allan Buckley, *Bert Solomon: A Rugby Phenomenon*, Mount Hawke: Truran, 2007.

414. Thomas, op.cit., 2004.

415. The importance of this is celebrated in Payton, op.cit., 1993. See also Jerry Clarke and Terry Harry (eds.), *Tales from Twickenham*, Redruth: Clarke and Harry, 1991, and Andy Seward, 'Cornish Rugby and Cultural Identity: A Socio-historical Perspective' in Payton (ed.), op.cit., 1997, pp.164-79.

416. John Hurst, 'Literature in Cornwall' in Ibid., p.299-302; Kent, op.cit., 2000.

417. See Mundic Nation and Hall for Cornwall, *D.M. Thomas: Hell Fire Corner*, programme, Truro: Hall for Cornwall, 2004.

418. Thomas has confirmed Macneill's importance in the production. In an e-mail to the author on 22 September 2008, Thomas observes that 'she was not only the director, but gave me great help preparing my script for the stage'.

419. See Mundic Nation and Hall for Cornwall, op.cit., p.11.

420. Ibid., p.12.

421. Ibid., p.13. For the significance of Hodge, see Kent, op.cit., 2007, pp.209-247.

422. Thomas, op.cit., 2003, p.7.

423. Ibid., p.6.

424. There is a strong thread of this in Thomas's poetry. See Thomas, op.cit., 1983, pp.49-51.

425. Thomas knows this culture intimately. He has edited the work of the poet John Harris. See D.M. Thomas (ed.), *Songs from the Earth: Selected Poems of John Harris*, Padstow: Lodenek Press, 1977.

426. Thomas, op.cit., 2003, p.7. Elements of this trans-national Cornish culture are found in A.L. Rowse, *A Cornish Childhood*, London: Anthony Mott, 1982 [1942].

427. Ibid., p.9.

428. Ibid., p.10.

429. Such frankness is not, for example, usually found in the work of Nick Darke. Cf. N.R. Phillips, *The Saffron Eaters*, Exeter: Devon Books, 1987; Alan M. Kent, *Electric Pastyland*, Wellington: Halsgrove, 2007.

430. The title of the play originates from the corner of the 'home' end at Redruth's ground. Hell Fire Corner was also the name of a road and rail junction outside of Ypres, Belgium during the First World War. This might indicate the term's origin at Redruth.

431. Thomas, op.cit., 2003, p.22.

432. Kershaw, op.cit.

433. Thomas, op.cit., 2004, p.97.

434. See Graham James, 'Play fails to live up to expectation' in *The West Briton*, 8 May 2004. James's review is unfairly critical.

435. Alan M. Kent, *Dreaming in Cornish*, Liskeard: Giss' On Books: 1998.

436. Alan M. Kent, *Out of the Ordinalia*, St Austell: Lyonesse Press, 1995, p.3.

437. Ordinalia Trust, *A Vision for the Future: An Inspiration from the Past*, Perranwell Station: Ordinalia Trust, 1996.

438. Kent, op.cit., 2005, p.25.

439. See Richard Beadle and Pamela M. King (eds.), *York Mystery Plays: A Selection in Modern Spelling*, Oxford, Clarendon Press, 1984; Otto Huber, Christian Stück and Ingrid Shafer (eds. and trs.), *Othmar Weis and Joseph Alois Daisenberger: Oberammergau: Passionspiel 2000*, Oberammergau: Gemeinde Oberammergau, 2000.

440. See Kent, op.cit., 2008, p.viii.

441. http://www.bishbashboshproductions.squarespace.com

442. Alan M. Kent, *Oogly es Sin: The Lamentable Ballad of Anthony Payne, Cornish Giant*, London: Francis Boutle Publishers, 2007. This played at the Soho Theatre London, as well as in Cornwall.

443. Ibid., p.12 and p.25. The play was nominated for a Sony Regional Drama Radio Award for 2007.

444. For background, see Richard McGrady, *Music and Musicians in Early Nineteenth-Century Cornwall: The World of Joseph Emidy – Slave, Violinist and Composer*, Exeter: University of Exeter Press, 1991.

445. Kent, op.cit., 2008, p.vi.

446. Ibid., p.10.

447. Ibid., p.vii. The company also consisted of Joanne Clare, Victoria Guy, Molly Weaver and director John Hoggarth. The play toured Cornwall on two runs in 2008 and played at the Camden People's Theatre, London in August 2008.

448. Ibid., p.30.
449. Ibid., p.viii.
450. Ibid., p.39. For a review, see *The Cornishman*, 13 November 2008, p.16.
451. Alan M. Kent, *Surfing Tommies*, London: Francis Boutle Publishers, 2009.
452. Ken George, *Flogholeth Krist / The Cornish Ordinalia – the missing play: The Childhood of Christ*, Cornwall: Kesva an Taves Kernewek, 2006.
453. Alan M. Kent, *Nativitas Christi / The Nativity: A New Cornish Mystery Play*, London: Francis Boutle Publishers, 2006.
454. See, for example, Ken George, *The Pronunciation and Spelling of Revived Cornish*, Cornwall: The Cornish Language Board, 1986.
455. See the argument in Richard McGrady, *Traces of Ancient Mystery: The Ballad Carols of Davies Gilbert and William Sandys*, Redruth: Institute of Cornish Studies, 1993.
456. George, op.cit., 2006, pp.162-3.
457. Kent, op.cit., p. 109.
458. See Kneehigh Theatre, op.cit., 2005, p.207.
459. Until recently, Grose lived all of his life in Truro, attending Richard Lander School and Truro College. After some study at Dartington College of Arts, Grose wrote a play for Grinning Gargoyle titled *Scorched*. Mike Shepherd and Nick Darke saw Grose perform in this, and offered him a job with Kneehigh Theatre. The RSC-funded youth theatre version of Darke's *Hell's Mouth* was influential in his development as a performer and writer.
460. An important actor in the company during this phase was Arran Hawkins.
461. See Kneehigh Theatre, *Quick Silver: A Cornish Western Pantomime*, programme, Truro: Kneehigh Theatre, 2002.
462. This was matching renewed interest overseas in Cornish heritage. Grose observes that 'Part of it is the fascination with migrations. I went to Real Del Monte in Mexico a few years ago to find the Cornish miners' cemetery. What amazes me is that our ancestors travelled by boat, had nothing, and were seeking work'. Interview with Alan M. Kent, January 2009.
463. See Emma Rice and Carl Grose, *Cymbeline*, London: Oberon Books, 2007.
464. http://www.o-region.co.uk. In 2004, Grose also developed the Tarantino-esque short film, *Kernow's Kick-Ass Kung-Fu Queens*. Short films continue to interest him as a writer and director.
465. Ibid.
466. Carl Grose, *Superstition Mountain*, unpublished playscript, 2008, pp.11-12. I am indebted to Carl Grose for letting me have sight of this script.
467. See Kent, op.cit., 2005 and 2007. St Day features heavily in these two texts. See also Myrna Combellack, *The Permanent History of Penaluna's Van*, Cornwall: Cornish Fiction, 2003. Grose says that he is 'really interested in keeping the

tourists out. I'm very interested in revealing the interior of the place. I much prefer the post-industrial landscapes the tourists don't get to see: Par Docks, Bugle, Nancegollan and St Day.' Interview with Alan M. Kent, January 2009.

468. Parker, op.cit., 2002, p.9.

469. See http://www.doollee.com/PlaywrightsM/murphy-anna-maria.html for a list of works. In March 2010, Murphy's play *Scummow Things Washed Up by the Sea* was broadcast by BBC Radio 4.

470. http://www.roguetheatre.co.uk.

471. Bec Applebee, "*Oh Mary*", programme, 2009.

472. See the critique in Kent, op.cit., 1998.

473. See the vision of the St Piran Trust at http://www.st-piran.com. This organisation wishes to make the oratory and relics of St Piran open to the public. The initial play was developed in 2000, co-ordinated by Howard Curnow, who had for many years helped to organise the annual pilgrimage across the dunes. Michael Truscott played Piran, with Will Coleman as one of the lead performers. In 2001, directorial control passed to Brian Odgers, but the play did not take place due to the Foot and Mouth Disease crisis. Odgers continued to direct for the next few years, but then was succeeded by Steve Jacobs. In 2007, the play was performed in torrential rain. The 2009 play was directed by Jim Carey. Aside from the initial production, Perran Tremewan played the role of Piran until 2008. In 2009 the role was played by Colin Retallack. I am indebted to Barbara and Tom Tremewan for their information here.

474. See *The Legend of St Piran,* leaflet, 2003. See also Bolingey Troyl Band, *Gwenognnnow Hag Oll*, St Agnes: Bolingey Troyl Band, 1998.

475. For a context, see Jonathan Howlett, 'Putting the Kitsch into Kernow' in Philip Payton (ed.), *Cornish Studies: Twelve*, Exeter: University of Exeter Press, 2004, pp.30-60.

476. For the life of St Piran, see Nicholas Orme (ed.), *Nicholas Roscarrock's Lives of the Saints of Cornwall and Devon*, Exeter: Devon and Cornwall Record Society, 1992, pp.105-8.

477. The Truro-based Skinner's Brewery presents St Piran as surfing on his millstone in their merchandising and promotions.

478. See Robert Morton Nance, A.S.D. Smith, and Graham Sandercock (eds. and trs.), *The Cornish Ordinalia, Third Play: Resurrection*, Cornwall: The Cornish Language Board, 1984, pp.160-1. This is a Unified spelling of Cornish.

CONCLUSION

Recycling the Plen-an-Gwarry – Coming Full Cycle and Full Circle?

'Heb dallathe na dowethva,
Fur wyre me ew'

['Without beginning nor end
very truly I am.']

The words of 'The Father in Heaven', from *The Creacion of the World,*
scribed by William Jordan, 1611[1]

'Cornwall, after flouting the stage for so long, has come back to it with a
rush. And no wonder when you consider how rooted [it] is in theatrical
tradition.'

From *Up From The Lizard* by J.C. Trewin, 1948[2]

As the research and writing of this book neared completion, I became aware
of the need to reflect on the diversity of theatrical practice taking place in
Cornwall at the end of the new century's first decade. In the month of
December 2008, I was pleased to see the Stiltskin Theatre Company present
their version of *Gogmagog* – one of Cornwall's oldest origin stories – in both
Cornwall and England.[3] That this narrative has lasted and is now being
presented as a drama is again testament to the tenacious nature of Cornish
culture. In the same month, I also witnessed Lostwithiel's annual Pageant
event. This piece of promenade para-theatre was instigated in the mid-1980s
by Catherine Rachel John,[4] but has now become a traditional part of the
town's mid-winter celebrations. Within its 'players' of St Petroc, shepherds,
kings and stars, accompanied by parading musicians, we see a continuity
stretching back into the medieval world. When the promenade walked past
Lostwithiel's Duchy Palace (not so long ago, the home of Cornwall's unique
jurisdiction and geo-political structure[5]), the layers of time suddenly
collapsed. High on the hill still sits Restormel Castle; though now contentiously owned by 'English Heritage',[6] its surrounding community is still

Fig. 126. Two twenty-first century shepherds, and a lamb, outside the Duchy Palace in Lostwithiel, 2008.

resistant to becoming like everywhere else. Many residents taking part in the event are part of a sustainability project for twenty-first-century living, *Transition Culture*, which is just one thread of Cornish local resilience, amongst many others.[7] Though inspired by a long distant past, the Pageant remains relevant in a new millennium. Meanwhile, far to the west, in the very same week (between 14 and 22 December 2008), the town of Penzance celebrated a 'revived' *Montol* [English: Winter Festival[8]] with guize dancers, mummers' plays, Penglaz (the town's Obby Oss), masks, traditional music and a bonfire high on Lescudjack Hill Fort to the north of the town. In 2009, St Ives Guisers [sic] presented a new adaptation of a Robert Morton Nance 'Christmas play' at St Ives Arts Club, while in Marazion a Cornish language class produced two shows to celebrate Christmas a pantomime in Cornish (*Hikka Chi An Hordh*) written by Yowann Parker; and a play by Penny Norman, *Nos Nadelik*. The topsy-turvy theatrical culture of former times still appeals today – bringing together ritual, landscape and community to celebrate the coming again of light at the mid-winter solstice.

While these events were happening in and around Lostwithiel and west Cornwall, at the Helford Theatre in Truro College, Final Year BTEC

National Diploma in Performing Arts students, who form the College's theatre company 'Stage Company Trucco', presented Timberlake Wertenbaker's 1987 play *Our Country's Good*.[9] This drama, about 'transportation' and the first prison colony in Australia, features two Cornish characters based on real people: John Arscott (tried at Bodmin Assizes in August 1783 for burglary and breaking and entering); and, more famously, Dabby (or Mary) Bryant, a Fowey fisherman's daughter (tried in Exeter in March 1786 for highway robbery).[10] Planning her escape from the colony at the end of Wertenbaker's play, Mary then fled northward in an open boat, sailing 3,254 miles in 69 days to the East Indies, only to be recaptured. Such was her notoriety and heroism, however, that, as Cook has detailed, she was eventually given a full pardon.[11] Bryant is a true Celtic drama queen, and the kind of no-nonsense stage Cornish woman we need to see more often. Anna Maria Murphy's *"Oh Mary"*, performed by Bec Applebee in 2009, is taking us in this direction.

Outside of Cornwall, in the same week, in that very centre-point of the English theatrical world – Stratford-upon-Avon – at The Courtyard Theatre, Kneehigh Theatre premiered their interpretation of *Don John* to great acclaim, before undertaking a national and international tour.[12] These are just a few tiny pieces of theatre in a fascinating ongoing history, where space, place and performance intersect, grow and learn from each other. This history began with a circle – the *plen-an-gwarry* at Perran Round – and it ends here with the completion of another circle of connected history and culture. Although elements of the theatrical continuum sometimes apparently disappear and subsequently seem lost to the mists of time, no sooner is that thought, than they suddenly re-emerge in new and exciting forms. But we should have confidence about this, for that is the way of theatre. We just need to trust it more: to assimilate, to challenge, to reinvigorate and to celebrate the human spirit in this land that is sometimes *Kernow*, sometimes Cornwall.

Although there is a great deal of theatrical activity in Cornwall, I would like to return to an observation that Mike Shepherd makes in his Preface at the start of this book, as to whether the Cornish people are actually bothered about theatre, identifying a kind of apathy amongst the population. Perhaps there would be even more theatre in Cornwall, if more people could be dragged out of their living rooms and away from their computer screens to see it. We have to remember that this observation is also borne from the life of an experienced performer who has struggled to develop audiences but who has also achieved remarkable theatre in Cornwall. Perhaps Cornish people *are* bothered about theatre, but are so accustomed to it, historically and culturally, that they view it as a given rather than a precious thing;

therefore, supported or not, it won't go away. It stubbornly persists despite local, 'national', Britain-wide and international changes. That said, Shepherd indicates that in the twenty-first century we shouldn't just passively accept this heritage and believe it will be around forever. It needs development, nurturing, support – and part of that support needs to come from the institutions of Cornwall.

Three in particular stand out from the rest as development opportunities. Although the Combined Universities of Cornwall at Tremough, Penryn, is an enormously important step forward to cultural development in Cornwall, it has yet to develop organically the kind of Cornu-centric theatre which this book has shown does exist in pockets, but needs to develop across a wider spectrum. The field of Cornish Studies needs to embrace and investigate further the theatrical, dance, operatic and performing arts traditions of Cornwall. Although literary and cultural studies have achieved a great deal in the past ten years, these fields remain ripe for development and research. Hopefully, more performance and theatrical work will arise from the move of Dartington College of Arts to the campus in Cornwall. This might even nurture a truly Cornish theatre school, with an international reputation that would help prevent (as in other fields) artistic and theatrical 'brain-drain' away from Cornwall. Another important institution is the Hall for Cornwall. Although there have been indicators of the potential of this centre, it seems that there is quite a lot more it could do in developing a true theatre of Cornwall. It has the historic impetus to generate work as important as, say, the Abbey Theatre in Dublin and yet, so far, it has failed in this endeavour. There are the companies, performers, actors, designers and writers to do the job, but currently not the economic will from the Hall for Cornwall. It should look to spearheading a Cornish National Theatre. Maybe this could happen. Who would have thought just ten years ago that the Cornish language would have official recognition and governmental support? Culture changes quickly, and perhaps it is high time for the Hall for Cornwall to move more speedily towards its original aims and objectives. Meanwhile, a third way is being considered: for some time, Kneehigh Theatre has been trying to develop a mobile alternative theatre and performance space. Tentatively titled *The Asylum*, this might just be the way forward for developing more exciting theatre. Described as 'shelter, refuge, sanctuary, madhouse, tent', it would be a tented-style structure that could be erected in one day, allowing it to be pitched on a variety of surfaces, in a variety of places.[13] Rooted in the tradition of circus and troubadour-style performance, this is perhaps akin to the way Footsbarn have developed their shows. It stands to be another highly innovative way of presenting theatre.

Some theatrical traditions of Cornwall are curiously absent. Given that places such as York and Coventry in England, and Oberammergau in Germany can mount regular productions of mystery play cycles, it seems strange that Cornwall's dramas are not performed more regularly, and indeed repackaged as major tourist events. Successive reinventions of the dramas (with alternative translations, writers and performers, perhaps mixing community groups with professionals) would provide Cornwall with a unique vision of itself, as well as a new kind of international awareness of its culture. The tourism and economic potential of Cornwall's Christmas dramatic tradition is also yet to be realised. Instead of looking to new technologies, facilities, attractions, and ways of working for the sustainability of communities, planners, perhaps decision-makers and arts-funders might reconsider what makes Cornwall distinctive in the first place.

As for cultural distinctiveness, the Cornish Gorsedd still has much to do. Although the ceremony itself is becoming more professional and more widely known,[14] the Gorsedd still does not adequately embrace theatrical culture – something of an irony considering that much of the Revival was based on Cornish derived from theatrical texts. The three-yearly Welsh–modelled *Esethvos Kernow* [Eisteddfod of Corwall] could be an important forum to

Fig. 127. Leaflet about Kneehigh Theatre's *The Asylum* project, 2009. Courtesy of Kneehigh Theatre.

nurture new dramatic work, but this has yet to happen. Although there have been haphazard attempts at developing an annual Gorsedd fringe, September's event has yet to embrace the kind of sustained festival that would facilitate cultural development and provide an opportunity for politically-aware young people to develop a new drama of Cornwall. By nature, it would seem, the Gorsedd is a conservative organisation. However, considering that a new generation of cultural activists is beginning to make headway in the institution, perhaps change could now occur. Given that theatre is Cornwall's natural creative medium, this would seem desirable.

Another absentee from the theatrical landscape of Cornwall is historical fiction. Considering the successful historical romantic construction of Cornwall in writings as diverse as those from Winston Graham, Susan Howatch, Rosamunde Pilcher and E.V. Thompson,[15] it is curious that there have been relatively few theatrical imaginings of their writings. Indeed, with a writer such as E.V. Thompson, whose writings have spanned major moments of 'dramatic' Cornish history,[16] why have not more of his novels been adapted? Perhaps it is their sheer epic nature which puts off dramatists. With Winston Graham, it is perhaps the defining vision of the *Poldark* series from BBC Television during the mid-1970s which means that any theatrical vision of them would be considered second-rate.[17] Still, it is a tempting proposition: the marshalling of a stage version of *Poldark* at the Hall for Cornwall? Surely this would be a cast-iron guarantee of a sell-out set of performances, alongside an international tour? The canonisation of Daphne du Maurier as a major British novelist, and a recent exhibition of Graham's life and work at the Royal Institution of Cornwall, indicate a rise in the cultural status of such authors, who should now perhaps be reconsidered in the theatre. Given technological developments in theatre (as witnessed in Kneehigh Theatre's *Brief Encounter*, and a recent London production of *The Woman in White*[18]), there is no reason why cinematic projection and special effects could not enhance the epic feel and stylisation of televised versions. For a generation, the television series *Poldark* defined an international vision of Cornishness.[19] Some forty years on, with a resilient, self-defining Cornwall – 'performing' devolution, if not yet gaining it politically – it would be interesting to look at the text again.

Two figures on the pan-British stage are also interesting to consider. These are Michael Grandage, and Thandiwe Adjewa 'Thandie' Newton. Both are important for different reasons. Grandage was born in Yorkshire in 1962, but was raised in Penzance, attending Humphry Davy Grammar School. Trained at the Central School of Speech and Drama, he is presently the artistic director of the influential Donmar Warehouse in London. Grandage has won numerous awards for his directorial work on *Frost/Nixon* and canonical drama such as *As You Like It*.[20] Although his career has focused on English texts, it would be interesting to speculate how, in the future, he might deal with Cornish-themed material. It would certainly be an interesting combination of directorial vision with place. Thandie Newton (b.1972) is an internationally-known film actress, the daughter of Nyasha (a Zimbabwean health-care worker) and Nick Newton (a white English artist). As the star of films such as *Mission Impossible II* and *Jefferson in Paris*, she has been prolific in talking about her childhood, partly spent in Penzance in Cornwall. As a mixed-race actress, her profile was raised by winning a BAFTA award in 2006 for Best Supporting Actress in *Crash*.[21] Though not predominantly a stage actress, she has shown by her success how far performers from Cornwall can go. Her presence on the world stage also reflects the move within Cornish theatre to begin examining non-white experience in a Celtic territory.[22]

Getting more Cornu-centric drama into the public realm is enormously important. Editors such as Tim Saunders, Simon Parker, Derek Williams and myself have made successful attempts to package the Cornish and Anglo-Cornish literary continuum for the twenty-first century public in ways previously unimagined.[23] That same energy is needed to gather up published and unpublished scripts and present them in anthologies of Cornish drama, so that they may be read and used in schools, colleges and universities, and performed by amateur theatrical groups.[24] There is the will to examine such work, but often a problem in accessing sometimes obscure texts. George Lillo's *Fatal Curiosity*, and Samuel Foote's *The Knights*, for example, ought to be much better known, but both are presently difficult to obtain.[25] Likewise, D.M. Thomas's *Hell Fire Corner* would make a interesting text for Advanced Level Theatre Studies in Cornwall, but it is unpublished.[26] There is also a need to present definitive versions of the historical canon of Cornish drama (in original spelling with translation), which have input not only from 'language experts' but also from cultural commentators and theatrical practitioners. This work is beginning to happen, and shows the scale and significance of the canon in world literature. Such work is important for challenging the general negativity shown towards Cornwall in the field of Celtic Studies. Further volumes exploring theatrical figures, institutions, texts and performers would also enhance this dimension of our understanding of Cornish, British and world history.

Importantly, the texts must also be claimed back by the people of Cornwall, away from the clutches of Celticists and Cornish-language enthusiasts. Landscape architect and eco-designer Andrew Clare has already begun this kind of exploration, designing an interpretative garden space on the former site of Glasney College which not only maps the former layout of the institution but also offers new, contemporary theatre space.[27] Through such initiatives the public can begin to appreciate anew the considerable contribution of this centre of learning, as well as find out more about Cornwall's theatrical heritage. Using eco-friendly building materials and an eye on contemporary design, Clare's plans point the way to a vibrant interpretation of the past. He has been inspired by medieval gardens,[28] but locates visionary theatre space (based on a maze design[29]) within a reconfigured Glasney College site, which reflects the cross design of the original church. The designs demonstrate his strong belief in site analysis, and his interest in the various user-groups. The gardens would contain medieval plants and medicinal herbs (thus making for a tactile and olfactory experience), but would also facilitate archaeological and heritage interpretation, as well as allowing for contemporary performance. Meanwhile, Philip Vaughn at the Mount Pleasant Eco Park, near the surfing town of Porthtowan, has been instrumental in constructing a modern amphitheatre there, made of recycled car tyres.[30] Sited at the top of Mount Pleasant, and looking across at the former mining landscape of Wheal Towan, the theatre makes an evocative and Cornu-centric site. Here then, we see an imagining of a 'green' *plen-an-gwarry*, indicative of not only recycled physicality but also recycled and reinterpreted culture with a 'sense of place'.[31] This sustainable

STAGE & OUTDOOR GALLERY

local theatre   school groups   miracle plays   live music   artwork display

Timber retaining walls

Rendered concrete blocks

Rendered concret water rill

Mosaic floor

GLASNEY HERITAGE GARDEN

ANDREW DAVID CLARE

Fig. 128. Design for a garden and theatre space on the former site of Glasney College, Penryn by Andrew Clare, 2008. Courtesy of Andrew Clare.

theatricality is clearly an important step forward. It lies only a few miles away from Perran Round.

As this physical world of performance is sustained, so must the needs of young people to create and develop within the theatre be supported. Since their inception in 2004, KEAP (Kernow Education Arts Partnership) have been providing a range of para-theatrical and theatrical opportunities for young people across Cornwall, from the primary, secondary and tertiary educational sectors, working with a wide range of practitioners. A flavour of such activity comes from KEAP's occasional magazine *The Big Picture*. At the Polperro Festival, Jo Tagney worked as a storyteller, allowing children in the local school to re-enact local legends through performance,[32] while poetry advocacy organisation 'Apples and Snakes' provided performance poetry in schools, hospitals and various outdoor venues.[33] Environmentally-themed performance took place at the gardens of Lanhydrock House, with Cornwall's Youth Dance Company presenting a work titled 'The Secret Life of Trees'.[34] Antony Waller, meanwhile, led an event titled 'The Edge' around Watergate Bay, connecting performance, environment and festival – this time celebrating surfing and the ocean.[35] Part of KEAP's work has been to help nurture events such as the Golowan Festival, as well as to encourage young people to develop new original plays for performance in primary schools.[36] In 2005, for example, while Cornwall Youth Theatre Company marked its 21st birthday,[37] the 'Ship of Dreams' performance project at Tregolls School in Truro celebrated Truro's maritime links,[38] Although the teaching of Cornish and Anglo-Cornish theatre has a long way to go in education in Cornwall, KEAP's emphasis on 'pride of place' shows a connection back to ritual, landscape and community that this book has made effort to explore. Cornwall's status as a theatrical centre has been given a great boost by the formerly London-centric National Youth Theatre holding open auditions for actors, designers, technicians and directors at Truro's Hall for Cornwall.[39] This shows from NYT a new awareness of 'peripheral Celtic Britain' being an exciting place for drama and performance. The KEAP Project has also promoted Cornwall and west Devon's status as a UNESCO World Heritage Site, which will surely offer new possibilities for drama. A flavour of this has come from 2008's *Imagineers* project which, as 'a celebration of man, machine and land', lit fires in the old stacks of engine houses to show what the landscape would once have looked like.[40] The mining heritage of Caradon Hill in east Cornwall was also considered in Simon Parker's script for a new community play, *Gonemena*, staged at the Sterts Theatre in June 2009.[41]

In these different but interconnected ways, a new generation of students, actors, directors, designers, technicians and writers will hopefully shape a new

Fig. 129. The *plen-an-gwarry* at Mount Pleasant Eco Park, composed of recycled car tyres.

drama of Cornwall. If some of the above happens in the next few years, then we will have come full circle: the theatre of Cornwall will be able to look at its past, operate in its present, but also look forward to a healthy and sustainable future. The cycle dramas at the backbone of the Cornish theatrical experience might be appreciated further, and stand in testament to a unique and important theatrical culture of Europe. If this happens, then we will truly understand the full cycle of space, place and performance over the centuries, emanating from a small, yet significant Celtic territory, whose identity continues to be asserted.[42] The theatre of Cornwall has overcome many difficulties and still faces many challenges in its evolution towards a combination of space, place and performance that will continue to challenge, delight and inspire audiences. J.C. Trewin rightly acknowledges that Cornwall is rooted in theatrical tradition. That has been the central argument of this book. Those roots continue to grow and develop, pushing ever deeper into the culture, and spreading dramatic branches ever outwards. If there have been moments when it has 'flouted the stage',[43] well, we can forgive it. Perhaps it is as strong now, in the twenty-first century, as it has ever been. The various theatrical creators of Cornwall have come back to it with a 'rush' that even wily Trewin may not have anticipated.

Fig. 130. A view of Perran Round as constructed for the Theatron Project. Courtesy of Drew Baker and Theatron Project, King's College, London.

In this way, the theatre of Cornwall speaks loudly to us. As the research for this book reached its conclusion, I was contacted by King's College London, who are developing Theatron,[44] a virtual reality tool for teaching and researching the subject of theatre history. Alongside the interpretation of such theatrical icons as the Theatre of Dionysis, the Globe Theatre, and the Paris Opera, was Perran Round at Perranzabuloe. Truly, it would seem, at long last, the theatre of Cornwall, is acknowledged in the pantheon of great world theatre. If the theatre of Cornwall could deliver a soliloquy about all of this, then it might choose the words of Helston's 1611 play, *The Creacion of the World*: *'Heb dallathe na dowethva, Fur wyre me ew'* ['Without beginning nor end, very truly I am.']⁴⁵ – just like the circle of a *plen-an-gwarry*. And so, Cornwall continues to create theatre, and we, as audience, continue to watch.

CONCLUSION: NOTES AND REFERENCES

1. Paula Neuss (ed. and tr.), *The Creacion of the World: A Critical Edition and Translation*, New York and London: Garland, 1983, pp.2-3.
2. J. C. Trewin, *Up from The Lizard*, London: Anthony Mott, 1982 [1948], pp.66-8.
3. See Lewis Thorpe (ed. and tr.), *Geoffrey of Monmouth: The History of the Kings of Britain*, Harmondsworth: Penguin, 1966, pp.72-3.
4. See Catherine Rachel John, *The Saints of Cornwall: 1500 Years of Christian Landscape*, Padstow: Tabb House, 2001 [1981]. Obviously, this performance is influenced by John's research interests.
5. George Harrison, *Substance of a Report on the Laws and Jurisdiction of the Stannaries in Cornwall*, London: Longman, Rees, Orme, Brown, Green and Longman, 1835. See also E. Trewin-Wolle (ed.), *Cornish Stannary Gazette*, No.1, Cornwall: Cornish Stannary Parliament, 1975.
6. See the observations in John Angarrack, *Breaking the Chains: Censorship, Deception and the Manipulation of Public Opinion in Cornwall*, Camborne: Stannary Publications, 1999, p.445-6.
7. Rob Hopkins, *The Transition Handbook: From Oil Dependency to Local Resilience*, Dartington: Green Books Ltd, 2008. The resilience alluded to is both green and political. See also Richard Heinberg, *Peak Everything: Waking Up to the Century of Decline in the Earth's Resources*, Forest Row: Clairview Books, 2007. The 'green' aspect of nationalistic resistance is found in the current policies of Mebyon Kernow, and occasional alliances with the Green Party in Cornwall. See Bernard Deacon, Dick Cole, and Gary Tregidga, *Mebyon Kernow and Cornish Nationalism*, Cardiff: Welsh Academic Press, 2003.
8. In his visit to Cornwall in 1700, Edward Lhuyd recorded *montol* or *An Vontol* as being Cornish for 'Winter Solstice'. See http://www.montol.co.uk. For the background to this visit, see Derek Williams, *Prying into Every Hole and Corner: Edward Lhuyd in Cornwall in 1700*, Redruth: Dyllansow Truran, 1993.
9. Timberlake Wertenbaker, *Our Country's Good*, London: Methuen, 1987. Wertenbaker's play was inspired by two texts: Robert Hughes, *The Fatal Shore: A History of the Transportation of Convicts to Australia, 1787-1868*, London: Vintage, 2003 [1986], and Thomas Keneally, *The Playmaker*, London: Serpentine Publishing, 1987.
10. See Stage Company Trucco, *Our Country's Good*, programme, Truro: Truro College, 2008. In the production, Arscott was played by Chris Blewett while Bryant was jointly played by Sarah Barker and Becca Halbert. The production was directed by Derekk Ross.
11. Judith Cook, *To Brave Every Danger: The Epic Life of Mary Bryant of Fowey*, London: Macmillan, 1993.

12. Http://www.kneehigh.co.uk.

13. See http://www.kneehigh.co.uk/asylum.

14. Embodied in Rod Lyon, *Gorseth Kernow: The Cornish Gorsedd – what it is and what it does*, Cornwall: Gorseth Kernow, 2008. The *Gorseth Kernow* website has also developed of late. See http://www.gorsethkernow.org.uk.

15. See, for example, Winston Graham, *The Poldark Omnibus*, London: The Bodley Head, 1991; Susan Howatch, *Penmarric*, London: Hamish Hamilton, 1971; Rosamunde Pilcher, *The Shell Seekers*, London: New English Library, 1988; E.V. Thompson, *Chase the Wind*, London: Macmillan, 1977.

16. See, for example, E.V. Thompson, *Ben Retallack*, London: Macmillan, 1977, and *Ruddlemoor*, London: Headline, 1995.

17. See Philip Dudley (dir.), *Poldark 1: Part One*, London: BBC Video, 1993 [1975]. There is a Poldark Appreciation Society.

18. This adaptation of Wilkie Collins' novel was by Andrew Lloyd Webber, David Zippel and Trevor Nunn. It played at the Palace Theatre, London from 2004-2006.

19. For commentary on this, see Nickianne Moody, 'Poldark Country and National Culture' in Ella Westland (ed.), *Cornwall: The Cultural Construction of Place*, Penzance: The Patten Press and the Institute of Cornish Studies, 1997, pp.129-36.

20. See Mark Kennedy, 'Director Michael Grandage Hits Broadway' in *The Huffington Post*, 28 April 2007. I am indebted to Jonathon Plunkett for drawing my attention to Grandage and Newton.

21. See Laura Barton, 'I was so incredibly self-conscious' in *The Guardian*, 28 May 2008.

22. Alan M. Kent, *The Tin Violin*, London: Francis Boutle Publishers, 2008.

23. See Tim Saunders (ed. and tr.), *Nothing Broken: Recent Poetry in Cornish*, London: Francis Boutle Publishers, 2006; *Scryfa*; Derek Williams, *Cornubia's Son: A Life of Mark Guy Pearse*, London: Francis Boutle Publishers, 2008; Alan M. Kent (ed.), *The Dreamt Sea: An Anthology of Anglo-Cornish Poetry 1928-2004*, London: Francis Boutle Publishers, 2004.

24. Rawe began this process earlier on. See Donald R. Rawe (ed.), *A Cornish Quintette: Five Original One Act Plays*, Padstow: Lodenek Press, 1973.

25. The only new published edition is Thomas Davies (ed.), *Lillo's Dramatic Works Vol. 2: Fatal Curiosity, Marina, Elmerick, or Justice Triumphant, Britannia and Batavia, Arden of Feversham*, Whitefish, Montana: Kessinger Publishing, 2008. A UK version is not available. See also Samuel Foote, *The Dramatic Works of Samuel Foote, Vol. I*, London: J. F. Rivington, C. Rivington, R. Baldwin, and S. Bladon, 1788. A modern edition does not exist.

26. D.M. Thomas, *Hell Fire Corner*, 2003.

27. See Andrew Clare, *Glasney: History, Heritage and Community*, BA (Hons) thesis in Garden Design, Arts and Environment, University College Falmouth, 2008.

28. See, for example, Sylvia Landsberg, *The Medieval Garden*, London: British Museum Press, 1996.

29. Note the Troy Town turf maze on the island of St Agnes in the Isles of Scilly, and three carved mazes in Rocky Valley, near Tintagel.

30. For a flavour of this, see http://www.mpecopark.co.uk/gallery. I am indebted to Andrew Clare for drawing my attention to this. For a context, see Kurt Gerard Heinlein, *Green Theatre: Promoting Ecological Preservation and Advancing the Sustainability of Humanity and Nature*, Berlin: VDM Verlag, 2007. See also Baz Kershaw, *Theatre Ecology: Environments and Performance*, Cambridge: Cambridge University Press, 2007. Another new *plen-an-gwarry* can be found at Palla Cross Farm, Frogpool, near Truro.

31. This reflects emergent literary and dramatic theory. See Greg Gerrard, *Ecocriticism*, London and New York: Routledge, 2004; Ursula K. Helse, *Sense of Place and Sense of Planet: The Environmental Imagination*, Oxford: Oxford University Press, 2008.

32. *The Big Picture*, Autumn, 2004, p.7.

33. Ibid., p.11.

34. Ibid., p.12.

35. Ibid., p.16-19. Such works fits into the observations made in Felicia Hughes-Freeland (ed.), *Ritual, Performance, Media*, London and New York, Routledge, 1998.

36. Ibid., pp.28-35.

37. Ibid., Summer, 2005, p.34. The long-term artistic director of this organisation is Dave Hunter.

38. Ibid., Spring, 2005, p.30.

39. http://www.nyt.org.uk.

40. *News from KEAP and RIO*, Summer, 2008, p.4. The producer of this event was Antony Waller, but it involved people from various organisations including The National Trust, King Edward Mine, Mineral Tramways, The Works, Hi8us Cornwall, KEAP, RIO (Real Ideas Organisation), The Cornwall Music Service and CUMPAS.

41. See 'Actors and 'gophers' wanted for mining play' in *Western Morning News*, 13 January 2009.

42. For a current context, see Martin Jones and George MacLeod, 'Regional spaces, spaces of regionalism: territory, insurgent politics and the English question' in *Transactions of the Institute of British Geographers*, 2004, pp.433-52. See also Joanie Willett, 'Cornish Identity: Vague Notion or Social Fact?' in Philip Payton, (ed.), *Cornish Studies: Sixteen*, Exeter: University of Exeter Press, 2008, pp.183-205.

43. Trewin, op.cit.

44. I am indebted here to Drew Baker of Theatron. See also *Maga: Cornish Language Partnership Newsletter*, Mis Hwevrer, 2009, p.3.

45. Neuss, op.cit.

BIBLIOGRAPHY

Manuscripts and Archive Collections

Arthur Quiller-Couch Archive, Trinity College, Oxford

BL: Additional MS. 32243

BL: Additional MS. 32244

BL: MS. Harl. MS. 1867

BL: MS. Harl. MS. 2252

Bodl. MSS. 28556-28557, Oxford

Borough Accounts, St Ives Guildhall

Charles Henderson Collection, Courtney Library, Royal Institution of Cornwall, Truro

Christopher Ebden, *Plan of the Assembly Rooms (High Cross, Truro): 14 designs submitted for the erection of the Old Assembly Rooms at Truro*, Royal Institution of Cornwall, Truro

Clark, Mr., *Theatre Collection*. Archive in the Courtney Library, Royal Institution of Cornwall, Truro

Constables List: Schedule B: *Constables List of the Borough of Truro*, Ref. N/80, 1803, Courtney Library, Royal Institution of Cornwall, Truro

Constables List: Schedule B: *Constables List of the Borough of St Clement*, Ref. N/73, 1803, Courtney Library, RIC, Truro

Bewnans Ke. MS. 23849D, NLW, Aberystwyth

Bewnans Meriasek. MS. Peniarth 105, NLW, Aberystwyth

Black Letter Pamphlet: News from Pe[n]rin in Cornwall of a most Bloody and un-exampled Murder, Quarto, Bodley, 4 M G29 (2), Oxford

Bodleian MS. Corn. e. 2, Oxford

Bodmin Manumissions in Bodmin Gospels, St Petroc's Gospels, BL: Add. MS.938, London

Diocese of Exeter: Statutes of Peter Quinell, 16/4

Donatus Glosses, BN MS. Lat. 13029 Paris [Bibliothèque Nationale]

Donatus Glosses, MS. Bodley 574, for 14 S.C. 2026 (3), Oxford

Gatley MS., Royal Institution of Cornwall, Truro

Glasney Cartulary. MS. Cornwall Records Office Dd R(S) 59

Gwreans an Bys. MS. Bodley 219, Oxford

Jenner Papers, Royal Institution of Cornwall, Truro

John of Cornwall, *Prophetia Merlini*. Cod. Ottobonianus Lat. 1474, Vatican

John Trembath Theatrical Archive, Newquay

Kneehigh Theatre Archive, Kneehigh Theatre, Truro

Life of St. Kea. MS. 23849D, NLW, Aberystwyth

Master B, Grossmith, Truro Theatre Poster, Rosewarne Collection R872-912, Royal
Institution of Cornwall, Truro

Mellors, C. *Sir Arthur Quiller-Couch 1863-1944: A List of Archive Material held at
Trinity College*, Oxford, 1991

Mrs Waylett, Truro Theatre Poster, Rosewarne Collection R872-912, Royal
Institution of Cornwall, Truro

Nance Collection, Royal Institution of Cornwall, Truro

Nicholas Roscarrock, *Lives of the Saints*. MS. Add. 3041, Cambridge

Nora Ratcliff, *Tristan of Cornwall: An Old Story Re-told*, unpublished MS., University
of Bristol Theatre Collection

Ordinalia. MS. Bodl. 791, Oxford

Pascon agan Arluth. BL: MS. Harley 1782

Papers of Charles Causley, EUL. MS. 50a, Exeter

Peniarth, MS. 428E, NLW

Prophetia Merlini, Cod. Ottobonianus Lat. 1474, Vatican

Reg Harris Archive, Lane Theatre, Newquay

Sir John Arundell's Stewards' Accounts: HK/17/1, Courtney Library, Royal
Institution of Cornwall, Truro

Taliesin MS. 3, Jesus College, Oxford

Thomas Shaw Methodism Collection, Courtney Library, Royal Institution of
Cornwall, Truro

Thurstan C. Peter Collection, Courtney Library, Royal Institution of Cornwall, Truro

Tobit-Glosses (Oxoniensis posterior) MS. Bodley 572, Oxford

Treatise on the Trial of Francis Tregian, St Mary's College, Oscott: MS. 545

Trioedd Ynys Prydian, MS, Peniarth 16, NLW, Aberystwyth

Vocabularium Cornicum, Cottonian or Old Cornish Vocabulary, BL: MS. Cotton
Vespasian A XIV, London

William Hals, *The Compleat History of Cornwall*, Truro, Courtney Library, Royal
Institution of Cornwall

Cornwall Record Office

CRO: AD43

CRO: AP/C/118/1

CRO: AR/21/21/2

CRO: AR/21/22

CRO: AR/26/2

CRO: B/Bod/20

CRO: B/Bod/233
CRO: B/Bod/244
CRO: B/Bod/314/1/6
CRO: B/Bod/314/2/12
CRO: B/Bod/314/2/15
CRO: B/Bod/314/2/20
CRO: B/Bod/314/2/21
CRO: B/Bod/314/2/26
CRO: B/Bod/314/3/10
CRO: B/Bod/314/3/21
CRO: B/Bod/314/3/22
CRO: B/Bod/314/3/32
CRO: B/Bod/314/3/39
CRO: B/Bod/314/3/51
CRO: B/Laus/135
CRO: B/Laus/143
CRO: B/Laus/147
CRO: B/Laus/170
CRO: B/Laus/173
CRO: B/Laus/174
CRO: B/Laus/175
CRO: B/Laus/176
CRO: B/Laus/177
CRO: B/Laus/178
CRO: B/Lis/266
CRO: B/Lis/268
CRO: B/Lis.272
CRO: B/WLooe/21/1
CRO: DD EN906/1
CRO: *Diary of Thomas Nicholl*, MSS.
CRO: Enys Memoranda, f.22
CRO: Penryn Borough Records Mayor's Cash Book, 1665-6 and 1668-9
CRO: P/7/5/1
CRO: P/192/5/1
CRO: P/19/5/1
CRO: P/36/8/1
CRO: P/36/81
CRO: PD/322/1
CRO: PD/322/2
CRO: X/50/5

Devon Record Office

DRO: Chanter 3.
DRO: Chanter 4
DRO: Chanter 11

Public Record Office

PRO: CI 46/388
PRO: E 31/122
PRO: SP 46/16

University of Bristol Theatre Collection Papers

BDD/00040
BDD/000274
BDD/C/000001
BDD/C/000002
BDD/D/000009
BDD/GW/081

Newspapers, Magazines and Journals

Activ für celtische Lexigraphie
An Baner Kernewek / The Cornish Banner
Annual Report of the Royal Cornwall Polytechnic Society
Anti-Jacobin Review
Antiquary
Antiquity
Archaeologia
Archaeologia Cambrensis
Architectural Review
Artswest
Big Picture
Calgary Herald
Cambridge Medieval Celtic Studies
Camborniana
Carn
Celtic Pen

Celtic Review
Chicago Daily Tribune
Comparative Drama
Cornish Archaeology / Hendhyscans Kernow
Cornish Buildings Group Newsletter
Cornish Guardian
Cornish Life
Cornish Magazine [Arthur Quiller-Couch (ed.)]
Cornishman
Cornish Review: First Series
Cornish Review: Second Series
Cornish Saints Series
Cornish Scene
Cornish Telegraph
Cornish World / Bys Kernowyon
Cornubian
Cornwall Gazette
Cornwall Gazette and Falmouth Packet
Cornwall Today, Yesterday and Dreckly
Brice's Weekly Journal
Daily Mirror
Daily News
Delyow Derow
Devon and Cornwall Notes and Queries
English Historical Review
Era
Evening Standard
Eythen
Figaro
Financial Times
Folklore
Folk Music Journal
Gentleman's Magazine
Grass Valley Union
Guardian
History Review
Huffington Post
Il Tempo Libero Economia E Società
Independent
Industrial Archaeology Review

International Journal of Heritage Studies
Journal of British Studies
Journal of the Cornish Methodist Historical Association
Journal of Medieval and Renaissance Studies
Journal of the Royal Institution of Cornwall
Maga
Mediaeval Studies
Medium Acvum
Meyn Mamvro
Midwestern Journal of Language and Folklore
Newquay Express
News from KEAP and RIO
Neuphilologische Mitteilungen
Notes and Queries
Nottingham Medieval Studies
Old Cornwall: Journal of the Old Cornwall Societies
Papers Presented to the Past and Present Conference on Popular Religion
Proceedings of the Modern Language Association of America
Proceedings of the Weslyan Historical Society
Radio Times
Report of the Royal Cornwall Polytechnic Society
Revels History of Drama in English
Review of English Studies
Revue Celtique
Royal Cornwall Gazette and Falmouth Packet
Scryfa
Shakespeare Quarterly
Sherbourne Mercury
Southern History
Speculum
Stage
Studia Celtica Japonica
Studi e Saggi Linguistici
Studi Medievali
Theatre Notebook: A Journal of the History and Technique of the British Theatre
Theatre Survey
Time Out
Times
Times Literary Supplement
Transactions of the Institute of British Geographers

Transactions of the Philological Society
Trivium
Tristania
Universal Magazine
Victorian Studies
West Briton and Cornwall Advertiser
West Briton
Western Morning News
Yorkshire Post

Posters, Playbills, Programmes and Publicity Leaflets

Abbey Theatre / Amharclann na Mainistreach, *Programme Autumn 08-Spring 09*, Dublin: Abbey Theatre / Amharclann na Mainistreach, 2008
Acorn Theatre, *Acorn October-December 2000*, Penzance: Acorn Theatre, 2000
    Acorn Autumn Season 2001, Penzance: Acorn Theatre, 2001
    Acorn January-March 2003, Penzance: Acorn Theatre, 2003
    Events Guide September-December, Penzance: Acorn Theatre, 2008
Applebee, Bec, "*Oh Mary*", programme, 2009
Blackheath Concert Halls, *Aesop* Flyer, Blackheath: Blackheath Concert Halls, 1991
British Drama League National Festival of Community Theatre booklet, 1971
Calumet Theatre, *Discover the Calumet Theatre in Historic Calumet, Michigan*, leaflet, 2002
Collingwood Selby, Francis, *Cornwall Drama Festival 1951 Programme*, Cornwall: Cornwall County Council, 1951
Combined Universities in Cornwall, *Higher Education Opportunities in Cornwall: Full and Part-time Courses 2003-2004*, Penryn: Combined Universities in Cornwall, 2003
Cornish Shakespeare Festival, *Cornish Shakespeare Festival Programme: Season 1935*, Cornwall: Cornish Shakespeare Festival, 1935
    Cornish Shakespeare Festival Programme: Season 1937, Cornwall: Cornish Shakespeare Festival, 1937
Cornwall County Council, *Historic Cornwall*, Truro: Cornwall County Council, 1997
Cornwall Heritage Trust, *To Safeguard Cornwall's Heritage*, Mevagissey: Cornwall Heritage Trust, n.d.
Dehwelans, *Dehwelans 2004: Festival of Cornwall, Souvenir Guide*, 2004
English Heritage, *English Heritage Events 1999*, London: English Heritage, 1999
George Square Theatre, *Aesop*, programme, Edinburgh: George Square Theatre, 1991
Gorseth Kernow, *Ceremonies of the Gorseth of the Bards of Cornwall*, n.d.
Foster, K. G. (ed.), *Piran Round, Perranporth: Souvenir Programme*, Cornwall: Cornwall County Council, 1969

Keay Theatre, *The Keay Events: September-December 2008*, St Austell: Keay Theatre, 2008

Kernow Productions, *The Last Voyage of Alfred Wallis*, programme, Falmouth: Falmouth Arts Centre, 1994

Keskerdh Kernow / Cornwall Marches On, *Keskerdh Kernow / Cornwall Marches On Souvenir Programme*, Truro: Keskerdh Kernow, 1997

Kneehigh Theatre, *The Ash Maid*, Truro: Kneehigh Theatre, 1994

  Figgie Hobbin, Truro: Kneehigh Theatre, 1994

  Quick Silver: A Cornish Western Pantomime, programme, Truro: Kneehigh Theatre, 2002

  Blast! Publicity Leaflet, Truro: Kneehigh Theatre, 2007

  Don John, programme, Truro: Kneehigh Theatre, 2008

Kneehigh Theatre and Theatre Royal, Plymouth, *Hans Christian Andersen's The Tinderbox*, programme, Truro and Plymouth, 1990

Lane Theatre, *Lane Theatre Newquay: 2008*, Newquay: Lane Theatre, 2008

Legend of St Piran, The, leaflet, 2003

Lowender Peran, *Lowender Peran: Festival of Celtic Culture*, Perranporth: Lowender Peran, 1994

Medieval Mystery Play Poster, 7 July 1996.

Mineral Point, *Eleventh Gathering of Cornish Cousins, September 27-30, 2001, Mineral Point, Wisconsin, Souvenir Programme*, 2001

Mundic Nation and Hall for Cornwall, *D.M. Thomas: Hell Fire Corner*, programme, Truro: Hall for Cornwall, 2004

Newquay Amateur Dramatic Society, *And A Size Larger*, publicity pamphlet, 1962

Newquay: New Theatre, *Into the Sun: A Revue in Four Editions*, souvenir programme, Newquay: New Theatre, 1954

  Into the Sun: A Revue in Three Editions, souvenir programme, Newquay: New Theatre, 1955

Restormel Borough Council, *The Daphne du Maurier Festival of Arts and Literature*, Cornwall: Restormel Borough Council, 1999

  The Daphne du Maurier Festival of Arts and Literature, Cornwall: Restormel Borough Council, 2000

  The Daphne du Maurier Festival of Arts and Literature, Cornwall: Restormel Borough Council, 2002

  The Daphne du Maurier Festival of Arts and Literature, Cornwall: Restormel Borough Council, 2003

  The Daphne du Maurier Festival of Arts and Literature, Cornwall: Restormel Borough Council, 2007

Shiva Theatre, *Meryasek*, programme, Cornwall: Shiva Theatre, 1980

South West Music Theatre, *The Ballad of Aucassin and Nicolette*, programme, Exeter: South West Music Theatre, 1978

South West Tourism, *The Film and TV Map*, Exeter: South West Tourism, n.d.

Stage Company Trucco, *Our Country's Good*, programme, Truro: Truro College, 2008

Sterts Theatre, *The Theatre on the Moor: Summer 2008*, Liskeard: Sterts Theatre, 2008

Tolmen Centre, *Constantine's Arts and Community Centre: September 2008-January 2009*, Constantine: Tolmen Centre, 2008

Tyr ha Tavas membership leaflet, c.1930

West Country Tourist Board, *West Country Writers*, Exeter: West Country Tourist Board, n.d.

Whiting, Kirsten, *Falmouth Festival of Literature and Arts*, Falmouth: Falmouth Festival of Literature and Arts, 2003

Books, Pamphlets and Articles

Ably, Mark, *Spoken Here: Travels Among Threatened Languages*, London: William Heinemann, 2003

Ackroyd, Peter, *The Life of Thomas More*, London: Chatto and Windus, 1998
    Shakespeare: The Biography, London: Chatto and Windus, 2005

Acton, Viv, 'Truro – Leisure and Entertainment' in Palmer, June (ed.), 1999

Acton, Viv and Carter, Derek, Operation *Cornwall 1940-1944*, Devoran: Landfall, 1994
    Cornish War and Peace: The Road to Victory and Beyond, Devoran: Landfall, 1995

Adair, John, *Puritans: Religion and Politics in Seventeenth-Century England and America*, Stroud: Sutton, 1998

Ainger, Michael, *Gilbert and Sullivan: A Dual Biography*, Oxford: Oxford University Press, 2002

Akhtar, Miriam and Humphries, Steve, *Far Out: The Dawning of New Age Britain*, Bristol: Sansom and Company, and Channel Four, 1999

Albery, Wyndam (ed.), *The Dramatic Works of James Albery, together with a Sketch of his Career, Correspondence Bearing Thereon, Press Notices, Casts, 2 Vols.*, London: Peter Davies, 1939

Alford, Violet *The Hobby Horse and other Animal Masks*, London: The Merlin Press, 1978

Alington, Gabriel, *The Hereford Mappa Mundi*, Leominster: Gracewing, 1996

Altree, Ann, 'The Georgian Theatre' in June Palmer and Ann Altree (eds.), 2005

Alvery, Ada *In Search of St James: Cornwall to Compestella – A Mediaeval Pilgrimage*, Redruth: Dyllansow Truran, 1989

Amderston, Celu, *Deepening the Power: Community Ritual and Sacred Theatre*, Vancouver, British Columbia: Beach Holme Publications, 1995

Anderson, Benedict, *Imagined Communities: Reflections on the Origin and Spread of Nationalism*, London and New York: Verso, 2006 [1983]

Andrews, Robert *The Rough Guide to Devon and Cornwall*, London: Rough Guides Ltd, 2007

Angarrack, John, *Breaking the Chains: Censorship, Deception and the Manipulation of Public Opinion in Cornwall*, Camborne: Stannary Publications, 1999
    Our Future is History: Identity, Law and the Cornish Question, Bodmin: Independent Academic Press, 2002
    Scat t'Larraps: Resist and Survive, Bodmin: Independent Academic Press, 2008

Arendt, Hannah and Zohn, Harry (eds. and trs.), *Walter Benjamin: Illuminations*, London: Fontana Press, 1973

Arnold, Matthew, *The Study of Celtic Literature*, London: Smith and Elder, 1867

Arthurson, Ian, *The Perkin Warbeck Conspiracy 1491-1499*, Stroud: Sutton, 1997

Ashbee, Paul, *Ancient Scilly: From the First Farmers to the Early Christians*, Newton Abbot: David and Charles, 1974

Ashby, Justine and Higson, Andrew (eds.), *British Cinema: Past and Present*, London and New York: Routledge, 2000

Ashcroft, Bill, Griffiths, Gareth and Tiffin, Helen, *The Empire Writes Back: Theory and Practice in Post-Colonial Literatures*. London: Routledge, 1989

Aubert, O.L., *Celtic Legends of Brittany*, Kerangwenn: Coop Breizh, 1993

Aughey, Arthur, *Nationalism, Devolution and the Challenge to the United Kingdom State*, London: Pluto Press, 2001

Backschneider, Paula (ed.), *Dictionary of Literary Biography, Volume 89: Restoration and Eighteenth-Century Dramatists*, Detroit: Gale Research, 1989

Badcock, W. *Historical Sketch of St Ives and District*, St Ives: W. Badcock, 1896

Baker, David J., *Between Nations: Shakespeare, Spenser, Marvell and the Question of Britain*, Stanford: Stanford University Press, 2001

Baker, Richard Anthony, *British Music Hall: An Illustrated History*, Stroud: Sutton Publishing, 2005

Bakere, Jane A., *The Cornish Ordinalia: A Critical Study*, Cardiff: University of Wales Press, 1980
    Glasney and Cornish Drama, Penryn: Friends of Glasney, 1989

Bakhtin, Mikhail, *Rabelais and His World*, Cambridge, Massachusetts, MIT Press, 1968 [1965]

Banks, Paul (ed.), *The Making of Peter Grimes*, Cambridge: The Boydell Press, 2000

Banks, R.A., *Drama and Theatre Arts*, London: Hodder and Stoughton, 1985

Barber, Antonia and Bayley, Nicola, *The Mousehole Cat*, London: Walker Books, 1990

Barber, C.L., *Shakespeare's Festive Comedy: A Study of Dramatic Form and its relation to Social Custom*, Oxford: Oxford University Press, 1959

Barber, Richard, *King Arthur in Music*, Cambridge: D.S. Brewer, 1993

Barham, Thomas Foster, *Abdallah*, or *The Arabian Martyr: A Christian Drama in Three Acts and in Verse*, London: J. Hatchford and Son, 1820
  Colonial Gardiner: A Christian Drama in Three Acts, London: Hatchard and Son, 1823
Barish, Jonas, *Ben Jonson and the Language of Prose Comedy*, Cambridge, Massachusetts: Harvard University Press, 1960
Baring-Gould, Sabine, *The Pennycomequicks: A Novel*, London: Collins, 1889
  Urith: A Tale of Dartmoor, London: Methuen, 1891
  In the Roar of the Sea, London: Methuen, 1892
  A Book of the West; Volume 1 – Devon, London: Methuen, 1899
Baring-Gould, Sabine and Sheppard, H. Fleetwood (eds.), *Songs from the West: Folksongs of Devon and Cornwall collected from the Mouths of the People*, London: Patey and Willis, 1889-1991
Barker, Katherine and Kain, Roger J.P., *Maps and History in South-West England*, Exeter: University of Exeter Press, 1991
Barnett, John, 'Lesser Known Stone Circles in Cornwall' in *Cornish Archaeology / Hendhyscans Kernow*, No. 19, 1980
  Prehistoric Cornwall: The Ceremonial Monuments, Wellingborough: Turnstone Press Limited, 1982
Barton, Laura, 'I was so incredibly self-conscious' in *The Guardian*, 28 May 2008
Bates, Brian, *The Real Middle Earth: Magic and Mystery in the Dark Ages*, London: Sidgwick and Jackson, 2002
Batten, Ben, 'The Cornish Ordinalia at Amersham' in *An Baner Kernewek / The Cornish Banner*, No. 110, 2002
Beadle, Richard, 'The York Cycle' in Beadle, Richard (ed.), 1994
  (ed.), *The Cambridge Companion to Medieval English Theatre*, Cambridge: Cambridge University Press, 1994
Beadle, Richard and King, Pamela M. (eds.), *York Mystery Plays: A Selection in Modern Spelling*, Oxford: Clarendon Press, 1984
Beart-Albrecht, Jan, 'Charles Causley' in *Artswest*, October, 1989
Beckett, Arthur (ed.), *The Sussex County Magazine*, Brighton: T.P. Beckett, 1927
Bédier, Joseph, *La Roman de Tristan*, Paris: Privately published, 1902-5
Beech, John (ed.), *Oral Literature and Performance Culture*, Edinburgh: John Donald, 2007
Beier, A.L., *Masterless Men: The Vagrancy Problem in England 1560-1640*, London: Methuen, 1985
Belloc, Hilaire and Rosenfield, Paul (eds. and trs.), *Joseph Bédier: The Romance of Tristan*, New York: Vintage, 1945
Bellow, John, 'On the Cornish Language' in *Report of the Royal Cornwall Polytechnic Society*, 1861

Benham, Patrick, *The Avalonians*, Glastonbury: Gothic Image, 1993

Benjamin, Walter, 'The Work of Art in the Age of Mechanical Reproduction' in Arendt, Hannah and Zohn, Harry (eds. and trs.), 1973

Bennett, David (ed.), *Multicultural States: Rethinking Difference and Identity*, London and New York: Routledge, 1998

Berridge, Peter and Roberts, Alison, 'The Mesolithic period in Cornwall' in *Cornish Archaeology / Hendhyscans Kernow*, No.25, 1986

Besant, Walter, *Armorel of Lyonesse: A Romance of Today*, Felinfach: Llanerch, 1993 [1890]

Betcher, Gloria J., 'Makers of Heaven and Earth: The Construction of Early Drama in Cornwall' in Davidson, Clifford (ed.), 1999

Betjeman, John, *Collected Poems*, London: John Murray, 1988

Bhabka, Homi K., 'Culture's in between' in Bennett, David (ed), 1998

Bickford-Smith, R.A.H., 'The Celtic Drama Revived: Buhaz Sant Gwennole at Morlaix' in *The Cornish Magazine*, November, 1899

Biddulph, Joseph, *A Handbook of West Country Brythonic: Old Devonian*, Pontypridd: Joseph Biddulph, n.d.

Billington, Michael, *State of the Nation: British Theatre Since 1945*, London: Faber and Faber, 2007

Bishop, Paul, *A Companion to Goethe's Faust, Parts 1 and 2*, New York: Camden House, 2006

Bleakley, Alan, 'Fires of Bel: The Celtic Midsummer' in *Meyn Mamvro*, No.2, 1986

Boase, George Clement, *Collectanea Cornubiensia: A Collection of Biographical and Topographical Notes relating to the County of Cornwall*, Truro: Netherton and Worth 1890

Boase, George Clement and Courtney, William Prideaux (eds.), *Bibliotheca Cornubiensis*, London: Longman, Green, Reader and Dyer, 1874, 1878 and 1882

Bond, Thomas, *Topographical and Historical Sketches of the Borough of East and West Looe in the County of Cornwall*, London: J. Nichols and Son, 1823

Borchmayer, Dieter, *Drama and the World of Richard Wagner*, Princton: Princeton University Press, 2003

Borlase, William, *Observations on the Antiquities Historical and Monumental of the County of Cornwall*, London: EP Publishing, 1973 [1754]

   The Natural History of Cornwall, Oxford: Oxford University Press, 1758

Borlase, William Copeland, *The Age of the Saints: A Monograph of Early Christianity in Cornwall with the Legends of the Cornish Saints*, Truro: Joseph Pollard, 1893

Bosanketh, Edward, *Tin*, Marazion: Justin Brooke, 1988 [1888]

Bottrell, William (ed.), *Traditions and Hearthside Stories of West Cornwall: First Series*, Penzance: W. Cornish, 1870 (ed.), *Traditions and Hearthside Stories of West Cornwall: Second Series*, Penzance: Beare and Son, 1873

(ed.), *Traditions and Hearthside Stories of West Cornwall: Third Series*, Penzance: F. Rodda, 1880

Bourke, Patricia, 'The Stained Glass Windows of the Church of St. Neot, Cornwall in *Devon and Cornwall Notes and Queries*, 33, 1974-8

Boussell du Bourg, Yann, 'Breton Mystery Theatre: An Enduring Legacy' in *The Celtic Pen*, Vol. 2, No. 10, 1996

Bowen, E.G., *Saints, Seaways and Settlements in the Celtic Lands*, Cardiff: University of Wales Press, 1969

Britain and the Western Seaways, London: Thames and Hudson, 1972

Boyes, Georgina, *The Imagined Village: Culture, Ideology and the English Folk Revival*, Manchester: Manchester University Press, 1993

(ed.), *Step Change: New Views on Traditional Dance*, London: Francis Boutle Publishers, 2001

Braasch, Barbara, *California's Gold Rush Country*, Medina, Washington: Johnston Associates International, 1996

Bradley, Ian, *Oh Joy! Oh Rapture! The Enduring Phenomenon of Gilbert and Sullivan*, Oxford: Oxford University Press, 1986

Bradshaw, Brendan and Morrill, John (eds.), *The British Problem c.1534-1707: State Formation in the Atlantic Archipelago*, Basingstoke: Macmillan, 1996

Braithwaite, R., *The Honest Ghost*, 1658

Brasher, Arthur, 'Sir Henry Irving's Childhood: The Great Actor's Reminiscences of Cornwall' in *The Cornish Magazine*, Vol. I, August, 1898

Bray, Donald, 'The Cornish Nightingale' in *Cornish Life*, Vol 5, No.1, 1978

Brendon, Piers (ed.), *Cornish Ballads and Other Poems: Robert Stephen Hawker*, St Germans: The Elephant Press, 1975

Hawker of Morwenstow, London: Anthony Mott, 1983 [1975]

Breton, H. Hugh, *Spiritual Lessons from Dartmoor Forest*, Newton Abbot: Forest Publishing, 1990 [1929 and 1930]

Brice, Andrew, 'The Exmoor Scolding' in *Brice's Weekly Journal*, No.52, 1727

Bristow, Colin, *Cornwall's Geology and Scenery*, St Austell: Cornish Hillside Publications, 1996

Brittain, F. (ed.), *Q Anthology: A Selection from the Prose and Verse of Sir Arthur Quiller-Couch*, London: J.M. Dent, 1948

Arthur Quiller-Couch: A Biographical Study of Q, Cambridge: Cambridge University Press, 1948

Broadhurst, Paul, *Sacred Shrines: In Search of the Holy Wells of Cornwall*, Launceston: Pendragon Press, 1991

Tintagel and the Arthurian Mythos, Launceston: Pendragon Press, 1992

'Stowe's Hill: A Ritual Centre' in *Meyn Mamvro*, No.20, 1993

Broadhurst, Paul and Miller, Hamish, *The Dance of the Dragon: An Odyssey into Earth Energies and Ancient Religion*, Launceston: Pendragon Press, 2000

Broadhurst, Paul and Heath, Robin, *The Secret Land: The Origins of Arthurian Legend and the Grail Quest*, Launceston: Mythos, 2009

Broadhurst, Paul and Trso, Gabriele, *The Green Man and the Dragon: The Mystery Behind the Myth of St George and the Dragon Power of Nature*, Launceston: Mythos, 2006

Bromley, Roger, *Narratives for a New Belonging: Diasporic Cultural Fictions*, Edinburgh: Edinburgh University Press, 2000

Brown, Callum G., *The Death of Christian Britain: Understanding Secularization 1800-2000*, London and New York: Routledge, 2001

Brown, H. Miles, *A Century for Cornwall: The Diocese of Truro 1877-1977*, Truro: Oscar Blackford, 1976

Brown, John Russell and Harris, Bernard (eds.), *Elizabethan Theatre*, London: Edward Arnold, 1974 [1966]

Brown, Tony and Stephens, Russell (eds.), *Nations and Relations: Writing Across the British Isles*, Cardiff: New Welsh Review, 2000

Browne, Austin L., *Corporation Chronicles: Being Some Account of the Ancient Corporation of East Looe and of West Looe in the County of Cornwall*, Plymouth: John Smith, 1904

Brown-Lawson, A., *John Wesley and the Anglican Evangelicals of the Eighteenth Century*, Durham: The Pentland Press, 1994

Bruch, Benjamin, 'Verse Structure and Musical Performance in *Bewnans Kê*' in *Journal of the Royal Institution of Cornwall*, 2006

Buck, M., Williams, M and Bryant, L., 'Housing the Cornish: Containing the crisis' in Payton, Philip (ed.), *Cornish Studies: One*, Exeter: University of Exeter Press, 1993b

Buckingham, James Silk, *Autobiography*, London: Longman, Brown, Green and Longmans, 1855

Buckingham, Leicester Silk, *Aggravating Sam: A Comic Drama, in 2 Acts [and in prose]*, London: Thomas Hailes Lacy, 1854

> *Take the Girl Away: A Comic Drama in Two Acts [and in prose]*, London: Thomas Hailes Lacy, 1855

> *Belphegor: A new and original, acrobatic, dramatic, epigrammatic and decidedly un-aristocratic burlesque*, London: Thomas Hailes Lucy, 1856

Buckley, Allen, *South Crofty Mine: A History*, Mount Hawke: Truran, 1997

> *The Story of Mining in Cornwall: A World of Payable Ground*, Fowey: Cornwall Editions, 2005

> *Bert Solomon: A Rugby Phenomenon*, Mount Hawke: Truran, 2007

Bullet, Gerald (ed.), *Silver Poets of the Sixteenth Century*, London: Dent, 1984

Burgh, Anita, *Daughters of a Granite Land 1: The Azure Bowl*, London: Chatto and Windus, 1989

Burton, Anthony, *Richard Trevithick: Giant of Steam*, London: Aurum Press, 2000

Burton, Rob, 'A Passion to Exist: Cultural Hegemony and the Roots of Cornish Identity' in Payton, Philip (ed.), 1997

Busby, Graham and Hambly, Zoë, 'Literary Tourism and the Daphne du Maurier Festival' in Payton, Philip (ed.), 2000

Butler, Angie, *The Giants*, Penzance: West Country Giants, 2001

Butterworth, Philip, 'Book-carriers: Medieval and Tudor Stage Conventions' in *Theatre Notebook*, 24, 1992

Cade, Rowena and Bates, Darrell, *A Short History of the Minack Theatre*, Porthcurno: The Minack Theatre, 1971

Cameron, Alasdair and Scullion, Adrienne (eds.), *Scottish Popular Theatre and Entertainment: Historical and Critical Approaches to Theatre and Film in Scotland*, Glasgow: Glasgow University Library Studies, 1995

Campanile, Enrico, 'Un Frammento Scenico Medio-Cornico' in *Studi e Saggi Linguistici*, Vol.3, 1963

Campbell, Gordon (ed.), *John Milton: The Complete Poems*, London: Dent, 1980

Campbell, Joseph, *The Hero with a Thousand Faces*, London: Fontana Press, 1993 [1949]

Carlton, Charles, *The Experience of the British Civil Wars*, London and New York: Routledge, 1992

Carr-Gomm, Philip (ed.), *The Rebirth of Druidry: Ancient Wisdom for Today*, London: Harper Collins, 2003

Carruthers, Gerard and Rawes, Alan (eds.), *English Romanticism and the Celtic World*, Cambridge: Cambridge University Press, 2003

Carter, Angela, *The Magic Toyshop*, London: Virago Press, 1981
Nights at the Circus, London: Chatto and Windus, 1984
Burning your Boats: Collected Short Stories, London: Vintage, 1996

Casier Quinn, Esther, *The Quest of Seth for the Oil of Life*, Chicago: Chicago University Press, 1962

Catling, Robert Mason and Rogers, J. Percival, *G.H. Doble: A Brief Memoir and Bibliography*, Exeter: Sidney Lee, 1949

Causley, Charles, *Runaway*, London: Curwen, 1936
The Conquering Hero, London: Curwen, 1937
Benedict: A Play in One Act, London: Muller, 1938
Farewell, Aggie Weston! Aldington: Hand and Flower Press, 1951
Hands to Dance and Skylark, London: Anthony Mott, 1983 [1951]
Survivor's Leave, Aldington: Hand and Flower Press, 1952

Union Street, London: Hart Davis, 1957

Figgie Hobbin, Harmondsworth: Puffin, 1985 [1970]

The Ballad of Aucassin and Nicolette: A Play in Three Acts, London: Viking, 1981

Collected Poems 1951-1975, London: Macmillan, 1975

The Gift of a Lamb: A Shepherd's Tale of the first Christmas, told as a verse play, London: Robson Books, 1978

Three Heads made of Gold, London: Robson Books, 1978

The Ballad of Aucassin and Nicolette: A Play in Three Acts, London: Viking, 1981

Early in the Morning, London: Viking Kestral, 1986

The Young Man of Cury, London: Macmillan, 1991

The Spirit of Launceston: A Celebration of Charles Causley's Poetry, Launceston: Launceston Calligraphers, 1994

Collected Poems for Children, London: Macmillan, 1996

Causley, Charles and Foreman, Michael, *The Merrymaid of Zennor*, London: Orchard Books, 1999

Cauveren, Sydney, *A.L. Rowse: A Bibliophile's Extensive Bibliography*, Maryland: The Scarecrow Press, 2000

Cave, Richard Allen (ed.), *W.B. Yeats: Selected Plays*, London: Penguin, 1997

Cawte, E.C., *Ritual Animal Disguise: A Historical and Geographical Study of Animal Disguise in the British Isles*, Cambridge: D.S. Brewer, 1978

Centlivre, Susannah, *The Wonder, or A Woman Keeps a Secret*, Canada: Broadview Press, 2001

Chambers, E.K. *The Mediaeval Stage*, Oxford: Oxford University Press, 1903

The English Folk Play, Oxford: Oxford University Press 1969 [1933]

Chambers, Harry (ed.), *Causley at 70*, Calstock: Peterloo Poets, 1987

Chandler, John H., *John Leland's Itinerary: Travels in Tudor England*, Stroud: Sutton, 1993

Chapman, Malcolm, *The Celts: The Construction of a Myth*, Basingstoke: Macmillan, 1992

Chatwin, Bruce, *The Songlines*, London: Jonathan Cape, 1987

Christie, Patricia M., 'Cornwall in the Bronze Age' in *Cornish Archaeology / Hendhyscans Kernow*, No.25, 1986

Chysauster and Carn Euny, London: English Heritage, 1993

Clark, Evelyn, *Cornish Fogous*, London: Methuen, 1961

Clarke, Jerry and Harry, Terry (eds.), *Tales from Twickenham*, Redruth: Clarke and Harry, 1991

Clemo, Jack, *Confession of a Rebel*, London: Chatto and Windus, 1949

The Shadowed Bed, Tring: Lion, 1986

Clifford, John (ed. and tr.), *Johann Wolfgang von Goethe: Faust*, London: Nick Hern Books, 2006

Climo, Shirley, and Venti, Anthony Bacon, *Magic and Mischief: Tales from Cornwall*, New York: Clarion Books, 1999

Coate, Mary, *Cornwall in the Great Civil War and Interregnum 1642-1660*, Truro: D. Bradford Barton, 1963 [1933]

Cobb, James Francis, *The Watchers on the Longships*, Redhill: Wells, 1876

Cockrell, Dale, *Demons of Disorder: Early Blackface Minstrels and Their World*, Cambridge: Cambridge University Press, 1997

Coe, Jon B. and Young, Simon, *The Celtic Sources for Arthurian Legend*, Felinfach: Llanerch, 1995

Coghill, Nevill 'The Basis of Shakespearean Comedy' in Ridler, Anne (ed.), 1963

Coleman, Will, *Tom and the Giant*, Cornwall: Brave Tales, 2005

   Lutey and the Mermaid, Cornwall: Brave Tales, 2005

   Madgy Figgy's Pig, Cornwall: Brave Tales, 2005

   Tales from Porth: The Box Set, Cornwall: Maga, 2008

Colley, Linda, *Britons: Forging the Nation 1707-1837*, New Haven and London: Yale University Press, 1992

Colley, S., *Life of the Rev. Thomas Collins*, London: Privately published, 1871

Collier, W.F., 'Wrestling: The Cornish and Devonshire Styles' in *The Cornish Magazine*, 1898

Collins, Wilkie, *Rambles beyond Railways, or Notes in Cornwall taken a-foot*, London: Westaway Books, 1948 [1851]

Colman, George, *John Bull, as Performed at the Theatre Royal, Covent Garden*, London: Longman, Hurst, Rees and Orme, 1806

   The Review, or The Wags of Windsor: A Musical Farce in Two Acts, London: J. Cawthorn and James Cawthorn, 1808

   The Poor Gentleman, Longman, 1810

Colquhoun, Ithel, *The Living Stones: Cornwall*, London: Owen, 1957

Combellack, Myrna (ed. and tr.), *The Camborne Play: A verse translation of Beunans Meriasek*, Redruth: Dyllansow Truran, 1988

   The Playing Place: A Cornish Round, Redruth: Dyllansow Truran, 1989

   The Permanent History of Penaluna's Van, Cornwall: Cornish Fiction, 2003

Combellack Harris, Myrna (ed.), *Cornish Studies for Schools*, Truro: Cornwall County Council, 1989

Combined Universities in Cornwall, *Higher Education Opportunities in Cornwall: Full and Part-time Courses 2003-2004*, Penryn: Combined Universities in Cornwall, 2003

Connolly, S.J. (ed.), *Kingdoms United? Great Britain and Ireland Since 1500: Integration and Diversity*, Dublin: Four Courts Press, 1999

Cook, Judith, *To Brave Every Danger: The Epic Life of Mary Bryant of Fowey*, London: Macmillan, 1993

Cooke, Ian McNeil, *Mermaid to Merrymaid: Journey to the Stones – Ancient Sites and Pagan Mysteries of Celtic Cornwall*, Penzance: Men-an-Tol Studio, 1987
  Mother and Sun: The Cornish Fogou, Penzance: Men-an-Tol Studio, 1993
Cooke, Ian McNeil and Straffon, Cheryl, 'The Celtic Year' in *Meyn Mamvro* No. 6, 1988
Cookson, Linda (ed.), *Christopher Marlowe: Doctor Faustus*, Harlow: Longman, 1984
Cope, Julian, *The Modern Antiquarian: A Pre-millennial Odyssey Through Megalithic Britain*, London: Thorsons, 1997
  Megalithic European: The 21st Century Traveller in Prehistoric Europe, London: Element Books, 2004
Cornish, John B. (ed.), *The Autobiography of a Cornish Smuggler: Captain Harry Carter of Prussia Cove 1749-1809*, Truro: D. Bradford Barton, 1971 [1894]
Cornwall, Julian, *Revolt of the Peasantry 1549*, London: Routledge, 1977
Cornwall Province of Freemasons, *Thread of Gold: Celebrating the Unbroken History of 250 Years of Freemasonry in the Province of Cornwall*, Cornwall: Cornwall Province of Freemasons, 2001
Couch, Jonathan, *The History of Polperro*, Clifton-upon-Teme: Polperro Heritage Press, 2004 [1871]
Couch, T.Q., 'Lanivet' in *Journal of the Royal Institution of Cornwall*, No.4, 1865
Courtney, Louise, *Half Century of Penzance 1825-1875 – from notes by J.S. Courtney*, Penzance: Beare and Son, 1878
Courtney, Margaret A. (ed.), *Cornish Feasts and Folklore*, Exeter: Cornwall Books, 1989 [1890]
Craig, Sandy (ed.), *Dreams and Deconstructions: Alternative Theatre in Britain*, Ambersgate: Amber Lane Press, 1980
Crane, Harvey, *Playbill: A History of the Theatre in the West Country*, Plymouth: Macdonald and Evans, 1980
Crawford, Robert, *Devolving English Literature*, Edinburgh: Edinburgh University Press, 2001
Crawford, T.D. 'The Composition of the Cornish *Ordinalia*' in *Old Cornwall*, 9, 1979-1985
  'Stanza Forms and Social Status in *Beunans Meriasek*' in *Old Cornwall*, 9, 1979-1985
Cross, Sally Joyce, 'Torturers as Tricksters in the Cornish *Ordinalia*' in *Neuphilologische Mitteilung*, 84, 1983
Crystal, David, *The Cambridge Encylopedia of The English Language*, Cambridge: Cambridge University Press, 1995
Cunliffe, Barry, *The Celtic World*, London: Bodley Head, 1979
  The Ancient Celts, Oxford: Oxford University Press, 1997
Curley, Michael, 'A New Edition of John of Cornwall's *Prophetia Merlini*' in *Speculum*, No.57, 1982

Dalley, Stuart, 'The Response in Cornwall to the Outbreak of the First World War' in Payton, Philip (ed.), 2003

Dames, Michael, *Merlin and Wales: A Magician's Landscape*, London: Thames and Hudson, 2002

Darke, Nick, 'The Body' (1983) in Kempe, Andy, *The Script Sampler*, Cheltenham: Nelson Thornes Ltd, 2002

    Ting Tang Mine and Other Plays, London: Methuen, 1987

    Plays: One, London: Methuen, 1999

    The Riot, London: Methuen, 1999

Davey, John and Lewis, Steve, *Edexcel AS Drama and Theatre Studies*, Harlow: Pearson, 2008

Davey, Merv, *Hengan: Traditional Folk Songs, Dances and Broadside Ballads collected in Cornwall*, Redruth: Dyllansow Truran, 1983

    "Guizing': Ancient Traditions and Modern Sensitivities' in Payton, Philip (ed.), 2006

Davey, Merv, Alison and Jowdy, *Scoot Dances, Troyls, Furrys and Tea Treats: The Cornish Dance Tradition*, London: Francis Boutle Publishers, 2009

Davey, Peter and Finlayson, David (eds.), *Mannin Revisited: Twelve Essays on Manx Culture and Environment*, Edinburgh: Scottish Society for Northern Studies, 2002

Davidson, Clifford (ed.), *The Saint Play in Medieval Europe*, Kalamazoo, Michigan: Medieval Institute Publications, 1986

    (ed.), *Material Culture and Medieval Drama*, Kalamazoo, Michigan: Western Michigan University Press, 1999

Davies, Ceri and Law, John E. (eds.), *The Renaissance and the Celtic Countries*, Oxford: Blackwell, 2005

Davies, Rupert, *Methodism*, Peterborough: Epworth Press, 1985 [1963]

Davies, Thomas (ed.), *Lillo's Dramatic Works Vol. 2: Fatal Curiosity, Marina, Elmerick, or Justice Triumphant, Britannia and Batavia, Arden of Feversham*, Whitefish, Montana: Kessinger Publishing, 2008

Davies, W., *Cornish Manuscripts in the National Library of Wales*, Aberystwyth: National Library of Wales, 1939.

Dawe, Richard, *Cornish Pioneers in South Africa: Gold and Diamonds, Copper and Blood*, St Austell: Cornish Hillside Publications, 1998

Dawson, James, *The Autobiography*, Truro: J. R. Netherton, 1865

Day, Brian, *A Chronicle of Celtic Folk Custom: A Day-to-Day Guide to Folk Traditions*, London: Hamlyn, 2000

Deacon, Bernard, "The hollow jarring of the distant steam engines': images of Cornwall between West Barbary and the Delectable Duchy, in Westland, Ella (ed.), 1997

'Proto-industrialization and Potatoes: A Revised Narrative for Nineteenth-Century Cornwall' in Payton, Philip (ed.), 1997

Cornwall: A Concise History, Cardiff: University of Wales Press, 2007

Deacon, Bernard, Cole, Dick and Tregidga, Garry, *Mebyon Kernow and Cornish Nationalism*, Cardiff: Welsh Academic Press, 2003

Deacon, Bernard, George, Andrew and Perry, Ronald, *Cornwall at the Crossroads: Living Communities or Leisure Zone?* Redruth: Cornish Social and Economic Research Group, 1988

Deane, Seamus (ed.), *Terry Eagleton, Fredric Jameson and Edward W. Said: Nationalism, Colonialism and Literature*, Minneapolis and London: University of Minnesota Press, 1990

Deane, Tony and Shaw, Tony, *Folklore of Cornwall*, Stroud: Tempus, 2003

A Cornish Christmas, Stroud: The History Press, 2008

de Mandach, André, 'Legend and Reality: Recent Excavation and Research in Cornwall concerning Tristan and Isolt' in *Tristania*, Vol.IV, No.2, 1979

Demuth, Avril, *The Minack Open-Air Theatre: A Symposium*, Newton Abbot; David and Charles, 1968

Denny, Neville, 'Arena Staging and Dramatic Quality in the Cornish Passion Play' in Denny, Neville (ed.), 1973

(ed.), *Medieval Drama*, London: Stratford-upon-Avon Studies 16, 1973

de Sélincourt, Audrey and Burn, A.R. (eds. and trs.), *Herodotus: The Histories*, Harmondsworth: Penguin, 1954

Dibdin, Thomas, *The Jew and the Doctor*, London: T.N. Longman and O. Rees, 1800

Dickens, A.G. and Carr, D., *The Reformation in England*, London: Hodder Arnold, 1967

Ditmus, E.M.R., *Tristan and Iseult in Cornwall*, Brockworth: Forrester Roberts, 1979

Dixon, John, *A Schooling in 'English': Critical Episodes in the Struggle to Shape Literary and Cultural Studies*, Milton Keynes: Open University Press, 1991

Doble, G.H., 'Saint Meriadoc: Bishop and Confessor' in *Cornish Saints Series*, No. 34, 1935

The Saints of Cornwall: Parts 1-5, Felinfach: Llanerch, 1997 [1960-1970]

Dodd, K.M., 'Another Elizabethan Theatre in the Round' in *Shakespeare Quarterly*, 21, 1970

Dollimore, Jonathan and Sinfield, Alan (eds.), *Political Shakespeare: New Essays in Cultural Materialism*, Manchester: Manchester University Press, 1985

Dominik, Mark, *Shakespeare and 'The Birth of Merlin'*, Beaverton, Oregon: Alioth Press, 1991

Douch, H. L., 'Household Accounts at Lanherne' in *Journal of the Royal Institution of Cornwall*, 2, 1, 1953-4

The Book of Truro, Chesham: Barracuda Books, 1977

Downing, George William, *The Great Hewas Mine, or The Humours of Cornwall: A Comedy in Five Acts and in Prose*, London: by C. Chapple, c.1816

Drabble, Margaret (ed.), *The Oxford Companion to English Literature*, Oxford: Oxford University Press, 1985

Drain, Richard (ed.), *Twentieth Century Theatre: A Sourcebook*, London and New York: Routledge, 1995

Drakakis, John (ed.), *Alternative Shakespeares*, London and New York: Methuen, 1985

DuBruck, Edelgard E. (ed.), *New Images of Medieval Women: Essays Towards a Cultural Anthropology*, Lampeter: The Edwin Mellen Press, 1989

Duffin, Anne, *Faction and Faith: Politics and Religion of the Cornish Gentry Before the Civil War*, Exeter: University of Exeter Press, 1996

du Maurier, Daphne, *Jamaica Inn*, London: Arrow Books, 1992 [1936]

    September Tide, London: Samuel French, 1994 [1949]

    Vanishing Cornwall, Harmondsworth: Penguin, 1972 [1967]

    Rule Britannia, London: Arrow Books, 1992 [1972]

    'East Wind' in Westland, Ella, 2007

Dunstan, Mike (ed.), *Tales from the White Mountains*, St Austell: Restormel Arts Clay Stories, 1993

Dunstan, Ralph (ed.), *Cornish Dialect and Folk Songs*, Truro: W. Jordan, 1932

During, Simon (ed.), *The Cultural Studies Reader*, London and New York: Routledge, 1993

Durkacz, Victor Edward, *The Decline of the Celtic Languages*, Edinburgh: John Donald Publishers Ltd, 1983

Dyer, Robert, *Nine Years of an Actor's Life*, London: Rees, Orme, Brown, and Co., 1833

Eames, David, 'Camborne's Repertory Theatre' in *The Cornish Review*, No.12, 1969

Eccles, Mark, 'Middleton's Birth and Education' in *Review of English Studies*, 7, 1933

Edmundson, Paul, *Twelfth Night: A Guide to the Text and its Theatrical Life*, Basingstoke: Palgrave Macmillan, 2005

Edwards, Gavin (ed.), *George Crabbe: Selected Poems*, Harmondsworth: Penguin, 1991

Edwards, Ray (ed. and tr.), *The Charter Fragment*, Sutton Coldfield: Kernewek Dre Lyther, 1991

    (ed. and tr.), *Pascon Agan Arluth / The Poem of Mount Calvary*, Sutton Coldfield: Kernewek Dre Lyther, 1993

    (ed. and tr.), *The Tregear Homilies*, Sutton Coldfield: Kernewek Dre Lyther, 1994

    'The Charter Fragment: Play or Poem?' in *The Celtic Pen*, Vol.2, No.1, 1995

    Notes on Meaning and Word Usage on Examination of Old Cornish Texts, Cornwall: Cornish Language Board, 1997

Eliade, Mircea, *Shamanism: Archaic Techniques of Ecstasy*, Princeton: Princeton University Press, 1972

Elliott-Binns, L.E., *Medieval Cornwall*, London: Methuen, 1955

Ellis, Peter Berresford, *The Cornish Language and its Literature*, London and Boston: Routledge and Kegan Paul, 1974

    The Celtic Revolution: A Study in Anti-Imperialism, Talybont: Y Lolfra, 1988 [1985]

    Celtic Inheritance, London: Contable, 1992

    The Celtic Dawn: A history of Pan-Celticism, London: Constable, 1993

    Celt and Saxon: The Struggle for Britain AD 410-937, London: Constable, 1993

    The Chronicles of the Celts: New Tellings of their Myths and Legends, London: Robinson, 1999

Embrey, P.G. and Symes, R.F., *Minerals of Cornwall and Devon*, London: British Museum, 1987

Evans, J. Gwenogvryn (ed.), *The Book of Taliesin*, Llanbedrog: Privately published, 1910

Evans, Malcolm, 'Deconstructing Shakespeare's Comedies' in Drakakis, John (ed.), 1985

Everett, David, 'Celtic Revival and the Anglican Church in Cornwall 1870-1930' in Payton, Philip (ed.), 2003

Everson, Michael, Weatherhill, Craig, Chubb, Ray, Deacon, Bernard and Williams, Nicholas, *Form and Content in Revived Cornish*, Westport: Evertype, 2007

Ewart, Shirley and George, Harold T., *Highly Respectable Families: The Cornish of Grass Valley, California 1854-1954*, Grass Valley: Comstock Bonanza Press, 1998

Faull, Jim, *The Cornish in Australia*, Melbourne: A.E. Press, 1983

Federation of Gouren, *Breton and Celtic Wrestling*, Brittany: Institut Culturel de Bretagne, 1985

Ferguson, John and Chisholm, Kitty (eds.), *Political and Social Life in the Great Age of Athens*, Bradford-on-Avon, Ward Lock Educational, 1978

Fielder, George, *Mineral Point: A History*, Madison: The State Historical Society of Wisconsin, 1997 [1962]

Filbee, Marjorie, *Celtic Cornwall*, London: Constable, 1996

Fisk, Deborah Payne (ed.), *The Cambridge Companion to English Restoration Theatre*, Cambridge: Cambridge University Press, 2000

Fitzpatrick, Joan, *Shakespeare, Spenser and the Contours of Britain: Reshaping the Atlantic Archipelago*, Hatfield: University of Hertfordshire Press, 2006

Fitzsimons, Raymond, *Edmund Kean*, London: Hamish Hamilton, 1976

Fletcher, Alan J., 'The N-Town Plays' in Beadle, Richard (ed.), 1994

    Drama, Performance and Polity in Pre-Cromwellian Ireland, Cork: Cork University Press, 2000

Foote, Samuel, *The Dramatic Works of Samuel Foote, Vols. I-IV*, London: J. F. Rivington, C. Rivington, R. Baldwin, and S. Bladon, 1788

Ford, John, *The Chronicle Historie of Perkin Warbeck: A Strange Truth – A Tragedy in Five Acts and Chiefly in Verse*, London: T.P. for Hugh Beeston, 1634

Forfar, W.B., *The Exhibition and Other Cornish Poems*, Truro: Netherton and Worth, n.d.

Forrest, John and Heaney, Michael, 'Charting Early Morris' in *Folk Music Journal*, 6, 2, 1991

Fowler, David C., 'The Date of the Cornish *Ordinalia*' in *Mediaeval Studies*, 23, 1961
  John Trevisa, Aldershot: Variorium, 1993
  The Life and Times of John Trevisa, Medieval Scholar, Seattle and London: University of Washington Press, 1995

Fox, Adam and Woolf, Daniel, *The Spoken Word: Oral Culture in Britain, 1500-1850*, Manchester: Manchester University Press, 2003

Fox, George Croker (ed. and tr.), *The Prometheus of Aeschylus and the Electra of Sophocles, translated from the Greek, with notes intended to illustrate the typical character of the former*, London: Darton and Harvey, 1835
  The Death of Demosthenes and other Original Poems, with the Prometheus and Agamemnon translated from the Greek, London: John Bohn, 1839

Frantzen, Allan J., *Speaking Two Languages: Traditional Disciplines and Contemporary Theory in Medieval Studies*, Albany: State University of New York Press, 1991

Frazer, Tony (ed.), *Poets of Devon and Cornwall: From Barclay to Coleridge*, Exeter: Shearsman Books, 2007

Fredrick, Alan S. (ed. and tr.), *Béroul: The Romance of Tristan*, Harmondsworth: Penguin, 1970

Fried, Harvey (ed.), *A Critical Edition of Brome's "The Northern Lasse"*, New York and London: Garland, 1980

Frost, D. H., '*Sacrament an Alter*: A Tudor Cornish Patristic Catena' in Payton, Philip (ed.), 2003
  'Glasney's Parish Clergy and the Tregear Manuscript' in Payton, Philip (ed.), 2007

Fudge, Crystan, 'Aspects of Form in the Cornish *Ordinalia* with special reference to 'Origo Mundi' in *Old Cornwall*, 8, 1973-79
  The Life of Cornish, Redruth: Dyllansow Truran, 1982

Fulton, Helen (ed.), *Medieval Celtic Literature and Society*, Dublin: Four Courts Press, 2005

Furness, Raymond, 'Wagner and Decadence' in Grimbert, Joan Tasker (ed.), 1995

Gantz , Jeffrey (ed. and tr.), *The Mabinogion*, Harmondsworth: Penguin, 1976
  (ed. and tr.), *Early Irish Myths and Sagas*, London: Penguin, 1981

Gardner, Jessica and Mortimer, Ian, *Modern Literary Papers in the University of Exeter Library: A Guide*, Exeter: University of Exeter Library, 2003

Garmonsway, G.N. (ed.), *The Anglo-Saxon Chronicle*, London: Dent, 1975 [1953]

Gendall, Jan, *Scat-Ups, Scabs, and Shagdowns: A Glossary of Cornish Community Nicknames*, Menheniot: Teere ha Tavas, 1995

'Fifteenth-Century Archery: New Perspectives' in *Journal of the Royal Institution of Cornwall*, 2008

Gendall, Richard, *1000 Years of Cornish*, Menheniot: Teere ha Tavaz, 1994

A Practical Dictionary of Modern Cornish, Part One: Cornish – English, Menheniot, Teere ha Tavza, 1997

George, Ken, *The Pronunciation and Spelling of Revived Cornish*, Cornwall: The Cornish Language Board, 1986

(ed. and tr.), *Bywnans Ke*, Cornwall: Kesva an Taves Kernewek, 2006

Flogholeth Krist / The Cornish Ordinalia – the missing play: The Childhood of Christ, Cornwall: Kesva an Taves Kernewek, 2006

Rol dewisys a eryow nowydh po kevys namenowgh, a-dhiworth Bywnans Ke, Cornwall: Cornish Language Board, 2006.

Gerrard, Greg, *Ecocriticism*, London and New York: Routledge, 2004

Gibbons, Anne, *Mary Stuart: A Tragedy from the German of Schiller*, London: A. Schloss, 1838

An Easter Offering, London; Edwards and Hughes, 1845

Gibson, Edmund (ed.), *Camden's Britannica*, Newton Abbot: David and Charles, 1975 [1695]

Gibson, Jacqueline and Griffiths, Gwyn (eds. and trs.), *The Turn of the Ermine: An Anthology of Breton Literature*, London: Francis Boutle Publishers, 2006

Gibson, James (ed.), *Chosen Poems of Thomas Hardy*, Basingstoke: Macmillan, 1975

Gilbert, Davies *Mount Calvary... Interpreted in the English Tongue... by John Keigwin*, London: J.B. Nichols, 1826

The Creation of the World with Noah's Flood, written in Cornish in the Year 1611 by Wm. Jordan, with an English Translation by John Keigwin, London, J.B. Nichols, 1827

The Parochial History of Cornwall, London: J.B. Nichols, 1838

Gilbert, Helen (ed.), *(Post) Colonial Stages: Critical and Creative Views on Drama, Theatre and Performance*, Hebden Bridge: Dangaroo Press, 1999

Gilbert, Helen and Tompkins, Joanne, *Post-Colonial Drama: Theory, Practice, Politics*, London and New York: Routledge, 1996

Gilbert, W.S. and Sullivan, Arthur, *The Complete Annotated Gilbert and Sullivan*, Oxford: Oxford University Press, 1996

Giles, Judy and Middleton, Tim (eds.), *Writing Englishness 1900-1950*, London: Routledge, 1995

Gill, Frederick C., *The Romantic Movement and Methodism: A Study of English Romanticism and the Evangelical Revival*, London: The Epworth Press, 1937

Gillespie, Jack (ed.), *Our Cornwall: The Stories of Cornish Men and Women*, Padstow: Tabb House, 1988

Ginever, F.A., 'The Tale of Camborne's Patron Saint' in *Camborniana*, 1897

Giot, Pierre-Roland, Guigon, Philippe and Merdrignac, Bernard, *The British Settlement of Brittany*, Stroud: Tempus, 2003

Glanville, Ian, *St Just's Point: Down Under Cornish Humour*, Bendigo, Victoria: Ian Glanville, n.d.

Glinert, Ed (ed.), *The Savoy Operas: The Complete Gilbert and Sullivan*, London: Penguin, 2006

Goodman, Liz (ed.), *Approaching Literature: Literature and Gender*, London: Routledge, 1996

Goodrich, Peter (ed.), *The Romance of Merlin: An Anthology*, New York and London: Garland, 1990

Graham, Winston, *The Poldark Omnibus*, London: The Bodley Head, 1991

Grantley, Darryl, 'Producing Miracles' in Neuss, Paula (ed.), 1983

Graves, Robert, *The White Goddess: A Historical Grammar of Poetic Myth*, London: Faber and Faber, 1961

Gray, J.M. (ed.), *Alfred, Lord Tennyson: Idylls of the King*, Harmondsworth: Penguin, 1983

Gray, Todd (ed.), *The Travellers' Tales: Cornwall*, Exeter: The Mint Press, 2000
 The Chronicle of Exeter, 1205-1772, Exeter: The Mint Press, 2005

Great Western Railway, *Cornwall's Legend Land*, Vols. 1 and 2, Penzance: Oakmagic Publications, 1997 [1922]

Green, Miranda, *Dictionary of Celtic Myth and Legend*, London: Thames and Hudson, 1992

Green, Thomas, 'Tom Thumb and Jack the Giant Killer: Two Arthurian Fairytales?' in *Folklore*, Vol. 118, No.2, 2007

Greenblatt, Stephen, *Renaissance Self-Fashioning: From More to Shakespeare*, Chicago: University of Chicago Press, 1980

Grene, David and Latimore, Richard (eds. and trs.), *Greek Tragedies, Volume 1*, Chicago: University of Chicago Press, 1960

Grene, Nicholas, *The Politics of Irish Drama: Plays in Context from Boucicault to Friel*, Cambridge: Cambridge University Press, 1999

Grene, Nicholas and Morash, Christopher (eds.), *Irish Theatre on Tour*, Dublin: Carysfort Press, 2005

Gries, Walter F. and Kinsey, Donald D., "Andsome 'Arry with the H'auburn 'Air' in Kent and McKinney (eds.) 2008

Griffiths, Debbie, *Guide to the Archaeology of Dartmoor*, Exeter: Devon Books, 1996

Grigg, Erik, 'The Medieval Cornish Bible: More Evidence' in Payton, Philip (ed.), 2008
 Beunans Meriasek / The Life of St Meriasek: A Study Guide, Cornwall: The Cornish Language Board, 2008

Grimbert, Joan Tasker (ed.), *Tristan and Isolde: A Casebook*, New York and London: Garland, 1995

Grimm, Jacob, Grimm, Wilhelm, Duffy, Carol Ann and Prachaticka, Marketa, *Rumpelstiltskin and other Grimm Tales*, London: Faber and Faber, 1999

Grooms, Chris, 'Trioedd Ynys Prydian' in John T. Koch (ed.), 2006

Grose, Carl and Murphy, Anna Maria, 'Tristan and Yseult' in Kneehigh Theatre, London: Oberon Books, 2005

Groves, James M. (ed.), *The Echunga Diaries: London to New Zealand by Sailing Ship, 1862*, Gormley, Ontario: Preston Lake Publishing, 2003

Gundry, Inglis, *Canow Kernow: Songs and Dances from Cornwall*, Cornwall: The Federation of Old Cornwall Societies, 1972

Gunther, R.T. (ed.), *Early Science in Oxford, Vol. XIV: Life and Letters of Edward Lhwyd* [sic], Oxford: Oxford University Press subscribers' edition, 1945

Guthkelch, A.C. (ed.), *The Miscellaneous Works of Joseph Addison*, 2 Vols, Vol. 1, London: C. Bell and Sons, 1914

Guthrie, A., 'The Plan-an-Gwarry, St. Just, Cornwall: Report on an Exploratory Excavation' in *Proceedings of the West Cornwall Field Club*, 2, 1, 1956-7

Gutman, Robert W., *Wagner: The Man, His Mind and His Music*, New York: Harcourt, Brace and World, 1968

Hadfield, Andrew, *Shakespeare, Spenser and the Matter of Britain*, London: Palgrave Macmillan, 2003

Haigh, Christopher, *English Reformations: Religion, Politics, and Society under the Tudors*, Oxford: Clarendon Press, 1993

Hale, Amy, 'Genesis of the Celto-Cornish Revival? L.C. Duncombe-Jewell and the Cowethas Kelto-Kernuak' in Payton, Philip (ed.), 1997

Hale, Amy, Kent, Alan M., and Saunders, Tim (eds. and trs.), *Inside Merlin's Cave: A Cornish Arthurian Reader 1000-2000*, London: Francis Boutle Publishers, 2000

Hall, Jim, 'Maximilla, the Cornish Montanist: The Final Scenes of Origo Mundi' in Payton, Philip (ed.), 1999

Hall, John *That Bloody Woman: The Turbulent Life of Emily Hobhouse*, Mount Hawke: Truran, 2008

Halliday, F.E. (ed.), *Richard Carew: The Survey of Cornwall*, London: Melrose, 1953
The Legend of the Rood, London: Gerald Duckworth, 1955

Halliwell, R., *Rambles in the West Country*, London: n.p.,1861

Hals, William, *The Compleat History of Cornwall*, Truro, c.1736

Hampton, Christopher (ed.), *A Radical Reader: The Struggle for Change in England 1381-1914*, Harmondsworth, Penguin, 1984

Hancock, Peter, *Cornwall at War, 1939-1945*, Tiverton: Halsgrove, 2006

Handford, S.A., and Gardner, Jane F. (eds. and trs.), *Caesar: The Conquest of Gaul*,Harmondsworth: Penguin, 1982

Happé, P. (ed.), *Medieval English Drama*, London: Macmillan, 1984

Hardie, Melissa (ed.), *A Mere Interlude: Some Literary Visitors to Lyonesse*, Penzance: The Patten Press, 1992

Hardy, Thomas, *A Pair of Blue Eyes*, Oxford: Oxford University Press, 1983 [1873]

    A Pair of Blue Eyes, Harmondsworth Penguin, 1986 [1873]

    The Return of the Native, Harmondsworth: Penguin, 1994 [1878]

    The Distracted Preacher and Other Tales, Harmondsworth: Penguin, 1979

    The Famous Tragedy of the Queen of Cornwall at Tintagel in Lyonesse, London: Macmillan, 1923

Hare, Arnold, *The Georgian Theatre in Wessex*, London: Phoenix House, 1958

Harris, J. Henry, *Cornish Saints and Sinners*, London: Jane Lane The Bodley Head Limited, 1906

Harris, John, *Luda: A Lay of the Druids*, London: Hamilton, Adams and Co., 1863

Harris, Markham (ed. and tr.), *The Cornish Ordinalia: A Medieval Dramatic Trilogy*, Washington D.C.: Catholic University of America Press, 1969

    (ed. and tr.) *The Life of Meriasek: A Medieval Cornish Miracle Play*, Washington D.C.: Catholic University of America Press, 1977

Harris, William Lewarne, 'In Search of the Sunken City: The Birth of a Celtic Opera' in *An Baner Kernewek / The Cornish Banner*, No. 59, 1990

Harrison, B., 'Religion and Recreation in Nineteenth-century England' in *Papers Presented to the Past and Present Conference on Popular Religion*, July, 1966

Harrison, George, *Substance of a Report on the Laws and Jurisdiction of the Stannaries in Cornwall*, London: Longman, Rees, Orme, Brown, Green and Longman, 1835

Harrison, Jim, *Legends of the Fall*, New York: Delacorte Press, 1979

Harrison, Tony, *The Mysteries*, London: Faber and Faber, 1985

    Theatre Works 1973-1985, Harmondsworth: Penguin, 1986

Hartnoll, Phyllis (ed.), *The Oxford Companion to the Theatre*, Oxford; Oxford University Press, 1995

Harvey, David C., Jones, Rhys, McInroy, Neil and Milligan, Christine (eds.), *Celtic Geographies: Old Culture, New Times*, London and New York: Routledge, 2002

Harvey, Graham and Hardman, Charlotte, *Paganism Today*, London: Thorsons, 1996

Harwood, Ronald, *All the World's a Stage*, London: Methuen, 1984

Hatcher, John, *Rural Economy and Society in the Duchy of Cornwall 1300-1500*, Cambridge: Cambridge University Press, 1970

Hatcher, John and Bailey, Mark, *Modelling the Middle Ages: The History and Theory of England's Economic Development*, Oxford: Oxford University Press, 2001

Hatto, A.T. (ed. and tr.), *Gottfried von Strassburg: Tristan, with the Tristan of Thomas*, Harmondsworth: Penguin, 1967

    (ed. and tr.), *Wolfram von Eschenbach: Parzival*, London: Penguin, 1980

Hawke, Andrew, 'A Lost Manuscript of the Cornish *Ordinalia*?' in Thomas, Charles (ed.), *Cornish Studies / Studhyansow Kernewk* 7, Redruth: Institute of Cornish Studies, 1979

Hayden, Cheryl, '1549 – The Rebels Shout Back' in Payton, Philip (ed.), 2008

Hays, Rosalind Conklin, and McGee, C.E. (Dorset) and Joyce, Sally L. and Newlyn, Evelyn S. (Cornwall) (eds.), *Records of Early English Drama: Dorset / Cornwall*, Toronto: University of Toronto and Brepols, 1999

Heath, Malcolm (ed. and tr.), *Aristotle: The Poetics*, London: Penguin, 1996

Hechter, Michael, *Internal Colonialism: The Celtic Fringe in British National Development, 1536-1966*, London: Routledge and Kegan Paul, 1975

Heinberg, Richard, *Peak Everything: Waking Up to the Century of Decline in the Earth's Resources*, Forest Row: Clairview Books, 2007

Heinlein, Kurt Gerard, *Green Theatre: Promoting Ecological Preservation and Advancing the Sustainability of Humanity and Nature*, Berlin: VDM Verlag, 2007

Helse, Ursula K., *Sense of Place and Sense of Planet: The Environmental Imagination*, Oxford: Oxford University Press, 2008

Henderson, Charles, *Parochial Antiquities*, Vol, V, 1915. MSS. in Charles Henderson Collection, Courtney Library, Royal Institution of Cornwall
Cornish Church Guide, Truro: D. Bradford Barton, 1964 [1925]
St Columb Major Church and Parish, Long Compton, n.p., 1930
'The Ecclesiastical Antiquities of the Four Western Hundreds of Cornwall' in *Journal of the Royal Institution of Cornwall*, 2, 3, 1955

Henderson, Thomas (ed.), *Sir Walter Scott: Minstrelsy of the Scottish Border*, London: George G. Harrap and Company Ltd, 1931

Hendra, Viv, *The Cornish Wonder: A Portrait of John Opie*, Mount Hawke: Truran, 2007

Heywood, Thomas, *An Apology for Actors*, London: Nicholas Okes, 1612

Higgins, Sydney, *Medieval Theatre in the Round: The Multiple Staging of Religious Drama in England*, Camerino, Italy: Laboratorio degli studi Linguistici, 1995
'The Action of St Meriasek – Day One' in Higgins, 1995
'The Action of St Meriasek – Day Two' in Higgins, 1995
'Creating the Creation: the staging of the Cornish medieval play *The Creation of the World* in Higgins, Sydney (ed.), 1996
(ed.), *European Medieval Drama 1996: Papers for the First International Conference on Aspects of European Medieval Drama*, Camerino: Universita Degli Studi Di Camerino – Centro Linguitico di Ateneo, 1996
(ed.), *European Medieval Drama 1997: Papers for the Second International Conference on Aspects of European Medieval Drama*, Camerino: Universita Degli Studi Di Camerino – Centro Linguitico di Ateneo, 1997

Hill, Christopher, *God's Englishman*, London: Weidenfield and Nicholson, 1970

Hill, Elizabeth Ann, *The Driftwood Fire*, London: Heinemann, 1996

Hill, Kerrow, *The Brontë Sisters and Sir Humphry Davy: A Sharing of Visions*, Penzance: Patten Press, 1994

Hoare, George and Stanhope Alan, *Towards a University in Cornwall*, Camborne: Cornwall College, 1998

Hobsbawm, Eric and Ranger, Terence (eds.), *The Invention of Tradition*, Cambridge: Cambridge University Press, 1992

Hocking, Joseph and Horton, R.E., *Shall Rome Reconquer England?* London: National Council of Evangelical Free Churches, 1910

Hocking, Silas K., *Alec Green: A Tale of Sea Life*, London: Frederick Warne and Company, 1878

    Sea Waif: A Tale of the Cornish Cliffs, London: Frederick Warne and Company, 1882

Holdsworth, Roger Victor (ed.), *Thomas Middleton and William Rowley, A Fair Quarrel*, London: Benn, 1974

Holguist, Michael, *Dialogism: Bakhtin and His World*, London and New York: Routledge, 2002

Holland, Kevin Crossley (ed.), *The Exeter Book Riddles*, Harmondsworth: Penguin, 1979

Holmes, A. W., *Out of this Fury*, London: Hutchinson, 1944

Holmes, Julyan (ed. and tr.), *An dhargan a Verdhin gan Yowaan Kernow*, Cornwall: Kesva and Tavaes Kernewek, 1998

Holroyd, Martin, *A Strange and Eventful History: The Dramatic Lives of Ellen Terry, Henry Irving and Their Remarkable Families*, London: Chatto and Windus, 2008

Hooper, E.G. Retallack (ed.), *Robert Morton Nance and A.S.D. Smith (eds. and trs.), Gwyrans an Bys*, Redruth: Dyllansow Truran, 1985

Hopkins, Rob, *The Transition Handbook: From Oil Dependency to Local Resilience*, Dartington: Green Books Ltd, 2008

Horner, Avril and Zlosnik, Sue, *Daphne du Maurier: Writing, Identity and the Gothic Imagination*, London: Palgrave Macmillan, 1998

Hosken, James Dryden, *Phaon and Sappho: A play (in five acts and song)*, Penzance: F. Rodda, 1891

    Verses by the way, London: Methuen, 1893

    A Monk's Love and Other Poems, London: James Dryden Hosken, 1895

    Christopher Marlowe: A Tragedy in Three Acts in Prose and Verse, and Belphegor: A Harlequinade in Doggerel, London: Henry and Co., 1896

    Poems and Songs of Cornwall, Plymouth: Mitchell, Burt and Co., 1906

    Shores of Lyonesse Poems: Dramatic Narrative and Lyrical, London: J.M. Dent and Sons Ltd c.1928

    Helston Furry Day, Helston: Helston Old Cornwall Society, 1931

Hosking, Phil, 'Kneehigh Theatre' in *Cornish World / Bys Kernowyon*, No. 11, 1996
'Sue Hill: Gifted Lady of Cornish Theatre' in *Cornish World / Bys Kernowyon*, No. 11, 1996
Howard, Douglas, 'Samuel Foote' in Backschneider, Paula (ed.), 1989
Howard, Leslie and Paris, Helen (eds.), *Performance and Place*, Basingstoke: Palgrave, 2006
Howatch, Susan, *Penmarric*, London: Hamish Hamilton, 1971
Howell, Mark A., 'Planning Provincial Theatres Under the 1757 Stage Licensing Act' in *Theatre Notebook: A Journal of the History and Technique of the British Theatre*, No. 3, 1989
Howlett, Jonathan, 'Putting the Kitsch into Kernow' in Payton, Philip (ed.), 2004
Huber, Otto, Stück, Christian and Shafer, Ingrid (eds. and trs.), *Othmar Weis and Joseph Alois Daisenberger: Oberammergau: Passionspiel 2000*, Oberammergau: Gemeinde Oberammergau, 2000
Hughes, Robert, *The Fatal Shore: A History of the Transportation of Convicts to Australia, 1787-1868*, London: Vintage, 2003 [1986]
Hughes-Freeland, Felicia (ed.), *Ritual, Performance, Media*, London and New York, Routledge, 1998
Hunt, Lindsay, *Brittany*, Windsor: AA Publishing, 1995
Hunt, Robert (ed.), *Popular Romances of the West of England: The Drolls, Traditions, and Superstitions of Old Cornwall (First Series)*, London: John Camden Hotten, 1865
Popular Romances of the West of England: The Drolls, Traditions, and Superstitions of Old Cornwall (Second Series), London: John Camden Hotten, 1865
Hurst, John, 'Literature in Cornwall' in Payton, Philip (ed.), 1993a 'A Poetry of Dark Sounds: The Manuscripts of Charles Causley' in Payton, Philip (ed.), 1999
Hutton, Patrick, *I would not be forgotten: The Life and Work of Robert Stephen Hawker*, Padstow: Tabb House, 2004
Hutton, Ronald, *The Pagan Religions of the Ancient British Isles: Their Nature and Legacy*, Oxford: Blackwell, 1991
The Rise and Fall of Merry England: The Ritual Year 1400-1700, Oxford: Oxford University Press, 1994
The Stations of the Sun: A History of the Ritual Year in Britain, Oxford: Oxford University Press, 1996
The Triumph of the Moon: A History of Modern Pagan Witchcraft, Oxford: Oxford University Press, 1999
Witches, Druids and King Arthur, London and New York: Hambledon, 2003
The Druids, London: Hambledon, 2007
Shamans: Siberian Spirituality and Western Imagination, London: Hambledon Continuum, 2007
I.M.G., *Old Kea Church*, Kea: Old Kea Church, 1991

Isaac, Peter, *A History of Evangelical Christianity in Cornwall*, Gerrards Cross: WEC Press, 2000

Ivey, W.F. (ed.), *A Dictionary of Cornish Dialect Words*, Helston: Helston Printers, 1976

Jackson, Julian, *The Fall of France: The Nazi Invasion of 1940*, Oxford: Oxford University Press, 2003

Jackson, Kenneth Hurlstone (ed. and tr.), *A Celtic Miscellany: Translations from the Celtic Literatures*, Harmondsworth: Penguin, 1971

Jackson, Russell, *Victorian Theatre: The Theatre in Its Time*, New York: New Amsterdam, 1994

Jacob, Valerie, *Tregonissey to Trenarren: The Cornish Years of A.L. Rowse*, St Austell: Valerie Jacob, 2001

Jago, F.W.P. (ed.), *The Ancient Language, and the Dialect of Cornwall, with an enlarged Glossary of Cornish Provincial Words*, Truro: Netherton and Worth, 1882

James, Graham, 'Play fails to live up to expectation' in *The West Briton*, 8 May 2004

James, Simon, *The Atlantic Celts: Ancient People or Modern Invention?* London: British Museum Press, 1999

Jamieson, Michael (ed.), *Three Comedies: Volpone, The Alchemist and Bartholomew Fair*, Harmondsworth: Penguin, 1966

Jenkin, A.K. Hamilton, *The Cornish Miner: An Account of his Life Above and Underground from Early Times*, Newton Abbot: David and Charles, 1972 [1927]

Jenkin, L.E.T., 'St Piran' in Combellack Harris, Myrna (ed.), *Cornish Studies for Schools*, Truro: Cornwall County Council, 1989

Jenkin, Richard, 'Modern Cornish Literature in the 20th Century' in *The Celtic Pen*, Vol. 1, No. 3, 1994

Jenkins, Chris, 'Traces of the Goddess Sillana' in *Meyn Mamvro*, No.35, 1998

Jenkins, Geraint H., *Facts, Fantasy and Fiction: Historical Vision of Iolo Morganwg*, Aberystwyth: University of Wales Centre for Advanced Wales and Celtic Studies, 1998

Jenner, Henry, *A Handbook of the Cornish Language: Chiefly in its Latest Stages with some account of its History and Literature*, London: David Nutt, 1904

    'The Cornish Drama' in *Celtic Review*, III, 1906-7

    'Perran Round and the Cornish Drama' in *The Seventy-Eighth Annual Report of the Royal Cornwall Polytechnic Society*, 1, 3, 1911

    'Some Possible Arthurian Place-Names in West Penwith' in *Journal of the Royal Institution of Cornwall*, 1912

    'The Tristan Romance and its Cornish Provenance' in *Journal of the Royal Institution of Cornwall*, No.14, 1914

    'The Fourteenth-Century Charter Endorsement' in *Journal of the Royal Institution of Cornwall*, No.20, 1915-16

    'The Bodmin Gospels' in *Journal of the Royal Institution of Cornwall*, No.70, 1922

'The Bodmin Manumissions' in *Journal of the Royal Institution of Cornwall*, No.71, 1924

'Tintagel Castle in History and Romance' in *Journal of the Royal Institution of Cornwall*, No.74, 1927

'King Teudar' in Roberts, Trelawney, Henderson, Charles, and Seldon, Leonard (eds.), 1928

'Cornwall: A Celtic Nation' in Williams, Derek R. (ed.), 2004

'The Sources for the Cornish Drama' in Jenner Papers, Royal Institution of Cornwall, Truro

Jenner, Henry and Taylor, Thomas, 'The Legend of the Church of the Holy Cross in Cornwall' in *Journal of the Royal Institution of Cornwall*, 20, 1917-1921

Jewell, Helen M., *The North-South Divide: The Origins of Northern Consciousness in England*, Manchester: Manchester University Press, 1994

John, Catherine Rachel, *The Saints of Cornwall: 1500 Years of Christian Landscape*, Padstow: Tabb House, 2001 [1981]

Johnson, John, *The Way to Get Married: And the Advantages and Disadvantages of the Marriage State, represented under the similitude of a dream*, Philadelphia: Johnson and Warner, 1810

Johnson, Trevor, "Time was Away': *A Pair of Blue Eyes* and the Poems of 1912-13' in Hardie, Melissa (ed.), 1992

Johnston, Dafydd, *The Literature of Wales*, Cardiff: University of Wales Press, 1994

Jones, Andy M., 'Settlement and ceremony: archaeological investigations at Stannon Down, St. Breward, Cornwall' in *Cornish Archaeology / Hendhyscans Kernow*, Nos 43-44, 2004-5

Jones, Anwen, *National Theatres in Context: France, Germany, England and Wales*, Cardiff: University of Wales Press, 2007

Jones, Dedwydd, 'The Father of Welsh Drama: Twm O'r Nant' in *The Celtic Pen*, Vol. 2, No. 1, 1994

Jones, Kelvin, *Witchcraft in Cornwall: An Account of Witchcraft, its Practice, its Customs and Condemnation*, St Just in Penwith: Sir Hugo Books, 1995

Jones, M. (ed.), *Traces of Ancestry: Studies in Honour of Colin Renfrew*, Vol. 2, Cambridge: McDonald Institute Monograph Series, 2004

Jones, Mari and Singh, Ishtla, *Exploring Language Change*, London: Routledge, 2005

Jones, Martin, and MacLeod, George, 'Regional spaces, spaces of regionalism: territory, insurgent politics and the English question' in *Transactions of the Institute of British Geographers*, 2004

Jones, Roger (ed.), *John Skinner: Westcountry Tour, being the Diary of a Tour through the Counties of Somerset, Devon and Cornwall in 1797*, Bradford upon Avon: Ex Libris Press, 1985

Jones, Thomas, 'The early evolution of the legend of Arthur' in *Nottingham Medieval Studies*, No.8, 1964

Kafka, Franz, *The Collected Novels*, Harmondsworth; Penguin, 1988

Karr, David S., 'Thoughts That Flash like Lightning: Thomas Holcroft, Radical Theatre, and the Production of Meaning in 1790s' London' in *Journal of British Studies*, No. 40, 2001

Kay-Robinson, Denys, *The First Mrs Thomas Hardy*, London: Macmillan, 1979

Keast, Horace, *The Catholic Revival in Cornwall 1833 to 1983*, Cornwall: The Catholic Advisory Council for Cornwall, 1983

Keating, Michael, *State and Regional Nationalism: Territorial Politics and the European State*, London: Harvester Wheatsheaf, 1988

Keith, Michael and Pile, Steve (eds.), *Place and the Politics of Identity*, London and New York, Routledge, 1993

Kelman, James, *How Late it Was, How Late*, London: Secker and Warburg, 1994

Kemp, David, *Art of Darkness Museum Guide*, St Ives: David Kemp, 1996

Kempe, Andy, *The Script Sampler*, Cheltenham: Nelson Thornes Ltd, 2002

Keneally, Thomas, *The Playmaker*, London: Serpentine Publishing, 1987

Kennedy, Edward Donald (ed.), *King Arthur: A Casebook*, London and New York: Routledge, 2002

Kennedy, F. Keith, *A Brief History of the Georgian Theatre Penzance*, Penzance: Union Hotel, n.d.

Kennedy, Mark, 'Director Michael Grandage Hits Broadway' in *The Huffington Post*, 28 April 2007

Kennedy, Neil, 'Meriasek' in Tim Saunders (ed. and tr.), 2006

Kent, Alan M., *Clay*, Launceston: Amigo, 1991

    Out of the Ordinalia, St Austell: Lyonesse Press, 1995

    'Art thou of Cornish crew? Shakespeare, *Henry V* and Cornish Identity' in Payton, Philip (ed.),1996

    Wives, Mothers and Sisters: Feminism, Literature and Women Writers of Cornwall, Penzance: The Jamieson Library, 1998

    Dreaming in Cornish, Liskeard: Giss 'On Books: 1998

    '"At the Far End of England...": Construction of Cornwall in Children's Literature' in *An Baner Kernewek / The Cornish Banner*, No.98, 1999

    (ed.), *Voices from West Barbary: An Anthology of Anglo-Cornish Poetry 1548-1928*, London: Francis Boutle Publishers, 2000

    The Literature of Cornwall: Continuity, Identity, Difference 1000-2000, Bristol: Redcliffe, 2000

    Pulp Methodism: The Lives and Literature of Silas, Joseph and Salome Hocking, St. Austell: Cornish Hillside Publications, 2002

    Love and Seaweed, St Austell: Lyonesse Press, 2002

"In Some State...': A Decade of the Literature and Literary Studies of Cornwall' in Payton, Philip (ed.), 2002

'Screening Kernow: Authenticity, Heritage and the Representation of Cornwall in Film and Television' in Payton, Philip (ed.), 2003

(ed.), *The Dreamt Sea: An Anthology of Anglo-Cornish Poetry 1928-2004*, London: Francis Boutle Publishers, 2004

Cousin Jack's Mouth-Organ: Travels in Cornish America, St Austell: Cornish Hillside Publications, 2004

"Drill Cores': A Newly-Found Manuscript of Cousin Jack Narratives from the Upper Peninsula of Michigan, USA' in Payton, Philip (ed.), 2004

Ordinalia: The Cornish Mystery Play Cycle – A Verse Translation, London: Francis Boutle Publishers, 2005

Assassin of Grammar, Penzance: Hypatia Publications, 2005

Proper Job, Charlie Curnow! Tiverton: Halsgrove, 2005

'Scatting it t'lerrups: Provisional Notes towards Alternative Methodologies in Language and Literary Studies in Cornwall' in Payton, Philip (ed.), 2005

"'Bringin' the Dunkey Down from the Carn": Cornu-English in Context 1549-2005' – A Provisional Analysis in Tristram, Hildegard L.C. (ed.), 2006

Nativitas Christi / The Nativity: A New Cornish Mystery Play, London: Francis Boutle Publishers, 2006

Stannary Parliament, St Austell: Lyonesse, 2006

Oogly es Sin: The Lamentable Ballad of Anthony Payne, Cornish Giant, London: Francis Boutle Publishers, 2007

'Some ancientry that lingers: Dissent, difference and dialect in the Cornish and Cornu-English Literature of Robert Morton Nance' in Thomas, Peter W. and Williams, Derek (eds.), 2007

"'Mozeying on down...": The Cornish Language in America' in Hildegard L.C. Tristram (ed.), 2007

Electric Pastyland, Wellington: Halsgrove, 2007

'Alex Parks, Punks and Pipers: Toward a History of Popular Music in Cornwall 1967-2007' in Payton, Philip (ed.), 2007

The Tin Violin, London: Francis Boutle Publishers, 2008

Druid Offsetting, St Austell: Lyonesse Press, 2008

Surfing Tommies, London: Francis Boutle Publishers, 2009

(ed.), *Charles Valentine Le Grice: Cornwall's 'Lost' Romantic Poet*, St Austell: Lyonesse, 2010

Kent, Alan M. and McKinney, Gage (eds.), *The Busy Earth: A Reader in Global Cornish Literature 1700-2000*, St Austell: Cornish Hillside Publications, 2008

Kent, Alan M. and Merrifield, Danny L.J., The *Book of Probus: Cornwall's Garden Parish*, Tiverton: Halsgrove, 2004

Kent, Alan M. and Saunders, Tim (eds. and trs.), *Looking at the Mermaid: A Reader in Cornish Literature 900-1900*. London: Francis Boutle Publishers, 2000

Kerman, Joseph, 'Wagner's Tristan und Isolde: Opera as Symphonic Poem' in Grimbert, Joan Tasker (ed.), 1995

Kerrigan, John, *Archipelagic English: Literature, History and Politics 1603-1702*, Oxford: Oxford University Press, 2008

Kershaw, Baz, *The Politics of Performance: Radical Theatre as Cultural Intervention*, London and New York: Routledge, 1992

    Theatre Ecology: Environments and Performance, Cambridge: Cambridge University Press, 2007

Killigrew, William, *Ayres and Dialogues for one, two and three voices*, London, 1653

    Four New Plays, viz. The Seege of Urbin, Selindra, Love and Friendship: tragy-comedies, Pandora, comedy, Oxford: Oxford University, printed by Henry Hall, 1666

    The Imperial Tragedy, taken out of a Latin play, and very much altered, by a Gentleman for his own diversion, London: William Wells and Robert Scott, 1669

    Three New Plays, viz. Selinda, Pandorea, Ormasdes, London, 1674

King, John, *Kingdoms of the Celts: A History and Guide*, London: Cassell, 1998

King, John Baragwanath, *The Coming of Arthur*, London: Erskine Macdonald, 1925

King, Stephen *The Tommyknockers*, London: Hodder 2008 [1987]

Kirby, Ernest T., *Dionysus: A Study of the Bacchae and the Origins of Drama*, Ann Arbor: University Microfilms Int., 1982

Kneehigh Theatre, *Tristan and Yseult, The Bacchae, The Wooden Frock, The Red Shoes*, London: Oberon Books, 2005

    The Reviews, Truro: Kneehigh Theatre, n.d.

    Peep Show, Truro: Kneehigh Theatre, n.d.

Knipping, Mark H and Oberle, Korinne K., *On the Shake Rag: Mineral Point's Pendarvis House, 1935-1970*, Mineral Point: The State Historical Society of Wisconsin and The Memorial Pendarvis Trust, 1990

Koch, John T. (ed.), *Celtic Culture: A Historical Encylopedia*, Vols. 1-5, Santa Barbara, California and Oxford: ABC Clio, 2006

Koch, John T. and Carey, John (eds. and trs.), *The Celtic Heroic Age: Literary Sources for Ancient Celtic Europe and Early Wales and Ireland*, Malden, Massachusetts: Celtic Studies Publications, 1995

Kowaleski, Maryanne, *Local Markets and Regional Trade in Medieval Exeter*, Cambridge: Cambridge University Press, 2003

Laing, Lloyd, *The Archaeology of Celtic Britain and Ireland c.AD 400-1200*, Cambridge: Cambridge University Press, 2006

Lake, Jeremy, Cox, Jo and Berry, Eric, *Diversity and Vitality: The Methodist and Nonconformist Chapels of Cornwall*, Truro: Cornwall Archaeological Unit, 2001

Langford, Paul, *A Polite and Commercial People: England 1727-1783*, Oxford: Clarendon Press, 1999

Landsberg, Sylvia, *The Medieval Garden*, London: British Museum Press, 1996

Langham, A.F., *The Island of Lundy*, Stroud: Sutton, 1994

Lankester, Edwin (ed.), *Memorials of John Ray, consisting of his life by Dr [William] Derham, biographical and critical notes by Sir J.E. Smith and Dupetit Thouers with his iterinaries, etc*, London: Ray Society, n.d

Lanyon, Andrew, *The First and Last Straw*, Cornwall: Andrew Lanyon, n.d.

Laughlin, Burgess, *The Aristotle Adventure: A Guide to the Greek, Roman and Latin Scholars who transmitted Artistotle's Logic to the Renaissance*, Flagstaff, Arizona: Albert Hale, 1995

Laviolette, Patrick, 'Cornwall's Visual Cultures in Perspective' in Payton, Philip (ed.), 2003

'Where Difference Lies: Performative Metaphors of Truth, Deception and Placelessness in the Cornish Peninsula' in Howard, Leslie and Paris, Helen (eds.), 2006

Lawrence, Robert G. (ed.), *Restoration Plays*, London: J.M. Dent and Sons, 1976

Laws, Peter, 'The Cornish Riviera – Architects and Builders Provide the Necessary Ingredient' in Mattingly, Joanna and Palmer, June (eds.), 1992

Leacroft, Richard, *The Development of the English Playhouse: An Illustrated Survey of the Theatre Building in England from Medieval to Modern Times*, London: Methuen, 1973

Leavis, F.R., *The Great Tradition*, London: Chatto and Windus, 1948

Lebègue, R., *Le Mystère des Actes des Apôtres. Contribution à l'étude de l'humanisme et du protestantisme français au XVIe siècle*, Paris, n.p.,1929

Lee, John (ed.), *The Works of Samuel Foote Esq*, London: Sherwood, Gilbert and Piper, 1830

'An Essay on the Life, Genius and Writings of the Author' in John Lee (ed.), 1830

Le Goffic, Ch. (ed.), *O.L. Aubert: Celtic Legends of Brittany*, Kerangwenn: Coop Breizh, 1999 [1993]

Leland, John, 'The Itinerary: So far as it relates to Cornwall' in Gilbert, Davies, 1838

Le Mat, Jean-Pierre, *The Sons of Ermine: A History of Brittany*, Belfast: An Clochán, 1996

Le Men, Gwenolé, 'Celtic Drama: Breton Popular Theatre' in *The Celtic Pen, Vol. 1, No. 1, 1993*

Leoussi, Athena S. and Grosby, Steven (eds.), *Nationalism and Ethnosymbolism: History, Culture and Ethnicity in the Formation of Nations*, Edinburgh: Edinburgh University Press, 2007

Levin, Richard, *The Multiple Plot in English Renaissance Drama*, Chicago: University of Chicago Press, 1971

Ley, Graham, *A Short Introduction to Greek Theatre*, Chicago: University of Chicago Press, 1991

Light, Alison, *Forever England: Femininity, Literature and Conservatism between the Wars*, London: Routledge, 1991

Löffler, Marion (ed.), *A Book of Mad Celts: John Wickens and the Celtic Congress of Caernarfon 1904*, Llandysul: Gomer, 2000

Longsworth, Robert, *The Cornish Ordinalia: Religion and Dramaturgy*, Cambridge, Massachusetts: Harvard University Press, 1967

Loughrey, Bryan and Taylor, Neil (ed.), *Thomas Middleton: Five Plays*, London: Penguin, 1988

Lovelock, John David, *The Function of Music in Greek Drama, and its influence on Italian Theatre, and Theatre Music of the Renaissance*, Milton Keynes: Open University Press, 1989

Loth, Joseph (ed.), *Vocubulaire Vieux-Breton*, Paris: Privately published, 1884
    De Nouvelles Théories sur l'origine du Roman Arthurian, Paris: Privately published, 1892

Lowerson, John, 'Celtic Tourism – Some Recent Magnets' in Payton, Philip (ed.), 1994

Lupack, Alan (ed.), *Modern Arthurian Literature: An Anthology of English and American Arthuriana from the Renaissance to the Present*, London and New York: Garland, 1992

Luzel, F.M., *Folktales from Armorica*, Felinfach: Llanerch, 1992 [c.1870]

Lyon, Rod, *Cornwall's Playing Places*, Nancegollan: Tavas an Weryn, 2001
    Cornish: The Struggle for Survival, Nancegollan: Tavas an Weryn, 2001
    Gorseth Kernow: The Cornish Gorsedd – what it is and what it does, Cornwall: Gorseth Kernow, 2008

MacKillop, James, *Dictionary of Celtic Mythology*, Oxford: Oxford University Press, 1998

Mackintosh, Ian, 'Rediscovering the Courtyard' in *Architectural Review*, April, 1984
    Architecture, Actor and Audience, London and New York: Routledge, 1993

Maclean, Magnus, *The Literature of the Celts*, London: Blackie and Son, 1908

Madam, F. and Craster, H.H.E. (eds.), *A Summary Catalogue of Western Manuscripts in the Bodleian Library*, Oxford: Clarendon Press, 1922-55

Magee, Bryan, *The Tristan Chord*, New York: Owl Books, 2002

Maguire, Jack, The *Power of Personal Storytelling: Spinning Tales to Connect with Others*, New York: Jeremy P. Tarcher, 2000

Maker, Lawrence, *Cob and Moorstone: The Curious History of some Methodist Churches*, London: Epworth Press, 1935

Malone, Caroline, *Neolithic Britain and Ireland*, Stroud: Tempus, 2001

Malone, Michael P., *The Battle for Butte: Mining and Politics on the Northern Frontier 1864-1906*, Helena: Montana Historical Society Press, 1981

Manning, Paul, 'Staging the State and the Hypostasization of Violence in the Medieval Cornish Drama' in Payton, Philip (ed.), 2005
'Jewish Ghosts, Knackers, Tommyknockers and other Sprites of Capitalism in Cornish Mines' in Payton, Philip (ed.), 2005
March, Caeia, *Reflections*, London: The Women's Press, 1995
March, Caeia and Straffon, Cheryl, 'The Search for Bride' in *Meyn Mamvro*, No. 21, 1993
'The Calendar of the Land: Ritual Landscapes of Bodmin Moor and Loughcrew' in *Meyn Mamvro*, No.24, 1994
Margolin, Reuben H. (ed.), *Bret Harte's Goldrush*, Berkeley: Heyday Books, 1997
Markley, Robert, 'The Canon and its Critics' in Fisk, Deborah Payne (ed.), 2000
Marsh, George D., and the Writers' Project of Montana, *Copper Camp: The Lusty Story of Butte, Montana, The Richest Hill on Earth*, Helena: Riverbend Publishing, 2002 [1943]
Marshall, Ian, *The Amazing Story of the Floral Dance*, Dobwalls; Songs of Cornwall, 2003
Marshalsay, Karen, *The Waggle of the Kilt: Popular Theatre and Entertainment in Scotland*, Glasgow: Glasgow University Library Studies, 1992
Mathew, David, *The Celtic Peoples and Renaissance Europe*, London, Sheed and Ward, 1933
Matthews, G. Forester, *The Isles of Scilly*, London: George Ronald, 1960
Matthews, J. H., *History of St Ives, Lelant, Towednack and Zennor*, St Ives Trust and St Ives Library, 2003 [1892].
Matthews, John and Matthews, Caitlin, *Taliesin: The Last Celtic Shaman*, Rochester, Vermont: Bear and Company, 2002
Mattingly, H. and Handford, S.A. (eds. and trs.), *Tacitus: The Agricola and the Germania*, Harmondsworth: Penguin, 1970
Mattingly, Joanna, 'The Medieval Parish Guilds of Cornwall' in *Journal of the Royal Institution of Cornwall*, 10, 3, 1989
Mattingly, Joanna and Palmer, June (eds.), *From Pilgrimage to Package Tour*, Truro: Royal Institution of Cornwall, 1992
Maufort, Marc, *Transgressive Itineraries: Postcolonial Hybridizations of Dramatic Realism*, Brussels: Peter Lang, 2004
May, Jo, *Fogou: A Journey into the Underworld*, Glastonbury: Gothic Image, 1996
Mayers, Lynne, *Balmaidens*, Penzance: The Hypatia Trust, 2004
McCaughran, Geraldine and Brassey, Richard, *Britannia: 100 Great Stories from British History*, London: Orion, 1999
McConkey, Kenneth, Risdon, Peter and Sheppard, Pauline, *Harold Harvey: Painter of Cornwall*, Bristol: Sansom and Company, 2001
McDonald, Marianne and Walton, Michael (eds.), *The Cambridge Companion to Greek and Roman Theatre*, Cambridge: Cambridge University Press, 2007

McGavin, John J., *Theatricality and Narrative in Medieval and Early Modern Scotland*, Aldershot: Ashgate, 2007

McGrady, Richard, *Music and Musicians in Early Nineteenth-Century Cornwall: The World of Joseph Emidy – Slave, Violinist and Composer*, Exeter: University of Exeter Press, 1991

> *Traces of Ancient Mystery: The Ballad Carols of Davies Gilbert and William Sandys*, Redruth: Institute of Cornish Studies, 1993

McKinney, Gage, *When Miners Sang: The Grass Valley Carol Choir*, Grass Valley: Comstock Bonanza Press, 2001

McMahon, Brendan, 'A Cornish Shaman' in *Meyn Mamvro*, No.28, 1995

> *The Princess Who Ate People: The Psychology of Celtic Myths*, Loughborough: Heart of Albion Press, 2006

McNeil Cook, Ian, *Mermaid to Merrymaid: Journey to the Stones – Ancient Sites and Pagan Mysteries of Celtic Cornwall*, Penzance: Men-an-Tol Studio, 1987

> *Mother and Sun: The Cornish Fogou*, Penzance: Men-an-Tol Studio, 1993

McNulty, Eugene, *The Ulster Literary Theatre and the Northern Revival*, Cork: Cork University Press, 2008

Mercer, Roger, 'The Neolithic in Cornwall' in *Cornish Archaeology / Hendhyscans Kernow*, No.25, 1986

Merton, Les, *Oall Rite Me Ansum! A Salute to Cornish Dialect*, Newbury: Countryside Books, 2003

Meyer, Robert T., 'The Liturgical Background of Medieval Cornish Drama' in *Trivium*, 3, 1968

> 'The Middle-Cornish Play: *Benuans Meriasek*' in *Comparative Drama*, 3, 1969

Michell, Frank, *Annals of an Ancient Cornish Town: Notes on the History of Redruth*, Redruth: Frank Michell, 1978 [1946]

> 'Redruth's Theatrical Past' in *The Cornish Review*, No.3, 1949

Michell, John, *The View over Atlantis*, London: Harper Collins, 1969

> *The Old Stones of Land's End*, London: Garnstone Press, 1974

Miles, Dillwyn, *The Secret of the Bards of the Isle of Britain*, Llandybie: Gwasg Dinefwr Press, 1992

Miller, Hamish and Broadhurst, Paul, *The Sun and the Serpent: An Investigation into Earth Energies*, Launceston: Pendragon Press, 1989

Millgate, Michael, *Thomas Hardy: His Career as a Novelist*, London: Bodley Head, 1971

> *Thomas Hardy: A Biography*, Oxford: Oxford University Press, 1985

Millington, Barry (ed.), *The Wagner Compendium: A Guide to Wagner's Life and Music*, London: Thames and Hudson, 2001

Millington, Peter, 'The Truro Cordwainers' Play: A "New" Eighteenth-Century Christmas Play' in *Folklore*, Vol. 114, No. 1, 2003

Mills, David, 'The Chester Cycle' in Beadle, Richard (ed.), 1994

Miners, Hugh, *Gorseth Kernow: The First 50 Years*, Cornwall: Gorseth Kernow, 1978 'Old Pagan Customs' in *Meyn Mamvro*, No. 3, 1986

Miners, Hugh and Crago, Treve, *Tolzethan: The Life and Times of Joseph Hambley Rowe*, Cornwall: Gorseth Kernow, 2002

Miners, Tom, 'The Mummers' Play in West Cornwall' in *Old Cornwall*, Vol. 1, 1925-1930

Mitchell, Bill, Shepherd, Mike, Rice, Emma, and Moore, Victoria, *Kneehigh Theatre*, Truro: Kneehigh Theatre, c.2005.

Mitchell, Emma, 'The Myth of Objectivity: The Cornish Language and the Eighteenth-Century Antiquarians' in Payton, Philip (ed.), 1998

Moffat, Alistair, *The Sea Kingdoms: The Story of Celtic Britain and Ireland*, London: Harper Collins, 2001

Molony, Eileen, *Folk Tales of the West*, London: Kaye and Ward, 1971

Moody, Nickianne. 'Poldark Country and National Culture' in Westland, Ella (ed.), 1997

Moor, J.R., 'Miracle Plays, Minstrels and Jigs' in *Proceedings of the Modern Language Association of America*, 48, 1933

Moore, David W., *The Other British Isles*, Jefferson, North Carolina and London: McFarland and Company, 2005

Moore, F. Frankfurt, *Tre Pol and Pen*, London: Society for Promoting Christian Knowledge, 1887

Moore, Helen (ed.), *Sir Thomas Malory: Le Morte Darthur*, London: Wordsworth Editions, 1996

Morash, Christopher, *A History of Irish Theatre 1601-2000*, Cambridge: Cambridge University Press, 2002

Morgan, Chris, 'The Rebellions of 1549 in Tudor England' in *History Review*, No.19, 1994

Morison, Samuel Elliot, *The European Discovery of America: The Northern Voyages AD 500-1600*, New York: Oxford University Press, 1971

Morpurgo, Michael and Foreman, Michael, *Arthur: High King of Britain*, London: Pavilion, 1994

Moyer, Patricia and Hull, Brenda (eds.), *Anne Treneer: School House in the Wind*, Exeter: University of Exeter Press, 1998 [1944]

Mufwene, Salikoko S., *The Ecology of Language Evolution*, Cambridge: Cambridge University Press, 2001

Muir, Kenneth (ed.), *William Shakespeare: King Lear*, London: Methuen, 1972

Mullins, Edwin, *Alfred Wallis: Cornish Primitive*, London: Pavilion Books, 1994

Mullins, Gerry and O'Keefe, Sean, *Dublin Nazi No.1: The Life of Adolf Mahr*, Dublin: Liberties Press, 2007

Munn, Pat, *The Story of Cornwall's Bodmin Moor*, Bodmin: Bodmin Books, 1972

Bodmin Riding and Other Similar Celtic Customs, Bodmin: Bodmin Books Limited, 1975

Murdoch, Brian (ed.), *The Medieval Cornish Poem of the Passion: A Bibliography*, Redruth: Institute of Cornish Studies, 1979

'Pascon Agan Arluth: The Literary Position of the Cornish Poem of the Passion' in *Studi Medievali*, Series 3, Vol.12, No.2, 1981

'Creation, Fall and After in the Cornish *Gwreans an Bys*: Some Comments on a Late Medieval Mystery Play' in *Studi Medievali*, Series 3, Vol.19, No.2, 1988

'The Holy Hostage: "*De filio mulieris*" in the Middle Cornish play *Beunans Meriasek*' in *Medium Aevum*, 158, 1989

Cornish Literature, Cambridge: D.S. Brewer, 1993

'The Cornish Medieval Drama' in Beadle, Richard (ed.), 1994

(ed.) *The Grin of the Gargoyle*, Sawtry: Dedalus 1995

'Is *John of Chyanhor* Really a 'Cornish *Ruodlieb*'?' in Payton, Philip (ed.), 1996

'Legends of the Holy Rood in Cornish Drama' in *Studia Celtica Japonica*. Vol. IX, 1997

'Rex David, Bersabe, and Syr Urry: A Comparative Approach to a Scene in the Cornish *Origo Mundi*' in Payton, Philip (ed.), 2004

Muret, Ernest (ed.), *Le Roman de Tristan par Béroul*, Paris: Firmin Didot et Compagnie, 1903

Murphy, Mary C. and Argetsinger, Gerald S., 'Samuel Foote' in Rollyson, Carl and Magill, Frank N. (eds.), 2003

Murphy, Peter E. *Tourism: A Community Approach*, New York and London: Routledge, 1985

Mustill, J.P., *Summer needs no brightening: An gof and the 1497 Cornish Rebellion*, Newmill: Blue Elvan Press, 1997

Nance, Robert Morton, 'A Redruth Christmas Play' in *Old Cornwall*, April, 1925

'A Guise-Dance play, St Keverne' in *Old Cornwall*, April, 1925

'What we stand for' in *Old Cornwall*, April, 1925

The Cornish Jury: A Dialect Dialogue for XII Characters, St Ives: St Ives Old Cornwall Society, 1926

'Tom Bawcock's Eve' in *Old Cornwall*, April 1927

Cornish for All: A Guide to Unified Cornish, Cornwall: Federation of Old Cornwall Societies, 1958 [1929]

An Balores, St Ives: James Lanham, 1932

'The Plen an Gwary or Cornish Playing-Place' in *Journal of the Royal Institution of Cornwall*, 24, 1935

'The Charter Endorsement in Cornish' in *Old Cornwall*, 1947

'Painted Windows and Miracle Plays' in *Old Cornwall*, 5, 1955 (ed.), *A New Cornish Dictionary / Gerlyver Noweth Kernewek*, Redruth: Dyllansow Truran, 1994 [1955]

The Cledry Plays: Drolls of Old Cornwall for Village Acting and Home Reading, Penzance: The Federation of Old Cornwall Societies, 1956

When was Cornish Last Spoken Traditionally? Truro: Royal Institution of Cornwall, 1973

'The Christmas Play of Saint George and the Turkish Knight' in Thomas, Peter W. and Williams, Derek (eds.), 2007

Nance, Robert Morton and Hooper, E.G.R., 'Notes on the *Beunans Meriasek* Manuscript' in *Old Cornwall*, 9, 1979-1985

Nance, Robert Morton and Smith, A.S.D. (tr.), *Bewnans Meryasek* (lines 759-1096), Camborne: Camborne Printing and Stationary Company, 1949

(tr.), *An Veven ha'y Map*, Cornwall: The Cornish Language Board, 1969 [n.d.]

(tr.), *An Tyr Marya* (R.D., lines 579-834), Cornwall: The Cornish Language Board, 1973 [1951]

(eds. and trs.), *Gwyrans an Bys*, Padstow, Federation of Old Cornwall Societies, 1959

(tr.), *Abram hag Ysak*, Marazion: Worden, n.d.

(tr.), *Sylvester ha'n Dhragon*, Marazion: Worden, n.d.,

Nance, Robert Morton, Smith, A.S.D., and Sandercock, Graham (eds. and trs.), *The Cornish Ordinalia, Second Play: Christ's Passion*, Cornwall: The Cornish Language Board, 1982

(eds. and trs.), *The Cornish Ordinalia, Third Play: Resurrection*. Cornwall: The Cornish Language Board, 1984

Nance, Robert Morton, Smith, A.S.D., Chubb, Ray, Jenkin, Richard and Sandercock, Graham (eds. and trs.), *The Cornish Ordinalia, First Play: Origo Mundi*. Cornwall: Agan Tavas, 2001

Neelands, Jonothan and Dobson, Warwick, *Drama and Theatre Studies*, London: Hodder and Stoughton, 2000

Neuss, Paula, 'The Staging of the 'Creacion of the World'' in *Theatre Notebook*, 33, 1979

'Memorial Reconstruction in a Cornish Miracle Play' in *Comparative Drama*, 5, 2, 1979

(ed. and tr.), *The Creacion of the World: A Critical Edition and Translation*, New York and London: Garland, 1983

(ed.) *Aspects of Early English Drama*, Cambridge and Totowa, New Jersey: D.S. Brewer, 1983

'The Staging of The Creacion of the World' in Happé, P. (ed.), *Medieval English Drama*, London: Macmillan, 1984

Newlyn, Evelyn S. (ed.), *Cornish Drama of the Middle Ages: A Bibliography*, Redruth: Institute of Cornish Studies, 1987

'Between the Pit and the Pedestal: Images of Eve and Mary in Medieval Cornish Drama' in DuBruck, Edelgard E. (ed.), 1989

'The Stained and Painted Glass of St. Neot's Church and the Staging of Middle Cornish Drama' in *Journal of Medieval and Renaissance Studies*, 24, 1994

'The Middle Cornish Interlude: Genre and Tradition' in *Comparative Drama*, 30, 2, 1996

'Middle Cornish Drama at the Millennium' in Higgins, Sydney (ed.), 1997

Newman, Paul, 'Soldiers, Saints and Kings: The Plays of Donald R. Rawe' in *The Cornish Review*, No.24, 1973

The Meads of Love: The Life and Poetry of John Harris (1820-84), Redruth: Dyllansow Truran, 1994

The Tregerthen Horror: Aleister Crowley, D.H. Lawrence and Peter Warlock in Cornwall, St Austell: Abraxas, 2005

Newquay Amateur Drama Society, Its First 21 Years, Newquay: Newquay Amateur Dramatic Society, 1952

Newquay Dramatic Society, *Lane Theatre Project, Newquay*, Newquay Dramatic Society, 1979

Nicol, Bran, *D.M. Thomas: Writers and Their Work*, Tavistock: Northcote House Publishers Ltd, 2002

Norfolk, Andy, 'Songlines: Legends in the Landscape' in *Meyn Mamvro*, No.62, 2007

Norris, Edwin (ed. and tr.), *The Ancient Cornish Drama*, London and New York: Blom, 1968 [1859]

North, David J., *Studies in the Phonology of West Penwith English*, Redruth: Institute of Cornish Studies, 1991

North, David J. and Sharpe, Adam, *A Word-Geography of Cornwall*, Redruth: Institute of Cornish Studies, 1980

North, Richard and Allard, Joe (eds.), *Beowulf and Other Stories: A New Introduction to Old English, Old Icelandic and Anglo-Norman Literatures*, Harlow: Pearson Longman, 2007

Ó Caiealláin, Gearóid, 'Irish Language Theatre: Drama Developments' in *The Celtic Pen*, Vol. 2, No. 1, 1994

O'Cleirigh, Jo, 'Milpreves – or Adder's Beads: A Possible Connection with the Druids' in *Meyn Mamvro*, No 1, 1986

Old Cornwall Societies, *Crying the Neck: A Harvest Celebration*, St Agnes: Federation of Old Cornwall Societies, n.d.

Oldwanton, Oliver, *A little Treatise called the Image of Idlenesse, containing certaine matters mooued between Walter Wedlock and Bawdin Bachelor, translated out of the Troyan or Cornish tung into English*, London: William Seres, 1574

Ollard, Richard, *A Man of Contradictions: A Life of A.L. Rowse*, London: Allen Lane, 1999 (ed.), *The Diaries of A.L. Rowse*, London: Allen Lane, 2003

Olson, Lynette, 'Tyranny in *Beunans Meriasek*' in Payton, Philip (ed.), 1997

Olson, Lynette and Preston Jones, Ann, 'An ancient cathedral of Cornwall? Excavated remains east of St German's Church', in *Cornish Archaeology / Hendhyscans Kernow*, Nos. 37-8, 1998-9

Ó Luain, Cathal (ed.), *For a Celtic Future: A Tribute to Alan Heusaff*, Dublin: The Celtic League, 1983

Olver, T. J., *An Account of the History of St. Stephen-in-Brannel*, St. Stephen-in-Brannel: St. Stephen-in-Brannel Church, n.d.

Orchard, W.G. (ed.), *A Glossary of Mining Terms*, Redruth: Dyllansow Truran, 1991

Ordinalia Trust, *A Vision for the Future: An Inspiration from the Past*, Perranwell Station: Ordinalia Trust, 1996

Orange, Hilary, 'Industrial Archaeology: Its Place within the Academic Discipline, the Public Realm and the Heritage Industry' in *Industrial Archaeology Review*, 30, 2, 2008

O'Reilly, Anne F., *Sacred Play: Soul-Journeys in Contemporary Irish Theatre*, Dublin: Carysfort Press, 2004

Orme, Nicholas, 'Education in the Medieval Cornish Play *Beunans Meriasek*' in *Cambridge Medieval Celtic Studies*, 25, 1993

    Exeter Cathedral As It Was: 1050-1550, Exeter: Devon Books, 1986

    (ed.), *Unity and Variety: A History of the Church in Devon and Cornwall*, Exeter: University of Exeter Press, 1991

    (ed.), *Nicholas Roscarrock's Lives of the Saints of Cornwall and Devon*, Exeter: Devon and Cornwall Record Society, 1992

    The Saints of Cornwall, Oxford: Oxford University Press, 2000

    Cornwall and the Cross: Christianity 500-1560, Chichester: Phillimore and Co., 2007

Osborne, John, *Look Back in Anger*, London: Faber and Faber, 1957

Owen, Elias, *Welsh Folk-Lore: A Collection of the Folk-Tales and Legends of North Wales*, Felinfach: Llanerch, 1996 [1887]

Owens, W.R. and Goodman, Lizbeth, 'Remaking the Canon: Aphra Behn's *The Rover*' in Owens and Goodman (eds.), 1996

    (eds.), *Approaching Literature: Shakespeare, Aphra Behn and the Canon*, London: Routledge, 1996

Padel, Oliver J. (ed. and trs.), *The Cornish Writings of the Boson Family*, Redruth: Institute of Cornish Studies, 1975

    'Review of *Gwryans an Bys* or *The Creacion of the World*' in *Old Cornwall*, 10, 1985

    A Popular Dictionary of Cornish Place-Names, Penzance: Alison Hodge, 1988

'Ancient Parishes with Possible Examples of the Plain-an-gwary' in Hays, Rosalind Conklin, McGee, C.E., Joyce, Sally L. and Newlyn, Evelyn S. (eds.), 1999

(ed.) *W.M.M. Picken: A Medieval Cornish Miscellany*, Chicester: Phillimore and Co., 2000

'Oral and literary culture in medieval Cornwall' in Fulton, Helen (ed.), 2005

Page, Norman, *Wilkie Collins: The Critical Heritage*, London and Boston: Routledge and Kegan Paul, 1974

Palmer, Jas. L., *The Cornish Chough through the Ages*, Cornwall: Federation of Old Cornwall Societies, n.d.

Palmer, John E., 'Bran the Blessed' in *Meyn Mamvro*, No.18, 1992

Palmer, June, *Truro in the Eighteenth Century: Interlocking Circles*, Truro: June Palmer, 1990

Searching for Glasney: The Evidence of the Records, Cornwall: Friends of Glasney Occasional Paper, 1991

(ed.), *Truro in the Age of Reform: 1815-1837*, Truro: June Palmer, 1999

Palmer, June and Altree, Ann (eds.), *Treasures of the Morrab: A Library that has more than Books*, Penzance: The Morrab Library, 2005

Palsson, Herman and Edwards, Paul (eds. and trs.), *The Orkneyinga Saga: The History of the Earls of Orkney*, London; Penguin, 2004

Palsson, Herman and Magnusson, Magnus (eds. and trs.), *King Harald's Saga from Snorri Sturluson's Heimskringla*, London: Penguin, 2005

Parker, Simon, *A Star on the Mizzen*, Liskeard: Giss' On Books, 1997

(ed.), *Cornwall Marches On! / Keskerdh Kernow*, Truro: Keskerdh Kernow, 1998

(ed.), *Chasing Tales: The Lost Stories of Charles Lee*, Linkinhorne: Giss 'On Books, 2002

Full as an Egg, Mount Hawke: Truran, 2006

Seven Stars: A Cornish Christmas Play for Voices, Linkinhorne: Hairy Bear Books, 2006

Parker, T.M., *The English Reformation to 1558*, Oxford: Oxford University Press, 1966

Parochial Church Council of Alternun, *St Nonna of Altarnon*, Alternun: Church of St Nonna, Altarnun, n.d

Parsons, David N., 'Classifying English Place-Names' in Parsons, David N. and Sims-Williams, Patrick (eds.), 2000

Parsons, David N. and Sims-Williams, Patrick (eds.), *Ptolemy: Towards a Linguistic Atlas of the Earliest Celtic Place-Names of Europe*, Aberystwyth: Department of Welsh, University of Wales, Aberystwyth, 2000

Pascoe, W. H., *Teudar: A King of Cornwall*, Redruth: Dyllansow Truran, 1985

Paul, Rodman W. (ed.), *A Victorian Gentlewoman: The Reminiscences of Mary Hallock Foote*, San Marino: Huntington Library, 2000 [1972]

Pawling, Christopher, *Popular Fiction and Social Change*, Basingstoke: Macmillan, 1984

Pawlyn, Tony, *The Falmouth Packets*, Mount Hawke: Truran, 2003

Payne, E.F.J. (ed. and tr.), *Arthur Schopenhauer: The World as Will and Representation*, Vols I and II, New York: Dover, 1967

Payne, Robin and Lewsey, Rosemarie, *The Romance of Stones*, Fowey: Alexander Associates, 1999

Payton, Philip, *The Cornish Miner in Australia: Cousin Jack Down Under*, Redruth: Dyllansow Truran, 1984

> *The Making of Modern Cornwall: Historical Experience and the Persistence of "Difference"*, Redruth: Dyllansow Truran, 1992
>
> (ed.), *Cornwall Since the War: The Contemporary History of a European Region*, Redruth: Institute of Cornish Studies and Dyllansow Truran, 1993a
>
> 'a… concealed envy against the English': a Note on the Aftermath of the 1497 Rebellions in Cornwall' in Payton, Philip (ed.), 1993b
>
> (ed.), *Cornish Studies: One*, Exeter: University of Exeter Press, 1993b
>
> (ed.), *Cornish Studies: Two*, Exeter: University of Exeter Press, 1994
>
> (ed.), *Cornish Studies: Three*, Exeter: University of Exeter Press, 1995
>
> *Cornwall*, Fowey: Alexander Associates, 1996
>
> "Reforming Thirties' and 'Hungry Forties': The Genesis of Cornwall's Emigration Trade' in Payton, Philip (ed.), 1996.
>
> (ed.), *Cornish Studies: Four*, Exeter: University of Exeter Press, 1996
>
> 'Identity, Ideology and Language in Modern Cornwall' in Tristram, Hildegard L.C. (ed.), 1997
>
> (ed.), *Cornish Studies: Five*, Exeter: University of Exeter Press, 1997
>
> (ed.), *Cornish Studies: Six*, Exeter: University of Exeter Press, 1998
>
> *The Cornish Overseas*, Fowey: Alexander Associates, 1999
>
> (ed.), *Cornish Studies: Seven*, Exeter: University of Exeter Press, 1999
>
> (ed.), *Cornish Studies: Eight*, Exeter: University of Exeter Press, 2000
>
> (ed.), *Cornish Studies: Ten*, Exeter: University of Exeter Press, 2002
>
> *A Vision of Cornwall*, Fowey: Alexander Associates, 2002
>
> 'I was before my time, caught betwixt and between': A L. Rowse and the Writing of British and Cornish History' in Payton, Philip (ed.), 2003
>
> (ed.), *Cornish Studies: Eleven*, Exeter: University of Exeter Press, 2003
>
> (ed.), *Cornish Studies: Twelve*, Exeter: University of Exeter Press, 2004
>
> (ed.), *Cornish Studies: Thirteen*, Exeter: University of Exeter Press, 2005
>
> *A.L. Rowse and Cornwall: A Paradoxical Patriot*, Exeter: University of Exeter Press, 2005
>
> (ed.), *Cornish Studies: Fourteen*, Exeter: University of Exeter Press, 2006
>
> 'John Betjeman and the Holy Grail: One Man's Celtic Quest' in Payton, Philip (ed.), 2007

(ed.), *Cornish Studies: Fifteen*, Exeter: University of Exeter Press, 2007

Making Moonta: The Invention of Australia's Little Cornwall, Exeter: University of Exeter Press, 2007

(ed.), *Cornish Studies: Sixteen*, Exeter: University of Exeter Press, 2008

Payton, Philip and Thornton, Paul, 'The Great Western Railway and the Cornish-Celtic Revival' in Payton, Philip (ed.), 1995

Peacock, Edward, 'On the Churchwardens' Accounts of the Parish of Stratton, in the County of Cornwall' in *Archaeologia*, 46, 1, 1880

Pearce, Keith and Fry, Helen (eds.), *The Lost Jews of Cornwall*, Bristol: Redcliffe, 2000

Pearce, Susan M., *The Kingdom of Dumnonia: Studies in History and Tradition in South West Britain AD 350-1150*, Padstow: Lodenek Press, 1978

Pearson, A., *Robert Hunt, F.R.S. (1807-1887)*, Cornwall: Federation of Old Cornwall Societies, 1976

Pellow, Sue, *A Wesley Family Book of Days*, Aurora: River Street Press, 1994

Penguin (eds.), *The Penguin Companion to Literature I*, Harmondsworth: Penguin, 1971

Penhallurick, Rob (ed.), *Debating Dialect: Essays on the Philosophy of Dialect Study*, Cardiff: University of Wales Press, 2000

Studying the English Language, Basingstoke: Palgrave Macmillan, 2003

Penhallurick, Roger, *Tin in Antiquity*, London: Institute of Metals, 1986

Pennick, Nigel, *Celtic Sacred Landscapes*, London: Thames and Hudson, 2000 [1996]

Perry, Margaret, 'Eminent Westcountryman, Honorary Cornishman' in *Journal of the Royal Institution of Cornwall*, 2000

Perry, Ronald, 'Celtic Revival and Economic Development in Edwardian Cornwall' in Payton, Philip (ed.), 1997

'The Changing Face of Celtic Tourism in Cornwall 1875-1975' in Payton, Philip (ed.), 1999

'The Making of Modern Cornwall: A Geo-Economic Perspective' in Payton, Philip (ed.), 2002

Perry, Ronald and Harradence, Hazel, *Silvanus Trevail: Cornish Architect and Entrepreneur*, London: Francis Boutle Publishers, 2008

Perry, Ronald and Thurlow, Charles, 'The 1913 China Clay Dispute: 'One and All or 'One – That's All'?' in Payton, Philip (ed.), 2006.

Peter, Richard and Barhurt Peter, Otto, *The History of Launceston and Dunheved in the County of Cornwall*, Plymouth: W. Brendon, 1885

Peter, Thurstan C., *The History of Glasney Collegiate Church*, Camborne: Camborne Printing and Stationary Co., 1903

The Old Cornish Drama, London, Elliot Stock, 1906

'Replies: St. George Mumming Play' in *Notes and Queries*, Series 12, Vol. I, 1916

Peters, Caradoc, *The Archaeology of Cornwall: The Foundations of our Society*, Fowey: Cornwall Editions, 2005

Pettitt, Tom, 'From Stage to Folk: A Note on the Passages from Addison's Rosamond in the "Truro" Mummer's Play' in *Folklore*, Vol. 114, No. 2, 2003

Phelps, Kenneth, *The Wormwood Cup – Thomas Hardy in Cornwall: A Study in Temperament, Topography and Timing*, Padstow: Lodenek Press, 1975

Philip, Neil (ed.), *The Penguin Book of English Folktales*, Harmondsworth: Penguin, 1992

Phillipps, K.C. *Westcountry Words and Ways*, Newton Abbot: David and Charles, 1976

    A Glossary of Cornish Dialect, Padstow: Tabb House, 1993

    (ed.), *The Cornish Journal of Charles Lee*, Padstow: Tabb House, 1995

Phillips, Andy, *Reclaiming Cornwall's Celtic Christian Heritage: A Study Guide*, Portreath: Spyrys a Gernow, 2006

    Lan Kernow: A Theology of Place for Cornwall, Portreath: Spyrys a Gernow, 2006

Phillips, N.R., *The Saffron Eaters*, Exeter: Devon Books, 1987

    Apocalyse Dreckly, Tiverton: Halsgrove, 2005

Picard, Barbara Leonie, *French Legends and Fairy Stories*, Oxford: Oxford University Press, 1992 [1955]

Pickard-Cambridge, Arthur W., *Dithyramb, Tragedy and Comedy*, Oxford: Clarendon Press, 1927

Pickering, David, *Encylopedia of Pantomime*, Andover: Gale Research International, 1993

Piette, J. R., 'Cornish Literature' in Penguin (eds.) 1971

Piggott, Stuart, 'The sources of Geoffrey of Monmouth' in *Antiquity*, No.25, 1941

    The Druids, London: Thames and Hudson, 1968

Pilcher, Rosamunde, *The Shell Seekers*, London: New English Library, 1988

Pinter, Harold, *Plays: One*, London: Methuen, 1977

Pitcher, John (ed.), *William Shakespeare: Cymbeline*, London: Penguin, 2005

Pite, Ralph, *Thomas Hardy: The Guarded Life*, London: Picador, 2006

Pittock, Murray G.H., *Celtic Identity and the British Image*, Manchester and New York: Manchester University Press, 1999

Pollard, A.W. and Redgrave, G.R. (comps), *Short Title Catalogue, 1475-1640*: 13309

Pollard, C.D. (ed.), *Joseph Henry Pearse: Cornish Drolls*, Felinfach: Llanerch, 1998

Pollard, Peggy, *Beunans Alysaryn*, St Ives: James Lanham, 1941

    Cornwall: Vision of England, London: Paul Elek, 1947

Polwhele, Richard, *The History of Cornwall*, London: Cadell and Davies, 1803

Pool, P.A.S., 'The Penheleg Ms' in *Journal of the Royal Institution of Cornwall*, III, 3, 1959

    (ed.), *The History of the Town and Borough of Penzance*, Penzance: The Corporation of Penzance, 1974 (ed.), *George Clement Boase: Reminiscences of Penzance*, Penzance: Penzance Old Cornwall Society, 1976

The Death of Cornish, Cornwall: Cornish Language Board, 1982

Poulson, Christine, *The Quest for the Grail: Arthurian Legend in British Art 1840-1920*, Manchester: Manchester University Press, 1999

Powys, John Cowper, *A Glastonbury Romance*, London: Penguin, 1999 [1932]

Preston-Jones, Ann, 'The Men an Tol reconsidered' in *Cornish Archaeology / Hendhyscans Kernow*, No.32, 1993

Price, Cecil, *The English Theatre in Wales*, Cardiff: University of Wales Press, 1948

Probert, John C.C., *A Sociology of Cornish Methodism*, Truro: Cornwall Methodist Historical Association, 1971

Worship and Devotion of Cornish Methodism, Redruth: John C.C. Probert, 1979

Pryce, Huw (ed.), *Literacy in Medieval Celtic Societies*, Cambridge: Cambridge University Press, 1998

Pryke, Richard, *Norman Garstin: Irishman and Newlyn Artist*, Reading: Spire Books, 2005

Pryor, Oswald, *Australia's Little Cornwall*, Adelaide: Rigby, 1962

Cornish Pasty, Adelaide: Rigby, 1966

Purinton, Marjean D., 'George Colman's *The Iron Chest* and *Bluebeard* and the Pseudoscience of Curiosity Cabinets' in *Victorian Studies*, Vol. 49, No.2, 2007.

Quayle, Eric and Foreman, Michael, *The Magic Ointment and Other Cornish Legends*, London: Anderson Press, 1986

Quiller-Couch, Arthur, *The Astonishing History of Troy Town*, London: Anthony Mott, 1983 [1888]

(ed.), *The Oxford Book of English Verse*, Oxford: Oxford University Press, 1900

Hetty Wesley, London: Harper and Brothers, 1903

From a Cornish Window, Cambridge: Cambridge University Press, 1906

Historical Tales from Shakespeare, London: Edward Arnold, 1910

Shakespeare's Workmanship, London: Henry Holt and Company, 1918

Studies in Literature Series III, Cambridge: Cambridge University Press, 1929

(ed.), *Charles Lee: Cornish Tales*, London: Dent, 1941

Quiller-Couch, Arthur and du Maurier, Daphne, *Castle Dor*, London: Dent, 1962

Quinn, Esther Casier, *The Quest of Seth for the Oil of Life*, Chicago: Chicago University Press, 1962

Radford, Maisie, 'Cornwall in Opera' in *The Cornish Review*, No. 2, 1966

Raithby, John, *The Statutes at Large of England and of Great Britain*, London: G. Agre and A. Strahan, 1806

Rastall, Richard, *The Heaven Singing: Music in Early English Religious Drama*, Cambridge: D.S. Brewer,1996

Minstrels Playing: Music in Early English Religious Drama II, Cambridge: D.S. Brewer, 2001

Rawe, Donald R., *Petroc of Cornwall*, Padstow: Lodenek Press, 1970
    Traditional Cornish Stories and Rhymes, Padstow: Lodenek Press, 1992 [1971]
    The Trials of St Piran, Padstow: Lodenek Press, 1971
    Padstow's Obby Oss and May Day Festivities: A Study in Folklore and Tradition,
    Padstow: Lodenek Press, 1990 [1971]
    Geraint: Last of the Arthurians. Padstow: Lodenek Press, 1972
    'A Skeleton in the Cupboard' in Rawe, Donald R. (ed.), 1973
    'The Happening at Botathen' in Rawe, Donald R. (ed.), 1973
    (ed.), *A Cornish Quintette: Five Original One Act Plays*, Padstow: Lodenek Press,
    1973
    The Creation of the World, Padstow: Lodenek Press, 1978
    The Mermaid of Padstow: Stories and Poems, Padstow: Lodenek Press, 1983
    A Prospect of Cornwall, London: Robert Hale, 1986
Rendall, Joan, 'Cornwall's Preaching Pits' in *Cornish Scene*, No.4, 1997
Reynolds, Frederick, *Plays: A Collection of Thirty 18th-Century English plays,
    Principally Comedies*, London: n.p., 2008
Rice, Emma, and Grose, Carl, *Cymbeline*, London: Oberon Books, 2007
Richards, Jeffrey, *Sir Henry Irving: A Victorian Actor and His World*, London:
    Hambledon Continuum, 2006
Riche, Claire, *The Lost Shrine of Liskeard / An Greva Gellys a Lyskerrys*, Liskeard: Saint
    Austin Press, 2002
Ricks, Christopher (ed.), *English Drama to 1710*, London: Penguin, 1987
Ridler, Anne (ed.), *Shakespeare Criticism: 1935-1960*, Oxford, Oxford University
    Press, 1963
Roberts, Forrester, *The Legend of Tristan and Iseult: The Tale and the Trail in Ireland,
    Cornwall and Brittany*, Gloucester: Forrester Roberts, 1998
Roberts, Trelawney, Henderson, Charles, and Seldon, Leonard (eds.), *Tre, Pol and
    Pen: The Cornish Annual*, London, 1928
Robins, Colin and Deacon, Bernard, *Merlin's Diner*, Tiverton: Cornwall Books, 1992
Robinson, F.N. (ed.), *The Complete Works of Geoffrey Chaucer*, Oxford: Oxford
    University Press, 1957
Roddis, Roland J., *Penryn: The History of an Ancient Cornish Borough*, Truro: D.
    Bradford Barton, 1964
Rogers, Ben, *Beef and Liberty: Roast Beef, John Bull and the English Nation*, London:
    Vintage, 2004.
Rogers, Eva C., *Dartmoor Legends*, London: The Pilgrim Press, 1930
Rollyson, Carl and Magill, Frank N. (eds.), *Critical Survey of Drama*, Vol 2, Pasadena,
    California: Salem Press, 2003
Rosen, Betty, *And None of it was Nonsense: The Power of Storytelling in School*, London:
    Mary Glasgow Publications, 1988

Rosenfeld, Sybil Marion, *Strolling Players and Drama in the Provinces 1660-1765*, London: Octagon Books, 1970

Rowe, Doc, *We'll Call once more unto your house*, Padstow: Doc Rowe, 1982

May Day: The Coming of Spring, Swindon: English Heritage, 2006

Rowe, J. Hambley, 'King Arthur's Territory' in *Journal of the Royal Institution of Cornwall*, No.76, 1929

Rowe, John, *Cornwall in the Age of the Industrial Revolution*, St Austell: Cornish Hillside Publications, 1993 [1953]

The Hard Rock Men: Cornish Immigrants and the North American Mining Frontier, Liverpool: Liverpool University Press, 1974

Rowe, Toni-Maree, *Cornwall in Prehistory*, Stroud: Tempus, 2005

Rowling, J.K., *Harry Potter and the Chamber of Secrets*, London: Bloomsbury, 1999

Rowse, A.L., *Tudor Cornwall*, Redruth: Dyllansow Truran, 1990 [1941]

A Cornish Childhood, London: Anthony Mott, 1982 [1942]

The Spirit of English History, London: Jonathan Cape, 1943

The English Spirit: Essays in History and Literature, London: Macmillan, 1944

The West in English History, London: Methuen, 1949

The England of Elizabeth: The Structure of Society, London: Macmillan, 1950

The Expansion of Elizabethan England, London: Macmillan, 1955

William Shakespeare: A Biography, London: Macmillan, 1963

A Cornishman at Oxford: The Education of a Cornishman, London: Jonathan Cape, 1965

Christopher Marlowe: A Biography, London: Macmillan, 1965

(ed.), *A Cornish Anthology*, Penzance: Alison Hodge, 1990 [1968]

The Cornish in America. Redruth: Dyllansow Truran, 1991 [1969]

The Elizabethan Renaissance: The Life of Society, London: Macmillan, 1971

The Elizabethan Renaissance, The Cultural Achievement, London: Macmillan, 1972

Shakespeare the Man, London: Macmillan, 1973

Shakespeare the Elizabethan, London: Weidenfeld and Nicholson, 1977

A Man of the Thirties, London: Weidenfeld and Nicolson, 1979

Shakespeare's Globe: His Intellectual and Moral Outlook, London: Weidenfeld and Nicholson, 1981

A Life: Collected Poems, Edinburgh: William Blackwood, 1981

Shakespeare's Characters: A Complete Guide, London: Methuen, 1984

The Little Land of Cornwall, Gloucester: Alan Sutton, 1987

A.L. Rowse's Cornwall: A Journey through Cornwall's Past and Present, London: Weidenfeld and Nicholson, 1988

Quiller-Couch: A Portrait of 'Q', London: Methuen, 1988

Discovering Shakespeare: A Chapter in Literary History, London: Weidenfeld and Nicholson, 1989

My View of Shakespeare, London: Duckworth, 1996

Rowse, A. L. and Harrison, G.B., *Queen Elizabeth and Her Subjects*, London: Allen and Unwin, 1935

Rowse, A.L. and Henderson, M. I. (eds.), *Charles Henderson: Essays in Cornish History*, Oxford: Clarendon, 1935

Roy, Rob, *Stone Circles: A Modern Builder's Guide to the Megalithic Revival*, White River Junction, Vermont and Totnes: Chelsea Green Publishing Company, 1999

Royle, Trevor, *Civil War: The Wars of the Three Kingdoms 1638-1660*, London: Abacus, 2006

Rozik, Eli, *The Roots of Theatre: Rethinking Ritual and Other Theories of Origin*, Iowa City: University of Iowa Press, 2002

Rudlin, John, *Commedia dell'Arte in the Twentieth Century: An Actor's Handbook*, London and New York: Routledge, 1994

Ruhrmund, Frank, *Penwith Poems*, Padstow: Lodenek, 1976

Rule, John, 'Methodism, Popular Beliefs and Village Culture in Cornwall 1800-50' in Storch, Robert (ed.), 1982

 'Idle Hands? Controlling non-Work Time in England c.1750-1815' in *Il Tempo Libero Economia E Società*, No. 26, 1995

 (ed.), *Cornish Cases: Essays in Eighteenth and Nineteenth Century Social History*, Southampton: Clio Publishing, 2006

Rump, Eric (ed.), *Richard Brinsley Sheridan: The School for Scandal and Other Plays*, Harmondsworth: Penguin, 1988

Russell, Paul, *An Introduction to the Celtic Languages*, Harlow: Longman, 1995

Rutt, Richard, 'Missa Propria Germani Episcopi and the Eponym of St. Germans' in *Journal of the Royal Insitution of Cornwall*, Vol. 7, 1977

 'Love and Tears at the Camborne Play' in *The Celtic Pen*, Vol. 2, No. 1, 1994

Ryan, W.G. (ed. and tr.), *The Golden Legend by Jacobus de Voragine*, Vols. 1 and 2, Chichester: Princetown University Press, 1993

Sandercock, Graham, *Meryasek yn Kernow*, Cornwall: Kesva an Taves Kernewek, 2000

Sandys, William, *Specimens of Cornish Provincial Dialect*, London: John Russell Smith, 1846

 'On the Cornish Drama' in *Journal of the Royal Institution of Cornwall*, 3, 1865

Saraga, Jessica, *Cromwell*, London: Batsford, 1990

Saunders, Tim, 'Cornish – Symbol and Substance' in Ó Luain, Cathal (ed.), 1983

 (ed. and tr.), *The Wheel: An Anthology of Modern Poetry in Cornish 1850-1980*, London: Francis Boutle Publishers, 1999

 (ed. and tr.), *Nothing Broken: Recent Poetry in Cornish*, London: Francis Boutle Publishers, 2006

Scavel an Gow, *Dream Atlas*, Linkinhorne: Giss 'on Books, 2002

Scawen, William, 'Antiquities Cornuontanic: The Causes of Cornish Speech's Decay' in Kent and Saunders (eds. and trs.), 2000

Schama, Patrick, 'A Hall for Cornwall: The Campaign to Provide a Cultural Centre for Cornwall and the Man Behind It' in *Cornish Scene*, No.15, n.d. (but c.1995)

Schmitz, Thomas A., *Modern Literary Theory and Ancient Texts*, Oxford: Blackwell, 2007

Schwartz, Sharon P., *Voices of the Cornish Mining Landscape*, Cornwall: Cornwall County Council, 2008

Scott, Walter Sidney, *Green Retreats: The Story of Vauxhall Gardens 1661-1859*, London: Odhams Press, 1955

Scrivers, Kevin and Smith, Stephen *Showmen of the Past: Hancocks of the West*, Telford: New Era Publications, 2006

Seddon, Richard, *The Mystery of Arthur at Tintagel*, London: Rudolph Steiner Press, 1990

Selwood, E.B., Durrance, E.M. and Bristow, C.M., *The Geology of Cornwall*, Exeter: University of Exeter Press, 1998

Semmens, Jason, 'Guising, Ritual and Revival: The Hobby Horse in Cornwall' in *Old Cornwall*, Volume 13, No. 52, 2005

   (ed.), *The Cornish Witch-finder: William Henry Paynter and the Witchery, Ghosts, Charms and Folklore of Cornwall*, Cornwall: The Federation of Old Cornwall Societies, 2008

Serjeantson, R.M., 'The Church and Parish Goods of St Columb Major, Cornwall' in *The Antiquary*, 33, 1897

Seward, Andy 'Cornish Rugby and Cultural Identity: A Socio-historical Perspective' in Payton, Philip (ed.), 1997

Seward, Jeff and Deb, 'The Riddle of the Mazes' in *Meyn Mamvro*, No. 5, 1988

Shakespeare, William, *Henry IV*

Shaw, George Bernard, *Plays Pleasant*, Harmondsworth: Penguin, 1985 [1898]

Shaw, Hilary, 'Celtic Drama: Cornish Miracle Plays' In: *The Celtic Pen*, Vol. 1, No. 1, 1993

Shaw, Thomas, *Saint Petroc and John Wesley: Apostles in Cornwall – An Examination of the Celtic Background of Cornish Methodism*, Cornwall: Cornish Methodist Historical Association, 1962

   The Bible Christians, London: Epworth Press, 1965

   A History of Cornish Methodism, Truro: D. Bradford Barton, 1967

   Gwennap Pit: John Wesley's Amphitheatre, a Cornish Pardon, Busveal: Busveal Methodist Church Council, 1992

   (ed.), *Book of Memories of Cornish Methodism: Parts One and Two*, Truro: Cornwall Methodist Historical Association, 1992 and 1994

Shepherd, David, *Bakhtin: Carnival and Other Subjects*, Amsterdam, Georgia: Rodophi B. V. Editions, 1993

Shepherd, Simon and Womack, Peter, *English Drama: A Cultural History*, Oxford: Blackwell, 1996

Shirley, James, *The Dramatic Works and Poems: Now First Collected, Vols. 1-3*, Boston: Adamant Media Corporation, 2005

Simmons, Jack (ed.), *A Devon Anthology*, London: Anthony Mott, 1983 [1971]

Sinfield, Alan, 'The Theatre and its Audiences' in Sinfield, Alan (ed.), 1983

(ed.), *Society and Literature 1945-1970*, London: Methuen, 1983

Skeat, Walter W. (ed.), *An Etymological Dictionary of the English Language*, Oxford: Oxford University Press, 1963

Slater, Cathy, 'Foots Barn Theatre' in *Cornish Review*, No.26, 1974

Smit, Tim, *Eden*, London: Chartered Institute of Personnel and Development, 2005

Smelt, Maurice, *101 Cornish Lives*, Penzance: Alison Hodge, 2006

Smiley, Jane and Kellogg, Robert (eds. and trs.), *The Sagas of the Icelanders: A Selection*, London: Penguin, 2000

Smith, A.S.D., *The Story of the Cornish Language: Its Extinction and Revival*, Camborne: Smith, 1947

Trystan hag Ysolt, Redruth: J. and M. Roberts, 1951

Smith, Edward, 'Reminiscences' in *The Cornishman*, 25 October, 1883

Smith, Laura, 'Madame Fanny Moody at Home: A Talk with the Cornish Nightingale' in Quiller-Couch, Arthur (ed.), *The Cornish Magazine*, Vol 1, 1898

Smyth, Joseph and Lyons, David, *Christmas Rime, or, The Mummer's own Book*, Belfast: Smyth and Lyons, 1803-18

Snell, Laurence, *The Suppression of the Religious Foundations of Devon and Cornwall*, Marazion, n.p.,1967

Solomon, Harry M., *The Rise of Robert Dodsley: Creating the New Age of Print*, Illinois, Southern Illinois University Press, 1996

Southern, Richard, *The Medieval Theatre in the Round: A Study of the Staging of The Castle of Perseverance, and related matters*, London: Faber and Faber, 1957

'The Lost Remains at King's Lynn' in *The Revels History of Drama in English*, 1975, No. 6

Southern, Richard and Brown, Ivor, *The Georgian Theatre, Richmond, Yorkshire*, Richmond: The Georgian Theatre, Richmond Trust, 1973

Southworth, John, *Fools and Jesters at the English Court*, Stroud: Sutton, 2003 [1998]

Sowell, C.R., 'The Collegiate Church of St Thomas of Glasney' in *Journal of the Royal Institution of Cornwall*, Vol. I, 1865

Spence, Elizabeth Isabella, *The Curate and His Daughter, a Cornish Tale*, London: Longman, Hurst, Rees, Orme and Brown, 1813

Spence, John E., *A Short Guide and History to the Church of St Germans*, St Germans: Privately published, 1966

Spriggs, Matthew, 'The Cornish Language, Archaeology and the Origins of English Theatre' in Jones, M. (ed.), 2004

'William Scawen (1600-1689) – A Neglected Cornish Patriot and Father of the Cornish Language Revival' in Payton, Philip (ed.), 2005

Stalmaszczyk, Piotr, *Celtic Presence: Studies in Celtic Languages and Literatures: Irish, Scottish Gaelic and Cornish*, ˏódê: ˏódê University Press, 2005

Stanier, Peter, *Cornwall's Literary Heritage*, Twelveheads: Twelveheads Press, 1992

Steiner, Rudolf, *The Druids: Esoteric Wisdom of the Ancient Celtic Priests*, Forest Row: Sophia Books, 2001

Stevenson, W.H., '*Dr Guest and the English Conquest of South Britain*' in *The English Historical Review*, Vol.17, No.68, 1902

Steward, Bob, *Where is St George?: Pagan Imagery in English Folk Song*, London: Blandford, 1988

Stewart, R.J., Coffey, Denise, and Hudd, Roy (eds.), *William Shakespeare and William Rowley: The birth of Merlin, or The childe hath found his father*, Shaftesbury: Element Books, 1989

Sticca, Sandro (ed .), *The Medieval Drama*, Albany: State University of New York Press, 1972

St Leger-Gordon, Ruth E., *The Witchcraft and Folklore of Dartmoor*, London: Robert Hale, 1965

Stock, James, *Star-Gazy Pie: Two Plays*, London: Nick Hern Books, 1995

Stokes, Whitley 'The Passion: A Middle Cornish Poem' in *Transactions of the Philological Society*, 1860-1

(ed. and tr.), *Gwreans an Bys: The Creation of the World*, London and Edinburgh: Williams and Norgate, 1864

(ed. and tr.), *The Life of Saint Meriasek, Bishop and Confessor: A Cornish Drama*, London: Trübner and Co., 1872

Old Breton Glosses, Calcutta: Privately published, 1879

'A Glossary to the Cornish Drama, *Beunans Meriasek*' in *Activ für celtische Lexigraphie*, 1, 1898-1900

Storch, Robert (ed.), *Popular Culture and Custom in Nineteenth-Century England*, London and Canberra: Croom Helm, 1982

Storry, Mike and Childs, Peter (eds.), *British Cultural Identities*, London and New York: Routledge, 1997

Stout, Adam, *Creating Prehistory: Druids, Ley Hunters and Archaeologists in Pre-War Britain*, Oxford: Wiley Blackwell, 2008

Stoyle, Mark, 'The dissidence of despair: Rebellion and identity in early modern Cornwall' in *Journal of British Studies*, 38, 4, 1999

West Britons: Cornish Identities and the Early Modern British State, Exeter: University of Exeter Press, 2002

Straffon, Cheryl, 'Rituals and Rites at Cornish Sites' in *Meyn Mamvro*, No.13, 1990
  Pagan Cornwall: Land of the Goddess, St Just-in-Penwith: Meyn Mamvro
  Publications, 1993
  The Earth Goddess: Celtic and Pagan Legacy of the Landscape, Poole: Cassell, 1997
  Fentynyow Kernow: In Search of Cornwall's Holy Wells, St Just-in-Penwith:
  Meyn Mamvro Publications, 1998
  'The Cornish Otherworld' in *Meyn Mamvro*, No.45, 2001
Strohm, Paul, *Theory and the Pre-Modern Text*, Minneapolis: University of Minnesota
  Press, 2000
Sturt, John, *Revolt in the West: The Western Rebellion of 1549*, Exeter: Devon Books,
  1987
Suckling, Nigel, *Faeries of the Celtic Lands*, London: Photographers' Press, 2007
Sutcliffe, Barry (ed.), *Plays by George Colman the Younger and Thomas Morton*,
  Cambridge: Cambridge University Press, 1983
Sutcliffe, Rosemary, *Tristan and Iseult*, London: The Bodley Head, 1971
Symons, Andrew C., 'John Harris – A Weaving of Traditions' in *An Baner Kernewek /
  The Cornish Banner*, No.82, 1995
  'She, 'Er and 'Un: Study II in Language and History' in *An Baner Kernewek /
  The Cornish Banner*, No. 94, 1998
  'Models of Language Transfer' in *An Baner Kernewek / The Cornish Banner*, No.
  96, 1999
  'Language Transfer in Cornwall' in *An Baner Kernewek / The Cornish Banner*,
  No. 127, 2007
Tagney, Joanna, 'The Hurlers: Sightlines to the Sun' in *Meyn Mamvro* No.66,
  2008
Tamplin, Ronald 'As New as it is Old' in Chambers, Harry (ed.), 1987
Tanner, Marcus, *The Last of the Celts*, New Haven and London: Yale University Press,
  2004
Taylor, Gary (ed.), *William Shakespeare: Henry V*, Oxford: Oxford University Press,
  1982
  Reinventing Shakespeare: A Cultural History from the Restoration to the Present,
  London: Vintage, 1991.
Taylor, Helen (ed.), *The Daphne du Maurier Companion*, London: Virago Press, 2007
Taylor, Thomas, *The Celtic Christianity of Cornwall: Divers Sketches and Studies*,
  Felinfach: Llanerch, 1995 [1916]
Tennyson, Alfred, Lord, *Enoch Arden &c*, London: Dodo Press, 2008 [1864]
Thieme, John, *Postcolonial Con-texts* [sic]*: Writing Back to the Canon*, London and
  New York: Continuum, 2001
Thomas, Charles, *Christian Antiquities of Camborne*, Cornwall: H.E. Warne, 1967
  'Piran Round and the Medieval Cornish Drama' in Foster, K. G. (ed.), 1969

(ed.), *Cornish Studies / Studhyansow Kernewk* 1-15, Redruth: Institute of Cornish Studies, 1973-1987

Exploration of a Drowned Landscape, London: Batsford, 1985

'Hardy and Lyonesse: Parallel Mythologies' in Hardie, Melissa (ed.), 1992

Tintagel: Arthur and Archaeology, London: English Heritage and Batsford, 1993

And Shall These Mute Stones Speak? Post-Roman Inscriptions in Roman Britain, Cardiff: University of Wales Press, 1994

Celtic Britain, London: Thames and Hudson, 1997

Christian Celts: Messages and Images, Stroud: Tempus, 1998

Penzance Market Cross, A Cornish Wonder re-wondered, Penzance: Penlee House Gallery and Museum, 1999

Thomas, Charles and Hardie, Melissa (eds.), *Dinah Craik: An Unsentimental Journey Through Cornwall 1884*, Penzance: Jamieson Library, 1988

Thomas, Charles and Mattingly, Joanna, *The History of Christianity in Cornwall: AD 500-2000*, Truro: Royal Institution of Cornwall, 2000

Thomas, D.M., *The Granite Kingdom*, Truro: D. Bradford Barton, 1970

(ed.), *Songs from the Earth: Selected Poems of John Harris*, Padstow: Lodenek Press, 1977

Birthstone, London: Gollancz, 1980

(ed. and trs.), *Alexander Pushkin: 'The Bronze Horseman' and Other Poems*, Harmondsworth: Penguin, 1982

The White Hotel, London: Viking, 1981

Selected Poems, Harmondsworth: Penguin, 1983

'Faithful Travelling' in Chambers, Harry (ed.), 1987

Memories and Hallucinations, Victor Gollancz, 1988

The Puberty Tree, Newcastle upon Tyne: Bloodaxe, 1992

Alexander Solzhenitsyn: A Century in His Life, London: Little, Brown and Company, 1998

Charlotte, London: Duckworth, 2000

Dear Shadows, Truro: Fal Publications, 2004

Bleak Hotel: The Hollywood Saga of the White Hotel, London: Quartet Books, 2008

Thomas, Dylan, *The Doctor and the Devils, and Other Scripts*, London: New Directions, 1970

Thomas, Graham and Williams, Nicholas (eds. and trs.), *Bewnans Ke: The Life of St Kea – A Critical Edition with Translation*, Exeter: University of Exeter Press, 2007

Thomas, M. Wynn, *Corresponding Cultures: The Two Literatures of Wales*, Cardiff: University of Wales Press, 1999

Thomas, Peter W., 'R.M. Nance's Spirituality and the Cornish Gorsedd' in *Journal of the Royal Institution of Cornwall*, 2008

Thomas, Peter W. and Williams, Derek (eds.), *Setting Cornwall on its Feet: Robert Morton Nance 1873-1959*, London: Francis Boutle Publishers, 2007

Thompson, E.V., *Chase the Wind*, London: Macmillan, 1977
Ben Retallack, London: Macmillan, 1977
Ruddlemoor, London: Headline, 1995

Thompson, Frank G. (ed.), *The Celt in the Seventies*, Belfast: The Celtic League, 1970

Thomson, Peter, *The Cambridge Introduction to English Theatre, 1660-1900*, Cambridge: Cambridge University Press, 2006

Thorpe, Lewis (ed. and tr.), *Geoffrey of Monmouth: The History of the Kings of Britain*, Harmondsworth: Penguin, 1966

Thorpe, Tony and Jarvis, Richard, *Inside Britain*, London: The Citizenship Foundation and Hodder Murray, 2007

Thurner, Arthur W., *Calumet Copper and People: History of a Michigan Mining Community, 1864-1970*, Hancock, Michigan: Turner, 1974
Strangers and Sojourners: A History of Michigan's Keweenaw Peninsula, Detroit: Wayne State University Press, 1994

Tibballs, Geoff, *The Wycliffe File: The Story of the ITV Detective Series*, London: Boxtree, 1995

Tickner, F.J. (ed.), *Earlier English Drama: From Robin Hood to Everyman*, London and Edinburgh: Thomas Nelson and Sons, 1929

Tiddy, R.J.E., *The Mummers' Play*, Oxford: Clarendon Press, 1923

Tilley, Christopher, 'Rocks as resources: landscapes and power reconsidered' in *Cornish Archaeology / Hendhyscans Kernow*, No.34, 1995

Tillyard, E.M.W., *The Elizabethan World Picture*, Harmondsworth: Penguin, 1988 [1943]

Todd, Arthur Cecil, *The Cornish Miner in America*, Spokane, Washington: Arthur H. Clark Co., 1995 [1967]
Beyond the Blaze: A Biography of Davies Gilbert, Truro: D. Bradford Barton, 1967
The Search for Silver: Cornish Miners of Mexico 1824-1947, St Austell: Cornish Hillside Publications, 2000 [1977]

Tolley, Clive, 'Old English Influence on *The Lord of the Rings*' in North, Richard and Allard, Joe (eds.), 2007

Tolstoy, Nikolai, *The Quest for Merlin*, London: Hamish Hamilton, 1985

Tomlin, E.W.F., *In Search of St Piran: An Account of his Monastic Foundation at Perranzabuloe, Cornwall, and its Place in the Western Celtic Church and Society*, Padstow Lodenek Press, 1982

Tonkin, Ronald E., *Chapters in the Life of Truro*, Truro: Echo Home Publishing, 2004

Tooby, Michael, *Tate St Ives: An Illustrated Companion*, London: Tate Gallery, 1993

Toorians, Lauran (ed.), *The Middle Cornish Charter Endorsement: The Making of a Marriage in Medieval Cornwall*. Innsbruck: Institut für Sprachwissenschaft der Universität Innsbruck, 1991

Toulson, Shirley, *The Celtic Alternative: A Reminder of the Christianity We Lost*, London: Century, 1987

Toy, H. Spencer, *The Methodist Church at Launceston*, Launceston: Launceston Wesleyan Methodist Church

Tregellas, John Tabois, *Cornish Tales*, Truro: Netherton and Worth, 1863

Tregidga, Garry, 'The Politics of the Celto-Cornish Revival, 1886-1939' in Payton, Philip (ed.), 1997

Tregidga, Garry and Crago, Treve, *Map Kenwyn: The Life and Times of Cecil Beer*, Cornwall: Gorseth Kernow, 2000

Trelawny, Jack, *Kernowland: The Crystal Pool*, Waltham Abbey: Campion Books, 2005

Tremain, Rose, *Restoration*, London: Hamish Hamilton, 1989

Tremaine, Hadley, 'Cornish Folk Speech in America' in *Midwestern Journal of Language and Folklore*, Vol. 6, No.1/2, 1980

Trenoodle, Uncle Jan, *Specimens of Provincial Cornish Dialect*, London: John Russell Smith, 1846

Trevelyan, G.M., *A Shortened History of England*, Harmondsworth: Penguin, 1965 [1942]

Trevenen Jenkin, Ann, *Notes on the Prayer Book Rebellion of 1549*, Leedstown: Noonvares Press, 1999

Trevose, Daniel, *Looking for Love in a Great City*, London: Cape, 1956

Trewin, J.C., *Up from The Lizard*, London: Anthony Mott, 1982 [1948]
(ed.), *Robert Stephen Hawker: Footprints of Former Men in Far Cornwall*, London: Westaway Books, 1948
Down to the Lion, London: Carroll and Nicholson, 1952
The Birmingham Repertory Theatre 1913-1963, London: Barrie and Rockliff, 1963
(ed.), *The Journal of William Charles Macready*, London: Longman, 1967 (ed.), *Theatre Bedside Book: An Anthology of the Stage*, Newton Abbot: David and Charles, 1974

Trewin-Wolle, E. (ed.), *Cornish Stannary Gazette*, No.1, Cornwall: Cornish Stannary Parliament, 1975

Trezise, Simon, "Off Wessex' or a Place in the Mind' in Hardie, Melissa (ed.), 1992
The West Country as a Literary Invention: Putting Fiction in its Place, Exeter: University of Exeter Press, 2000

Tribby, William L., 'The Medieval Prompter: A Reinterpretation' in *Theatre Survey*, Vol. 5, No. 1, 1964

Tristram, Hildegard L.C. (ed.), *The Celtic Englishes*, Heidelberg: Universitätsverlag Winter, 1997
(ed.), *The Celtic Englishes IV: The Interface between English and the Celtic Languages*, Potsdam: Potsdam University Press, 2006

(ed.), *The Celtic Languages in Contact*, Potsdam: Potsdam University Press, 2007

Tschirschky, Malte W., 'The Medieval 'Cornish Bible'' in Payton, Philip (ed.), 2003

Die Erfindung der keltischen Nation Cornwall: Kultur, Identität und ethnischer Nationalismus in der britischen Peripherie, Heidelberg: Universitätsverlag Winter, 2006

Turk, Frank A. and Combellack, Myrna M., 'Doctoring and Disease in Medieval Cornwall: Exegetical Notes on Some Passages in *Beunans Meriasek*' in Thomas, Charles (ed.), 1976-1977

Turley, Simon, *Seeing Without Light*, Cardigan: Parthian, 2005

Turner, Victor, *From Ritual to Theatre: The Human Seriousness of Play*, New York: Performance Arts Journals Publications, 1987

Tydeman, William, *The Medieval European Stage 500-1550*, Cambridge: Cambridge University Press, 2001

University of Oxford (ed.), *The Historical Register of the University of Oxford, completed to the end of Trinity Term, 1888*, Oxford; Clarendon Press, 1888

Unsworth, Barry, *Morality Play*, London: Hamish Hamilton, 1995

Losing Nelson, London: Hamish Hamilton, 1999

Val Baker, Denys, *Britain's Art Colony by the Sea*, Bristol: Sansom and Company, 2000 [1959]

The Minack Theatre, Cornwall: G. Ronald, 1960

The Timeless Land: The Creative Spirit in Cornwall, Bath: Adams and Dart, 1973

The Spirit of Cornwall, London: W.H. Allen, 1980

A View from Land's End: Writers against a Cornish Background, London: William Kimber, 1982

Vere, B.D., *King Arthur: His Symbolic Story in Verse*, Tintagel: King Arthur's Hall, 1930

Vickers, Stanley and King, Diana (eds.), *The du Maurier Companion*, Fowey: Fowey Rare Books, 1997

Vincent, John A.C., 'The Glasney Cartulary' in *Journal of the Royal Institution of Cornwall*, Vol.6, 1878-81

Waites, Bernard, Bennett, Tony and Martin, Graham (eds.), *Popular Culture: Past and Present*, London: Croom Helm, 1982

Wakelin, Martyn F., *Language and History in Cornwall*, Leicester: Leicester University Press, 1975

Walke, Bernard, *Twenty Years at St Hilary*, London: Anthony Mott, 1982 [1935]

Plays from St Hilary, London: Faber and Faber, 1939

Walling, R.A.J., *The Story of Plymouth*, London: Westaway Books, 1950

Wallis, John (ed.), *The Bodmin Register: Containing Collections Relative to the Past and Present State of the Parish of Bodmin*, Bodmin, 1827-38

Walsh, Thomas, *History of the Irish Heirarchy*, New York: D. & J. Sadlier and Co., 1854

Ward, A.W. and Waller, A. (eds.), *The Cambridge History of English Literature, V: The Drama to 1642 Pt 1*, Cambridge University Press, 1970 [1910]

Wasson, John M. (ed.), *Records of Early English Drama: Devon*, Toronto: University of Toronto and Brepols, 1986

Watkins, Alfred, *The Old Straight Track*, London: Abacus, 1994 [1925]

Watkins, D.H., *Trystan hag Ysolt*, Camborne: An Lef Kernewek, 1973

Watts, Ian, *Myths of Modern Individualism: Faust, Don Quixote, Don Juan, Robinson Crusoe*, Cambridge: Cambridge University Press, 1996

Weatherhill, Craig, *Cornovia: Ancient Sites of Cornwall and Scilly*, Penzance: Alison Hodge, 1989 [1985]

    The Lyonesse Stone, Padstow: Tabb House, 1991

    Cornish Place Names and Language, Wilmslow: Sigma, 1995

    'The Riddle of the Fogous' in *Meyn Mamvro*, No 1, 1986

    'Epona's Children' in *Meyn Mamvro*, No. 33, 1997

Weatherhill, Craig, and Devereux, Paul, *Myths and Legends of Cornwall*, Wilmslow: Sigma, 1998 [1994]

Wedlock, Walter, see Oldwanton, Oliver

Weight, Richard, *Patriots: National Identity in Britain 1940-2000*, London: Macmillan, 2002

Welch, Robert (ed.), *W.B. Yeats: Writings on Irish Folklore, Legend and Myth*, London: Penguin 1993

Wertenbaker, Timberlake, *Our Country's Good*, London: Methuen, 1987

Wesley, John, *Journal*, London: Everyman, 1906

West, Alick, *Crisis and Criticism and Literary Essays*, London: Lawrence and Wishart, 1975

Westland, Ella (ed.), *Cornwall: The Cultural Construction of Place*, Penzance: The Patten Press and the Institute of Cornish Studies, 1997

    Reading Daphne: A guide to the writing of Daphne du Maurier for readers and book groups, Mount Hawke: Truran, 2007

    'Rule Britannia' in Taylor, Helen (ed.), 2007

Whetter, James, *Cornwall in the Seventeenth Century: An Economic Survey of Kernow*, Padstow: Lodenek Press, 1974

    Scryow Kernewek / Cornish Essays 1971-76, Gorran: CNP Publications, 1977

    The History of Falmouth, Gorran: Lyfrow Trelyspen, 2004 [1981]

    The History of Glasney College, Padstow: Tabb House, 1988

    'The Search for Gorran's Playne-an-Gwarry' in *Old Cornwall*, Vol.11, No.4, 1993

    The Bodrugans: A Study of a Cornish Medieval Knightly Family, Gorran: Lyfrow Trelyspen, 1995

    'Play recalls rebellion' in: *An Baner Kernewek / The Cornish Banner*, No. 88, 1997

Cornwall in the 13th Century: A Study in Social and Economic History, Gorran: Lyfrow Trelyspen, 1998

Cornish People in the 18th Century, Gorran: Lyfrow Trelyspen, 2000

'Charterhouse Theatre Company is performing a cycle of Mystery Plays' in *An Baner Kernewek / The Cornish Banner*, No. 104, 2001

Dr A.L. Rowse: Poet, Historian, Lover of Cornwall, Gorran: Lyfrow Trelyspen, 2003

Essays Ancient and Modern, Gorran: Lyfrow Trelyspen, 2005

'The Life and Work of Bernard Walke' in *An Baner Kernewek / The Cornish Banner*, No. 123, 2006

White, Hugo, *One and All: A History of the Duke of Cornwall's Light Infantry, 1702-1959*, Padstow: Tabb House, 2006

Whitfield, H.J., *Scilly and its Legends*, London: Timpkin, Marshall and Co., 1852

Whiting, Robert, *The Blind Devotion of the People: Popular Religion and the English Reformation*, Cambridge: Cambridge University Press, 1989

Whitley, H. Michell, 'The Church Goods of Cornwall at the Time of the Reformation' in *Journal of the Royal Institution of Cornwall*, 7, 1881-2

Whitlock, Ralph, *The Folklore of Devon*, London: B.T. Batsford Ltd, 1977

Whittaker, John, *The Ancient Cathedral of Cornwall Historically Surveyed*, London: Stockdale, 1804

Wickham, Glynne, 'The Staging of Saint Plays in England' in Sticca, Sandro (ed.), 1972

'The Beginnings of English Drama: Stage and Drama till 1660' in Ricks, Christopher (ed.), 1987

The Medieval Theatre, Cambridge: Cambridge University Press, 1987

Wiles, David, *The Early Plays of Robin Hood*, Cambridge: Cambridge University Press, 1981

Greek Theatre Performance: An Introduction, Cambridge: Cambridge University Press, 2000

Wilhelm, James J. (ed. and tr.), *The Romance of Arthur: An Anthology of Medieval Texts in Translation*, New York and London: Garland, 1994

Willett, Joanie, 'Cornish Identity: Vague Notion or Social Fact?' in Payton, Philip (ed.), 2008

Willett, John, *The Theatre of Bertolt Brecht*, London: Methuen, 1959

Williams, Derek, *Prying into Every Hole and Corner: Edward Lhuyd in Cornwall in 1700*, Redruth: Dyllansow Truran, 1993

'Henry Jenner: The Years of Fulfilment' in *An Baner Kernewek / The Cornish Banner*, No.85, 1996

'Robert Morton Nance' in *An Baner Kernewek / The Cornish Banner*, No. 88, 1997

'The Ordinalia Company's production of *The Passion* at St. Just-in-Penwith' in *An Baner Kernewek / The Cornish Banner*, No. 106, 2001

(ed.), *Henry and Katharine Jenner: A Celebration of Cornwall's Culture, Language and Identity*, London: Francis Boutle Publishers, 2004

(ed.), *A Strange and Unquenchable Race: Cornwall and the Cornish in Quotations*, Mount Hawke: Truran, 2007

Cornubia's Son: A Life of Mark Guy Pearse, London: Francis Boutle Publishers, 2008

Williams, Douglas, *Festivals of Cornwall*, St Teath: Bossiney Books, 1987

Williams, Glanmore and Jones, Robert Owen (eds.), *The Celts and the Renaissance: Traditions and Innovation*, Cardiff: University of Wales Press, 1990

Williams, J. E. Caerwyn (ed.), *Ifor Williams: The Poems of Taliesin: Mediaeval and Modern Welsh*, Dublin: Dublin Institute for Advanced Celtic Studies, 1968

(ed.), *Literature in Celtic Countries*, Cardiff: University of Wales Press, 1971

Williams, N.J.A., *Cornish Today: An Examination of the Revived Language*, Sutton Coldfield: Kernewek dre Lyther, 1995

Testament Noweth agan Arluth ha Savyour Jesu Cryst, Redruth: Sprys a Gernow, 2002

'The Cornish Englyn' in Payton, Philip (ed.), 2007

Williams, Raymond, *The Country and the City*, St Albans: Paladin, 1975 [1973]

Problems in Materialism and Culture: Selected Essays, London and New York: Verso, 1980

Williams, Robert, 'Cornish Literature' in *Archaeologia Cambrensis*, 3, 15, 1869

Williamson, Duncan, *The Broonie, Silkies and Fairies*, Edinburgh: Canongate, 1985

Tales of the Seal People, Edinburgh: Canongate, 1992

Wilson, Jerome, 'A Modern Cornish Miracle Play' in *The Celtic Pen*, Vol. 2, No. 2, 1994

Wilson, Michael, *Storytelling and Theatre: Contemporary Professional Storytellers and their Art*, London: Palgrave Macmillan, 2005

Wilson, Philip, *Celtic Fairy Tales for Children*, Bath: Parragon, 1999

Wilson, R.M., *The Lost Literature of Medieval England*, London: Methuen, 1952

Wilson, Scott, *Cultural Materialism: Theory and Practice*, Oxford: Blackwell, 1995

Wiltshire, Rex, *Copper to Gold: A History of Wallaroo – South Australia – 1860-1923*, Wallaroo: Corporation of the Town of Wallaroo, 1983

Wingfield, Deborah, *Penryn: Archaeology and Development – A Survey*, Redruth Institute of Cornish Studies and Cornwall Committee for Rescue Archaeology, 1979

Wolff, Janet, *The Social Production of Art*, Basingstoke: Macmillan, 1992 [1981]

Wood, Briar, "The Words Are There Before Us': A Reading of Twentieth-Century Anglo-Cornish Poems Written by Women' in Payton, Philip (ed.), 2006

Woodhouse, Harry, *Cornish Bagpipes: Fact or Fiction?* Redruth: Dyllansow Truran, 1994
  (ed.), *The Cornish Passion Poem*, Cornwall: Gorseth Kernow, 2007
Wooding, Jonathan, *St Meriasek and King Tudor in Cornwall*, Sydney: n.p.,1992
Woodley, Helen, 'Where Stones touch the Sky' in *Meyn Mamvro*, No.4, 1987
Woolf, Charles, *An Introduction to the Archaeology of Cornwall*, Truro: D. Bradford
  Barton, 1970
Wootton, Brenda, *Pantomime Stew*, Hayle: Sue Luscombe, 1994
Wootton, George, *Thomas Hardy: Towards a Materialist Criticism*, Lanham: Rowan
  and Littlefield, 1985
Wyrall, Everard, *The History of the Duke of Cornwall's Light Infantry 1914-1919*,
  London: Methuen, 1939
Yeats, W.B., *Writings on Irish Folklore, Legend and Myth*, London: Penguin, 1993
  Selected Plays, London: Penguin, 1997
Youings, Joyce 'The South-Western Rebellion of 1549' in *Southern History*, 1, 1979
Young, Robert J.C., *The Idea of English Ethnicity*, Oxford: Blackwell, 2008
Young, Simon, *A.D. 500: A Journey through the Dark Isles of Britain and Ireland*,
  London: Phoenix Books, 2006 [2005]
Zipes, Jack, *Creative Storytelling: Changing Communities/Changing Lives*, London and
  New York: Routledge, 1995

Unpublished Sources

Berry, Eric, 'The Old Theatre, Penzance: Preliminary Findings for Sensitivity Study',
  2006, unpublished notes in the Hypatia Trust Archive
Clare, Andrew, *Glasney, History, Heritage and Community*, BA (Hons) thesis in
  Garden Design, Arts and Environment, University College Falmouth, 2008
Combellack-Harris, Myrna May, *A Critical Edition of Beunans Meriasek*, University of
  Exeter, Ph.D. thesis, 1985
Denny, Neville (dir.), *Performance Texts for the Cornish Ordinalia*, 1969
George, Ken, *A Phonological History of Cornish*, University of Western Brittany, Brest,
  Ph.D thesis, 1984
Graves, Eugene Val Tassel (ed.), *Vocabularium Cornicum: The Old Cornish Vocabulary*,
  University of Columbia, Ph.D. thesis, 1962
Grose, Carl, *Superstition Mountain*, unpublished playscript, 2008
Harding, Jacqueline Anne, *John Harris (1820-1884), 'The Cornish Miner Poet': An
  Exploration of the Cultural Construction of Place and the Creation of Cornish Identity*,
  Open University, MA Dissertation, 2008
Harris, Phyllis Pier, *Origo Mundi, First play of the Cornish mystery cycle, the Ordinalia: a
  new edition*, University of Washington: Ph.D. thesis, 1964

Higgins, Sydney, *Medieval Staging in Cornwall with Special Reference to St. Meriasek*, University of Bristol, M.Phil. thesis, 1974

Hill, Sue and Mitchell, Bill, *The Annual Governor's Lecture*, University College Falmouth, 2007

Kent, Alan M., *The Implication of Texts in History: The Rise, Development and Some Applications of Cultural Materialism*, University of Exeter M.Phil. thesis, 1991

Lipscombe, Miss Daniella, Letter from Territory Co-ordinator West, English Heritage: South-West Region to Dr Melissa Hardie, The Hypatia Trust, New Mill, Penzance, 9/2/2007

Lloyd, Trevor, 'Alexander the Pig: Shakespeare and the Celts', unpublished paper read at Sixth Australian Celtic Conference, 2007

Love, Ian, *Hic Descendit Deus Pater: Miracle Play Performance in Late Mediaeval Cornwall*, University of Cambridge, BA Dissertation, 2002

Neuss, Paula, *The Creacion of the World*, University of Toronto, Ph.D. Dissertation, 1970

Plunkett, Jonathon, *A Name Perpetual*, 1997

Plunkett, Jonathon, Southern, Janine, Parker, Simon and Vince, S., *To Catch a Tale*, Callington Writers' Group, 2001

Pollard, Peggy, *Synta Acherontia: Gwary-myr* in Nance Collection, Box 10, Royal Institution of Cornwall, n.d.

　　　Synt Tanbellan: A tryfle in one Scene in Nance Collection, Box 10, Royal Institution of Cornwall, n.d.

Rawe, Donald R., *Hawker of Morwenstow*, 1975

　　　Murder at Bohelland, 1991

　　　The Last Voyage of Alfred Wallis, 1994

Renton Howard Wood Levin Partnership, *The Georgian Theatre, Union Hotel: A Feasibility Study for the Reconstruction*, 1989

Shepherd, Mike and Grose, Carl, *Blast!*, 2007

Smith, Sarah, *Hall for Cornwall: Some Memories*, 2007

Symons, Andrew C., *Trevisa: Further Reflections*, unpublished paper, 2008

Thomas, Charles, *Canon Doble: An Appreciation Fifty Years On: Address in Wendron Church April 30, 1995* – typescript copy in the Courtney Library, Royal Institution of Cornwall, 1995

Thomas, D.M., *Hell Fire Corner*, unpublished script, 2003

Turley, Simon, *Where Are You Gone, Jimmy Trevenna?* 1996

Waverley, Peter, 'The Lost Georgian Theatre', Article in the Hypatia Trust Archive, n.d.

Willett, Joanie, *Liberal Ethnic Nationalism, Universality and Cornish Identity*, unpublished paper, 2008

Williams, N.J.A., *The Language of Bewnans Ke*, unpublished paper, 2008.

Audio and Audio-Visual Sources

Adams, John (dir.), *Kneehigh Theatre: Imagination Burning*, Penzance: Three S Films, 1997

Cowling, Johnny, *Off the Back of a Lorry – Live at Carnglaze Caverns*, Cornwall: Turn it Around Records, 2007

Darke, Nick and Darke, Jane, *The Wrecking Season*, Porthcothan: Boatshed Films, 2004

    The Art of Catching Lobsters, Porthcothan: Boatshed Films, 2005

De Heer, Rolf (dir.), *Ten Canoes*, Los Angeles: Universal Pictures, 2007

Dudley, Philip (dir.), *Poldark 1: Part One*, London: BBC Video, 1993 [1975]

Jethro, *From Behind the Bushes – Live!*, London: Universal Pictures UK, 1994

    Live! What Happened Was…, London: Universal Pictures UK, 1995

    The Beast of Bodmin Moor, London: Universal Pictures UK, 1997

    Says Bull'cks to Europe!, London: Universal Pictures UK 2000

    Rule Britannia! London: Universal Pictures UK, 2001

    Live at Jethro's: Back of Beyond, London: Universal Pictures UK, 2007

Lawrence, Trev *Songs, Poems and Legends: A Cornish Miscellany*, Paul: Sentinel, 1989

Minghella, Dominic (dir.), *Robin Hood*, London: BBC, 2006

Nunn, Trevor (dir.), *Twelfth Night*, London: Fine Line Features, 1996

Ordinalia Company, *Ordinalia: The Full Cycle*, Penzance: Three S Films, 2004

Reynolds, Kevin (dir.), *Robin Hood: Prince of Thieves*, Los Angeles: Warner Bros, 1991

    (dir.), *Tristan and Isolde*, Los Angeles: 20th Century Fox, 2006

Scott, Bill (dir.), *An Dewetha Gweryow Dolly Pentreath / The Last Words of Dolly Pentreath*, Cornwall: Wild West Films, 1994

    (dir.), *The Saffron Threads*, Cornwall: Wild West Films, 1995

    (dir.), *Splatt Dhe Wertha / Plot for Sale*, Cornwall: Wild West Films, 1997

Sharp, Ian (dir.), *Robin of Sherwood*, Bristol: HTV/Goldcrest, 1984

Sir Arthur Quiller-Couch Memorial Fund Committee, *Q: A Great Cornishman*, Truro: Sir Arthur Quiller-Couch Memorial Fund Committee, 2008

Stone, Oliver (dir.) *Alexander*, Los Angeles: Warner, 2004

Weatherhill, Craig, *Legends of Cornwall*, Tiverston: Halsgrove, 1998

Musical Sources

Barenboim, Daniel (cond.), *Tristan und Isolde*, Berlin: Teldec, 1995

Bolingey Troyl Band, *Gwenogennow Hag Oll*, St Agnes: Bolingey Troyl Band, 1998

Celtic Legend, *Tristan and Isolde*, France: Well Played Music, 2005

Gwaryoryon, *Three Drunken Maidens*, Cornwall: Gwaryoryon, 1996

Kneehigh Theatre, *Scat t'Larraps*, Truro: Kneehigh Theatre, 1999
Luxon, Benjamin and Moyer, Frederick, *Enoch Arden: Opus 38, Melodrama for Narrator and Piano. Poetry by Alfred, Lord Tennyson. Music by Richard Strauss*, Cornwall: JRI Recordings, 2002
O'Connor, Mike, *Tristan and Iseult*, Wadebridge: Lyngham House, n.d
Pyba, *Ilow Koth a Gernow / The Ancient Music of Cornwall*, Withiel: Pyba, 1999
Sowena, *A Month of Sundays*, St. Agnes: Sowena, 1999

World-Wide Web Sources

Author's note: these sites were consulted during the preparation of this book but, given the nature of the World-Wide Web, some of the references may not remain accessible.

http://abrax7.stormloader.com/donrawe.htm
http://freepages.genealogy.rootsweb.ancestry.com
http://members.fortunecity.com/gerdewnansek
http://www.acornartscentre.co.uk
http://www.admin.ox.ac.uk/po/news/2005-06/jun/15.shtml http://www.antony-waller.com/imagineers
http://www.applause.org.uk
http://www.asnc.cam.ac.uk/resources
http://www.bbc.co.uk/cornwall
http://www.bedlamtc.co.uk
http://www.bewnanske.co.uk
http://www.bishbashboshproductions.squarespace.com
http://www.carrickleisureservices.org.uk
http://www.cornish-theatre-collective.co.uk
http://www.cornwall.ac.uk/thekeay
http://www.cornwall24.co.uk
http://www.crbo.co.uk/event
http://www.creativeskills.org.uk/CaseStudies/PaulineSheppard
http://www.curtainup.com/midsummerfootsbarn.html
http://www.dmthomasonline.com
http://www.doollee.com/PlaywrightsM/murphy-anna-maria.html
http://www.doollee.com/PlaywrightsS/SheppardPauline.htm
http://www.dressinggranite.net/background
http://www.erbzine.com/mag18/jocko.htm
http://www.falmouth.ac.uk/138/the-college-8/dartingtons-merger-with-ucf-206.html

http://www.footsbarn.com
http://www.georgiantheatreroyal.co.uk
http://www.gorsethkernow.org.uk
http://www.gutenberg.org/dirs/etex04/wglf210.txt
http://www.gutenberg.org/ebooks/16625
http://www.hallforcornwall.co.uk
http://www.home.vicnet.net.au~caov/language/pasties.htm
http://www.johnnycowling.com/biog.htm
http://www.kent.ac.uk/sffva/invisible
http://www.kernewek.org.
http://www.kidzrus.net
http://www.kneehigh.co.uk
http://www.letrs.indiana.edu/cgi-bin/eprosed
http://www.llgc.org.uk/drych
http://www.llgc.org.uk/drych/drych_s074.htm
http://www.minack.com
http://www.miracletheatre.co.uk
http://www.montol.co.uk
http://www.mpecopark.co.uk
http://www.nls.uk/playbills
http://www.nyt.org.uk
http://www.o-region.co.uk
http://www.roguetheatre.co.uk
http://www.staps.co.uk
http://www.sterts.co.uk
http://www.st-piran.com
http://www.tech.org/~cleary/fairq/html
http://www.theartofcatchinglobsters.com
http://www.thewreckingseason.com
http://www.twainquotes.com/Travel1891/Dec1891.html
http://www.vortigernstudies.org.uk
http://www.wildworks.biz
http://www.worldwidewords.org/weirdwords/ww-pan2.htm
http://www.youtube.com/

CHRONOLOGY

BCE: Before Common Era
* indicates a text written in Cornish

10000-3500 BCE	Hunter-gatherer rituals
3500-2700 BCE	Portal dolmen (quoits) burial ceremonies
2700-1500 BCE	Proto-theatrical processions Megalithic erection
1500-200 BCE	Forts, enclosures and roundhouses Celts reach island of Britain Early storytelling Para-theatrical practices Fogous
200 BCE-400 CE	Dumnonia Roman presence in Cornwall Adoption of Christianity

400   The Age of Saints begins

550   *The Dialogue of Arthur and Eliud* – Taliesin

700   Anglo-Saxon intrusion into south-west British peninsula

838   Combined Cornish and Danish army fight Anglo-Saxons at Hingston Down

878   Death of King Dungarth
880   Life of St Pol de Leon by Urmonek, a monk from Landévennec

930   *Armes Prydain [The Prophecy of Britain]*
931   'Cornish' driven out of Exeter
936   Athelstan fixes border between his Saxon empire and the 'west wealhas'
960   *The Bodmin Manumissions*

1000	*The Old Cornish Vocabulary**
1086	*Domesday Book*

1136	*The History of the Kings of Britain* – Geoffrey of Monmouth
1150	*The Prophecy of Merlin* – John of Cornwall
	The Romance of Tristan – Béroul

1260	Birth of William de Grenfild?
1265	Founding of Glasney College, Penryn

1320	Robert Luc de Cornubia, Oxford
	Godfrey of Cornwall alive
1338	Monks of Tywardreath warned about watching 'worldly shows'
c.1342	Birth of John Trevisa
1350	Girard of Cornwall
1362	John Trevisa at Exeter College, Oxford
1380	*The Charter Endorsement* – fragment of drama?*

1400	Birth of Michael Tregury
1402	Death of John Trevisa
1415	Battle of Agincourt
1450?	The *Ordinalia**
	Possible lost *Flogholeth* drama*
1450	Original *Bewnans Ke* – but scribe wrote present copy c.1500*
1451	John Pascoe, rector of Camborne – possible playwright?
1466	Costume- and disguise-making by the Arundells at Lanherne
1477	Henry Bodrugan employs minstrels
1478	Possible date for St Goran play at Gorran
1485	*Le Morte D'Arthur* – Thomas Malory
1490	John Nans, vicar of Gwennap – possible playwright?
1497	Rebellion led by Michael Joseph 'An Gof' and Thomas Flamank
1498	A play performed at Sancreed

1500	Alexander Penhylle, rector at Illogan and Camborne – possible playwright?
	Lost Corpus Christi Play at Bodmin
c.1504	*Bewnans Meriasek* – Radolphus [or Ricardus] Ton?*
1531	Lost play featuring Queen of Gall at Launceston.
1537	A pilgrimage to Treguier, Brittany by a party of Cornishmen
	St George's Riding at Lostwithiel
1539	Dissolution of Bodmin Priory

1548   Dissolution of Glasney College, Penryn
1549   'Christmas Game' reference in Articles of Rebels
        Act of Uniformity
1553   Robin Hood play at Millbrook in East Cornwall
1565   *The Image of Idleness* – Oliver Oldwanton
1566   Last mention of Corpus Christi play at Bodmin
1572   Lost interlude performed at St Ives
1573   Possible Suzanna Play at St Breock
1574   *The Image of Idleness* – Oliver Oldwanton
1575   Lost five days of drama at St Ives
        An interlude is performed at Golden, near Probus
1587   Samson play performed in Penryn
1589   Lost Robin Hood play at St Columb Major
1591   *Harry of Cornwall* play in London – Lord Strange's Men
1595   Another performance of lost Robin Hood play at St Columb Major
1599   *Henry V* – William Shakespeare

1602   Observations on Gwary Miracle plays by Richard Carew
1604   Interlude at Liskeard on Whit Monday
1605   *King Lear* – William Shakespeare
1611   *The Creacion* [sic] *of the World* – scribed by William Jordan*
        Cymbeline: King of Britain – William Shakespeare
1615   Young men still performing a play in St Columb Major
1615   *A Fair Quarrel* – Thomas Middleton and William Rowley
1620   Lost rhyme/drama of St Columb's Legend translated by Mr Williams –
        mentioned by Nicholas Roscarrock
1622   *The Birth of Merlin, or The Childe Hath Found His Father* – William
        Shakespeare and William Rowley
1632   *The Northern Lasse* – Richard Brome
1633   King and Queen of the Summer Games in St Ives still operating
1634   *The Chronicle History of Perkin Warbeck: A Strange Truth* – John Ford
1639   *The Phoenix in her Flames* – William Lower
1642   Start of the War of Five Nations (Civil War)
1654   *The Innocent Lady* – William Lower, from the French of Rene de Ceriziers
1655   *Polyeuctes the Martyr* – William Lower, from Piere Corneille
        The Innocent Lord – William Lower
1656   *The Triumphant Lady* – William Lower
        Horatius, A Roman Tragedy – William Lower
1657   *The Three Dorothies, A Comedy* – William Lower
1659   *The Enchanted Lovers* – William Lower

1660	Restoration of Charles II
1661	*The Noble Ingratitude* – William Lower
	The Amorous Fantasme – William Lower
1666	Mr Tomblyn has a stage in Penryn
1667	Two Cornish-language writers: Richard Angwyn and Pendarvis recorded
	John Ray's *Itinerary*
1669	Tumblers and acrobats in Penryn
1680	*Antiquities Cornuontanic: The Causes of Cornish Speech's Decay* – William Scawen
1720	Birth of Samuel Foote in Truro
1727	*The Exmoor Scolding* – Andrew Brice
1736	*The Fatal Curiosity* – George Lillo
1747	*The Diversions of the Morning* – Samuel Foote, Haymarket
1748	*An Auction of Pictures* – Samuel Foote, Haymarket
	The Knights – Samuel Foote, Drury Lane
1752	*Taste* – Samuel Foote, Drury Lane
1753	*An Englishman in Paris* – Samuel Foote, Drury Lane
1756	*The Englishman returned from Paris* – Samuel Foote, Covent Garden
1757	*The Author* – Samuel Foote, Drury Lane
1760	*The Minor* – Samuel Foote, Haymarket
1762	*The Lyar* – Samuel Foote, Covent Garden
	The Orators – Samuel Foote, Haymarket
1763	*The Mayor of Garret* – Samuel Foote, Haymarket
	Birth of Charles Incledon
1764	*The Patron* – Samuel Foote, Haymarket
1765	*The Commissary* – Samuel Foote, Haymarket
1768	*The Devil on Two Sticks* – Samuel Foote, Haymarket
1770	*The Lame Lover* – Samuel Foote, Haymarket
1771	*The Maid of Bath* – Samuel Foote, Haymarket
1772	*The Nabob* – Samuel Foote, Haymarket
1773	*Piety in Patterns* – Samuel Foote, Haymarket
	The Bankrupt – Samuel Foote, Haymarket
	White Is the Man? – Hannah Cowley
1774	*The Cozeneers* – Samuel Foote, Haymarket
1776	*On the Expiration of the Cornish Language* – Daines Barrington
	A Trip to Calais – Samuel Foote, Haymarket
	The Wheel of Fortune – Richard Cumberland
1777	Death of Samuel Foote
1787	Opening of the Penzance Theatre and Truro Assembly-Room Theatre

1788   Truro Cordwainers' Play

1790   Charles Incledon's success at Covent Garden

1802   *Blue-Beard, Pizarro, Perouse* and *The Shipwreck* at Falmouth

        The Poor Gentleman at Falmouth – Samuel Fisher in lead role

        The Wonder at Falmouth – Susannah Centlivre

1803   *Alexander the Great,* or *The Rival Queens* at Truro

        The Two Recruits at Truro – Character of a Cornish Miner

1804   *The Rivals* and *Tragedy of Edward the Black Prince* at Penzance

        Speed the Plough at Falmouth – Thomas Morton

        The Iron Chest – George Colman

1805   *John Bull* – George Colman

        Performance interrupted in Penzance by the announcement of Horatio

        Nelson's death

        The Birth-Day and *The Shipwrecked Sailor* at Falmouth

        The Lady of the Rock at Falmouth – Thomas Holcroft

1806   *Hamlet* at Falmouth

1807   *Raising the Wind* at Truro

        Love's Systems – William Vone

1813   *The Tragedy of King Lear and His Three Daughters* at Falmouth

1816   Publication of *The Great Hewas Mine, or The Humours of Cornwall* by

        George William Downing

1817   Death of Samuel Fisher

1824   Truro Theatre reopens under James Dawson

1826   Death of Charles Incledon

1827   *Tragedy of Jane Shore* and *The Cornish Miners* at Truro

1828   *Tom Thumb the Great* at Truro

        Edmund Kean in Redruth

1829   Droll-tellers Anthony James and Billy Foss operating in West Cornwall

1831   Closure of the Penzance Theatre

1833   *Nine Years of an Actor's Life* – Richard Dyer

1836   *The Daughter: A Play in Five Acts* – James Sheridan Knowles

1838   *Jocko, The Brazilian Ape* and *The Wreck Ashore* at Truro

        Birth of Sir Henry Irving

1845   Devonport-based Mr Doel starts to present drama in Cornwall

1846   Birth in Exeter of Charles Algernon Sidney Vivian, Cornu-American

        theatrical entrepreneur and performer

1849   Henry Irving leaves Cornwall to train as an actor in London

        The False Petition – John Westland Marston and Bayle Bernard, at Royal

        Surrey Theatre

Birth of Henry Jenner

1851   *The Curate's Daughter* – visit by Wilkie Collins to Sans Pareil Theatre, Redruth

1854   *Aggravating Sam, A Comic Drama, in 2 Acts [and in prose]* – first dramatic success of Leicester Silk Buckingham

1856   *The Dream at Sea: A Drama in Three Acts* – John Baldwin
       The Fractious Man – Henry Curling

1857   Justus H. Rathbone's drama group on the Keweenaw Peninsula of Northern Michigan

1859   *The Ancient Cornish Drama* – translation of *Ordinalia* by Edwin Norris

1862   Birth in Redruth of Richard Jose

1863   *The Quest of the Sangraal* – Robert Stephen Hawker
       Birth of Arthur Quiller-Couch

1864   *Kiddle-a-wink: A Cornish Drama* – Brownlow Hill, at Victoria Theatre, London.

1865   *Popular Romances of the West of England: The Drolls, Traditions, and Superstitions of Old Cornwall* – Robert Hunt
       Tristan and Isolde – Richard Wagner
       Publication of James Dawson's *Autobiography*

1866   Revival of performances at Truro Assembly-Room Theatre

1867   *Faw Fee Fo Fum, or Harlequin Jack, the Giant Killer* – Edward Leman Blanchard, at Drury Lane
       Nobody's Child – Watis Phillips, at Surrey Theatre

1868   Arrival of touring theatre star Alice Kingsbury in Grass Valley, California

1869   *The Home Wreck* – Joseph Stirling Coyne and J. Denis Coyne, at Surrey Theatre
       The Shadow of a Crime – Charles Smith Cheltnam, at Theatre Royal, Belfast

1870   *Traditions and Hearthside Stories of West Cornwall: First Series* – William Bottrell

1871   *Watch and Wait* – James Albery, at Surrey Theatre

1872   Formation of Amateur Dramatic Club in Wallaroo
       The Cornish Brothers – H. Pomeroy Gilbert, at Paignton

1873   Birth of Robert Morton Nance

1874   *Queen Mab* – G.W. Godfrey, at The Haymarket, London

1875   *Jack the Giant Killer and Tom Thumb or Harlequin King Arthur and the Knights of the Round Table* – Frank W. Green
       The History of Joseph and His Brethren – Joseph Hill, at St Stithians
       First recorded performance in Butte City, Montana

1879   *The Pirates of Penzance, or Love and Duty* – W.S. Gilbert and Arthur Sullivan

1880   Corporation clampdown on guizing tradition in Penzance

Owsley's Hall opened in Butte City, Montana
1882   *Parsifal* – Richard Wagner
1884   *Over the Cliff* – Alfred Farthing Robbins, at the Theatre Royal, Great Grimsby
        The Wreckers – R. Dodson, at Her Majesty's Theatre, Carlisle
1887   *Ruddigore, or The Witch's Curse* – W.S. Gilbert and Arthur Sullivan
        Gipsy Gabriel – William Park and William Hogarth, at Theatre Royal, Bradford
        Our Joan – Herman Merivale and Cecil Dale, in the USA and at the Prince of Wales's Theatre, Birmingham
1888   *Forgery* – J. Carne Ross, at St John's Hall, Penzance
        Golden Goblin – Frank Maryat, at the Theatre Royal, Croydon
        The Loadstone – T. Edgar Pemberton and W.H. Vernon. at the Lyceum Theatre, London
1890   Guizing still active in St Ives
1891   *Phaon and Sappho* – James Dryden Hosken
1895   *The Bishop of Eucalyptus* – Arthur Quiller-Couch
1896   Fanny Moody performs in South Africa
        Christopher Marlowe: A Tragedy in Three Acts in Prose and Verse, and Belphegor: A Harlequinade in Doggerel – James Dryden Hosken
1898   *The Cornish Magazine* – Arthur Quiller-Couch
1899   *Historical Tales from Shakespeare* – Arthur Quiller-Couch

1900   Opening of the Calumet Theatre, Calumet, Northern Michigan
1902   *The Literature of the Celts* – Magnus Maclean
1904   *A Handbook of the Cornish Language* – Henry Jenner
        Cornwall admitted to the Celtic Congress
1905   Death of Henry Irving
1906   *From a Cornish Window* – Arthur Quiller-Couch
1907   *Sally's Shiners: A Droll of Smuggling Days* – Robert Morton Nance
1908   Birth of J.C. Trewin – theatre critic
        The Kite in the Castle: A Legend of Lamorna – Robert Morton Nance
1909   *The Wreckers* – Ethel Smyth and Henry Brewster
        Formation of the Redruth Amateur Operatic Society

1912   Founding of the Truro Amateur Operatic and Dramatic Society
        Arthur Quiller-Couch appointed Chair of English at the University of Cambridge
1914   Opening of the Opera House, at Mineral Point, Wisconsin
        Start of the First World War

	It's Hard To be Toogood – Arthur Quiller-Couch
1917	Birth of Charles Causley
1918	End of the First World War

1920	*Duffy: A Tale of Trove* – Robert Morton Nance
	The Tragedy of the Chrononhotonthologos: being the most Tragical Tragedy that was ever Tragedied by any Company of Tragedians – Robert Morton Nance
	Founding of first Old Cornwall Society at St Ives
1923	*The Famous Tragedy of the Queen of Cornwall at Tintagel in Lyonesee* – Thomas Hardy
	Demolition of the Truro Assembly-Room Theatre
1924	*The Christmas Play of Saint George and the Turkish Knight* – Robert Morton Nance
1925	*The Coming of Arthur* – John Baragwanath King
1926	*Bethlehem* – Bernard Walke
	Tom and the Giant: A Christmas Play – Robert Morton Nance
	John Knill – Robert Morton Nance
1927	*Newquay Theatre* built
	Revival of Tom Bawcock's Eve – Robert Morton Nance
1928	First 'revived' Gorseth Kernow*
1929	*A Midsummer Night's Dream* – Penzance Orchestral Society and Rowena Cade's actors
	Opening of permanent *Cosy Nook* Theatre in Newquay

1930	*King Arthur: His Symbolic Story in Verse* – B.D. Vere
	Plays from St Hilary – Bernard Walke (but published in 1939)
1932	*An Balores / The Chough* – Robert Morton Nance*
	The Tempest – first performance at the Minack Theatre
1934	*Iernin* – George Lloyd and William Lloyd
	First Cornish Shakespeare Festival, opened by Arthur Quiller-Couch
1936	*Runaway* – Charles Causley
1937	J.C. Trewin joins *The Observer* newspaper
	The Conquering Hero – Charles Causley
	New Theatre opened in Newquay
	This Sceptred Isle – Arthur Quiller-Couch
1938	*Benedict* – Charles Causley
1939	*Rebecca* – adaptation by Daphne du Maurier
	Journey of the Magi – Charles Causley
	Tristan and Isolt – John Masefield, at the Minack Theatre

Start of the Second World War

1940   *Beunans Alysaryan* – Peggy Pollard*
        Death of Bernard Walke
1941   *Synt Avaldor* – Peggy Pollard*
1942   *Synt Tanbellan* – Peggy Pollard*
        Bewnans Meriasek – English language version in Redruth
1043   *Synta Acherontia* – Peggy Pollard*
1944   Death of Arthur Quiller-Couch
1945   *The Years Between* – Daphne du Maurier
        End of the Second World War
1946   Studio Theatre opens in Camborne
1948   *How Pleasant to Know Mrs Lear* – Charles Causley
        Birth of Geoff Rowe (Jethro) at St Buryan
        The Contemporary Players in Truro
        The Merlin Theatre opens in Mousehole
1949   Discovery of *The Tregear Homilies*
        September Tide – Daphne du Maurier
        Formation of the Little Theatre, Perranporth
        Redruth Amateur Operatic Society perform *Tears from their Eyes* in the
        West End
        International Youth Drama Course at Restormel Castle, Lostwithiel
        The Minack Theatre re-opens

1950   *Bewnans Meriasek* – a section performed by Camborne-Redruth Theatre
        Group
1951   Foundation of *Mebyon Kernow*
        Cornish Drama Festival
        Tristan of Cornwall – Nora Ratcliff
        The Work of Our Hands – Phyllida Garth
        Women of Cornwall – Patricia Donahue
        The Cliff Edge – Patricia Donahue
        The Boy from Egypt – Wallace Nichols
        The Wesley Tapestry – Christian Michell
        St Petroc's Festival Play – Dorothy Miles and Patricia Deeman
        The Carn Remembers – Eileen R. Speek
        The Pilgrim Stone – Michael Toms
        Aunt Saul's Recipe – Constance Cleminson
        The Mermaid of Zennor – Pearl Peirson
        The Stranger – Edith M. Jolly

Richard Trevithick – Helena Jones

Trystan hag Ysolt – A.S.D. Smith

1952   *Down to the Lion* – J.C. Trewin

Arthur of Britain – Nora Ratcliff

1955   *St Ursula* – Cornish Religious Drama Fellowship, at the Minack Theatre

1956   *The Cledry Plays: Drolls of Old Cornwall for Village Acting and Home Reading* – Robert Morton Nance (but originally from 1920s)

1959   Christmas Play – St Mawgan Church

Death of Robert Morton Nance

1960   Richard Southern visits remains of the Penzance Theatre

1961   *Trelyans Sen Powl / The Conversion of St Paul* – N.J.A. Williams*

1962   *Castle Dor* – Arthur Quiller-Couch and Daphne du Maurier

1964   *Morvoren* – Philip Cannon

The Tinners of Cornwall – Inglis Gundry

Initial version of St Petroc drama – Donald R. Rawe

1965   *The Logan Rock* – Inglis Gundry

1967   *The Creacion of the World* – Roland Conrad Miller, Hoxton Street, London

1969   *Ordinalia* – Neville Denny and Bristol University, Perran Round

1970   *Petroc of Cornwall* – Donald R. Rawe

1971   *The Trials of St Piran* – Donald R. Rawe

Founding of Footsbarn Theatre

Perran Cherrybeam – Footsbarn Theatre

The Net – Nora Ratcliff, at the Minack Theatre

1972   *Geraint: Last of the Arthurians* – Donald R. Rawe

Giant – Dave Johnson and Footsbarn Theatre

1973   *A Skeleton in the Cupboard* – Donald R. Rawe

The Happening at Botathen – Donald R. Rawe

Wheal Judas – Burness Bunn

The Christmas Widow – Burness Bunn

Shadows of Men – Gwen Powell-Jones

Tristan and Isolde – Footsbarn Theatre

Opening of the Redannick Theatre, Truro

Trystan hag Ysolt – D.H. Watkins

1974   *John Tom* – Footsbarn Theatre

The Legends of King Arthur – Exeter University Drama Department, at the Minack Theatre

1975   *Hawker of Morwenstow* – Donald R. Rawe

1977   *The Life of Meriasek: A Medieval Cornish Miracle Play* – translation by
Markham Harris
Never Say Rabbit in a Boat – Nick Darke
Low Tide – Nick Darke

1978   *The Ballad of Aucassin and Nicolette* – Charles Causley, Exeter Festival

1979   *My Cousin Rachel* – adaptation of the du Maurier novel, by Diana Morgan
The Little Photographer – adaptation of the du Maurier short story, by
Derek Hoddinott
Origo Mundi – formation of Miracle Theatre Company
Summer Trade – Nick Darke

1980   *The Doctor and the Devils* – Charles Causley
Meryasek – Shiva Theatre
Awful Knawful – First Kneehigh Theatre Show

1981   *The Catch* – Nick Darke
The Mystery Machine –Kneehigh Theatre

1982   *The Burning Boy: A Miracle Play for Music Theatre* – Charles Causley,
unperformed
King Arthur – Shiva Theatre, at the Minack Theatre

1983   *The Body* – Nick Darke
Meriask – Pauline Sheppard
Skungpoomery – Kneehigh Theatre

1984   *The Earth Turned Inside Out*, Nick Darke and Restormel Borough Council
Footsbarn Theatre leave Great Britain

1985   *Tregeagle (Version 1)* – Kneehigh Theatre
Mass New Year's Eve Fancy Dress celebrations at Newquay and St Ives

1986   Performance of *Bewnans Meriasek* at St Paul's Church, Truro

1988   *The Camborne Play* – Myrna Combellack, a verse translation of *Bewnans
Meriasek*
Sun and Shadow – Stuart Delves and Kneehigh Theatre

1989   The Treworgey Tree Fayre
Tregeagle (Version 3) – Kneehigh Theatre

1990   Death of J.C. Trewin
Ting Tang Mine – Nick Darke, Kneehigh Theatre
The Mermaid – Bedlam Theatre Company of Cornwall
The Tinderbox – Charles Causley and Kneehigh Theatre
Badger's Cross – Pauline Sheppard, Acorn Theatre, Penzance

1991   *Aesop: A New Opera* – Charles Causley, National Youth Music Theatre
Murder at Bohelland – Donald R. Rawe

A Mere Interlude – Theatre Rotto, Penzance
1992   *St Meriasek and King Tudor in Cornwall* – University of Sydney
Trystan and Yseult – Bedlam Theatre Company of Cornwall
Aesop: A New Opera – Charles Causley
Hell's Mouth – Nick Darke
Dogs – Pauline Sheppard and Cornwall Theatre Company
1993   *A Parcel of Rogues* – Miracle Theatre Company
Danger My Ally – Nick Darke, Kneehigh Theatre
Tin – Pauline Sheppard
1994   *The Bogus* – Nick Darke, Kneehigh Theatre
The Last Voyage of Alfred Wallis – Donald R. Rawe
Smuggler's Moon – Bedlam Theatre Company of Cornwall
Rebecca – adaptation of the du Maurier novel by Clifford Williams
The Tempest – Miracle Theatre
1995   *Figgie Hobbin* – Kneehigh Theatre
Star-Gazy Pie and Sauerkraut – James Stock, Royal Court Theatre Upstairs
Duffy and the Devil – Bedlam Theatre Company of Cornwall
The Scapegoat – Miracle Theatre Company
1996   *Cherry of Zennor* – Bedlam Theatre Company of Cornwall
Dressing Granite – Pauline Sheppard
Tregeagle (Version 4) – Kneehigh Theatre
Where Are You Gone, Jimmy Trevenna? – Simon Turley
1997   *The King of Prussia* – Nick Darke, Kneehigh Theatre
Tin – Rory Wilton, and Bedlam Theatre Company of Cornwall
A Name Perpetual – Jonathon Plunkett
Our Little Town – Pauline Sheppard
The Fall of Robin Hood – Miracle Theatre Company
A Star on the Mizzen – Simon Parker
Bohelland – Justin Chubb, Cornish Theatre Collective
1998   *One and All* – Bedlam Theatre Company of Cornwall
Pete Townsend and Friends Benefit Concert for Kneehigh Theatre at Hall
for Cornwall
Judas Worm – Justin Chubb, Cornish Theatre Collective
Dreaming in Cornish – Alan M. Kent
1999   *The Riot* – Nick Darke, Kneehigh Theatre
The Governor of Sombrero Rock – Bedlam Theatre Company of Cornwall
Southern Comfort – Justin Chubb, Cornish Theatre Collective

2000   *Hell's Mouth* – Nick Darke and Kneehigh Theatre
The Watched – Bedlam Theatre Company of Cornwall

Discovery of *Bewnans Ke* in Wales

2001   *Roger Salmon, Cornish Detective* – Kneehigh Theatre, Geevor Tin Mine

The Passion – The Ordinalia Company's production at St. Just-in-Penwith

The Beggar's Opera – Miracle Theatre Company

Mapbeth – Son of the Grave, Cornish Theatre Collective

2002   *She Doesn't Like Pasties* – Peter Trevorah, at Bendigo Cornish Festival*

Quick Silver – Carl Grose, Kneehigh Theatre

2003   *Tristan and Yseult* – Kneehigh Theatre, Restormel Castle

Death of Charles Causley

2004   *Hell Fire Corner* – D.M. Thomas, Hall for Cornwall

Ordinalia – Pauline Sheppard and the Cornish Theatre Collective

Kernow Eduation Arts Project begins

2005   *Tin & Fishes* – Pauline Sheppard

Tristan and Yseult – Kneehigh Theatre, national and international Tour

Ordinalia: The Cornish Mystery Play Cycle – Alan M. Kent, a verse translation of *Ordinalia*

Laughing Gas – Nick Darke and Carl Grose, o-region

2006   *Flogholeth Krist* – Ken George*

Nativitas Christi / The Nativity – Alan M. Kent

Seven Stars: A Cornish Christmas Play for Voices – Simon Parker

2007   *Oogly es Sin* – Alan M. Kent, BishBashBosh Productions,

Blast! – Kneehigh Theatre

The Zig Zag Way – Pauline Sheppard

2008   Announcement of merger of Dartington College of Arts and University College Falmouth

Designation of Cornwall and West Devon as a UNESCO World Heritage Site

Below – C-scape Dance Company and Anna Maria Murphy

The Tin Violin – Alan M. Kent, BishBashBosh Productions

A Midsummer Night's Dream – Footsbarn Theatre in London

2009   *Surfing Tommies* – Alan M. Kent, BishBashBosh Productions

Gonemena – Simon Parker

Superstition Mountain – Carl Grose, o-region

"Oh Mary" – Anna Maria Murphy

Hansel & Gretel, a wonder tale – Kneehigh Theatre

2010   *A Mere Interlude* – Alan M. Kent, Bish Bash Bash Productions

The Asylum – Kneehigh Theatre

INDEX

John Bull: An Englishman's Fireside
43, 395, 432, 465-9, 492, 494,
512, 668, 928
Coleman, Will 82, 325, 729, 748, 766,
826, 831, 841
Collier, Jeremy 364, 426
Collins, Wilkie 170, 438, 482, 488,
853, 929
Colquhoun, Ithel 70-1
Colshull family 229
Combellack, Myrna 52, 142, 244, 247,
252, 317, 563, 934
Combined Universities of Cornwall
312, 319, 701, 845
Community 26, 35, 36, 40, 42-3, 52,
55, 62, 65-7, 72, 75, 77, 79, 88,
91-3, 95, 97, 99, 100, 105-7,
111, 115, 119-23, 135, 150, 152,
157, 159, 174, 187, 201, 207,
216, 222, 227, 234, 245, 248,
250, 256-7, 264, 277, 289-90,
360, 367, 396, 408, 439, 450-1,
495, 513, 530, 534, 539, 543,
545, 549, 555, 557, 559, 562-5,
583, 585, 593, 597, 609, 614,
629, 634-5, 650, 652, 654, 670,
672, 692, 700, 702-5, 712,
720-4, 731, 738, 745-8, 751,
753, 760-6, 768, 771-4, 777-8,
782, 784, 788, 792, 794, 796,
812-3, 825, 837, 842-3, 846,
850, 854
Congreve, William 364
Constantine [*place*] 183, 769, 773
Constantine [*Saint, and Emperor*] 183,
234, 237, 240-5,
Continuum 25, 27, 33, *35*, 36-40, 43,
57, 69, 80, 88, 92, 120, 150-1,
195, 239, 248, 263, 280, 294-6,
361, 439, 455, 458, 464, 471,
478, 481, 489-90, 494, 496,
507-8, 515, 519, 531, 536,
538-9, 541, 543, 548, 550,
554-5, 563, 586-7, 597-9, 629,
632, 635-6, 640-2, 654, 665,

669-72, 700, 705, 719, 721-2,
725, 730, 746, 758, 761, 766, 848
Cook, Jon Paul 720, 821
Cope, Julian 70
Corineus 83, 329, 353
Cornish Gorsedd 64, 72, 90-2, 114,
131, 589, *597*, 609, *616*, 642,
647, 670, 673, 732, 758, 846
Cornish identity 27, 40, 125, 155, 294,
334, 350, 372, 469, 563, 565,
622, 634, 666, 670, 672, 704,
740, 764, 768, 774, 784, 812
Cornish language 26, 29-30, 40, 80, 89,
106, 118, 120, 122, 135, 150-1,
158, 166, 193, 226, 229, 248-50,
257, 274-7, 282, 294-7, 325,
330, 355-7, 360, 367-9, 389,
419-20, 428, 506, 534-9, 563,
565, 575, 585-6, 596-9, 613-4,
620, 621-9, 631, 635, 646, 648,
679, 683, 686, 691, 701, 705,
707-9, 738, 767, 785, 804, 814,
843, 845, 848, 927, 930
Late Cornish 289
Middle Cornish 113-4, 117, 159,
161, 165, 186, 188, 193, 229,
248, 252-3, 261
Old Cornish 77, 85, 110-1, *112*,
115, 117, 120, 144, 220, 369,
538, 683, 925
Revived Cornish 585
Unified Cornish 307, 325, 585,
598-9, 626
Cornish Language Board 626
Cornish-language drama 29, 40, 125,
151, 226, 248, 250, 282, 294-6,
325, 360, 368-9, 536, 538-9, 709
Cornish literature 29, 31-2, 47, 109,
245, 554, 575, 626, 760
Cornish Nationalism 661, 704, 720
Cornish Nationalist Party 702
Cornish Record Office 266
Cornish Review 28, 705, 819
Cornish Revival 30, 35, 495, 512, 596,
599, 628, 661, 670